MW01609892

BUSINESS STATISTICS

Courseware Edition

Alan H. Kvanli I Robert J. Pavur I Kellie B. Keeling

CENGAGE
Learning™

Australia • Brazil • Japan • Korea • Mexico • Singapore • Spain • United Kingdom • United States

CENGAGE
Learning™

BUSINESS STATISTICS: Courseware Edition

Executive Editors:
Maureen Staudt
Michael Stranz

Senior Project Development Manager:
Linda deStefano

Marketing Specialist:
Courtney Sheldon

Senior Production/Manufacturing Manager:
Donna M. Brown

PreMedia Manager:
Joel Brennecke

Sr. Rights Acquisition Account Manager:
Todd Osborne

Source 1:
Title: Concise Managerial Statistics
Authors: Kvanli, Keeling, Pavur

© 2006 Cengage Learning. All rights reserved.

Source 2:
Title: Introduction to Business Statistics, Text Only
Authors: Alan H. Kvanli, Robert J. Pavur, Kellie Keeling

© 2002 Cengage Learning. All rights reserved.

ALL RIGHTS RESERVED. No part of this work covered by the copyright herein may be reproduced, transmitted, stored or used in any form or by any means graphic, electronic, or mechanical, including but not limited to photocopying, recording, scanning, digitizing, taping, Web distribution, information networks, or information storage and retrieval systems, except as permitted under Section 107 or 108 of the 1976 United States Copyright Act, without the prior written permission of the publisher.

For product information and technology assistance, contact us at
Cengage Learning Customer & Sales Support, 1-800-354-9706

For permission to use material from this text or product,
submit all requests online at **cengage.com/permissions**
Further permissions questions can be emailed to
permissionrequest@cengage.com

This book contains select works from existing Cengage Learning resources and was produced by Cengage Learning Custom Solutions for collegiate use. As such, those adopting and/or contributing to this work are responsible for editorial content accuracy, continuity and completeness.

Compilation © 2010 Cengage Learning
ISBN-13: 978-1-111-40020-0

ISBN-10: 1-111-40020-2

Cengage Learning
5191 Natorp Boulevard
Mason, Ohio 45040
USA

Cengage Learning is a leading provider of customized learning solutions with office locations around the globe, including Singapore, the United Kingdom, Australia, Mexico, Brazil, and Japan. Locate your local office at:
international.cengage.com/region

Cengage Learning products are represented in Canada by Nelson Education, Ltd.
For your lifelong learning solutions, visit **www.cengage.com/custom**
Visit our corporate website at **www.cengage.com**

Printed in the United States of America

Custom Contents

chapter

A First Look at Statistics and Data Collection

Statistics in Action
Online Surveys: E-xpress Yourself

Online surveys are proliferating on the World Wide Web. In a recent online survey by Direct Marketing Services, results showed that 68 percent of participating consumers have also participated in a telephone, mall, or mail survey. The other 32 percent indicated that they were now responding only to online surveys. This survey consisted of more than 2,000 randomly selected men and women aged 18 or older who were polled by Direct Marketing Services through Opinion Place on America Online. The vice president of research services at Direct Marketing Services proclaims, "Our research concludes that online surveys are reaching the same consumer groups that traditional research methods are targeting, but with more success."

Telephone and mail surveys have traditionally been conducted by corporations and newspapers, such as the *Wall Street Journal*, to obtain quick feedback from the general population. These procedures have benefited business decision makers in a variety of business fields, including marketing, finance, accounting, management, and information systems. However, a challenge for those involved in conducting survey research is to ensure that the quality of surveys on the Internet is at least at the same level as the traditional approaches of collecting data. Only by fully understanding the benefits and drawbacks of this non-traditional method can the potential of online surveys be fully exploited.

When you have completed this chapter, you will be able to examine the results of a poll and discuss such questions as

- What is the *population* of interest?

- Can the respondents of the poll be viewed as a *random sample*?

- What is the *level of measurement* of the data collected?

- What is meant by a *statistic*?

1

1.1

A FIRST LOOK AT STATISTICS

Many people probably think a statistician is someone who figures batting averages during a baseball game broadcast. You might wonder how we can devote an entire textbook to compiling numbers and making simple calculations. Surely it cannot be that complicated!

Statistics is the science comprising rules and procedures for collecting, describing, analyzing, and interpreting numerical data. The applications of statistics are evident everywhere. Hardly a day goes by in which we are not bombarded by such statements as these:

Results show that Crest toothpaste helps prevent tooth decay.

The chance of rain tomorrow is 30%.

The state court has ruled that the XYZ Company is guilty of age discrimination in its termination procedure.

Smoking causes lung cancer, heart disease, and emphysema, and may complicate pregnancy.

Or how about:

American companies are continuing to place more emphasis on quality improvement in an attempt to offer better products that can be delivered on time at less cost.

Besides using statistics to inform the public, statisticians help businesses make forecasts for planning and decision making.

The use of statistics began as early as the first century A.D., when governments used a census of people, land, and properties for tax purposes. Census taking was gradually extended to include such local events as births, deaths, and marriages. The *science* of statistics, which uses a sample to predict or estimate some characteristics of a population, began its development during the nineteenth century.

Use of statistical methods has undergone a dramatic change as computers and powerful calculators have entered the research environment. Companies can store and manipulate large collections of data, and once-formidable statistical calculations are reduced to a few keystrokes. Sophisticated computer software allows users merely to specify the type of analysis desired and input the necessary data. This textbook concentrates on three of these software packages: Excel (a spreadsheet package developed by Microsoft), MINITAB (a statistical computer package originally designed at Penn State University specifically for students), and SPSS (a large-scale statistical software package designed to integrate and analyze marketing, customer, and operational data).

Although most statistical functions are performed by professional statisticians, it might be your job to draw a valid conclusion from a statistical report. In addition, you might be asked to perform a statistical analysis. Although you might elect to obtain outside assistance, you will need to know when to consult a statistician and how to tell him or her what you need.

So welcome to the world of uncertainty. Statistical methods offer you a way of evaluating an uncertain future by using limited information to assess the likelihood of future events occurring. But despite the best intent of statistical measurements, it is important to remember that an event with a high chance of occurring might, in fact, not occur at all. Anyone who has changed plans because of a 90% chance of rainy weather only to sit home on a sunny day can attest to this fact.

USING THE COMPUTER 1.2

Use of statistical methods has undergone a dramatic change as computers and powerful calculators have entered the everyday business environment. Companies can store and manipulate large collections of data so that once-formidable statistical calculations are reduced to a few keystrokes. Sophisticated windows-based software allows users merely to specify the type of analysis required and input the necessary data. This textbook concentrates on three of these software packages: Excel, MINITAB, and SPSS. Excel is a spreadsheet package developed by Microsoft, whereas MINITAB and SPSS are true statistical software systems. We briefly describe these three software products.

Microsoft Excel

Excel is a spreadsheet program that can be used to access, process, analyze, display, and share information for running a business. Excel continues to make the existing functionality easier to use while offering a wide array of tools for making the more advanced tasks less complex and more intuitive. Excel was not designed to be a statistical package; however, it does offer a number of built-in statistical functions and analysis procedures. To overcome Excel's statistical shortcomings, the CD that accompanies this textbook contains a number of Excel macros. These are programs written by the authors that operate within Excel and provide a number of graphical and analytical procedures that are not included in the standard (off-the-shelf) Excel package. For more information on implementing these macros, consult the *Introduction to Excel* file in the textbook CD.

MINITAB

MINITAB is a widely used statistical analysis package, originally developed in 1972 at Penn State University to help professors teach basic statistics. Over the years, MINITAB has grown into a powerful and accurate, yet easy-to-use, set of statistical tools. MINITAB is used by a number of Fortune 500 companies and by more than 4,000 colleges and universities worldwide. In 2001, *Scientific Computing and Instrumentation,* a publication covering computing and analytical instrument technology, named MINITAB as the winner in the Reader's Choice Awards Statistical Software category. For first-time users, an *Introduction to MINITAB* is provided in the textbook CD.

SPSS

SPSS is a large-scale statistical software package designed to integrate and analyze marketing, customer, and operational data. CRM Magazine's 2003 CRM (Customer Relationship Management) Leader Awards recognized SPSS in the Analytics category as "One to Watch." The letters *SPSS* originally meant "Statistical Package for the Social Sciences." As the system evolved from its academic roots in the late 1960s into a leading enterprise analytical solutions provider, the company simply began using *SPSS Inc.* for the company name and *SPSS* for the original product. Today, SPSS provides solutions that discover what customers want and predict what they will do. Although this might appear to be intimidating to the first-time user of SPSS, rest assured that, like many windows-based programs, this statistical package is very easy to use. *An Introduction to SPSS* is included with the textbook CD.

1.3

USES OF STATISTICS IN BUSINESS

Modern businesses have more need to predict future operations than did those of the past, when businesses were smaller. Small-business managers often can solve problems simply through personal contact. Managers in large corporations, however, must try to summarize and analyze the various data available to them. They do this by using modern statistical methods.

Here we list six areas of business that rely on statistical information and techniques:

1. *Quality improvement.* Statistical quality-control procedures can help to assure high product quality and enhance productivity.

2. *Product planning.* Statistical methods are used to analyze economic factors and business trends and to prepare detailed sales budgets, inventory-control systems, and realistic sales quotas.

3. *Forecasting.* Statistics are used to predict sales, productivity, and employment trends.

4. *Yearly reports.* Annual reports for stockholders are based on statistical treatment of the many cost and revenue factors analyzed by the business comptroller.

5. *Personnel management.* Statistical procedures are used in such areas as age- and sex-discrimination lawsuits, performance appraisals, and workforce-size planning.

6. *Market research.* Corporations that develop and market products or services use sophisticated statistical procedures to describe and analyze consumer purchasing behavior.

1.4

SOME BASIC DEFINITIONS

Statistics has specialized definitions for terms crucial to statistical reasoning. In **descriptive statistics,** you collect and describe data. If you analyze the data and make decisions or estimates based on information obtained from the data, you are using **inferential statistics.**

Descriptive statistics are used to describe a large set of data. For example, you can reduce the set of data values to one or more single numbers, such as the average of 150 test scores, or you can construct a graph that represents some feature of the data.

You use inferential statistics to form conclusions about a large group—a population—by collecting a portion of it—a sample. Thus, a **population** is the set of all possible measurements (generally pertaining to a group of people or objects) that is of interest. A **sample** is the portion of the population from which information is gathered.

Another way to distinguish between a population and a sample is to view a population as the set of values you would obtain if you observed a particular **variable** indefinitely. For example, this variable could be the total of two dice, and the *population* would consist of the dice totals when the two dice are rolled time and time again. To gain insight into this population, you could observe this variable, say, 100 times; that is, roll the dice 100 times and record the resulting totals. This set of *observations* of

FIGURE

1.1

Population versus
a sample.

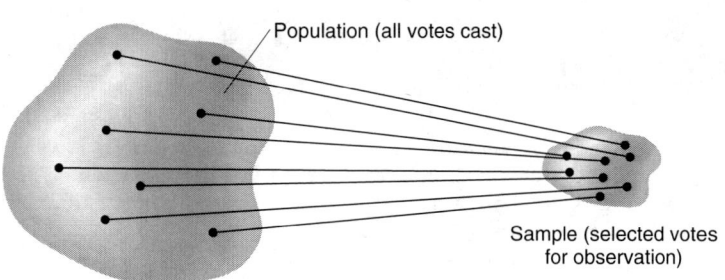

Population (all votes cast)

Sample (selected votes
for observation)

the corresponding variable (total of two dice) results in a *sample*. Consequently, you can view a sample as a set of values obtained by observing a variable of interest a finite number of times. Such variables are actually called *random variables* and will be explored further in Chapters 5 and 6.

The analyst decides what the population is. Typically, the population is so large that it would be nearly impossible to obtain information about every item in it. Instead, we obtain information about selected population members and attempt to draw a conclusion about all members. In other words, we attempt to infer something about the population using information about only some of the members of this population.

To make an early prediction of the election results for governor of California, for example, analysts could use a sample of voters leaving the voting booths, as illustrated in Figure 1.1. The population is all the votes cast in the election. To make a valid statistical inference using a sample, it is crucial that the sample *represent* the population; that is, the values in the sample must be representative (typical) values in the population. One way to make sure the sample is representative is to collect a sample of size *n*, where each set of *n* people has the same chance of being selected for the sample. This is a **simple random sample** (Figure 1.1). It is akin to drawing names out of a hat; each name in the hat has the same chance of being pulled out. Thus, if our population is all votes cast on the day of the gubernatorial election, a sample of votes cast in only one city would not be representative, because we would have no guarantee that these votes would represent the votes of the entire state. A random sample obtained across the entire state would better represent this population.

As another illustration, assume that Calcatron, a producer of electronic calculators, orders 50,000 components from GLC. Calcatron instructs GLC that it will accept the shipment if an outside laboratory that randomly selects 100 components from the batch finds that fewer than 3 are defective. Calcatron relies on inferential statistics; it infers that the population of components is of satisfactory quality if the sample is satisfactory. Note that it is possible that the sample could contain fewer than 3 defective components even if the population contains, say, 80% defective parts. Whenever we attempt to infer something about a population from a sample, there is always a chance of drawing an incorrect conclusion. The only way of being 100% sure is to examine the entire population. Such a sample is called a **census.**

In the Calcatron example, there are two proportions of interest. The first proportion, the proportion of defective components in the *population,* is referred to as a **parameter.** The second proportion, the proportion of defective components in the *sample,* is referred to as a **statistic.** In general, any value describing a population (such as the average or a particular proportion) is a parameter. Parameters typically are unknown and are estimated using the corresponding statistic derived from a statistical sample. In the chapters to follow we will examine a number of sample statistics and their corresponding population parameters.

1.5 DISCRETE AND CONTINUOUS NUMERICAL DATA

Proper use of numerical data can be a great aid in making a critical decision. However, using an improper technique or bad data can lead you down the wrong path. Generally, the technique we use to analyze data in statistics depends on the nature of the data. We can distinguish between two types of numerical data.

How do the following two sets of numbers differ?

3, 5, 2, 1, 4, 4, 3, 5, 5, 1, 2, 4

4.31, 11.62, 5.37, 1.55, 3.71, 6.88, 7.23, 9.52, 2.36, 7.42, 6.11, 4.85

The primary difference is that the values in the first data set consist of *counting numbers,* or *integers.* Such data are **discrete.** For example, these data may be the coded responses from 12 people who answered a particular question in a marketing survey where 1 = strongly agree, 2 = agree, 3 = uncertain, 4 = disagree, and 5 = strongly disagree. Note that discrete data may contain a decimal point. Nevertheless, discrete data have *gaps* in their possible values. For example, if you throw a single die twice and record the average of the two throws, the possible values are 1, 1.5, 2, 2.5, 3, 3.5, 4, 4.5, 5, 5.5, and 6. If you repeatedly averaged two throws of the die, you would obtain discrete data.

Examples of discrete data that have integer values are the number of automobiles that arrive at a drive-up window over a 5-minute period, the number of children in your family, and the total of the two numbers appearing on a throw of two dice. Note that although the first two have infinite (theoretically, at least) possible values, the data are discrete. Your family cannot have 2.5 children.

Now consider the second data set. These data might represent the weights of 12 parcels received at a post office. A list of all the possible values of package weights would be long—if our scale were completely accurate, the list would be infinite and any value would be possible. Such data are **continuous:** *any value* over some particular range is possible. There are no gaps in possible values for continuous data. For example, although we may say Sandra is 5.5 feet tall, we mean her height is about 5.5 feet. In fact, it might be 5.50372 feet. Height data are continuous. Or consider the contents of a coffee cup filled by a vending machine. Will the machine release exactly 6 ounces every time? Certainly not. In fact, if you were to observe the machine fill five such cups and measure the contents to the nearest .001 ounce, you might observe values of 6.031, 5.932, 5.871, 6.353, and 5.612 ounces. Here again, any value between, say, 5.5 ounces and 6.5 ounces is possible: these are continuous data. *Data such as weights, heights, age (actual), and time are generally continuous data and will be used in the examples in the chapters to follow.*

It is important to remember that *discrete data* can be the result of observing a *continuous variable.* For example, actual age is a continuous variable, but if a recorded age is the age at the last birthday, the data will be discrete. Very often, measurements on a continuous variable (such as height in inches) result in discrete data. However, discrete data can also be the result of observing a discrete variable, such as the number of traffic tickets a person has received during the past three years.

To simplify matters, remember that you can use these guidelines in most applications in a business environment:

• Discrete data are the result of *counting* something (such as the number of defective parts or the number of scratches on a newly painted door panel).

• Continuous data are the result of *measuring* something (such as weight or length of time to complete a task).

1.6

LEVEL OF MEASUREMENT FOR NUMERICAL DATA

In addition to classifying numerical data as discrete or continuous, we can also classify these data according to their level of measurement. We will discuss them in order of strength, beginning with the weakest. **Nominal data** are really not numerical at all but are merely labels or assigned values. Examples include gender (1 = male, 2 = female), manufacturer of automobile (1 = General Motors, 2 = Ford, 3 = Toyota), or color of eyes (1 = blue, 2 = green, 3 = brown). Assigning a numerical code to such data is merely a convenience so that, for example, one can store the information in a computer. Therefore, it makes no sense to perform calculations with such numbers, such as finding their average. What would it mean to claim that "the average eye color is 2.73"? This statement is meaningless. Generally, we are interested in the *proportion* of such data in each category. Consider Calcatron's shipment, in which each component is either defective or not defective. We could assign the code 1 = defective, 0 = not defective. The parameter of interest here is p, where p = proportion of defective components in the population of 50,000 components. If Calcatron believes p is too large, it will not accept the shipment. We will consider what is "too large" in Chapter 10.

Ordinal data can be arranged in order such as worst to best, or F to A (grades on an exam). A classic example of ordinal data is the result of a 100-meter dash, where 10 people compete and 1 = the fastest (the winner), 2 = the runner-up, and so on, with 10 = the slowest. Here, the *order* of the values is important (3 finished before 4) but the *difference* of the values is not. For example, $2 - 1 = 1$ and $10 - 9 = 1$, but this does not imply that 1 and 2 were just as close in the final results as were 9 and 10.

The difference between values of **interval data** *does* have meaning. It is meaningful to add and average such data. The classic example is *temperature,* where it is true that the difference in heat between 60° F and 61° F is the same as that between 80° F and 81° F. Many of the techniques used to analyze data in statistics require data that are at least of this strength.

Ratio data differ from interval data in that there is a definite *zero point* that indicates that nothing exists for the variable being measured. To decide if your data are interval or ratio, ask yourself whether twice the value is twice the strength. For example, is 100° F twice as hot as 50° F? The answer is no, so these data are interval. Is a 4-acre field twice as large as a 2-acre field? The answer is yes, so these are ratio data. Here the zero point is a field of 0 acres. An important distinction between interval and ratio data is that for interval data, a value of zero (such as 0° F) is an arbitrary point and does not reflect an absence of the characteristic of interest (such as temperature). Typically, data consisting of areas, counts, volumes, and weights are ratio data. These four levels of measurement are summarized in Table 1.1.

TABLE

1.1

Summary of data levels of measurement.

Property	Level of Measurement			
	Nominal	**Ordinal**	**Interval**	**Ratio**
Order of data is meaningful	N	Y	Y	Y
Difference between data values is meaningful	N	N	Y	Y
Zero point represents total absence	N	N	N	Y

7

FIGURE

1.2
─────
Classifications of
numerical data.

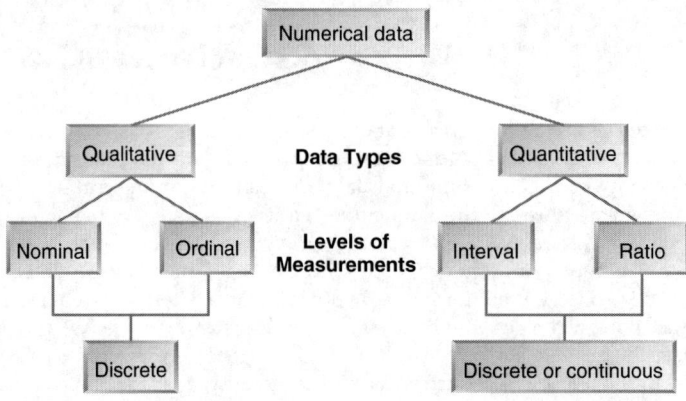

EXAMPLES OF DISCRETE DATA	
1.	Nominal: Ownership status of resident dweller (1 = own, 2 = rent)
2.	Ordinal: Level of customer satisfaction (1 = very dissatisfied, 2 = somewhat dissatisfied, 3 = somewhat satisfied, 4 = very satisfied)
3.	Interval: Person's score on IQ test
4.	Ratio: Number of defective lightbulbs in a carton
EXAMPLES OF CONTINUOUS DATA	
1.	Interval: Actual temperature, °F
2.	Ratio: Weight of packaged dog food

Comments

1. When deciding whether data are interval or ratio, the good news is that techniques used in statistics generally do not distinguish between these two data types; that is, these techniques can be used on interval *or* ratio data.

2. Interval and ratio data are often referred to as **quantitative data** because such data consist of values that naturally take on numerical (quantitative) values (such as age or weight).

3. Nominal and ordinal data can be grouped together under the heading **qualitative data** because they consist essentially of labels that are either unordered (nominal data) or ordered (ordinal data).

A summary of the various data classifications is shown in Figure 1.2. Notice that discrete data can result from any of the four levels of measurement, whereas continuous data can be only interval or ratio.

X Exercises 1.1–1.6

1.1 Give an example of a population of interest to a business manager. Do you think that a business manager would prefer to select a sample from this population or take a census? Why?

1.2 What differentiates ratio data from data that are only interval?

1.3 To generalize the results of a statistical study, what type of statistics is more useful—descriptive statistics or inferential statistics?

1.4 Nielsen Media Research is a popular TV ratings company. This company estimates the number of viewers tuned in to TV programs during specified rating periods.

These estimates are computed from a relatively small random sample of homes selected across the United States. For example, the TV broadcast of the 2003 Academy Awards was estimated to have 37 million viewers with an estimated 25.5% of the TV sets tuned into this program.

    a. To obtain completely accurate figures on the number of viewers and percent share of the homes viewing this program, Nielsen Media Research would need to obtain a census. A disadvantage to using a sample is that only an estimate can be obtained. What are the advantages of obtaining a sample in this case?

    b. What level of measurement would you classify the figures provided to Nielsen Media Research?

    c. What impact do you think these statistics have on advertisers?

(Source: "Nielsen Ratings," *USA Today*, March 24, 2003.)

1.5 Classify each of the following variables as being either qualitative or quantitative and as having nominal, ordinal, interval, or ratio level of measurements:

    a. The time that a chief executive officer spends at work

    b. The ordered preference that investors have for different investment funds for retirement purposes

    c. The state where an individual was born

    d. The average temperature for the summer months in Chicago

    e. The ranking of computer stores with respect to their competitors, based on sales

1.6 An executive within the automotive industry wished to determine the proportion of used import automobiles with odometers that showed less miles than their recorded reading in Japan. A random sample of Japanese imported automobiles revealed that 24% of the odometers had readings that were less than that recorded before being shipped to the United States.

    a. What is the population of interest?

    b. What is the difference between numerical facts and statistics? What does the value of 24% represent?

    c. What type of data is the value of the odometer setting?

    d. Why would a sample be used in this study? Explain.

1.7 OBTAINING A SAMPLE

When it comes time to obtain sample data, a key decision you will need to make is whether to gather data that are obtained in a *random* manner or are obtained using a more deliberate selection procedure. Samples generated using the latter method are *nonrandom samples* and are often referred to as *nonprobability samples*. There are many situations, such as an exploratory study, where you simply want to gain insight into a population of interest rather than make a statistical decision or estimate.

Nonrandom Sampling

You can use a variety of procedures for obtaining a **nonrandom sample** with little or no attention paid to randomization. For example, you may wish to restrict your sample to hand-picked individuals who satisfy a certain requirement, such as individuals over age 50 who have recently been laid off from their jobs. This section will consider three nonrandom sampling strategies: convenience sampling, judgment sampling, and quota sampling.

1. *Convenience sampling.* A **convenience sample** is obtained just as the name implies—in a convenient manner. You may elect to use a group of friends, fellow students in your marketing class, shoppers at a local mall, and so on. Individuals for such a sample are selected based on their presumed resemblance to the population of interest (potential customers of your new product or service) and their ready availability. Such a sample can be extremely valuable in gaining insight into a new idea or the sentiment of a much larger population. If a convenience sample of 20 coworkers indicates that 19 of these 20 people think your idea is not a good one, it's probably time to go back to the drawing board. On the positive side, many a good idea has been born by obtaining information through a convenience sample.

2. *Judgment sampling.* For situations where you want to handpick individuals who satisfy certain requirements or who you believe have expertise regarding the population, a **judgment sample** often works very well. The earlier illustration of laid-off workers over age 50 is an example of a judgment sample, and this group of people may provide excellent insight into problems facing middle-aged employees. Other examples of judgment samples would include divorced individuals or voting districts likely to represent the opinions of the entire state or nation. A certain city may be selected to test market a new product since it is believed that potential customers within this city have buying behaviors that are typical of a much larger population.

3. *Quota sampling.* Quota sampling is a form of nonrandom sampling that is a bit more deliberate in an attempt to obtain a sample that is representative of the entire population. To illustrate this technique, if you know that 60 percent of the registered voters in a particular community are women, you may, in a sample of 100 voters, restrict your sample to 60 women and 40 men. In this way, your sample is a miniature of the population.

Once the criteria have been determined, a judgment sampling technique can then be used to make the sample selection. The sample may in fact not represent the population if care is not taken in obtaining a representative cross-section of people satisfying the sample criteria. Despite this defect of quota sampling, it remains a very popular technique among opinion pollsters, market researchers, and other researchers because it is usually less expensive than obtaining a random sample and takes less time.

Random Sampling

When using a *simple random sample* (usually referred to as a **random sample**), you will need to make sure that every sample of size *n* has the same chance of being selected. One method of doing this is to use a computer to generate random numbers between 1 and *N*, where *N* is the size of the population. For example, you might want to select a set of six numbers between 1 and 50 for a lottery ticket. Here, *n* is 6, and *N* is 50. We will illustrate this procedure in the next section. The main advantage of using a random sample is that the sample results can be extended to estimating something of interest in the population. Furthermore, you can measure and control how reliable this estimate is. *The use of simple random samples will be the primary focus of the chapters to follow.*

The main advantage of random sampling is that you can generalize beyond the sample itself. A result derived from such a sample (such as a recovery amount estimated from an audit) is legally defensible in a court of law. Just the opposite holds for the results of a nonrandom sample—you cannot safely generalize to the entire population, and the results are *not* legally defensible. The main advantages behind the use of nonrandom sampling are that (1) data are more easily obtained, (2) such data may provide you with enough information to make a decision with much less expense, and (3) data from a nonrandom sample can be used as an informal base of knowledge in preparation for a later sample based on random sampling.

Generating a Set of Random Numbers

When obtaining a simple random sample, you will need to generate your sample using a set of random values. A simple method is to utilize a computer-generated list of random digits to determine your sample elements.

To illustrate the process of generating a set of random numbers, consider a situation in which an auditor is responsible for obtaining a random sample of 50 hospital records from a list of 1,000 records, numbered sequentially from 1 to 1,000. For this procedure to work, it is vital that you be able to list sequentially all of the population elements from 1 to 1,000.

Procedures for generating random numbers for each of the three computer packages are explained in the end-of-chapter appendices. The output using Excel is shown in Figure 1.3(a), where column A contains the original data and column B contains the values in increasing order. Column A will likely contain values with a decimal point. These values can be converted to integer values by highlighting column A and repeatedly clicking on the **Decrease**

FIGURE

1.3

Computer-generated Random Numbers (a) Excel output (b) MINITAB output (c) SPSS output.

(a) Book1

	A	B
1	871	108
2	800	233
3	239	239
4	548	251
5	336	336
6	548	525
7	525	548
8	233	548
9	251	800
10	108	871

(b) Worksheet 1 *

	C1	C2
1	794	127
2	221	221
3	127	357
4	844	424
5	543	543
6	922	610
7	718	718
8	610	794
9	357	844
10	424	922

(c)

	counter	values
1	1	142
2	2	44
3	3	622
4	4	154
5	5	715
6	6	928
7	7	579
8	8	263
9	9	725
10	10	38

Decimal icon ( ) until all values are rounded to the nearest integer. To obtain column B, highlight the values in column A and click on **Edit ➤ Copy.** Select cell B1 and click on **Edit ➤ Paste.** Highlight column B and click on the **Sort Ascending** icon ( ).

The values in Figure 1.3(b) were generated using MINITAB. To obtain the sorted values in column C2, click on **Manip ➤ Sort.** Type C1 in the first box, C2 in the second box, C1 in the top **Sort by column** box, and **OK.**

The values in Figure 1.3(c) were generated using SPSS. The values are rounded to the nearest integer by clicking on the **Variable View** tab and setting **Decimals** to zero. To sort the data, click on **Data ➤ Sort cases.** Click on **values,** the right arrow button , and **OK.**

X Exercises 1.7–1.11

1.7 Primary sources are those where data are obtained from "hands-on" experience, such as questionnaires or designed experiments. Secondary sources represent sources containing data collected as part of a regularly scheduled data collection procedure, such as government reports or industry financial statements. Would telephone interviews conducted during a class project to obtain data on the satisfaction of college graduates with their first job be an example of primary or secondary data?

1.8 A sports medicine researcher wants to determine if there was a difference among athletes who were primarily runners, swimmers, or cyclists with regard to the amount of muscle discomfort experienced during their activities. Does this researcher need to obtain random samples of athletes from each category? What effect would a convenience sample have on the results of the experiment?

1.9 To obtain information, primary or secondary sources are used. For each of the following statements, indicate the company's most likely source of information.

 a. "The majority of the employees of our company are willing to work in self-directed work teams to achieve a 10% reduction in administrative cost."

 b. "Last year, the 4.2 million tons of steel imported by the United States had a significant impact on the earnings of all American steel companies, including our own."

 c. "Our company conducted a poll of 1,000 of its employees. The poll indicates that the company's president enjoys increasing popularity among all employees of the company."

 d. "The Value Line Survey has recently given our company the highest ranking for price appreciation."

1.10 The sales of luxury-car maker BMW were 220,000 units during the first quarter of 2001 versus 200,000 units during the first quarter of 2000. With the economic slowdown in the United States during 2001, high-level management at BMW was concerned that this upward trend would not continue because demand for mid-price cars of the American auto makers had already slipped. Suppose management selected four dealerships in the New York City and Boston metropolitan areas to sample prospective buyers to determine if they planned to delay purchase of a luxury car due to a slowdown in the economy. Would you consider this to be a convenience sample? How do you think management should randomly select dealerships to conduct a survey?

(Source: "BMW's Net Helped by Robust U.S. Sales," *The Wall Street Journal*, August 8, 2001, p. A8.)

1.11 [DATA SET EX1-11] *Variable Description:*

ZipCodes: A list of Zip codes from the Memphis Metropolitan area

A property manager in Memphis is interested in the average rental price for a three-bedroom house. The property manager takes note of the latest surveys showing the average housing costs by renters for a three-bedroom house. In 2001, this cost was $549. However, the property manager believes that this cost might be higher in the Memphis metropolitan area. The manager decides to do a survey of homes in selected areas of Memphis to determine the cost of renting a three-bedroom home. From the list of 70 Zip codes in this data set, the manager will first select 20 at random and then select five three-bedroom homes that are being rented within these 20 zip codes .

a. Explain why a random sample of 20 Zip codes would be better than using the first 20 Zip codes in the list of 70 Zip codes.

b. Use computer software to determine a random sample of these Zip codes. In Excel, click on **Tools ➤ Data Analysis ➤ Random Number Generation** and choose the uniform distribution. In MINITAB, click on **Calc ➤ Random Data ➤ Uniform.** In SPSS, click on **Data ➤ Select Cases ➤ Random Sample** and select 20 out of the 70 cases.

(Source: "How Much Renting Costs," *USA Today*, July 11, 2001, p. 1A.)

 # Summary

Decision making using statistical procedures continues to grow in popularity, because calculators and computers make it easy to avoid "seat-of-the pants" decisions by analyzing sample results in a scientific manner. Contemporary applications (e.g., should a particular company accept an outside shipment of components based on a sample of these components?) can be found in a variety of business disciplines.

The science of statistics comprises a set of rules and procedures used to describe numerical data or to make decisions based on these data. The group of measurements that are of interest define the population. The portion of a population selected for observation is a sample. Descriptive statistics is concerned only with collecting and describing data. Inferential statistics is used when tentative conclusions about a population are drawn on the basis of data contained in a representative sample.

Numerical data are either discrete or continuous. A further classification of data is their level of measurement (nominal, ordinal, interval, or ratio). Nominal data are the weakest data, and ratio data are the strongest.

Most statistical methods assume that a simple random sample of size n has been collected. Nonrandom samples (convenience samples, judgment samples, and quota samples) are samples selected in a convenient or deliberate manner, with little or no attention paid to randomization. Random numbers can be easily generated using a computer package, such as Excel, MINITAB, or SPSS.

 ## On the CD

Section 1.8: Business Research Questions in Practice
Section 1.9: Designing and Coding a Questionnaire
Exercises 1.12–1.20

X Review Exercises 1.21–1.33

1.21 An operations manager at a semiconductor company is interested in the satisfaction level of the firms that buy computer chips from the company. Approximately 1,000 firms buy chips from this company. The manager has developed a satisfaction scale from 1 to

100 for the respondents to mark their level of satisfaction with the company's products. This scale is to be included on a survey to a sample of 100 firms that buy from this firm.

    a. What is the population of interest?
    b. How can a random sample be selected?
    c. What is the parameter of the population that is of interest?
    d. What is the statistic corresponding to the parameter requested in part (c)?

1.22 Referring to Exercise 1.7, are the following data sources primary or secondary?

    a. Data collected during a manufacturing process to determine the proportion of defective items produced
    b. Data published by the U.S. Bureau of Census in *Statistical Abstracts of the United States*
    c. Data collected by management to determine the acceptability of a new policy by its employees
    d. Data published in *Standard & Poor's* on the financial liabilities of energy service companies

1.23 America Online raised the price of its flagship online service by 9% during the summer of 2001, potentially adding hundreds of millions of dollars to its annual revenues. Management was concerned that some of its online users would start to seek out its lower-priced competitors. The chief executive officer was interested in estimating the percentage of users who thought that this increase would cause them to discontinue using its online service. A survey could be conducted to estimate this percentage.

    a. What is the population of interest?
    b. How might a random sample of users be selected for a survey?
    c. Do you think a convenience sample or a random sample would be a better way to obtain an estimate of the percentage of users that would likely discontinue the online service?

(Source: "America Online Boots Price for Flagship Service," *Wall Street Journal,* May 23, 2001, p A3.)

1.24 Financial planning is a dynamic process that starts with the identification of an individual's specific goals. Personal data are gathered to determine the extent to which a person can achieve these goals. In a recent survey, more than 50% of working individuals identified extensive travel as a specific goal during their golden years and approximately 60% identified a particular hobby that they want to pursue. List some questions that you believe may help individuals think about goals for retirement. For example, how much do you plan on spending for travel during your retirement? For which of your questions would you consider the response to be descriptive? Which of your responses would allow you to calculate a numerical average?

(Source: "Great Expectations for Aging," *USA Today,* August 7, 2001, p. 1D.)

1.25 Determine whether each of the following groups of people or objects represents a population or a sample.

    a. A list of 500 employees of General Motors (*Hint:* Could this be either a sample or a population? Explain.)
    b. Forty students who were randomly stopped and questioned on a university campus
    c. Two hundred people who were selected randomly from a telephone book to receive a marketing questionnaire
    d. The list of all possible choices of 2 cards from a deck of 52 cards
    e. A batch of electronic parts ready for inspection

1.26 Typically after live presidential candidate debates on network television, there appears a phone number for viewers to call and state which candidate performed the best. Would this be considered a simple random sample? a convenience sample? Why?

1.27 Dr. Ronald Kessler, a researcher at Harvard Medical School, reports that health conditions of workers cost industry 2.5 billion days each year. Besides fighting increases in health care costs, employers are concerned about how health care education can help improve the day-to-day efficiency of their workers. Assume that a health care professional was contracted to collect information from workers at an automotive assembly factory.

The following items are examples of questions. What type of data and which level of measurement would you classify each response? Explain how descriptive statistics might be used to summarize the findings.

    a. How many times do you perform physical fitness exercise per week?
    b. Approximately how many times do you see a doctor per year?
    c. Do you fall asleep easily at night and sleep soundly?
    d. Do you enjoy your current work (always, sometimes, usually not, never)?
    e. Do you consume less than two glasses of water per day, at least two but less than four, or at least four?
    f. How many pounds do you think you should lose to be considered healthy?

(Source: "Programs Aim to Keep Staffers Healthy and on the Job," *Dallas Morning News,* June 21, 2001, p. 1D.)

1.28 Upscale retailer Neiman Marcus announced in the summer of 2001 that it hoped to profit from adding a store at the newly constructed 1.3-million-square-foot retail center in San Antonio's North Star mall. Tourists spend an average of $1,083 per trip to San Antonio. Neiman Marcus would like to lure these tourists to its new store after they are finished viewing the sights. Suppose that a random sample of tourists visiting the Alamo were selected to answer the following questions. Classify each of the requested data items as either qualitative or quantitative and give the appropriate level of measurement.

    a. How often do you believe you will visit San Antonio over the next three years?
    b. Is the amount of money that you will spend in San Antonio during your visit less than $500, at least $500 but less than $1,000, at least $1,000 but less than $1,500, at least $1,500 but less than $2,000, or more than $2,000?
    c. How much time will you spend shopping during your visit?
    d. What is the name of the store that you are most likely to go shopping in while visiting San Antonio?
    e. Rank your three most favorite activities during this trip.

(Source: "Elegant Ideas," *Dallas Morning News,* June 14, 2001, p. 1D.)

1.29 At the end of 2000, Apple, the erstwhile leading supplier of computers to schools, realized that it grossly overestimated demand for the pricey Power Macintosh G4 Cube. Revenues slumped by 57% for the year. In 2001, Apple had a new hot product, the Titanium Power-Book laptop, or TiBook. Suppose you are working for the marketing department of Apple and are asked to conduct a sample survey on how satisfied purchasers are with the new product.

    a. What is the population of interest?
    b. Describe a procedure to select a random sample.
    c. Write three questions for the survey to gather information on demographics and three questions to gather information on how satisfied the customer is with the product.
    d. What incentive might be appropriate to encourage customers to complete the survey?
    e. What follow-up action might achieve a higher response rate?

(Source: "Steve Jobs: The Graying Price of a Shrinking Kingdom," *Fortune,* May 14, 2001, pp. 118–131.)

1.30 Marketing researchers often use a list for drawing simple random samples of consumers to assess a new product. To illustrate one way of selecting a random sample from a list of members, perform the following procedure. In Excel, type a 1 in A1 and a 2 in A2. Highlight both A1 and A2. Now drag the handle on the highlighted region down to row 100. Think of the 100 numbers as representing 100 consumers on a list. Click on **Tools ➤ Data Analysis ➤ Sampling.** Now select the 100 numbers in the first column for input (A1: A200) and click on Random and type in 10. Select an output cell (say, B1). Then click **OK.** Note that the 10 numbers displayed represent a random sample from the population of 100 members.

1.31 **[DATA SET EX1-31]** *Variable Description:*
Rank: Ranking of companies with 1 assigned to the fastest growing
Company: Name of Company
Revenue: Annual Revenue

Fortune (www.fortune.com) publishes annually the fastest-growing companies. This data set contains a list of 100 of the fastest-growing small companies having annual revenue of less than $200 million. Use random numbers to select 20 companies and record their ranks. Do the ranks appear to be random? Can you think of another way to select 20 companies at random that uses a more systematic approach?

1.32 [DATA SET EX1-32] *Variable Description:*
Question: Question with response categories
NumberOfResponses: Number of responses to each category

A leading Web infrastructure software company, named Zend Technologies Ltd., serves as a leader in sales for PHP (acronym for Hypertext Preprocessor). This data set is adapted from a survey obtained from its Web site *(www.zend.com)*. What is the level of measurement for each of the questions? Why? Can you think of two additional questions for the survey that would contain either ordinal or ratio data?

1.33 Look at the issues that are in the news at *www.pollingreport.com*. For example, pollsters are interested in such topics as whether the U.S. government should allow illegal immigrants to work in the United States. Explain what data collection technique you would use to collect information on these issues: Telephone, mail, e-mail, and/or door-to-door. Discuss the advantages and disadvantages of each technique with respect to time, cost, and reliability.

Computer Exercises Using the Databases

Exercise 1—Appendix F

For each of the variables defined in the database of household financial variables, determine if the corresponding data would be classified as discrete or continuous.

Exercise 2—Appendix F

For each of the variables in the database of household financial variables, what is the highest level of measurement for the corresponding data?

Exercise 3—Appendix F

For each of the variables defined in the database of household variables, would you classify the corresponding data as qualitative or quantitative?

Exercise 4—Appendix G

Answer exercises 1 through 3 for each variable defined in the database using the financial variables on companies.

Insights from Statistics in Action

Online Surveys: E-xpress Yourself

The introductory case study in Statistics in Action discussed the ever-increasing use of the Internet as a means of obtaining survey information from customers and Web site visitors. This survey method provides for faster data collection at a much lower cost. Using the concepts introduced in this chapter, answer the following questions.

1. Suppose that the manager at Direct Marketing Services wishes to construct a survey on the experiences that consumers have after the purchase of a Chevrolet Suburban. List two questions, one with a qualitative response and one with a quantitative response, for each of the following areas in which a dealership might be interested: (1) financing of the vehicle by purchaser, (2) information about a purchaser's previously owned vehicles, (3) satisfaction with the purchase experience, and (4) satisfaction with the vehicle.

2. Suppose that a health care administrator wishes to obtain information on the service provided by a children's health center. What do you think the population of interest would be? Give an example of discrete and continuous data that could be obtained from a survey requesting information on the service provided by the health center.

3. Here are some questions that a *Wall Street Journal* poll might use in a survey. Which level of measurement would you classify each response?

   a. Are you a voting citizen?
   b. What is your mortgage payment?
   c. How much money have you saved in a Roth IRA?
   d. How long have you owned your home?
   e. Would you say that your confidence in the current government administration is 1, very high; 2, somewhat high; 3, low; or 4, very low?

   f. List your favorite three TV commercials.
   g. Rank your favorite three TV commercials in the order in which you believe that they are creative.

4. Suppose that a major hotel chain has a Web site that allows visitors to rate the services of its facilities. List examples of questions for this survey that would be useful to the hotel chain's management. What is the level of measurement for the responses to each of these questions?

Source: "Poll Position," *The Washington Post*, August 1, 2004, p. W.08. "The Wall Street Journal/NBC News Poll," *The Wall Street Journal*, April 14, 2003, p. A4. "The 2000 Internet Survey," *Mortgage Banking*, vol. 61, no. 1, 2000, pp. 42–53. "Study: On-Line Surveys Effective," *Direct Marketing*, vol. 61, no. 7, 1998, p. 8.

Appendix

Generating Random Numbers

Excel

A set of random numbers can be obtained using Excel's Analysis ToolPak. Using this add-in, select the **Tools** menu from the menu bar. Select **Data Analysis ➤ Random Number Generation** and then click OK. The following dialog box will appear. The 10 indicates the number of random numbers you wish to generate for each random variable. If the dialog box is filled in as given in this example, 10 random numbers between 1 and 1,000 for one random variable will be generated with the results appearing in column A and starting in cell A1. These random numbers will include decimals. In Excel 2003, the decimal can be removed by using the **Decrease Decimal** icon. The output will look like that given in Figure 1.3(a).

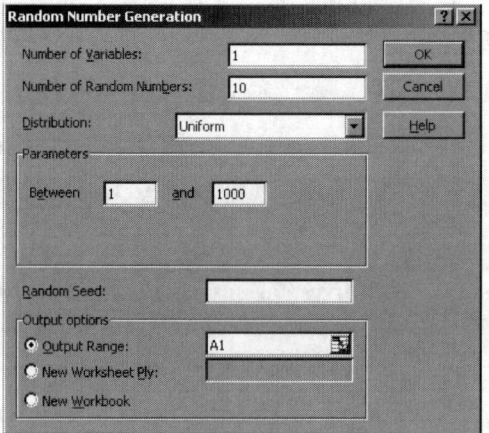

Minitab

A set of random numbers can be generated in MINITAB by using the **Calc** menu on the menu bar. Select **Random Data ➤ Integer** and the following dialog box will appear. If the dialog box is filled in as given in this example, 10 random numbers between 1 and 1,000 for one random variable will be generated in column C1. These numbers will be integers, so no adjustment is necessary to remove decimals. The output will look like that given in Figure 1.3(b).

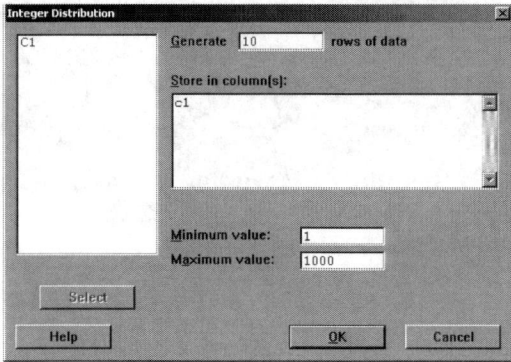

SPSS

To generate 10 random values between 1 and 1,000, begin by typing 1 through 10 in the first column of a blank data worksheet and name this variable "counter." Click on **Transform ➤ Compute.** In the following **Compute Variable** screen, type **Value** in the **Target Variable** box. From the list on the right-hand-side, double-click on RV.UNIFORM(min,max) and replace the question marks in what appears in the **Numeric Expression** box with 1 and 1,000. Click on **OK.** The result is the screen in Figure 1.3(c). To get 10 random *integers* between 1 and 1,000, click on the **Variable View** tab and set the number of decimal places (in the column labeled Decimals) equal to zero for the Value variable.

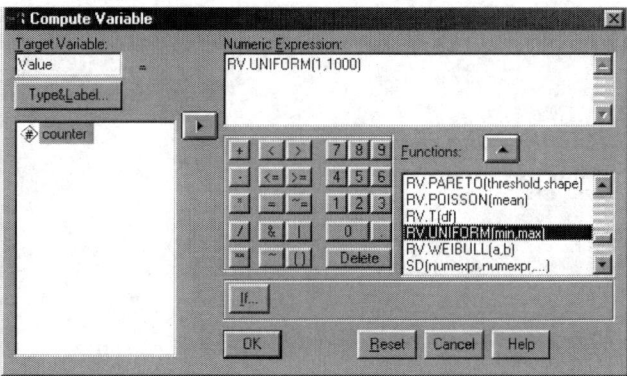

chapter

2

Data Presentation Using Descriptive Graphs

Statistics in Action
Lean Philosophy Drives Productivity Growth

Productivity growth, usually defined as getting more output from every hour worked, has been identified as key to sustaining the economy and raising living standards. Both service and manufacturing companies are giving managers and workers special incentives in an effort to encourage company output and reward gains in productivity. Companies have realized that output is a team effort. As a consequence, 86% of companies in the service sector have an output award initiative in place for workers, while 68% of the manufacturing companies have similar programs.

Some of the biggest gains in productivity have resulted from management decisions that often seem brilliant in hindsight. For example, AutoNation USA's used car megastores, where haggling and hassling are not allowed and salespeople are trained in communication instead of intimidation, made the difficult decision to overhaul its used-car megastores by coupling them with new-car franchises. That resulted in AutoNation's employment being reduced from 47,100 to 33,000 over a couple of years. The action increased revenue per employee by 82%. When PepsiCo sold its restaurant operations (Taco Bell, Pizza Hut, and KFC restaurants), its employment was reduced by 74% with only a 25% drop in assets. Although its revenue did decrease, its revenue per worker showed an increase in productivity by 33%.

When you have completed this chapter, you will be able to examine the total productivity gains of major corporations and discuss these questions:

- How can productivity figures be presented graphically in a form that is easy to understand?

- What does the *frequency distribution* of productivity figures reveal?

- How can *bar charts* be used to describe the average productivity for various industries?

- What makes certain graphs *deceptive?*

FREQUENCY DISTRIBUTIONS

We need to reduce a large set of data to a much smaller set of numbers that can be more easily comprehended. If you have recorded the population sizes of 500 randomly selected cities, there is no easy way to examine these 500 numbers visually and learn anything. It would be easier to examine a condensed version of this set of data, such as that presented in Table 2.1.

This type of summary, called a **frequency distribution,** consists of classes (such as "10,000 and under 15,000") and frequencies (the number of data values within each class). The last class (50,000 and over) is referred to as an **open-ended class.** Such a class is useful whenever the first or last class contains one or more unusually large or small values. What do you gain using a frequency distribution? You reduce 500 numbers to 10 classes and frequencies. You can study the frequency distribution in Table 2.1 and learn a great deal about the shape of this data set. For example, approximately 50% of the cities in your sample have a population between 20,000 and 35,000. Also, only 1% of the cities contain 50,000 people or more.

A frequency distribution is typically condensed from data having an interval or ratio level of measurement. When you construct a frequency distribution for continuous data, you need to decide how many classes to use (10 in Table 2.1) and the class width (5,000 in Table 2.1).

There is no "correct" number of classes (K) to use in a frequency distribution. However, you can best condense a set of data by using between 5 and 20 classes. The usual procedure is to choose what you think would be an adequate number of classes and to construct the resulting frequency distribution. A quick look at this distribution will tell you if you have reduced the data too much (not enough classes; K is too small) or not enough (too many classes; K is too large). One indication that K is too small is that a large portion of your data (say, nearly 50%) lies in one class. If you observe a number of empty classes, or many classes with a frequency of 1 or 2, this may indicate that K is too large. If you have a very large set of data, you can use a larger number of classes than you would for a smaller data set. Whenever you construct frequency distributions using a computer, select several different values of K and look at the effects of the different choices.

Class Number	Size of City	Frequency
1	Under 10,000	4
2	10,000 and under 15,000	51
3	15,000 and under 20,000	77
4	20,000 and under 25,000	105
5	25,000 and under 30,000	84
6	30,000 and under 35,000	60
7	35,000 and under 40,000	45
8	40,000 and under 45,000	38
9	45,000 and under 50,000	31
10	50,000 and over	5
		500

TABLE

2.1

Frequency distribution of the population of 500 cities.

Having chosen a value for K, the next step is to examine

$$\frac{\text{range}}{\text{number of classes}} = \frac{H - L}{K}$$

where H = the highest value in your data and L = the lowest value in your data. Round the result to a value that provides an easy-to-interpret frequency distribution. This is the *class width (CW)*. The width of each class should be the same. Later we will discuss possible exceptions to this rule for the first and last classes.

DEFINITION

Class width *(CW)* = the value of $\dfrac{H - L}{K}$ rounded (up or down) to a value that is easy to interpret.

Suppose that, for a particular set of data, you have elected to use $K = 10$ classes in your frequency distribution and that $H = 106$ and $L = 10$. Then

$$\frac{H - L}{K} = \frac{106 - 10}{10} = 9.6$$

The desirable class width to use here is $CW = 10$.

Here are some additional examples of rounding to determine the class width:

$\dfrac{H - L}{K}$	Rounded Value (the *CW*)
89.6	100
1.38	1.5
48.2	50
12.4	10

Now let us use the 50 salaries in Table 2.2 to construct a frequency distribution of the salaries, using six classes. Our first step should be to arrange the data from smallest to largest. This arrangement is called an **ordered array.** Both the original data and the ordered data are *raw data,* because they are not grouped into classes. The ordered salaries are listed in Table 2.3. Using the ordered data, $H = 43.8$ and $L = 32.8$. Since $K = 6$, we compute *CW:*

$$\frac{43.8 - 32.8}{6} = 1.83$$

The best choice for class width is $CW = 2$.

There are two rules to remember in selecting the first class: This class must contain L, your lowest data value, and it should begin with a value that makes the frequency distribution easy to interpret. Because $L = 32.8$, our first class should begin with 32, that is, $32,000. The resulting frequency distribution is shown in Table 2.4, which also shows each **relative frequency,** where

$$\text{Relative frequency} = \frac{\text{Frequency}}{\text{Total number of values in data set}}$$

TABLE

2.2

Starting salaries for graduating business majors at Bellaire College.

Major	No. of Graduating Students	Starting Salary (thousands of dollars)						
Accounting	26	41.5	39.4	40.9	35.9	37.4	39.5	40.3
		39.3	41.6	36.6	41.1	35.7	43.7	37.0
		41.3	40.6	38.0	42.4	35.7	41.4	39.2
		36.8	39.3	43.8	38.5	43.0		
Information systems	10	36.3	35.6	36.2	38.1	34.8	38.1	35.7
		36.5	39.5	37.9				
Marketing	14	34.3	36.8	33.8	35.0	37.8	38.7	37.2
		32.8	38.2	37.0	39.7	38.8	35.2	36.2

TABLE

2.3

Fifty starting salaries for business majors at Bellaire College, presented as original data and as an ordered array.

Raw Data					Ordered Array				
41.5	39.4	40.9	35.9	37.4	32.8	33.8	34.3	34.8	35.0
39.5	40.3	39.3	41.6	36.6	35.2	35.6	35.7	35.7	35.7
41.1	35.7	43.7	37.0	41.3	35.9	36.2	36.2	36.3	36.5
40.6	38.0	42.4	35.7	41.4	36.6	36.8	36.8	37.0	37.0
39.2	36.8	39.3	43.8	38.5	37.2	37.4	37.8	37.9	38.0
43.0	36.3	35.6	36.2	38.1	38.1	38.1	38.2	38.5	38.7
34.8	38.1	35.7	36.5	39.5	38.8	39.2	39.3	39.3	39.4
37.9	34.3	36.8	33.8	35.0	39.5	39.5	39.7	40.3	40.6
37.8	38.7	37.2	32.8	38.2	40.9	41.1	41.3	41.4	41.5
37.0	39.7	38.8	35.2	36.2	41.6	42.4	43.0	43.7	43.8

For example, in class 2 the relative frequency is .18; this class contains 9 of the 50 values. The advantage of using relative frequencies is that the reader can tell immediately what percentage of the data values lies in each class.

Comments

Often a set of data contains one or two very small or very large numbers quite unlike the remaining data values. Such values are called **outliers.** It is generally better to include these values in one or two open-ended classes. The distribution in Table 2.1 contains two open-ended classes: class 1 (under 10,000) and class 10 (50,000 and over). *You may need an open-ended class if your data set includes one or more outliers or your current frequency distribution has too many empty classes on the low or high end.*

The highest and lowest values describing a class are the **class limits.** For example, in Table 2.4, the lower class limit of class 2 is 34, and the upper class limit is 36. The **class midpoints** are those values in the center of the class.* Each midpoint, in a sense, *represents* its class. These values often are used in a statistical graph, as well as for calculations performed on the information contained within a frequency distribution. The midpoint of class 2 in Table 2.4 is $(34 + 36)/2 = 35$.

*Class midpoints are often referred to as *class marks*.

TABLE				
2.4	**Class Number**	**Class**	**Frequency**	**Relative Frequency**
Frequency distribution of starting salaries using six classes.	1	32 and under 34	2	.04
	2	34 and under 36	9	.18
	3	36 and under 38	13	.26
	4	38 and under 40	14	.28
	5	40 and under 42	8	.16
	6	42 and under 44	4	.08
			50	1.00

CONSTRUCTING A FREQUENCY DISTRIBUTION

1. Gather the sample data.
2. Arrange the data in an ordered array.
3. Select the number of classes to be used.
4. Determine the class width.
5. Determine the class limits for each class; begin by assigning to the first class a lower class limit that will make the frequency distribution easy to interpret.
6. Count the number of data values in each class (the class frequencies).
7. Summarize the class frequencies in a frequency distribution table.

X Exercises 2.1–2.7

Understanding the Mechanics

2.1 The following frequency table indicates the number of individuals with a minimum balance in their checkbook at a local bank.

Minimum Balance in Dollars	Frequency
0 and under 1,000	1,200
1,000 and under 2,000	1,500
2,000 and under 3,000	2,500
3,000 and under 4,000	2,300
4,000 and under 5,000	500
5,000 and under 6,000	50
6,000 and under 7,000	10
7,000 and under 8,000	2

a. What is the class width?
b. What are the class limits?
c. Calculate the group relative frequencies of each group.

2.2 The monthly down time in minutes for a Web site for 24 months is as follows. Construct a frequency distribution with seven classes.

30	25	14	45
68	32	12	15
27	35	44	57
5	25	46	33
17	51	47	44
29	32	38	54

2.3 A random sample of two-bedroom condominium apartments at Vera Beach, Florida, revealed that the asking price of units on the market varied from $111,000 to $224,000. A frequency distribution of the asking price of the condominiums is needed.

a. Set up class limits if 5 classes are desired.
b. Set up class limits if 6 classes are desired.
c. Set up class limits if 12 classes are desired.

Applying the New Concepts

2.4 The percentages of increase in the property tax of 26 randomly selected homes in a certain subdivision of Memphis, Tennessee, are as follows.

5.10	7.35	13.34	18.19	9.12
9.89	10.45	12.89	17.91	.51
3.42	8.34	11.12	14.51	7.25
12.35	11.89	14.10	29.1	14.91
11.89	17.89	15.30	26.1	19.80
18.45				

a. Construct a relative frequency distribution with six classes.

b. From the relative frequency distribution, determine what proportion of homes had an increase of more than 15% in property tax.

c. What interpretation can you give to the shape of the distribution?

2.5 The U.S. Office of Employment Projections conducted a population survey to determine the characteristics about the work force. In its survey, a tabulation was performed to state the number of multiple job holders (in thousands) and their respective weekly earnings. The results are presented below.

Weekly Earnings	Number of Multiple Job Holders
$0 and under $211	1,462
$211 and under $334	1,295
$334 and under $493	1,354
$493 and under $730	1,297
$730 and higher	1,288

a. What do you achieve by tabulating the data in the form of a frequency distribution?

b. Form a relative frequency distribution.

c. What proportion of the multiple job holders were making $493 or more per week?

Using the Computer

2.6 [DATA SET EX2-6] *Variable Description:*

Insurance Company: Name of life and health insurance company

Revenue: Revenue in millions of dollars for 2003

The annual revenues in 2003 for 13 top global life and health insurance companies are displayed on the *Fortune* Web site *(www.fortune.com)*. Construct a relative frequency histogram using seven classes and comment on the shape of the distribution.

2.7 [DATA SET EX2-7] *Variable Description:*

Company: A company in the portfolio of the Money Index of Stocks

P/E: Price-to-earnings ratio

Money magazine tracks the performance of its Money Index of Stocks. In addition to the performance of the stocks in this index, *Money* also keeps track of the price-to-earnings (P/E) ratios. By definition, a P/E ratio is simply the price of the common stock divided by its earnings per share. Investors use this measure as one gauge of risk. For example, a company with disappointing sales and a P/E greater than 100 may experience a substantial downturn because of the high expectations for that stock.

a. Display the data using a frequency histogram. Use a class width of 5 and let 15 be the lower endpoint of the first class.

b. Repeat part a, but use a class width of 7. How has the shape of the histogram changed?

c. What do you hope to accomplish by displaying the data in the form of a histogram?

(Source: "The Truth About P/E . . . ," *Money*, September 14, 2004.)

HISTOGRAMS AND STEM-AND-LEAF DIAGRAMS

2.2

Histograms

After you complete a frequency distribution, your next step will be to construct a picture of these data values using a histogram. A **histogram** is a graphical representation of a frequency distribution. It describes the shape of the data. You can use it to answer quickly such questions as, are the data symmetric? and, where do most of the data values lie? For the frequency distribution in Table 2.4, the corresponding histogram is illustrated in Figure 2.1. The height of each bar represents the frequency of that particular class, and the bars must be adjoining (no gaps).

Avoid constructing a "squashed" histogram by using the vertical axis wisely. The top of this axis (15 in Figure 2.1) should be a value close to your largest class frequency (14). Notice also that, for this example, you obtain a more concise picture by starting the horizontal axis at 32 rather than at zero and putting a scale break ($\sqrt{}$) before the 32 mark.

FIGURE

2.1

Frequency histogram for the frequency distribution shown in Table 2.4. Of 50 salaries, 27 were between $36,000 and $40,000, with 12 people receiving $40,000 or more.

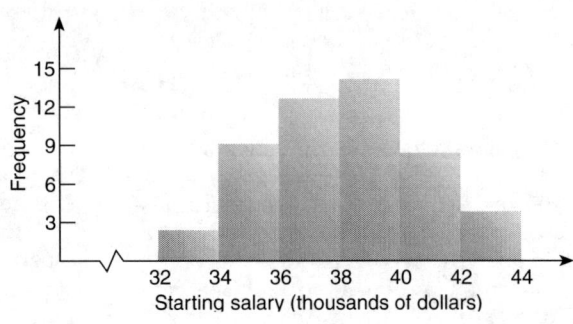

FIGURE

2.2

Relative frequency histogram for the frequency distribution in Table 2.4. This histogram shows that 54% (26% plus 28%) of the salaries were between $36,000 and $40,000, and 24% (16% plus 8%) of the people received $40,000 or more.

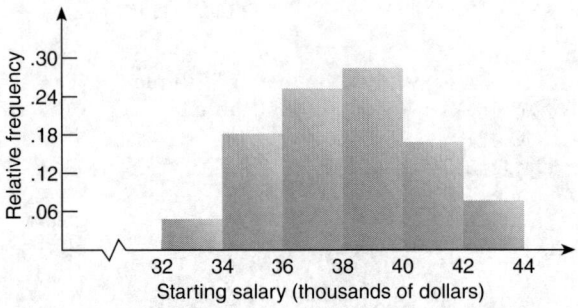

A histogram can be constructed using the relative frequencies rather than the frequencies. A *relative frequency histogram* of the salary distribution in Table 2.4 is shown in Figure 2.2. Notice that the shape of a frequency histogram (Figure 2.1) and its corresponding relative frequency histogram (Figure 2.2) are the same. One advantage of using a relative frequency histogram is that the units on the vertical axis are always between zero and one, so the reader can tell at a glance what percentage of the data lies in each class.

Most standard statistical packages will construct a histogram of your sample data. Using the Excel macro provided with this textbook,* or using MINITAB or SPSS, you can control the number of classes and the class width in your histogram. The Excel histogram in Figure 2.3 can be obtained by clicking on **KPK Data Analysis ➤ Quantitative Data Charts/Tables ➤ Histogram/Freq. Charts** and following the instructions contained in the end-of-chapter Excel appendix. Inputs for the MINITAB histogram (Figure 2.4) and the SPSS histogram (Figure 2.5) are also described in the end-of-chapter appendices. To obtains Excel's version of the histogram in Figure 2.1, refer to the input screen described in the end-of-chapter Excel appendix and click on **Number of Classes** (enter "6") and

---

*An Excel macro is a set of instructions that greatly simplifies an Excel graph or statistical procedure. These macros will be invisible to you but are available whenever you click on **KPK Data Analysis** in the menu bar at the top of your Excel screen.

FIGURE

2.3

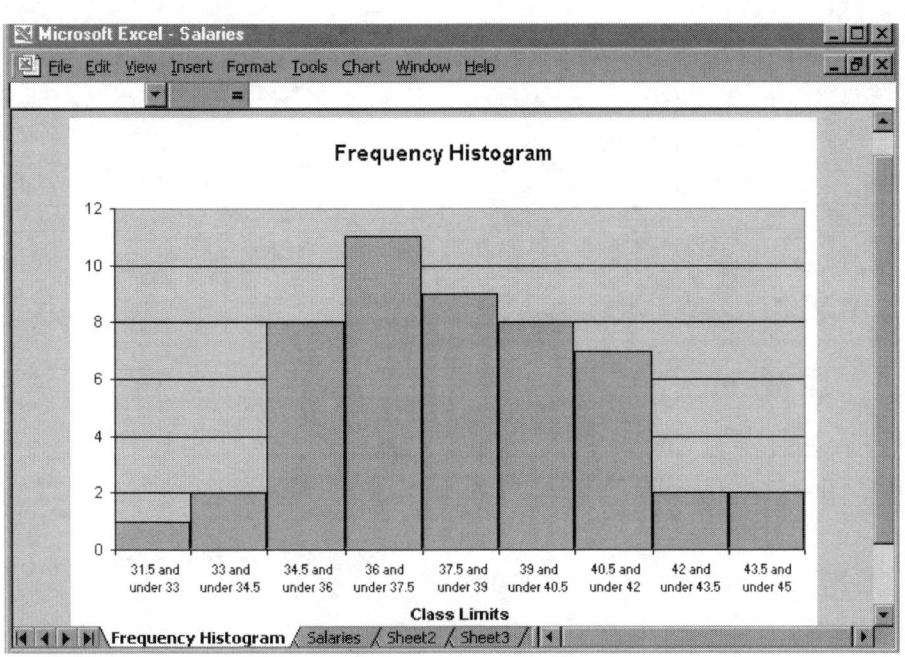

FIGURE

2.4

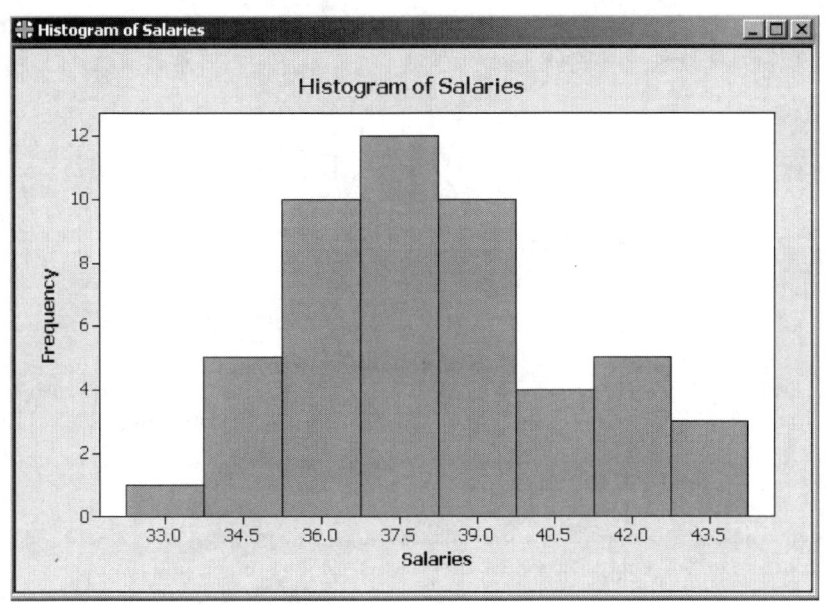

FIGURE

2.5

SPSS histogram for the salary data in Table 2.3.

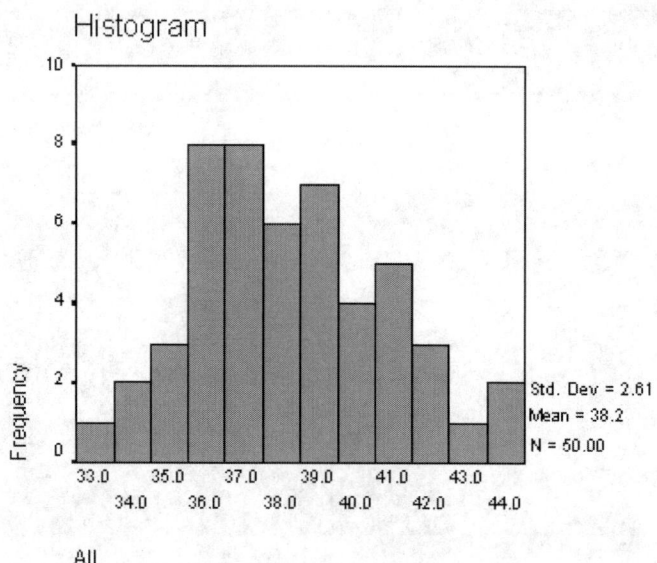

FIGURE

2.6

Excel spreadsheet created by KPK Data Analysis procedure where number of classes is 6 and class width is 2.

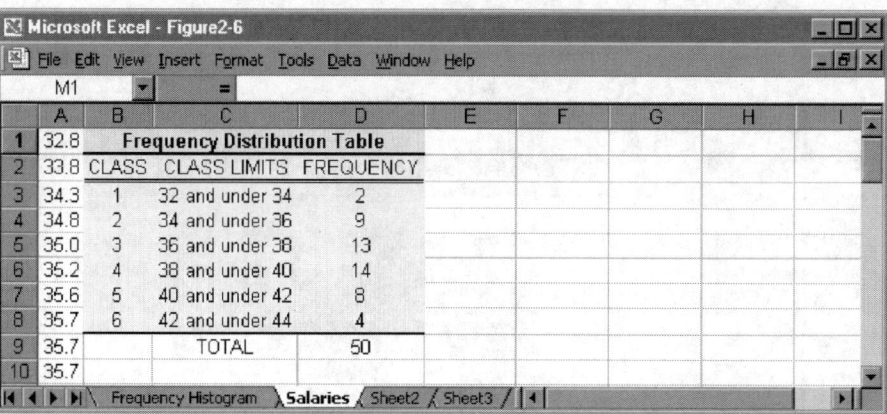

Class Width (enter "2"), followed by **OK.** You should see the the frequency distribution in Figure 2.6, and the histogram will be an Excel version of the histogram in Figure 2.1.**

Stem-and-Leaf Diagrams

Stem-and-leaf diagrams were originally developed by John Tukey (pronounced Too'key) of Princeton University. They are extremely useful in summarizing reasonably sized data sets (under 150 values as a general rule) and, unlike histograms, result in no loss of information. By this we mean that it is possible to retrieve the original data set from a stem-

---

**The Excel frequency distribution and histogram provided by the KPK Data Analysis procedure attempts to derive an easy-to-interpret table and graph, as stressed in the chapter discussion. As a result, a lot of rounding to "nice numbers" takes place, and the final frequency distribution and histogram may contain slightly more (or less) classes than you specified. If you specified a class width, it will not be changed.

FIGURE

2.7

Stem-and-leaf
diagram for after-
tax profits.

Stem	Leaf (unit = .1)
2	3 4 7
3	4 4 6 8
4	1 5 7
5	1 9

TABLE

2.5

Ordered array
of aptitude test
scores for
50 applicants.

22	44	56	68	78
25	44	57	68	78
28	46	59	69	80
31	48	60	71	82
34	49	61	72	83
35	51	63	72	85
39	53	63	74	88
39	53	63	75	90
40	55	65	75	92
42	55	66	76	96

and-leaf diagram, which is not the case when using a histogram—some of the information in the original data is lost when a histogram is constructed. Nevertheless, histograms provide the best alternative when attempting to summarize a large set of sample data.

To illustrate the construction of a stem-and-leaf diagram, suppose that a study reports the after-tax profits of 12 selected companies. The profits (recorded as cents per dollar of revenue) are as follows:

$$3.4 \quad 4.5 \quad 2.3 \quad 2.7 \quad 3.8 \quad 5.9 \quad 3.4 \quad 4.7 \quad 2.4 \quad 4.1 \quad 3.6 \quad 5.1$$

The stem-and-leaf diagram for these data is shown in Figure 2.7. Each observation is represented by a *stem* to the left of the vertical line and a *leaf* to the right of the vertical line. For example, the stems and leaves for the first and last observation would be:

Stem	Leaf (unit = .1)		Stem	Leaf (unit = .1)
3	4		5	1

In a stem-and-leaf diagram, the stems are put *in order* to the left of the vertical line. The leaf for each observation is generally the last digit (or possibly the last two digits) of the data value, with the stem consisting of the remaining first digits. The leaf values are generally arranged in ascending order. The value 562 could be represented as 5|62 or as 56|2 in a stem-and-leaf diagram, depending on the range of the sample data. If the diagram is rotated counterclockwise, it has the appearance of a histogram and clearly describes the shape of the sample data.

To illustrate this diagram, suppose that the personnel manager at Texas Industries has administered an aptitude test to 50 applicants. The ordered data are shown in Table 2.5; the corresponding stem-and-leaf diagram is shown in Figure 2.8. From this diagram we observe that the minimum score is 22, the maximum score is 96, and the largest group of scores is between 60 and 69. Also, the five leaves in stem row 3 indicate that five people scored at least 30 but less than 40. The three leaves in stem row 9 tell us at a glance that three people scored 90 or better.

For larger data sets, you may want to consider spreading out the stem column by repeating the stem value two or three times. To illustrate, the same 50 test scores are used

FIGURE

2.8

Stem-and-leaf
diagram for
aptitude test
scores.

Stem	Leaf (unit = 1)
2	2 5 8
3	1 4 5 9 9
4	0 2 4 4 6 8 9
5	1 3 3 5 5 6 7 9
6	0 1 3 3 3 5 6 8 8 9
7	1 2 2 4 5 5 6 8 8
8	0 2 3 5 8
9	0 2 6

FIGURE

2.9

Stem-and-leaf
diagram for
aptitude test
scores using
repeated stems.

Stem	Leaf (unit = 1)
2	2
2	5 8
3	1 4
3	5 9 9
4	0 2 4 4
4	6 8 9
5	1 3 3
5	5 5 6 7 9
6	0 1 3 3 3
6	5 6 8 8 9
7	1 2 2 4
7	5 5 6 8 8
8	0 2 3
8	5 8
9	0 2
9	6

to construct another stem-and-leaf diagram in Figure 2.9, where each stem value is repeated twice. The first stem value contains leaves between 0 and 4, the second stem contains
leaves between 5 and 9.

Statistical Software Application Use DATA2-1

EXAMPLE
2.1

**Using Statistical Software to Construct a Histogram
and a Stem-and-Leaf Diagram**

In a production process, certain requirements referred to as *specification limits* are often
imposed on the product. For example, the inside diameter of a certain machined part must
be between 10.1 millimeters and 10.3 millimeters. The value 10.1 is the lower specification
(spec) limit, and 10.3 is the upper spec limit. These spec limits can be written as $10.2 \pm .1$
millimeters. Any part with an inside diameter outside these limits is called *nonconforming*
and is considered unacceptable.

By gathering a sample and constructing a histogram and stem-and-leaf diagram, production personnel can learn a great deal about a process—in particular, whether the process is capable of meeting these specifications. The Boston plant of Allied Manufacturing produces these parts. As an Allied employee, you have obtained a sample of 100 machine part diameters, contained in column A. What can you conclude about this production process?

Solution

Input instructions for generating an Excel, MINITAB, or SPSS stem-and-leaf diagram are contained in the end-of-chapter appendix. The Excel-generated stem-and-leaf diagram is shown in Figure 2.10(a). The MINITAB and SPSS diagrams are in Figures 2.10(b) and 2.10(c). Since any part with a diameter over 10.3 is nonconforming, the stem-and-leaf diagram makes it clear that the process is struggling to meet specifications and is shifted too far to the right. With this diagram, you are able to see the 17 values (underlined in Figure 2.10(a)) that are exceeding the upper spec limit—not possible using a histogram, where the data are condensed into classes.

A suggestion would be for Allied to try shifting the process to the left by whatever means are available, such as making a machine adjustment or changing raw material. With such a change, the process will be more capable of meeting the required specifications.

Histograms and stem-and-leaf diagrams are simple yet powerful tools for analyzing and improving product quality.

FREQUENCY POLYGONS

2.3

Although a histogram does demonstrate the shape of the data, perhaps the shape can be more clearly illustrated by using a **frequency polygon.** Here, you merely connect the centers of the tops of the histogram bars (located at the class midpoints) with a series of straight lines. The resulting multisided figure is a frequency polygon. Figure 2.11 is an example that uses the frequency distribution of salaries in Table 2.4. From this graph, observe that 27 (out of 50) salaries are between $36,000 and $40,000, with 12 people receiving $40,000 or more.

To obtain the Excel-generated frequency polygon in Figure 2.11(a), begin by entering the 50 salaries into column A of the spreadsheet. Next, click on **KPK Data Analysis ➤ Quantitative Data Charts/Tables ➤ Histogram/Freq. Charts.** Set the number of classes equal to 6 and the class width equal to 2 in the **Classes** section. Finally, click on the checkbox alongside **Frequency Polygon.** The instructions for generating the SPSS frequency polygon in Figure 2.11(b) are contained in the end-of-chapter SPSS appendix.

Comments

The polygon can also be constructed from the relative frequency histogram. The shape will not change, but the units on the vertical axis will now represent relative frequencies. The polygon must begin and end at zero frequency (as in Figure 2.11). To accomplish this, imagine a class at each end of the corresponding histogram that is empty (contains no data values). Begin and end the polygon with the class midpoints of these imaginary classes. Thus, your vertical axis *must* begin at zero. This need not be true for the horizontal axis.

How do you handle an open-ended class? The easiest way is to construct a frequency polygon of the closed classes and place a footnote at each open-ended class location indicating the frequency of that particular class. Figure 2.12 demonstrates this, using the city size data from Table 2.1.

Frequency polygons are usually better than histograms for comparing the shape of two (or more) different frequency distributions. For example, Figure 2.13 demonstrates at a glance that salaries at Texcom Electronics are higher (for the most part) for management personnel who have a college degree.

Both histograms and frequency polygons represent the actual number of data values in each class. Suppose

FIGURE

2.10

(a) Stem-and-leaf diagram generated using KPK Data Analysis for Example 2.1. (b) MINITAB stem-and-leaf diagram for Example 2.1. (c) SPSS stem-and-leaf diagram for Example 2.1.

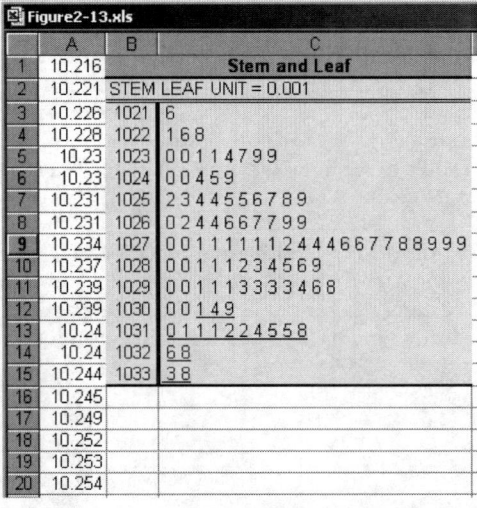

(a)

Character Stem-and-Leaf Display

```
Stem-and-leaf of C1        N  = 100
Leaf Unit = 0.0010


      1  1021 6
      4  1022 168
     12  1023 00114799
     17  1024 00459
     27  1025 2344556789
     37  1026 0244667799
    (21) 1027 001111112444667788999
     42  1028 00111234569
     31  1029 001113333468
     19  1030 00149
     14  1031 0111224558
      4  1032 68
      2  1033 38
```

(b)

DIAMETER

```
DIAMETER Stem-and-Leaf Plot

 Frequency    Stem &  Leaf

     1.00     1021 .  6
     3.00     1022 .  168
     8.00     1023 .  00114799
     5.00     1024 .  00459
    10.00     1025 .  2344556789
    10.00     1026 .  0244667799
    21.00     1027 .  001111112444667788999
    11.00     1028 .  00111234569
    12.00     1029 .  001113333468
     5.00     1030 .  00149
    10.00     1031 .  0111224558
     2.00     1032 .  68
     2.00     1033 .  38

 Stem width:      .010
 Each leaf:       1 case(s)
```

(c)

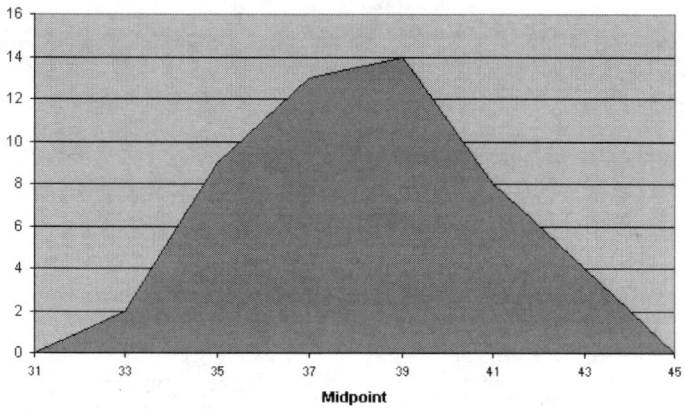

Frequency Polygon

(a)

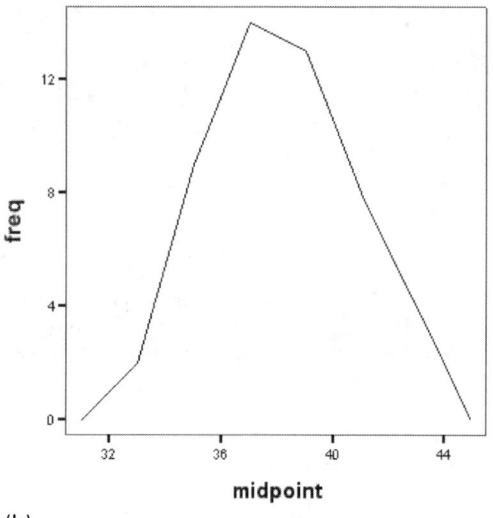

(b)

FIGURE

2.11

(a) Excel frequency polygon using KPK Data Analysis and Table 2.4. (b) SPSS frequency polygon for Table 2.4.

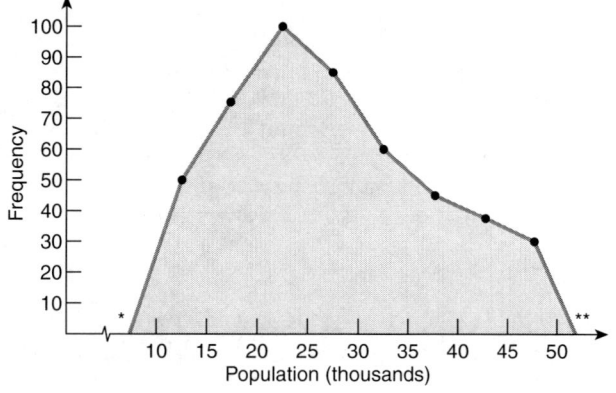

* 4 cities had populations of less than 10,000.
** 5 cities had populations of 50,000 or greater.

FIGURE

2.12

Frequency polygon using footnotes to handle open-ended classes. The data are from Table 2.2

FIGURE

2.13

Frequency polygon showing annual salaries for Texcom Electronics management personnel. Higher salaries are observed in the college degree sample.

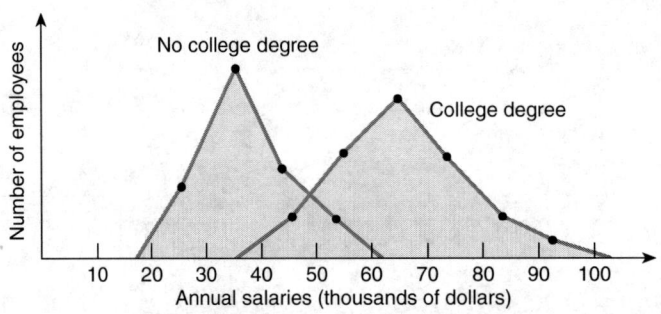

TABLE

2.6

Summary of starting salaries from Table 2.3, including the cumulative frequencies and cumulative relative frequencies

Class Number	Class	Frequency	Cumulative Frequency	Relative Frequency	Cumulative Relative Frequency
1	32 and under 34	2	2	.04	.04
2	34 and under 36	9	11	.18	.22
3	36 and under 38	13	24	.26	.48
4	38 and under 40	14	38	.28	.76
5	40 and under 42	8	46	.16	.92
6	42 and under 44	4	50	.08	1.00
		50		1.00	

that your annual salary is one of the values contained in a sample of 250 salaries. One question of interest might be, what fraction of the people in the sample have a salary *less than* mine? Such information can be displayed using a statistical graph called an *ogive.*

2.4 CUMULATIVE FREQUENCIES (OGIVES)

Another method of examining a frequency distribution is to list the number of observations (data values) that are *less than* each of the class limits rather than how many are *in* each of the classes. You are then determining **cumulative frequencies.** Table 2.6 shows the cumulative frequencies for the frequency distribution in Table 2.4. Notice that you can determine cumulative frequencies (column 4) or cumulative relative frequencies (column 6). The results in Table 2.6 can be summarized more easily in a simple graph called an **ogive** (pronounced oh'-jive). The ogive is useful whenever you want to determine what percentage of your data lies *below* a certain value. Figure 2.14 is constructed by calculating the following:

2 values (2/50 = .04) are less than $34,000

2 + 9 = 11 values (11/50 = .22) are less than $36,000

11 + 13 = 24 values (24/50 = .48) are less than $38,000, and so on.

The ogive allows you to make such statements as, "Twenty-two percent of the salaries were less than $36,000," and, "Fifty percent of the salaries were under $38,100."

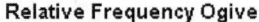

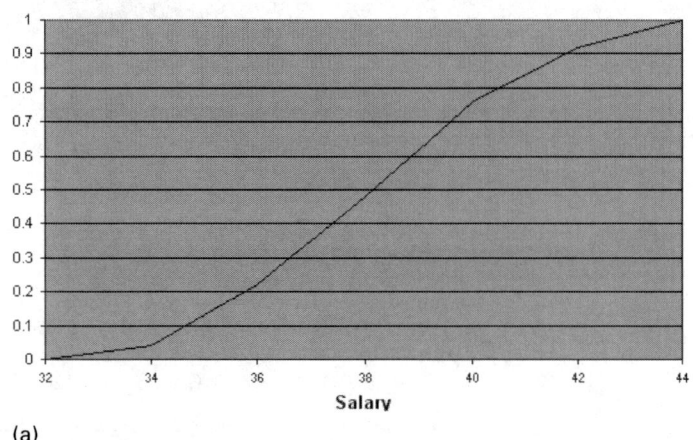

(a)

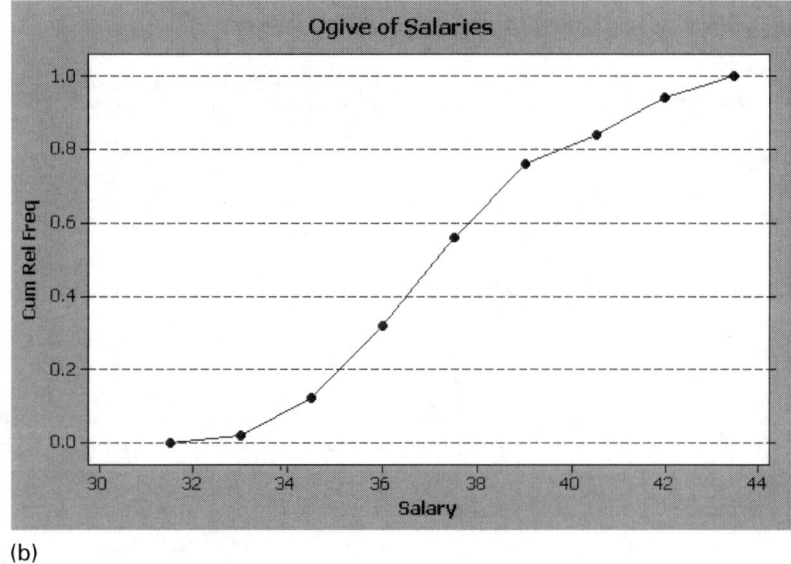

(b)

FIGURE 2.14

(a) Excel ogive (cumulative relative frequencies) using KPK Data Analysis and Table 2.6.
(b) MINITAB ogive (cumulative relative frequencies) using data in Table 2.2.

You always begin at the lower limit of the first class (32 here). The cumulative relative frequency at that point is always 0, because the number of data values less than this number is 0. You always end at the upper limit of the last class (44 here). The cumulative relative frequency at the upper limit is always 1, because all the data values are less than this upper limit. This ogive value would be n = the number of data values ($n = 50$ here) if you are constructing a frequency ogive rather than a relative frequency ogive. *However, the shape of the ogive is the same for both procedures.*

To obtain the Excel generated ogive in Figure 2.14(a), begin by entering the 50 salaries into column A of the spreadsheet. Next, click on **KPK Data Analysis ➤ Quantitative Data Charts/Tables ➤ Histogram/Freq. Charts.** Set the number of classes equal to 6 and the class width equal to 2 in the **Classes** section. Finally, click on the checkbox alongside **Relative Frequency Ogive.** The instructions for generating the MINITAB ogive in Figure 2.14(b) are contained in the end-of-chapter MINITAB appendix.

X Exercises 2.8–2.26

Understanding the Mechanics

2.8 The distribution of the salaries of 100 employees at a small consulting firm are as follows.

Salary	Number of Employees
$30,000 and under $40,000	10
$40,000 and under $50,000	25
$50,000 and under $60,000	30
$60,000 and under $70,000	20
$70,000 and under $80,000	15

  a. Construct a relative frequency distribution.
  b. Construct a relative frequency histogram.
  c. Construct a relative frequency polygon.
  d. Construct a cumulative relative frequency distribution.
  e. Construct a relative frequency ogive.

2.9 The number of vacant seats on a sample of 40 flights is as follows.

Number of Vacant Seats	Number of Flights with Vacant Seats
0–4	15
5–9	10
10–14	8
15–19	5
20–24	2

  a. Construct a frequency histogram.
  b. Describe the shape of the histogram.
  c. Construct a cumulative frequency distribution.
  d. Construct a frequency polygon.
  e. Construct an ogive.

2.10 The monthly repair costs for videocassette recorders (VCR) returned within the past three years for malfunction problems are as follows, in dollars.

73.20	99.60	72.80	102.97	87.45	92.45
89.75	63.70	112.60	68.40	96.75	68.70
80.57	93.80	115.90	89.98	77.93	82.50
84.67	99.75	103.65	63.71	74.39	110.90
69.45	88.70	107.40	86.90	82.25	74.80
88.69	113.30	67.50	87.50	92.57	94.45

  a. Convert the data into an ordered array using six classes.
  b. Construct a relative frequency distribution. Start the first class at $60.00.
  c. Construct a relative frequency histogram.
  d. Construct a cumulative frequency distribution.
  e. Draw a stem-and-leaf diagram.

2.11 The response times to emergency maintenance problems at an assembly plant for 27 randomly selected emergency calls are as follows, in hours.

1.21	1.87	2.35	4.16	1.50	1.30	2.78	3.71	2.80
1.80	2.60	3.30	4.30	3.10	1.80	3.07	2.19	1.67
2.89	4.25	1.10	2.25	3.94	4.22	1.73	2.54	3.27

  a. Arrange the observations in increasing order of magnitude.
  b. Present the data in the form of a frequency distribution. Use seven classes.
  c. Construct a cumulative frequency distribution.
  d. Construct an ogive.
  e. Draw a stem-and-leaf diagram.

2.12 Construct the cumulative frequency distribution for the frequency distribution in Exercise 2.1. Draw the corresponding ogive.

2.13 Construct a frequency histogram and a frequency polygon for the number of times that employees accessed the World Wide Web in Exercise 2.2. Describe the shape of the two charts.

2.14 Form a stem-and-leaf diagram of the following 18 weekly sales. Sales are in units of $1,000.

3.6	2.7	6.2
3.6	8.0	7.1
5.4	5.2	6.4
4.3	7.3	5.3
3.9	5.7	4.2
6.1	5.5	4.0

Applying the New Concepts

2.15 The price of an alternator for a Buick LeSabre was priced at various auto parts outlet stores throughout the Dallas and Ft. Worth Metroplex. The resulting prices are as follows, in dollars.

95	86	89	105	89	99	78	110	113	87
77	96	115	103	86	95	94	106	99	99
83	76	99	94	102	99	104	93	101	94

Use a stem-and-leaf diagram to describe the distribution of the data. What is the most commonly quoted price?

2.16 A quality-control engineer has been gathering a sample of cylinders that have completed the manufacturing process. The cylinders must be manufactured such that the inside diameter is between 10.6 centimeters and 11.0 centimeters. These two limits are called the specification limits. Any cylinder with an inside diameter outside of these limits is called nonconforming and is considered a defective cylinder.

The engineer can make a machine adjustment to shift the process to the right or left. How far and in what direction should the process be shifted to minimize the number of nonconforming cylinders?

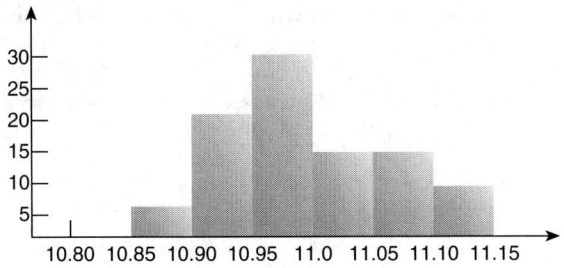

2.17 A county library's records show the following information regarding the number of patrons who used the library during the past 30 days.

100, 87, 44, 53, 17, 34, 88, 67, 31, 40, 98, 77, 55, 41, 73, 62, 88, 28, 70, 51, 82, 44, 32, 50, 33, 49, 59, 67, 79, 84

   a. Construct a cumulative frequency distribution.
   b. Convert the cumulative frequency distribution in part a into an ogive graph.
   c. The number of patrons attending the library was less than what value 80% of the time?

2.18 The following is a frequency distribution of the number of daily automobile accidents reported for a month in Newark, New Jersey.

Accidents Per Day	Frequency
0–3	12
4–7	10
8–11	7
12–15	1
16–19	1

   a. Construct a cumulative relative frequency distribution for the data.
   b. What percentage of the time do eight or more daily accidents occur?
   c. Construct a cumulative frequency distribution for the data.
   d. Compare the shape of the distributions in parts a and c.

Using the Computer

2.19 **[DATA SET EX2-19]** *Variable Description:*

Name: Name of money-losing company

Loss: Amount of money that the company lost in millions of dollars

The top money-losing global companies in 2003 are displayed on the *Fortune* Web site *(www.fortune.com)*. Construct a relative frequency ogive with eight classes. What percentage of the selected companies lost less than $1,500 million?

2.20 **[DATA SET EX2-20]** *Variable Description:*

Name: Name and title of entrepreneurs

Wealth: Net worth in millions of dollars from owning company stock

The wealth of top entrepreneurs for 2003 is displayed on the *Fortune* Web site *(www.fortune.com)*. Construct a relative frequency histogram and comment on the shape of the distribution for these selected entrepreneurs.

2.21 **[DATA SET EX2-21]** *Variable Description:*

Company: Name of a fast-growing company

TotalReturn: Three-year total return

Total return from owning stocks of several of the fastest-growing companies in 2003 is displayed on the *Fortune* Web site *(www.fortune.com)*. Construct a relative frequency ogive and determine the percentage of companies with a total return of at least 60%.

2.22 **[DATA SET EX2-22]** *Variable Description:*

Company: Name of a fast-growing company

Growth: Revenue growth in percentage

Revenue growth for several of the fastest-growing U.S. companies in 2003 is displayed on the *Fortune* Web site *(www.fortune.com)*. Construct a frequency polygon histogram and comment on the shape of the distribution for these selected companies.

2.23 **[DATA SET EX2-23]** *Variable Description:*

Company: Name of a Fortune 500 company

Score: Average rating for Most Admired Company, with 10 as highest score

Ratings for the Most Admired Company contest in 2003 are displayed on the *Fortune* Web site *(www.fortune.com)*. Construct a relative frequency polygon and comment on the shape of the distribution for these selected companies.

2.24 **[DATA SET EX2-24]** *Variable description:*

PhoneTime: Total daily times spent on the telephone by an employee (in hours).

The manager of a marketing firm wished to determine the distribution of the total daily time that the firm's 50 employees spend on the telephone. Data were collected for a randomly selected day.

   a. Use the command **KPK ➤ Quantitative ➤ Histogram** to construct a histogram of the data.
   b. Select a class width of 1 hour. What happens to the shape of the frequency distribution?

2.25 **[DATA SET EX2-25]** *Variable Description:*

YearMonth: Year and month that electricity consumption is recorded

ElectricConsump: California's Monthly Electricity Consumption (in millions of MWh)

California lawmakers are assessing whether to expand restraints on the wholesale price of electricity in the state.

Currently, controls become effective when California's energy reserves slip below 7% of demand. For lawmakers to decide how frequently controls should go into effect, consumption data are studied to determine the distribution of usage.

a. Using a relative frequency polygon, describe the distribution of consumption for the data from years 1998 and 1999. Use a class width of two.

b. Repeat part a for the years 1998 to 2001 and compare the shapes of both distributions. Can you conclude that the distribution of usage has shifted during the 1998 to 2001 period?

(Source: "White House Looks Isolated in Its Opposition to Energy Price Caps," *Wall Street Journal*, June 14, 2001, p. A22.)

2.26 [DATA SET EX2-26] *Variable Description:*

HourlyComp91-95: Quarterly percent increases in hourly wage compensation from 1991 through 1995.

HourlyComp96-00: Quarterly percent increases in hourly wage compensation from 1996 through 2000.

Quarterly increases in wage compensation have varied according to the economic climate. The 1990s have seen an upward trend in productivity. During this period, quarterly increases in hourly wages nationwide have varied approximately between 2% and 5%. This decade has seen exceptional economic performance with low inflation.

a. Compare the distribution of quarterly percent increases for the time period 1991 to 1995 and 1996 to 2000 by forming two histograms (if using the KPK macros, click on the Stacked Histogram option).

b. Construct two separate relative frequency polygons for the time periods in part a. Use a class width of one. Do you prefer the relative frequency polygons or the histograms to represent the distribution of the data?

c. Construct an ogive using the combined data from 1991 through 2000. How would you interpret this graph?

(Source: "Fed's Meyer Warns of Inflation, Joblessness," *Wall Street Journal*, June 7, 2001, p. A2.)

2.5 BAR CHARTS

Histograms, frequency polygons, and ogives are used for data having an interval or ratio level of measurement. For data having a *nominal* level, we use a **bar chart.** For situations producing a sample of *ordinal* level data with a reasonable set of possible values (such as 1 = strongly agree, 2 = agree, . . . , 5 = strongly disagree), a bar chart can be used to summarize the sample. A bar chart is similar to a histogram, in that the height of each bar is proportional to the frequency of that class. Such a graph is most helpful when you have many categories to represent.

Consider the data in Table 2.2. If you are interested in the number of business graduates in each of the three disciplines (accounting, information systems, and marketing), a bar chart will do a good job of summarizing this information (Figure 2.15). This figure shows that 26 were accounting majors; the smallest group consisted of the information systems majors (20%). Notice that a gap is inserted between each of the bars in a bar chart. The data here are nominal, so the length of this gap is arbitrary.

FIGURE

2.15

Bar chart showing the number of this year's graduating business majors at Bellaire College in each of the three disciplines.

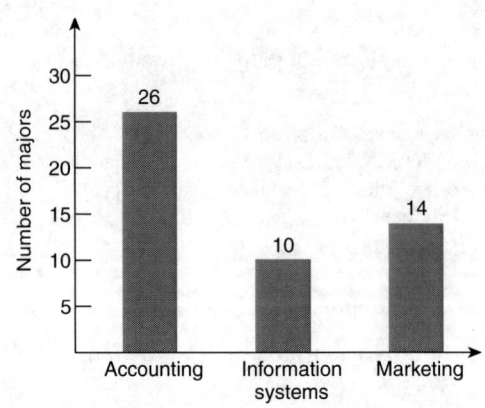

Figure 2.16 is an example of a bar chart in which the bars are constructed horizontally rather than vertically. This form enables you to label each category *within* the bar.

EXAMPLE
2.2

The head of Quality Assurance at Microtech (a fictional company) has categorized company costs related to quality improvement into three categories: prevention, appraisal, and failure. These three costs for the past fiscal year were:

Prevention costs: $ 3,600
Appraisal costs: $38,400
Failure costs: $78,000

She wants to demonstrate at a glance the small amount spent on prevention measures and the large amount spent on failure costs (largely due to warranty claims but also due to having to rework defective components). Construct a bar chart to illustrate this information.

Solution

The bar chart consists of three boxes (bars), where the height of each box represents the dollar amount for that category. It is shown in Figure 2.17. This bar chart is a rather dramatic illustration that many more dollars are being spent in the failure cost category than in the other two categories—in particular, for prevention costs. Such a chart can have a tremendous impact in a business presentation.

FIGURE

2.16

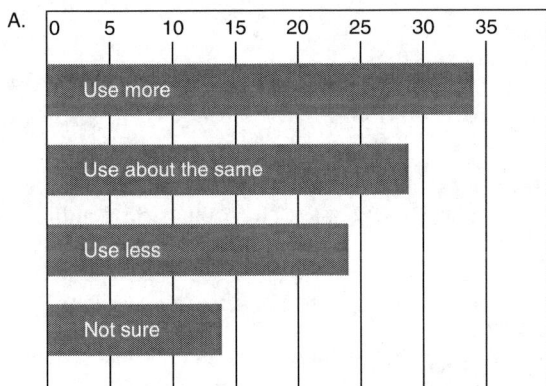

Q. If the price of natural gas goes down by 25% in the next few years, would you and your family use more or less?

Bar chart drawn horizontally; note that it is easy to place labels within the boxes.

FIGURE

2.17

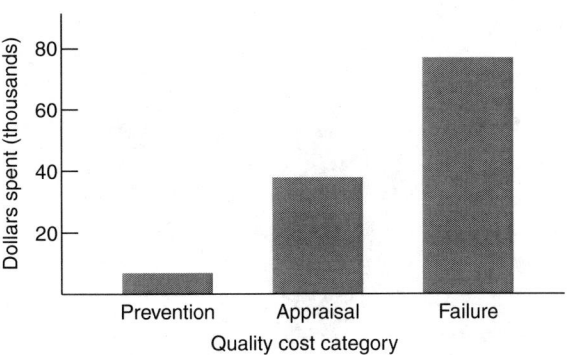

Bar chart of quality costs for Microtech (Example 2.2).

2.6

PIE CHARTS

An alternative to the bar chart for nominal or ordinal data is the **pie chart.** This graph is used to split a particular quantity into its component pieces, typically at some specified point in time or over a specified time span. It is a convenient way of representing percentages or relative frequencies (rather than frequencies). Figure 2.18 shows a pie chart of the major discipline for the 50 graduates in Table 2.2. The chart makes it easy to compare relative sizes of each class. Figure 2.18 shows that accounting majors were 52 percent of the graduates. Information systems majors made up the smallest percentage, at 20 percent. To construct a pie chart, draw a line from the center of the circle to the outer edge. Then construct the various pieces of the pie chart by drawing the corresponding angles. For example, the accounting majors represent 52% of the total number of business graduates (26 out of 50), so angle A in Figure 2.23 is 52% of 360°, or 187.2°. Angle B is 20% of 360°, or 72°, and angle C represents the remaining portion.

Statistical Software Application Use DATA2-3

E X A M P L E
2.3

Using Statistical Software to Construct a Bar Chart and Pie Chart

The manager of Freedman Furniture Store has compiled a list of the types of written customer complaints during the past three months. The complaints have been categorized as follows:

Type	Coded Value
Error in billing	1
Rudeness by store personnel	2
Late delivery	3
Question not answered during telephone inquiry	4
Other	5

The total complaints for the three months is 75 and the coded values (1s, 2s, . . . , 5s) are contained in a column in DATA2-3. Construct the corresponding bar chart and pie chart and discuss the results.

Solution   To obtain the Excel bar chart and pie chart in Figure 2.20, click on the **Open** icon (![Open icon]) and open the file **DATA2-3.** You should see 75 integers, 1 through 5. You can see the first 8 values in column A of Figure 2.19. Next, click on **KPK Data Analysis ➤ Qualitative Data**

FIGURE
2.18

Pie chart showing the percentage of this year's graduating business majors at Bellaire College in each of the three disciplines.

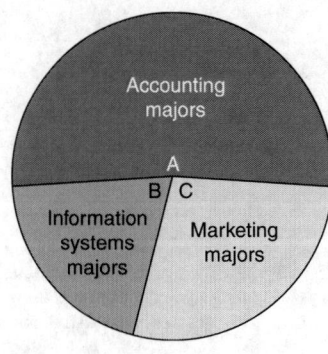

Charts ➤ Bar Chart. For the input range enter A1:A75, and for the output range enter B1. You should then see the bar chart table in Figure 2.19 (columns B and C) and the bar chart in Figure 2.20. Repeat this sequence and use **Pie Chart** in place of **Bar Chart,** entering D1 for the output range. This produces the pie chart table in Figure 2.19 (columns D and E) and the corresponding pie chart in Figure 2.20. To make the output easier to interpret, replace the integers 1 through 5 using the labels "Billing," "Rudeness," "Late," "Not Answered," and "Other" in cells B3 through B7 and cells D3 through D7 as shown in Figure 2.19. By doing this, you also change the labels on the graphs to the ones shown in Figure 2.20.* The SPSS bar chart and MINITAB pie chart are shown in Figure 2.21.

Both charts make it very clear that the bulk of the customer complaints during this three-month period (42 out of 75) are related to billing errors, with rudeness by store personnel a distant second (14 out of 75). The quality of service at Freedman would be greatly improved if the billing department would make a serious effort to eliminate the billing errors.

FIGURE

2.19

Excel spreadsheet after running **KPK Data Analysis ➤ Qualitative Data Charts ➤ Bar Chart and Pie Chart.**

	A	B	C	D	E	F	G	H
1	1	Bar Chart		Pie Chart				
2	2	CATEGORY	FREQUENCY	CATEGORY	FREQUENCY			
3	1	Billing	42	Billing	42			
4	3	Rudeness	14	Rudeness	14			
5	1	Late	8	Late	8			
6	1	Not Answered	6	Not Answered	6			
7	2	Other	5	Other	5			
8	1							

Microsoft Excel - Data2-3 · File Edit View Insert Format Tools Data KPK Data Analysis Window Help · M1 · Bar Chart / Pie Chart \ DATA2-3 /

FIGURE

2.20

Excel bar chart and pie chart created by KPK Data Analysis for Example 2.3.

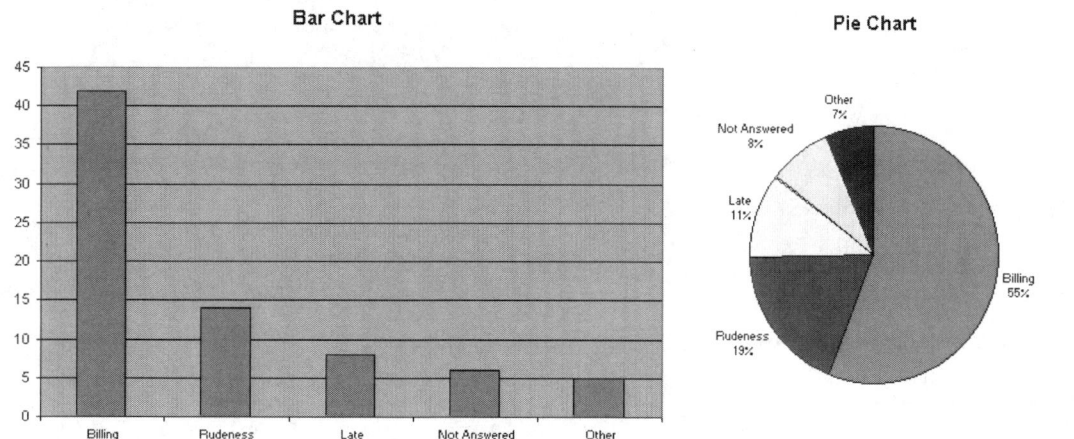

---

*When you clicked on **KPK Data Analysis ➤ Qualitative Data Charts,** you might have noticed another option called Pareto chart. This particular graph modifies the bar chart to distinguish the few important categories (one, in this example) from the categories with low relative frequencies. This chart will be illustrated in the exercises at the end of this section.

FIGURE

2.21

(a) SPSS bar chart for Example 2.3.
(b) MINITAB pie chart for Example 2.3.

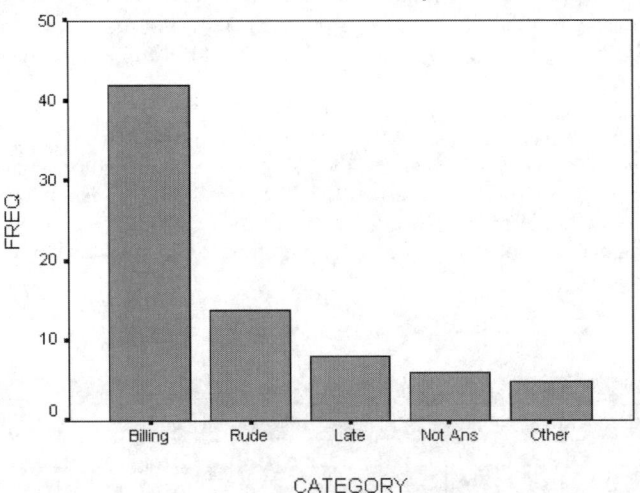

(a)

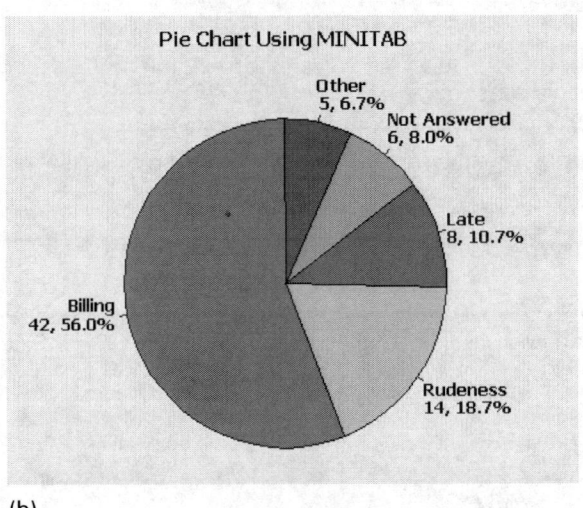

(b)

X Exercises 2.27–2.50

Understanding the Mechanics

2.27 The ratings of a conference speaker were marked E (excellent), G (good), F (fair), or P (poor). Construct a bar chart and a pie chart to represent the following ratings provided by the audience.

E F E G P G E G F P E G G F G
G G E P F G G G E G G G E G G

2.28 An electronics firm has the following percentages of its employees with different educational backgrounds. Construct a pie chart to display the data.

Highest Educational Degree	Percentage of Employees
High school degree	5
Associate degree	20
College degree	50
Masters degree	15
Doctorate degree	10

2.29 A survey of 200 households revealed the following results on how residential homeowners feel about a proposed increase in property tax.

Category	Number of Households
Strongly agree	23
Agree	30
Neutral	10
Disagree	90
Strongly disagree	27
Not sure	20

a. Draw a bar graph.

b. Change the numbers to relative percentages and construct a bar graph.

c. Draw a pie chart.

Applying the New Concepts

2.30 The following sport-utility vehicles (SUVs) are listed in rank order according to their performance rating by *Consumer Reports* on handling and driving tests. Construct relative frequency distributions with a class width of 5,000 and a class width of 3,000 to display the distribution of the costs of top ranked SUVs. Which class width do you think should be used to display these prices? Why?

Vehicle	Price
Acura MDX	39,450
Lexus RX300	42,961
Mercedes-Benz ML320	40,270
Ford Explorer XLT	32,600
Nissan Pathfinder LE	34,724
Jeep Grand Cherokee LTD V8	37,950
Toyota 4Runner SR5	33,395
GMC Envoy SLE	33,320
Dodge Durango SLT Plus	34,745
Land Rover Discovery	40,395
Jeep Grand Cherokee Laredo	33,030

(Source: "Luxury-brand SUVs Top List," *USA Today*, August 8, 2001, p. 6B.)

2.31 Office investment sales brokers bring together investors and investment opportunities in office real estate. These brokers provide counseling to all parties in an investment interchange involving office space. Their careful market and financial analysis and negotiations help lead to successful purchasing decisions of office space. The following office investment sales brokers are listed by total dollar volume of transactions during the year 2000.

Broker	Total Amount in Millions of Dollars Transacted
Cushman & Wakefield, Inc.	931.0
CBRichard Ellis	741.5
Insignia/ESG	735.4
Eastdil Realty Company	671.3
NewMark & Company Real Estate, Inc.	395.2
Eastern Consolidated Properties	281.8
Clarion Partners	210.0
Kennedy-Wilson Properties, Ltd.	207.5
Helmsley-Spear, Inc.	174.1
Murray Hill Properties/TCN	59.5

a. Summarize the data in the form of a pie chart.

b. Omit the companies Cushman & Wakefield, Inc and CBRichard Ellis and construct a pie chart.

c. Describe how your findings change from part a to part b.

(Source: "Top 10 Office Investment Sales Brokers," *Wall Street Journal*, August 1, 2001, p. B7.)

2.32 Small-company stocks funds are prone to periodic bursts of hot performance. Consider the five small-company mutual funds and their performance, as listed below.

Small-Company Mutual Fund	Performance over the Past 12 Months	Performance over the Past 5 Years
Babson Enterprises II	31.8%	119%
Eclipse Equity	33.8%	131%
Fasciano	25.3%	133%
Gabelli Small Cap Growth	36.8%	123%
Nicholas Limited Edition	30.0%	119%

(Source: "Hot Small-Company Funds," *USA Today*, February 20, 1998, p. 4B.)

Construct a bar chart for the 12-month performance and another bar chart for the 5-year performance. Comment on the differences in the two charts.

2.33 Many developing countries receive loans or loan guarantees from the U.S. Export-Import Bank. These loans help some of these countries to have economies that are growing faster than that of the United States. Ten important recipients of large loans from the Export-Import Bank are listed below with their current amount borrowed.

Country	Amount (in Billions of Dollars)
Brazil	3.9
Russia	1.5
Indonesia	3.5
Argentina	2.3
Philippines	2.2
Turkey	2.0
Mexico	5.4
China	4.1
India	1.5

(Source: "U.S. Ex-Im Bank Is Beating the Drum in China," *Wall Street Journal*, June 20, 1997, p. A12.)

To analyze this data, a Pareto diagram is used. A Pareto diagram summarizes the findings of categorical responses so that the few important categories are distinguished from the numerous categories with low-relative frequencies. A Pareto diagram is a vertical bar chart with the categories placed in descending rank order of their bar heights. A cumulative graph is plotted with the bar chart. The scale on the right-hand side displays the cumulative percentages. The left-hand axis shows the amount of loans borrowed by a country. The 100% figure on the right-hand axis corresponds to the total amount of loans borrowed by all the countries.

a. What conclusions can be drawn from the Pareto diagram?

b. What information is available through a Pareto diagram that is not available from a bar chart or pie chart?

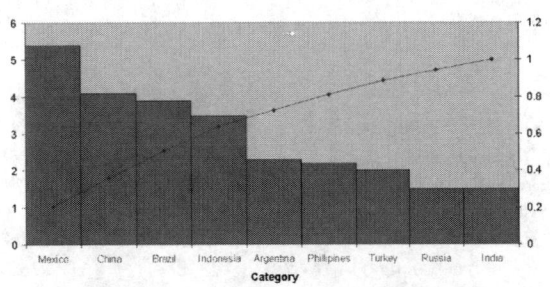

Pareto Chart

2.34 An operations manager interviewed 200 employees to find out what their excuses were for being late to work. The results were: 20 due to traffic, 35 due to family stress, 10 due to weather, 75 due to health reasons, and 60 due to dropping off children at school. Construct and interpret a Pareto diagram of these data (see Exercise 2.33).

2.35 A successful businessperson receives the following yearly incomes (in dollars) from seven business partnerships.

Business Partnership	Yearly Income
A	23,160
B	30,070
C	32,732
D	35,900
E	37,304
F	43,608
G	60,014
	Total 262,788

Express the yearly incomes from each partnership as a percentage of the businessperson's total income, and summarize this information using a pie chart.

2.36 The Backstreet Boys were among the leaders of the wave of pop music boy bands that took America by storm at the beginning of this century. The popularity of bands is sometimes fickle in the world of pop music. *Airplay Monitor*, a trade publication, estimates the number of listeners who hear a given record. The following song titles by the Backstreet Boys illustrate that not all of their songs made it to the top of the charts. However, the figures do reveal that a couple of their hits reached an audience of more than 70 million.

Backstreet Boys' Songs	Audience (in Millions)
"All I Have to Give"	38.5
"I Want It That Way"	80.4
"Larger Than Life"	43.7
"Show Me the Meaning of Being Lonely"	75.8
"The One"	35.3
"Shape of My Heart"	48.1
"The Call"	24.6
"More Than That"	33.7

a. Construct a Pareto diagram for the audience size for each song. What songs account for most of the audience listening?

b. Construct a pie chart to display the proportion of the audience size for each song. What conclusions can you make from viewing this chart that are similar to those revealed by the Pareto diagram?

(Source: "Charting the Teen-Pop Audience," *USA Today*, July 20, 2001, p. 1F.)

2.37 Consumer electronic companies are competing to become leaders in marketing home entertainment products. Many of these companies are counting on new life with the introduction of MP3 and DVD players, plasma screen, and high-definition televisions that are Web-ready. The following is a list of consumer electronic companies and their current share of that market.

Brand	Market Share
General Electric	4.6
Orion	3.9
Panasonic	6.4
Philips	11.0
RCA	12.5
Samsung	4.2
Sanyo	15.4
Sharp	3.9
Sony	10.8
Zenith	4.2

a. Display these data using a bar chart. Is it obvious who the big four companies are in consumer electronics?

b. Use a pie chart to display the market share of the consumer electronic companies. Try both the regular pie chart and a three-dimensional pie chart. Which of the two pie charts do you prefer? Explain.

(Source: "Zenith Sees Its Future in Digital TV," *USA Today*, July 20, 2001, p. 7B.)

2.38 According to the *www.pollingreport.com* Web site, in December 2003, the following data represent how much adults have heard or read about changes to Medicare. Construct a side-by-side bar chart and interpret the graph.

	Great Deal	Moderate Amount	Not Much	Nothing at All
All adults	12%	41%	36%	11%
65 and older	21%	52%	22%	5%

2.39 According to the *www.pollingreport.com* Web site, in December 2003, the following data represent the percentage of individuals who expect to receive Social Security benefits after retiring. Construct and interpret a pie chart for each group.

	Yes	No	Not Sure
18–29 years old	58%	36%	6%
46–55 years old	75%	18%	7%

2.40 According to the *www.pollingreport.com* Web site, in June of 2003, the following data represent the percentage of Republicans and Democrats that believe the new tax cut was either a good thing or a bad thing. Construct and interpret a side-by-side bar chart.

	Good Thing	Bad Thing	Not Sure
Republicans	70%	16%	14%
Democrats	38%	51%	11%

2.41 According to the *www.pollingreport.com* Web site, in November 2003, the following data represent the percentage of individuals concerned about getting the flu. Construct a pie chart and a bar chart and compare.

Very Concerned	Somewhat Concerned	Not Too Concerned	Not at All Concerned
29%	33%	21%	17%

2.42 According to the *www.pollingreport.com* Web site, the percentage of adults who believe that investing in the stock market is a good/bad idea follows for two time periods. Construct a pie chart for each time period and compare.

Time Period	Good Idea	Bad Idea	No Opinion
January 2004	53%	43%	4%
June 2002	31%	63%	6%

2.43 BEA Systems is one of the world's leading e-business infrastructure software companies. This company paid for an advertisement in the *Wall Street Journal* showing that 80% of the Fortune 500 companies prefer BEA when it comes to e-business platforms. The advertisement used a three-dimensional pie chart to show that the remaining choices are IBM at 6% and "others" at 11%. Construct both a regular pie chart and a three-dimensional pie chart to display this information. Do you think that BEA's use of the three-dimensional chart was a good marketing strategy?

(Source: "The World's #1 E-business Software Platform," *Wall Street Journal*, July 19, 2001, p. B5.)

2.44 A mutual fund has its assets spread over seven sectors of the economy. The following data are the total value (in millions of dollars) of the stocks in which the fund is invested for each sector.

Stock	Value
Electronics and electrical equipment	2.116
Aerospace and defense	10.375
Food and beverage	4.864
Utilities	2.713
Insurance and finance	6.538
Health care	3.675
Oil and gas	1.532

a. Express the amount invested in each sector of the economy as a percent.
b. Summarize the list in a pie chart.

2.45 Construct and interpret a Pareto diagram for the dollar volume of transactions in Exercise 2.31.

2.46 An independent oil firm recently hired 10 engineers, five geologists, three accountants, one statistician, four computer scientists, and one chemist. Present these data in the form of a pie chart.

Using the Computer

2.47 [DATA SET EX2-47] *Variable Description:*

Question: Which database is your favorite in relation to PHP development?

NumberOfResponses: Number of responses to each category

A leading Web infrastructure software company, named Zend Technologies Ltd, serves as a leader in sales for PHP (acronym for Hypertext Preprocessor). This data set is adapted from a survey obtained from its Web site (*www.zend.com*). Construct and interpret a bar chart for the database choices.

2.48 [DATA SET EX2-48] *Variable Description:*

Question: In what computer languages do you feel most proficient?

NumberOfResponses: Number of responses in each category

For the survey provided by Zend Technologies Ltd in Exercise 2.47, construct and interpret a Pareto chart for the responses to the question on the computer language in which a Web developer feels most proficient.

2.49 [DATA SET EX2-49] *Variable Description:*

Question: What is your country of origin?

NumberOfResponses: Number of responses for several countries

For the survey provided by Zend Technologies Ltd in Exercise 2.48, construct and interpret a Pareto chart for the responses to the country of origin.

2.50 [DATA SET EX2-50] *Variable Description:*

Manufacturer: Automotive Company producing vehicles in Mexico

VehiclesProduced: Number of vehicles produced in year 2000 in Mexico

VehiclesExported: Number of vehicles exported from Mexico in year 2000

The cost of manufacturing vehicles in Mexico is very attractive to automakers. Global carmakers build approximately 1.9 million vehicles in Mexico. Of these, nearly

76% are exported, primarily to the United States. Although General Motors is the largest manufacturer of vehicles in Mexico, DaimlerChrysler exports the most vehicles. Automotive analysts examine both the number of vehicles produced and the number exported to determine the potential market share of each company.

a. For the data on vehicles produced in Mexico, construct a bar chart displaying the amount produced by each company.

b. Repeat part a using a pie chart.

c. Construct a bar chart displaying the number of vehicles exported from Mexico.

d. Repeat part d using a pie chart.

e. Do you prefer the bar charts or the pie charts for displaying the data? Explain.

f. What differences do the charts reveal for the automotive companies with respect to number of vehicles produced and number of vehicles exported?

(Source: "DaimlerChrysler Tops in Mexico Exports," *USA Today*, August 8, 2001, p. 2B.)

2.7   DECEPTIVE GRAPHS

You might be tempted to be creative in your graphical displays by using, for example, a three-dimensional figure. Such originality is commendable, but does your graph accurately represent the situation? Consider Figure 2.22, which someone drew in an attempt to demonstrate that there are twice as many men as women in management positions. The artist constructed a box for the category "men" twice as high—but also twice as deep—as that for the category "women." The result is a rectangular solid for men that is, in fact, four times the volume of the one for women. The illustration is misleading—it appears that there are four times as many men as women in management.

The use of deceptive graphs is eloquently described in Edward Tufte's *The Visual Display of Quantitative Information.** Tufte asks the question, "Why do artists draw graphics that lie, and why do the major newspapers publish them?" His answers range from the artists' lack of quantitative skills to attempts to make statistical data less boring. Tufte's basic premise is that statistical graphs should tell the truth. He describes the most common *graphical lies* and how to avoid them. He mentions that simpler graphs are often better and that oftentimes a pretty graph is the least informative. This book is highly recommended for anyone who is in the business of producing or interpreting statistical information.

When data values correspond to specific time periods—such as monthly sales or annual expenditures—the resulting data collection is a **time series**. A time series is repre-

FIGURE 2.22

The illustrator wished to show that there are twice as many men as women in management positions. However, box B is twice the height *and* twice the depth of box A and thus is four times the volume.

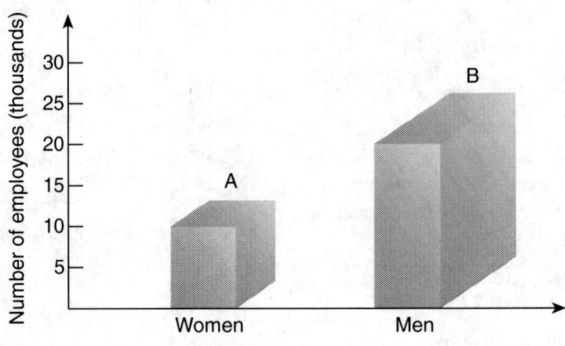

*Edward Tufte, *The Visual Display of Quantitative Information*, 2nd ed. (Chesire, Connecticut: Graphics Press, 2001).

sented graphically by using the horizontal axis for the time increments. For example, Figure 2.23 contains a return-on-investment time series for two mutual funds, plotted over a six-year period. A glance at this figure might lead you to believe that mutual fund A is performing nearly twice as well as mutual fund B. A closer look, however, reveals that *the vertical axis does not start at zero;* such a construction can seriously distort the information contained in such a graph. The 2001 return for fund A appears to be roughly twice that for fund B. However, the actual returns are 15.8% for fund A and 14.5% for fund B. Granted, fund A is outperforming fund B, but not nearly as dramatically as Figure 2.23 seems to indicate. Also, fund B is not as "unstable" as Figure 2.23 would indicate, since the return only fluctuates between 14% and 15%.

Such examples, and many others, are contained in an entertaining and enlightening book by Darrell Huff titled *How to Lie with Statistics.** Other deceptive graphs include bar charts similar to those in Figure 2.24. Here, you may be tempted to conclude that there is a significant difference in bar heights, either because the vertical axis does not begin at zero (left side) or because the bars are chopped in the middle without a corresponding adjustment of the vertical axis (right side). *As an observer, beware of such trickery. As an illustrator, do not intentionally mislead your reader by disguising the results through the use of a misleading graph.* This practice tends to give statisticians a bad name!

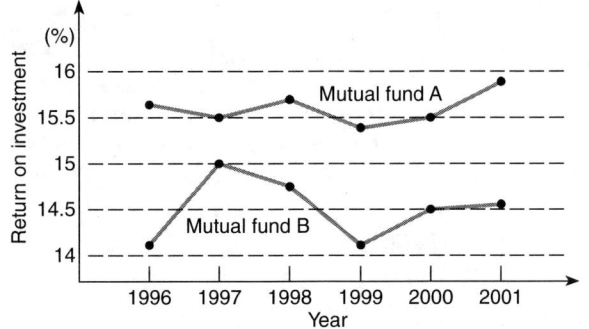

FIGURE

2.23

Time-series graph of the performance of two mutual funds. The graph is misleading because the vertical axis does not start at zero.

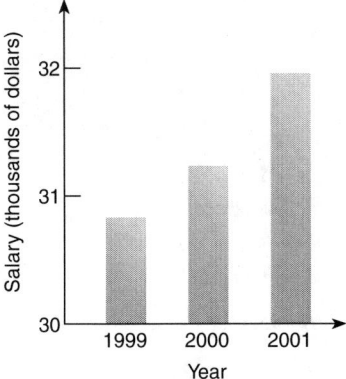
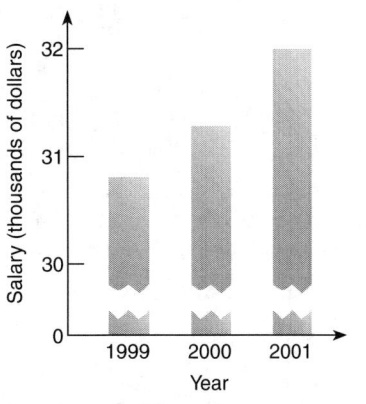

FIGURE

2.24

Two misleading bar charts. The vertical axis of the left-hand chart does not begin at zero, and the bars in the right-hand chart are chopped without a corresponding adjustment in the vertical axis.

*Darrell Huff, *How to Lie with Statistics* (New York: Norton, 1954 [and 1993 by Darrell Huff with Irving Geis, illustrator]). Other discussions are included in *How to Lie With Charts* by Gerald Jones (Alameda, CA: Sybex, 1995), and "How to Display Data Badly" by Howard Wainer, *The American Statistician* (May 1984).

✓ Summary

This chapter examined methods of summarizing and presenting a large set of data using a graph. You begin by placing the sample data in order, from smallest to largest (an ordered array). The next step is to summarize the data in a frequency distribution, which consists of a number of classes (such as "150 and under 250") and corresponding frequencies.

The data summary can then be displayed using an appropriate graph. Five kinds of graphs were discussed: the histogram, stem-and-leaf diagram, ogive, bar chart, and pie chart. Histograms and stem-and-leaf diagrams are graphical representations of a frequency distribution and are generally used for data having an interval or ratio level of measurement. A stem-and-leaf diagram does not condense the sample data into classes, but, rather, represents each value in an easy-to-read graph. An excellent way to indicate the shape of the data values is to use a frequency polygon, which is constructed by replacing the bars in the histogram with straight lines connecting the midpoints at the top of each bar. An ogive allows you to make a statement such as "40% of the data values are less than 500." When the data are nominal or ordinal, a bar chart or pie chart provides an excellent graphical summary.

What's Next?

The next chapter examines a variety of numerical measures that describe the sample data. Rather than reducing the data to a graph, we will reduce the data to one or more numbers (numerical measures) that give us some information about the data.

X Review Exercises 2.51–2.59

2.51 Buying a portable CD player with a snazzy appearance and sharp sound quality is important to most consumers. However, a buyer should assess the hassle of frequent battery changes before buying a player. Portable CD players consume AA batteries at an amazing rate. Not only is this expensive, but it is a nuisance if the consumer does not have a back-up supply. *Consumer Reports* rated the battery life of the following portable CD models.

Model	Battery Life (Hours)
Sony D-MJ95	26
Sony D-SJ17CK	29
Sony D-SJ01	33
Sony D-EJ611	26
Sony D-SJ15	25
Panasonic SL-SX280	23
Aiwa XP-SP911	23
Panasonic SL-SW869V	23
Aiwa XP-V713	20
Panasonic SL-CT470	12
Philips AZ9213	17
RCA RP-2360FM	10
RCA RP-2300	12

a. Construct a stem-and-leaf display. Do you notice any outliers?
b. Construct a frequency distribution using a class width of 5.
c. Interpret the shape of the distribution.

(Source: "Portable CD Players," *Consumer Reports*, July 2001, p. 43.)

2.52 Compare and contrast bar charts and histograms. For what type of data do you use each of these diagrams?

2.53 Some business leaders and scientists are concerned about the effect that greenhouse gases have on global warming and how sensitive the Earth's climate is to a buildup of greenhouse gases. The most industrialized nations are studying how much each country should reduce carbon dioxide emissions. Construct bar charts for the percentage contribution by that country to global dioxide emissions and for the per capita emissions. Compare the two charts. Interpret the two bar charts.

Country	Percentage Contribution to Global Dioxide Emission	Per Capita Emissions (Metric Tons)
United States	24.8%	5.6
Russia	6.5%	2.7
Japan	5.0%	2.4
Germany	3.7%	2.8
United Kingdom	2.5%	2.6
Canada	2.5%	4.9

(Source: "Who Pollutes the Most," *USA Today*, July 16, 2001, p. 2A.)

2.54 When money is allowed to grow in a tax-deferred retirement account for several decades, the results can be impressive. Consider the following results.

Starting Age	Investment Value at Age 65 When Investing $500 Annually
20	$221,238
30	$ 96,216
40	$ 39,890

Starting Age	Investment Value at Age 65 When Investing $1,000 Annually
20	$442,475
30	$192,431
40	$ 79,781

Construct a bar chart for the investment values at age 65 for the case where an investor saves $500 annually and for the case where an investor saves $1,000 annually. Compare the two charts. How will an investor who saves $1,000 annually starting at age 30 fare against an investor who starts at age 20 and saves $500 annually?

(Source: "A Little Can Go a Long Way," *Stages: The Fidelity Investments Magazine of Personal Finance*, Winter 1998, pp. 22–23.)

2.55 [DATA SET EX2-55] *Variable Description:*

City: Name of City in which rental car is rented

WeeklyEconomyRate: The weekly rate to rent a car (in dollars)

Many car-rental companies offer special weekly rates on economy cars. During 2004, these weekly rates by Avis, Budget, and Hertz have seen an average increase of $20 per week. Consider this data set to contain a sample of Hertz's weekly economy rate at 18 locations (three of which are in Canada). Construct and compare a relative frequency histogram with nine classes and a stem-and-leaf diagram.

(Source: "Car-Rental Companies Hike Rates," *Kiplinger's Personal Finance*, May 2004, p. 99)

2.56 [DATA SET EX2-56] *Variable Description:*

Occupation: Occupation of immigrants

Percentage: Percentage of immigrants in each occupation category

The federal government estimates that only 4% of the illegal immigrants crossing the Texas border are apprehended. Congress has considered a plan to give this population legal status as temporary workers, but not full citizenship. Construct and compare a bar chart and a pie chart for the occupations of these immigrants.

(Source: "Preying On Human Cargo," *Forbes*, June 7, 2004, p. 74)

2.57 [DATA SET EX2-57] *Variable Description:*

Automotive Company: Name of automobile manufacturer

December Sales: Number of automobile sales in December 2001

In the wake of the September 11, 2001, terrorist attacks, automakers offered incentives to boost sales and invigorate the economy. As a result, 2001 sales almost matched the record levels of 2000. Construct and interpret a Pareto diagram (see Exercise 2.33) to summarize this data set.

(Source: "U.S. Car, Truck Sales Eased in December," *Wall Street Journal*, January 4, 2002, p. A4.)

2.58 [DATA SET EX2-58] *Variable Description:*

LongTermHealthFacility: Name of company providing long-term care

Ownership: Public or private

NetRevenue: Net revenue for year 2000 for long-term health care provider

More than 60% of people age 65 or older will require long-term care during their lifetime. Medicare and Medicaid typically pay only a fraction of the costs of long-term health care. Managers of long-term health facilities must keep costs low at these facilities so that people seeking assisted living can afford the facility. Those companies that manage to keep their costs very low typically generate higher net revenue. Compare histograms of net revenue for 2000 for publicly owned and privately owned long-term providers. What differences do you notice from viewing these two histograms?

(Source: "Post-Acute-Care Companies Ranked by 2000 Net Revenue," *Modern Healthcare*, July 9, 2001, p. 29.)

2.59 [DATA SET EX2-59] *Variable Description:*

Company: Forty randomly selected retail stores

2001April: Percent change in sales over prior year's April time period

2001June: Percent change in sales over prior year's June time period

Retail store sales are an important economic indicator for the financial position of the consumer. Economists watch changes in retail sales from one year to the next to determine the robustness of the economy. Using a sample of retail stores, data were obtained for the percentage increase in sales from the prior year. Compare the percentages of change in retail store sales for the April and June time periods in 2001. Use a relative frequency histogram. Comment on the similarities of the shape of the distribution for these two time periods.

(Source: "April Comps Beat Forecasts, Rise 3.8%," *Chain Store Age*, June 2001, p. 136.)

Computer Exercises Using the Databases

Exercise 1—Appendix F

Select 50 observations at random from the database. Using a convenient statistical package, construct a frequency histogram and a stem-and-leaf diagram on the variable HPAYRENT (house payment or house/apartment rent). Using this same set of observations, construct separate frequency histograms and stem-and-leaf diagrams on the variable HPAYRENT for those who own their residence and for those who rent their residence. Comment on the shapes of the frequency histograms.

Exercise 2—Appendix F

Choose at random 30 observations from families living in the NE sector and then choose another 30 observations at random from families living in the SW sector. Using a convenient statistical computer package, construct frequency histograms and stem-and-leaf diagrams on the variable INCOME1 (income of principal wage earner) for each group of 30 observations, and comment on the frequency distribution of each.

Exercise 3—Appendix G

Select 100 observations at random from the database. Construct a frequency distribution and a histogram of the values of the variable ASSETS (current assets). Construct a stem-and-leaf diagram. What do you observe from these two graphs?

Exercise 4—Appendix G

Repeat Exercise 3 using the variable LIABIL (current liability).

Insights from Statistics in Action
Lean Philosophy Drives Productivity Growth

The Statistics in Action discussion at the beginning of the chapter emphasized the importance of measuring gains in company productivity and the reasons behind record-ed productivity gains for several large companies. To gain more insight into figures describing productivity gains, consider the data from 70 corporations contained in data set StatInActChap2 and answer the following questions.

1. You would like to include a descriptive graphic with a report discussing the distribution of the productivity gains for these 70 corporations. Present this graphic. How would you describe the shape of the frequency distribution of the productivity gains?

2. Construct a histogram for only the companies listed as being part of the energy industry. Repeat this for the companies listed as being part of the banking or insurance industry. Compare these two graphs.

3. Find the separate average productivity gain for the corporations in each of the following industries by summing the productivity gains and dividing by the total number of corporations in that industry: aerospace, banking, energy, insurance, merchandiser, and pharmaceutical. Present a bar graph of these industries showing the average productivity gain for each.

4. Construct a histogram of the productivity gains for all the corporations except those in energy. Compare this to the histogram that you obtained in Question 1.

5. Change the class width on the histogram in Question 1 and determine if the shape of the histogram is sensitive to the value assigned to the class width.

Source: "In Some States, Foreign Trade Means Jobs," *The Wall Street Journal*, September 20, 2004, p. A.2. "A Who's Who of Productivity," *USA Today*, August 30, 2001, p. 1B. "Companies Pay Out For Productivity Gains," *Information Week*, October 30, 2000.

Appendix
Data Analysis with Excel, MINITAB, and SPSS

Histograms

To obtain a histogram in Excel, use the Excel KPK Data Analysis macro. Click on **KPK Data Analysis ➤ Quantitative Data Charts/Tables ➤ Histograms/Freq. Charts** to obtain the following dialog box. Assume that the 50 salaries presented in Table 2.2 are listed in the first 50 rows of column A and that the output is to start in cell B1. Check **Frequencies** and **Frequency Histogram** to display a frequency histogram. To obtain the resulting histogram in Figure 2.1, enter 6 for the **Number of Classes** and 2 for the **Class Width** and then click **OK.**

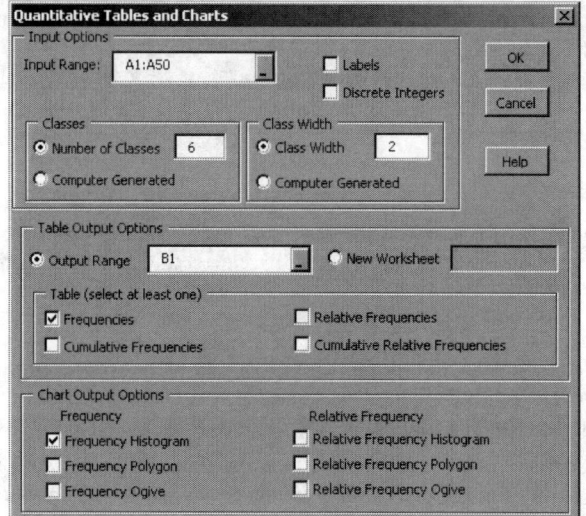

Stem-And-Leaf Diagrams

To obtain the stem-and-leaf diagram in Figure 2.10(a), for Example 2.1, click on **KPK Data Analysis ➤ Quantitative Data Charts/Tables ➤ Stem and Leaf Plots** and enter the range containing the data (say, A1:A100) into the **Input Range.** Select a cell (C1) to display the output.

Frequency Polygons and Ogives

To obtain a polygon or ogive in Excel, use the Excel KPK Data Analysis macro. Click on **KPK Data Analysis ➤ Quantitative Data Charts/Tables ➤ Histograms/Freq. Charts.** The same dialog box as in the section above on obtaining a histogram will appear. Simply select polygon or ogive in the chart output options to obtain the charts as given in Figures 2.11(a) and 2.14(a). Use relative frequencies to keep the vertical axis between 0 and 1.

Bar Charts and Pie Charts

To obtain a bar chart in Excel, either the Excel KPK Data Analysis macros or the Excel Chart Wizard can be used. If the category frequencies are listed in a column, the Excel Chart Wizard should be used. If the frequencies of the categories are not available, then the Excel KPK macros should be used. For example, the observations in file DATA2-3.xls indicate the category in which each complaint is classified. **Click KPK Data Analysis ➤ Qualitative Data Charts ➤ Bar Chart.** The following dialog box displays the **Input Range** and **Output Range.** Click **OK** and a bar chart will appear with the numbers 1, 2, 3, 4, and 5 for the category labels. Replace these integers in the frequency table by the category labels as in the following table. The labels on the bar chart will change to these category names. To obtain a pie chart, repeat this process by clicking **KPK Data Analysis ➤ Qualitative Data Charts ➤ Pie Chart.** Change the labels the same way.

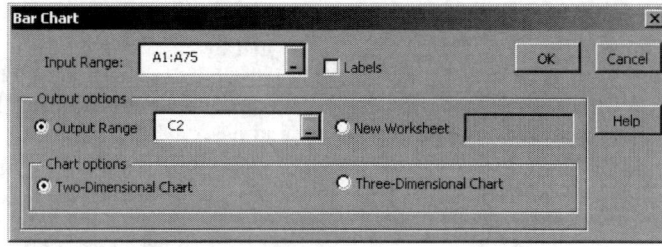

Bar Chart	
CATEGORY	FREQUENCY
Error in billing	42
Rudeness	14
Late delivery	8
Not Answered	6
Other	5

MINITAB

Histograms

The MINITAB procedure to construct a histogram will be illustrated with the salary data in Table 2.2. Click on **Graph ➤ Histogram ➤ Simple** and then click **OK.** Several options are available in the dialog box, which will appear next. Click on **Scale** and then check each box under the low option for the vertical *(y)* and horizontal *(x)* axes. By checking these boxes, the frequencies and the midpoints of the histogram will be displayed, as in Figure 2.4.

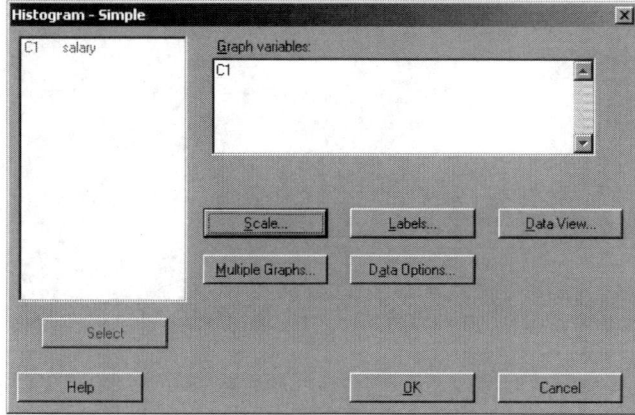

Stem-and-Leaf Diagrams

The MINITAB procedure to construct a stem-and-leaf diagram will be illustrated with the diameter data in Example 2.1. Click on **Graph ➤ Stem-and-Leaf** and this dialog box will appear. If the **OK** button is clicked, the stem-and-leaf diagram will assign the leaves the least significant digit, which is .001 in this example.

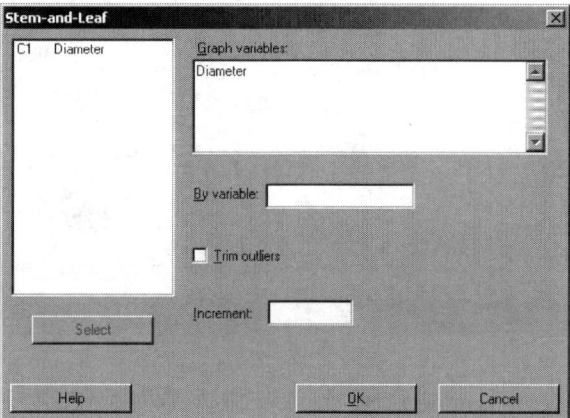

Frequency Polygons and Ogives

To obtain a relative frequency polygon or ogive for the data in Table 2.6, first put the midpoints of each interval in column 1 including the empty classes at each end. Next, put the relative frequencies in column 2 including a zero for the empty classes at each end. To obtain the cumulative frequencies, either type these into column 3 or use the Calculator to obtain these numbers. To use the Calculator, click **Calc ➤ Calculator.** Then put C3 in the box for storing the output from the calculator, select partial sums under **Functions,** type C2 in place of "number" for Pars(number) in the **Expression** box and click **OK.** The C3 column will contain the cumulative frequencies. To obtain a relative frequency polygon, click on **Graph ➤ Scatterplot ➤ With Connect Lines** and the shown dialog box will appear. Put C2 (Rel Freq) under Y variables and C1 under X variables. The relative frequency polygon graph will appear. If C3 is used instead of C2 for the Y variable, the cumulative relative frequency ogive in Figure 2.14(b) will appear. When plotting the ogive, you can delete the right-hand empty class (as in Figure 2.14(b)).

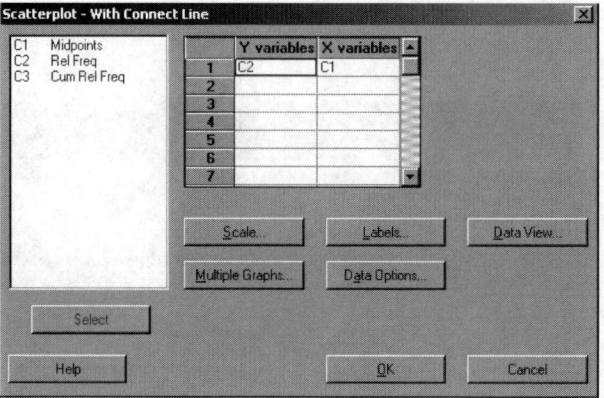

Bar Charts and Pie Charts

To obtain a bar chart, click on **Graph ➤ Bar Chart ➤ Simple** and click **OK,** and the following dialog box will appear. Using the file DATA2-3.mtw, select the categorical variable C1. Click on **Bar Chart Options** to select **Decreasing Y** if it is desired to show the categories with the highest frequencies first. To change the labels on the bar chart, right-click on the *x* axis and select **Edit X Scale.** The following dialog box will appear. Click on the **Labels ➤ Specified** and fill in the label names.

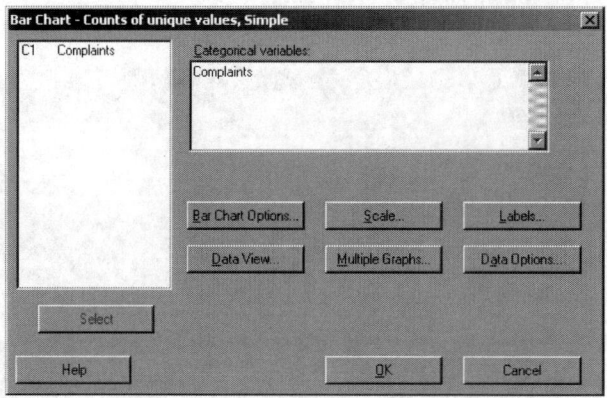

To obtain the pie chart for the file DATA2-3.mtw complaint data, first click on **Data ➤ Code ➤ Numeric to text** and the following dialog box will appear. For the values 1, 2, 3, 4, and 5, assign new names as given in Example 2.3. Note that these relabeled data are placed in column 2 in the dialog box.

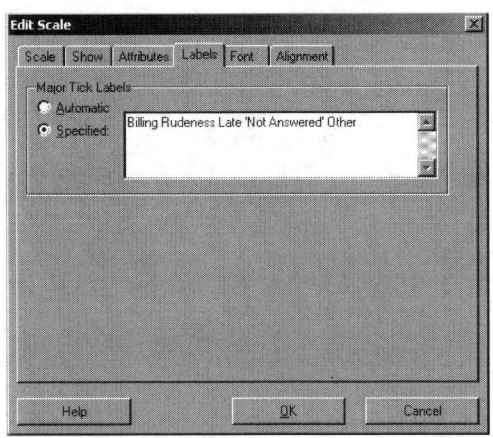

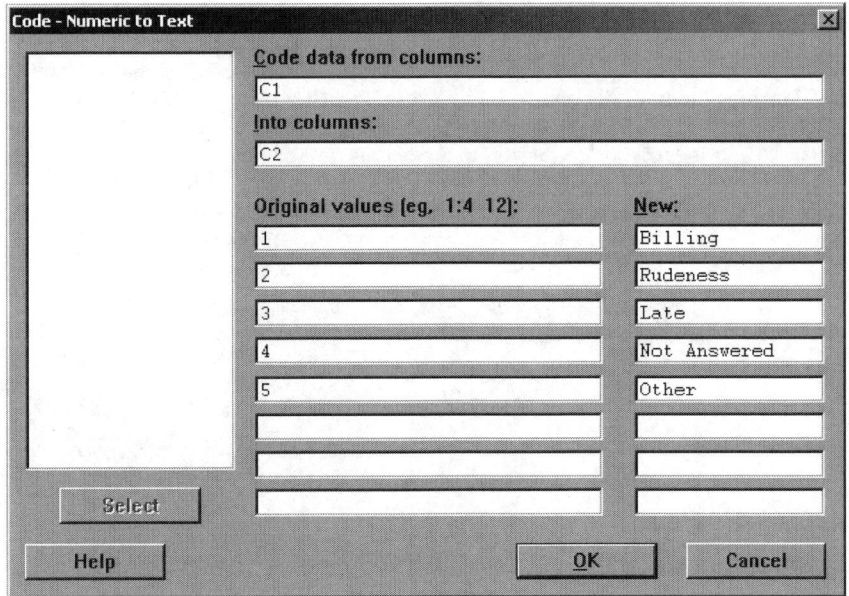

Click on **Graph ➤ Pie** to obtain the following dialog box and select column 2 as the categorical variable. Click **OK,** and a pie chart will appear. To obtain the pie chart in Figure 2.21(b), click on the legend, and hit the delete key to remove it. Then right-click on the pie chart and select **Edit Pie ➤ Slice Labels** and select **Category Name, Frequency,** and **Percent.** If larger labels are desired, click on the **Font** tab and change the font size.

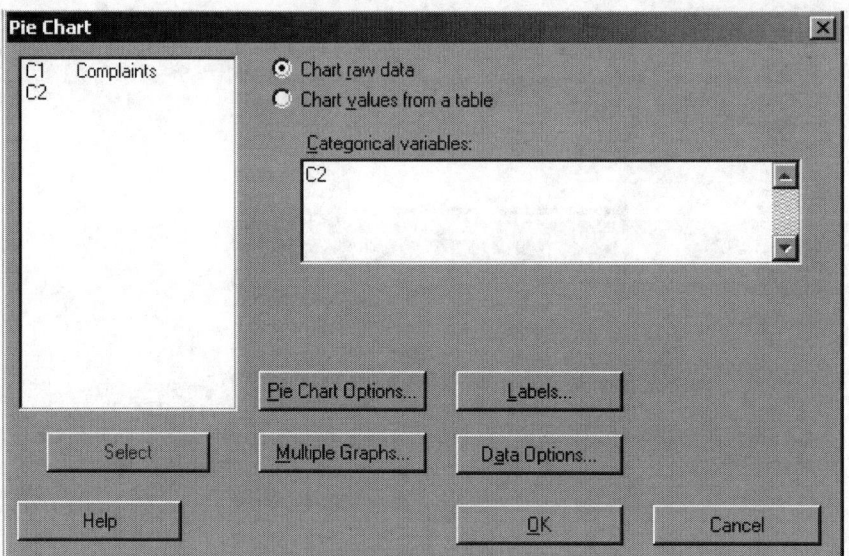

SPSS

Histograms and Stem-and-Leaf Plots

The SPSS procedure will be illustrated using the salary data in Table 2.2. When using SPSS, the class boundaries are defined with "less than or equal to" limits rather than "under" limits. For example, the first class using six classes of salaries would be "32 and less than or equal to 34" rather than "32 and under 34," as described in this chapter. Missing data are automatically omitted. To construct a histogram using SPSS, click on **Analyze ➤ Descriptive Statistics ➤ Explore.** In the dialog shown, click on the variable name (salaries) and the top pointer button to move this variable into the **Dependent List** box. In the **Display** frame, select **Statistics** (summary statistics only), **Plots** (plots only), or **Both.** Click on the **Plots** button and select **Stem-and-leaf** and/or **Histogram** in the window that appears. Click on **Continue** to return to the screen above. Finally, click on **OK.**

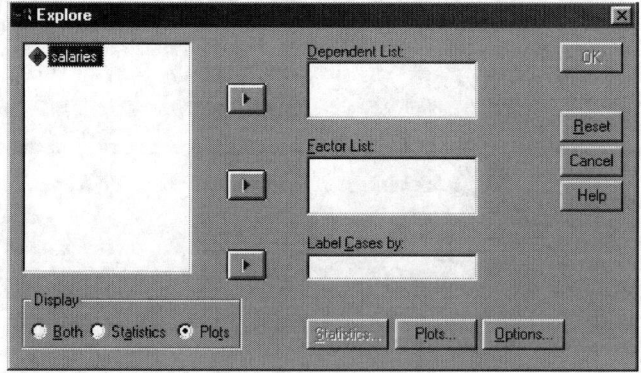

The resulting histogram and stem-and-leaf plot are displayed in Figure 2.5 and Figure 2.10(c). Another option for creating histograms is to use the Interactive Histograms feature in SPSS. The class width or number of classes for a histogram can be specified. To use this feature, click on **Graphs ➤ Interactive ➤ Histogram.** In the following dialog box, click on **salaries** in the left box and drag it into the indicated box. Next, click on the **Histogram** tab. In the **Interval Size** frame, unselect the box that says "Set interval size automatically." Set the **Number of Intervals** value (or **Width of Intervals** value) equal to the

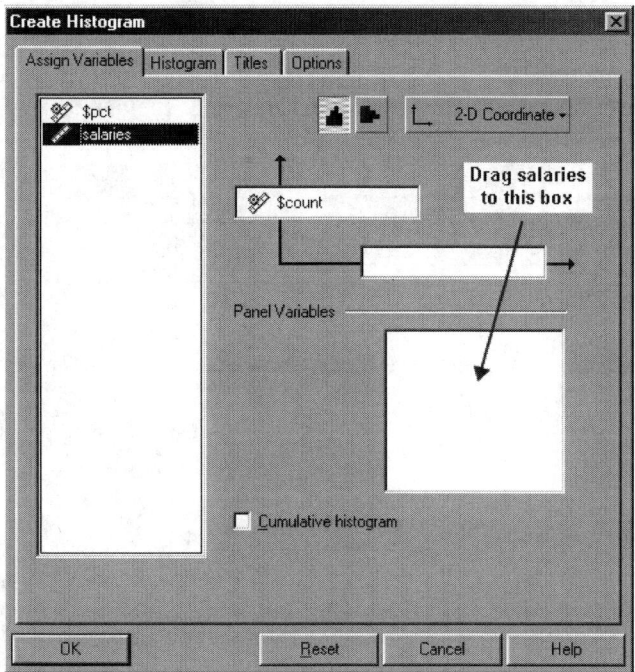

desired value. *Note:* To obtain a relative frequency histogram, replace $count with $pct by dragging the $pct label into the box now containing $count.

Frequency Polygon

To construct a frequency polygon with SPSS, you must put the class midpoints and frequencies into a data window. Be sure to add a class at each end having a zero frequency. The resulting data window for the salary data in Table 2.6 using six classes is shown.

	midpoint	freq
1	31	0
2	33	2
3	35	9
4	37	14
5	39	13
6	41	8
7	43	4
8	45	0

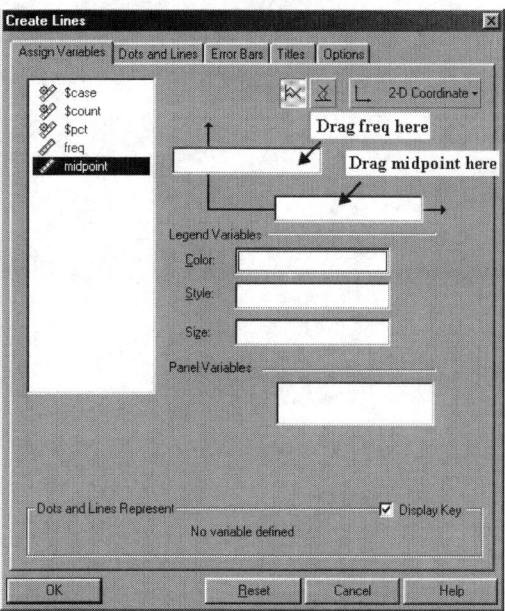

Click on **Graphs ➤ Interactive ➤ Line** and drag the variable names (freq and midpoint) into the appropriate boxes (refer to Create Lines dialog box). Click on **OK** and the graph as presented in Figure 2.11(b) will appear.

Bar Charts and Pie Charts

To illustrate the construction of bar charts and pie charts, the data consisting of the frequency of complaints in Figure 2.19 (using data set DATA2-3.sav) will be used. Begin by putting the category names and frequencies in the first two columns.

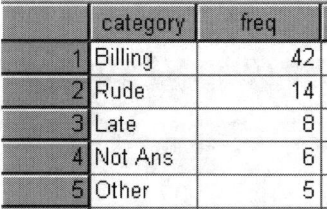

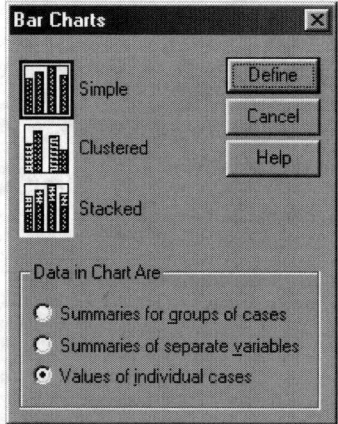

Click on **Graphs ➤ Bar** and select **Simple** and **Values of individual cases** as shown in the window. Click on **Define.**

In the following window, select the freq variable and click on the top pointer to move this variable into the **Bars Represent** box. Select the category variable and click on the lower pointer to move this variable into the **Variable** box inside the Category Labels frame. The graph title (Bar Chart of Complaints) can be specified by clicking on the **Titles** button. Click on **OK** to obtain the bar chart. The procedure to construct a pie chart is similar. To construct the pie chart, click on **Graphs ➤ Pie.**

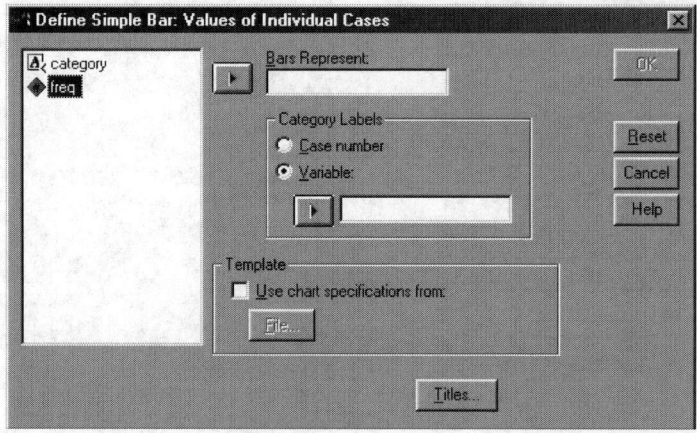

chapter

3

Data Summary Using Descriptive Measures X

Statistics in Action
Semiconductor Business: When the Chips Are Down

What do personal computer upgrades, increased automobile production, and Christmas gaming toys have in common? These products are each fueled by the technological wonder called the *semiconductor*. Companies such as Intel and Texas Instruments have been major players in supplying industry with semiconductors to further advance the high-technology revolution. This revolution has resulted in hard-to-be-seen chips making many difficult tasks seem effortless, ranging from operating a coffee maker to controlling the space shuttle. The most sophisticated chip is a microprocessor, whose transistors can execute hundreds of millions of instructions per second.

Chips are essentially a commodity. A case in point was the project proposed by Cypress Semiconductor Corporation of San Jose, California. In early 1996, Cypress had a ground-breaking ceremony at Round Rock, Texas, for its Fab V facility. In fact, then-governor George Bush was in attendance. However, in late 1996 the chip business went into a dramatic decline. Cypress was forced to put the project on indefinite hold.This Fab V facility eventually became known as the "Slab V" facility, as Cypress stopped investing money into the project.

Countries such as Taiwan have dramatically increased their consumption of semiconductors. In the past six years the consumption of semiconductors, as a percentage of total world consumption, has doubled for the country of Taiwan. This is in contrast to Japan, which had approximately 30% of the world's consumption of semiconductors in the early 1990s and now has less than 18%. These figures illustrate how business cycles worldwide can make the market for semiconductors dynamic and volatile.

When you have completed this chapter, you will be able to examine data illustrating the consumption of semiconductors internationally and discuss these questions:

- What class of *descriptive measures* could be used to compare the percentage of semiconductor consumption by several key global players?

- For each global player, what measure would you use to describe the *middle* of the data collected over a 10-year period?

- For each global player, what measure would you use to describe the *variation* in the data over a 10-year period?

- Are the figures illustrating consumption of semiconductors *skewed*?

3.1

VARIOUS TYPES OF DESCRIPTIVE MEASURES

A **descriptive measure** is a *single* number computed from the sample data that provides information about the data. The class of descriptive measures described here consists of four types. Which one you select depends on what you want to measure:

1. *Measures of central tendency.* These answer the questions, where is the "middle" of my data? and, which data value occurs most often?

2. *Measures of variation.* These answer the questions, how spread out are my data values? and, how much do the data values jump around?

3. *Measures of position.* These answer the questions, how does my value (score on an exam, for example) compare with all the others? and, which data value was exceeded by 75% of the data values? by 50%? by 25%?

4. *Measures of shape.* These answer the questions, are my data values symmetric? and, if not symmetric, just how nonsymmetric (skewed) are the data?

3.2

MEASURES OF CENTRAL TENDENCY

The purpose of a **measure of central tendency** is to determine the center of your data values, or possibly the most typical data value. Some measures of central tendency are the *mean, median, midrange,* and *mode.* We will illustrate each of these measures using as data the number of accidents (monthly) reported over a particular five-month period:

accident data: 6, 9, 7, 23, 5

The Mean

The **mean** is the most popular measure of central tendency. It is merely the average of the data. The mean is easy to compute and explain, and it has several mathematical properties that make it more advantageous to use than the other three measures of central tendency.

Business managers often use a mean to represent a set of values. They select one value as typical of the whole set of values, such as average sales, average price, average salary, or average production per hour. In economics, the term *per capita* is a measure of central tendency. The income per capita of a certain district, the number of clothes washers per capita, and the number of televisions per capita are all examples of a mean.

The *sample mean,* $\bar{x}$ (read "x bar"), is equal to the sum of the data values divided by the number of data values. For the accident data set,

$$\bar{x} = \frac{6+9+7+23+5}{5} = 10.0$$

In general, let an arbitrary data set be represented as

$$x_1, x_2, x_3, \ldots, x_n$$

where n is the number of data values. (In the accident data set, $x_1 = 6$, $x_2 = 9$, $x_3 = 7$, $x_4 = 23$, $x_5 = 5$, and n is 5.) Then,

$$\bar{x} = \frac{x_1 + x_2 + \ldots + x_n}{n} = \frac{\Sigma x}{n} \qquad \textbf{3.1}$$

The symbol Σ (sigma) means "the sum of." In this case, the sample mean, $\bar{x}$, is the sum of the x values divided by n.* When dealing with discrete data, the sample mean is often *not* an integer (such as 10, here) and should *not* be rounded to an integer. For example, remove the last value (5) from the accident data set. The sample mean is now

$$\bar{x} = \frac{6 + 9 + 7 + 23}{4} = 11.25$$

In subsequent chapters, we will be concerned with the mean of the *population*. The symbol of the population mean is μ (mu). For a population consisting of N elements, denoted by

$$x_1, x_2, x_3, \ldots, x_N$$

the *population mean* is defined to be

$$\mu = \frac{x_1 + x_2 + \cdots + x_N}{N} = \frac{\Sigma x}{N} \qquad \textbf{3.2}$$

Population: $x_1, x_2, \ldots, x_N$

Population mean = $\mu = \dfrac{x_1 + x_2 + \cdots + x_N}{N} = \dfrac{\Sigma x}{N}$

Sample values (selected from the population): $x_1, x_2, \ldots, x_n$, where $n \leq N$

Sample mean = $\bar{x} = \dfrac{x_1 + x_2 + \cdots + x_n}{n} = \dfrac{\Sigma x}{n}$

The Median

The **median (Md)** of a set of data is the value in the center of the data values when they are arranged from smallest to largest. Consequently, it is in the center of the ordered array.

Using the accident data set, the median is found by first constructing an ordered array:

5, 6, 7, 9, 23

The value that has an equal number of items to the right and the left is the median. Thus, $Md = 7$.

---

*In another application of this symbol, we square each of the sample values and sum these values. For the accident data, this operation would be written as

$$\begin{aligned} \Sigma x^2 &= 5^2 + 6^2 + 7^2 + 9^2 + 23^2 \\ &= 25 + 36 + 49 + 81 + 529 \\ &= 720 \end{aligned}$$

For these data, then, $\Sigma x = 50$ and $\Sigma x^2 = 720$

In general, if n is *odd*, Md is the center data value of the ordered set:

$$Md = \left(\frac{n+1}{2}\right)\text{st ordered value}$$

Here, the median is the $(5 + 1)/2 = 3$rd value in the ordered array. Note that for these data, the *position* of the median is 3, and the *value* of the median is 7. If n is *even*, Md is the average of the two center values of the ordered set. Thus, the median of the array, 3, 8, 12, 14 is $(8 + 12)/2 = 10.0$.

In our accident data set, one of the five values (23) is much larger than the remaining values—it is an outlier. Notice that the median ($Md = 7$) was much less affected by this value than was the mean ($\bar{x} = 10$). *When dealing with data that are likely to contain outliers (for example, personal incomes or prices of residential housing), the median usually is preferred to the mean as a measure of central tendency, since the median provides a more "typical" or "representative" value for these situations.*

Finally, note that newspaper and magazine articles often refer to both the mean and the median as an "average" value. Care must be taken not to always interpret this word as representing the sample mean unless this is specified in the discussion.

The Midrange

Although less popular than the mean and median, the **midrange (*Mr*)** provides an easy-to-grasp measure of central tendency. Notice that it also is severely affected (even more than $\bar{x}$) by the presence of an outlier in the data. In general:

$$Mr = \frac{L+H}{2}$$

3.3

where L = smallest (lowest) value in the sample and H = largest (highest) value in the sample. Using the accident data set, $L = 5$, $H = 23$, and

$$Mr = \frac{5+23}{2} = 14.0$$

Compare this to $\bar{x} = 10$ and $Md = 7$.

The Mode

The **mode (*Mo*)** of a data set is the value that occurs more than once and the most often. The mode is not always a measure of central tendency; this value need not occur in the "center" of your data. One situation in which the mode is the value of interest is the manufacturing of clothing. The *most common* hat size is what you would like to know, not the *average* hat size. Can you think of other applications where the mode would provide useful information? Consider situations where your sample consists of nominal data.

Note that there is no mode for our accident data set because all values occur only once. Instead, consider this data set:

4, 8, 7, 6, 9, 8, 10, 5, 8

$Mo = 8$ (occurs three times).

There may be more than one mode if several numbers occur the same (and the largest) number of times. This is the only exception to our earlier statement that a descriptive measure consists of a *single* number.

FIGURE

3.1
____

Dot plot, along with
several measures
of central tendency
for a sample
of 10 housing
construction times.
See text for
application.

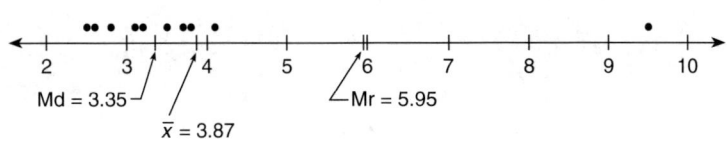

Construction time (months)

E X A M P L E

3.1

A sample of 10 was taken to determine the typical completion time (in months) for the construction of a particular model of Brockwood Homes:

4.1, 3.2, 2.8, 2.6, 3.7, 3.1, 9.4, 2.5, 3.5, 3.8

We find the mean completion time as follows:

$$\bar{x} = \frac{4.1 + 3.2 + \cdots + 3.8}{10} = \frac{38.7}{10} = 3.87 \text{ months}$$

Notice that there is an outlier in the data, namely, 9.4 months. To be safe, you should double-check this figure to make sure that it is, in fact, correct—that is, that there was no mistake in recording or transcribing this value. In the presence of one or two outliers, the median generally provides a more reliable measure of central tendency, so we construct an ordered array:

2.5, 2.6, 2.8, 3.1, 3.2, 3.5, 3.7, 3.8, 4.1, 9.4

Consequently, since n is even,

$$Md = \frac{3.2 + 3.5}{2} = 3.35 \text{ months}$$

Also, the midrange is given by

$$Mr = \frac{2.5 + 9.4}{2} = 5.95 \text{ months}$$

This value is severely affected by the presence of the outlier; the midrange value of nearly 6 months is a poor measure of central tendency for this application.

Finally, no mode exists because there are no repeats in the data values. These results are summarized in the graph in Figure 3.1, a *dot plot*. Each data value is represented as a dot on the horizontal line. The outlier of 9.4 is very obvious when the data are displayed in this type of plot.

E X A M P L E

3.2

In Chapter 2, we examined the starting salaries of the 50 business majors at Bellaire College. The data are presented in Tables 2.2 and 2.3. Dataset DATA3-2 contains these 50 sorted salaries, stored in a single column (column A in Figure 3.2) and also by type of major (columns B, C, and D). After opening this file, you should see columns A through D in

FIGURE

3.2

File DATA3-2 and the four measures of central tendency using Excel's descriptive statistics (midrange added).

	A	B	C	D	E	F
1	**All**	**Accounting**	**Info. Systems**	**Marketing**	***All***	
2	32.8	35.7	34.8	32.8		
3	33.8	35.7	35.6	33.8	Mean	38.202
4	34.3	35.9	35.7	34.3	Standard Error	0.368555
5	34.8	36.6	36.2	35.0	Median	38.05
6	35.0	36.8	36.3	35.2	Mode	35.7
7	35.2	37.0	36.5	36.2	Standard Deviation	2.606075
8	35.6	37.4	37.9	36.8	Sample Variance	6.791629
9	35.7	38.0	38.1	37.0	Kurtosis	-0.48144
10	35.7	38.5	38.1	37.2	Skewness	0.267932
11	35.7	39.2	39.5	37.8	Range	11
12	35.9	39.3		38.2	Minimum	32.8
13	36.2	39.3		38.7	Maximum	43.8
14	36.2	39.4		38.8	Sum	1910.1
15	36.3	39.5		39.7	Count	50
16	36.5	40.3			Midrange	38.3
17	36.6	40.6				

Figure 3.2. Determine the mean, median, and midrange for the entire class of graduating business majors and for each of the three disciplines (accounting, information systems, and marketing). What can you conclude about the "typical" starting salaries for these three groups at Bellaire?

Solution

To obtain the various statistics in Figure 3.2 using Excel, use the Excel Descriptive Statistics command. To obtain this command, click on **Tools ➤ Data Analysis ➤ Descriptive Statistics ➤ OK.*** *You can ignore the shaded cells for now; they'll be covered later in the chapter.* To obtain the midrange, type "Midrange" in cell E16 and enter "=(F12+F13)/2" in cell F16. This uses Excel's formula capability and merely averages the minimum and maximum values in cells F12 and F13.

To derive the same set of statistics for the three disciplines, enter "B1:D27" for the input range and for the output range, enter "G1." This results in columns G through L shown in Figure 3.3. The midranges can be obtained by: (1) highlighting cells E16 and F16 by dragging the mouse across these two cells, (2) finding the fill handle in cell F16 (the small square in the lower right corner) and placing the cursor over the fill handle (you should see a black "+"), and (3) dragging the fill handle through L16. You should now see the midrange label and the corresponding value for each of the three majors.

Since there appear to be no unusual values (outliers)[†] in each of the three sets of salaries, we will examine the means. The mean average starting salary for these 50 business graduates is $38,202. The accounting graduates had the largest mean starting salary ($39,612), followed by the information systems graduates ($36,870) and the marketing graduates ($36,536). For this graduating class at Bellaire, on the average, accounting graduates received a starting salary approximately $3,000 higher than for the other two disciplines.

Often the choice of which measure of central tendency to use is affected by the level of measurement (nominal, ordinal, interval, ratio) of the sample data. For interval/ratio data, you can use any of these four measures. For ordinal data, the difference between

---

*For additional input instructions, refer to the end-of-chapter Excel appendix.

[†]The subject of outliers will be discussed in more detail in Section 3.7.

FIGURE

3.3

The four measures of central tendency using Excel's Descriptive Statistics on the three samples (midrange added).

	G	H	I	J	K	L
1	*Accounting*		*Info. Systems*		*Marketing*	
2						
3	Mean	39.61154	Mean	36.87	Mean	36.53571
4	Standard Error	0.479946	Standard Error	0.461652	Standard Error	0.552776
5	Median	39.45	Median	36.4	Median	36.9
6	Mode	35.7	Mode	38.1	Mode	#N/A
7	Standard Deviation	2.447256	Standard Deviation	1.459871	Standard Deviation	2.068298
8	Sample Variance	5.989062	Sample Variance	2.131222	Sample Variance	4.277857
9	Kurtosis	-0.96244	Kurtosis	-0.65336	Kurtosis	-0.87532
10	Skewness	-0.06037	Skewness	0.444149	Skewness	-0.29774
11	Range	8.1	Range	4.7	Range	6.9
12	Minimum	35.7	Minimum	34.8	Minimum	32.8
13	Maximum	43.8	Maximum	39.5	Maximum	39.7
14	Sum	1029.9	Sum	368.7	Sum	511.5
15	Count	26	Count	10	Count	14
16	Midrange	39.75	Midrange	37.15	Midrange	36.25

TABLE

3.1

Summary of levels of measurement and appropriate measure of central tendency. A "Y" indicates this measure can be used with the corresponding level of measurement.

Measure of Central Tendency	Level of Measurement			
	Nominal	Ordinal	Interval	Ratio
Mean			Y	Y
Median		Y	Y	Y
Midrange			Y	Y
Mode	Y	Y	Y	Y

data values has no meaning, so only the mode and median are appropriate. For nominal data (such as hair color), the sample mode is the only measure of central tendency that should be used. These comments are summarized in Table 3.1.

X Exercises 3.1–3.11

Understanding the Mechanics

3.1 The following five numbers were obtained from a random sample: 48, 4, 12, 8, 24.
  a. Find the mean, median, and midrange.
  b. Divide the five numbers by 4. Find the mean, median, and midrange.

3.2 The following are two ordered sets of data each with a sample size of 6:

Set 1:	2	4	6	6	8	10
Set 2:	2	2	6	8	14	80

a. By simply observing the ordered figures, would you say that data set one is "symmetric" about the value of 6? Without computing, what do you think the mean, median, mode, and midrange are for data set 1? Compute these measures and compare to the answer you provided.

b. Would you consider the value of 80 to be unusually large for data set 2? Do you think that this might make the mean and median rather different? Compute the mean, median, mode, and midrange. Do the mean and median differ as much as you expected?

Applying the New Concepts

3.3 Select five different values between 1 and 20 such that
  a. The mean is smaller than the median.
  b. The mean is larger than the median.

3.4 The number of automobiles that are serviced daily by EZ Service Stations are recorded as follows for 30 days.

50	45	50	51	42	49	80	42	52	49
48	50	88	49	42	50	50	48	50	46
50	51	52	49	49	50	51	40	50	42

  a. Calculate the mean, median, mode, and midrange.
  b. Interpret each statistic in part a. Which measure of central tendency appears to be most appropriate? Why?

3.5 Several years ago, the office occupancy costs, which include rents, real estate taxes, and operating expenses, were sky-high in Japan. Recently, the costs have fallen. The average occupancy costs have slid from $130 to $95 in Tokyo. Interpret this information. Does this imply that the median occupancy costs have decreased by this amount?

(Source: "Less of a Gulf in Office Rents," *Business Week,* June 16, 1997, p. 28.)

3.6 A traveling salesperson in Canada records the number of kilometers his Ford Taurus can drive on a full tank of gas. The following data give the kilometers traveled on a full tank of gas until the gas gauge indicated "empty."

640	620	640	521	655	605	638	678	630	650
420	595	670	633	628	660	595	670	640	630

  a. Calculate the mean, median, and mode.
  b. Which value appears to be more appropriate as a measure of central tendency?
  c. Recalculate the mean, median, and mode with the value of 420 kilometers omitted. Compare your answers to part a.

Using the Computer

3.7 [DATA SET EX3-7] *Variable Description:*

Insurance Company: Name of life and health insurance company

Revenue: Revenue in millions of dollars for 2003

The annual revenues in 2003 for 13 top global life and health insurance companies are displayed on the *Fortune* Web site *(www.fortune.com).* Compute the mean and median. Which observation affects the value of the mean the most if omitted?

3.8 [DATA SET EX3-8] *Variable Description:*

Company: Name of a Fortune 500 company

Score: Average rating for Most Admired Company with 10 as highest score

Ratings for the Most Admired Company contest in 2003 are displayed on the *Fortune* Web site *(www.fortune.com).* Compare the mean, median, mode, and midrange for the score variable.

3.9 [DATA SET EX3-9] *Variable Description:*

Company: Name of a fast-growing company

Growth: Revenue growth in percentage

Revenue growth for several of the fastest-growing U.S. companies in 2003 is displayed on the *Fortune* Web site *(www.fortune.com).* Compare the mean, median, mode, and midrange for the variable growth.

3.10 [DATA SET EX3-10] *Variable Description:*

Company: Name of a fast-growing company

TotalReturn: Three-year total return in percentage

Total return from owning stocks of several of the fastest-growing companies in 2003 is displayed on the *Fortune* Web site *(www.fortune.com).* Which measure or measures of central tendency would you select to explain to a manager the center of the data? Why?

3.11 [DATA SET EX3-11] *Variable Description:*

Company: Selected Fortune 500 companies

CEOComp: Total compensation for the year 2000 for CEOs

Chief executive officers (CEOs) of Fortune 500 companies typically receive a compensation package worth many millions. Sometimes these packages are so unbelievably large that share holders publicly criticize top management and the company's compensation committee. Of course, most CEOs still seem to believe they are worth every dollar they get.
  a. Find the mean, median, and midrange of the total compensation for CEOs of the selected companies.
  b. Remove the CEO pay for Citigroup and General Electric and repeat part a. Compare these statistics to those obtained in part a.
  c. Suppose that these compensation packages were to be compared to those of Japanese firms. To make a comparison, the amount of compensation could be converted into yen. Assuming that 1 dollar is equal to 120 yen, what do you think the new mean and median would be for the total compensation in units of yen for the CEOs of the selected companies?
  d. Transform the compensation figures by multiplying them by 120 to obtain equivalent figures in yen and find the mean and median. Compare the computed values to your values in part c.

(Source: "CEO Pay: Whoosh!" *Fortune,* June 25, 2001, p. 78.)

MEASURES OF VARIATION

Measures of central tendency, such as the mean, are certainly useful. However, the use of any single statistic to describe a complete distribution fails to reveal important facts.

Homogeneity refers to the degree of similarity within a set of data values. For example, the values in data set 1 (sunrise times for 10 randomly selected days in May) are much more homogeneous than the values in data set 2 (current batting averages for the starting lineup of the Cincinnati Reds.)

Data set 1: 6:20, 6:20, 6:20, 6:21, 6:21, 6:22, 6:22, 6:24, 6:26, 6:27
Data set 2: .115, .190, .224, .245, .256, .259, .279, .294, .331

The more homogeneous a set of data is, the better the mean will represent a typical value. **Variation** is the tendency of data values to scatter about the mean, $\bar{x}$. If all the data values in a sample are identical, then the mean provides perfect information, the variation is zero, and the data are perfectly homogeneous. This is rarely the case, however, so we need a measure of this variation that will increase as the scatter of the data values about $\bar{x}$ increases.

Knowledge of variation can sometimes be used to control the future variability of your data values. Industrial production operations maintain quality control by observing and measuring the variation of the units produced. If there is too much variation in the production process, the causes are determined and corrected using an inspection control procedure.

Commonly used measures of variation are the *range, variance, standard deviation,* and *coefficient of variation.* Such measures are meaningful only when computed from *interval* or *ratio* data. To illustrate the various variation measures, we will use the accident data from the previous section: 6, 9, 7, 23, 5.

The Range

The simplest measure of variation is the **range** of the data, which is the numerical difference between the largest value *(H)* and the smallest value *(L)*. For the accident data,

$$\text{range} = H - L = 23 - 5 = 18$$

The range is a rather crude measure of variation, but it is an easy number to calculate and contains valuable information for many situations. Stock reports generally give prices in terms of their ranges, citing the high and low prices of the day. The value of the range is strongly influenced by an outlier in the sample data.

The Variance and Standard Deviation

By far the most commonly used measures of variation are the **variance** and **standard deviation.** Both measures describe the variation of the sample values about the sample mean, $\bar{x}$. Using the accident data, the sample mean is $\bar{x} = 10$. To calculate the sample variance, you begin by finding (1) the distance from each sample value to the mean, (2) the square of these distances, and (3) the sum of the squared distances. The closer the sample values are to $\bar{x} = 10$, the smaller this sum will be. Figure 3.4 illustrates the distance from the second sample value (6) to the mean, $\bar{x}$. The calculations necessary to compute the variance are as follows.

FIGURE

3.4

This presentation of the accident data shows their variation.

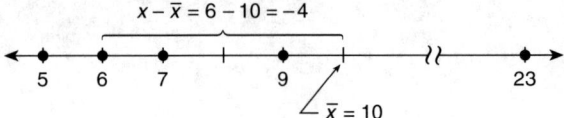

$x - \bar{x} = 6 - 10 = -4$

$\bar{x} = 10$

Data Value (x)	$(x - \bar{x})$	$(x - \bar{x})^2$
5	−5	25
6	−4	16
7	−3	9
9	−1	1
23	13	169
	$\Sigma(x - \bar{x}) = 0$	$\Sigma(x - \bar{x})^2 = 220$

So, $\Sigma(x - \bar{x})^2 = 220$.

The obvious thing to do next would be to find the average of these squared deviations:

$$\frac{\Sigma(x - \bar{x})^2}{n}$$

One use of this particular statistic in subsequent chapters is an *estimator*. In particular, we will need to estimate the variation within an entire population, using sample data collected from the population. However, a better estimator is obtained by dividing the sum of the squared deviations by $n - 1$ rather than by n. This leads to the **sample variance, s^2**. In general,

DEFINITION

$$s^2 = \frac{\Sigma(x - \bar{x})^2}{n - 1}$$

3.4

Using the accident data,

$$s^2 = \frac{220}{5 - 1} = \frac{220}{4} = 55.0$$

The square root of the variance is referred to as the **sample standard deviation, s**. In general,

$$s = \sqrt{\frac{\Sigma(x - \bar{x})^2}{n - 1}}$$

3.5

Using the accident data,

$$s = \sqrt{55.0} = 7.416$$

As previously mentioned, the sample variance, s^2, is used to estimate the variance of the entire population. The symbol for the population variance is s^2 (read as sigma squared). For a population consisting of N elements,

$$x_1, x_2, x_3, \ldots, x_N$$

the population variance is defined to be

$$\sigma^2 = \frac{\Sigma(x - \mu)^2}{N}$$

3.6

where μ is the population mean, defined in equation 3.2.

As we saw, the *population* variance can be obtained by dividing the sum of the squared deviations about μ by the population size N. The *sample* variance is calculated by dividing the sum of the squared deviations about $\bar{x}$ by the sample size (n) minus one. Had we chosen to divide by n rather than by $n - 1$, the resulting estimator would (on the average) underestimate σ^2. For this reason, we use $n - 1$ in the denominator of s^2.

Population: $x_1, x_2, \ldots, x_N$

$$\text{Population variance} = \sigma^2 = \frac{(x_1 - \mu)^2 + \cdots + (x_N - \mu)^2}{N}$$

$$= \frac{\Sigma(x - \mu)^2}{N}$$

$$\text{Population standard deviation} = \sigma = \sqrt{\frac{\Sigma(x - \mu)^2}{N}}$$

Sample values (selected from the population): $x_1, x_2, \ldots, x_n$, where $n \leq N$

$$\text{Sample variance} = s^2 = \frac{(x_1 - \bar{x})^2 + \cdots + (x_n - \bar{x})^2}{n - 1} = \frac{\Sigma(x - \bar{x})^2}{n - 1}$$

$$\text{Sample standard deviation} = s = \sqrt{\frac{\Sigma(x - \bar{x})^2}{n - 1}}$$

Now consider what the units of measurement are for s and s^2. The units of s are the same as the units on the data. If the data are measured in pounds, the units of s are pounds. Consequently, the units of the variance, s^2, would be (pounds)^2—a rather difficult unit to grasp, at best. For the accident data, $s = 7.416$ accidents and $s^2 = 55$ (accidents)^2.

Comments

The units of measurement for s are the same as the units of measurement on the mean ($\bar{x}$)—namely, the units of measurement for the sample values. As a result, we are able to combine the sample standard deviation and the sample mean and ask questions such as, "How many of the sample values are less than $\bar{x} + s$?" or "How many of the sample values lie between $\bar{x} - s$ and $\bar{x} + s$?" Such questions will be discussed in Section 3.6.

There is another way to compute the sample variance. Using equation 3.4 to compute the value of s^2 may have appeared easy enough, but the computation was helped in part by the fact that the sample mean, $\bar{x}$, was an integer (10). When $\bar{x}$ is not an integer, it is easier to find s^2 using

COMPUTING FORMULA FOR s^2

$$s^2 = \frac{\Sigma x^2 - (\Sigma x)^2 / n}{n - 1}$$

3.7

As before, the standard deviation is the square root of the variance. To illustrate the use of equation 3.7, consider the accident data:

x	x^2
5	25
6	36
7	49
9	81
23	529
50	720

So, $n = 5$, $\Sigma x = 50$, $\Sigma x^2 = 720$. Consequently, using equation 3.7

$$s^2 = \frac{720 - (50)^2 / 5}{5 - 1}$$

$$= \frac{720 - 500}{4} = 55.0 \qquad \text{(as before)}$$

Also

$$s = \sqrt{55.0} = 7.416 \qquad \text{(as before)}$$

Finally, you may wish to interpret the magnitude of the value of s or s^2—that is, whether your value of s (or s^2) is large. This is difficult to determine because the values of s and s^2 depend on the magnitude of the data values. In other words, large data values generally lead to large values of s. For example, which of the following two data sets exhibits more variation?

Data set 1: 5, 6, 7, 9, 23   (accident reports)

Data set 2: 5,000, 6,000, 7,000, 9,000, 23,000   (seating capacity of five football stadiums)

As we have already seen, for data set 1, $\bar{x} = 10.0$ and $s = 7.416$. For data set 2, the mean and standard deviation are $\bar{x} = 10,000$ and $s = 7,416$.

Do these results mean that data set 2 has a great deal more variation, given that its standard deviation is 1,000 times that of data set 1? Another look at the values reveals that the large value of s for data set 2 is due to the large values within this set. In fact, considering the size of the numbers within each data set, the *relative* variation within each group of values is the same. So comparing the standard deviations or variations of two data sets is not a good idea unless you know that their mean values ($\bar{x}$) are approximately equal. The next section deals with another statistical measure that will allow you to compare the relative variation within two data sets.

The Coefficient of Variation

Consider again our two data sets, which appear to have the same variation (relative to the size of the data values) yet have vastly different standard deviations:

Data set 1: 5, 6, 7, 9, 23   ($\bar{x} = 10$, $s = 7.416$)

Data set 2: 5,000, 6,000, 7,000, 9,000, 23,000   ($\bar{x} = 10,000$, $s = 7,416$)

To compare their variation, we need a measure of variation that will produce the same value for both of them. The solution here is to measure the standard deviation in terms of the mean; that is, what percentage of $\bar{x}$ is s? This measure of variation is the **coefficient of variation, CV.** In general, for samples containing non-negative values,

$$CV = \frac{s}{\bar{x}} \cdot 100$$

For our example data sets:

$$\text{Data set 1:} \quad CV = \frac{7.416}{10} \cdot 100 = 74.16$$

$$\text{Data set 2:} \quad CV = \frac{7,416}{10,000} \cdot 100 = 74.16$$

So our conclusion here is that both data sets exhibit the same relative variation; s is 74.16% of the mean for both sets. As a final word here, we must point out that for data sets with *extreme* variation, it is possible to obtain a coefficient of variation larger than 100%.

EXAMPLE 3.3

To review the various measures of variation, let's use the data on housing construction time in Example 3.1.

Completion time: 4.1, 3.2, 2.8, 2.6, 3.7, 3.1, 9.4, 2.5, 3.5, 3.8 (months)

First, compute the range:

$$H - L = 9.4 - 2.5 = 6.9 \text{ months}$$

To find the variance and the standard deviation, first determine

$$\Sigma x = 4.1 + 3.2 + \ldots + 3.8 = 38.7$$

and

$$\Sigma x^2 = (4.1)^2 + (3.2)^2 + \ldots + (3.8)^2 = 186.25$$

Hence,

$$s^2 = \frac{186.25 - (38.7)^2 / 10}{10 - 1}$$

$$= \frac{186.25 - 149.77}{9} = 4.05 \text{ (months)}^2$$

and

$$s = \sqrt{4.05} = 2.01 \text{ months}$$

To calculate the coefficient of variation, use the previously obtained values of s and $\bar{x}$, where

$$CV = \frac{2.01}{3.87} \cdot 100 = 51.9$$

The sample standard deviation is 51.9% of the sample mean.

Statistical Software Application Use DATA3-4

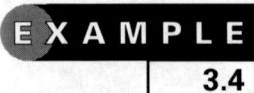

Using Statistical Software to Compute Various Sample Statistics

Example 2.1 introduced a sample of inside diameters for 100 machined parts produced at the Boston facility of Allied Manufacturing. This sample is also contained in Excel file DATA3-4. The machined part is supposed to have an inside diameter of 10.2 millimeters, with specification (spec) limits of 10.1 to 10.3 millimeters. Prior to examining this sample, you received word that the Toronto facility of Allied obtained a random sample of their parts, which have the same specs. Their sample produced a mean of 10.191 millimeters and a standard deviation of 0.0448 millimeter. Determine the sample mean, range, standard deviation, and coefficient of variation of the Boston sample. Comment on this sample. In particular, do these parts appear to be better than the Toronto parts?

Solution   The Excel output using the descriptive statistics command is shown in Figure 3.5(a). Enter A1:A101 for the input range and B1 for the output range. Be sure to click on the checkboxes for **Labels in First Row** and **Summary Statistics.** The coefficient of variation in cells B16 and C16 is not part of the initial output but can be easily obtained by entering "Coeff. of Variation" in cell B16 and "=(C7/C3)*100" in cell C16.

Instructions for obtaining the MINITAB descriptive statistics in Figure 3.5(b) and the SPSS descriptive statistics in Figure 3.5(c) are contained in the end-of-chapter appendices.

FIGURE

3.5

(a) Descriptive statistics for 100 machined parts (inside diameter) using Excel.
(b) Descriptive statistics for 100 machined parts (inside diameter) using MINITAB.
(c) Descriptive statistics for 100 machined parts (inside diameter) using SPSS.

	A	B	C	D
1	Diameter	*Diameter*		
2	10.216			
3	10.221	Mean	10.27539	←
4	10.226	Standard Error	0.002668	
5	10.228	Median	10.276	
6	10.23	Mode	10.271	
7	10.23	Standard Deviation	0.026681	←
8	10.231	Sample Variance	0.000712	
9	10.231	Kurtosis	-0.3467	
10	10.234	Skewness	-0.01021	
11	10.237	Range	0.122	←
12	10.239	Minimum	10.216	←
13	10.239	Maximum	10.338	←
14	10.24	Sum	1027.539	
15	10.24	Count	100	
16	10.244	Coeff. of Variation	0.259659	←
17	10.245			

⏮ ◀ ▶ ⏭ \DATA3-4\

(a)

Descriptive Statistics: Diameter

Variable	N	Mean	StDev	Minimum	Q1	Median	Q3	Maximum
Diameter	100	10.275	0.0267	10.216	10.257	10.276	10.293	10.338

(b)

Descriptives

Descriptive Statistics

	N	Range	Minimum	Maximum	Sum	Mean	Std. Deviation	Variance
DIAMETER	100	.122	10.216	10.338	1027.539	10.27539	.02668	.000712
Valid N (listwise)	100							

(c)

The coefficient of variation can easily be computed by dividing the standard deviation by the mean and multiplying by 100.

Using any of the three computer outputs, the smallest sample value is 10.216, the largest value is 10.338, and the range is 10.338 – 10.216 = .122 millimeter. This machined part is supposed to have an inside diameter of 10.2 millimeters. The specification limits were from 10.1 to 10.3 millimeters; that is, these parts are of acceptable quality only if the diameter is between these two values. The sample mean of 10.275 is much larger than 10.2 millimeters, so the conclusion here would be the same as in Example 2.1: The process is off center and needs adjustment. The standard deviation for the Boston sample is 0.0267, and the coefficient of variation is 0.260. Consequently, the sample standard deviation is 0.26% of the sample mean.

To compare the Boston and Toronto samples, consider the following summary information:

	$\bar{x}$	s
Boston	10.275	.0267
Toronto	10.191	.0448

Based on this information, is the Boston process better or worse than the Toronto process? The answer is *both!* The Boston process is worse based on the value of $\bar{x}$, since this indicates that this process is 0.075 (10.275 – 10.2) millimeter off center, whereas for the Toronto sample, the production process is 0.009 (10.2 – 10.191) millimeter off center. However, the Boston process is more consistent, since the standard deviation ($s = 0.0267$ millimeter) is much smaller than for the Toronto sample ($s = 0.0448$ millimeter). So you have mixed results here—the Boston process has less variation but is producing parts having inside diameters that are too large, on the average.

So far, you can reduce a set of sample data to a number that indicates a typical or average value (a measure of central tendency) or one that describes the amount of variation within the data values (a measure of variation). The next section examines yet another set of statistics—measures of position.

X Exercises 3.12–3.21

Understanding the Mechanics

3.12 From 50 collected data points, the statistics Σx and Σx^2 are calculated to be 20 and 33, respectively. Compute the sample mean, sample variance, sample standard deviation, and coefficient of variation.

3.13 Find the range, standard deviation, and coefficient of variation for each of the following data sets and comment on your results:

a. 2	4	6	8	10
b. 20	40	60	80	100
c. .02	.04	.06	.08	.10

3.14 The values of the difference between the data values and the sample mean are –5, 1, –3, 2, 3, and 2.
  a. Do these values add to 0? Should they?
  b. What is the variance of the data?
  c. What is the standard deviation?

Applying the New Concepts

3.15 The scores for team 1 were 70, 60, 65, and 69. The scores for team 2 were 72, 58, 61, and 73. Compare the coefficients of variation for these two teams.

3.16 The prices of two stocks are shown to vary over a 12-month period. Describe the variability of the stocks. Which stock appears to be more stable? Why?

Month	Stock A	Stock B
Jan	10	30
Feb	11	33
Mar	12	36
Apr	11	32
May	15	45
June	18	49
Jul	13	37
Aug	16	48
Sept	11	33
Oct	10	30
Nov	9	33
Dec	13	39

3.17 Using the number of automobiles serviced in Exercise 3.4, compute the standard deviation. Remove the two largest and two smallest observations and recompute. How do you explain your results?

3.18 Using the kilometers data for the trips made by a Ford Taurus in Exercise 3.6, compute the coefficient of variation for these data. What are the units of this measure?

3.19 Apparel sales in summer are difficult for apparel retailers because shoppers are usually looking for summer discounts. The July sales for six large apparel retailers for July 2001 are as follows:

Apparel Retailer	Sales in Millions
Gap	948.0
Limited	612.3
TJX	745.0
Kohl's	466.3
Talbots	106.6
AnnTaylor	84.9

a. From observing the data, what would you guess is the mean and standard deviation?
b. Compute the mean and the standard deviation.
c. Remove the apparel retailers with the largest and smallest sales. How do you believe the mean and standard deviation of the sales will change with the removal of these figures?
d. Compare the calculated mean and standard deviation with the values that you guessed. What characteristics about the data give you a clue as to what the mean and standard deviation might be?

(Source: "Discounts in Demand: Shoppers Sought Bargains in July," *Wall Street Journal,* August 10, 2001, p. B3.)

Using the Computer

3.20 [DATA SET EX3-20] *Variable Description:*

YearMonth: Year and months ranging from January 1982 to August 2001

CPI: The consumer price index

CPILessE&G: The consumer price index excluding energy and food

Economists use the Consumer Price Index (CPI) to obtain insights into the effects of inflation on purchases made by consumers. The CPI is a measure of the average change in prices over time in a market basket of goods and services. This measure is also computed excluding energy and food since these two categories can change dramatically.

a. Compute the mean and standard deviation for the CPI for the time period from January 1982 to August 2001.
b. Repeat part a using the CPI excluding energy and food.
c. Compute the coefficient of variation for the CPI and for CPI excluding energy and food. Discuss your findings when comparing these two measures.

(Source: "Taming Inflation," *Wall Street Journal,* August 17, 2001, p. A2.)

3.21 [DATA SET EX3-21] *Variable Description:*

TimeTV: Total daily time in minutes spent watching TV

Marketing managers are interested in TV viewership to attract company advertising. Viewers are customers for many products. To justify the millions of dollars spent on advertising, marketing departments must assess the percentage of the population that TV advertisement will reach as well as the likelihood of a viewer seeing the advertisement. One hundred adult viewers were sampled, and their total daily time in minutes spent watching TV for that day was recorded.

a. Find the mean and standard deviation of TimeTV. (Excel: Use the **Insert Function ➤ Statistical.**) Compute the coefficient of variation and variance from these values.
b. Convert the values of TimeTV to hours by dividing by 60. How do you think the mean, standard deviation, and variance will change?
c. Compute the mean, standard deviation, and variance of the values of TimeTV in units of hours. Compare these results to your answer in part b. Is this what you expected?

3.4   MEASURES OF POSITION

Suppose that you think you are drastically underpaid compared with other people with similar experience and performance. One way to attack the problem is to obtain the salaries of these other employees and demonstrate that *comparatively* you are way down the list. To evaluate your salary compared with the entire group, you would use a measure of position. *Measures of position* are indicators of how a particular value fits in with all the other data values. Two commonly used measures of position are (1) a percentile (and quartile), and (2) a z-score.

To illustrate these measures, we suppose that the personnel manager of Texon Industries has administered an aptitude test to 50 applicants. The ordered data are shown in Table 3.2. The mean of the data is $\bar{x} = 60.36$, and the standard deviation is $s = 18.61$. Ms. Jenson received the score of 83. She wishes to measure her performance in relation to all the applicant scores. We will return to this illustration in Example 3.5.

TABLE

3.2

22	44	56	68	78
25	44	57	68	78
28	46	59	69	80
31	48	60	71	82
34	49	61	72	83
35	51	63	72	85
39	53	63	74	88
39	53	63	75	90
40	55	65	75	92
42	55	66	76	96

Ordered array of aptitude test scores for 50 applicants ($\bar{x} = 60.36$, $s = 18.61$).

Percentiles

A **percentile** is the most common measure of position. The value of, for example, the 35th percentile is essentially the value that exceeds 35% of all the data values. More precisely, the 35th percentile is that value (say, P_{35}) such that at most 35% of the data values are less than P_{35} and at most 65% of the data values are greater than P_{35}. We will use the Texon Industries applicant data to determine the 35th percentile. Which data value is located 35% of the way between the first and last locations? Here the number of data values is $n = 50$ and the percentile is $P = 35$. We define the *position* of the 35th percentile as follows:

$$n \cdot \frac{P}{100} = 50 \cdot .35 = 17.5$$

To satisfy the more precise definition of a percentile, whenever $n \cdot P/100$ is *not* a counting number, it should be rounded *up* to the next counting number. So, 17.5 is rounded up to 18, and the 35th percentile is the 18th value *of the ordered values*. Referring to Table 3.2, the 35th percentile is $P_{35} = 53$.

In general, to find the *location* of the *P*th percentile, determine $n \cdot P/100$ and use one of the following two location rules.

Location rule 1. If $n \cdot P/100$ is *not* a counting number, round it *up*, and the *P*th percentile will be the value in this position of the ordered data.

Location rule 2. If $n \cdot P/100$ *is* a counting number, the *P*th percentile is the average of the number in this location (of the ordered data) and the number in the next largest location.

Now we can use the applicant data to determine the 40th percentile. Here $n \cdot P/100 = (50)(.4) = 20$. Then, using the second rule,

$$P_{40} = 40\text{th percentile} = \frac{(20\text{th value}) + (21\text{st value})}{2}$$

$$= \frac{55 + 56}{2} = 55.5$$

Notice here that the 40th percentile is *not* one of the data values but is an average of two of them. Now work out the 50th percentile yourself. What measure of the central tendency uses the same procedure? From our previous discussion, you should realize that *the 50th percentile is the median.*

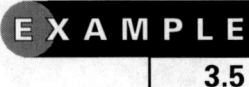

3.5

Solution

Recall that Ms. Jenson received a score of 83. What is her percentile value?

Her value is the 45th largest value (out of a total of 50). An initial guess of her percentile would be:

$$P = \frac{45}{50} \cdot 100 = 90$$

However, due to the percentile rules used here, this guess may be slightly incorrect. Your next step should be to examine this value of P, along with the next two smaller values. The following calculations of $P = 88$, $P = 89$, and $P = 90$ reveal that Ms. Jenson's score is the 89th percentile.

P	$\dfrac{n \cdot P}{100}$	Pth Percentile
88	$50 \cdot .88 = 44$	$(82 + 83)/2 = 82.5$
89	$50 \cdot .89 = 44.5$	45th value = 83
90	$50 \cdot .90 = 45$	$(83 + 85)/2 = 84$

3.6

Solution

What is the 50th percentile for the applicant data in Table 3.2?

Here, $n \cdot P/100 = 50 \cdot .5 = 25$. The 50th percentile is an average of the 25th and 26th ordered data values:

$$P_{50} = 50\text{th percentile} = \frac{61 + 63}{2} = 62$$

Quartiles

Quartiles are merely particular percentiles that divide the data into quarters, namely:

$$Q_1 = \text{1st quartile} = \text{25th percentile } (P_{25})$$

$$Q_2 = \text{2nd quartile} = \text{50th percentile} = \text{median } (P_{50})$$

$$Q_3 = \text{3rd quartile} = \text{75th percentile } (P_{75})$$

They are used as benchmarks, much like the use of A, B, C, D, and F on examination grades. Using the applicant data in Table 3.2, we can determine the first quartile by first calculating:

$$n \cdot \frac{P}{100} = (50)(.25) = 12.5$$

This result is rounded up to 13, and $Q_1 = $ 13th ordered value = 46.

$$Q_2 = \text{median} = 62$$

from Example 3.6. Finally, for Q_3,

$$n \cdot \frac{P}{100} = (50)(.75) = 37.5$$

This is rounded up to 38, and Q_3 = 38th ordered value = 75.

Another measure commonly used in conjunction with quartiles is the **interquartile range *(IQR)*,** defined as

$$IQR = Q_3 - Q_1$$

In the applicant data, the interquartile range is

$$IQR = 75 - 46 = 29$$

Consequently, the middle 50% of the data are between 46 and 75.

Strictly speaking, the interquartile range is a measure of variation, since it can be expected to increase as the data become more spread out. It is not a commonly used measure of variation, although it is certainly easy to compute (much like the range of a sample data set). Its primary disadvantage is that it measures the spread within the middle of the data, not within the entire data set. The interquartile range can be illustrated in a simple graph called a box plot, discussed in Section 3.7.

z-Scores

Another measure of position is a sample z-score, which is based on the mean ($\bar{x}$) and standard deviation of the data set. Like a percentile, a z-score determines the relative position of any particular data value x; it is expressed in terms of the number of standard deviations above or below the mean. The z-score of x is defined as

$$z = \frac{x - \bar{x}}{s}$$

3.9

Recall from Example 3.5 that Ms. Jenson had a score of 83 on the test. For this data set, $\bar{x}$ = 60.36 and s = 18.61. Her score of 83 is the 89th percentile. The corresponding z-score is

$$z = \frac{83 - 60.36}{18.61} = 1.22$$

This z-score means that Ms. Jenson's score of 83 is 1.22 standard deviations to the *right* of the mean, or above the group's average. Thus, if z is positive, it indicates how many standard deviations x is to the right of the mean.

A negative z-score implies that x is to the *left* of the mean. Again referring to Table 3.2, what is the z-score for the individual who obtained a total of 35 on the aptitude examination?

$$z = \frac{35 - 60.36}{18.61} = -1.36$$

This individual's score is 1.36 standard deviations to the left of the mean, or below the group's average.

The process of subtracting the mean and dividing by the standard deviation is referred to as *standardizing* the sample data, and the corresponding z-value is the *standardized* value. So Ms. Jensen's raw score is 83, and her standardized score is 1.22, indicating that her raw score is 1.22 standard deviations to the right of the mean. For a typical sample, you can expect nearly all of the standardized values to lie between –3 and 3 (the z-scores range from –3 to 3). This will be discussed further in Section 3.6.

EXAMPLE 3.7

Example 3.4 contained data listing 100 measurements for the inside diameter of a certain machined part. The specification limits for this part are 10.1 millimeters (the lower spec limit, or LSL) and 10.3 millimeters (the upper spec limit, or USL). Any part falling outside this range is said to be nonconforming and is not of acceptable quality. Of interest here is the following question: What is the z-score for both the LSL and the USL, and which z-score has the smaller absolute value?

Solution

The z-score for each of these limits is found by subtracting the sample mean and dividing by the standard deviation. In Example 3.4, the sample mean was found to be $\bar{x} = 10.275$ and the sample standard deviation was $s = .0267$. The z-score for the USL (10.3) is

$$\frac{10.3 - 10.275}{.0267} = .94$$

and the z-score for the LSL is

$$\frac{10.1 - 10.275}{.0267} = -6.55$$

The absolute values of these two z-scores are .94 and 6.55. The minimum of these two absolute values is .94, indicating that the nearer spec limit is the upper spec limit and that the sample mean is .94 standard deviations away from this limit. *A general rule here is that to consistently produce products of acceptable quality, the minimum absolute value of these two z-scores should be at least 3.* In this case, the product is not capable of meeting these specifications—a result consistent with Examples 2.1 and 3.4.

3.5   MEASURES OF SHAPE

A basic question in many applications is whether your data exhibit a *symmetric* pattern. **Measures of shape** include measures of skewness and kurtosis.

Skewness

The histogram in Figure 3.6 demonstrates a perfectly symmetric distribution. When the data are symmetric, the sample mean, $\bar{x}$, and the sample median, Md, are the same. As the data tend toward a nonsymmetric distribution, referred to as skewed, the mean and median drift apart. The easiest method of determining the degree of *skewness* present in your sample data is to calculate a measure referred to as the **Pearson's coefficient of skewness, Sk.** Its value is given in Equation 3.10:

$$Sk = \frac{3(\bar{x} - Md)}{s}$$

3.10

where s is the standard deviation of the sample data.

3.6

Histogram
constructed with
symmetric data.
The mean, median,
and mode are
equal.

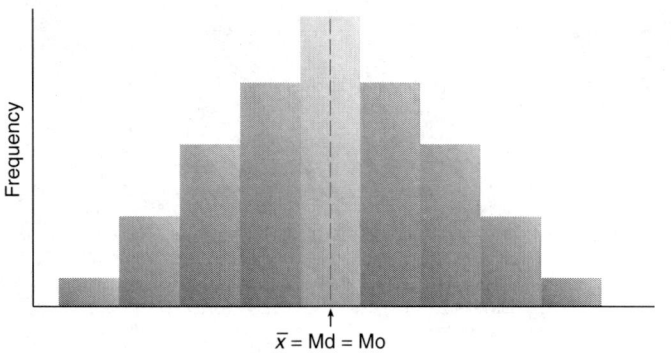

$\bar{x}$ = Md = Mo

3.7

Histogram
showing right
(positive) skew.

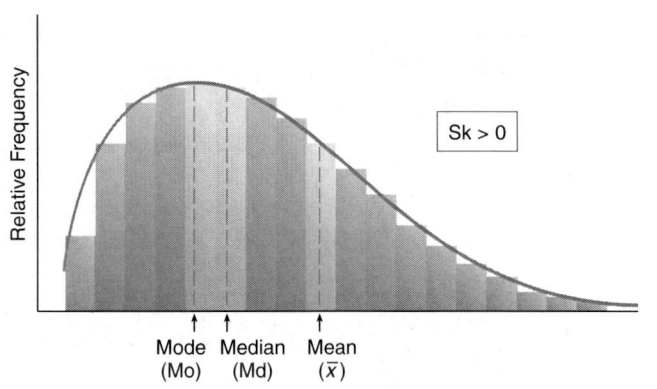

Sk > 0

Mode Median Mean
(Mo)   (Md)   ($\bar{x}$)

The value of *Sk* ranges from –3 to 3.* If the data are perfectly symmetric (a rare event), *Sk* = 0, because $\bar{x}$ = *Md*. For Figure 3.6, *Sk* is zero. If the mean is larger than the median, then *Sk* is positive, and we say that the data are *skewed right*. Consequently, for data that are skewed right, *values above the mean occur less frequently than values below the mean.* This merely means the data exhibit a pattern with a right tail, as illustrated in Figure 3.7. We know the mean is affected by extreme values, so we would expect the mean to move toward the right tail, above the median, resulting in a positive value of *Sk*. Similarly, if the mean is smaller than the median, then *Sk* is negative and the data are *skewed left*. As a result, in a negatively skewed sample, *values above the mean occur more frequently than values below the mean.* Figure 3.8 shows a data distribution exhibiting a left tail and negative skew.

Excel, SPSS, and MINITAB use a slightly more complicated measure of skewness. This involves finding the *z*-score for each data value, cubing each *z*-score, and then summing the results (that is, $(z\text{-score})_1^3 + (z\text{-score})_2^3 + (z\text{-score})_3^3 + \ldots$). This measure of skewness will be written as *Sk'* and uses the formula given below.

*One proof of this statement can be found in Colm Art O'Cinneide, "The Mean is Within One Standard Deviation of Any Median," *The American Statistician* 44, no. 4 (1990), p. 292.

3.8

Histogram
showing left
(negative) skew.

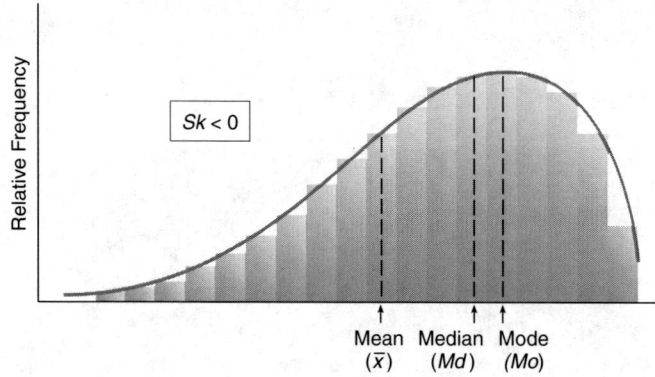

$$Sk' = \frac{n}{(n-1)(n-2)} \Sigma \left(\frac{x - \bar{x}}{s} \right)^3 = \frac{n}{(n-1)(n-2)} \Sigma(z - score)^3$$

3.11

Similar to the Pearson's skewness measure, this measure of skewness will be positive for samples that are skewed right (Figure 3.7) and negative for samples that are skewed left (Figure 3.8).

Examples 3.4 and 3.7 were concerned with the inside diameters of 100 machined parts. To examine the symmetry of the data, we can use the various statistics in Figure 3.5. The Pearson's measure of skewness is

$$Sk = \frac{3(10.27539 - 10.276)}{.02668} = -.069$$

This is nearly zero, and we conclude that the data are nearly symmetric and a histogram of these 100 values would resemble the one in Figure 3.6. According to Figure 3.5(a), the Excel measure of skewness is $Sk' = -.0102$ (in cell C10). This same skewness value could be calculated using MINI TAB or SPSS. Since this skewness measure is nearly zero, we again conclude that the data are nearly symmetric.

Kurtosis

Sk measures the tendency of a distribution to stretch out in a particular direction. Another measure of shape, referred to as the **kurtosis,** measures the *peakedness* of your distribution. The calculation of this measure is a bit cumbersome, and the kurtosis value is not needed in the remaining text material.* Briefly, this value is large if there is a high frequency of observations near the mean and in the tails of the distribution.

---

*Using Excel, you can click on **Help ➤ Statistical Functions,** and type "kurtosis." The formula used by Excel is in this discussion.

X Exercises 3.22–3.33

Understanding the Mechanics

3.22 The number of defects in 10 rolls of carpets are

| 3 | 2 | 6 | 0 | 1 | 3 | 2 | 1 | 0 | 4 |

   a. What are the 75th percentile and the 50th percentile?
   b. What are the mean and standard deviation?
   c. What is the coefficient of skewness?

3.23 Assume that the sum of 10 observations is 10, that the sum of the squares of 10 observations is 20, and that the median is 1.5. What is the coefficient of skewness?

3.24 The percentage of unemployed workers in each of 20 randomly selected cities are as follows.

| 3.1 | 4.5 | 8.2 | 1.4 | 6.3 | 1.8 | 2.4 | 8.8 | 1.9 | 2.4 |
| 5.4 | 3.8 | 7.2 | 3.8 | 4.6 | 7.2 | 2.5 | 4.8 | 3.7 | 4.2 |

   a. Calculate the 20th percentile.
   b. Calculate the 40th percentile.
   c. Calculate the 60th percentile.
   d. Calculate the 80th percentile.
   e. Calculate the interquartile range.

3.25 From a random sample, the mean is 50 and the sample standard deviation is 5.
   a. What is the z-score if an observation's value is 40?
   b. What is the z-score if an observation's value is 65?
   c. What is the value of an observation with a z-score of 1?
   d. What is the value of an observation with a z-score of –2.5?

3.26 The time (in minutes) that it takes 20 people to complete a task follows.

| 30 | 35 | 51 | 65 | 22 | 35 | 44 | 55 | 30 | 50 |
| 40 | 60 | 64 | 38 | 52 | 68 | 38 | 53 | 62 | 49 |

   a. Find the interquartile range.
   b. Find the mean of the data.
   c. Find the standard deviation of the data.
   d. Find the coefficient of skewness.

Applying the New Concepts

3.27 The following data were obtained from a survey requesting 30 different families to list their weekly expenditure on food.

105	85	72	59	130	120	95	83	78	91
64	106	86	87	78	108	145	102	86	74
72	103	94	63	73	89	75	88	107	101

   a. Calculate the 20th percentile.
   b. Calculate the 80th percentile.
   c. Calculate the interquartile range.

   d. Calculate the mean, median, standard deviation, and coefficient of skewness.
   e. Write up a brief description of the survey's results, and interpret each of the values of the statistics.

3.28 Consider the following grades recorded on an aptitude test.

70	15	42	21	73	45	22	71	20	74
74	53	74	86	52	19	77	84	73	54
87	90	71	53	21	71	75	72	12	47

   a. Calculate each of the quartiles and the coefficient of skewness to describe the distribution of the data.
   b. What observations would you consider to be unusually low or high? Why?
   c. How would you evaluate a student who scored 75 on the exam?

3.29 Select five numbers between 0 and 10.
   a. Calculate the standard deviation of these five numbers.
   b. Form the z-scores for these five numbers.
   c. What do you think is the standard deviation of the z-scores? Calculate the standard deviation of the z-scores.

3.30 Using the number of automobiles serviced in Exercise 3.4, compute the coefficient of skewness and interpret this measure.

Using the Computer

3.31 **[DATA SET EX3-31]** *Variable Description:*

Name: Name of money-losing company

Loss: Amount of money that the company lost in millions of dollars

The top money-losing global companies in 2003 are displayed on the *Fortune* Web site (*www.fortune.com*). Compute the coefficient of skewness. How would you interpret this measure in explaining characteristics of the data distribution to a manager?

3.32 **[DATA SET EX3-32]** *Variable Description:*

Checkfee: Fee that financial institution charges for a checking account with no minimum

Bank and financial institutions have been steadily increasing checking fees for no-minimum checking accounts. A sample of 75 banks and financial institutions that offer checking accounts with no minimum balance required was selected in the Toronto metropolitan area. Data are presented in units of Canadian dollars.
   a. What are the mean, median, and standard deviation, coefficient of skewness, and the interquartile range? How would you interpret these statistics?

b. Convert the data to U.S. dollars. Use the conversion 1 Canadian dollar equals .70 U.S. dollars. Calculate the statistics in part a. How do these values change?

3.33 [DATA SET EX3-33] *Variable Description:*

District: Forty school districts in North Texas

Graduates: Number of high school graduates in the year 2000

State funding and salary structure in school districts depend on a formula that takes into account the number of students. Because the number of students varies greatly across the school districts of North Texas, educational administrators face a considerable challenge in providing all school districts with the necessary resources to provide a quality education to their students.

a. Obtain a histogram of the number of high school graduates for the year 2000. Would you conclude that the data are skewed?

b. Use the mean, median, and standard deviation to compute Pearson's coefficient of skewness. Does this number confirm your conclusion in part a?

c. Delete the five districts with the largest values from the list of the number of high school graduates for 2000. Recompute the coefficient of skewness. Did you think that the coefficient of skewness would change by this much?

(Source: "High School Attrition," *The Dallas Morning News*," May 20, 2001, p. 17A.)

3.6

INTERPRETING $\bar{x}$ AND s

Now that you have gone through several pencils determining the sample mean and standard deviation, what can you learn from these values? The type of question that you can answer is, how many of the data values are within two standard deviations of the mean?

Take a look at the aptitude test scores in Table 3.2. Here $\bar{x} = 60.36$ and $s = 18.61$, and so we obtain

$$\begin{aligned} \bar{x} - s &= 60.36 - 18.61 \\ &= 41.75 \end{aligned} \qquad \begin{aligned} \bar{x} + s &= 60.36 + 18.61 \\ &= 78.97 \end{aligned}$$

$$\begin{aligned} \bar{x} - 2s &= 60.36 - 37.22 \\ &= 23.14 \end{aligned} \qquad \begin{aligned} \bar{x} + 2s &= 60.36 + 37.22 \\ &= 97.58 \end{aligned}$$

$$\begin{aligned} \bar{x} - 3s &= 60.36 - 55.83 \\ &= 4.53 \end{aligned} \qquad \begin{aligned} \bar{x} + 3s &= 60.36 + 55.83 \\ &= 116.19 \end{aligned}$$

Examine these data and observe that (1) 33 out of the 50 values (66%) lie between $\bar{x} - s$ and $\bar{x} + s$; (2) 49 out of the 50 values (98%) lie between $\bar{x} - 2s$ and $\bar{x} + 2s$; and (3) 50 out of the 50 values (100%) lie between $\bar{x} - 3s$ and $\bar{x} + 3s$. Or, put another way: (1) 66% of the data values have a z-score between −1 and 1; (2) 98% have a z-score between −2 and 2, and (3) 100% have a z-score between −3 and 3.

What can we say in general for any data set? First, **Chebyshev's inequality** is usually conservative but makes *no assumption* about the population from which you obtained your data. Following are the components of Chebyshev's inequality.

CHEBYSHEV'S INEQUALITY

For any data set:

1. At least 75% of the data values are between $\bar{x} - 2s$ and $\bar{x} + 2s$. At least 75% of the data values have a z-score between −2 and 2.
2. At least 89% of the data values are between $\bar{x} - 3s$ and $\bar{x} + 3s$. At least 89% of the data values have a z-score between −3 and 3.
3. In general, at least $(1 - 1/k^2) \times 100\%$ of your data values lie between $\bar{x} - ks$ and $\bar{x} + ks$ (have z-scores between $-k$ and k) for any $k > 1$.

FIGURE

3.9

A bell-shaped (normal) population.

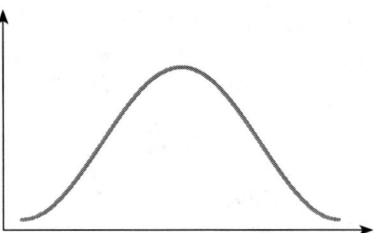

TABLE

3.3

Summary of percentages of sample values by interval, using data from Table 3.2.

Between	Actual Percentage	Chebyshev's Inequality Percentage	Empirical Rule Percentage
$\bar{x} - s$ and $\bar{x} + s$	66% (33 out of 50)	—	≈ 68%
$\bar{x} - 2s$ and $\bar{x} + 2s$	98% (49 out of 50)	≥75%	≈ 95%
$\bar{x} - 3s$ and $\bar{x} + 3s$	100% (50 out of 50)	≥89%	≈ 100%

Note that if $k = 1$, then $1 - 1/k^2 = 0$; so Chebyshev's inequality provides no information on the number of data values to expect between $\bar{x} - s$ and $\bar{x} + s$.

The other type of statement is called the **empirical rule.** We make a key assumption here; namely, that the population from which you obtain your sample has a *bell-shaped distribution*; that is, it is symmetric and tapers off smoothly into each tail. Such a population is called a **normal population** and is illustrated in Figure 3.9. Thus, the data set should have a skewness measure, *Sk,* near zero and a histogram similar to that in Figure 3.6. The empirical rule has three components.

EMPIRICAL RULE

Under the assumption of a bell-shaped population:*
1. Approximately 68% (roughly two-thirds) of the data values lie between $\bar{x} - s$ and $\bar{x} + s$ (have z-scores between –1 and 1).
2. Approximately 95% (19 out of 20) of the data values lie between $\bar{x} - 2s$ and $\bar{x} + 2s$ (have z-scores between –2 and 2).
3. Approximately 99.7% (nearly all) of the data values lie between $\bar{x} - 3s$ and $\bar{x} + 3s$ (have z-scores between –3 and 3).

Returning to Table 3.2, we can summarize our previous results along with the information provided by Chebyshev's inequality and the empirical rule. The actual percentages of the sample values in each interval, as well as the percentages specified using each of the two rules, are shown in Table 3.3.

---

*Strictly speaking, the empirical rule applies to population values (substituting μ for $\bar{x}$ and σ for s). However, this rule works very well for large samples having an approximate bell-shaped histogram.

As you can see, Chebyshev's inequality is very conservative, but it always works. The empirical rule predicted results close to what was observed. For these data, the median is $Md = 62$ (see Example 3.6), and so Pearson's measure of skewness is

$$Sk = \frac{3(60.36 - 62)}{18.61} = -.26$$

Recalling that this measure ranges from –3 to 3, we could call this skewness measure *close to zero,* and so it is not surprising that the empirical rule was quite accurate, since we are dealing with a nearly symmetric set of data.

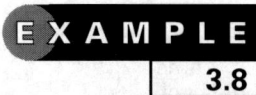

3.8

In a random sample of 200 automobile insurance claims obtained from Landmark Insurance Company, $\bar{x} = \$615$ and $s = \$135$.

1. What statement can you make using Chebyshev's inequality?

2. If you have reason to believe that the population of all insurance claims is bell-shaped (normal), what does the empirical rule say about these 200 values?

Solution 1

Chebyshev's inequality provides information regarding the number of sample values within a specified number of standard deviations of the mean. For $k = 2$, we have:

$$\bar{x} - 2s = 615 - 2(135) = \$345$$
$$\bar{x} + 2s = 615 + 2(135) = \$885$$

We conclude that at least 75% of the sample values lie between \$345 and \$885 and have z-scores between –2 and 2. Because $.75 \cdot 200 = 150$, this implies that at least 150 of the claims are between \$345 and \$885.

For $k = 3$,

$$\bar{x} - 3s = 615 - 3(135) = \$210$$
$$\bar{x} + 3s = 615 + 3(135) = \$1,020$$

and we conclude that at least 8/9 (89%) of the data values are between \$210 and \$1,020. Here, $8/9 \cdot 200 = 177.8$, so at least 178 of the claims are between \$210 and \$1,020.

Solution 2

If the distribution of automotive claims at Landmark Insurance Company is believed to be bell-shaped, the empirical rule allows us to draw stronger conclusions. In particular, for $k = 1$, we have

$$\bar{x} - s = 615 - 135 = \$480$$
$$\bar{x} + s = 615 + 135 = \$750$$

and we conclude that approximately 68% of the data values ($.68 \cdot 200 = 136$) are between \$480 and \$750 and have z-scores between –1 and 1.

For $k = 2$,

$$\bar{x} - 2s = \$345$$
$$\bar{x} + 2s = \$885$$

and we conclude that approximately 95% of the data values ($.95 \cdot 200 = 190$) will lie between \$345 and \$885.

X Exercises 3.34–3.45

Understanding the Mechanics

3.34 A random sample of observations has a sample mean of 20 and a standard deviation of 5. Use Chebyshev's inequality to find the following intervals:
 a. An interval that has at least 75% of the data within it
 b. An interval that has at least 89% of the data within it

3.35 A random sample from a bell-shaped population yields a mean of 100 and a standard deviation of 20. Calculate the following intervals:
 a. An interval that has approximately 68% of the data values within it
 b. An interval that has approximately 99.7% of the data values within it

Applying the New Concepts

3.36 A manager notices that the mean weight of a bag of grain from a recent shipment is 50 pounds, with a standard deviation of 3. At least what percentage of values can the manager say will lie within 4 standard deviations of the mean?

3.37 The following random sample of annual salaries was recorded. Units are in thousands of dollars.

50 52 48 46 32 51 47 20 53 49

 a. Calculate the mean and standard deviation.
 b. Using Chebyshev's inequality, between what two bounds will at least 75% of the data lie?
 c. Using Chebyshev's inequality, between what two bounds will at least 89% of the data values lie?
 d. Are the percentage of values within the bounds in parts b and c from these data consistent with Chebyshev's inequality?

3.38 The sample mean is 120 and the standard deviation is 30 for a random sample of 300 observations.
 a. At least how many observations are expected to lie between 60 and 180?
 b. Under the assumption that the data are from a bell-shaped population, how many observations are expected to lie between 60 and 180?

3.39 Refer to the data in Exercise 3.4 on the number of automobiles serviced daily by EZ Service Station. Calculate the percentage of observations between 1, 2, and 3 standard deviations of the mean. Could these data be considered to have been collected from a normal population?

3.40 An increasing number of foreign carriers are allowing their cockpit crews to take short, planned naps on long-haul flights. These planned naps are intended to counteract the effects of fatigue. Currently, the Federal Aviation Administration does not allow domestic carriers to nap, even on overseas flights. Suppose that it is known that on approximately 95% of the flights between Tokyo and Sydney, pilots nap between 30 minutes and 1 hour, with the average being 45 minutes. Assuming that the empirical rule can be used, what is the standard deviation of the time spent napping by the pilots?

(Source: Adapted from "Nap Time," *Wall Street Journal*, May 8, 1998, p. W6.)

3.41 Refer to the data in the weekly expenditure on food by various families in Exercise 3.27. Between what two values would you expect at least 75% of the data to fall? How many observations actually lie within this interval?

3.42 Approximately how many standard deviations from the mean will at least 55% of the data values lie for any population? Note that this number is not an integer value.

Using the Computer

3.43 [**DATA SET EX3-43**] *Variable Description:*

WeeklyRate: The weekly rate to rent a car (in dollars)

Special weekly rates at 18 national locations of Hertz's car rentals are provided in this data set. Between what two bounds will at least 75% of the data lie? What about at least 89%?

3.44 [**DATA SET EX3-44**] *Variable Description:*

Servtime: Amount of time that it takes to be served the main course at Anthony's Restaurant

The manager of Anthony's Restaurant is interested in examining the total wait time that customers spend in the restaurant before being served their main course. A random sample of 75 parties was observed and their total wait time in minutes was recorded.
 a. Plot a histogram of the data. Would you conclude that the data appear to be bell-shaped?
 b. Use the mean and standard deviation functions to compute intervals such that the mean is in the center of the interval and the distance from the mean to either endpoint is two standard deviations. Use an appropriate rule to approximate the percentage of data values within this interval.

3.45 [**DATA SET EX3-45**] *Variable Description:*

MMbal: Balance in money market fund

A local bank offers a money market fund that pays above average interest rates provided the investor maintains a minimum balance of $10,000. A vice president of the bank has a random sample of 200 accounts examined and their balances were recorded.
 a. Find the mean and standard deviation of MMbal. Compute ranges in which at least 75% and 89% of the data will lie.
 b. Sort the data. (Excel: Use **Data ➤ Sort.**) Determine how many observations actually fall outside the ranges computed in part a. Compare these to the minimum numbers expected by Chebyshev's inequality.

BOX PLOTS

Exploratory data analysis (EDA) is a recently developed set of tools for providing easy-to-construct pictures that summarize and describe a sample. Two popular diagrams that fall under this category are *stem-and-leaf diagrams* (introduced in Chapter 2) and *box plots*. Section 2.2 gave several illustrations of stem-and-leaf diagrams. These graphs provide a representation of the *entire* sample and, unlike histograms, do not condense the data into classes. This section discusses box plots that are graphical illustrations of the quartile measures of position discussed in Section 3.4.

A **box plot** is a graphical representation of a set of sample data that illustrates the lowest data value *(L)*, the first quartile (Q_1), the median (Q_2, Md), the third quartile (Q_3), the interquartile range *(IQR)*, and the highest data value *(H)*.

In Section 3.4, the following values were determined for the aptitude test scores in Table 3.2:

$$L = 22 \qquad\qquad Q_3 = 75$$
$$Q_1 = 46 \qquad\qquad IQR = 75 - 46 = 29$$
$$Q_2 = Md = 62 \qquad\qquad H = 96$$

A box plot of these values is shown in Figure 3.10. The ends of the box are located at the first and third quartiles, with a vertical bar inserted at the median. Consequently, the length of the box is the interquartile range. If the data are symmetric, the median bar should be located at the center of the box. *Consequently, the bar location indicates the skewness of the data: If located in the left half of the box, the data are skewed right. If located in the right half, the data are skewed left.*

Box plots provide a very easy method of detecting outliers in a set of sample data. First, we define the two *inner fences*. The lower inner fence is the first quartile minus 1.5 times the interquartile range, and the upper inner fence is the third quartile plus 1.5 times the interquartile range.

Any value smaller than the lower inner fence or larger than the upper inner fence will be classified as an outlier. Using the aptitude test scores in Table 3.2, we get

$$\text{lower inner fence} = 46 - (1.5)(29) = 2.5$$
$$\text{upper inner fence} = 75 + (1.5)(29) = 118.5$$

Since none of the data values are less than 2.5 or larger than 118.5, we conclude that this sample contains no outliers.

Extreme outliers are identified by defining *outer fences*. The lower outer fence is the first quartile minus 3 times the interquartile range and the upper outer fence is the third quartile plus 3 times the interquartile range.

FIGURE

3.10

Box plot for 50 aptitude test scores (data in Table 3.2).

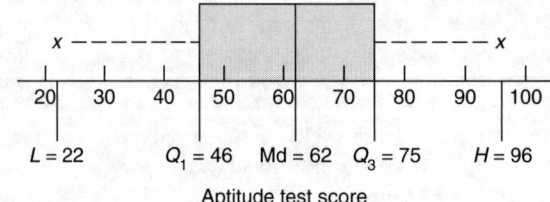

Aptitude test score

FIGURE

3.11

Excel spreadsheet using the KPK Data Analysis box plot (data are 75 residential appraisals).

	A	B	C
1	211	**Values of Box Plot Parameters**	
2	205	PARAMETER	VALUE
3	212	First Quartile	174
4	205	Median	206
5	235	Third Quartile	230
6	182	IQR	56
7	232	Minimum	151
8	184	Maximum	410
9	225	Upper Inner Fence	314
10	157	Lower Inner Fence	90
11	155	Upper Outer Fence	398
12	241	Lower Outer Fence	6

FIGURE

3.12

Excel box plot created using KPK Data Analysis (data are 75 residential appraisals).

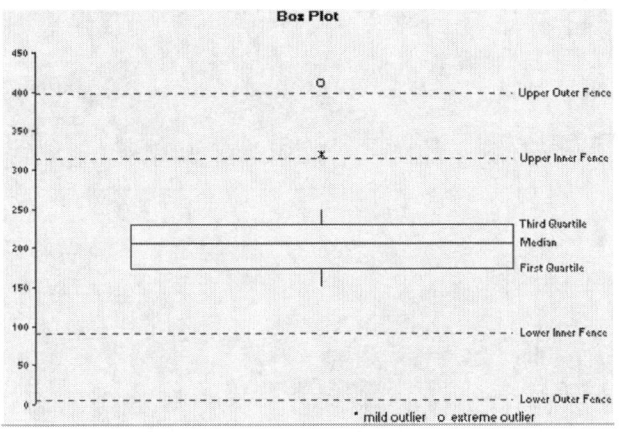

Any value less than the lower outer fence or greater than the upper outer fence are **extreme outliers.** We expect *less than one-hundreth of 1%* of the sample values from a bell-shaped population to lie outside the outer fence. Sample values that lie beyond an inner fence but inside the outer fence are **mild outliers.** For a sample from a bell-shaped population, we expect *less than 1%* of the values to lie outside the inner fences. The sample in Table 3.2 contains no values beyond the inner fences (mild outliers), and, as a result, contains no extreme outliers.

The dotted lines on a box plot, called the **whiskers,** connect the highest and lowest data values *contained within the inner fences* to the ends of the box. Thus, approximately 25% of the data values will lie in each whisker and in each portion of the box.

Excel does not have a data analysis tool to construct a box plot, but the set of KPK data analysis macros supplied with this textbook does have this feature. The spreadsheet in Figure 3.11 is a result of (1) entering (loading) the data into column A, and (2) clicking on **KPK Data Analysis ➤ Quantitative Data Charts/Tables ➤ Box Plot.** In Figure 3.11, the data in column A consist of 75 residential appraisals (in thousands of dollars) having a median value of $206,000. After clicking on **Box Plot** you should see a small input screen. Enter "A1:A75" as the input range and enter "B1" in the output range box. The resulting box plot is shown in Figure 3.12 where the median value ($206,000) is represented by the line inside the box. Any mild outlier is represented by the symbol ✳ and extreme outliers are represented using the symbol **O.** The sample of residential appraisals contains one mild outlier and one extreme outlier. A closer look at the data revealed one appraised value of $320,000 (the mild outlier) and one value of $410,000 (the extreme outlier). The extreme outlier is equal to the maximum value in cell C8, Figure 3.11.

FIGURE

3.13

(a) MINITAB box plots of 50 job applicants (sample 1) and 100 current employees (sample 2).
(b) SPSS box plots of 50 job applicants (sample 1) and 100 current employees (sample 2).

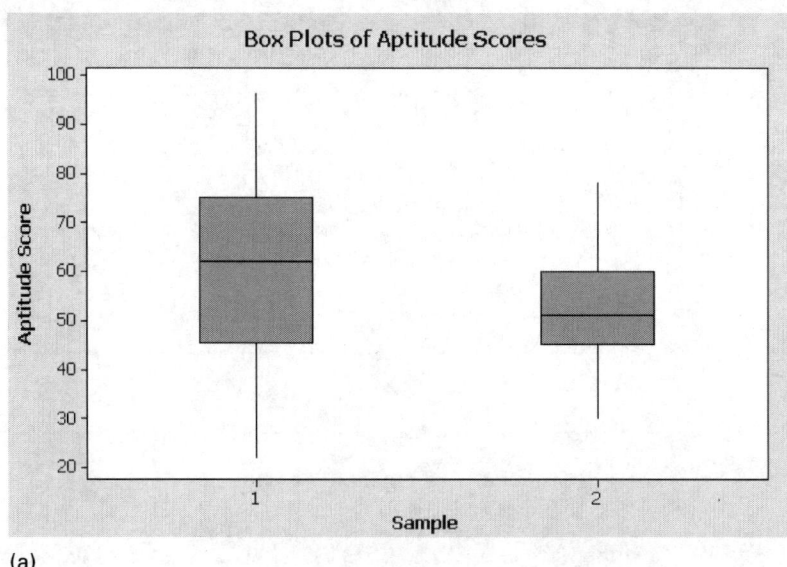

(a)

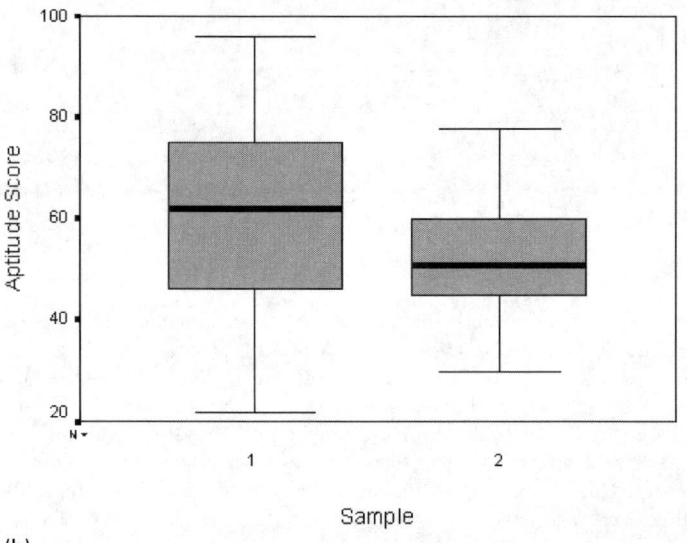

(b)

E X A M P L E

3.9

The personnel manager of Texon Industries is interested in comparing the aptitude scores from the 50 job applicants (Table 3.2) with those of 100 people randomly selected from people currently employed at Texon. Both box plots are shown in Figure 3.13, which illustrates the ability of MINITAB and SPSS to put two box plots in the same graph. What conclusions can be drawn?

At least four observations can be made:

1. The median of each group is represented by the line within the corresponding box. The median score of the job applicants [sample (1)] is roughly 62 – 50 = 12 points higher than for the sample of 100 current employees [sample (2)].

2. The range for sample (1), using Table 3.2, is 96 – 22 = 74 points. The range for sample (2) is 80 – 30 = 50 points. The middle 50% for sample (1), as indicated by the ends of the box, covers a spread of roughly 30 points. The corresponding spread for sample (2) is 15 points. *Conclusion:* There is much more variation in the job applicant scores.

3. The job applicant scores have a slight left skew (the median line is slightly above center in the box), whereas for sample (2), the scores contain a heavy right skew, since the median line is considerably below center, and the right whisker is quite long. Consequently, the sample of current employees contains a higher concentration of scores at the low end.

4. After examining the box plots, we could conclude that, based on the aptitude test scores, there are some very good and some not-so-good applicants (a lot of variation in scores), but that overall this group outscored the sample of current employees.

X Exercises 3.46–3.52

Understanding the Mechanics

3.46 Construct a box plot using only the following information about a data set with 30 observations.

First Quartile	=	25
Second Quartile	=	50
Third Quartile	=	75
Lowest Value	=	1
Largest Value	=	100

3.47 From the MINITAB box plot displayed below, approximate the following:

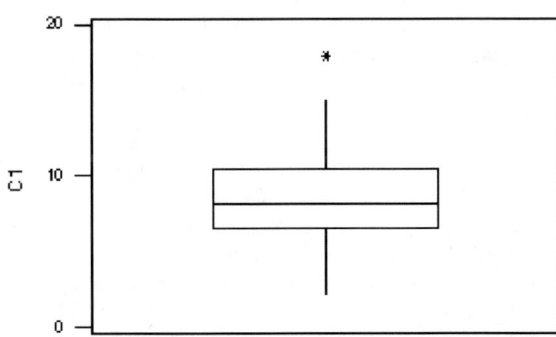

a. First quartile
b. Median
c. Third quartile
d. Any mild outliers
e. Any extreme outliers

3.48 The following is a sample of size 10:

15   20   12   30   25   33   70   24   32   22

a. Find the first, second, and third quartiles.
b. What are the largest and smallest values?
c. Construct a box plot and comment on the shape of the distribution.

Applying the New Concepts

3.49 The manager of a small restaurant wished to determine how long the average customer had to wait to be served during the lunch hour. At the lunch hour on a particular typical day, 20 customers experienced the following waiting times (in minutes):

5.5, 10.3, 7.5, 8.1, 6.8, 11.0, 10.2, 9.0, 7.0, 5.8, 12.5, 7.5, 6.0, 13.7, 5.5, 14.0, 7.0, 6.9, 6.3, 7.4

a. Construct a box plot of the data.
b. Should the manager feel comfortable in advertising that if meals are not served in 10 minutes or less, the customer eats for free?

3.50 Refer to the weekly expenditure on food by 30 different families in Exercise 3.27. Construct a box plot for these data. How many outliers would you expect if these data were from a normal population?

Using the Computer

3.51 [DATA SET EX3-51] *Variable Description:*

Show: Television program

Rating: Nielsen rating of selected television programs

The name Nielsen Media Research is synonymous with television ratings and audience estimates. The ratings provide an estimate of audience size and composition for television programmers and commercial advertisers. These ratings are used as a barometer of people's viewing habits. For May 14 and May 15, a sample of television programs and their ratings by Nielsen Media Research are provided. Use a box plot to describe the distribution of the data.

(Source: "Nielsen Ratings," *USA Today,* May 23, 2001, p. 6D.)

3.52 [DATA SET EX3-52] *Variable Description:*

OccRateNorth: Occupancy rate of Holiday Hotel North

OccRateSouth: Occupancy rate of Holiday Hotel South

To better manage two hotels in the north and south side of Atlanta, the managers decide to collect 60 days of data representing the occupancy rate in percentage. Staff and resources could be more proportionally divided between the two hotels based on projected occupancy rates.

a. Construct box plots—one for each hotel's occupancy rate.

b. Compare and contrast the distribution of each hotel. Which hotel has fewer outliers?

3.8 DESCRIBING BIVARIATE DATA

So far we have discussed methods of reducing a set of values for one variable to a graph (such as a histogram) or a numerical measure (such as a mean). A variable here is a characteristic of the population being measured or observed. For example, the variable of interest might be an individual's height or income. The sample then consists of random observations of the variable describing a given population.

In this section we discuss the situation in which the population and sample consist of measurements not of *one* variable but of *two*. As a result, we not only can describe each variable individually—we can also describe how the two variables (such as height and weight) are related. The relationship between the two variables can be described using a simple graph or a numerical measure (statistic).

Bivariate Data

With **bivariate data,** each observation consists of data on two variables. For example, you obtain a sample of people and record their ages *(X)* and liquid assets *(Y)*. Or, for each month, you record the average interest rate *(X)* and the number of new housing starts *(Y)*. These data are *paired*.

Suppose that a real-estate developer is interested in determining the relationship between family income *(X,* in thousands of dollars) of the local residents and the square footage of their homes *(Y,* in hundreds of square feet). A random sample of 10 families is obtained with the following results:

Income *(X)*	32	36	55	47	38	60	66	44	70	50
Square footage *(Y)*	16	17	26	24	22	21	32	18	30	20

Bivariate data can be represented graphically using a **scatter diagram.** In this graph, each observation is represented by a point, where the *x*-axis is always horizontal and the *y*-axis is vertical. A scatter diagram of the real-estate data is shown in Figure 3.14(a). The underlying pattern here appears to be that larger incomes *(X)* are associated with larger home sizes *(Y)*. In this example, X and Y have a **positive (direct) relationship.** A **negative (inverse) relationship** occurs when Y decreases as X increases—for example, when Y is the demand for a particular consumer product and X is the selling price.

We next try to determine whether we can estimate this relationship by means of a straight line. One possible line is sketched in Figure 3.14(b); it passes among these points and has a positive slope. In Chapter 11 we will determine the equation of the line that best slices through these points. To measure the strength of the linear relationship between these two variables, we first determine the coefficient of correlation.

Coefficient of Correlation and Covariance

It is often difficult to determine whether a *significant* linear relationship exists between X and Y by inspecting a scatter diagram of the data. A second procedure is to include a *measure* of this linearity—the sample coefficient of correlation. It is computed from the

FIGURE

3.14

Scatter diagram of real-estate data. (a) Scatter diagram of sample data. (b) Line through sample data.

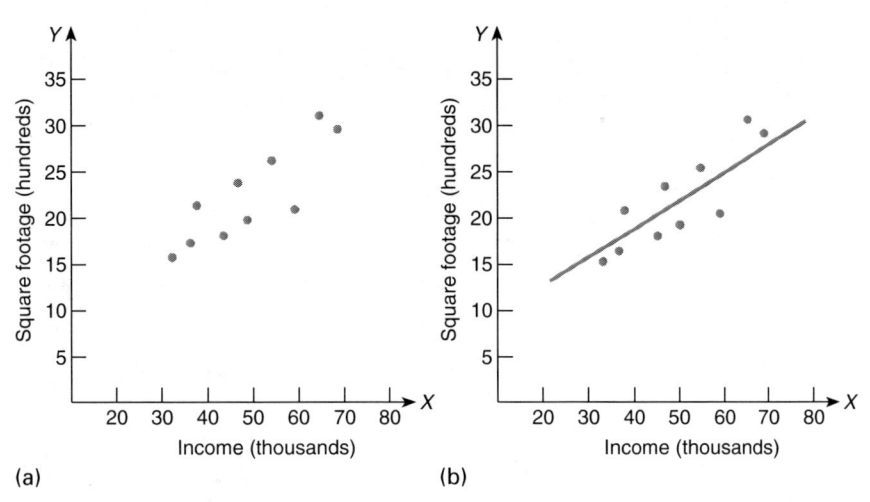

sample data by combining these pairs of values into a single number, written as *r*. The sample **coefficient of correlation, r,** measures the strength of the linear relationship that exists within a sample of *n* bivariate data. Its value is given by

$$r = \frac{\Sigma(x - \bar{x})(y - \bar{y})}{\sqrt{\Sigma(x - \bar{x})^2}\sqrt{\Sigma(y - \bar{y})^2}}$$

3.12

The coefficient of correlation is often referred to as the *Pearson coefficient of correlation,* named after Karl Pearson, a famous British statistician around the turn of the twentieth century. The coefficient of skewness in equation 3.10 is also named after Karl Pearson.

The following are some important properties of the sample correlation coefficient, *r*.

- *r* ranges from −1.0 to 1.0.

- The larger |*r*| (absolute value of *r*) is, the stronger is the linear relationship.

- *r* near zero indicates that there is no linear relationship between *X* and *Y*, and the scatter diagram typically (although not necessarily) appears to have a shotgun effect, as in Figure 3.15(a). Here, *X* and *Y* are uncorrelated.

- *r* = 1 or *r* = −1 implies that a perfect linear pattern exists between the two variables in the sample; that is, a single line will go *through* each point. Here we say that *X* and *Y* are *perfectly correlated,* as illustrated in Figures 3.15(b) and 3.15(c).

- Values of *r* = 0, 1, or −1 are rare in practice. Several other values of the correlation coefficient are illustrated in Figures 3.15 (d), 3.15(e), and 3.15(f).

- The sign of *r* tells you whether the relationship between *X* and *Y* is a positive (direct) or negative (inverse) one.

- The value of *r* tells you very little about the slope of the line through these points (except for the sign of *r*). If *r* is positive, the line through these points has positive slope, and similarly, this line will have negative slope if *r* is negative. However, a set of data with *r* = .9 will not necessarily have a steeper line passing through it than will a set of data with *r* = .4. All you observe in the first data set (with *r* = .9) is a set of points that is very close to some straight line but with positive slope, but you know nothing (except for the sign) about the slope of this line. See Figure 3.16, where both sets of data have an *r* value of .9.

FIGURE

3.15

Scatter diagrams for various values of the sample correlation coefficient.

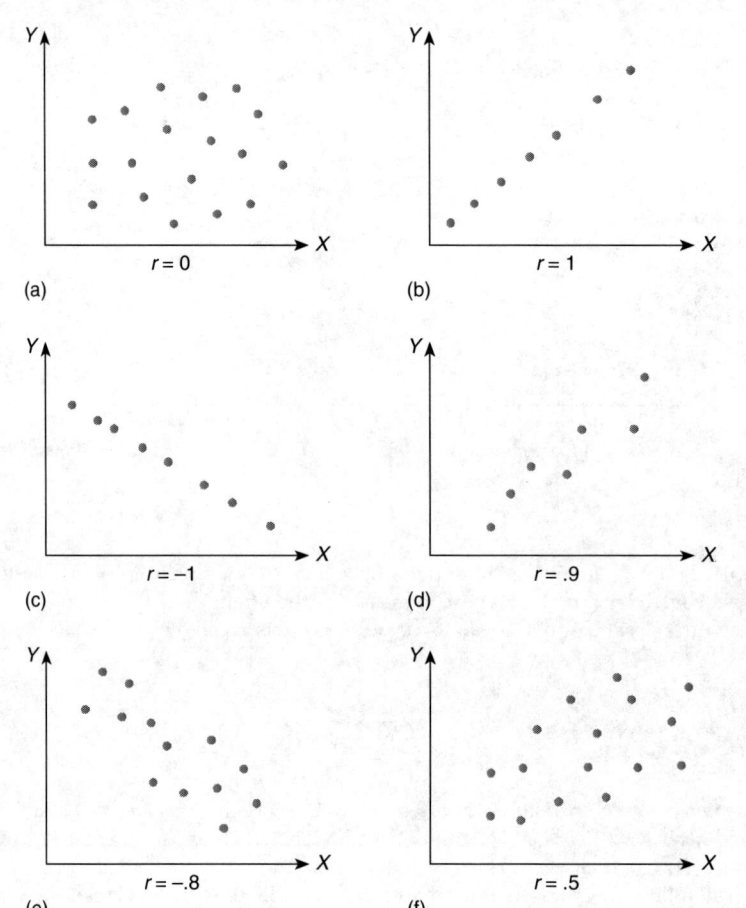

(a) $r = 0$

(b) $r = 1$

(c) $r = -1$

(d) $r = .9$

(e) $r = -.8$

(f) $r = .5$

FIGURE

3.16

Although (a) has a large slope and (b) has a small slope, both are scatter diagrams for r = .9.

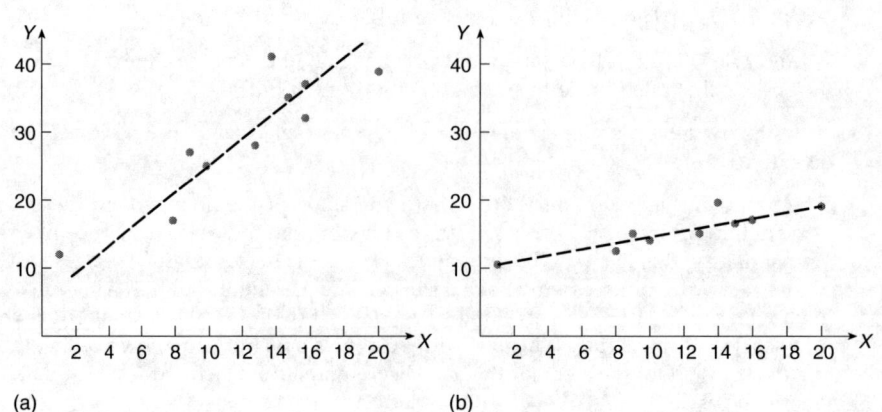

(a)

(b)

If the numerator in equation 3.12 is divided by $n-1$, another often-used measure of association—called the **covariance** between X and Y—is obtained. Consequently, the sample covariance between X and Y, cov(X,Y), is defined by equation 3.13.

$$\text{cov}(X,Y) = \frac{1}{n-1}\Sigma(x-\bar{x})(y-\bar{y})$$

3.13

To see how the sample covariance and sample correlation *(r)* are related, let

$$s_X = \text{standard deviation of the } X \text{ values} = \sqrt{\frac{\Sigma(x-\bar{x})^2}{n-1}}$$

$$s_Y = \text{standard deviation of the } Y \text{ values} = \sqrt{\frac{\Sigma(y-\bar{y})^2}{n-1}}$$

Then

$$r = \text{sample correlation between } X \text{ and } Y$$

$$= \frac{\text{cov}(X,Y)}{s_X s_Y}$$

3.14

EXAMPLE 3.10

Determine the sample covariance and sample correlation coefficient for the real-estate data in Figure 3.14.

Solution

The calculations for the covariance are summarized below.

Family	X (Income)	Y (Square Footage)	$(X-\bar{X})$	$(Y-\bar{Y})$	$(X-\bar{X})(Y-\bar{Y})$
1	32	16	−17.8	−6.6	117.48
2	36	17	−13.8	−5.6	77.28
3	55	26	5.2	3.4	17.68
4	47	24	−2.8	1.4	−3.92
5	38	22	−11.8	−0.6	7.08
6	60	21	10.2	−1.6	−16.32
7	66	32	16.2	9.4	152.28
8	44	18	−5.8	−4.6	26.68
9	70	30	20.2	7.4	149.48
10	50	20	0.2	−2.6	−0.52
					527.2

The value of 527.2 in the bottom-right corner is the value of $\Sigma(x-\bar{x})(y-\bar{y})$. Consequently, the sample covariance between X and Y from equation 3.13 is

$$\text{cov}(X,Y) = \frac{527.2}{9} = 58.58$$

The standard deviation of the 10 X values (32, 36, . . ., 50) can found using equation 3.5 and is equal to 12.865. The standard deviation of the 10 Y values (16, 17, . . ., 20) can also be obtained using equation 3.5 and is equal to 5.400. From equation 3.14, the sample correlation is equal to

$$r = \frac{58.58}{(12.865)(5.400)} = .843$$

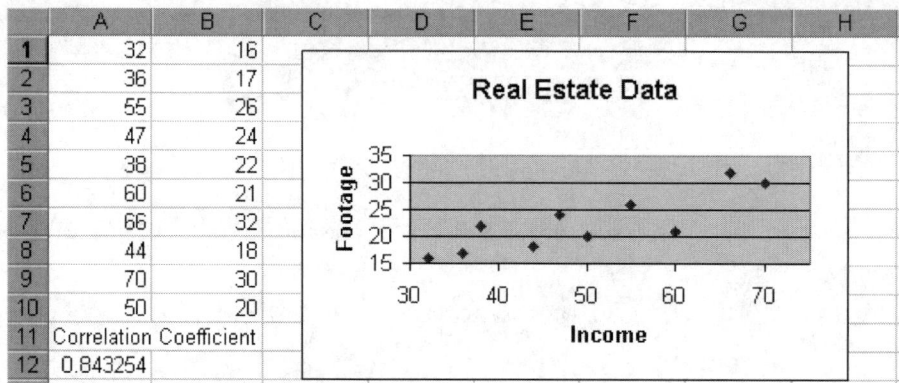

FIGURE

3.17

Excel-generated scatter diagram and correlation coefficient for the real estate data.

The covariance and correlation always have the *same sign*. Consequently, if large values of X are associated with large values of Y, then both the covariance and correlation are positive. Similarly, both values are negative whenever large values of X are associated with small values of Y.

The correlation between two variables is used more often than the covariance because r always ranges from –1 to 1. The covariance, by contrast, has no limits and can assume any value. Furthermore, the units of measurement for a covariance are difficult to interpret. For example, the previously calculated covariance is 58.58 (thousands of dollars) times (hundreds of square feet), a somewhat meaningless unit of measurement. So, in a sense, the correlation is a scaled version of the covariance and has no units of measurement (a nice feature). To illustrate, the sample correlation between body weight and height will be the same whether you use the metric or the English systems to obtain the sample data. The covariance will *not* be the same for these two situations. The covariance does have its applications, however—particularly in financial analyses, such as determining the risk associated with a number of interrelated investment opportunities.

The easiest way to construct a scatter diagram and calculate the sample correlation coefficient is to use Excel, MINITAB, or SPSS. The steps required to carry this out are contained in the end-of-chapter appendix. The Excel solution is contained in Figure 3.17. In cell A11, "Correlation Coefficient" was entered and this value (.843) was computed in cell A12 by clicking on **Insert ➤ Function ➤ Statistical ➤ CORREL.** The MINITAB and SPSS solutions are in Figures 3.18 and 3.19, respectively.

X Exercises 3.53–3.60

Understanding the Mechanics

3.53 For the following data set compute the coefficient of correlation and explain whether the relationship is positive or negative.

X	1	4	7	9	12
Y	2	10	12	15	28

3.54 The following data on age and health expenses (in thousands of dollars) are collected on a sample of six individuals. Compute the coefficient of correlation.

Age	35	43	48	50	52	55
Health Expenses	2.3	3.6	3.8	4.0	4.5	4.9

3.55 Draw a scatter plot of the following scores for two tests and provide an estimate of the strength of the linear relationship.

Test Score 1	60	55	88	45	90
Test Score 2	48	45	30	50	20

Applying the New Concepts

3.56 Eight observations were collected on the distance (in miles) traveled by a commercial airline and the corresponding coach fare. Draw a scatter plot. Compute the coefficient of correlation and explain what this value represents.

FIGURE

3.18

MINITAB-generated scatter diagram and correlation coefficient for the real-estate data.

Correlations: Income, Footage

Pearson correlation of Income and Footage = 0.843

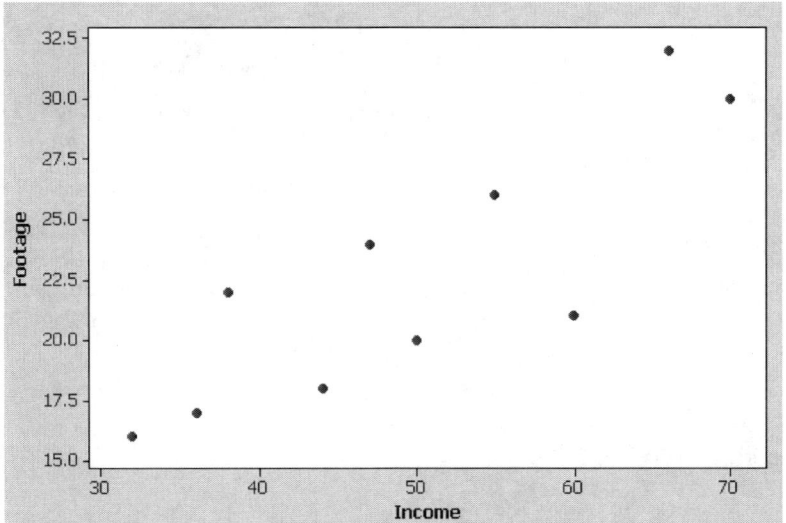

FIGURE

3.19

SPSS-generated scatter diagram and correlation coefficient for the real-estate data.

Correlations

		INCOME	FOOTAGE
INCOME	Pearson Correlation	1.000	.843
	Sig. (2-tailed)	.	.002
	N	10	10
FOOTAGE	Pearson Correlation	.843	1.000
	Sig. (2-tailed)	.002	.
	N	10	10

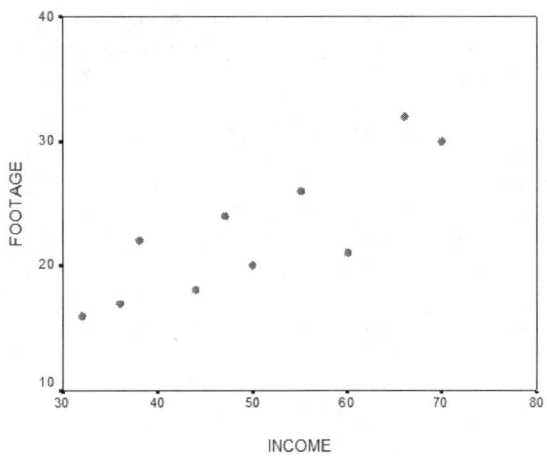

Distance	300	400	450	500	550	600	800	1,000
Price Charged($)	140	220	230	250	255	288	350	480

3.57 A production manager was interested in the relationship between cost and profit (in units of thousands of dollars) on the production of six special orders. Draw a scatter plot of the data and interpret the coefficient of correlation.

Cost	2.1	2.6	3.0	3.2	3.5	4.0
Profit	3.6	3.4	2.9	2.7	2.6	2.0

3.58 A financial planner was interested in the relationship between age and retirement funds of a company's employees. Seven employees were selected. Interpret the coefficient of correlation for these data. Retirement funds are in units of thousands of dollars.

Age	30	35	40	45	50	55	60
Retirement Funds	100	30	200	50	450	300	200

Using the Computer

3.59 **[DATA SET EX3-59]** *Variable Description:*

2004 Loans: Amount of mortgage loans in 2004 (millions of dollars)

2003 Loans: Amount of mortgage loans in 2003 (millions of dollars)

Twenty major mortgage institutions were selected, and the amount of mortgage refinancing was recorded for 2003 and 2004. Draw a scatter plot of the data and interpret the coefficient of correlation.

3.60 **[DATA SET EX3-60]** *Variable Description:*

CEO_Compens: Total compensation of the CEO in thousands of dollars

CompanyProfit: Annual company after-tax profit in millions of dollars

A random sample of 50 chief executive officers (CEOs) was selected to determine the relationship between total compensation and company profits. Interpret the strength of the linear relationship.

✓ Summary

This chapter has introduced you to some of the more popular descriptive measures used to describe a set of sample values. Measures of central tendency are used to describe a typical value within the sample and include the mean, the median, the mode, and the midrange. To measure the variation within a set of sample data, we use measures of variation, which include the range, the variance, the standard deviation, and the coefficient of variation.

Percentiles and quartiles are measures of position and indicate the relative position of a particular value. The first quartile (Q_1), the second quartile (Q_2), and the third quartile (Q_3) are the 25th, 50th, and the 75th percentiles, respectively. The difference between the first and third quartiles is the interquartile range (IQR). Measures of position include the sample z-scores, which indicate how many standard deviations each sample value is from the sample mean. Finally, the shape of a data set can be described using various measures of shape. Two such measures are the sample skewness and kurtosis.

Exploratory data analysis provides easy-to-construct, yet very powerful, graphs that summarize and describe a set of sample data. The box plot introduced in this chapter can be used to illustrate the data symmetry and presence of any sample outliers.

The two most commonly used measures are the sample mean and standard deviation. These two statistics can be used together to describe the sample data by applying Chebyshev's Inequality or the Empirical Rule. The latter procedure draws a stronger conclusion about the concentration of the data values but assumes that the population of interest is bell-shaped.

When dealing with a pair of variables (say, X and Y), we generally are interested in determining whether the variables are related in some manner. If a linear relationship exists within the sample data, both the direction (positive or negative) and the strength of this linear relationship can be measured using the sample coefficient of correlation, r. Another commonly used measure of association between two variables is the sample covariance.

Summary of Formulas

Measures of Central Tendency

1. Sample mean is

$$\bar{x} = \frac{\Sigma x}{n}.$$

2. Population mean is

$$\mu = \frac{\Sigma x}{N}.$$

3. Midrange is

$$Mr = \frac{L+H}{2}.$$

Measures of Variation

1. Range is $H - L$.
2. Sample variance is

$$s^2 = \frac{\Sigma(x-\bar{x})^2}{n-1}$$

$$= \frac{\Sigma x^2 - (\Sigma x)^2/n}{n-1}$$

3. Population variance is

$$\sigma^2 = \frac{\Sigma(x-\mu)^2}{N}.$$

4. Sample standard deviation is

$$s = \sqrt{\frac{\Sigma(x-\bar{x})^2}{n-1}}$$

$$= \sqrt{\frac{\Sigma x^2 - (\Sigma x)^2/n}{n-1}}$$

5. Population standard deviation is

$$\sigma = \sqrt{\frac{\Sigma(x-\mu)^2}{N}}.$$

6. Coefficient of variation is

$$CV = \frac{s}{\bar{x}} \cdot 100.$$

Measures of Position

1. Sample z-score is

$$z = \frac{x-\bar{x}}{s}.$$

Measures of Shape

1. Pearson's coefficient of skewness

$$Sk = \frac{3(\bar{x}-Md)}{s}$$

2. Excel, SPSS, and MINITAB coefficient of skewness

$$Sk' = \frac{n}{(n-1)(n-2)}\Sigma\left(\frac{x-\bar{x}}{s}\right)^3$$

$$= \frac{n}{(n-1)(n-2)}\Sigma(z\text{-}score)^3$$

Box Plots

1. Interquartile range is $\quad IQR = Q_3 - Q_1.$
2. Lower inner fence is $\quad Q_1 - 1.5 \cdot IQR.$
3. Upper inner fence is $\quad Q_3 + 1.5 \cdot IQR.$
4. Lower outer fence is $\quad Q_1 - 3 \cdot IQR.$
5. Upper outer fence is $\quad Q_3 + 3 \cdot IQR.$

Bivariate Data

1. Sample covariance $= \text{cov}(X,Y) = \dfrac{1}{n-1}\Sigma(x-\bar{x})(y-\bar{y})$

2. Sample coefficient of correlation $= r =$
$$\frac{\Sigma(x-\bar{x})(y-\bar{y})}{\sqrt{\Sigma(x-\bar{x})^2}\sqrt{\Sigma(y-\bar{y})^2}} = \frac{\text{cov}(X,Y)}{s_X s_Y} \text{ where } s_X =$$

standard deviation of the X values and $s_Y =$ standard deviation of the Y values.

X Review Exercises 3.61–3.78

3.61 Compute the mean, standard deviation, and coefficient of skewness for the following production data. Explain what these measures represent.

230	300	600	250	325	200	300

3.62 Use a box plot to describe the distribution of the following data.

4	10	25	30	50	70	80	40	50	60

3.63 Construct a histogram for the following data. Would you say that the data appear to be bell-shaped? Between what two bounds would approximately 95% of the data be expected to lie?

23	35	46	50	57
44	55	69	72	48
52	58	61	30	56
63	68	41	70	57

3.64 The daily number of defective items for shift 1 for a one-week period were 12, 20, 10, 15, and 20. The daily number of defective items for shift 2 for the same weekly period were 8, 12, 20, 10, and 5. Compare the coefficients of variation for these two shifts.

3.65 The earnings-per-share growth (in percentage) for a portfolio of 10 stocks are as follows. Compute the z-score for each stock. Suppose that an observation is considered to be unusual if it has a z-score greater than 2 or less than –2. Would you consider any of the observations to be unusual?

30	20	7	200	25	35	18	34	40	15

3.66 Between what two bounds would at least 89% of the following waiting times (in minutes) at a bank lie?

10	3	16	20	2	18	4	9	7	25	6	5	4	11	6	2	15	10	2	5

3.67 The lowest fare between Dallas/Fort Worth and Chicago as displayed by two travel Web sites during the first of each month over a year are as follows. Construct a scatter plot and interpret the coefficient of correlation.

Web site A	270	250	240	290	310	220	230	285	275	248	270	290
Web site B	240	260	270	310	280	200	250	285	260	250	265	275

3.68 Consider a sample of observations:

10	15	30	25

Transform these values into z-scores. What is the mean and standard deviation of the z-scores? Show that the mean of any set of z-scores is always equal to zero.

3.69 Answer the questions below for the following data set:

.7, 1.5, 1.5, 1.8, 1.9, 2.1, 2.4, 2.5, 2.8, 2.9, 2.9, 3.3, 3.7, 3.8, 3.9, 4.0, 4.1, 4.3, 4.9, 5.0, 5.4, 6.1

  a. Do the data appear to be bell-shaped?
  b. Calculate the coefficient of skewness.
  c. Using the empirical rule, estimate the range of values within which about 68% of the data values are expected to lie.

3.70 An operations manager records the salvage value (in dollars) of a machine over 7 years. What is the coefficient of correlation of this value with time?

Time (in years)	1	2	3	4	5	6	7
Salvage Value	10,000	9,500	8,600	8,000	7,100	5,800	4,500

3.71 The mean rate charged by the CPAs in a certain city is about $75 per hour, with a standard deviation of $15. Assuming that the data came from a normal population, estimate the range of rates within which about 95% of the CPA's charges are expected to lie.

3.72 The z-score is -1.50, the mean is 45, and $x = 15$. What is the value of the variance?

3.73 A manufacturing plant requires one of its suppliers to provide aluminum sheets that have a special coating that is between 1.5 and 4.5 millimeters in depth. A shipment of 800 coated aluminum sheets was delivered to the plant. The supervisor at the plant was told that the mean depth of the coating was 3.0 millimeters, with a standard deviation of .5. If there are more than 100 aluminum sheets with a coating thickness outside of the range 1.5 to 4.5 millimeters, the plant supervisor will not accept the shipment. What decision should the supervisor make?

3.74 The mean GMAT score of the 65 applicants who were accepted into the MBA program of Xavier Business School was 520 with a standard deviation of 25. About how many applicants scored between 470 and 570 on the GMAT?

3.75 **[DATA SET EX3-75]** *Variable Description:*

ETF: Name of exchange traded fund

ExpenseRatio: Expense ratio for selected exchange traded funds

Exchange traded funds (ETF) allow investors to buy a portfolio of securities as easily as buying a single security. A major advantage is the low expense ratio. Compute three descriptive measures to summarize these data.

3.76 Form a stem-and-leaf diagram of the expense ratios in Exercise 3.75. Remove any observations that appear to be outliers and repeat the analysis.

3.77 **[DATA SET EX3-77]** *Variable Description:*

JobArr: Number of job orders arriving at a manufacturing plant

A production facility manufactures air compressors for automobiles. The facility tries to accommodate special orders that arrive on a daily basis. Allowing capacity for the special orders is important to the planning process. For 120 working days, the number of job orders have been recorded.
  a. Plot a histogram and a box plot of the data.
  b. How would you describe the data?
  c. Find the mean and standard deviation of the data. From these values, compute the coefficient of skewness. Does the value of this measure appear to be consistent with your description in part b?

3.78 **[DATA SET EX3-78]** *Variable Description:*

MarketExp: Travel expenses for the marketing department

R&DExp: Travel expenses for the research and development department

The vice president of a semiconductor company wished to compare the distribution of travel expenses in two departments, the marketing department and the research and development department. The travel expenses of 120 persons from the marketing department and 150 persons from the research and development department are listed under MarketExp and R&DExp, respectively, in dollars.
  a. Form a box plot for the expenses of each department.
  b. Form a histogram for the expenses of each department.
  c. Do the data from either department appear to be bell-shaped?
  d. Contrast the distributions of the two departments.

Computer Exercises Using the Databases

Exercise 1—Appendix F

Randomly select 100 observations of variable INCOME1 (income of principal wage earner) from the database.

a. Use a convenient statistical computer package to determine the various descriptive measures that describe the distribution of INCOME1.

b. What are the actual proportions of observations that are between ±2.0 and ±3.0 standard deviations of the mean of the data set? Are these proportions consistent with:
   (i)   Chebyshev's inequality?
   (ii) the empirical rule?

c. Construct a box plot of this sample. What do you observe from this graph?

Exercise 2—Appendix G

Randomly select 100 observations of the variable SALES from the database.

a. Use a convenient statistical computer package to find the mean, median, range, variance, coefficient of variation, and coefficient of skewness for this variable.

b. Construct a box plot, and use this graph to describe your sample of SALES values.

Insights from Statistics in Action

Semiconductor Business: When the Chips Are Down

The Statistics in Action section at the beginning of this chapter discussed the cyclical nature of the semiconductor business and the worldwide players in this market (primarily, the United States and Japan). Data for the following questions are listed in StatIn-ActChap3.xls. These data contain the consumption of semiconductors by key global companies as a percentage of world consumption. The percentages are presented for the 10-year period from 1994 to 2003.

1. For each of the global players, find the mean and the median over the 10-year period for the consumption of semiconductors. For which global player is the difference between the mean and the median the largest?

2. By looking at the data, which global players do you think would exhibit the largest standard deviation for the percentage of semiconductor consumption over this 10-year period? Find the standard deviations. Which global player has the largest standard deviation?

3. Using the formula for Pearson's coefficient of skewness in the text, find the skewness of the data for each global player over this 10-year period. Which global players have a positive coefficient of skewness and which have a negative?

4. Which yearly figure do you think most influenced the coefficient of skewness for the United States? Eliminate this figure and recalculate the mean, median, and standard deviation. By how much does the coefficient of skewness change?

5. Find the coefficient of variation for each of the global players over this 10-year period. Which global player exhibits the least variation using this measure?

Source: "Top Chip Makers Report Strong Revenue Gains," *The Wall Street Journal*, September 10, 2004, p. 1. "The Semi Swing," *Red Herring*, June 15, 2001, pp. 142–144. "All Eyes Turn Toward South," *Electronic Business*, July 2000, pp. 104–112.

Data Analysis with Excel, MINITAB, and SPSS

Excel

Descriptive Statistics

To obtain the descriptive statistics illustrated in Figure 3.5(a) using Excel, click on **Tools ➤ Data Analysis ➤ Descriptive Statistics.** The Descriptive Statistics dialog box will appear. Insert the cells for the **Input Range,** check **Labels in first row** if the column label is included, and insert the location of the **Output Range.** Select **Summary statistics** and click **OK** to obtain the output in Figure 3.5(a) using the Diameter data.

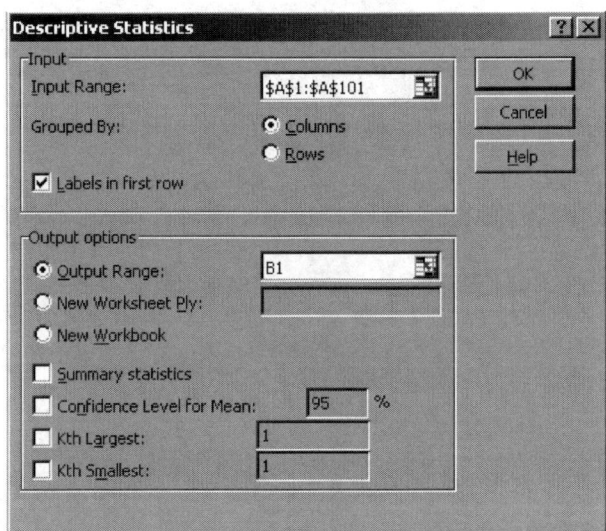

Box Plots

To obtain a box plot of 75 residential appraisals as illustrated in Figure 3.12, click on **KPK Data Analysis ➤ Quantitative Data Charts/Tables ➤ Box Plot** and fill in the **Input Range** and **Output Range** as displayed in the Box Plot dialog box.

Scatter Diagrams and Correlation

To obtain a scatter diagram of the real estate data plotted in Figure 3.17, first put the income and footage data in adjacent columns. The data for the X axis should be placed before the data for the Y axis. Highlight the data in these two columns. Click on the **Chart Wizard ➤ Scatter** and the following dialog box will appear. Click on **Next** to obtain the next dialog box to put in the title and labels for the X and Y axes. Click on any of the tabs at the top of this dialog box to enhance the display of the scatter plot. Click **Next** again to select whether to place the graph in the current worksheet or on a separate worksheet. Then, click **Finish** to display the graph.

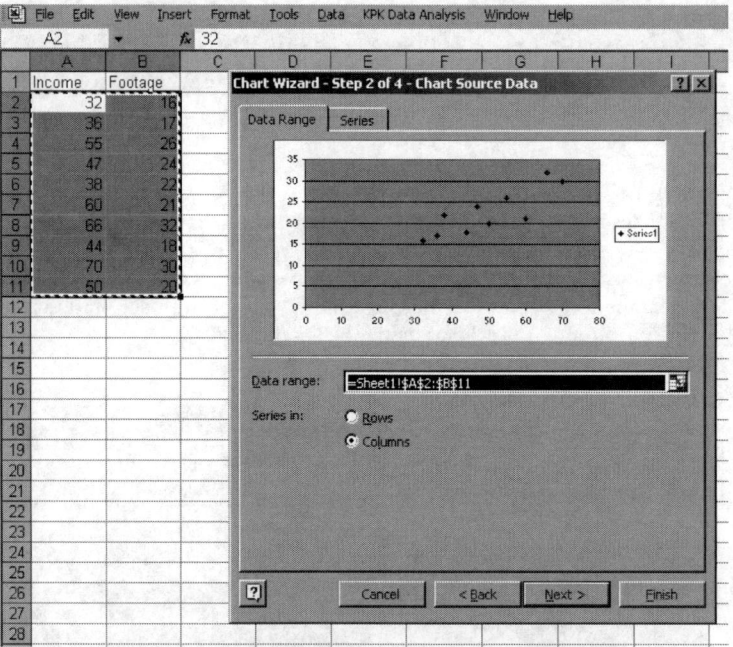

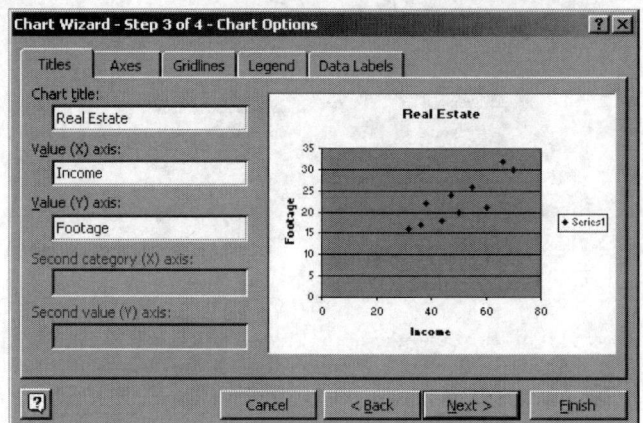

To obtain the correlation between two variables, click on **Insert ➤ Function** to obtain the **Insert Function** dialog box. Select **Statistical** for the category and **CORREL** for the function and click **OK** to obtain the CORREL Function Arguments dialog box. Next, select the ranges for the variables in **Array1** and **Array2**. The value of the correlation (.843) appears in the dialog box. Selecting **OK** displays the value of the correlation on the spreadsheet. To obtain a covariance value, replace CORREL with COVAR in the preceding discussion. Note: Excel divides by n rather than $n - 1$ in equation 3.13 when computing this value. To obtain the value using equation 3.13 multiply Excel's covariance value by $n/(n-1)$.

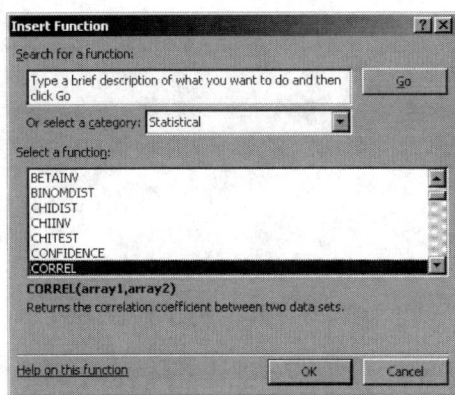
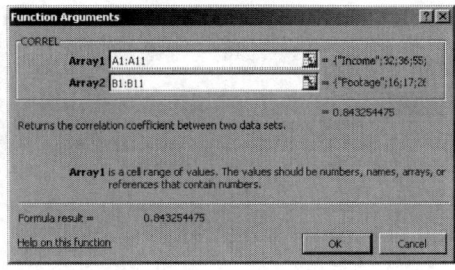

MINITAB

Descriptive Statistics

To obtain the descriptive statistics illustrated in Figure 3.5(b) using MINITAB, click on **Stat ➤ Basic Statistics ➤ Display Descriptive Statistics.** The **Display Descriptive Statistics** dialog box will appear. Click on each of the input variables and then on **Statistics.** The Descriptive Statistics—Statistics dialog box will appear. Select those statistics you wish to see appear and then click on **OK** on each dialog box to obtain the output in Figure 3.5(b).

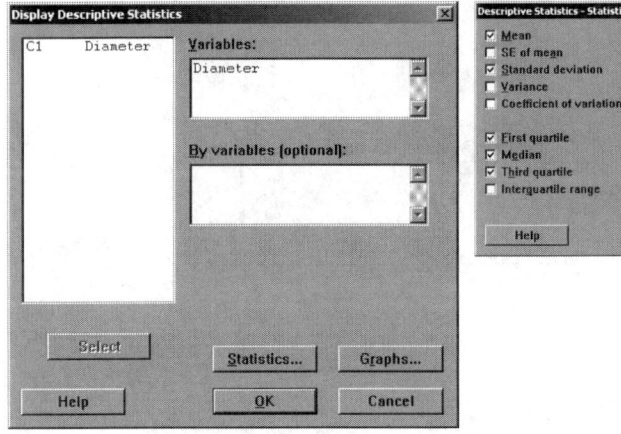
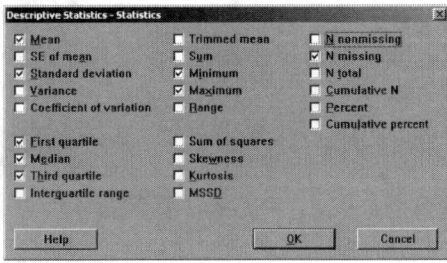

Box Plots

To obtain single or multiple box plots using MINITAB, click on **Graph ➤ Boxplot** and select either **One Y Simple** or **Multiple Y's Simple.** If two columns of data are to be graphed, as in Figure 3.13(a), select **Multiple Y's Simple** and select the variables as in the following dialog box. Click on **Data View** to select options for the box plot.

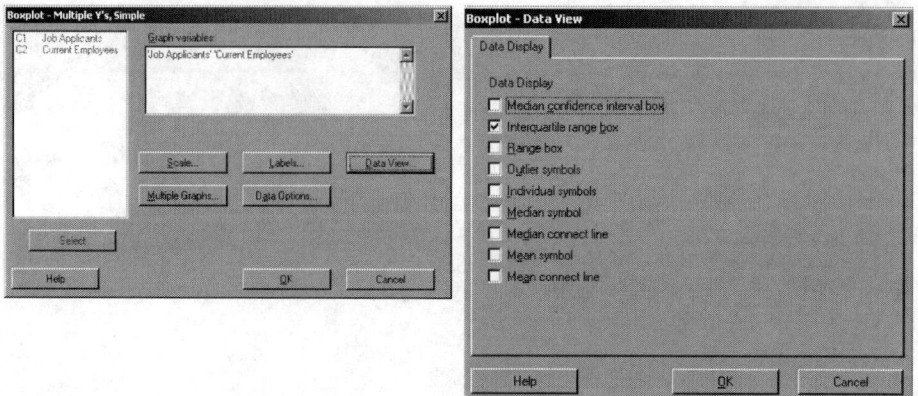

Scatter Diagrams and Correlation

To obtain a scatter diagram of the real estate data plotted in Figure 3.18, click on **Graph ➤ Scatter ➤ Simple.** The **Scatterplot – Simple** dialog box will appear. Select the *Y* and *X* variables. Click on the **Scale** or **Labels** buttons to enhance the graph by using titles or showing the ticks on the *X* and *Y* axes.

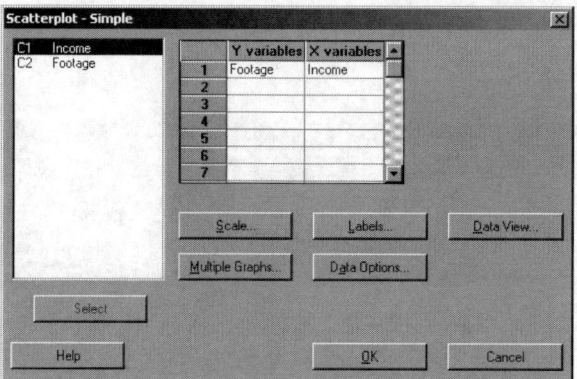

To obtain the correlation between two variables, click on **Stat ➤ Basic Statistics ➤ Correlation.** The Correlation dialog box will appear. Select the variables and click **OK.**

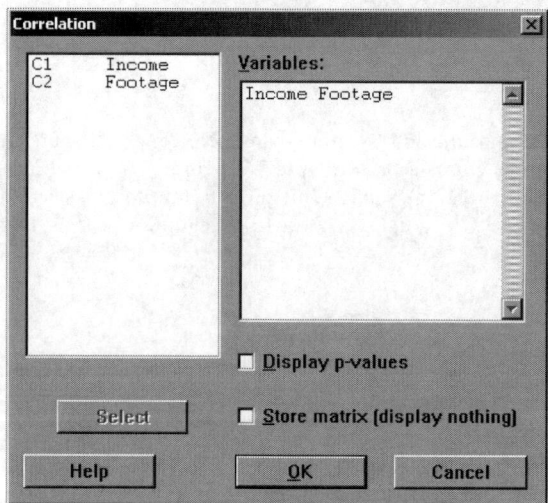

SPSS

Descriptive Statistics

To display the output in Figure 3.5(c) with SPSS, click on **Analyze ➤ Descriptive Statistics ➤ Descriptives.** In the **Descriptives** dialog box, select the Diameter variable and click on **Options.** In the **Descriptives:Options** window, click on the boxes corresponding to the desired descriptive statistics. Then click **Continue** and **OK.**

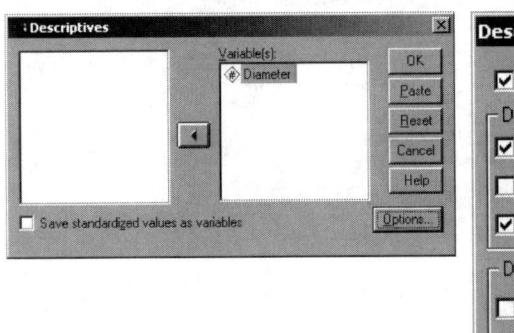
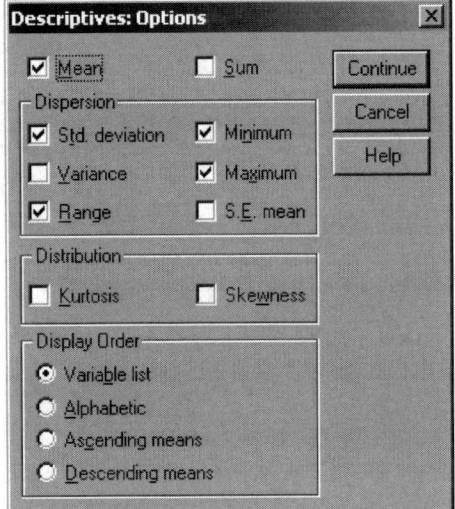

Box Plots

To obtain a box plot from the aptitude test scores of 50 applicants listed in Table 3.2, click on **Graphs ➤ Boxplot.** In the window, click on **Simple** and **Summaries of separate variables.** Click on **Define.** Select the variable and click on the pointer to move this variable into the **Boxes Represent** box. Click on **OK** to view the box plot. For multiple box plots, move several variables into the **Boxes Represent** box.

	scores	var	var	var	var
1	22				
2	25				
3	28				
4	31				
5	34				
6	35				
7	39				
8	39				
9	40				
10	42				
11	44				
12	44				
13	46				
14	48				

Scatter Diagrams and Correlation

To obtain a scatter diagram of the real estate data plotted in Figure 3.19, click on **Graphs ➤ Scatter ➤ Simple ➤ Define.** The **Simple Scatterplot** dialog box will appear. Select the variables for the Y and X axes. Click on **Titles** to enhance the graph with a title or subtitle and then click **OK** to obtain the scatter diagram.

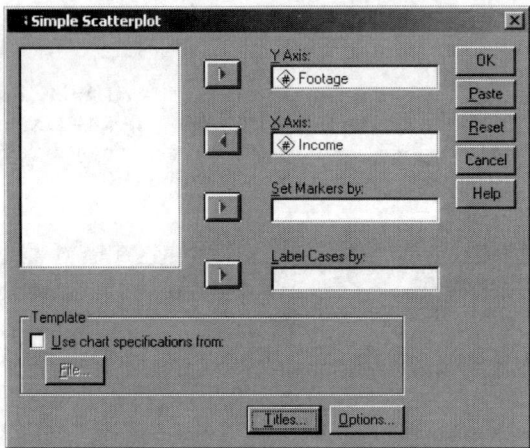

To obtain the correlation between two variables, click on **Analyze ➤ Correlate ➤ Bivariate** to obtain the Bivariate Correlations dialog box. Select Pearson for the choice of correlation coefficient. Click **OK** to display the correlation.

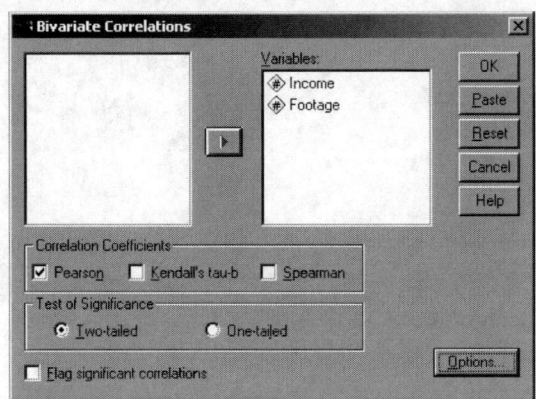

chapter

4

Time Series Analysis and Forecasting X

Statistics in Action
Forecasting Underlying Economic Trends: Oh CPI, Why Did You Lie?

The Consumer Price Index (CPI) is arguably the world's most quoted economic index. It has a profound ripple effect in economic decision making. A large leap in the CPI raises the specter of the Federal Reserve taking action to check inflation. This index affects pay-raise decisions, Social Security benefit decisions, standard deductions as determined by the Internal Revenue Service, stipends for food stamps, and rates on bank loans. The CPI frequently is called a cost-of-living index, but it is not a complete cost-of-living measure. The index reflects changes in the prices of goods and services commonly purchased in the marketplace.

The CPI is determined by the Bureau of Labor Statistics through an extensive survey of approximately 40,000 consumers. Information on consumer buying habits is collected on purchases in the following areas: food, housing, apparel, transportation, medical care, recreation, education, and communication. Economists often criticize the use of the CPI as not being an accurate index because it is sometimes temporarily jolted by changes due to spikes in oil prices or rapid changes in one sector of the economy. For example, real estate in certain "hot areas" of the country might make the index look higher than it would be without the housing component. Some economists refer to the *core CPI*, which removes the more volatile sectors of the economy from the computation. However, economists realize that even their modified indexes are still far from perfect and give misleading results.

Cyclical companies are firms whose earnings are strongly tied to the business cycle. These companies use the CPI and other economic indicators to forecast their earnings and make business decisions with regard to hiring or laying off employees. Examples of cyclical companies include General Motors, International Paper, and Caterpillar. Many economic indexes, including the CPI, are adjusted to remove the effect of seasonal influences. Seasonal influences are those that occur at the same time and in about the same magnitude every year. These indexes may also be affected by cycles in the economy. Examples of such cycles are presidential cycles, global changes in demand, and changes in demographics. Economists often use indexes that are seasonally adjusted or that have the effect of certain cycles removed. Policy makers and economic analysts need good current measures of the underlying economic trends to forecast patterns in the economy. An incorrect economic decision by a major corporation could result in overwhelming losses or in lost opportunities.

This chapter examines data in the form of a time series—that is, a variable, such as the CPI, recorded across time. When you have completed this chapter, you will be able to

- Describe and measure seasonal, trend, and cyclical components of variables such as the CPI.
- Make simple forecasts considering the trend and seasonal components.
- Compare the change in the price or value of certain items between any two time periods using an index number.

4.1

COMPONENTS OF A TIME SERIES

A **time series** represents a variable observed across time. The time increment can be years, quarters, months, or even days. The values of the time series can be presented in a table or illustrated using a scatter diagram. Usually, the points in the graph are connected by straight lines, making it easier to detect any existing patterns; such a graph is called a *line graph*.

The time series for the power-consumption in Pine Bluff, Texas, is shown in Figure 4.1 where it can be seen that the power-consumption values increase steadily from one year to the next. This long-term movement in the time series is called a *trend*. These values exhibit a definite increasing trend (or growth). Trend is only one of several components that describe the behavior of any time series. The components of a time series are

- Trend (*TR*)

- Seasonal variation (*S*)

- Cyclical variation (*C*)

- Irregular activity (*I*)

The purpose of time series analysis is to describe a particular data set by estimating the various components that make up this time series. We examine each of these components individually, although time series data usually contain a mixture of all four. This section will *not* attempt to measure these components, but rather will introduce you to the nature of each component. The remainder of this chapter demonstrates methods of capturing and measuring these individual components.

Trend (*TR*)

The **trend** is a steady increase or decrease in the time series. If a particular time series is neither increasing nor decreasing over its range of time, it contains *no trend*. The trend reflects any long-term growth or decline in the observations. For example, a trend may be due to inflation, increases in the population, increases in personal income, market growth or

FIGURE

4.1

Power consumption in Pine Bluff.

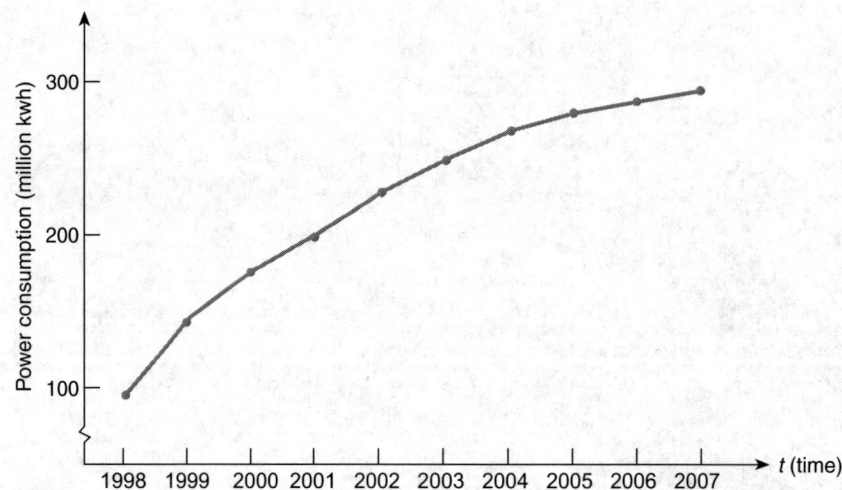

FIGURE

4.2

Number of employees at Video-Comp (an example of linear trend).

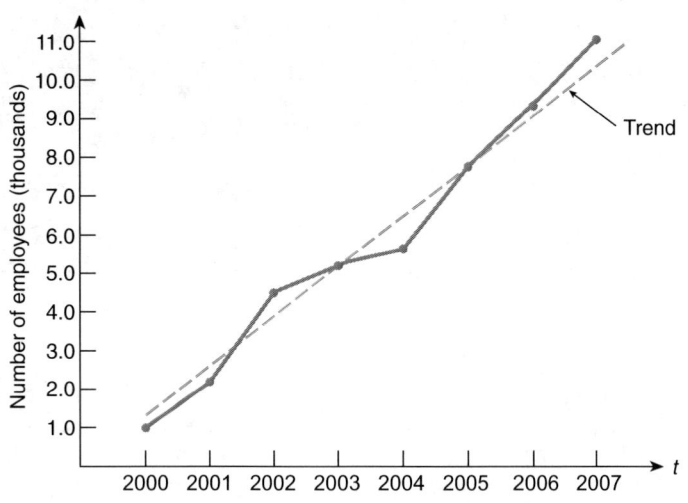

decline, or changes in technology. Each of these factors could have a long-term effect on the variable of interest and would be reflected in the trend in the corresponding time series.

This long-term growth or decay pattern can take a variety of shapes. If the rate of change in Y from one time period to the next is relatively constant, the trend is a **linear trend:**

$$TR = b_0 + b_1 t$$

(for some b_0 and b_1), where the predictor variable is time t.

When the time series appears to be slowing down or accelerating as time increases, then a nonlinear trend may be present. It may be a **quadratic trend**

$$TR = b_0 + b_1 t + b_2 t^2$$

or a **decaying trend**

$$TR = b_0 + b_1 \left(\frac{1}{t} \right) \quad \text{or} \quad TR = b_0 + b_1 e^{-t}$$

These trend equations can be derived from the linear regression equations developed in Chapter 13 (for linear or decaying trend) and Chapter 14 (for quadratic trend). The linear trend equation is an application of *simple* linear regression, whereas the quadratic trend uses a *multiple* regression equation using two predictors, t and t^2. Simple linear regression techniques also can be used to derive b_0 and b_1 for the decaying trend equations, where values of t are replaced by the values of $1/t$ or e^{-t} in the data input.

The number of employees from 2000 to 2007 at Video-Comp, an expanding microcomputer-software firm, are recorded in the following table and illustrated in Figure 4.2.

Year	Number of Employees (Thousands)
2000	1.1
2001	2.4
2002	4.6
2003	5.4
2004	5.9
2005	8.0
2006	9.7
2007	11.2

4.3

(a) Increasing linear trend: $TR = b_0 + b_1 t$ $(b_1 > 0)$.
(b) Decreasing linear trend: $TR = b_0 + b_1 t$ $(b_1 < 0)$.

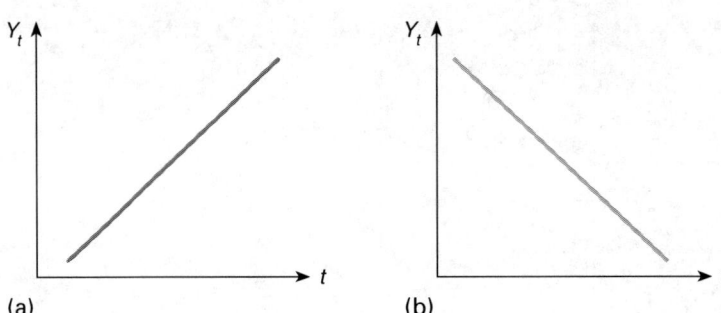

(a)   (b)

The underlying long-term growth trend in this time series appears to be nearly *linear*, as represented by the trend line in Figure 4.2. To determine the equation of this line, we use the technique of simple linear regression, where X = the predictor variable = time and Y = the number of employees. We can estimate the existing trend using

$$\hat{y}_t = b_0 + b_1 t$$

where t represents the time variable and y_t is the value of Y at time period t. Here b_0 and b_1 are the least squares regression coefficients for a straight line predictor. The procedure of deriving these least squares estimates is developed later in the chapter. Figure 4.3 shows an *increasing* linear trend (y_t increases over time) and a decreasing linear trend (y_t decreases over time).

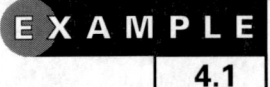

EXAMPLE 4.1

What type of trend exists in the power-consumption data (Figure 4.1)?

Solution   Although this time series increases steadily, *it increases at a decreasing rate*; it starts off with large increases from one time period to the next, but these increments gradually become smaller. When the growth is linear, the values increase at a nearly constant rate. Figure 4.1 is an illustration of *quadratic trend*, where the time series randomly fluctuates about a quadratic (or curvilinear) level over time. This trend is captured by the equation

$$\hat{y}_t = b_0 + b_1 t + b_2 t^2$$

To derive these estimates, we use the multiple linear regression approach discussed in Chapter 14 (curvilinear models). Section 4.2 demonstrates this technique.

The four types of quadratic trend are summarized in Figure 4.4.

Seasonality (S)

Seasonal variation, or **seasonality,** refers to periodic increases or decreases that occur *within a calendar year* in a time series. They are very predictable because they occur every year. When a time series consists of annual data (as in Figure 4.1), you cannot see what is going on within each year. Data reported in annual increments therefore cannot be used to examine seasonality. Seasonality may or may not exist; annual increment data are not in a form that will show whether it does.

When time series data are quarterly or monthly, seasonal variation may be evident. For example, if the power-consumption data were available for each month over these

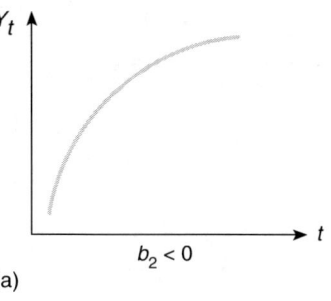

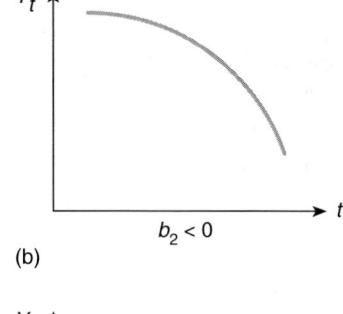

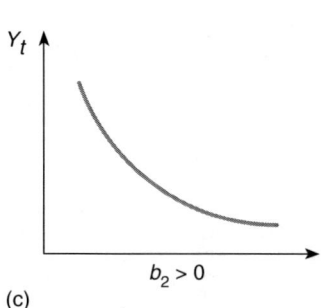

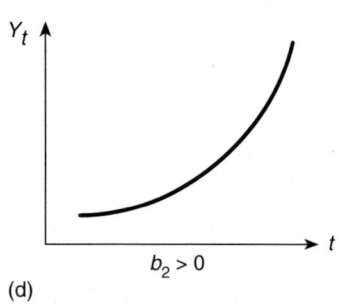

FIGURE 4.4

Quadratic trend.
(a) Y increases at a decreasing rate.
(b) Y decreases at an increasing rate.
(c) Y decreases at a decreasing rate.
(d) Y increases at an increasing rate.

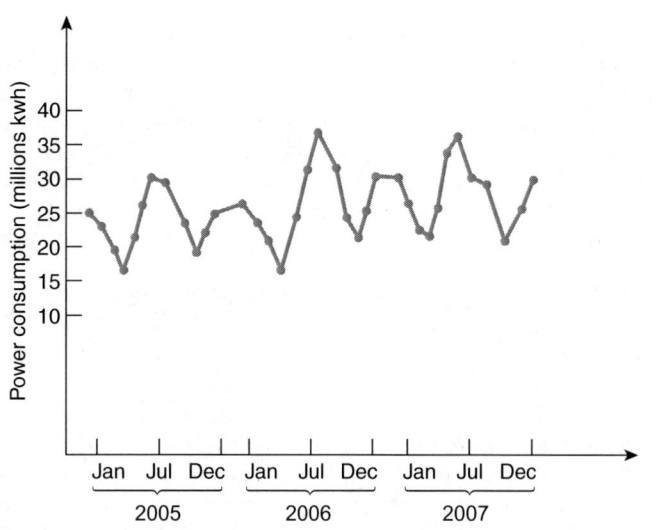

FIGURE 4.5

Illustration of seasonal variation. These are monthly observations; compare with annual data in Figure 4.1.

10 years, then the resulting time series would contain $12 \cdot 10 = 120$ observations. A plot of monthly data for the last 3 years (36 observations) is shown in Figure 4.5. The seasonal effects here consist of the following characteristics:

- Extremely high power consumption during the hot summer months (July and August)

- Very high consumption during the coldest part of the winter (December and January)

- Gradually declining consumption during the spring, reaching a low level in April and then increasing until July

- Gradually declining power consumption during the fall, but beginning to increase in November

4.6

A time series
containing trend
and seasonal
variation.

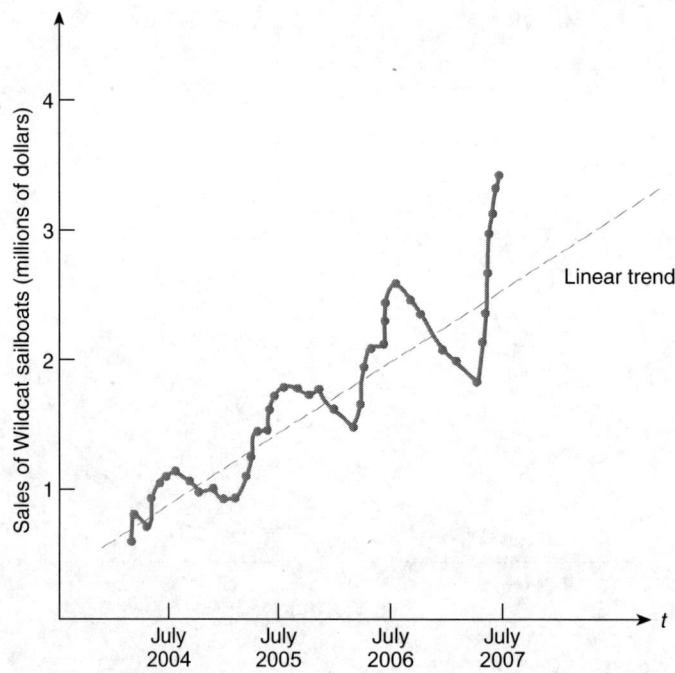

The key is that these movements in the time series follow the same pattern each year and so probably are due to seasonality. An analysis of seasonal variation is often a crucial step in planning sales and production. Just because your sales drop from one month to the next does not necessarily mean that it is time to panic. If a review of past observations indicates that sales *always* drop between these two months, then quite likely there is no cause for concern. On the production side, if sales always are extremely high in December, then you will need to increase production in the months prior to December so that you will have the necessary inventory level for this peak month. Measurement of this seasonal component is discussed later.

As mentioned earlier, a time series often contains the effect of trend and seasonality (as well as cyclical and irregular activity). The sales of Wildcat sailboats, illustrated in Figure 4.6, contain a strong linear trend as well as definite seasonal variation. In particular, the highest sales occur in the summer months of each year.

As manager of Wildcat Enterprises, would you be concerned that the sales of these boats in December 2007 were lower than those in July 2007? There may or may not be a problem; this seasonal pattern exists in Figure 4.6 despite an overall growth. More data would be required to determine whether the December sales were lower than expected for that month. What would you think if sales in July 2008 were lower than those in July 2007? This event should definitely concern you. This is a year-to-year comparison, and seasonal variation or not, we would expect the sales for July 2008 to be larger than for July 2007 if the long-term growth trend in Figure 4.6 is still present. Lower sales in July 2008 would indicate a possible leveling off or a drop in boat sales in 2008.

Cyclical Variation (*C*)

Cyclical variation describes a gradual cyclical movement about the trend; it is generally attributable to business and economic conditions. The length of a cycle is the *period* of that cycle. The period of a cycle can be measured from one *peak* to the next, one *trough* (valley) to the next, or from the time value at which the cycle crosses the horizontal line (where no cyclic activity exists) to the value where it completes the cycle and returns to this point.

FIGURE

4.7

The cycle can be measured from P_1 to P_2, from V_1 to V_2, or from Z_1 to Z_2.

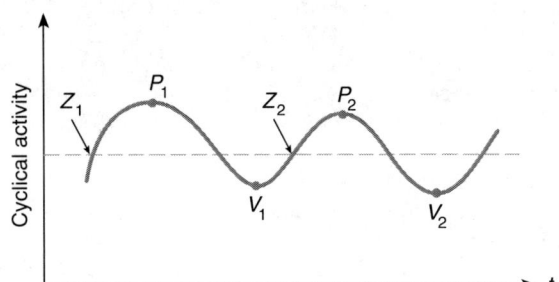

FIGURE

4.8

Annual taxes paid by Lindale Textiles (illustration of cyclical activity; Example 4.2).

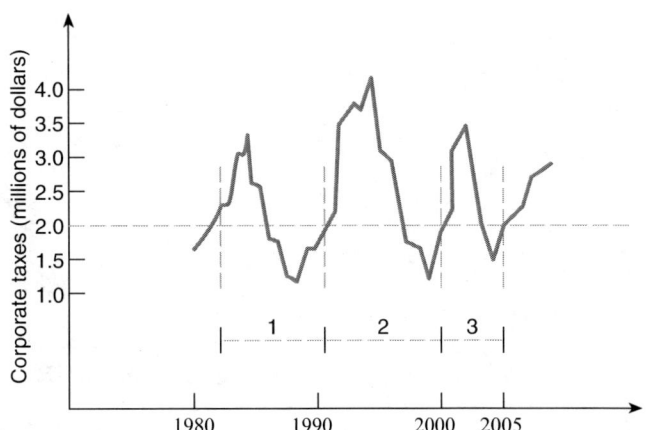

Figure 4.7 shows that the cycle length can be measured from P_1 to P_2, from V_1 to V_2, or from Z_1 to Z_2. In the illustrations to follow, we use the Z_1 to Z_2 approach.

In business applications, cycles typically are long-term movements, with periods ranging from 2 to 10 years. The primary difference between the cyclical and seasonal factors is the period length. Seasonal effects take place *within* one year, whereas the period for cyclical activity is usually *more than* one year.

Cyclical activity need not follow a definite, recurrent pattern. The cycles generally represent conditions within the economy, where a peak occurs at the height of an expansion (prosperity) period and is generally followed by a period of contraction in economic activity. The low point (trough) of each cycle usually takes place at the low point of an economic recession or depression. This low point is then followed by a gradual increase during the recovery period.

EXAMPLE

4.2

The annual corporate taxes paid by Lindale Textiles (a clothing manufacturer) over a 25-year period are shown in Figure 4.8. How many cycles do you observe?

Solution

The year 1982 began a cycle lasting approximately eight years. There are three cycles contained within the time series, which ends in the midst of an up cycle. Notice that the cycle lengths are not the same.

Irregular Activity (*I*)

Irregular activity consists of what is left over after accounting for the effect of any trend, seasonality, or cyclical activity. These values should consist of noise, much like the error term in the linear regression models discussed in the previous chapters. *The irregular activity should contain no observable or predictable pattern.* An extremely large irregular component can be caused by a measurement error in the variable. Such an outlier should always be checked to ensure its accuracy.

The irregular component (1) measures the random movement in your time series and (2) represents the effect introduced by unpredictable rare events, such as earthquakes, oil embargoes, or strikes.

If a noticeable jump in the resulting irregular components (when plotted across time) can be attributed to a particular rare event, you may wish to eliminate such data from the time series. You can then examine the remaining data to measure more accurately the other time series components.

Combining the Components

The time series components can be combined in various ways to describe the behavior of a particular time series. One method is to describe the time series variable, y_t, as a *sum* of these four components

$$y_t = TR_t + S_t + C_t + I_t$$

This is called the **additive structure.** The implication here is that any seasonal effects are additive from one year to the next. For example, if the seasonal effect of December for a time series representing sales is an increase of 250 units over the average yearly sales, then this same increase will occur each year regardless of the sales volume. Whether the average yearly sales are 1,000 units or 10,000 units, December should show a sales volume of approximately 1,250 (the first case) or 10,250 (the latter case).

Better success has been achieved by describing a time series using the **multiplicative structure,** where

$$y_t = TR_t \cdot S_t \cdot C_t \cdot I_t$$

Here, the seasonal effect increases or decreases according to the underlying trend and cyclical effect. Using the previous illustration, the difference between the December sales and the yearly average will be *higher* for the latter case (where the yearly average is 10,000 units). For example, for the first case, the December sales might be 1,250 (a 25% increase over the yearly average) and, for the latter situation, it might be 12,500 (also a 25% increase). This result follows from the implication in the multiplicative structure that as the sales increase from one year to the next, the changes in volume due to seasonality also increase. For our illustration, this shift was 250 units for the first case and 2,500 units for the second case.

X Exercises 4.1–4.6

Applying the New Concepts

4.1 Assume that a new company believes that its future sales will best be described by a multiplicative structure with respect to trend, seasonality, cyclical variation, and irregular activity.

  a. Describe how seasonality affects sales over time if the trend is increasing.

  b. Describe how cyclical variation affects sales over time if the trend is increasing.

4.2 The following data set shows the number of manufactured mobile homes (in thousands) since 1996. With low interest rates for most of the 1990s, mobile homes have had tough competition from the traditional home market. Plot the number of mobile homes versus time and describe the trend.

Year	1996	1997	1998	1999	2000	2001
Mobile Homes						
Manufactured	370	360	355	345	252	220

(Source: "Sliding Shipments," *Los Angeles Times,* June 11, 2001, p. L1.)

4.3 Construction in the housing industry usually appears to peak in the middle of the summer and to bottom out around January. If the number of new housing starts are the same for the month of March and the month of July in a particular year, of what concern would these figures be to housing construction companies? Would they be pleased, worried, or indifferent? Why?

4.4 The end-of-year inventory levels, in dollars, of West Coast Distributing are given in the following table. Estimate the period of the cyclical component by graphing the data.

Year	Inventory	Year	Inventory
1995	80	2002	80
1996	75	2003	83
1997	71	2004	80
1998	73	2005	77
1999	82	2006	79
2000	76	2007	84
2001	78		

4.5 To which of the four components of a time series would each of the following influences on housing starts contribute?

   a. Presidential election year
   b. Start of the school year in September
   c. Long-term growth of the housing industry
   d. Shortage of lumber because of a strike

4.6 Describe in words both the trend and the seasonal components for the following sales figures (in thousands of dollars). (*Hint:* Draw a graph for each.)

Month	2006	2007	Month	2006	2007
Jan	1.2	2.2	July	2.9	3.8
Feb	1.4	2.4	Aug	3.2	4.0
Mar	1.3	2.3	Sept	2.5	3.5
Apr	1.5	2.4	Oct	2.4	3.0
May	1.5	2.5	Nov	2.3	2.8
June	2.3	3.5	Dec	2.1	2.5

4.2 MEASURING TREND: NO SEASONALITY

Suppose that you have a time series containing trend and cyclical activity but no seasonality. For example, the employment data in Figure 4.2 are annual and so contain no seasonality. The same is true for the annual power-consumption data in Figure 4.1. When data are collected on a yearly basis, we are not concerned with any seasonality in the data; we need data from quarterly or shorter intervals to identify any seasonality. Yearly data may have trend *(TR)*, cyclical activity *(C)*, or irregular activity *(I)*. If we observe a strong linear trend (as in Figure 4.2) or a quadratic trend (Figure 4.4), we can estimate it using the least squares technique developed in Chapters 11 and 12. We use simple linear regression for linear trends and multiple linear regression for quadratic trends.

Linear Trend

We begin by *coding* the variable to make the calculations (or computer input) easier.

We can find an equation for the trend line in Figure 4.2 passing through the eight observations in the time series. The least squares trend line through these eight values is sketched in Figure 4.9. The equation of the trend line is

$$\hat{y}_t = TR_t = b_0 + b_1 t$$

where t represents the time variable. For this equation, TR_t represents the trend component of the sample observation at time period t and is simply a new name for the trend effect that this equation allows us to estimate.

We could use $t = 2000, 2001, \ldots$ to represent time, but a much simpler method is to code the data, as illustrated in Figure 4.9. By using $t = 1, 2, \ldots$, the estimate, $\hat{y}_t$ is not

FIGURE

4.9

Least squares
trend line using
coded time data
(compare with
Figure 4.2)
$\hat{y}_t = b_0 + b_1 t$.

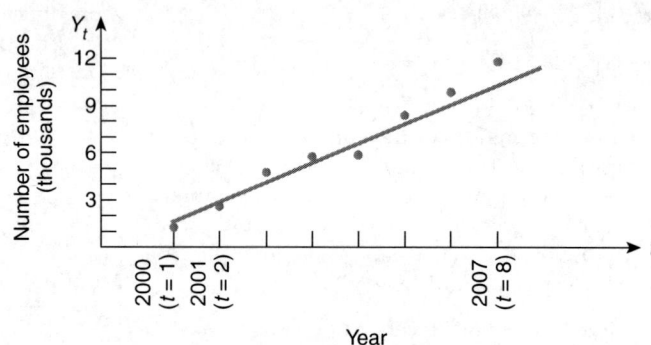

affected and the calculations are easier. You are able to code the predictor variable, t, because the sample values are equally spaced—they are all one year apart. As we saw in Chapter 13, this equal spacing does not occur in all simple regression applications. Continuing the scheme in Figure 4.9, $t = 9$ represents the year 2008, and the estimated number of employees for 2008 (using trend only) is

$$\hat{y}_9 = b_0 + b_1(9)$$

To derive the "best" line through the time series data, we use the least squares estimates discussed in Chapter 13; the independent variable here is time, t.

t	y_t	
1	1.1	$(= y_1)$
2	2.4	$(= y_2)$
3	4.6	•
4	5.4	•
5	5.9	•
6	8.0	
7	9.7	
8	11.2	

The necessary calculations are

$$\Sigma y_t = 1.1 + 2.4 + \cdots + 11.2 = 48.3$$

$$\Sigma t y_t = (1)(1.1) + (2)(2.4) + \cdots + (8)(11.2) = 276.3$$

In Chapter 13, when we regressed the variable Y on a single variable X, the estimate for the slope of the least squares line (from equation 13.8) was given by

$$b_1 = \frac{\text{SCP}_{XY}}{\text{SS}_X} = \frac{\Sigma xy - (\Sigma x)(\Sigma y)/n}{\Sigma x^2 - (\Sigma x)^2/n}$$

where n was the number of sample observations. To determine a linear trend line for a time series, this equation becomes

$$b_1 = \frac{\Sigma t y_t - (\Sigma t)(\Sigma y_t)/T}{\Sigma t^2 - (\Sigma t)^2/T}$$

where T = the number of observations in the time series.

The sample estimate of the intercept is

$$b_0 = \bar{y} - b_1 \bar{x} = \bar{y}_t - b_1 \bar{t}$$

where $\bar{y}_t = (y_1 + y_2 + \ldots + y_T)/T$.

Because the time variable, t, *always* is $1, 2, \ldots, T$, there is an easier way to calculate $\Sigma t, \Sigma t^2, \bar{t}, b_0$, and b_1.

$$\Sigma t = 1 + 2 + \cdots + T \qquad \text{4.1}$$
$$= \frac{T(T+1)}{2}$$

$$\Sigma t^2 = 1 + 4 + \cdots + T^2 \qquad \text{4.2}$$
$$= \frac{T(T+1)(2T+1)}{6}$$

$$\bar{t} = \frac{\Sigma t}{T} = \frac{T+1}{2} \qquad \text{4.3}$$

$$b_1 = \frac{12B - 6(T+1)A}{T(T^2 - 1)} \qquad \text{4.4}$$

$$b_0 = \frac{A}{T} - b_1\left(\frac{T+1}{2}\right) \qquad \text{4.5}$$

where $A = \Sigma y_t$ and $B = \Sigma t y_t$

We use these equations to derive the least squares line in Figure 4.9. By the previous results, $A = 48.3$ and $B = 276.3$. So we can now calculate

$$b_1 = \frac{12B - 6(T+1)A}{T(T^2 - 1)}$$
$$= \frac{12(276.3) - 6(9)(48.3)}{8(64 - 1)} = \frac{707.4}{504} = 1.4036$$

and

$$b_0 = \frac{A}{T} - b_1\left(\frac{T+1}{2}\right)$$
$$= \frac{48.3}{8} - (1.4036)\left(\frac{9}{2}\right) = 6.0375 - 6.3162 = -.279$$

The trend line for this time series is

$$\hat{y}_t = -.279 + 1.404t$$

We conclude that the number of employees appears to increase at the rate of 1,404 per year, on the average.

The trend line is derived using the same least squares procedure discussed in Chapter 13—you can use the computer instructions contained in the simple linear regression illustrations. A computer solution using Excel is shown in Figure 4.10. Enter the values 1 though 8 in column A and the time series values in column B.* To

---

*You can generate $1, 2, \ldots, 8$ in column A by typing "1" in cell A1 and "2" in cell A2, highlighting these two cells, and dragging them through cell A8. This technique will be especially useful for very long time series.

FIGURE

4.10

Excel solution of least squares trend line.

	A	B	C	D	E	F	G	H
1	1	1.1	SUMMARY OUTPUT					
2	2	2.4						
3	3	4.6	Regression Statistics					
4	4	5.4	Multiple R	0.992				
5	5	5.9	R Square	0.985				
6	6	8.0	Adjusted R Square	0.982				
7	7	9.7	Standard Error	0.462				
8	8	11.2	Observations	8				
9								
10			ANOVA					
11				df	SS	MS	F	Significance F
12			Regression	1	82.741	82.741	388.388	1.10669E-06
13			Residual	6	1.278	0.213		
14			Total	7	84.019			
15								
16				Coefficients	Standard Error	t Stat	P-value	
17			Intercept	-0.279	0.360	-0.775	0.468	
18			X Variable 1	1.404	0.071	19.708	1.10669E-06	

obtain the linear trend equation, click on **Tools ➤ Data Analysis ➤ Regression**. Enter B1:B8 as the **Input Y Range,** A1:A8 as the **Input X Range,** and C1 as the **Output Range.** The regression coefficients in cells D17 and D18 agree with the previously derived trend equation.

Figure 4.10 contains the t statistic; you may be tempted to use it to determine whether time is a significant predictor of Y = number of employees. However, to use this statistic, you must assume that the errors about the trend line are completely *independent* of one another and contain *no observable pattern*. Do not forget that there may well be considerable cyclical activity about the trend line, and this cyclical activity will be contained in the residuals of the regression analysis. Thus, there probably will be a cyclical pattern to these residuals, so the assumption of complete independence is not met. The errors are therefore *autocorrelated* and any test of hypothesis is invalid.

This situation poses no serious problems at this point, however, because *our intent is simply to describe the time series by measuring the various components, and not to perform a statistical test of hypothesis.* If, however, the residuals about the trend line appear to be extremely large, it suggests that a linear trend component is not appropriate.

Quadratic Trend

The nature of a **quadratic trend** is illustrated in Figure 4.4. This type of trend is common for a time series that increases or decreases rapidly and then gradually levels off over the observed values. We discussed a similar situation in Chapter 14, where a quadratic model of the form

$$\hat{Y} = b_0 + b_1 X + b_2 X^2$$

was used to capture a curvilinear relationship between two variables. We use exactly the same technique to describe a quadratic trend; now X is replaced by time, t.

The power-consumption time series in Figure 4.1 indicates that as time increases, the amount of power consumption (y_t) also increases, but at a decreasing rate. More specifically, the increase for 2000 to 2001 is 18; for 2001 to 2002 is 12 (12 < 18); for 2002 to 2003 is 8 (8 < 12); and for 2003 to 2004 is 5 (5 < 8).

When you observe a series where the *changes* from one year to the next are not (approximately) constant but seem to be either increasing or decreasing with time, these changes indicate a quadratic trend. The equation of this curvilinear (quadratic) trend is

$$\hat{y}_t = b_0 + b_1 t + b_2 t^2$$

FIGURE
4.11

Excel solution for quadratic trend (power consumption data).

A	B	C	D	E	F	G	H	I
95	1	1	SUMMARY OUTPUT					
145	2	4						
174	3	9	Regression Statistics					
200	4	16	Multiple R	0.999				
224	5	25	R Square	0.998				
245	6	36	Adjusted R Square	0.997				
263	7	49	Standard Error	3.579				
275	8	64	Observations	10				
283	9	81						
288	10	100	ANOVA					
				df	SS	MS	F	Significance F
			Regression	2	37777.952	18888.976	1474.903	6.46E-10
			Residual	7	89.648	12.807		
			Total	9	37867.600			
				Coefficients	Standard Error	t Stat	P-value	
			Intercept	58.600	4.209	13.922	2.33E-06	
			X Variable 1	44.0485	1.758	25.058	4.11E-08	
			X Variable 2	-2.1212	0.156	-13.620	2.71E-06	

To derive the least squares estimates b_0, b_1, and b_2, we use the multiple linear regression procedure of Chapter 14.

What would be the input to a computer program (such as Excel, SPSS, or MINITAB) for the power-consumption data? For the regression program, you have two predictor variables, $X_1 = t$ and $X_2 = t^2$. The resulting data configuration looks like this:

y_t	t	t^2	
95	1	1	(for 1998)
145	2	4	(for 1999)
174	3	9	(for 2000)
200	4	16	$\vdots$
224	5	25	
245	6	36	
263	7	49	
275	8	64	
283	9	81	(for 2006)
288	10	100	(for 2007)

Figure 4.11 contains the Excel solution for the quadratic trend equation. To obtain this equation, click on **Tools ➤ Data Analysis ➤ Regression.** You should enter the time series values in column A (as in Figure 4.11) and the values 1 though 10 in column B. To obtain column C, enter =B1*B1 in cell C1 and drag this cell through cell C10. Enter A1:A10 as the **Input Y Range,** B1:C10 as the **Input X Range,** and D1 as the **Output Range.** The regression coefficients in cells E17:E19 provide the quadratic trend equation

$$y_t = 58.6 + 44.0485t - 2.1212t^2$$

To illustrate the use of this equation, the actual value for the second time period is $y_2 = 145$ and the predicted value is

$$\hat{y}_2 = 58.6 + 44.0485(2) - 2.1212(2)^2 = 138.21$$

A First Look at Forecasting: Extending the Trend

Whenever a time series contains very little seasonality (such as *annual* data, which have *no* seasonality) and a strong trend, an easy method of providing future forecasts is to project the observed growth pattern, as measured by the trend equation, into the future. For example, if a city's tax revenues have increased steadily by approximately $15,000 per year over the past 10 years, it seems reasonable to expect that this pattern will continue, at least for a short time. (Of course, assuming that such a growth will continue indefinitely is a hazardous gamble, at best!)

The process of extending a trend equation is called *forecasting*, or *extrapolation*. The following examples illustrate that extending a straight-line trend equation can provide useful estimates of future values. A quadratic trend equation is, however, useful only *within* the range of the sample data, that is, for *interpolation*.

Section 4.8 will take a closer look at this forecasting procedure and Section 4.9 discusses another popular forecasting technique, referred to as simple exponential smoothing.

EXAMPLE 4.3

Using the trend line from Figure 4.9, estimate the number of employees in 2008.

Solution $t = 9$ corresponds to the year 2008, so the *forecast* for this year is

$$\hat{y}_9 = -.279 + 1.404(9) = 12.357$$

that is, 12,357 employees.

As mentioned earlier, the basic assumption when using the trend line to determine a forecast is that this same pattern *will continue* into the future. This may or may not be true. Very often a time series will increase at a more or less constant rate and then begin to level off. One example is the sales of an innovative product. Such a time series will grow from one year to the next as people think that they just have to have this product, but eventually a saturation point is reached and the sales grow at a much smaller rate. If the historical data used to determine the trend line are collected during the growth stage, then you will stop short of and miss the "slowing down" of the time series, severely overestimating the sales. This problem is not a flaw in the technique; any time series model makes predictions by capturing the pattern(s) in the past observations and extending this pattern beyond the last year of the data. It does, however, place a great deal of responsibility on the person who uses the data to predict beyond the data range. If you do not know what underlying factors are driving the trend, serious errors can result.

Very often, a nonlinear growth rate can be described accurately by including a quadratic term in the trend equation. However, using such an equation to forecast *future* values is not a reliable procedure, as the following example demonstrates.

EXAMPLE 4.4

Using the trend equation from Figure 4.11

$$\hat{y}_t = TR_t = 58.6 + 44.0485t - 2.1212t^2$$

what is your forecast for the power consumption during 2008? during 2009? Use only the trend equation.

Solution The year 2008 corresponds to $t = 11$ (the last year of your data is $t = 10$ for 2007). Your forecast for 2008 is

$$\hat{y}_{11} = 58.6 + 44.0485(11) - 2.1212(11)^2 = 286.46$$

that is, 2,864,600 kilowatt-hours. For the year 2009, your forecast is

$$\hat{y}_{12} = 58.6 + 44.0485(12) - 2.1212(12)^2 = 281.72$$

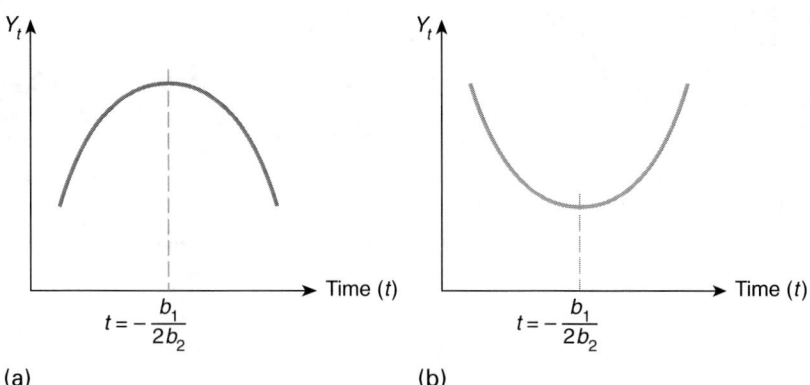

FIGURE

4.12

Illustration of how quadratic trend equations will reverse direction. The quadratic trend equation is $y_t = b_0 + b_1 t + b_2 t^2$, where (a) $b_2 < 0$ and (b) $b_2 > 0$.

The sermon we delivered about projecting a trend line beyond the range of the data applies to a quadratic trend as well: by forecasting with such an equation, you assume that this quadratic (curved) pattern observed in the time series observations will continue.

In addition, there is another danger when forecasting with a quadratic trend equation. Every such equation looks like Figure 4.12(a) or (b). In other words, the curve reaches a peak or trough at $t = -b_1/(2b_2)$ and then reverses direction. This change in direction is generally not seen in the sample data and produces trend estimates that are contrary to the pattern seen in the sample data. For example, rather than producing trend estimates that "slow down" with increasing time, the estimates after a certain point [namely, after $t = -b_1/(2b_2)$] will reverse direction.

The forecasts for power consumption (Example 4.4) for 2008 and 2009 provide a good illustration of this problem. Notice that the predicted value for 2008 is less than the actual value for 2007, despite a steadily increasing pattern in the time series data. Even worse, the year 2009 estimate is less than that for 2008. These values imply that the trend equation is decreasing during the years after 2007. We see that the trend equation forecasts appear to be poor estimates—we have no reason to suspect a downturn in the amount of power consumption in these future years. The trend is appropriately described by the quadratic curve, but only within the range of the data. This curve will peak at $t = -44.0485/2(-2.1212) = 10.38$ (between 2007 and 2008) and then begin to decline. Because we have no reason to believe that the demand for electrical power will decrease, the quadratic equation is no longer appropriate outside the range of the sample data.

To describe the trend *within* the years of your time series data, the quadratic trend equation may work well. However, remember that, as a *forecasting procedure, it is very dangerous; do not use it for this purpose.*

X Exercises 4.7–4.16

Understanding the Mechanics

4.7 The following table displays annual observations from 1999 to 2004.

Year	Time (t)	y_t	ty_t
2002	1	30	
2003	2	120	
2004	3	180	
2005	4	220	
2006	5	280	
2007	6	320	
	$\Sigma t =$	$\Sigma y_t =$	$\Sigma ty_t =$

a. Complete the table.
b. Determine the least squares line.
c. What is the predicted value for the year 2005?

4.8 Using the following statistics, fit a linear trend line for time periods $t = 1, 2, \ldots, 10$.

$$\Sigma y_t = 1300, \Sigma ty_t = 7484$$

Applying the New Concepts

4.9 Explain why a prediction equation with a quadratic trend may be dangerous to use in forecasting even though a quadratic trend fits the historic data very well.

4.10 The amount of money deposited into savings accounts at a local bank has grown steadily over the years, as the following data indicate (deposits are the amount of money in savings accounts at the end of the year, in units of $100,000):

Year	Deposits	Year	Deposits
2000	2.1	2004	10.3
2001	4.2	2005	13.3
2002	6.4	2006	14.9
2003	8.5	2007	16.7

a. Does it appear that a quadratic trend exists in the data?
b. Calculate the equation you would use to describe the trend.

4.11 An insurance company would like to find the trend line for the amount of insurance sold annually (in millions of dollars) across time. The variable time is represented by t and is equal to 1, 2, . . ., 8 for the past eight years. The following statistics were collected:

$$\Sigma ty_t = 394.5 \qquad \Sigma y_t = 29.4$$

Find the trend line for these time series data.

4.12 Due to rising competition from overseas, an electronics firm has been losing its share of the market. The following data show the percent of the market that the firm has captured for the past seven years.

Year	Share of Market
2001	4.7
2002	4.3
2003	3.9
2004	3.8
2005	3.6
2006	3.0
2007	2.9

a. Does the trend appear to be linear?
b. Find the equation to estimate the trend for the time series data.
c. What would be your estimate of the electronics firm's share of the market in 2008?

4.13 High-speed Internet broadband has rapidly expanded over the past 10 years. The following data show the number of total households using broadband (in millions) from 1997 to 2003. Using a quadratic estimate of the trend, what is your estimate of the total number of households using broadband in 2004?

Year	1997	1998	1999	2000	2001	2002	2003
Households	.1	.6	1.8	5.2	10.4	15.7	21.4

(Source: "Facing Its Demons," Forbes, July 21, 2003, p. 42.)

4.14 Qualcom developed Code Division Multiple Access (CDMA) technology. This technology is now the choice for the leading wireless network operators in North America. The following data represent the number of CDMA subscribers (in millions).

Quarter	Q1 2001	Q2 2001	Q3 2001	Q4 2001
Subscribers	90	96	103	111

	Q1 2002	Q2 2002	Q3 2002	Q4 2002
Subscribers	120	127	135	147

What is your estimate of the number of subscribers for Q1 of 2003 using a linear trend line?

(Source: "Qualcomm CDMA Technology," Forbes, July 21, 2003, p. 116.)

Using the Computer

4.15 **[DATA SET EX 4-15]** Variable Description:

Year: Year from 1981 to 2000

PC_Shipments: Number of personal computer shipments in millions worldwide

The first personal computer (PC) was introduced in 1981 by IBM. Since then, there have been many players in this fast-growing market. The number of PC shipments in 1981 was 2 million. That compares to 138 million in 2000.
a. Plot the number of shipments versus time. Do you think that a linear trend or a quadratic trend is a better fit?
b. Estimate the number of PC shipments in 2001 using an appropriate trend equation.

(Source: "Worldwide PC Shipments," USA Today, August 8, 2001, p. 3B.)

4.16 **[DATA SET EX 4-16]** Variable Description:

Year: Year from 1982 to 2007

Bonus: Annual bonus in thousands of dollars

A new vice president of a local bank is interested in examining the annual bonuses paid to her predecessors. She also realizes that stockholders of the bank are concerned about exorbitant bonuses. Do you believe that a linear or quadratic trend is present? What are the estimates of the expected annual bonuses for 2008 and 2009?

MEASURING CYCLICAL
ACTIVITY: NO SEASONALITY

Practically every time series in a business setting contains a certain amount of cyclical activity. Cyclical activity is a gradual movement about the trend. It is generally due to economic or other long-term conditions. The overall U.S. economy tends to fluctuate through "good times" and "bad times," producing (rather unpredictable) upward and downward variation about the long-term growth or decline in a time series.

One way of describing the cyclical activity component is to represent it as a fraction of the trend. This procedure provides accurate measures of the cyclical activity provided the time series contains *little irregular activity*. Assuming that each time series observation is the *product* of its components, then

$$y_t = TR_t \cdot C_t \cdot I_t$$

because we are dealing with data containing no seasonality.

If we represent a small irregular activity component as i_t (rather than I_t), then a time series containing little irregular variation (noise) can be written as

$$y_t = TR_t \cdot C_t \cdot i_t$$

The cyclical components are then obtained by dividing each observation, y_t, by its corresponding estimate using trend only, $\hat{y}_t$.

$$\text{ratio of data to trend} = \frac{y_t}{\hat{y}_t} = \frac{\cancel{TR_t} \cdot C_t \cdot i_t}{\cancel{TR_t}} = C_t \cdot i_t$$

where y_t = actual time series observation at time period t and $\hat{y}_t = TR_t$ = the estimate of y_t using trend only. Notice that the resulting ratios still contain some irregular activity. (A method of reducing the irregular activity within these values is illustrated in Section 4.6.)

An estimate of the cyclical components can be obtained by ignoring the irregular activity components in these ratios and defining

$$C_t \cong \frac{y_t}{\hat{y}_t}$$

4.6

Assuming that we are dealing with data containing no seasonality (such as annual data), equation 4.6 provides a convenient method of determining the cycles present in the data. If $C_t > 1$, the actual y_t is larger than that predicted by trend alone. Consequently, this value is somewhere in a cycle *above* the trend line. A similar argument indicates a cycle below the trend line whenever $C_t < 1$ (Figure 4.13).

FIGURE

4.13

A complete cycle within a time series.

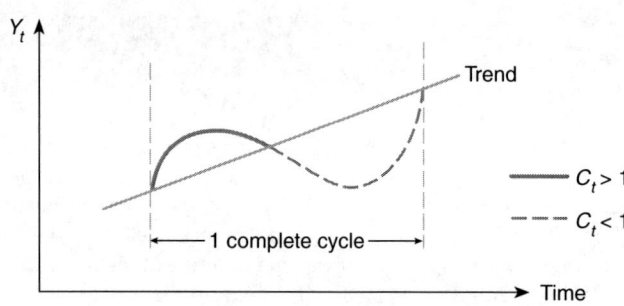

TABLE

4.1

Trend and cyclical activity (Example 4.5).

t	y_t	$\hat{y}_t$	$y_t/\hat{y}_t$
1	1.1	1.125	.978
2	2.4	2.529	.949
3	4.6	3.933	1.169
4	5.4	5.337	1.012
5	5.9	6.741	.875
6	8.0	8.145	.982
7	9.7	9.549	1.016
8	11.2	10.953	1.022

The third column is the trend component, and the fourth column is the cyclical component as a fraction of the trend.

E X A M P L E

4.5

For the data in Figure 4.9, we determined a least squares trend line for the number of employees (y_t) over an eight-year period at Video-Comp. We observed a linear trend with the corresponding equation

$$\hat{y}_t = -.279 + 1.404t$$

where $t = 1$ represents 2000, $t = 2$ is for 2001, and so on. Determine and graph the cyclical activity over this period.

Solution

We can obtain Table 4.1 by using the preceding trend line. Here $\hat{y}_1 = -.279 + 1.404(1) = 1.125$, $\hat{y}_2 = -.279 + 1.404(2) = 2.529$, and so on.

To examine the cyclical activity, we can describe each component as a percentage of the trend. For example, in Table 4.1, during the first time period, the actual number of employees is 97.8% of the trend value: C_1 is .978. An illustration of the trend and cyclical activity is shown in Figure 4.14. The cycles fluctuate about the trend line. Between the years $t = 2$ (2001) and $t = 3$ (2002), $y_t = \hat{y}_t$ and a cycle begins. This cycle is completed somewhere between $t = 6$ (2005) and $t = 7$ (2006), where, once again, $y_t = \hat{y}_t$. As discussed earlier, you can also measure cycles from peak to peak or from trough to trough.

The summary of the cyclical variation (components) over the eight years is contained in Table 4.1 and Figure 4.15. The four-year cycle we described is more evident in this

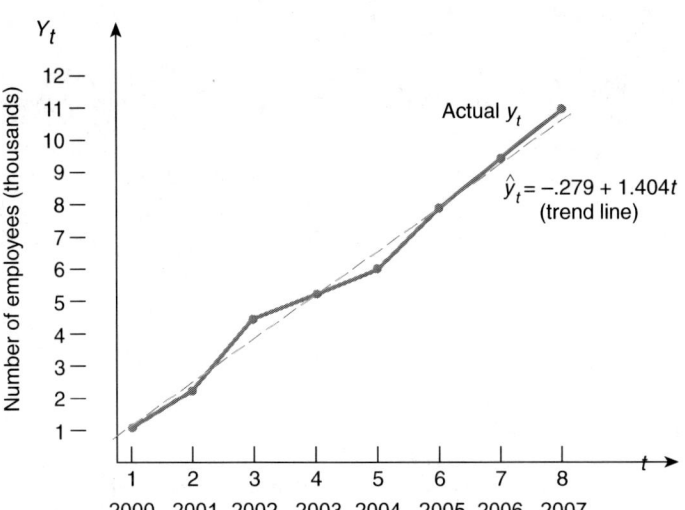

FIGURE

4.14

Cyclical activity about a trend line (Example 4.5).

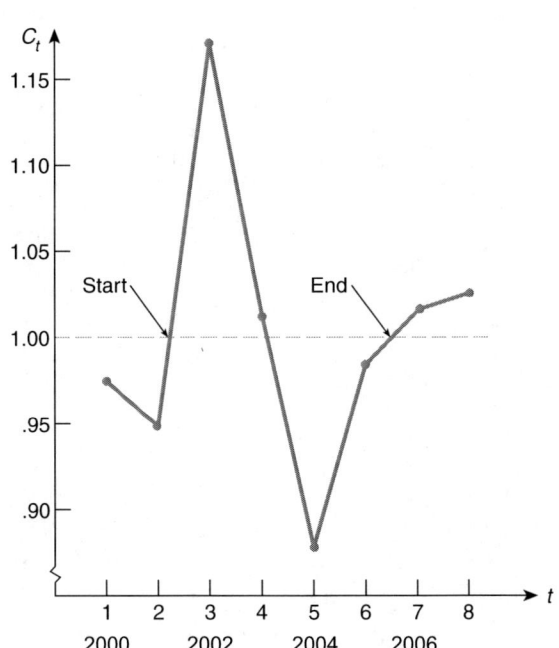

FIGURE

4.15

Cyclical components (Example 4.5).

graph. The graph clearly indicates the beginning of the cycle, where $C_t = 1$. The cycle's peak occurs at $t = 3$ (2002), the trough is at $t = 5$ (2004), and the cycle is finally complete when C_t is again equal to 1, toward the end of 2005.

In summary, cyclical variation represents an upward or downward movement about the overall growth or decline (that is, the trend) in the time series data. Such cycles typically last more than one year. For annual data, these components can be estimated by dividing each observation (y_t) by its corresponding estimate using the trend equation ($\hat{y}_t$).

X Exercises 4.17–4.26

Understanding the Mechanics

4.17   The following time series data are presented with the predicted values using the trend line. Find the cyclical components.

t	y_t	$\hat{y}_t$
1	1.0	1.493
2	2.0	2.752
3	5.0	4.012
4	5.5	5.271
5	6.0	6.530
6	8.0	7.790
7	10.0	9.049
8	11.0	10.309
9	11.3	11.568
10	11.8	12.827

4.18 Estimate the length of the cycle for each of the following three time series.

a. t	C_t	b. t	C_t	c. t	C_t
1	1.0	1	.3	1	3.1
2	.9	2	.7	2	2.2
3	1.7	3	1.3	3	1.2
4	.8	4	2.0	4	.9
5	1.5	5	1.5	5	.6
6	.9	6	.8	6	.3
7	1.4	7	.4	7	.7
8	.8	8	.9	8	.9
9	1.6	9	1.2	9	1.3
10	.7	10	2.4	10	1.8
		11	1.6	11	4.0
		12	.8	12	2.5
		13	.5	13	1.0
				14	.6

Applying the New Concepts

4.19   A food-store chain has the following record for yearly sales volume (in hundreds of thousands of dollars) for the past 9 years.

Year	Sales Volume	Year	Sales Volume
1999	7	2004	17
2000	15	2005	12
2001	10	2006	8
2002	5	2007	17
2003	11		

   a. Find the trend line.
   b. Find the cyclical components.
   c. Estimate the period of the cycle.

4.20   Residential Construction of America has been growing over the long term. Because the construction company is sensitive to cyclical variations in the economy,

the level of employment for the company changes from year to year, as can be seen by the following data:

Year	Full-Time Employees (in Hundreds)	Year	Full-Time Employees (in Hundreds)
1995	2.4	2002	11.7
1996	9.2	2003	17.3
1997	11.1	2004	23.1
1998	8.5	2005	28.7
1999	10.5	2006	29.3
2000	6.8	2007	25.2
2001	5.4		

   a. Find the trend line.
   b. Find the cyclical components.
   c. Estimate the period of the cycle.

4.21 Few objects convey wealth and power like a private airplane and many companies are presently using them. Casket salesmen for Hillenbrand Industries, Inc., use them to escort funeral directors when visiting showrooms. Lumber buyers for The Home Depot based in Atlanta fly on private airplanes to purchase inventory at out-of-the-way mills. Corning, Inc.'s technicians use them to shuttle between the company's headquarters in upstate New York and its optical-fiber plant in Wilmington, North Carolina. The following data illustrate the number of U.S. companies from 1988 to 1998 that operated turbine-powered aircraft in units of thousands.

Year	Number of U.S. Companies Operating Turbine-Powered Aircraft
1988	7.1
1989	6.7
1990	6.6
1991	6.5
1992	6.6
1993	6.7
1994	6.8
1995	7.8
1996	7.4
1997	7.5
1998	8.0

   a. Find the trend line.
   b. Determine the cyclical activity.
   c. Does the period of the cycle appear to be longer or shorter than five years?

(Source: "Not Just for Highfliers, Corporate Planes Take Off," *The Wall Street Journal*, January 8, 1999, p. B1.)

4.22 Estimate the cyclical components using the data in Exercise 4.12.

4.23 A production manager is interested in the competitiveness of his company in manufacturing air conditioning compressors for automobiles. Data are collected over a

10-year period, and the compressor cost per unit compressor is recorded. Determine the cyclical components for each year. Do you believe that the length of the cycle is longer than three years?

Year	Dollar Cost per Unit Compressor	Year	Dollar Cost per Unit Compressor
1998	100.4	2003	104.3
1999	103.6	2004	107.8
2000	105.2	2005	101.6
2001	102.3	2006	98.4
2002	99.8	2007	103.1

4.24 The United States is very important as a market for other countries. Since 1991, U.S. imports as a percentage of the rest of the world's gross domestic product (GDP) has increased. The following table illustrated the growth in U.S. imports from 1985 to 2000.
  a. Estimate the trend line. How would you interpret the slope of this line?
  b. Estimate the cyclical components and approximate the period of the cycle.

Year	Imports as a Percentage of World GDP	Year	Imports as a Percentage of World GDP
1985	2.5	1993	3.3
1986	1.9	1994	3.5
1987	2.2	1995	4.0
1988	2.4	1996	3.6
1989	2.6	1997	4.0
1990	3.2	1998	4.5
1991	2.8	1999	4.8
1992	3.1	2000	6.0

(Source: "Magnet," *The Wall Street Journal*, July 17, 2001, p. 1A.)

Using the Computer

4.25 [DATA SET EX4-25] *Variable Description:*

Year: Year from 1991 to 2007

Applicants: Number of applicants for supervisory positions

The manager of a division of an original equipment manufacturer (OEM) for a large technology company wishes to understand the cyclical nature of the division's hiring. Determine the length of the cycles for this data set.

4.26 [DATA SET EX4-26] *Variable Description:*

Year: Year from 1984 to 2000

NewVehicleSales: U.S. new vehicle sales in millions

Sales of new vehicles have undergone several downturns. During the Arab oil embargo of 1973, during the OPEC price increase in the early 1980s, and during the Gulf War in 1991, sales of new vehicles were very slow.
  a. Estimate the trend equation for the sales of new vehicles from 1984 to 2000.
  b. Estimate the approximate period of the cycle for sales of new vehicles between 1984 and 2000.

(Source: "Auto Sales During National Crises," *USA Today*, September 20, 2001, p. 2B.)

4.4

TYPES OF SEASONAL VARIATION

Seasonality causes another type of variation about the trend in a time series. Seasonality generally is present when the data are quarterly or monthly. It can also occur for weekly or even daily data. For example, recurrent daily effects can be expected to occur in the check-processing volume in a bank. *Seasonality* is any recurrent, constant source of variation caused by events at the particular time of year rather than by any long-term influence (as in cyclical activity). For example, one would expect to sell more snowmobiles in January than in July. In a sense, the seasonal variation appears as a cycle within a year; we do not refer to this as cyclical variation, however, due to its recurrent nature.

We will discuss two types of seasonal variation: additive and multiplicative.

Additive Seasonal Variation

One encounters **additive seasonal variation** when the amount of the variation due to seasonality *does not depend on the level* y_t. This type of seasonal variation is illustrated in Figure 4.16,

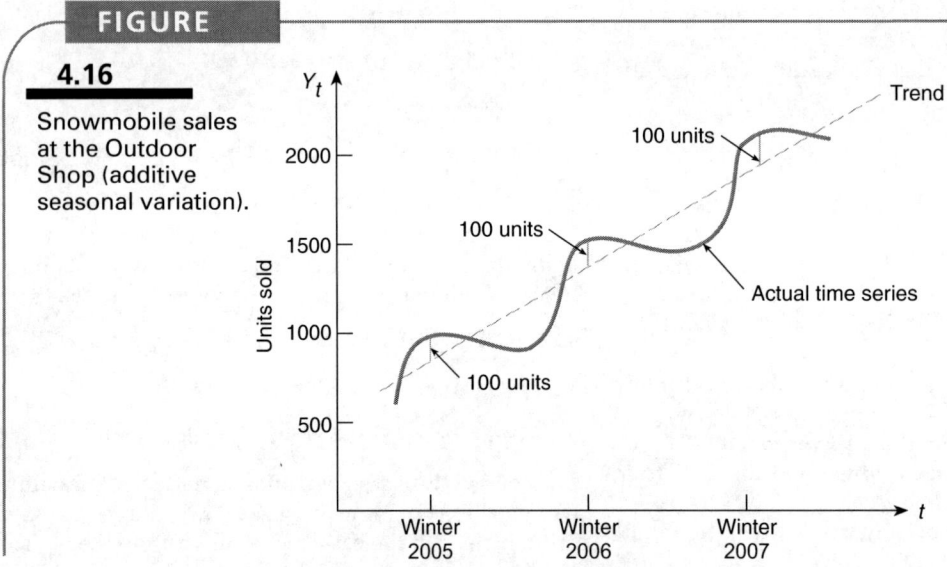

FIGURE

4.16

Snowmobile sales at the Outdoor Shop (additive seasonal variation).

which shows the sales of snowmobiles over a three-year period at the Outdoor Shop. Notice that the amount of variation for each of the winter quarters remains the same (100 units), even as the unit sales increase over the three years. For an actual application, we assume an additive effect of seasonality if these increments are of nearly the same magnitude over the observed time series.

Assume that the sales data for Jetski snowmobiles from sales area 1 were recorded quarterly over the five-year period from 2003 through 2007. The following trend line was derived:

$$TR_t = \hat{y}_t = 100 + 20t$$

The seasonal indexes for a seasonal time series represent the incremental effect of the seasons alone, apart from any trend or cyclical activity. For the Jetski data in sales area 1, these indexes were found to be

$$S_1 = +60 \text{ (winter quarter)} \qquad S_3 = -40 \text{ (summer quarter)}$$
$$S_2 = +30 \text{ (spring quarter)} \qquad S_4 = -20 \text{ (fall quarter)}$$

In a time series decomposition (where we actually derive these seasonal indexes), additive seasonal variation assumes that the seasonal index for, say, the winter quarter is the *same* for each year. Using the additive model, this implies that the store will sell 60 more Jetski units in the winter quarter than would be predicted by trend alone during any year. This implies that $S_1 = S_5 = S_9 = \ldots = +60$.

To estimate y_t using only the trend and seasonality, we *add* the two corresponding components.

t (Time)	$TR_t + S_t$ (Sales Estimate)
1 (winter 2003)	$[100 + 20(1)] + 60 = 180$
2 (spring 2003)	$[100 + 20(2)] + 30 = 170$
3 (summer 2003)	$[100 + 20(3)] - 40 = 120$
4 (autumn 2003)	$[100 + 20(4)] - 20 = 160$
5 (winter 2004)	$[100 + 20(5)] + 60 = 260$
6 (spring 2004)	$[100 + 20(6)] + 30 = 250$
7 (summer 2004)	$[100 + 20(7)] - 40 = 200$
8 (autumn 2004)	$[100 + 20(8)] - 20 = 240$
$\vdots$	$\vdots$

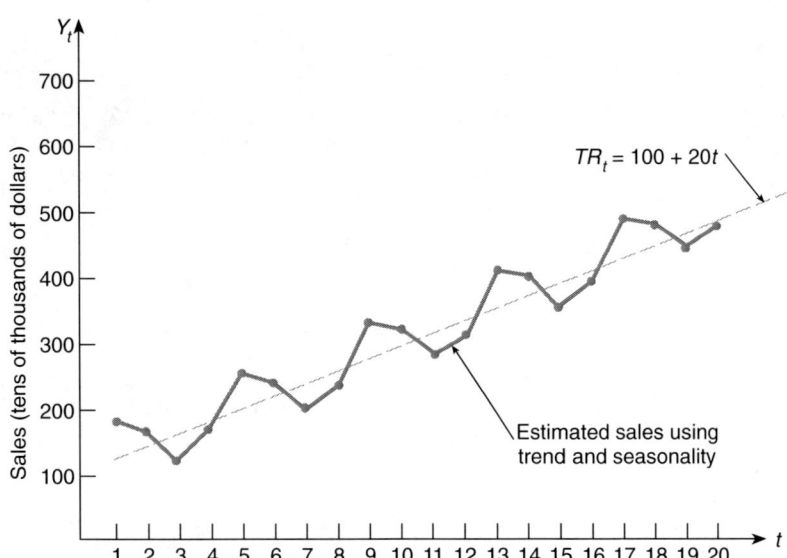

FIGURE

4.17

Jetski sales from sales area 1 (additive seasonal variation).

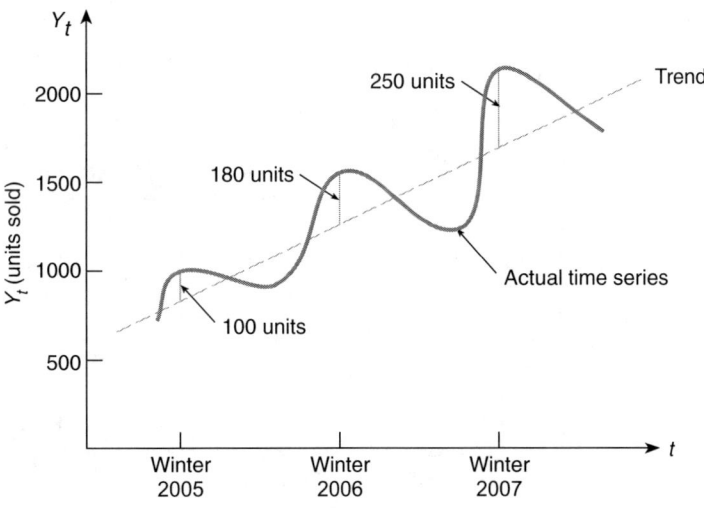

FIGURE

4.18

Heat-pump sales at Handy Home Center (an illustration of multiplicative seasonal variation).

A graph of the estimated sales is shown in Figure 4.17. Notice that as the overall level of sales increases, the deviation from the trend line (due to seasonality) remains the same. If the past observations in the time series indicate that higher levels of sales produce wider seasonal fluctuations, this is an indication of multiplicative seasonal variation.

Multiplicative Seasonal Variation

Figure 4.6 shows **multiplicative seasonal variation** in the time series for the sale of Wild-cat sailboats. Notice that in each successive year, the difference between the actual value and the trend value for July is larger. In multiplicative seasonal variation, the seasonal fluctuation is *proportional* to the trend level for each observation. Figure 4.18 is a general illustration of multiplicative seasonability; it shows the sales of heat pumps over a three-year period at Handy Home Center.

Considering only the effects of trend and seasonality, an estimate for a time series observation is given by

$$\text{estimate of } y_t = TR_t \cdot S_t$$

As in additive seasonal variation, the seasonal indexes, S_t, remain constant from one year to the next. When dealing with quarterly data, this means that $S_1 = S_5 = S_9 = \ldots$, $S_2 = S_6 = S_{10} = \ldots$, and so on. The next section discusses a method for determining these indexes for the case of multiplicative seasonality.

EXAMPLE 4.6

Suppose that the sales of Jetski snowmobiles from sales area 2 contain multiplicative seasonal effects with trend $= TRt = 100 + 20t$ (as before) and these seasonal indexes:

$$S_1 = 1.4 \text{ (winter quarter)}$$
$$S_2 = 1.2 \text{ (spring quarter)}$$
$$S_3 = 0.6 \text{ (summer quarter)}$$
$$S_4 = 0.8 \text{ (autumn quarter)}$$

Determine the estimated sales using the trend and seasonal components.

Solution

The calculations for the first two years are

t (Time)	$TRt \cdot St$ (Estimate)
1 (winter 2003)	$[100 + 20(1)](1.4) = 168$
2 (spring 2003)	$[100 + 20(2)](1.2) = 168$
3 (summer 2003)	$[100 + 20(3)](\,.6) = 96$
4 (autumn 2003)	$[100 + 20(4)](\,.8) = 144$
5 (winter 2004)	$[100 + 20(5)](1.4) = 280$
6 (spring 2004)	$[100 + 20(6)](1.2) = 264$
7 (summer 2004)	$[100 + 20(7)](\,.6) = 144$
8 (autumn 2004)	$[100 + 20(8)](\,.8) = 208$
$\vdots$	$\vdots$

A graph of the estimated sales over a five-year period is shown in Figure 4.19. Notice that seasonal patterns do exist, but (unlike additive variation) these fluctuations increase as the sales level rises. For a time series representing sales, this type of variation seems to make sense. If the volume of sales doubles, it is reasonable to expect a larger effect due to seasonality than occurred previously.

Remember that in practice, few time series exhibit exact additive or multiplicative seasonal effects. However, you can classify a great many time series as essentially belonging to one or the other of these two classes.

In the discussion to follow, we assume that any seasonality in the time series is *multiplicative*. Most analysts (including those in the U.S. Census Bureau) have had better success describing time series in this manner. The decomposition method to be discussed assumes that each observation is the *product* of its various components. So, the *component structure* is assumed to be

$$y_t = TR_t \cdot S_t \cdot C_t \cdot I_t$$

4.7

FIGURE

4.19

Jetski sales from
sales area 2
(multiplicative
seasonal
variation).

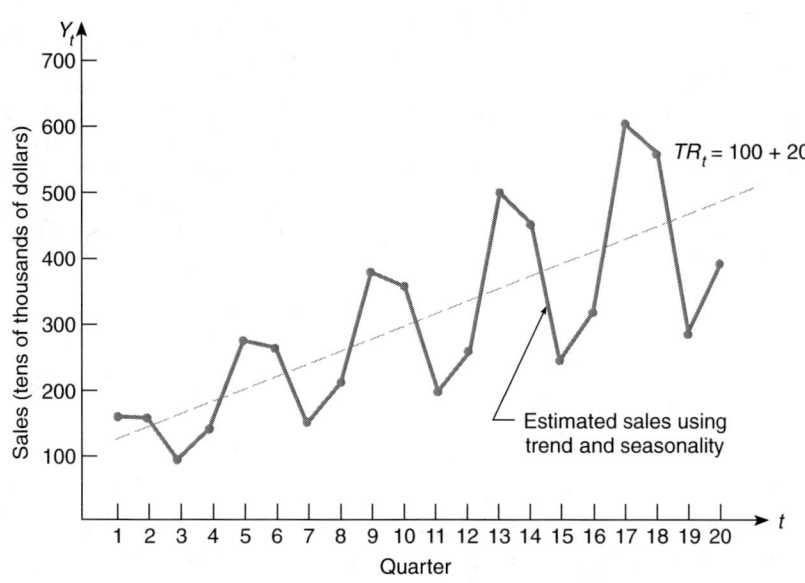

where the components representing seasonality, trend, cyclical variation, and noise are
multiplied by one another.*

Four-Step Procedure (Multiplicative Components)

Based on the multiplicative component structure in equation 4.7, the following four-step procedure can be used to decompose a time series containing the effects of all four components.

Step 1.   *Determine a seasonal index, S_t, for each time period.* For quarterly data, this involves
determining four such indexes, S_1, S_2, S_3, and S_4. When the time series contains
monthly observations, 12 seasonal indexes ($S1$ through S_{12}) must be calculated,
one for each month.

Step 2.   *Deseasonalize the data.* This step is often referred to as *adjusting for seasonality*; the
seasonal component is eliminated. Because we are using a multiplicative struc-
ture, we divide each observation by its corresponding seasonal index. So

$$\text{deseasonalized observation} = d_t = \frac{y_t}{S_t}$$

where

$$S_t = \begin{cases} S_1, \ S_2, \ S_3, \ \text{or } S_4 & \text{(quarterly data)} \\ S_1, \ S_2, \dots, \ \text{or } S_{12} & \text{(monthly data)} \end{cases}$$

---

*Similar methods for determining the components of a time series containing additive seasonality
also exist. For a fuller discussion of such techniques, see B. L. Bowerman and R. T. O'Connell,
Forecasting and Time Series: An Applied Approach, 3d ed., Pacific Grove, California: Brooks/Cole,
a part of Cengage Lerning, 2000.

Because $y_t = TR_t \cdot S_t \cdot C_t \cdot I_t$,

$$d_t = \frac{y_t}{S_t} = \frac{TR_t \cdot \cancel{S_t} \cdot C_t \cdot I_t}{\cancel{S_t}} = TR_t \cdot C_t \cdot I_t$$

Step 3. *Determine the trend component, TR_t.* The trend is estimated by passing a least squares line through the *deseasonalized* data. The technique is identical to that discussed in Section 4.2 (which assumed no seasonality), except that we use the d_t values rather than the original time series. This process is illustrated in the next section.

Step 4. *Determine the cyclical component, C_t.* You obtain C_t by first dividing each deseasonalized observation, d_t, by the corresponding trend value from step 3. So the cyclical estimates are derived by first calculating (for each time period)

$$\frac{d_t}{\hat{d}_t} = \frac{d_t}{TR_t} = \frac{\cancel{TR_t} \cdot C_t \cdot I_t}{\cancel{TR_t}} = C_t \cdot I_t$$

Notice that the resulting series contains cycles and irregular activity (but no trend or seasonality). A method for reducing the irregular component in these ratios is discussed in Section 4.6. The resulting values are the cyclical components, $C_{\cdot t}$.

We do not use the cyclical components to attempt to forecast future values of the time series because their behavior (and period) generally cannot be predicted. The cyclical components can be used in forecasting if one is willing to assume a particular phase in the business cycle. If one assumes, for example, that the cycle is in the midst of an upturn, a value of C_t (such as $C_t = 1.2$) can be assigned to this particular time period. In the discussion to follow, the cyclical components are obtained strictly as a means of *describing* the cyclical activity within a recorded time series.

X Exercises 4.27–4.34

Understanding the Mechanics

4.27 Assuming additive seasonal variation, find the estimate of y_t for $t = 1, 2, 3, 4$. These time periods represent four quarters.

$$TR_t = 21 + 4.5t$$

$$S_1 = 12 \qquad S_3 = -8$$
$$S_2 = 6 \qquad S_4 = -4$$

4.28 Assuming multiplicative seasonal variation, find the estimates of y_t for $t = 1, 2, 3, 4$. These time periods represent four quarters.

$$TR_t = 100 - 3t$$

$$S_1 = .82 \qquad S_3 = 1.30$$
$$S_2 = .64 \qquad S_4 = 1.24$$

Applying the New Concepts

4.29 For a six-year period (2002 to 2007) quarterly sales data (in thousands) were used to arrive at the following trend line and seasonal indexes.

$$TR_t = 35 + 2.3t \qquad \text{for } t = 1, 2, \ldots, 24$$

$$S_1 = -8.7 \qquad S_3 = 8.4$$
$$S_2 = 2.5 \qquad S_4 = 3.1$$

Estimate the sales figures for the four quarters in 2006 using an additive equation containing only the trend and seasonality components.

4.30 Advanced Digital Components has experienced rapid growth during the past several years. The quarterly data for the past four years give the following trend line and seasonal indexes. Sales units are in tens of thousands.

$$TR_t = 0.85 + 0.8t \qquad \text{for } t = 1, 2, \ldots, 16$$

$$S_1 = 0.82 \qquad S_3 = 1.20$$

$$S_2 = 1.36 \qquad S_4 = 0.62$$

Estimate the sales figures for the four quarters in the most recent year using a multiplicative equation containing only the trend and seasonality components.

4.31 Monthly data from the years 2002 through 2007 were used to find the following trend line and seasonal indexes:

$$TR_t = 1.3 + 0.5t \qquad \text{for } t = 1, 2, \ldots, 60$$

$S_1 = 0.5$	$S_4 = 1.3$	$S_7 = 2.4$	$S_{10} = 0.2$
$S_2 = 0.8$	$S_5 = 1.1$	$S_8 = 3.1$	$S_{11} = 0.2$
$S_3 = 0.6$	$S_6 = 1.4$	$S_9 = 0.3$	$S_{12} = 0.1$

Assuming a multiplicative model containing only the trend and seasonality components, estimate the data for the 12 months of 2006.

4.32 The manager of a local utility company is interested in estimating the deseasonalized quarterly usage of electric power consumption by the average household. Using deseasonalized data, the manager wants to see if a clear pattern exists. Average electrical usage is collected quarterly from 2005 through 2007 in units of millions of kilowatt hours. Assume that the data are subject to additive seasonal variation and that the seasonal indexes are $S_1 = 12.4$, $S_2 = -5.8$, $S_3 = 7.2$, and $S_4 = -6.8$. Deseasonalize the data and determine if any patterns are revealed in these seasonally adjusted values.

Year	Quarter	Electrical Usage
2005	1	62
	2	46
	3	61
	4	49
2006	1	66
	2	52
	3	67
	4	55

Year	Quarter	Electrical Usage
2007	1	76
	2	60
	3	75
	4	63

Using the Computer

4.33 [DATA SET EX4-33] *Variable Description:*

Year: Year from 1992 to 2000

Quarter: Quarter denoted by 1, 2, 3, or 4.

FDI_Japan: Foreign direct investment (in billions of dollars) in Japan

Japan's gross domestic product has shown little growth in recent years. However, a bright spot in its economy is that foreign direct investment (FDI) in the country has been soaring during this time period. This increase shows that investors have faith that Japan's economy will rebound. Assume that the seasonal indexes are $S_1 = 1.0$, $S_2 = 1.18$, $S_3 = .90$, and $S_4 = .92$. If FDI in Japan is subject to multiplicative seasonal variation, what are the deseasonalized FDI figures per quarter from 1992 to 2000?

(Source: "Japanese Economy Is Showing Fresh Signs of Weakness," *The Wall Street Journal*, June 8, 2001, p. A13.)

4.34 [DATA SET EX4-34] *Variable Description:*

Year_Quarter: Year and quarter from the first quarter of 1996 to the fourth quarter of 2000

HourlyComp: Percentage increase in hourly compensation

During the expanding economy and low unemployment rate from 1996 to 2000, the percentage increase in hourly compensation rose. Assuming additive seasonality, calculate the deseasonalized hourly compensation, given the following seasonal indexes: $S_1 = .2$, $S_2 = .3$, $S_3 = -3$, and $S_4 = -.2$.

(Source: "Fed's Meyer Warns to Inflation, Joblessness," *The Wall Street Journal*, June 7, 2001, p. A2.)

4.5

MEASURING SEASONALITY

Seasonality often is present in time series data collected over months or quarters. This effect is observed when, for example, some months are always higher than the average for the year. For example, if the recorded values of the time series indicate that July sales are 25% higher than the average monthly sales for the year, the July index should be 1.25 using the multiplicative structure.

TABLE

4.2

Time series with
quarterly
observations.

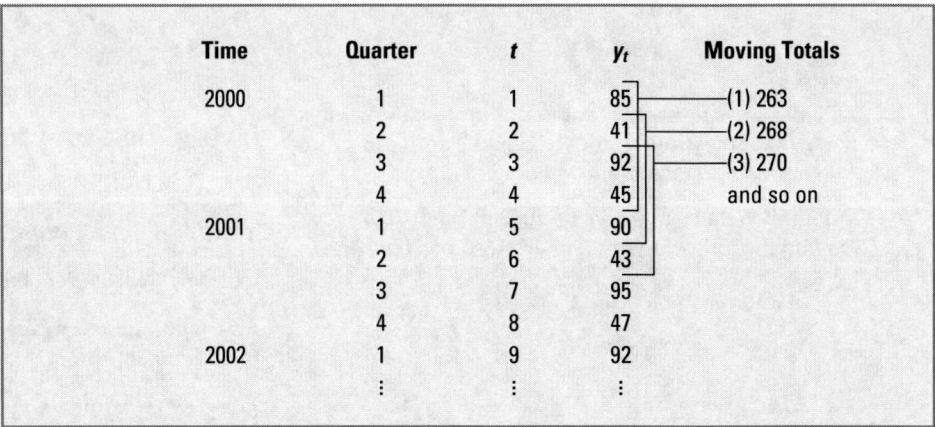

Time	Quarter	t	y_t	Moving Totals
2000	1	1	85	(1) 263
	2	2	41	(2) 268
	3	3	92	(3) 270
	4	4	45	and so on
2001	1	5	90	
	2	6	43	
	3	7	95	
	4	8	47	
2002	1	9	92	
	⋮		⋮	⋮

To conduct a time series analysis for a particular time series, we derive a seasonal index for each period during the year (4 for quarterly data, 12 for monthly data). We begin by developing a new series that contains *no seasonality*. This new series is obtained from the original time series and consists of the *centered moving averages*. Using the information calculated from the centered moving averages, we proceed through the four steps outlined in Section 4.4. This section describes how to calculate the centered moving averages and describes the first two steps (determining the seasonal indexes and deseasonalizing the data) in more detail. Example 4.9 then illustrates how the four-step procedure can be applied.

Centered Moving Averages

The **centered moving averages** provide an excellent way of isolating the seasonal components from the original time series. In addition to containing no seasonality, the centered moving averages are *smoother* (contain less irregular activity) than the original time series. Consequently, the moving averages give you a clearer picture of any existing trend within a time series containing significant seasonality and irregular activity. Other methods of smoothing a time series will be discussed in Section 4.9.

To illustrate the calculation of a moving average, consider a time series containing quarterly observations, as shown in Table 4.2.* Here,

$$(1) = \text{sum of } y_1 \text{ through } y_4$$
$$= 85 + 41 + 92 + 45 = 263$$
$$(2) = \text{sum of } y_2 \text{ through } y_5$$
$$= 41 + 92 + 45 + 90 = 268$$
$$(3) = \text{sum of } y_3 \text{ through } y_6$$
$$= 92 + 45 + 90 + 43 = 270$$

and so on.

Because each total contains four observations (one from each quarter), any quarterly seasonal effects have been removed. Consequently, there is no seasonality in the moving totals 263, 268, 270, and so on, in Table 4.2.

---

*An example using monthly data is given in Section 4.6.

The first moving total in Table 4.2 is equal to $y_1 + y_2 + y_3 + y_4$. If we were to position this total in the center of these values, it would lie between $t = 2$ and $t = 3$, at $t = 2.5$. The second moving total is equal to $y_2 + y_3 + y_4 + y_5$; again, we position this total in the center between $t = 3$ and $t = 4$, at $t = 3.5$.

We then add the first two moving totals. Notice that four values went into each of these totals, so that a total of *eight* values makes up this sum. The sum of the first two moving totals is $263 + 268 = 531$. The average for the eight months in the first two moving totals is $531/8 = 66.38$. This is a *centered moving average*. The position of this centered moving average is midway between $t = 2.5$ and $t = 3.5$, at $t = 3$. We therefore conclude that 66.38 is the centered moving average corresponding to $t = 3$.

EXAMPLE 4.7

Continue the procedure using Table 4.2 and determine the centered moving average for (1) $t = 4$ and (2) $t = 5$.

Solution 1

Here we obtain

$$268 = y_2 + y_3 + y_4 + y_5$$

(positioned at $t = 3.5$) and

$$270 = y_3 + y_4 + y_5 + y_6$$

(positioned at $t = 4.5$). So the average of the eight numbers making up $268 + 270 = 538$ would be positioned midway between 3.5 and 4.5, at $t = 4$. Consequently, the centered moving average for $t = 4$ is

$$\frac{268 + 270}{8} = 67.25$$

Solution 2

Proceeding as before,

$$270 = y_3 + y_4 + y_5 + y_6$$

(positioned at $t = 4.5$) and

$$273 = y_4 + y_5 + y_6 + y_7$$

(positioned at $t = 5.5$). Therefore, the centered moving average for $t = 5$ is

$$\frac{270 + 273}{8} = 67.88$$

Assume quarterly sales data at Video-Comp were recorded over a four-year period. We now want to determine the centered moving averages for these data, shown in Table 4.3. There appears to be a definite seasonal effect within this time series; the highest sales occur in the fourth quarter of each year. Table 4.4 shows the centered moving averages for these data. The *first moving total* is

$$139 = y_1 + y_2 + y_3 + y_4$$
$$= 20 + 12 + 47 + 60$$

TABLE

4.3

Sales data for Video-Comp (millions of dollars).

Year	Quarter 1	Quarter 2	Quarter 3	Quarter 4
2004	20	12	47	60
2005	40	32	65	76
2006	56	50	85	100
2007	75	70	101	123

TABLE

4.4

Moving averages for Video-Comp sales data.

Year	Quarter	t	y_t	Moving Total	Centered Moving Average	Ratio to Moving Average
2004	1	1	20	—	—	—
	2	2	12		—	—
	3	3	47	139	37.25	1.26
	4	4	60	159	42.25	1.42
2005	1	5	40	179	47.00	.85
	2	6	32	197	51.25	.62
	3	7	65	213	55.25	1.18
	4	8	76	229	59.50	1.28
2006	1	9	56	247	64.25	.87
	2	10	50	267	69.75	.72
	3	11	85	291	75.13	1.13
	4	12	100	310	80.00	1.25
2007	1	13	75	330	84.50	.89
	2	14	70	346	89.38	.78
	3	15	101	369	—	—
	4	16	123	—	—	—

Its actual location is $t = 2.5$; it is positioned between $t = 2$ and $t = 3$. Similarly, the next moving total is centered at $t = 3.5$ and so appears between $t = 3$ and $t = 4$ in the table. This total is

$$159 = y_2 + y_3 + y_4 + y_5$$
$$= 12 + 47 + 60 + 40$$

Each moving total is centered midway between the values making up this total. For example, the last moving total, 369, is centered between $t = 14$ and $t = 15$, at $t = 14.5$. Here,

$$369 = y_{13} + y_{14} + y_{15} + y_{16}$$
$$= 75 + 70 + 101 + 123$$

The centered moving average at time t is the average of the moving total immediately preceding this time value and the total immediately following it. This means that, for $t = 3$,

$$37.25 = \frac{139 + 159}{8}$$

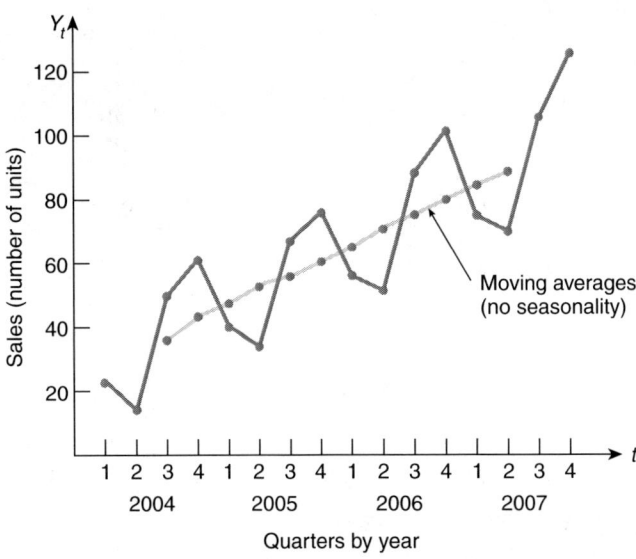

FIGURE

4.20

Smoothing a time series using moving averages (Video-Comp sales data).

For $t = 4$,

$$42.25 = \frac{159 + 179}{8}$$

and so on. Consequently, for $t = 3$, $y_3 = 47$ and the centered moving average is 37.25.

This procedure produces 12 centered moving averages; we are unable to compute this value for $t = 1, 2, 15,$ or 16. Notice that the first two of these values of t are for quarters 1 and 2, whereas the remaining two correspond to quarters 3 and 4. In general, if our time series contains T observations, we can derive $T - 4$ centered moving averages using quarterly data or $T - 12$ averages for monthly data.

The moving totals and centered moving averages are formed by summing over the four quarters (seasons), so there is no seasonality present in these values. Furthermore, the irregular component has been reduced because averages always contain less random variation (noise) than do the individual values making up these averages. Representing this reduced irregular activity component as i_t (rather than I_t), we can represent a centered moving average at time t as

$$\text{centered moving average at time } t = TR_t \cdot C_t \cdot i_t$$

Because of this averaging procedure, the moving averages contain much less irregular activity and so are much "smoother" than the original time series. This procedure thus is referred to as *smoothing* the time series to get a clearer picture of any existing trend as well as of its shape (straight line or curve).

The centered moving averages in Table 4.4 show a steadily increasing trend. Because the differences between any two adjacent moving averages are nearly the same, this trend is very *linear*. The trend is more apparent in Figure 4.20, which contains the original data with the moving averages.

To determine the four quarterly seasonal indexes, the first step is to divide each observation, y_t, by its corresponding centered moving average; the result is shown in the last column in the table.

TABLE

4.5

Ratios for each quarter.

Year	Quarter 1	Quarter 2	Quarter 3	Quarter 4
2004	—	—	1.26	1.42
2005	.85	.62	1.18	1.28
2006	.87	.72	1.13	1.25
2007	.89	.78	—	—
Total	2.61	2.12	3.57	3.95
Average	0.870	0.707	1.190	1.317

$$\text{for } t = 3: \quad \text{ratio} = 47/37.25 = 1.26 \quad \text{(belongs to quarter 3, 2004)}$$
$$\text{for } t = 4: \quad \text{ratio} = 60/42.25 = 1.42 \quad \text{(belongs to quarter 4, 2004)}$$
$$\vdots$$
$$\text{for } t = 14: \quad \text{ratio} = 70/89.38 = .78 \quad \text{(belongs to quarter 2, 2007)}$$

When we divide y_t by its corresponding centered moving average, we obtain

$$\text{ratio} = \frac{y_t}{\text{centered moving average}} = \frac{\mathcal{TR}_t \cdot S_t \cdot \mathcal{C}_t \cdot I_t}{\mathcal{TR}_t \cdot \mathcal{C}_t \cdot i_t}$$
$$= S_t \cdot I_t$$

Consequently, these ratios contain the seasonal effects as well as the irregular activity (noise) components. The following discussion illustrates how you can reduce the effect of the irregular activity factor by combining these ratios into a set of four seasonal indexes, one for each quarter.

Computing a Seasonal Index

The purpose of a **seasonal index** is to indicate how the time series value for each quarter (or month) compares with the average for the year. The following discussion will assume that we are dealing with a time series containing quarterly data. In the next section, we illustrate this procedure using monthly data.

We begin by collecting the ratios to moving average, placing each of them in its respective quarter. In Table 4.4, we see that 1.26 belongs to quarter 3, 1.42 to quarter 4, .85 to quarter 1, and so on. Table 4.5 is the result. Notice that there are three ratios for each quarter. In general, you always will obtain (total number of years − 1) ratios under each quarter (or month). The time series in this example contains four years; therefore, it has three ratios. To obtain a typical ratio for each quarter, you have at least three options:

1. Determine an average (mean) of these ratios.

2. Find the median of these values.

3. Eliminate the largest and smallest ratio within each quarter and compute a mean of the remaining ratios; this is called a *trimmed mean*.

We will follow the first procedure and calculate a mean ratio for each quarter, as illustrated in Table 4.5. When the time series contains five or more years of data, a trimmed mean offers you protection against an outlier ratio dominating the index for this quarter. Using the median ratios also helps guard against this type of situation.

A Final Adjustment

The last step in computing the seasonal indexes is to make sure that the four computed ratio averages *sum to 4* (or 12, for monthly indexes). This is accomplished by (1) adding the four averages computed in the table (call this SUM) and (2) multiplying each average by 4/SUM. The modified average obtained in this process is the seasonal index for that quarter.

EXAMPLE 4.8

Solution

Using Table 4.5, determine the four seasonal indexes.

First,

$$SUM = .870 + .707 + 1.190 + 1.317 = 4.084$$

This means that we need to multiply each of the four averages in Table 4.5 by 4/4.084 = .9794.

Quarter	Seasonal Index
1	(0.870)(.9794) = 0.852
2	(0.707)(.9794) = 0.692
3	(1.190)(.9794) = 1.166
4	(1.317)(.9794) = 1.290
	4.0

On the one hand, the indexes for quarters 1 and 2 are below 1.0, so the sales during these quarters typically are below the yearly average. On the other hand, quarters 3 and 4 have seasonal indexes of 1.166 and 1.290, so the sales for these quarters are higher than the average for the year.

This procedure for determining seasonal effects works well, provided the ratios in Table 4.5 are reasonably *stable*. In Table 4.5, all the ratios for quarter 2 are small (near .7) and all the ratios for quarter 4 are large (near 1.3). If strong seasonality is present, such will be the case.

Seasonal indexes can be updated as you obtain an additional year's observations on the variable of interest. You have the option of deleting the most distant year's observations prior to recalculating these values. This procedure leads to seasonal indexes that change slowly over the years.

Thus, the procedure for calculating seasonal indexes based on a determination of centered moving averages is as follows:

1. Derive the *moving totals* by summing the observations for 4 (quarterly data) or 12 (monthly data) consecutive time periods.

2. Average and center the totals by finding the *centered moving averages*.

3. Divide each observation by its corresponding centered moving average.

4. Place the ratios from step 3 in a table headed by the 4 quarters or 12 months.

5. For each column in this table, determine the mean of these ratios; these are the unadjusted seasonal indexes.

6. Make a final adjustment to guarantee that the final seasonal indexes sum to 4 (quarterly data) or 12 (monthly data); these adjusted means are the seasonal indexes.

Deseasonalizing the Data

To remove the seasonality from the data, we **deseasonalize** the time series. The resulting series contains no seasonal effects and consists of the trend, cyclical activity, and, of course, irregular activity. We write deseasonalized data as d_t.

TABLE

4.6

Deseasonalized sales.

Year	t	y_t	Seasonal Index (S_t)	Deseasonalized Values
2004	1	20	.852	23.47
	2	12	.692	17.34
	3	47	1.166	40.31
	4	60	1.290	46.51
2005	5	40	.852	46.95
	6	32	.692	46.24
	7	65	1.166	55.75
	8	76	1.290	58.91
2006	9	56	.852	65.73
	10	50	.692	72.25
	11	85	1.166	72.90
	12	100	1.290	77.52
2007	13	75	.852	88.03
	14	70	.692	101.16
	15	101	1.166	86.62
	16	123	1.290	95.35

$$d_t = \frac{y_t}{\text{corresponding seasonal index}}$$

$$= \frac{TR_t \cdot \cancel{S_t} \cdot C_t \cdot I_t}{\cancel{S_t}} = TR_t \cdot C_t \cdot I_t$$

The deseasonalized sales values from Table 4.3 are contained in Table 4.6. These values contain trend, cyclical effects, and irregular activity. Notice how the trend is much more apparent in the deseasonalized values than in the original time series.

In Table 4.6, we obtained deseasonalized values for all 16 of the original observations, including the two quarters on each end. We can use the "new" deseasonalized series to determine the *trend* and *cyclical components* of the original time series. This will be illustrated in the next section, where we apply the four-step procedure: (1) computing seasonal indexes, (2) deseasonalizing the data, (3) computing the trend components from the deseasonalized time series (d_t), and finally (4) calculating the cyclical activity.

Comments

Monthly values in the *Wall Street Journal* and other business publications are often stated as "seasonally adjusted." This simply means these values have been deseasonalized to reflect "real" changes in the variable. For example, the number of unemployed workers always increases in May because college students are looking for summer or long-term employment. To determine if there has actually been an increase in the unemployment rate, a deseasonalized (seasonally adjusted) value is generally quoted in the article or news release.

X Exercises 4.35–4.44

Understanding the Mechanics

4.35 Complete the following table.

Year	Quarter	t	y_t	Moving Total	Centered Moving Average	Ratio to Moving Average
2006	1	1	10			
	2	2	6	—		
	3	3	23	69		
	4	4	30	79		
2007	1	5	20	88		
	2	6	15	95		
	3	7	30	101		
	4	8	36	—		

4.36 Find the deseasonalized values for the following monthly time series data.

Year	t	y_t	Seasonal Index (S_t)
2007	1	20	1.12
	2	19	.98
	3	17	.96
	4	16	.93
	5	15	.92
	6	11	.90
	7	18	1.05
	8	19	1.06
	9	20	1.07
	10	22	1.05
	11	19	.96
	12	18	1.00

Applying the New Concepts

4.37 Explain why a moving average is a smoothing technique.

4.38 The following table presents the ratio to moving average figures for sales at Zano Systems, a supplier of photocopy machines. Find the seasonal indexes.

Year	Quarter 1	Quarter 2	Quarter 3	Quarter 4
2002			.88	.87
2003	1.14	1.25	.83	.86
2004	1.19	1.22	.94	.88
2005	1.23	1.35	.90	.72
2006	1.16	1.32	.94	.81
2007	1.10	1.21		

4.39 The following table presents the ratio to moving average figures for the cost of a bushel of grapefruit in a certain county in Florida. Find the seasonal indexes.

Year	Jan	Feb	Mar	Apr	May	June
2003						
2004	.90	.87	.95	.93	1.00	1.04
2005	.87	.84	.81	.88	1.01	1.02
2006	.81	.75	.82	.89	1.05	1.04
2007	.87	.81	.77	.98	1.01	1.06

Year	July	Aug	Sept	Oct	Nov	Dec
2003	1.06	1.10	1.12	1.02	1.03	.99
2004	1.08	1.14	1.15	1.06	1.04	.97
2005	1.01	1.15	1.07	1.03	1.00	.90
2006	1.10	1.21	1.18	1.10	1.07	.97
2007						

4.40 The sale of grass sod is a seasonal business. Green Garden Supplies does most of its business in May, June, July, and August. The following table presents their monthly sales (in thousands of dollars). Find the seasonal indexes. For what month is the seasonal index the largest?

Year	Jan	Feb	Mar	Apr	May	June
2003	.1	.1	1.2	2.2	4.1	4.5
2004	.1	.2	1.4	2.0	4.0	4.2
2005	.1	.2	1.3	2.2	4.3	4.4
2006	.1	.3	1.4	2.3	4.4	4.6
2007	.1	.3	1.5	2.3	4.6	4.8

Year	July	Aug	Sept	Oct	Nov	Dec
2003	5.5	5.3	3.5	1.1	.2	.1
2004	5.3	5.0	3.2	1.0	.1	.1
2005	5.6	5.3	3.5	1.1	.2	.1
2006	5.8	5.5	3.7	1.3	.3	.1
2007	6.0	5.6	3.7	1.4	.4	.1

4.41 The following table represents the ratio to moving average figures for the number of people below the poverty level in a certain county. Find the seasonal indexes.

Year	Quarter 1	Quarter 2	Quarter 3	Quarter 4
2003			.84	.83
2004	1.12	1.29	.91	.89
2005	1.17	1.24	.92	.90
2006	1.15	1.30	.92	.88
2007	1.13	1.26		

4.42   The amount of beverage sold at Chesapeake Restaurant varies according to the time of the year. The manager would like to know which quarter is most affected by seasonal variation. Business at Chesapeake Restaurant has steadily increased over the past four years. What advice can you give the manager? The following data are in units of thousands of dollars.

Year	Quarter	Beverage Sales
2004	1	22
	2	21
	3	26
	4	27
2005	1	25
	2	24
	3	29
	4	30
2006	1	29
	2	28
	3	35
	4	37
2007	1	34
	2	33
	3	40
	4	42

Using the Computer

4.43 [DATA SET EX 4-43] Variable Description:

Year: Year from 1998 to 2001

Month: One through twelve for the months of the year

JoblessFemale: Percentage of unemployed females who are married and in the civilian labor force

Unemployment among married females is typically higher than unemployment among married males. From 1998 to 2001, the strong economy has produced a much tighter job market and, therefore, the difference in the unemployment rates of married males and females has narrowed. Find the seasonal indexes for the percentage of unemployed females who are married and in the civilian labor force.

4.44 [DATA SET EX 4-44] Variable Description:

Year: Year from 1988 to 2003

Quarter: Quarter denoted by 1, 2, 3, or 4

Assets: Assets of Banks (in billions of dollars)

The federal reserve bank of St. Louis reports the assets of all banks whose allowance for Loan and Lease Losses (ALLL) exceeds their nonperforming assets. Using quarterly data from 1988 to 2003, compute the seasonal indexes from these data and interpret their values.

(Source: http://research.stlouisfed.org/fred2/series/LLRNPT/83.)

4.6   A TIME SERIES CONTAINING SEASONALITY, TREND, AND CYCLES

During the summer of 2008, the owner of an import/export company decided to investigate the past behavior of U.S. retail sales figures for the years 2004 through 2007. He collected the data in Table 4.7 using monthly figures released by the U.S. Department of Commerce. He suspected that these data would indicate high retail trade during December (due to holiday sales) with much lower activity during January and possibly February. For the remaining months, he had no idea whether seasonal effects would be present. He also suspected there would be a steadily increasing trend due to inflation and population growth.

The four-step procedure for decomposing (a gruesome term, we'll admit) a time series into the seasonal, trend, and cyclical components was introduced in Section 4.4. We demonstrate this method of describing a time series by using the monthly retail trade data in Example 4.9.

TABLE

4.7

Total U.S. retail
sales (excluding
motor vehicle and
parts dealers)
(billions of dollars).

	2004	2005	2006	2007
Jan	220.458	231.134	253.084	264.342
Feb	217.362	227.910	247.107	256.234
Mar	240.615	258.297	280.039	293.112
Apr	242.168	257.794	276.634	284.152
May	251.154	266.893	293.456	309.461
Jun	245.942	265.450	287.487	299.831
Jul	249.349	263.898	282.706	296.300
Aug	250.073	274.253	294.334	306.475
Sep	240.047	263.754	274.788	283.135
Oct	251.036	272.449	280.158	297.128
Nov	258.980	278.908	290.971	313.157
Dec	314.591	334.955	348.342	360.089

Source: U.S. Department of Commerce, Bureau of the Census, *Current Business Report*. These
reports are only available electronically using Internet address www.census.gov/mrts/www/mrts.html.

Microsoft Excel Application Use DATA4-9

A Time Series Decomposition Using Excel

EXAMPLE

4.9

The U.S. monthly retail data for 2004 to 2007 are contained in Table 4.7 and in data set
DATA4-9. Perform a time series decomposition of these data, and discuss the results.

Solution

Begin by entering the 48 observations into column A. Click on **KPK Data Analysis ➤
Time Series Analysis ➤ Decomposition.** Select 12 as the number of time periods per
year, and enter A1:A48 in the **Input Range** box, B1 in the **Output Range** box, and 2004 in
the **First Year** box. Also, click on A Single Column since the data are stored in a single column (column A). The resulting output will be contained in five sheets, labeled **Components, Cyclical, Trend, Seasonal,** and **Plots.**

Step 1.   *Determine the seasonal indexes.* The first step is to determine the moving totals and
centered moving averages for the 48 observations in Table 4.7. This portion of
the output is in the sheet labeled **Seasonal** and will be identical to the results
contained in Table 4.8. Notice that when using monthly data, there is no
monthly average for $t = 1$ through $t = 6$ (January through June 2004) and for $t =
43$ through 48 (July through December 2007). The first moving total is

$$2,981.775 = y_1 + y_2 + \ldots + y_{12}$$

$$= 220.458 + 217.362 + \ldots + 314.591$$

This value is positioned midway between $t = 1$ and $t = 12$, that is, at $t = 6.5$
(between $t = 6$ and $t = 7$). The next moving total is

$$2,992.451 = y_2 + y_3 + \ldots + y_{13}$$

$$= 217.362 + 240.615 + \ldots + 231.134$$

TABLE

4.8

Moving averages and ratios to moving average for U.S. monthly retail sales data. This output is contained in the Excel sheet labeled **Seasonal.**

Year	Month	t (1)	y_t (2)	Moving Total (3)	Centering Moving Average (4)	Ratio to Moving Average (5)
2004	Jan	1	220.458			
	Feb	2	217.362			
	Mar	3	240.615			
	Apr	4	242.168			
	May	5	251.154			
	Jun	6	245.942			
				2981.775		
	Jul	7	249.349		248.926	1.002
				2992.451		
	Aug	8	250.073		249.810	1.001
				3002.999		
	Sep	9	240.047		250.987	0.956
				3020.681		
	Oct	10	251.036		252.375	0.995
				3036.307		
	Nov	11	258.980		253.681	1.021
				3052.046		
	Dec	12	314.591		255.150	1.233
				3071.554		
	⋮					
2007	Jan	37	264.342		290.436	0.910
				3492.025		
	Feb	38	256.234		291.508	0.879
				3504.166		
	Mar	39	293.112		292.362	1.003
				3512.513		
	Apr	40	284.152		293.417	0.968
				3529.483		
	May	41	309.461		295.048	1.049
				3551.669		
	Jun	42	299.831		296.462	1.011
				3563.416		
	Jul	43	296.300			
	Aug	44	306.475			
	Sep	45	283.135			
	Oct	46	297.128			
	Nov	47	313.157			
	Dec	48	360.089			

which is centered at $t = 7.5$ (between $t = 7$ and $t = 8$). So the first *centered moving average* is positioned midway between $t = 6.5$ and $t = 7.5$, at $t = 7$. This is

$$248.926 = (2{,}981.775 + 2{,}992.451) / 24$$

Notice that we divide by 24, because 24 observations went into the sum of these two moving totals.

TABLE

4.9

Summary of ratios.
This output is in
the Excel sheet
labeled **Seasonal**.

				Month (Period)								
Year	Jan	Feb	Mar	Apr	May	Jun	Jul	Aug	Sep	Oct	Nov	Dec
2004							1.002	1.001	0.956	0.995	1.021	1.233
2005	0.901	0.883	0.993	0.984	1.012	1.000	0.988	1.020	0.975	1.000	1.017	1.213
2006	0.911	0.884	0.997	0.982	1.039	1.014	0.993	1.031	0.960	0.976	1.010	1.204
2007	0.910	0.879	1.003	0.968	1.049	1.011						
Average	0.907	0.882	0.997	0.978	1.033	1.008	0.994	1.017	0.963	0.990	1.016	1.216

The final centered moving average is

$$296.462 = (3{,}551.669 + 3{,}563.416) / 24$$

and corresponds to $t = 42$.

The Excel output and Table 4.8 also contain each ratio to moving average (column 2 divided by column 4). To illustrate:

$$1.002 = 249.349 / 248.926 \quad 1.001 = 250.073 / 249.810$$

and so on. These ratios are summarized in the top portion of the **Seasonal** Excel spreadsheet (under **Summary of Ratios**) and in Table 4.9, both of which also contain the average of the three values for each time period.

The final step is to adjust each of these averages in Table 4.9 so they sum to 12 (because there are 12 time periods per year). Here,

$$\text{SUM} = .907 + .882 + \ldots + 1.216 = 12.004$$

and so

$$S_1 = \text{seasonal index for January}$$

$$= .907\left(\frac{12}{12.004}\right) = .907$$

$$S_2 = \text{seasonal index for February}$$

$$= .882\left(\frac{12}{12.004}\right) = .882$$

$$\vdots$$

$$S_{12} = \text{seasonal index for December}$$

$$= 1.216\left(\frac{12}{12.004}\right) = 1.216$$

The final collection of seasonal indexes is

Month	Seasonal Index	Month	Seasonal Index
Jan.	.907	July	.994
Feb.	.882	Aug.	1.017
Mar.	.997	Sept.	.963
Apr.	.978	Oct.	.990
May	1.033	Nov.	1.016
Jun	1.008	Dec.	1.216

TABLE

4.10

Deseasonalized
monthly retail
sales values. This
output is in the
Excel sheet labeled
Trend.

Year	Month	t	y_t	S_t	$d_t = \dfrac{y_t}{S_t}$
2004	Jan	1	220.458	0.907	243.093
	Feb	2	217.362	0.882	246.559
	Mar	3	240.615	0.997	241.306
	Apr	4	242.168	0.978	247.667
	May	5	251.154	1.033	243.169
	Jun	6	245.942	1.008	243.967
	Jul	7	249.349	0.994	250.874
	Aug	8	250.073	1.017	245.886
	Sep	9	240.047	0.963	249.211
	Oct	10	251.036	0.990	253.601
	Nov	11	258.980	1.016	255.013
	Dec	12	314.591	1.216	258.700
	⋮				
2007	Jan	37	264.342	0.907	291.483
	Feb	38	256.234	0.882	290.652
	Mar	39	293.112	0.997	293.954
	Apr	40	284.152	0.978	290.605
	May	41	309.461	1.033	299.622
	Jun	42	299.831	1.008	297.424
	Jul	43	296.300	0.994	298.112
	Aug	44	306.475	1.017	301.343
	Sep	45	283.135	0.963	293.944
	Oct	46	297.128	0.990	300.164
	Nov	47	313.157	1.016	308.360
	Dec	48	360.089	1.216	296.115

The sum of these seasonal indexes $(S_1 + S_2 + \ldots + S_{12})$ is 12.000. Due to rounding, this sum might not be exactly 12 on occasion, and this is perfectly acceptable.

We observe (1) a large seasonal index for December $(S_{12} = 1.216)$, indicating large retail trade for this month, (2) low indexes for January and February, and (3) very little seasonality for any of the remaining months.

Step 2. *Deseasonalize the data.* We obtain the deseasonalized values (which contain no seasonality) by dividing each observation by its corresponding seasonal index. These values are contained in the Excel spreadsheet labeled **Trend** (under the column labeled D(t)) and are partially shown in Table 4.10. The trend is more apparent now because the deseasonalized values tend to increase over time.

Step 3. *Determine the trend components.* A common method for estimating trend (and the one we use) is to construct a least squares trend line (or curve) through the deseasonalized data. From the moving averages in the Excel output (under the column **Centered Average** in the sheet labeled **Seasonal**), also shown in Table 4.8, it appears that a straight line trend equation will be appropriate; these values tend to increase at a fairly steady rate.

The calculations for the trend line are identical to those discussed in Section 4.2, using the d_i values in place of the original observations, y_i. A summary of these calculations is given in Table 4.11. The least squares line through the deseasonalized data is contained at the top of the Excel sheet labeled **Trend** and is given by

$$TR_t = \hat{d}_t = b_0 + b_1 t$$

TABLE

4.11

Calculations for trend line (U.S. monthly retail sales data).

t	d_t	$t \cdot d_t$
1	243.093	243.093
2	246.559	493.117
3	241.306	723.919
4	247.667	990.669
⋮		
45	293.944	13227.462
46	300.164	13807.565
47	308.360	14492.898
48	296.115	14213.512
	13,140.476	334,415.306

where

$$b_1 = \frac{12B - 6(T+1)A}{T(T^2 - 1)}$$

where now

$$A = \Sigma d_t = 13,140.476 \text{ and } B = \Sigma t d_t = 334,415.316$$

$$= \frac{12(334,415.306) - 6(49)(13,140.476)}{48(2,304 - 1)} = \frac{63,610\,740}{100,544} = 1.35406$$

and

$$b_0 = \frac{A}{T} - b_1\left(\frac{T+1}{2}\right)$$

$$= \frac{13,140.476}{48} - (1.35406)\frac{49}{2} = 273.760 - 33.175 = 240.585$$

Consequently, the equation of the trend equation is given by

$$TR_t = \hat{d}_t = 240.585 + 1.354t$$

This equation agrees with the Excel result and implies that, apart from seasonal fluctuations, U.S. retail sales are increasing at an average rate of $575 million each month. A graph of the deseasonalized data and corresponding trend line is shown in Figure 4.21.

Step 4. *Determine the cyclical activity.* We begin by following the procedure outlined in Section 4.3. We divide each deseasonalized observation by the corresponding trend value:

$$\frac{d_t}{TR_t} = \frac{d_t}{\hat{d}_t} = \frac{\cancel{TR_t} \cdot C_t \cdot I_t}{\cancel{TR_t}} = C_t \cdot I_t$$

The resulting values contain cyclical effects as well as an irregular activity component. One method of reducing the irregular effect is to compute a series of

FIGURE

4.21

Deseasonalized data and trend line (monthly U.S. retail sales).

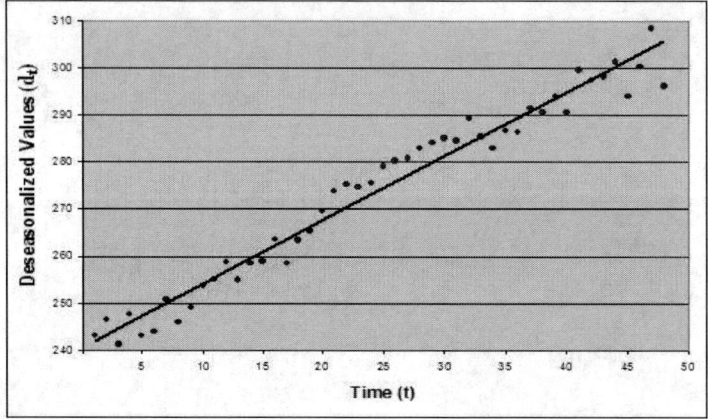

TABLE

4.12

Calculating the cyclical components for the U.S. monthly retail sales data.

t	d_t	$\hat{d}_t$	$\dfrac{d_t}{\hat{d}_t}$ $(= C_t \cdot I_t)$	Three-Month Moving Average (C_t)
1	243.093	$240.585 + 1.354(1) = 241.939$	1.0048	—
2	246.559	$240.585 + 1.354(2) = 243.293$	1.0134	1.002
3	241.306	$240.585 + 1.354(3) = 244.647$	0.9863	1.002
4	247.667	$240.585 + 1.354(4) = 246.002$	1.0068	0.992
5	243.169	$240.585 + 1.354(5) = 247.356$	0.9831	0.990
6	243.967	$240.585 + 1.354(6) = 248.710$	0.9809	0.989
⋮	⋮	⋮	⋮	⋮

three-period moving averages on the $C_t \cdot I_t$ values. This procedure greatly reduces the irregular activity effect, and the moving averages provide a much better estimate of the cyclical components. The choice of a three-period moving average is somewhat arbitrary; however, when we use an odd number of terms, the moving averages need not be centered.

A partial solution, using the first six rows of the Excel output under the column **Ratio** in the sheet labeled **Seasonal,** is shown in Table 4.12. We see that the cyclical component for $t = 2$ is C_2, where

$$C_2 = (1.0048 + 1.0134 + 0.9863)/3 = 1.002$$

and the cyclical component for $t = 3$ is

$$C_3 = (1.0134 + 0.9863 + 1.0068)/3 = 1.002$$

Similarly,

$$C_4 = (0.9863 + 1.0068 + 0.9831)/3 = 0.992$$

TABLE

4.13

Cyclical components (monthly U.S. retail sales data). This output is in the Excel sheet labeled **Cyclical**.

Year	Month	t	d_t	$\hat{d}_t$	$\dfrac{d_t}{\hat{d}_t}$ $(= C_t \cdot I_t)$	Three-Month Moving Average (C_t)
2004	Jan	1	243.093	241.939	1.0048	—
	Feb	2	246.559	243.293	1.0134	1.002
	Mar	3	241.306	244.647	0.9863	1.002
	Apr	4	247.667	246.002	1.0069	0.992
	May	5	243.169	247.356	0.9831	0.990
	Jun	6	243.967	248.710	0.9809	0.989
	Jul	7	250.874	250.064	1.0032	0.987
	Aug	8	245.886	251.418	0.9780	0.989
	Sep	9	249.211	252.772	0.9859	0.987
	Oct	10	253.601	254.126	0.9979	0.994
	Nov	11	255.013	255.480	0.9982	1.001
	Dec	12	258.700	256.834	1.0073	0.998
	⋮					
2007	Jan	37	291.483	290.686	1.0027	0.996
	Feb	38	290.652	292.040	0.9952	1.000
	Mar	39	293.954	293.394	1.0019	0.994
	Apr	40	290.605	294.748	0.9859	1.000
	May	41	299.622	296.102	1.0119	0.999
	Jun	42	297.424	297.456	0.9999	1.003
	Jul	43	298.112	298.810	0.9977	1.000
	Aug	44	301.343	300.164	1.0039	0.992
	Sep	45	293.944	301.518	0.9749	0.990
	Oct	46	300.164	302.872	0.9911	0.993
	Nov	47	308.360	304.226	1.0136	0.991
	Dec	48	296.115	305.580	0.9690	—

and

$$C_5 = (1.0068 + 0.9831 + 0.9809)/3 = 0.990$$

The complete set of smoothed cyclical values is contained in the Excel sheet labeled **Cyclical** (under the column titled **C(t)**). These components are partially reproduced in Table 4.13 (far right column) and plotted in Figure 4.22. There appears to be a some cycic activity, although not very pronounced since the cyclic components range from 0.987 to 1.016 (a very narrow range). Cyclic components larger than one are observed between August 2005 and September 2006 indicating stronger retail trade than predicted using the trend line through the deseasonalized data.

Once the steps in the previous sections have been completed, the various components can be combined for any specified value of t.

FIGURE

4.22

Plot of cyclical activity (monthly U.S. retail sales data).

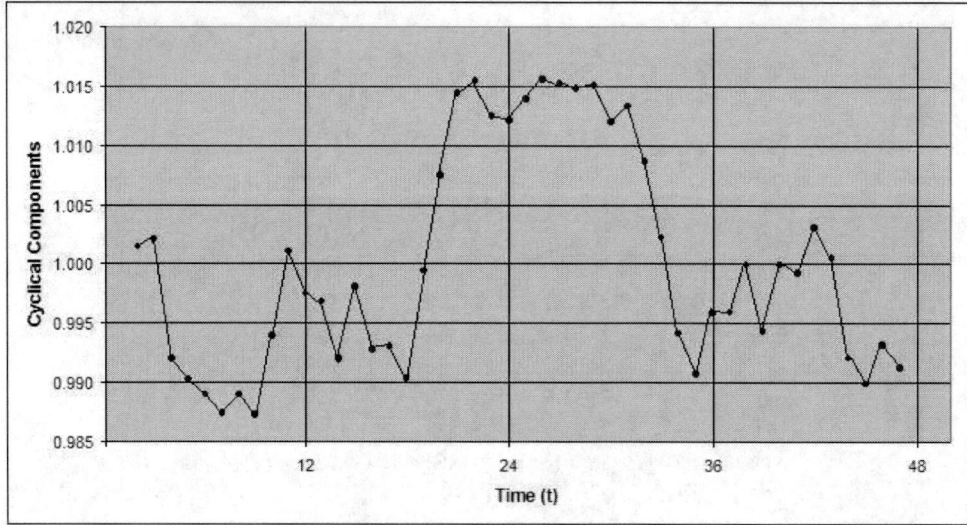

EXAMPLE

4.10

Determine the four components for (1) September 2004 and (2) June 2007.

Solution 1   The value of t for September 2004 is $t = 9$. The seasonal index for September is $S_9 = .963$. The trend component (second column of numbers in Table 4.13) is $TR_9 = 252.772$. The cyclical component (far right column of Table 4.13) is 0.987. Therefore,

$$S_9 \cdot TR_9 \cdot C_9 = (.963)(252.772)(0.987) = 240.255$$

The actual observation for September 2004 is $y_9 = 240.047$. Since $y_9 = S_9 \cdot TR_9 \cdot C_9 \cdot I_9$,

$$I_9 = \frac{y_9}{S_9 \cdot TR_9 \cdot C_9} = \frac{240.047}{240.255} = 0.999$$

and the final decomposition is

$$y_9 = 240.047 = S_9 \cdot TR_9 \cdot C_9 \cdot I_9 = (.963)(252.772)(0.987)(0.999)$$

Solution 2   For $t = 42$ (June 2007), we have S_{42} = seasonal index for June = $S_6 = 1.008$. Also, $TR_{42} = 297.456$ and $C_{42} = 1.003$, from Table 4.3. Consequently,

$$I_{42} = \frac{y_{42}}{S_{42} \cdot TR_{42} \cdot C_{42}} = \frac{299.831}{300.735} = .997$$

The combined decomposition for this observation is

$$y_{42} = 299.831 = S_{42} \cdot TR_{42} \cdot C_{42} \cdot I_{42} = (1.008)(297.456)(1.003)(.997)$$

The components for all but the first and last observations are contained in the Excel spreadsheet labeled **Components** under the heading **Time Series Components**. The same components are partially shown in Table 4.14.

TABLE

4.14

Time series
components for
U.S. retail sales
data. This output is
in the Excel sheet
labeled
Components.

Year	Month	y_t	TR_t	S_t	C_t	I_t
2004	Jan	220.458	241.939	0.907		
	Feb	217.362	243.293	0.882	1.002	1.012
	Mar	240.615	244.647	0.997	1.002	0.984
	Apr	242.168	246.002	0.978	0.992	1.015
	May	251.154	247.356	1.033	0.990	0.993
	Jun	245.942	248.710	1.008	0.989	0.992
	Jul	249.349	250.064	0.994	0.987	1.016
	Aug	250.073	251.418	1.017	0.989	0.989
	Sep	240.047	252.772	0.963	0.987	0.999
	Oct	251.036	254.126	0.990	0.994	1.004
	Nov	258.980	255.480	1.016	1.001	0.997
	Dec	314.591	256.834	1.216	0.998	1.010
	⋮					
2007	Jan	264.342	290.686	0.907	0.996	1.007
	Feb	256.234	292.040	0.882	1.000	0.995
	Mar	293.112	293.394	0.997	0.994	1.008
	Apr	284.152	294.748	0.978	1.000	0.986
	May	309.461	296.102	1.033	0.999	1.013
	Jun	299.831	297.456	1.008	1.003	0.997
	Jul	296.300	298.810	0.994	1.000	0.997
	Aug	306.475	300.164	1.017	0.992	1.012
	Sep	283.135	301.518	0.963	0.990	0.985
	Oct	297.128	302.872	0.990	0.993	0.998
	Nov	313.157	304.226	1.016	0.991	1.023
	Dec	360.089	305.580	1.216		

Summary of Time Series Decomposition

The time series decomposition procedure allows you to examine the presence of the following:

* Trend (a long-term growth or decline)

* Seasonality (a within-year recurrent pattern)

* Cyclical activity (upward or downward variation about the trend)

The remaining component (what is left after removing the effect of these three factors) is irregular activity. Having determined these four components, you are able to describe a particular time series by carefully examining and plotting the calculated components.

A partial summary of the components for the U.S. retail sales time series is contained in Table 4.14. The irregular activity components $(I)_t$ are determined by continuing the procedure in Example 4.10. Graphs of these components are shown in Figure 4.23. These four graphs will be on the Excel sheet labeled **Plots** when using **KPK Data Analysis ▶ Time Series Analysis ▶ Decomposition**. Notice that the graph of the irregular activity components contains no obvious pattern, as we would expect. By combining the various graphs of the time series components into a single set of graphs (Figure 4.23), we can tell

FIGURE

4.23

Excel plots of monthly U.S. retail sales data using **KPK Data Analysis ➤ Time Series Analysis ➤ Decomposition.**

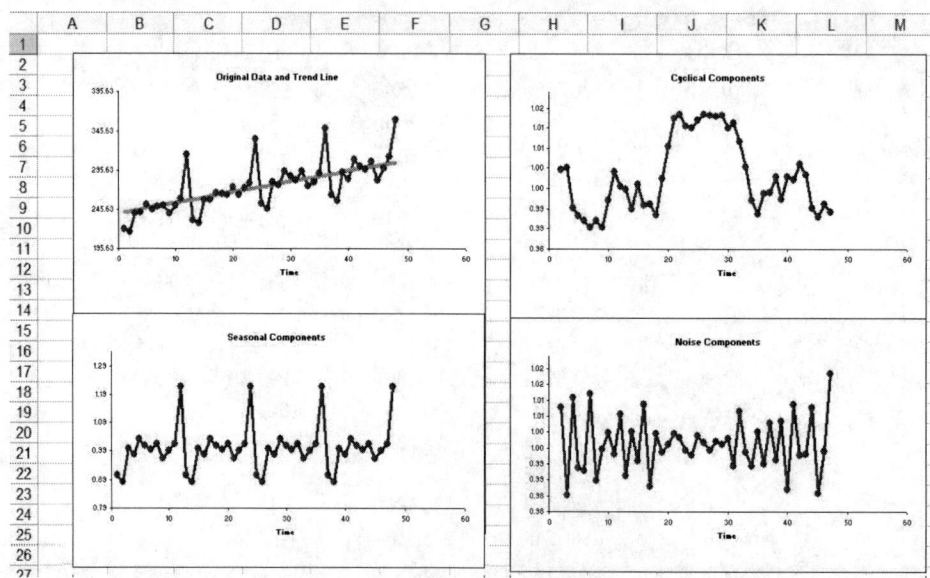

at a glance what is the nature of the series. We can reach at least three conclusions from this figure:

1. There is a strong linear trend that increases over the four-year period.

2. There is a strong retail sales peak each December, followed by weak sales in January and February.

3. There is very little cyclic activity between Jan 2004 and Dec 2007. Retail trade for 2007 ends in the midst of a downward turn.

X Exercises 4.45–4.52

Understanding the Mechanics

4.45 For the month of January 2007, a researcher finds that the seasonal index is 1.2, the trend value is 100, and the cyclical component is .90. What is the irregular component if the actual observation for January 2007 is 110?

4.46 Given the following ratio to moving averages, determine the seasonal indexes.

Year	Month	Ratio to Moving Average	Year	Month	Ratio to Moving Average
2005	July	1.046	2007	Jan	.856
	Aug	1.057		Feb	.826
	Sept	.993		Mar	.969
	Oct	1.015		Apr	.952
	Nov	.996		May	1.021
	Dec	1.217		June	1.011
2006	Jan	.851		July	1.019

Year	Month	Ratio to Moving Average	Year	Month	Ratio to Moving Average
2005	Feb	.858	2006	Aug	1.071
	Mar	.978		Sept	1.005
	Apr	.968		Oct	1.088
	May	1.010		Nov	1.026
	June	1.011		Dec	1.218
	July	1.020	2007	Jan	.881
	Aug	1.051		Feb	.843
	Sept	1.195		Mar	.982
	Oct	1.012		Apr	.956
	Nov	1.038		May	1.012
	Dec	1.252		June	1.003

Applying the New Concepts

4.47 The gross domestic product (GDP) is defined as the output of goods and services produced by labor and property located in the United States. GDP is the broadest measure of the health of the U.S. economy. The following table illustrates the deseasonalized percentage quarterly change in GDP from 1997 to 2000 and the value of the trend component for each quarter. Determine the cyclical components for the four quarters of 1999 using a multiplicative model.

Year	Quarter	Deseasonalized GDP Increase	Trend Component
1997	1	4.763	5.185
	2	7.247	5.047
	3	4.376	4.909
	4	2.113	4.771
1998	1	6.603	4.633
	2	2.825	4.495
	3	4.376	4.357
	4	5.056	4.219
1999	1	3.464	4.081
	2	2.088	3.943
	3	4.91	3.805
	4	6.264	3.667
2000	1	2.381	3.529
	2	7.001	3.391
	3	1.494	3.253
	4	1.434	3.115

(Source: "U.S. Economy Slows," *USA Today,* July 30, 2001, p. 1B.)

4.48   The amount of monthly business that an automotive repair shop receives can be described by the following trend line and seasonal indexes for the time periods January 2004 ($t = 1$) to the present. Sales are in units of thousands of dollars.

$$TR_t = 12 + .5t$$

$$S_1 = .90, S_2 = .84, S_3 = 1.00, S_4 = 1.00, S_5 = 1.02,$$

$$S_6 = 1.04, S_7 = 1.00, S_8 = 1.00, S_9 = 1.00, S_{10} = .99,$$

$$S_{11} = 1.00, S_{12} = 1.21$$

Assume that no cyclical component is present ($C_t = 1.0$). Given the following set of actual sales for the first six months of 2007, calculate the irregular activity component for the first six months of 2007.

	2007					
	Jan	**Feb**	**Mar**	**Apr**	**May**	**Jun**
Sales	10.6	10.5	12.0	12.5	12.9	12.8

Using the Computer

4.49 **[DATA SET EX4-49]** *Variable Description:*

Year: Years from 2004 through 2007

Months: Months are numbered from 1 through 12

Membership: The monthly membership

The membership of a local spa fluctuates seasonally. The manager of the spa is interested in knowing what the trend line is for the spa's membership. The membership data are recorded monthly. Estimate the trend line and use it to predict the deseasonalized membership for January 2008.

4.50 **[DATA SET EX4-50]** *Variable Description:*

Year: Year from 1998 to 2003

Month: Month denoted by 1, 2, . . . 12

CC: Consumer Credit (in millions of dollars)

The Federal Reserve Board reports the amount of Consumer Credit (CC) at major institutions holding consumer credit. The deseasonalized consumer credit is provided in the variable CC. Estimate the trend line and use it to predict the deseasonalized consumer credit for January 2004.

(Source: *www.economagic.com.*)

4.51 **[DATA SET EX4-51]** *Variable Description:*

Year: Years from 2002 through 2007

Quarter: Quarters are numbered from 1 through 4

LoanApp: Number of loan applications

The manager of a branch bank is having difficulty in staffing. A good measure of banking business is the number of loan applications received quarterly. Quarterly data are collected from 2002 through 2007. Plot the original data and the trend line. Also plot the noise components over time and determine if any pattern is apparent in this plot.

4.52 **[DATA SET EX4-52]** *Variable Description:*

Year: Years from 2003 through 2007

Quarter: Quarters are numbered from 1 through 4

Enroll: Enrollment in a retirement education seminar

A stock brokerage firm offers a free retirement seminar on a quarterly basis. Since many of the participants in the seminar will invest in financial products offered by the firm, the manager of the brokerage firm wishes to determine the trend and seasonal components of the enrollment. Plot the trend line using the deseasonalized data. Also construct a plot of the seasonal components.

4.7

TIME SERIES FORECASTING

Forecasting procedures come in a variety of shapes and colors. You can arrive at a sales forecast by simply assembling a panel of experts and arriving at a collective guess or by constructing a highly complex statistical model that attempts to predict the future using past data. In the broadest sense, forecasting methods can be classified as **qualitative** (the panel of experts procedure) or **quantitative** (the statistical forecasting procedure). Quantitative forecasting can be carried out using two different approaches, namely, *regression* models (with several predictor variables) or **time series** models, which utilize past observations of the dependent variable to arrive at forecasted values.

Qualitative Forecasting

There are many instances when a qualitative approach to forecasting is appropriate. When no past data are available, it is impossible to construct a quantitative model to predict future values. This situation can occur when you intend to introduce a new product and no past sales data exist. Furthermore, when you introduce this product, it becomes a guessing game as to what the response will be from competitors in the field. Will they respond to your entry into the market? When will they respond? Will they lower their price to increase the demand for their product? Will they attempt to copy your product, and how soon can this be accomplished? Such questions do require expert opinion.

One popular method of qualitative forecasting is the **Delphi method.** With this procedure, you assemble individuals from the sales force and the market research staff and ask them to supply their predictions based on their knowledge of the area. This can be accomplished through a questionnaire or any other written set of specific questions. After this step, members of the team are informed as to the responses of the entire group and asked to reevaluate their opinions based on this new information. In this way, members of the team may be able to arrive at a *best-educated* prediction of competitor response to their market entry. Of course, it is also entirely possible that no collective agreement will be reached after several rounds of this process.

We do not pursue qualitative forecasting methods in this chapter. The interested reader is referred to the text by Bowerman and O'Connell (see the Further Reading section at the end of the chapter) for additional qualitative procedures. The remainder of this section focuses on the use of quantitative forecasting techniques.

Quantitative Forecasting

With a quantitative forecasting procedure, you predict future behavior of a dependent variable using information from previous time periods. This can be accomplished in one of two ways: using a *regression* model or using a *time series* model.

Regression Models. The multiple regression approach consists of using regression models where variation of the dependent variable is explained using several independent (predictor) variables. One main advantage of this approach is that you can measure the effect of changes in one or more of the predictor variables. Furthermore, this type of model is generally easily understood by those individuals responsible for making the final forecast decision, since it is clear which variables are assumed to have an effect on the value of the dependent variable. A drawback of this type of model as a forecasting instrument is that to predict future values of the dependent variable, it is necessary to predict future values of the predictor variables, which, in many instances, may be as uncertain as future values of the dependent variable.

Time Series Models. A time series forecast is made by capturing the patterns that exist in the past observations and extending them into the future. Consider the annual data reflecting

4.24

Sales for Clayton Corporation.

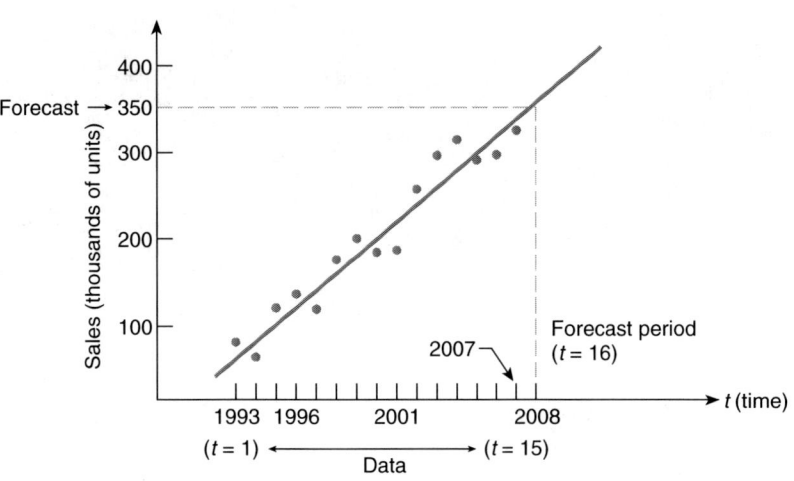

the sales of the Clayton Corporation between 1993 and 2007, shown in Figure 4.24. The data reflect a strong linear trend, as shown by the line passing through the points. To estimate the sales for the year 2008, one simple method would be to extend this line to 2008, as illustrated in Figure 4.24. By graphically extending this line and observing the estimated value, we obtain

$$\hat{y}_{16} = \text{forecast for the year } 2008 \cong 350$$

that is, 350,000 units. This procedure, along with methods of dealing with trend and seasonality, is discussed in Section 4.8.

At first glance, it might appear that time series forecasting is easier to apply than are multiple regression models. After all, there is no need to search for a reliable set of predictor variables. It is true that time series predictors can be simple and straightforward. *However, extracting the complex and interrelated structure of an observed time series often requires sophisticated and complex prediction equations.* In sections 4.8 and 4.9, we examine two fairly simple time series forecast models.

Remember that any quantitative forecasting technique can never replace the forecast of individuals (or teams of people) who uses their expertise and knowledge of unpredictable future events (such as strikes, wars, or market shifts) to make forecasts. Rather, the quantitative forecast is one tool the forecaster uses. A forecast is an excellent baseline that can be modified by informed judgment.

4.8

PROJECTING THE LEAST SQUARES TREND EQUATION

A Time Series Containing Trend

For data containing a strong linear or curvilinear trend, one method of predicting future values of the time series is to extend the trend line (or curve) into the forecast periods. This method was illustrated in Figure 4.24, where the data from 1993 to 2007 demonstrated a very strong linear growth over those 15 years.

Suppose that a simple linear regression analysis is performed on these data, using the 15 sales values as the dependent variable and $t = 1, 2, \ldots, 15$ as the predictor variable (as

FIGURE

4.25

Quarterly sales at
Video-Comp.

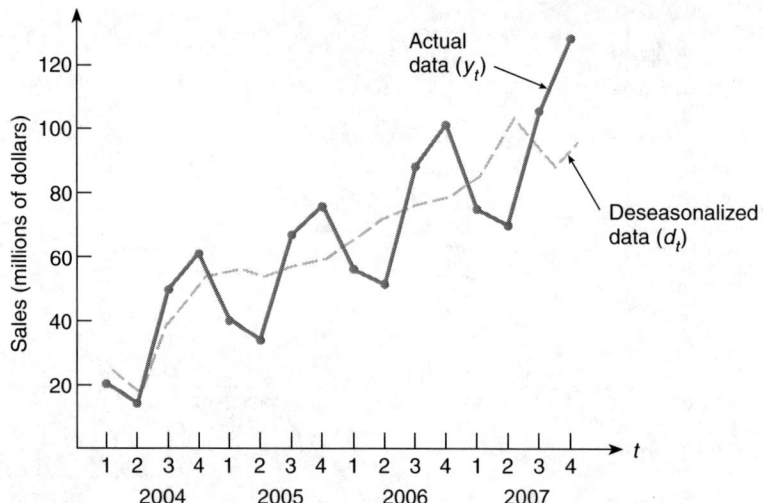

discussed in Section 4.2). The resulting least squares line, shown in Figure 4.24, turns out to be

$$\hat{y}_t = 32 + 20t$$

The estimated forecast for the year 2008 in the earlier discussion was $\hat{y}_{16} = 350$. This value was determined simply by extending the least squares line into this time period and "eyeballing" the estimate for 2008. The actual forecast is

$$\hat{y}_{16} = 32 + 20(16) = 352$$

So, our estimate of sales for the year 2008 is 352,000 units, based on the linear trend equation.

You could also have obtained this trend equation in Excel by clicking on **KPK Data Analysis ➤ Time Series Analysis ➤ Forecasting ➤ Trend Only** after entering the 15 sales values in column A.

A Time Series Containing Trend and Seasonality

The previous procedure can be adapted to situations in which the time series contains significant trend *and* seasonality. Such a situation can occur when the data are monthly or quarterly, with seasonal fluctuations about a linear or curvilinear trend.

The quarterly sales for Video-Comp over a four-year period (2004–2007) were contained in Table 4.3 in Section 4.5 and illustrated in Figure 4.25. The deseasonalized sales figures (often called *seasonally adjusted* sales) were summarized in Table 4.6 and also graphed in Figure 4.25. Notice that the extreme seasonal fluctuations of the original time series were removed when these values were divided by the appropriate seasonal index. The indexes for this application were derived in Example 4.8 and they indicated low sales for the first two quarters, above-average sales for the third quarter, and extremely high sales during the fourth (holiday) quarter. The corresponding indexes were

$$S_1 = .852 \qquad S_3 = 1.166$$
$$S_2 = .692 \qquad S_4 = 1.290$$

To forecast future values when using seasonal data, you once again determine the least squares line (or curve), except that now you use the *deseasonalized data (say, d_t)* as your dependent variable. Once you have calculated the trend forecast, you obtain your final forecast by multiplying this deseasonalized estimate by the corresponding seasonal index. So the procedure for extending trend and seasonal components is:

1. Calculate the deseasonalized (seasonally adjusted) data from the original time series $(y_1, y_2, \ldots, y_T)$. Call these values $d_1, d_2, \ldots, d_T$.

2. Construct a least squares line through the deseasonalized data, where $(t = 1, 2, \ldots, T)$.

$$\hat{d}_t = b_0 + b_1 t$$

3. Calculate the forecast for time period $T + 1$ using

$$\hat{y}_{T+1} = (\hat{d}_{T+1}) \cdot (\text{seasonal index for } t = T + 1)$$
$$= [b_0 + b_1(T + 1)] \cdot (\text{seasonal index for } t = T + 1)$$

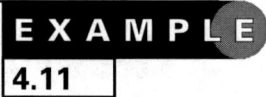

E X A M P L E

4.11

Solution

Using the Video-Comp data, what would be your forecast for the first-quarter sales for 2008? second-quarter sales?

The trend line through the deseasonalized data is contained in Figure 4.27 and illustrated in Figure 4.26. To obtain this solution, enter the 16 deseasonalized values in column A and click on **KPK Data Analysis ➤ Time Series Analysis ➤ Forecasting**. Select the **Trend with Seasonality** option and enter 2 as the **Number of Forecast Periods**, select 4 as the **Number of Periods per Year**, enter A1:A16 as the **Input Range**, and B1 as the **Output Range**. After clicking on **Continue**, select **Linear** in the **Trend** frame and enter the four seasonal indexes (.852, .692, 1.166, 1.290) by repeatedly entering a value and then clicking on the **Next Period** button. The resulting output is shown in Figure 4.27. The least squares trend line is

$$\hat{d}_t = 19.372 + 5.037t$$

This equation tells us that, apart from seasonal variation, the sales at Video-Comp are increasing by approximately $5 million each quarter. Using this equation and Figure 4.26, your deseasonalized forecast for the first quarter of 2008 (time period 17) is

$$\hat{d}_{17} = 19.372 + 5.037(17)$$
$$= 105.00$$

Now, the sales for the first quarter of each year are lower than the yearly average, as reflected in the seasonal index of $S_1 = .852$ (from Example 4.8). Consequently, your actual forecast for this time period is contained in cell C21 (Figure 4.27) and is equal to

$$\hat{y}_{17} = \hat{d}_{17} \cdot (\text{seasonal index for quarter 1})$$
$$= 105.00 \cdot .852$$
$$= 89.5 \text{ (million dollars)}$$

This procedure can be used to forecast any future time period. For the second quarter of 2008, the estimated sales will be

$$\hat{y}_{18} = \hat{d}_{18} \cdot (\text{seasonal index for quarter 2})$$
$$= [19.372 + 5.037(18)] \cdot .692$$
$$= (110.04)(.692) = 76.2 \text{ (million dollars)}$$

FIGURE

4.26

Trend line through deseasonalized data (quarterly sales, Video-Comp).

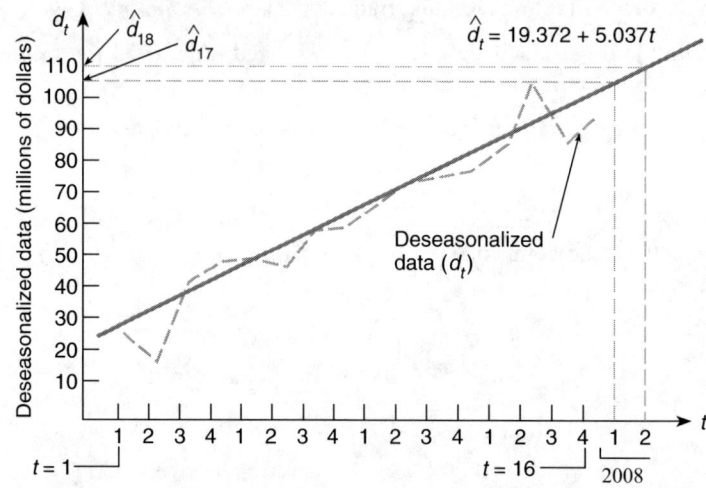

FIGURE

4.27

Excel solution for deseasonalized trend line and forecasting two periods ahead.

	A	B	C	D	E	F	G
1	23.47	Linear Trend with Seasonality Model is Y(t) = 19.372 + 5.037t					
2	17.34	t	Y(t)	Yhat	Residual		Seasonal Factors
3	40.31	1	23.47	24.409	-0.939		0.852
4	46.51	2	17.34	29.446	-12.106		0.692
5	46.95	3	40.31	34.484	5.826		1.166
6	46.24	4	46.51	39.521	6.989		1.290
7	55.75	5	46.95	44.559	2.391		
8	58.91	6	46.24	49.596	-3.356		
9	65.73	7	55.75	54.634	1.116		
10	72.25	8	58.91	59.671	-0.761		
11	72.90	9	65.73	64.709	1.021		
12	77.52	10	72.25	69.746	2.504		
13	88.03	11	72.9	74.784	-1.884		
14	101.16	12	77.52	79.821	-2.301		
15	86.62	13	88.03	84.859	3.171		
16	95.35	14	101.16	89.896	11.264		
17		15	86.62	94.934	-8.314		
18		16	95.35	99.971	-4.621		
19							
20		Forecasts					
21		17	89.467				
22		18	76.152				

Do these estimates seem reasonable? Look at the observed (2004–2007) and forecast (2008) values for the first and second quarters:

Year	First-Quarter Sales	Second-Quarter Sales
2004	20	12
2005	40	32
2006	56	50
2007	75	70
2008	89.5	76.2

The forecast for the first quarter 2008 seems to be about what we would expect, based on the past first-quarter sales. The predicted sales value for the second quarter of 2008 seems to be on the low side, with an increase of only 6.2 from the second quarter of 2007. Remember, however, that this forecasting techniques contains the effect of *all* the quarters observed over the four years. By examining the past sales during the second quarter only, we are ignoring the remaining quarters, and perhaps an explanation for this seemingly low forecast lies in these values.

Exercises 4.53–4.57

Understanding the Mechanics

4.53 Several sets of quarterly data have been gathered over a 3-year period from 2005 to 2007. Find the forecasts for the four quarters of 2008 for each of the following models. Assume $t = 1, 2, \ldots$

a. $\hat{d}_t = 5.2 + .8t$, $S_1 = .81$, $S_2 = .93$, $S_3 = 1.19$, $S_4 = 1.07$

b. $\hat{d}_t = 10.5 + 5t$, $S_1 = .66$, $S_2 = 1.08$, $S_3 = 1.19$, $S_4 = 1.07$

c. $\hat{d}_t = 50 - 2t$, $S_1 = 1.10$, $S_2 = 1.16$, $S_3 = .90$, $S_4 = .84$

Applying the New Concepts

4.54 For what type of data do you think the least squares trend line would be more reliable than the naïve forecast procedure? For what type of data do you think that the naïve forecast procedure would be more reliable than the least squares trend line?

4.55 The Learning Company sells educational material to households online. The company usually receives many online requests during the third and fourth quarters, which have seasonal indexes of 1.6 and 1.7, respectively. The quarterly number of online requests (deseasonalized) resulting in sales are presented below. Find the least squares trend line for the deseasonalized data and find the forecast for the number of online requests resulting in sales during the third and fourth quarters of 2005.

Year	Quarter 1	Quarter 2	Quarter 3	Quarter 4
2003	69	56	60	57
2004	68	65	68	71
2005	75	72	69	74
2006	72	79	80	81
2007	78	85	88	90

Using the Computer

4.56 [DATA SET EX4-56] *Variable Description:*

Year: Year starting in 2004 through 2007

Month: Numbered from 1 through 12 for the twelve months of the year

HousePermits: Number of new housing permits issued to build houses (deseasonalized)

A real estate developer is interested in forecasting the number of new housing permits issued for the first three months of 2005. She knows that the seasonal indexes for those three months are .7, .6, and 1.1. Monthly deseasonalized data have been collected from 2001 through 2004. Find the least squares trend line for the deseasonalized data and find the forecasts that the developer needs.

4.57 [DATA SETS EX4-57] *Variable Description:*

Year: Year starting in 1996 and ending in 1999

Quarter: Numbered from 1 to 4 for each of the four quarters of the year

PretaxProf: Deseasonalized pretax profit per quarter

The German software company, SAP, benefited from the year-2000 computer problem. In addition, the company is the biggest maker of enterprise-resource-planning software, known as ERP. The company's programs automate manufacturing, human resources, and other nuts-and-bolts functions to give companies insight into the profitability of their internal operations according to "European Software Highflier SAP Comes Back to Earth" (*The Wall Street Journal*, Jan. 6, 1999, p. B8). Like most high-tech companies, the profits depend on cycles in the economy. Assume that deseasonalized pretax profit (converted into U.S. dollars from German marks) is collected from 1996 through 1999. If the quarterly indexes are .7, 1.0, .8, and 1.5, respectively, for quarters 1 through 4, what is the forecast of pretax profit for the four quarters of the year 2000?

4.9

SIMPLE EXPONENTIAL SMOOTHING

In Section 4.5, we introduced the concept of smoothing a time series by computing a set of centered *moving averages.* The moving averages were used to derive the various seasonal indexes, but they also provided a "new" time series with considerably less random variation (irregular activity) and no seasonality. Because the moving average series was much smoother, it provided a clearer picture of any existing trend or cyclical activity.

Another method of smoothing a time series, which also serves as a forecasting procedure, is **exponential smoothing.** Unlike moving averages, this technique uses all the preceding observations to determine a smoothed value for a particular time period. The

FIGURE

4.28

Illustration of a
stationary time
series.

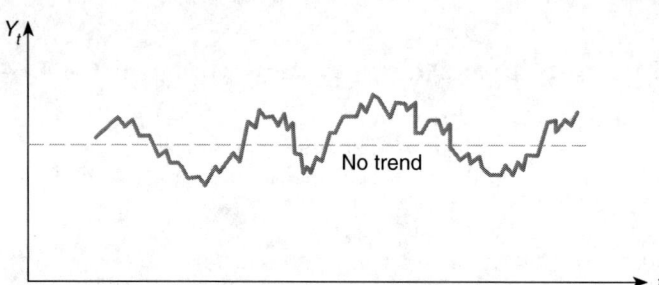

method described in this section is called *simple* (or single) *exponential smoothing* and works
well for a time series containing *no trend* (Figure 4.28). A time series (such as the one in
this figure) is said to be **stationary** if the data exhibit no trend and the variance about the
mean ($\bar{y}_t$) remains constant over time. *Simple exponential smoothing generally will track the
original time series well, provided this series is stationary.* Techniques exist for extending the
simple exponential smoothing procedure to a series containing trend and seasonality.

The simplest way to determine a smoothed value for time period t using exponential
smoothing is to find a weighted sum of the actual observation for this time period, y_t, and
the previous smoothed value, S_{t-1}.

> S_t = smoothed value for time period, t
> $= Ay_t + (1 - A)S_{t-1}$ $t = 2, 3, 4, \ldots$

4.8

where A is any number between 0 and 1.

The value of A is the **smoothing constant.** Small values of A produce smoothed values giving less weight to the corresponding observation, y_t. You should use such values
(say, $A < .1$) for a volatile time series containing considerable irregular activity (noise). In
this way, you give more weight to the previous smoothed value, S_{t-1}, rather than to the
original observation, y_t. You can use larger values of A for a more stable time series.

The smoothing procedure used here begins by setting the first smoothed value, S_1,
equal to the first observation, y_1. So,

$$S_1 = y_1$$

Then,

$$S_2 = Ay_2 + (1 - A)\, S_1$$
$$= Ay_2 + (1 - A)y_1$$
$$S_3 = Ay_3 + (1 - A)S_2$$
$$S_4 = Ay_4 + (1 - A)S_3$$

and so on.

The average attendance (y_t, in thousands) for major events held at the Jefferson
County Civic Center for the past 13 years is contained in Table 4.15. We determine the
exponentially smoothed values using three smoothing constants, $A = .1$, $A = .5$, and $A = .9$.

The actual time series and the three smoothed series are shown in Table 4.15 and
Figure 4.29. For $A = .1$,

$$S_1 = y_1 = 5.0$$
$$S_2 = (.1)y_2 + (.9)S_1$$
$$= (.1)(8.0) + (.9)(5.0) = 5.3$$

FIGURE

4.29

Smoothed values
for attendance
data (Table 4.15).

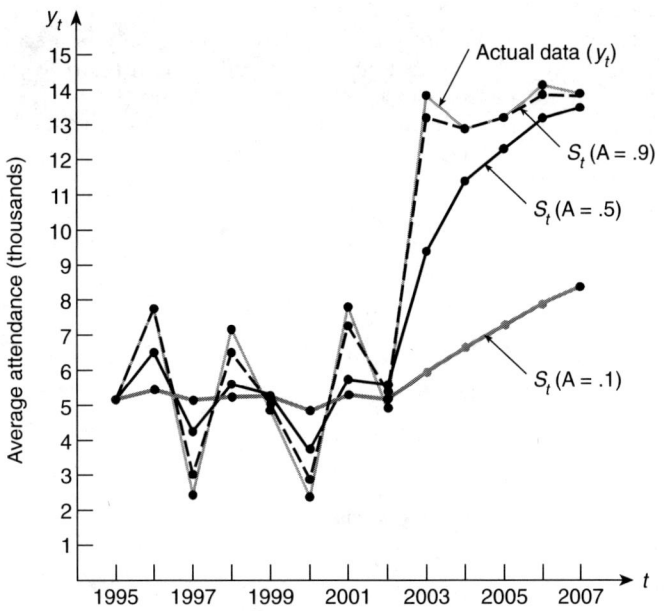

TABLE

4.15

Actual and
smoothed values
for attendance at
Jefferson Civic
Center.

Year	t	y_t	$S_t (A = .1)$	$S_t (A = .5)$	$S_t (A = .9)$
1995	1	5.0	5.0	5.0	5.0
1996	2	8.0	5.3	6.5	7.7
1997	3	2.1	4.98	4.3	2.66
1998	4	7.1	5.19	5.7	6.66
1999	5	4.8	5.15	5.25	4.99
2000	6	2.0	4.84	3.62	2.30
2001	7	7.8	5.13	5.71	7.25
2002	8	5.0	5.12	5.36	5.23
2003	9	14.1	6.02	9.73	13.21
2004	10	13.0	6.72	11.36	13.02
2005	11	13.5	7.39	12.43	13.45
2006	12	14.2	8.07	13.32	14.12
2007	13	14.0	8.67	13.66	14.01

$$S_3 = (.1)y_3 + (.9)S_2$$

$$= (.1)(2.1) + (.9)(5.3) = 4.98$$

and so on.

Notice that the average attendance, y_t, had a significant jump in 2003, when (it turns out) the facility was completely refurnished, providing better seating and more accessible snack booths. With the small value of $A = .1$, the smoothed values did not "track" the original series very well after this point. In general, when you use exponential smoothing with a small smoothing constant, the resulting series will be slow to detect any turning points or shifts in the observed values. However, such values of A provide considerable smoothing, as is evident from the values between the years 1995 and 2002.

The large value of $A = .9$ provides much better tracking (see Figure 4.29) but not much smoothing. Larger smoothing constants are more useful for a time series that does not contain a great deal of random fluctuation. Using $A = .5$ offers a compromise between these two extreme smoothing constants. The KPK Data Analysis macros can be used to compare the tracking ability of different values of A, in an effort to determine the best smoothing constant for a particular series.

To see why this procedure is called *exponential smoothing,* we look at how each smoothed value is obtained. First, $S_1 = y_1$. Then,

$$S_2 = Ay_2 + (1 - A)S_1$$
$$= Ay_2 + (1 - A)y_1$$
$$S_3 = Ay_3 + (1 - A)S_2$$
$$= Ay_3 + (1 - A)[Ay_2 + (1 - A)y_1]$$
$$= Ay_3 + A(1 - A)y_2 + (1 - A)^2 y_1$$
$$S_4 = Ay_4 + (1 - A)S_3$$
$$= Ay_4 + (1 - A)[Ay_3 + A(1 - A)y_2 + (1 - A)^2 y_1]$$
$$= Ay_4 + A(1 - A)y_3 + A(1 - A)^2 y_2 + (1 - A)^3 y_1$$

In general,

$$S_t = Ay_t + A(1 - A)y_{t-1} + A(1 - A)^2 y_{t-2} + \ldots + A(1 - A)^{t-2} y_2 + (1 - A)^{t-1} y_1$$

For example, if $A = .5$, then

$$S_t = .5y_t + .25y_{t-1} + .125y_{t-2} + .062y_{t-3} \ldots$$

Therefore, each smoothed value is actually a weighted sum of *all the previous observations.* Because the more recent observations have the largest weight, they have a larger effect on the smoothed value. Notice that the weights on the observations are decreasing exponentially. Except for observation y_1, the weight given to a particular observations is some constant (namely, $1 - A$) *times* the weight given to the preceding observation. That is why this procedure is called exponential smoothing.

Forecasting Using Simple Exponential Smoothing

The naïve forecasting procedure is a simple forecasting procedure that predicts the time series value for tomorrow using the actual value for today. In other words, $\hat{y}_{t+1} = y_t$. The exponential smoothing process is similar, except now the forecast for tomorrow is the smoothed value from today. In general,

$$\hat{y}_{t+1} = S_t \qquad t = 1, 2, 3, \ldots$$

4.9

For the special case where $A = 1$, we have

$$\hat{y}_{t+1} = S_t = 1y_t + (1 - 1)S_{t-1} = y_t$$

and the exponential smoothing forecast is the same as that provided by the naive predictor. Because A is considerably less than 1 in practice, the smoothed forecast makes use of all the past observations, rather than only the most recent measurement.

FIGURE
4.30

	A	B	C	D	E	F
1	5.0	Simple Exponential Smoothing (A = .1)				
2	8.0	t	Y(t)	SM(t)	Yhat	Residual
3	2.1	1	5.0	5.000		
4	7.1	2	8.0	5.300	5.000	3.000
5	4.8	3	2.1	4.980	5.300	-3.200
6	2.0	4	7.1	5.192	4.980	2.120
7	7.8	5	4.8	5.153	5.192	-0.392
8	5.0	6	2.0	4.838	5.153	-3.153
9	14.1	7	7.8	5.134	4.838	2.962
10	13.0	8	5.0	5.120	5.134	-0.134
11	13.5	9	14.1	6.018	5.120	8.980
12	14.2	10	13.0	6.717	6.018	6.982
13	14.0	11	13.5	7.395	6.717	6.783
14		12	14.2	8.075	7.395	6.805
15		13	14.0	8.668	8.075	5.925

Forecasts and residuals using Excel and KPK Data Analysis to do simple exponential smoothing on attendance data ($A = .1$).

EXAMPLE
4.12

Using simple exponential smoothing with $A = .1$, what are the predicted values and residuals for the attendance data in Table 4.15?

Solution

Suppose the year is 1995 ($t = 1$) and you want a forecast for 1996 ($t = 2$). You need the smoothed value for 1995: $\hat{y}_2 = S_1 = 5.0$. Next, the year is 1996 and you need a forecast for 1997. Here, $\hat{y}_3 = S_2 = 5.3$ (from Table 4.15).

To obtain an Excel solution, enter the 13 time series values in column A. Click on **KPK Data Analysis ➤ Time Series Analysis ➤ Forecasting** and select **Simple Exponential Smoothing.** Enter 0 as the **Number of Forecast Periods,** A1:A13 as the **Input Range,** and B1 as the **Output Range.** After clicking on **Continue,** select **Smoothing Constant(s) Will be Provided** and enter .1 as the smoothing constant (A). You will obtain the output in Figure 4.20 after clicking on **Continue.**

How well does this forecasting procedure perform here? We cannot use Figure 4.29 to compare the $\hat{y}$'s and the y's because, for each time period t, we have plotted y_t and S_t. The predicted value at t, however, is $\hat{y}_t = S_{t-1}$, not S_t. So we need to shift the smoothed values in Figure 4.29 one period to the right. This is shown in Figure 4.31, which contains a plot of the values in Figure 4.30 for $A = .1$.

As we might expect from Figure 4.31, the residuals using this method are quite large from 2003 on because this value of A produces smoothed values that fail to adapt to the shift that occurred in 2003. This series was not a good one for simple exponential smoothing because of this sudden shift. However, between the years 1996 and 2002 (a relatively stationary set of observations), the smoothed time series contains much less noise using $A = .1$ and gives a clear indication of the lack of any trend.

Simple exponential smoothing is a popular method of forecasting, particularly when there are hundreds or perhaps thousands of forecasts to be updated for each time period. Such is the case for many inventory-control systems, which are used to predict future demand levels for each item in inventory by means of a computerized forecasting procedure. Simple exponential smoothing often is used for such situations because each forecast, $\hat{y}_{t+1}$, requires only two values: the current observation, y_t, and the previous smoothed value, S_{t-1}. There is no need to store all the previous observations. *Computationally, this procedure is very simple and requires less computer time than do more sophisticated forecasting techniques.*

Exponential smoothing can also be used to capture trend and seasonality. *Holt's two-parameter linear exponential smoothing* allows you to estimate separately the smoothed value of the time series as well as the average trend gain at each point in time by using two equations and two smoothing constants. An extension of Holt's method, *Winters' linear*

FIGURE

4.31

Predicted versus actual values for attendance data (Table 4.15).

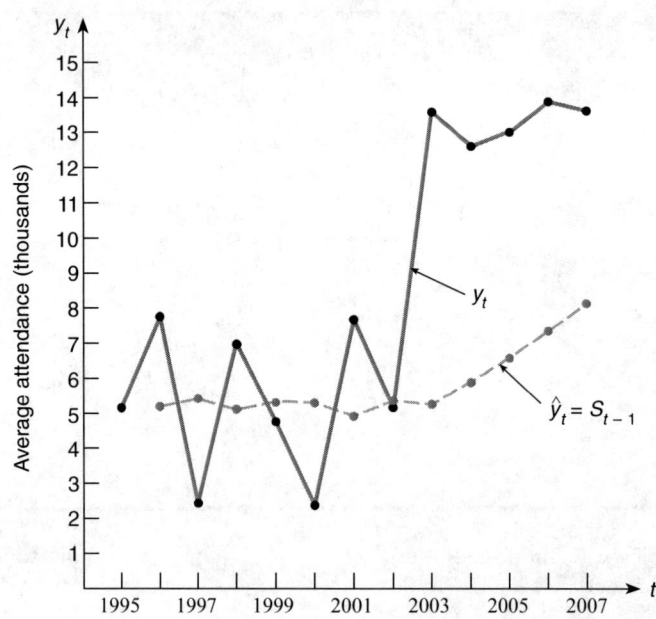

and seasonal exponential smoothing, offers additional flexibility. This three-parameter technique (i.e., there are three smoothing constants) not only smooths the past observation and trend estimates (as in Holt's method) but also provides smoothed seasonality factors for each time period. These (and many other) forecasting methods are explained in the text by Bowerman and O'Connell in the Further Reading section at the end of the chapter.

X Exercises 4.58–4.62

Understanding the Mechanics

4.58 Calculate the smoothed values for the following time series data. Use simple exponential smoothing with the smoothing constant equal to .1 and also with the smoothing constant equal to .3.

Year	t	y_t	S_t $(A = .1)$	S_t $(A = .3)$
1993	1	2	2	2
1994	2	3		
1995	3	2		
1996	4	5		
1997	5	8		
1998	6	7		
1999	7	5		
2000	8	8		
2001	9	10		
2002	10	9		
2003	11	8		
2004	12	10		
2005	13	7		
2006	14	9		
2007	15	7		

Applying the New Concepts

4.59 Direct TV offers its customers 225 channels via its satellite TV system and the option of paying per movie viewed with up to 55 movie choices per day. The number of customers subscribing to Direct TV has grown slowly over the past two years.

Year	Month	Direct TV Customers in Millions
2000	July	8.3
	August	9.0
	September	8.5
	October	8.8
	November	8.9
	December	9.0
2001	January	9.8
	February	10.1
	March	9.6
	April	10.3
	May	10.0
	June	10.1

a. Using simple exponential smoothing with $A = .1$, find the residual for April, May, and June of 2001.

b. Repeat part a with $A = .3$ and compare the residuals for April, May and June 2001.

(Source: "Satellite TV Leaders," *USA Today*, August 7, 2001, p. 3B)

4.60 The Federal Reserve Board reports the ratio of U.S. retail inventories to sales as a leading indicator of the health of the economy. The following ratios are provided for the year 2003. Using simple exponential smoothing with $A = .2$, predict the ratio of U.S. retail inventories to sales for January of 2004.

Month	Jan	Feb	Mar	Apr	May	Jun
Ratio	.84	.90	.84	.84	.78	.82

Month	Jul	Aug	Sep	Oct	Nov	Dec
Ratio	.78	.78	.85	.84	.85	.77

(Source: *www.economagic.com*.)

Using the Computer

4.61 **[DATA SET EX4-61]** *Variable Description:*

Year 1991 to 2007

ProductivityIndex: An index to measure the overall productivity of a paper plant

The plant manager has developed a productivity index measuring plant productivity for plants that manufacture paper products. This measure has been recorded yearly and fluctuates with the demand for paper products and the number of employees hired. Use simple exponential smoothing with $A = .15$, to forecast the productivity index for the year 2008.

4.62 **[DATA SET EX4-62]** *Variable Description:*

Year: Year from 1992 to 2007

RefinanceNum: Number of home loans refinanced

The trend in interest rates over the past decade has been generally downward. So as mortgage interest rates dip, homeowners consider refinancing home loans. Suppose that the manager of First State Bank in Denton, Texas, is interested in forecasting the number of homeowners refinancing their home mortgage for a better interest rate. Using simple exponential smoothing with $A = .2$, predict the number of homeowners refinancing at First State Bank in the years 2006 and 2007 and comment on the accuracy.

4.10

INDEX NUMBERS

How many times have you heard a remark such as, "Fifteen years ago we could have bought that house for $70,000. Now it's worth $180,000." Or "My weekly grocery bill used to be $25. Today, it's almost $100." Many people like to talk about the prices back in the "good old days," but were goods and services actually less expensive in those days?

Perhaps a particular item consumed a greater proportion of the typical consumer's consumable income (purchasing power) in years past. To compare effectively the change in the price or value of a certain item (or group of items) between any two time periods, we use an index number. An **index number** (or index) measures the change in a particular item (typically a product or service) or a collection of items between two time periods.

The average hourly wages for production employees at Kessler Toy Company in 1990, 1995, 2000, and 2005 are shown in Table 4.16. Suppose we wish to compare the average wages for 1995, 2000, and 2005 with those for 1990. By computing a ratio for each pair of wages (expressed as a *percentage* of the 1990 wage), we obtain the following set of index numbers:

$$\text{index number for 1995:} \quad \left(\frac{8.50}{7.05}\right) \cdot 100 = 120.6$$

$$\text{index number for 2000:} \quad \left(\frac{10.90}{7.05}\right) \cdot 100 = 154.6$$

$$\text{index number for 2005:} \quad \left(\frac{12.50}{7.05}\right) \cdot 100 = 177.3$$

TABLE

4.16

Average hourly wage of production employees at Kessler Toy Company.

	1990	1995	2000	2005
Wage	$7.05	$8.50	$10.90	$12.50
Index (base = 1990)	100	120.6	154.6	177.3

TABLE

4.17

Prices of four items in 1990 and 2005.

Item	1990	2005
Eggs	.75 (doz.)	1.35 (doz.)
Chicken	.95 (lb)	1.79 (lb)
Cheese	.89 (lb)	1.85 (lb)
Auto battery	$31.00 (each)	$55.00 (each)

When calculating an index number, we follow standard practice—round to the nearest tenth (as in Table 4.16) and omit the percent sign. For this application, all wages were compared to those in 1990, the *base year*. The index number for the base year is always 100.

When each index number uses the same base year, the resulting set of values is an **index time series.** An index time series is a set of index numbers determined from the same base year. The purpose of such a time series is to measure the yearly values in *constant* units (dollars, people, and so on). Because these values define a time series, they can be analyzed and decomposed by using the methods described previously. Our purpose in this section is simply to describe how to *construct* a time series of this type.

Price Indexes

Index numbers are derived for a variety of products (goods or services) as well as locations. For example, you may wish to compare the relative costs of consumer items in Los Angeles and Minneapolis if you are considering a move. Such information is readily available or can be determined from a number of business publications or government reports. The Department of Labor and the Bureau of Labor Statistics release reports (many of them monthly) on the price and quantity of many consumer items and agricultural commodities. Often these are recorded for specific U.S. cities, providing geographical comparisons.

We focus our attention on comparison of *prices* from one year to the next; such comparisons are **price indexes.** The most popular of these indexes is the Consumer Price Index (CPI), which combines a large number (thousands) of prices for consumer goods (such as food and housing) and family services (such as health care and recreation) into a single index. It is often called the cost-of-living index.

A price index that includes more than one item is an **aggregate price index.** We examine two methods of calculating an aggregate price index.

Say we wish to measure the change in the prices of several items from 1990 to 2005, using a single price index. Table 4.17 shows four items; 1990 is the base year. Let P_0 denote the price for a particular item in the base year (1990) and P_1 represent this price during the reference year (2005). So

$$\sum P_0 = \text{sum of sampled prices for 1990}$$

$$= .75 + .95 + .89 + 31 = \$33.59$$

and

$$\Sigma P_1 = \text{sum of sampled prices for 2005}$$
$$= 1.35 + 1.79 + 1.85 + 55 = \$59.99$$

The ratio of these sums represents the **simple aggregate price index** for this application.

$$\text{simple aggregate price index} = \left(\frac{\Sigma P_1}{\Sigma P_0}\right) \cdot 100$$

4.10

For our example,

$$\text{index} = \left(\frac{59.99}{33.59}\right) \cdot 100 = 178.6$$

It might be tempting to conclude that, based on the prices of these four items, all prices increased by 78.6% between 1990 and 2005. Two problems arise here. The first is whether these sampled items are *representative* of the population of all price changes over this eight-year period. This is not a new problem—the same concern arose when we first introduced statistical sampling.

The second problem is that this index does not take into account the amounts of these items that are typically purchased by consumers. A significant change in the price for any single item will have a dramatic effect on the simple aggregate index, regardless of the demand for this product. The increase of $24 in the price of an automobile battery dominated the computed value of the aggregate price index; however, a typical consumer will spend much more annually on chicken than on car batteries. *The simple aggregate price index assumes that equal amounts of each item are purchased.*

For this reason, the next step is to include a measure of the quantity (*Q*) of each item in the price index. (We discuss methods of selecting the item quantities later.) The resulting index is known as a **weighted aggregate price index.**

$$\text{weighted aggregate price index} = \left(\frac{\Sigma P_1 Q}{\Sigma P_0 Q}\right) \cdot 100$$

4.11

EXAMPLE 4.13

Assume that a representative family each year purchases 1 automobile battery and each month consumes 6 dozen eggs, 15 pounds of chicken, and 8 pounds of cheese. Using 1990 as the base year and equation 4.11, determine the weighted aggregate price index for 2005. Use the data in Table 4.17.

Solution

The choice of time units on the quantities, *Q*, is arbitrary, but it is essential that we be consistent across all items. Converting the family purchases to annual units, we have $6 \cdot 12 = 72$ dozen eggs, $15 \cdot 12 = 180$ pounds of chicken, $8 \cdot 12 = 96$ pounds of cheese, and 1 car battery (Table 4.18).

The weighted aggregate price index for 2005 (using 1990 as the base year) is

$$\text{index} = \left(\frac{\Sigma P_1 Q}{\Sigma P_0 Q}\right) \cdot 100 = \left(\frac{652}{341.44}\right) \cdot 100 = 191.0$$

In this index, the increase of 91% between 1990 and 2005 is not as severely affected by the price change for the car battery as was the simple aggregate price index, which ignored annual demand for each item. All widely used business price indexes are based on some variation of the weighted aggregate price index in equation 4.11.

TABLE 4.18							
Calculated aggregate price index.		**1990**			**2005**		
Item	P_0	Q	P_0Q	P_1	Q	P_1Q	
Eggs	.75	72	$ 54.00	1.35	72	$ 97.20	
Chicken	.95	180	171.00	1.79	180	322.20	
Cheese	.89	96	85.44	1.85	96	177.60	
Auto battery	31.00	1	31.00	55.00	1	55.00	
			$\Sigma P_0Q = 341.44$			$\Sigma P_1Q = 652.00$	

Selection of the Quantity, Q

Because the weights in a weighted aggregate price index usually reflect the quantities consumed, a problem arises when these quantities cannot be assumed to remain constant over the time span of the index. In Example 4.13, the same quantities, Q, were applied to both time periods, so we are assuming an equal demand for the two years.

We have two options here: (1) Use the quantities for the base year (1990, here) and (2) use the quantities for the reference year (2005, here). The first method is the **Laspeyres index**; the second is the **Paasche index.**

$$\text{Laspeyres index} = \left(\frac{\Sigma P_1 Q_0}{\Sigma P_0 Q_0} \right) \cdot 100$$

4.12

where Q_0 represents a base-year quantity.

$$\text{Paasche index} = \left(\frac{\Sigma P_1 Q_1}{\Sigma P_0 Q_1} \right) \cdot 100$$

4.13

where Q_1 represents a reference-year quantity.

Each of these indexes has strengths and weaknesses. The main advantage of the Laspeyres index is that the same base-year quantities apply to all future reference years. This greatly simplifies updating of this index, particularly given that most aggregate business indexes contain a large number of items. Its main disadvantage is that it tends to give more weight to those items that show a dramatic price increase. When a particular commodity's price increases sharply, it is typically accompanied by a decrease in the demand (measured by Q) for this item, or perhaps another item may be substituted by the consumer. The Laspeyres index fails to adjust for this situation. The advantages of this index outweigh its disadvantages, however, and it is more popular than the Paasche index.

The complexity of updating the reference-year quantities for the Paasche index make it difficult (and often impossible) to apply. Furthermore, because it reflects *both* price and quantity changes, we cannot use it to reflect price changes between two time periods. Its obvious advantage is that it uses current-year quantities, which provide a more realistic and up-to-date estimate of total expense.

We have seen that there is no completely reliable and accurate method of describing aggregate price changes. All such indexes include inaccuracies introduced by using a sample of items in the index as well as by the quantities to be used for weighting. Nevertheless, we treat such an index like any other sample estimate: We use the index as an estimate of relative price changes and realize that it is subject to a certain amount of error.

Comments

1. The most widely used Laspeyres index is the Consumer Price Index (CPI), which is based on thousands of items, ranging from the price of housing to medical expenditures. The CPI is used as a measure of inflation and the cost of living in the United States. It is published monthly and is utilized by the federal government (and some private companies), which bases payment (or salary) adjustments on increases or decreases in the CPI. For example, Social Security payments and retirement benefits for federal civil service employees are tied to this index.

2. The CPI can be used to *deflate* a time series, providing a better comparison of dollar amounts across time. A value is deflated by *dividing* the actual dollar amount for this time period by the corresponding value of the CPI and then multiplying by 100. For example, if your current hourly wage is $18 and the CPI for this year is 150, then the deflated amount is (18/150)(100) = $12. Consequently, the $12 amount can be compared to the hourly wage for the base year (or any other deflated wage value) to determine if there has been a change in real wages. This technique can also be applied to the Gross National Product (GNP) to detect real changes in the total value of goods and services.

Ⓧ Exercises 4.63–4.72

Understanding the Mechanics

4.63 The following data are the selling prices of a particular chemical.

Year	1995	2000	2002	2004	2007
Price	24	28	34	44	50

a. Construct an index time series for the years 1995, 2000, 2002, 2004, and 2007 using 1995 as the base year.
b. Repeat part a using 2000 as the base year.

4.64 Consider the following prices and quantities of four items.

	2000		2007	
	P_0	Q_0	P_1	Q_1
Item 1	1.50	60	3.00	50
Item 2	2.00	100	2.25	90
Item 3	1.70	80	2.00	100
Item 4	4.00	20	3.50	50

a. Construct the Laspeyres index.
b. Construct the Paasche index.

Applying the New Concepts

4.65 A typical family in Jackson, Mississippi, had the following weekly buying patterns in 2000 and 2007 (prices are in dollars). Use 2000 as the base year.

Item	2000 Unit Price	2000 Quantity	2007 Unit Price	2007 Quantity
Meat	1.03	2	1.25	2
Milk	.97	3	1.19	2
Fish	.98	2	1.05	3
Oranges	.65	3	.75	4
Bread	.40	1	.62	2

a. Find the simple aggregate price index.
b. Construct the Laspeyres index.
c. Construct the Paasche index.

4.66 Explain the meaning, including the advantages and disadvantages, of the Paasche and Laspeyres weighted indexes. Comment on whether the indexes can be used as a representation of buying pattern.

4.67 The following table reflects the typical family's buying habits per 6 months on repairs for the family car. Use 2000 as the base year.

Item	2000 Price	2000 Quantity	2007 Price	2007 Quantity
Lube job	3.50	2	5.00	1
Oil change	9.50	3	13.00	2
Tune-up	29.95	1	39.95	1
New tires	35.95	2	49.00	2

a. Find the simple aggregate price index.
b. Construct the Laspeyres index.
c. Construct the Paasche index.

4.68 A conglomerate is considering buying one or more of three companies. The closing prices of the stocks of these three companies for the years 1999 to 2007 are:

Year	Better Foods	Friendly Insurance	Chock Full of Computer Chips
1999	13.500	20.125	39.25
2000	13.750	20.250	35.50
2001	14.250	20.500	31.75
2002	15.125	21.750	34.25
2003	15.500	21.500	37.75
2004	16.000	21.750	39.75
2005	16.125	22.500	40.00
2006	16.250	23.750	39.50
2007	16.750	23.500	42.25

Find an appropriate index to measure the change in the price of these three stocks for the years 2002, 2003, 2005, and 2007 using 1999 as the base year.

4.69 Suppose that, for a certain basket of goods, the Paasche index for 2007 is 115 and the Laspeyres index is 97. Assuming that the base year is 2000, interpret the meaning of the value of the two indexes.

4.70 The number of housing starts for four counties for the years 2005, 2006, and 2007 is as follows:

County	2005	2006	2007
Brooks	1304	1505	1580
Litton	1264	1759	1987
Riverbed	1135	1443	1565
Tannon	1401	1605	1615

a. Compare the housing starts for Litton county for the years 2006 and 2007 using 2005 as the base year.
b. Compare the aggregate of housing starts for the years 2006 and 2007 for the four counties using 2005 as the base year.

4.71 Resource-based industries are an important component of the Canadian economy. The following table illustrates the quantity (consumption in thousands of kilograms) and selling price (in Canadian dollars) of three minerals commonly mined in Canada.

	Quantity		Price	
Mineral	**1998**	**2002**	**1998**	**2002**
Zinc	131	143	1.65	1.92
Copper	190	265	3.16	3.20
Nickel	21	22	14.04	10.29

a. Calculate the Laspeyres index for 2002 using 1998 as the base year.
b. Calculate the Paasche index for 2002 using 1998 as the base year.
c. Compare the two indexes.

4.72 Indexes are often confusing to investors. For example, the Dow Jones Industrial Average (DJIA) is a price-weighted index incorporating a multiplier that changes over time. In December 1997, the multiplier could be interpreted to mean that a gain in the DJIA of 3.93 would result from a gain of one dollar in any one of the 30 companies that make up the DJIA. But the price-weighted DJIA also means that higher-priced stocks have a bigger impact than lower-priced stocks. Say that hypothetically an investor had bought equal dollar amounts of each Dow stock at the close of the market one day. The next day, if the Dow's 15 highest-priced stocks had each declined 5% and the 15 lowest-priced stocks each gained 5%, the DJIA would have declined 197 points or 1.5% for the day. How would the investor have fared? Does this explain how the DJIA can be confusing for investors who may not understand how a price-weighted index works?

(Source: "The Numbers Game," *Stages: The Fidelity Investments Magazine of Personal Finance,* Winter 1998, p. 21.)

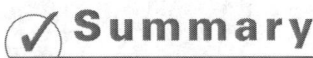 Summary

A variable recorded over time is a time series. You obtain a sample of values for this variable by recording its past observations. The process of using the patterns of past data to predict future values is called forecasting. Because a sample of past observations is not a random one, it is extremely difficult (if not impossible) to obtain any tests of hypothesis or confidence intervals. Consequently, we resort to describing the past observations by deriving the components of the time series. This process is called time series decomposition. The components of a time series are (1) trend (a long-term growth or decline in the observations—either **linear, quadratic,** or **decaying,** (2) **seasonality** (within-year recurrent fluctuations), (3) **cyclical activity** (upward and downward movements of various lengths about the trend), and (4) **irregular activity** (what remains after the other three components have been removed).

We described methods of estimating these components for a time series. We first specify how we believe the components interact with one another, thus describing the time series variable, y_t. The **additive structure** assumes that each observation is the *sum* of its components. In particular, this structure implies that seasonal fluctuations during a particular year are not affected by the base volume for that year. In the **multiplicative structure,** each value of y_t is the *product* of the four components. In this framework, the seasonal fluctuation for a specific month (or quarter) is more apt to be a constant *percentage* of the base volume for that year; for example, sales in December might be 35% higher than the average (base) sales for that particular year. The multiplicative structure was assumed for practically all of the illustrations in this chapter and is used more commonly in practice. The Bureau of the Census uses a variation of this procedure for their time series decomposition analyses.

There are two types of seasonal variation: **additive seasonal variation,** in which the amount of variation due to seasonality does not depend on the level y_t, and **multiplicative seasonal variation,** in which the variation is proportional to the trend level for each observation.

Seasonality can be isolated from an original time series using **centered moving averages.** We described a four-step procedure for deriving time series components for a particular time series, based on the multiplicative structure:

(1) determine a **seasonal index** for each month or quarter (monthly or quarterly data); (2) **deseasonalize** the data by dividing each observation by its corresponding seasonal index; (3) determine the **trend components** by deriving a least squares line or quadratic curve through the deseasonalized values; and (4) determine the **cyclical components** by, for each time period, dividing each deseasonalized value by its estimate using the trend equation and smoothing these values by computing three-period moving averages.

Forecasting methods can be divided into two broad categories: qualitative procedures and quantitative techniques. When arriving at a qualitative forecast, expert opinion is used to arrive at a best-educated estimate of future behavior. One such method is the Delphi method, which requires input from a team of experts. Each team member is then informed as to the responses from all other members and asked to reevaluate his or her opinion in light of this information. This process is continued for several rounds until each member of the team feels confident in his or her final decision.

Quantitative forecasting, the main emphasis of this chapter, dealt with two (sometimes overlapping) sets of procedures: time series techniques and multiple linear regression on time series data. **Time series procedures** attempt to capture the past behavior of the time series and use this information to predict future values. No external predictors are considered; only the past observations are used to describe and predict the future value of the time series variable. Time series methods include, (1) **projecting the least squares trend line,** which extracts and extends the trend and seasonal components, and (2) **simple exponential smoothing,** which reduces randomness and forecasts future values by using the **smoothed** values.

Simple exponential smoothing works best when the time series contains neither trend nor seasonality.

An **index time series,** often used by business analysts, is a time-related sequence of index numbers in which each value is a measure of the change in a particular item (or group of items) from one year to the next. **Price indexes** are used to compare prices over time.

An **aggregate price index** is used to compare the relative price of a set of items for any year to the price during the base year. The index for the base year always is 100. The prices for the items can be averaged **(simple aggregate price index)** or weighted by the corresponding quantity of each item **(weighted aggregate price index).** Methods of selecting these quantities include using base-year quantities (the **Laspeyres index**) or using the reference-year quantities (the **Paasche index**). The most popular Laspeyres index in practice is the Consumer Price Index (CPI).

Further Reading

Bowerman, B. L., and R. T. O'Connell. *Forecasting and Time Series: An Applied Approach,* 3rd ed. Pacific Grove, Calif.: Brooks/Cole, a part of Cengage Learning 2000.

Brockwell, P. J., and R. A. Davis. *Introduction to Time Series and Forecasting,* 2nd ed. New York: Springer-Verlag, 2002.

Hanke, J., A. Reitsch, and D. W. Wichern. *Business Forecasting,* 7th ed. Upper Saddle River, NJ: Prentice Hall, 2001.

Kvanli, A., R. Pavur, and K. Keeling. *Introduction to Business Statistics: A Microsoft Excel Integrated Approach,* 6th ed. Mason, OH: South-Western, a part of Cengage Learning2003.

Makridakis, S., S. C. Wheelwright, and R. J. Hyndman. *Forecasting: Methods and Applications,* 3rd ed. New York: Wiley, 1997.

Yaffee, R. A., and M. McGee. *An Introduction to Time Series Analysis and Forecasting: With Applications of SAS and SPSS.* Burlington, Mass.: Academic Press, 2000.

Summary of Formulas

Linear Trend Line

$$\hat{y}_t = b_0 + b_1 t$$

where

$$t = 1, 2, \ldots, T$$

$$b_1 = \frac{\Sigma t y_t - (\Sigma t)(\Sigma y_t)/T}{\Sigma t^2 - (\Sigma t)^2/T} = \frac{12B - 6(T+1)A}{T(T^2-1)}$$

$$b_0 = \bar{y}_t - b_1 \bar{t} = \frac{A}{T} - b_1\left(\frac{T+1}{2}\right)$$

where $A = \Sigma y_t$ and $B = \Sigma t y_t$

Deseasonalized Value of y_t

$$d_t = \frac{y_t}{\text{corresponding seasonal index}}$$

Simple Aggregate Price Index

$$\left(\frac{\Sigma P_1}{\Sigma P_0}\right) \cdot 100$$

Weighted Aggregate Price Index

$$\left(\frac{\Sigma P_1 Q}{\Sigma P_0 Q}\right) \cdot 100$$

Laspeyres Index

$$\left(\frac{\Sigma P_1 Q_0}{\Sigma P_0 Q_0}\right) \cdot 100$$

where Q_0 represents a base-year quantity.

Paasche Index

$$\left(\frac{\Sigma P_1 Q_1}{\Sigma P_0 Q_1}\right) \cdot 100$$

where Q_1 represents a reference-year quantity.

Forecasting Models

1. Using seasonality and trend:

$$\hat{y}_{t+1} = [b_0 + b_1(t + 1)]$$
$$\cdot \text{ (seasonal index for period } t + 1)$$

2. Simple exponential smoothing:

$$\hat{y}_{t+1} = S_t$$

where

$$S_t = Ay_t + (1 - A)S_{t-1}$$
$$0 < A < 1.$$

X Review Exercises 4.73–4.88

4.73   Each of the following influences on the variation in profits of a national chain of department stores would contribute to which of the four components of a time series?
  a. The long-term growth of the economy
  b. The resignation of top managers in the company
  c. Annual demand in spring and summer for garden equipment
  d. The closing of several other department stores

4.74 A manufacturer of tractors has built a record number of tractors for every year for the past seven years. Given in thousands, the figures show the number of tractors built from 2001 to 2007.

Year	Tractors Built
2001	10.75
2002	11.78
2003	12.59
2004	13.4
2005	14.3
2006	15.7
2007	16.8

Find the least squares prediction equation that you would use to forecast the trend. What would you estimate the number of tractors built in 2008 to be?

4.75 Luz Chemicals, which manufactures a special-purpose baking soda, is interested in estimating the equation of the trend line for their monthly sales data (in tons) for the year 2007.

Month	Baking Soda Sales	Month	Baking Soda Sales
Jan.	28	July	34
Feb.	33	Aug.	34
Mar.	39	Sept.	35
Apr.	33	Oct.	36
May	38	Nov.	31
June	31	Dec.	37

a. Without considering the seasonality present in the monthly sales, estimate the trend line equation.

b. Using the equation obtained in part a, estimate the sales (in tons) for the month of February 2008.

4.76   Telemex, a supplier of telephone systems, has experienced moderate to rapid growth over a 12-year period. The data show the annual sales figures (in tens of thousands of dollars).

Year	Sales	Year	Sales
1996	3.1	2002	18.8
1997	6.3	2003	18.4
1998	10.5	2004	20.0
1999	10.2	2005	21.3
2000	11.5	2006	29.0
2001	14.7	2007	28.3

a. Find the trend line.
b. Find the cyclical components.
c. Graph the data and estimate the period of the cycle.

4.77 U.S. households have adopted the Internet at a slightly slower pace than what was observed for television. Perhaps this is partly due to the Internet being an active pursuit and television watching being a passive pursuit. The following data display the percent of households that have adopted the Internet from 1992 to 2001. Find the least squares trend line and compute the cyclical components of the percent of households that have adopted the Internet.

Year	Households with Internet	Year	Households with Internet
1992	1	1997	25
1993	5	1998	35
1994	8	1999	46
1995	13	2000	54
1996	24	2001	59

(Source: "Adoption Rate of Internet by Consumers Is Slowing," *The Wall Street Journal*, July 16, 2001, p. B8.)

4.78   Suppose that for the month of January 2007, the marketing department of a firm finds that the seasonal index is 1.20, the trend line value is $17,000 in sales, and the cyclical component is .79. What is the irregular component if the actual sales figure for January 2007 is $16,500?

4.79 In Chinese cities, a small but growing middle class of first-time home and car buyers is powering the country's growth. China experienced rapid growth during the early 1990s and now is seeing more moderate growth in its economy. The following data illustrate the year-to-year percentage change in its gross domestic product (GDP) from 1990 to 2001.
a. Plot these data. Would you suggest using a linear or quadratic trend line to fit the data?
b. Determine the cyclical components.

Year	China's GDP Change	Year	China's GDP Change
1990	4.0	1996	9.7
1991	9.0	1997	9.0
1992	14.0	1998	8.0
1993	13.5	1999	7.0
1994	12.5	2000	8.0
1995	10.5	2001	7.9

(Source: "China Says GDP Growth Slowed," *The Wall Street Journal*, July 18, 2001, p. 14A.)

4.80 The following table lists the number of building permits per month for nonresidential construction during the four-year period 2004 through 2007 in Parkins, Nebraska.

Year	Jan	Feb	Mar	Apr	May	June	July	Aug	Sept	Oct	Nov	Dec
2004	21	22	23	24	25	28	29	30	27	26	20	20
2005	21	24	23	25	26	25	29	32	32	27	20	18
2006	17	18	21	24	22	28	29	30	27	26	22	20
2007	17	21	23	23	24	29	31	22	28	22	21	29

   a. Determine the seasonal indexes.
   b. Determine the cyclical components for 2004 using a three-month moving average.
   c. Determine the irregular component for July of 2004.

4.81 The average monthly utility bill for residents of the small community of Ridgecrest for the years 2004 through 2007 is:

Year	Jan	Feb	Mar	Apr	May	June	July	Aug	Sept	Oct	Nov	Dec
2004	190	180	179	130	135	145	148	153	145	153	170	185
2005	197	193	185	150	151	159	163	165	160	159	180	185
2006	215	205	193	175	171	179	185	184	180	180	173	190
2007	235	225	205	180	182	190	195	198	188	185	195	201

   a. Determine the seasonal indexes.
   b. Determine the trend.
   c. Determine the cyclical components for 2005 using a three-period moving average.
   d. Determine the irregular components for June and July 2005.

4.82 The weekly buying pattern of a typical family in a suburb of Atlanta, Georgia, for 2000 and 2007 follows.

Item	2000 Unit Price	2000 Quantity	2007 Unit Price	2007 Quantity
Chicken	2.40	1	2.75	2
Milk	1.02	3	1.19	2
Bread	.39	2	.45	2
Ground beef	1.59	3	1.89	2
Tomatoes	.39	2	.78	2

Using 2000 as the base year,
   a. Find the simple aggregate price index.
   b. Calculate the Laspeyres index.
   c. Calculate the Paasche index.
   d. Compare the indexes in parts b and c.

4.83   An operations manager has ordered four types of chemicals over the past five years. The price and quantity purchased by the manager in 2000 and 2007 are as follows.

Chemical	2000 Unit Price	2000 Quantity	2007 Unit Price	2007 Quantity
Citric acid	10.70	50	11.80	52
Manganese sulphate	25.75	25	29.6	23
Sodium bichromate	4.25	110	4.30	150
Sodium chlorite	7.50	75	8.10	100

   a. Using 2000 as the base year, find the Laspeyres index.
   b. Using 2000 as the base year, find the Paasche index.

4.84 [DATA SET EX4-84] *Variable Description:*

Year_Quarter: Year and quarter from the first quarter of 1990 to the fourth quarter of 2000

Productivity: Percentage growth rate in productivity

High-growth periods are usually associated with a wave of innovations such as electricity or the motor vehicle. The advances in the Internet have increased the productivity of the U.S. economy in recent years. The growth rate in productivity has ranged from slightly less than 1% to slightly more than 3% during the past decade.

a. Use the trend line and the seasonal components to forecast productivity for the four quarters of 2001.

b. During what time period does the noise component show high variability?

(Source: *"Fed's Meyer Warns of Inflation, Joblessness,"* *The Wall Street Journal,* June 7, 2001, p. A2.)

4.85 **[DATA SET EX4-85]** *Variable Description:*

Year: Year from 2002 to 2003

Month: Month denoted by 1, 2, . . . 12

HS: Housing Starts Consumer Credit (in millions of dollars)

Housing was a heroic performer throughout 2002 and 2003, with credit due to historically low interest rates. The Census Bureau reports housing starts (HS) monthly. The variable HS is the number of new privately owned housing units started during each month of 2002 and 2003. Using simple exponential smoothing with $A = .2$, predict housing starts for January 2004.

(Source: *www.economagic.com.*)

4.86 **[DATA SET EX4-86]** *Variable Description:*

Year: Year from 1996 to 2003

Month: Month denoted by 1, 2, . . . 12

PMI: Purchasing Managers Index

The Institute for Supply Management (ISM) publishes the Purchasing Managers Index (PMI) monthly. The ISM surveys more than 300 purchasing managers nationwide who represent 20 different industries to compute this index. A PMI index over 50 indicates that manufacturing is expanding, while anything below 50 means that the industry is contracting. Estimate the trend line and use it to predict the deseasonalized PMI for January 2004.

(Source: *www.ism.ws/ISMReport/PMIndex.cfm.*)

4.87 **[DATA SET EX4-87]** *Variable Description:*

Year: Year from 1988 to 2003

Month: Month denoted by 1, 2, . . . 12

PPI: Producer Price Index

The producer price index (PPI) is an index that measures inflation in wholesale goods. The producer price index tracks the prices of food, metals, lumber, oil, and gas, as well as many other commodities. Estimate the trend line and use it to predict the deseasonalized PPI for January 2004.

(Source: *research.stlouisfed.org/fred2/series/PPIACO.*)

4.88 **[DATA SET EX4-88]** *Variable Description:*

Time: Monthly data over 25 months, numbered 1 through 25

Y1: Data collected from sales of Business A

Y2: Data collected from sales of Business B

The data on sales from Business A and Business B were collected to determine if sales exhibited additive variation or multiplicative variation. Plots of these data are presented below. What type of variation do these plots exhibit? Draw a trend line for each time series. Estimate the length of the cycle.

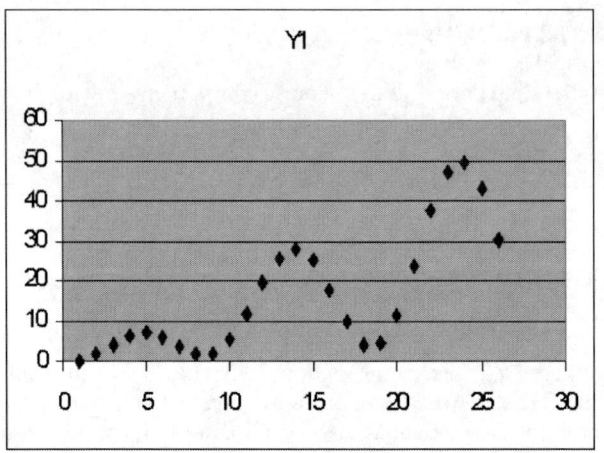

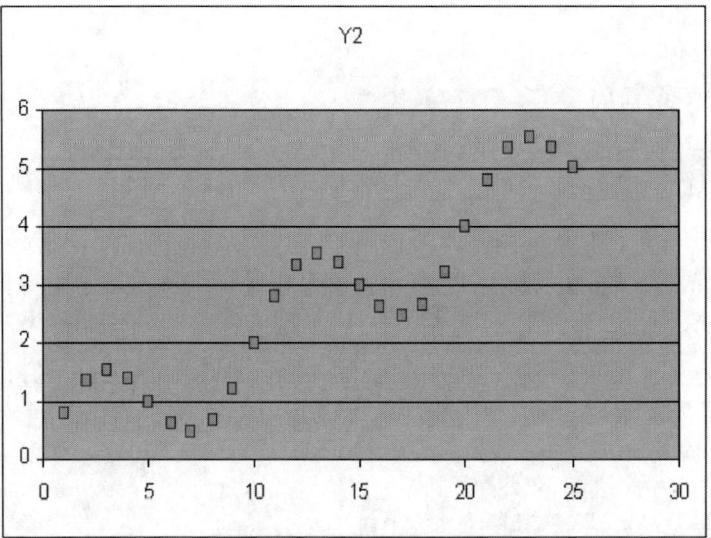

Insights from Statistics in Action

Forecasting Underlying Economic Trends: Oh CPI, Why Did You Lie?

The Statistics in Action introductory case study mentioned that companies use the CPI and other economic indicators to forecast their earnings and make business decisions with regard to the future direction of the company. There are several economic indexes, such as the Producer Price Index (PPI) for measuring inflation during the production process and the Employment Cost Index (ECI) for measuring inflation in the labor market. However, the CPI is the index that gets most of the attention when determining inflation experienced by consumers in their day-to-day living expenses. Future val-

ues for economic indexes are important in negotiating government budgets, setting wage guidelines, and determining benefits.

To interpret fluctuations in the economic indexes such as the CPI, the trend, seasonal, and cyclical components of these indexes are analyzed. Economists often rely on the trend component to gain insight into the direction that inflation is headed. Eleven years of monthly data on the CPI are listed in StatInActChap16.xls. These figures have not been adjusted for seasonality or cyclical activity in the data.

1. Plot the CPI index from 1991 to 2001 in a time series graph. Relying on your own judgment and not a statistical procedure, comment on the trend of the index and the existence of seasonality.

2. Assuming that the seasonality is multiplicative in nature, determine the seasonal indexes, deseasonalize the data, determine the trend components, determine the cyclical activity, and compute the noise (irregular) components.

3. For what years is there more variability in the noise components of the CPI?

4. Find deseasonalized forecasts of the CPI for the four months of 2002 using only the trend equation. Use the seasonal indexes to adjust the deseasonalized forecasts.

5. How far into the future do you think that a researcher could predict with this model and still obtain accurate forecasts? What type of economic events do you think could make the forecasts invalid for predicting the CPI?

(Source: "Gradual Fed Rate Hikes Expected," *Los Angeles Times*, June 16, 2004, p. C1. "Inflation Is Back," *The Wall Street Journal*, April 15, 2004, p. A14. "Inflation and Prices," *Economic Trends*, March 2001, p. 2.)

Appendix

Data Analysis with Excel, MINITAB, and SPSS

Excel

Time Series Decomposition

To obtain the four-step procedure for the decomposition of times series, click on **KPK Data Analysis ➤ Time Series Analysis ➤ Decomposition** to display the **Time Series Decomposition** dialog box. For the monthly retail data used in Example 4.9, select 12 for the **Periods Per Year** and select **A Single Column** to describe how the data are stored. Enter A1:A48 for the **Input Range,** B1 for the **Output Range,** and enter 2004 for the **First year.** Click **OK** and five sheets of output will be displayed, including the plots.

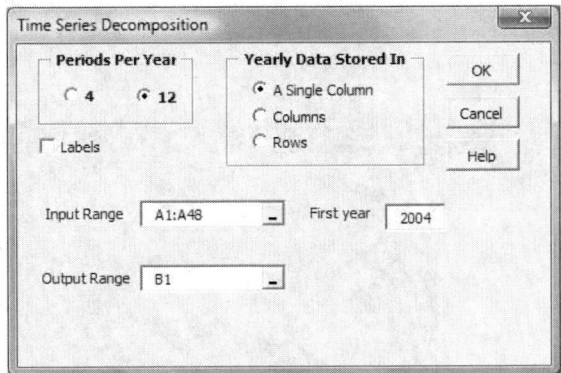

Simple Exponential Smoothing

To use the simple exponential smoothing procedure, click on **KPK Data Analysis ➤ Time Series Analysis ➤ Forecasting** to display the **Time Series Forecasting** dialog box. For the attendance data used in Example 4.12, select **Simple Exponential Smoothing,** 0 for the **Number of Forecast Periods,** A1:A13 for the **Input Range,** B1 as the **Output Range,** and click on **Continue.** The **Input for Exponential Smoothing** dialog box will appear. Enter .1 in the box designated as **Values of Smoothing Constants** and select **Smoothing Constant(s) will be provided.** Click **OK** to obtain the output in Figure 4.30. Note that the **Time Series Forecasting** dialog box also provides options to obtain forecasting results for a model with a **Trend Only** or **Trend With Seasonality.** Excel does have a built-in exponential smoothing procedure, which may be used as well. Click on **Tools ➤ Data Analysis ➤ Exponential Smoothing.** In the resulting dialog box, the damping factor is the same as the smoothing constant for simple exponential smoothing.

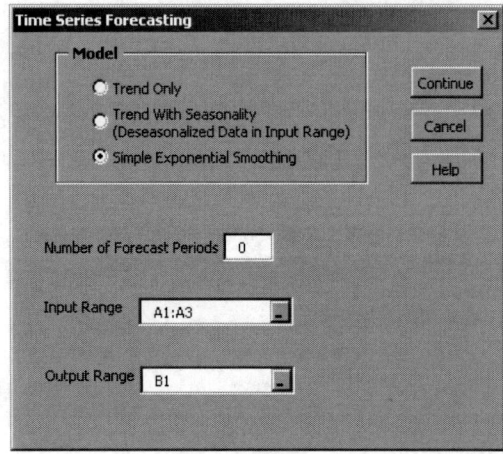

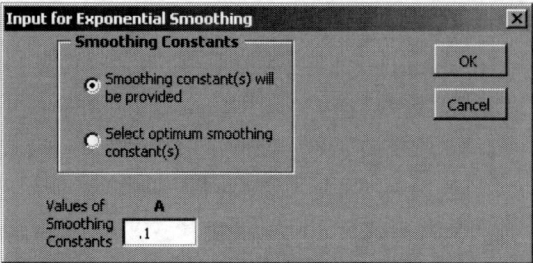

MINITAB

Time Series Decomposition

MINITAB uses a different procedure than the Excel KPK macros or SPSS to determine the trend and seasonal components. Also, it does not determine a cyclical component in the decomposition of a time series. The **Decomposition** dialog box is obtained by clicking on **Stat ➤ Time Series ➤ Decomposition.** For the monthly retail data in Example 4.9, select **Sales** (in column C1) for **Variable, 12** for **Seasonal length, Multiplicative** for **Model Type,** and **Trend plus seasonal** for **Model Components. Time** may be clicked to use a time variable. Click on **Options** to center a **Title.** Also, in the **Options** dialog box, since the observations start in period 1, into the **First obs. is in seasonal period** box. Click on **Storage** to store the components of the decomposition. To display either a **Summary table,** a **Summary table and results table,** or **Display nothing,** click on **Results.** Click on **OK** to display the output.

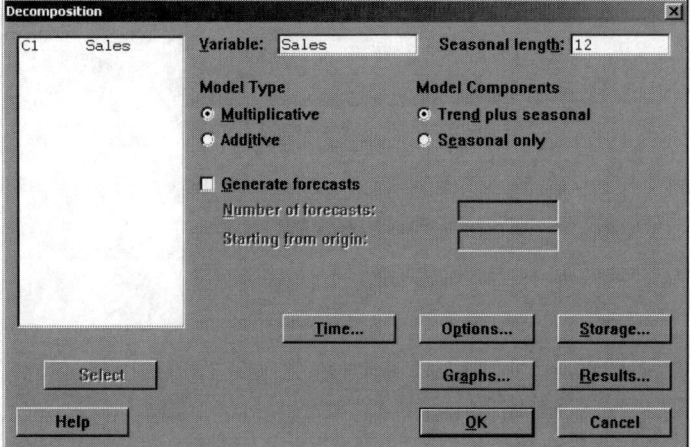

Simple Exponential Smoothing

To use the simple exponential smoothing procedure in Minitab, click on **Stat ➤ Time Series ➤ Single Exp Smoothing.** For the attendance data used in Example 4.12, select the **Variable** from the columns in which the data are stored. Enter .1 in the **Use** input box. The buttons on the **Single Exponential Smoothing** dialog box function similar to those on the **Decomposition** dialog box.

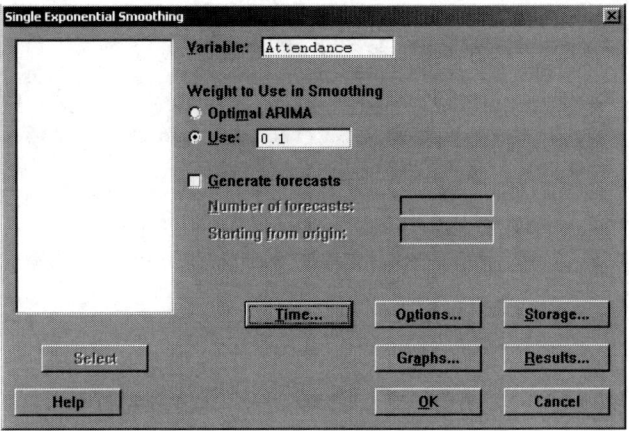

SPSS

Time Series Decomposition

The time series decomposition procedure used by SPSS will be illustrated using the U.S. monthly retail data discussed in Example 4.9. Enter the data in the first column and name this variable data. Click on **Data ➤ Define Dates ➤ Year, months.** Enter 2004 in the **Year** box and click on **OK.** This will create three additional columns, as shown.

Data	YEAR_	MONTH	DATE_
134.74	2004	1	JAN 2004
130.26	2004	2	FEB 2004
148.50	2004	3	MAR 2004
145.70	2004	4	APR 2004
156.60	2004	5	MAY 2004
150.92	2004	6	JUN 2004
153.20	2004	7	JUL 2004
156.78	2004	8	AUG 2004

Click on **Analyze ➤ Time Series ➤ Seasonal Decomposition.** Move the data variable into the **Variable(s)** box and click on **OK** to obtain the output. SPSS calculates the seasonal indexes in a slightly different manner from KPK Macros. Consequently, the values differ slightly from those displayed in Example 4.9. Four additional columns are created in the data window as a result of this procedure. The irregular/noise components (I_t) are contained in the err_1 column. The seasonal components (S_t) are in the saf_1 column. The deseasonalized values (y_t/S_t) are in the sas_1 column. SPSS does not separate out the trend and cyclical components. Rather, column stc_1 contains the $TR_t \times C_t$ components. Consequently, each y_t value is the product of the corresponding values in the stc_1, saf_1, and err_1 columns.

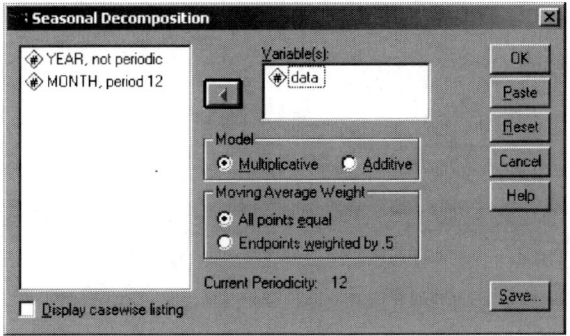

Simple Exponential Smoothing

Click on **Analyze ➤ Time Series ➤ Exponential Smoothing** to obtain the **Exponential Smoothing** dialog box in SPSS. For the attendance data used in Example 4.12, enter the column variable with the attendance data into **Variables** and click on **Simple.** Click on **Parameters** to obtain the **Exponential Smoothing: Parameters** dialog box. Enter .1 for the **Value** under **General (Alpha)** and click on **Automatic** to have SPSS select the starting value. The initial starting value for the **Automatic** option is the average of the time series values. After clicking on **Continue** and **OK,** two additional columns, FIT_1 and ERR_1, will appear in the SPSS Data Editor, displaying the forecasting results.

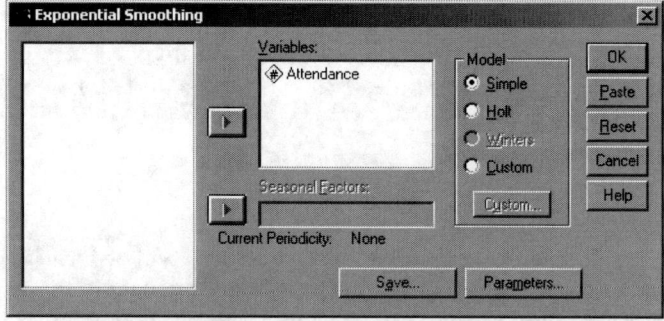

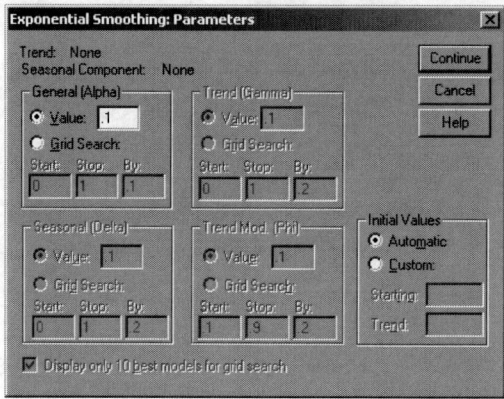

chapter 5

Probability Concepts

Statistics in Action
Cable and DSL Connections: Wired for Speed

With high-speed Internet connections, users can watch video online or download software and other data-rich files in a matter of seconds. In addition to offering speed, broadband access provides a continuous "always on" connection (no need to dial-up) and a "two-way" capability to both receive (download) and transmit (upload) data at high speeds. One high-speed Internet application that has held considerable promise is video-on-demand services. Five major Hollywood studios—MGM Home Entertainment Group, Paramount Pictures, Sony Pictures Entertainment, Universal Studios and Warner Bros.—announced plans in August 2001 to deliver this service.

In 2001, high-speed Internet connections were still a small proportion, at about 8 million or 12% of all ISP subscribers. However, in large metropolitan areas such as Boston, Dallas, Los Angeles, and New York, the percent of Internet subscribers connected to high-speed Internet technology is approximately 25%. It is exciting that there are all kinds of new and amazing Web technologies.

Research firms are forecasting that cable modem and Digital Subscriber Line (DSL) use is expected to grow steadily over the next five years. They differ on whether cable or DSL will maintain the greatest share. The growth will be driven largely by a range of widely available technologies, as well as by content and services.

Research firms believe that the future of high-speed Internet access is full of uncertainty, as competing companies and industries try to anticipate technological advances, market conditions, consumer preferences, and even cultural and societal trends. When you have completed this chapter, you will be able to examine the market for broadband Internet and discuss such questions as

- How can market share be understood in terms of probabilities?

- What is the probability that a high-speed Internet consumer will select cable or DSL?

- How can the probability that a high-speed Internet consumer makes a monthly purchase online be revised if the type of connection that the consumer purchased is known?

179

5.1   EVENTS AND PROBABILITY

An activity for which the outcome is uncertain is an **experiment.** An experiment need not involve mixing chemicals in the laboratory; it could be as simple as throwing two dice and observing the total of the faces turned up. At the completion of an experiment, a measurement of some kind is obtained. An **event** consists of one or more possible outcomes of the experiment; it is usually denoted by a capital letter.* The following are examples of experiments and some corresponding events:

- *Experiment:* Rolling two dice; *events:* A = rolling a total of 7, B = rolling a total greater than 8, C = rolling two 4s.

- *Experiment:* Taking a CPA exam; *events:* A = pass, B = fail.

- *Experiment:* Observing the number of arrivals at a drive-up window over a 5-minute period; *events:* A_0 = no arrivals, A_1 = one arrival, A_2 = two arrivals, and so on.

When you estimate a **probability,** you are estimating the probability *of an event.* For example, when rolling two dice, the probability that you will roll a total of 7 (event A) is the probability that event A occurs. It is written **$P(A)$.** The probability of any event is always between 0 and 1, inclusive.

NOTATION

$P(A)$ = probability that event A occurs

Classical Definition of Probability

Suppose a particular experiment has n possible outcomes and event A occurs in m of the n outcomes. The **classical definition** of the probability that event A will occur is

$$P(A) = m/n$$

5.1

This definition assumes that all n possible outcomes have the same chance for occurring. Such outcomes (events) are said to be **equally likely,** and each has probability $1/n$ of occurring. If this is not the case, the classical definition does not apply.

Consider the experiment of tossing a nickel and a dime into the air and observing how they fall. Event A is observing one head and one tail. The possible outcomes are (H = head, T = tail):

Nickel	Dime
H	H
H	T
T	H
T	T

Thus, there are two (m = 2) outcomes that constitute event A of the four possible outcomes (n = 4). These four outcomes are equally likely, so each occurs with probability 1/4. Consequently,

$$P(A) = 2/4 = .5$$

---

*The set of all possible outcomes of an experiment is often referred to as the *sample space.*

Relative Frequency Approach

Another method of estimating a probability is referred to as the **relative frequency** approach. It is based on observing the experiment n times and counting the number of times an event (say, A) occurs. If event A occurs m times, your estimate of the probability that A will occur in the future is

$$P(A) = m/n$$

5.2

Suppose that a particular production process has been in operation for 250 days; 220 days have been accident-free. Let A = a randomly chosen day in the future is free of accidents. Using the relative frequency definition, then

$$P(A) = 220/250 = .88$$

Subjective Probability

Another type of probability is **subjective probability.** It is a measure (between 0 and 1) of your belief that a particular event will occur. A value of one indicates that you believe this event will occur with complete certainty.

Examples of situations requiring a subjective probability follow:

• The probability that the Dow Jones closing index will be below 8500 at some time during the next 6 months.

• The probability that your newly introduced product will capture at least 10% of the market.

• The probability that an audited voucher will contain an error.

• The probability that your recently married cousin, divorced five times already, will once again go down alimony lane.

Although no two people may agree on a particular subjective probability, these probabilities are governed by the same rules of probability, which are developed later in the chapter.

5.2

BASIC CONCEPTS

Datacomp recently conducted a survey of 200 selected purchasers of their newly introduced laptop computer to obtain a gender-and-age profile of its new customers. A summary by gender revealed

Class	Frequency
Male	120
Female	80
	200

and a summary by age resulted in the following frequency distribution (note that 30–45 includes the 30 and 45 year olds):

Class	Frequency
Under 30	100
30–45	50
Over 45	50
	200

TABLE

5.1

Datacomp survey
of microcomputer
purchasers.

| | Age (Years) | | | |
Sex	< 30 (U)	30–45 (B)	> 45 (O)	Total
Male (M)	60	20	40	120
Female (F)	40	30	10	80
Total	100	50	50	200

These two categories (gender and age) can be summarized *together* in a **contingency,** or **cross-tab, table,** shown in Table 5.1. The numbers within the table represent the frequency, or number of individuals, within each pair of subcategories, and so the contingency table allows you to see how these two categories interact.

There are 60 purchasers who are male *and* under 30; 10 purchasers are female *and* over 45. One person from the total group of 200 is to be selected at random to receive a free software package. We can define the following events:

$$M = \text{a male is selected}$$

$$F = \text{a female is selected}$$

$$U = \text{the person selected is under 30}$$

$$B = \text{the person selected is between 30 and 45}$$

$$O = \text{the person selected is over 45}$$

Because there are 200 people, there are 200 possible outcomes to this experiment. All 200 outcomes are equally likely (the person is randomly selected), so the classical definition proves an easy way of determining probabilities.

Marginal Probability

The probability of any one single event used to define the contingency table is a **marginal probability.** When you use a contingency table, you can obtain the marginal probabilities by merely counting. For example, of the 200 purchasers, 120 are males. So the probability of selecting a male is

$$P(M) = 120/200 = .6$$

Similarly,

$$P(F) = 80/200 = .4$$

$$P(U) = .5$$

$$P(B) = .25$$

$$P(O) = .25$$

Notice that $P(O) = 50/200 = .25$, which implies that (1) if you repeatedly selected a person at random from this group, 25% of the time the person selected would be over 45 years of age, and (2) 25% of the people in this group are over 45 years old. So a probability here is simply a *proportion*.

The **complement** of an event A is the event that A does *not* occur. This event is denoted by $\bar{A}$. For example, A = it rains tomorrow, $\bar{A}$ = it does not rain tomorrow; or A = stock market rises tomorrow, $\bar{A}$ = stock market does not rise tomorrow.

In our Datacomp survey, $P(M) = .6$, and so

$$P(\bar{M}) = P(F) = .4$$

Notice that $P(M) + P(\bar{M}) = .6 + .4 = 1.0$. In general, for any event A, either A or $\bar{A}$ must occur. Consequently,

$$P(A) + P(\bar{A}) = 1$$

and so

$$P(\bar{A}) = 1 - P(A)$$

Written another way,

$$P(A) = 1 - P(\bar{A})$$

How can we determine what proportion of the purchasers are age 45 or younger?

$$P(\bar{O}) = 1 - P(O) = 1 - .25 = .75$$

Joint Probability

What if we wish to know the probability of selecting a purchaser who is female *and* under age 30? Such a person is selected if events F *and* U occur. This probability is written $P(F$ and $U)$ and is referred to as a **joint probability.**[*] There are 40 purchasers who are female and under 30, so

$$P(F \text{ and } U) = 40/200 = .2$$

What proportion are males between 30 and 45? This is the same as

$$P(M \text{ and } B) = 20/200 = .1$$

because 20 out of 200 satisfy both requirements.

Probability of A or B

In addition to calculating joint probabilities involving two events, we can also determine the probability that *either* of the two events will occur. In our discussion, "either A or B" will refer to the event that A occurred, B occurred, or both occurred. This probability is written as

$$P(A \text{ or } B)$$

for any two events A and B.[†]

Now we will calculate the probability of selecting someone who is a male *or* under 30 years of age. This is $P(M$ or $U)$. How many people qualify? There are 120 males and there are 100 people under 30. Is the answer $(120 + 100)/200 = 1.1$? You should realize that

---

[*]The joint probability of events A and B is often written as $P(A \cap B)$, read as "the probability of A intersect B."
[†]The probability $P(A$ or $B)$ can be written as $P(A \cup B)$, read as "the probability of A union B."

this is not correct, because *a probability is never greater than 1.* What is the mistake here? The problem is that the 60 males under age 30 were counted *twice.* How many purchasers are male or under 30? The answer is the 120 males plus the 40 females under age 30. So

$$P(M \text{ or } U) = (120 + 40)/200 = .8$$

What is *P(F or B)?* In Table 5.1, the 80 females and 20 of the males qualify. So,

$$P(F \text{ or } B) = (80 + 20)/200 = .5$$

Conditional Probability

Suppose that someone has some inside information about who has been selected from the group of 200 purchasers. This person informs you that the selected individual is under 30 years of age; that is, event U occurred. Armed with this information, we can calculate the probability that the selected person is a male. Given that event U occurred, we have immediately narrowed the number of possible outcomes from 200 to the 100 people under age 30. Each of these 100 people is equally likely to be chosen, and 60 of them are male. So the answer is $60/100 = .6$.

Whenever you are given information and are asked to find a probability based on this information, the result is a **conditional probability.** This probability is written as

$$P(A \mid B)$$

where B is the event that you know occurred and A is the uncertain event whose probability you need, given that event B has occurred. The vertical line indicates that the occurrence of event B is given, so the expression is read as the "probability of A given B." In the example, $P(M \mid U) = .6$.

Suppose that you were given *no information* about U and were asked to find the probability that a male is selected. This is a marginal probability. We earlier determined that $P(M) = .6$. For our example, note that

$$P(M) = P(M \mid U) = .6$$

This means that being given the information that the person selected is under 30 has *no effect* on the probability that a male is selected. In other words, whether U happens has no effect on whether M occurs. Such events are said to be independent. *Thus, events* A *and* B *are independent if the probability of event* A *is unaffected by the occurrence or nonoccurrence of event* B.

There are a number of ways to demonstrate that any two events A and B are independent.

DEFINITION

Events A and B are **independent** if and only if:
1. $P(A \mid B) = P(A)$ (assuming $P(B) \neq 0$), or
2. $P(B \mid A) = P(B)$ (assuming $P(A) \neq 0$), or
3. $P(A \text{ and } B) = P(A) \cdot P(B)$.

5.3 5.4 5.5

You need not demonstrate all three conditions. If one of the equations is true, they are all true; if one is false, they are all false (in which case A and B are not independent). Events that are not independent are **dependent** events.

In our example, are events F and O independent? We previously showed that

$$P(O) = 50/200 = .25$$

Since $P(O|F) = 10/80 = .125$ then $P(O) \neq P(O|F)$ and these events are dependent. Put another way, if someone informs you that event F (a female) has occurred, this *does* have an effect on whether the person selected is over 45 years of age. If you are told that F occurred, the probability that the selected person is over 45 *drops* from .25 to .125. These events do affect each other and so are dependent events.

We could also approach this by showing that $P(F|O)$ is not the same as $P(F)$:

$$P(F|O) = 10/50 = .2$$
$$P(F) = 80/200 = .4$$

These are not the same values, so events F and O are not independent.

The final option is to show that $P(F \text{ and } O)$ is not the same as $P(F) \cdot P(O)$. This follows because

$$P(F \text{ and } O) = 10/200 = .05$$
$$P(F) \cdot P(O) = (.4)(.25) = .1$$

In our discussion of joint probabilities, we showed that

$$P(F \text{ and } U) = 40/200 = .2$$

Consequently, events F and U *can both occur* because their joint probability is not zero.

How would you calculate $P(F \text{ and } M)$? One cannot be both a male and a female, so $P(F \text{ and } M) = 0$. Because events M and F cannot both occur, these events are said to be *mutually exclusive*.

DEFINITION

Events A and B are **mutually exclusive** if A and B cannot both occur simultaneously. To demonstrate that two events A and B are mutually exclusive, you must show that their joint probability is zero: $P(A \text{ and } B) = 0$.

EXAMPLE 5.1

The quality-improvement department of Lectron has selected 10 devices for testing purposes. Which of these outcomes are mutually exclusive?

A = exactly one device is defective

B = more than two devices are defective

C = fewer than four devices are defective

Solution

A and B are mutually exclusive events—they cannot both occur.
A and C are *not* mutually exclusive—if A occurs, so does event C.
B and C are *not* mutually exclusive—if three devices are defective, both events B and C will occur.

By *not mutually exclusive,* we do not mean that both of these events *must* occur, only that both *could* occur. Also, be sure to distinguish between the terms *mutually exclusive* and *independent.* Loosely, mutually exclusive means that they cannot both occur and independent means that one event occurring has no effect on the other. For example, when drawing a single card from a deck of 52 playing cards, the events K = drawing a king and H = drawing a heart are *not* mutually exclusive since they can both occur, namely when drawing the king of hearts. However, they *are* independent, since $P(K) = 4/52 = 1/13$

(there are four kings out of 52 cards), and $P(K|H) = 1/13$ (there are 13 hearts and one of them is a king). Consequently, knowing that a heart was selected has *no effect* on whether this card was a king, and so these events are independent.

SUMMARY OF PROBABILITY DEFINITIONS

1. *Experiment.* An experiment is any process that yields a measurement (observation).
2. *Outcome.* An outcome is any particular result of an experiment.
3. *Event.* An event consists of one or more possible outcomes of an experiment.
4. *Complement.* The complement of event A is the event that A does not occur. This is written $\bar{A}$
5. *Mutually exclusive events.* Two events are mutually exclusive if they cannot both occur simultaneously.
6. *Independent events.* Two events are independent if the probability of one event occurring is unaffected by the occurrence or nonoccurrence of the other.
7. *Probability.* A probability is a measure of the likelihood that an event will occur when the experiment is performed.
8. *Marginal probability.* A marginal probability is the probability that any one single event used to define a contingency table will occur.
9. *Joint probability.* The joint probability of events A and B is the probability that both A and B will occur. This is written as $P(A \text{ and } B)$.
10. *Conditional probability.* The conditional probability of A given B is the probability that event A occurs given that event B occurs. This is written $P(A|B)$.

X Exercises 5.1–5.15

Understanding the Mechanics

5.1 Assume that there are only four distinct possible outcomes in an experiment: A, B, C, and D. Explain what is incorrect about each of the following sets of assigned probabilities.
  a. $P(A) = .25$ $P(B) = 1.25$ $P(C) = .50$ $P(D) = .25$
  b. $P(A) = .15$ $P(B) = .01$ $P(C) = .01$ $P(D) = .01$
  c. $P(A) = .40$ $P(B) = .40$ $P(C) = .40$ $P(D) = .40$

5.2 Consider an experiment of randomly selecting a card from a deck of 52 cards.
  a. What is the probability of selecting a queen?
  b. What is the probability of not selecting a queen?
  c. What is the probability of selecting the queen of hearts?
  d. Is the event of selecting a queen mutually exclusive from the event of selecting a heart?

5.3 Let A and B be two events such that $P(A \text{ or } B) = .60$, $P(A \text{ and } B) = .10$, $P(A|B) = .25$, $P(B|A) = .333$, $P(\bar{A}) = .70$, and $P(\bar{B}) = .60$.
  a. What is the joint probability of events A and B?
  b. What is the probability of event A conditioned on the occurrence of event B?

  c. What is the probability of either event A or event B occurring?
  d. What is the probability that event A does *not* occur?

5.4 The probability of A occurring is .3 and the probability of B occurring is .5.
  a. What is the probability of both A and B occurring if A and B are mutually exclusive?
  b. What is the probability of A occurring given that B is known to occur if A and B are independent?
  c. What is the probability of B occurring given that A is known to occur if A and B are independent?

Applying the New Concepts

5.5 Let A represent freshmen and B represent both juniors and seniors at a community college with various undergraduate programs. Are A and B mutually exclusive? What is the complement of A? Are the complement of A and the complement of B mutually exclusive?

5.6 Four hundred randomly sampled automobile owners were asked whether they selected the particular make and model of their present car mainly because of its appearance or because of its performance. The results were as follows:

Owner	Appearance	Performance	Totals
Male	95	55	150
Female	85	165	250

a. What is the probability that an automobile owner buys a car mainly for its appearance?

b. What is the probability that an automobile owner buys a car mainly for its appearance and the automobile owner is a male?

c. What is the probability that a female automobile owner purchases the car mainly because of its appearance?

5.7 A quality-control engineer summarized the frequency of the type of defect with the manufacturing of a certain motor. The following table shows which of three shifts was responsible for the type of defect.

Type of Defect

Shift	Misaligned Component	Missing Component	Measurement Outside of Specification Limits	Other	Total
1	23	13	12	14	62
2	15	15	18	12	60
3	5	11	10	2	28

a. What is the probability that a defective motor will have a measurement outside of its specification limits?

b. What is the probability that a defective motor was not produced by Shift 1?

c. What is the probability that a defective motor produced by Shift 3 does not have a misaligned component?

d. What is the probability that a defective motor has a misaligned component or was produced by Shift 1?

5.8 The employment center at a university wanted to know the proportion of students who worked and also the proportion of those who lived in the dorm. The following data were collected:

Work Situation

Living Arrangements	Full Time	Part Time	Do not Work	Total
In dorm	19	22	20	61
Not in dorm	25	9	5	39
				100

a. What is the probability of selecting a student at random who works either full or part time?

b. What is the probability that a student who works lives in the dorm?

c. What is the probability that a student either works full time or does not live in the dorm?

d. Is the event that a student lives in the dorm independent of the event that a student works full time? Discuss what your answer means.

5.9 An investment newsletter writer wanted to know in which investment areas her subscribers were most interested. A questionnaire was sent to 331 randomly selected professional clients, with the following results:

Investment Area

Business	Stocks	Bonds	Commercial Paper	Commodities	Stock Options	Total
Doctors	30	25	15	2	0	72
Lawyers	29	34	12	0	5	80
Bankers	50	35	29	5	10	129
Others	21	14	10	3	2	50
						331

a. What is the probability that an investment client is neither a doctor nor a lawyer?

b. What is the probability that an investment client is a banker and that the investment client's main investment interest is in commodities?

c. If an investment client's main investment interest is commodities, what is the probability that he or she is a banker?

d. What is the probability that an investment client's main investment interest is not in stock options?

e. Let A be the event that an investment client is a lawyer. Let B be the event that an investment client's main investment interest is in commodities. Are the events A and B mutually exclusive?

5.10 If events A and B are mutually exclusive, is the occurrence of event A affected by the occurrence of event B? Can one say that if two events are mutually exclusive, they are not independent?

5.11 Computer-controlled cameras are being used experimentally to ticket automobile drivers for speeding and running red lights. These devices are operated by private firms and have an incentive to pull in as many drivers as they can. Although approximately 70% of the motorists stoically accept and pay these tickets, others resent this procedure and fight the tickets. Assume that the actions of 200 motorists who received a ticket from a computer-controlled camera produced the following results.

Traffic Violation	Pay Ticket	Fight Ticket
Run Red Light	40	20
Speeding	100	40

a. What is the probability of selecting a person at random who receives a speeding ticket?

b. What is the probability or selecting a person at random who receives a speeding ticket and fights the ticket?

c. What is the probability that a person, selected at random, either receives a speeding ticket or pays for the traffic violation ticket?

d. What is the probability that a person, selected at random, does not run a red light and does not fight the traffic violation ticket?

(Source: "Speeders, Say Cheese," *Time*, vol. 158, no. 11, September 17, 2001, p. 32.)

5.12 In Exercise 5.11, list two events that are not independent. Explain.

5.13 In Exercise 5.11, list events that have a joint probability of zero. List a combination of events that have an "or" probability equal to one.

5.14 Public confidence in charitable groups is roughly 10 percentage points lower today than it was in the 2001. Assume that the following table represents a survey of 100 charitable donors. These donors indicated whether their confidence in charitable groups was high or low.

	Have High Confidence	Have Low Confidence
Male	13	25
Female	20	42

a. What is the probability that a charitable donor was a male who had high confidence or a female that had low confidence?

b. What is the probability that a female charitable donor has high confidence?

c. What is the probability that a charitable donor who had low confidence was a female?

(Source: "Public Confidence in Charitable Groups Sags," *The Wall Street Journal*, Sep 14, 2004, p. D2)

5.15 Employers have expanded benefits for workers over the past several years to make recruiting easier and to increase morale. Among the benefits have been full or partial school tuition reimbursement and up to three months leave of absence unrelated to the Family Medical and Leave Act. The following table illustrates employee benefit programs provided by 200 randomly selected companies.

	At Least 3 Months of Leave Allowed	Less than 3 Months of Leave Allowed
No Tuition Reimbursement	10	15
Partial Tuition Reimbursement	60	50
Full Tuition Reimbursement	50	15

a. What is the probability that a company will offer partial or full tuition reimbursement?

b. What is the probability that a company will not offer full tuition reimbursement and will offer at least three months of leave?

c. What is the probability that a company that allows at least three months of leave will provide partial or full tuition reimbursement?

d. Are the events of no tuition reimbursement and at least three months of leave allowed mutually exclusive? If not, what would have to occur to make them mutually exclusive?

(Source: "Employers Expand Benefits," *USA Today*, June 28, 2001, p. 1B.)

5.3 GOING BEYOND THE CONTINGENCY TABLE

Our Datacomp survey served as an intuitive introduction to probability definitions. The classical approach was used to derive probabilities by dividing the number of outcomes favorable to an event by the total number of (equally likely) outcomes. Not all probability problems, however, are concerned with randomly selecting an individual from a contingency table.

When dealing with two or more events in general, one approach is to illustrate these events by means of a **Venn diagram.** A Venn diagram representing any two events A and B is shown in Figure 5.1.

In a Venn diagram, the probability of an event occurring is its corresponding area. This might sound complicated, but it really is not. The Venn diagram for $P(A) = .4$ is shown in Figure 5.2(a). The area of the rectangle is 1; it represents all possible outcomes. The shaded area is the complement of A, namely, $\bar{A}$. Here, $P(\bar{A}) = 1 - P(A) = 1 - .4 = .6$. No effort is made to construct a circle with an area of .4; it is simply labeled .4. The shaded area then represents $\bar{A}$, and the corresponding area must be .6.

Figure 5.2(b) shows $P(A \text{ and } B)$, and Figure 5.3(a) shows $P(A \text{ or } B)$.

If A and B are mutually exclusive (they cannot both occur), then $P(A \text{ and } B) = 0$. For example, an auto dealer has data that indicate that 20% of all new cars ordered contain a red interior and 25% have a blue interior. Only one interior color is allowed. Let A be the event that a red interior is selected and B be the event that a blue interior is selected. A Venn diagram for this situation is shown in Figure 5.3(b).

FIGURE

5.1

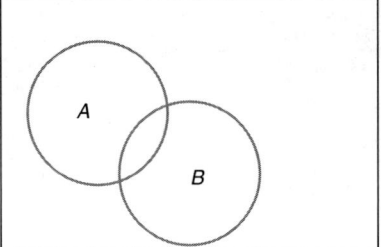

Venn diagram for events *A* and *B*. The rectangle represents all possible outcomes of an experiment.

FIGURE

5.2

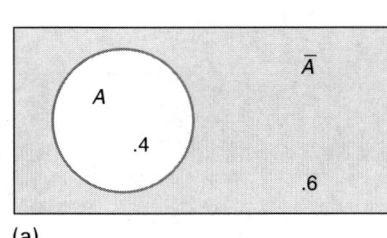

(a)

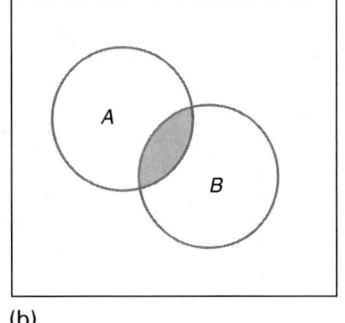

(b)

(a) Venn diagram for *P(A)* = .4. (b) *P(A and B)*. The points in the shaded area are in *A* and *B*.

FIGURE

5.3

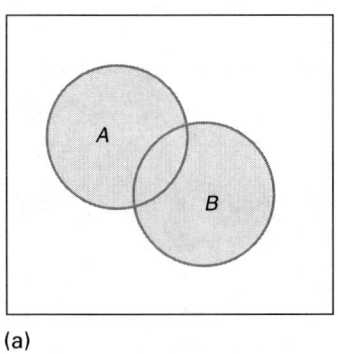

(a)

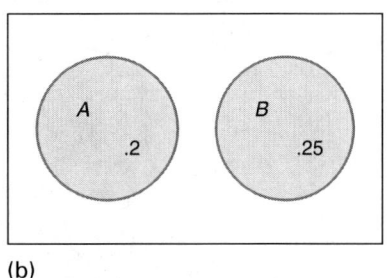

(b)

(a) *P(A or B)*. The points in the shaded area are in *A* or *B*. (b) Venn diagram of mutually exclusive events. *P(A and B)* = 0. *P(A or B)* = *P(A)* + *P(B)* = .2 + .25 = .45.

Each person can select only one color, so events *A* and *B* are mutually exclusive, and the resulting circles do not overlap in the Venn diagram. What is the probability that a person selects red *or* blue? This is *P(A or B)* and is represented by the shaded area in the circles in Figure 5.3(b). The Venn diagram allows us to see clearly that this shaded area is *P(A)* + *P(B)* = .2 + .25 = .45. In other words, 45% of the people will purchase either red or blue interiors. We thus have the following rule.

SPECIAL CASE

If events *A* and *B* are *mutually exclusive,* then
$$P(A \text{ or } B) = P(A) + P(B)$$

4.6

FIGURE

5.4

$P(Q) = 4/52; P(H) = 13/52.$

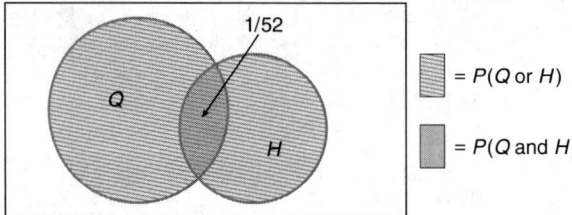

This rule does *not* work when A and B can both occur, but there is an easy way to devise another solution. By adding $P(A) + P(B)$, we do not obtain $P(A \text{ or } B)$ because we have counted $P(A \text{ and } B)$ *twice*. So we need to subtract $P(A \text{ and } B)$ to obtain the actual area corresponding to $P(A \text{ or } B)$. This is the **additive rule of probability.**

ADDITIVE RULE

For *any* two events, A and B,
$$P(A \text{ or } B) = P(A) + P(B) - P(A \text{ and } B)$$

5.7

Notice that if A and B are mutually exclusive, then $P(A \text{ and } B) = 0$, and we obtain the previous rule; namely, that $P(A \text{ or } B) = P(A) + P(B)$.

E X A M P L E

5.2

Draw a single card from a deck of 52 playing cards. Let Q be the event that the card is a queen and H be the event that the card is a heart. What is $P(Q \text{ or } H)$?

Solution

First, determine $P(Q \text{ and } H)$. $P(Q \text{ and } H)$ is the probability of selecting a queen of hearts from the deck. There is only one such card, so

$$P(Q \text{ and } H) = 1/52$$

A Venn diagram for this situation is shown in Figure 5.4. Using the additive rule, the proportion of draws (probability) on which a queen *or* a heart will be selected from the deck is

$$P(Q \text{ or } H) = P(Q) + P(H) - P(Q \text{ and } H)$$
$$= 4/52 + 13/52 - 1/52$$
$$= 16/52$$

Refer back to the Datacomp survey data in Table 5.1. Does the additive rule work here also? It does—this rule works for *any* two events—but it certainly is a hard way to solve this problem. Suppose we want to find the probability (from our previous example) that the person selected is a male or is under age 30. By inspection, we previously found that

$$P(M \text{ or } U) = 160/200 = .8$$

FIGURE

5.5

A Venn diagram illustrating a conditional probability.

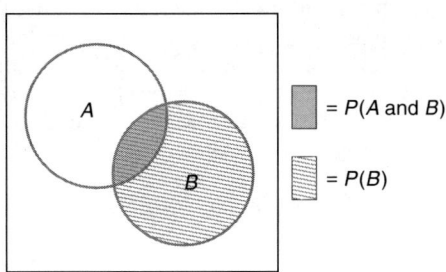

Using the additive rule, we obtain the same result:

$$P(M \text{ or } U) = P(M) + P(U) - P(M \text{ and } U)$$

$$= 120/200 + 100/200 - 60/200$$

$$= 160/200 = .8$$

Rules for Conditional Probabilities

Using the Datacomp survey data, we found that the probability the person selected is a male *(M)*, given the information that the person selected is under 30 *(U)*, was $(M \mid U) = .6$. Our reasoning here was: (1) There are 100 people under 30 years of age, (2) 60 of them are male, (3) each of these 100 people is equally likely to be selected, and so (4) the result is $60/100 = .6$. Notice that

$$P(U) = 100/200 = .5$$

$$P(M \text{ and } U) = 60/200 = .3$$

$$P(M \mid U) = P(M \text{ and } U)/P(U) = .3/.5 = .6$$

This procedure for finding a conditional probability applies to *any* two events. Use the Venn diagram in Figure 5.5 to determine $P(A \mid B)$. Given the information that event *B* occurred, we are immediately restricted to the lined area *(B)*. What is the probability that a point in *B* is also in *A* (that is, event *A* occurs)? A point is also in *A* if it lies in the shaded area, and

$$P(A \mid B) = \frac{\text{shaded area}}{\text{striped area}}$$

$$= \frac{P(A \text{ and } B)}{P(B)}$$

This is the rule for conditional probabilities.

RULE FOR CONDITIONAL PROBABILITIES

For any two events, *A* and *B*,

$$P(A \mid B) = \frac{P(A \text{ and } B)}{P(B)} \qquad (P(B) \neq 0) \qquad 5.8$$

and

$$P(B \mid A) = \frac{P(A \text{ and } B)}{P(A)} \qquad (P(A) \neq 0) \qquad 5.9$$

Independent Events

In the Datacomp example, equations 5.3, 5.4, and 5.5 provided a summary of how to demonstrate that two events are independent. One need demonstrate only that one of these equations holds to verify independence. These three methods of proving independence apply to *any two events*, not just to contingency table applications.

To summarize, events A and B are *independent* if any of the following statements can be verified:

$$P(A \mid B) = P(A)$$
$$P(B \mid A) = P(B)$$
$$P(A \text{ and } B) = P(A) \cdot P(B)$$

In many situations, it is unnecessary (or impossible) to prove independence of two events. However, one can often argue convincingly that two events are independent or dependent without resorting to a mathematical proof. Consider these events:

A = Procter & Gamble's new laundry detergent will capture at least 5% of the market next year

and

B = General Motors will introduce a new line of compact automobiles next year

Whether event B happens should have no effect on whether event A occurs. So $P(A \mid B) = P(A)$, and these events are independent. Next, change event A to: Toyota automobile sales will drop next year. Now whether event B occurs could very well have an effect on whether event A occurs. It is not safe to assume that $P(A \mid B) = P(A)$—it seems reasonable that $P(A \mid B)$ is *larger* than $P(A)$. Notice that we have not discussed the values of $P(A)$ and $P(A \mid B)$. The probability values are not necessary to show that the events are dependent. The important thing is that $P(A \mid B) \neq P(A)$, so these events are clearly dependent events.

Multiplicative Rule

The rule for conditional probabilities in equations 5.8 and 5.9 can be rewritten as

MULTIPLICATIVE RULE

For any two events A and B,
$$P(A \text{ and } B) = P(A \mid B) \cdot P(B)$$

5.10 5.11

This is the **multiplicative rule of probability.** Using equation 5.5, we also have the following rule for two independent events.

SPECIAL CASE

For any two independent events A and B,
$$P(A \text{ and } B) = P(A) \cdot P(B)$$

5.12

You may be wondering how we can use the same equation to define the rule for $P(A \mid B)$ (equation 5.8) and the rule for $P(A$ and $B)$ (equation 5.10). This is not a bad question! It appears that we have used the same rule twice to make two different statements—and, in fact, we have. However, for any application you encounter, either $P(A \mid B)$ or $P(A$ and $B)$ must be provided or can be determined without resorting to formulas. We can clarify this using our card-drawing example:

$$Q = \text{select a queen}$$

$$H = \text{select a heart}$$

Here $P(Q$ and $H)$ (the probability of selecting a queen of hearts) is 1/52. No formulas were necessary to determine this, only a little head scratching.

Now, what is $P(Q \mid H)$? Using equation 5.8,

$$P(Q \mid H) = P(Q \text{ and } H)/P(H)$$

$$= (1/52)/(13/52)$$

$$= 1/13$$

Replacement in Sampling

Assume that you select a card from a deck, examine it, and then discard it. You then select another card. This procedure is called *sampling without replacement.* Let

$$A = \text{selecting a queen on the first draw}$$

$$B = \text{selecting a queen on the second draw}$$

What is the probability of drawing two queens [$P(A$ and $B)$]? If you selected a queen on the first draw, then, of the 51 cards remaining, three are queens. So $P(B \mid A) = 3/51$. Again, we used no formulas.

Next, we use the multiplicative rule, equation 5.11:

$$P(A \text{ and } B) = P(B \mid A) \cdot P(A)$$

$$= \left(\frac{3}{51}\right) \cdot \left(\frac{4}{52}\right) \cong .0045$$

Notice that $P(A) = 4/52$ because there are four queens available on the first draw. So you would expect to draw two queens from a card deck about 45 times out of 10,000, if you are drawing without replacement.

Now suppose you select a card from a deck but replace it before selecting the second card. This procedure is called *sampling with replacement.* What is $P(B \mid A)$? There are still 52 cards in the deck when you select your second card, and four of these are queens. So

$$P(B \mid A) = 4/52 = P(B)$$

If event A occurs, the probability of a queen on the second draw is unaffected. This probability is 4/52 *whether or not A* occurs; these events are now independent. For this situation,

$$P(A \text{ and } B) = P(A \mid B) \cdot P(B)$$

$$= P(A) \cdot P(B) \qquad \text{(since they are independent)}$$

$$= 4/52 \cdot 4/52 = .0059$$

The probability of getting two queens is higher when drawing cards with replacement—not a surprising result.

Using Statistical Software to Construct a Contingency Table

A quality engineer at Microtek obtained a random sample of 200 electrical components produced over a one-week period. Each component was inspected and classified as (1) OK, (2) OK after the component was reworked (repaired), or (3) scrap (unusable). The engineer also made note of which of the three Microtek plants produced the component: Memphis, Miami, or Pittsburgh. The sample information was stored in two columns in dataset DATA4-3, where

City = the city producing the component: 1 = Memphis
                                          2 = Miami
                                          3 = Pittsburgh

Quality = the component quality: 1 = OK
                                        2 = OK after rework
                                        3 = scrapped

Construct a contingency table. (i) If a component is selected at random, determine the probability that this component is OK and produced in Miami. (ii) What percentage of the reworked components in the sample were produced in Memphis?

Solution

The instructions for creating a contingency table for this example are contained in the end-of-chapter appendix. For the Excel output in Figure 5.6(a), the city names were entered in cells C4, C5, and C6 and the quality labels were entered in cells D3, E3, and F3. The MINITAB contingency table is shown in Figure 5.6(b). In each cell, the first value is the cell count, the second value is the row percentage, the third value is the column percentage, and the fourth value is the table percentage. To obtain the SPSS output in Figure 5.6(c), double-click somewhere inside the contingency table. Double-click on the **1** under CITY and the city name (Memphis) can be entered to replace this number. Repeat for the other two cities (Miami and Pittsburgh). Similarly, by double-clicking on the **1** under QUALITY, the word OK can be substituted for this number. This can be repeated for the other two QUALITY values (OK-Rework and Scrapped).

Solution to (i)

Thirty-five of the 200 components (in cell D5) are OK and produced in Miami, and so

$$P(\text{OK and Miami}) = 35/200 = .175$$

That is, 17.5% of the components are OK and produced in Miami.

Solution to (ii)

There are 50 reworked components in the sample, 15 of which were produced in Memphis. Consequently,

$$P(\text{Memphis}\mid\text{reworked}) = 15/50 = .3$$

That is, 30% of the reworked components were produced in Memphis.

5.4   APPLYING THE CONCEPTS

Thus far, we have described methods of solving probabilities for one or two events using formulas or contingency tables. This section will use the concepts discussed in Sections 5.2 and 5.3 to derive various probabilities. Here we are going to leave our Data-comp example to consider some other probabilities. Some examples will present more

5.6

(a) Excel contingency table for Example 5.3.
(b) MINITAB contingency table for Example 5.3.
(c) SPSS contingency table for Example 5.3.

	A	B	C	D	E	F	G	H
1	City	Quality	Contingency Table					
2	2	2		Quality				
3	1	1	City	OK	OK-Rework	Scrapped	Grand Total	
4	2	2	Memphis	60	15	5	80	
5	1	1	Miami	35	20	10	65	
6	2	3	Pittsburgh	25	15	15	55	
7	1	1	Grand Total	120	50	30	200	
8	2	2						
9	1	1						

DATA4-3

(a)

```
        Rows: City     Columns: Quality

                    1          2          3        All

         1         60         15          5         80
                75.00      18.75       6.25     100.00
                50.00      30.00      16.67      40.00
                30.00       7.50       2.50      40.00

         2         35         20         10         65
                53.85      30.77      15.38     100.00
                29.17      40.00      33.33      32.50
                17.50      10.00       5.00      32.50

         3         25         15         15         55
                45.45      27.27      27.27     100.00
                20.83      30.00      50.00      27.50
                12.50       7.50       7.50      27.50

       All        120         50         30        200
                60.00      25.00      15.00     100.00
               100.00     100.00     100.00     100.00
                60.00      25.00      15.00     100.00
```

(b)

CITY * QUALITY Crosstabulation
Count

		QUALITY			Total
		OK	OK-Rework	Scrapped	
CITY	Memphis	60	15	5	80
	Miami	35	20	10	65
	Pittsburgh	25	15	15	55
Total		120	50	30	200

(c)

than one solution to show how the problem can be solved using either formulas or contingency tables.

These examples are set up as word problems. *The most important step in solving a word probability problem is to set up the problem correctly.* Your first step should always be to define the events clearly, using capital letters. If you do not recall the correct formula to use, refer back to Section 5.2 and 5.3.

In a particular city, 20% of the people subscribe to the morning newspaper, 30% subscribe to the evening newspaper, and 10% subscribe to both. Determine the probability that an individual from this city subscribes to the morning newspaper, the evening newspaper, or both.

E X A M P L E

5.4

Using the Formulas

Solution   Your initial step should be to define

$$M = \text{person subscribes to the morning newspaper}$$
$$E = \text{person subscribes to the evening newspaper}$$

We do not need to define another event for a person subscribing to both newspapers, as we shall see.

We now have

$$P(M) = .2$$
$$P(E) = .3$$

The probability that a selected individual subscribes to the morning *and* the evening newspaper is given as .10. This a *joint* probability:

$$P(M \text{ and } E) = .1$$

We want to find the probability of *M* or *E*. Using the additive rule,

$$P(M \text{ or } E) = P(M) + P(E) - P(M \text{ and } E)$$
$$= .2 + .3 - .1$$
$$= .4$$

So 40% of the people in this city subscribe to at least one of the two newspapers.

Suppose we also know that 1/3 of the evening newspaper subscribers are also morning newspaper subscribers. How can you translate this statement into a probability? We can restate the preceding sentence as "Given that a randomly selected individual subscribes to the evening newspaper, the probability that this person also subscribes to the morning newspaper is 1/3." In other words, this is a *conditional* probability:

$$P(M \mid E) = 1/3$$

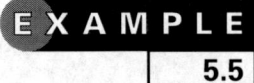

5.5

Referring to the subscription data in Example 5.4, what percentage of the evening subscribers do not subscribe to the morning newspaper?

Solution 1   A Venn diagram for this problem is shown in Figure 5.7. Notice that *M* (the morning subscribers) is made up of two components: (1) those people in *E* (the evening subscribers) and (2) those not in *E*. Since $P(M \text{ and } E) = .1$, the area of *M* that is striped is

$$P(M) - P(M \text{ and } E) = P(M \text{ and } \bar{E})$$
$$= .2 - .1 = .1$$

Similarly, the area of *E* that is striped is

$$P(E) - P(M \text{ and } E) = P(\bar{M} \text{ and } E)$$
$$= .3 - .1 = .2$$

FIGURE

5.7

Venn diagram for
Example 5.5.

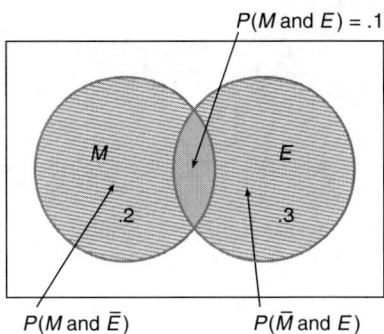

$P(M \text{ and } E) = .1$

$P(M \text{ and } \bar{E})$ $P(\bar{M} \text{ and } E)$

Our question could be stated, "Given that a person subscribes to the evening newspaper, what is the probability that this person does not subscribe to the morning newspaper?" This is the *conditional* probability

$$P(\bar{M} \mid E)$$

Look at the Venn diagram. You know that E occurred, so the outcome is in the E circle. What is the probability that the outcome is not in M? We know that the total area of E is .3 and that the area that is not in M but is in E is .2. So

$$P(\bar{M} \mid E) = .2/.3 = 2/3$$

Another approach here is to utilize the formulas in the section by noting that given event E has occurred, either event M occurs or it doesn't. Consequently,

$$P(\bar{M} \mid E) = 1 - P(M \mid E)$$
$$= 1 - [P(M \text{ and } E)]/P(E)$$
$$= 1 - (.1/.3) = 2/3$$

Using a Contingency Table

Solution 2

Although Example 5.4 made no mention of a random sample, a useful device here is to imagine that a random sample of, say, $n = 100$ people is obtained (actually, any sample size (*n*) could be used). Next, construct a contingency table like the one in Section 5.2, by *assuming that the population percentages given in the problem apply to these 100 people.* In Example 5.4, we would assume that 20% of the sample (20 people) subscribe to the morning newspaper and 30% of the sample (30 people) subscribe to the evening newspaper. So far, the contingency table would be

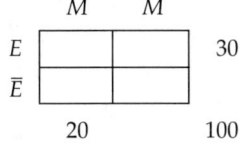

	M	$\bar{M}$	
E			30
$\bar{E}$			
	20		100

Since the sample size is 100, the totals for $\bar{M}$ and $\bar{E}$ are 80 and 70, respectively, producing the following table:

	M	$\bar{M}$	
E			30
$\bar{E}$			70
	20	80	100

The final piece of information is that 10% of the people (10 people) subscribe to *both* newspapers. So 10 people are in the cell in the upper-left corner, corresponding to E and M, and the table is now

	M	$\bar{M}$	
E	10		30
$\bar{E}$			70
	20	80	100

By using the row and column totals, the remaining cells can be filled in.*

	M	$\bar{M}$	
E	10	20	30
$\bar{E}$	10	60	70
	20	80	100

Once the table is filled in, probabilities become very easy to derive via the approach used in Section 5.2. To illustrate, the solution to Example 5.4 is

$$P(M \text{ or } E) = \frac{10 + 10 + 20}{100} = \frac{40}{100} = .4$$

The conditional probability in Example 5.5 is

$$P(\bar{M} \mid E) = \frac{20}{30} = 2/3$$

since there are 30 people who subscribe to the evening newspaper *(E)*, 20 of whom do not subscribe to the morning newspaper *(M̄)*.

HELPFUL HINTS FOR PROBABILITY APPLICATIONS

Using the Formulas
1. Define each event using capital letters.
2. Translate each statement into a probability. Does a particular statement tell you *P(A)? P(B)? P(A and B)? P(A or B)? P(A|B)? P(B|A)?*
3. Determine the answer by identifying the probability rule that applies and by using a Venn diagram. Using both allows you to check your logic and your arithmetic.

---

*This procedure is easier to apply and explain if the sample size *(n)* is chosen so that all numbers in the contingency table are counting numbers (integers).

Using a Contingency Table
1. Select *any* sample size, say, $n = 100$ or 1000.
2. Using the information given, fill in the row and column totals.
3. Using the final piece of information given, fill in the appropriate cell and complete the contingency table.
4. Determine the answer by dividing the proper value by the appropriate total.

In a certain northeastern state that is going through financial difficulties, it is believed that 5% of the banks will fail. It is known that the deposits of 90% of the banks in this state are insured by the Federal Depository Insurance Company (FDIC). It is also believed, from past experience, that 3% of the banks protected by FDIC will fail. A bank examiner employed by the federal government would like to know three things:

EXAMPLE 5.6

1. What is the probability that, for a randomly chosen bank, the bank has deposits protected by FDIC and the bank will fail?

2. What is the probability that, for a randomly chosen bank, the bank has deposits covered by FDIC or the bank will fail?

3. What percentage of the banks that go under have deposits protected by FDIC?

Using the Formulas

The first step is to define appropriate events:

Solution 1

$$A = \text{bank has deposits protected by FDIC}$$
$$B = \text{bank will fail}$$

We now translate each of the statements into a probability. We have the following marginal probabilities:

$$P(A) = .90$$
$$P(B) = .05$$

The last statement in the problem can be written as "Given that a bank has accounts protected by FDIC, the probability that the bank will fail is .03." So this is a conditional probability; namely,

$$P(B \mid A) = .03$$

What does question 1 ask for? $P(A \text{ or } B)$? $P(A \mid B)$? $P(A \text{ and } B)$? The examiner wishes to know the probability that a bank is protected by FDIC *and* will fail. This is $P(A \text{ and } B)$. Using the multiplicative rule,

$$P(A \text{ and } B) = P(B \mid A) \cdot P(A)$$
$$= (.03)(.90) = .027$$

For question 2, we wish to know the probability that A or B occurs. By the additive rule,

Solution 2

$$P(A \text{ or } B) = P(A) + P(B) - P(A \text{ and } B)$$
$$= .90 + .05 - .027 = .923$$

Thus, 92.3% of the banks are covered by the FDIC, will fail, or both.

Solution 3

Question 3 can be phrased as, "Given that a bank has failed, what is the probability that this bank has deposits protected by FDIC?" This is $P(A \mid B)$.

$$P(A \mid B) = [P(A \text{ and } B)]/P(B) = .027/.05 = .54$$

Therefore, 54% of those banks that fail have deposits protected by FDIC.

Using a Contingency Table

To obtain a table containing all counting numbers, a sample size of $n = 1,000$ is selected here. Remember that any sample size can be used with this approach. Five percent of the banks failed ($.05 \times 1,000 = 50$ banks) and 90% of the banks are insured by FDIC ($.90 \times 1,000 = 900$ banks). Filling in the remaining row and column totals, we get the following table:

	FDIC	$\overline{\text{FDIC}}$	
FAIL			50
$\overline{\text{FAIL}}$			950
	900	100	1000

Finally, 3% of the banks *protected by FDIC* failed. There are 900 banks protected by FDIC, so we find $.03 \times 900 = 27$ banks.* Thus, 27 of the banks are protected by FDIC and failed. This value goes into the upper left cell and the table is

	FDIC	$\overline{\text{FDIC}}$	
FAIL	27		50
$\overline{\text{FAIL}}$			950
	900	100	1000

Filling in the remaining cells, we get the following completed contingency table:

	FDIC	$\overline{\text{FDIC}}$	
FAIL	27	23	50
$\overline{\text{FAIL}}$	873	77	950
	900	100	1000

Solution 1

$$P(\text{FDIC and FAIL}) = 27/1,000 = .027$$

Solution 2

$$P(\text{FDIC or FAIL}) = \frac{27 + 873 + 23}{1,000} = \frac{923}{1,000} = .923$$

Solution 3

$$P(\text{FDIC} \mid \text{FAIL}) = 27/50 = .54$$

since 50 of the banks failed, 27 of which are protected by FDIC.

---

*A sample size of $n = 100$ would have produced a value of 2.7 here. The problem can still be solved using $n = 100$, but is easier to explain using counting numbers in each cell; hence, $n = 1000$ was selected.

X Exercises 5.16–5.35

Understanding the Mechanics

5.16 The probability of event A is .5 and the probability of event B is .2.
   a. If $P(A$ and $B)$ is .1, what is $P(A$ or $B)$?
   b. If the probability of A given B is .5, what is the $P(A$ and $B)$?
   c. If $P(A$ and $B)$ is .2, what is the probability of B given A?

5.17 Let $A = \{1, 3, 5, 7, 9\}$ and $B = \{4, 5, 6\}$. An experiment results in any number between 1 and 10, inclusively, being randomly selected.
   a. Draw a Venn diagram.
   b. Find $P(A$ and $B)$.
   c. Find $P(\bar{A}$ and $\bar{B})$.
   d. Find $P(\bar{A}\,|\,B)$.

5.18 The probabilities of the independent events A and B are .3 and .6, respectively.
   a. What is the probability of A or B?
   b. What is the probability of A and B?
   c. What is the probability of A given B?
   d. What is the probability of B given A?
   e. What is the probability of neither A nor B occurring?

5.19 An experiment has the following outcomes and probabilities:

Outcome	Probability
2	.1
4	.2
6	.4
8	.2
10	.1

Let $A = \{2, 6, 8\}$ and $B = \{6, 8, 10\}$.
   a. Find the probability that either A or B occurs.
   b. Find the probability that B occurs if A occurs.
   c. Find the probability that A occurs and B does not occur.
   d. Find the probability that A occurs if B does not occur.

5.20 The probabilities of the independent events A and B are .4 and .5, respectively. Find the following probabilities.
   a. The probability of A and B occurring.
   b. The probability of A but not B occurring.
   c. The probability of A or B occurring.
   d. The probability of A or not B occurring.
   e. The probability of A occurring given that B has occurred.
   f. The probability of A occurring given that B has not occurred.

5.21 Assume that events A, B, C, and D are mutually exclusive and are the only possible events of an experiment. What is $P(C$ or $D)$ if $P(A) = .2$ and $P(B) = .3$?

5.22 Assume that $P(A) = .6$, $P(B) = .2$, and $P(A\,|\,B) = .1$, what is the $P(\bar{A}$ or $B)$?

5.23 Assume that events A and B are mutually exclusive and that $P(A) = .2$ and $P(B) = .3$. What is $P(A\,|\,\bar{B})$?

5.24 Let event A be multiples of 2 between 1 and 20 and B be multiples of 3 between 1 and 20, inclusively. Assume that each number is equally likely. Draw Venn diagrams of the events. What is $P(A$ or $B)$?

5.25 If $P(A) = P(B) = .5$ and $P(A$ or $B) = .8$, can A and B be mutually exclusive? Explain.

5.26 If $P(A) = P(B) = .5$ and $P(A$ and $B) = .25$, are A and B independent? Explain.

5.27 Explain the difference between $P(A$ and $B)$ and $P(A\,|\,B)$ in your own words.

Applying the New Concepts

5.28 Brokerage firms receive awards for their analysts' stock-picking abilities. The following security firms were the top eight firms in terms of investment research for the year 2000.

Security Firms	Total Awards
Salomon Smith Barney	39
Merrill Lynch	28
Morgan Stanley	25
Lehman Brothers	24
Goldman Sachs	22
A. G. Edwards	21
Credit Suisse First Boston	21
J. P. Morgan Chase	20

   a. What is the probability that an award selected at random from the above list is either to Salomon Smith Barney or to Merrill Lynch?
   b. What is the probability of selecting an award at random from the above list that is not to Credit Suisse First Boston and not to J. P. Morgan Chase?
   c. What is the probability of selecting an award at random from the above list that is to Credit Suisse First Boston or to J. P. Morgan Chase if it is selected from those not at Salomon Smith Barney and not at Merrill Lynch?

(Source: "Salomon Takes Top Spot Among Firms," *The Wall Street Journal*, June 26, 2001, p. R16.)

5.29 At a semiconductor plant, 60% of the workers are skilled and 80% of the workers are full-time. Ninety percent of the skilled workers are full-time.
   a. What is the probability that an employee selected at random is a skilled full-time employee?

b. What is the probability that an employee selected at random is a skilled worker or a full-time worker?

c. What percentage of the full-time workers are skilled?

5.30 Assessment of colleges of business have become increasingly important as the environment is characterized by rising costs and scarce resources. In addition, business schools face the challenge of producing capable graduates who can meet the job-related demands of employers. In a survey of deans of colleges of business, approximately 90% of the deans said they would use the results of the survey to make curriculum changes. Of the deans that said they would make curriculum changes, 40% said that they would make these changes to meet changing requirements of industry.

a. What is the probability that a dean, selected at random from the survey, responds that the assessment results were used for curriculum changes and were used to make changes to meet the changing requirements of industry?

b. What is the probability that a dean, selected at random from the survey, responds that the assessment results were used for curriculum changes and were not used to make changes to meet the changing requirements of industry?

(Source: "A Survey of Assessment Practices in Schools of Business," Central Business Review, vol. 19, no. 1, 2000, pp. 13–18.)

5.31 For every person who visits the leasing office of an apartment community near a certain university, there is an 80% chance that the person will lease an apartment if the person is a student and a 50% chance that the person will lease an apartment if the person is not a student. If two people, one of whom is a student and the other of whom is not, enter the office, what are the chances of leasing an apartment to at least one of the two people? What assumption did you have to make here?

Using the Computer

5.32 **[DATA SET EX5-32]** Variable Description:

Year-Quarter: Time period ranging from the first quarter of 1990 to the first quarter of 2001.

Productivity: Each quarter is categorized as having high or low productivity.

HourlyPayIncreases: Each quarter is categorized as having large or small hourly pay increases.

Higher productivity in the economy usually translates into higher increases in hourly compensation to workers. However, management often delays increasing compensation to show profits for the company. For the period 1990 to 2001, productivity is labeled as high for each quarter if the annualized economic growth is at least 2%. In addition, the amount of pay increase during that quarter is labeled

large if the hourly compensation is at least 4% on an annualized basis.

a. Construct a contingency table with the rows showing the categories of high and low productivity and the columns showing the categories of small or large pay increases. (Excel: Use Contingency Table option in KPK Data Analysis Menu.)

b. Suppose that a quarter is randomly selected, what is the probability that this quarter has high productivity growth and has a large pay increase?

c. If a quarter has high productivity, what is the probability that the quarter has a small pay increase?

d. Are the events of productivity and amount of hourly pay increase independent? Explain.

(Source: "Fed's Meyer Warns of Inflation, Joblessness," The Wall Street Journal, June 7, 2001, p. A2.)

5.33 **[DATA SET EX5-33]** Variable Description:

Month: January through December

Year: 1998, 1999, and 2000

ElecConsumption: "High" and "Low" for California's monthly electricity consumption

Construct a contingency table using Year as the row categories and "High" and "Low" usage as the column categories. What is the probability that a month selected at random for the year 1998 shows "High" consumption? What if the year is 1999? 2000?

(Source: "White House Looks Isolated in Its Opposition to Energy Price Caps," The Wall Street Journal, June 14, 2001, p. A22)

5.34 People are often amazed when they find someone who was born on the same day as themselves. To keep the solution simple, assume in this problem that leap years can be ignored and that all years have 365 days. Also, assume that the probability of being born on any day of the year is the same for all days of the year.

a. If two persons are selected at random, what is the probability that these two persons were born on the same day? (Hint: For one person, there are 365 distinct birthdays. For two people, there are 364 different ways that the second could have a birthday without matching the first.)

b. If three persons are selected at random, what is the probability that at least two of the three persons were born on the same day?

c. In general, the probability that at least two of n people have the same birthday is given by the formula:

Probability $= 1 - (365/365)(364/365) \ldots ((365 - n + 1)/365)$

Use the formula to determine the probability that at least two people out of a class of 40 people have the same birthday.

d. The following graph displays the probability of having at least two people having the same birthday. For what number of people is the probability of a match at least .20?

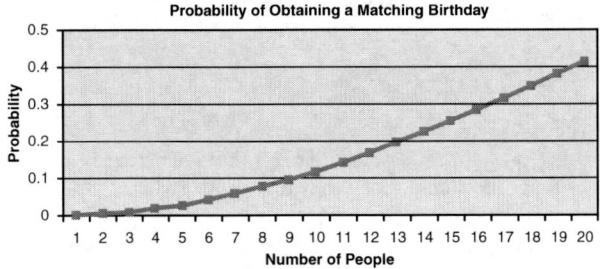

e. Construct a similar graph but extend the graph to 60 people. For what number of people is the probability of obtaining at least one match at least .9?

5.35 [Simulation Exercise] The birthday problem in Ex 5.34 considers the probability of at least two individuals having the same birthday. Additional questions can be asked in the birthday problem. For example, how likely are matches of three, four, or even five? Coincidences fascinate people. Suppose you were in a large class and you found three individuals born on the same day. Would you say that is to be expected, or would you perhaps resort to some sort of cosmic conclusion? A simulation of the birthday problem can help to answer these type of questions. On the KPK menu, select the **Birthday Problem** by clicking on **Simulation Exercises.** Enter the number of people in a group and discover what type of birthday matches can be expected through a simulation of birthday dates.

a. How large of a group of people would you say is necessary to have at least a 50-50 chance that three individuals have the same birthday? Does the simulation support it?

b. How large of a group of people would you say is necessary to have at least a 50-50 chance that four individuals have the same birthday? Does the simulation support it?

c. Enter 100 people for the group size. Perform the simulation 20 times and count how many times there are at least three individuals with the same birthday. Is this estimate of the probability of a three-way match what you might have expected?

d. What type of birthday matches do you think could reasonably occur with a group of 2,000 individuals? What does the simulation say?

BAYES' RULE USING TREE DIAGRAMS

5.5

Another useful device for determining probabilities is a **tree diagram.** Notice in Example 5.6 that both marginal probabilities $P(\text{FDIC})$ and $P(\text{Fail})$ were known; that is, the percentage of banks protected by FDIC was known (90%) and the percentage of banks that would fail was known (5%). The contingency table approach illustrated in the previous section works well for this situation.

Suppose instead that one of the marginal probabilities is missing, say, $P(\text{Fail})$, but that we *do* know three things:

1. 90% of the banks are protected by FDIC (and 10% are not).

2. 3% of the banks protected by FDIC will fail.

3. 23% of the banks not protected by FDIC will fail.

So we can write

$$P(\text{FDIC}) = .90$$

$$P(\overline{\text{FDIC}}) = .10$$

$$P(\text{Fail} \mid \text{FDIC}) = .03$$

$$P(\text{Fail} \mid \overline{\text{FDIC}}) = .23$$

This information can be summarized in the following picture, which we refer to as a tree diagram.

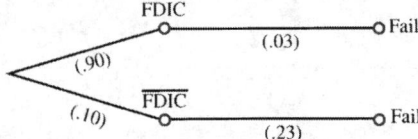

Each number in parentheses is the probability associated with that particular branch. For example, .03 is the probability of a bank failing *given* that it is protected by FDIC, and so this value is placed on the Fail branch corresponding to FDIC.

To find the remaining marginal probability, $P(\text{Fail})$, the following rule is used.

RULE #1 WHEN USING A TREE DIAGRAM

The probability of the event on the right side (say, event *B*) of the tree is equal to the sum of the paths; that is, all probabilities along a path leading to event *B* are multiplied, and then summed over *all* paths leading to *B*.

For the preceding tree diagram, Rule #1 states that

$$P(\text{Fail}) = (.90)(.03) + (.10)(.23)$$

$$= .027 + .023 = .05$$

Consequently, we conclude that 5% of the banks will fail, the same value provided in Example 5.6.

Another question of interest might be, given that a bank fails, what is the probability that it is protected by FDIC? Or put another way, what percentage of banks that fail are protected by FDIC? This can be written

$$P(\text{FDIC} \mid \text{Fail})$$

Recall that earlier we were given that $P(\text{FDIC}) = .90$; that is, 90% of the banks are protected by FDIC. For this probability we were given no conditions at all; it is referred to as a **prior probability.** Now we are asked to determine the probability of this event having been given some information, namely that the bank failed. The probability $P(\text{FDIC} \mid \text{Fail})$ is called a **posterior probability** and is always a conditional probability; in particular, we are given that the event on the right side of the tree diagram (Fail) did, in fact, occur. Since FDIC lies on the first branch and $\overline{\text{FDIC}}$ lies on the second branch, we are asked to determine the probability that we got to event Fail along the first path, given that event Fail occurred.

The tree diagram used in this example has two paths. In general, there can be any number of paths, as illustrated in Figure 5.8.

To determine a posterior probability, written as $P(E_i \mid B)$ for some i, we use the following rule, usually referred to as **Bayes' rule** (named after Thomas Bayes, an English Presbyterian minister and mathematician).

RULE #2 FOR TREE DIAGRAMS (BAYES' RULE)

The posterior probability for the *i*th path is

$$P(E_i \mid B) = \frac{i\text{th path}}{\text{sum of paths}}$$

where the "sum of paths" is found using Rule #1.

FIGURE

5.8

General form of a
tree diagram.

To illustrate:

$$P(\text{FDIC} \mid \text{Fail}) = \frac{\text{1st path}}{\text{sum of paths}}$$

since FDIC lies on the first path. By "1st path" we mean the product of all probabilities along this path. So

$$P(\text{FDIC} \mid \text{Fail}) = \frac{(.9)(.03)}{(.9)(.03) + (.1)(.23)}$$

$$= \frac{.027}{.05} = .54$$

Consequently, 54% of the banks that fail are protected by FDIC (the same result obtained in Example 5.6).

EXAMPLE

5.7

Zetadyne Corporation produces electrical components utilizing three nonoverlapping work shifts. It is known that 50% of the components are produced during shift 1, 20% during shift 2, and 30% during shift 3. A further look at product quality reveals that 6% of the components produced during shift 1 are defective. The corresponding percentage for shift 2 is 8%. Shift 3, the late-night shift, produces a relatively large percentage, 15%, of defective components. Determine the following:

1. What percentage of all components is defective?

2. Given that a defective component is found, what is the probability that it was produced during shift 3?

The tree diagram for this example is

Solution 1

Using Rule #1, we find that

$$P(\text{Defective}) = \text{sum of paths}$$
$$= (.5)(.06) + (.2)(.08) + (.3)(.15)$$
$$= .030 + .016 + .045$$
$$= .091$$

Consequently, 9.1% of the components produced are defective.

Solution 2   We know that $P(\text{shift 3})$ is .3; that is, 30% of the components produced are produced during shift 3. This is a *prior probability*. To determine the *posterior probability*, $P(\text{shift 3} \mid \text{defective})$, we use Rule #2.

$$P(\text{shift 3} \mid \text{defective}) = \frac{\text{third path}}{\text{sum of paths}}$$
$$= \frac{(.3)(.15)}{.091}$$
$$= \frac{.045}{.091} = .495$$

So approximately half of the defective components produced are produced during shift 3. This means that once a component is identified as defective, the probability that it came from shift 3 increases from .3 (the prior probability) to .495 (the posterior probability).

X Exercises 5.36–5.43

Understanding the Mechanics

5.36 Construct a tree diagram to find the probability of B.
  a. Assume that the probability of A is .8, the probability of B given that A occurs is .05, and the probability of B given that A does not occur is .25.
  b. Assume that the probability of A is .6, the probability of B given that A occurs is .20, and the probability of B given that A does not occur is .40.

5.37 Using the given probabilities, construct a tree diagram to find $P(B)$.
  a. $P(E_1) = .4$, $P(E_2) = .1$, $P(E_3) = .5$, $P(B \mid E_1) = .2$, $P(B \mid E_2) = .6$, $P(B \mid E_3) = .4$
  b. $P(E_1) = .6$, $P(E_2) = .1$, $P(E_3) = .1$, $P(E_4) = .2$, $P(B \mid E_1) = .3$, $P(B \mid E_2) = .4$, $P(B \mid E_3) = .1$, $P(B \mid E_4) = .1$

5.38 Using the given probabilities, construct a tree diagram to find $P(E_1 \mid B)$.
  a. $P(E_1) = .4$, $P(E_2) = .6$, $P(B \mid E_1) = .5$, $P(B \mid E_2) = .3$
  b. $P(E_1) = .35$, $P(E_2) = .25$, $P(E_3) = .2$, $P(E_4) = .2$ $P(B \mid E_1) = .2$, $P(B \mid E_2) = .4$, $P(B \mid E_3) = .2$, $P(B \mid E_4) = .1$

Applying the New Concepts

5.39 Many organizations, including military and defense-related companies, require their employees to be screened for drugs. Some employees are concerned that a *false positive* may be recorded from the screening; that is, employees who are not drug abusers may incorrectly test positive. Assume that 10% of a certain population are drug abusers. Suppose that the probability of a "false positive" is 0.5% and that the probability of a correct positive on someone who is under the influence of certain drugs is 99.9%. What is the probability that a person who tests positive is really a drug user?

5.40 Sixty percent of individual investors blamed themselves for stock portfolio losses during the bear market of 2001. Of those investors that blame themselves for their personal losses, 40% had a loss of more than 30%. Of those individual investors who did not blame themselves for their portfolio losses, 60% had a loss of more than 30%.
  a. What is the probability that an individual investor had a loss of more than 30%?
  b. What is the probability that a randomly selected individual investor with a loss of more than 30% takes the blame for his/her portfolio losses?

(Source: "Investors: We Messed Up," *USA Today*, July 17, 2001, p. 1B.)

5.41 A large manufacturing company is in the process of training its personnel in quality-control procedures. At present, 40% of the assembly lines use control charts, 40% use inspection techniques, and 20% do not use any method for controlling quality. The assembly lines that use control charts have a 1% defective rate. The assembly lines that use inspection techniques have a 5% defective rate. The assembly lines that do not use any quality-control techniques have a 12% defective rate. What is the probability that an item produced by this company is defective?

5.42 Suppose that in Exercise 5.41, the assembly lines that use inspection techniques had only a 1% defective rate rather than a 5% rate. What is the probability that a produced item is defective?

5.43 Materials for a food-processing plant are supplied by four companies. The following table lists the percentage of defective items from each company and the percentage of materials supplied by that company to the food-processing plant.

	Percentage of Materials Supplied	Percentage of Defective Materials
Supplier 1	40	2
Supplier 2	5	10
Supplier 3	20	8
Supplier 4	35	3

a. Determine the percentage of all materials that are defective.

b. Given that a material supplied to the plant is defective, what is the probability that it came from supplier 3?

Summary

This chapter has examined methods of dealing with uncertainty by applying the concept of probability. An activity that results in an uncertain outcome is called an *experiment*; the possible outcomes are *events*. The complement of an event consists of all outcomes not in this event. Uncertainty is measured in terms of the probabilities of events. To determine the value of a particular probability, we used the classical approach, the relative frequency method, or the subjective probability approach.

Events can be summarized together in a contingency (cross-tab) table. The numbers in the table represent frequencies within each pair of subcategories, so comparisons can be made. When examining more than one event, say A and B, several types of probabilities can be derived, including a joint probability, a conditional probability, or the probability of event A or event B occurring. The probability of a single event, such as P(the person selected is a female) or P(an individual subscribes to the *Wall Street Journal*), is a marginal probability.

Two events are said to be independent if the occurrence of the one event has no effect on the probability that the other event occurs. If two events can never both occur, they are said to be mutually exclusive. An effective method of determining a probability in complicated situations is to use a Venn diagram. Another useful method for structuring a decision problem is to use a tree diagram.

Summary of Formulas

1. Additive rule

$$P(A \text{ or } B) = P(A) + P(B) - P(A \text{ and } B)$$

Special case: If A and B are *mutually exclusive*,

$$P(A \text{ or } B) = P(A) + P(B)$$

2. Multiplicative rule

$$P(A \text{ and } B) = P(A \mid B) \cdot P(B)$$
$$= P(B \mid A) \cdot P(A)$$

Special case: If A and B are *independent*

$$P(A \text{ and } B) = P(A) \cdot P(B)$$

3. Conditional probability

$$P(A \mid B) = \frac{P(A \text{ and } B)}{P(B)}$$

4. Independence: Two events A and B are independent if one of the following can be shown:

$$P(A \mid B) = P(A)$$
$$P(B \mid A) = P(B)$$
$$P(A \text{ and } B) = P(A) \cdot P(B)$$

5. Mutually exclusive: Two events A and B are mutually exclusive if P(A and B) is zero.

6. Posterior probability (Bayes' Rule) For any event E_i, the posterior probability of event E_i, given that the final event B occurred is

$$P(E_i \mid B) = \frac{i\text{th path}}{\text{sum of paths}}$$

where the sum of paths is obtained by multiplying all probabilities along a path leading to event B and summing the results over all paths leading to event B.

X Review Exercises 5.44–5.62

5.44 Let the events *A*, *B*, and *C* consist of the integers from 1 to 10, 5 to 15, and 10 to 20, respectively. Suppose that the integers from 1 to 20 are equally likely to occur. Draw a Venn diagram and illustrate the probability of *A* or *B* occurring and also the probability of *A* and *B* occurring.

5.45 Assuming that the probabilities of *A*, *B*, and *C* are .4, .3, and .1, respectively, what is the joint probability of *A* and *B* if $P(A \mid B) = .4$?

5.46 In Exercise 5.45, what is the probability of *A* or *B* if *A* and *B* are independent?

5.47 In Exercise 5.45, are there any events besides *A*, *B*, and *C* that are possible? Why?

5.48 If the probability of mutually exclusive events *A* and *B* are .2 and .4, respectively, what is $P(\bar{A} \text{ and } B)$?

5.49 In Exercise 5.48, what is $P(A \mid \bar{B})$?

5.50 The probability of two mutually exclusive events is equal to the sum of their probabilities. This rule extends to more than two events. If $P(A) = P(B) = P(C) = .2$, what is the $P(A \text{ or } B \text{ or } C)$?

5.51 The probability of two independent events is equal to the product of their probabilities. This rule extends to more than two events. If $P(A) = P(B) = P(C) = .2$, what is the $P(A \text{ and } B \text{ and } C)$?

5.52 In Exercise 5.45, if all three events are mutually exclusive, what is the $P(A \text{ or } B \text{ or } C)$?

5.53 In Exercise 5.45, if all three events are independent, what is the probability of *A* and *B* and *C*?

5.54 A study by Clayton/Curtis/Cottrell found significant numbers of consumers in the mood for breakfast foods at dinner. This may be because many adults are sufficiently awake to enjoy the eggs and bacon if they are eating them at 7:00 P.M. rather than at 7:00 A.M. Assume that the following table shows the results of a survey of teenagers, working adults, and retired adults and their likelihood of ordering breakfast-type meals at a restaurant for dinner.

	Very Likely	Somewhat Likely	Somewhat Unlikely	Not at All Likely
Teenager	12	20	15	53
Working Adults	10	25	20	45
Retired Adults	5	15	20	60

Consider the following events.
A: {A person is a working adult or a retired adult}
B: {A person is very likely or somewhat likely to order a breakfast-type meal at dinner time}
C: {A person is not a retired adult}
D: {A person is not at all likely to order a breakfast-type meal at dinner time}
  a. Find the probability of each event.
  b. Find $P(A \text{ and } B)$, $P(A \mid B)$, and $P(B \mid A)$.
  c. What is $P(A \text{ or } D)$ and $P(A \text{ and } D)$?
  d. Which events are mutually exclusive?

(Adapted from "A Toast to Consumers Who Want a Change of Pace," *Adweek*, March 24, 1997, p. 21.)

5.55 A marketing-research group conducted a survey to find out where people did their holiday shopping. Out of a group of 110 randomly selected shoppers, 70 said that they shopped exclusively at the local mall, 30 said that they shopped exclusively in the downtown area, and 10 said that they shopped both at the local mall and in the downtown area.

    a. What is the probability that a customer shops both at the local mall and in the downtown area?

    b. What proportion of customers who shop at the local mall also shop in the downtown area?

    c. What is the probability that a customer shops downtown but not at the local mall?

5.56 An electronics firm decides to market three different software packages for its personal computers. The marketing analyst gives each of the three packages an 80% chance of success. The outcomes for each of the software packages are independent.

    a. What is the probability that all three will be a success?

    b. What is the probability that only two of the packages will be a success?

    c. What is the probability that none will be successful?

5.57 Thousands of counterfeit software manufacturing sites exist worldwide. Law enforcement officials believe that approximately 40% of all software used in business is counterfeit. Suppose that an auditor selects three software packages from small business companies in Europe, say companies A, B, and C.

    a. What is the probability that either company A or company B has a counterfeit copy?

    b. What is the probability that company A has a counterfeit copy and that company C does not have a counterfeit copy?

    c. What is the probability that none of the three companies has a counterfeit copy?

    d. What is the probability that at least one of the three companies has a counterfeit copy?

    e. What is the probability that either all three companies have a counterfeit copy or none of them have a counterfeit copy?

(Source: "Piracy on Rise," *USA Today*, August 1, 2001, p. 2B.)

5.58 The Internet, as a marketing medium, offers many challenges to marketers. Knowing the Internet population's demographic profile is critical to advertisers. From a survey, the following information on the age of Internet users and how often they viewed Internet advertising was compiled.

Age	No More than Once a Month	Several Times a Month	Once a Week	Several Times a Week	Every Day
18–24	24	7	20	19	10
25–34	33	18	23	27	20
35–44	33	9	14	29	19
45–54	19	5	14	12	10
55–64	17	1	3	7	3

    a. What is the probability that an Internet user is between 18 and 24 years of age and reads Internet advertising at least once a week?

    b. What is the probability that an Internet user reads Internet advertising no more than once a month or is between 45 and 64 years of age?

    c. What is the probability that an Internet user reads Internet advertising at least several times a week if that person is between 18 and 34 years of age?

    d. Are age and frequency of viewing Internet advertising independent? Explain.

(Source: "Survey of Internet Users' Attitudes toward Internet Advertising," *Journal of Interactive Marketing*, vol. 13, no. 3, 2001, pp. 34–54.)

5.59 "We've noticed a big increase in the number of Americans coming into our store," said Richard Montgomery, manager of Eaton's at Yorkdale Mall in Toronto. But the biggest change is the number of Canadian shoppers looking for deals at home instead of south of the border. "It's the Canadian consumer that's making the difference." Since the beginning of October 1997 to April 1998, the Canadian dollar has fallen from 73 cents per

U.S. dollar to below 70 cents per U.S. dollar. Assume that the table below is from a sample of Americans and Canadians that shopped at Yorkdale Mall in Toronto.

	Shopping at Mall Because of Weak Canadian Dollar	Shopping at Mall Because of Reasons Other Than the Weak Canadian Dollar
American	55	45
Canadian	60	140

a. What is the probability that a person selected at random from the sample is an American who is shopping at the mall for reasons other than the weak Canadian dollar?

b. What is the probability that a Canadian person selected at random from the sample is shopping at the mall because of the weak Canadian dollar?

(Adapted from "Lower C$ Prompts U.S. Bargain Hunting," *The Financial Post*, January 2, 1998, p. 6.)

5.60 A defective iPod is inspected by two service representatives. If one representative has a 50% chance of finding the defect, and the other has a 60% chance, what is the probability that at least one will find the defect if both check the iPod independently? What is the probability that neither will spot the defect?

5.61 During the first six months of 2003, most airlines experienced an improvement in the number of flight delays. This improvement was due in part to smarter flight scheduling and a reduction in the number of flights. The percentages of late arrivals for American, Delta, and Southwest were approximately 20%, 18%, and 15%, respectively.

a. Suppose that the probability of either a Delta or Southwest airline flight being delayed is .33. Would this indicate that the event of a Delta airline flight being delayed is independent of a Southwest airline being delayed?

b. Assuming independence of flight delays among airlines, what is the probability that for three randomly selected flights, one from American, Delta, and Southwest airlines, that none of the three flights experienced delays?

(Source: "Airlines Beat Punctuality Record," *USA Today*, August 7, 2003.)

5.62 Much controversy was stirred by Marilyn VosSavant's response to whether contestants on a game show should switch their random selection of a door with a possible prize behind it when the host gives additional information. The following is a basic description of the game as described in *Ask Marilyn*: "Suppose you're on a game show and you're given a choice of three doors. Behind one door is a car; behind the others are goats. You pick a door—say, Number 1—and the host, who knows what's behind each door, opens another door—say, Number 3—which has a goat behind it. He then says to you, 'Do you want to keep door Number 1 or switch doors?' Is it to your advantage to switch your choice?" Marilyn's response is, "Yes, you should switch. The first door has a 1/3 chance of winning, but the second has a 2/3 chance." Marilyn received letters from numerous mathematicians that described her response as being absurd. In particular, one comment was: "I am in shock that after being corrected by at least three mathematicians, you still do not admit your mistake."

a. Pair up with another student and label three paper cups Number 1, Number 2, and Number 3. While one student (the contestant) is not looking, the other student (the host) generates a number between 1 and 3 using the following Excel commands:

Put the numbers 1, 2, and 3 in cells A1, A2, and A3.

Type = 1/3 in cells B1, B2, and B3.

Click on **Tools ➤ Data Analysis ➤ Random Number Generator.**

Type into the user form:

   1 for the number of variables;

   1 for the number of random numbers;

   Discrete for distribution;

A1:B3 for value and probability input range; and
C1 for output range.

The host puts a key under the cup corresponding to the random integer generated. The contestant then randomly selects a cup using the same Excel commands. The host then lifts a losing cup. Let's say that the contestant never switches. Then the contestant lifts his or her cup. Keep a tally of the contestant's wins. Repeat this game 100 times.

b. Perform the game in part a, except have the contestant switch cups each time.

c. Compare the number of wins in parts a and b. Do you believe Marilyn's response is correct?

d. Give a convincing argument that either supports Marilyn's response or supports the contention that there is no advantage in switching doors.

(Adapted from "Ask Marilyn," *The Dallas Morning News,* by Marilyn VosSavant, February 17, 1991.)

Computer Exercises Using the Databases

Exercise 1—Appendix F

Select a random sample of 100 observations from the database. Using the relative frequency approach of finding a probability value, find the probability that a family owns its home.

Exercise 2—Appendix G

Generate 200 random numbers from a uniform distribution and use them to select 200 observations from the database. Using the relative frequency approach, find the probability that a company has an A bond rating. Also find the probability that a company has a B bond rating.

Insights from Statistics in Action

Cable and DSL Connections: Wired for Speed

The Statistics in Action case study presented at the beginning of this chapter introduced the concept of viewing a market share as a probability. For example, if the cable industry has a 50% market share of the consumers of high-speed Internet access, then the following probability can be used to express this:

P(Select cable modem for Internet connection | a consumer decides to have high speed Internet access) = .50

So market share can be thought of as a conditional probability. Suppose that the market share for cable, DSL, and other (satellite and wireless) are as follows. Since advertisers are highly interested in the proportion of individuals that purchase online, probabilities of making an online purchase are given. The proportion of individuals that purchase online are presented conditioned on the type of high-speed Internet connection they have.

	Proportion of High-Speed Internet Users
Using cable for Internet connection	50%
Using DSL for Internet connection	40%
Using other (satellite & wireless) for Internet connection	10%
Make a purchase online once a month given that user has a cable connection	20%
Make a purchase online once a month given that user has a DSL connection	40%
Make a purchase online once a month given that user has a satellite or wireless connection	25%

1. Should the proportions of the market share for high-speed Internet consumers using cable, DSL, or other sum to one? Should the proportions of those consumers who

make a monthly purchase online given their type of high-speed connection also sum to one? Why?

2. What is the probability that a high-speed Internet consumer has a cable connection and also makes a monthly purchase online? What is the probability that the consumer has a DSL connection and makes a monthly purchase online? What is the probability that the consumer has a satellite or wireless connection and makes a monthly purchase online?

3. What is the probability that a high-speed Internet consumer will make a monthly purchase online?

4. Suppose that it is known that a high-speed Internet consumer makes a monthly purchase online. What is the probability that the consumer has a cable connection? A DSL connection? A satellite or wireless connection?

Source: "Coming Soon: Movies You Rent on the Web – And Then Download," *The Wall Street Journal,* August 30, 2004, p. B1. "The Coming DSL Debacle," *Business Communications Review,* June 2001, vol. 31, no. 6, p. 6. "Broadband Internet Access," *Red Herring,* October 1, 2001, p. 34

Appendix

Data Analysis with Excel, MINITAB, and SPSS

Excel

Contingency Table

To construct a contingency table, click on **KPK Data Analysis ➤ Qualitative Data Charts ➤ Contingency Table.** The Create Contingency Table dialog box will appear. For the input row range and input column range, the first cell is considered a label for the category. For the City and Quality data in Example 5.3, insert the data range as given in the dialog box. After clicking **OK,** the contingency table in Figure 5.6(a) will appear. Enter the city names in place of the numbers under the **City** column and enter the quality labels in place of the numbers under the **Quality** heading.

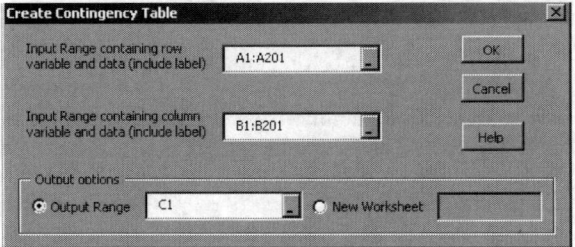

MINITAB

Contingency Table

To construct a contingency table, click on **Stat ➤ Tables ➤ Cross Tabulation and Chi-square.** For the City and Quality data in Example 5.3, select **City** for the rows categorical variable and **Quality** for the column categorical variable. Select the options under **Display.** Click **OK,** and the resulting contingency table will be Figure 5.6(b).

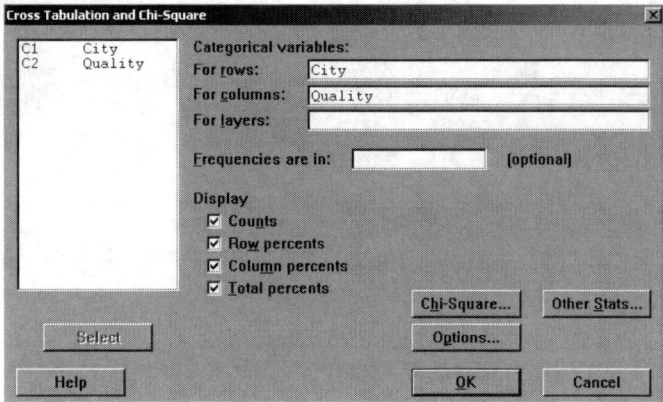

SPSS

Contingency Table

To construct a contingency table, click on **Analyze ➤ Descriptive Statistics ➤ Crosstabs.**
For the City and Quality data in Example 5.3, select **City** for the **Row** variable and **Quality**
for the **Column** variable in the **Crosstabs** dialog box. Click the **Cells** button if row, column, or total percentages are desired. Click **OK** to obtain Figure 5.6(c). By double-clicking
inside the table and then double-clicking the row and column numbers, the city names
and quality labels can be entered.

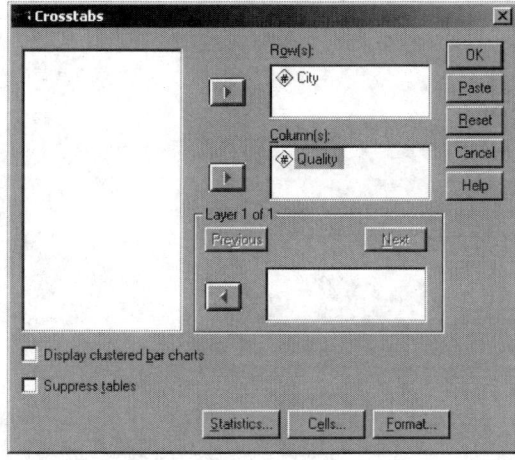

chapter

Discrete Probability Distributions

Statistics in Action
AACSB Accreditation: A Commitment to Excellence in Business Education

The Association to Advance Collegiate Schools of Business (AACSB) is a not-for-profit corporation of approximately 900 members representing colleges, universities, and business and professional organizations committed to excellence in business education. Business schools nationwide strive to obtain AACSB accreditation, considered to be the premier accreditation for colleges of business. More than 400 business schools have affirmed their commitment to academic excellence and to continuous improvement by receiving accreditation.

The accreditation process uses the tools of quality management that emphasize examining and improving the *process*. Colleges of business must perform a self assessment that involves defining customers, improving the processes used to deliver services to customers, and reviewing their school's strengths, limitations, and opportunities, with the ultimate purpose of improving educational effectiveness. Participation in the accreditation process affirms the school's responsibility for the quality of education offered and demonstrates its commitment to continuous improvement. In this accreditation process, deans and faculty members have to ask themselves: Is the business school doing its job? Is research in the ivory tower relevant or simply fuzzy and pretentious?

Each college of business participating in the accreditation process can define its school's mission and can identify competencies that it views as important to its mission. Typical competencies include communication skills, professional knowledge, critical thinking, problem solving, technology/computer usage, interpersonal skills, knowledge and comprehension, global issues, professional integrity/ethics, and lifelong learning. Approximately 90% of the schools participating in this process use the assessment process to monitor the effectiveness of their programs. At least 75% of the schools participating in this accreditation believe that the stakeholders are the faculty, employers, current students, and the business community.

With each college of business being able to establish its own mission, the accreditation process is sometimes full of uncertainties. Deans often obtain information from other universities to better understand how their schools stack up. When you have completed this chapter, you will be able to

- Examine the mean and standard deviation for measurements of the importance of competencies considered necessary for a quality business education.

- Understand how to obtain a probability that a certain number of randomly selected schools of business will use the results of the assessment process to make changes in their curriculum.

- Understand what is meant by a discrete probability distribution when viewing the proportions of importance ratings rendered by deans on competencies deemed to be part of a quality business education.

RANDOM VARIABLES

What Is a Random Variable?

Whenever an experiment results in a numerical outcome, such as the total value of two dice, we can represent the various possible outcomes and their corresponding probabilities much more conveniently by using a *random variable,* the topic of this chapter. Suppose that your company manufactures a product that is sometimes defective and is returned for repair during the warranty period in 10% of the cases. An excellent way of describing the chance that 3 of 20 products will be returned before the warranty runs out is to use the concept of a random variable.

Random variables can be classified into two categories: discrete and continuous. This chapter introduces both but concentrates on the discrete type. Several commonly used discrete random variables will be discussed, as will methods of describing and applying them.

DEFINITION

A **random variable** is a function that assigns a numerical value to each outcome of an experiment.

In Chapter 3 we used various statistics (numerical measures) to describe a set of sample data. For example, the sample mean and standard deviation provide measures of a "typical" value and variation within the sample, respectively. Similarly, we will use a random variable and its corresponding distribution of probabilities to describe a *population.* Just as a sample has a mean and standard deviation, so does the population from which the sample was obtained. We will use the basic concepts from Chapter 4 to derive probabilities related to a random variable. Random variables can be both *discrete* (counting something) or *continuous* (measuring something). This chapter focuses on discrete random variables and continuous random variables will be discussed in Chapter 6.

Discrete Random Variables

The probability laws developed in the previous chapter provide a framework for the discussion of random variables. We will still be concerned about the probability of a particular event; often, however, some aspect of the experiment can be easily represented using a random variable. The result of a simple experiment can sometimes be summarized concisely by defining a discrete random variable to describe the possible outcomes.

Flip a coin three times. The possible outcomes for each flip are heads (H) and tails (T). Since there are three coin flips, there are $2 \cdot 2 \cdot 2 = 8$ possible results. These are TTT, TTH, THT, HTT, HHT, HTH, THH, and HHH. Let

A = event of observing 0 heads in 3 flips (TTT)

B = event of observing 1 head in 3 flips (TTH, THT, HTT)

C = event of observing 2 heads in 3 flips (HHT, HTH, THH)

D = event of observing 3 heads in 3 flips (HHH)

We wish to find $P(A)$, $P(B)$, $P(C)$, and $P(D)$.

Consider one outcome, say, HTH. Since the coin flips are independent,

$P(\text{HTH})$ = (probability of H on 1st flip) · (probability of T on 2nd flip) · (probability of H on 3rd flip)

$= (1/2) \cdot (1/2) \cdot (1/2) = 1/8$

This same argument applies to all eight outcomes. These outcomes are all equally likely, and each occurs with probability 1/8.

Event *A* occurs only if you observe TTT. It has the probability of occurring one time out of eight:

$$P(A) = 1/8$$

Event *B* will occur if you observe HTT, TTH, or THT. It would be impossible for HTT and TTH *both* to occur, so *P(HTT and TTH) = 0*. *This is true for any combination of these three outcomes, so these three events are all mutually exclusive. Consequently,*

$$P(B) = P(\text{HTT or TTH or THT})$$
$$= P(\text{HTT}) + P(\text{TTH}) + P(\text{THT})$$
$$= 1/8 + 1/8 + 1/8 = 3/8$$

By a similar argument,

$$P(C) = 3/8 \quad \text{(using HHT, HTH, THH)}$$
$$P(D) = 1/8 \quad \text{(using HHH)}$$

The variable of interest in this example is *X*, defined as

$$X = \text{number of heads out of three flips}$$

We defined all the possible outcomes of *X* by defining the four events *A, B, C,* and *D*. This method works but is cumbersome. Consider having to do this for 100 flips of a coin! A more convenient way to represent probabilities is to examine the value of *X* for each possible outcome.

Outcome	Value of X	
TTT	0	1 outcome
THT	1	
TTH	1	3 outcomes
HTT	1	
HHT	2	
HTH	2	3 outcomes
THH	2	
HHH	3	1 outcome

Each outcome has probability 1/8, so the probability that *X* will be 0 is 1/8, written:

$$P(X = 0) = P(0) = 1/8$$

The probability that *X* will be 1 is 3/8, written:

$$P(X = 1) = P(1) = 3/8$$

The probability that *X* will be 2 is 3/8, written:

$$P(X = 2) = P(2) = 3/8$$

The probability that *X* will be 3 is 1/8, written:

$$P(X = 3) = P(3) = 1/8$$

Notice that

$$P(X = 0) + P(X = 1) + P(X = 2) + P(X = 3) = 1/8 + 3/8 + 3/8 + 1/8 = 1$$

because 0, 1, 2, and 3 represent *all the possible values of X.*

The values and probabilities for this random variable can be summarized by listing each value and its probability of occurring.

$$X = \begin{cases} 0 \text{ with probability } 1/8 \\ 1 \text{ with probability } 3/8 \\ 2 \text{ with probability } 3/8 \\ 3 \text{ with probability } 1/8 \end{cases}$$

This list of possible values of X and the corresponding probabilities is a **probability distribution.**

In any such formulation of a problem, the variable X is a *random variable.* Its value is not known in advance, but there is a probability associated with each possible value of X. Whenever you have a random variable of the form

$$X = \begin{cases} x_1 \text{ with probability } p_1 \\ x_2 \text{ with probability } p_2 \\ x_3 \text{ with probability } p_3 \\ \vdots \\ x_n \text{ with probability } p_n \end{cases}$$

where $x_1, \ldots, x_n$ is the set of possible values of X, then X is a **discrete random variable.** In the coin-flipping example, $x_1 = 0$ and $p_1 = 1/8$; $x_2 = 1$ and $p_2 = 3/8$, $x_3 = 2$ and $p_3 = 3/8$, and $x_4 = 3$ and $p_4 = 1/8$.

Other examples of a discrete random variable include the following:

X = the number of cars that drive up to a bank within a five-minute period ($X = 0, 1, 2, 3, \ldots$).

X = the number of people out of a group of 50 who will suffer a fatal accident within the next 10 years ($X = 0, 1, 2, \ldots, 50$).

X = the number of people out of 200 who make an airline reservation and then fail to show up ($X = 0, 1, 2, \ldots, 200$).

X = the number of calls arriving at a telephone switchboard over a two-minute period ($X = 0, 1, 2, 3, \ldots$).

Notice that, for each example, the discrete random variable is *a count* of the number of people, calls, accidents, and so on that can occur.

X Exercises 6.1–6.8

Understanding the Mechanics

6.1 In a batch of circuit boards there are two boards that need to be returned to the factory, three boards that need repair but do not need to be sent back to the factory, and three boards that are in good working condition.

  a. What is the probability that a circuit board selected at random needs to be returned to the factory?

  b. What is the probability that a circuit board is in good working condition?

6.2 A manager can either hire or not hire an applicant after an interview. Let H represent "hire" and N represent "not hire." Suppose that both outcomes are equally likely. Let X equal the number of Ns after two interviews.

  a. List all possible outcomes from two interviews. List these as pairs. Are each of these pairs of outcomes equally likely.

  b. What is $P(X = 0)$? $P(X = 1)$? $P(X = 2)$?

6.3 Consider a deck of 52 cards with 13 hearts, 13 spades, 13 clubs, and 13 diamonds and assume that a card is drawn at random. Define a random variable X to be 1 if a heart is drawn, 2 if a spade is drawn, and 3 if either a club or a diamond is drawn.
  a. List the values of X and their probabilities.
  b. What is the probability that X is greater than 1?
  c. What is the probability that X is either 1 or 3?

6.4 State the values that the following random variables can assume. Classify each random variable as either discrete or continuous.
  a. The percentage change in the S&P 500.
  b. The number of small businesses that fail each month in Chicago.
  c. The number of cases heard daily in a Common Pleas Court.
  d. The time that it takes a family to decide on purchasing a new home.
  e. The number of times that a manufacturing process needs readjustment during a week.

6.5 Let a random variable be the number of daily accidents that can occur in a manufacturing plant. Would this random variable follow a discrete distribution? Describe what a plausible probability distribution might look like for this random variable.

6.6 Is there any limit on the number of values that a discrete random variable can have? If a random variable had many possible values, would some of the probabilities need to be very small? Explain.

6.7 List two continuous and two discrete random variables that would be of interest to a business manager.

6.8 Let a random variable X be the sum of two discrete random variables. Is X discrete?

Representing Probability Distributions for Discrete Random Variables

There are three popular methods of describing the probabilities associated with a discrete random variable X:

1. List each value of X and its corresponding probability.

2. Use a histogram to convey the probabilities corresponding to the various values of X.

3. Use a function that assigns a probability to each value of X.

Remember our coin-flipping example, in which X = number of heads in three flips of a coin. We can list each value and probability:

$$X = \begin{cases} 0 \text{ with probability } 1/8 \\ 1 \text{ with probability } 3/8 \\ 2 \text{ with probability } 3/8 \\ 3 \text{ with probability } 1/8 \end{cases}$$

This works well when there is only a small number of possible values for X; it would not work well for 100 flips of a coin.

Using a histogram also is a convenient way to represent the shape of a discrete distribution having a small number of possible values. For this situation, you construct a histogram in which the height of each bar is the probability of observing that value of X (Figure 6.1). It is easier to determine the shape of the probability distribution by using such a chart. The distribution in Figure 6.1 is clearly symmetric and concentrated in the middle values.

Using a function (that is, an algebraic formula) to assign probabilities is the most convenient method of describing the probability distribution for a discrete random variable. For any given application of such a random variable, however, this function may or may not be known. Later in the chapter we identify certain useful discrete random variables, each of which has a corresponding function that assigns these probabilities.

The function that assigns a probability to each value of X is called a **probability mass function (PMF).** Denoting a particular value of X as x, this function is of the form

6.1

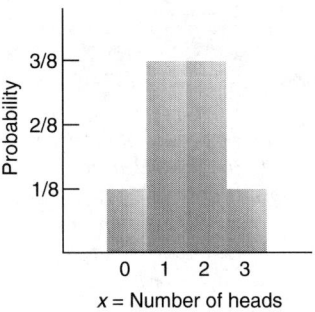

A histogram representation of a discrete random variable, where $X =$ number of heads in three coin flips.

$P(X = x) =$ some expression (usually containing x)
that produces the probability of observing x

$= P(x)$

Not every function can serve as a PMF. There are two requirements for a PMF function:

1. $P(x)$ is between 0 and 1 (inclusively) for each x

2. $\Sigma P(x) = 1$

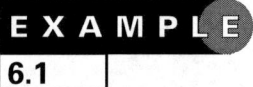

E X A M P L E

6.1

Consider a random variable X having possible values of 1, 2, or 3. The corresponding probability for each value is:

$$X = \begin{cases} 1 \text{ with probability } 1/6 \\ 2 \text{ with probability } 1/3 \\ 3 \text{ with probability } 1/2 \end{cases}$$

Determine an expression for the PMF.

Consider the function

Solution

$$P(X = x) = P(x) = x/6 \qquad \text{for } x = 1, 2, 3$$

This function provides the probabilities

$$P(X = 1) = P(1) = 1/6 \qquad \text{(OK)}$$
$$P(X = 2) = P(2) = 2/6 = 1/3 \qquad \text{(OK)}$$
$$P(X = 3) = P(3) = 3/6 = 1/2 \qquad \text{(OK)}$$

This function satisfies the requirements for a PMF: Each probability is between 0 and 1, and $P(1) + P(2) + P(3) = 1/6 + 1/3 + 1/2 = 1$. Consequently, the function

$$P(x) = x/6 \qquad \text{for } x = 1, 2, 3 \qquad \text{(and zero elsewhere)}$$

is the PMF for this discrete random variable.

EXAMPLE

6.2

6.2

You roll two dice, a red die and a blue die, and decide to let X represent the total of the two dice. Consequently, the possible values for X range from 2 (one on the red die, one on the blue die) to 12 (six on the red die, six on the blue die). Since there are 6 possible outcomes for the red die and 6 possible outcomes for the blue die, there are 36 equally likely outcomes here. The value of $X = 2$ occurs only one way (one on the red die, one on the blue die), so its probability is 1/36. The value $X = 3$ can occur two ways (one on the red die, two on the blue die or two on the red die, one on the blue die). The value of X with the highest probability is $X = 7$, since this can occur six ways. Can you list them? Start with one on the red die, six on the blue die, and end with six on the red die, one on the blue die. As a result, $P(X = 7) = P(7) = 6/36$. A summary of the probabilities is shown below. Notice they add to 1, as they should.

x	2	3	4	5	6	7	8	9	10	11	12
$P(x)$	1/36	2/36	3/36	4/36	5/36	6/36	5/36	4/36	3/36	2/36	1/36

Consider the expression

$$P(x) = \frac{6 - |x - 7|}{36} \quad \text{for } x = 2, 3, \dots, 12 \quad \text{(and zero elsewhere)}$$

where $|\ |$ represents the absolute value of a number. See if you can demonstrate that this function is a bona fide PMF for this example. (It is). Do not worry about where this expression came from, but do verify that it works. The truth of the matter is that often PMFs are derived by trial and error.

Notice that a probability mass function provides a theoretical model of the population by describing the chance of observing any particular value of the random variable. *You can view the population as what you would obtain if you observed the corresponding random variable indefinitely.*

X Exercises 6.9–6.19

Understanding the Mechanics

6.9 Which of the following probability mass functions are valid? Why?

a. x	$P(x)$	b. x	$P(x)$
–2	.4	10	–.1
–3	.4	20	.9
4	.2	30	.2

c. x	$P(x)$	d. x	$P(x)$	e. x	$P(x)$
1	.1	0	.1	100	.3
2	.2	5	.6	120	.3
3	.3	7	.1	300	.3
4	.4	9	.1	500	.3

6.10 Let $P(X = x)$ be equal to .125 for x equal to 10, 20, 30, 40, 50, 60, 70, or 80 and zero elsewhere. Why is this function a probability mass function?

6.11 Is the following function a probability mass function? Why?

$P(X = x) = x/30$ for $x = 0, 10,$ and 20 (and zero elsewhere)

6.12 Is the following function a probability mass function? Why?

$$P(X = x) = \frac{3}{4(3 - x)! x!} \text{ for } x = 0, 1, 2, 3$$

6.13 Is the following function a probability mass function? Why?

$$P(X = x) = \frac{\sqrt{x}}{9} \text{ for } x = 4, 9, 16 \quad \text{(and zero elsewhere)}$$

Applying the New Concepts

6.14 There are three electrical components that a quality-control inspector needs to inspect. One of the components does not function. Suppose that the inspector only chooses two randomly and that the random variable X represents the number of components not working.

  a. List all possible outcomes.
  b. Find the probability mass function for X.

6.15 A quality manager receives shipments of probe cards from three suppliers—say, suppliers A, B, and C. Probe cards are complex, multilayer printed circuit boards with some electrical points of contact smaller than a human hair. Suppose that the manager receives two boxes of probe cards from supplier A, which are believed to be of substandard quality. The manager receives four boxes of probe cards from supplier B, which are considered to be of good quality. From supplier C, the manager receives six boxes of very high quality probe cards. Suppose that a probe card is selected at random from this shipment. Define the random variable X to be 1, 2, or 3 if the probe card was manufactured by supplier A, B, or C, respectively. Verify that the following function is the probability mass function of X.

$$P(X = x) = x/6 \quad \text{if } x = 1, 2, 3 \quad \text{(and zero elsewhere)}$$

6.16 A real estate broker needs to advertise two townhouses, two duplexes, and two single-family homes. However, the broker decides to choose at random only one of the six properties for open house on a certain weekend. Let the random variable X take on the value 1 if a townhouse is chosen, 2 if a duplex is chosen, and 3 if a single-family home is chosen. Write the probability mass function of X.

6.17 Suppose that in Exercise 6.16, the random variable X is assigned the value of 2 if a townhouse is chosen, 4 if a duplex is chosen, and 6 if a single-family home is chosen. Write the probability mass function of X.

6.18 An investor has two investments, A and B. The investor believes that investment A is equally likely to increase by \$1,000 or to decrease by \$1,000 by the end of the year. The investor also believes that investment B is equally likely to increase by \$2000 or decrease by \$2,000 by the end of the year. Let X represent the total amount of change in investments A and B. Assume that these investments perform independent of each other. Find the probability mass function of X.

6.19 [**Simulation Exercise**] What happens if you roll two dice many times? How can you analyze this situation? To find the distribution of the sum of the values appearing on each dice roll a computer simulation can be created. On the KPK menu, select the **Sum of Dice Problem** by clicking on **Simulation Exercises.**
   a. Enter the number of times you think that you need to roll a pair of dice to determine the distribution. Continue to increase the number selected until the shape of the graph appears to stabilize.
   b. What is the probability of the most frequently occurring value for the sum of two dice? Does this agree with the solution to Example 6.2?
   c. Using the values from the simulation, what is the probability that the sum of dice will be between 5 and 8, inclusively? Does this agree with the solution to Example 6.2?

6.2

MEAN AND VARIANCE OF DISCRETE RANDOM VARIABLES

Mean of Discrete Random Variables

Chapter 3 introduced you to the mean and variance of a set of sample data consisting of n values. Suppose that these values were obtained by observing a particular random variable n times. The sample mean, $\overline{X}$, represents the *average* value of the sample data. In this section, we determine a similar value, the **mean of a discrete random variable,** written as μ. The value of μ represents the average value of the random variable if you were to observe this variable over an indefinite period of time.

Reconsider our coin-flipping example, where X is the number of heads in three flips of a coin. Suppose you flip the coin three times, record the value of X, flip the coin three times again, record the value of X, and repeat this process 10 times. Now you have 10 observations of X. Suppose they are

2, 1, 1, 0, 2, 3, 2, 1, 1, 3

The mean of these data is the *statistic* $\overline{X}$, where

$$\overline{x} = \frac{2+1+1+ \cdots +1+3}{10}$$

$$= 1.6 \text{ heads}$$

If you observed X *indefinitely*, what would X be on the average?

$$X = \begin{cases} 0 \text{ with probability } 1/8 \\ 1 \text{ with probability } 3/8 \\ 2 \text{ with probability } 3/8 \\ 3 \text{ with probability } 1/8 \end{cases}$$

So 1/8 of the time you should observe the value 0; 3/8 of the time, the value 1; 3/8 of the time, the value 2; and 1/8 of the time, the value 3. In a sense, each probability represents the *relative frequency* for that particular value of X. So the average value of X is

$$(0)(1/8) + (1)(3/8) + (2)(3/8) + (3)(1/8) = 1.5 \text{ heads}$$

Notice that X cannot be 1.5; this is merely the value of X on the average.

DEFINITION

The average value of the discrete random variable X (if observed indefinitely) is the mean of X. The symbol for this parameter is μ.

We found that $\mu = 1.5$ by multiplying each value of X by its corresponding probability and summing the results:

$$\mu = 1.5 = 0 \cdot P(0) + 1 \cdot P(1) + 2 \cdot P(2) + 3 \cdot P(3)$$

This procedure applies to any discrete random variable, and so we define*

$$\mu = \Sigma \, xP(x) \qquad \text{6.1}$$

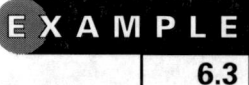

EXAMPLE 6.3

A personnel manager in a large production facility is investigating the number of reported on-the-job accidents over a period of one month. We define the random variable

$$X = \text{number of reported accidents per month}$$

Based on past records, she has derived the following probability distribution for X:

$$X = \begin{cases} 0 \text{ with probability } .50 \\ 1 \text{ with probability } .25 \\ 2 \text{ with probability } .10 \\ 3 \text{ with probability } .10 \\ 4 \text{ with probability } .05 \\ \hline 1.00 \end{cases}$$

---

*μ is often referred to as the *expected* value of the random variable, X, and is written $\mu = E(X)$.

During 50% of the months there were no reported accidents, 25% of the months had one accident, and so on. (Notice that deriving an algebraic expression for the PMF for this distribution would be extremely difficult. This poses no problem, however.)

What is the mean (average value) of X?

Solution

Using equation 6.1,

$$\mu = (0)(.5) + (1)(.25) + (2)(.1) + (3)(.1) + (4)(.05)$$

$$= .95$$

There is .95 (nearly 1) accident reported on the average per month.

Variance of Discrete Random Variables

We previously considered 10 observations of the random variable that counted the number of heads in three flips of a coin. These data were 2, 1, 1, 0, 2, 3, 2, 1, 1, 3. We used the notation from Chapter 3 to define the mean of these data, and we obtained $\bar{x} = 1.6$. The variance of these data, using equation 3.4, is $s^2 = .933$. Since s^2 describes a sample, it is a statistic.

Once again, consider observing X indefinitely. For this situation, the average value of X is defined as the mean of X, μ. When we observe X indefinitely, this particular variance is defined to be the variance of the random variable, X, and is written σ^2 (read as "sigma squared").

$$\sigma^2 = \text{variance of the discrete random variable, } X$$

The **variance of a discrete random variable,** X, is a parameter describing the variation of the corresponding population. It is the average (expected) value of $(X - \mu)^2$ if X were observed indefinitely, and it can be obtained by using one of the following expressions, which are mathematically equivalent:*

$$\sigma^2 = \Sigma(x - \mu)^2 \cdot P(x)$$

$$\sigma^2 = \Sigma x^2 P(x) - \mu^2$$

6.2 6.3

Equation 6.3 generally provides an easier method of determining the variance and will be used in all of the examples to follow. For the coin-flipping example,

$$\sigma^2 = \Sigma\, x^2 P(x) - \mu^2$$

$$= [(0)^2 \cdot (1/8) + (1)^2 \cdot (3/8) + (2)^2 \cdot (3/8) + (3)^2 \cdot (1/8)] - (1.5)^2$$

$$= 3 - 2.25 = .75$$

So our final results would be:

Using the Sample of 10 Observations		For the Random Variable, X (Indefinite Number of Observations)	
$\bar{x} = 1.6$	$s^2 = .933$	$\mu = 1.5$	$\sigma^2 = .75$
mean	variance	mean	variance
statistics		parameters	

---

*Using the expectation notation, σ^2 is the expected value of $(X - \mu)^2$ and can be written $\sigma^2 = E(X - \mu)^2$ or $\sigma^2 = E(X^2) - [E(X)]^2$.

In Chapter 3, the square root of the variance, s, was defined to be the standard deviation of the data. The same definition applies to a random variable. The **standard deviation of a discrete random variable,** X, is denoted σ, where:

$$\sigma = \sqrt{\Sigma(x-\mu)^2 \cdot P(x)}$$

$$\sigma = \sqrt{\Sigma x^2 P(x) - \mu^2}$$

5.4   5.5

6.4

Determine the variance and standard deviation of the random variable concerning on-the-job accidents in Example 6.3.

Solution

A convenient method of determining both the mean and variance of a discrete random variable is to summarize the calculations in tabular form:

x	$P(x)$	$x \cdot P(x)$	$x^2 \cdot P(x)$
0	.5	0	0
1	.25	.25	.25
2	.1	.2	.4
3	.1	.3	.9
4	.05	.2	.8
	1.00	.95	2.35

So,

$$\mu = \Sigma\, xP(x) = .95 \text{ accident}$$

and

$$\sigma^2 = \Sigma\, x^2 P(x) - \mu^2 = 2.35 - (.95)^2$$
$$= 1.45$$

Also

$$\sigma = \sqrt{1.45} = 1.20 \text{ accidents}$$

X Exercises 6.20–6.27

Understanding the Mechanics

6.20 Find the mean and standard deviation for the random variable X with the following distributions.

a. x	$P(x)$	b. x	$P(x)$	c. x	$P(x)$
0	.2	−3	.1	1	.1
1	.6	0	.3	2	.1
2	.2	3	.6	3	.4
				4	.3
				5	.1

6.21 For each of the following probability mass functions, determine the mean and standard deviation.

a. $P(X = x) = x/60$ for $x = 20$ and 40 (and zero elsewhere)

b. $P(X = x) = \sqrt{x}/11$ for $x = 4$, 16, and 25 (and zero elsewhere)

6.22 A random variable has possible values of 20, 21, 22, 23, and 24 that are equally likely to occur.

a. What is the probability that the random variable is less than 23?

b. What is the mean of the random variable?

c. What is the standard deviation of the random variable?

Applying the New Concepts

6.23 Suppose that a coin is flipped three times. Define the random variable X to be equal to twice the number of heads that appear. Determine the mean and variance of X.

6.24 An investment will return $500, $1,000, $2,000, or $5,000 with probabilities of .5, .2, .2, and .1, respectively. Compute the mean and standard deviation of the return.

6.25 The probabilities that 0, 1, 2, or 3 orders will be made daily at a particular Web site are .6, .2, .1, and .1, respectively. What are the mean and standard deviation of the number of daily orders at the Web site?

6.26 The accessibility that business professionals have to information technology creates the potential for misuse of this technology. Business professionals were asked to give their perceived importance of two ethical issues. Scenario 1 says that a programmer uses company equipment for personal use. Scenario 2 says that an employee uses proprietary software without paying the fee.

Importance of the Issue	Scenario 1	Scenario 2
Very important	.16	.61
Undecided	.18	.21
Not very important	.66	.18

a. Code very important, undecided, and not very important as having the values 1, 2, and 3. Find the mean and standard deviation for Scenario 1.
b. Repeat part a for Scenario 2.
c. Compare and interpret the statistics found in parts a and b.

(Source: "Making Ethical Decisions," *Communications of the ACM*, vol. 43, no. 12, December 2000, p. 66.)

6.27 The probabilities of a retailer discounting merchandise after Christmas by 20%, 30%, 40%, and 50% are .1, .4, .4, and .1, respectively. What are the mean and standard deviation of the discount percentage?

6.3   BINOMIAL DISTRIBUTION

The random variable X representing the number of heads in three flips of a coin is a special type of discrete random variable, a **binomial random variable.** We next list the conditions for a binomial random variable in general and as applied to our coin-flipping example:

A Binomial Situation

1. Your experiment consists of n repetitions, called *trials.*

2. Each trial has two mutually exclusive possible outcomes (or can be considered as having two outcomes) referred to as *success* and *failure.*

3. The n trials are *independent.*

4. The probability of a success for each trial is denoted p; the value of p remains the same for each trial.

5. The random variable X is the number of *successes* out of n trials.

For the Example in Section 6.1

1. $n = 3$ (flips of a coin).

2. Success = head, failure = tail (this is arbitrary).

3. The results on one coin flip do not affect the results on another flip.

4. p = the probability of flipping a head on a particular trial = 1/2.

5. X = the number of heads out of three flips.

You encounter a binomial random variable when a certain experiment is repeated many times (n trials), the trials are independent, and each experiment results in one of two mutually exclusive outcomes. For example, a randomly selected individual is either male or female, is on welfare or is not, will vote Republican or will not, and so on.

The two outcomes for each experiment are labeled as *success* or *failure.* A success need not be considered good or desirable. Instead, it depends on what you are counting at the completion of the n trials. If, for example, the object of the experiment is to determine the probability that 3 people out of 20 randomly selected individuals *are* on welfare, then a success on each of the $n = 20$ trials is the event that the person selected on each trial *is* on welfare.

EXAMPLE 6.5

In Example 5.4, it was noted that 30% of the people in a particular city read the evening newspaper. Select four people at random from this city. Consider how many of these four people read the evening paper. Does this situation satisfy the requirements of a binomial situation? What is your random variable here?

Solution   Refer to conditions 1 through 5 in our list for a binomial situation.

1. There are $n = 4$ trials, where each trial consists of selecting one individual from this city.

2. There are two outcomes for each trial. We are interested in counting the number of people, out of the four selected, who *do* read the evening paper, so define

$$\text{success} = \text{read the evening newspaper}$$
$$\text{failure} = \text{do not read the evening newspaper}$$

3. The trials are independent because the people are selected randomly.

4. p = probability of a success on each trial = .3.

5. The random variable here is X, where

$$X = \text{number of successes in } n \text{ trials}$$
$$X = \text{number of people (out of four) who read the evening newspaper}$$

All the requirements are satisfied. Thus, X is a binomial random variable (it is also discrete).

Counting Successes for a Binomial Situation

How many ways are there of getting two heads out of four flips? There are six: HHTT, HTHT, HTTH, THHT, THTH, and TTHH. In general, there is an expression that counts the number of ways of getting k successes in n trials. This expression is

$$_nC_k = \frac{n!}{k!(n-k)!}$$

where $k! = (k)(k-1)(k-2)\cdots(1)$. The expression $_nC_k$ is referred to as the **combination function** and is equal to 1 whenever $k = 0$ or $k = n$, since 0! is defined to be 1. Consequently, the number of ways of getting two heads out of four flips would be

$$_4C_2 = \frac{4!}{2!(4-2)!} = \frac{(4)(3)(2)(1)}{(2)(1)(2)(1)} = \frac{24}{4} = 6$$

Suppose a state lottery system requires the purchaser to select six lottery numbers between 1 and 50 with no repeat numbers allowed. The number of combinations here is the number of ways of selecting six values out of the 50 possible values and is equal to

$$_{50}C_6 = \frac{50!}{6!(50-6)!} = \frac{(50)(49)(48)(47)(46)(45)\,(44!)}{6!\,(44!)} = \frac{(50)(49)(48)(47)(46)(45)}{(6)(5)(4)(3)(2)(1)} = 15,890,700$$

(Note that in this equation, $(n - k)!$ will cancel out in the numerator and denominator so that you only have to multiply $n \cdot (n - 1) \cdot (n - 2) \cdots (n - k + 1)$ to arrive at the numerator, and the denominator will reduce to $k!$.) Consequently, your chances of winning this lottery with the purchase of one ticket are 1 in 15,890,700; that is, $\dfrac{1}{_{50}C_6} = .000000063$—not exactly great odds.

Once again, let X equal the number of heads out of three flips. Here X is a binomial random variable, with $p = .5$. Consider any value of X, say, $X = 1$. Then the probability of any one outcome where $X = 1$, such as HTT, is $1/8$ and the number of ways of getting one head (success) out of three flips (trials) is $_3C_1 = 3$. Consequently, the probability that X will be 1 is:

$$P(1) = {_3C_1}(1/8) = 3/8$$

The resulting *probability mass function* (PMF) for this situation can be written as

$$P(x) = {_3C_x} \cdot (1/8) \qquad \text{for } x = 0, 1, 2, 3 \qquad \text{(and zero elsewhere)}$$

Using this function, we obtain the same results as before:

$$P(0) = {_3C_0}(1/8) = 1 \cdot (1/8) = 1/8$$
$$P(1) = {_3C_1}(1/8) = 3 \cdot (1/8) = 3/8$$
$$P(2) = {_3C_2}(1/8) = 3 \cdot (1/8) = 3/8$$
$$P(3) = {_3C_3}(1/8) = 1 \cdot (1/8) = \underline{1/8}$$
$$1$$

EXAMPLE 6.6

In Example 6.5, the binomial random variable X is the number of people (out of four) who read the evening newspaper. Also, there are $n = 4$ trials (people) with $p = .3$ (30% of the people read the evening newspaper). Let S denote a success and F a failure. Then define:

$$S = \text{a person reads the evening newspaper}$$
$$F = \text{a person does not read the evening newspaper}$$

What is the probability that exactly two people (out of four) will read the evening paper?

Solution

This is $P(X = 2)$, or $P(2)$. Consider any one result where $X = 2$, such as SFSF. Since the trials are independent, the probability of this result is (probability of S on first trial) $\cdot$ (probability of F on second trial) $\cdot$ (probability of S on third trial) $\cdot$ (probability of F on fourth trial) which is

$$(.3)(.7)(.3)(.7) = (.3)^2(.7)^2$$

Also note that the probability of *each* result with two S's and two F's ($X = 2$) also is $(.3)^2(.7)^2 = p^2(1 - p)^2$. How many ways can we get two successes out of four trials? This is:

$$_4C_2 = \frac{4!}{2!2!} = 6$$

So the final result here is

$$P(2) = (\text{number of ways of getting } X = 2)(\text{probability of each one})$$
$$= {_4C_2}(.3)^2(.7)^2$$
$$= (6)(.09)(.49) = .265$$

FIGURE

6.2

Probability mass function for $n = 4$, $p = .3$.

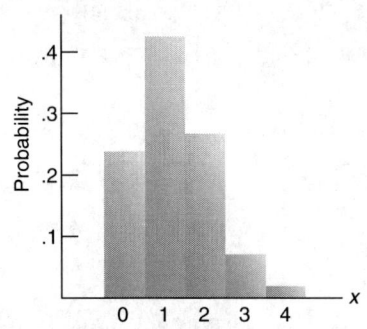

x = Number of evening newspaper subscribers

So 26.5% of the time, exactly two people out of four will read the evening newspaper.

We can extend the results of Example 6.6 to obtain the PMF for a binomial random variable:

$$P(x) = {}_nC_x p^x (1-p)^{n-x} \quad \text{for } x = 0, 1, 2, \ldots, n \quad \text{(and zero elsewhere)} \quad 6.6$$

where n is the number of trials and p is the probability of a success for each trial.

For the newspaper example, $x = 2$, $n = 4$, and $p = .3$. The complete list of probabilities for this example is:

$$X = \begin{cases} 0 \text{ with probability } {}_4C_0 \,(.3)^0\,(.7)^4 = .240 \\ 1 \text{ with probability } {}_4C_1 \,(.3)^1\,(.7)^3 = .412 \\ 2 \text{ with probability } {}_4C_2 \,(.3)^2\,(.7)^2 = .265 \\ 3 \text{ with probability } {}_4C_3 \,(.3)^3\,(.7)^1 = .076 \\ 4 \text{ with probability } {}_4C_4 \,(.3)^4\,(.7)^0 = .008 \\ \hline \phantom{0 \text{ with probability } {}_4C_0 \,(.3)^0\,(.7)^4 = {}} 1.001 \end{cases}$$

Note that the total value may be slightly greater or less than 1.0, because of rounding. A graphical representation of this PMF is shown in Figure 6.2.

Using Binomial Table A.1

The binomial PMFs have been tabulated in Table A.1 for various values of n and p. The maximum number of trials in this table is $n = 20$. For binomial situations where $n > 20$, we suggest the use of a computer package, such as Excel, SPSS, or MINITAB.

For the evening newspaper illustration in Example 6.6, $n = 4$ and $p = .3$. To find $P(2)$, locate $n = 4$ and $x = 2$. Go across the table to $p = .3$ and you will find the corresponding probability. This probability is .265. Similarly, $P(0) = .240$, $P(1) = .412$, $P(3) = .076$, and $P(4) = .008$, as before.

The probability that no more than two people will read the evening paper is written $P(X \leq 2)$, where

$$P(X \leq 2) = P(X = 0) + P(X = 1) + P(X = 2)$$

$$= P(0) + P(1) + P(2)$$

$$= .240 + .412 + .265$$

$$= .917$$

FIGURE

6.3

Shape of the
binomial
distribution.

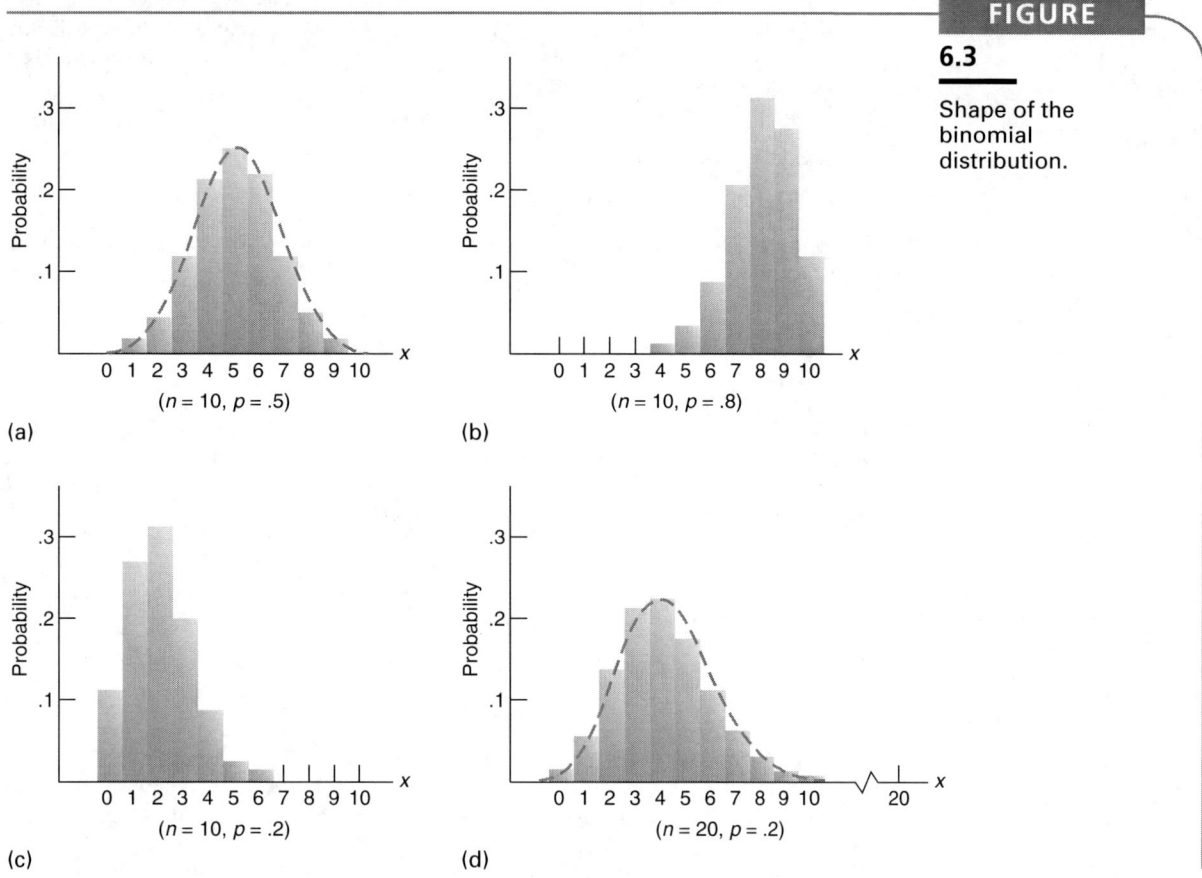

This is a *cumulative probability* and is obtained by summing $P(x)$ over the appropriate values of X.

Using Binomial Table A.2

Cumulative binomial probabilities are tabulated in Table A.2 for the same values of n and p used in Table A.1. The value in this table corresponding to $n = 4$, $x = 2$, and $p = .3$ is .916. Since this is a *cumulative* probability, then $P(X \leq 2) = .916$. Note that this value agrees with the previous result, except in the third decimal place. In general, using this table for cumulative probabilities will provide slightly more accurate results than summing the values in Table A.1.

Shape of the Binomial Distribution

Figure 6.3 contains a graphical representation of four binomial distributions. In particular, notice these three relationships hold:

1. When $p = .5$, the shape is perfectly *symmetrical* and resembles a bell-shaped (normal) curve.

2. When $p = .2$, the distribution is *skewed right*. This skewness increases as p decreases.

3. For $p = .8$, the distribution is *skewed left*. As p approaches 1, the amount of skewness increases.

Compare Figure 6.3(c) and (d). Notice that, in both cases, p is .2; however, the number of trials increased from $n = 10$ in (c) to $n = 20$ in (d). For the larger value of n, the shape of

229

this distribution is nearly bell-shaped, *despite the small value of* p. *This suggests that, regardless of the value of* p, *the shape of a binomial distribution approaches a bell-shaped distribution as the number of trials* (n) *increases.* For large sample sizes, we can approximate binomial probabilities using a bell-shaped (normal) curve.

In summary, the shape of a binomial distribution is

- Skewed left for $p > 1/2$ and small n

- Skewed right for $p < 1/2$ and small n

- Approximately bell-shaped (symmetric) if p is near $1/2$ or if the number of trials is large

Mean and Variance of Binomial Random Variables

In Example 6.6, we examined the binomial random variable X representing the number of people (out of four) who read the evening newspaper. If you select four people, observe X, select four more people, observe X, and repeat this procedure indefinitely, what will X be on the average? This is the mean of X, where, using equation 6.1,

$$\mu = \Sigma\, xP(x)$$
$$= (0)(.240) + (1)(.412) + (2)(.265) + (3)(.076) + (4)(.008)$$
$$= 1.2 \text{ people}$$

Also, using equation 6.3, the variance of X is

$$\sigma^2 = \Sigma\, x^2 P(x) - \mu^2$$
$$= [(0)^2(.240) + (1)^2(.412) + (2)^2(.265) + (3)^2(.076) + (4)^2(.008)] - (1.2)^2$$
$$= 2.28 - 1.44 = .84$$

and so σ = standard deviation of $X = \sqrt{.84} = .92$ people. (Watch the units.)

The good news is that there is a convenient shortcut for finding the mean and variance of a binomial random variable. For this situation, you need not use equations 6.1 and 6.3. Instead, for any binomial random variable,

$$\mu = np$$

6.7 6.8

How these expressions were derived is certainly not obvious, but let us verify that they work for Example 6.6. Here $n = 4$ and $p = .3$, so

$$\mu = (4)(.3) = 1.2 \qquad \text{(OK)}$$
$$\sigma^2 = (4)(.3)(.7) = .84 \qquad \text{(OK)}$$

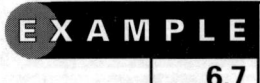

If you repeat Example 6.6 using $n = 50$ people (rather than $n = 4$ people), how many evening newspaper readers will you observe on the average?

Solution Now, X is the number of people (out of 50) who read the evening paper. Consequently,

$$\mu = np = (50)(.3) = 15$$

So, on the average, X will be 15 people. For this situation, the variance of X is

$$\sigma^2 = np(1 - p) = (50)(.3)(.7) = 10.5$$

Also,

$$\sigma = \sqrt{10.5} = 3.24 \text{ people}$$

EXAMPLE 6.8

Airline overbooking is a common practice. Many people make reservations on several flights due to uncertain plans and then cancel at the last minute or simply fail to show up. Eagle Air is a small commuter airline. Its planes hold only 15 people. Past records indicate that 20% of the people making a reservation do not show up for the flight. We will assume that all reservations are independent; that is, each reservation is for one person, and these reservations are made independent of one another.

Suppose that Eagle Air decides to book 18 people for each flight.

1. Determine the probability that on any given flight, at least one passenger holding a reservation will not have a seat.

2. What is the probability that there will be one or more empty seats for any one flight?

3. Determine the mean and standard deviation for this random variable.

Solution 1

The binomial random variable for this situation is X = the number of people (out of 18) who book a flight and actually do appear. For this binomial situation, $n = 18$ (18 reservations are made) and $p = 1 - .2 = .8$ (the probability that any one person will show up). At least one passenger will have no place to sit if X is 16 or more. Using Table A.1,

$$P(X \geq 16) = P(X = 16) + P(X = 17) + P(X = 18)$$
$$= .172 + .081 + .018 = .271$$

We see that if the airline follows this policy, 27% of the time one or more passengers will be deprived of a seat—not a good situation.

This result could also be obtained using Table A.2:

$$P(X \geq 16) = 1 - P(X < 16) = 1 - P(X \leq 15)$$
$$= 1 - .729 = .271.$$

Solution 2

We want to find the probability that the number of people who actually arrive (X) is 14 or less. Using Table A.2 (where $n = 18$, $p = .8$),

$$P(X \leq 14) = .499$$

With this booking policy, the airline will have flights with one or more empty seats approximately one-half of the time.

Solution 3

The mean of X is

$$\mu = np = (18)(.8) = 14.4 \text{ people}$$

which implies that the average number of people who book a flight and do appear is 14.4. The standard deviation of X is

$$\sigma = \sqrt{np(1-p)} = \sqrt{(18)(.8)(.2)} = 1.70 \text{ people}$$

EXAMPLE 6.9

It is estimated that 1 out of 10 vouchers examined by the audit staff employed by a branch of the Department of Health and Human Services will contain an error. Define X to be the number of vouchers in error out of 20 randomly selected vouchers.

1. What is the probability that at least three vouchers will contain an error?

2. What is the probability that no more than one contains an error?

3. Determine the mean and standard deviation of X.

Solution 1

The random variable X satisfies the requirements for a binomial random variable with $n - 20$ and $p = .1$. For this situation, a "success" is defined to be that a voucher contains an error. The probability that at least three vouchers will contain an error is the probability that X is *3 or more*, which is

$$P(X \geq 3) = 1 - P(X < 3)$$
$$= 1 - P(X \leq 2)$$
$$= 1 - .677 \text{ (using Table A.2)}$$
$$= .323$$

Consequently, the probability that at least three vouchers will contain an error is .323.

Solution 2

The chance that no more than one voucher is in error is the probability that X is *1 or less*, which is

$$P(X \leq 1) = P(0) + P(1) = .392 \text{ (using Table A.2)}$$

So this event will occur with probability .392.

Solution 3

The mean of the random variable X is

$$\mu = np = (20)(.1) = 2 \text{ vouchers}$$

and the standard deviation of X is

$$\sigma = \sqrt{np(1-p)} = \sqrt{(20)(.1)(.9)} = 1.34 \text{ vouchers}$$

This implies that, on the average, the audit staff will encounter two vouchers containing an error (out of 20 randomly selected vouchers).

One situation that requires the use of a binomial random variable is **lot acceptance sampling,** in which you decide whether to accept or send back a lot (batch) of many electrical components, machine parts, or whatever.

Using Statistical Software to Determine Binomial Probabilities

In an earlier section titled "Using the Binomial Table," we mentioned that this table contains only values of $n \leq 20$. Excel offers a simple way of finding binomial probabilities for any sample size (n)—in particular, for values of n greater than 20. Excel can be used to calculate an individual probability [such as $P(X = 3)$] or a cumulative probability [such as $P(X \leq 3)$]. This will be illustrated in the next example.

EXAMPLE 6.10

A shipment of 2,500 calculator chips arrives at Cassidy Electronics. The contract specifies that Cassidy will accept this lot if a sample size of 100 from the shipment has no more than one defective chip. What is the probability of accepting the lot if, in fact, 5% of the lot (125 chips) are defective?

Solution

This is approximately a binomial situation:

1. There are $n = 100$ trials.

2. Each trial has two outcomes:

$$success = chip\ is\ defective$$

$$failure = chip\ is\ not\ defective$$

(*Note:* Since the object is to count the number of *defective* chips in the shipment, a success on each trial (chip) will be that the chip is defective. As mentioned earlier, a success need not be a desirable event.)

3. p = probability of a success = .05*

4. The random variable here is X = number of successes out of n trials = number of defective chips out of 100. Cassidy accepts the lot of chips if X is 0 or 1. The corresponding probability is a cumulative probability:

$$P(\text{accept}) = P(X \leq 1)$$

$$= P(0) + P(1)$$

To determine binomial probabilities using Excel, click on **Insert** and select **Function.** Click on **Statistical** under **Function Category,** and click on **BINOMDIST** under **Function Name.** You should then see the input screen shown in Figure 6.4. Panel A of Figure 6.4 is what you would enter to determine $P(X = 0)$, and Panel B provides $P(X = 1)$. Notice that "false" was entered in the box labeled **Cumulative** since individual probabilities were

---

*If the lot size is large (2,500 here) and the sample size is relatively small (100 here), then the value of p is nearly, although not completely, unaffected by the previous trials. For example, if 5% of the chips are defective, then on the first trial, p is 125/2,500 = .05. On the second trial, p is either 125/2,499 = .05002 (if the first chip was nondefective) or 124/2,499 = .04962 (if the first chip was defective). We typically ignore this minor problem in lot sampling from large populations, but this is why at the start of the solution we mentioned that this is "approximately a binomial situation."

FIGURE

6.4

Using Excel to find individual probabilities (panels a and b) or cumulative probabilities (panel c).

BINOMDIST

Number_s	0	= 0
Trials	100	= 100
Probability_s	.05	= 0.05
Cumulative	false	= FALSE

= 0.005920529

Returns the individual term binomial distribution probability.

Cumulative is a logical value: for the cumulative distribution function, use TRUE; for the probability mass function, use FALSE.

Formula result = 0.005920529   OK   Cancel

(a)

BINOMDIST

Number_s	1	= 1
Trials	100	= 100
Probability_s	.05	= 0.05
Cumulative	false	= FALSE

= 0.03116068

Returns the individual term binomial distribution probability.

Cumulative is a logical value: for the cumulative distribution function, use TRUE; for the probability mass function, use FALSE.

Formula result = 0.03116068   OK   Cancel

(b)

BINOMDIST

Number_s	1	= 1
Trials	100	= 100
Probability_s	.05	= 0.05
Cumulative	true	= TRUE

= 0.037081209

Returns the individual term binomial distribution probability.

Cumulative is a logical value: for the cumulative distribution function, use TRUE; for the probability mass function, use FALSE.

Formula result = 0.037081209   OK   Cancel

(c)

desired. From Panels A and B, we also learn that $P(X \leq 1) = P(X = 0) + P(X = 1) = .0059 + .0312 = .0371$. Consequently, there is about a 4% chance that a sample of size 100 from this population will contain zero or one defective chip (the lot will be accepted).

The easiest way to find $P(X \leq 1)$ is to use Panel C in Figure 6.4 where "true" was entered in the **Cumulative** box and the result .0371 (rounded) appears. To summarize: enter "false" in the **Cumulative** box for individual probabilities and "true" for cumulative probabilities. The procedures for generating binomial probabilities using MINITAB and SPSS are explained in the end-of-chapter appendix.

The concept of lot acceptance sampling was originally presented in Section 1.4 of Chapter 1 to illustrate the distinction between a population and a sample. It also serves as a brief introduction to the area of inferential statistics, discussed at length in Chapter 8. In Example 6.10, we inferred something about a population (the lot of 2,500 chips) using a sample (the 100 chips selected for testing). The sample does not include all elements of the population, so there is a risk of making an incorrect decision, such as (1) accepting the lot of chips when in fact it should be rejected or (2) rejecting the lot of chips when in fact it was satisfactory. *Such possibilities for error always exist when a statistical sample is used as a basis for an assertion about a population.*

X Exercises 6.28–6.41

Understanding the Mechanics

6.28 Using the binomial probabilities in Table A.1, find the following probabilities for a binomial random variable X.
   a. $P(X = 2)$, $n = 4$, $p = .2$
   b. $P(X = 7)$, $n = 9$, $p = .8$
   c. $P(X = 4)$, $n = 10$, $p = .5$
   d. $P(X = 0)$, $n = 20$, $p = .1$

6.29 Find the probabilities of the following events for a binomial random variable with $n = 10$ and $p = .5$.
   a. exactly 2 successes
   b. more than 2 successes
   c. no more than 2 successes
   d. less than 2 successes
   e. at least 2 successes

6.30 For a binomial random variable with $n = 5$ and $p = .25$, compute the following.
   a. $P(X = 1)$
   b. $P(X \geq 1)$
   c. $P(X \leq 3)$
   d. $P(1 \leq X \leq 3)$

6.31 What is the probability that a binomial random variable with $n = 21$ and $p = .1$ does not exceed 1?

Applying the New Concepts

6.32 A lawyer estimates that 40% of the cases in which she represented the defendant were won. If the lawyer is presently representing 10 defendants in different cases, what is the probability that at least 5 of the cases will be won? What are you assuming here?

6.33 A market-research firm has discovered that 30% of the people who earn between $25,000 and $50,000 per year have bought a new car within the past two years. In a sample of 12 people earning between $25,000 and $50,000 per year, what is the probability that between 4 and 10 people, inclusive, have bought a new car within the past two years?

6.34 Web site visitors are often loath to disclose personal information when making a purchase on the Internet. Despite safeguards that have been in place, approximately 60% of all consumers who make purchases on the Internet do not feel comfortable giving their credit card number. Suppose that X is a random variable that represents the number of Web site purchasers that do not feel comfort-able typing their credit card number online from a sample of 20 purchasers.
   a. Why is X a binomial random variable?
   b. What is the probability that X is less than six?
   c. Would you consider the event of X less than six to be unusual?
   d. What value would you expect X to be on average? What is the standard deviation of X?

(Source: "Why Do You Ask," *The Wall Street Journal*, June 25, 2001, p. R17.)

6.35 According to the Consumer Aerosol Products Council, when adults were asked if it is true or false that aerosol cans may use CFC propellants (which eat the earth's ozone), approximately three in 10 adults knew that it was false. CFCs were banned in almost all sprays 20 years ago. However, 37% of the adults still believed the answer to be true.
   a. For a random sample of 10 adults, what do you think the probability is that fewer than three adults know that the answer is false? Compute it.
   b. For a random sample of 10 adults, what do you think the probability is that fewer than three believe that the answer is true (the incorrect answer)? Compute it.
   c. What is the mean number of sampled adults that you would expect to say that the answer is false [part a] and to say that the answer is true [part b]?

(Source: "Do Spray Cans Use CFCs?" *USA Today*, April 22, 1998, p. 1A.)

6.36 Sun Microsystems has approximately 50% of the high-end Unix machines, with its closest competitor being IBM. Suppose that 15 corporations were in the market to purchase a high-end Unix machine. Assume that these corporations listened to sales pitches by all the major players selling high-end Unix machines.
   a. What is the mean and standard deviation of the number of corporations that purchase a Unix machine from Sun Microsystems?
   b. What is the probability that exactly eight corporations purchase a Unix machine from Sun Microsystems?
   c. What is the probability that between 5 and 10 corporations, inclusively, purchase a Unix machine from Sun Microsystems?

(Source: "IBM Unveils High-End Computer Server," *The Wall Street Journal*, October 4, 2001, p. B7.)

6.37 Let the random variable X represent the number of correct responses on a multiple choice test that has 15 questions. Each question has five multiple choice answers.

  a. What is the probability that the random variable X is greater than 8 if the person taking the test randomly guesses?

  b. What is the mean value of X if the person randomly guesses?

  c. What is the standard deviation of X if the person randomly guesses?

  d. Estimate the probability that X will fall within the limits $\mu \pm 2\sigma$.

6.38 The *Professional Technician* recommends stocks each month. If 40% of the stocks recommended advance at least 20%, what is the probability that of the five stocks most recently recommended, at least three will advance at least 20%?

6.39 The manager of a retail store knows that 10% of all checks written are "hot" checks. Of the next 25 checks written at the retail store, what is the probability that no more than three checks are hot?

6.40 Mergers and slow periods in the economy often spell layoffs at many companies. Many employees count on two or three months of severance pay to carry them over to the next job. However, job searches can sometimes take longer than 6 months. A survey of workers who have been with companies for more than a year revealed that only 30% of the workers would be financially secure if they lost their job for 6 months to a year. Let X represent the number of employees out of a sample of 80 who would feel financially secure if they lost their job for 6 months to a year.

  a. What is the probability that at least 30 employees out of 80 would be financially secure if they lost

their job for 6 months to a year? (In Excel, click on **Insert Function ➤ Statistical ➤ Binomdist.** In SPSS, click on **Transform ➤ Compute ➤ CDF.BINOM(q,n,p).** In MINITAB, click on **Calc ➤ Probability Distributions ➤ Binomial.**)

  b. Do a "what if" analysis by changing the probability to .4 and to .5 and rework part a.

(Source: "How Long Workers Believe That They Would Be Financially Secure If They Lost Their Jobs," *USA Today,* June 5, 2001, p. 1B.)

6.41 Home ownership in the United States soared to its highest level in the late 1990s. The average percentage of the population owning a home is 66.2%. However, that rate varies from state to state. For example, in New York, approximately 50% of the population own their home and in Indiana, the home ownership rate is about 70%.

  a. Supposing that 100 families were randomly selected from New York, what is the probability that at least 50 families own their home. Use a statistical computer package.

  b. Supposing that the 100 families in part a were from Indiana, what would the probability be?

  c. If the 100 families in part a were from across the United States, what would the probability be?

  d. What is the expected number of families that are owners from New York, Indiana, and across the United States in a random sample of 100 families?

  e. Which sample (from New York, Indiana, or across the USA) would you expect to have the highest standard deviation? Compute the standard deviations and compare.

(Source: "Homeownership Gets Sweeter, Hits Record," *USA Today,* May 23, 2001, p. 2B.)

6.4

POISSON DISTRIBUTION

The Poisson distribution, named after the French mathematician Simeon Poisson, is useful for counting the number of times a particular event occurs over a specified period of time. It also can be used for counting the number of times an event (such as a manufacturing defect) occurs over a specified area (such as a square yard of sheet metal) or in a specified volume. *We will restrict our discussion to counting over time, although any unit of measurement is permissible.*

The random variable X for this situation is the number of occurrences of a particular event over a specified period of time. The possible values are 0, 1, 2, 3, . . . For X to be a **Poisson random variable** over a given interval of time, the occurrences of this event need to occur *randomly*, as summarized by the following three conditions:

1. *The number of occurrences in one interval of time is unaffected by the number of occurrences in any other nonoverlapping time interval. That is, the variables are statistically independent. For example, what took place between 3:00 and 3:20 P.M. is unaffected by what took place between 9:00 and 10:00 A.M.*

236

2. *The expected (or average) number of occurrences over any time period is proportional to the size of this time interval.* For example, we would expect half as many occurrences between 3:00 and 3:30 P.M. as between 3:00 and 4:00 P.M.

This condition also implies that the probability of an occurrence must be constant over any intervals of the same length. A situation in which this is usually *not* true is at a restaurant from 12:00 noon to 12:10 P.M. and 2:00 to 2:10 P.M. Due to the differences in traffic flow for these two intervals, we would not expect the arrivals between, say, 11:30 A.M. and 2:30 P.M. to satisfy the requirements of a Poisson situation.

3. *Events cannot occur exactly at the same time.* More precisely, there is a unit of time sufficiently small (such as one second) that no more than one occurrence of an event is possible during this time.

Here are some situations that usually meet these conditions:

- The number of arrivals at a local bank over a five-minute interval.
- The number of telephone calls arriving at a switchboard over a one-minute interval.
- The number of daily accidents reported along a 20-mile stretch of an intercity toll road.
- The number of trucks in a fleet that break down over a one-month period.

For each situation, the (discrete) random variable X is the number of occurrences over the time period T. If all the assumptions are satisfied, then X is a Poisson random variable. Define μ to be the expected (or average) number of occurrences over this period of time.* For any application, the value of μ must be specified or estimated in some manner. The Poisson PMF for X follows.

POISSON PROBABILITY MASS FUNCTION

X = number of occurrences over time period T.

$$P(x) = \frac{\mu^x e^{-\mu}}{x!} \quad \text{for } x = 0, 1, 2, 3, \dots$$

where μ = expected number of occurrences over T and e = 2.71828.**

6.15

Mean and Variance of a Poisson Random Variable

Once again, we could use the definition of the mean and variance of a discrete random variable in equations 6.1 and 6.3. However, this is not necessary. It is fairly easy to show, using equation 6.7, that

$$\text{mean of } X = \Sigma\, xP(x)$$

$$= \mu$$

This is hardly a surprising result, given how μ was originally defined. Also,

$$\text{variance of } X = \sigma^2$$

$$= \Sigma\, x^2 P(x) - \mu^2$$

$$= \mu$$

So, *both the mean and the variance of the Poisson random variable X are equal to μ.* Recall that the Poisson random variable is the number of occurrences of a particular event (such

---

*The symbol λ (lambda) often is used to denote this parameter.
**To see additional decimal places for e, enter 1 in your calculator and press the e^x key. We will use e again in Chapter 6.

as a traffic accident) over a given time period (such as an hour). If the time period is doubled to two hours, then the mean of the "new" Poisson random variable is twice the original mean; if the time period is halved to 30 minutes, the corresponding mean is halved, and so on. This is illustrated in the next two examples.

EXAMPLE 6.11

Applications of a Poisson Random Variable

Handy Home Center specializes in building materials for home improvements. They recently constructed an information booth in the center of the store. Define X to be the number of customers who arrive at the booth over a five-minute period. Assume that the conditions for a Poisson situation are satisfied with

$$\mu = 4 \text{ customers over a 5-minute period}$$

A graph of the Poisson probabilities for $\mu = 4$ is contained in Figure 6.5.

1. What is the probability that over any five-minute interval, exactly four people arrive at the information booth?

2. What is the probability that more than one person will arrive?

3. What is the probability that exactly six people arrive over a 10-minute period?

Solution 1 First, this probability is not 1, because $\mu = 4$ is the *average* number of arrivals over this time period. The actual number of arrivals over some five-minute period may be fewer than four, more than four, or exactly four. The fraction of time that you observe exactly four people is, using Table A.3,

$$P(4) = \frac{4^4 e^{-4}}{4!} = .1954$$

If you stand in the booth for many five-minute periods, 19.5% of the time you will observe four people arrive.

FIGURE 6.5

Poisson probabilities for $\mu = 4$.

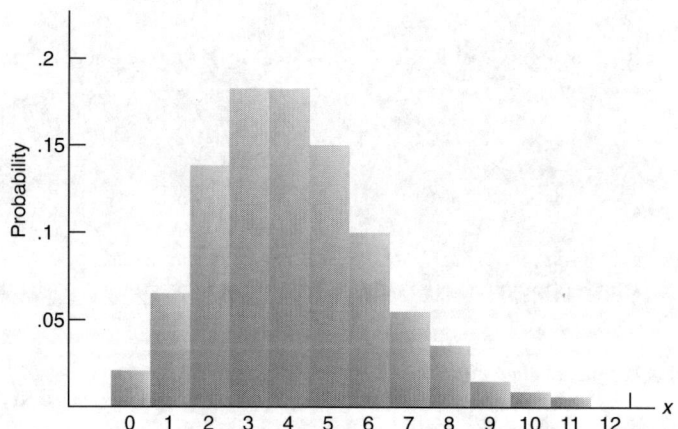

This is $P(X > 1) = P(X \geq 2)$. We could try

$$P(X \geq 2) = P(X = 2) + P(X = 3) + \cdots$$
$$= P(2) + P(3) + \cdots$$
$$= .1465 + .1954 + \cdots$$

There is an infinite number of terms here, however, so this is *not* the way to find this probability. A much better way is to use the fact that these probabilities sum to 1. Consequently,

$$P(X \geq 2) = 1 - P(X < 2)$$
$$= 1 - P(X \leq 1)$$
$$= 1 - [P(0) + P(1)]$$
$$= 1 - \left[\frac{4^0 e^{-4}}{0!} + \frac{4^1 e^{-4}}{1!} \right]$$
$$= 1 - [.0183 + .0733] = .9084$$

For this time interval,

μ = expected (average) number of people over a 10-minute time period

$\mu = 8$ (we expect four people over a 5-minute period)

Therefore, the probability of observing six people over a 10-minute period is

$$\frac{8^6 e^{-8}}{6!} = .1221$$

using Table A.3.

The Poisson distribution is widely used in the area of quality control for describing the number of nonconformities observed in a sampling unit. A *nonconformity* is defined as a failure to conform to a particular specification, such as "no scratches on a strip of sheet metal" or "no leaks in an automobile radiator." If a sampling unit is a square yard of sheet metal, then the number of nonconformities might be the number of observed scratches. Or if the sampling unit is a radiator, the number of nonconformities is the number of observed leaks. If the occurrences of a nonconformity are relatively rare (compared to the number that could occur if everything went wrong), then the Poisson distribution typically works well to describe the random variable X = number of nonconformities per sampling unit, as illustrated in the following example.

E X A M P L E 6.12

A certain process produces 100-foot-long sheets of vinyl composed of a simulated wood grain top layer and a black bottom layer. A blemish (nonconformity) occurs when the black layer shows through or the wood grain pattern is not distinct. A 10-foot sample is obtained by trimming the end of a roll, at which point the number of blemishes is observed and recorded. It is believed that the number of blemishes per sample follows a Poisson distribution with an average of two blemishes per 10-foot sample. Determine the probability that:

1. There will be no blemishes observed in a 10-foot sample.

2. There will be more than eight blemishes observed if a 30-foot sample is used.

FIGURE

6.6

Using Excel to determine Poisson probabilities for Example 6.12.

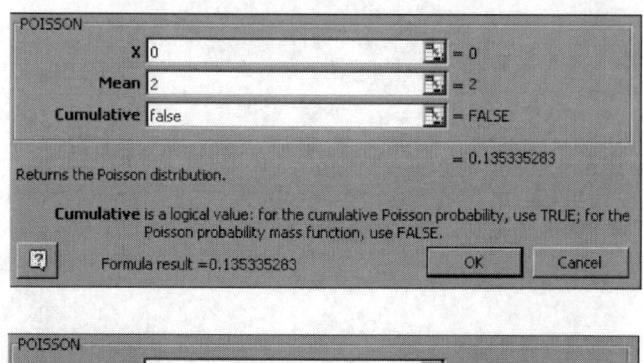

Solution 1   The Poisson variable X for this situation is the number of observed blemishes. The average number of observed blemishes in a 10-foot sample is two, so

$$P(X=0)=\frac{2^0 e^{-2}}{0!}=.1353$$

using Table A.3. This result means that 13.5% of the 10-foot samples will contain no blemishes.

Solution 2   The average number of blemishes in a 30-foot sample is six, given that the average is two for a 10-foot sample. Therefore, using Table A.3 with $\mu = 6$,

$$P(X>8)=1-P(X\le 8)$$

$$=1-\left[\frac{6^0 e^{-6}}{0!}+\frac{6^1 e^{-6}}{1!}+\cdots+\frac{6^7 e^{-6}}{7!}+\frac{6^8 e^{-6}}{8!}\right]$$

$$=1-(.0025+.0149+\cdots+.1377+.1033)=.153$$

We can expect more than eight blemishes in a 30-foot sample about 15% of the time.

Using Statistical Software to Determine Poisson Probabilities

To find a Poisson probability using Excel: (1) click on **Insert** and select **Function,** (2) click on **Statistical** under **Function Category,** and (3) click on **POISSON** under **Function Name.** The Poisson probabilities in Example 6.12 are calculated using Excel in Figure 6.6. The top panel is used to find $P(X = 0)$, where the mean of X is 2. Notice that "false" is entered in the **Cumulative** box since an individual probability is desired. The formula result of .1353 will appear in the current active cell in the Excel spreadsheet and agrees with Solution 1 in Example 6.12.

The bottom panel of Figure 6.6 is used to determine $P(X > 8)$ for the situation posed in the second part of Example 6.12, where the mean of X is now 6. To find $P(X > 8)$, remember that $P(X > 8)$ is the same as $1 - P(X \le 8)$. According to the Excel output, $P(X \le 8)$ is .847, and so $P(X > 8)$ is $1 - .847 = .153$, which agrees with Solution 2 in Example 6.12. To find the cumulative probability $P(X \le 8)$, enter "true" in the **Cumulative** box.

The procedure for generating Poisson probabilities using MINITAB and SPSS are explained in the end-of-chapter appendix.

X Exercises 6.42–6.56

Understanding the Mechanics

6.42 Let X be a Poisson random variable with a mean of 4. What is the probability that X is greater than 4? Less than 4? Equal to 4?

6.43 A Poisson random variable, X, has a mean of 8. What is the probability that X exceeds 7? Is no more than 7?

6.44 What is the probability that a Poisson random variable, X, is between 2 and 6, inclusively? Assume that the mean is 3.

6.45 If X is distributed as a Poisson random variable, what is the probability that X is equal to 0 assuming that the mean is 2? What is the probability if the mean is 5?

6.46 What is the probability that a Poisson random variable is greater than 9 if the mean is 7.2? What is this probability if the mean is 4.4?

6.47 What is the probability that a Poisson random variable is either less than 2 or greater than 5 assuming that the mean is equal to 3.5?

6.48 If a Poisson random variable has a standard deviation of 4, what is the mean?

Applying the New Concepts

6.49 After business professionals, cellphone companies are targeting the under-20 segment of the population as the next most lucrative market segment. Teenagers judge the coolness of their cell phones by the ring tones, the quality of pictures, and instant messaging. Assume that an average number of cellphones sold weekly by The Cellphone Store for use by individuals less than 20 years of age is 10. The owner believes that the Poisson distribution can be used to approximate the probability of the number of cellphones sold weekly to this segment of the population.
   a. What is the probability that at least eight phones are sold weekly to the under-20 population?
   b. What is probability that no more than 12 phones are sold weekly to the under-20 population?
   c. What is the mean and standard deviation of the number of cellphones sold to the under-20 group?

   d. Does it make sense to use the Poisson distribution to approximate the probability of the sales to the under-20 group?

(Source: "Back to School: It's Not About the Clothes," *The Wall Street Journal*, August 27, 2004, p. W1.)

6.50 The vice president of a bank wishes to provide banking service so that the probability of the number of waiting customers being greater than 8 is less than .07. Would this condition be satisfied if the number of waiting customers is a Poisson random variable with a mean of 5?

6.51 Some analysts believe that the number of Internet surfers clicking on a Web site has a Poisson distribution. Suppose that the number of times that the University of North Texas's (UNT) home page is accessed over the noon hour has an average rate of 10 times per hour. The Web master of this home page wants to determine various probabilities. Assuming that the number of times this Web page is accessed during the noon hour is Poisson distributed, find the following probabilities.
   a. What is the probability that no more than 10 Internet users will access the UNT home page during the noon hour?
   b. What is the probability that the number of Internet users accessing the UNT home page will exceed 15 during the noon hour?

6.52 California has the highest compliance of use of shoulder belts by the vehicle's front-seat occupants. On a 10 mile stretch of I-10 near Los Angeles, traffic officers estimate that approximately 1,000 cars pass every 15 minutes during the evening rush hour. Suppose that the average number of vehicles not complying with seat-belt laws is 10 during this period of time.
   a. Does it appear reasonable to assume that the number of vehicles not complying with seat-belt laws during the evening traffic follows a Poisson distribution?
   b. What is the likelihood during a particular 15-minute period that at least eight vehicles do not comply with the seat-belt laws?

(Source: "Seat Belt Use Highest in California," *USA Today*, June 28, 2001, p. 1A.)

6.53 The auto parts department of an automotive dealership sends out an average of eight special orders daily. The number of special orders is assumed to follow a Poisson distribution.

    a. What is the probability that for any day, the number of special orders sent out will be more than four?

    b. What is the standard deviation of the number of special orders sent out daily?

6.54 A city averages 10 business bankruptcies per year. Compute the interval $\mu - 2\sigma$ to $\mu + 2\sigma$ assuming that the number of yearly bankruptcies is a Poisson random variable.

6.55 A certain manufacturer sells a machine that has numerous moving parts. A quality-control inspector counts the number of moving parts that are misaligned as the number of nonconformities for a particular machine. It is believed that the number of nonconformities per machine follows a Poisson distribution, with an average of three nonconformities per machine.

    a. Determine the probability that the quality-control inspector finds no more than one nonconformity on a particular machine selected at random.

    b. What is the standard deviation of the number of nonconformities per machine.

6.56 On the eve of filing its anticipated initial public offering (IPO), Google had a half billion dollars in cash. Google has surpassed Yahoo as a cash generator. Suppose that Google averages 30 million visitors per day. Assume that the conditions of a Poission distribution are satisfied.

    a. What is the probability that less than 35 million visitors per day visit Google? (In Excel, click on **Insert Function ➤ Statistical ➤ Poisson**. In SPSS, click on **Transform ➤ Compute ➤ CDF.POISSON(q,mean)**. In MINITAB, click on **Calc ➤ Probability Distribution ➤ Poisson**.)

    b. What is the probability that more than 50 million visitors per day visit Google?

    c. Would the event of more than 50 million visitors per day at Google be considered unusual?

    d. What is the standard deviation of the number of visitors per day that visit Google?

(Source: "The Little Search Engine That Could," *The Wall Street Journal*, May 5, 2004, p. A14.)

 # Summary

When an experiment results in a numerical outcome, a convenient way of representing the possible values and corresponding probabilities is to use a random variable. If the possible values of this variable can be listed, along with the probability for each value (e.g., you are counting something), this variable is said to be a discrete random variable. Conversely, if any value of this variable can occur over a specific range (e.g., you are measuring something), then it is a continuous random variable. This chapter concentrated on the discrete type, whereas Chapter 6 discusses the continuous random variable.

For a discrete random variable, the set of possible values and corresponding probabilities is a probability distribution. There are several ways of representing such a distribution, including a list of each value and its probability, a histogram, or an expression called a probability mass function (PMF), which is a numerical function that assigns a probability to each value of the random variable.

The mean of a discrete random variable, μ, is the average value of this variable if observed over an indefinite period. The variance of a discrete random variable, σ^2, is a measure of the variation for this variable. The standard deviation, σ, also measures this variation and is the square root of the variance.

Two popular discrete random variables used in a business setting are the binomial and Poisson random variables. A binomial random variable counts the number of successes out of n independent trials. The Poisson random variable is used for situations in which you observe the number of occurrences of a particular event over a specified period of time or space.

 # Summary of Formulas

Any Discrete Random Variable, X

1. Mean = $\mu = \Sigma x P(x)$

2. Variance = $\sigma^2 = \Sigma (x - \mu)^2 P(x) = \Sigma x^2 P(x) - \mu^2$

3. Standard deviation = $\sigma = \sqrt{\Sigma(x-\mu)^2 P(x)} = \sqrt{\Sigma x^2 P(x) - \mu^2}$

Binomial Distribution

1. X = the number of successes out of n independent trials. Each trial results in a success (with probability p) or a failure (with probability $1 - p$).

2. PMF is $P(X = x) = P(x) = {}_nC_x p^x (1 - p)^{n - x}$ for $x = 0, 1,$ . . . , n.

3. Mean = $\mu = np$.
4. Variance = $\sigma^2 = np(1-p)$ and standard deviation = $\sigma = \sqrt{np(1-p)}$.
5. Probabilities for the binomial random variable are provided in Table A.1 and Table A.2.

2. PMF is $P(x) = (\mu^x e^{-\mu})/(x!)$ for $x = 0, 1, 2, \ldots$
3. Mean = μ
4. Variance = μ
5. Probabilities for the Poisson random variable are provided in Table A.3.

Poisson Distribution

1. X = the number of occurrences of a particular event over a certain unit of time, length, area, or volume.

X Review Exercises 6.57–6.69

6.57 Which of the following is a property of a discrete probability distribution?
  a. The probability for every value of a random variable is positive and not greater than .9.
  b. The sum of the probabilities for the values of a random variable is 1.
  c. The probabilities for any two different values of a random variable are different.
  d. At least one of the values of a random variable has a probability equal to .5.

6.58 A random variable is equal to 0, 5, or 10 with probabilities of .2, .6, and .2, respectively. What is the coefficient of variation of this random variable?

6.59 A manager has four employees with 0, 1, 3, and 4 years of job experience. The manager will assign two of the employees at random to a team. Define X to be equal to the total number of years of job experience for the two selected employees.
  a. What values can X assume?
  b. What is the probability mass function of X?
  c. What is the mean of X?
  d. What is the standard deviation of X?

6.60 Compute the mean of X if the PMF of X is $P(x) = (6 - |x-7|)/36$ for $x = 2, 3, \ldots, 12$ (see Example 6.2).

6.61 A supervisor believes that a new worker installs the wrong electrical component 30% of the time. The supervisor randomly selects 20 components installed by the new worker. The supervisor finds one incorrectly installed component. Is this a likely occurrence if the supervisor's belief is correct? What assumptions are necessary?

6.62 Let the variable X be equal to –1 if stock XYZ declines, 0 if stock XYZ remains unchanged, and 1 if stock XYZ increases in price. If $P(X = x)$ is equal to $(x+2)/6$, what are the mean and standard deviation of X?

6.63 What is the probability that at least 5 out of the next 10 customers makes a purchase if 60% of the customers make a purchase? What assumptions are you making?

6.64 In Exercise 6.63, compute to $\mu - 2\sigma$ to $\mu + 2\sigma$. What is the probability that an observation falls outside of this interval?

5.65 A Gallup Poll of 1,025 adults revealed that 20% of Americans do not own a credit card. However, the majority of adults own at least two credit cards. Define a random

243

variable X to be equal to the number of credit cards owned by an adult. The probability mass function is as follows:

X: Number of Credit Cards Owned	P(x)
0	.20
1	.20
2	.15
3	.13
4	.10
5	.06
6	.07
7	.05
8	.04

a. From viewing the probability mass function, what do you think the mean and standard deviation are for the number of credit cards owned by Americans?
b. Find the mean and standard deviation and compare to your answer in part a.

(Source: "Most Americans Have One or Two Credit Cards," *USA Today*, June 1, 2001, p. 1A.)

6.66 Blair's Moving Company loads an average of three boxes of damaged merchandise daily. What is the probability that exactly three boxes of damaged merchandise are shipped daily? What is the standard deviation of the number of boxes of damaged merchandise that are shipped daily? Assume a Poisson distribution.

6.67 According to Consumer Reports Travel Letter, which asked 840 travel agents about airline fares for 12 of the most popular routes for leisure travel, not all travel agents are providing their customers with the cheapest fare. For the airline route from Chicago to Santa Ana, only 50% of the agencies provided the cheapest fare.

a. If a traveler contacted eight travel agencies, how many would you expect to provide the cheapest airfare for the Chicago to Santa Ana route?
b. What is the standard deviation of the number of agencies that provide the cheapest airfare for this route assuming that eight travel agencies were contacted?
c. What is the probability that none of the travel agencies from the eight randomly selected provide the cheapest airfare for this route? Would this be unusual?
d. What assumptions are you making in answering parts a, b, and c?

(Source: "Playing 'Fare'," *Consumer Reports*, July 2001, p. 8.)

6.68 According to CAP Ventures, Inc., a leading consulting and market research firm, approximately 26% of all documents printed for business purposes, from in-house employee manuals to glossy marketing brochures, are thrown away without ever seeing the light of day. For example, in a run of 5,000 sales brochures, roughly 1,300 are expected to be lost due to damage or neglect or perhaps discarded because they are considered outdated.

a. Using a statistical computer package, find the probability that for 1,000 copies of a brochure, that no more than 250 are never read. (In Excel, click on **Insert Function ➤ Statistical ➤ Binomdist**. In SPSS, click on **Transform ➤ Compute ➤ CDF.BINOM(q,n,p)**. In MINITAB, click on **Calc ➤ Probability Distributions ➤ Binomial**.)
b. Do a "what if" analysis in part a by using the proportion of copies never read to be .28, .30, and .32. Is the probability changing as much as you would have expected?
c. Do a "what if" analysis in part a by using the proportion of copies never read to be .24, .22, and .20. Do these probabilities seem reasonable to you?

(Source: "From Copies to Customized Business Solutions," *Forbes*, September 3, 2001, pp. 81–83.)

6.69 Many e-commerce sites find that the percentage of Web site visitors who actually make a final purchase is disappointingly small. The average percentage of all e-tailing sites is only about 5%. However, J. C. Penney's Web site has been averaging close to 10%. One problem that visitors to e-tailing sites often encounter is finding the product that they wish to purchase. One estimate of the number of clicks that it takes visitors to find their product is 10. However, after finding their product, Web site visitors frequently do not make the purchase.

a. What is the probability that at least 5 of 50 Web site visitors to J.C. Penney's Web site will actually make a purchase?

b. Do a "what if" analysis in part a by changing the probability that any one person will make a final purchase to be .13, .15, .20.

c. What is the probability that a Web site visitor takes more than 8 clicks to find the product that they wish to find? Assume that the average is 10 clicks. What distribution are you using to solve for this probability? Explain.

d. What is the standard deviation of the number of clicks it takes to find the product on the Web site in part c?

(Source: "Making the Sale," *The Wall Street Journal*, September 24, 2001, p. R6.)

Computer Exercises Using the Databases

Exercise 1—Appendix F

Generate 100 random numbers, and select a sample of 100 observations from the database. Consider the variable FAMLSIZE (family size). Let p represent the proportion of observations in your set of 100 observations in which the family size is no greater than 2. If you randomly select 10 observations (with replacement) from the 100 possible, what is $P[X \leq 5]$, where X is the number of observations (out of 10) in which the family size is no greater than 2? What type of random variable is X?

Note: The MINITAB procedure here is

MTB > SAMPLE 10 FROM Cxx, PUT INTO Cyy;
SUBC > REPLACE.

where the 100 values of FAMLSIZE are in column Cxx and the 10 selected values are in column Cyy.

Exercise 2—Appendix F

Estimate the proportion of homeowners in a randomly selected set of 100 observations. From this set of 100 observations, select with replacement a random set of 10 observations. Can this be considered a binomial experiment

with $n = 10$ and p equal to the proportion of homeowners in the set of 100 observations? Estimate the probability that the number of homeowners in the set of 10 observations is greater than or equal to 5.

Exercise 3—Appendix G

Select 200 observations at random from the database. Let p be the proportion of companies with a positive net income. If you were randomly to select (with replacement) 15 observations from the 200 possible, what would be the probability of selecting at least nine companies with a positive net income?

Exercise 4—Appendix G

For the 200 observations in Exercise 3, let p equal the proportion of companies in which the number of employees exceeds 10,000. If you were randomly to select 15 observations (with replacement) from the 200 possible, what would be the probability of selecting at least seven companies in which the number of employees exceeds 10,000?

Insights from Statistics in Action
AACSB Accreditation: A Commitment to Excellence in Business Education

From surveys, assume that the following table represents the proportion of ratings by deans on their view of the importance of each of eight top competencies. That is, the proportions represent probabilities that a dean

will respond on a scale of 1 = Strongly Agree to 5 = Strongly Disagree in response to the statement: Improvement in this competency is crucial to receiving AACSB accreditation.

Competency/Response	Strongly Agree	Agree	Neither Agree Nor Disagree	Disagree	Strongly Disagree
Communication skills	.40	.40	.16	.04	.00
Professional knowledge	.35	.30	.20	.12	.03
Critical thinking	.40	.30	.25	.03	.02
Problem solving	.30	.32	.23	.10	.05
Technology computer usage	.45	.25	.10	.16	.04
Knowledge and comprehension	.33	.28	.19	.15	.05
Global issues	.25	.35	.15	.10	.15
Professional integrity/ethics	.26	.22	.12	.30	.10

1. For the eight competencies listed above, what are the means and standard deviations? What two competencies have the highest means? What two competencies have the highest standard deviations? Are these what you would expect from viewing the probabilities presented in the table?

2. If 10 business schools were selected at random, what is the probability that at least five of the business school deans agree or strongly agree that improvement in technology and computer usage is crucial to their school receiving accreditation?

3. Suppose that 20 business schools were selected at random. What is the probability that at least 15 of these schools have deans that agree or strongly agree that improvement in communications skills is crucial to their school receiving accreditation?

4. From question 3, how many business schools would you expect to have deans that agree or strongly agree that improvement in communication skills is crucial to receiving accreditation at their school? What is the standard deviation?

5. For 20 business schools selected from Michigan, suppose it is known that 15 agree or strongly agree that improvement in the global issues competency is crucial to their business school receiving accreditation. If 8 of these 20 business schools were selected with replacement, what is the probability that all eight schools agree or strongly agree that improvement in the global issues competency is crucial to their accreditation?

(Source: "Can School Oversight Adequately Assess Department Outcomes," *Journal of Education for Business*, 2004, vol. 79, no. 3, p. 157. "Ranking the International Business Schools," *Management International Review*, 2004, vol. 44, pp. 213–229. "The Relationship Between Student Evaluations of Teaching and Faculty Evaluations," *Journal of Education for Business*, March/April 2001, vol. 76, issue 4, p. 189.)

Appendix

Data Analysis with Excel, MINITAB, and SPSS

Calculating Binomial and Poisson Probabilities with Excel

To obtain binominal probabilities, first click on **Insert ➤ Function** to obtain the **Insert Function** dialog box. Select **Statistical** under **Category** and **BINOMDIST** under **Function.** Then click **OK** to obtain the **Function Arguments** dialog box for the binomial distribution. Insert the number of successes, number of trials, probability of a success, and True or False for the **Cumulative** distribution in the four edit boxes, respectively. Note that False for the **Cumulative** distribution yields the probability mass function value for the number of successes. The resulting probability is displayed in the dialog box. Clicking **OK** displays this probability in the spreadsheet.

To obtain Poisson probabilities, select **POISSON** from the **Insert Function** dialog box under the **Statistical** category. In the **POISSON** dialog box, insert the value of the Poisson random variable, the mean, and True or False for the **Cumulative** distribution in the three

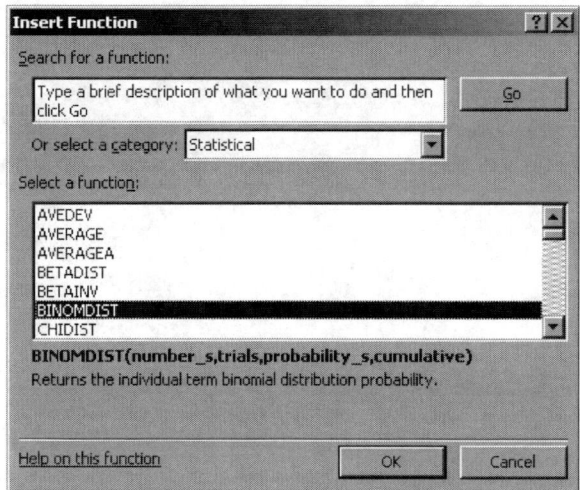

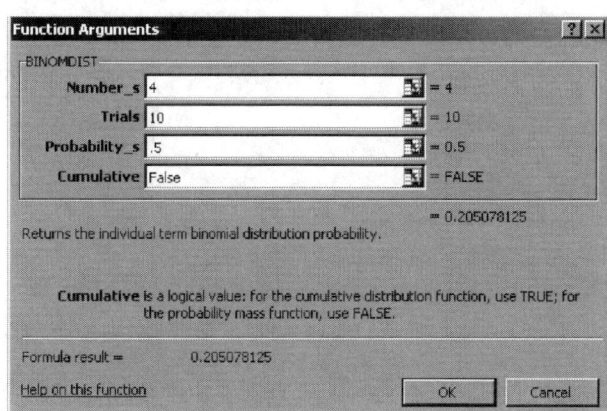

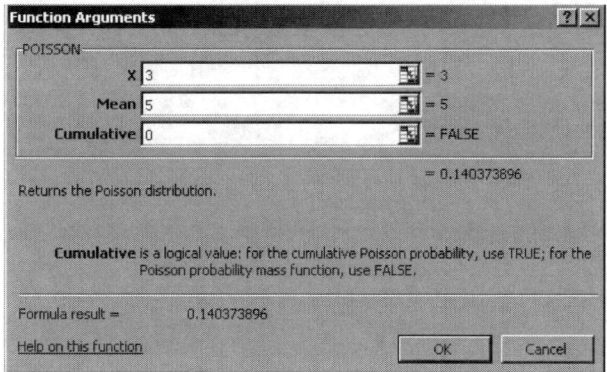

edit boxes, respectively. The resulting probability will appear in the dialog box. Click **OK** to display this probability in the spreadsheet.

Calculating Binomial and Poisson Probabilities with MINITAB

To obtain binominal probabilities, first enter values of the binomial random variable in a column, say C1. Click **Calc ➤ Probability Distributions ➤ Binomial** to obtain the **Binomial Distribution** dialog box. Select either **Probability** for a value of the probability mass

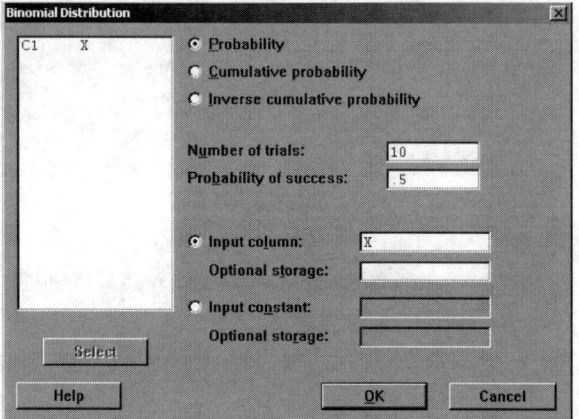

function or **Cumulative probability.** Enter the **Number of Trials** and **Probability of success** in the respective boxes. Enter the column (C1), which has values of the binomial random variable. Click **OK** to retrieve the probabilities. To obtain Poisson probabilities, follow the same procedure, except select **Poisson** from the menu of probability distributions under **Calc.**

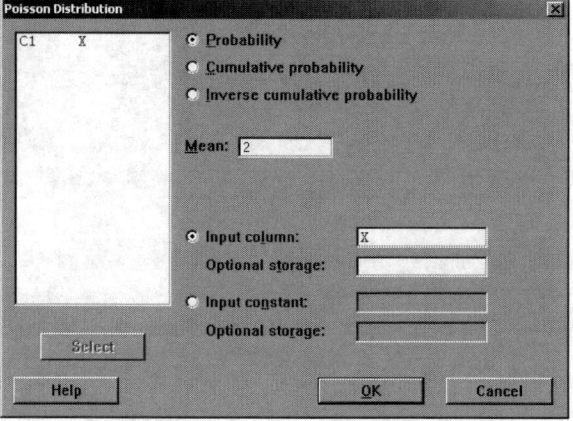

Calculating Binomial and Poisson Probabilities with SPSS

Probabilities and cumulative probabilities can be calculated for binomial and Poisson distributions using SPSS. The following discussion will demonstrate how to construct the columns of probabilities.

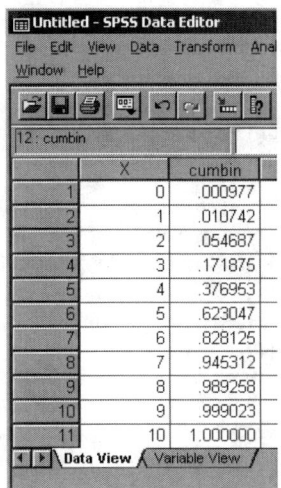

Binomial Probabilities

Consider a binomial situation with $n = 10$ and $p = .5$. Begin by entering 0 through 10 in the first column of the data worksheet (shown). After clicking on the **Variable View** tab, change the name of this variable to x and set the number of decimal places equal to zero. SPSS does not allow the direct calculation of equal-to binomial probabilities (contained in Table A.1), only cumulative probabilities (contained in Table A.2). However, by first determining the cumulative probabilities, SPSS can easily calculate the equal-to probabilities.

Click on **Transform ➤ Compute.** Enter the variable name "cumbin" in the **Target Variable** box. Find the function name CDF.BINOM(q,n,p) inside the function list box and double-click on it. Replace the question marks that appear inside the **Numeric Expression** box with x, 10, and .5 as shown in the dialog box. Here, q refers to the name of the variable in the first column, n is the sample size, and p is the probability of a success on each trial. By clicking on **OK,** the column containing the cumulative binomial probabilities (cumbin) appears in the data window. Click on the **Variable View** tab and set the number of decimal places for this variable equal to six or whatever accuracy is desired.

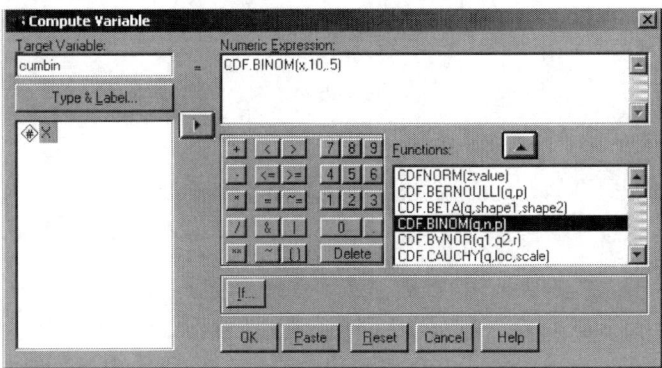

249

To create the equal to probabilities, click on **Transform ➤ Compute.** In the **Target Variable** box, enter "probbin" and inside the **Numeric Expression** box, enter "cumbin - lag(cumbin)." Click on **OK.** To complete the probbin column containing the equal-to binomial probabilities, enter the value from the top row of the cumbin column (i.e., .000977) into the top row of the probbin column. Set the number of decimal places for the probbin variable equal to the desired level of accuracy.

Poisson Probabilities

Consider a Poisson situation having a mean of 2.0. The preceding procedure can be used to determine both cumulative and equal to Poisson probabilities. The function to use here is CDF.POISSON(q,mean) where q is replaced with the name of the variable in the first column (x) and "mean" is replaced by the value 2. Enter "cumpois" in the **Target Variable** box and click on **OK.** The equal-to Poisson probabilities are obtained (as before) by clicking on **Transform ➤ Compute.** In the **Target Variable** box, enter "probpois" and inside the **Numeric Expression** box, enter "cumpois - lag(cumpois)." Enter the value from the top row of the cumpois column (i.e., .135335) into the top row of the probpois column and set the number of decimal places for both columns equal to the desired level of accuracy.

chapter

7

Continuous Probability Distributions X

Statistics in Action
Examining Unethical Behavior: More Fun than Decent People Think Should Be Legal

Many assume the pursuit of profit is the reason for being in business. Some even assume it is a right. Upper-level managers are often faced with decisions that involve ethical considerations. For example, should a company purchase supplies at a discount price or pay full price for more environmentally responsible supplies? Company representatives have a responsibility to their customers to provide them with accurate information concerning, for example, pricing. At the same time, they have a responsibility to meet the profit goals of their organization. Balancing duties and responsibilities can be a challenge for aggressive managers. The scandal surrounding the mass shredding of Enron documents by Arthur Andersen, auditors for the bankrupt U.S. energy giant, revealed that senior executives cannot balance company duties with ethical responsibilities.

Surveys of U.S. business employees reveal that at least one in three workers observed behavior that violated the organization's ethics standards. One in eight business workers have, in fact, felt pressure to compromise their organization's ethics standards. Withholding needed information, using intimidating behavior toward other employees, and willfully misrepresenting information in reports are some of the behaviors that ethical people would consider unacceptable. The vast amount of statistical data available to businesses creates the potential for misuse of statistics. An unethical person might use only selective data to make a point. A manager might want to ignore the validity of certain assumptions necessary for the proper use of a statistical procedure. Business per-

sonnel need to be aware of the ethical pitfalls that can occur even in the field of statistics.

Research examining ethical behavior indicates that business decisions vary by type of ethical situation. When an ethical issue is perceived as being very important, business professionals are more inclined to follow the business code of ethics. To measure ethical behavior, researchers have developed vignettes describing a situation in which a business decision is made. Respondents, who first read these vignettes, rate the scenario on an acceptable—unacceptable scale.

Chapter 5 introduced you to discrete random variables. Such variables, when observed, produce a countable number of distinct values. In this chapter, continuous random variables will be studied. These random variables are often used in measurements and can assume any value across a range of numbers. In examining the ethical behavior of business professionals, variables, such as the proportion of vignettes considered ethically acceptable and scores used to rate an individual's ethical perception, are considered *continuous variables*. When you have completed this chapter, you will be able to

- Recognize the distribution of normally distributed data as well as uniformly and exponentially distributed data.

- Standardize data by forming the corresponding z values.

- Determine the probability of a continuous random variable being between two specified values.

7.1

CONTINUOUS RANDOM VARIABLES

The concept of a continuous random variable was introduced in Chapter 5. What distinguishes a discrete random variable from one that is continuous is the presence of *gaps* in the possible values for a discrete random variable. To illustrate, X = total of two dice is a discrete random variable; there are many gaps over the range of possible values, and a value of 10.4, for example, is not possible. One can list the possible values of a discrete variable, along with the probability that each value will occur.

Determining probabilities for a continuous random variable is quite different. For such a variable, any value over a specific range is possible. Therefore, we are unable to list all the possible values of this variable. Probability statements for a continuous random variable (such as X) are not concerned with specific values of X (such as the probability that X will equal 50) but rather, deal with probabilities over a range of values, such as the probability that X is *between* 40 and 50, *greater than* 65, or *less than* 20, for example.

Such probabilities can be determined by first making an assumption regarding the nature of the population involved. We assume that the population can be described by a curve having a particular shape—such as normal, uniform, or exponential. Once this curve is specified, a probability can be determined by finding the corresponding area under this curve. As an illustration, Figure 7.1 shows a particular curve (called the normal curve) for which the probability of observing a value of X between 20 and 60 is the area under this curve between these two values. *The entire range of probability is covered using such a curve, since, for any continuous random variable, the total area under the curve is equal to 1.*

The following sections examine the normal, uniform, and exponential distributions, since these are the most widely encountered random variables in practice. The graphs and descriptive statistics discussed in the previous chapters can help determine if one of these random variables might be appropriate for a particular situation. If a histogram of the sample data appears nearly flat, the population might be represented by a uniform random variable. If the histogram is symmetric with decreasing tails at each end, a normal random variable may be in order. If the sample histogram steadily decreases from left to right, the population of all possible values perhaps can be described using an exponential random variable. In the first two cases, the mean and median should be nearly equal (the population is symmetric), providing a skewness measure near zero. For the exponential case, the median should be less than the mean with a corresponding positive measure of skewness.

FIGURE

7.1

Finding a probability for a continuous random variable.

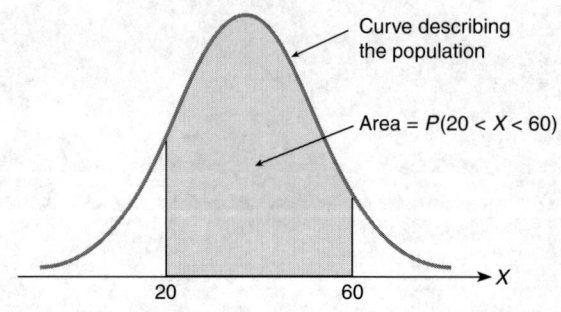

NORMAL RANDOM VARIABLES

The normal distribution is the most important of all the continuous distributions. You will find that this distribution plays a key role in the application of many statistical techniques. When attempting to make an assertion about a population, oftentimes a major assumption (based on sample evidence) is that the population has a normal distribution.

When discussing measurements such as height, weight, thickness, or time, the resulting population of all measurements often can be assumed to have a probability distribution that is normal if evidence obtained from the sample supports this assumption.

A histogram constructed from a large *sample* of such measurements can help determine whether this assumption is realistic. Assume, for example, that data were collected on the length of life of 200 high-intensity Everglo light bulbs. Let X represent the length of life (in hours) of an Everglo bulb. One thing we are interested in is the *shape* of the distribution of the 200 lifetimes. Where are they centered? Are they symmetric? The easiest way to approach such questions is to construct a histogram of the 200 values, as illustrated in Figure 7.2. This histogram indicates that the data are nearly symmetric and are centered at approximately 400.

The curve in Figure 7.2 is said to be a **normal curve** because of its shape. A normal curve is characterized by a *symmetric, bell-shaped appearance,* with tails that "die out" rather quickly. We use such curves to represent the *assumed population* of all possible values. This example contained 200 values observed in a *sample.* Consequently:

1. A histogram represents the shape of the sample data.

2. A smooth curve represents the assumed shape (distribution) of the population.

If all possible values of a variable X follow an assumed normal curve, then X is said to be a **normal random variable,** and the population is **normally distributed.**

When you assume that a particular population follows a normal distribution, you assume that X, an observation randomly obtained from this population, is a normal random variable. Based on the histogram in Figure 7.2, it appears to be a reasonable assumption that the smooth curve describing the population of *all* Everglo bulbs can be approximated using a normal curve centered at 400 hours. Therefore, we will assume that X is a normal random variable, centered at 400 hours.

There are two numbers used to describe a normal curve (distribution); they tell where the curve is centered and how wide it is. The center of a normal curve is called the *mean* and is represented by the symbol μ (mu). The width of a normal curve can be described using the *standard deviation,* which is represented by the symbol σ (sigma). These descriptions are

FIGURE

7.2

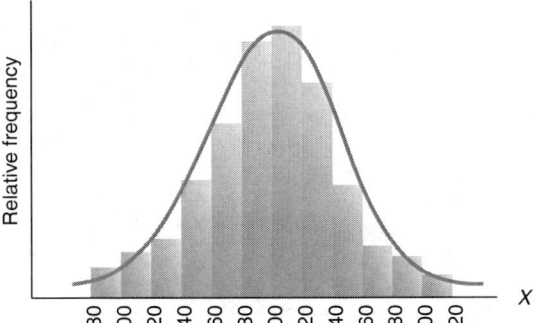

Histogram of 200 Everglo light bulb lifetimes (in hours). The curve represents all possible values (population). The histogram represents the sample (200 values).

FIGURE

7.3

Distribution of the lifetime of Everglo bulbs showing the mean ($\mu = 400$), the standard deviation ($\sigma = 50$), and the inflection point *(P)*.

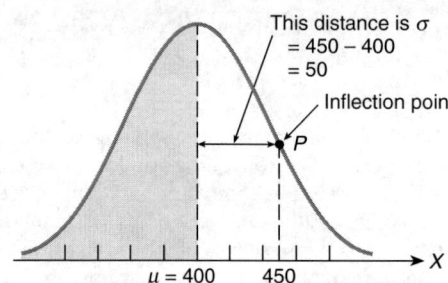

illustrated in Figure 7.3, which shows the normal curve representing the lifetime of Everglo light bulbs. Another way of stating this situation is: X is a normal random variable with $\mu = 400$ hours and $\sigma = 50$ hours. Notice that the units of μ and σ are the same as the units of the data (hours).

In Figure 7.3, there is a point P on the normal curve. Above this point P, the curve resembles a bowl that is upside down, and below P the curve is "right side up." In calculus, this point is referred to as an *inflection point*. The distance between vertical lines through μ and P is the value of σ.

Because μ and σ represent the location and spread of the normal distribution, they are called *parameters*. The parameters are used to define the distribution completely. The values of μ and σ of a normal population are all you need to distinguish it from all other normal populations that have the same bell shape but different location and/or variability. The values of the parameters must be specified in order to make probability statements regarding X. As a result, there are infinitely many normal curves (populations), one for each pair of values of μ and σ.

In Chapter 5, we discussed the mean of (say) 10 observations of the random variable X, written as $\bar{X}$. If you were to observe X indefinitely, then you could obtain the mean of the population, μ. The same concept applies to continuous random variables; for the Everglo example, $\bar{X}$ represents the mean of the 200 bulbs (the sample) and μ is the mean of all Everglo bulbs (the population).

Mean		Standard Deviation	
Sample	**Population**	**Sample**	**Population**
$\bar{X}$	μ	s	σ
the average of the sample	the average of the population	the standard deviation of the sample	the standard deviation of the population

In our Everglo example, the average lifetime of all bulbs is *assumed* to be $\mu = 400$ hours. The standard deviation of the population, σ, just like s, is a measure of *variability*. The larger σ is, the more variation (jumping around) we would see if X were observed indefinitely. For both the sample and the population, the square of the standard deviation is referred to as the variance. It is another measure of the variability of X. The *variance* of a random variable, X, is represented by σ^2.

Consider whether the sample average ($\bar{X}$) of the 200 values in our example is the *same* as μ. It is not. Do not confuse the average lifetime of all light bulbs (μ) with the average lifetime of just 200 bulbs ($\bar{X}$). This is an important distinction in statistics. However, if our assumed normal distribution (with $\mu = 400$ and $\sigma = 50$) is correct, then $\bar{X}$ most often will be "close to" μ. We examine this again in Chapter 7.

The curve in Figure 7.3 is an illustration of a normal random variable with a mean of 400 hours and a standard deviation of 50 hours. We can compare normal curves that may differ in mean, standard deviation, or both. The normal curves in Figure 7.4 indicate that,

7.4

Two normal curves with unequal means and equal standard deviations.

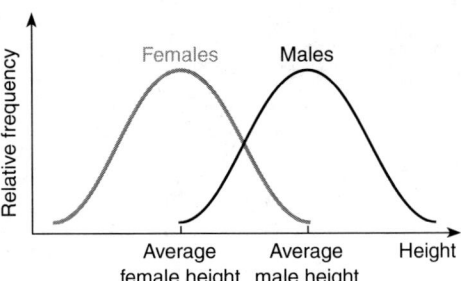

7.5

Two normal curves with equal means and unequal standard deviations.

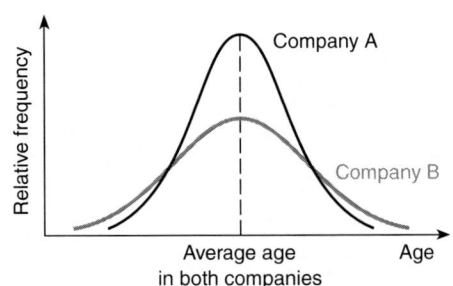

on the average, males are taller than females. The mean of the male curve is to the right of the mean of the female curve. The male heights "jump around" about as much as female heights. In other words, there is about the same amount of *variation* in male and female heights because the standard deviation of each curve is the same; that is, each curve is equally wide.

In Figure 7.5, the two normal curves represent the ages of the employees at two large companies. Two things appear to be true, based on the figure:

1. The average age of employees for the two companies is the same.

2. The ages in Company B have more variability. This simply means that there are more old people and more young people in Company B than in Company A.

7.3

DETERMINING A PROBABILITY
FOR A NORMAL RANDOM VARIABLE

So you have assumed that the lifetime of an Everglo light bulb is a normal random variable with $\mu = 400$ and $\sigma = 50$. Now what? This brings us back to the subject of probability. Before we describe probabilities for a normal random variable, consider one important property of *any* normal curve (or of any curve representing a continuous random variable, for that matter)—namely, that the total area under the curve is 1 (see Figure 7.6). When we described the normal curve as bell-shaped, we also determined that it was symmetrical. If the halves are identical, then the probability above the mean (μ) is equal to .5 and is the same as the probability below the mean. Thus, in Figure 7.3 the shaded area is equal to the nonshaded area under the curve.

FIGURE

7.6

Area under a
normal curve.

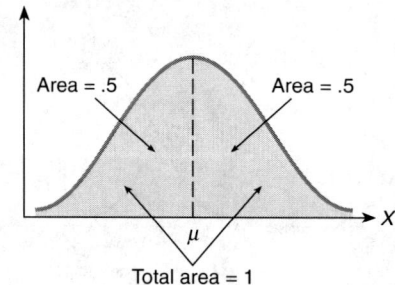

FIGURE

7.7

Normal curve for
Everglo light bulbs
showing
$P(X < 360)$. The
shaded area is the
percentage of time
that X will be less
than 360.
(X = lifetime of
Everglo bulb.)

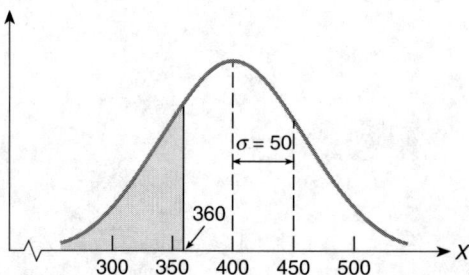

Returning to the Everglo bulb example, what percentage of the time will the burnout time, X, be less than 360? This probability is written as

$$P(X < 360)$$

We discuss how to determine this area (a simple procedure) later in the chapter, but for now, just remember that when dealing with a normal random variable, a *probability* is represented by an *area* under the corresponding normal curve. The value of $P(X < 360)$ is illustrated in Figure 7.7. It appears that roughly 20% of the total area has been shaded, so we can conclude that (1) roughly 20% of the Everglo bulbs will burn out in less than 360 hours, and (2) the probability that X is less than 360 is approximately .2.

7.4 FINDING AREAS UNDER THE STANDARD NORMAL CURVE

We begin our discussion by finding the area under a special normal curve—namely, one that is centered at 0 ($\mu = 0$) and has a standard deviation of 1 ($\sigma = 1$). This random variable is typically represented by the letter Z and is referred to as the **standard normal random variable.** As Figure 7.8 demonstrates, Z is as likely to be negative as positive; that is, $P(Z \leq 0) = P(Z \geq 0) = .5$. Although you probably never will observe a random variable like Z in practice, it is a useful normal random variable. In fact, an area under *any* normal curve (as in Figure 7.7) can be determined by finding the corresponding area under the standard normal curve.

FIGURE

7.8

Standard normal curve.

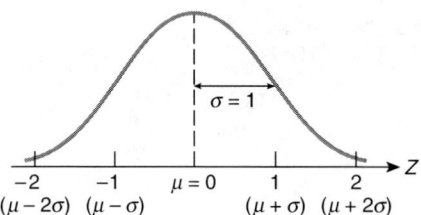

FIGURE

7.9

Shaded area = .4474, from Table A.4.

To derive the area under the standard normal curve requires the use of integral calculus. Unfortunately, the integral of the function describing the standard normal curve does not have a simple (closed form) expression. By using excellent approximations of this integral, however, we can tabulate these areas—see Table A.4 and Figure 7.9.

For example, suppose we want to determine the probability that a standard normal random variable will be between 0 and 1.62. This is written as

$$P(0 < Z < 1.62)$$

The value of this probability is obtained from Table A.4, which contains the area under the curve between the mean of zero and the particular value of Z. The far left column of Table A.4 identifies the first decimal place for Z, and you read across the table to obtain the second decimal place.

In our example, we find the intersection between 1.6 on the left and .02 on the top, because $Z = 1.62$. Look at Table A.4; the value .4474 is the *area* between 0 and 1.62. In other words, the probability that Z will lie between 0 and 1.62 is .4474.

You can begin to see why it is a good idea to sketch the curve and shade in the area when dealing with normal random variables. It gives you a clear picture of what the question is asking and cuts down on mistakes.

EXAMPLE

7.1

What is the probability that Z will be greater than 1.62?

Solution

We wish to find $P(Z > 1.62)$. Examine Figure 7.10. The area under the right half of the Z curve is .5, so, using our value from Table A.4, the desired area here is

$$.5 - .4474 = .0526$$

So the probability that Z will exceed 1.62 is .0526.

What if we wish to know the probability that Z is equal to a particular value, such as $P(Z = 1.62)$? There is no area under the curve corresponding to $Z = 1.62$, so

$$P(Z = 1.62) = 0$$

FIGURE

7.10

The shaded area represents the probability that Z will be greater than 1.62 [$P(Z > 1.62)$].

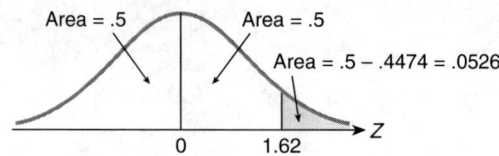

FIGURE

7.11

Area under the Z curve for $P(Z < 1.62)$.

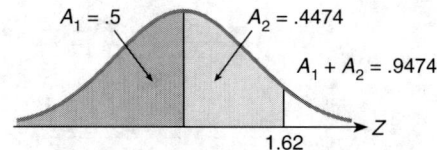

FIGURE

7.12

Area under the Z curve for $P(1.0 < Z < 2.0)$.

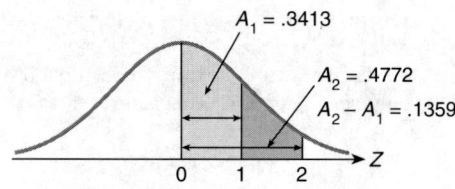

In fact,

$$P(Z = \text{any value}) = 0$$

One nice thing about this fact is that $P(Z \geq 1.62)$ is the *same* as $P(Z > 1.62)$ (i.e., .0526). So putting the equal sign on the inequality ($\geq$ or $\leq$) has *no* effect on the resulting probability.

By looking at the Z curve in Figure 7.11, you can see that

$$P(Z < 1.62) = .5 + .4474 = .9474$$

As before, this also is $P(Z \leq 1.62)$.

Figure 7.12 shows $P(1.0 < Z < 2.0)$ (areas from Table A.4). We see that

$$P(1.0 < Z < 2.0) = P(0 < Z < 2.0) - P(0 < Z \leq 1.0)$$

$$= .4772 - .3413$$

$$= .1359$$

By subtracting the two areas, we find that the probability that Z will lie between 1.0 and 2.0 is .1359.

We use Figure 7.13 and Table A.4 to determine $P(-1.25 < Z < 1.15)$:

$$P(-1.25 < Z < 1.15) = P(-1.25 < Z < 0) + P(0 < Z < 1.15)$$

$$= A_1 + A_2$$

FIGURE
7.13

Area under the
Z curve for
$P(-1.25 < Z < 1.15)$.

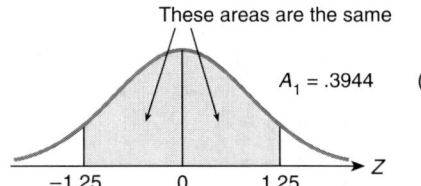

$A_1 = .3944$ $A_2 = .3749$

$A_1 + A_2 = .7693$

−1.25   0   1.15

FIGURE
7.14

Z curce for
$P(0 < Z < 1.25) =$
$P(-1.25 < Z < 0)$.

These areas are the same

$A_1 = .3944$ (See Figure 7.13)

−1.25   0   1.25   Z

FIGURE
7.15

Area under the
Z curve for
$P(Z < -1.45)$.

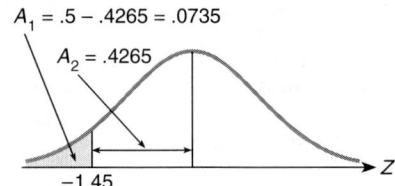

$A_1 = .5 - .4265 = .0735$

$A_2 = .4265$

−1.45   Z

Using the symmetry of the Z curve and Figure 7.14, the area of A_1 is the same as $P(0 < Z < 1.25)$ and thus is .3944. The area of A_2, from Table A.4, is .3749. So we add A_1 and A_2:

$$.3944 + .3749 = .7693$$

Finally, we can determine $P(Z < -1.45)$ using Figure 7.15. This can be written as $P(Z < 0) - P(-1.45 < Z < 0)$, that is, $.5 - A_2$. Using the symmetry of the Z curve, the area between 0 and −1.45 is $A_2 = .4265$ (from Table A.4). As a result, Z will be less than (or equal to) −1.45 approximately 7.35% of the time.

Finding the Z Value for a Specified Area. This is the reverse of what we have discussed so far. Here, you will be given the area and asked to determine the value of Z having this specified area. For example, for what value of Z (say, z) is the following statement true?

$$P(Z \geq z) = .03$$

The value of z is the one having a right-tailed area (due to the ≥ in this statement) of .03. This is illustrated in Figure 7.16. The value of z having a right tail of .03 is the value of z having a shaded area in Table A.4 of $.5 - .03 = .47$. By examining this table, we see that the value closest to .47 is .4699 (belonging to 1.88). Consequently, $z = 1.88$.

Another example: For what value of Z (say, z) is the following statement true?

$$P(Z \leq z) = .2$$

259

FIGURE

7.16

Value of *Z* having
a right-tailed area
of .03.

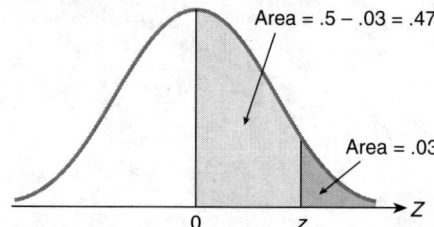

FIGURE

7.17

Value of *Z* having
a left-tailed area
of .2.

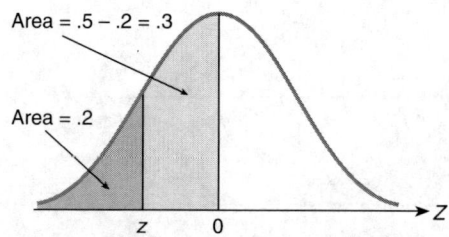

This is a left-tailed area of .2 due to the ≤ (see Figure 7.17). The *z* having this left-tailed area is the negative of the *z* having a shaded area in Table A.4 of .5 − .2 = .3. Examining this table, we see that the value closest to .3 is .2995, belonging to .84. We know that *z* is negative because it is to the left of zero, and so *z* = −.84.

X Exercises 7.1–7.10

Understanding the Mechanics

7.1 Draw a normal curve with the following values for μ and σ.
  a. $\mu = 0, \sigma = 1$
  b. $\mu = 4, \sigma = 1$
  c. $\mu = 4, \sigma = 3$
  d. $\mu = -4, \sigma = 3$

7.2 Find the area under the standard normal distribution between the following *Z* values.
  a. $Z = 0$ and $Z = 1$
  b. $Z = 0$ and $Z = 2$
  c. $Z = 0$ and $Z = .55$
  d. $Z = 0$ and $Z = -1.52$

7.3 For a random variable that has a standard normal distribution, find the following probabilities.
  a. The probability that the random variable is between −2 and 0.
  b. The probability that the random variable is between −1.66 and −1.00.
  c. The probability that the random variable is between −1.15 and 2.15.

7.4 Find the following probabilities. Sketch the corresponding area.
  a. $P(0 \le Z \le .5)$
  b. $P(Z \le .5)$
  c. $P(Z \le -.5)$
  d. $P(Z \ge .5)$
  e. $P(-.5 \le Z \le .5)$

7.5 For a standard normal random variable *Z*, what is the probability that:
  a. *Z* is less than 1.23.
  b. *Z* is less than or equal to 1.23.
  c. *Z* is at least −1.23.
  d. *Z* is between the mean and 1.96.
  e. *Z* is less than −1.5 or greater than .62.

7.6 Find the value of *z* for the following probability statements, and sketch the corresponding area.
  a. $P(0 \le Z \le z) = .4901$
  b. $P(z \le Z \le 0) = .2324$
  c. $P(Z \le z) = .8888$
  d. $P(Z \ge z) = .2090$
  e. $P(Z \ge z) = .7910$

7.7 Find the value of z for the following probability statements, and sketch the corresponding area.

    a. $P(-1.0 \leq Z \leq z) = .6898$
    b. $P(1.0 \leq Z \leq z) = .0072$
    c. $P(-2.0 \leq Z \leq z) = .0164$
    d. $P(-2.0 \leq Z \leq z) = .9544$
    e. $P(z \leq Z \leq 2.0) = .9544$

Applying the New Concepts

7.8 An educational testing service administers a national test to measure the reading comprehension of third-grade students. Only standardized scores are reported. The scores are approximately normally distributed. The testing service classifies scores above the 90th percentile as outstanding, between the 70th and 90th percentile as above average, between the 30th percentile and 70th percentile as average, between the 10th percentile and the 30th percentile as below average, and below the 10th percentile as poor. Find the z-scores corresponding to the 90th, 70th, 30th, and 10th percentiles.

7.9 A production manager uses z values to identify observations that appear to be unusually large or small. The manager identifies a z value as being unusually large if the $P(Z > z) < .01$. A z value is considered to be unusually small if $P(Z < z) < .01$. (To use the cumulative probability function in Excel, click on **Insert ➤ Function** then click on **Statistical ➤ NORMSDIST(z).** In SPSS, click on **Transform ➤ Compute ➤ CDF.NORMAL(q,mean, stddev)** and in MINITAB, click on **Calc ➤ Probability Distributions ➤ Normal** and select cumulative distribution.)

    a. Is a value of z equal to 2.0 considered unusually large?
    b. Is a value of z equal to 3.4 considered unusually large?
    c. Is a value of z equal to -1.8 considered unusually small?
    d. Is a value of z equal to -3.8 considered unusually small?

7.10 A researcher represents outcomes from an experiment using z values. The researcher is interested in the z values that correspond to the 50th, 75th, and 90th percentiles. Find these z values. (In Excel, click on **Insert ➤ Function,** then click on **Statistical ➤ NORMINV.** In SPSS, click on **Transform ➤ Compute ➤ IDF.NORMAL (p,mean,stddev)** and in MINITAB, click on **Calc ➤ Probability Distributions ➤ Normal** and then select inverse cumulative probability.)

7.5

AREAS UNDER ANY NORMAL CURVE

Take another look at the histogram of the 200 Everglo light bulb lifetimes in Figure 7.2. A normal curve with $\mu = 400$ hours and $\sigma = 50$ hours was used to describe the population of *all* Everglo lifetimes. So X = Everglo lifetime is a normal random variable with $\mu = 400$ and $\sigma = 50$.

What happens to the shape of the data if we take each of the 200 lifetimes in this example and subtract 400 (that is, subtract μ)? As you can see in Figure 7.18, the histogram (and corresponding normal curve) is merely "shifted" to the left by 400. It resembles the normal curve for X, except the "new" mean is 0. The random variable defined by $Y = X - 400$ has these characteristics:

- It is a normal random variable.

- It has a mean equal to zero.

- It has a standard deviation equal to that of X, that is, 50.

Figure 7.19 shows what happens to the shape of 200 Y values if each of them is *divided* by 50 (that is, by σ). Notice the horizontal axis in the histogram and the corresponding normal curve. The resulting normal curve resembles a normal curve with a mean of 0 and a standard deviation equal to 1.

Thus, if X is a normal random variable with mean 400 and standard deviation 50, then the random variable defined by

$$Z = \frac{X - 400}{50}$$

FIGURE

7.18

Histogram
obtained by
subtracting
μ = 400 (compare
with Figure 7.2).

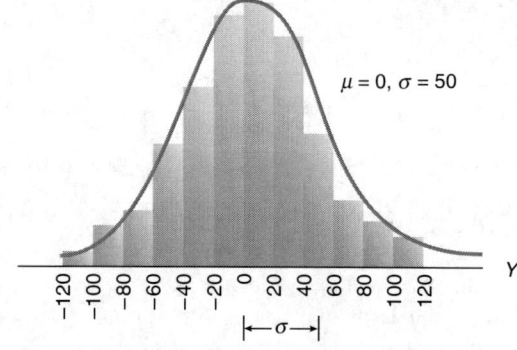

$\mu = 0, \sigma = 50$

FIGURE

7.19

Histogram
obtained by
subtracting μ and
dividing by σ
(compare with
Figures 7.2 and
7.18).

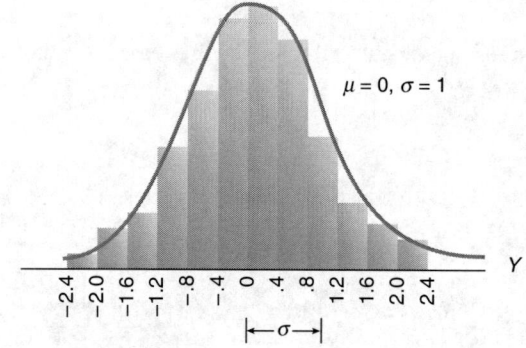

$\mu = 0, \sigma = 1$

has these characteristics:

• It is a normal random variable.

• It has a mean equal to zero.

• It has a standard deviation equal to 1.

In general, for *any normal* random variable X,

$$Z = \frac{X - \mu}{\sigma}$$

is a **standard normal random variable.** This procedure of subtracting μ and dividing by σ is referred to as **standardizing** the normal random variable X. *It allows us to determine probabilities for any normal random variable by first standardizing it and then using Table A.4. So the standard normal distribution turns out to be much more important than you might have expected!*

E X A M P L E

7.2

The normal curve in Figure 7.7 represented the lifetime of all Everglo bulbs, with μ = 400 hours and σ = 50 hours. What percentage of the bulbs will burn out in less than 360 hours? Or, put another way, what is the probability that any particular bulb will last less than 360 hours?

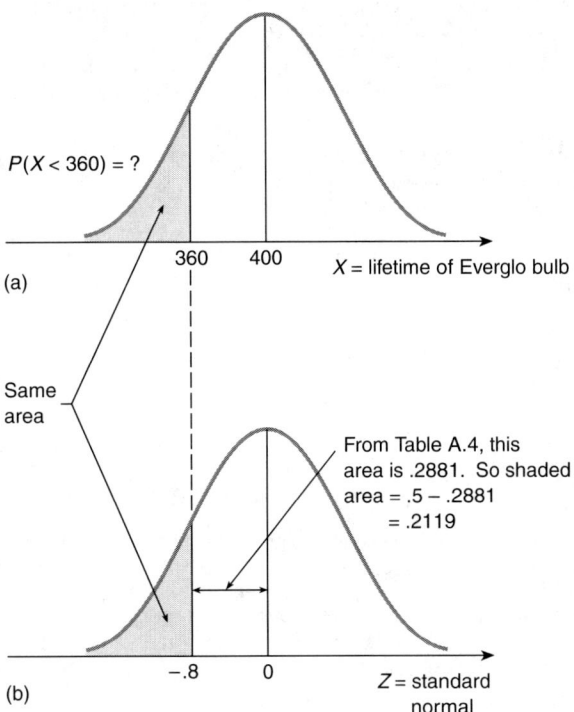

FIGURE

7.20

Compare the areas
for (a) the *X* and
(b) the *Z* normal
curves to find
P(*X* < 360).

Solution

This probability is written as

$$P(X < 360)$$

This random variable is continuous, so $P(X < 360) = P(X \leq 360)$. To determine the probability, you need to standardize this variable:*

$$P(X < 360) = P\left(\frac{X - 400}{50} < \frac{360 - 400}{50} \right)$$

$$= P(Z < -.8)$$

where $Z = (X - 400)/50$ (Figure 7.20).

Earlier, by examining Figure 7.7, we estimated this area to be roughly 20%. The actual area, from Figure 7.20, is .2119; that is, it is 21.19% of the total area. The conclusion here is that

$$P(X < 360) = .2119$$

and so 21% of all Everglo bulbs will have a lifetime of less than 360 hours.

---

*Since 400 is subtracted from *both* sides of the inequality and *both* sides are divided by 50, the events described by the original inequality $P(X < 360)$ and the standardized inequality $P(Z < -.8)$ are the same.

Interpreting Z

What does a Z value of $-.8$ imply in Example 7.2? It simply means that 360 is .8 standard deviations to the left of the mean (Z is negative). So

$$\mu - .8(\sigma) = 400 - .8(50) = 360$$

Recall that a z-score was defined in exactly the same way in Chapter 3 using a sample mean $(\overline{X})$ and standard deviation (s). In this chapter, we use the population mean (μ) and standard deviation (σ). In general:

1. A *positive* value of Z designates how many standard deviations (σ) X is to the *right* of the mean (μ).

2. A *negative* value of Z designates how many standard deviations X is to the *left* of the mean.

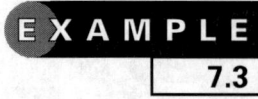

The funds dispensed daily by an automatic teller machine (ATM) in a Denver grocery store are believed to be normally distributed with a mean of $3,700 and a standard deviation of $625. The machine is programmed to notify the store manager if the daily dollar volume is very low (less than or equal to $2,000) or unusually high (greater than or equal to $5,000). What percentage of the time will the daily dollar volume *not* be in either of these two conditions?

Solution   This probability can be written as

$$P(2000 < X < 5000)$$

Using the standardization procedure:

$$P(2000 < X < 5000) = P\left(\frac{2000 - 3700}{625} < \frac{X - 3700}{625} < \frac{5000 - 3700}{625} \right)$$

$$= P(-2.72 < Z < 2.08)$$

where Z once again represents the *standardized* normal random variable, which for this example is defined by

$$Z = \frac{X - 3700}{625}$$

Refer to Table A.4 and Figure 7.21 and note that the shaded areas in Figure 7.21(a) and (b) are both equal to .4967 + .4812 = .9779. As a result, the manager can expect no notification of unusual activity approximately 98% of the time.

Also note two other values:

1. The value of $5,000 is 2.08 standard deviations to the right of the mean, since $Z = 2.08$ and $5000 = 3700 + (2.08)(625)$.

2. The value of $2,000 is 2.72 standard deviations to the left of the mean, since $Z = -2.72$ and $2000 = 3700 - (2.72)(625)$.

FIGURE

7.21

(a) The probability
that *X* is between
$2,000 and $5,000.
(b) The probability
that *Z* is between
−2.72 and 2.08.

(a)

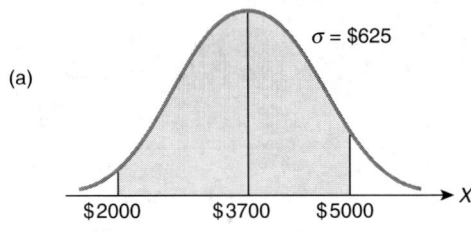

(b)

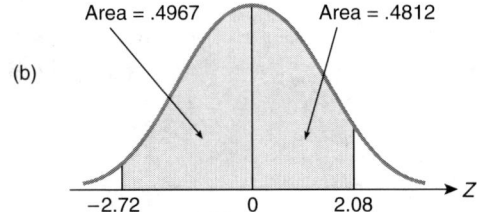

FIGURE

7.22

The normal curve
for policyholder
lifetimes. *X* = age
at death (in years).

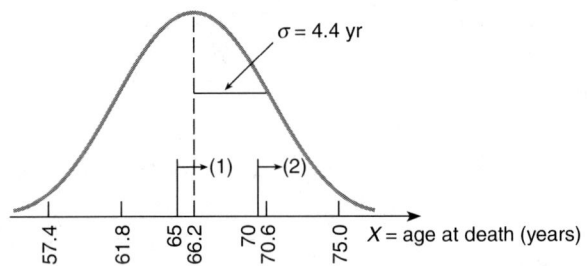

E X A M P L E

7.4

Actuarial scientists in an insurance company formulate insurance policies that will be both profitable and marketable. For a particular policy, the lifetimes of the policyholders follow a normal distribution with $\mu = 66.2$ years and $\sigma = 4.4$ years. One of the options with this policy is to receive a payment following the 65th birthday and a payment every five years thereafter.

1. What percentage of policyholders will receive at least one payment using this option?

2. What percentage will receive two or more payments?

3. What percentage will receive exactly two payments?

The normal curve for the policyholder lifetimes is shown in Figure 7.22. To receive at least one payment, the policyholder must live beyond 65 years of age. So we need to determine (see Figure 7.23):

Solution 1

$$P(X > 65) = P[(X - 66.2)/4.4 > (65 - 66.2)/4.4]$$
$$= P(Z > -.27) = .1064 + .5$$
$$= .6064$$

So nearly 61% of the policyholders will receive at least one payment.

FIGURE

7.23

Z curve for
$P(Z > -.27)$.

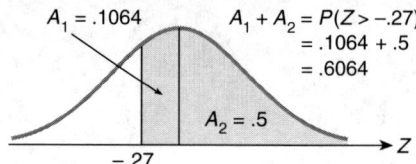

FIGURE

7.24

Z curve for
$P(Z > .86)$.

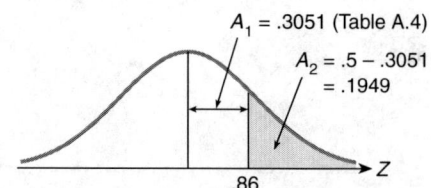

FIGURE

7.25

Z curve for
$P(.86 < Z < 2.00)$.

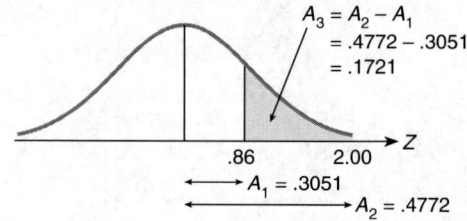

Solution 2   Because the policyholder receives a payment every five years, he or she will receive two or more payments provided he or she lives to be older than 70 years of age. Thus, the probability of two or more payments is determined in this way (see Figure 7.24):

$$P(X > 70) = P[(X - 66.2)/4.4 > (70 - 66.2)/4.4]$$

$$= P(Z > .86) = .5 - .3051$$

$$= .1949$$

Thus, 19.5% of the policyholders will survive long enough to collect two payments.

Solution 3   To receive exactly two payments, the policyholder must live longer than 70 years and less than 75 years. This probability is

$$P(70 < X < 75)$$

Using the same standardization procedure (see Figure 7.25):

$$P(70 < X < 75) = P[(70 - 66.2)/4.4 < (X - 66.2)/4.4 < (75 - 66.2)/4.4]$$

$$= P(.86 < Z < 2.00)$$

$$= .4772 - .3051 = .1721$$

So 17.21% of the policyholders will receive exactly two payments.

Applications Where the Area Under a Normal Curve Is Provided

Another twist to dealing with normal random variables is a situation where you are given the area under the normal curve and asked to determine the corresponding value of the variable. This is a common application of a normal random variable. For example, the manufacturer of a product may want to determine a warranty period during which the product will be replaced if it becomes defective, so that at most 5% of the items are returned during this period. Or, in a grocery store on any given day, the demand for a freshly made food item may or may not exceed the supply. The owner may want to determine how much to supply each day, such that the demand (a normal random variable) will exceed this value 10% of the time (in other words, the customers will be disappointed no more than 10% of the time).

EXAMPLE 7.5

Referring to Example 7.2, after how many hours will 80% of the Everglo bulbs burn out? Recall that $\mu = 400$ and $\sigma = 50$.

Solution

The first step here is to sketch this curve [Figure 7.26(a)] and estimate the value of X (say x_0) so that

$$P(X < x_0) = .8$$

Because .8 is larger than .5, x_0 must lie to the *right* of 400.

Next, find the point on a standard normal *(Z)* curve such that the area to the left is also .8 [Figure 7.26(b)]. Using Table A.4, the area between 0 and .84 is .2995. This means that

$$P(Z < .84) = .5 + .2995$$

$$= .7995$$

$$= .8 \quad \text{(approximately)}$$

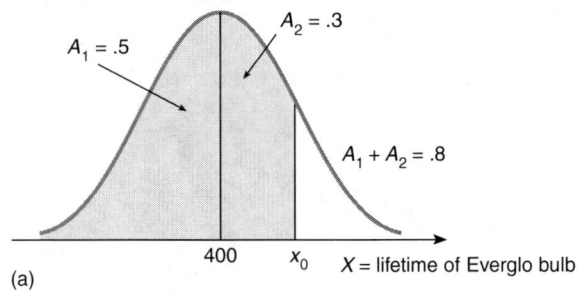

(a)

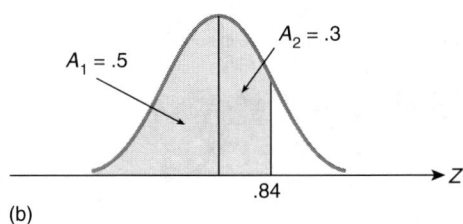

(b)

FIGURE 7.26

(a) $P(X < x_0) = .8$.

(b) $P(Z < .84) = .8$.

By standardizing X, we conclude that

$$\frac{x_0 - 400}{50} = .84$$

$$x_0 - 400 = (50)(.84) = 42$$

$$x_0 = 400 + 42 = 442$$

So 80% of the Everglo bulbs will burn out within 442 hours.

EXAMPLE 7.6

A bakery shop sells loaves of freshly made French bread. Any unsold loaves at the end of the day are either discarded or sold elsewhere at a loss. The demand for this bread has followed a normal distribution with $\mu = 35$ loaves and $\sigma = 8$ loaves.

How many loaves should the bakery make each day so that they can meet the demand 90% of the time?

Solution

The normal random variable X here is the demand for French bread (measured in loaves) [Figure 7.27(a)]. To meet the demand 90% of the time, the bakery must determine an amount, say x_0 loaves, such that:

$$P(X \leq x_0) = .90$$

Proceeding as before, examine a Z curve and find the value having an area to the left equal to .90 [Figure 7.27(b)]. Using Table A.4:

$$P(0 \leq Z \leq 1.28) = .4 \qquad \text{(more accurately, .3997)}$$

which means that

$$P(Z \leq 1.28) = .4 + .5 = .9$$

FIGURE 7.27

(a) $P(X \leq x_0) = .90$.

(b) $P(Z \leq 1.28) = .90$.

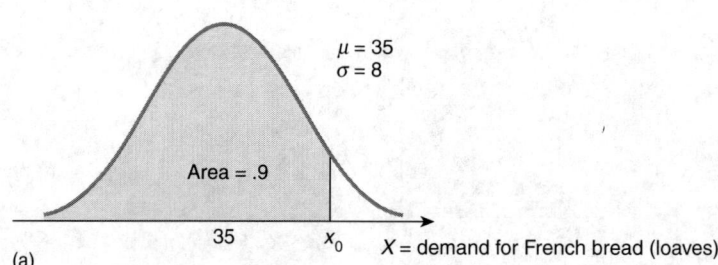

(a)

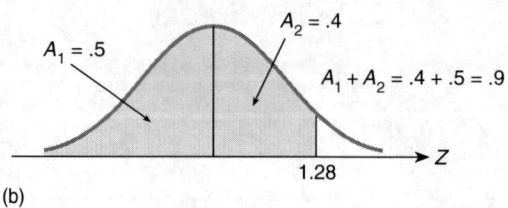

(b)

So

$$\frac{x_0 - 35}{8} = 1.28$$

and

$$x_0 = 35 + (1.28)(8) = 45.24$$

To be conservative, round this value up to 46 loaves. By stocking 46 loaves each day, the bakery will meet the demand for this product 90% of the time.

ANOTHER LOOK AT THE EMPIRICAL RULE

In Chapter 3, the empirical rule specified that when sampling from a bell-shaped distribution (which means a normal distribution), three guidelines apply:

1. Approximately 68% of the data values should lie between $\bar{X} - s$ and $\bar{X} + s$.

2. Approximately 95% of them should lie between $\bar{X} - 2s$ and $\bar{X} + 2s$.

3. Approximately 99.7% of them should lie between $\bar{X} - 3s$ and $\bar{X} + 3s$.

Nothing was said at that time about the origin of these numbers. They actually came directly from Table A.4. To see this, consider Figure 7.28, in which

$$P(-1 < Z < 1) = .68$$

This implies that, for any normal random variable X,

$$P[-1 < (X - \mu)/\sigma < 1] = .68$$

That is,

$$P[(\mu - \sigma) < X < (\mu + \sigma)] = .68$$

As a result, for a set of data from a normal population where $\bar{X}$ is the sample mean and s is the sample standard deviation, we would expect approximately 68% of the data to lie between $\bar{X} - s$ and $\bar{X} + s$.

FIGURE

7.28

Z curve for $P(-1 \leq Z \leq 1) \cong .68$.

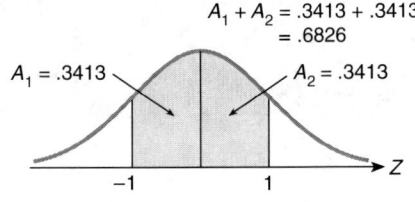

Similarly, $P(-2 < Z < 2) = .4772 + .4772 = .9544$, so you can expect (approximately) 95% of the data points from a normal (bell-shaped) population to lie between $\bar{X} - 2s$ and $\bar{X} + 2s$.

Finally, $P(-3 < Z < 3) = .4987 + .4987 = .9974$, which leads to the third conclusion of the empirical rule.

7.7

USING STATISTICAL SOFTWARE TO DETERMINE AREAS AND VALUES HAVING A SPECIFIED AREA FOR NORMAL POPULATIONS

The calculations demonstrated in Sections 7.4 and 7.5 to determine areas under a normal curve or determine a value of a normal random variable having a specified area can be done very easily using Excel, SPSS, and MINITAB. In Example 7.2, the area to the left of 360 was determined for a normal curve with a mean of 400 and a standard deviation of 50. To find this area (probability) using Excel, click on **Insert** and select **Function.** Click on **Statistical** under **Function Category** and click on **NORMDIST** under **Function Name.** Fill in the entries as in the top panel of Figure 7.29. Entering "true" in the last box indicates that you want the area to the *left* of 360, and you will always enter "true" in this box for all the applications in this textbook. The formula result is .2119 and agrees with Example 7.2.

FIGURE

7.29

Illustration of Excel functions NORMDIST (Example 7.2) and NORMINV (Example 7.5).

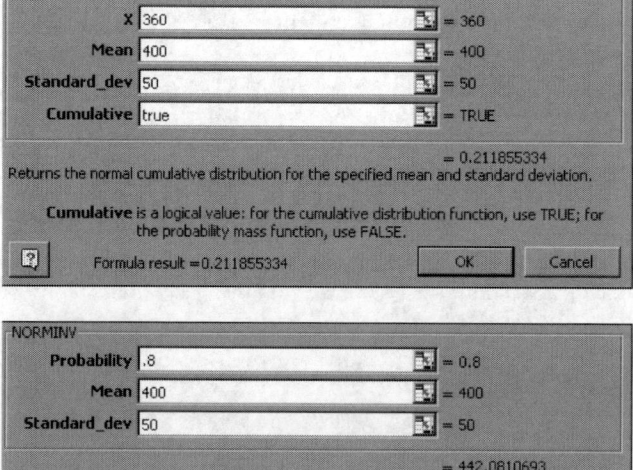

Comment

Whenever you need to find P(X > some value), use Excel's **NORMDIST** function as described here and subtract the result from one. For example, the probability that the bulb lifetime (X) in Example 7.2 exceeds 360 hours is 1 – .2119 = .7881. Remember, Excel always determines the area to the left of the specified value of X.

The bottom panel of Figure 7.29 illustrates Excel's **NORMINV** function and repeats the solution to Example 7.5. The **NORMINV** function finds the value of X having a specified area to the left of this value. Using the Excel solution in Figure 7.29, 80% of the Everglo bulbs will burn out within 442 hours—that is, P(X ≤ 442) = .8, where X is normally distributed with a mean of 400 hours and a standard deviation of 50 hours.

Statistical Software Application Use DATA7-7

Using Statistical Software to Find Areas Under a Normal Curve

EXAMPLE
7.7

In Chapter 3 (Example 3.4) we examined a sample of 100 inside diameters of a machined part produced at the Boston facility of Allied Manufacturing. Earlier discussion of this sample in Chapter 2 (Example 2.1) mentioned that for this part to be acceptable, the diameter must be between 10.1 mm (the lower spec limit) and 10.3 mm (the upper spec limit). Any part outside these spec limits is said to be nonconforming. The targeted diameter is 10.2 mm.

This same data set is contained in DATA6-7. Determine the mean and standard deviation of this sample and compute the sample Z scores for the two spec limits. Assuming the population is normal, with mean $\bar{x}$ and standard deviation s, what proportion of the population will lie outside the spec limits—that is, be nonconforming? What can you say about this process?

In Figure 7.30 you see the descriptive statistics calculated using SPSS. These agree with the statistics calculated using Excel shown in Figure 3.5(a), which also contains the first 16 rows of data set DATA6-7. The SPSS descriptive statistics in Figure 7.30 can be obtained by clicking on **Analyze ➤ Descriptive Statistics ➤ Descriptives** and selecting the diameter variable.

Solution

The area to the left of the lower spec limit of 10.1 mm is illustrated in Figure 7.31 and uses Excel's **NORMDIST** function (refer to Figure 7.29). This area is 2.46843E-11; that is, 2.45579 with the decimal point moved 11 spaces to the left. This number is nearly zero, so we will treat it as zero. The MINITAB output in Figure 7.32 indicates that the area to the left of the upper spec limit (10.3 mm) is .8218. Consequently, the area to the right of this spec limit is 1 – .8218 = .1782. The MINITAB solution in Figure 7.32 is obtained by clicking on **Calc ➤ Probability Distributions ➤ Normal.** Click on the button next to **Cumulative probability,** enter the mean (10.27539) and the standard deviation (.026681), enter 10.3 as the **Input constant,** and click on **OK.**

FIGURE
7.30

The descriptive statistics obtained using SPSS.

Descriptives

Descriptive Statistics

	N	Minimum	Maximum	Mean	Std. Deviation
DIAMETER	100	10.216	10.338	10.27539	.026681
Valid N (listwise)	100				

FIGURE

7.31

Area to the left of
the lower spec
limit using Excel.

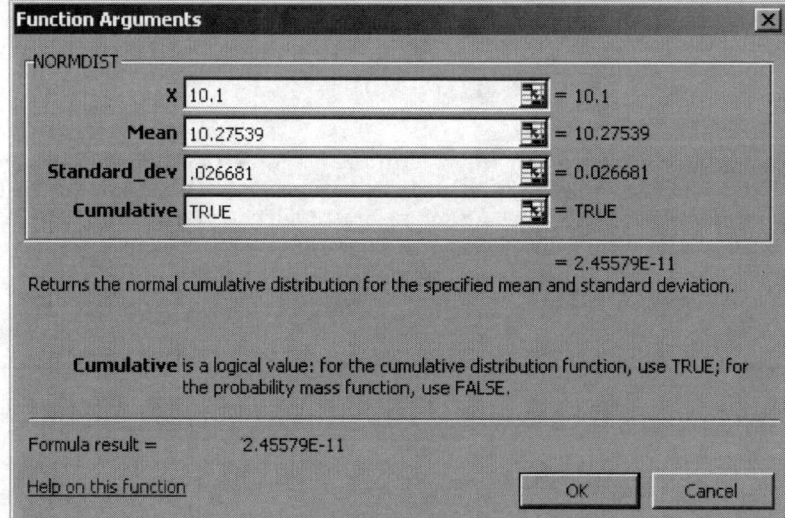

FIGURE

7.32

Area to the right of
the upper spec
limit using
MINITAB.

Cumulative Distribution Function

```
Normal with mean = 10.2754 and standard deviation = 0.0266810

        x       P( X <= x)
   10.3000       0.8218
```

Conclusion   The total tail area outside the spec limits is $0 + .1782 = .1782$. For this population, we can expect 17.82% of the parts to be nonconforming. As a reminder, this percentage is approximate, since we have estimated the population parameters (μ and σ) using the corresponding sample statistics ($\bar{x}$ and s). It is interesting to note that in Example 2.1, it was determined that 17% of the 100 values in this sample were outside the spec limits. Our observations regarding this process remain the same as in earlier examples that examined the process: The z-score for the upper spec limit is $(10.3 - 10.27539)/.026681 = .922$, which indicates that this process is shifted too far to the right (both z-scores should be at least 3 in absolute value) and is producing parts that are too large in diameter. An adjustment to the process that shifts the mean toward the stated target of 10.2 mm will reduce the percentage of parts exceeding the upper spec limit (now an estimated 17.82%).

X Exercises 7.11–7.25

Understanding the Mechanics

7.11 Let X be a random variable with a normal distribution having a mean of 30 and a standard deviation of 20.
  a. What is the probability that X is less than 10?
  b. What is the probability that X is greater than 70?
  c. What is the probability that X is between 20 and 40?

7.12 Find the value of x if the random variable X is normally distributed with mean 50 and standard deviation 6.
  a. $P(X \geq x) = .0655$
  b. $P(X \leq x) = .8686$
  c. $P(40 \leq X \leq x) = .6715$
  d. $P(x \leq X \leq 50) = .3531$

Applying the New Concepts

7.13 High-Tech, Inc., produces an electronic component, GX-7, that has an average life span of 4,500 hours. The life span is normally distributed with a standard deviation of 500 hours. The company is considering a 3,800 hours' warranty on GX-7. If this warranty policy is adopted, what proportion of GX-7 components should High-Tech expect to replace under warranty?

7.14 The estimated miles-per-gallon (on the highway) ratings of a class of trucks are normally distributed with a mean of 12.8 and a standard deviation of 3.2. What is the probability that one of these trucks selected at random would get
   a. between 13 and 15 miles per gallon?
   b. between 10 and 12 miles per gallon?

7.15 The yearly cost of dental claims for the employees of D. S. Inc. is normally distributed with a mean of $75 and a standard deviation of $30. At least what yearly cost would be expected for 40% of the employees?

7.16 Housing has become more affordable over the past couple of decades, thanks to low inflation and low interest rates. Soon-to-be buyers participating in the National Association of Home Builders' 2001 buyer-preference survey indicated that they typically spent between six months and a year to buy a home. Suppose that the distribution of the time that it takes to buy a home can be approximated by a normal distribution with a mean of nine months and a standard deviation of three months.
   a. What is the probability that a home buyer selected at random spends less than a year to buy a home?
   b. At least what amount of time would 60% of the home buyers be expected to spend looking for a home to buy?

(Source: "Most Shoppers Take Six Months to a Year to Find a New Home," *Los Angeles Times*, October 14, 2001.)

7.17 Credit cards with low APRs might not offer low international charges to credit-card providers making a transaction abroad. The average international charge is 2.46% on standard credit cards, 2.55% on gold cards, and rising to 2.65% on platinum cards. Few credit-card users compare credit cards based on their international charges. Suppose that the standard deviation of the percent charge when using a credit card overseas is .6%. Assume that the international charges by credit-card companies can be approximated by a normal distribution.
   a. What is the probability that a credit-card company charges more than 3% for international transactions with a standard credit card?
   b. Repeat part a for a gold credit card.
   c. Repeat part a for a platinum credit card.
   d. Compare your findings in parts a, b, and c.

(Source: "Credit Cards," *The Times* (London, England), August 11, 2001, p. 2.)

7.18 The thickness of a manufactured sheet of metal is believed to follow a normal distribution with a mean of .30 inches and a standard deviation of .02 inches. The lower spec limit is 2.5 standard deviations to the left of the mean. The upper spec limit is 3.0 standard deviations to the right of the mean. Nonconforming sheets of metal have thicknesses outside of these two spec limits. What proportion of the sheets of metal are nonconforming?

7.19 The vice president of a computer networking equipment company named Force10 Networks travels upwards of 100,000 miles a year visiting clients who purchase his networking equipment. To save time, he started booking business jets with charter brokers. He claims that he can make five stops across the country in just two days and that this same trip on a commercial airline would take at least a week with delays and connecting flights. However, companies that charter the use of a small jet can average around $1,800 per flight hour. Assume that the distribution of the cost of a flight hour by companies that charter small jets is approximately normally distributed with a mean of $1,800 and a standard deviation of $200.
   a. What is the probability that a randomly selected jet broker charges less than $2,000?
   b. What is the probability that a randomly selected jet broker charges less than $1,200? Would you consider this to be an unusual occurrence?

(Source: "A Jet You Can Call Your Own," *BusinessWeek*, October 8, 2001, p. 120.)

7.20 The vice president of Offshore Oil and Gas, a consulting firm, notices that the average length of time that a consultant spends on the telephone with a client at any one time is 40 minutes with a standard deviation of 18 minutes. Assuming that the length of such conversations is normally distributed, what percent of the consultant's phone calls would take longer than 50 minutes?

7.21 A production manager is analyzing quality data from a manufacturing process. Sometimes the manager knows certain probabilities but is missing information on the mean or standard deviation. Assume that the manager knows that the proportion of values less than 19.8 is .975.
   a. What is the mean of the process if the standard deviation is known to be 5?
   b. What is the standard deviation of the process if the mean is known to be 15.88?

7.22 As a result of new attractions and marketing, the operating income of Disney World increased by 20% in the first half of 2004. Hotels at Walt Disney World Village charge considerably more than local hotels, particularly during the summer months. The average rate for a room at the Courtyard by Marriott at Walt Disney World Village is $310. Assume that the distribution of the cost of a room at the Courtyard over a year can be approximated by a normal distribution with a mean of $130 and a standard deviation of $20.

    a. What is the probability that the cost of a room on a randomly selected day is at least $115?

    b. What is the probability that the cost of a room on a randomly selected day is between $110 and $150?

    c. Between what two numbers, centered at $130, will the cost of a room be 80% of the time?

(Source: "Disney Theme Parks, Cable Networks Thrive," *The Wall Street Journal*, August 11, 2004, p. A3)

Using the Computer

7.23 [DATA SET EX6-23] *Variable Description:*

Refunddamage: Amount of refund to customers who return damaged merchandise.

A store manager recorded the refund to customers on 100 returned items that were sold to the customer and found to be damaged. The manager knows that historically the average refund is $70 with a standard deviation of $20 on such merchandise.

    a. The manager would like to know the probability of randomly receiving a refund that is at least as large as the amount in **Refunddamage.** For very small probabilities, the manager may suspect that customers have damaged very expensive goods and returned them. The manager treats these refunds as unusual. Find these probabilities. In Excel, put the values of **Refunddamage** in column A, starting in A1. Then type into cell B1 "=1-NORMDIST (A1,70,20,1)." Drag this cell down to B100.

    b. How many of the probabilities obtained in part a are less than .01? Do you think that the manager should consider these refunds as unusual?

7.24 [DATA SET EX6-24] *Variable Description:*

RentResident: Amount of monthly profit from residential rent homes

RentCommercial: Amount of monthly profit from rent paid on commercial buildings

A realtor owns numerous residential and commercial buildings and collects rent on these properties. The realtor selects 100 months over the past several years and lists the monthly profit in thousands of dollars for these properties. These values are listed in the variables **RentResident** and **RentCommercial,** in thousands of dollars.

    a. Plot a histogram of the data in **RentResident** and also of the data in **RentCommercial.** Would you say that the data are approximately normally distributed? Find the mean and the variance for each of the variables.

    b. What type of distribution do you believe the sum of **RentResident** and **RentCommercial** would have? What do you think the resulting mean and variance would be?

    c. Plot a histogram of the sum of **RentResident** and **RentCommercial.** Does the distribution appear to be approximately normally distributed? Find the mean and variance. Compare these results to your answers in part b. Is the variance of the sum equal to the sum of the variances?

7.25 To gain insight into how the standard deviation changes the shape of a normal distribution, first generate 200 observations from a normal distribution with a mean of 0 and standard deviation of 1. Then, generate two more sets of 200 observations changing the standard deviation to 3 and to 5. Construct three frequency histograms and compare the heights and widths of the histograms and comment on how the standard deviation changes the shape of a normal distribution. (In Excel, click on **Tools ➤ Data Analysis ➤ Random Number Generation** and select the Normal distribution to generate the random values. Use the Stacked Histogram option in the KPK menu to form a stacked histogram for the data sets. In SPSS, click on **Transform ➤ Compute ➤ RV.NORM(q, mean, std-dev)** to generate the random values. In MINITAB, click on **Calc ➤ Random Data ➤ Normal** to generate the random values.)

7.8

OTHER CONTINUOUS DISTRIBUTIONS

The normal distribution is one example of a continuous distribution. A normal random variable X is a continuous random variable; that is, over some specific range, *any* value of X is possible. We used X to represent the lifetime of an Everglo bulb to illustrate a continuous random variable because any value between 280 hours and 520 hours (see Figure 7.2) is possible. In fact, any value less than 280 or more than 520 is also possible, although not likely to occur.

In the Everglo example, a normal distribution seemed appropriate because the histogram of 200 sample bulbs in Figure 7.2 revealed a concentration of burnout times in the "middle" and not nearly as many burnout times around 300 or 500. These features give the normal curve its mound in the center and tails on each end.

There are many continuous distributions that do not resemble a normal curve in appearance. For example, consider the following two situations, in which a random variable, X, ranges from 1 to 10.

Situation 1. The chance that X is between 1.0 and 1.5

$$= \text{the chance that } X \text{ is between 1.5 and 2.0}$$
$$= \text{the chance that } X \text{ is between 2.0 and 2.5}$$
$$\vdots$$
$$= \text{the chance that } X \text{ is between 9.0 and 9.5}$$
$$= \text{the chance that } X \text{ is between 9.5 and 10.0}$$

Situation 2. The larger X is, the less likely it is to occur. Thus, the chance that X is between 1.0 and 1.5

$$> \text{the chance that } X \text{ is between 1.5 and 2.0}$$
$$> \text{the chance that } X \text{ is between 2.0 and 2.5}$$
$$\vdots$$
$$> \text{the chance that } X \text{ is between 9.0 and 9.5}$$
$$> \text{the chance that } X \text{ is between 9.5 and 10.0}$$

These two cases can be represented by two other frequently occurring continuous distributions. Situation 1 can be represented by a uniform random variable; situation 2 could be described using an exponential random variable.

Although there are other random variables that apply to these two situations, the uniform and exponential distributions fit many of the applications encountered in business.

Uniform Distribution

Consider spinning the minute hand on a clock face. Define a random variable X to be the stopping point of the minute hand. It seems reasonable to assume, for example, that the probability that X is between 2 and 4 is *twice* the probability of observing a value of X between 8 and 9. In other words, the probability that X is in any particular interval is *proportional* to the width of that interval.

A random variable of this nature is a **uniform random variable.** The values of such a variable are evenly distributed over some interval because the random variable occurs *randomly* over this interval. Unlike the normal random variable, values of the uniform random variable do not tend to be concentrated about the mean.

Assume that the manager of Dixie Beverage Service is concerned about the amount of soda that is released by the dispensing machine that the company is now using. He is considering the purchase of a new machine that electronically controls the cutoff time and is supposed to be very accurate. The present machine cuts off mechanically, and he suspects that the device shuts off the fluid flow *randomly* anywhere between 6 and 8 ounces. To test the present system, a sample of 150 cups is taken from the machine, and the amount of soda released into each cup is recorded. The relative frequency histogram made from these 150 observations is shown in Figure 7.33.

Would you be tempted to describe the population of *all* cup contents using a normal curve? We hope not, because there is no evidence of a declining number of observations in the tails. A word of warning here: though we often have a tendency to think of all continuous random variables as being normally distributed, as this application demonstrates

FIGURE

7.33

Relative frequency histogram of a sample of 150 cups of soda.

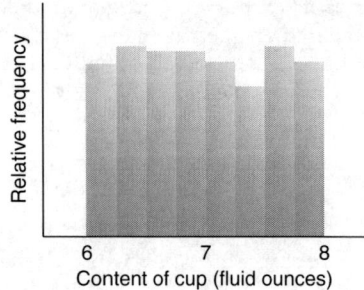

FIGURE

7.34

Uniform distribution for X = soda content (compare with Figure 7.33).

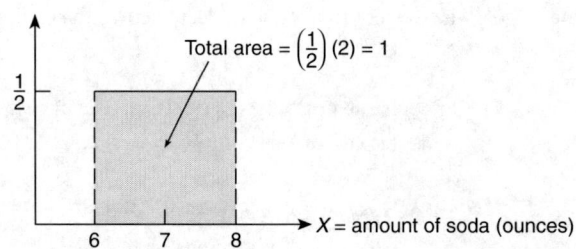

FIGURE

7.35

Total area of a uniform distribution.

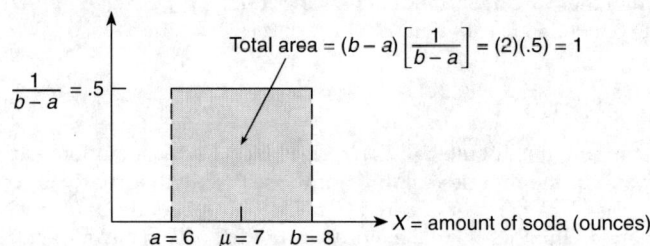

this is certainly not the case. Instead, this distribution is a flat or uniform distribution. The random variable X = cup contents is a uniform random variable. The corresponding smooth curve describing the population is shown in Figure 7.34. Notice that the total area here is given by a rectangle, and, as is true of all continuous random variables, this total area must be 1. The area of a rectangle is given by (width) · (height). By making the height of this curve (a straight line, actually) equal to .5, the total area is

$$(8 - 6)\,(.5) = 1.0$$

In general, the curve defining the probability distribution for a uniform random variable is as shown in Figure 7.35. The total area is

$$(b - a)\left[\frac{1}{b - a}\right] = 1.0$$

FIGURE

7.36

The probability
that X exceeds 7.5.
The shaded area
represents the
percentage of cups
containing more
than 7.5 ounces.

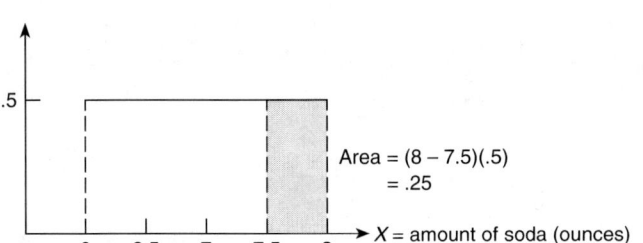

Mean and Standard Deviation

Refer to Figure 7.35. The mean (μ) of X is the value midway between a and b, namely,

$$\mu = \frac{a+b}{2}$$

The standard deviation (σ) of X is, as before, a measure of how much variation there would be in X if you were to observe it indefinitely. Unlike the standard deviation of a normal distribution, σ for a uniform distribution is hard to represent graphically as a particular distance on the probability curve. Its value, however, is given by

$$\sigma = \frac{b-a}{\sqrt{12}}$$

Determining Probabilities

As it is for all continuous random variables, a probability based on a uniform random variable is determined by finding an area under a curve. Suppose, for example, the manager of Dixie Beverage Service would like to know what percentage of the cups will contain more than 7.5 ounces, using the current machines. In Figure 7.36, the shaded area is a rectangle, so its area is easy to find:

$$\text{area} = (\text{width}) \cdot (\text{height}) = (8 - 7.5) \cdot .5 = .25$$

So 25% of the cups will contain more than 7.5 ounces.

EXAMPLE

7.8

What is the probability that a cup will contain between 6.5 and 7.5 ounces? What is the average content?

Solution

The first result is the same as the percentage of cups containing between 6.5 and 7.5 ounces. Based on Figure 6.37, we conclude that

$$P(6.5 < X < 7.5) = .5$$

The average cup content (mean of X) is

$$\mu = \frac{6+8}{2} = 7 \text{ ounces}$$

FIGURE

7.37

The probability
that X is between
6.5 and 7.5.

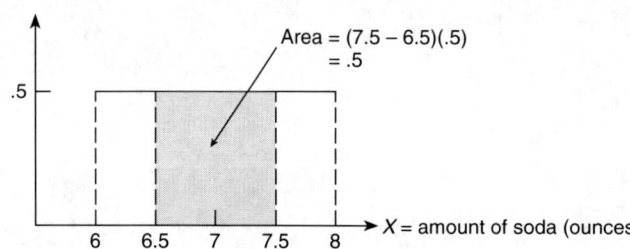

The standard deviation of X is

$$\sigma = \frac{8-6}{\sqrt{12}} = 0.58 \text{ ounce}$$

Notice that, as with the normal random variable, the probability that X is equal to any particular value is zero. So,

$$P(X = 6.5) = P(X = 7.5) = 0$$

As a result,

$$P(6.5 \le X \le 7.5) = P(6.5 < X < 7.5) = .5$$

Simulation is an area of statistics that relies heavily on the uniform distribution. In fact, the uniform distribution is the underlying mechanism for this often-complex procedure. So, although not as many "real-world" populations have uniform distributions as have normal ones, the uniform distribution is extremely important in the application of statistics.

Exponential Distribution

The final continuous distribution we will discuss is the *exponential distribution.* Similar to the uniform random variable, the **exponential random variable** is used in a variety of applications in statistics. One application is observing the time between arrivals at, for example, a drive-up bank window. Another situation that often fits the exponential distribution is observing the lifetime of certain components in a machine.

Chapter 6 discussed the Poisson random variable, which often is used to describe the *number* of arrivals over a specified time period. If the random variable Y, representing the number of arrivals over period T, follows a Poisson distribution, then X, representing the *time between* successive arrivals, will be an *exponential random variable.* The exponential random variable has many applications when describing any situation in which people or objects have to wait in line. Such a line is called a *queue.* People, machines, or telephone calls may wait in a queue.

The Exponential Random Variable. The shape of the exponential distribution is represented by a curve that steadily decreases as the value of the random variable, X, increases. Thus, the larger X is, the probability of observing a value of X at least this large decreases exponentially. This type of curve is illustrated in Figure 7.38.

Determining Probabilities. Determining areas for exponential random variables is not as simple as for uniform ones, but it is easier than for normal random variables because exponential probabilities can be derived on a calculator.

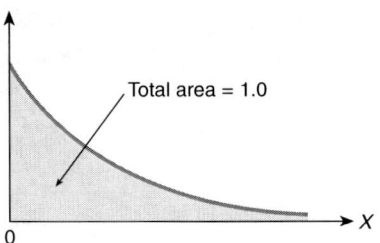

FIGURE

7.38

Curve showing the distribution of an exponential random variable.

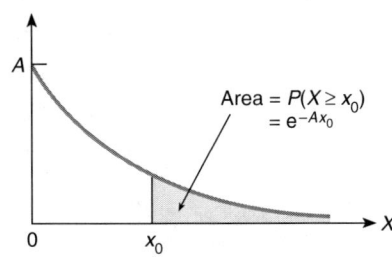

FIGURE

7.39

Curve used for determining a probability for an exponential random variable.

As Figure 7.39 illustrates, for an exponential random variable, X, the probability that X exceeds or is equal to a specific value, x_0, is

$$P(X \geq x_0) = e^{-Ax_0}$$

The parameter A is related to the Poisson random variable we used when discussing arrivals. In fact, the Poisson distribution for arrivals per unit time and the exponential distribution for time *between* arrivals provide two alternative ways of describing the same thing. For example, if the number of arrivals per unit time follows a Poisson distribution with an average of $A = 6$ per hour, then an alternate way of describing this situation is to say that the time between arrivals is exponentially distributed with mean time between arrivals equal to $1/A = 1/6$ hour (10 minutes).

In general, $1/A$ is the average (mean) value of the exponential random variable, X. It is also equal to the standard deviation of X. So,

$$\mu = 1/A$$

$$\sigma = 1/A$$

In applications using this distribution, the value of A either will be given or can be estimated in some way.

EXAMPLE

7.9

The owner of the Downtown Haircut Emporium believes the best way to run his barbershop is to rely on walk-in customers and not to schedule appointments. From past experience, the arrival of customers follows a Poisson distribution with an average arrival rate of $A = 4$ customers per hour.

1. If the owner just witnessed the arrival of a customer, what is the probability that there will be a new arrival within 30 minutes?

2. If X represents the time between successive arrivals, what are the mean and standard deviation of X?

FIGURE

7.40

Curve showing the
probability that
X exceeds .5
$[P(X > .5)]$.

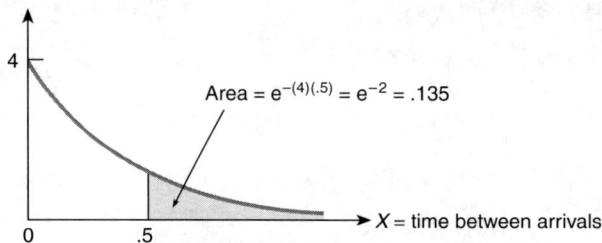

Solution 1 To determine this probability, we must first convert 30 minutes to .5 hour, since the arrival rate is 4 *per hour*. The desired probability then is $P(X \le .5)$. Referring to Figure 7.40, the probability that X *exceeds* .5 is

$$P(X > .5) = P(X \ge .5)$$
$$= e^{-(4)(.5)}$$
$$= e^{-2}$$
$$= .135$$

Consequently, $P(X \le .5) = 1 - .135 = .865$, and so 86.5% of the time, the time between successive arrivals will not exceed 30 minutes.

Solution 2 Both the mean and standard deviation of X (the time between successive arrivals) are $1/A = 1/4$ hour (15 minutes).

X Exercises 7.26–7.41

Understanding the Mechanics

7.26 Let X be a uniformly distributed random variable over the range from 10 to 20. What are the following probabilities?
  a. $P(X < 15)$
  b. $P(X > 15)$
  c. $P(X < 12)$
  d. $P(X > 12)$

7.27 What is the mean and standard deviation of a random variable that is uniformly distributed between 100 and 200?

7.28 Let X be an exponentially distributed random variable with a rate of 2 per hour.
  a. What is the mean of X?
  b. What is the standard deviation of X?
  c. Find $P(X > 1 \text{ hour})$.

7.29 What is the probability that an exponentially distributed random variable with a rate of 4 per hour is less than .6?

7.30 For a random variable that is uniformly distributed between 5 and 10, find the probability that the random variable is:
  a. between 6 and 8.
  b. greater than 7.
  c. less than 9.

7.31 Let X be a random variable with a uniform distribution between 55 and 70.
  a. What is the probability that X is between $\mu - \sigma$ and $\mu + \sigma$?
  b. Find the value of x such that the $P(X \le x) = .80$.

7.32 Suppose that the distribution of a random variable X is approximately exponential with a mean of 10.
  a. What is $P(X \ge 8)$?
  b. What is $P(X \le 11)$?
  c. What is $P(6 \le X \le 10)$?
  d. What is the standard deviation of X?

Applying the New Concepts

7.33 The rate at which a swimming pool is filled is uniformly distributed between 20 and 26.3 gallons per minute.
- **a.** What is the probability that the filling rate at any one time is between 21.3 and 24.6 gallons per minute?
- **b.** What is the mean rate at which the swimming pool is filled?
- **c.** What is the standard deviation of the rate at which the swimming pool is filled?

7.34 Suppose that customers arrive at a bank to either deposit money or withdraw money. Assume that the interarrival time (time between arrivals) is exponentially distributed with a mean of four minutes.
- **a.** What is the probability that the interarrival time is greater than five minutes?
- **b.** What is the probability that the interarrival time is between one minute and four minutes?
- **c.** What is the standard deviation of the interarrival time?

7.35 The time intervals (in operating hours) between successive failures of air conditioning equipment in certain aircraft is believed to follow an exponential distribution. Assume that the mean time between failures is 300 hours. What is the probability that air conditioning equipment in a particular aircraft will fail after 200 operating hours?

7.36 From surveys, Holiday Inn knew that guests found the bathrooms at its hotels to be dirty. If the company shifted from tubs to shower stalls, it would mean much less dingy grout and an end to dark showers and discolored shower curtains. Moreover, consultants estimate that the cleaning time required for each guest room would fall to 13 minutes on average from the current 23 minutes required for guest rooms with tubs. That translates into a savings of $150 per room per year in maintenance costs.
- **a.** Assume that the time to clean a guest room is uniformly distributed between 15 and 31 minutes for guest rooms with bathtubs. What is the standard deviation of the time that it takes to clean a guest room that has a tub?
- **b.** What is the probability that a guest room with a tub is cleaned in less than 25 minutes?

(Adapted from "Shower or Bath? It's a Hotel's Tough Call," The Wall Street Journal, May 14, 1998, p. B1.)

7.37 Yellow Rose taxi company estimates that it makes an average of $415 in profits per day. Assuming that the daily profit follows an exponential distribution, what is the probability that on a given day at least $500 in profits will be made?

7.38 The president of Bright-Light Candles estimates that the average burning time of their "medium-K" candles is 40 hours. Assuming that burning time follows an exponential distribution, calculate the probability that a given medium-K candle will burn for at least 50 hours?

7.39 AT&T recently offered an exclusive rebate program with Nokia, a Finnish telecommunications equipment company, on the Nokia 8260 wireless phone. These phones sold for $39.99 after rebate, weigh only 3.4 oz each, and have standard extended-life batteries with a mean life of 200 hours of standby time. Assuming that the extended-life batteries have a life that is exponentially distributed with a mean of 200 hours, what is the probability that an extended-life battery will last longer than 200 hours?

(Source: http://store.yahoo.com/1800mobiles/.)

Using the Computer

7.40 A production manager believes that the insulating effectiveness of a certain padding has a life span that is exponentially distributed with a mean equal to three years. The manager would like to know the reliability of this material. The reliability of a product is often measured by the formula 1 minus the cumulative exponential distribution evaluated at a specified time period. (To use the cumulative exponential distribution in Excel, click on the paste function, then click on **Statistical ➤ EXPONDIST** and enter $1/\mu$ for the lambda value where μ is the population mean. In SPSS, click on **Transform ➤ Compute ➤ CDF.EXP(q, scale)** and enter $1/\mu$ for the value of the scale. In MINITAB, click on **Calc ➤ Probability Distributions ➤ Exponential** and then select cumulative probability.)
- **a.** What is the reliability of the padding after 4 years?
- **b.** What is the reliability of the padding after 5 years? Compare this reliability to that in part a.
- **c.** After how many years would the reliability be .1?

7.41 **[DATA SET EX7-41]** Variable Description:

BotErr: Error in manufacturing bottom half of rod

TopErr: Error in manufacturing top half of rod

A quality-control engineer is monitoring the production of a metal rod that is made in two parts. The bottom (steel) part is manufactured to a length of 1 meter. The top (aluminum) part is also manufactured to a length of 1 meter. The errors in manufacturing these rods are recorded for 400 observations in variables BotErr and TopErr.
- **a.** Plot a histogram of BotErr and a histogram of TopErr. Which of the following distributions most closely fits this data: normal, exponential, or uniform?
- **b.** Define the variable TotalErr to be equal to BotErr + TopErr. Plot a histogram of the data for this variable. What is the approximate shape of the distribution?

Summary

A random variable that can assume any value over a specific range is a continuous random variable. Many business applications have continuous probability distributions that can be approximated using a *normal, uniform,* or *exponential random variable.* Each of these distributions has a unique curve that can be used to determine probabilities by finding the corresponding area under this curve. The normal distribution is characterized by a bell-shaped curve with values concentrated about the mean. The uniform distribution (curve) is flat; values of this random variable are evenly distributed over a specified range. The exponential distribution has a shape that steadily decreases as the value of the random variable increases. Any calculator with an e^x key can be used to derive probabilities for the exponential distribution.

We discussed examples illustrating the shape of each distribution. The exact curve for a particular random variable is specified using one or two *parameters* that describe the corresponding population. As in the case of a discrete random variable, the population consists of what you would obtain if the random variable was observed indefi-

nitely. The resulting average value and standard deviation represent the *mean* and *standard deviation* of the random variable and corresponding population.

There are infinitely many normal random variables, one for each mean (μ) and positive standard deviation (σ). If $\mu = 0$ and $\sigma = 1$, this normal random variable is the standard normal random variable, Z. Consequently, there is only *one* normal random variable of this type. Table A.4 gives the probabilities (areas) under the standard normal curve. You can also use this table to determine a probability for any normal random variable if you first standardize the variable by defining $Z = (X - \mu)/\sigma$. For this situation, Z represents the number of standard deviations that X is to the right (Z is positive) or left (Z is negative) of the mean.

A uniform random variable is one in which the values of such a variable are evenly distributed over some interval because the random variable occurs *randomly* over this interval. Simulation is an area of statistics that relies heavily on the uniform distribution. An exponential random variable is useful for situations that have a time component, such as when people or objects are waiting in a line (*queue*).

 # Summary of Formulas

1. Standardizing a normal random variable *(X)*

$$Z = \frac{X - \mu}{\sigma}$$

2. Uniform distribution

$$\mu = \frac{a+b}{2} \quad \text{and} \quad \sigma = \frac{b-a}{\sqrt{12}}$$

$$P(X \le x_0) = \frac{x_0 - a}{b - a} \quad \text{for } a \le x_0 \le b$$

3. Exponential distribution

$$P(X \le x_0) = 1 - e^{-Ax_0} \quad \text{for } x_0 \ge 0$$

$$\text{where } A = 1/\mu, \mu = \frac{1}{A}, \text{ and } \sigma = \frac{1}{A}.$$

X Review Exercises 7.42–7.63

7.42 Let the random variable X be normally distributed with mean 10 and standard deviation 2. Without computing any probabilities, explain why the following probabilities are equal.

$$P(8 < X < 10) = P(8 \le X \le 10) = P(10 \le X \le 12) = P(10 < X < 12)$$

7.43 What is the probability that a random variable is greater than its mean if its distribution is as follows?
  a. Normal
  b. Uniform
  c. Exponential

7.44 If Z is a random variable with a standard normal distribution, what value represents the 95th percentile of the distribution?

7.45 If the random variable X has a uniform distribution between 0 and 20, find the value x such that the probability that X is less than x is .25.

7.46 Assume that the expenditure of a family of four at Six Flags over Texas for food, souvenirs, and parking is approximately normally distributed with a mean of $150 and a standard deviation of $25. What percentage of four-member families will have an expenditure:
  a. greater than $200?
  b. less than $125?
  c. between $100 and $200?

7.47 Refer to Exercise 7.46. Determine the expenditure by a family of four, say x, such that
  a. 50% of the time the expenditure is less than x.
  b. 20% of the time the expenditure is greater than x.
  c. 80% of the time the expenditure is less than x.

7.48 Which distribution, the normal or exponential distribution, would be most suitable for approximating the distributions of the following quantities.
  a. The time between arrivals at a bank drive-up window.
  b. The heights of seniors in a high school class.
  c. The time between placement and execution of a market order on the New York Stock Exchange.

7.49 An operations manager decides on the amount of inventory to keep on hand based on demand. The manager wishes to know what value demand will exceed 30% of the time.
  a. If demand is normally distributed with a mean of 400 and a standard deviation of 100, what is this value?
  b. If demand is uniformly distributed between 200 and 600, what is this value?

7.50 Wireless service is much more reliable than it was several years ago. However, blocked calls remain a fact of life for wireless carriers and users. Figures from various industry sources put the average percentage of blocked calls at nearly 2% per carrier on a per-market basis. Blocked calls are defined technically as calls where users fail to access the network due to network congestion or other capacity shortcomings. Assume that the percentage of blocked calls per user is approximately normally distributed with a mean of 2% and a standard deviation of a half percent. What percentage of the users of wireless service experience blocked calls that are in excess of 2.5% of their calls?

(Source: "Blocked Out," *Wireless Review*, vol. 18, September 16, 2001, pp. 36–37.)

7.51 Automotive analysts contend that a weak Japanese yen enables Japanese automakers to keep a lid on the price of vehicles sold in the United States because it is cheaper for them to develop and build autos at home. U.S. automakers must cut costs when the yen reaches a very high level. Suppose that an analyst believes that for 2002, the value of the yen to the dollar will follow approximately a normal distribution with a mean of 130 yen to the dollar and a standard deviation of 5 yen to the dollar. Find the values, symmetrical about the mean of 130, between which the price of yen to the dollar should lie 60% of the time.

(Adapted from "Another Strike Against GM," *USA Today*, June 16, 1998, p. 4B, and U.S. dollar table, *The Wall Street Journal*, January 14, 2002, p. C1.)

7.52 The Forbes Web site *(www.forbes.com)* tracks the job approval ratings for at least 50 chief executive officers (CEOs) by allowing individuals to vote each month on their CEO performance. Suppose that these ratings are approximately normally distributed with a mean of 50 and a standard deviation of 15. Using the normal distribution, what percent of the CEOs receive an extreme rating defined as either over 85 or less than 15?

7.53 The examination committee of the Institute of Chartered Accountants passes only 20% of those who take the examination. If the scores follow a normal distribution with an average of 72 and a standard deviation of 18, what is the passing score?

7.54 The shelf life of cookies made by a small bakery is considered to be exponentially distributed with a mean equal to three days. What percentage of the boxes of cookies placed on the shelf today would still be considered marketable after 2.75 days?

7.55 The time that a certain drug has an effect on a normal human being is considered to be exponentially distributed when a standard dose is taken. If the average length of time that the drug has an effect is 30 hours, what is the probability that any given normal person will be affected by the drug for at least 32 hours? What is the standard deviation for the length of time that the drug affects a person?

7.56 One class of hedge funds is the equity-market-neutral hedge fund. This class of funds balances investments among carefully researched long and short positions, and it averaged 6% for 2003. These neutral funds are less volatile than hedge funds that can invest in emerging markets and distressed debt. Suppose that an investor has compiled performance records on hundreds of these market-neutral funds and found that their returns were approximately uniformly distributed between 0% and 12% for 2003. What percentage of the funds performed within one standard deviation of 6%?

(Source: Adapted from "Hedge Funds Post Solid Returns," *The Wall Street Journal*, January 2, 2004, p. R2)

7.57 In a 1965 issue of *Electronics* magazine, Mr. Moore published an article articulating the concept that underpins what has become known as Mr. Moore's Law: The power of a silicon chip will double every 18 to 24 months. Because this accelerates the pace of technological change, marketing analysts estimate that the lifespan of a personal computer purchased by the typical consumer is exponentially distributed. Suppose we assume that the mean life span is two years. What is the probability that the lifespan of a personal computer exceeds three years?

7.58 Vail Resorts in Colorado has expanded many low-price options for tourists, but does not remind visitors about the slow moving highway to Vail. Skiers can pay a fraction of peak-season prices by scheduling trips in November and December. For example, four people can share a two-bedroom condo for $50 to $80 during November and December, whereas from January to March the prices vary from $100 to $150. Assuming a uniform distribution for the peak season prices, what percentage of the condos are priced at more than one standard deviation above the mean during the peak season?

(Source: "In Colorado, Traffic on the Interstate Is at a Peak," *New York Times*, September 19, 2004, p. 5.3)

7.59 The revenue from a movie theatre's concessions may easily determine whether a theatre remains profitable. If the average expenditure at the concession stand is $6 with a standard deviation of $2, between what two values centered around the mean will 60% of the purchases lie. Assume that purchases are normally distributed.

7.60 Lead times between ordering a product and the delivery of the product are considered to be approximately normally distributed. What value will the lead time be less than 40% of the time? Assume that the average lead time is 72 hours with a standard deviation of 5 hours?

7.61 The District of Columbia (D.C.) passed a law that prohibits anyone driving in D.C. from talking on a cell phone without a hands-free device. If the average accident rate for a

D.C. driver using a cell phone is .25 accidents per year, what is the probability that a driver who uses a cell phone in D.C. will be involved in an accident within the next two years? Assume that the length of time between car accidents is exponentially distributed.

(Source: "Drive Now, Talk Later—or Use Earpiece," The Washington Post, Washington, D.C., July 1, 2004, p. B1)

7.62 **[DATA SET EX7-62]** Variable Description:

Company: Name of a Fortune 500 company

Score: Average rating for Most Admired Company with 10 as highest score

Ratings for the America's Most Admired Company contest are displayed on the Fortune Web site (www.fortune.com). A sample of these ratings is provided in this data set. Determine the percentage of observations that are within one standard deviation of the mean. Repeat this for two standard deviations. Would you say that these percentages are close to those stated by the empirical rule for the normal distribution?

7.63 Data were collected from two computer service divisions of a large semiconductor company. In division A, the salaries were approximately normally distributed with a mean of $5,000 per month and a standard deviation of $1,000 per month. In division B, the salaries were approximately normally distributed with a mean of $7,000 and a standard deviation of $1,500 per month. In Excel, type in the two rows displayed below, with the upperleft most cell starting in cell A1.

	A	B	C	D	E	F	G
1	0	=NORMDIST(A1,D2,E2,0)	=NORMDIST(A1,F2,G2,0)	mean1	std1	mean2	std2
2	0.25	=NORMDIST(A2,D2,E2,0)	=NORMDIST(A2,F2,G2,0)	5	1	7	1.5

Now highlight the first two rows of columns A, B, and C. Drag these rows down through the 41st row. Highlight columns A and B from row 1 to row 41. Click on **Chart Wizard ➤ Scatter Plot with Data Values Connected by Smooth Lines ➤ Next ➤ Series.** Add series two by first clicking on the **Add** button and then entering the range of values in column A into **X Values** and the range of values in column C into **Y Values.** The resulting graph presented below will be displayed.

   a. The units in the plot are in thousands of dollars. What range of salaries appears to be at least somewhat likely to occur in both groups?
   b. If an employee is selected at random from division A, what is the probability that the employee's salary falls within the range in part a?
   c. Do a "what if" analysis by changing the mean values in cells D2 and F2. What mean salaries for divisions A and B would allow almost no overlap in salaries?

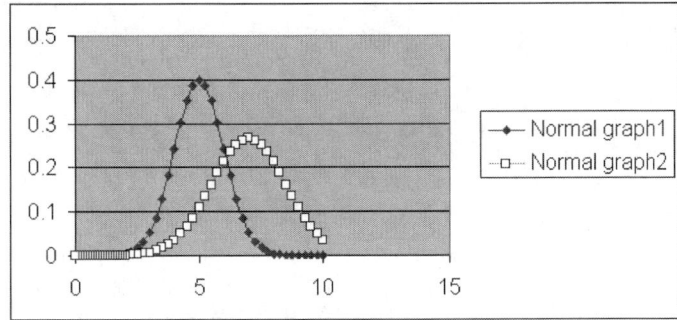

285

Computer Exercises Using the Databases

Exercise 1—Appendix F

Select 100 observations at random from the database and use a convenient statistical computer package to estimate the mean and standard deviation of the variable HPAYRENT (house payments or apartment/house rents). Find the percentage of the observations between $\bar{x} \pm s$, $\bar{x} \pm 2s$, and $\bar{x} \pm 3s$. Comment on whether these percentages support the conclusion that the data come from a normally distributed population.

Exercise 2—Appendix F

Select 150 observations at random from the database and, with reference to the variable OWNORENT, calculate the proportion of those observations that indicate the house is owned rather than rented. If a random sample of 20 observations were chosen from this set of 150 observations with replacement, what is the probability that more than half of the homes in the sample of 20 are owned by their occupants?

Exercise 3—Appendix G

Select 100 observations at random from the database on the variable EMPLOYEES (number of employees). Use a convenient statistical computer package to construct a histogram. What type of distribution does the histogram approximate? normal? uniform? exponential? none of these?

Exercise 4—Appendix G

Repeat Exercise 3 using the variable SALES.

Insights from Statistics in Action

Examining Unethical Behavior: More Fun than Decent People Think Should Be Legal

In the Statistics in Action discussion at the beginning of this chapter, we examined the question of measuring the ethical behavior of business professionals. Often, vignettes are used to determine if an individual would act in a professional way. Some examples of these vignettes are the following:

- *Vignette 1.* A programmer who works for a bank decides to modify a bank's accounting system to hide his overdrawn account and thus avoid an overdraft charge. After making a deposit, the programmer corrects his modification.

- *Vignette 2.* A business manager receives software ordered from a mail-order company but also finds another software package sent in error. The extra software is not listed on the invoice. The manager decides to keep the extra software without paying for it.

- *Vignette 3.* An employee uses the company's copier to make copies for a friend who does not work for the company.

Suppose that a researcher investigating ethical behavior surveys 100 business professionals from each of three groups: the under-30-years-old group, the at-least-30-years-old-but-less-than-50-years-old group, and the at-least-50-years-old group. The researcher uses 50 vignettes and records the proportion of vignettes that each respondent says he/she would not act in the same way because the behavior is ethically unacceptable. Use the data contained in StatInActChap6.xls to answer the following questions.

1. Plot a histogram of the data for each age group. In practice, the distribution of data never conforms exactly to a particular distribution. However, approximate distributions are often used to conveniently describe the distributions and to find probabilities. What continuous distribution approximates the distribution of each of these data sets?

2. Find the sample mean and sample standard deviation of each of the distributions and compare. If a distribution is approximately uniform, compute the mean and standard deviation provided by the formulas for the uniform distribution and compare these to the sample mean and sample standard deviation.

3. For the under-30-years-old group, calculate the z score for a value of .98. Interpret this value.

4. Using the approximate distribution found in question 1, determine the probability that a respondent found at least 40 percent of the vignettes ethically unacceptable for the at-least-30-years-old-but-less-than-50-years-old group.

5. Repeat question 4 using the at-least-50-years-old group and compare the probabilities.

(Source: "Strategic Importance Of Business Ethics: Case Studies Of Abuse," *Journal of Global Business*, 2004, Vol. 15, p. 37. "Andersen Chiefs Say Shredding Was Shared," *The Financial Times*, Jan 25, 2002, p. 1. "Making Ethical Decisions," *Communications of the ACM*, 2000, Vol. 43, No. 12, p. 66–71.)

Appendix

Data Analysis with Excel, MINITAB, and SPSS

Excel

Calculating Normal Probabilities

Click **Insert ➤ Function.** Select **NORMDIST** from the **Insert Function** dialog box to compute cumulative normal distribution probabilities. If the normal distribution is the standard normal distribution, use **NORMSDIST.** Select **NORMINV** to find the value of the normal random variable given the cumulative distribution. The function **NORMSINV** is used for the standard normal distribution. Fill in the dialog boxes for **NORMDIST** and **NORMINV** as illustrated in Figure 7.29.

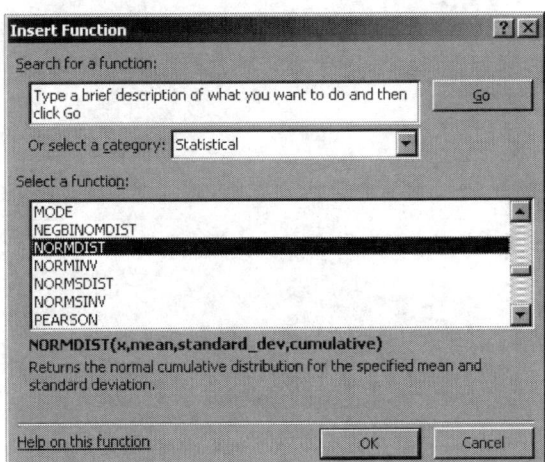

Calculating Exponential Distribution Probabilities

Select **EXPONDIST** from the **Insert Function** dialog box to compute cumulative exponential distribution probabilities. In the **Function Arguments** dialog box for the exponential distribution, enter the value of the random variable (2, for this example), the reciprocal of the mean (.5), and "True" for the three edit boxes, respectively. Note that the probability is .632.

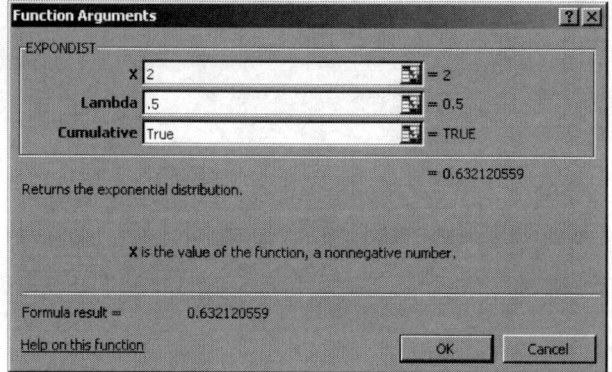

MINITAB

Calculating Normal and Exponential Distribution Probabilities

To obtain normal probabilities, first enter values of the normal random variable in a column, say C1. Click **Calc ➤ Probability Distributions ➤ Normal** to obtain the **Normal Distribution** dialog box. Select **Cumulative probability.** Enter the **Mean** and the **Standard deviation** in the respective edit boxes. Enter the column (C1) which has values of the normal random variable. Click **OK** to retrieve the cumulative probabilities. Use the **Inverse cumulative probability** option to find the value of a normal random variable for a given cumulative probability value. To obtain exponential distribution probabilities, follow the same procedure, except select **Exponential** from the list of probability distributions in the **Calc** menu. In the **Exponential Distribution** dialog box, set the **Threshold** to zero and enter the value of the mean into the **Scale** edit box.

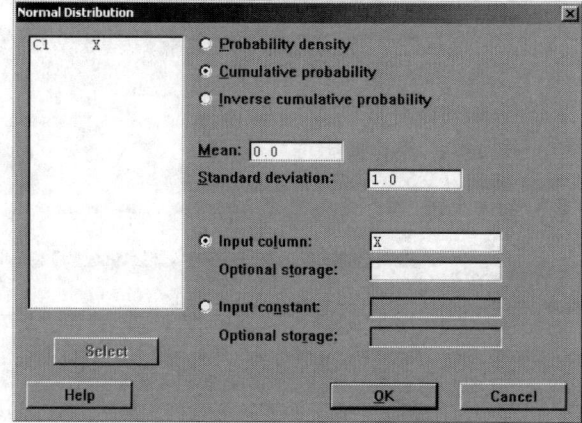

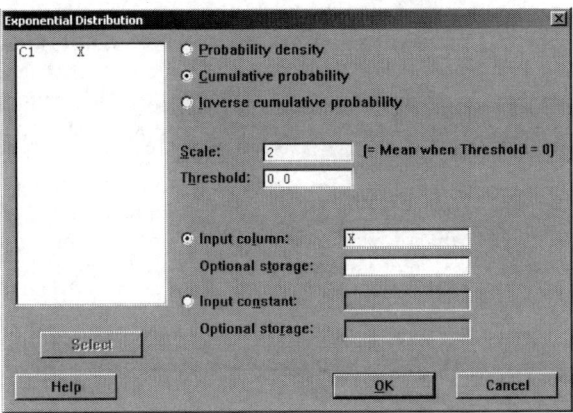

SPSS

Calculating Normal Probabilities

Cumulative probabilities can be calculated for a number of continuous distributions in SPSS. The examples below will illustrate how to find cumulative probabilities for a specified value of (1) the standard normal random variable *(Z)* and (2) any normal random variable *(X)*. A cumulative probability is defined as $P(X \leq x)$; that is, the area to the left of *x* under the continuous curve (normal here) describing the random variable, *X*.

The following discussion will demonstrate how to obtain the cumulative probabilities for a standard normal random variable and for any normal distribution, as displayed in the data window.

	z	cumz	x	cumx
1	1.75	.96	487.50	.96
2				

To obtain a cumulative probability for the standard normal random variable *(Z)*, enter the value of Z (say, 1.75) as shown above. Click on the Variable View tab and name this variable "z." Click on **Transform ➤ Compute.** Enter the variable name "cumz" in the **Target Variable** box. Find the function name CDFNORM(zvalue) inside the function list box and double click on it. Replace the question mark inside the **Numeric Expression** box with "z." Click on **OK.** In the data window, click on the **Variable View** tab and set the number of decimal places for variable cumz to two. *Note:* The z column can contain more than one value of Z. The corresponding number of cumulative probabilities will be determined in the cumz column.

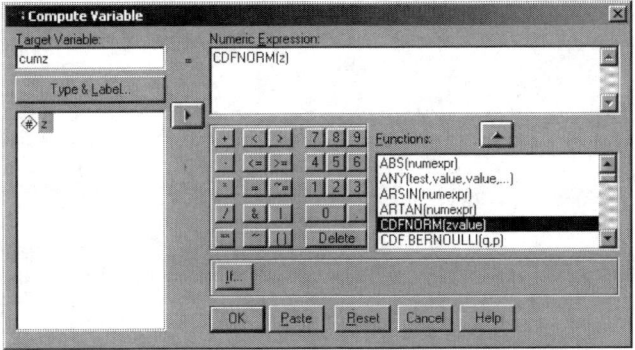

To obtain a cumulative probability for any normal random variable *(X)*, enter the value of X (say, 487.5) in one of the cells. Click on the **Variable View** tab and name this variable "*x*." Click on **Transform ➤ Compute.** Enter the variable name "cumx" in the **Target Variable** box. Find the function name CDF.NORM(q,mean,stddev) inside the function list box and double-click on it. Replace the question marks inside the **Numeric Expression** box, as shown. This assumes the normal random variable X has a mean of 400 hours and a standard deviation of 50. Click on **OK.** In the data window, click on the **Variable View** tab and set the number of decimal places for variable cumx to two. *Note:* The *x* column can contain more than one value of X. The corresponding number of cumulative probabilities will be determined in the cumx column.

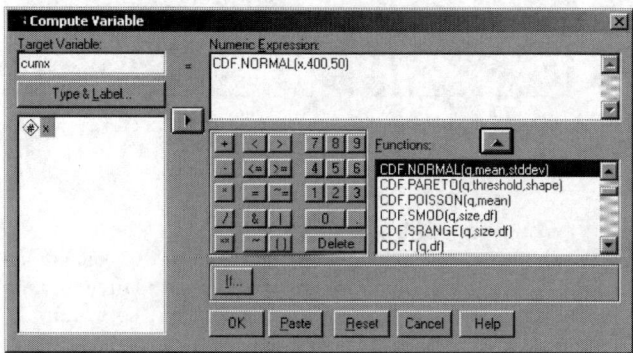

Calculating Exponential Distribution Probabilities

To obtain one or more cumulative exponential probabilities, enter the value(s) of X starting in the upper left cell. Click on the **Variable View** tab and name this variable "*x*." Follow the same procedure as above for computing the cumulative normal distribution probabilities, except select the function name CDF.EXP(q,scale). Enter the reciprocal of the mean for the scale value.

chapter

8

Statistical Inference and Sampling X

Statistics in Action
Traffic Congestion Takes Its Toll

It's not your imagination. According to a national study of 18 years of traffic data from 68 urban areas, traffic congestion is getting worse, and it is costing us billions in lost time and excess fuel costs. In fact, the amount of time drivers spend stuck in traffic has tripled since 1982, climbing from an average per driver of 11 hours a year to over 46 hours a year in 2003. Of course, in certain cities, the amount of time stuck in traffic greatly exceeds these figures. A thriving economy can compound a city's traffic problems, causing productivity to decline as people spend more time on the roads. Los Angeles's traffic is a major cost to its economy. An estimated $12.5 billion in congestion costs puts Los Angeles at the top of the list of cities with the worst traffic congestion.

In some research studies, survey data are collected to obtain a better understanding of the behavior of drivers. These data contain information on where the drivers live, work, and drop off their kids. These studies assist traffic planners in deciding whether to construct more freeways, to implement HOV (high occupancy vehicle) lanes, or to be more creative in coming up with solutions. In addition, these studies show that the behavior of drivers during rush hour can be unpredictable. If one car slows and moves on, it forces the next car to overreact, and the next, and the next, in a giant ripple effect, which can last long after the first car went merrily on its way. That is why one often spends an hour in a traffic jam, and then returns to normal speed, without ever seeing any sign of what caused the problem.

One solution to relieving traffic congestion has been mass transit. For example, Dallas Area Rapid Transit has operated light rail and commuter rail trains for about eight years. Mass transit is only one part of the solution to traffic congestion. Another solution to relieving traffic gridlock is an instant traffic monitoring system. This system gives updates to the public on the radio and updates a Web site illustrating bottlenecks.

Texas, which has the largest state highway system in the nation, is now only spending 8% of its budget on new construction. This is in contrast to the days when it spent 30% of its budget on new construction. Data collected in surveys from drivers on their driving patterns, frequency of delays, and costs of various options are helping states such as Texas to spend transportation dollars more wisely. When you have completed this chapter, you will be able to

- Use the average time spent by a random sample of motorists on freeways as an estimate of the average time spent by all motorists on freeways.

- Discuss the reliability of the estimate of the average time spent in traffic and construct and interpret an interval in which the average time spent in traffic by the population of interest might reasonably lie.

- Discuss how many motorists should be included in a random sample so that the estimated time spent in traffic is within a certain margin of error.

8.1

RANDOM SAMPLING AND THE DISTRIBUTION OF THE SAMPLE MEAN

In Chapter 3, you learned how to calculate the mean of a sample, $\bar{X}$. This sample is drawn from a population having a particular distribution, such as normal, exponential, or uniform. If you were to obtain another sample (you probably will not, as most decisions are made from just one sample), would you get the same value of $\bar{X}$? Assuming that the new sample was made up of different individuals than was the first sample, then almost certainly the two $\bar{X}$'s would not be the same. So, $\bar{X}$ itself is a random variable. We will demonstrate that if a sample is large enough, $\bar{X}$ is very nearly *normally* distributed regardless of the shape of the sampled population. That is, if you were to obtain many large samples, calculate the resulting $\bar{X}$'s, and then make a histogram of these $\bar{X}$'s, *this histogram would always approximately resemble a bell-shaped (normal) curve.*

Simple Random Samples

In Chapter 1, the concept of a simple random sample was introduced. The mechanics of obtaining a random sample range from drawing names out of a hat to using a computer to generate lists of random numbers. For extremely large populations, one is often forced to select individuals (elements) from the population in a *nearly* random manner.

The underlying assumption behind a random sample of size n is that any sample of size n has the same chance (probability) of being selected. To be completely assured of obtaining a random sample from a *finite* population, you should number the members of the population from 1 to N (the population size) and, using a set of n random numbers, select the corresponding sample of n population elements for your sample.

This procedure was described in the Chapter 1 appendix and is often used in practice, particularly when you have a sampling situation that needs to be legally defensible, as is the case in many statistical audits. However, for situations in which the population is extremely large, this strategy may be impractical, and instead you can use a sampling plan that is nearly random. Several other sampling procedures are discussed in the last section of this chapter.

The main point of all this lengthy discussion is that practically all the procedures presented in subsequent chapters relating to decision making and estimation assume that you are using a random sample. In the chapters that follow, the word *sample* will mean *simple random sample.*

Estimation

The idea behind statistical inference has two components:

1. The *population* consists of everyone of interest. By "everyone" we mean measurements taken from all people, machine parts, daily sales, or whatever else you are interested in measuring or observing. The mean value (for example, average height, average income) of everyone in this population is μ and generally is not known.

2. The *sample* is randomly drawn from this population. Elements of the sample thus are part of the population—but certainly not all of it. The exception to this is a *census*, a sample that consists of the entire population.

The sample values should be selected randomly, one at a time, from the entire population. Figure 8.1 emphasizes our central point—namely, an unknown population **parameter** (such as μ = the mean value for the entire population) can be **estimated** using the corresponding sample statistic (such as $\bar{X}$ = the mean of your sample).

It makes sense, doesn't it? It would be most desirable to know the average value for everyone in the population, but in practice this is nearly always impossible. It may take

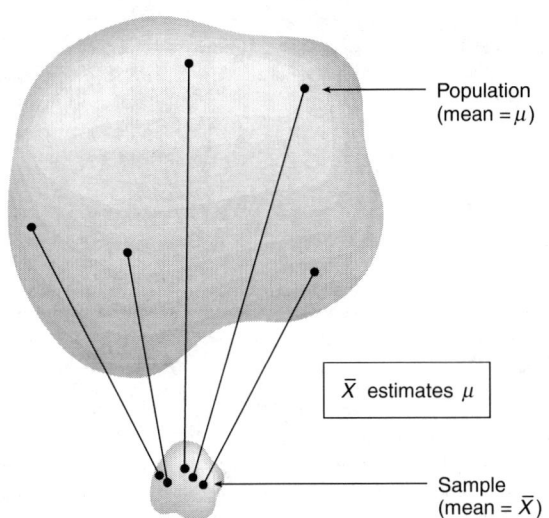

FIGURE

8.1

The sample mean, $\bar{X}$, is used to estimate the population mean, μ. In general, sample statistics are used to estimate population parameters.

too much time or money, we may not be able to obtain values for them all even if we want to, or the process of measuring the individual items may destroy them (such as measuring the lifetime of a light bulb). In many instances, estimating the population value using a sample estimate is the best we can do.

EXAMPLE

8.1

In Example 6.3, the funds dispensed daily by an automatic teller machine (ATM) were believed to follow a normal distribution with a mean of $\mu = \$3,700$ and a standard deviation of $\sigma = \$625$. There is no way of *knowing* that μ is \$3,700 unless the population of all daily dispersements is examined. Assume that

$$X = \text{daily funds released by this ATM}$$

Solution

is a normal random variable, but do not assume anything about the mean and standard deviation. Ignoring the standard deviation, estimating the mean, μ, involves obtaining a random sample of daily dispersements. Suppose you obtain a random sample of size $n = 10$, with the following results (in dollars):

3,880   3,460   3,530   4,240   3,470   3,770   3,990   4,550   3,310   2,300

What is the estimate of μ, based on these values?

Solution

The sample mean is $\bar{x} = \$3,650.00$. Thus, based on these 10 sample values, our best estimate of μ is $\bar{x} = \$3,650.00$.*

Distribution of $\bar{X}$

Referring to Example 8.1, the value of $\bar{X}$ would almost certainly change if you were to obtain another sample. The question of interest here is, if we *were* to obtain many values of

*The notation $\hat{\mu}$ is commonly used in place of $\bar{x}$ to denote an *estimate* of μ. For this example, the estimate of μ is $\hat{\mu} = \$3,650.00$.

$\bar{X}$, how would they behave? If we observed values of $\bar{X}$ indefinitely, where would they center; that is, what is the **mean** of the distribution for the random variable, $\bar{X}$? Is the variation of the $\bar{X}$ values more, less, or the same as the variation of individual observations? This variation is measured by the **standard deviation** of the distribution for $\bar{X}$.

In Example 7.2, it was assumed that the average lifetime of an Everglo light bulb was $\mu = 400$ hours, with a population standard deviation of $\sigma = 50$ hours. This result does not imply that if you obtain a random sample of these bulbs, the resulting sample mean, $\bar{X}$, always will be 400. Rather, a little head scratching should convince you that $\bar{X}$ will not be exactly 400, but $\bar{X}$ should be **approximately** 400.

Statistical Software Application Use DATA8-2

Determining the Distribution of the Sample Mean

Twenty samples of 10 Everglo bulbs each and the calculated $\bar{X}$'s for each sample are shown in Table 8.1. The data are contained in columns 1 to 20 in dataset DATA7-2. For now we will assume that the population parameters are $\mu = 400$ hours and $\sigma = 50$ hours (Figure 8.2). (1) Using Excel, determine the mean and standard deviation of the means of these 20 samples. What do you observe here? (2) Construct a histogram of these 20 means. What can you say about the "shape" of the $\bar{X}$ values?

Solution 1

Rather than using Excel to determine the 20 means one at a time, use the Excel KPK Data Analysis. First you must open file DATA7-2. Then click on **KPK Data Analysis ➤ Means and CIs for Multiple Samples.** Enter "A1:T10" as the **Input Range,** "50" as the **Population Std. Dev.,** and "U1" as the **Output Range.** Make sure the button alongside **Means** at the bottom of the form is selected. The output from this macro is shown in Figure 8.3 and does not include the frequency distribution in cells W1:Y11. Examining cell V24, we conclude that the average of the 20 sample means is 402.89 hours, and so the $\bar{X}$ values appear to be centered approximately at $\mu = 400$ hours. Look at the 20 standard deviations in Table 8.1. These values are in the neighborhood of $\sigma = 50$, as they should be. However, the standard deviation of the 20 $\bar{X}$ values (contained in cell V25) is 12.78, so we conclude that the $\bar{X}$ values have much less variation than the individual observations in each of the samples.

Solution 2

To obtain the frequency distribution of the twenty sample means in Figure 8.3 and corresponding histogram, click on **KPK Data Analysis ➤ Quantitative Data Charts/Tables ➤ Histogram/Freq. Charts.** You will then see the input form for this macro (see Figure 2.3 on page 25). For the **Input Range,** enter "V3:V22," and for the **Output Range,** enter "W1." Also, click on the circle to the left of **Number of Classes** and enter "7" in the text box. Finally, click on the check box for **Frequencies** in the **Table** list and the check box for **Frequency Histogram** in the **Chart Output Options** list. This will result in the frequency distribution table shown in Figure 8.3 and the histogram in Figure 8.4 (obtained by clicking on the **Frequency Histogram** tab at the bottom of your spreadsheet). Notice that the procedure produced eight classes, rather than the requested seven. As mentioned in earlier chapters, this Excel macro creates a frequency distribution containing an easy-to-interpret class width and classes, and very often will modify the intended number of classes to achieve this.

Based on the histogram in Figure 8.4 and the solution to (1), it seems reasonable to assume that the values of $\bar{X}$ follow a normal distribution centered at $\mu = 400$ hours but one that is much narrower than the population of individual lifetimes described in Figure 8.2.

In the previous example, we observed that the values of $\bar{X}$ were centered about the mean of the population, μ. In addition, the standard deviation of the $\bar{X}$ values was

TABLE

8.1

Twenty samples of 10 Everglo bulbs.

Sample 1	Sample 2	Sample 3	Sample 4	Sample 5
308	431	416	373	354
419	448	361	451	385
389	380	389	329	449
432	371	497	460	419
362	387	400	481	483
302	410	489	350	396
440	400	406	431	317
430	426	333	356	457
375	381	307	410	404
383	361	375	353	480
$\bar{x}=384.0$	399.5	397.3	399.4	414.4
$s=49.30$	28.54	60.51	53.99	54.25

Sample 6	Sample 7	Sample 8	Sample 9	Sample 10
404	372	449	403	354
390	404	389	350	446
390	493	397	565	343
454	344	428	354	458
386	396	374	358	404
385	441	502	412	468
384	373	365	441	416
351	438	402	340	340
392	360	416	359	409
396	367	316	446	408
$\bar{x}=393.2$	398.8	403.8	402.8	404.6
$s=25.45$	46.10	50.32	68.93	46.28

Sample 11	Sample 12	Sample 13	Sample 14	Sample 15
329	429	461	448	457
473	286	399	386	432
336	382	416	375	425
356	380	378	488	391
385	423	359	447	429
365	388	408	429	448
419	329	393	377	416
448	438	374	380	429
459	423	440	372	414
449	378	454	408	315
$\bar{x}=401.9$	385.6	408.2	411.0	415.6
$s=54.12$	47.91	34.60	40.12	39.73

Sample 16	Sample 17	Sample 18	Sample 19	Sample 20
491	439	331	418	428
353	336	427	422	368
375	425	445	341	445
536	419	420	485	429
447	346	401	442	475
415	408	389	470	437
322	392	363	404	475
350	409	439	370	458
453	313	352	539	308
343	334	346	435	408
$\bar{x}=408.5$	382.1	391.3	432.6	423.1
$s=71.46$	45.28	41.35	56.78	51.48

FIGURE

8.2

Assumed
distribution of
Everglo bulb
lifetimes.

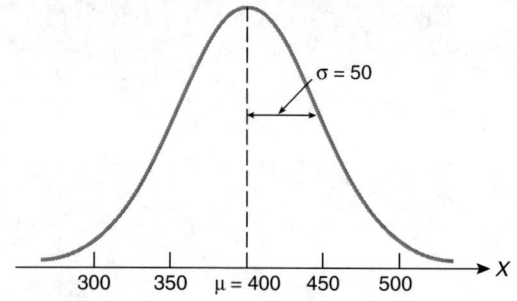

FIGURE

8.3

Sample means
created using **KPK
Data Analysis ➤
Means and CIs for
Multiple Samples.**

	Q	R	S	T	U	V	W	X	Y
					Multiple Samples			**Frequency Distribution Table**	
					SAMPLE	MEANS	CLASS	CLASS LIMITS	FREQUENCY
1	439	331	418	428	1	384.00	1	377 and under 384	1
2	336	427	422	368	2	399.50	2	384 and under 391	2
3	425	445	341	445	3	397.30	3	391 and under 398	3
4	419	420	485	429	4	399.40	4	398 and under 405	7
5	346	401	442	475	5	414.40	5	405 and under 412	3
6	408	389	470	437	6	393.20	6	412 and under 419	2
7	392	363	404	475	7	398.80	7	419 and under 426	1
8	409	439	370	458	8	403.80	8	426 and under 433	1
9	313	352	539	308	9	402.80		TOTAL	20
10	334	346	435	408	10	404.60			
11					11	401.90			
12					12	385.60			
13					13	408.20			
14					14	411.00			
15					15	415.60			
16					16	408.50			
17					17	382.10			
18					18	391.30			
19					19	432.60			
20					20	423.10			
21									
22					SUMMARY FOR X-BARs				
23					Mean	402.89			
24					St. Dev.	12.78			

Frequency Histogram   DATA7-2

FIGURE

8.4

Excel histogram of
20 sample means.

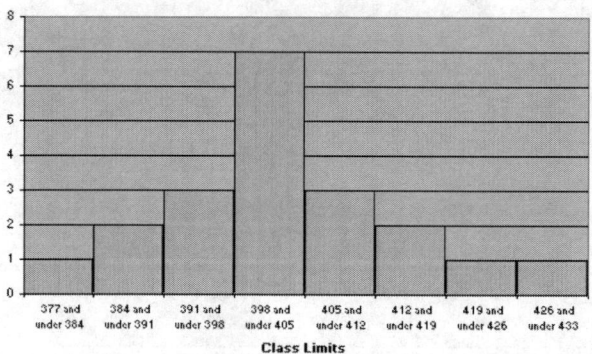

Frequency Histogram

considerably less than the standard deviation of the population, σ. In general, what can you say about the mean and standard deviation of the random variable $\bar{X}$? This is summarized as follows:

Mean of the random variable $\bar{X}$ is

$$\mu_{\bar{X}} = \mu$$

Standard deviation of the random variable $\bar{X}$ is

$$\sigma_{\bar{x}} = \frac{\sigma}{\sqrt{n}}$$

8.1

8.2

For the previous example, $\mu = 400$, $\sigma = 50$, and $n = 10$. As a result, the mean and standard deviation of the $\bar{X}$ values, if samples of size 10 were obtained *indefinitely*, are

$$\mu_{\bar{x}} = 400 \quad \text{and} \quad \sigma_{\bar{x}} = \frac{50}{\sqrt{10}} = 15.81$$

Recall that the mean and standard deviation of the 20 observed $\bar{X}$ values was 402.89 and 12.78, respectively. These values will tend toward 400 and 15.81 if we were to take additional samples of size 10. These results are summarized in Figure 8.5, where $\mu_{\bar{X}} = 400$ and $\sigma_{\bar{X}} = 15.81$.

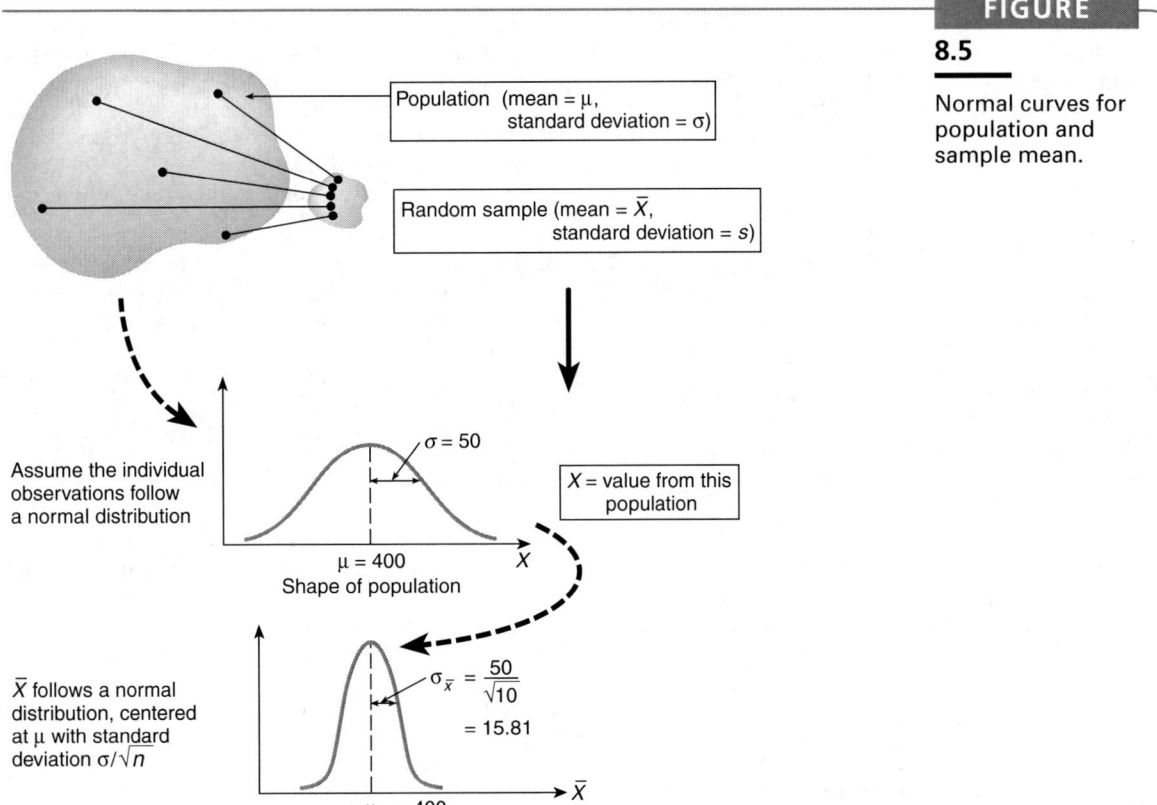

FIGURE

8.5

Normal curves for population and sample mean.

8.2

THE CENTRAL LIMIT THEOREM

In the previous example, we observed that the shape of the $\bar{X}$ curve was approximately normal. This is not a surprising result, considering that the population from which the samples were obtained followed an assumed normal curve; that is, the random variable X = lifetime of Everglo bulb is a normal random variable. What may surprise you is that the random variable $\bar{X}$ follows an approximate normal curve *regardless* of the shape of the population curve, *provided large samples are obtained*. This is summarized in the **Central Limit Theorem.**

CENTRAL LIMIT THEOREM

When obtaining large samples (generally $n > 30$) from any population, the sample mean $\bar{X}$ will follow an approximate normal distribution.

Based on the Central Limit Theorem and equations 8.1 and 8.2, whenever large samples are obtained from *any* population, the sample mean, $\bar{X}$, will follow an approximate normal distribution with mean μ and standard deviation $\sigma/\sqrt{n}$. In practice, you are likely to obtain your one and only sample of size n. However, these results allow you to make probability statements regarding $\bar{X}$, as illustrated in the examples to follow.

Comments

1. Not having to know the shape of the sampled population for large samples makes the Central Limit Theorem a very strong tool in statistics. For example, if you repeatedly took large samples from a population with an exponential distribution (look ahead to Figure 8.11), the resulting $\bar{X}$'s would follow a *normal* (not an exponential) curve.

2. Based on equations 8.1 and 8.2, the mean of $\bar{X}$ is μ and the standard deviation of $\bar{X}$ is $\sigma/\sqrt{n}$ for *any* sample size n. However, for $\bar{X}$ to be approximately normally distributed, a large value of n is necessary if the population is not assumed to be normally distributed.

3. What constitutes a "large" sample depends on the shape of the population. For populations that are fairly symmetrical, a sample size of 20 may suffice. Government auditors often deal with populations containing a large percentage of values equal to zero. For such populations (and other highly skewed populations), sample sizes of several hundred may be required for the sample mean to be approximately normally distributed. For typical populations encountered in a business setting, a sample size larger than 30 ($n > 30$) generally provides an approximate normal distribution for the sample mean.

4. If the population from which you are sampling is a normal population, the Central Limit Theorem isn't necessary. For this situation, the random variable $\bar{X}$ is *exactly* normally distributed, with mean μ and standard deviation $\sigma/\sqrt{n}$. For Example 8.2, we can say that the random variable $\bar{X}$ follows an exact normal distribution with mean = 400 and standard deviation $50/\sqrt{10}$ = 15.81.

Basically, equations 8.1 and 8.2 along with the Central Limit Theorem state that the normal curve (distribution) for $\bar{X}$ is centered at the same value as the population distribution but has a much smaller standard deviation. Notice that as the sample size, n, increases, $\sigma/\sqrt{n}$ decreases, and so the spread relative to the mean of the $\bar{X}$ curve (that is, the variation in the $\bar{X}$ values) decreases. In the Everglo bulb example, if we repeatedly obtained samples of size 100 (rather than 10), the corresponding $\bar{X}$ values would lie even closer to $\mu_{\bar{X}} = 400$ because now $\sigma_{\bar{X}}$ would equal $50/\sqrt{100}$ = 5 (see Figure 8.6).

For the 20 values of $\bar{X}$ in Table 8.1, it was assumed that the population mean was *known* to be $\mu = 400$, so each of the $\bar{X}$ values estimates μ with a certain amount of error. The more variation in the $\bar{X}$ values, the more error we encounter using $\bar{X}$ as an estimate of μ.

FIGURE

8.6

Normal curves for
the sample mean
(n = 10, 20, 50,
100).

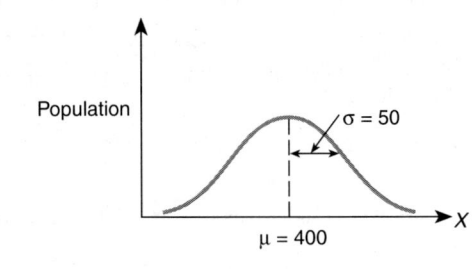

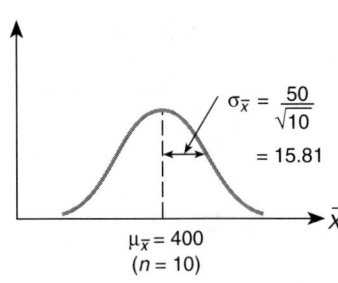

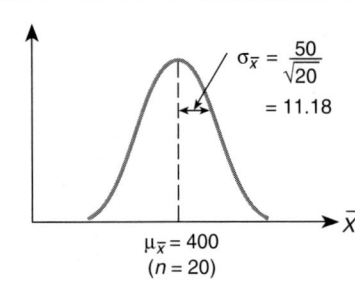

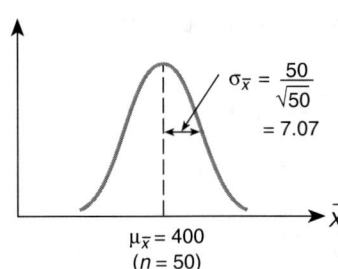

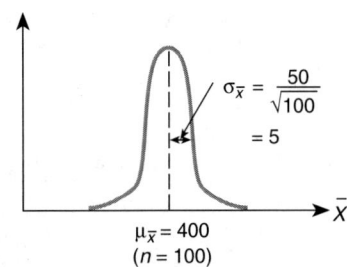

Consequently, the standard deviation of $\bar{X}$ also serves as a measure of the error that will be encountered using a sample mean to estimate a population mean. The standard deviation of the $\bar{X}$ distribution is often referred to as the **standard error** of $\bar{X}$.

Standard error of $\bar{X}$ = standard deviation of the probability distribution for $\bar{X}$

$$= \frac{\sigma}{\sqrt{n}}$$

The previous discussion has described the probability distribution of the sample mean, $\bar{X}$. This distribution is referred to as the *sampling distribution* of $\bar{X}$.

DEFINITION

The probability distribution of a sample statistic is its **sampling distribution.**

To summarize this section: For large samples, the sampling distribution of $\bar{X}$ is approximately normal, centered at μ, with a standard deviation (standard error) of $\sigma/\sqrt{n}$, regardless of the shape of the sampled population.

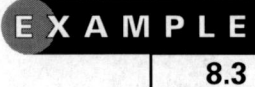

Electricalc has determined that the assembly time for a particular electrical component is normally distributed with a mean of 20 minutes and a standard deviation of 3 minutes.

1. What is the probability that an employee in the assembly division takes longer than 22 minutes to assemble one of these components?

2. What is the probability that the average assembly time for 15 such employees exceeds 22 minutes?

3. What is the probability that the average assembly time for 15 employees is between 19 and 21 minutes?

Solution 1

The random variable X here is the assembly time for a component. It is assumed to be a normal random variable, with $\mu = 20$ minutes and $\sigma = 3$ minutes (Figure 8.7). We wish to determine $P(X > 22)$. Standardizing this variable and using Table A.4, we obtain

$$P(X > 22) = P\left[\frac{X - 20}{3} > \frac{22 - 20}{3}\right]$$

$$= P(Z > .67)$$

$$= .5 - .2486 = .2514$$

Therefore, a randomly chosen employee will require longer than 22 minutes to assemble the component with probability .25.

Solution 2

Figure 8.7 does *not* apply to this question, because we are concerned with the *average* time for 15 employees, not an individual employee. Using comment 4 on page 224, we know that the curve describing $\bar{X}$ (an average of 15 employees) is normal with

$$\text{mean} = \mu_{\bar{X}} = \mu = 20 \text{ minutes}$$

$$\text{standard deviation (standard error)} = \sigma_{\bar{x}} = \frac{\sigma}{\sqrt{n}}.$$

$$= \frac{3}{\sqrt{15}} = .77 \text{ minutes}$$

(See Figure 8.8.)

FIGURE

8.7

Assembly time for the population of electrical components. (See Example 8.3.)

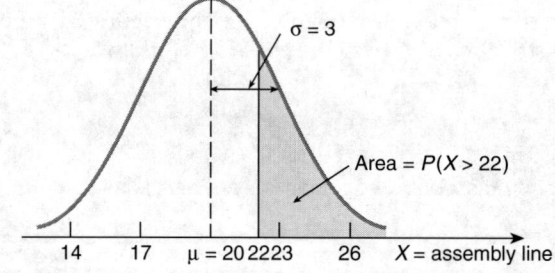

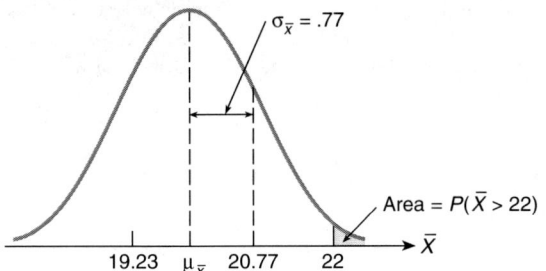

8.8

Curve for $\bar{X}$ = average of 15 employees' assembly times. Shaded area shows $P(\bar{X} > 22)$.

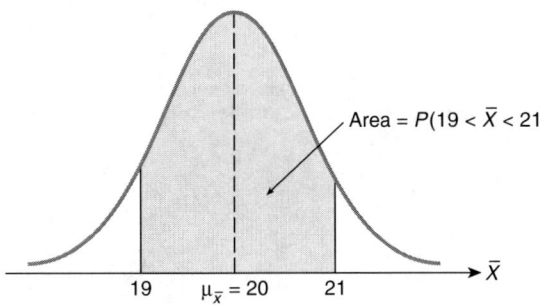

8.9

Curve for average assembly time of 15 employees. Shaded area shows $P(19 < \bar{X} < 21)$.

This procedure is the same as in solution 1, except now the standard deviation of this curve is .77 rather than 3:

$$P(\bar{X} > 22) = P\left[\frac{\bar{X} - 20}{.77} > \frac{22 - 20}{.77}\right]$$

$$= P(Z > 2.60)$$

$$= .5 - .4953 = .0047$$

So an average assembly time for a sample of 15 employees will be more than 22 minutes with less than 1% probability; that is, it is very unlikely that an average of 15 assembly times will exceed 22 minutes.

The curve for this solution is shown in Figure 8.9. We wish to find $P(19 < \bar{X} < 21)$.

Solution 3

$$P(19 < \bar{X} < 21) = P\left[\frac{19 - 20}{.77} < \frac{\bar{X} - 20}{.77} < \frac{21 - 20}{.77}\right]$$

$$= P(-1.30 < Z < 1.30)$$

$$= .4032 + .4032 = .8064$$

Thus, a sample of 15 employees will produce an average assembly time between 19 and 21 minutes with probability about .81.

In Example 8.3, it was assumed that the individual assembly times followed a normal distribution. *However, remember that the strength of the Central Limit Theorem is that this assumption is not necessary for large samples.* We can answer questions 2 and 3 for *any* population whose mean is 20 minutes and standard deviation is 3 minutes, provided we take a *large* sample ($n > 30$). In this case, the normal distribution of $\bar{X}$ may not be exact, but it provides a very good approximation.

A Look at the Sampling Distribution of $\bar{X}$ for Normal Populations

The Central Limit Theorem tells us that $\bar{X}$ tends toward a normal distribution as the sample size increases. If you are dealing with a population that has an assumed normal distribution (as in Example 8.3), then $\bar{X}$ is normal regardless of the sample size. However, as the sample size increases, the variability of $\bar{X}$ decreases, as is illustrated in Figure 8.6. This means that for large sample sizes, if you were to get many samples and corresponding values of $\bar{X}$, these values of $\bar{X}$ would be more concentrated around the middle, with very few extremely large or extremely small values.

Look at Figure 8.6, which illustrates the assumed normal distribution of all Everglo bulbs. We know (using Table A.4) that 95% of a normal curve is contained within 1.96 standard deviations of the mean. For a sample size of n = 10 from a normal population with $\mu = 400$ and $\sigma = 50$, $\sigma_{\bar{X}} = 15.81$. Now,

$$\mu_{\bar{X}} - 1.96\sigma_{\bar{X}} = 400 - 1.96(15.81) = 369.0$$

and

$$\mu_{\bar{X}} + 1.96\sigma_{\bar{X}} = 400 + 1.96(15.81) = 431.0$$

Thus, if we repeatedly obtain samples of size 10, 95% of the resulting $\bar{X}$ values will lie between 369.0 and 431.0.

This result and the corresponding results using $n = 20$, 50, and 100 are contained in Table 8.2, which reemphasizes that for larger samples, you are much more likely to get a value of $\bar{X}$ that is close to $\mu = 400$. In practice, you typically do not know the value of μ. However, by using a larger sample size, you are more apt to obtain an $\bar{X}$ that is a good estimate of the unknown μ.

TABLE 8.2

Sample from a normal population with $\mu = 400$ and $\sigma = 50$; 95% of the time, the value of $\bar{X}$ will be between $\mu_{\bar{X}} - 1.96\, \sigma_{\bar{X}}$ and $\mu_{\bar{X}} + 1.96\sigma_{\bar{X}}$. Refer to Figure 8.6 for the values of $\sigma_{\bar{X}}$.

Sample Size	$\sigma_{\bar{X}}$	$\mu_{\bar{X}} - 1.96\sigma_{\bar{X}}$	$\mu_{\bar{X}} + 1.96\sigma_{\bar{X}}$	Conclusion
$n = 10$	15.81	369.0	431.0	95% of the time, the value of $\bar{X}$ will be between 369.0 and 431.0
$n = 20$	11.18	378.1	421.9	95% of the time, the value of $\bar{X}$ will be between 378.1 and 421.9
$n = 50$	7.07	386.1	413.9	95% of the time, the value of $\bar{X}$ will be between 386.1 and 413.9
$n = 100$	5	390.2	409.8	95% of the time, the value of $\bar{X}$ will be between 390.2 and 409.8

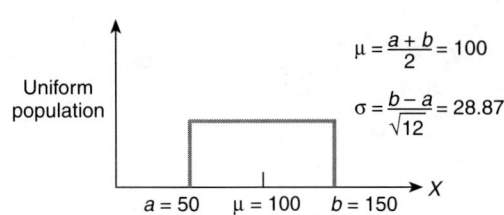

FIGURE

8.10

Distribution of $\bar{X}$ for a uniform population.

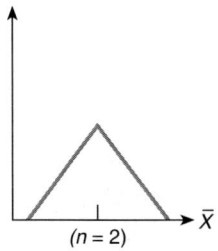

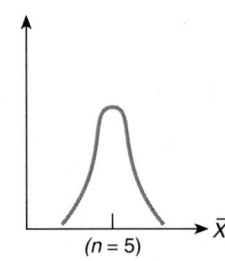

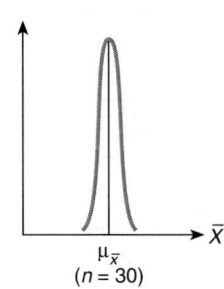

For $n = 30$, $\mu_{\bar{x}} = \mu = 100$

$$\sigma_{\bar{x}} = \frac{\sigma}{\sqrt{n}} = \frac{28.87}{\sqrt{30}} = 5.27$$

Applying the Central Limit Theorem to Nonnormal Populations

The real strength of the Central Limit Theorem is that $\bar{X}$ will tend toward a normal random variable regardless of the shape of your population. You need a large sample to obtain a nearly normal distribution for $\bar{X}$. See Comment 3 on p. 224. The Central Limit Theorem also holds when sampling from a discrete population.

Figures 8.10, 8.11, and 8.12 illustrate the distribution of $\bar{X}$ for three nonnormal populations. Notice that the uniform population (Figure 8.10) is at least symmetric about the mean, so the distribution of the sample mean, $\bar{X}$, tends toward a normal distribution for much smaller sample sizes. The U-shaped distribution (Figure 8.12) is another continuous distribution. It is characterized by many small and large values, with few values in the middle. This distribution is symmetric about the mean, but its shape is opposite to that of a normal distribution. Here, $\bar{X}$ requires a large sample ($n \geq 30$) to attain an approximate normal distribution.

X Exercises 8.1–8.9

Understanding the Mechanics

8.1 A sample of $n = 100$ observations from a normal population is drawn. The population mean is 500 and the population standard deviation is 200. Find the following.
  a. $P(\bar{X} > 480)$
  b. $P(460 < \bar{X} < 480)$
  c. $P(\bar{X} < 530)$

8.2 A population has a mean of 200 and a standard deviation of 50. Let $\bar{X}$ be used to estimate the mean of the population from a random sample of size 100. Find the following probabilities.
  a. $P(\bar{X} \leq 205)$
  b. $P(\bar{X} \geq 190)$
  c. $P(195 \leq \bar{X} \leq 210)$
  d. $P(188 \leq \bar{X} \leq 198)$

FIGURE

8.11

Distribution of $\bar{X}$ for an exponential population.

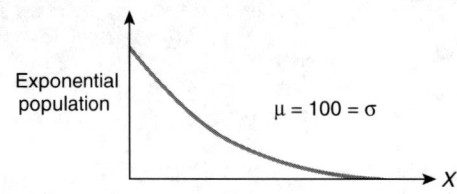

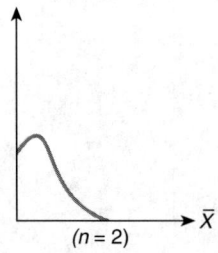
$(n = 2)$

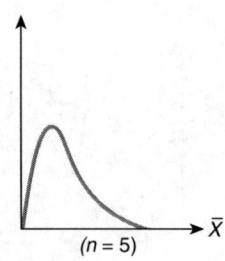
$(n = 5)$

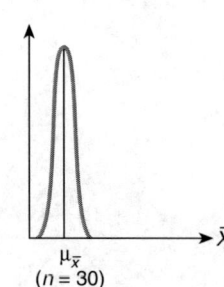
$\mu_{\bar{x}}$
$(n = 30)$

For $n = 30$, $\mu_{\bar{x}} = \mu = 100$

$$\sigma_{\bar{x}} = \frac{\sigma}{\sqrt{n}} = \frac{100}{\sqrt{30}}$$

$$= 18.26$$

FIGURE

8.12

Distribution of $\bar{X}$ for a U-shaped population.

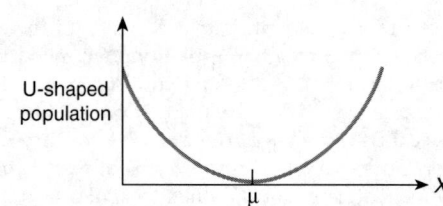

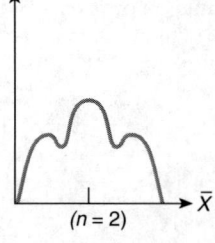
$(n = 2)$

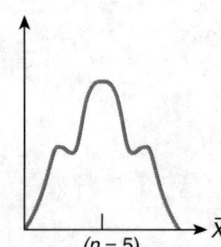
$(n = 5)$

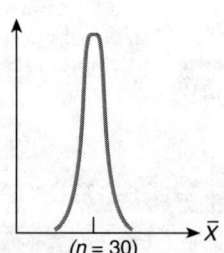
$(n = 30)$

Applying the New Concepts

8.3 Surveys indicate that an adult between the ages of 20 and 30 years of age spends a mean of four hours per day either watching TV or listening to the radio. The standard deviation of the amount of time spent doing these activities is one hour.

a. If a sample of 50 adults between the ages of 20 and 30 years of age was drawn, what does the Central Limit Theorem tell us about the distribution of the sample mean of the time spent by the adults either watching TV or listening to the radio?

b. If the sample size were to increase to 100, how would this change the distribution of the sample mean of the time spent by the adults either watching TV or listening to the radio?

8.4 Five machines produce electronic components. The number of components produced per hour is normally distributed with a mean of 25 and a standard deviation of 4.

   a. What percentage of the time does a machine produce more than 27 components per hour?
   b. What percentage of the time is the average rate of output of the five machines more than 27 components per hour?

8.5 A quality engineer knows from past data that in a shipment lot, the number of wire cables that have tensile strengths below the lower specification limit follows a Poisson distribution with a mean of 50. For a sample of 45 shipment lots, what is the probability that the sample mean for the number of wire cables with tensile strengths below the lower specification limit exceeds 53?

8.6 The average length of actual running time (excluding advertisements) for television feature films is 1 hour and 40 minutes, with a standard deviation of 15 minutes. If a sample of 49 TV feature films is taken at random, what is the probability that the average running time for this group is 1 hour and 45 minutes or more?

8.7 The Labor Department measures the changes in a set list of food, clothing, housing, energy, and medical costs to calculate the consumer price index. The government uses the time span from October to September each year to figure increases in Social Security benefits based on this index. For 2002, the estimated average Social Security check is $850 due to an increase in this index. Assume that the population standard deviation is $240.

   a. A random sample of 64 Social Security recipients is selected. What is the probability that the average Social Security check for this sample is between $820 and $880?
   b. Suppose that in part a the sample size is increased to 100. Do you think the probability would increase or decrease? Find the probability and compare.

(Source: "Social Security Checks to Rise 2.6%," *The New York Times*, October 20, 2001, p. C1.)

8.8 California's olive-oil industry may never match the glorious success of the wine industry. However, California olive-oil producers have expanded to approximately 120 producers statewide. This compares to tens of thousands of olive-oil producers in Europe, mostly concentrated in Spain and Italy. Olive-oil analysts say that the California producers are able to compete with European olive-oil producers by marketing their product as a perishable commodity that is ideally made, bought, and consumed locally, and that California olive oil has its own distinctive taste. These analysts estimate that the average price that California consumers pay for a 350-milliliter bottle of olive oil is $21, with a standard deviation of $2.40.

   a. What is the probability that the average price paid by a random sample of 36 olive-oil-buying consumers in California is less than $22?
   b. Do a what-if analysis by changing the standard deviation to $3.00 and answering part a. Do you think that the probability will increase or decrease? Why?

(Source: "California Dreaming," *Los Angeles Times*, October 17, 2001, p. H1.)

8.9 [Simulation Exercise] The Central Limit Theorem is important to statistical analysis because it says that the sample mean will tend toward a normal random variable regardless of the shape of the population. To demonstrate this theorem using Excel, click on **KPK menu ➤ Simulation Exercises ➤ Central Limit Theorem.**

   a. Select values of .1 for the probability of each of the numbers from 1 through 10. Click on the button to start the simulation. Comment on the histogram shapes for sample sizes of 2, 5, 10, 20, and 50. Would you say that the sample mean tends toward a normal random variable quickly as the sample size increases for this population?
   b. Select values of .4, .1, .1, and .4 for the values 1, 2, 9, and 10 and zeros for the remaining values. Repeat part a using this very nonnormal population.
   c. Try other population shapes and discover for which shapes the sample mean tends quickly toward a normal random variable as the sample size increases.

8.3

CONFIDENCE INTERVALS FOR THE MEAN OF A NORMAL POPULATION (σ KNOWN)

Return to the situation where we have obtained a sample from a normal population with unknown mean, μ. We first consider a case in which we know σ, the standard deviation of the normal random variable (Figure 8.13). (The situation where both μ and σ are unknown is dealt with in the next section.)

FIGURE

8.13

An example where the standard deviation σ is known but the mean μ is unknown.

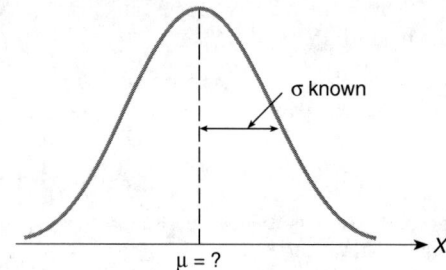

FIGURE

8.14

Distribution of $\bar{X}$ if μ = 20 minutes.

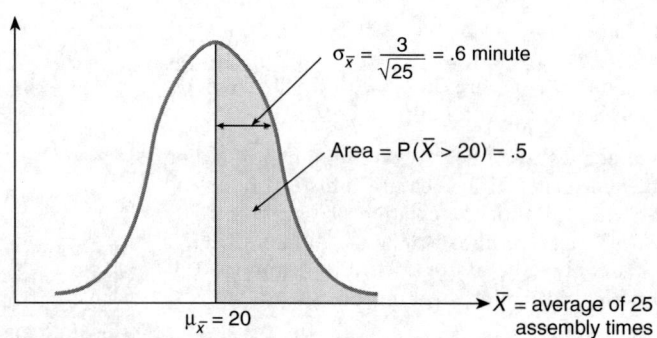

We know that to estimate μ, the average of the entire population, we obtain a sample from this population and calculate $\bar{X}$, the average of the sample. The sample mean, $\bar{X}$, is the estimate of μ and is also called a **point estimate,** because it consists of a single number.

In Example 8.3, it was assumed that the assembly time for a particular electrical component followed a normal distribution, with μ = 20 minutes and σ = 3 minutes. What if μ is not known for *all* workers? A random sample of 25 workers' assembly times was obtained with the following results (in minutes):

22.8, 29.3, 27.2, 30.2, 24.0, 23.2, 22.9, 30.3, 27.1, 31.2, 27.0, 32.0, 28.6, 24.1, 28.9, 26.8, 26.6, 23.4, 25.1, 26.6, 25.7, 28.1, 31.5, 24.8, 25.2

Based on these data,

$$\text{estimate of } \mu = \text{ sample mean, } \bar{X}$$

$$= \frac{22.8 + 29.3 + \cdots + 25.2}{25} = 26.9 \text{ minutes}$$

Is this large value of $\bar{X}$ (= 26.9) due to random chance? We know that 50% of the samples drawn will have $\bar{X}$ larger than 20, even if μ = 20 (Figure 8.14). Or is this value large because μ is a value larger than 20? In other words, does this value of $\bar{X}$ provide just cause for concluding that μ is larger than 20? We tackle this type of question in Chapter 9.

How accurate is a derived estimate of the population mean, μ? The accuracy depends, for one thing, on the sample size. We can measure the precision of this estimate by constructing a **confidence interval.** By providing the confidence interval, one can make such statements as "I am 95% confident that the average assembly time, μ, is

FIGURE

8.15

$P(-1.96 \le Z \le 1.96)$
$= .95$.

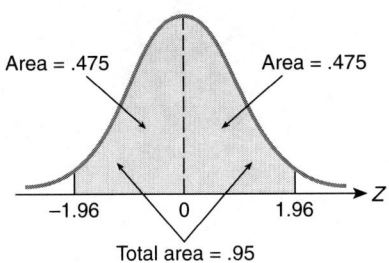

Area = .475   Area = .475

-1.96 0   1.96   → Z

Total area = .95

between 25.7 minutes and 28.1 minutes." For this illustration, (25.7, 28.1) is called a 95% confidence interval for μ. The following discussion demonstrates how to construct such a confidence interval.

Using comment 4 on page 224, we know that $\bar{X}$ is a normal random variable with

$$\mu_{\bar{X}} = \mu$$

$$\sigma_{\bar{X}} = \frac{\sigma}{\sqrt{n}}$$

where μ and σ represent the mean and standard deviation of the population. To standardize $\bar{X}$, you subtract the mean (μ) of $\bar{X}$ and divide by the standard deviation ($\sigma/\sqrt{n}$) of $\bar{X}$. Consequently,

$$Z = \frac{\bar{X} - \mu}{\sigma/\sqrt{n}}$$

is a standard normal random variable. Consider the following statement and refer to Figure 8.15:

$$P(-1.96 \le Z \le 1.96) = .95$$

so

$$P\left(-1.96 \le \frac{\bar{X} - \mu}{\sigma/\sqrt{n}} \le 1.96\right) = .95$$

After some algebra and rearrangement of terms, we get

$$P\left(\bar{X} - 1.96\frac{\sigma}{\sqrt{n}} \le \mu \le \bar{X} + 1.96\frac{\sigma}{\sqrt{n}}\right) = .95$$

How does the last statement apply to a *particular* sample mean, $\bar{x}$? Consider the interval

$$\left(\bar{x} - 1.96\frac{\sigma}{\sqrt{n}}, \bar{x} + 1.96\frac{\sigma}{\sqrt{n}}\right)$$

8.3

FIGURE

8.16

$1.28 = Z_{.1}$,
$1.645 = Z_{.05}$, and
$1.96 = Z_{.025}$.

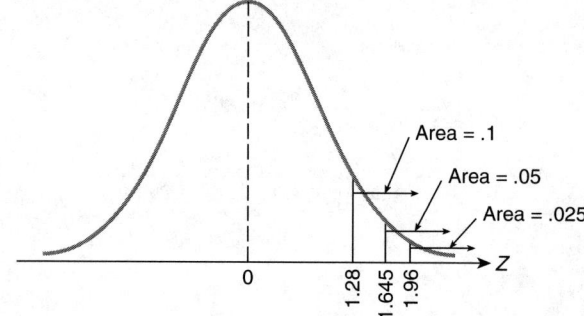

Using the values from our assembly-time example, we have $\bar{x} = 26.9$, $\sigma = 3$, and $n = 25$. The resulting 95% confidence interval is

$$\left(26.9 - 1.96 \cdot \frac{3}{\sqrt{25}}, 26.9 + 1.96 \cdot \frac{3}{\sqrt{25}} \right)$$

or

$$(25.72, 28.08)$$

Since μ is unknown, we do not *know* whether μ lies between 25.72 and 28.08 minutes. However, if you were to obtain random samples repeatedly, calculate $\bar{x}$, and determine the intervals defined by equation 8.3, then 95% of these intervals would contain μ and 5% would not. For this reason, formula 8.3 is called a **95% confidence interval** for μ. Using our assembly-time illustration, we are 95% confident that the average assembly time, μ, lies between 25.72 and 28.08 minutes.

Notation. Let Z_a denote the value of Z such that the area *to the right* of this value is equal to a. How can we determine $Z_{.025}$, $Z_{.05}$, and $Z_{.1}$ (Figure 8.16)? Using Table A.4, $Z_{.025} = 1.96$, $Z_{.05} = 1.645$, and $Z_{.1} = 1.28$.

When defining a confidence interval for μ, we can define a 99% confidence interval, a 95% confidence interval, a 90% confidence interval, or whatever. The specific percentage represents the **confidence level**. The *higher* the confidence level, the *wider* the confidence interval. The confidence level is written as $(1 - \alpha) \cdot 100\%$, where $\alpha = .01$ for a 99% confidence interval, $\alpha = .05$ for a 95% confidence interval, and so on. Thus, a $(1 - \alpha) \cdot 100\%$ confidence interval for the mean of a normal population, μ, is

$$\left[\bar{x} - Z_{\alpha/2}\left(\frac{\sigma}{\sqrt{n}} \right), \bar{x} + Z_{\alpha/2}\left(\frac{\sigma}{\sqrt{n}} \right) \right]$$

8.4

According to the Central Limit Theorem, formula 8.4 provides an approximate confidence interval for the mean of any population, provided the sample size, n, *is large (see Comment 3 on page 224).*

Comment

The end-of-chapter appendix will demonstrate how to compute this confidence interval using Excel and MINITAB. SPSS does not compute a confidence interval for the population mean when the population standard deviation is known.

Determine a 90% and a 99% confidence interval for the average assembly time of all work-ers using the 25 observations given on page 232.

The sample mean here was $\bar{x} = 26.9$. The population standard deviation is assumed to be 3 minutes. The resulting 90% confidence interval for the population mean μ is

Solution

$$26.9 - Z_{.05}\left(\frac{3}{\sqrt{25}}\right) \quad to \quad 26.9 + Z_{.05}\left(\frac{3}{\sqrt{25}}\right)$$

$$= 26.9 - 1.645\left(\frac{3}{\sqrt{25}}\right) \quad to \quad 26.9 + 1.645\left(\frac{3}{\sqrt{25}}\right)$$

$$= 26.9 - .99 \quad to \quad 26.9 + .99$$

$$= 25.91 \text{ minutes} \quad to \quad 27.89 \text{ minutes}$$

The 99% confidence interval for μ is

$$26.9 - Z_{.005}\left(\frac{3}{\sqrt{25}}\right) \quad to \quad 26.9 + Z_{.005}\left(\frac{3}{\sqrt{25}}\right)$$

$$= 26.9 - 2.575\left(\frac{3}{\sqrt{25}}\right) \quad to \quad 26.9 + 2.575\left(\frac{3}{\sqrt{25}}\right)$$

$$= 26.9 - 1.54 \quad to \quad 26.9 + 1.54$$

$$= 25.36 \text{ minutes} \quad to \quad 28.44 \text{ minutes}$$

Consequently, we are 90% confident that the mean assembly time for all workers is between 25.91 and 27.89 minutes. We are also 99% confident that this parameter is between 25.36 and 28.44 minutes, based on the results of this sample. Notice that the width of the interval increases as the confidence level increases when using the same sample data.

Discussing a Confidence Interval

The narrower your confidence interval, the better, for the same level of confidence. Suppose Electricalc spent $50,000 investigating the average time necessary to assemble their electrical components. Part of this study included obtaining a confidence interval for the average assembly time, μ. Which statement would Electricalc prefer to see?

1. I am 95% confident that the average assembly time is between 2 minutes and 50 minutes.

2. I am 95% confident that the average assembly time is between 25 minutes and 27 minutes.

The information contained in the first statement is practically worthless, and that's $50,000 down the drain. The second statement contains useful information; μ is narrowed down to a much smaller range.

Given the second statement, can you tell what the corresponding value of $\bar{X}$ was that produced this confidence interval? For any confidence interval for μ, $\bar{X}$ (the estimate of μ) is always *in the center*. So $\bar{X}$ must have been 26 minutes.

For the 90% confidence interval in Example 8.4, the following conclusions are valid:

1. I am 90% confident that the average assembly time for the population (μ) lies between 25.91 and 27.89 minutes.

2. If I repeatedly obtained samples of size 25, then 90% of the resulting confidence inter-vals would contain μ and 10% would not. (Question from the audience: Does this confidence interval [25.91, 27.89] contain μ? Your response: I don't know. All I can say is that this procedure leads to an interval containing μ 90% of the time.)

3. I am 90% confident that my estimate of μ (namely, $\bar{x} = 26.9$) is within .99 minute of the actual value of μ.

Here .99 is equal to $1.645 \cdot (\sigma/\sqrt{n})$. This quantity is referred to as the **margin of error, E.**

$$E = \text{margin of error} = Z_{\alpha/2}\left(\frac{\sigma}{\sqrt{n}}\right)$$

8.5

Be careful! The following statement is *not* correct: The probability that μ lies between 25.91 and 27.89 is .90. What is the probability that the number 27 lies in this confidence interval? How about 24? The answer to the first question is 1, and to the second, 0, because 27 lies in the confidence interval and 24 does not. So what is the probability that μ lies in the confidence interval? Remember that μ is a fixed number; we just do not know what its value is. It is *not* a random variable, unlike its estimator, $\bar{X}$. As a result, this probability is either 0 or 1, not .90. Therefore, remember that once you have inserted your sample results into formula 8.4 to obtain your confidence interval, the word *probability* can no longer be used to describe the resulting confidence interval.

EXAMPLE 8.5

Refer to the 20 samples of Everglo bulbs in Table 8.1. Using sample 1, what is the resulting 95% confidence interval for the population mean, μ? Assume that σ is 50 hours.

Solution

Here, $n = 10$ and $\bar{x} = 384.0$. The confidence level is 95%, so $Z_{\alpha/2} = Z_{.025} = 1.96$ (from Table A.4). Therefore, the resulting 95% confidence interval for μ is

$$384.0 - 1.96\left(\frac{50}{\sqrt{10}}\right) \quad \text{to} \quad 384.0 + 1.96\left(\frac{50}{\sqrt{10}}\right)$$

$$= 384.0 - 31.0 \quad \text{to} \quad 384.0 + 31.0$$

$$= 353.0 \quad \text{to} \quad 415.0$$

So we are 95% confident that μ lies between 353 and 415 hours. Also, we are 95% confident that our estimate of μ ($\bar{x} = 384.0$) is within 31.0 hours of the actual value.

X Exercises 8.10–8.21

Understanding the Mechanics

8.10 A random sample of 100 observations is obtained from a normally distributed population with a standard deviation of 10. What is a 95% confidence interval for the mean of the population if the sample mean is 40?

8.11 Find the 90% confidence interval for the mean of a normally distributed population using the following data. Assume a standard deviation of 5.

50 43 65 52 45 60 38 62 53 49

8.12 Fifty observations are randomly selected from a normally distributed population with a population standard deviation of 25. The sample mean is 175.
  a. Find a 90% confidence interval for the mean.
  b. Find a 95% confidence interval for the mean.
  c. Find a 99% confidence interval for the mean.

Applying the New Concepts

8.13 The monthly advertising expenditure of Discount Hardware Store is normally distributed with a standard deviation of $100. If a sample of 10 randomly selected months yields a mean advertising expenditure of $380 monthly, what is a 90% confidence interval for the mean of the store's monthly advertising expenditure?

8.14 In analyzing the operating cost for a huge fleet of delivery trucks, a manager takes a sample of 25 cars and calculates the sample mean and sample standard deviation. Then he finds a 95% confidence interval for the mean cost to be $253 to $320. He reasons that this interval contains the mean operating cost for the fleet of delivery trucks because the sample mean is contained in the interval. Do you agree? How would you interpret this confidence interval?

8.15 The perfectionist owner of Kwik Kar Kare has reduced an oil-change job to a science and wants to keep it that way. The owner constantly monitors the performance of the staff. This week, 15 oil-change jobs were sampled with a sample mean of 9.8 minutes per job. Experience has shown that the times follow a normal distribution, and the standard deviation of the population is known to be 1.2 minutes. Based on this week's sample, construct a 90% confidence interval for the population mean (average time for an oil-change job).

8.16 Brazil was Latin America's leading economic power by the 1970s. In the past, this country has also had one of the highest inflation rates in Latin America. In an attempt to regain investor confidence, the Brazilian government has increased interest rates and has worked to establish a sound fiscal policy to keep inflation under control. In 2001, a random sample of locations across the country revealed that the average year-to-year increase in food prices was 6%. Assume that the standard deviation of the increase in food prices is known to be 1.75%. Construct a 99% confidence interval for the population mean using
  a. a sample size of 30.
  b. a sample size of 60.
  c. a sample size of 120.

(Source: "Brazil Inflation Slows Sharply," The Financial Times, October 5, 2001, p. 13.)

8.17 A quality-control engineer is concerned about the breaking strength of a metal wire manufactured to stringent specifications. A sample of size 25 is randomly obtained, and the breaking strengths are recorded. The breaking strength of the wire is considered to be normally distributed with a standard deviation of 3. Find a 95% confidence interval for the mean breaking strength of the wire.

26, 27, 18, 23, 24, 20, 21, 24, 19, 27, 25, 20, 24, 21, 26, 19, 21, 20, 25, 20, 23, 25, 21, 20, 21

8.18 Federal law requires GTE to allow competing long-distance carriers to use its infrastructure, and it regulates how much GTE can charge for the service. To compensate for the lost revenue from federal regulations related to long-distance access charges, GTE asked the Idaho Public Utilities Commission for permission to approve hikes in basic monthly rates. Commission members scheduled public meetings and sought written comments from customers before making a decision. Suppose that the standard deviation of charges to business customers by GTE in Idaho is $10. A concerned business association surveyed 20 business members to collect data on the monthly charges paid to GTE to reveal how high current charges were. Construct a 90% confidence interval on the average business customer's monthly bill to GTE using the data below. What assumption is necessary for this to be a reliable confidence interval?

| 35 | 45 | 57 | 21 | 46 | 78 | 52 | 32 | 24 | 81 |
| 34 | 29 | 45 | 51 | 33 | 26 | 46 | 37 | 40 | 34 |

(Adapted from "GTE Requests Rate Increase in North Idaho," Spokane Spokesman-Review, May 30, 1998, p. B2.)

8.19 As the sample size increases, would a confidence interval given by equation 8.8 get smaller or larger? For a given random sample, would the confidence interval given by equation 8.4 for a 90% confidence interval be wider or narrower than that obtained using an 80% confidence level?

Using the Computer

8.20 **[DATA SET EX8-20]** Variable Description:

LuggageCharge: Fee for shipping suitcases owned by domestic travelers

Virtual Bellhop, based in Volo, Illinois, picks up, ships, and delivers packages for any domestic traveler. With the increase in baggage restrictions and security at airports, this company is experiencing a substantial increase in business for shipping air travelers' suitcases. Assume that the standard deviation for the fee charged for suitcases is $11.60.

  a. Find a 95% confidence interval for the mean fee charged for shipping suitcases owned by domestic travelers. (In Excel, click on **KPK Data Analysis ➤ One Population Inference,** select Population Mean (z statistic), and use 5 for the alpha level (this value is the percentage value for one minus the confidence level) and enter 11.60 for the standard deviation. In MINITAB, click on **Stat ➤ Basic Statistics ➤ 1-Sample Z,** select confidence interval, and type in 95 for the confidence level. SPSS does not have an option to directly compute a mean confidence interval using the normal distribution. However, the menu obtained from clicking on **Transform ➤ Compute** features the mean function and the cumulative normal distribution function that can be used to calculate the confidence interval.)
  b. Change the standard deviation to $16.00 in part b. How much has the length of the confidence interval changed?

(Source: "Don't Check That Bag. Ship It," The New York Times, October 21, 2001, p. 8I.)

8.21 **[DATA SET EX8-21]** Variable Description:

SATscoresNorthTexas: SAT scores from seniors across north Texas

In Texas, about 52% of the graduating seniors took the SAT, compared with 44 percent nationally. These scores are closely monitored to detect trends in education.

Assume that this data set consists of randomly selected SAT scores from high school seniors across north Texas. Compare 90% and 99% confidence intervals for the mean SAT score for north Texas. Assume a population standard deviation of 150.

(Source: "McKinney Students Beat SAT Averages," The Dallas Morning News, September 30, 2004, p. 7B.)

 8.4

CONFIDENCE INTERVALS FOR THE MEAN OF A NORMAL POPULATION (σ UNKNOWN)

If σ is unknown, it is impossible to determine a confidence interval for μ using formula 8.4 because we are unable to evaluate the standard error $\sigma/\sqrt{n}$. Let us take another look at how we estimate the parameters of a normal population.

When a population mean is unknown, we can estimate it using the sample mean. The logical thing to do if σ is unknown is to replace it by its estimate, the standard deviation of the sample, s. But consider what happens when

$$\frac{\bar{X} - \mu}{\sigma/\sqrt{n}}$$

is replaced by

$$\frac{\bar{X} - \mu}{s/\sqrt{n}}$$

This is no longer a standard normal random variable, Z. However, it does follow another identifiable distribution, the t **distribution.** Its complete name is Student's t distribution, named after W. S. Gosset, a statistician in a Guinness brewery who used the pen name Student. The distribution of

$$\frac{\bar{X} - \mu}{s/\sqrt{n}}$$

will follow a t distribution, provided the population from which you are obtaining the sample is normally distributed.

The t Distribution

The t distribution is similar in appearance to the standard normal (Z) distribution in that it is symmetric about zero. Unlike the Z distribution, however, its shape depends on the sample size, n. Consequently, when you use the t distribution, you must take into account the sample size. This is accomplished by using **degrees of freedom,** df. For this application using the t distribution,

$$\text{degrees of freedom} = df = n - 1$$

The value of $df = n - 1$ can be explained by observing that for a given value of $\bar{X}$, only $n - 1$ of the sample values are free to vary. For example, in a sample of size $n = 3$, if $\bar{x} = 5.0$,

FIGURE

8.17

The *t* distribution.

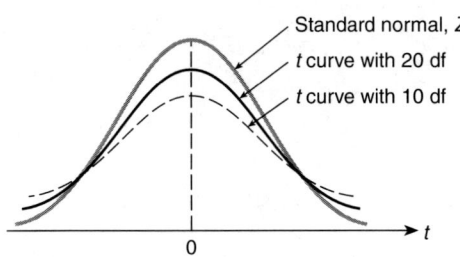

Standard normal, *Z*

t curve with 20 df

t curve with 10 df

0 → *t*

$x_1 = 2$, and $x_2 = 7$, then x_3 must be 6 because this is the only value providing a sample mean equal to 5.0.

Two *t* distributions are illustrated in Figure 8.17. Notice that the *t* distributions are symmetrically distributed about zero but have wider tails than does the standard normal, *Z*. Observe that as *n* increases, the *t* distribution tends toward the standard normal, *Z*. In fact, for *n* > 30, there is little difference between these two distributions. Values having a specified tail area under a *t* curve are provided in Table A.5 for various df. So, for large samples (*n* > 30), it does not matter whether σ is known (*Z* distribution, Table A.4) or σ is unknown (*t* distribution, Table A.5) because the *t* and *Z* curves are practically the same. For this reason, the *t* distribution often is referred to as the *small-sample distribution* for $\bar{X}$. The *Z* table can be used as an approximation even if σ is unknown, provided *n* is larger than 30. *Remember, however, that a more accurate confidence interval is always obtained using the* t *table when the sample standard deviation* (s) *is used in the construction of this interval.*

Using the *t* distribution, then, a $(1 - \alpha) \cdot 100\%$ confidence interval for μ is

$$\bar{x} - t_{\alpha/2, n-1}\left(\frac{s}{\sqrt{n}}\right) \quad \text{to} \quad \bar{x} + t_{\alpha/2, n-1}\left(\frac{s}{\sqrt{n}}\right)$$

8.9

where $t_{\alpha/2, n-1}$ denotes the *t* value from Table A.5 using a *t* curve with $n - 1$ df and a right-tail area of $\alpha/2$.

Do you remember our sample of 25 assembly times that produced a point estimate for μ having a value of $\bar{x} = 26.9$ minutes? This estimate was used in Example 8.4, where it was assumed that the population standard deviation was σ = 3, in constructing a confidence interval for μ. Furthermore, the assembly times were assumed to follow a *normal* distribution.

Suppose that we do not know σ, either. Then the point estimate of the population standard deviation is

$$s = \sqrt{\frac{(22.8^2 + 29.3^2 + \cdots + 25.2^2) - (22.8 + 29.3 + \ldots + 25.2)^2/25}{24}}$$

$$= \sqrt{\frac{18,285.14 - (672.6)^2/25}{24}}$$

$$= \sqrt{7.896} = 2.81 \text{ minutes}$$

Using Table A.5 to find a 90% confidence interval for μ, you first determine that

$$t_{\alpha/2, n-1} = t_{.05, 24} = 1.711$$

313

The resulting 90% confidence interval is

$$26.9 - 1.711\left(\frac{2.81}{\sqrt{25}}\right) \quad \text{to} \quad 26.9 + 1.711\left(\frac{2.81}{\sqrt{25}}\right)$$

$$= 26.9 - .96 \quad \text{to} \quad 26.9 + .96$$

$$= 25.94 \quad \text{to} \quad 27.86$$

Using these data, we are 90% confident that the estimate for the mean of this normal population ($\bar{x} = 26.9$) is within .96 minute of the actual value. Comparing this result with Example 8.4, we notice little difference in the two 90% confidence intervals. Their agreement is due mostly to the fact that the estimate of σ ($s = 2.81$) is very close to the assumed value of $\sigma = 3$.

EXAMPLE 8.6

The output voltage of power supplies manufactured by Clark Products is believed to follow a normal distribution. Of primary concern to the company is the average output voltage of a particular power supply unit, believed to be 10 volts. Eighteen observations taken at random from this unit are

10.85, 11.40, 10.81, 10.24, 10.23, 9.49, 9.89, 10.11, 10.57, 11.21, 10.10, 11.22, 10.31, 11.24, 9.51, 10.52, 9.92, 8.33

What is the 95% confidence interval for the average output voltage for this power supply unit?

Solution

Your point estimate of σ is $s = .7667$ volt. Also, your point estimate of μ is $\bar{x} = 10.3306$ volts. A 95% confidence interval for the average output voltage (μ) is

$$10.3306 - t_{.025,17}\left(\frac{.7667}{\sqrt{18}}\right) \quad \text{to} \quad 10.3306 + t_{.025,17}\left(\frac{.7667}{\sqrt{18}}\right)$$

$$= 10.3306 - 2.11\left(\frac{.7667}{\sqrt{18}}\right) \quad \text{to} \quad 10.3306 + 2.11\left(\frac{.7667}{\sqrt{18}}\right)$$

$$= 10.3306 - .3813 \quad \text{to} \quad 10.3306 + .3813$$

$$= 9.949 \quad \text{to} \quad 10.712$$

We are 95% confident that the average output voltage of this power supply unit is between 9.949 and 10.712 volts. Notice here that the margin of error is

$$E = 2.11\left(\frac{.7667}{\sqrt{18}}\right) = .3813 \text{ volt}$$

which implies that we are 95% confident that $\bar{X}$ is within .3813 volt of the actual average voltage.

Deriving Confidence Intervals Using Statistical Software

Confidence intervals can easily be computed using the three computer packages. Detailed input instructions for obtaining the computer outputs in Figure 8.18 are contained in the end-of-chapter appendix. The Excel output in Figure 8.18(a) was generated using KPK Data Analysis by clicking on **One Population Inference** and selecting **Population mean**

FIGURE
8.18

(a) Excel 95% confidence interval using KPK Data Analysis; (b) 95% confidence interval using MINITAB; and (c) 95% confidence interval using SPSS

B	C	D	E
t Test for Population Mean			
Number of Observations	18		
Sample Standard Deviation	0.766715		
Sample Mean	10.330556		
95% CI for Pop. Mean	9.949276	to	10.711835

(a)

One-Sample T: voltage

```
Variable   N    Mean    StDev   SE Mean      95% CI
voltage    18  10.3306  0.7667  0.1807   (9.9493, 10.7118)
```

(b)

One-Sample Test

	t	df	Sig. (2-tailed)	Mean Difference	95% Confidence Interval of the Difference Lower	Upper
VOLTAGE	57.164	17	.000	10.3306	9.9493	10.7118

Test Value = 0

(c)

with est. std. dev. (t statistic) in the top box. The value of **Alpha** is 100 minus the confidence level (95%); that is, 5%. The MINITAB interval in Figure 8.18(b) can be obtained by clicking on **Stat ➤ Basic Statistics ➤ 1-Sample t.** Figure 8.18(c) contains the SPSS confidence interval obtained by clicking on **Analyze ➤ Compare Means ➤ One-Sample T test.** The only portion of this output that is of interest at this point is the highlighted portion in the right-hand side. For both MINITAB and SPSS, the default confidence level is 95% but can be changed by clicking on the **Options** button. All three computer-generated intervals agree with the solution to Example 8.6.

X Exercises 8.22–8.33

Understanding the Mechanics

8.22 For a t distribution with 20 degrees of freedom, what is the t value such that the following are true?
- **a.** 90% of the area under the t distribution is to the right of the t value.
- **b.** 10% of the area under the t distribution is to the right of the t value.
- **c.** 5% of the area under the t distribution is to the left of the t value.

8.23 A t distribution has 30 degrees of freedom.
- **a.** Find the area to the right of 2.750.
- **b.** Find the area to the left of 1.697.
- **c.** Find the area to the left of −1.310.
- **d.** Find the area between −2.042 and 2.042.

8.24 A random sample of size 20 is selected from a normally distributed population. The sample mean is 50 and the sample standard deviation is 10.
- **a.** Find a 90% confidence interval for the population mean.
- **b.** Find a 95% confidence interval for the population mean.
- **c.** Find a 99% confidence interval for the population mean.

Applying the New Concepts

8.25 The manager of a gift shop would like to estimate the average retail price of a particular greeting card by its competitors. A random sample of 20 retail stores in a 100-mile radius of the store was selected. The sample mean and standard deviation were $2.05 and $0.40, respectively. Find a 99% confidence interval for the mean price of the greeting card.

8.26 The mean monthly expenditure on gasoline per household in Middletown is determined by selecting a random sample of 36 households. The sample mean is $68, with a sample standard deviation of $17.

a. What is a 95% confidence interval for the mean monthly expenditure on gasoline per household in Middletown?

b. What is a 90% confidence interval for the mean monthly expenditure on gasoline per household in Middletown?

8.27 Second Federal Savings and Loan would like to estimate the mean number of years in which 30-year mortgages are paid off. Eighteen paid-off 30-year mortgages are randomly selected, and the numbers of years in which the loans were paid in full are

19.6, 20.8, 29.6, 6.3, 3.1, 10.6, 30.0, 21.7, 10.5, 26.3, 10.7, 6.1, 7.3, 12.6, 9.8, 27.4, 20.1, 10.8

Assuming that the number of years in which 30-year mortgages are paid off is normally distributed, construct an 80% confidence interval for the mean number of years in which the mortgages are paid off.

8.28 An apartment-finder service would like to estimate the average cost of a one-bedroom apartment in Kansas City. A random sample of 41 apartment complexes yielded a mean of $310 with a standard deviation of $29. Construct a 90% confidence interval for the mean cost of one-bedroom apartments in Kansas City.

8.29 People are conscious of fuel economy, global warming, and safety rollovers, but they still seem to love their sport-utility vehicles (SUVs). In fact, despite the problems with recalled Firestone tires, the Ford Explorer remains the best selling SUV. Automobile analysts are curious as to how much consumers are willing to pay for an SUV. A random sample of 10 recently sold SUVs was obtained for this purpose and the results are as follows:

SUV	Selling Price
Acura MDX	$39,450
Mercedes-Benz ML320	$40,270
Ford Explorer XLT	$32,600
Nissan Pathfinder LE	$34,724
Jeep Grand Cherokee LTD V8	$37,950
Toyota 4Runner SR5	$33,395
GMC Envoy SLE	$33,320
Dodge Durango SLT	$34,745
Land Rover Discovery	$40,395
Jeep Grand Cherokee Laredo 6	$33,030

a. Find a 99% confidence interval for the mean price that consumers are willing to pay for a new SUV.

b. Repeat part a using a 90% confidence interval. Compare and interpret the 90% and 99% confidence intervals.

(Source: "New Explorer Passes Magazine's Test," USA Today, August 8, 2001, p. 6B.)

8.30 An investment advisor believes that the return on interest-sensitive stocks is approximately normally distributed. A sample of 24 interest-sensitive stocks was selected, and their yearly return (including dividends and capital appreciation) was as follows (in percentages):

11.1, 12.5, 13.6, 9.1, 8.7, 10.6, 12.5, 15.6, 13.8, 8.0, 10.9, 7.6, 5.2, 1.2, 12.8, 16.7, 13.9, 10.1, 9.6, 10.8, 11.6, 12.3, 12.9, 11.6

Find a 90% confidence interval for the mean yearly return on interest-sensitive stocks.

Using the Computer

8.31 [DATA SET EX8-31] Variable Description:

Name: Name of money-losing company

Loss: Amount of money that the company lost in millions of dollars during 2003

Assume this data set consists of a sample of money-losing global companies in 2003 (data sampled from www. fortune.com). Construct a 95% confidence interval for the mean loss. Remove companies Telefonica and UFJ Holdings and reconstruct this confidence interval. Compare the lengths of the two confidence intervals.

8.32 [DATA SET EX8-32] Variable Description:

Company: Name of a fast-growing company

Score: Three-year total return

This data set contains a sample of the fastest-growing companies in America from Fortune's Web site (www. fortune.com). Construct 90% and 99% confidence intervals for the mean three-year return of these companies during 2003. Compare the lengths of the confidence intervals.

8.33 [DATA SET EX8-33] Variable Description:

BookshelfSpeakers: Brand model of bookshelf loudspeaker

Accuracy: Score by Consumer Reports on the reproduction of sound by the speaker

Consumer Reports rates speakers on accuracy. Consider the 23 speakers scored in this sample to be a random sample of bookshelf loudspeakers. Find the 95% confidence interval for the average accuracy of bookshelf loudspeakers and give two interpretations of this interval.

(Source: "Loudspeakers," Consumer Reports, August 2001, p. 36.)

DETERMINING THE NECESSARY SAMPLE SIZE

Sample Size for Known σ

How large a sample do you need? This is often difficult to determine, although a carefully chosen *large* sample generally provides a better representation of the population than does a smaller sample. Acquiring large samples can be costly and time-consuming. Why obtain a sample of size $n = 1,000$ if a sample size of $n = 500$ will provide sufficient accuracy for estimating a population mean? This section will show you how to determine what sample size is necessary when the margin of error, E, is specified in advance.

In Example 8.5, we assumed that the lifetime of Everglo bulbs is normally distributed with standard deviation $\sigma = 50$ hours but unknown mean μ. Based on the results of sample 1 from Table 8.1, we concluded that we were 95% confident that the estimate of μ ($\bar{x} = 384.0$) was within 31.0 hours of the actual value of μ for $n = 10$. How large a sample is necessary if we want our point estimator ($\bar{x}$) to be within 15 hours of the actual value of μ, with 95% confidence? The value 15 here is the margin of error, E, defined in equation 8.5. We would like the estimate of μ (that is, $\bar{x}$) to be within 15 of the actual value, so

$$E = 15 = Z_{\alpha/2}\left(\frac{50}{\sqrt{n}}\right)$$

Because the confidence level is 95%, $Z_{\alpha/2} = Z_{.025} = 1.96$. Consequently,

$$15 = (1.96)\frac{50}{\sqrt{n}}$$

$$\sqrt{n} = \frac{(1.96)(50)}{15} = 6.53$$

Squaring both sides of this statement produces

$$n = (6.53)^2 = 42.68$$

To be a bit conservative, this number should always be rounded *up*. So a sample size of $n = 43$ will produce a confidence interval with $E \leq 15$ hours. Your point estimate of μ ($\bar{x}$), will then be within 15 hours of the actual value, with 95% confidence.

This sequence of steps can be summarized by the following expression:

$$n = \left[\frac{Z_{\alpha/2} \cdot \sigma}{E}\right]^2$$

8.7

Sample Size for Unknown σ

Equation 8.7 works if σ is known, but it does not apply to situations where both μ and σ are unknown. There are two approaches to the latter situation.

A Preliminary Sampling

If you have already obtained a small sample, you have an estimate of σ, namely, the sample standard deviation, s. Replacing σ by s in equation 8.7 gives you the desired sample

Chapter 8   Statistical Inference and Sampling

size, n. Assuming that the resulting value of n is greater than 30, the $Z_{\alpha/2}$ notation in equation 8.7 is still valid because the actual t distribution here will be closely approximated by the standard normal distribution.

When you do obtain the confidence interval using the larger sample, the resulting margin of error, E, may not be exactly what you originally specified, because the new sample standard deviation will not be the same as that belonging to the smaller original sample.

In Example 8.6, Clark Products obtained 18 observations of the output voltages for a particular power supply unit. For these data,

$$\bar{x} = 10.3306 \text{ volts}$$

$$s = .7667 \text{ volt}$$

How large a sample would they need for $\bar{X}$ to be within .2 volt of the actual average output voltage with 95% confidence?

Solution   Based on the results of the original sample, $s = .767$, so

$$n = \left[\frac{Z_{\alpha/2} \cdot s}{E}\right]^2 = \left[\frac{(1.96)(.7667)}{.2}\right]^2 = 56.5$$

We round this number up to 57. Consequently, they would need 57 observations to make a statement with this much precision, that is, within .2 volt. Of course, they already have 18 observations that can be included in the larger sample.

Obtaining a Rough Approximation of σ

We know from the empirical rule and Table A.4 that 95.4% of the population will lie between $\mu - 2\sigma$ and $\mu + 2\sigma$. Because $(\mu + 2\sigma) - (\mu - 2\sigma) = 4\sigma$, this is a span of 4 standard deviations. One method of obtaining an estimate of σ is to ask a person who is familiar with the data to be collected these questions:

1. What do you think will be the highest value in the sample *(H)?*

2. What will be the lowest value *(L)?*

The approximation of σ is then obtained by assuming that $\mu + 2\sigma = H$ and $\mu - 2\sigma = L$, so

$$H - L = (\mu + 2\sigma) - (\mu - 2\sigma) = 4\sigma$$

Consequently,

$$\sigma \cong \frac{H - L}{4}$$

8.8

In other words, a rough approximation of σ is the *anticipated range* $(H - L)$ divided by 4. This (somewhat conservative) estimate of σ can be used in equation 8.7 to determine the necessary sample size, n.

EXAMPLE 8.8

The manager of quality assurance for a division that produces hair dryers is interested in the average number of switches that can be tested by the division's employees. Assuming that the number of switches that are tested each hour by an employee follows a normal distribution (centered at μ), the manager wants to estimate μ with 90% confidence. Also, this estimate must be within one unit (switch) of μ. The manager estimates that H is 45 switches and L is 25 switches. How large a sample will be necessary?

Solution

Based on $H = 45$ switches and $L = 25$ switches,

$$\sigma \cong \frac{45 - 25}{4} = 5 \text{ switches}$$

The sample size necessary to obtain a margin of error of $E = 1$ is

$$n = \left[\frac{(1.645)(5)}{1} \right]^2 = 67.7$$

Thus, a sample size of 68 should produce a value of E close to one switch. The value will not be exactly one because the sample standard deviation, s, probably will not be exactly 5. Estimating σ in this manner, however, produces a value that is in the neighborhood of σ.

X Exercises 8.34–8.43

Understanding the Mechanics

8.34 Assume that a 90% confidence interval on the mean is to be constructed with a maximum error of E. The population standard deviation is equal to 50. How large a sample is required if:

    a. $\bar{X}$ is to be within 10 units of the population mean.
    b. $\bar{X}$ is to be within 15 units of the population mean.
    c. $\bar{X}$ is to be within 5 units of the population mean.

8.35 A pilot study yielded the following random sample of 15 observations from a normally distributed population.

69 50 74 40 24 50 49 60 52 44 49 52 39 47 48

    a. Using the sample standard deviation as an estimate for the population standard deviation, what is the necessary sample size for the sample mean to be within 3 units of the population mean with 95% confidence?
    b. Repeat part a using the highest and lowest values of the observations to estimate the population standard deviation.

Applying the New Concepts

8.36 The Chamber of Commerce of Tampa, Florida, would like to estimate the mean amount of money spent by a tourist to within $100 with 95% confidence. If the amount of money spent by tourists is considered to be normally distributed with a standard deviation of $200, what sample size would be necessary for the Chamber of Commerce to meet its objective in estimating this mean amount?

8.37 Security Savings and Loan Association's manager would like to estimate the mean deposit by a customer into a savings account to within $500. If the deposits into savings accounts are considered to be normally distributed with a standard deviation of $1,250, what sample size would be necessary to be 90% confident?

8.38 If a sample size of 70 was necessary to estimate the mean of a normal population to within 1.2 with 90% confidence, what is the approximate value of the standard deviation of the population?

8.39 The marketing agency for computer software of Personal Micro Systems would like to estimate with 95% confidence the mean time that it takes for a beginner to learn to use a standard software package. Past data indicate that the learning time can be approximated by a normal distribution with a standard deviation of 20 minutes. How large a sample size should the marketing agency choose if the mean time to learn to use the software package is to be estimated within 8 minutes with 90% confidence?

8.40 In an effort to lure vacationers to exotic locations, several vacation packages to world-class golf destinations, such as Scotland, New Zealand, and Maui, are offered by the major airlines and vacation agencies. The prices range from $1,200 to $4,000. Suppose that a travel agency wished

319

to obtain a 90% confidence interval on the mean price of an exotic golf vacation offered by numerous vacation agencies throughout the United States. What sample size would be necessary to estimate the mean price to within $250?

(Source: "Charting a Course for World-Class Tee Times," *USA Today*, April 17, 1998, p. D1.)

8.41 A chemist at International Chemical would like to measure the adhesiveness of a new wood glue. From past experiments, a measure used to indicate adhesiveness has ranged from 7.3 to 11.1 units. To be 98% confident, how large a sample would be necessary to estimate the mean adhesiveness to within 0.5 units?

8.42 For the Canadian government and casino operators, gambling has provided the basis for a very profitable marriage. Some 14 million visitors come to Canada annually, many to gamble at the casinos. The lion's share of that action is in Central Canada, which has five glitzy casinos—Niagara Falls, Windsor, and Casino Rama near Oril-

lia in Ontario and Hull and Montreal in Quebec. A survey at one of these casinos revealed that the Canadian households that gamble spend between $100 and $3,200 annually in gambling. What sample size would be necessary to estimate the average amount spent by Canadian households that visit the casinos so that the estimate of the average is within $150 with 95% confidence.

(Source: "Two Niagara Falls: A Study in Contrasts," *The Wall Street Journal*, March 3, 2004, p. B4.)

8.43 Pollsters often determine the sample size of their survey so that a prespecified margin of error will be achieved. One factor affecting the margin of error is the confidence level. To understand how the sample size increases as the confidence level increases to maintain a specified margin of error, determine the sample size for $s = 10$, $E = 1$, and for confidence levels of 86%, 88%, 90%, 92%, 94%, 98%, and 99%. Compare the sample sizes as the confidence level increases. To find the z value used in the sample size formula, use a statistical computer package.

On the CD . . .
Section 7.6: Bootstrap Confidence Intervals
Exercises 7.44–7.53
Section 7.7: Other Sampling Procedures
Exercises 7.54–7.59

Summary

This chapter introduced you to statistical inference, an extremely important area of statistics. Inference procedures were used to estimate a certain parameter (such as the population mean, μ, or the population standard deviation, σ) by using the corresponding sample statistic. The Central Limit Theorem states that for large samples, the sample mean, $\bar{X}$, follows an approximate normal distribution. The strength of the Central Limit Theorem is that no assumptions need to be made concerning the shape of population, provided the sample is large (generally, $n > 30$). The probability distribution of a sample statistic is its sampling distribution. Consequently, according to the Central Limit Theorem, the sampling distribution of $\bar{X}$ is approximately normal for large sample sizes, regardless of the shape of the sampled population.

The sample mean, $\bar{X}$, provides a point estimate of the population mean and a confidence interval for μ mea-

sures the precision of the point estimate. If the population standard deviation (σ) is known, the standard normal table is used to derive the confidence interval. If σ is unknown, the t table is used to derive the confidence interval. For situations where is σ unknown and the sample size is greater than 30, approximate confidence intervals for the population mean can be constructed using the standard normal table. A summary of this procedure is contained in Figure 8.19.

The sample size n necessary to achieve a desired accuracy can be obtained by specifying the desired margin of error (E). An estimate of the population standard deviation is required in the sample size calculation and can be estimated from a preliminary sample or obtained using a rough approximation (the estimated sample range divided by four).

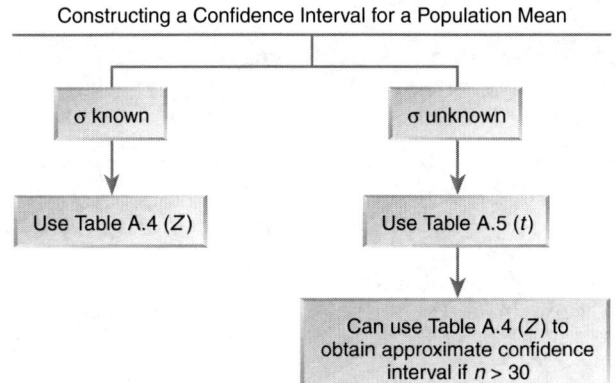

Constructing a Confidence Interval for a Population Mean

σ known → Use Table A.4 (Z)

σ unknown → Use Table A.5 (t)

Can use Table A.4 (Z) to obtain approximate confidence interval if $n > 30$

FIGURE

8.19

The correct table to use for constructing a confidence interval for a population mean.

✓ Summary of Formulas

1. Standard error of $\bar{X}$ (simple random sample):

$$\frac{\sigma}{\sqrt{n}}$$

2. Estimated standard error of $\bar{X}$ (simple random sample):

$$\frac{s}{\sqrt{n}}$$

3. Confidence interval for a population mean (large simple random sample, σ known):

$$\bar{X} \pm Z_{\alpha/2}\frac{\sigma}{\sqrt{n}}$$

4. Confidence interval for the mean of a normal population (simple random sample, σ unknown):

$$\bar{X} \pm t_{\alpha/2,n-1}\frac{s}{\sqrt{n}}$$

5. Necessary sample size (simple random sample):

$$n = \left[\frac{Z_{\alpha/2}\cdot\sigma}{E}\right]^2$$

where E is the specified margin of error.

Additional Bootstrap Readings

1. Biddle, G.C., C.M. Bruton, and A.F. Siegel, "Computer-Intensive Methods in Auditing: Bootstrap Difference and Ratio Estimation," *Auditing: A Journal of Practice & Theory,* vol. 3, no. 3, Fall 1990, pp. 92–114.

2. Davison, A.C., and D.V. Hinkley, *Bootstrap Methods and Their Application,* Cambridge, UK: Cambridge University Press, 1997.

3. Efron, B., "Nonparametric Estimates of Standard Error: The Jackknife, the Bootstrap, and Other Resampling Methods," *Biometrika,* 1981, pp. 589–99.

4. Efron, B., and R.J. Tibshirani, *An Introduction to the Bootstrap,* New York: Chapman & Hall, 1993.

X   Review Exercises 8.60–8.74

8.60 After taking a random sample of 40 customers and asking them the amount of time they spend shopping at a particular store, a 95% confidence interval is computed to be 10 to 32 for the average time spent shopping. An analyst can correctly make which of the following statements?

   a. I am 95% confident that the average time that a customer spends shopping is between 10 and 32 minutes.
   b. The probability is .95 that the midpoint of the interval is equal to the population mean.
   c. The mean of the population is between 10 and 32.
   d. If I repeatedly obtained samples of size 40, then 95% of the resulting confidence intervals would contain the mean time that customers spend shopping.

8.61 In a survey on the quality of customer service at Car Toys, customers were asked to rate the service on a scale from 1 to 10, with 10 being that a customer was completely satisfied with the service. Assume that the distribution of the responses can be approximated by a normal distribution with a mean of 7 and a standard deviation of 1.

   a. What is the probability that an individual customer gives a rating of at least 8?
   b. In a random sample of 10, what is the probability that the average rating is at least 8?

8.62 In August 2000, new car prices were on average 11% lower than they were the year before. In August 2001, the price of new cars was again lower, but not by as much. The prices were approximately 5.6% lower in 2001. Suppose that an automobile analyst wished to obtain information on how much lower a new medium-sized car was selling for in Richmond, Virginia. The following data are the results of a random sample of 20 new cars that were sold in August 2001. These figures represent the decrease in the 2001 selling price (in percentage) compared to the 2000 ceiling price.

| 4.1 | 5.3 | 5.8 | 6.7 | 4.8 | 7.3 | 6.5 | 5.1 | 7.2 | 5.2 |
| 6.7 | 8.1 | 3.5 | 5.2 | 6.1 | 4.2 | 3.2 | 6.8 | 3.8 | 7.1 |

   a. Compute a 90% confidence interval for the mean decrease in the price of a new medium sized car selling in Richmond, Virginia. Interpret the confidence interval.
   b. What could you do to obtain a narrower confidence interval?
   c. What sample size is necessary to estimate the sample mean with 90% confidence such that it is within .2 of the actual decrease in selling price on a year-to-year basis?

(Source: "News Digest," *The Financial Times,* September 27, 2001, p. 10.)

8.63 A quality-assurance manager uses a random sample of size 25 to construct a 95% confidence interval on the average weight of a bag of dry feed. This interval is found to be 49.9174 to 50.0826.

   a. What is the point estimate of the average weight of a bag of dry feed?
   b. What is the sample standard deviation of the weight of a bag of dry feed?

8.64 Although high school teachers in some states, such as Connecticut, New Jersey, and New York, earn average salaries topping $50,000 for a nine-month year, teachers' salaries in states such as North Dakota and Oklahoma hover around $30,000. To estimate the mean salary of a high school teacher in Connecticut to within $1,000 with 99% confidence, what sample size is necessary? Assume that the range of high school teachers' salaries in Connecticut is $30,000 to $60,000.

(Source: "Schools Discount the Need to Boost Teachers' Salaries," *USA Today,* August 8, 2001, p. 12A.)

8.65 A random variable is found to range from a high of 50 to a low of 25 from past data. The distribution of the random variable can be approximated by a normal distribution. To estimate the mean of the random variable to within 2.1, what sample size would be necessary in selecting a random sample to achieve a 99% confidence level?

8.66 The tensile strength of a high-powered copper coil used in giant power transformers is believed to follow a normal distribution. A sample of 14 high-powered copper coils yields the following tensile strength (in units of thousands of pounds per square inch). Construct a 90% confidence interval for the mean tensile strength of copper coils.

6.1, 2.6, 3.5, 4.3, 3.1, 5.2, 3.6, 3.5, 5.4, 4.2, 3.2, 2.8, 4.0, 3.7

8.67 The manager of a cafe would like to estimate the proportion of days that the cafe sells out of their daily baked breads. If a 1 is recorded for a day when the baked breads are sold out and a 0 when the baked breads are not sold out, a proportion of days when the breads are sold out can be computed by summing the 1's and 0's and dividing by the total number of days. What is the approximate distribution of the estimate of the proportion of days when the daily baked breads are sold out? (Hint: What does the Central Limit Theorem say?)

8.68 A financial planner knows that 40% of construction workers do not have a retirement plan. Suppose that the financial planner mails retirement literature to a random sample of 100 construction workers. Using the Central Limit Theorem, the sample proportion of workers not having a retirement account can be thought of as a sample mean and its distribution can be approximated by the normal distribution for large sample sizes. What is the probability that the proportion not having a retirement plan exceeds .5? Use $p = .40$ as the mean of the sample proportion and use $p \cdot (1 - p)/n$ as the variance of the proportion. (Note that the variance of the sample proportion is the variance of a binomial random variable divided by the sample size.)

8.69 An auditor is interested in the average account balance for a large number of accounts at a computer software company. If the standard deviation of the accounts is known to be $800, what sample size would the auditor need to select to estimate the mean account balance to within $200 with 95% confidence?

8.70 A market analyst is interested in the average purchase amount of groceries by customers at an organic online supermarket Web site. If the standard deviation of the amount purchased is $25, how many customers would need to be randomly sampled to estimate the mean purchase to within $6 with 99% confidence?

8.71 [**DATA SET EX8-71**] Variable Description:

City: Name of city in which rental car is rented

Weekly Economy Rate: The weekly rate to rent a car (in dollars)

Many car-rental companies offer special weekly rates on economy cars. A sample of Hertz's weekly economy rate at 18 locations (3 of which are in Canada) is presented in this data set. Construct a 90% confidence interval for the mean weekly rate and interpret this interval.

(Source: www.Travelocity.com)

8.72 [**DATA SET EX8-72**] Variable Description:

2004 Loans: Amount of mortgage loans in 2004 (millions of dollars)

2003 Loans: Amount of mortgage loans in 2003 (millions of dollars)

Twenty major mortgage institutions were selected and the amount of mortgage refinancing was recorded for 2004 and 2003. Construct a 95% confidence interval for the average mortgage loan for each of these years and compare.

8.73 [**DATA SET EX8-73**] Variable Description:

LaptopBatteryLife: the number of hours that a laptop computer will function.

Most computer laptops use a rechargeable lithium-ion battery. However, with brighter computer displays and more powerful chips, batteries are not lasting any longer than they did on older computer laptop models. To determine the average number of hours of use that a college student gets on a laptop before the batteries fail, 51 students were randomly selected, and values of the variable LaptopBatteryLife were recorded. Find a 90% confidence interval for the mean battery lifetime. Use a t distribution. Repeat, using the normal distribution with $\sigma = 1.202583$, and compare the two confidence intervals.

8.74 To understand how the required sample size changes with a change in the maximum error for a confidence interval, plot n against the values of $E = 8, 9, 10, \ldots, 20$, when the population standard deviation is equal to 100, and the confidence level is 95%. The plot should look like the one displayed below. Comment on the relationship between n and E. In Excel, type in $8, 9, 10, \ldots, 20$ in cells A1 through A13. In cell B1, enter =(1.96*100/A1)^2. Drag B1 through B13. Then click on the **Chart Wizard** to form a line graph.

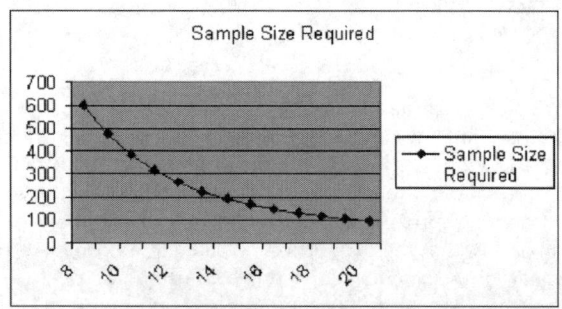

Computer Exercises Using the Databases

Exercise 1—Appendix F

Select the first 500 observations of the database as the population of interest. Estimate the mean of HPAYRENT (house payment or house/apartment rent) for this population by taking a simple random sample of size 40. Also estimate the mean by taking a stratified sample proportional to the size of the two strata. Let stratum 1 be the group of observations in which a secondary wage earner (variable INCOME2) has a positive income, and let stratum 2 be the group of observations in which there is no secondary wage earner. Compare the confidence intervals on mean house payment/rent (HPAYRENT) for both the simple random sample and the stratified random sample.

Note: The necessary steps to select the first 500 rows when using SPSS are

Data ➤ Select Cases ➤ Based on time or case range ➤ Range ➤ First case = 1, Last case = 500

To obtain the simple random sample of size 40, the steps are

Data ➤ Select Cases ➤ Select variable HPAYRENT ➤ Random sample of cases (Unselected Cases are Deleted) ➤ Sample ➤ Exactly 40 cases from the first 500 cases ➤ Continue ➤ OK

The MINITAB procedure to select the first 500 rows is

MTB ➤ COPY C1–C9 INTO C11–C19;
SUBC ➤ USE ROWS 1:500.

To obtain the simple random sample of size 40, use

MTB ➤ RANDOM 40 FROM C17, PUT INTO C20

Exercise 2—Appendix F

Select a simple random sample of 32 observations from the database. Calculate a 95% confidence interval on the mean income of the principal wage earner (variable INCOME1). Select another simple random sample of size 60 from this database. Calculate a 95% confidence interval on the mean income of the principal wage earner. Comment on the widths of these two confidence intervals.

Exercise 3—Appendix G

Generate 20 random samples of size 10 using the data for the variable ASSETS (current assets). For each sample determine the sample mean. Construct a histogram of these 20 sample means. Also find the mean and the variance of these 20 values. Repeat this procedure for samples of size 25 and 40. Does the Central Limit Theorem appear to be operating correctly here? Discuss.

Insights from Statistics in Action

Traffic Congestion Takes Its Toll

The Statistics in Action introductory case study discussed the problem of excessive time spent on the freeways at major U.S. cities. To estimate the average time spent by motorists on the freeways in the morning and evening rush hours in Dallas, Texas, a random sample of 200 motorists is selected. Use the data set listed in StatIn- ActChap7 to answer the following questions. This data set consists of responses to two questions: (1) What is the typical amount of time you spend traveling to downtown Dallas each morning? (2) What is the typical amount of time you spend traveling home each evening? Units are given in minutes.

1. Should a census be taken instead of a random sample to obtain the average time spent by motorists driving in the morning and in the evening rush hours? For what reasons would the researcher want to use a random sample instead of a census? Construct a histogram of the sampled data. Comment on the shape of the distribution of the sampled data.

2. Find two 99% confidence intervals—one for the average time that motorists spend driving in the morning and one for the average time motorists spend driving in the evening.

3. Interpret the confidence intervals in question 2. If you repeatedly obtained samples of 200 and constructed 99% confidence intervals, what general statement can you make about the true average time that motorists in Dallas spend driving in the morning and the evening?

4. What sample size would be necessary for the sample mean time spent driving in the morning to be within 2 minutes of the population average time that motorists in Dallas spend driving in the morning? What sample size would be necessary for the sample size to be within 1 minute of the population average?

5. Repeat question 4 for the time spent driving in the evening and compare sample sizes.

(Source: "D.C. Area Traffic Heavier, Costlier," *The Washington Post*, September 8, 2004, p. A1. "Been in an Accident? Dallas Police Say, 'Move that wreck," *Dallas Morning News*, September 29, 2004, p. A1. "Plans to Raise Road Funds on the Table," *Dallas Morning News*, February 5, 2001, p. 17A.)

Data Analysis with Excel, MINITAB, and SPSS

Appendix

Excel

Confidence Intervals for the Mean with Known Population Standard Deviation

To obtain a confidence interval for the mean with known population standard deviation, click **KPK Data Analysis ➤ One Population Inference.** For the example with the data consisting of 25 assembly times in section 8.3 entered in A1:A25, select **Population mean (z statistic)** for the test in the drop-down list box, enter **A1:A25** for the **Input Range, 3** for the **Population Standard Deviation,** and **5** for the **Alpha** since a 95% confidence level is desired in this example. Select **Confidence Interval** for **Method, C2** (or some other location) for the **Output Range,** and click **OK** to print the confidence interval output.

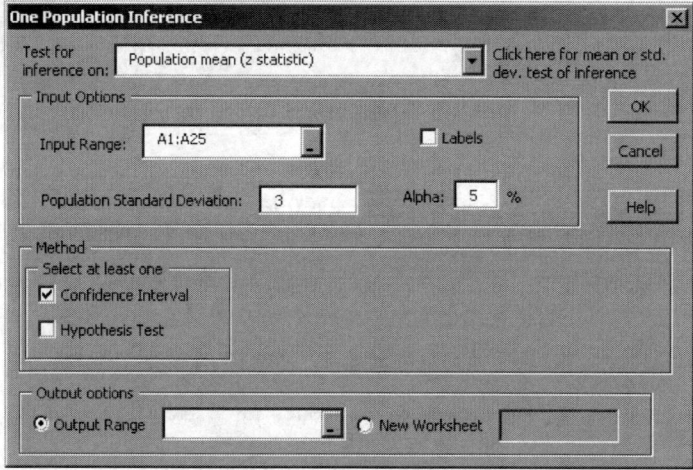

Confidence Intervals for the Mean with Unknown Population Standard Deviation

To obtain a confidence interval for the mean with unknown population standard deviation, click **KPK Data Analysis ➤ One Population Inference.** Follow the same procedure for the case in which the population standard deviation is known except select **Population mean with est. std. dev. (t statistic)** for the test in the drop-down list box. With this option, an edit box for the population standard deviation will not appear.

MINITAB

Confidence Intervals for the Mean with Known Population Standard Deviation

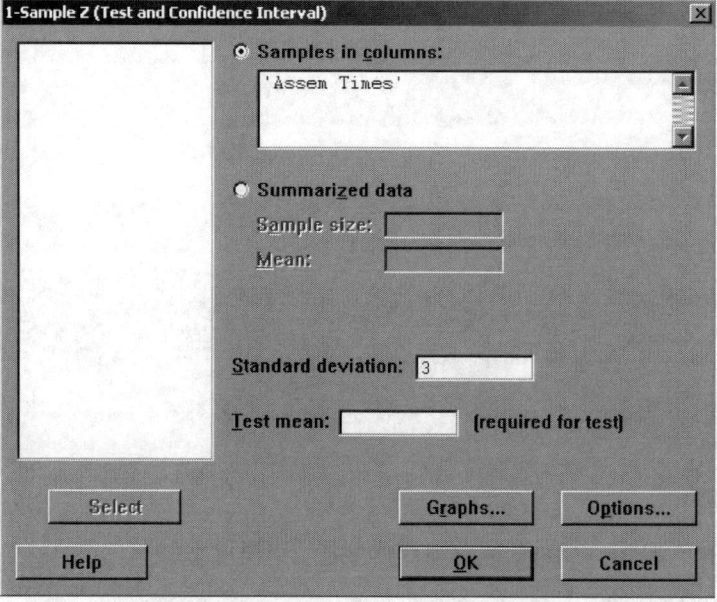

To obtain a confidence interval for the mean with known population standard deviation, click **Stat ➤ Basic Statistics ➤ 1-Sample Z.** Using the 25 assembly times in section 8.3 in C1 as an example, select **C1** for the **Samples in columns** and enter **3** for the population **Standard deviation** in the dialog box. Click on **Options** and enter **95** for the **Confidence level** in the **Options** dialog box. Select **not equal** as the option for **Alternative** to compute both upper and lower limits of the confidence interval. Click **OK** for the output.

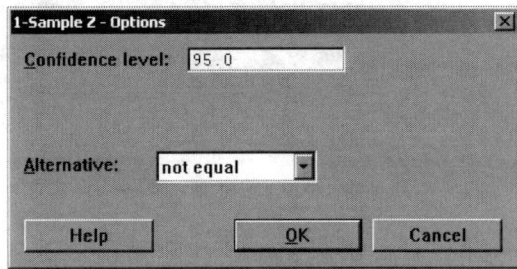

Confidence Intervals for the Mean with Unknown Population Standard Deviation

To obtain a confidence interval for the mean with unknown population standard deviation, click **Stat ➤ Basic Statistics ➤ 1-Sample t.** Follow the same procedure for the case in which the population standard deviation is known. With this option, an edit box for the population standard deviation will not appear.

SPSS

Confidence Intervals for the Mean with Unknown Population Standard Deviation

To illustrate the construction of a confidence interval for a population mean, consider the output voltage of the 18 power supplies in Example 8.6. Enter these values in the first column of the data window. Click on the **Variable View** tab and name this variable "voltage." To obtain the confidence interval, click on **Analyze ➤ Compare Means ➤ One-Sample T Test.** Click on the pointer button to move the variable voltage into the **Test Variable(s)** box. To set the confidence level, click on **Options** and enter 95 in the Confidence Interval box (this is the default value). Click **OK** and note that the right-hand side of the output displays the confidence interval. (SPSS does not compute confidence intervals for the case in which the standard deviation is known.)

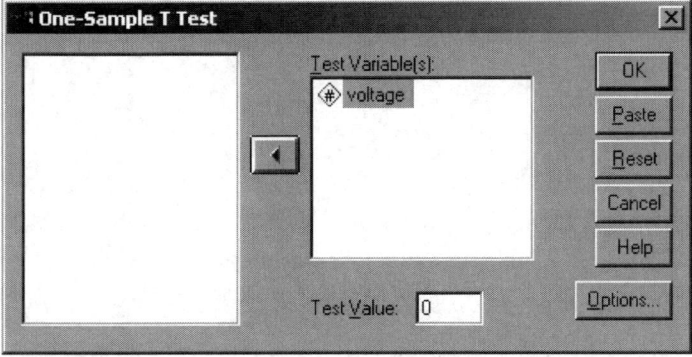

Quality Improvement X

Statistics in Action
Business Excellence: Banking on Six Sigma to Keep Quality Job One

During 2000, surveys by Consumer Reports and J. D. Power & Associates revealed that overall quality and customer satisfaction for Ford cars lagged the competition. This was a reversal from the 1980s, when Ford had a substantial lead in quality. In fact, Dr. W. Edwards Deming was recruited to jump-start Ford's quality movement. Commitment to Deming's principles of total quality management is credited for a series of home runs at Ford, including the aerodynamic Taurus-Sable's rise to best-selling car in America and Ford's achievement as the most profitable American auto company during the 1980s. Ford's hard-won reputation for quality was tarnished by a series of setbacks, from the controversy over deadly rollovers of Ford Explorers equipped with Firestone tires to costly recalls of several models.

What is Ford's chief executive officer (CEO) counting on to put Ford back on track? *Six Sigma.* Employees understand that sigma is a Greek symbol representing a statistical unit that measures how much something varies from perfection. Most U.S. companies operate at Three Sigma—about 66,800 defects per million opportunities. Six Sigma quality is virtually flawless—3.4 defects per million opportunities.

Ford's approach is quality oriented, but with a bottom-line orientation, whereas the total quality management approach of the 1980s focused primarily on improving processes with the thought that profits automatically follow. A typical project is assigned to a manager who has to improve processes 70 percent and produce $250,000 in cost savings. Middle managers, known as Black Belts, are committed to working on quality-improvement projects for two years. Ford's CEO painfully realizes that consistency is the ultimate test of any quality program—and, perhaps, Ford's greatest failing. He believes that had Ford stuck with total quality management, it might have avoided many of the problems that have plagued the company. As the years rolled by, the concept faded into the background at Ford. Its champions retired and were replaced by executives who had other priorities. U.S. automakers had so much confidence that they felt they had achieved quality and didn't need to focus on it anymore.

When you have completed this chapter, you will have a firm grasp in understanding how quality improvement tools can provide a company with a greater competitive advantage. When you have completed this chapter, you will be able to

- Discuss the essential concepts behind total quality management (TQM) and the Malcolm Baldrige National Quality Award.
- Construct control charts that monitor the stability of a process.
- Determine if a particular process is capable of meeting the corresponding process specifications.

9.1

A FIRST LOOK AT QUALITY IMPROVEMENT

What if you could be 99% mistake-free in your job? How about 99.9%? In many job areas, that is just good enough to get you a place in the unemployment line. Because if 99.9% was good enough, then . . .

- 22,000 checks per hour would be deducted from the wrong bank accounts.
- Two million documents would be lost by the IRS this year.
- 12 babies born today would be given to the wrong parents.
- 18,322 pieces of mail would be mishandled in the next hour.
- 20,000 drug prescriptions would be written incorrectly this year.

It should be clear from these statistics that there is a great need to ensure quality in our goods and services.

Previous chapters have introduced you to various statistical measures, such as the sample mean (a measure of *location*) and the sample range (a measure of *dispersion* or *variation*). When examining a population, knowledge of these measures can tell you a great deal about the population. For example, if your company advertises 10-pound bags of dog food but a large random sample of bags produces an average ($\bar{x}$) of 8.7 pounds, the company will undoubtedly encounter many angry consumers and may well be out of the dog food business if the sample is representative of all bags being produced.

Similarly, too much variation in the bag weights would indicate that the *production process* is too erratic. The company would then lose money due to dissatisfied customers (whose bags weigh under 10 pounds) or excess product being packaged (in bags that weigh over 10 pounds). Ideally, this production process could be fine-tuned to always produce 10-pound bags with no variation, but realistically, such a goal is nearly impossible. Our example, however, points out the need to be *on target* and *consistent*.

In part, *quality improvement is the study of variability*. Recently, it has received a great deal of national attention, as more and more companies are facing competitors who focus on quality and offer less expensive, more reliable products. This chapter will examine the human side of quality management along with many of the popular tools for implementing quality standards in manufacturing and service industries. Many of the statistical measures and procedures from the earlier chapters will be used to develop simple, yet powerful, methods of monitoring and controlling process location and variation.

9.2

QUALITY IMPROVEMENT: THE PAST, PRESENT, AND FUTURE

Rarely a day goes by in which we are not bombarded by such statements as, "Quality is our most important job at Company A," or "Company B is a leader in quality." It is safe to say that a focus on quality is taking over U.S. business; however, using the word *quality* in one's advertising is not what this movement is all about. Rather, the focus on quality represents a change in the entire corporate culture, from the top on down, ranging from a dramatic change in how we manage and treat company employees all the way to using statistical methods to monitor and improve a production or service process.

New ideas within U.S. business organizations generally encounter a great deal of resistance. The "Doing business as usual" and "If it ain't broke, don't fix it" philosophies have prevailed, we would argue, for too long. New ideas require change. Change means more work, and we all seem to have enough work. American manufacturing organizations were first to notice that, in fact, many parts of their businesses were broken. As they began to lose an ever-increasing share to overseas competition, they began to take a closer look at their manufacturing processes and management styles. It has become clear to an increasing number of both manufacturing and service organizations that what worked in the past may not be the ideal path for the twenty-first century.

At the dawn of the twentieth century, most of the products in the marketplace today didn't even exist. There were no airplanes, televisions, computers—or even bottled soft drinks. As we began to efficiently mass produce goods, organizations were created that contained multilayered management hierarchies under top-down control, as exemplified by General Motors in the 1920s. The General Motors model consisted of semiautonomous divisions (Chevrolet, Buick, Oldsmobile, Cadillac, and Pontiac) managing their own affairs while headquarters maintained financial control over the organization as a whole.

Today, nearly every business organization reflects these roots to some degree, and it was in this world that the quality profession developed. Their early efforts focused on creating statistical tools to help produce mass quantities of nearly identical goods. Prior to the late 1970s, *quality* meant *quality control*. In fact, the original name of the American Society for Quality was the American Society for Quality Control. Quality efforts encompassed inspection, conformance, and sorting out defects. Little effort was placed on monitoring work processes or preventing problems. Inspection—both incoming and outgoing—and 100% testing were the predominant methods of controlling quality.

Quality improvement hit center stage in the 1970s, when U.S. industry was faced with increased competition from the Japanese on the basis of product quality, price, and overall product reliability. In the 1980s, defect prevention (largely spearheaded by the U.S. automotive industry) rapidly evolved and expanded. The early results were favorable, spurring additional expansion of the quality movement.

The word *quality* began to fall into disfavor in the early 1990s as evidenced by the fact that many organizations seemed to be talking less about their quality improvement programs. There were a number of reasons behind this phenomenon:

- There were oftentimes bitter memories for many employees from the 1980s when quality initiatives were popular, leading employees to believe that they would have control over their work and be able to work on problems of significance to the organization.
- Senior leaders within the organization had little training in the concepts and tools behind an effective and comprehensive quality improvement program. Consequently, under stress they fell back into old habits and management approaches.
- When leaders were under pressure to achieve rapid results, they often abandoned quality initiatives that typically took time to implement before producing a gain in the corporate bottom line.

However, a large number of organizations were quiet on the subject of quality improvement simply because quality control and statistical process control (SPC) had already become integrated into the business strategy. These concepts moved from being new ideas into an accepted part of the organizational strategy. Quality concepts, tools, and methods were intertwined with the work of the organization, and use of this methodology became part of the job.

Even as we continue to use command-and-control techniques in our organizations, the emphasis in the twenty- rst century is shifting toward allowing greater freedom. Layer after layer of bureaucracy and hierarchy is being stripped away, allowing for ever-increasing creativity and productivity. It has taken organizations a long time to realize that the level of external customer satisfaction is related to the level of employee satisfaction. This is especially true for industries such as health care and retail trade, where the customer is an integral part of the work process. As a result, discussion of quality improvement can no longer set aside the social, psychological, and emotional needs of employees.

Total Quality Management

This concept forms the basis of the **total quality management (TQM)** movement that has produced positive results for many U.S. manufacturing and service organizations. The TQM approach represents a basic change for many businesses in how they view employees, competition, training, and business strategies. What these businesses have discovered is that we live at a time when changes are occurring constantly and institutions that do not allow reaction to such changes have dif culty surviving.

What is TQM? There are a number of de nitions of TQM in the literature, but essentially, TQM embraces a management philosophy that will allow a rm to meet or surpass customer expectations. TQM focuses on continuous quality improvement, teamwork, and paying close attention to the voice of the customer. TQM is an integrated management system that involves everyone in the organization (as well as outside suppliers) and uses quantitative methods to monitor and continuously improve the quality of a process.

Despite TQM being a hot topic for the past 15 years, it has its critics. Unrealistic expectations, lack of understanding, quick- x mentality, and competition from other tools are some reasons why many rms have soured on TQM. It was expected to turn lead into gold and reverse poor performance. Often TQM efforts were measured against short-term nancial performance. When short-term improvements did not materialize, many rms became disillusioned.

Proponents of TQM examine these arguments and are quick to point out that the case against TQM is based on haphazard studies that merely report managers' perceptions about whether TQM had a signi cant nancial impact on their organizations. Such studies are rarely based on objective data and statistically valid analyses. They also maintain that while most rms will claim they have implemented TQM, few are doing it effectively. Effectively implementing TQM means that the key principles of TQM—such as focus on customer satisfaction, employee involvement, and continuous improvement—are well accepted, practiced, and deployed within a rm.

Six Sigma

The most recent player in the quality improvement arena is the implementations of Six Sigma. Six Sigma goes beyond the more customer-focused, employee empowerment (but often vague) tools proposed by TQM. However, the primary goal of Six Sigma is to improve customer satisfaction and as a result, profitability. The Six Sigma philosophy forces a company to focus on the bottom line by requiring a clearly visible return on investment and requires companies to make strides in reducing waste and system failure rates. The Six Sigma approach requires companies to concentrate on improving systems on a project-by-project and a process-by-process basis.

In short, it is a very structured approach to solving problems and requires companies to make decisions based on sound statistical methods and cold hard facts.

Six Sigma has become the quality improvement standard and is the most effective method for improving business and organizational performance. The term Six Sigma originated at Motorola in the mid-1980s. Due to sagging sales and increased Japanese competition, Motorola instigated the Six Sigma philosophy that essentially attempted to improve quality to a level of only 3.4 defects per million opportunities (see Insights from Statistics in Action at the end of this chapter for more details).

Implementation of Six Sigma involves a five-phase improvement cycle, referred to as DMAIC (pronounced "duh-MAY-ick"). DMAIC is an acronym for the following five activities:

- **D**efine the problem and requirements
- **M**easure key internal processes and determine the capability of each process
- **A**nalyze the data collected and search out opportunities for improvement
- **I**mprove the target process
- **C**ontrol the process and correct problems

DMAIC essentially is a data-driven quality strategy for improving processes and has become the standard guide for Six Sigma process-improvement projects.

Six Sigma utilizes a "belt" system to indicate an employee's level of Six Sigma training and involvement. These include Master Black Belts (in-house coaches that devote 100% of their time to Six Sigma), Black Belts (work under Master Black Belts and concentrate on Six Sigma project execution), Green Belts (work under Black Belts and are involved in Six Sigma implementation along with other job responsibilities), and Yellow Belts (employees trained in Six Sigma but have not completed a Six Sigma project).

Six Sigma provides companies with a methodology and philosophy for minimizing mistakes and maximizing value. The quality improvement philosophy is that all business organizations and individuals have room to improve. When used properly, the Six Sigma approach can dramatically reduce costs, improve efficiency, and maximize customer satisfaction in all operations within the company.

As a final comment, those executives that are not totally in favor of a Six Sigma culture point out that a Six Sigma focus needs to also consider the importance of innovation and customer relationships. The structured and systematic nature of a Six Sigma program may make it difficult to adapt to the changing strategic needs of a business that has successfully cut costs and improved profitability

Some Key Definitions

As we have seen, the term quality means slightly different things to different people. We will define a quality product or service to be one that meets or surpasses the needs and expectations of the customer; that is, quality means general excellence in the eyes of the customer. However, as Deming was quick to point out, "It will not suffice to have customers who are merely satisfied. A satisfied customer may switch. . . . It is necessary to innovate, to predict the needs of the customer, to give him more." It is important to understand that quality improvement does not just apply to businesses. It also works in nonprofit organizations, such as schools, health care and social services, and government agencies. Here are other key terms that will be used in the sections to follow.

Process. Any combination of people, machinery, material, and methods that is intended to produce a product or service.

Quality Characteristics. Features of a product that describe its fitness for use, such as length, weight, taste, appearance, reliability. For a service organization these could include promptness of service (e.g., check-in time at a hotel, response time to a police call), number of customer complaints, or level of employee attitude.

Statistical Process Control (SPC). The application of statistical quality-control methods to measuring and analyzing the variation found in processes.

Control Chart. A statistical chart used to monitor various aspects of a process (such as the process average) and to determine if the process is in control (stable) or out of control (unstable).

9.3 THE MALCOLM BALDRIGE NATIONAL QUALITY AWARD AND ISO 9000 REGISTRATION

Malcom Baldrige Award

The **Malcolm Baldrige National Quality Award** (MBNQA) was established by Congress in 1987. The award was named after the former Secretary of Commerce, who was killed in a rodeo accident earlier the same year. The MBNQA was modeled, in part, after the Deming Award, named after W. Edwards Deming, presented annually in Japan for more than 45 years to the organization that best demonstrates dramatic quality improvement. After the MBNQA was created, 37 countries, Puerto Rico, and Western Europe developed national quality awards, many of which were modeled after the Baldrige award. In 1998, Baldrige Awards were expanded to include nonprofit education and health care sectors. Not-for-profit organizations (including government agencies) were added in 2007.

Organizations can request copies of the MBNQA criteria and application forms by contacting the Baldrige organization Web site at www.quality.nist.gov. The 1,000th applicant was received in 2005. Recent winners of the MBNQA, through 2004, are listed in Table QI.1. There can be at most two winners each year within each of three business categories-manufacturing companies, small businesses, and service companies. Federal Express was the first service company winner in 1990; in 1992, AT&T became the only company to win two Baldrige awards in the same year. Also, 1992 marked the first time two service companies won the award. In 1997, Xerox joined the group of two-time winners, and in 1994, AT&T became the only three-time winner. The examination process includes on-site visits for those companies passing an initial screening. As you can see from Table QI.1, there need not be an MBNQA winner within all three categories if the Baldrige examiners find no company in a particular category (such as manufacturing companies, 2006 and 2007, and service companies, 2007) that meet the rather strict, yet very objective, criteria.

The MBNQA was established to raise awareness about quality management in the United States, and to recognize U.S. companies that have a world-class system for managing their operations and people and for satisfying their customers. A company applying for this award must provide evidence, in minute detail, describing its achievements and improvements in the following areas:

- Leadership
- Strategic planning
- Customer and market focus
- Measurement, analysis, knowledge management
- Workforce focus
- Process management
- Results

Each of these seven categories receives a score, ranging from 85 (strategic planning, customer and market focus, workforce focus, and process management) to 450 (results). The total score is 1,000 points. Figure QI.1 also contains a breakdown of the points within each category. For example, the 85 points within category 3 (customer and market focus) is broken down into two subcategories: customer and market knowledge (40 points) and customer relationships and satisfaction (45 points).

TABLE

9.1

Recent Winners of the Malcolm Baldrige National Quality Award for Manufacturing Companies, Service Companies, and Small Business.

	Manufacturing Companies	Small Business	Service Companies
1995	Armstrong World Industries Building Products Operations Corning Telecommunications Products Division		
1996	ADAC Laboratories	Custom Research, Inc. Trident Precision Manufacturing, Inc.	Dana Commercial Credit Corp.
1997	3M Dental Products Division Solectron Corp.		Merrill Lynch Credit Corp. Xerox Business Services

TABLE

9.1

	Manufacturing Companies	Small Business	Service Companies
1998	Boeing Airlift and Tanker Programs Solar Turbines, Inc.	Texas Nameplate Co. Inc.	
1999	STMicroelectronics, Inc.— Region Americas	Sunny Fresh Foods	BI Ritz-Carlton Hotel Company, L.L.C. Operations Management International, Inc.
2000	Dana Corporation— Spicer Driveshaft Division	Los Alamos National Bank	
2001	Clarke American Checks, Inc.	Pal's Sudden Service	
2002	Motorola Commercial, Government & Industrial	Branch-Smith Printing Division	
2003	Medrad, Inc.	Stoner, Inc.	Boeing Aereospace Support Caterpillar Financial Services Corp., U.S.
2004	The Bama Companies, Inc.	Texas Nameplate Company, Inc.	
2005	Sunny Fresh Foods, Inc. Sector	Park Place Lexus	DynMcDermott Petroleum Operations
2006		MESA Products, Inc.	Premier, Inc.
2007		PRO-TEC Coating Co.	

FIGURE

9.1

Categories and maximum points awarded for the Malcolm Baldrige National Quality Award.

Examination Categories		Points
1.0 Leadership		120
1.1 Senior leadership	70	
1.2 Governance and Social responsibilities	50	
2.0 Strategic planning		85
2.1 Strategy development	40	
2.2 Strategy deployment	45	
3.0 Customer and market focus		85
3.1 Customer and market knowledge	40	
3.2 Customer relationships and satisfaction	45	
4.0 Measurement, analysis, knowledge management		90
4.1 Measurement, analysis, and improvement of organizational performance	45	
4.2 Management of information, information technology, and knowledge	45	
5.0 Workforce focus		85
5.1 Workforce engagement	45	
5.2 Workforce environment	40	
6.0 Process management		85
6.1 Work systems design	35	
6.2 Work process management and improvement	50	
7.0 Results		450
7.1 Product and service outcomes	100	
7.2 Customer-focused outcomes	70	
7.3 Financial and market outcomes	70	
7.4 Workforce-focused outcomes	70	
7.5 Process effectiveness outcomes	70	
7.6 Leadership outcomes	70	

The seven categories and their characteristics are described as follows.

Category 1: Leadership
- How the organization's senior leaders address values and performance expectations
- empowerment, innovation, learning, and organizational directions

Category 2: Strategic Planning
- The organization's strategic development process, including how the organization develops strategic objectives, action plans, and related human resource plans
- How plans are deployed and how performance is tracked

Category 3: Customer and Market Focus
- How the organization determines requirements, expectations, and preferences of customers and markets
- How the organization builds relationhips with customers and determines their satisfaction

Category 4: Measurement, Analysis, Knowledge Management
- The organization's performance measurement system
- How the organization analyzes performance data and information

Category 5: Workforce Focus
- How the organization enables employees to develop and utilize their full potential, aligned with the organization's objectives
- The organization's efforts to build and maintain a work environment and an employee support climate conducive to performance excellence, full participation, as well as personal and organizational growth

Category 6: Process Management
- The key aspects of the organization's process management, including customer-focused design as well as product and service delivery
- The supplier and partnering processes involving all work units

Category 7: Results
- The organization's performance and improvement in key business area -- customer satisfaction, product and service performance, financial and marketplace performance, human resource results, supplier and partner results, and operational performance
- Performance relative to competitors

The Baldrige criteria can be used to quantify and measure the more human attributes of your organization, such as attitudes, perceptions, emotions, values, motivation, and morale. The guiding force behind such changes must be the corporate managers. However, successful implementation of this program does not depend entirely on management expertise, but also on the cooperation of other people, including line operators, vendors, customers, and the CEO, who interact within the organizational system.

Few awards or programs have affected U.S. business as the Baldrige Award has. Initiated in obscurity, it has rapidly become a glittering prize for executives, who see it as an of cial recognition of their behind-the-scenes efforts to improve quality. Companies considering applying for this award must examine their motives carefully. If this is merely an attempt for the company to look good, and management is not fully aligned with the values of quality, the application process and resulting disappointment can have a serious negative (and often costly) effect on the organization.

An important point to be made here is that the principal bene t of the application process is the internal changes required, not the award itself, as Baldrige winners are quick to point out. Companies are using these criteria as a self-assessment tool. Whether or not they win the award, such quality-driven companies undoubtedly will be better able to survive and thrive in an increasingly competitive and quality-conscious marketplace.

ISO 9000 Registration

As the emerging global economy invites new and expanded international trade and business, corporations are nding that continued success requires doing business beyond the borders of their host country. As new worldwide markets bring together once foreign customers and companies, standardized business practice will facilitate successful business relations. Industry standards and practices unique to individual countries and continents become a problem when expanding markets, much like a language barrier.

Acknowledging, controlling, and reducing process variation lies at the heart of most quality-control endeavors. Conflicting business practices among various international industries represent one possible source of variation. In response to this problem, the International Organization for Standards for Quality Management issued the **ISO 9000 standards** as a series of guidelines. Revised in 2000, the ISO 9000 standards now represent the worldwide benchmark standards for process quality systems. ISO 9000 does not specify how business and industry processes must be performed but instead defines required actions that must be carried out within those processes to ensure quality products. Businesses and corporations that subscribe to ISO practices operate their systems in like fashion. In this sense, ISO 9000 significantly reduces process variation among companies in the worldwide business community. A newer version (ISO 9001:2008) is due to be released in late 2008 and early reports indicate that the standard will not be substantially changed from its 2000 version.

The ISO 9000 set of standards contains the following three core documents.

1. ISO 9000:2000. "Quality Management Systems—Fundamentals and vocabulary." This document describes quality management system fundamentals and terminology.

2. ISO 9001:2000. "Quality Management Systems—Requirements." This document de nes the requirements and is used to demonstrate an organization's capability to provide products or services that meet customer and applicable regulatory requirements.

3. ISO 9004:2000. "Quality Management Systems—Guidelines for Performance Improvement." This document provides guidance on quality management systems for those organizations that wish to move beyond the requirements of ISO 9001:2000.

The intent of ISO 9001:2000 is to shift an organization's focus from functional management thinking to process management thinking. It is structured to facilitate the idea that all processes are linked within the company.

ISO 9001 requires companies to establish and maintain procedural control by concentrating on procedure documentation. Employee training and awareness in quality procedures is required and documented. ISO 9000 mandates that ISO registered businesses have written procedures that are understood and followed by all company employees. ISO requires a documented and established system as well as universal conformance to that system.

Registration to ISO 9001 standards is increasingly becoming a prerequisite for doing business. Nonregistered companies are often blocked from entering the competition. The European business community led the adoption of ISO standards and is now nearly an exclusively ISO community. Major U.S. corporations are following suit. Required ISO registration of suppliers is commonplace, and in many instances an invitation to bid on a contract is predicated upon ISO registration. ISO 9000 registration requires application to a register, quality system documentation reviews, pre-assessment to identify noncompliant procedures, nal assessment and registration or corrective action, and periodic surveillance audits for verifying continued compliance.

It is worth noting that ISO 9001 registration does not necessarily imply that the registered companies have good product quality. The ISO standards do not require a company to supply references to quality results or customer satisfaction. A registered company is not required to document attempted improvements in the product quality. As a result, ISO 9001 registration does not mean that all registered companies have similar levels of product quality.

Comparing the Baldrige Award and ISO 9001 Registration

Quite often, the Baldrige Award criteria and the ISO 9001 standards are considered to be equivalent in their purpose and content. Such is not the case, however, because there are many notable differences. In particular, the Baldrige Award depends heavily on results, continuous improvement, and customer satisfaction, whereas ISO 9001 registration is less outcome-oriented. ISO 9001 helps companies determine what is needed to maintain an efficient quality conformance system and certifies that consistent business processes are being applied. The Baldrige Award is just that—an award or form of recognition. On the other hand, ISO 9001 registration provides customers with some assurance that a registered supplier has a documented quality system in place and is following it. Although many companies are using the Baldrige Award and ISO 9000 standards compatibly, there is no guarantee that an ISO registration will translate into a high Baldrige Award assessment score. In fact, ISO 9000 registration covers less than 10 percent of the Baldrige Award criteria.

X Exercises 9.1–9.8

9.1 Perform a search on the World Wide Web for information that compares and contrasts basic points of agreement and differences between TQM and Six Sigma.

9.2 Although Six Sigma is most commonly associated with reducing defects in the manufacturing process, this methodology improves other business processes and outcomes. List two additional bene ts that may be derived from the implementation of Six Sigma.

9.3 Cite the appropriate term associated with each of the following de nitions.

c. Top management must signal a commitment to quality values by being responsible members of society through ful lling their societal or public obligations.

d. Firms should be able to establish that their levels of quality meet or exceed those of direct product/service competitors.

9.5 If a rm is unsuccessful in winning the Baldrige Award, its efforts will have been wasted. Do you agree or disagree with this statement, and why?

9.6 What are the three documents in the ISO 9000 set of

a. A feature/characteristic of a product or service that imparts its tness for use.

b. A chart used to monitor and control some aspect of a process.

c. A combination of people, machinery, material, and methods used to produce a product or service.

9.4 For each of the following statements, indicate to which of the seven MBNQA categories the statement corresponds.

a. Companies should have well-de ned programs for developing their employees and involving them in quality-improvement activities.

b. Firms must have well-established and well-documented systems for collecting and analyzing data concerning product/service quality.

standards? Which of these would be used to demonstrate an organization's capability of providing quality products or services?

9.7 Roughly half of the MBNQA point total comes from which category? Consider a company or business you have worked for (in any capacity) prior to or during your college years. How does this category apply to this company, and what advice would you offer the company to improve in this area?

9.8 Do you see the seven examination categories for the MBNQA as distinct and nonoverlapping? Would you expect efforts within certain categories to have an impact on improvement efforts in other categories? If so, which categories?

9.4 QUALITY-IMPROVEMENT TOOLS

This textbook has emphasized the use of statistical graphs for examining sample data. This is especially important in the quality area, where such graphs allow you to understand the reasons for quality problems and to nd solutions for eliminating them. They provide a means of conveying information that is more easily understood by a group of people, such as those attending a staff meeting or a team assigned to examine a particular quality problem. They allow you to see an entire process or to focus on a particular problem area within the process.

Recall that we de ned a *process* as any combination of people, machinery, material, and methods intended to produce a product or service. The use of statistical graphs can provide you with various recordings of this process, ranging from an instant snapshot, such as a **histogram,** to charts recorded over time. This latter category of graphs includes control charts, the subject of the remaining sections of this chapter. Histograms, introduced in Chapter 2, provide a summary of a set of sample data, constructed by condensing the data into classes (groups) and constructing bars of height equal to the frequency (or relative frequency) of each class.

Another popular quality-improvement tool, the **Pareto chart,** was introduced in the Chapter 2 exercises (see Exercises 2.33, 2.34, and 2.57). This is an enhanced bar chart useful for identifying quality problems with the largest impact, and for displaying the relative importance of different categories of information. Another statistical graph in the category of quality-improvement tools is the scatter diagram (discussed in Chapters 3 and 11). The scatter diagram is useful whenever your sample observations contain information on two variables, say X = percent of steel used in a rubber tire mixture and Y = corresponding tire durability.

Two other methods of graphing a process include the **owchart** and the **cause-and-effect diagram** (also known as the fishbone or Ishikawa diagram). The best way to understand a process is to draw a picture of it—that is basically what a owchart is. The purpose of a cause-and-effect diagram is to examine a phase of the process in more detail and to relate causes and effects within the process.

Flowcharts

When a product moves down an assembly line, the process flow is readily apparent, so a flowchart likely is not necessary. However, if the flow of material during a production process is unpredictable (as in a job-shop manufacturing facility), or is not flowing smoothly, such a chart can be very useful in studying the process. While not statistical in nature, a flowchart can often identify key areas where a data collection and/or analysis would be beneficial. A popular use of flowcharts is to analyze the delivery of a service for which the flow of paper and sequence of actions may not be readily apparent.

Flowcharts should be used as a first-step examination of a process. In this way, all people who work in the process can understand it. Better understanding leads to more suggestions for improvement and more enthusiasm, because employees can see better how they fit into the overall picture. The flowchart provides a basic diagram of the entire process and so leads to better communication among everyone involved. Let's examine an example.

Metro Delivery Service provides package delivery services in a large metropolitan area. It has a money-back guarantee that any package brought to any of its dropoff stations will be delivered to anywhere within its area in 90 minutes or less. Metro achieved initial success with its innovative use of bicycles and motorbikes for delivering small packages. The bulk of its business, however, consists of delivering larger packages requiring an automobile or van. Lately, the owner of Metro had noticed a lack of consistency in meeting the 90-minute deadline. Metro management immediately began to blame the problem on what it perceived to be a careless attitude among the company drivers. However, the owner of Metro had attended several quality-improvement seminars and suspected that company performance could best be improved by making changes to the process itself.

A team of employees from all phases of the delivery process was formed and charged with taking a systematic look at the entire delivery process, beginning with a customer's arrival at a dropoff station and ending with the package's delivery. The flowchart in Figure 9.2 was the result.

The chart is basic and doesn't provide a great deal of detail. Nevertheless, it is a good starting point for the team to begin discussing the various operations and potential bottlenecks (the points at which the flow is constricted) within the delivery process. Final versions of a flowchart most often are very detailed, so that each employee can see precisely where his or her job fits into the flow of the entire process.

The symbols used in Figure 9.2 consist of rectangular boxes ($\square$) and diamond boxes ($\diamond$). The rectangles represent each step of the process; the diamonds are points where a decision must be made, typically requiring a yes or no response. A decision point does occur in this flowchart, because the dispatch supervisor must determine whether a driver is available at the time a package is due to leave the station.

The quality-improvement team at Metro was able to use this flowchart to discuss the delivery operation and to study potential problem areas. Their next concern was to explore why a package arrived late at its destination—a topic best examined using a cause-and-effect diagram.

Cause-and-Effect Diagrams

Cause-and-effect diagrams are often called fishbone diagrams or *Ishikawa diagrams,* named after their originator, Dr. Kaoru Ishikawa. In the 1940s, Ishikawa found that many Japanese plant personnel were overwhelmed by the many factors that could influence the outcome of a particular process. He created this very powerful diagram to represent the relationships between potential problems and their sources.

The basic form of a cause-and-effect diagram is shown in Figure 9.3. It has three features:

1. A horizontal arrow with the problem to be studied in a box at its far right

2. Major branches off the horizontal arrow representing the primary (main) causes contributing to this problem

3. Additional arrows within each major branch making up the secondary causes that contribute to the main problem within that major branch

If you examine the shape of Figure 9.3, you will see that it does indeed resemble the skeleton of a fish, which is why *fishbone diagram* is the more popular name for this chart. Although Figure 9.3 shows only two levels of arrows off the horizontal arrow (primary and secondary causes), this procedure of subdividing the possible causes can be continued for additional levels in Step 3 until all variables have been accounted for.

The team at Metro Delivery Service began by identifying four primary causes for the late delivery of a package: taking the order; assigning the driver to the order; traffic conditions; and the delivery vehicle. Secondary causes within each of these primary branches were brainstormed; the result of this effort was the cause-and-effect diagram in Figure 9.4. While developing this chart, the individuals on the team discovered (1) there was a feeling that everyone was working together (a true "team spirit"); (2) the chart enabled them to discuss the delivery process better; and (3) they were able to view the entire delivery process as a system rather than as a collection of disjointed activities.

A final word regarding this example: The logical next step for Metro would be to observe the process (obtain sample data) and construct a Pareto chart for each

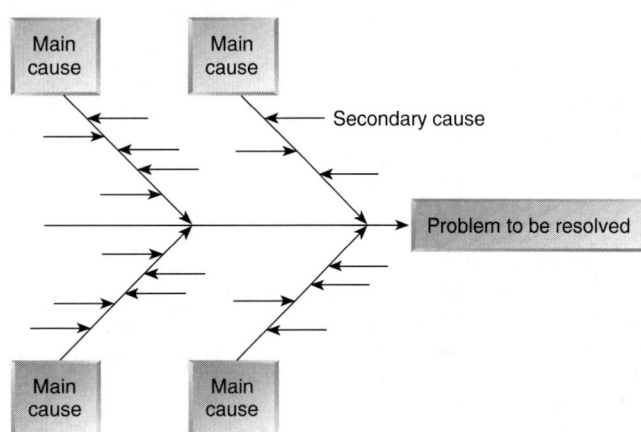

FIGURE

9.3

Basic structure of a cause-and-effect diagram.

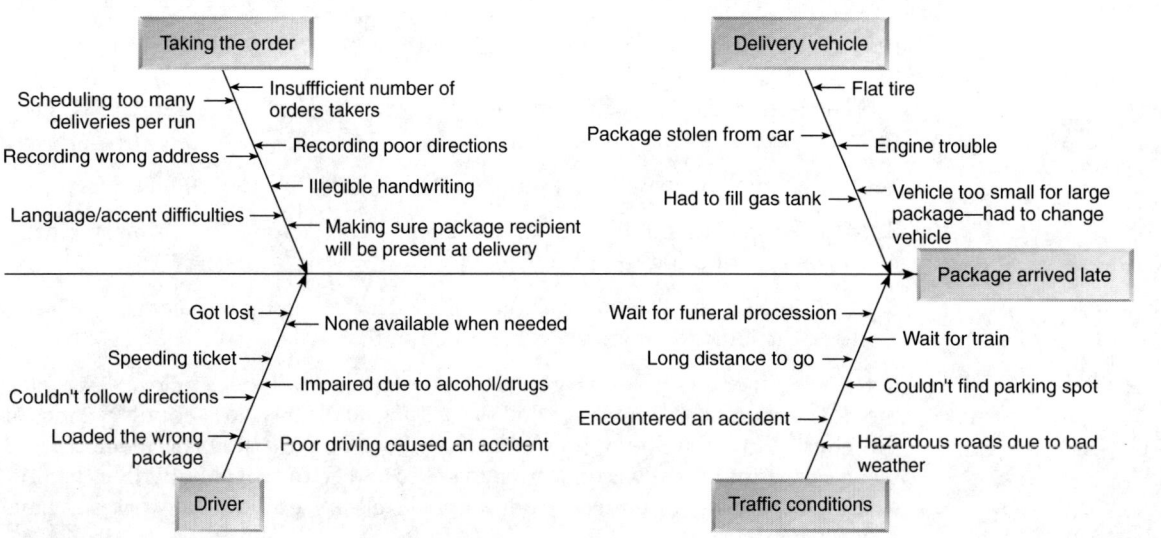

FIGURE

9.4

Cause-and-effect diagram for Metro Delivery Service.

of the four major branches, summarizing the frequency of secondary causes within each branch. In this way, they could attack the problem by putting their resources into those areas that would bring about the greatest improvement in performance.

X Exercises 9.9–9.19

9.9 Describe reasons for using each of the following graphical quality improvement tools. What information does each graph best present?
  a. Pareto chart
  b. Fishbone diagram
  c. Flowchart
  d. Control chart
  e. Scatter diagram

9.10 For each of the following scenarios, select the graphical tools noted in Exercise 9.9 as the most appropriate for analyzing the given scenario. Explain the reasons for each of your selections.
  a. A university is interested in the relationship between a student's grade point average and the student's starting salary after graduating from college. The university's assessment office has interviewed students prior to and after earning a degree. How can this office show this relationship?

  b. An appliance manufacturer maintains records for all warranty services performed. Data analysis for warranty service related to their stoves and ovens has revealed cooking temperature problems generate over 60 percent of the warranty calls. The service manager wishes to investigate possible causes for the temperature problems. What analysis should the manager next perform?

  c. A production supervisor has listed all operations required in a manufacturing facility for each product. The supervisor wishes to examine methods for streamlining production. How should the supervisor compile and present the operations?

  d. A restaurant manager notices that the catering service provided by the restaurant has received numerous complaints. Problems occur during recording of orders as well as with delivery of the food. What type of chart should the manager use to understand the many factors that could influence the quality of the catering service?

e. Every hour an inspector randomly selects five bearings and measures their inside and outside diameters. The inspector wishes to investigate the ability of the manufacturing process to produce dimensionally acceptable bearings. What graphical technique should be used?

9.11 Create a flowchart showing the steps that a customer would follow to apply for a mortgage loan. Include decision symbols that ask the following questions: (1) Is this a small loan or a large loan? (2) Do I qualify for the loan? (3) Will the home appraise for more than the loan amount? (4) Is the proposed down payment sufficient? (5) Will the loan be granted?

9.12 Six sigma can be applied to any industry, not just the manufacturing sector. The goal can still be to reduce errors to 3.5 parts per million. For example, St. Joseph Health Center, a hospital in suburban St. Louis, decided to use corporate improvement techniques in a patient model because many procedures are repetitive. Although process control charts may be of little use in improving these procedures, statistical quality control techniques can help to identify problem areas. Identifying instances of error or difficulty when providing health care permits the use of Pareto analysis for identifying improvement opportunities. Assume that 10 problematic areas and the number of occurrences were recorded over a 10-week period.

Areas Needing Improvement	Number of Occurrences
Waiting Time in Emergency room over 30 min	11
Infections while in Intensive Care Unit	21
Time to retrieve X-rays from technician more than an hour	4
Evaluation by social worker taking more than 90 minutes	9
Insufficient number of nurses on duty	27
Medical imaging equipment malfunctioning	10
Doctors and nurses not following hospital policy	32
Patient complaining about services and facilities	12
Inadequate orientation for new/visiting doctors and nurses	14
Incorrect dose of medicine administered	13

Construct a Pareto chart for the above data and prioritize only the major areas needing improvement.

(Source: "Running a Hospital Like a Factory, in a Good Way," *The New York Times*, February 22, 2004, p. 3.4.)

9.13 Review Web home pages of major corporations, such as Ford and IBM. Create categories for items that are missing from their home page. For example, does the home page have a search index? Is there online help? Is there an FAQ section? Is there a copyright and privacy statement? Is there contact information? Is there a link to financial news about the company? Is there a link to career information for jobs within the company? Which of these categories has the highest frequency of missing items? Which categories appear to have very few missing items?

9.14 The process of purchasing a new car can be very frustrating to the careful buyer. Construct a fishbone diagram to show potential causes of a car buyer being frustrated with the car-buying process. Consider the initial stage of viewing a car and the final stage of negotiating a contract on a car. Pursue each line of causality back to its root cause. Consider grafting relatively empty branches onto others.

9.15 Construct a fishbone diagram to show the potential causes of a customer being unsatisfied with a meal served at a fine restaurant. Consider root causes, starting with the chef, management, training of employees, and the facility. Split up any overcrowded branches.

9.16 Toyota Motor Corporation is North America's most efficient car manufacturer. The company used 6.4 fewer hours of labor per vehicle than did GM to build a vehicle in 2004. That labor gap translates into about $300 to $500 a car. Suppose that an automotive manager at GM wished to construct a fishbone diagram to study the factors influencing productivity. The manager identified four key performance factors: Manufacturing Equipment, Personnel, Management, and Customer Feedback. Construct a fishbone diagram to solve the problem of increasing productivity using these four primary causes. Create several secondary causes within these primary causes on the fishbone diagram. For example, under management, possible secondary causes could be increasing employee productivity incentives and negotiating supplier contracts.

(Source: "GM's Productivity Growth Does Little for Woes," *The Wall Street Journal*, June 3, 2005, p. B.3.)

9.17 It so happens that pizza is the preferred food of most college students. Chances are good that you are a pizza expert. Create a flowchart of the process that the local pizzeria must go through to make and deliver your pizza. Include decision symbols that ask the following questions: (1) Does the local pizzeria accept online orders? (2) How long will it be until they can deliver your pizza? (3) Is the delivered pizza what you ordered? (4) What form of payment will the delivery person accept? After creating this flowchart, see if you can determine what potential bottlenecks exist in the pizza making/delivery process.

9.18 A major crisis facing education today is the dropout rate for high school students. As a concerned citizen, you have volunteered to help examine this problem and to try to identify root causes of student dropout.

a. Construct a fishbone diagram where the primary causes are Students, Faculty/Staff, Curriculum, and Family.

b. For the Student branch, what are some possible secondary causes (e.g., low self-esteem and peer pressure)?

c. For the Faculty/Staff branch, possible secondary causes are disinterest of teachers and class size. What are some others?

d. Secondary causes for the Curriculum branch might include lack of basic skills and language barriers. Can you think of other causes?

e. Possible secondary causes for the Family branch are lack of parental interest in education and truancy not being monitored. What are some others?

9.19 In November 2001, new telephone codes went into effect for long-distance phone calls in Mexico. Authorities did not announce the new dialing arrangement until the month before the new codes became effective. Under the new system, a long-distance phone call from Dallas to Mexico City will require 15 digits. Under this new system, phone calls to Mexico's three largest cities require an extra two digits, but to the rest of the country an extra three digits are needed. Many customers have phoned the operator complaining about the new system. Even operators were not sure of the correct phone numbers in some cases. The following table categorizes causes of problems with the new system. Using the information in this table, construct a cause-and-effect diagram that can be used to improve the implementation of the new telephone codes in Mexico.

Main Causes of Delay in Making Long Distance Call	Elements of Each Main Cause
Customer	**a.** Customer did not receive information about the new telephone codes. **b.** Customer was unfamiliar with dialing to Mexico. **c.** Customer incorrectly dialed the new telephone code.
	d. Customer knew of the new telephone codes but thought that the old code would still work.
Operator	**a.** Operator gave customer wrong advice on how to dial using the new telephone codes. **b.** Operator kept getting a busy signal when trying to connect the customer to the phone line using the new telephone code. **c.** Customer did not give operator enough information to dial the phone number. **d.** Operator connected customer to a phone connection other than the one he/she requested.
Hardware	**a.** There was a hardware malfunction. **b.** Third party interfered with the phone connection.
Language	**a.** Operator could not understand the language in which the customer was speaking. **b.** Explanation given by operator was too complicated.

(Source: "Mexico's New Dialing Codes Could Confuse Phone Callers," *Dallas Morning News*, October 31, 2001, p. 10D.)

STATISTICAL PROCESS CONTROL, PROCESS VARIATION, AND CONTROL CHARTS

A **process** is a combination of resources such as people, machines, or material that lead to a specific product. **Statistical Process Control** (SPC) was previously defined as the application of statistical quality-control methods to measuring and analyzing the variation found in processes. Before a company can successfully implement SPC techniques, it is important that all workers (including management) have a clear understanding of process variation and the value of reducing variation and keeping it reduced. SPC is not a tool to steer a process, but is a means of gaining process understanding to reduce process variation.

Variation exists in every process and in nearly every sample of measurements. Even the best automatic machine tools cannot make every unit exactly the same. Along with machine inconsistencies, process variation is introduced due to people, materials, production methods, and the environment, for example. These sources of variation also are the key components of any cause-and-effect (fishbone) diagram.

Consequently, the measured quality of a manufacturer's product is always subject to a certain amount of variation as a result of chance. We refer to this situation as a *stable* system of *chance causes* of variation. Variation within this stable pattern is random and inevitable. Variation *outside* this stable pattern is another matter. Once discovered, causes for such variation (called *assignable causes*) should be searched out and corrected. Detection of such variation is a key objective of quality control, and is the subject of the remaining sections in this chapter.

For a production process, one of the goals of a quality-improvement program is to reduce the variability in the process, with an eye toward eliminating this process variation—an impossible task, but a goal, nonetheless. By keeping a close watch on process variation and not overreacting to chance variation, a company can bring about dramatic improvements in product quality and a reduction of line stoppages, scrap, and rework. This can be illustrated in a very striking and entertaining way using a favorite device of Dr. W. Edwards Deming—the funnel experiment.*

The Deming Funnel Experiment

The **funnel experiment** was often used by Dr. Deming in his lectures to illustrate that reacting to chance (random) variation has an adverse effect on overall process variation. Despite the good intentions of a machine operator to "fix" the system and move it closer to the process target, such manipulations only make matters worse. In fact, the more diligent the operator, the worse the result.

The device used by Deming was a funnel, mounted on a stand, that is placed directly over a target having a bull's-eye directly in the center, illustrated in Figure 9.5a. A marble is dropped through the funnel, hits the target, and rolls a short distance away. The target bull's-eye represents the process target (such as a stated length or weight), and the final resting place of the marble represents the value of the final product. The direction and distance from the bull's-eye represent random variation within the manufacturing process. Despite the operator's best efforts, the marble will not come to rest directly on the bull's-eye each time.

Strategy 1. The recommended strategy would be not to react to this random variation and not to move the funnel. The diligent operator, on the other hand, could measure the distance and direction that the marble strayed from the bull's-eye and move the funnel that distance in the opposite direction. Two possible alternative strategies here would be the following.

---

*Dr. W. Edwards "Ed" Deming was a famous twentieth-century U.S. statistician who was best known for his confrontive style when delivering his typically unflattering message to corporate executives up until shortly before his death in 1993. For many years, he was largely ignored in the United States. In 1950 he took his message to Japan and was very instrumental in turning Japanese industry into a world economic power. In appreciation, the Japanese government created the Deming Prize to commemorate his contribution and to promote the continuous development of quality improvement in Japan. The prize was established in 1950 and annual awards are still given every year.

FIGURE

9.5

Deming funnel experiment (panel *a*) and MINITAB
simulation output using control strategies 1, 2, and 3 (panels *b, c,* and *d*).

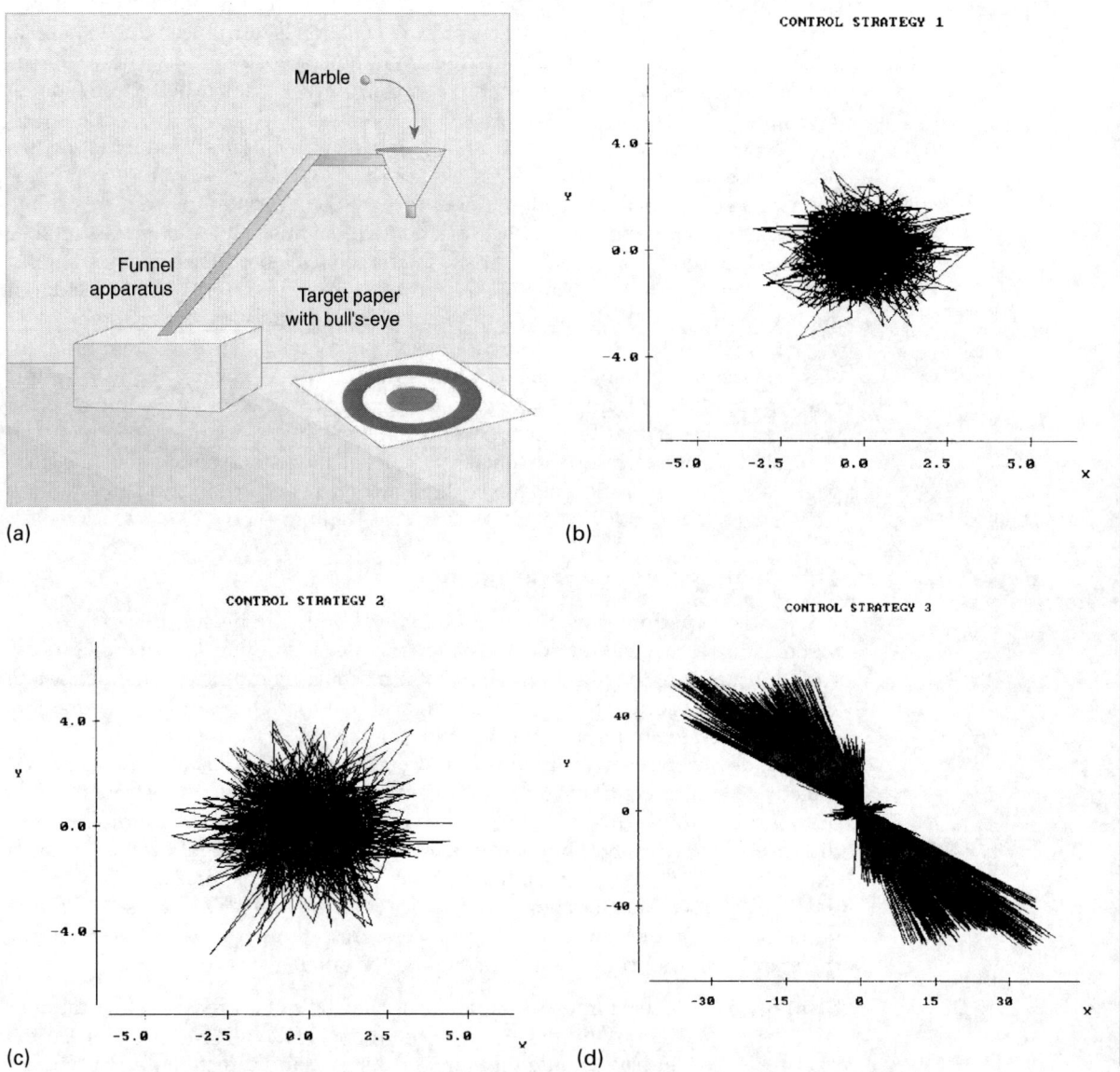

Strategy 2. Measure the distance from the marble's resting place to the bull's-eye.
Move the funnel an equal distance, but in the opposite direction. This
will be called the "error relative to the previous position" strategy.

Strategy 3. Measure the distance from the marble's resting place to the bull's-eye.
Move the funnel this distance, in the opposite direction, starting at
the bull's-eye. This procedure could be called the "error relative to
the bull's-eye" strategy.

A sequence of MINITAB commands was used to simulate this funnel experiment 1000 times; the results are given in Figure 9.5.* The bull's-eye is in the center of each graph, at the point $X = 0$, $Y = 0$. Control strategy 1 is where we do not react to chance variation and the funnel is not moved (no machine adjustments are made in an attempt to fix the process). Figure 9.5*b* is an illustration of this strategy, with, as expected, a certain amount of random variation. Parts *c* and *d* represent the outcome of strategies 2 and 3, respectively. The result of strategy 2 is stable but contains more variation than the "leave it alone" strategy (strategy 1)—in fact, it can be shown that the variation within this process is *twice* that in part *b*. The error relative to the bull's-eye strategy (strategy 3) used in part *d* is unstable, contains a great deal of variation, and resembles a bow tie. The error associated with this strategy will eventually wander off to infinity.

The point of the funnel experiment is to make clear that a machine operator can only be held accountable for what is under his or her control. If the goal is to reduce process variation, then we can *improve the process* by building a better funnel or by moving the funnel closer to the target. It is management's responsibility to examine the process carefully and to provide resources and training for making process improvements. As Deming, and others, have said, "Attack the system, not the employee."

Control Charts

In a sense, **control charts** form the foundation of the inspection side of Statistical Process Control. These charts were first introduced by W. A. Shewhart at Bell Telephone Laboratories in 1924. Essentially, control charts allow you to monitor a process (usually, but not necessarily, a manufacturing process) to determine if the process is **in control** or **out of control.** A process is *in control* if the observed variation is due to inherent or natural variability. This variability is the cumulative effect of many small, essentially uncontrollable, causes. A process is *out of control* if a relatively large variation is introduced that can be traced to an *assignable cause.* Such causes are generally the result of an improperly adjusted machine, an operator error, or defective raw material.

It is important to note that a process may be in control yet entirely unsatisfactory. For example, your process of producing 10-pound bags of dog food might be perfectly in control, with little variation, yet a closer look might reveal that the process appears to be centered at 8.7 pounds, which would certainly be unacceptable to dog owners who check the weight of the bags.

During the in-control state, we say that the variation is due to **chance cause.** Such variation can be reduced by careful analysis of the process, but it can never be completely eliminated. On the other hand, variation during an out-of-control state is due to one or more **assignable causes.** Such causes are avoidable and cannot be overlooked.

The purpose of the control chart is to detect the presence of an out-of-control state, during which a large portion of the process output will not be conforming to requirements. If an assignable cause can be determined, corrective action is taken and an attempt is made to return the process to an in-control state. As Figure 9.5 illustrates, while a process is believed to be in control it should not be

---

*This sequence of MINITAB commands (a MINITAB macro) is in the MINITAB Macros folder in the textbook CD. If the file has been copied into say, C:\Temp, then type EXECUTE "C:\Temp\funnel" while in MINITAB. The result will be modified versions of Figure 9.5*b, c,* and *d.* This macro is a revised version of the one in the *MINITAB Users' Group Newsletter,* 14, October 1991.

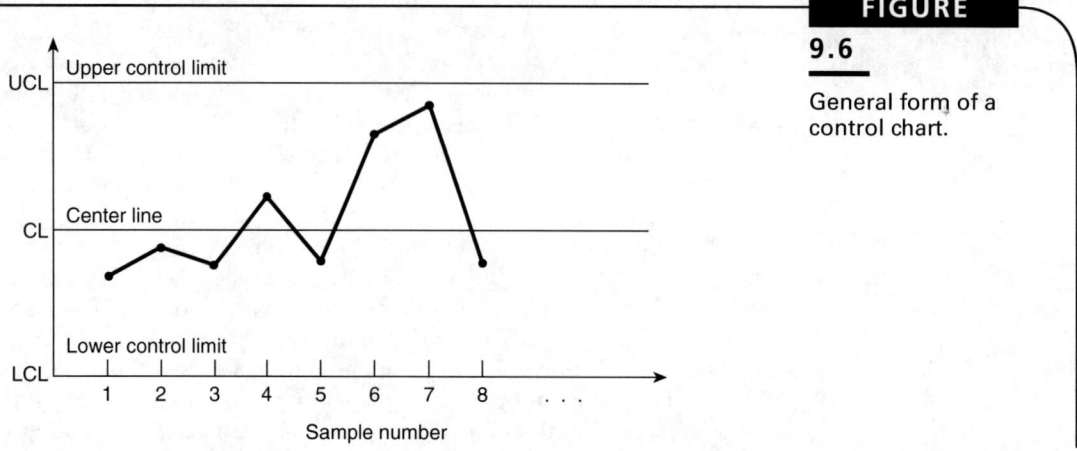

FIGURE

9.6

General form of a
control chart.

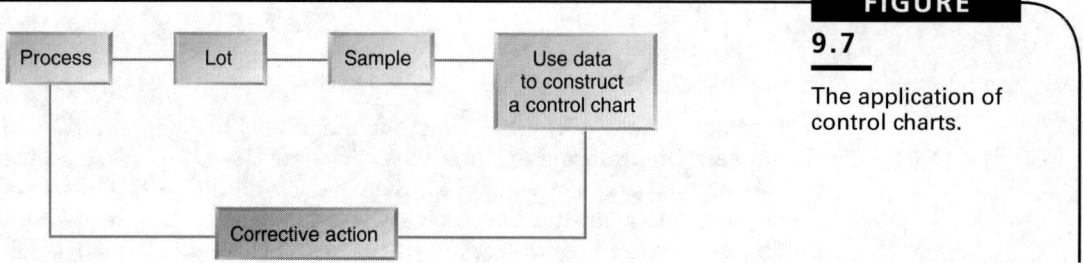

FIGURE

9.7

The application of
control charts.

adjusted or tampered with, since such well-meaning adjustments generally result in an *increase* in process variation.

The general form of a control chart is shown in Figure 9.6. The chart contains a **center line (CL),** which represents the average value of the quality characteristic corresponding to the in-control state. The other two horizontal lines are the *control limits;* the **upper control limit** (UCL) and the **lower control limit** (LCL) are the same distance from the center line. *These limits are chosen so that if the process is in control, nearly all the plotted points will be between the two control limits.* For example, a plotted point might represent the average weight of a sample of five filled coffee cans. As long as the plotted averages fall within the control limits, the process is determined to be in control, with only chance variation present. The process of using a control chart to monitor and improve process quality is shown in Figure 9.7.

When measuring a *quality characteristic* such as the weight of a filled coffee can, the resulting data are referred to as **variables data.** Conversely, when counting the number of solder defects in the coffee can, such data are referred to as **attribute data.** Chapter 1 referred to variables data as *continuous* data and to attribute data as *discrete* data. The type of control chart that is needed for a particular situation depends on what quality characteristic is being measured and what type of data is being collected. For the filled weight of the coffee cans, we would undoubtedly be interested in the average weight of each sample of five cans and would construct a control chart referred to as an $\bar{X}$ **chart** ($\bar{X}$ is read as "X bar"). We would also want to maintain a control chart for the *variation* within each sample. The control chart to use for this situation would be an **R chart,** where R represents the sample range.

Because control charts are typically used to monitor *small* samples, the sample range is generally used to measure sample variation. The range is easier to calculate than is the sample standard deviation (s), and provides nearly as much information about the sample variation for sample sizes under 10. For sample sizes of 10 or more, the sample standard deviation should be used to measure sample variation, producing $\bar{X}$ and s charts. For a more thorough discussion of these charts, refer to the book by D. C. Montgomery in the list of Further Reading later in the chapter.

One cautionary note regarding the use of control charts: Most processes cannot be expected to remain stable over an extended period of time. A change in raw materials, tooling, or work shifts or any other major change in process operating conditions can change the process distribution. New control limits should be determined if the control chart is to retain its effectiveness.

9.6
CONTROL CHARTS FOR VARIABLES DATA: THE $\bar{X}$ AND R CHARTS

Variables data are obtained by observing a continuous variable, which has *no gaps* in the values it can have, over the range of possible values. A corresponding control chart could be constructed for controlling and analyzing a process whose quality characteristic is a continuous variable, such as weight, length, or concentration.

The first step is to obtain data for construction of the control chart. A number of preliminary samples (say, *m* of these) is obtained, each of size *n*, when the process is thought to be in control. Typically, *m* ranges from 20 to 25, and the sample size, *n*, is 4, 5, or 6. Define $\bar{X}_1, \bar{X}_2, \ldots, \bar{X}_m$ to be the *m* sample averages. Also define $R_1, R_2, \ldots, R_m$ to be the *m* sample ranges.

For example, suppose the quality characteristic is the weight of a filled coffee can produced by International Food Products. The first three samples are (data in ounces):

Sample	Data	$\bar{X}$	R
1	19.8, 20.1, 20.2, 19.9, 20.0	20.00	20.2 − 19.8 = .4
2	20.3, 19.9, 19.8, 19.8, 20.1	19.98	20.3 − 19.8 = .5
3	20.0, 19.7, 20.2, 19.8, 19.7	19.88	20.2 − 19.7 = .5

For these samples, $\bar{X}_1 = 20.00$, $\bar{X}_2 = 19.98$, $\bar{X}_3 = 19.88$, $R_1 = .4$, $R_2 = .5$, and $R_3 = .5$. These results and those for the next 17 samples are shown in Table 9.2.

In the quality-control context, the population consists of the *process* values. Thus we speak of the process mean, the process standard deviation, and so on. The best estimator of μ, the process mean, is

$$\bar{\bar{X}} = \frac{\bar{X}_1 + \bar{X}_2 + \cdots + \bar{X}_m}{m}$$

9.1

TABLE

9.2

Preliminary sample results.

Sample	1	2	3	4	5	6	7	8	9	10
$\bar{X}$	20.00	19.98	19.88	19.94	20.04	20.06	20.02	19.82	20.02	20.06
R	.4	.5	.5	.4	.6	.3	.4	.4	.5	.7
Sample	11	12	13	14	15	16	17	18	19	20
$\bar{X}$	19.94	19.86	19.90	20.12	19.92	20.04	20.06	19.98	19.88	20.08
R	.4	.3	.2	.5	.5	.4	.3	.5	.6	.4

For our coffee-can filling example, the process consists of taking empty coffee cans and filling them with a prescribed amount of coffee. The quality characteristic is the filled weight of the can. The estimate of the process average is

$$\bar{\bar{X}} = \frac{20.00 + 19.98 + \cdots + 20.08}{20}$$

$$= \frac{399.60}{20} = 19.98 \text{ ounces}$$

We also need an estimate of the process standard deviation (σ). As mentioned earlier, there is more than one way to estimate this parameter, but because the sample sizes are small (under 10), the best way to proceed is to use the sample ranges (R) and carry out the following steps:

1. Determine the average of the m values of R. Call this $\bar{R}$.

2. Select the value of d_2 from Table 9.3 using the corresponding sample size, n.

3. Estimate σ using

$$\hat{\sigma} = \frac{\bar{R}}{d_2}$$

9.2

For the coffee-can illustration,

$$\bar{R} = \frac{.4 + .5 + \cdots + .4}{20}$$

$$= \frac{8.8}{20} = .44$$

Using Table 9.3, the estimate of the process standard deviation is

$$\hat{\sigma} = \frac{\bar{R}}{d_2} = \frac{.44}{2.326} = .189 \text{ ounce}$$

In Chapter 7, a procedure was outlined for constructing a confidence interval for the population mean using the results of a *single* sample. When constructing a control chart for the process average, a similar procedure is followed using the

TABLE

9.3

Factors for constructing on R chart.

n	d_2	d_3	D_3	D_4
2	1.128	.853	0	3.267
3	1.693	.888	0	2.574
4	2.059	.880	0	2.282
5	2.326	.864	0	2.114
6	2.534	.848	0	2.004
7	2.704	.833	.076	1.924
8	2.847	.820	.136	1.864
9	2.970	.808	.184	1.816
10	3.078	.797	.223	1.777

results of *multiple* samples (*m* of them). The center line and control limits are defined below:

$$\text{UCL} = \overline{\overline{X}} + 3\frac{\hat{\sigma}}{\sqrt{n}} = \overline{\overline{X}} + 3\frac{(\overline{R}/d_2)}{\sqrt{n}}$$

$$\text{Center Line} = \overline{\overline{X}}$$

$$\text{LCL} = \overline{\overline{X}} - 3\frac{\hat{\sigma}}{\sqrt{n}} = \overline{\overline{X}} - 3\frac{(\overline{R}/d_2)}{\sqrt{n}}$$

Notice that the control limits take on the appearance of a confidence interval where the value 3 replaces the value previously obtained from the standard normal (Z) table or the *t* table. The resulting control limits are referred to as the **three-sigma control limits.** It should be mentioned that the value 3 can be changed to fit the quality requirements of the process. Essentially, using this value produces control limits that will be exceeded approximately 27 times in 10,000 (.0027) if the process average and variation remain stable. Assuming a normal (or nearly normal) process, the value .0027 is obtained by finding the combined tail area under a standard normal curve outside ±3 (see Figure 9.8). In Chapter 7, a confidence interval for a population mean was constructed using a single sample. Control limits in a control chart are derived using many small samples instead of a single larger sample. Tying these two topics together, it may be helpful for you to view an $\overline{X}$ chart as a 99.7% confidence interval for the population mean derived using many small samples. Here, 99.7% is $(1 - .0027) \times 100\%$, where .0027 is the probability of a sample mean lying outside the control limits if the process is on target (centered correctly) and remains stable.

For the coffee-can illustration, $\overline{\overline{X}} = 19.98$ and $\hat{\sigma} = .189$, so the control limits would be

$$\text{UCL} = 19.98 + 3\frac{.189}{\sqrt{5}} = 19.98 + .25 = 20.23$$

$$\text{Center Line} = 19.98$$

$$\text{LCL} = 19.98 - 3\frac{.189}{\sqrt{5}} = 19.98 - .25 = 19.73$$

The control chart is shown in Figure 9.9. Notice that all 20 of the sample means are within the control limits, indicating that the control chart is ready for

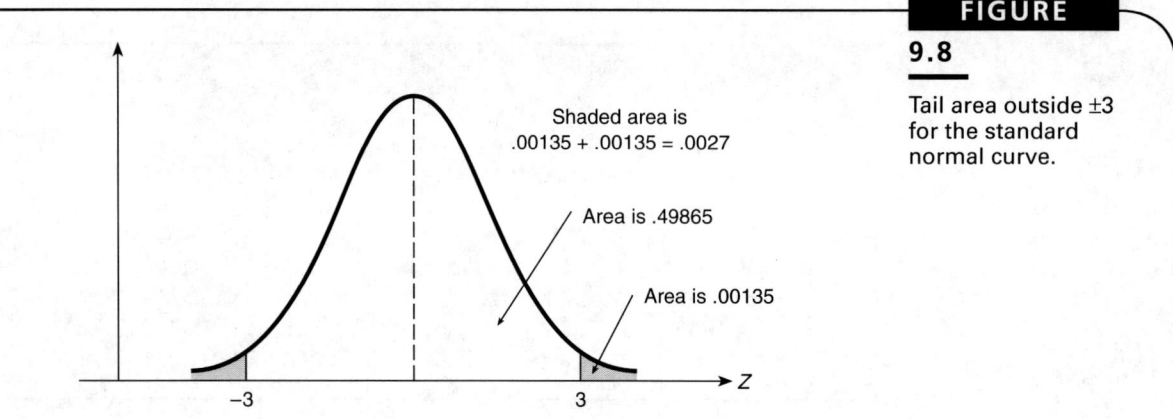

FIGURE

9.8

Tail area outside ±3 for the standard normal curve.

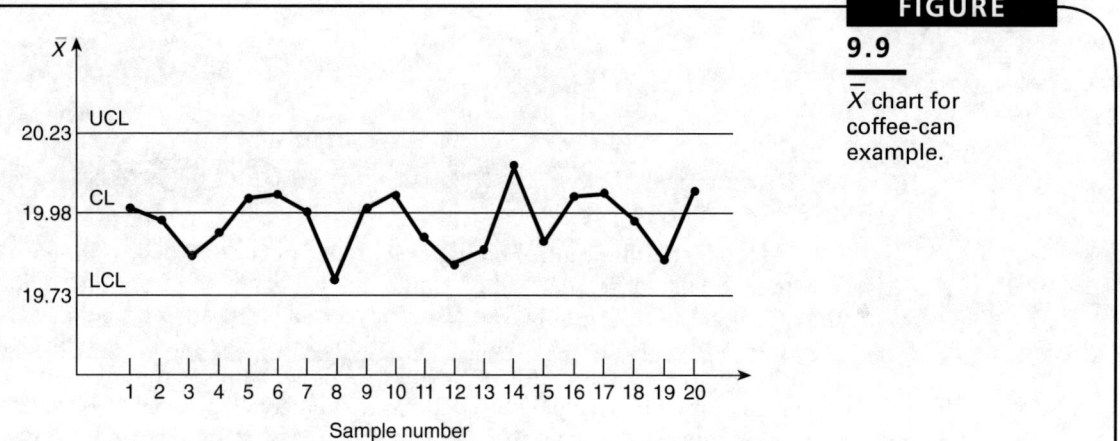

FIGURE

9.9

$\overline{X}$ chart for coffee-can example.

use. If one or more of the sample means falls outside the control limits, a search should be made to determine whether there is an assignable cause behind these extreme sample values. If such a cause is found, this sample should be removed and the control limits (including the center line) should be rederived.

The R Chart

To monitor the process variability, we use an R chart to plot values of the sample range, R. As we do with the $\overline{X}$ chart, we conclude that the sample *variability* is out of control when a sample range falls outside the control limits of the R chart. If the sample range falls within the control limits, the process variation is in control, that is, stable. Note that it is possible for a sample range to be out of control while the corresponding sample mean ($\overline{X}$) is well in control; that is, a sample can contain extreme variation but be centered properly.

The center line for the R chart is the average ($\overline{R}$) of the m ranges. For the summary data in Table 9.2, we have already determined that $\overline{R} = .44$. The three-sigma control limits are derived by again adding and subtracting three times the estimated standard deviation of $\overline{R}$, say, $s_{\overline{R}}$. The value of $s_{\overline{R}}$ can be derived using

$$s_{\overline{R}} = \overline{R}\left(\frac{d_3}{d_2}\right)$$

9.4

where the values of d_2 and d_3 are provided in Table QI.3.

The control limits for the R chart are

$$\text{UCL} = \overline{R} + 3s_{\overline{R}} = \overline{R} + 3\overline{R}\left(\frac{d_3}{d_2}\right) = \left(1 + 3\frac{d_3}{d_2}\right)\overline{R}$$

$$\text{LCL} = \overline{R} - 3s_{\overline{R}} = \overline{R} - 3\overline{R}\left(\frac{d_3}{d_2}\right) = \left(1 - 3\frac{d_3}{d_2}\right)\overline{R}$$

By defining

$$D_3 = 1 - 3\frac{d_3}{d_2} \quad \text{and} \quad D_4 = 1 + 3\frac{d_3}{d_2}$$

9.5

the R chart can be defined using

$$\text{UCL} = D_4\overline{R}$$
$$\text{Center line} = \overline{R}$$
$$\text{LCL} = D_3\overline{R}$$

9.6

Comments

1. Values of D_3 and D_4 are provided in Table 9.3.

2. Because a sample range is never negative, D_3 is defined to be zero whenever the expression in equation (9.5) is negative, that is, for $n = 2, 3, 4, 5,$ and 6.

For our previous example, in which the quality characteristic is the filled weight of a coffee can, the limits for the R chart are easily found:

$$\text{UCL} = (2.114)(.44) = .93$$
$$\text{Center line} = .44$$
$$\text{LCL} = 0$$

This R chart is shown in Figure 9.10. Note that all the sample ranges appear to be in control, so the R chart is ready for use. If future range values fall within these limits, we conclude that the process variation is in control. Our procedure is the same as for the $\overline{X}$ chart: If any of the values in Figure 9.10 had fallen outside the control limits, a search would have been made for an assignable cause (or causes) for these sample points. Samples for which such a cause is found should be removed and the R chart derived again.

FIGURE

9.10

R chart for the coffee-can example.

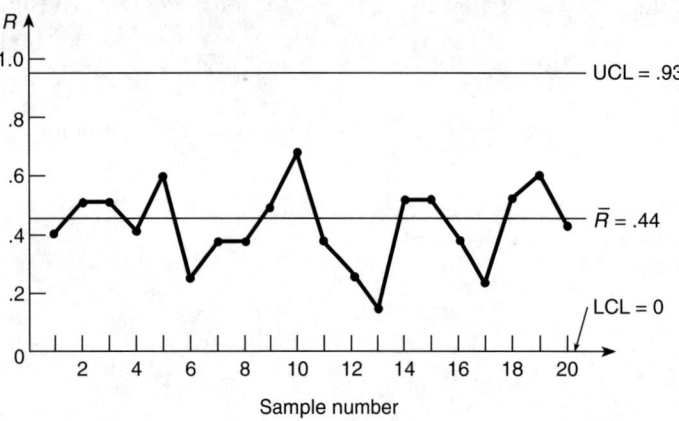

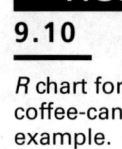

Following the construction of the control charts using the data in Table 9.2 (shown in Figures 9.9 and 9.10), samples of five filled coffee cans were obtained every half hour over a three-hour period. The data for these samples are as follows (in ounces).

Sample	Data
1	19.9, 19.7, 19.9, 20.2, 20.3
2	20.1, 20.3, 19.6, 19.8, 19.5
3	19.9, 20.1, 20.3, 19.9, 19.9
4	20.1, 19.9, 20.0, 20.1, 20.3
5	20.0, 19.5, 19.5, 20.1, 20.2
6	19.7, 19.8, 20.3, 19.7, 20.1

Using the proper control charts, determine whether the process location and variability are in control during this three-hour period.

Solution

The first step is to find the sample averages and ranges.

Sample	1	2	3	4	5	6
$\overline{X}$	20.00	19.86	20.02	20.08	19.86	19.92
R	.6	.8	.4	.4	.7	.6

Each sample mean is plotted in the $\overline{X}$ chart and each sample range in the R chart. Both charts are shown in Figure 9.11. Because all points in the two charts are within the control limits, we conclude that the process is in control (stable) and that no adjustments to the process are necessary.

Steps for Making $\overline{X}$ and R Charts

1. Collect m samples of data, each of size n (in our first example, $m = 20$ samples of $n = 5$ observations each).

2. Compute the average of each subgroup ($\overline{X}_1, \overline{X}_2, \overline{X}_3, \ldots, \overline{X}_m$).

3. Compute the range for each subgroup ($R_1, R_2, R_3, \ldots, R_m$).

FIGURE

9.11

Control charts for
Example 9.1.

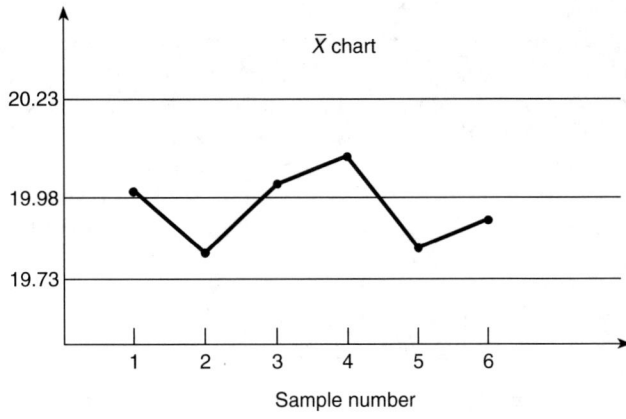

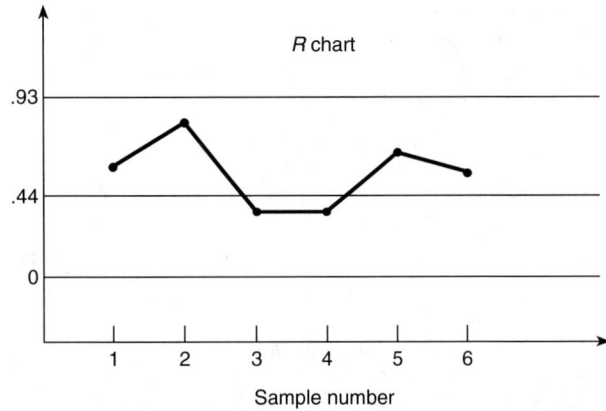

4. Find the overall mean, $\overline{\overline{X}}$, where $\overline{\overline{X}}$ is the average of the m values of $\overline{X}$.

5. Find the average range, $\overline{R}$, where $\overline{R}$ is the average of the m values of R.

6. To estimate σ (say, $\hat{\sigma}$), compute $\overline{R}/d_2$, where d_2 can be found using Table 9.3.

7. Compute the 3-sigma control limits for the $\overline{X}$ control chart:

$$\text{UCL} = \overline{\overline{X}} + 3\frac{\hat{\sigma}}{\sqrt{n}}$$

$$\text{CL} = \overline{\overline{X}}$$

$$\text{LCL} = \overline{\overline{X}} - 3\frac{\hat{\sigma}}{\sqrt{n}}$$

8. Compute the 3-sigma control limits for the R control chart.

$$\text{UCL} = D_4\overline{R} \qquad \text{(using Table 9.3)}$$
$$\text{CL} = \overline{R}$$
$$\text{LCL} = D_3\overline{R} \qquad \text{(using Table 9.3)}$$

9. Construct the control charts by plotting the $\overline{X}$ and R points for each subgroup on the same vertical line.

Pattern Analysis for $\overline{X}$ Charts

So far, our discussion of control charts has focused on determining out-of-control conditions by identifying a point beyond the three-sigma control limits on the $\overline{X}$ or R charts. For $\overline{X}$ charts, a closer look at the pattern of the control chart points (all of which may be within the control limits) may also reveal a process that is out of control and requiring attention. For example, six points in a row, all increasing or decreasing, indicates an out-of-control process, possibly due to a gradual wearing down of a machine part or due to operator fatigue. While the process may be not outside the control limits, it can be improved by identifying and eliminating this source of variation (an assignable cause).

Pattern analysis is concerned with recognizing systematic or nonrandom patterns in an $\overline{X}$ control chart and identifying the source of such process variation. To help us detect nonrandom patterns in $\overline{X}$ charts, we divide each chart into zones:

- *Zone A* contains the area between the two- and the three-sigma limits, both above and below the center line.
- *Zone B* contains the area between the one- and the two-sigma limits, both above and below the center line.
- *Zone C* contains the area between the center line and the one-sigma limit, both above and below the center line.

Specific patterns indicating nonrandom variation can be summarized as follows:*

Pattern	Description
1	One point beyond zone A
2	Nine points in a row in zone C or beyond, all on one side of the center line
3	Six points in a row, all increasing or all decreasing
4	Fourteen points in a row, alternating up and down
5	Two out of three points in a row in zone A or beyond
6	Four out of five points in a row in zone B or beyond (on one side of center line)
7	Fifteen points in a row in zones C (above or below center line)
8	Eight points in a row beyond zones C (above or below center line)

These patterns are illustrated in Figure 9.12, where A, B, and C refer to zones A, B, and C. Note that pattern 1 illustrates what we have, up to this point, identified as an out-of-control state.

We will not attempt in this discussion to interpret the causes behind these nonrandom patterns; rather, these patterns should point out to you that *there is more to control chart inspection than looking for points outside the control limits.* The ability to interpret a particular pattern in terms of assignable causes requires a great deal of experience and knowledge of the process. For more information on pattern interpretation, see the textbook by Montgomery listed in the Further Reading section at the end of this chapter.

MINITAB and Excel KPK Data Analysis will search for the eight patterns. The instructions for carrying out this analysis are contained in the end-of-chapter appendix. If either package does detect a pattern, the sample at which the pattern is completed is flagged by placement of a value (1 for pattern 1, 2 for pattern 2, and so forth) directly above or below the plotted point.

---

*There is no general agreement about the set of nonrandom patterns. This set is used by MINITAB and the Excel macros within KPK Data Analysis.

FIGURE

9.12

Eight patterns requiring a search for assignable causes due to nonrandom variation. The dotted lines indicate the nonrandom pattern.

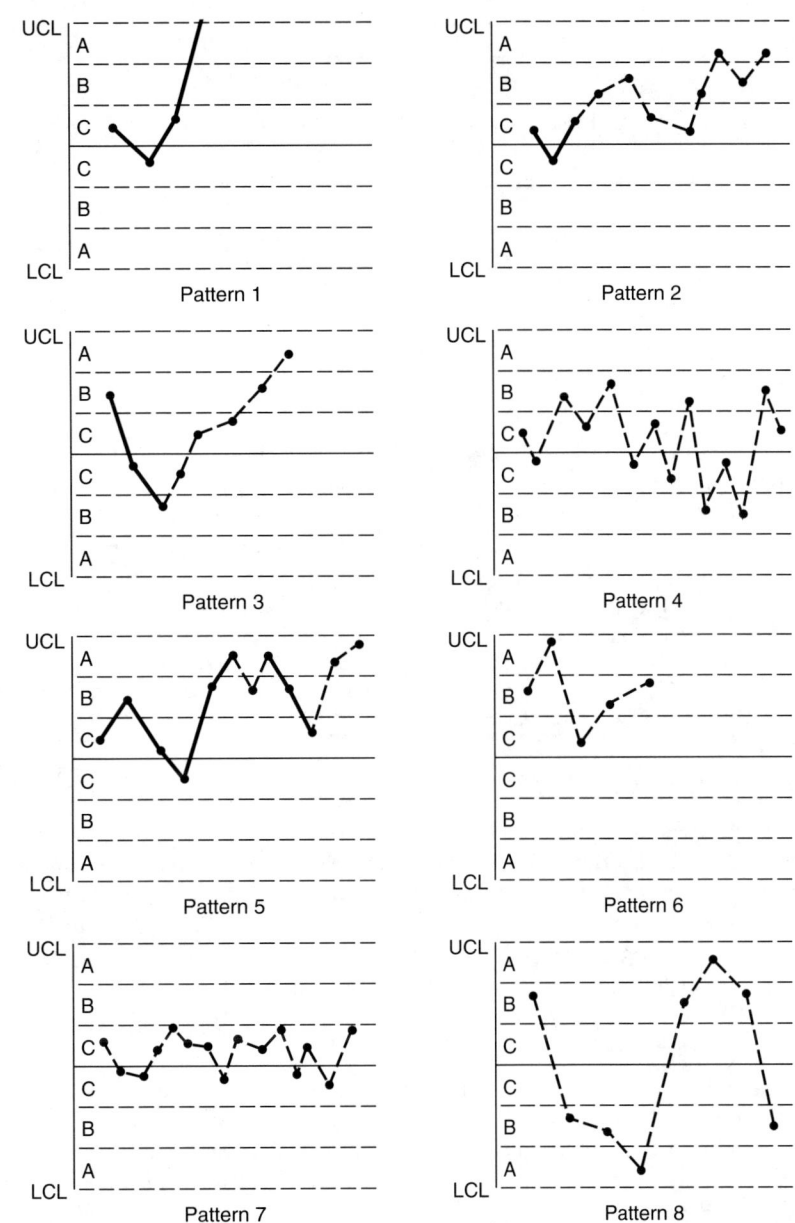

Suppose that Home Security Protection is a company that installs and maintains home security systems. It is interested in monitoring the number of calls that come into its office as a result of a home system triggering an alarm because of an intruder or false alarm. The company obtains a sample of 50 consecutive days and records the number of calls between midnight and 6 A.M., 6 A.M. and noon, noon and 6 P.M., and 6 P.M. and midnight—a total of four observations for each of the

FIGURE

9.13

MINITAB X̄ chart
with zones A, B,
and C, containing
three nonrandom
patterns.

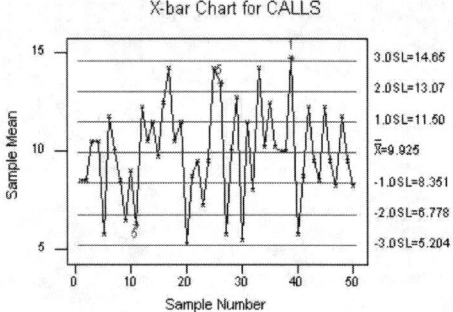

X-bar Chart for CALLS

50 days. The resulting X̄ chart is shown in Figure 9.13, where several nonrandom patterns are detected. The glaring pattern occurs in sample 39, where the plotted mean lies above the upper control limit (pattern 1). Two instances of pattern 5 (two out of three points in a row in zone A or beyond) are observed in samples 9, 10, 11 and in samples 24, 25, 26. Home Security Protection clearly has a process that is not in control, and it should take a closer look at what assignable causes are contributing to this excessive variation.

Statistical Software Application Use DATA9-2

Software-Generated X̄ and R Charts

The control charts in Figures 9.9 and 9.10 were derived for the 20-ounce cans of ground coffee produced by International Food Products. Management decided to repeat this procedure on their 50-ounce coffee cans, sold mostly to restaurants and hospitals. Twenty samples of five cans each were obtained every 30 minutes, and the resulting 100 observations are contained in a single column. Analyze these data by first constructing an R chart and, if in control, then constructing the X̄ chart. Are these control charts ready for use?

Solution

Excel does not have the capability of constructing control charts using its built-in graphical tools, but they are easily constructed using the KPK Data Analysis Excel macros. To obtain the R chart and X̄ chart, click on **KPK Data Analysis ➤ Quantitative Data Charts/Tables ➤ Control Charts.** Enter "5" in the **Sample Size** box. By selecting the **R Chart** option, you will obtain the output in B1:C5 in Figure 9.14 along with the R chart on a separate sheet. When selecting the **X Bar Chart option,** you will obtain the output in E1:G16 and the X̄ chart on another sheet.

The R chart in Figure 9.15 was generated using SPSS by clicking on **Graphs ➤ Control ➤ X-Bar, R, s.** Click on **Define** and select **X-Bar and range** in the **Charts** frame. With SPSS, you will need to build a column containing the sample number (explained in the end-of-chapter appendix). All 20 of the sample ranges lie between the upper control limit of 1.918 and the (inactive) lower control limit of zero. From a variability standpoint, this process is in control. In general, if the R chart signals an out-of-control process, there is no point in continuing and attempting to interpret the corresponding X̄ chart.

9.14

Excel spreadsheet using KPK Data Analysis for Example 9.2.

	A	B	C	D	E	F	G
1	49.89	**R Chart**			**X-Bar Chart**		
2	50.13	Limit	Value		Limit	Value	
3	49.73	UCL	1.917724		UCL	50.542959	
4	50.77	CL	0.907000		CL	50.019800	
5	49.26	LCL	0.000000		LCL	49.496641	
6	49.85						
7	50.39					**Pattern Analysis**	
8	50.09				Test	Result	Data Points
9	50.35				1	Passed	
10	50.49				2	Passed	
11	51.23				3	Passed	
12	50.41				4	Passed	
13	50.06				5	Passed	
14	49.96				6	Passed	
15	50.29				7	Passed	
16	50.06				8	Passed	
17	50.40						

9.15

R Chart using SPSS for Example 9.2.

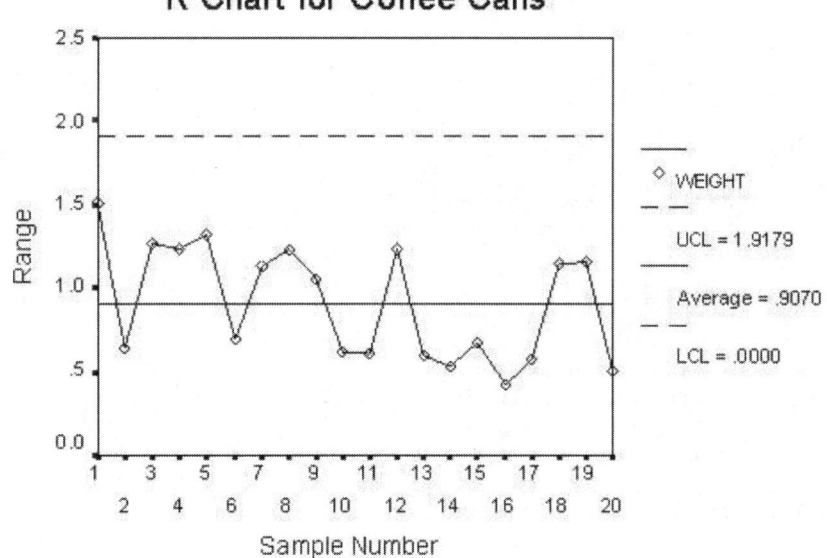

R Chart for Coffee Cans

The MINITAB $\overline{X}$ chart in Figure 9.16 was obtained by clicking on **Stat ➤ Control Charts ➤ Xbar.** Enter "5" in the **Subgroup size** box and click on **Tests** to have MINITAB search for the eight patterns in Figure 9.12. None of the sample means exceed the upper control limit of 50.54 or are below the lower control limit of

FIGURE

9.16

$\bar{X}$ Chart using MINITAB for Example 9.2.

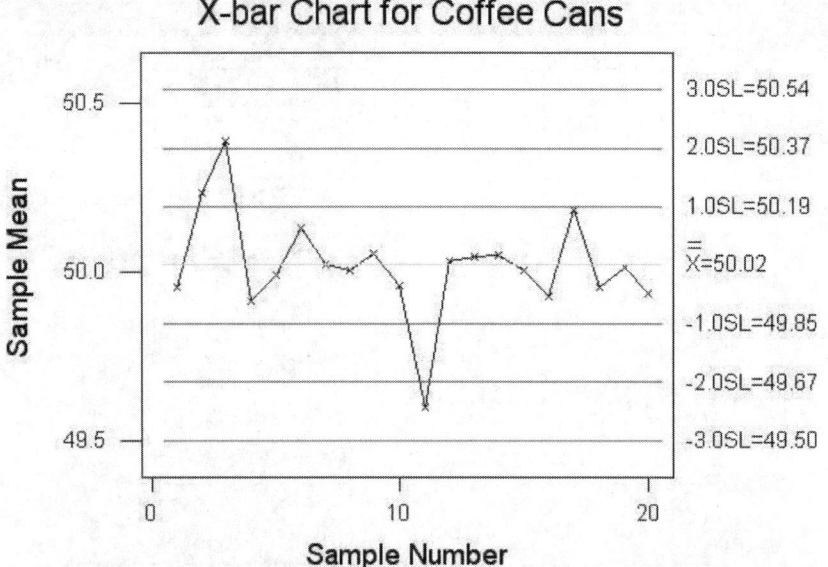

X-bar Chart for Coffee Cans

49.50. According to the Excel 5 [output] in Figure 9.14 and the MINITAB $\bar{X}$ chart in Figure 9.16, there are no nonrandom patterns. Consequently, the R chart and $\bar{X}$ chart for this process are ready to use.

X Exercises 9.20–9.32

Understanding the Mechanics

9.20 Thirty samples of size 5 are drawn from a process. The mean of the sample means for the batches of size 5 is equal to 130 and the mean of the sample ranges is equal to 10.

    a. Find the center line and control limits for the $\bar{X}$ chart.

    b. Find the boundaries for the A, B, and C zones of the $\bar{X}$ chart.

    c. Find the center line and control limits for the R chart.

    d. Would the process be in control for the following set of future sample means?

| 125.7 | 126.5 | 128.0 | 129.7 | 132.3 | 134.5 |

9.21 Construct an $\bar{X}$ and R chart for the following data, assuming a sample size of 5.

Sample Number	Sample Mean	Sample Range
1	380	27
2	420	28
3	435	31
4	425	42
5	422	33
6	433	36
7	430	18
8	445	42
9	430	38
10	409	38
11	403	33
12	418	28
13	400	22
14	401	25
15	409	35
16	450	70

Sample Number	Sample Mean	Sample Range
17	429	31
18	490	85
19	412	21
20	500	95

9.22 Samples of ve cups of beer are taken at ve-hour intervals from various depths in the brew kettle, and the alcohol content, as a percentage of volume, is measured. The following table relates the sample means and ranges for the last 10 samples.

Sample	Mean	Range	Sample	Mean	Range
1	2.8	0.9	6	3.3	0.2
2	4.2	0.2	7	2.9	0.9
3	3.7	0.6	8	2.7	0.3
4	3.9	1.1	9	3.4	0.5
5	2.6	0.5	10	2.8	1.0

a. Construct an R chart that can be used to control the alcohol content of the beer.

b. Construct an $\overline{X}$ chart that can be used to control the alcohol content of the beer.

c. Perform a pattern analysis of the $\overline{X}$ chart from part b by checking for nonrandom patterns.

9.23 The range of eight samples of the time in minutes for a compound to harden are collected. Each sample consists of 10 time measurements. Construct and interpret an R chart using the following ranges: 12.6 12.0 13.9 16.2 14.2 14.4 9.9 12.1 2.3. 8.3.

Applying the New Concepts

9.24 Concerned with reducing costs, a delivery manager uses control charts for monitoring gas mileage of delivery eet vehicles. Each week the manager randomly selects mileage and fuel records for ve vehicles. The eet of delivery vehicles consists of identical make and model trucks. Data for 25 weeks follow:

Week	Miles per Gallon
1	12.3, 13.1, 10.2, 11.6, 12.2
2	9.3, 10.5, 13.1, 12.2, 10.3
3	11.3, 12.6, 9.9, 10.6, 11.4
4	12.0, 11.3, 10.2, 10.6, 11.6
5	11.2, 12.3, 10.9, 11.5, 11.8
6	13.1, 12.2, 11.8, 11.2, 9.4
7	11.2, 11.7, 10.8, 10.1, 12.4
8	12.6, 11.3, 10.4, 11.7, 13.2
9	11.5, 12.6, 9.7, 10.5, 10.7
10	13.1, 12.7, 11.6, 12.3, 12.8
11	12.3, 11.2, 11.6, 13.4, 9.4
12	11.3, 12.6, 9.8, 10.7, 11.1
13	10.4, 11.3, 12.3, 12.6, 11.9
14	12.4, 13.5, 10.8, 11.6, 10.7
15	13.1, 12.0, 10.9, 11.8, 11.1
16	11.5, 11.3, 12.2, 10.9, 11.8
17	11.3, 12.6, 12.1, 10.9, 11.8
18	12.4, 10.7, 9.6, 13.6, 11.1
19	11.5, 12.3, 12.2, 11.8, 11.6
20	11.3, 10.8, 11.4, 12.0, 11.9
21	12.6, 10.2, 13.5, 12.1, 12.8
22	10.9, 11.4, 10.5, 13.2, 12.7
23	13.2, 12.8, 11.9, 12.7, 13.1
24	9.4, 11.6, 12.8, 13.0, 12.3
25	12.2, 11.5, 12.9, 10.6, 10.1

a. Construct an R chart for gasoline mileage.

b. Construct an $\overline{X}$ chart for gasoline mileage.

c. Comment on any nonrandom patterns in the $\overline{X}$ chart.

9.25 A drill press operator selects samples of eight bronze bushings and measures and records the internal diameter of the bushings at 15-minute intervals for the rst two hours of her shift. The following are the sample ranges of the internal diameter measurements:

Sample	Range (in.)	Sample	Range (in.)
1	.016	5	.007
2	.014	6	.010
3	.012	7	.012
4	.010	8	.013

a. Construct an R chart using these data.

b. What are your observations concerning the pattern of these data?

9.26 The drill press operator in Exercise 9.25 continues to sample eight bushings for the next two hours of her shift and gathers the following internal diameter sample ranges:

Sample	Range (in.)	Sample	Range (in.)
1	.013	5	.019
2	.015	6	.021
3	.015	7	.022
4	.018	8	.023

a. What pattern has emerged during the last two hours of operation?

b. What are the likely consequences if nothing is done to correct the process?

c. What are some possible causes for the new pattern of variation?

Using the Computer

9.27 [DATA SET EX9-27] Variable description:

Day: Days are numbered 1 through 20

8AM: Percentage of resin at 8 A.M.

10AM: Percentage of resin at 10 A.M.

2PM: Percentage of resin at 2 P.M.

4PM: Percentage of resin at 4 P.M.

ArtLine Inc., sells everything from lawn amingos to patio furniture and many decorative items for deck support posts. The company manufactures a material named "polystone," a resin and crushed rock combination to create decorative squirrels and birds. Suppose that the amount of resin in the "polystone" must not vary too much or the decorative items will either not be durable or will not have a decorative image. The quality manager uses control charts that are constructed from four daily samples of polystone to measure the percentage of resin: 8 A.M., 10 A.M., 2 P.M., and 4 P.M. Construct an appropriate chart using the four daily measurements as one sample. Interpret the chart. (Note that the data must be reformatted into one column to use the control chart option in the KPK macros.)

(Source: "Fencing Lessons," The Washington Post, July 22, 2004, p. H03.)

9.28 Repeat Exercise 9.27 using the two morning gures for each day as the sample. Also, construct another control chart using the two afternoon gures as the sample. Compare and interpret these two charts.

9.29 [DATA SET EX9-29] Variable description:

DelivTimes: Time in minutes that it takes to deliver a pizza

The owner of Pizza New York has built a solid business by promising timely and consistent home delivery service. She maintains a control chart procedure for monitoring these delivery times and searches for an assignable cause whenever an out-of-control condition appears. The data recorded in the variable DelivTimes are the delivery times for 200 trips over 50 randomly selected days, with four trips observed on each day. Use appropriate control charts to determine if this process is out of control.

9.30 [DATA SET EX9-30] Variable description:

BoltLen: Length of a bolt produced for a military aircraft

A quality engineer is interested in the precision of the production of bolts for a tactical military aircraft. A special computerized instrument is used to measure the exact length of the bolts. Forty samples of size 10 each are randomly selected, and the length is recorded in centimeters. The ideal length is 9 centimeters.
   a. Construct an $\bar{X}$ chart and an R chart.
   b. What is the rst indication (if any) of the process being out of control?

9.31 [DATA SET EX9-31] Variable description:

BatteryLife: Life of a 12-volt battery in hours from accelerated life testing

The production plant manager has used control charts to monitor the quality of 12-volt batteries manufactured at the plant. A sample of three 12-volt batteries is selected every hour. These batteries are subjected to an accelerated life testing procedure. The life of each of the 120 samples of batteries of size 3 is recorded in BatteryLife. Construct the necessary charts to determine if you have any reservations about this process based on these charts.

9.32 Assume that a manufacturing process produces axle shafts having a mean diameter of 3.5 inches and a standard deviation of .01 inches. If the axle diameter from this process is a normally distributed random variable and 20 samples of 10 axles are periodically checked, estimate the upper and lower process control limits. Now use Excel's random number generator to produce 20 samples of 10 axles from a normal distribution having a mean of 3.5 and a standard deviation equal to .01. Construct an $\bar{X}$ chart for these observations and compare the control limits to the ones you estimated above.

9.7

CONTROL CHARTS FOR ATTRIBUTE DATA:
THE p AND c CHARTS

Many quality characteristics cannot be measured. In these situations, an item is typically classi ed as either conforming or nonconforming, where the word conforming implies that the item conforms to speci cations imposed upon the process (such as no surface scratches). Such quality characteristics are called attributes. The data gathered on these characteristics consist of counts or values based on counts, such as proportions. Examples of such data would be the proportion of nonconforming computer chips in a container of 200 chips (monitored using a p chart) or the number of blemishes in a square yard of sheet metal (monitored using a c chart).

Control Chart for the Proportion Nonconforming: The p Chart

The proportion nonconforming is defined as the number of nonconforming items in a population divided by the population size. It is denoted by p, and it corresponds to the binomial parameter p discussed in Chapters 5 and 10, where (as in Chapter 10) the value of p is unknown. Consequently, the process involved must satisfy the assumptions behind a binomial situation, described in Chapter 5, Section 4. When using a **p chart**, we concentrate on the parameter p and observe when this proportion appears to be out of control. If an item is judged on more than one quality characteristic, it is said to be nonconforming if the item does not conform to standard on one or more of these characteristics.

The reasons for using a p chart include the following:

1. Quality measurements are not possible.

2. Quality measurements are possible, but not practical (such as determining the atmospheric pressure at which an electrical component is destroyed).

3. Many characteristics on each part are being judged during inspection.

4. The main question of interest is, "will the process be able to produce conforming products over time?"

The construction of a p chart is done in basically the same way as for an $\overline{X}$ or an R chart. A collection of samples (usually, 20 to 25) is obtained while the process is believed to be in control. Let T_i be the number of nonconforming items in the ith sample, and let n be the sample size. The resulting proportion nonconforming is $p_i = T_i/n$. For example, if sample 4 contains 150 items, 3 of which are nonconforming, then $n = 150$, $T_4 = 3$, and $p_4 = 3/150 = .02$.

The five-step procedure for constructing a p chart follows, and is illustrated in the next example.

Steps for Making p Charts (Constant Sample Size)

1. Collect m samples of data (typically, 20 to 25), each of size n.

2. Determine the proportion nonconforming for each sample. Call this value p_i.

$$p_i = \frac{T_i}{n}$$

where T_i is the number of nonconforming items in sample i and n is the sample size.

3. Find $\bar{p}$, the overall proportion nonconforming.

$$\bar{p} = \frac{\text{total number of nonconforming units}}{\text{total sample size}}$$

That is,

$$\bar{p} = \frac{\sum T_i}{mn}$$

Note: $\bar{p}$ is merely the average of the m values of p_i.

4. Compute the 3-sigma control limits:

$$\text{UCL} = \bar{p} + 3\sqrt{\frac{\bar{p}(1-\bar{p})}{n}}$$

$$\text{CL} = \bar{p}$$

$$\text{LCL} = \bar{p} - 3\sqrt{\frac{\bar{p}(1-\bar{p})}{n}}$$

9.7

5. Draw in the control lines and plot the values of p_i.

EXAMPLE

9.3

Repeated samples of 150 coffee cans are inspected to determine whether a can is out of round (the cylindrical shape of the can has been distorted) or whether it contains leaks due to improper construction. Such a can is said to be nonconforming, and p represents the proportion of nonconforming cans in the population. Twenty preliminary samples (150 cans each) are obtained.

Sample Number	Number of Nonconforming Cans	p_i
1	7	.047
2	4	.027
3	1	.007
4	3	.020
5	4	.027
6	8	.053
7	10	.067
8	5	.033
9	2	.013
10	7	.047
11	6	.040
12	8	.053
13	0	.000
14	9	.060
15	3	.020
16	1	.007
17	4	.027
18	5	.033
19	7	.047
20	2	.013
	96	

Construct the p chart for these data.

Solution

Steps 1 and 2 have been completed. The next step is to determine the overall proportion nonconforming, $\bar{p}$, which is found by dividing the total number of nonconforming items (96) by the total sample size ($20 \cdot 150 = 3,000$). Consequently,

$$\bar{p} = \frac{96}{3000} = .032$$

The control limits are then easily derived:

$$UCL = .032 + 3\sqrt{\frac{(.032)(.968)}{150}} = .075$$

Center line = .032

$$LCL = .032 - 3\sqrt{\frac{(.032)(.968)}{150}} = -.011 \quad (\text{set } LCL = 0)$$

Because a negative proportion is impossible, the LCL is set equal to zero and is inactive. A p chart can easily be constructed using Excel (with KPK Data Analysis), MINITAB, or SPSS. To obtain the p chart summary in Figure 9.17, click on **KPK Data Analysis ➤ Quantitative Data Charts/Tables ➤ Control Charts.** Select **p Chart,** select **counts** in the **Type of Input Data** frame, and enter "150" in the **Sample Size** box. The MINITAB p chart in Figure 9.18 was obtained by clicking on **Stat ➤ Control Charts ➤ P** and entering "150" in the **Subgroup size** box. Based on the p chart in Figure 9.18, we conclude that the process is in control and that the p chart is ready to use.

FIGURE

9.17

Summary of p chart in Excel using KPK Data Analysis (Example 9.3).

	A	B	C	D
1	7		p Chart	
2	4		Limit	Value
3	1		UCL	0.075
4	3		CL	0.032
5	4		LCL	0.000
6	8			

FIGURE

9.18

MINITAB p chart for Example 9.3.

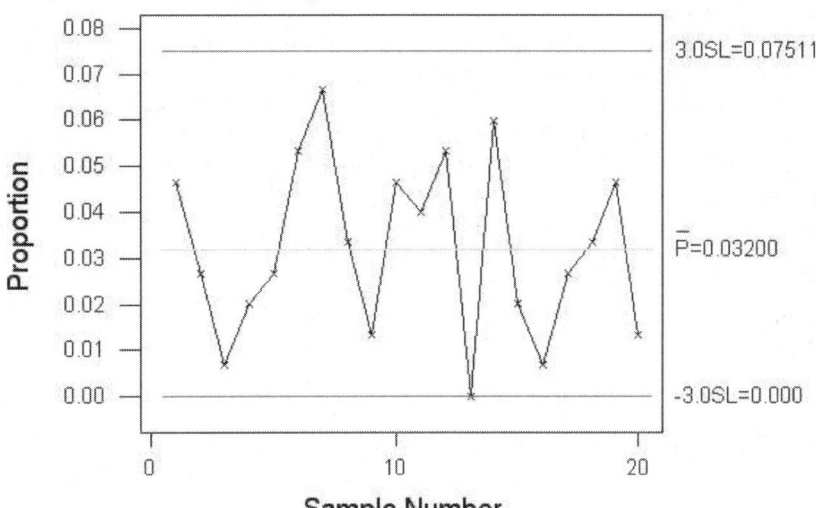

P Chart for Coffee Cans

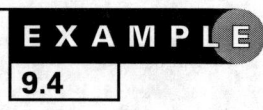

Continuing with Example 9.3, the next five coffee can samples (each of size 150) produced 5, 2, 11, 6, and 8 nonconforming cans, respectively. Do the sample proportions indicate that the process is in control for each of these samples?

Solution

The five sample proportions are

$$5/150 = .033$$
$$2/150 = .013$$
$$11/150 = .073$$
$$6/150 = .040$$
$$8/150 = .053$$

Each of these proportions falls within the control limits in Figure 9.17, so the conclusion would be that the process is in control during this period.

Notice that the third sample came close to exceeding the upper control limit of .075, and it might be tempting to react and start tampering with the process to fix it. But this action would defeat the purpose of a control chart, because we conclude that the occurrence of 11 nonconforming cans is due simply to chance variation and no process adjustment is called for. As was pointed out in the Deming funnel experiment discussion, such well-meaning overadjustments result in *increased* process variation rather than improved product quality.

Control Chart for Number of Nonconformities: The c Chart

The p chart dealt with monitoring the proportion (or in a sense, the number) of *nonconforming units* in a sample of n units. Because it is quite possible for a unit to have more than one nonconformity, we must also consider the *number of nonconformities per unit*. The **c chart** can be used for controlling a single type of nonconformity or for controlling all types of nonconformities without distinguishing between types. Situations in which a c chart could be used would include monitoring the number of scratches on a CRT casing, the number of minor blemishes on a rubber tire, the number of loose bolts on a manufactured assembly, and so forth.

The assumption behind the process is that the number of nonconformities occurring in a unit satisfies the assumptions behind the Poisson process, described in Chapter 5, Section 4. An important characteristic of the Poisson random variable is that the mean and variance are identical, and so the standard deviation is the square root of the mean. Therefore, the control chart for the number of nonconformities per unit (say, c) is easy to construct. The method for constructing a c chart is described in the following five-step procedure.

Steps for Making a c Chart

1. Collect m samples of data (typically, 20 to 25 units), where each sample is obtained by observing a single unit.

2. Determine the number of nonconformities for the ith unit. Call this value c_i.

3. Find the *average* number of nonconformities per unit, $\bar{c}$, where

$$\bar{c} = \frac{\sum c_i}{m}$$

366

4. Compute the 3-sigma control limits:*

$$UCL = \bar{c} + 3\sqrt{\bar{c}}$$
$$\text{Center line} = \bar{c}$$
$$LCL = \bar{c} - 3\sqrt{\bar{c}}$$

5. Construct the control chart by drawing in the control lines and plotting the values of c_i.

EXAMPLE 9.5

An automobile assembly worker is interested in monitoring and controlling the number of minor paint blemishes appearing on the outside door panel on the driver's side of a certain make of automobile. The following data were obtained, using a sample of 25 door panels.

Panel	1	2	3	4	5	6	7	8	9	10	11	12	13	14
Number of Paint Blemishes	1	0	3	3	1	2	5	0	2	1	2	0	8	0

Panel	15	16	17	18	19	20	21	22	23	24	25
Number of Paint Blemishes	2	1	4	0	2	4	1	1	0	2	3

Construct the control chart for this situation and determine whether all the plotted points are in control.

Solution

The average number of nonconformities (minor paint blemishes) for the sample of 25 door panels is $\bar{c}$ where

$$\bar{c} = \frac{1 + 0 + 3 + \cdots + 2 + 3}{25}$$

$$= \frac{48}{25} = 1.92$$

The limits and center line for the resulting c chart are

$$UCL = 1.92 + 3\sqrt{1.92} = 6.08$$

$$\text{Center line} = 1.92$$

$$LCL = 1.92 - 3\sqrt{1.92} = -2.24 \quad (\text{set } LCL = 0)$$

Because the Poisson variable is never negative, the LCL is set equal to zero here and is inactive.

A c chart can easily be constructed using Excel (with KPK Data Analysis), MINITAB, or SPSS. To obtain the Excel c chart summary in Figure 9.19, click on **KPK Data Analysis ➤ Quantitative Data Charts/Tables ➤ Control Charts ➤ c Chart.** The SPSS c chart in Figure 9.20 was obtained by clicking on **Graphs ➤ Control ➤ c, u.** Be sure to check the box next to **Cases are subgroups** in the **Data Organization** frame and click on **Define.** Enter "1" as the **Constant** in the **Sample Size** frame and click on c **(Number of nonconformities)** in the **Chart** frame. Referring to the c chart in Figure 9.20, notice that the thirteenth sample contains an

---

*If the mean of the process is known, its value may be substituted for $\bar{c}$ in the control limits and center line.

FIGURE

9.19

Summary of *c* chart
in Excel using
KPK Data Analysis
(Example 9.5).

	A	B	C	D
1	1		c Chart	
2	0		Limit	Value
3	3		UCL	6.077
4	3		CL	1.920
5	1		LCL	0.000
6	2			

FIGURE

9.20

SPSS *c* chart for
Example 9.5.

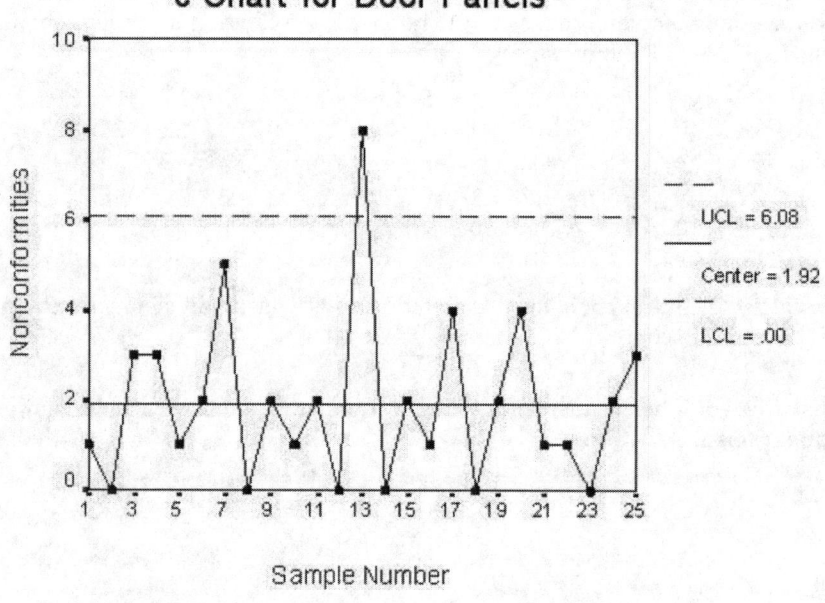

c Chart for Door Panels

out-of-control observation. If control limits for current or future production are to be meaningful, they must be based on data from a process that is *in control*.

The next step here would be to examine the thirteenth observation to determine if an assignable cause can be located. If it can, the observation should be removed, the control limits recomputed (using 24 samples), and the procedure continued until all observations are in control. If no assignable cause is found, you have one of two choices: (1) retain this observation and keep the control limits, or (2) drop this observation, assuming that an assignable cause exists but was not identified.

It was discovered that defective paint was used during sample number 13 in Example 9.5. Because this is a legitimate assignable cause, the observation was emoved from the sample. Construct the modified control limits for the *c* chart, and determine if the control chart is ready for use.

EXAMPLE

9.6

Solution   Removing the thirteenth observation produces a new total of $48 - 8 = 40$ and an average of

$$\bar{c} = \frac{40}{24} = 1.67$$

The resulting control limits are

$$UCL = 1.67 + 3\sqrt{1.67} = 5.55$$

$$\text{Center line} = 1.67$$

$$LCL = 1.67 - 3\sqrt{1.67} = -2.21 \quad (\text{set } LCL = 0)$$

Reviewing the 24 samples, all of the number of nonconformities fall within the revised control limits, so the c chart has been established.

Comments

1. At first glance, it might seem strange that lower control limits are used for p charts and c charts. After all, why should we be concerned when, say, a sample proportion (p_i) falls below the lower control limit? Keep in mind that a plotted point outside a control limit does not necessarily indicate that something *bad* happened, merely that something *unusual* occurred. Whether this point lies above the UCL or below the LCL, a search should be made for an assignable cause. Perhaps this small proportion is due to extremely good raw material or to a change in operator skill/ attitude. In either case, management should investigate the reasons behind this unusual event.

2. Any control chart should be modified when it appears that a substantial decrease in variability has produced a process that is more consistent. As product quality improves, the definition of what is in control should also change to reflect the new standards resulting from the improved process. One always hopes that *this year's control limits will not be acceptable on next year's control chart.*

X Exercises 9.33–9.44

Understanding the Mechanics

9.33 The p chart and c chart are commonly used when quality measurements are not practical. How do these charts differ? Which chart uses the assumption of a Poisson process to obtain its control limits? Which chart is appropriate for observing the proportion of nonconforming items?

9.34 Indicate whether a p or c chart would be appropriate for controlling the following:
  a. The number of defective fuses in a sample of 25.
  b. The number of defective sectors on a disk drive.
  c. The number of times that a computer software program malfunctions in a month.
  d. The number of overripe tomatoes in a carton of 50 tomatoes.
  e. The number of knots on a sheet of paneling.

9.35 Fifty samples of 100 items each were inspected for an in-control process. In the 50 samples, a total of 250 items were found to be defective.

  a. What is an estimate of the proportion of defective items?
  b. What are the upper and lower control limits for a p chart?

9.36 Surface defects have been counted on 18 circular steel plates. Using the following data, set up the appropriate control chart and comment on whether the process is in control.

Plate	1 2 3 4 5 6 7 8 9 10 11 12 13 14 15 16 17 18
No. of non-conformities	1 4 0 3 2 5 1 0 8 1 1 3 5 2 4 2 1 3

Applying the New Concepts

9.37 Consider a hospital that uses control charts for monitoring patient sedation. After administering sedation, nurses record their impressions of the patients at 10- to 15-minute intervals. Patients who were asleep or awake and pain free were considered acceptable and

369

ful lled the objective of conscious sedation. Other patient conditions were deemed unacceptable. Twenty-five entries each day over a 15-day period are given below:

							Day							
1	2	3	4	5	6	7	8	9	10	11	12	13	14	15

Unacceptable

17	7	5	9	5	14	5	0	6	7	13	14	8	5	0

p

.680	.280	.200	.360	.200	.560	.200	0.00	.240	.280	.520	.560	.320	.200	0.00

a. Construct a p chart using these data.

b. Is this process in control?

c. What assignable cause might be the cause of any out-of-control observations? What should the hospital do?

9.38 Six operators produce boots at a leather goods manufacturing facility. Each day 50 pairs of boots are inspected from each worker and the number of defects is recorded. Data collected during the past two weeks follow.

Operator	Mon.	Tue.	Wed.	Thu.	Fri.	Total
Steve	2	1	2	2	2	
	0	2	1	2	3	17
Mary	1	3	0	2	1	
	4	2	0	0	2	15
Carlos	2	0	1	0	1	
	2	0	2	1	1	10
John	4	4	5	5	6	
	4	3	4	5	6	46
Andrew	2	1	1	0	2	
	2	1	1	0	2	12
Bethany	2	0	0	1	3	
	2	1	0	0	2	11

a. Construct an appropriate type of control chart for the number of defects using the 10 data points for the two-week period. Note that 300 pairs of boots are inspected each day.

b. Can the process be considered as in control?

c. Construct Pareto charts for the number of defects by worker.

d. What corrective measures do you suggest?

9.39 Web design experts believe that the greatest mistake exhibited by Web sites today is poor information architecture. Research strongly indicates that 80% of usability problems are directly related to the structure of a Web site. Poor structure causes broken links and error messages that don't tell users what to do next. Suppose that a company has a large intranet Web site and uses software to detect broken links and error messages. Assume that this software is run weekly at the company and the numbers of broken links and error messages obtained from going to a location linked to a Web page are noted. These data are presented for 14 weeks.

eek	1	2	3	4	5	6	7	8	9	10	11	12	13	14
Broken Links	2	1	0	1	3	0	0	0	1	3	4	5	8	4

a. What type of control chart is appropriate to use in this instance? Why?

b. Construct the appropriate control chart for these data. Is this process in control?

(Source: "Giving Web Users a Break," Marketing Magazine, 106, no. 37, September 2001, p. 13.)

9.40 As the purchasing manager, you are in charge of ensuring that shipments of transducers from a new supplier are acceptable. You are to construct a control chart using the rst 30 samples of 20 transducers and count the number of nonconforming transducers in each sample of 20. The supplier believes that the average proportion of nonconforming transducers is 0.10.

a. Obtain the rst 30 samples of size 20 by generating 30 values of a binomial random variable. In Excel, select **Tools ➤ Data Analysis ➤ Random number generation.** Generate 30 binomial random numbers with the probability of a nonconforming item being 0.1. Construct a p chart.

b. Suppose the supplier's proportion of nonconforming transducers shifts to 0.20. Generate 30 binomial random numbers with a probability of a nonconforming item being 0.2. How long does it take the control chart in part a to indicate that the process is out of control?

Using the Computer

9.41 [DATA SET EX9-41] Variable description:

NumAirBubbles: Number of air bubbles in the production of picture windows

A quality engineer is interested in the quality of picture windows produced at his plant. Every ftieth window produced is selected, and a sample of 40 windows is obtained where the number of air bubbles is recorded. Construct a control chart to determine those samples where the chart indicates that the process is out of control.

9.42 [DATA SET EX9-42] Variable description:

NumAbsences: Number of absences per day from a plant with 200 employees

The production manager of a plant is concerned about the effect that too many absences may have on the productivity of a plant. The manager does not mind some absences per day, as employees may use sick time, personal leave, or comp time. If too few absences are occurring, this might indicate that in the future too many employees will be absent on the same day. Also many absences are sometimes followed by very few absences. The manager would like to gain insight into the process from a control chart of the number of absences per day from a total of 200 employees over 30 working days. What conclusions can you reach?

370

9.43 [DATA SET EX9-43]   Variable description:

NumErrAcct: Number of errors found in purchase orders

A manager of an accounting of ce is concerned that pur-chase orders may contain too many errors and hence result in excessive returned merchandise. To gain insight into the process in which purchase orders are lled out, 35 purchase orders are randomly selected and the num-ber of errors is recorded in the variable NumErrAcct. What control chart is appropriate for this situation? Con-struct this chart and discuss the results.

9.44 [DATA SET EX9-44]   Variable description:

SuppA: Number of defective cases in sampled batch of 150 cases from supplier A

SuppB: Number of defective cases in sampled batch of 120 cases from supplier B

A recording studio and production company use two suppliers for their clear plastic cassette tape cases. A case is considered defective if it is scratched, cloudy, cracked, or otherwise unusable. Data from 50 samples collected from each of the two suppliers are recorded in the vari-ables SuppA and SuppB.

a. Construct the appropriate control chart for each of the two suppliers.

b. Do either of these two processes indicate an out-of-control condition?

c. Comment on the performance of the two suppliers. Which would you prefer to use?

9.8 PROCESS CAPABILITY

We have dealt with control charts that monitor a process to determine whether it is operating in control. But the term "in control" merely indicates that the process is performing within natural variation as measured by past performance t is entirely possible that the process might be in control but not be capable of meeting the process requirements, referred to as **speci cation limits.**

For example, suppose the process that produces piston rings is operating in control, with the inside diameter of the rings centered at 12.1 cm with a standard deviation of .03 cm. However, the product speci cations state that in order to be of acceptable quality, the piston rings must have an inside diameter between 11.95 and 12.05 cm. The value 11.95 is called the lower spec limit (LSL) and 12.05 is the upper spec limit (USL). From this information, we would have to conclude that the piston rings process is incapable of meeting the required speci cations (specs) (see Figure 9.21).

In Figure 9.21, the difference between 12.19 and 12.01 is 6 standard devia-tions (estimated) and is referred to as the **process spread:**

$$\text{process spread} = 6\hat{\sigma}$$

9.9

For this illustration, $6\tilde{\sigma} = 12.19 - 12.01 = .18$ cm.

A visual method of checking process capability is to obtain a fairly large sam-ple and plot a histogram against the required spec limits. In the preceding exam-ple, the quality characteristic of interest is the inside diameter of a piston ring; suppose that the histogram of inside diameters looks like the one in Figure 9.22. Visually, it is clear that the process is centered at a value much too large and that the process is not capable of meeting the required speci cations.

This section will introduce three descriptors of **process capability** that measure how well the process is conforming to the required speci cations. We will move away from a subjective visual assessment of process capability toward an objec-tive measure that is based on facts (sample information) rather than opinion.

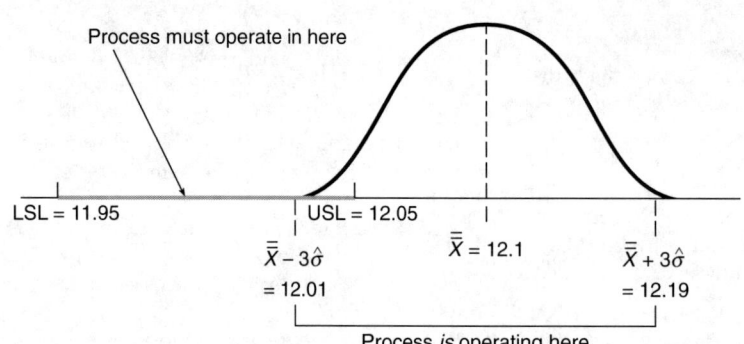

FIGURE

9.21

Spec limits versus process performance.

Process must operate in here

LSL = 11.95

USL = 12.05

$\bar{\bar{X}} - 3\hat{\sigma}$
= 12.01

$\bar{\bar{X}}$ = 12.1

$\bar{\bar{X}} + 3\hat{\sigma}$
= 12.19

Process *is* operating here

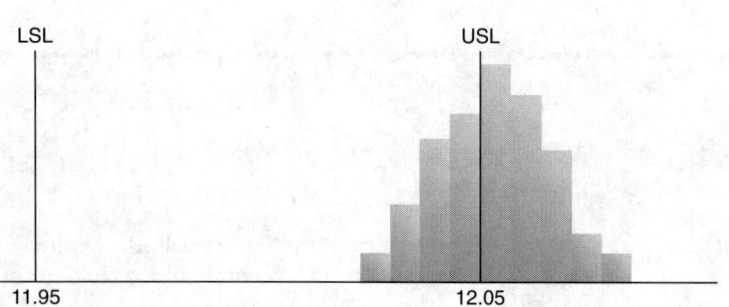

FIGURE

9.22

Visual inspection of process capability.

LSL

USL

11.95

12.05

Process Capability Ratios, C_p and C_{pk}

When computing the first measure (C_p), there are three assumptions:

1. The process output is centered within specification.

2. The process is normally distributed.

3. The process is stable (in control).

The measure C_p is simply a comparison of the process capability with the specifications, and it is a valid indicator *only* if the above assumptions are true. It is clear from Figure 9.22 that assumption 1 is violated for the piston ring illustration, because the process is centered at a value much larger than 12 cm (the center of the spec limits).

Determining the ratio C_p is similar to comparing the width of a car driving down the center of a road to the width of the road, where the width of the car is the process spread, $6\hat{\sigma}$, and the width of the road is the width of the process specs (USL – LSL). The process capability ratio C_p for a two-sided spec limit is found by dividing these two widths:

$$C_p = \frac{USL - LSL}{6\hat{\sigma}}$$

9.10

Often, process specifications are one-sided, specifying only a lower spec limit (for example, the bursting strength of a glass bottle) or an upper spec limit (for example, the number of missing rivets in an aircraft assembly). For these situations, we compare the distance between the sample mean and the spec limit with three standard deviations:

$$C_p = \frac{USL - \overline{X}}{3\hat{\sigma}} \qquad \text{(upper spec limit only)}$$

$$C_p = \frac{\overline{X} - LSL}{3\hat{\sigma}} \qquad \text{(lower spec limit only)}$$

EXAMPLE 9.7

The specification limits for the filled weight of a coffee can are 20 ± 1 (ounces); that is, the USL is 21 ounces and the LSL is 19 ounces. A sample of 100 cans provides a mean of 19.98 ounces and an estimated standard deviation of 0.189 ounce. Determine the capability ratio, C_p.

Solution

The process spread is $(6)(.189) = 1.134$ ounce. The value of C_p can be found from equation 12.10:

$$C_p = \frac{21 - 19}{1.134} = 1.76$$

EXAMPLE 9.8

The bursting strength of a particular soft-drink container has a lower spec limit of 200 psi (pounds per square inch). A sample of 100 containers produced a sample mean of 226 psi and a standard deviation of 11.3 psi. What is the capability ratio, C_p?

Solution

Using equation 9.12,

$$C_p = \frac{226 - 200}{3(11.3)} = \frac{26}{33.9} = .77$$

Interpreting C_p

A general rule for interpreting C_p is as follows:*

$C_p \geq 1.33$	good
$1 \leq C_p < 1.33$	adequate
$C_p < 1$	inadequate

For Example 9.7, the value of $C_p = 1.76$ would be in the "good" category, and we would conclude that the *potential* capability of the coffee-can process to meet the product specs is very good, with little chance of producing a nonconforming (out-of-spec) product. The term *potential* is needed here, because *no attention has been paid to where the process is centered when determining this capability ratio.* The C_{pk} capability ratio (discussed next) considers this very important aspect of the process performance.

---

*A more precise interpretation of C_p should consider whether the process is new or existing and whether the quality characteristic is of critical importance (such as one related to consumer safety). See the reference by Montgomery in the Further Reading section for more detail.

A value of $C_p = .77$ was determined for Example 9.8, indicating that this process has a tendency to operate dangerously close to the lower spec limit. We can expect that an unsatisfactory number of containers will have a bursting strength below the lower spec limit of 200 psi.

Consideration of Process Location: Use of C_{pk}

When determining the C_p ratio, we used the analogy of comparing the width of a car (the process spread) to the width of the road (the difference between the spec limits), while *assuming* that the car is traveling down the center of the road. The C_p ratio is a measure of potential capability.

The C_{pk} process capability ratio not only compares the width of the car to the width of the road but also questions whether the car is on or off the center stripe. This ratio examines the distance from the process center to the *nearest* spec limit (assuming both an upper and a lower spec limit), as illustrated in Figure 9.23.

There are four assumptions behind the use of the C_{pk} ratio:

1. The process may or may not be centered in spec.

2. The process is normally distributed.

3. The process is stable.

4. Control charts will be used to monitor the process over time.

Procedure for Finding C_{pk}.

1. Determine $R_L = \dfrac{\overline{X} - \text{LSL}}{3\hat{\sigma}}$

2. Determine $R_U = \dfrac{\text{USL} - \overline{X}}{3\hat{\sigma}}$

3. C_{pk} = Minimum of R_L and R_U

Referring to Example 9.7, we have $x = 19.98$ ounces, $\hat{\sigma} = .189$ ounce, LSL = 19 ounces, and USL = 21 ounces. Consequently,

$$R_L = \frac{19.98 - 19}{3(.189)} = 1.73$$

$$R_U = \frac{21 - 19.98}{3(.189)} = 1.80$$

and so C_{pk} is the minimum of 1.73 and 1.80, that is, $C_{pk} = 1.73$.

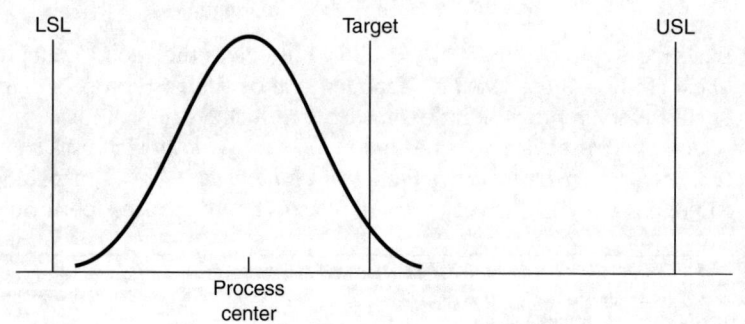

FIGURE

9.23

The C_{pk} ratio considers the distance from the process center to the nearest spec limit.

374

The value of C_{pk} will always be less than or equal to the corresponding value of C_p. *A generally acceptable value of* C_{pk} *is 1.* Consequently, the coffee-can process in Example 9.7 is well centered and operating well within the upper and lower spec limits.

Taking C_{pk} One Step Further. If the process is capable ($C_{pk} > 1$),

1. Monitor the process.

2. Pursue continuous improvement.

If the process is not capable ($C_{pk} \leq 1$),

1. Monitor the process.

2. Pursue continuous improvement.

3. Invest time, money, and resources to reduce process variation.

4. Consider removing this product from production.

Although the fourth statement under $C_{pk} \leq 1$ may appear to be a bit drastic, it is worthy of serious consideration, given the present world of increasing product quality requirements and consumer quality demands.

Consideration of the Process Target: Use of C_{pm}

When using the C_p ratio or the C_{pk} ratio, we divide by either $3s$ or $6s$, where s is the sample standard deviation. The value of s is a measure of the variation about the process mean (center). An alternative here is to replace s with an estimate of the variation about the process *target* (T), assumed here to be midway between the upper spec limit and the lower spec limit; that is, $T = (\text{USL} + \text{LSL})/2$. Denoting this estimate by s', then,

$$
\begin{aligned}
s' &= \sqrt{\frac{\Sigma(x - T)^2}{n - 1}} \\
&= \sqrt{\frac{\Sigma(x - \bar{x})^2}{n - 1} + \frac{n(\bar{x} - T)^2}{n - 1}} \\
&= \sqrt{s^2 + \frac{n(\bar{x} - T)^2}{n - 1}}
\end{aligned}
$$

9.13

Consider the ratio defined by

$$
C_{pm} = \frac{\text{USL} - \text{LSL}}{6s'}
$$

9.14

This index will decrease as s' increases, due to a shift from the process target. When the process variance (s^2) changes and the process mean drifts from T concurrently, the C_{pm} index has the ability to detect these changes. We suggest you interpret the C_{pm} index using the same guidelines for interpreting the C_p ratio discussed previously. In particular, this implies that a C_{pm} ratio less than 1 is an indicator of a process that cannot adequately meet the process specifications.

Determine the C_{pm} ratio for the coffee-can illustration in Example 9.7.

EXAMPLE
9.9
Solution

The sample size is $n = 100$, the target value is $T = 20$ ounces, the sample mean is $\bar{x} = 19.98$ ounces, and the sample standard deviation is $s = .189$ ounce. Consequently,

$$s' = \sqrt{.189^2 + \frac{100(19.98 - 20)^2}{99}} = .1901$$

and

$$C_{pm} = \frac{21 - 19}{6(.1901)} = \frac{2}{1.141} = 1.75$$

Since $1.75 > 1.33$, we once again conclude that this process is capable of meeting the process specifications.

Determining the Percent Nonconforming

Another method of measuring process capability is to estimate the number of nonconforming units, that is, those outside the spec limits. The basic assumption behind this procedure is that we have reason to believe that the process is *normally distributed*. If there is reason to doubt this assumption (such as, when a process has been shown to be out of control), then the results of this section are unreliable. There is nothing new about the procedure we will use here, since we learned in Chapter 6 that the percent nonconforming can be determined by finding the corresponding area under a normal curve. The mean and standard deviation are estimated using the sample statistics, again assuming that the process is in control during the collection of this sample. This procedure is illustrated in the following example.

EXAMPLE
9.10

Solution

A machine is used to fill plastic containers of motor oil, each of which is supposed to contain 32 fluid ounces. The process specs are $32 \pm .5$ fluid ounces. A sample of 75 containers produces a mean of $\bar{x} = 31.92$ fluid ounces and a standard deviation of $s = .16$. Describe the process capability.

The sample standard deviation is the estimated process standard deviation, that is, $\hat{\sigma}$. First we determine the process capability ratio C_{pk}.

$$R_L = \frac{31.92 - 31.5}{3(.16)} = \frac{.42}{.48} = .88$$

$$R_U = \frac{32.5 - 31.92}{3(.16)} = \frac{.58}{.48} = 1.21$$

Consequently,

$$C_{pk} = \text{minimum of } .88 \text{ and } 1.21$$
$$= .88$$

which is an unacceptable value.

To find the value of C_{pm}, we use equation 9.13 to calculate the variation about the process target, $T = 32$. This is

$$s' = \sqrt{(.16)^2 + \frac{75(31.92 - 32)^2}{74}} = .179$$

The resulting ratio is

$$C_{pm} = \frac{32.5 - 31.5}{6(.179)} = .93 < 1$$

So, both the C_{pk} and C_{pm} ratios indicate a process incapable of meeting process specifications. The small value of C_{pm} is due to the variation about the process center, as measured by $s = .16$, and the slight drift from the process target equal to $\bar{x} - T = 31.92 - 32 = -.08$.

To estimate the percent nonconforming, we examine the tails of a normal curve outside the lower and upper spec limits of 31.5 and 32.5. These tail areas are shaded in Figure 9.24, where the curve is centered at $\bar{x} = 31.92$ with a standard deviation of $\hat{\sigma} = .16$.

The standardized values for the spec limits are

$$\text{standardized LSL} = \frac{31.5 - 31.92}{.16} = -2.62$$

$$\text{standardized USL} = \frac{32.5 - 31.92}{.16} = 3.62$$

The proportion nonconforming will be

(the proportion to the left of –2.62 under a Z curve)

+ (the proportion to the right of 3.62 under a Z curve)

= .0044 + .0002 (approximately) = .0046

So, an estimated .46% of the oil containers will be nonconforming. At first glance, this appears to be a reasonably "small" number. However, when discussing the proportion of units nonconforming, it is common to talk in terms of number of units nonconforming *per million* units produced. For this example, the estimated number of nonconforming oil containers per million produced is (.0046)(1,000,000) or 4,600, a number that should be large enough to get management's attention.

FIGURE

9.24

Tail areas represent the proportion of nonconforming units.

C_{pk}	Number of Nonconforming Units per Million Produced
.5	133,614
.75	24,448
1.00	2,700
1.30	96
1.50	6.8
2.00	.002

TABLE

9.4

Determining the number of nonconforming units per million produced using C_{pk}.

The expected number of nonconforming units per million produced, *provided the process is centered in the specs*, can be estimated roughly from the value of C_{pk} using Table 9.4. This table is constructed using the procedure discussed in the previous example.

Because Table 9.4 assumes the process is centered exactly on target (midway between the spec limits), it provides a measure of the potential number of nonconforming units per million produced, given the variation of the process. Because the process in the previous example was very nearly centered on target (32 fluid ounces) with a C_{pk} of .88, we would expect Table 9.4 to provide a crude estimate of the number nonconforming, namely, between 2,700 and 24,448. The actual number of nonconforming units per million produced was estimated to be 4,600.

☒ Exercises 9.45–9.55

Understanding the Mechanics

9.45 What phenomena do process capability indices measure? If a process is in control, does that imply that the process is capable of meeting process requirements? Explain.

9.46 How does the measure of process capability C_{pm} differ from both C_p and C_{pk}?

9.47 For each of the following well-centered processes (i.e., A–D), a sample of size 325 is collected and the standard deviation of the process estimated. Calculate C_p, and indicate whether you believe the process capability to be "good," "adequate," or "inadequate."

Process	Specifications	Sample Standard Deviation
A	0.65 ± 0.07	0.030
B	29.3 ± 2.5	0.740
C	99.5 ± 7.2	1.110
D	0.25 ± 0.02	0.006

9.48 For each of the following processes (i.e., A–D), a sample of size 400 is collected in order to estimate the process mean and variability.

Process	Specifications	Mean	Sample Standard Deviation
A	124.0 ± 8.5	117.6	2.560
B	0.66 ± 0.08	0.67	0.022
C	89.2 ± 2.0	90.0	0.720
D	0.13 ± 0.03	0.132	0.009

a. Indicate which measure of process capability (C_p vs. C_{pk}) appears the more appropriate to use for each process, and state why.

b. Compute the appropriate measure of process capability for each process.

c. Using Table 9.4, estimate the number of nonconforming units per million for processes B and D.

9.49 Verify in equation 9.13 that

$$\frac{\Sigma(x-T)^2}{n-1} = s^2 + \frac{n(\bar{x}-T)^2}{n-1}$$

Applying the New Concepts

9.50 A process used to fill small cartridges with CO_2 has an upper specification limit of 250 psi (i.e., pounds per square inch). A sample of 150 CO_2 cartridges produces a sample mean of 228.8 psi and a standard deviation of 6.2 psi.

a. What is the capability ratio C_p for this process?

b. What proportion of the CO_2 cartridges will exceed the upper specification limit?

9.51 Answer the following questions using the data from Exercise 9.50.

a. Assuming that the process target is 225 psi, compute C_{pm}, considering only the upper specification limit.

b. Assuming that the process target is 229 psi, compute C_{pm}, considering only the upper specification limit.

c. What happens to C_{pm} as the process mean and target converge (i.e., get closer to one another), given a constant process variability?

9.52 Printed circuit boards are manufactured using several processes. One process applies an etch-resist ink to a panel that is composed of a copper-clad laminate. The etch-resist ink is printed on the panel by passing a squeegee over a screen that contains a template of the desired circuit image. The size of the image that is printed on the panel is a critical factor. If the image is either too large or too small, substantial problems in component assembly are encountered. Consider the specification of the height of the image to be 1.34 ± .04 mm. A sample of 300 printed circuit boards is randomly collected. The sample mean was found to be 1.35 with a standard deviation of .009 mm.

a. What is the value of C_p for this process? How would you interpret this value?

b. What is the value of C_{pk} for this process? How would you interpret this value?

c. Using Table 9.4, estimate the number of nonconforming units per million for this process.

(Source: "Process Capability: A Criterion for Optimizing Multiple Response Product and Process Design," IIE Transactions, 33, 2001, pp. 497–509.)

9.53 A decision must be made between two experimental processes for producing silicon chips. The specification limits on the thickness of the chips is .125 ± .003 mm. Samples of 500 chips are drawn from experimental runs

for each process, and means and standard deviations are recorded:

Process	Sample Mean	Sample Standard Deviation
A	0.1254	0.0008
B	0.1231	0.0003

a. Which of the two processes is better centered?

b. Calculate C_{pk} for both processes.

c. Which process do you recommend, and why?

9.54 Three processes in your manufacturing facility have been producing unacceptably high numbers of nonconforming parts. You have drawn normally distributed samples of 375 from each process. The sample means and standard deviations are as follows:

Process	Specifications	Sample Mean	Sample Standard Deviation
A	51.0 ± 1.2	51.2	1.1
B	102.5 ± 8.9	108.1	2.3
C	3.4 ± 0.5	3.7	0.4

a. Calculate the z-scores for the specification limits and the spread between specification limits (in standard deviations) for each process.

b. The plant manager wants to know your thoughts regarding this predicament. Considering the calculated z-scores and spreads, do you believe that the problem is attributable to improper centering of the process, excessive process variability, or both? Discuss your answer for each process individually.

9.55 [DATA SET EX9-55] Variable Description:

Diameter: The diameter of a fastening hole for an aluminum body cover

A random sample of 15 fastening holes for an aluminum body cover was recorded in a Ford manufacturing plant to determine the process capability. The diameters of these holes are given in units of millimeters. Specification limits are 8.975 ± .105 mm. The target value is 8.975 mm. Determine the capability indices for this process. What are your recommendations?

(Source: "Simple Process Capability," Quality, February 2001, pp. 34–38.)

 # Summary

American manufacturing and service industries are continuing to undergo an evolution that emphasizes quality. The need for tools to monitor quality has sparked a renewed interest in the everyday application of statistical thinking. Decisions are routinely based on facts gathered from sample data.

This chapter has examined both the management and the statistical sides of quality improvement. **Total Quality Management (TQM)** is a customer-focused management strategy that emphasizes a respect for employees and a constant effort at improving product or service quality. The most recent quality improvement movement is the implementation of **Six Sigma.** Six Sigma provides companies with a methodology and philosophy for minimizing mistakes and maximizing value by dramatically reducing costs, improving efficiency, and maximizing customer satisfaction in all operations within a company. A **quality product or service** is one that meets or surpasses the needs and expectations of the customer.

Companies in the United States demonstrating a high degree of quality emphasis both internally and externally are recognized each year through the **Malcolm Baldrige National Quality Award** (MBNQA). Recipients of this award have exhibited and documented that they have a world-class system for managing their operations/employees and satisfying their customers. The **ISO 9000 standards** require businesses to provide evidence of the establishment of a quality system that is understood and followed by all company employees. Registration to ISO 9000 standards increasingly is becoming a prerequisite for doing business. The Baldrige Award criteria are more customer focused, whereas ISO 9000 registration provides a common basis for assuring buyers that specific (documented) quality practices are being followed by their suppliers.

A **process** can be any combination of resources, such as people, machines, and/or material that lead to a product or service. **Statistical process control** (SPC) is the application of statistical procedures intended to measure, analyze, and control this process.

To monitor a process, you must first define what it is you wish to measure or count. For measurement data, what you are measuring is the *quality characteristic* and such measurements result in **variables data.** Examples of variables data include the weight or length of a manufactured unit. When counting, you obtain **attribute data,** such as the number of nonconformities per unit.

Two of the quality-improvement tools were explained in Chapter 2, namely, the **histogram** and **Pareto chart.** Two additional tools for describing a process were introduced in this chapter, the flowchart and the cause-and-effect diagram. A **flowchart** is a diagram of an entire process that can be used to view the process as a system and allow you to search for potential problem areas or opportunities for improvement. The **cause-and-effect diagram** can be used to represent the relationships between potential problems within a process and their possible causes.

Another quality-improvement tool, a **control chart,** can be set up to monitor a process to determine whether it is **in control** (stable) or **out of control** (unstable). Provided the plotted points for a control chart stay within the **upper control limit** (UCL) and the **lower control limit** (LCL), the process is exhibiting natural variation and is said to be in control. The **center line (CL)** represents the average value of the quality characteristic corresponding to the in-control state. If a plotted point exceeds either of the limits, a search is made for an **assignable cause,** that is, an explanation (such as defective raw material) for this extreme value in the control chart. Control charts for variables data consist of the $\overline{X}$ **chart** for monitoring the process center and the R **chart** for monitoring the process variation. For attribute data, the most commonly used control charts are the p **chart** for observing and controlling the proportion of nonconforming units and the c **chart** for the number of nonconformities per unit.

Control charts enable the front-line worker to distinguish between random variation (**chance cause**) and that due to an assignable cause. One of Deming's main points is that a process should not be "tampered with" when it is exhibiting chance variation. This was illustrated using his **funnel experiment,** which demonstrated how such manipulations will actually have an adverse effect on process variation. Systematic and nonrandom patterns can be detected in an $\overline{X}$ control chart by conducting a **pattern analysis.**

For most production situations, a process must conform to certain requirements referred to as **specification limits.** These may be imposed by an outside purchaser or internally by the company's engineering staff. The ability of the process to conform to these specifications is the **process capability.** If a large percentage of the units produced can be expected to lie outside the spec limits, we would conclude that the process is not capable of performing to specification. Measures of process capability consist of the C_p ratio, which does not consider where the process is centered, the C_{pk} ratio, which does, and the C_{pm} ratio, which includes the effect of a drift away from the process target. The C_p ratio measures how well the process *should* perform (the difference of the spec limits) compared with how well the process *is* performing (the **process spread,** defined as six standard deviations).

Summary of Formulas

Control Charts

1. $\overline{X}$ Chart:

$$\text{UCL} = \overline{\overline{X}} + 3\frac{\hat{\sigma}}{\sqrt{n}}$$

$$\text{CL} = \overline{\overline{X}}$$

$$\text{LCL} = \overline{\overline{X}} - 3\frac{\hat{\sigma}}{\sqrt{n}}$$

where $\overline{\overline{X}} = \sum \overline{X}_i/m$ and $\hat{\sigma} = \overline{R}/d_2$ (values of d_2 provided in Table 9.3).

2. R chart:

$$\text{UCL} = D_4\overline{R}$$

$$\text{CL} = \overline{R}$$

$$\text{LCL} = D_3\overline{R}$$

(values of D_3 and D_4 provided in Table 9.3).

3. p chart:

$$\text{UCL} = \overline{p} + 3\sqrt{\frac{\overline{p}(1-\overline{p})}{n}}$$

$$\text{CL} = \overline{p}$$

$$\text{LCL} = \overline{p} - 3\sqrt{\frac{\overline{p}(1-\overline{p})}{n}}$$

4. c chart:

$$\text{UCL} = \overline{c} + 3\sqrt{\overline{c}}$$

$$\text{CL} = \overline{c}$$

$$\text{LCL} = \overline{c} - 3\sqrt{\overline{c}}$$

where $\overline{c}$ = average number of nonconformities per unit.

Process Capability

1. Process spread: $6\hat{\sigma}$ where $\hat{\sigma} = s$ (sample standard deviation).

2.
$$C_p = \frac{\text{USL} - \text{LSL}}{6\hat{\sigma}} \qquad \text{(two-sided spec limit)}$$

$$C_p = \frac{\text{USL} - \overline{X}}{3\hat{\sigma}} \qquad \text{(upper spec limit only)}$$

$$C_p = \frac{\overline{X} - \text{LSL}}{3\hat{\sigma}} \qquad \text{(lower spec limit only)}$$

3. C_{pk} = minimum of R_L and R_U where

$$R_L = \frac{\overline{X} - \text{LSL}}{3\hat{\sigma}} \qquad R_U = \frac{\text{USL} - \overline{X}}{3\hat{\sigma}}$$

4. $C_{pm} = \dfrac{\text{USL} - \text{LSL}}{6s'}$ where

$$s' = \sqrt{s^2 + \frac{n(\overline{x} - T)^2}{n-1}}$$

and T = process target = $(\text{USL} + \text{LSL})/2$.

Further Reading

Cianfrani, Charles, *ISO 9001:2000 Explained,* Milwaukee, Wis.: American Society for Quality, 2001.

Crosby, Philip, *Quality and Me: Lessons from an Evolving Life,* San Francisco: Jossey-Bass, 1999.

———, *Quality Is Still Free: Making Quality Certain in Uncertain Times,* New York: McGraw-Hill, 1996.

Deming, W. Edwards, *Out of the Crisis,* Cambridge, Mass.: MIT Press, 2000.

Eckes, George, *Six Sigma for Everyone,* New York: McGraw-Hill, 2003.

George, Michael, David Rowlands, and Bill Kastle, *What is Lean Six Sigma?*, New York: McGraw-Hill, 2004.

Juran, J. M., *Juran on Leadership for Quality,* New York: Free Press, 1989.

———, *Juran on Quality by Design,* New York: Free Press, 1992.

———, *Quality Control Handbook,* 5th ed., New York: McGraw-Hill, 1999.

Juran, J.M., and Frank M. Gryna, *Quality Planning and Analysis,* 4th ed., New York: McGraw-Hill, 2001.

Kane, V. E., "Process Capability Indices," *Journal of Quality Technology,* 18, no. 1, 1986: 41.

Kanholm, Jack, *ISO 9000:2000 New Requirements,* Pasadena, Calif.: AQA Press, 2000.

Ketola, Jeanne, and Kathy Roberts, *ISO 9000:2000 in a Nutshell,* Chico, Calif.: Paton Press, 2001.

Montgomery, D. C., *Introduction to Statistical Quality Control,* 4th ed., New York: Wiley, 2000.

Pyzdek, Thomas, *The Six Sigma Handbook,* New York: McGraw-Hill, 2003.

Rosander, A. C., *Deming's 14 Points Applied to Services,* Houston: Marcel-Dekker, 1991.

Shewhart, W. A., "Quality Control Charts," *Bell System Technical Journal,* 1926.

Walton, Mary, *The Deming Management Method,* New York: Perigee Books, 1988.

Information on the Malcolm Baldrige National Quality Award: Malcolm Baldrige National Quality Award Office, NIST, Administration Bldg., Rm. A537, Gaithersburg, MD 20899-0001, (301) 975-2036. Website is http://www.quality.nist.gov.

X Review Exercises 9.56–9.73

9.56 What is the difference between chance causes and assignable causes? Explain the objective of control charts with respect to these two causes.

9.57 Typically, p charts and c charts plot proportions and counts, respectively. If a sample proportion or count falls below the lower control limit, then management needs to search for an assignable cause. Because having fewer nonconforming units/nonconformities is a desirable outcome, why is this important?

9.58 Under what conditions would C_p, C_{pk}, and C_{pm} all be equal?

9.59 Briefly explain, in one sentence each, the seven categories of the Malcolm Baldrige National Quality Award. Which categories carry the most points during the examination phase of a company?

9.60 Control charts have upper and lower limits just as confidence intervals have upper and lower endpoints. Explain the similarity between the calculation of the limits for control charts and the endpoints of a confidence interval.

9.61 Differentiate between specification limits and control limits. Is there a measure that conveys the relationship between the two? Explain.

9.62 Classify the following as attribute or variables data:
  a. The weight of a bat manufactured for professional baseball
  b. The number of broken links on a Web home page
  c. The number of defective sectors on a hard drive manufactured for personal computers
  d. The voltage output of a transformer
  e. The thickness of a razor manufactured for shaving

9.63 Explain the primary difference between the measures of process capability C_p and C_{pm}. Which do you think will usually be larger? Why?

9.64 The speci cation limits for the tear strength of a cardboard container are 150 ±2 ft-lb. A normally distributed sample of 100 containers yields a mean tear strength of 150.3 ft-lb with a standard deviation of 0.7 ft-lb.

   a. Calculate C_{pk}.
   b. Estimate the number of containers nonconforming per million by using Table 9.4.
   c. Calculate the number of containers nonconforming per million.

9.65 Health care executives are using statistical process control to provide insight into medical group performance. One of the primary care performance indicators that they are charting is the net revenue per relative value unit (RVU) production from a full-time equiv-alent provider. The upper and lower control limits for the average value per month are 84 and 48, respectively. Using the eight patterns for detecting assignable causes, at what point would you consider the process to be out of control, using the following 18 values?

Month	1	2	3	4	5	6	7	8	9
RVU	55	67	72	73	77	85	44	64	65

Month	10	11	12	13	14	15	16	17	18
RVU	74	61	66	60	59	66	67	64	76

(Source: "The Synergistic Effect of Linking Statistical Process Control and Pro t and Loss," Journal of Health Care Finance, 27, no. 3, Spring 2001, pp. 64–75.)

9.66 Indicate whether an $\bar{X}$, R, p, or c chart would be the best for controlling
   a. the number of defective resistors in a container of 500 resistors
   b. the mean cranking amperage of a sample of car batteries
   c. the discrepancy in time it takes to perform an identical oil change
   d. the number of scratches and other imperfections in an 8-foot × 4-foot sheet of paneling
   e. the mean length of a sample of bolts
   f. the number of nonconforming sprocket sets in a container of 250

9.67 A number of graphical tools for quality improvement were mentioned in this chapter. The following statements correspond to one of these tools. Identify the graphical tool asso-ciated with each statement.
   a. This tool shows the relationship, if any, between two variables.
   b. This tool graphically illustrates a process by showing the activities engaged in and decisions made.
   c. This tool can be used to monitor and control a process over time.
   d. This tool is used to identify the quality problem(s) with the largest impact.
   e. This tool shows the main/subcauses responsible for a quality problem.

9.68 Hillerich & Bradsby crafts each professional bat to be within ±.0003 inches in ve key diameters: barrel, midbarrel, midhandle, handle, and knob. Assume that the target diame-ter of the midhandle is .75000 inches and that a random sample of 20 bats yields a sample mean of .75003 with a standard deviation of .00005.
   a. What is the value of C_p for this process? How would you interpret this value?
   b. What is the value of C_{pm} for this process? How would you interpret this value?
   c. What is the value of C_{pk} for this process? How would you interpret this value?
   d. Using Table 9.4, estimate the number of nonconforming units per million for this process.

(Source: "Making Bats for the Pros," Quality Progress, 34, no. 8, August 2001, p. 30.)

9.69 [DATA SET EX9-69] Variable description:

Sample Number: Samples are numbered from 1 to 20

Breaking Strength1 through Breaking Strength4: the breaking points of a single strand of fabric in a sample of size 4

During most fabric production processes, fabric tensile and tear strength are checked before the weaving of fabric. Control charts have replaced many inspection procedures in an attempt to produce quality fabric. Quality-control procedures are conducted during every phase of the production process, from the fiber opening to the spinning and weaving. Twenty samples of size four are selected from a fabric production process. Develop appropriate control charts to determine whether this process is in control. What are your recommendations?

(Source: "Box-Chart: Combining *X*-bar and *S* Charts," *Total Quality Management*, July 2000, p. 857.)

9.70 The lower specification limit for an inflatable air bladder to be used in an automobile seat is 230 psi. A sample of 100 bladders failed at a mean of 236.1 psi with a standard deviation of 1.8 psi.
   a. Calculate the process capability ratio C_p.
   b. What proportion of the air bladders will fail at less than 230 psi?

9.71 The Palmer House, a landmark Chicago hotel, periodically receives complaints from guests regarding low water pressure. To remedy the problem, the engineering department can adjust the flow of water, therefore water pressure, to the various floors of the hotel. Management wishes to establish a control chart to control the number of complaints about low water pressure. It is decided that the number of complaints received per day will be recorded by floor of the hotel. The following are the number of complaints received per floor (10 in all) for the last two days.

Sample	Complaints	Sample	Complaints	Sample	Complaints
1	3	8	2	15	4
2	1	9	1	16	4
3	0	10	0	17	0
4	2	11	4	18	2
5	5	12	3	19	2
6	0	13	2	20	1
7	2	14	1		

   a. What type of chart is appropriate to use in this instance?
   b. Construct the appropriate control chart.
   c. Plot the data and control limits. Is this process in control or out of control?

9.72 Rural ambulance and rescue squads are largely staffed by volunteer emergency medical technicians (EMTs). As the number of rural jobs decline and EMTs begin commuting to work in more populated areas, ambulance and rescue services find it increasingly difficult responding to all calls. The chief of one such rural squad used control charts to gain a better understanding of her community's need for service and to improve the squad's ability to respond to all calls. The following control chart shows the number of daily calls for which the squad was unable to respond ("dropped calls") over a seven-week period. Comment on any patterns that you observe. What recommendations would you make? (*Hint:* Look for a cyclical pattern.) Note that this example illustrates that control charts are useful to service organizations as well as to manufacturing-oriented organizations.

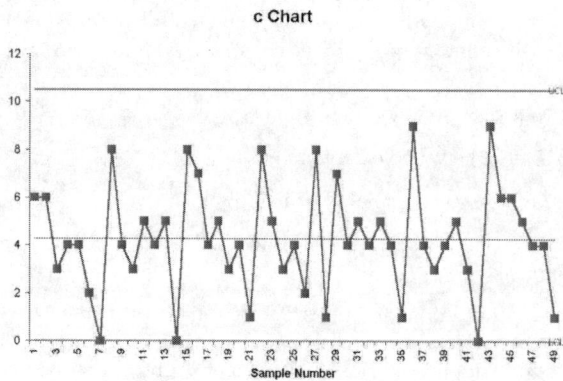

c Chart

9.73 [DATA SET EX9-73] Variable description:

WidthCircuit: The width of a circuit path in a computer chip (in microns)

A computer chip manufacturer monitors the quality of its computer chips by selecting a batch of 10 computer chips and measuring the width of the circuit path. If this path is too wide or too narrow, the computer CPU might malfunction. Is there a pattern that might indicate that the following $\bar{X}$ chart, in which 30 batches were sampled, is out of control? Construct an R chart and explain if there is a similar indication that the process is out of control.

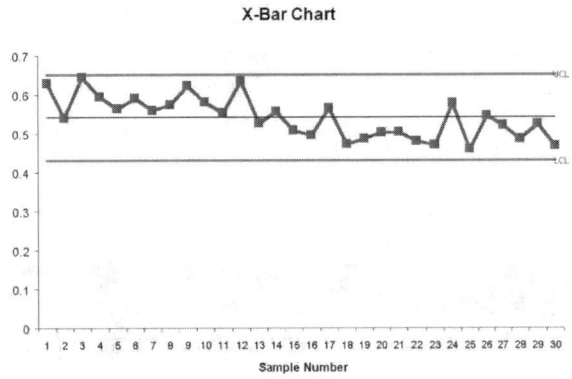

X-Bar Chart

Insights from Statistics in Action

Business Excellence: Banking on Six Sigma to Keep Quality Job One

At the beginning of this chapter, the Statistics in Action case study discussed the efforts of Ford Motor Company to implement the six-sigma concept in its production processes. In essence, this policy states that a single-sided spec limit is at least six standard deviations (sigmas) away from the mean, allowing for a 1.5 sigma shift for the process average. For a K-sigma quality process, one would subtract 1.5 from the value of K and then examine the standard normal (Z) curve to the right of $K - 1.5$. For example, for a six-sigma policy, examine the area to the right of $6 - 1.5 = 4.5$ under the Z curve. This is .0000034, which translates to 3.4 nonconforming parts per million, or "being 99.9997% perfect." Similarly, for $K = 4$, the number of nonconforming items in a four-sigma plan is $P(Z > 2.5) \times 10^6 = 6,210$ parts per million.

As explained in "Six Sigma's Missing Link" in Quality Progress, K-sigma plans can be implemented for service industries as well. The example used in that article is one involving mortgage customers who expect their applications to be processed in 10 days after ﬁling. Suppose all the defects (loans in a monthly sample taking more than 10 days to process) are counted and it is determined that 150 loans in the 1,000 applications processed in that month do not meet this customer requirement. Now, 150/1,000 defects translates into 850/1,000 defect-free applications. Let $z_{.85}$ represent the z value such that 85% of the area to its left is equal to .85. From a normal distribution table or using the inverse normal probability function on a statistical computer program, $z_{.85}$ can be found to be 1.036. Adding 1.5 to 1.036 gives a process sigma of 2.5, which is well below the value of 6 for a six-sigma plan.

1. Consider a process in which an electronic component is measured in units of 1/128 inch. The process target is 31 units and the speciﬁcation limits are set at $31 - 16 = 15$ and $31 + 16 = 47$. If

this process was on target (that is, the sample mean is midway between the spec limits) and the standard deviation of the process was 5.33, what is C_{pk}? From Table 9.4, what is the estimate of the number of nonconforming units per million?

2. To achieve six-sigma quality, C_{pk} must be equal to 1.54. What would the standard deviation have to be for the process in question 1 to achieve six-sigma quality?

3. Suppose that the sample mean is 33.5 in question 1 and that the process target is midway between the specification limits. What is the value of C_{pm}? How would you interpret this value?

4. A six-sigma policy translates into 3.4 nonconforming parts per million and a four-sigma policy translates into 6,210 nonconforming parts per million. How many nonconforming parts per million would there be for a five-sigma program?

5. Suppose that a hotel manager is monitoring the number of complaints that customers have about their rooms. If 1,000 customers are sampled and it is determined that five customers had legitimate complaints, at what process sigma level would the hotel be operating?

(Source: "Ford Revamps Its Vehicle Development System," *The New York Times*, February 20, 2003, p. C3; "Ford Embraces Six Sigma," *The New York Times*, June 13, 2001, p. C5; "Six Sigma's Missing Link," *Quality Progress*, November 2000, p. 77.)

Data Analysis with Excel, MINITAB, and SPSS

Appendix

EXCEL

$\bar{X}$ and R Control Charts

The $\bar{X}$ and R control charts can be constructed using the KPK Data Analysis macros. Click **KPK Data Analysis ➤ Quantitative Data Charts/Tables ➤ Control Charts.** Use the **Select a chart** drop-down box on the displayed **Control Charts** dialog box to select X-Bar chart or R chart. The dialog box is essentially the same for both of these charts. For the data in Example 9.2, the observations are listed in the **Input Range** (a1:a100) with a value of 5 entered in the **Sample Size.** The Output Range is selected to be starting in cell E1. An optional Chart Title may be entered. Clicking **OK** results in the output in Figure 9.14. This procedure must be repeated using the R chart option in the **Select a chart** drop-down box to obtain the output for the R chart.

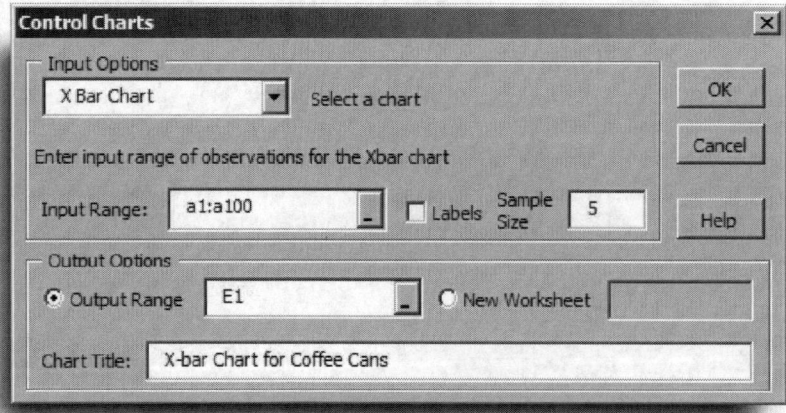

386

p and c Control Charts

The construction of p and c charts is basically the same as for the $\bar{X}$ and R control charts. The data for a p chart—either number of nonconforming units or proportion of nonconforming units—must be in column format. For a c chart, the number of non-conformities must also be in a column format. Click **KPK Data Analysis ➤ Quantitative Data Charts/Tables ➤ Control Charts.** Use the **Select a chart** drop down box to select p chart or c chart. For the p chart, an additional frame will be displayed for the **Type of Input Data.** Select either **counts** or **proportions.** The dialog box is basically the same for both of these charts. Click **OK** to display the selected chart.

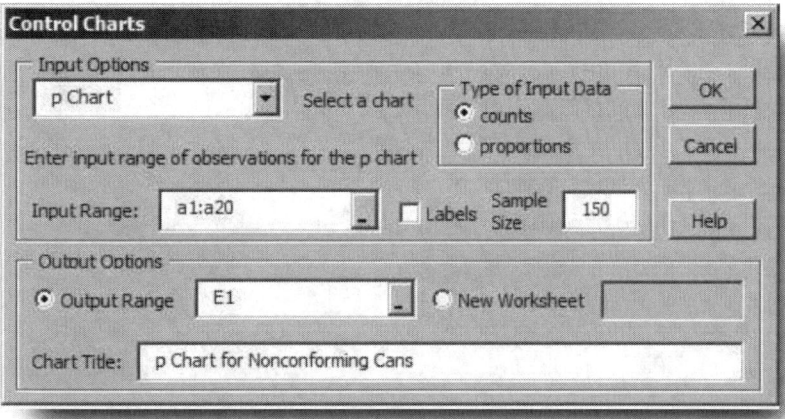

MINITAB

$\bar{X}$ and R Control Charts

Data may be listed in either column or row format. Click **Stat ➤ Control Charts ➤ Variable Charts for Subgroups ➤ Xbar-R Chart** to obtain the dialog box for the **Xbar-R Charts.** The drop-down edit box allows one to select the data format. The

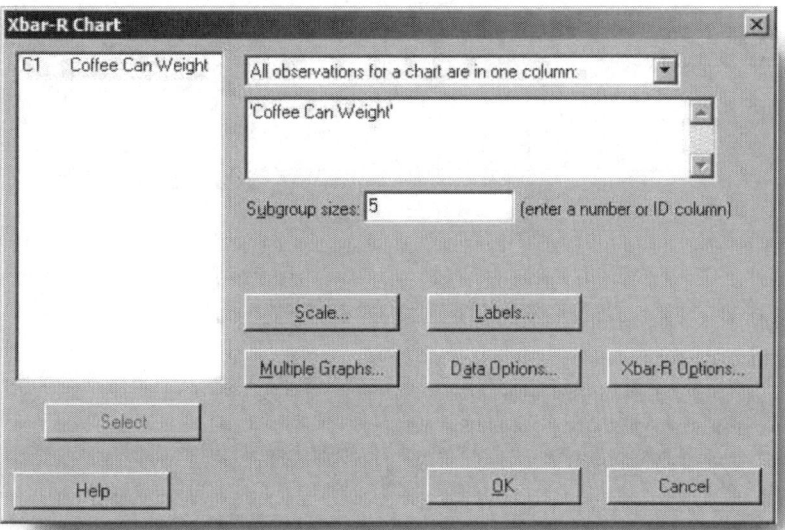

default is for the observations to be in one column. Enter the column variable/label for the column in the edit box. The sample size needs to be entered in the **Subgroup sizes** edit box. Click on the **Labels** button to include an optional title for the control chart. Click on **Xbar-R Options ➤ Tests** to detect any of eight patterns that indicate a process to be out of control.

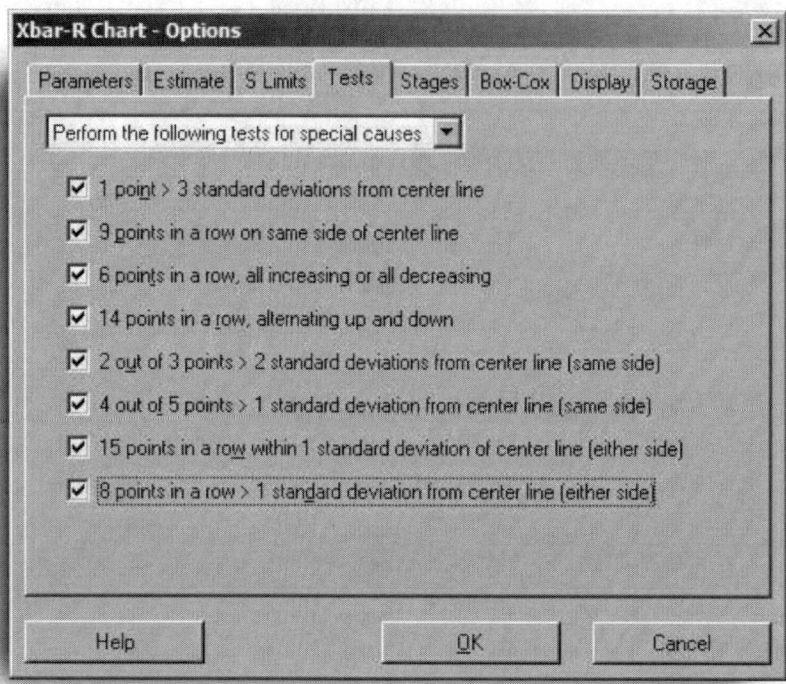

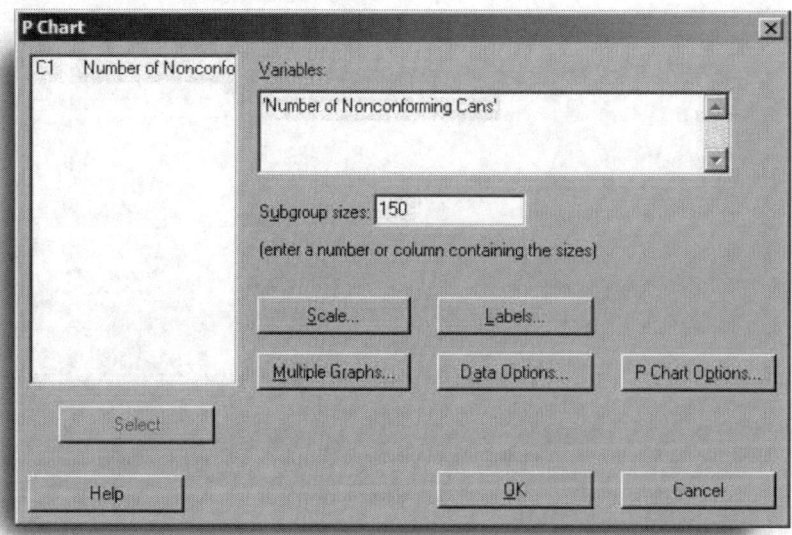

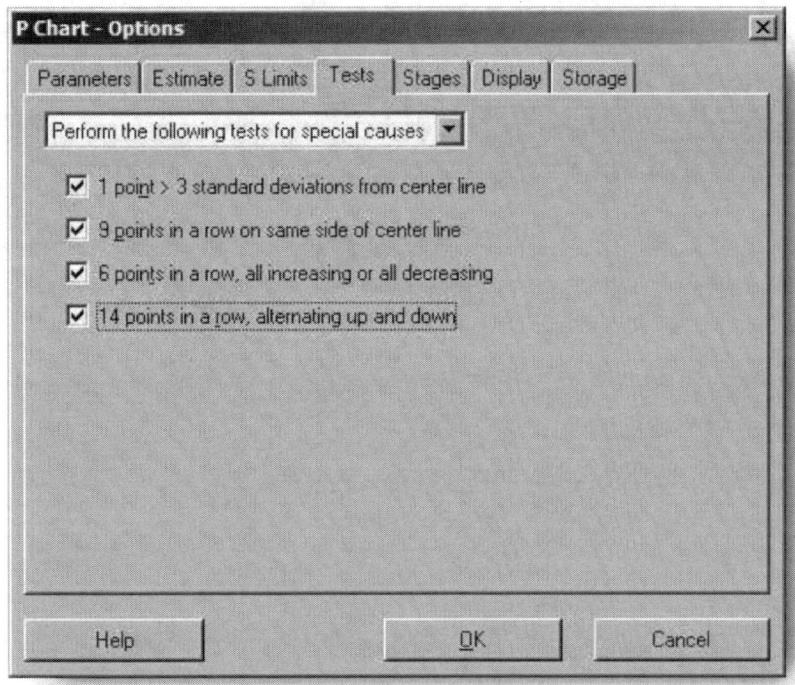

Control Charts ➤ Attributes Charts. Then select either **P** or **C**. In the **P Chart** dialog box, enter the variable name/column number in the **Variables** edit box and the sample size in the **Subgroup sizes** edit box. Click the **Data Options** button if data need to be specified as being in row format. Click the **Labels** button to add an optional title to the control chart. Click the **P Chart Options** ➤ **Tests** button to display data patterns to indicate that a process is out of control. Selecting **C** as one of the **Attribute Charts** displays a similar dialog box to construct a *c* chart.

SPSS

*X*bar and *R* Control Charts

For the coffee can weights in Example 9.2, enter the weights in the first column (named "Weight"). The subgroup size is five for this example because five measurements were obtained in each of the 20 samples. Consequently, enter five values of "1," five values of "2," . . . , five values of "20" in the second column (named "Group"). To obtain any of the control charts, first click **Graphs** ➤ **Control**. In the **Control Charts** dialog box, select **X-Bar, R, s** for an *X*-bar and *R* chart. Select **Cases are units** in the **Data Organization** frame. Click on **Define** and enter the variable labeled Weight in the **Process Measurement** edit box and the variable labeled Group in the **Subgroups Defined by edit** box as illustrated in the **X-Bar, R, s: Cases Are Units** dialog box. In the **Charts** frame, select the option **X-bar and range**. After clicking on **OK**, the *X*-bar and *R* charts will appear.

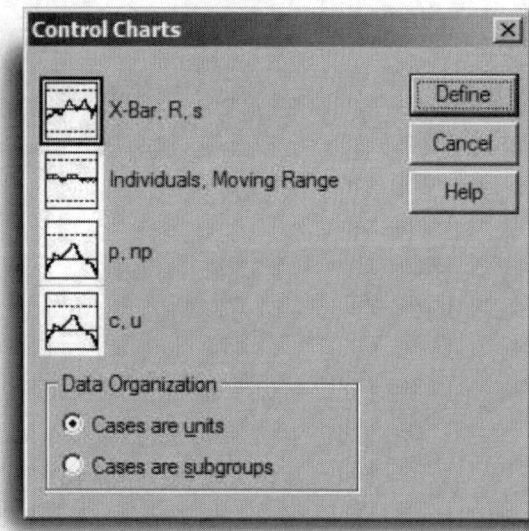

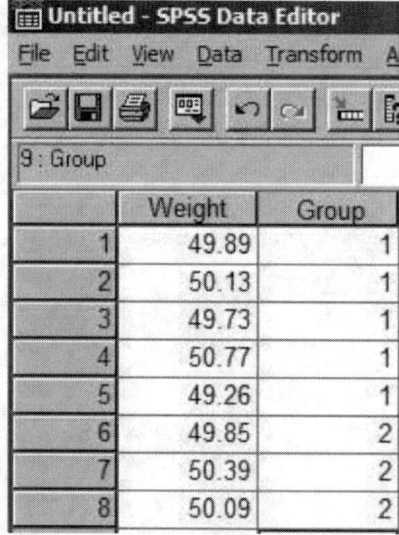

	Weight	Group
1	49.89	1
2	50.13	1
3	49.73	1
4	50.77	1
5	49.26	1
6	49.85	2
7	50.39	2
8	50.09	2

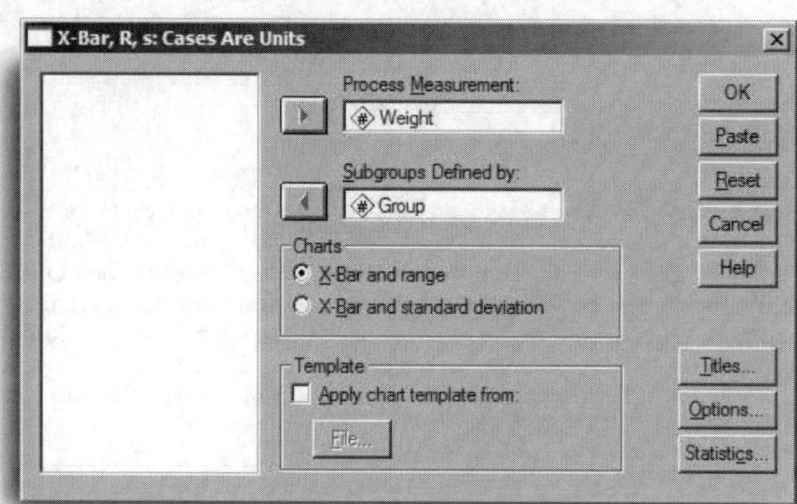

p Charts

Consider the data used in Example 9.3. Enter the number of nonconforming cans in each of the samples (7, 4, 1, . . . , 2) in the first column and name this column "Cans." In the next column, enter the sample number and label this column as Group. To construct the corresponding p chart, click on **Graphs ➤ Control ➤ p, np.** Be sure to check the box alongside **Cases are subgroups** in the **Data Organization** frame of the **Control Charts** dialog box. Click on **Define.** The **p, np: Cases Are Subgroups** dialog box will appear. Move the variable labeled Cans into the **Number Nonconforming** box and variable labeled Group into the **Subgroups Labeled by** edit box. In the **Sample Size** frame, enter 150 for the value of the **Constant** because this is the sample size. Select the **p (Proportion nonconforming)** option button. After clicking on **OK,** the p chart will appear.

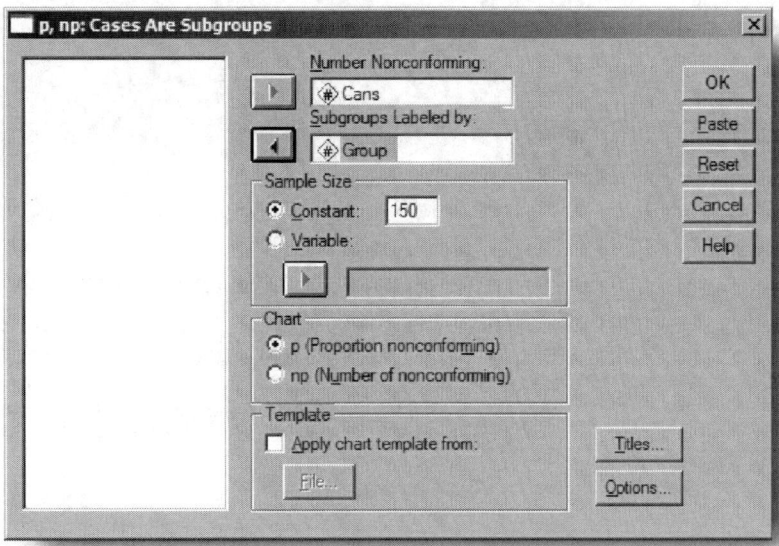

c Charts

Consider the data used in Example 9.5. Enter the number of paint blemishes for each of the door panels (1, 0, 3, . . . , 3) in the first column and name this column "Blemishes." In addition, create a column for the variable "Panel" with data values 1, 2, . . . , 25. To construct the corresponding c chart, click on **Graphs ➤ Control ➤ c, u.** Be sure to select the option alongside **Cases are units** in the **Data Organization** frame. Click on **Define.** Move the variable labeled "Blemishes" into the **Characteristic** edit box and "Panel" into the **Subgroups Defined by** edit box. Select **c (Number of nonconformities)** in the **Chart** frame. After clicking on **OK,** the *c* chart will appear.

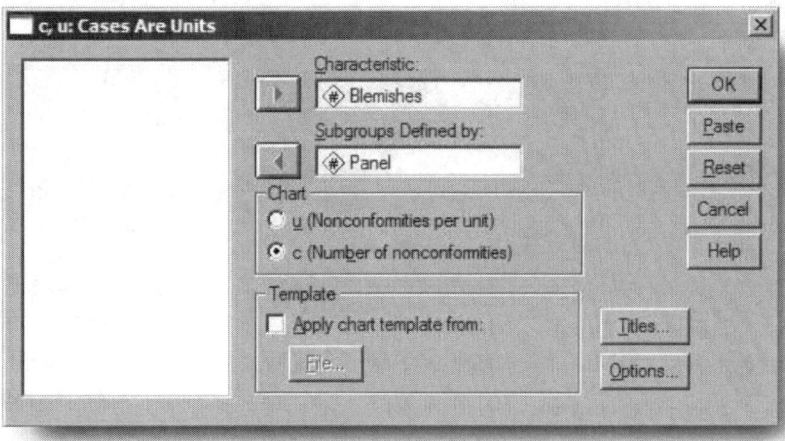

chapter

10

Hypothesis Testing for the Mean of a Population

Statistics in Action
Hillerich & Bradsby Company: Hitting the Quality Mark

The crack of the bat as a home run leaves the park. The sound of a hockey stick meeting the puck on a slap shot. The ping as an iron makes contact with a golf ball to create the perfect shot. These sounds are music to the ears of Hillerich & Bradsby (H & B) executives. The Louisville, Kentucky-based manufacturer, best known for producing Louisville Slugger baseball bats, provides a variety of baseball, hockey, and golf equipment to amateur and professional athletes worldwide.

In the pro bat business, quality means wood craftsmanship and personal service. H & B's Louisville Slugger Division sells around 1 million wooden bats and has approximately 70% of the professional bat market.

H & B has discovered that athletes can be very demanding when choosing equipment. Producing a bat requires many decisions by operators and managers. Billets, from which bats are manufactured, arrive at the Louisville plant weighing 80 to 100 ounces. If a shipment has billets with an average weight outside of this range, the shipment is typically returned. When finished, the bats weigh 30 to 35 ounces.

Quality control is important in the production of wooden bats. There is a chance that the billets have defects hidden inside the wood; high-tech imaging of billet interiors is not considered cost-effective. Computer monitors are able to tell whether a bat is out of spec or if it is drifting away from centerline. But the operator must move through the turning, branding, and sanding process quickly because billets and turned bats lose moisture quickly. Moisture control is critical to meeting weight specifications. Some pros have

asked that their bats be measured in quarter ounces. Lighter bats are more apt to be damaged on impact, especially if the batter connects with the ball somewhere other than the center of percussion. But because it is possible to hit better with a thin, lighter bat, most batters are willing to trade durability for performance.

H & B's top managers have learned to use statistical analysis in their decision making. After a certain number of bats are manufactured, operators randomly sample bats to check for weight and length specifications. If the average weight of a sample is more than the target weight, is it safe to assume that the average weight has increased for all bats recently turned? The answer is, not necessarily. Now, if it can be shown that this average weight is *significantly* more than the target weight, the operator should be very concerned about whether bats are being produced outside of specs and should recheck the setup of the machinery.

Producing bats that provide the look and feel that customers want is what has allowed H & B to capture such a large portion of the professional bat market. The use of statistical analysis in their operations keeps the company competitive. When you have completed this chapter, you will be able to

- Determine what is meant by "significantly greater" or "significantly different."

- Understand the types of error that can result when trying to infer something about a population when using a sample.

- Determine the role that sample size plays on the probability that one of the types of error will occur.

HYPOTHESIS TESTING ON THE MEAN OF A POPULATION (σ KNOWN)

A newspaper article claims that the average height of adult males in the United States is not the same as it was 50 years ago; it claims the average height is now 5.9 feet (approximately 5'11"). Your firm manufactures clothing, so the value of this population mean is of vital interest to you. To investigate the article's claim, you randomly select 75 males and measure their heights.* The average of the 75 heights is $\bar{x} = 5.79$ feet. From past experience, the population standard deviation (σ) is assumed to be 0.4 feet.

Let μ represent the population average (mean) of all U.S. male heights. We do have a point estimate of μ; $\bar{x} = 5.79$ feet is an estimate of μ. Keep in mind that the actual value of μ is unknown (although it *does exist*) and will remain that way. What we can do is estimate μ using the sample data. This situation can be summarized by considering the following pair of hypotheses:

Null Hypothesis	Alternative Hypothesis
H_0: μ = 5.9	H_a: μ ≠ 5.9

H_0 asserts that the value of μ that has been claimed to be correct is in fact correct. H_a asserts that μ is some value other than 5.9 feet. The alternative hypothesis typically contains the conclusion that the researcher is attempting to demonstrate using the sample data. In our height example, if you do not believe that the average height is 5.9 feet and you expect the data to demonstrate that μ has some other value, H_a is μ ≠ 5.9.

DEFINITION

1. *Null hypothesis* (H_0). A statement (equality or inequality) concerning a population parameter; the researcher wishes to discredit this statement.
2. *Alternative hypothesis* (H_a). A statement in contradiction to the null hypothesis; the researcher wishes to support this statement.

The task of all hypothesis testing is to either **reject H_0** or **fail to reject H_0**. Notice that we do not say "reject H_0 or accept H_0." This is an important distinction.

In our study of male heights, the (point) estimate of μ is $\bar{x} = 5.79$ feet. Should we reject H_0, given that it claims that μ is 5.9? First of all, the sample mean, $\bar{X}$, is a continuous random variable. What is the probability that *any* continuous random variable is equal to a certain value? In particular, what is the probability that $\bar{X}$ is exactly equal to 5.9 feet? The answer to both questions is zero. Thus, we see that we cannot reject H_0 simply because $\bar{X}$ is not equal to 5.9 feet. What we do is allow H_0 to stand, provided $\bar{X}$ is "close to" 5.9 feet, and reject H_0 otherwise. To define what "close" means, we need to take an in-depth look at what happens when you test hypotheses.

---

*The size of this sample is unrealistically small (yet large, statistically).

Type I and Type II Errors

Because the sample does not consist of the entire population, there always is the possibility of drawing an incorrect conclusion when inferring the value of a population parameter using a sample statistic. When testing hypotheses, there are two types of possible errors:

Type I Error. A **Type I error** occurs if you rejected H_0 when in fact it is true. For example, a Type I error would occur if you were to reject the claim (hypothesis) that the population mean is 5.9 feet when in fact it really is true.

Type II Error. A **Type II error** occurs if you fail to reject H_0 when in fact H_0 is not true. For example, a Type II error occurs if you fail to reject the hypothesis that the population mean is 5.9 feet when in fact the mean is *not* 5.9 feet.

	Actual Situation	
Conclusion	H_0 **True**	H_0 **False**
Fail to reject H_0	Correct decision	Type II error
Reject H_0	Type I error	Correct decision

For any test of hypothesis, define

$$\alpha = \text{probability of rejecting } H_0 \text{ when } H_0 \text{ is true}$$

$$= P(\text{Type I error})$$

$$\beta = \text{probability of failing to reject } H_0 \text{ when } H_0 \text{ is false}$$

$$= P(\text{Type II error})$$

For any test of hypothesis, you would like to have control over n (the sample size), α (the probability of a Type I error), and β (the probability of a Type II error). However, in reality, you can control only two of these: n and α, n and β, or α and β. *In other words, for a fixed sample size, you cannot predetermine both α and β.*

Suppose you decide to set $\alpha = .02$. Then the procedure you use to test H_0 versus H_a will reject H_0 when it is true with a probability of .02. You may wonder why we do not set $\alpha = 0$, so that we would never have a Type I error. The thought of never rejecting a correct H_0 sounds appealing, but the bad news is that β (the probability of a Type II error) is then equal to 1; that is, you will *always* fail to reject H_0 when it is false. If we set $\alpha = 0$, then the resulting test of H_0 versus H_a will automatically fail to reject H_0: $\mu = 5.9$ whenever μ is, in fact, any value other than 5.9 feet. If, for example, μ is 7.5 feet (hardly the case, but interesting), we would still fail to reject H_0—not a good situation at all. We therefore need a value of α that offers a better compromise between the two types of error probabilities.

The value of α you select depends on the relative importance of the two types of error. For example, consider the following hypotheses and decide if the Type I error or the Type II error is the more serious: You have just been examined by a physician using a sophisticated medical device, where the hypotheses under consideration are as follows:

H_0: you do not have a particular serious disease

H_a: you do have the disease

$\alpha = P(\text{rejecting } H_0 \text{ when it is true})$

$\quad = P(\text{device indicates that you have the disease when you do not have it})$

$\beta = P(\text{fail to reject } H_0 \text{ when in fact it is false})$

$\quad = P(\text{device indicates that you do not have the disease when you do have it})$

For this situation, the Type I error (measured by α) is not nearly as serious as the Type II error (measured by β). Provided the treatment for the disease does you no serious harm if you are well, the Type I error is not serious. But the Type II error means you fail to receive the treatment even though you are ill.

We never set β in advance, only α. This will allow us to carry out a test of H_0 versus H_a. *The smaller α is, the larger β is. Consequently, if you want β to be small, you choose a large value of α.* For most situations, the range of acceptable α values is .01 to .1.

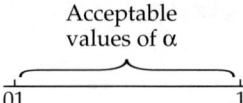

Acceptable
values of α

.01   .1

For the medical-device problem, you could choose a value of α near .1 or possibly larger, due to the seriousness of a Type II error. On the other hand, if you are more worried about Type I errors for a particular test (such as rejecting an expensive manufactured part that really is good), a small value of α is in order. What if there is no basic difference in the effect of these two errors? If there is no significant difference between the effects of a Type I error versus a Type II error, researchers often choose α = .05.

Performing a Statistical Test

The claim that the average adult male height is 5.9 feet resulted in the following pair of hypotheses:

$$H_0: \mu = 5.9$$

$$H_a: \mu \neq 5.9$$

We decide to use a test that carries a 5% risk of rejecting H_0 when it is correct; that is α = .05. In hypothesis testing, α is referred to as the **significance level** of your test. Using $n = 75$, $\bar{x} = 5.79$ ft, and σ = .4 ft, we wish to carry out the resulting statistical test of H_0 versus H_a. We decided to let H_0 stand (not reject it) if $\bar{X}$ was "close to" 5.9 feet. In other words, we will reject H_0 if $\bar{X}$ is "too far away" from 5.9 feet. We write this as follows:

$$\text{reject } H_0 \text{ if } |\bar{X} - 5.9| \text{ is "too large"}$$

or, by standardizing $\bar{X}$, we can

$$\text{reject } H_0 \text{ if } \left| \frac{\bar{X} - 5.9}{\sigma/\sqrt{n}} \right| \text{ is "too large"}$$

We rewrite the last statement as

$$\text{reject } H_0 \text{ if } \left| \frac{\bar{X} - 5.9}{\sigma/\sqrt{n}} \right| > k, \text{ for some } k$$

What is the value of k? Here is where the value of α has an effect. If H_0 is true and the sample size is large, then using the results of section 7.2, $\bar{X}$ is approximately (or exactly) a normal random variable with*

$$\text{mean} = \mu = 5.9 \quad \text{and} \quad \text{standard deviation} = \frac{\sigma}{\sqrt{n}}$$

---

*Section 7.2 states that $\bar{X}$ is *exactly* normally distributed for any sample size provided you have reason to believe the population being sampled is normally distributed. Also according to section 7.2, the distribution for $\bar{X}$ is *approximately* normal for large sample sizes, regardless of the shape of the sampled population. See Comment 3 on p. 224.

FIGURE

10.1

The shaded area
represents the
significance
level, α.

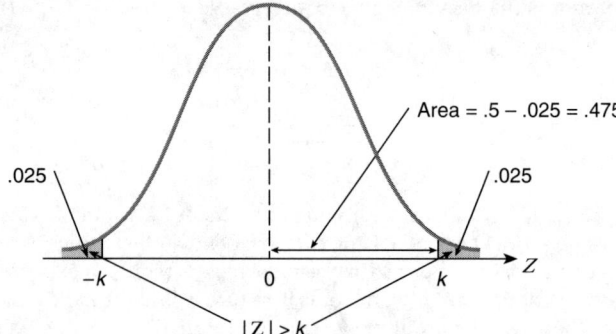

So, if H_0 is true, $(\overline{X} - 5.9)/(\sigma/\sqrt{n}$) is approximately (or exactly) a standard normal random variable, Z. In this case, we reject H_0 if $|Z| > k$, for some k. Suppose α = .05. Then,

$$.05 = \alpha = P(\text{rejecting } H_0 \text{ when it is true})$$

$$= P\left(\left|\frac{\overline{X} - 5.9}{\sigma/\sqrt{n}}\right| > k, \text{ when } \mu = 5.9\right)$$

$$= P(|Z| > k)$$

To find the value of k that satisfies this statement, consider Figure 10.1. When $|Z| > k$, either $Z > k$, or $Z < -k$, as illustrated. Since $P(|Z| > k) = .05$, the total shaded area is .05, with .025 in each tail due to the symmetry of this curve. Consequently, the area between 0 and k is .475, and, using Table A.4, k = 1.96. So our test of H_0 versus H_a is

$$\text{reject } H_0 \text{ if } \left|\frac{\overline{X} - 5.9}{\sigma/\sqrt{n}}\right| > 1.96$$

and fail to reject H_0 otherwise. So,

$$\text{reject } H_0 \text{ if } \frac{\overline{X} - 5.9}{\sigma/\sqrt{n}} > 1.96$$

or

$$\text{reject } H_0 \text{ if } \frac{\overline{X} - 5.9}{\sigma/\sqrt{n}} < -1.96$$

This test will reject H_0 when it is true 5% of the time. This means that there is a 5% risk of making a Type I error.

Using the sample data, we obtained n = 75, and $\overline{x}$ = 5.79 feet. The population standard deviation was assumed to be 0.4 feet. Is $\overline{x}$ = 5.79 feet far enough away from 5.9 feet for us to reject H_0? This was not at all obvious at first glance; it may have seemed that this value of $\overline{X}$ is "close enough to" 5.9 for us not to reject H_0. Such is not the case, however, because

$$Z = \frac{\overline{X} - 5.9}{\sigma/\sqrt{n}} = \frac{5.79 - 5.9}{.4/\sqrt{75}} = -2.38 = Z^*$$

where Z* is the *computed value* of Z.

FIGURE

10.2

Distribution of $\bar{X}$ if H_0 is true (H_0: μ = 5.9′).

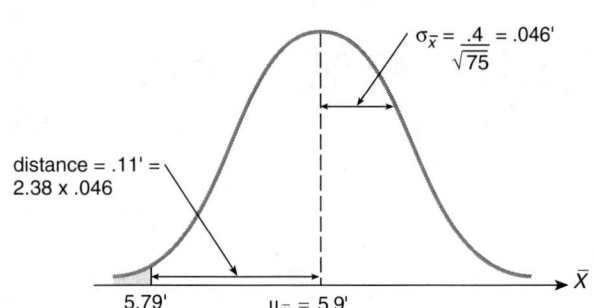

Conclusion. Because $-2.38 < -1.96$, we reject H_0. Based on the sample results and a value of α = .05, the average population male height (μ) is not equal to 5.9 feet.

Another way of phrasing this result is to say that if H_0 is true (that is, if μ = 5.9 feet), the value of $\bar{X}$ obtained from the sample (5.79 feet) is 2.38 standard deviations to the left of the mean using the normal curve for $\bar{X}$ (Figure 10.2). Because a value of X this far away from the mean is very unlikely (that is, with probability less than α = .05), our conclusion is that H_0 is not true, and so we reject it.

Comment

When testing μ = (some value) versus μ ≠ (some value), the null hypothesis, H_0, always contains the =, and the alternative hypothesis, H_a, always contains the ≠. In our example, this resulted in splitting the significance level, α, in half and including one-half in each tail of the test statistic, Z. Consequently, a test of H_0: μ = (some value) versus H_a: μ ≠ (some value) is referred to as a **two-tailed test.**

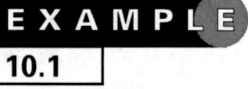

EXAMPLE

10.1

Solution

Using the data from our example of male heights, what would be the conclusion using a significance level α of .01?

The only thing that we need to change from our previous solution is the value of k. Now,

$$P(|Z| > k) = \alpha = .01$$

as shown in Figure 10.3. Using Table A.4, $k = 2.575$, and the test is (see Figure 10.4):

$$\text{reject } H_0 \text{ if } Z > 2.575 \quad \text{or} \quad Z < -2.575$$

What is the computed value of Z? Our data values have not changed, so the value of this expression is the same: $Z^* = -2.38$.

The region defined by values of Z to the right of 2.575 and to the left of -2.575 in Figure 10.4 is the **rejection region.** The value of k (2.575) defining this region is the **critical value.** Z^* fails to fall in this region, so we fail to reject H_0. In other words, for α = .01, the value of $\bar{X}$ is "close enough" to 5.9 to let H_0 stand; there is insufficient evidence to conclude that μ is different from 5.9 feet.

Clearly then, the choice of the significance level, α, is a delicate matter. It is important to remember that a value of α must be selected prior to obtaining the sample and should reflect the impact of a Type I versus a Type II error.

FIGURE

10.3

The shaded area is $\alpha = .01$.

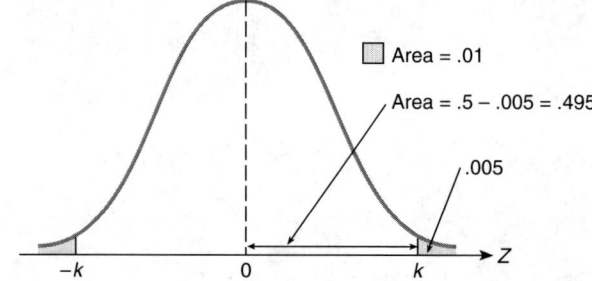

Area = .01

Area = $.5 - .005 = .495$

.005

$-k$ 0 k Z

FIGURE

10.4

We reject H_0 if Z^* falls within either tail—the rejection region for $\alpha = .01$.

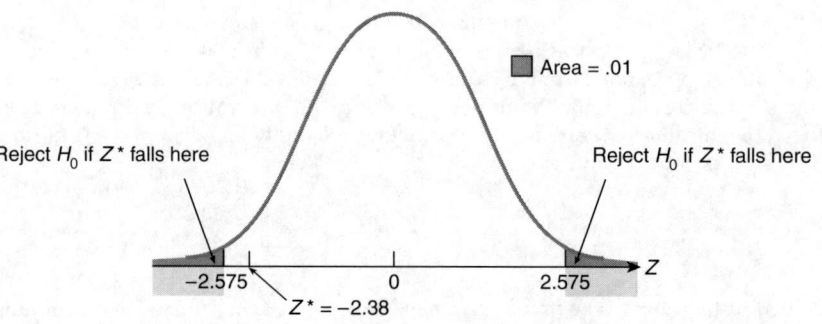

Area = .01

Reject H_0 if Z^* falls here

Reject H_0 if Z^* falls here

-2.575 0   2.575   Z

$Z^* = -2.38$

Accepting H_0 or Failing to Reject H_0

It may appear that there is no difference between "accepting" and "failing to reject" a null hypothesis, but there *is* a difference between these two statements. When you test a hypothesis, H_0 is *presumed innocent* until it is demonstrated to be guilty. In Example 10.1, using $\alpha = .01$ we failed to reject H_0. Now, how certain are we that μ is *exactly* 5.9 feet? After all, our estimate of μ is 5.79 feet. Clearly, we do not believe that μ is precisely 5.9 feet. There simply was not enough evidence to *reject* the claim that $\mu = 5.9$ feet.

For any hypothesis-testing application, the only hypothesis that can be *accepted* is the alternative hypothesis, H_a. Either there is sufficient evidence to *support H_a* (we reject H_0) or there is not (we fail to reject H_0). The focus of our attention is whether there is sufficient evidence within the sample data to conclude that H_a is correct. By failing to reject H_0, we are simply saying that the data do not allow us to support the claim made in H_a (such as $\mu \neq 5.9$ feet) and not that we accept the statement made in H_0 (such as $\mu = 5.9$ feet).

THE FIVE-STEP PROCEDURE FOR HYPOTHESIS TESTING

The discussion up to this point has concentrated on hypothesis testing on the unknown mean of a particular population. We want to emphasize that the shape of the parent population is not important, provided you have a large sample. In other words, the population may be a normal (bell-shaped) one or it may not—it simply does not matter for large samples. If you have reason to believe that the population being sampled is normally distributed, then any sample size will suffice. Once the level of significance (α) has been determined, there are five steps when attempting to reject or failing to reject a claim regarding the population mean, μ:

Step 1.   *Set up the null hypothesis, H_0, and the alternative hypothesis, H_a.* If the purpose of the hypothesis test is to test whether the population mean is equal to a particular value (say, μ_0), the "equal hypothesis" always is stated in H_0 and the "unequal hypothesis" always is stated in H_a.

Step 2.   *Define the test statistic.* The test statistic will be evaluated, using the sample data, and the known population standard deviation to determine if the data are compatible with the null hypothesis. For tests regarding the mean of a population when σ is known, the test statistic is approximately (or exactly) a standard normal random variable given by the equation

$$Z = \frac{\bar{X} - \mu_0}{\sigma/\sqrt{n}}$$

where μ_0 is the value of μ specified in H_0.

Step 3.   *Define a rejection region,* having determined a value for α, the significance level. In this region the value of the test statistic will result in rejecting H_0.

Step 4.   *Calculate the value of the test statistic, and carry out the test.* State your decision: to reject H_0 or to fail to reject H_0.*

Step 5.   *Give a conclusion,* in the terms of the original problem or question. This statement should be free of statistical jargon and should merely summarize the results of the analysis.

10.1

Steps 1 through 5 apply to all tests of hypothesis in this and subsequent chapters. The form of the test statistic and rejection region change for different applications, but the sequence of steps always is the same.

Everglo light bulbs are advertised as lasting 400 hours on the average. As manager of the quality assurance department, you need to examine this claim closely. If the average lifetime is, in fact, less than 400 hours, you can expect at least a half-dozen government watchdog agencies knocking on your door. If the light bulbs last longer than the 400 hours (on the average) claimed, you want to revise your advertising accordingly. From past experience, you have reason to believe the lifetime population is normally distributed with a standard deviation of 40 hours. To check this claim, you have tested the lifetimes of 25 bulbs, each under the same circumstances (power load, room temperature, and so on). The results of this sample are $n = 25$ and $\bar{x} = 420$ hours. In addition, σ is assumed to be 40 hours. What conclusion would you reach using a significance level of .1?

Step 1.   *Define the hypotheses.* We will test H_0: $\mu = 400$ H_a: $\mu \neq 400$.

Solution

Step 2.   *Define the test statistic.* The proper test statistic for this problem is

$$Z = \frac{\bar{X} - 400}{\sigma/\sqrt{n}}$$

Step 3.   *Define the rejection region.* The steps for finding the rejection region are shown in Figure 10.5. We conclude:

reject H_0 if $Z > 1.645$ or $Z < -1.645$

---

*An alternative to Steps 3 and 4 is to examine a number referred to as the *p-value*. The derivation of the *p*-value is explained in section 10.3. When using Excel, MINITAB, or SPSS, the resulting *p*-value will be contained in the computer output.

FIGURE

10.5

See Example 10.2;
the rejection
region is
$|Z| > 1.645$.

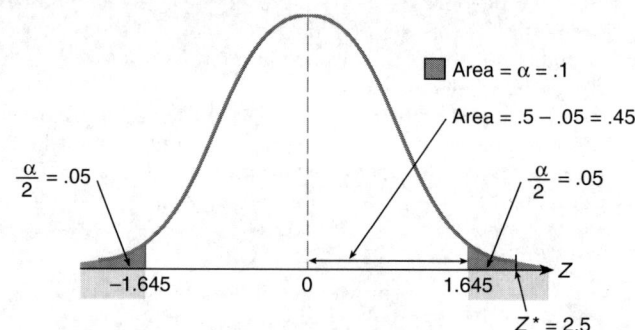

Step 4. *Calculate the value of the test statistic and carry out the test.* The computed value of Z is

$$Z^* = \frac{420 - 400}{40/\sqrt{25}} = \frac{20}{8} = 2.5$$

Since 2.5 > 1.645, our decision is to reject H_0. In Figure 10.5, Z^* falls in the rejection region.

Step 5. *State a conclusion.* Based on the sample data, there is sufficient evidence to conclude that the average lifetime of Everglo bulbs is not 400 hours.

Comments

In Example 10.2, $\bar{X}$ was "far enough away from" 400 for us to reject the claim that the average lifetime is 400 hours (H_0). However, remember that you cannot decide what is "far enough away from" without also considering the value of the standard deviation ($\sigma = 40$ hours in Example 10.2). This is why the value of σ is a vital part of the test statistic. Essentially, when the population contains much variation (σ is large), the sample mean ($\bar{X}$) is a less reliable estimator of the population mean and it is more difficult for $\bar{X}$ to be significantly different than the hypothesized value (400, in the previous value).

Examine the test statistic in Example 10.2. Observe that for *small* σ, it is "easier" to reject H_0. As σ becomes smaller, the absolute value of the test statistic, Z, becomes larger, and the test statistic is more likely to be in the rejection region for a given value α.

Confidence Intervals and Hypothesis Testing

What is the relationship, if any, between a 95% confidence interval and performing a *two-tailed* test using $\alpha = .05$? There is a very simple relationship here: When testing $H_0: \mu = \mu_0$ versus $H_a: \mu \neq \mu_0$ using the five-step procedure and a significance level, α, H_0 will be rejected if and only if μ_0 lies outside the $(1 - \alpha) \cdot 100\%$ confidence interval for μ.

The five-step procedure and the confidence interval procedure always lead to the same result. In fact, you can think of a confidence interval as that set of values of μ_0 that would not be rejected by a *two-tailed test* of hypothesis.

In our example involving heights of U.S. males, a sample of 75 heights produced $\bar{x} = 5.79$ feet where the population standard deviation was assumed to be .4 feet. The resulting 95% confidence interval for μ is

$$\bar{X} - k\left[\frac{\sigma}{\sqrt{n}}\right] \quad \text{to} \quad \bar{X} + k\left[\frac{\sigma}{\sqrt{n}}\right]$$

What is the value of k? For large sample sizes, the standard normal table (Table A.4) gives us the probability points we need. The value of k that provides a 95% confidence interval here is the *same* value of k that provides a two-tailed area under the Z curve equal to $1 - .95 = .05$. In other words, we use the same k value that we used in a two-tailed test of H_0 versus H_a—namely, $k = 1.96$. The resulting 95% confidence interval for μ is

$$\bar{X} - 1.96\left(\frac{\sigma}{\sqrt{n}}\right) \quad \text{to} \quad \bar{X} + 1.96\left(\frac{\sigma}{\sqrt{n}}\right)$$

$$= 5.79 - 1.96\left(\frac{.4}{\sqrt{75}}\right) \quad \text{to} \quad 5.79 + 1.96\left(\frac{.4}{\sqrt{75}}\right)$$

$$= 5.79 - .09 \quad \text{to} \quad 5.79 + .09$$

$$= 5.70 \quad \text{to} \quad 5.88$$

The value of μ we are investigating here is $\mu = 5.9$ feet, and the corresponding hypotheses are $H_0: \mu = 5.9$ and $H_a: \mu \neq 5.9$. For $\alpha = .05$, our result using the two-tailed test was to reject H_0. Using the confidence interval procedure, we obtain the same result because 5.9 does not lie in the 95% confidence interval.

Thus, if you already have computed a confidence interval for μ, you can tell at a glance whether to reject H_0 for a two-tailed test, provided the significance level, α, for the hypothesis test and the confidence level, $(1 - \alpha) \cdot 100\%$, match up.

EXAMPLE 10.3

Repeat the example involving the heights of U.S. males, but using a 99% confidence interval. Is the result the same as in Example 10.1, where we failed to reject $H_0 : \mu = 5.9$ using $\alpha = .01$?

Solution

Using $\alpha = .01$, we failed to reject H_0 because the absolute value of the test statistic did not exceed the critical value of $k = 2.575$. The corresponding 99% confidence interval for μ is

$$\bar{X} - 2.575\left(\frac{\sigma}{\sqrt{n}}\right) \quad \text{to} \quad \bar{X} + 2.575\left(\frac{\sigma}{\sqrt{n}}\right)$$

$$= 5.79 - 2.575\left(\frac{.4}{\sqrt{75}}\right) \quad \text{to} \quad 5.79 + 2.575\left(\frac{.4}{\sqrt{75}}\right)$$

$$= 5.79 - .12 \quad \text{to} \quad 5.79 + .12$$

$$= 5.67 \quad \text{to} \quad 5.91$$

Because 5.9 does (barely) lie in this confidence interval, our decision is to fail to reject H_0—the same conclusion reached in Example 10.1.

The Power of a Statistical Test

Up to this point, the probability of a Type II error, β, has remained a phantom— we know it is there, but we don't know what it is. One thing we can say is that a *wide* confidence interval for μ means that the corresponding two-tailed test of H_0 versus H_a has a *large* chance of failing to reject a false H_0; that is, β is large. Now,

$$\beta = P(\text{fail to reject } H_0 \text{ when } H_0 \text{ is false})$$

which means that

$$1 - \beta = P(\text{rejecting } H_0 \text{ when } H_0 \text{ is false})$$

The value of $1 - \beta$ is referred to as the **power** of the test. Since we like β to be small, we prefer the power of the test to be large. Notice that $1 - \beta$ represents the probability of making a *correct* decision in the event that H_0 is false, because in this case we *should* reject it. The more powerful your test is, the better.

Determining the power of your test (hence, β) is not difficult. We will illustrate this procedure for the previous two-tailed test of $H_0: \mu = \mu_0$ versus $H_a: \mu \neq \mu_0$, for some μ_0.

In Example 10.2 we looked at the data on Everglo light bulbs, where the hypotheses were $H_0: \mu = 400$ hours and $H_a: \mu \neq 400$ hours. Assume that the actual population standard deviation is known to be $\sigma = 40$ hours. For this situation, our test statistic is (using a sample size of $n = 25$):

$$Z = \frac{\bar{X} - 400}{\sigma/\sqrt{n}} = \frac{\bar{X} - 400}{40/\sqrt{25}}$$

$$= \frac{\bar{X} - 400}{8}$$

Proceeding as in Example 10.2, using $\alpha = .10$, we reject H_0 if $Z > 1.645$ or $Z < -1.645$, that is, if $|Z| > 1.645$. So reject H_0 if $(\bar{X} - 400)/8 > 1.645$ [same as $\bar{X} > 400 + (1.645)(8) = 413.16$] or if $(\bar{X} - 400)/8 < -1.645$ [same as $\bar{X} < 400 - (1.645)(8) = 386.84$]. This way of representing the rejection region is illustrated in Figure 10.6, using the shaded area under curve A. The power of this test is

$$1 - \beta = P(\text{rejecting } H_0 \text{ if } H_0 \text{ is false})$$

$$= P(\text{rejecting } H_0 \text{ if } \mu \neq 400)$$

What is the power of this test if μ is not 400 but is 405? What you have here is a value of $1 - \beta$ for *each* value of $\mu \neq 400$.

Recall that we reject H_0 if $\bar{X} > 413.16$ or $\bar{X} < 386.84$. The probability of this occurring if $\mu = 405$ is illustrated as the lined area under curve B in Figure 10.6. Now, if $\mu = 405$ and $\sigma = 40$ (assumed), then

$$Z = \frac{\bar{X} - 405}{40/\sqrt{25}} = \frac{\bar{X} - 405}{8}$$

FIGURE

10.6

The shaded area is the probability of rejecting H_0 if $\mu = 400$ (that is, $\alpha = .10$), and the striped area is the probability of rejecting H_0 if $\mu = 405$ (that is, the power of the test $1 - \beta$ when $\mu = 405$).

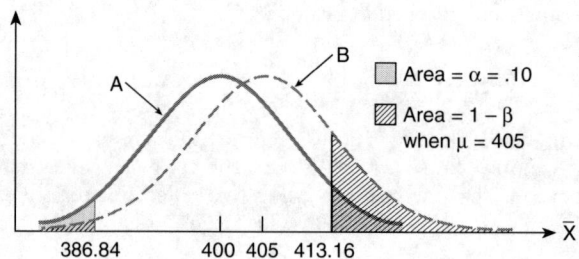

□ Area = α = .10

▨ Area = $1 - \beta$ when $\mu = 405$

is a standard normal random variable. So, in Figure 10.6, the striped area to the right of 413.16 is

$$P(\bar{X} > 413.16) = P\left[\frac{\bar{X} - 405}{8} > \frac{413.16 - 405}{8}\right]$$

$$= P\left[Z > \frac{8.16}{8}\right]$$

$$= P(Z > 1.02)$$

$$= .5 - .3461$$

$$= .1539$$

Also, the striped area to the left of 386.84 is

$$P(\bar{X} < 386.84) = P\left[\frac{\bar{X} - 405}{8} < \frac{386.84 - 405}{8}\right]$$

$$= P(Z < -2.27)$$

$$= .5 - .4884$$

$$= .0116$$

Adding these two areas, we find that, if $\mu = 405$, the power of the test of H_0: $\mu = 400$ versus H_a: $\mu \neq 400$ is

$$1 - \beta = .1539 + .0116 = .1655$$

This means that if $\mu = 405$, the probability of making a Type II error (not rejecting H_0) is $\beta = 1 - .1655 = .8345$ (rather high).

This procedure is summarized in the following box. Notice that in the previous discussion, $Z_{\alpha/2} = Z_{.05} = 1.645$, $z_1 = 1.645 - (405 - 400)/40/\sqrt{25} = 1.02$, and $z_2 = -1.645 - (405 - 400)/40/\sqrt{25} = -2.27$.

POWER OF TEST FOR H_0: $\mu = \mu_0$ VERSUS H_a: $\mu \neq \mu_0$

1. Determine

$$z_1 = Z_{\alpha/2} - \frac{\mu - \mu_0}{\sigma/\sqrt{n}}$$

and

$$z_2 = -Z_{\alpha/2} - \frac{\mu - \mu_0}{\sigma/\sqrt{n}}$$

where $Z_{\alpha/2}$ is the value of Z from Table A.4 having a right-tailed area of $\alpha/2$ and μ is the specific value of the population mean (405 in Figure 10.6).

2. Power of test = $P(Z > z_1) + P(Z < z_2)$.

FIGURE

10.7

Power curve for
H_0: $\mu = 400$ versus
H_a: $\mu \neq 400$.

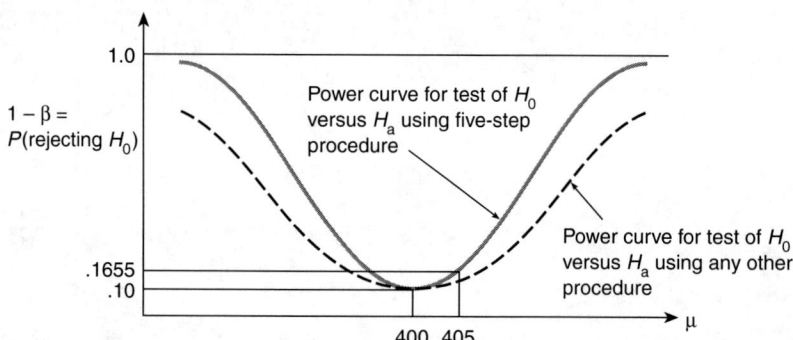

The power of your test increases (β decreases) as μ moves away from 400, as illustrated in Figure 10.7. Using the five-step procedure, which uses the test statistic $Z = (\bar{X} - 400)/(\sigma/\sqrt{n})$, the resulting **power curve** is the solid-line curve in Figure 10.7. It is symmetric, and its lowest point is located at $\mu = 400$. For this value of μ, H_0 is actually true, so that a Type II error was not committed. Nevertheless, the value on the power curve corresponding to $\mu = 400$ is always

$$P(\text{rejecting } H_0 \text{ if } \mu = 400) = \alpha = .10 \text{ (for this example)}$$

The *steeper* your power curve is, the better. You are more apt to reject H_0 as μ moves away from 400—certainly a nice property. If we assume that the sampled population is normally distributed, Figure 10.7 illustrates that the power curve using the five-step procedure lies above (is steeper than) the power curve for any other testing procedure. To illustrate briefly another testing procedure, rather than basing the test statistic on the sample mean $\bar{X}$, we could derive a test statistic using the sample *median*. The resulting power curve for this procedure would lie *below* the one using $\bar{X}$, indicating that the test using the sample median is less powerful and thus inferior. So, in this sense, the five-step procedure defines the best (most powerful) test of H_0: $\mu = \mu_0$ versus H_a: $\mu \neq \mu_0$.

X Exercises 10.1–10.16

Understanding the Mechanics

10.1 A manager randomly samples 50 containers of juice. The manager is concerned that the containers may be filled to an amount different from 24 ounces.
   a. Develop a suitable null and alternative hypothesis.
   b. How can the manager make a Type I error?
   c. How can the manager make a Type II error?
   d. Will the hypothesis test procedure prove that the containers are filled to an amount different from 24 ounces?

10.2 State if an error is made in the following situations and, if so, what type of error.
   a. The null hypothesis is true and the calculated value of the test statistic falls in the rejection region.
   b. The null hypothesis is true and the calculated value of the test statistic does not fall in the rejection region.
   c. The alternative hypothesis is true and the calculated value of the test statistic falls in the rejection region.
   d. The alternative hypothesis is true and the calculated value of the test statistic does not fall in the rejection region.

10.3 Are the following statements true or false? Explain.
   a. As the significance level increases, the probability of a Type I error increases.
   b. As the power increases, the probability of a Type II error decreases.
   c. As the significance level increases, the size of the rejection region increases.
   d. The probability of a Type I error and the probability of a Type II error always sum to 1.

Applying the New Concepts

10.4 State the null and alternative hypotheses for the following situations.
  a. A federal auditor believes that a health care company has overcharged its patients.
  b. The editor of a magazine believes that the mean income of subscribers to its magazine is $75,000.
  c. An operations manager must maintain machines that produce 50 pound bags of fertilizer.
  d. A manufacturer believes that the average life of its competitor's battery is less than 10 hours.

10.5 The mean of a normally distributed population is believed to be equal to 50.1. A sample of 36 observations is taken, and the sample mean is found to be 53.2. The alternative hypothesis is that the population mean is not equal to 50.1. Complete the hypothesis test, assuming that the population standard deviation is equal to 4. Use a .05 significance level.

10.6 More people are choosing to get married in the Caribbean as the cost of a traditional wedding increases. In fact, weddings in the Caribbean, with the cost of travel, can cost the bride's father between $5,000 and $10,000. As an additional benefit, the wedding can roll right into the honeymoon. While the disadvantage of such far-away weddings is difficult for many relatives and close friends, the savings over a $25,000 to $30,000 traditional wedding can make the decision easy. Suppose that a Caribbean resort wished to promote its location as a low-cost alternative to the traditional wedding and advertised that the average wedding with travel expenses is $7,500. To confirm this figure, 50 previously held weddings on the Caribbean island are randomly sampled. The data are presented below in dollars. Using a .05 significance level, is there sufficient evidence to indicate that the average cost of a wedding in the Caribbean differs from $7,500? Assume the population standard deviation is equal to $1096.31.

6,300	8,400	9,000	7,400	7,000	8,100	6,500	8,400
7,700	7,300	5,800	9,700	6,800	6,400	8,300	7,700
5,100	5,800	8,700	9,500	7,800	8,000	7,200	7,500
6,500	9,700	7,400	7,800	6,700	8,900	7,500	8,700
7,700	6,900	7,100	8,200	6,400	7,600	8,700	7,800
9,600	9,200	7,700	5,700	7,900	8,800	9,000	7,300
8,300	8,100						

(Source: "Here Come the Isles: Exotic Ways to Wed," *USA Today*, June 19, 1998, p. 4D.)

10.7 "Most things in the movie business are disappointments," said Ben Feingold, president of the Columbia TriStar Motion Picture Group. "DVD isn't one of them." Industry figures show that the average price of DVD players, expected to be in 25 million homes by the end of the year, is about $180, down from about $500 when the format was introduced in 1997. Suppose that a retail analyst randomly samples 25 retail stores in a certain geographical area and records a sample mean of $193. The retail analyst would like to test whether the average price of DVD players in this region differs from $180.
  a. What is the null and alternative hypotheses?
  b. Assume that the population standard deviation of the cost of DVD players is $30. Is there evidence that the average price for a DVD player in this region differs from $180? Use a 1% significance level.
  c. What would your answer be in part b if the sample size were 50?
  d. What assumption are you making about the distribution of the data for the hypothesis test procedure to be valid?

(Source: "Choosing Bells or Whistles," *The New York Times*, October 26, 2001, p. E27.)

10.8 A crime reporter was told that, on the average, 3,000 burglaries per month occurred in his city. The reporter examined past data, which were used to compute a 95% confidence interval for the number of burglaries per month. The confidence interval was from 2,176 to 2,784. At a 5% level of significance, do these data tend to support the alternative hypothesis, H_a: $\mu \neq 3,000$?

10.9 The greatest variation in real estate prices is in California, where recently there was a difference of more than $1 million between a home in Palo Alto and one in Bakersfield. In Palo Alto, the typical four-bedroom, 2,200-square-foot house was appraised at about $1.2 million in 2001, whereas a similar home in Bakersfield was appraised at $200,000. Suppose that a realtor randomly sampled 50 homes in Palo Alto in 2005 and found a 95% confidence interval for the average appraised value of a home in Palo Alto to be .91 to 1.08 million. Assume that the appraised values of homes in Palo Alto are normally distributed. Is there sufficient evidence to indicate that the average price of a home in Palo Alto is different from $1.2 million in 2005? Use a 5% significance level.

(Source: "Palo Alto Tops Realtor List of Most Expensive Markets," *Los Angeles Times*, August 19, 2001, p. K13.)

10.10 The life span of an electronic chip used in a high-powered microcomputer is estimated to be 625.35 hours from a random sample of 40 chips. The life of an electronic chip is considered to be normally distributed with a population variance of 400 hours.
  a. Find a 90% confidence interval for the mean life of the electronic chips.
  b. Is the true mean life of the electronic chips different from 633 hours? Use a 10% significance level.

10.11 The $450 million Stade de France, built specifically for the 1998 World Cup soccer championship, has 80,000 seats with no pillars or obstructed views. Soccer is so popular that the global television audience will outdraw that of the Olympics. Tickets sold through travel agencies were priced up to $600 for early matches before the World Cup championship. Suppose that a travel agency wished to know the mean selling price of the early matches. A random sample revealed a mean of \$430. Historical data revealed a population standard deviation of \$130.

    a. Find an interval with a 90% confidence level for estimating the true mean selling price for the early matches. Assume a sample size of 100.

    b. Is there sufficient evidence to indicate that the true mean selling price for the early matches differs from \$500? Use a 10% significance level.

(Source: "Frank Talk About State-of-the-Art Stadium," *USA Today*, May 12, 1988, p. 8C.)

10.12 The hypotheses for a situation are

$$H_0: \mu = 20$$

$$H_a: \mu \neq 20$$

If the population of interest is normally distributed, what is the power of the test for the mean if μ is actually equal to 22? Assume that a sample of size 49 is used and the population standard deviation is 4.2. Use a significance level of .05.

10.13 The manager of Technology Solutions wishes to market a Wonder Card to transition a personal computer to a household multimedia center. The manager samples 25 stores to test the null hypothesis that the mean price that retailers would market the card is \$200 using a 10% significance level. The manager knows that the population standard deviation is \$40. What is the power of this test if the true population mean is \$215? How would this power change if the null hypothesis was that the mean is equal to \$160?

10.14 An electro-optical firm currently uses a laser component in producing sophisticated graphic designs. The time it takes to produce a certain design with the current laser component is 70 seconds, with a standard deviation of 8 seconds. A new laser component is bought by the firm because it is believed that the time it takes this laser to produce the same design is not equal to 70 seconds; the new component also has a standard deviation of 8 seconds. The research-and-development department is interested in constructing the power curve for testing the claim that the time it takes to produce the same design by the new laser component is not equal to 70 seconds. Graph the power function for a sample of size 25 and a significance level of .05.

Using the Computer

10.15 **[DATA SET EX10-15]** Variable Description:

ATMwithdrawal: Amount of euro currency withdrawn

The most convenient way for tourists to get euro currency is through an ATM machine. Bank managers are interested in the average withdrawals from these machines. Assume a population standard deviation of 50 euros.

    a. Using a histogram, describe the shape of the data.

    b. Using a significance level of 5%, test that the average withdrawal differs from 150 euros.

    c. Construct a 95% confidence interval for the average withdrawal. Can this interval be used to obtain the conclusion in part b? Explain.

10.16 **[DATA SET EX10-16]** Variable Description:

Decibels: Decibels produced by power tools at a plant

Prolonged exposure to noise louder than 85 decibels can impair hearing. A plant manager wishes to determine if there is evidence that the average number of decibels produced by plant power tools differs from 85. Using the Decibels data, what is your conclusion at the 1% significance level? Assume a population standard deviation of 2 decibels. Repeat this analysis with a standard deviation of 2.5 decibels and compare the results.

10.2

ONE-TAILED TEST FOR THE MEAN OF A POPULATION (r KNOWN)

There are many situations in which you are interested in demonstrating that the mean of a population is larger or smaller than some specified value. For example, as a member of a consumer-advocate group, you may be attempting to demonstrate that the average weight of a bag of sugar for a particular brand is not 10 pounds (as specified on the bag) but is in fact less than 10 pounds. Because the situation that you (the researcher) are attempting to demonstrate goes into the alternative hypothesis, the resulting hypotheses would be $H_0: \mu \geq 10$ and $H_a: \mu < 10$. Remember that we said it is standard practice always to put the equals *sign in the null hypothesis.* In the testing procedure only the *boundary value* is important, and so the hypotheses may be written as

$$H_0: \mu = 10$$

$$H_a: \mu < 10$$

In this way, we can identify the distribution of $\bar{X}$ when H_0 is true—namely, $\bar{X}$ is approximately a normal random variable centered at 10 with standard deviation $\sigma/\sqrt{n}$. Because the focus of our attention is on H_a (can we support it or not?), which of the two ways you use to write H_0 is not an important issue. The procedure for testing H_0 versus H_a is the same regardless of how you state H_0.

The resulting test is referred to as a **one-tailed test,** and it uses the same five-step procedure as the two-tailed test. The only change we make is to modify the rejection region: All the error is in a single tail.

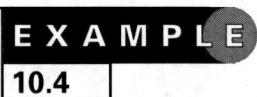

E X A M P L E

10.4

A foreign car manufacturer advertises that its newest model, the Bullet, rarely stops at gas stations. In fact, it claims its EPA rating for highway driving is at least 32.5 mpg. However, the results of a recent independent study determined the miles per gallon (mpg) for 50 identical models of the Bullet, with these results: $n = 50$ and $\bar{x} = 30.4$ mpg. From past experience, the population standard deviation is known to be 5.5 mpg. This report failed to offer any conclusion, and you have been asked to interpret these results by someone who has always felt that the 32.5 figure is too high. What would be your conclusion using a significance level of $\alpha = .05$?

Solution

Step 1.   *An important point to be made here is that* H_0 *and* H_a *(as well as* α*) must be defined before you observe any data. In other words, do not let the data dictate your hypotheses;* this approach would introduce a serious bias into your final outcome. For this application, we want to demonstrate that the population mean, μ, is less than 32.5 mpg, and so this goes into H_a. The appropriate hypotheses then are H_0: $\mu \geq 32.5$ and H_a: $\mu < 32.5$.

Step 2.   The test statistic for a one-tailed test is the same as that for a two-tailed test, namely,

$$Z = \frac{\bar{X} - \mu_0}{\sigma/\sqrt{n}}$$

Here,

$$Z = \frac{\bar{X} - 32.5}{\sigma/\sqrt{n}}$$

Step 3.   What happens to Z when H_a is true? Here we would expect $\bar{X}$ to be less than 32.5 (because μ is), so the value of Z should be negative. Consequently, our procedure will be to reject H_0 if Z lies "too far to the left" of 0; that is,

$$\text{reject } H_0 \text{ if } Z = \frac{\bar{X} - 32.5}{\sigma/\sqrt{n}} < k \quad \text{for some } k < 0$$

Since $\alpha = .05$, we will choose a value of k (the critical value) such that the resulting test will reject H_0 (shoot down the mpg claim) when it is true, with a 5% risk of an incorrect decision. This amounts to defining a rejection region in the *left tail* of the Z curve, the shaded area in Figure 10.8. Using Table A.4, we see that the critical value is $k = -1.645$, and the resulting test of H_0 versus H_a is

$$\text{reject } H_0 \text{ if } Z = \frac{\bar{X} - 32.5}{\sigma/\sqrt{n}} < -1.645$$

Step 4.   Using the sample results, the value of the test statistic is

$$Z^* = \frac{30.4 - 32.5}{5.5/\sqrt{50}} = -2.70$$

Because $-2.70 < -1.645$, the decision is to reject H_0.

Step 5.   The results of this study support the claim that the average mileage for the Bullet is *less than* 32.5 mpg. This result would provide just cause for claiming false advertising by the auto manufacturer.

One-Tailed Test or Two-Tailed Test?

The decision to use a one-tailed test or a two-tailed test depends on what you are attempting to demonstrate. For example, when the quality-control department of a manufacturing facility receives a shipment from one of its vendors and wants to determine if the product meets minimal specifications, a one-tailed test is appropriate. If the product does not meet specifications, it will be rejected. This type of problem was first encountered in Chapter 5, where we examined lot acceptance sampling. Here, the product is *not* checked to see whether it *exceeds* specifications, because any product that exceeds specifications is acceptable.

By contrast, the vendors who supply the products would generally run two-tailed tests to determine two things. First, they must know if the product meets the minimal specifications of their customers before they ship it. Second, they must determine whether the product greatly exceeds specifications because this can be very costly in production (making a product that uses too much raw material costs them extra money).

The testing of electric fuses is a classic example of a two-tailed test. A fuse must break when it reaches the prescribed temperature or a fire will result. However, the fuse must not break before it reaches the prescribed temperature or it will shut off the electricity when there is no need to do so. Therefore, the quality-control procedures for testing fuses must be two-tailed.

FIGURE

10.8

The one-tailed rejection region is $Z < -1.645$. We reject H_0 if $Z = (\bar{X} - 32.5)/(\sigma/\sqrt{n}) < -1.645$.

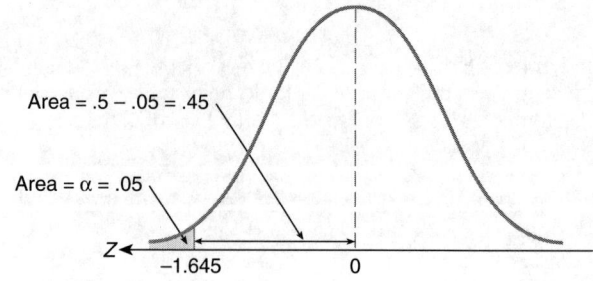

Area $= .5 - .05 = .45$

Area $= \alpha = .05$

-1.645 0

Using Statistical Software to Calculate the Large-Sample Test Statistic for Testing a Population Mean

EXAMPLE

10.5

The mean consumption of electricity for the month of June at the Southern States Power Company (SSPC) historically has been 918 kilowatt-hours per residential customer. Based on past experience, the population standard deviation is assumed to be σ = 175 kilowatt-hours. As part of its request for a rate increase, SSPC is arguing that the power consumption for June of the current year is substantially higher. To demonstrate this, they hired an independent consulting firm to examine a random sample of 60 customer accounts. The sample results, contained in data set DATA8-5, consist of the 60 kilowatt-hours for June of the current year. Can you conclude that the average consumption for all users during June of this year (denoted by μ) is larger than 918? Use α = .01.

Solution

Step 1.   The hypotheses here are $H_0: \mu \leq 918$ and $H_a: \mu > 918$.

Step 2.   The correct test statistic is

$$Z = \frac{\bar{X} - 918}{\sigma/\sqrt{n}}$$

Step 3.   For this situation, what happens to Z if H_a is true? The value of $\bar{X}$ should then be larger than 918 (on the average), resulting in a positive value of Z. So we

$$\text{reject } H_0 \text{ if } Z = \frac{\bar{X} - 918}{\sigma/\sqrt{n}} > k \quad \text{for some } k > 0$$

Examine the standard normal curve in Figure 10.9, where the area corresponding to α is the shaded part of the **right tail**; using Table A.4, the critical value is k = 2.33. The test of H_0 versus H_a will be

$$\text{reject } H_0 \text{ if } Z > 2.33$$

Step 4.   To carry out the test of hypothesis using Excel, begin by opening file DATA8-5. Click on **KPK Data Analysis ➤ One Population Inference** and specify the input range as A1:A61, since there are 60 data values and cell A1 contains the label "KW-Hours" (be sure to click on the box alongside **Labels**). Enter 175 as the **Population Standard Deviation** and 1% as **Alpha**. Select **Hypothesis Test** and **Right-tail test**. Enter 918 as the **Hypothesized Value of Mean**. By specifying the

FIGURE

10.9

One-tailed
rejection region;
reject H_0 if $Z > 2.33$.

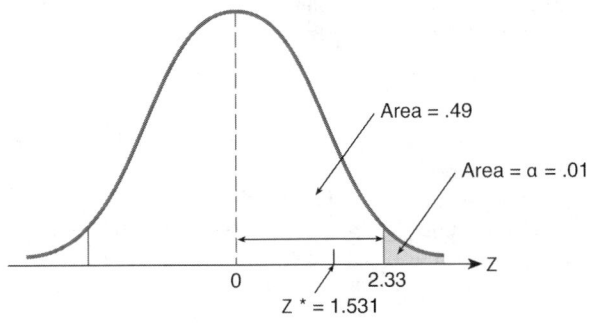

FIGURE

10.10

Excel spreadsheet
and output using
**KPK Data Analysis
➤ One Population
Inference.**

	A	B	C
1	KW-Hours	**Z Test for Population Mean**	
2	1128.89		KW-Hours
3	976.81	Number of Observations	60
4	936.20	Population Std. Deviation	175.0
5	1107.81	Sample Mean	952.58
6	951.89	Ho:μ ≤ 918	Ha:μ > 918
7	501.65	Z*	1.531
8	1161.07	P[Z ≥ Z*]	0.0629
9	997.04	Z Critical, α = 0.01	2.3263
10	775.58		

FIGURE

10.11

MINITAB output
using **Stat ➤ Basic
Statistics ➤
1-Sample Z.**

One-Sample Z: KW-Hours

```
Test of mu = 918 vs > 918
The assumed standard deviation = 175
```

					99% Lower		
Variable	N	Mean	StDev	SE Mean	Bound	Z	P
KW-Hours	60	952.580	173.915	22.592	900.022	1.53	0.063

output range as B1 (upper-left corner), you obtain the output shown in Figure 10.10. The computed value of the test statistic is

$$Z^* = \frac{952.58 - 918}{175/\sqrt{60}} = 1.531$$

Because 1.531 < 2.33 (the value in cell C9), the decision is to fail to reject H_0. A valuable piece of information, the *p-value* for the test of hypothesis, is contained in cell C8. It will be discussed in Section 10.3.

This analysis can also be carried out using MINITAB. To carry out the one-tailed Z test, refer to the instructions in the end-of-chapter appendix. The highlighted portion of the MINITAB output in Figure 10.11 contains the computed Z statistic, $Z^* = 1.53$. The other highlighted value (.063) is the corresponding *p*-value. Calculating and interpreting *p*-values will be explained in the next section and this particular *p*-value will be reexamined in Example 10.6.

Step 5.   At the .01 significance level, there is insufficient evidence to support the power company's claim that the power consumption for June has increased.

Comments

1. This result is very much tied to the value of α. Using α = .10 in Example 10.5, we would obtain the *opposite* conclusion—which you may find somewhat disturbing. You often hear the expression, that "statistics lie." This is not true—statistics are merely mistreated, either intentionally or accidentally. One can often obtain the desired conclusion by choosing the value of α that produces the desired conclusion. We therefore reemphasize that you must choose α by weighing the seriousness of a Type I versus a Type II error *before* seeing the data. A partial remedy for this dilemma is discussed in Section 10.3.

2. To calculate the power of a one-sided test, refer to the box on page 265. We modify this procedure for a one-sided test as outlined in the following boxes.

3. A summary of the procedure for carrying out a large-sample test on a population mean for known σ is contained in the box titled "Tests on a Population Mean (σ Known)."

POWER OF TEST FOR H_0: $\mu \leq \mu_0$ VERSUS H_a: $\mu > \mu_0$

1. Determine

$$z_1 = Z_\alpha - \frac{\mu - \mu_0}{\sigma/\sqrt{n}}$$

where Z_α is the value of Z from Table A.4 having a right-tailed area of α and μ is the specific value of the population mean.
2. Power of the test is $P(Z > z_1)$

POWER OF TEST FOR H_0: $\mu \geq \mu_0$ VERSUS H_a: $\mu < \mu_0$

1. Determine

$$z_2 = -Z_\alpha - \frac{\mu - \mu_0}{\sigma/\sqrt{n}}$$

where Z_α is the value of Z from Table A.4 having a right-tailed area of α and μ is the specific value of the population mean.
2. Power of the test is $P(Z < z_2)$

TESTS ON A POPULATION MEAN (σ KNOWN)

Two-Tailed Test

$$H_0: \mu = \mu_0$$
$$H_a: \mu \neq \mu_0$$
$$\text{reject } H_0 \text{ if } |Z^*| > Z_{\alpha/2}$$

where Z^* is the computed value of $Z = \frac{\bar{X} - \mu_0}{\sigma/\sqrt{n}}$ $(Z_{\alpha/2} = 1.96 \text{ for } \alpha = .05)$.

One-Tailed Test

$H_0: \mu \leq \mu_0$	$H_0: \mu \geq \mu_0$
$H_a: \mu > \mu_0$	$H_a: \mu < \mu_0$
reject H_0 if $Z^* > Z_\alpha$	reject H_0 if $Z^* < -Z_\alpha$
$(Z_\alpha = 1.645 \text{ for } \alpha = .05)$	$(-Z_\alpha = -1.645 \text{ for } \alpha = .05)$

411

X　Exercises 10.17–10.26

Understanding the Mechanics

10.17 Set up the null hypothesis and the alternative hypothesis for each of the following situations.

   a. An automotive analyst believes that the miles per gallon on a new model is less than what the company is advertising. A random sample of data is taken to support the analyst's belief.

   b. A phone company claims that the average customer pays less than $30 a month. A random sample of data is taken to verify this claim.

   c. A marketing research firm believes that the average number of hours per week that Americans watch television differs from 15 hours a week. A sample of data is taken to support this belief.

10.18 A random sample of 64 observations was selected. Test that the mean of the population is less than 106 using a significance level of .05. The population variance is believed to be 32 and the sum of the sample values is 6,592.

10.19 A random sample of 49 observations from a normal population yields a sample mean of 85. The population standard deviation is 14 and the significance level is 5%.

   a. Test the claim that the population mean differs from 81.

   b. Test the claim that the population mean is greater than 85.

Applying the New Concepts

10.20 The Federal Reserve board made eight interest-rate cuts on its benchmark short-term rates during 2001. However, credit cards have averaged around 14%, with the lowest credit cards charging around 8%. A financial analyst believes that the average rate on credit cards that charge monthly fees is lower than the national average of all credit cards. A random sample of 49 different credit cards that charged monthly fees revealed a sample mean of 13.5%. Assume a population standard deviation of 1.4%. Test the financial analyst's belief that the average rate charged by credit cards with monthly fees is less than 14%. Use a 5% significance level.

(Source: "Credit Card Fees," Kiplinger's Personal Finance Magazine, vol. 55, no. 11, November 2001, p. 101.)

10.21 H&M hires a pool of financial consultants who are members of the National Association of Personal Financial Advisors to discuss portfolio recommendations with its clients. The manager of H&M believes that another financial consultant should be hired if the average phone consultation exceeds 350 seconds. A random sample of 100 phone calls revealed a mean of 375 seconds. The population standard deviation is 150 seconds. Should another financial consultant be hired? Use a 5% significance level.

10.22 A movie theater complex will raise its ticket price if the average ticket price of theaters in southern California exceeds $7.50. A random sample of 36 theaters resulted in a mean of $7.80. The population standard deviation is $1.00. What conclusion can be made at the 10% significance level? How about at the 5% significance level?

10.23 In an attempt to get AIDS drugs to thousands of HIV-infected people in Africa, Asia, and South America, several major pharmaceutical companies slashed their prices, in some cases by 50% to 75%. The manager of a medical center working under the United Nations' AIDS program is interested in the average cost of widely used anti-HIV drugs in the South African region. The manager believes that the cost is less than $280 per month. Assume that the costs of these anti-HIV drugs are approximately normally distributed with a standard deviation of $100. What is the power of the statistical test to test the manager's belief if the sample size is 35 and the true mean cost is $240 for the anti-HIV drugs in South Africa? Use a significance level of .05.

(Source: "AIDS Medicine Will Cost Less in Poor Nations," The Wall Street Journal, June 23, 1998, p. B1.)

10.24 Following the September 11, 2001, terrorist attack, U.S. flags of all sorts were glued, clipped, and taped to American vehicles as a sign of patriotism. Several months later, these flags had been badly beaten by the elements. One man, Tom Fucigna, has made it his mission to pick up flags that lay alongside the interstate. Suppose that Tom claims that the average number of flags that he picks up is greater than 15. The population standard deviation of the number of flags that he picks up is known to be 2.5. Assume that an observer wished to test Tom's claim using a sample size of 35 days and a significance level of 5%. What is the power of the hypothesis test to test this claim if the true average number of flags that Tom picks up is 16?

(Source: "Oh, Say, Can You See That Your Car Flag Is Now a Bit Ragged?" The Wall Street Journal, January 21, 2002, p. A1.)

Using the Computer

10.25 **[DATA SET EX10-25]** Variable Description:

CartridgLife: Number of pages that a cartridge can be used to print

An office supply company would like to advertise that its new and improved ink jet cartridges last longer than the previous ones. From past tests, the old cartridges had a life of 2,375 pages with a standard deviation of 250 pages. The company believes that the life of the new ink jet cartridges will be longer than the old cartridges and that the standard deviation of the life of the new cartridges is the same. A random sample of 100 new cartridges were used in a study and their life is recorded in variable CartridgLife in units of pages.

    a. Using a significance level of .10, is there sufficient evidence that the new cartridges last longer?

    b. Explain how practical and statistical significance are important in determining whether the company should advertise the new cartridges as lasting longer?

    c. Should the standard deviation also have decreased to really have an improved cartridge? Explain.

10.26 [Simulation Exercise] A rejection of a null hypothesis is affected by four factors: (1) the value of the mean when the alternative hypothesis is true; (2) the sample size; (3) the population standard deviation; (4) the significance level. In Excel, click on **KPK Data Analysis ▶ Simulation Exercises ▶ Hypothesis Testing** to discover through a simulation game how these factors affect rejecting the null hypothesis. This game assumes that H_0: $\mu \leq 50$. Fifty simulations using randomly generated data are performed and a visual display of the value of the test statistic and whether it falls in the rejection or nonrejection region is presented.

    a. In the dialog box, enter 50 for the true value of the population mean under the alternative hypothesis. This situation is the case where the null hypothesis is true. Now enter 25 for the sample size, 20 for the σ, and 5 for the alpha level. What is the percent rejected? Repeat this five times. On average, there should be approximately 5% rejections.

    b. In part a, change the value of μ under the alternative to 53, 55, 58, and 60. How does the number of rejections change?

    c. Select 53 for the value of μ under the alternative. Enter 25 for the sample size and 5 for the alpha level. Change σ to 10, 15, 20, 25, and 30. How does the percentage of rejections change as the value of the population standard deviation increases?

    d. Select 53 for the value of μ under the alternative. Enter 20 for the value of σ and 5 for the alpha level. Change the sample size to 25, 50, 75, and 100. How does the percentage of rejections change as the value of the sample size increases?

    e. Select 53 for the value of μ under the alternative. Enter 20 for the value of σ and 25 for the sample size. Change the alpha level to 1, 5, 10, and 20. How does the percentage of rejections change as the significance level increases?

10.3 REPORTING TESTING RESULTS USING A *p*-VALUE

In Example 10.1, we noted that for one value of α we rejected H_0, and for another (seemingly reasonable) value of α we failed to reject H_0. Is there a way of summarizing the results of a test of hypothesis that allows you to determine whether these results are barely significant (or insignificant) or overwhelmingly significant (or insignificant)? Did we barely reject H_0, or did H_0 go down in flames?

A convenient way to summarize your results is to use a *p*-value, often called the *observed* α or *observed significance level*.

> The ***p*-value** is the value of α at which the hypothesis test procedure changes conclusions based on a given set of data. It is the largest value of α for which you will fail to reject H_0.

Consequently, the *p*-value is the point at which the five-step procedure leads us to switch from rejecting H_0 to failing to reject H_0 for a given set of data.

Determining the *p*-Value

The *p*-value for *any* test is determined by replacing the area corresponding to α by the area corresponding to the *computed* value of the test statistic. In our discussion and Example 10.1, using $\alpha = .05$ you reject H_0 and using $\alpha = .01$ you fail to reject H_0. We know that the *p*-value here is between .01 and .05. For this example, the computed value of the test

10.12

Rejection regions
for $\alpha = .01, .05$.

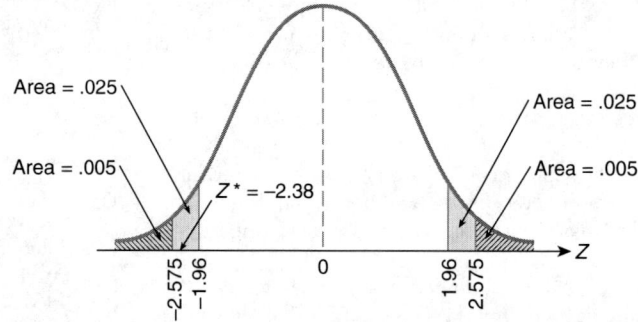

10.13

p-value is
determined by
replacing the area
corresponding to α
(see Figure 10.12)
by the area
corresponding to
Z^*. Here $Z^* =$
-2.38, and the
p-value $= 2 \cdot$
$.0087 = .0174$ (total
shaded area).

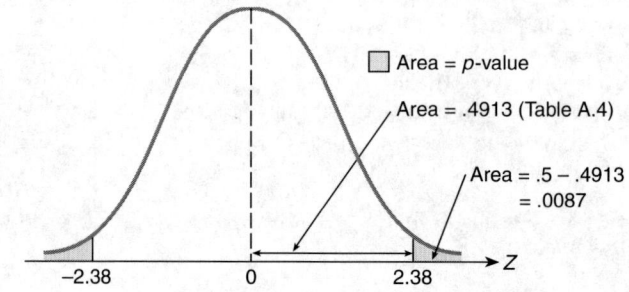

statistic was $Z^* = -2.38$, where the hypotheses are H_0: $\mu = 5.9$ feet and H_a: $\mu \neq 5.9$ feet. The Z curve for this situation is shown in Figure 10.12.

For which value of α does the testing procedure change the conclusions here? In Figure 10.12, if you were using a predetermined significance level α, you would split α in half and put $\alpha/2$ into each tail. So the total tail area represents α. Using Figure 10.13, we reverse this procedure by finding the *total* tail area corresponding to a two-tailed test with $Z^* = -2.38$; we add the area to the left of -2.38 (.0087) to that to the right of 2.38 (also .0087). This total area is .0174, which is the p-value for this application. Thus, if you choose a value of $\alpha > .0174$ (such as .05), you will reject H_0. If you choose a value of $\alpha < .0174$ (such as .01), you will fail to reject H_0.

PROCEDURE FOR FINDING THE p-VALUE

1. For H_a: $\mu \neq \mu_0$

$$p = 2 \cdot (\text{area outside of } Z^*)$$

Reason: When using a significance level α, the value of α represents a *two*-tailed area.

2. For H_a: $\mu > \mu_0$

$$p = \text{area to the right of } Z^*$$

Reason: When using a significance level α, the value of α represents a *right*-tailed area.

3. For H_a: $\mu < \mu_0$

$$p = \text{area to the left of } Z^*$$

Reason: When using a significance level α, the value of α represents a *left*-tailed area.

What is the *p*-value for Example 10.5?

The results of the sample were $n = 60$ and $\bar{x} = 952.58$ kilowatt-hours. Also, σ was assumed to be 175 kilowatt-hours. The corresponding value of the test statistic was

$$Z^* \approx \frac{952.58 - 918}{175/\sqrt{60}} = 1.53$$

The alternative hypothesis is H_a: $\mu > 918$, so the *p*-value will be the area to the *right* of the computed value, 1.53, as illustrated in Figure 10.14. Notice that the inequality in H_a determines the *direction* of the tail area to be found. The *p*-value here is .0630, which is consistent with the results of Example 10.5, where we concluded that for $\alpha = .01$, you fail to reject H_0 and for $\alpha = .10$, you reject H_0. That is, the *p*-value is between .01 and .10.

Interpreting the *p*-value

We will consider two ways of using the *p*-value to arrive at a conclusion. The first is the *classical approach* that we have used up to this point: We choose a value for α and base our decision on this value. When using a *p*-value in this manner, the procedure is as follows:

reject H_0 if *p*-value $< \alpha$

fail to reject H_0 if *p*-value $\geq \alpha$

The second approach is a *general rule of thumb* that applies to most business applications of hypothesis testing on μ. We previously stated that typical values of α range from .01 to .10, implying that for most applications we will not see values of α smaller than .01 or larger than .1. With this in mind, the following rule can be defined:

reject H_0 if the *p*-value is small ($p < .01$)

fail to reject H_0 if the *p*-value is large ($p > .1$)

Consequently, if $.01 \leq$ *p*-value $\leq .1$, the data are *inconclusive*.

FIGURE

10.14

p-value for
$Z^* = 1.53$.

The advantage of this approach is that you avoid having to choose a value of α; the disadvantage is that you may arrive at an inconclusive result.

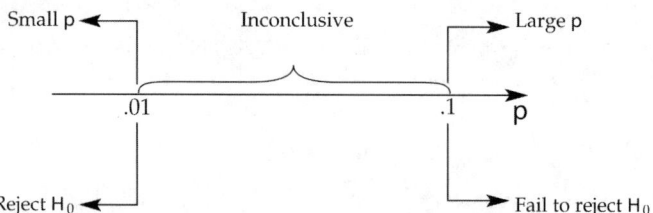

Now for a brief disclaimer: This rule does not apply to all situations. If a Type I error would be extremely serious and you prefer a very small value of α using the classical approach, then you can lower the .01 limit. Similarly, you might raise the .1 limit if the Type II error is extremely critical and you prefer a large value for α. However, this rule gives a working procedure for most applications in business.

What can you conclude if the p-value is p = .0001? This value is extremely small compared with any reasonable value of α. So we would strongly reject H_0. Consequently, if you are making an investment decision based on these results, for example, you can breathe a little easier. This data set supports H_a overwhelmingly. However, if p = .65, this value is large compared with any reasonable value of α. Without question, we would fail to reject H_0.

There is yet one other interpretation of the p-value, summarized in the following box.

ANOTHER INTERPRETATION OF THE p-VALUE

1. For a two-tailed test where $H_a: \mu \neq \mu_0$ the p-value is the probability that the value of the test statistic, Z^*, will be at least as large (in absolute value) as the observed Z^*, if μ is in fact equal to μ_0.
2. For a one-tailed test where $H_a: \mu > \mu_0$, the p-value is the probability that the value of the test statistic, Z^*, will be at least as large as the observed Z^*, if μ is in fact equal to μ_0.
3. For a one-tailed test where $H_a: \mu < \mu_0$, the p-value is the probability that the value of the test statistic, Z^*, will be at least as small as the observed Z^*, if μ is in fact equal to μ_0.

In Example 10.6, we determined the p-value to be .0630; the computed value of the test statistic was $Z^* = 1.53$; the hypotheses were $H_0: \mu \leq 918$ and $H_a: \mu > 918$. So the probability of observing a value of Z^* as large as 1.53 (that is, $Z^* \geq 1.53$) if μ is 918 is p = .0630.

Based on this description of the p-value, if p is small, conclude that H_0 is not true and reject it. We obtain precisely the same result using the classical and rule-of-thumb options of the p-value. Small values of p favor H_a, and large values favor H_0.

Statistical Software Application Use DATA10-7

Using Statistical Software to Calculate the Z Statistic and Corresponding p-Value

In Examples 2.1, 3.4, and 7.8 we examined the inside diameter of a certain machined part produced by Allied Manufacturing having specification (spec) limits of 10.1 millimeters (the lower limit) and 10.3 millimeters (the upper limit). Your advice to Allied was that, based on the sample of 100 diameters, the process was producing parts that were, on the average, too large, with a large percentage of the parts exceeding the upper spec limit. The quality-improvement team at Allied took your advice and attempted to modify the manufacturing process to produce parts that were closer to the target diameter of 10.2 millimeters. After this modification, another sample of 100 parts was obtained (stored in data set DATA8-7). The population standard deviation is assumed to be .035 millimeter. They would like to know whether there is sufficient evidence to indicate that the average diameter (μ) differs from 10.2 millimeters. In particular, four questions require answers:

1. What is your conclusion based on the corresponding *p*-value, using $\alpha = .05$?

2. Without specifying a value of α, what would be your conclusion based on the calculated *p*-value?

3. How should you interpret the *p*-value for this application?

4. What can you advise Allied about the current manufacturing process?

Solution 1

Begin by opening dataset DATA8-7. The first 9 values are visible in column A of Figure 10.15. To carry out the test of hypothesis, click on **KPK Data Analysis ➤ One Population Inference.** The resulting output is contained in Figure 10.15 (cells B1:C9).

The calculated value of the test statistic is $Z^* = 2.92$. The *p*-value for this two-tailed test is equal to $p = .0035$, as illustrated in Figure 10.16. This graphical output was produced using **KPK Data Analysis** by clicking on **Graphical Display of Test** after first clicking on **Hypothesis Test** in the **One Population Inference** window. Because *p* is less than $\alpha = .05$, we reject H_0 and conclude that the mean diameter is not 10.2 millimeters. Put another way, the sample mean $\bar{x} = 10.2102$ is *significantly different* from 10.2—certainly not obvious at first glance.

This analysis can also be carried out using MINITAB. To carry out the two-tailed Z test, refer to the instructions in the end-of-chapter appendix. The MINITAB output in Figure 10.17 contains the computed Z statistic, $Z^* = 2.92$, and the corresponding *p*-value of .003.

Solution 2

We use the general rule of thumb for interpreting the *p*-value. Since $p = .0035$, this value is small ($<.01$) and so we reject H_0. Although this is the same conclusion reached in Solution 1, this is not always the case.

Solution 3

We can make the following statements:

1. The significance level at which the conclusion indicated by the testing procedure changes is $\alpha = .0035$.

2. The largest significance level for which we fail to reject the null hypothesis is $\alpha = .0335$.

3. The probability of observing a value of the test statistic as large (in absolute value) as the one obtained (that is, ≥ 2.92), is .0035 if, in fact, the population mean is 10.2 millimeters.

FIGURE

10.15

	A	B	C
1	Diameter	**Z Test for Population Mean**	
2	10.158		Diameter
3	10.244	Number of Observations	100
4	10.202	Population Std. Deviation	0.035
5	10.206	Sample Mean	10.2102
6	10.257	Ho:$\mu = 10.2$	Ha:$\mu \neq 10.2$
7	10.149	Z^*	2.923
8	10.202	2 * P[$\mathbf{Z} \geq |Z^*|$] two tail	0.0035
9	10.237	$|Z$ Critical $|, \alpha = 0.05$	1.960
10	10.220		

Excel spreadsheet and output using **KPK Data Analysis ➤ One Population Inference.**

FIGURE
10.16

Illustration of the *p*-value for Example 10.7 using **KPK Data Analysis.**

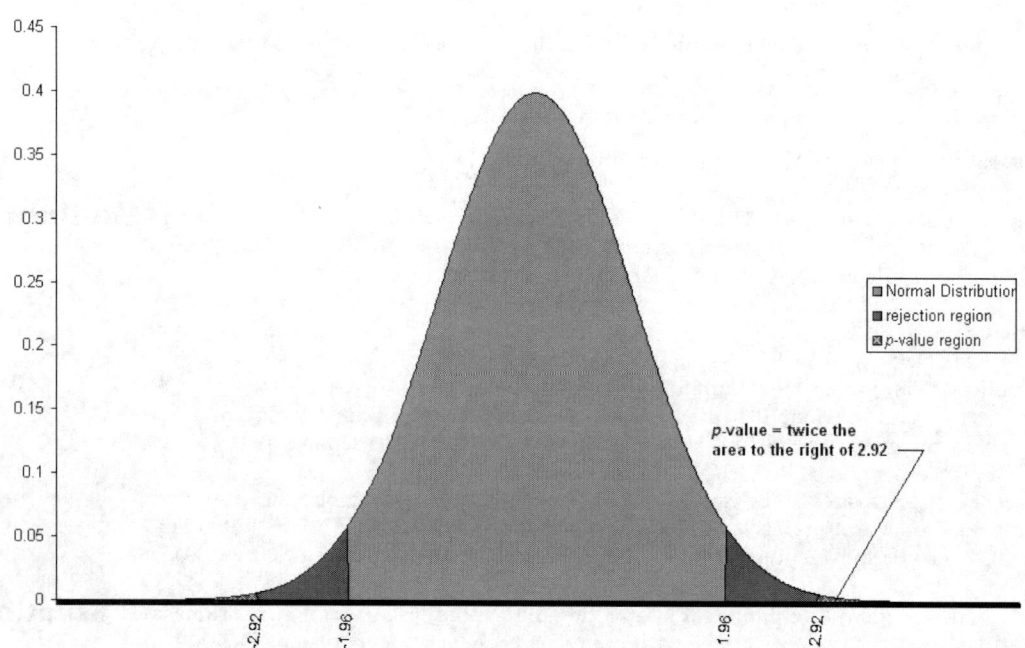

Rejection Region and *P*-value Region

p-value = twice the area to the right of 2.92

Legend:
- Normal Distribution
- rejection region
- *p*-value region

Solution 4   Prior to the quality-improvement effort, the mean diameter was 10.275 millimeters and 17% of the sample exceeded the upper spec limit. In one sense, the quality of the process has been improved, since the estimated mean of the new process (10.2102) is much closer to 10.2 than before, and none of the sample values lie outside the spec limits of 10.1 millimeters and 10.3 millimeters.

We also observe additional variation in this sample, since the sample standard deviation has increased from .0267 (before the quality-improvement effort) to .0334 (refer to Figure 10.17).* Overall, the team should be commended for improving the process. But based on Solution 1, efforts should be made to move the process even closer to 10.2 millimeters and to reduce the process variation.

Practical versus Statistical Significance

Researchers often calculate what appears to be a conclusive result without considering the practical significance of their findings. For example, consider a situation similar to the one described in Example 10.4; this time, a sample of 3,000 Bullets, tested under normal highway conditions, results in a sample average of $\bar{x} = 32.23$ mpg, where, as before, the population standard deviation is assumed to be 5.5 mpg. Advertising for this car claims that the mpg under test conditions is at least 32.5 mpg. Is there sufficient evidence to reject this claim?

---

*Section 9.4 will allow you to determine if there is a *significant* change in the variation for the before and after processes (populations).

FIGURE

10.17

MINITAB output using **Stat ➤ Basic Statistics ➤ 1-Sample Z.**

One-Sample Z: Diameter

```
Test of mu = 10.2 vs not = 10.2
The assumed standard deviation = 0.035


Variable    N     Mean    StDev   SE Mean      95% CI            Z      P
Diameter   100   10.2102  0.0334  0.0035   (10.2034, 10.2171)   2.92  0.003
```

FIGURE

10.18

p-value for $Z^* = -2.69$.

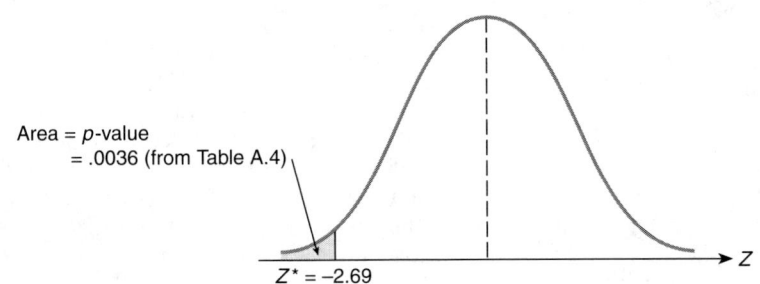

Area = *p*-value
= .0036 (from Table A.4)

$Z^* = -2.69$

The hypotheses are H_0: $\mu \geq 32.5$ and H_a: $\mu < 32.5$. The value of the test statistic is

$$Z^* = \frac{\bar{X} - 32.5}{\sigma/\sqrt{n}} = \frac{32.23 - 32.5}{5.5/\sqrt{3000}} = -2.69$$

The *p*-value here is the area to the left of –2.69 under the Z curve, as illustrated in Figure 10.18. This value (from Table A.4) is .0036. Based on this small *p*-value, we reject H_0 and conclude (as we did in Example 10.4) that the mpg for these cars under normal highway conditions is less than 32.5. Statistically speaking, this is correct, and the data do provide sufficient evidence to support the statement that their mpg claim is overstated. As a consumer, however, how concerned would you be that the sample average ($\bar{x} = 32.23$) is (only) .27 mpg under the advertised level? In other words, in a practical sense, how misleading is the Bullet advertising?

What we have seen is that $\bar{X}$ is far enough away from 32.5 (in a statistical sense) to conclude that μ is less than 32.5 mpg. However, perhaps in the eyes of a consumer about to invest $25,000 in a new car, this value of $\bar{X}$ is really "close enough" to 32.5.

Moral: It is possible for a statistically significant result to be of no particular practical significance, depending on the context of the analysis.

X Exercises 10.27–10.36

Understanding the Mechanics

10.27 State the conclusion to testing the null hypothesis assuming each of the following situations.
  a. *p*-value = .10 and significance level is .05
  b. *p*-value = .02 and significance level is .05
  c. *p*-value = .40 and significance level is .10
  d. *p*-value = .001 and significance level is .01

10.28 Using the rule of thumb for *p*-values, what is your conclusion in testing the null hypothesis if the *p*-value is .001? .80? .05?

10.29 Test H_0: $\mu = 10$ versus H_a: $\mu \neq 10$ using the rule of thumb for *p*-values. Assume that $\bar{x} = 12$, $\sigma = 4$, and $n = 36$.

10.30 Test H_0: $\mu \leq 50$ versus H_a: $\mu > 50$ using the rule of thumb for *p*-values. Assume that $\bar{x} = 51$, $\sigma = 4$, and $n = 49$.

10.31 Test $H_0 : \mu = 100$ versus $H_1 : \mu \neq 100$ using the rule of thumb for p-values. Assume that $\bar{x} = 102$, $\sigma = 6$, and $n = 64$.

Applying the New Concepts

10.32 The producer of Take-a-Bite, a snack food, claims that each package weighs 175 grams. A representative of a consumer advocate group selected a random sample of 70 packages. From this sample, the mean is 172 grams. The population standard deviation is known to be 8 grams. Find and interpret the p-value for testing that the mean weight of Take-a-Bite is less than 175 grams.

10.33 A marketing-research analyst is interested in examining the statement made by the makers that brand A cigarettes contain less than three milligrams of tar. The marketing-research analyst randomly selected 60 cigarettes and found the mean amount of tar to be 2.75 milligrams. The population standard deviation is known to be 1.5 milligrams. Do the data support the claim? Find the p-value.

10.34 Alice Chang and her husband Jau Huang are the co-founders of a multimedia software start-up company named CyberLink, based in Taiwan. These founders are interested in the average number of hours that engineers would be willing to work for the company if they were given a small salary but a large quantity of stock with the anticipation that an initial public offering would yield a nice return. A consultant advised the founders that engineers would be willing to work an average of 70 hours per week under those terms. The idea that they could get rich in a short period of time is very enticing to many engineers in Taiwan. Suppose that a sample of 50 start-up companies was randomly selected and the number of hours that the typical engineer worked was recorded.

  a. Does a sample mean of 62 hours and a population standard deviation of 20 hours indicate that the average work time that an engineer would be willing to work for a start-up company differs from 70 hours a week? Interpret the p-value.

  b. From the p-value in part a, would you expect a 99% confidence interval for the mean number of weekly hours that an engineer would be willing to work for a start-up company to include 70? Find a 99% confidence interval for this mean.

(Source: "Taiwan Doesn't Shield Firms: Only Strong Survive," The Wall Street Journal, June 23, 1998, p. 2B.)

Using the Computer

10.35 **[DATA SET EX10-35]** Variable Description:

CostGoods: Cost of goods by shoplifters

A manager of a New York retail store believes that the average cost of goods shoplifted by those customers that have shoplifted is greater than $75. A random sample of 60 customers that have shoplifted is selected, and the selling price of the goods shoplifted was recorded. Assume the population standard deviation is $23.75.

  a. Test that the average cost of goods shoplifted among the population of shoplifters at the retail store is greater than $75. Use the general rule of thumb concerning the p-value to arrive at a conclusion.

  b. How would you interpret the results of the hypothesis test in part a for the manager?

10.36 **[DATA SET EX10-36]** Variable Description:

StressIndex: Stress index for managers

An industrial psychologist has a stress test that is used to determine the amount of stress that managers are under. A value of 80 or higher indicates "high stress." The industrial psychologist believes that the managers at a large, profitable pharmaceutical firm are not under "high stress" and that the average stress index is less than 80 for managers of the company. A random sample of 50 managers is selected, and their stress index was recorded. Assume that the population standard deviation is $10.15.

  a. Test that the data support the industrial psychologist's belief.

  b. What conclusion would you reach if the significance level was .10? .05? .01?

10.4

HYPOTHESIS TESTING ON THE MEAN OF A NORMAL POPULATION (σ UNKNOWN)

Our approach to hypothesis testing for applications where the population standard deviation, σ, is unknown (the usual situation) uses the same technique we used for dealing with confidence intervals on the mean of a population: we switch from the standard normal distribution, Z, to the t distribution. In this section, we have reason to believe that the population has a normal distribution.

Certain variations from a normal population are permissible with this hypothesis test. If a test of hypothesis is still reliable when slight departures from the assumptions are encountered, the test is said to be robust. If you believe the parent population to be reason-

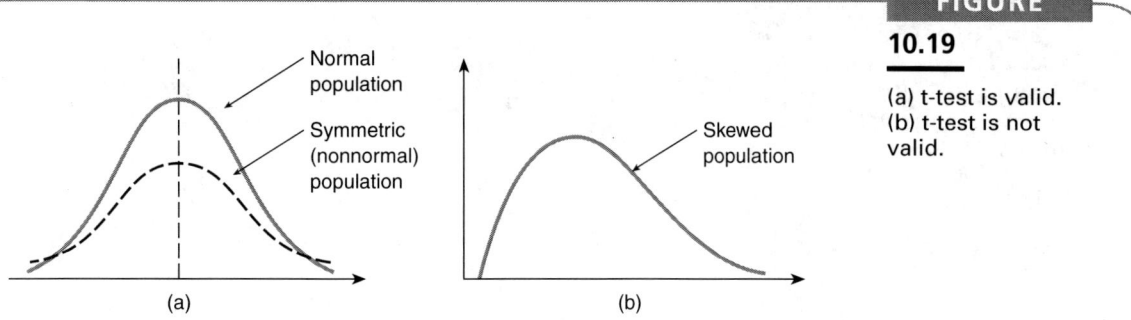

FIGURE

10.19

(a) t-test is valid.
(b) t-test is not valid.

ably symmetric, the level of your confidence interval and Type I error (α) will be quite accurate, even if the population has heavy tails (unlike the normal distribution), as shown in Figure 10.19(a). However, the testing procedure in this section is *not* robust for populations that are heavily skewed (see Figure 10.19(b)). For larger sample sizes, a histogram of your data often can detect whether a population is heavily skewed in one direction.

To reemphasize, the discussion in this section assumes a normal population. In other words, if X is an observation from this population, then X is a normal random variable with unknown mean μ. Also, we assume that σ is unknown. (If σ is known, the resulting test statistic is $Z = (\bar{X} - \mu_0)/(\sigma/\sqrt{n})$, and the five-step procedure of Section 10.1 allows you to do hypothesis testing on μ.)

The only distinction between situations where σ is known and unknown is the identification of the test statistic. Using the discussion from Chapter 8, if we define the test statistic as

$$t = \frac{\bar{X} - \mu_0}{s/\sqrt{n}}$$

10.2

we now have a t distribution with $n - 1$ degrees of freedom (df). The procedure to use for testing $H_0: \mu = \mu_0$ and $H_a: \mu \neq \mu_0$ is the same five-step procedure, except that the rejection region is defined using the t table (Table A.5) rather than the Z table (Table A.4). This procedure also applies to a one-tailed test.

You may recall from Example 7.6 that Clark Products manufactures a power supply with an output voltage that is believed to be normally distributed with a mean of 10 volts. During the design stage, the quality-engineering staff recorded 18 observations of the output voltage of a particular power supply unit. They decide to use a significance level of .05, since the implications of making a Type I error (rejecting a correct H_0) and a Type II error (failing to reject an incorrect H_0) appear to be the same. Is there evidence to indicate that the average output voltage is not 10 volts?

Solution

Step 1. When a question is phrased "Is there evidence to indicate that . . . ," what follows is the *alternative hypothesis*. For this application then, the alternative hypothesis is that the mean is unequal to 10 volts, and the resulting hypotheses are $H_0: \mu = 10$ and $H_a: \mu \neq 10$.

Step 2. The test statistic here is

$$t = \frac{\bar{X} - 10}{s/\sqrt{n}}$$

10.20

t distribution; the rejection region is the lightly shaded area to the right of 2.11 and to the left of –2.11, for Example 10.8.

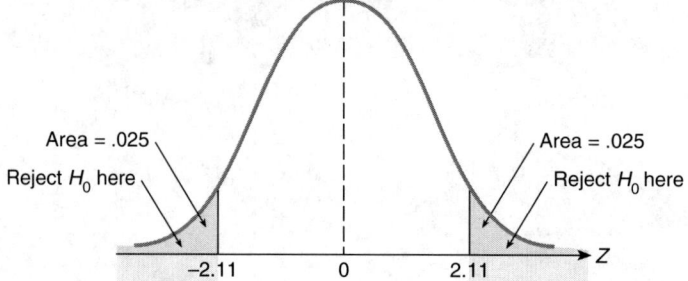

10.21

t curve with 17 df. The *p*-value is twice the area to the right of *t** = 1.83, so we can say only that it is between .05 and .10.

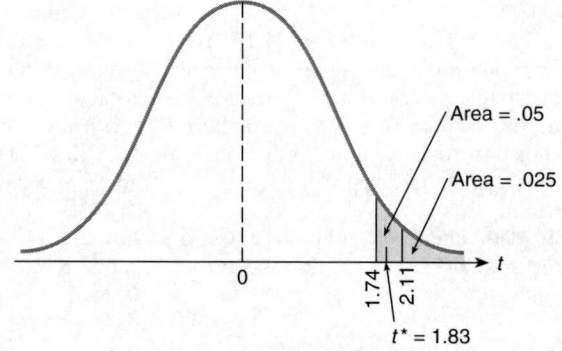

Step 3. Using a significance level of .05 and Figure 10.20, the corresponding two-tailed procedure is to

$$\text{reject } H_0 \text{ if } |t| > t_{.025,17} = 2.11$$

because df = $n - 1 = 17$.

Step 4. For these data, $n = 18$, $\bar{x} = 10.331$ volts and $s = .767$ volt. The value of the test statistic is

$$t = \frac{10.331 - 10}{.767/\sqrt{18}} = 1.83$$

Because 1.83 < 2.11, we fail to reject H_0.

Step 5. There is insufficient evidence to indicate that the average output voltage is different from 10 volts.

What is the *p*-value in Example 10.8, and what can we conclude based on this value? We run into a slight snag when dealing with the *t* distribution, because we are not able to determine precisely the *p*-value. You can see this in Figure 10.21, using Table A.5 (17 df). The *p*-value is twice the area to the right of *t** = 1.83. The best we can do here is to say that *p* is *between* (2)(.025) and (2)(.05), that is, between .05 and .10. (*Note:* A reliable computer package or sophisticated calculator will provide the exact *p*-value. Using Excel, SPSS, or MINITAB, this value is *p* = .0847.)

Using the classical approach and $\alpha = .05$ we *can* say that p is greater than .05, despite not knowing p exactly. Consequently, we fail to reject H_0. *This procedure always produces the same result as the five-step procedure, and calculating the p-value can replace Steps 3 and 4 in this procedure.*

Suppose we choose not to select a significant level (α) but prefer to base our conclusion strictly on the calculated p-value. We use the rule of thumb and decide whether p is small ($<.01$), large ($>.1$), or in between. Despite not having an exact value of p, we can say that this p-value falls in the inconclusive range. These data values do not provide us with any strong conclusion. One approach available to Clark Products is to obtain some additional data.

EXAMPLE 10.9

An auditing firm was hired to determine if a particular defense plant was overstating the value of their inventory items. It was decided that 15 items would be randomly selected. For each item, the recorded amount, the audited (exact) amount, and the difference between these two amounts (recorded–audited) were determined. Of particular interest was whether it could be demonstrated that the average difference exceeds $25, in which case the defense plant would be subject to a loss of contract and financial penalties. The following 15 differences were obtained (in dollars):

$$17, 35, 31, 22, 50, 42, 56, 23, 27, 38, 20, 25, 43, 45, 21$$

So $n = 15$, $\bar{x} = \$33.00$, and $s = \$12.15$. Set up the appropriate hypotheses and test them using a significance level of $\alpha = .05$. The population of differences is believed to be normally distributed.

Solution

Step 1. The hypotheses are H_0: $\mu \leq 25$ and H_a: $\mu > 25$, where μ is the average difference between the recorded and audited amounts for *all* the inventory items.

Steps 2, 3.

$$\text{reject } H_0 \text{ if } t = \frac{\bar{X} - 25}{s/\sqrt{n}} > t_{.05,14} = 1.761$$

where the df $= n - 1 = 14$.

Step 4. The calculated t is

$$t^* = \frac{33 - 25}{12.15/\sqrt{15}} = 2.55$$

Because 2.55 exceeds the tabulated value of 1.761, we reject H_0. Also, the p-value (using Table A.5 and 14 df) is the area to the right of 2.55. It is between .01 and .025, so it is less than $\alpha = .05$, and so (as before) we reject H_0.

Step 5. These data indicate that the defense plant is overstating the value of their inventory items by more than $25.

To obtain the Excel solution shown in Figure 10.22, enter the 15 values in cells A1:A15. Next, click on **KPK Data Analysis ➤ One Population Inference** and select **Population Mean with Est. Std. Dev. (t statistic).** Enter "A1:A15" for the **Input Range,** but don't click on the **Labels** box (unless you inserted a label in cell A1). Enter 5 in the **Alpha** box (this is the default value), click on **Hypothesis Test** and **Right-Tail Test,** and enter "25" for the **Hypothesized Value of Mean** and "B1" for the **Output Range.** To obtain a graphical display of the p-value (similar to that in Figure 10.16), click on **Graphical Display of Test.** The

FIGURE

10.22

Excel spreadsheet
and output using
**KPK Data Analysis
➤ One Population
Inference.**

	A	B	C
1	Diameter	**t Test for Population Mean**	
2	17		Diameter
3	35	Number of Observations	15
4	31	Sample Standard Deviation	12.148
5	22	Sample Mean	33.000
6	50	Ho:μ ≤ 25	Ha:μ > 25
7	42	T*	2.551
8	56	P[T ≥ T*]	0.0115
9	23	T Critical, α = 0.05	1.761
10	27		
11	38		
12	20		
13	25		
14	43		
15	45		
16	21		

FIGURE

10.23

MINITAB output
using **Stat ➤ Basic
Statistics ➤ 1-
Sample t.**

One-Sample T: Difference

Test of mu = 25 vs > 25

```
                                                   95%
                                                  Lower
Variable     N     Mean    StDev   SE Mean   Bound    T      P
Difference   15   33.0000  12.1479  3.1366   27.4755  2.55  0.012
```

FIGURE

10.24

SPSS output using
**Analyze ➤
Compare Means ➤
One-Sample
T Test.**

One-Sample Test

	t	df	Sig. (2-tailed)	Mean Difference	95% Confidence Interval of the Difference Lower	Upper
			Test Value = 25			
DIFFEREN	2.551	14	.02309	8.00	1.27	14.73

p-value here is .012 and is in agreement with the solution to Example 10.9—namely that the p-value is between .01 and .025.

The MINITAB solution using **Stat ➤ Basic Statistics ➤ 1-Sample t** is shown in Figure 10.23. The SPSS output using **Analyze ➤ Compare Means ➤ One-Sample T Test** is contained in Figure 10.24. As discussed in the end-of-chapter appendix, the p-value must be divided by two for a one-tailed test. Consequently, the resulting p-value here is .02309/2 = .0115, which agrees with the Excel and MINITAB solutions.

424

SMALL-SAMPLE TESTS ON A NORMAL POPULATION MEAN

Two-Tailed Test

$$H_0: \mu = \mu_0$$

$$H_a: \mu \neq \mu_0$$

$$\text{reject } H_0 \text{ if } |t^*| > t_{\alpha/2,\, n-1}$$

where n = sample size and t^* is the computed value of

$$t = \frac{\bar{X} - \mu_0}{s/\sqrt{n}}$$

One-Tailed Test

$$H_0: \mu \leq \mu_0 \qquad\qquad H_0: \mu \geq \mu_0$$

$$H_a: \mu > \mu_0 \qquad\qquad H_a: \mu < \mu_0$$

$$\text{reject } H_0 \text{ if } t^* > t_{\alpha,\, n-1} \qquad \text{reject } H_0 \text{ if } t^* < -t_{\alpha, n-1}$$

X Exercises 10.37–10.46

Understanding the Mechanics

10.37 Find the t statistic and carry out the statistical test for the following situations in sampling data from a normally distributed population. Use a significance level of .05.
   a. $H_0: \mu = 50$, $H_a: \mu \neq 50$, $\bar{x} = 56$, $s = 24$, $n = 15$
   b. $H_0: \mu \leq 50$, $H_a: \mu > 50$, $\bar{x} = 56$, $s = 24$, $n = 15$
   c. $H_0: \mu \geq 113.7$, $H_a: \mu < 113.7$, $\bar{x} = 111.6$, $s = 2.5$, $n = 30$
   d. $H_0: \mu = 85$, $H_a: \mu \neq 85$, $\bar{x} = 78$, $s = 25$, $n = 25$

10.38 Find the p-value for the following situations, with calculated test statistics given by t^*.
   a. $H_0: \mu = 72.5$, $H_a: \mu \neq 72.5$, $t^* = 2.72$, $n = 12$
   b. $H_0: \mu \leq 72.5$, $H_a: \mu > 72.5$, $t^* = 2.72$, $n = 12$
   c. $H_0: \mu = 180.7$, $H_a: \mu \neq 180.7$, $t^* = 1.3$, $n = 41$
   d. $H_0: \mu \leq 180.7$, $H_a: \mu > 180.7$, $t^* = 1.3$, $n = 41$

10.39 The following data were sampled from a normally distributed population. At the 10% significance level, is there evidence to indicate that the mean of the population differs from 16?

12	15	14	19	15	20	16

Applying the New Concepts

10.40 Easy-Fly Airline took a random sample of 25 flights to determine if the mean time it takes for luggage to reach the travelers departing from a flight is less than 15 min-

utes. The sample mean was found to be 13.8 minutes with a standard deviation of four minutes.
   a. Using a significance level of .05, what conclusion can be reached based on the random sample?
   b. What assumption about the data is necessary for the hypothesis test to be valid in this situation?

10.41 The Hungarian-born executive Zsolt Rummy, chairman of Zoltek Company, claims that his company is the world's largest producer of carbon fiber, the strong yet lightweight material used in everything from aircraft to golf clubs. To maintain profitability, the cost of producing carbon fiber is very important. Zoltek has production lines in both Texas and Hungary. A financial analyst interested in estimating the earnings of the company wants to test that the cost of producing a pound of carbon differs from its average cost of $6 per pound last year. Twenty days are randomly selected from the first six months of 2005, and the cost per pound of carbon is recorded. The data are presented below. Using a .05 significance level, what conclusion can the financial analyst make? Assume that the distribution of the cost per pound of carbon can be approximated by a normal distribution.

6.3	6.8	7.5	6.0	5.3	6.2	5.4	7.3	6.1	6.4
6.1	6.5	5.7	6.3	7.2	6.9	6.2	7.0	5.9	6.1

(Source: "Zoltek Touts Potential for Carbon Fiber; Its Shares Reflect Immediate Concerns," *The Wall Street Journal*, June 12, 1998, p. B11.)

10.42 The National Retail Federation in Washington conducted a telephone survey of 1,000 adults in early October 2001 and found that approximately 55% of the respondents planned to do some type of Halloween decorating. The Federation claims that households spend an average of $45 on Halloween candy, costumes, and decorations. The Federation says that the Halloween market generates almost $7 billion in sales. Suppose that a local retail manager wished to determine if the average household in the local area planned to spend more than $45. A random sample of 25 households yielded a mean of $52 with a standard deviation of $18. Do the data support the belief that the average household in the local area spends more than $45 in preparation for Halloween at a significance level of .01?

(Source: "Many Households Plan a Traditional Halloween," *The New York Times*, October 14, 2001, p. 8L.)

10.43 A fitness-center manager believes that "virtual" trainers on the Web charge more than $50 per year. Test this belief assuming $\bar{x} = \$62$, $s = \$15$, and $n = 16$. Use the p-value to support your conclusion.

10.44 In an effort to control cost, a quality-control inspector is interested in whether the mean number of ounces of sauce dispensed by bottle-filling machines differs from 16 ounces. From the bottling process, the inspector collects the following measurements.

16.3, 16.2, 15.8, 15.4, 16.0, 15.6, 15.5, 16.1, 15.9, 16.1

Test at a .05 significance level that the bottle-filling machines need adjusting.

Using the Computer

10.45 **[DATA SET EX10-45]** Variable Description:

Expend: Expenditure per night by guests sharing the same room

The manager at the Ocean Breeze Hotel believes the average expenditure per night for guests sharing the same room is greater than $200. A random sample of 25 rooms was selected, and the expenditure by the guests per night was recorded.

a. Test the manager's belief that the average expenditure for guests sharing the same room is greater than $200. At what significance level can the null hypothesis be rejected?

b. What assumption are you making about the sampled population?

10.46 **[DATA SET EX10-46]** Variable Description:

Time: Time, in minutes, to correct a defective aluminum sheet

A quality inspector is interested in the average time it takes to correct defective sheets of aluminum manufactured at the plant. A random sample of 25 sheets of defective aluminum sheets was selected, and the time to correct the defect was recorded.

a. Suppose that the quality inspector believes the average time to correct a defective sheet of aluminum is different from 20 minutes, a time given in a recent report on the operations of the company. Test the quality inspector's belief. Use the general rule of thumb for interpreting the p-value.

b. Construct a histogram and determine if the data can be assumed to come from an approximately normal population.

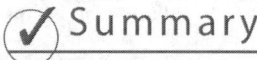

Summary

In Chapter 8 you were introduced to the topic of statistical inference through discussion of the concept using a confidence interval when estimating a population parameter. This chapter presented the other side of statistical inference—hypothesis testing regarding population parameters.

For testing against a hypothetical value of the population mean (μ), we introduced a procedure that used the standard normal (Z) distribution when the population standard deviation (σ) is known and the t distribution for the usual situation where σ is unknown. Both tests used a five-step procedure that derived a value of the test statistic and reached a conclusion.

The two hypotheses under investigation are the null hypothesis, H_0, and the alternative hypothesis, H_a. Two specific errors are of great concern when you use the hypothesis-testing procedure. A Type I error occurs in the event you reject a null hypothesis when in fact it is true; a Type II error occurs when you fail to reject a null hypothesis when in fact it is not true. The probability of a Type I error is the significance level and is written as α. The probability of a Type II error is written as β. For each possible value of the population mean (μ), the power of a statistical test is defined as $1 - \beta$ and is equal to the probability of rejecting H_0 when it is in fact false.

To define a test of hypothesis, you select a value of α that considers the cost of rejecting a correct H_0 and failing to reject an incorrect H_0. Hypotheses can be two-tailed (such as H_0: $\mu = 50$ versus H_a: $\mu \neq 50$) or one-tailed (such as H_0: $\mu \leq 50$ versus H_a: $\mu > 50$).

A hypothesis test should always include a *p*-value that measures the strength of the conclusion. *We encourage you to get used to examining the p-value in your computer output because it saves you the effort of having to calculate the value of the test statistic and refer to a Z or t table.*

Summary of Formulas

1. Test statistic for hypothesis testing on a population mean:

$$Z = \frac{\bar{X} - \mu_0}{\sigma/\sqrt{n}} \quad \text{(when } \sigma \text{ is known)}$$

or,

$$t = \frac{\bar{X} - \mu_0}{s/\sqrt{n}} \quad \text{(when } \sigma \text{ is unknown). Here df} = n - 1.$$

2. Power of a test for H_0: $\mu = \mu_0$ versus H_a: $\mu \neq \mu_0$ (σ known):

$$\text{Power} = P(Z > z_1) + P(Z < z_2)$$

where Z is the standard normal random variable,

$$z_1 = Z_{\alpha/2} - \frac{\mu - \mu_0}{\sigma/\sqrt{n}}$$

$$z_2 = -Z_{\alpha/2} - \frac{\mu - \mu_0}{\sigma/\sqrt{n}}$$

and μ is the specified value of the population mean.

3. Power of a test for H_0: $\mu \leq \mu_0$ versus H_a: $\mu > \mu_0$ (σ known):

$$\text{Power} = P(Z > z_1)$$

where Z is the standard normal random variable and

$$z_1 = Z_{\alpha} - \frac{\mu - \mu_0}{\sigma/\sqrt{n}}$$

4. Power of a test for H_0: $\mu \geq \mu_0$ versus H_a: $\mu < \mu_0$ (σ known):

$$\text{Power} = P(Z < z_2)$$

where Z is the standard normal random variable and

$$z_2 = -Z_{\alpha} - \frac{\mu - \mu_0}{\sigma/\sqrt{n}}$$

X Review Exercises 10.47–10.61

10.47 Which of the following can be an acceptable alternative hypothesis? Why?
a. H_a: $\mu = 10$
b. H_a: $\mu \neq 10$
c. H_a: $\mu \leq 10$
d. H_a: $\mu > 10$

10.48 A production manager will shut down her production line if the bags of dry feed are overfilled or underfilled. The production operation is designed to produce bags weighing 25 pounds. The manager periodically takes a random sample of 20 bags to decide whether the production line should be shut down so that adjustments can be made to the machinery.
a. What null and alternative hypotheses should the production manager use?
b. What conclusion would the manager make if she failed to reject the null hypothesis?
c. What conclusion would the manager make if she rejected the null hypothesis?

10.49 Which of the following statements are true about a hypothesis test? Explain.
  a. A smaller significance level decreases the probability of a Type I error.
  b. If the p-value is less than the significance level, then the null hypothesis is rejected.
  c. A Type II error can be more serious than a Type I error.
  d. The power of a test decreases as the sample size increases.
  e. A Type I error and a Type II error are the only ways that a wrong conclusion can occur.

10.50 The manager of Lone Star Restaurant believes that the average wait time for the Saturday evening meal is 30 minutes. To test this belief, the manager selects 50 customers at random and computes the average wait time to be 34 minutes. Assume a population standard deviation of 12 minutes.
  a. Find a 99% confidence interval for the mean wait time of a customer.
  b. Do the data indicate that the mean wait time differs from 30 minutes at the 1% significance level?

10.51 Calculate the power of the test for the mean of a normally distributed population with known population variance for the following situations, assuming that the true population mean is 10 and the known population standard deviation is 3.1. Use a significance level of .05.
  a. $H_0: \mu = 11$, $H_a: \mu \neq 11$, $n = 14$.
  b. $H_0: \mu = 9.5$, $H_a: \mu \neq 9.5$, $n = 25$.
  c. $H_0: \mu = 8$, $H_a: \mu \neq 8$, $n = 40$.

10.52 A supervisor is interested in whether a new machine will produce a batch of cylinders more quickly than the current machines do. A trial test of 23 batches of cylinders on the new machine yielded a sample mean of 8.5 minutes. The population standard deviation is known to be 1.2 minutes. The old machine is known to have a mean time of 9 minutes. Assume that the time required to produce a batch of cylinders follows a normal distribution.
  a. Assuming a significance level of .10, what managerial conclusion can be given in testing that the mean time for the new machine is less than 9 minutes?
  b. Explain how statistical significance and practical significance play a role in determining decisions made by the supervisor with regard to the new machine.

10.53 A manufacturer of drugs and medical products claims that a new antiinflammatory drug will be effective for four hours after the drug is administered in the prescribed dosage. A random sample of 50 volunteers demonstrated that the average effective time is 3.70 hours. The population standard deviation is known to be .606 hours. Use the p-value criteria to determine if there is sufficient evidence to support the hypothesis that the mean effective time of the drug differs from four hours.

10.54 Indicate what the p-values are for the following situations, in which the mean of a normally distributed population is being tested.
  a. $H_0: \mu = 31.6$, $H_a: \mu \neq 31.6$ (population variance is known), $Z^* = 2.16$
  b. $H_0: \mu = 4.07$, $H_a: \mu \neq 4.07$ (population variance is known), $Z^* = -1.35$
  c. $H_0: \mu = 87.6$, $H_a: \mu \neq 87.6$ (population variance is unknown), $t^* = 2.51$, $n = 15$
  d. $H_0: \mu = 195.3$, $H_a: \mu \neq 195.3$ (population variance is unknown), $t^* = -1.71$, $n = 25$

10.55 A&G car rental agency samples 64 cars rented at Chicago O'Hare Airport and records the average mileage to be 260 miles. Assume a population standard deviation of 40 miles. Use a Z-test to test that the average mileage differs from 250 at a significance level of 5%. Does the conclusion change if a t test is used and the sample standard deviation is 40 miles?

10.56 The vice president of academic affairs at a small private college believes that the average full-time student who lives off campus spends about $300 per month for housing. A random sample of 200 full-time students living off campus spent an average of $305 per month. Assume that the population standard deviation is $70 a month.
  a. Find the p-value to determine whether there is sufficient evidence to indicate that a full-time student spends more than $300 per month on housing.
  b. Would you reject the null hypothesis for the test in part a if $\alpha = .01$? if $\alpha = .05$? if $\alpha = .10$?

10.57 According to a survey of American adults by the Travel Industry Association, 98 million people have enjoyed a "high adventure" trip in the past five years. For example, high adventurers are willing to spend several thousands of dollars to explore Minnesota's Northwoods by dogsled, on snowshoes, and skis over a five-day period. Other high adventurers prefer a 12-day ski and mountaineering expedition to the Torngat Mountains, the tallest mountain range in northeastern Canada. Suppose that a marketing analyst is interested in the average travel expenses of these high adventurers and believes that their average expense is approximately $4,000. A random sample of 100 households taken by the marketing analysts yielded a sample mean of $4,500. Assume that the population standard deviation is $1,600.

    a. Find a 99% confidence interval for the mean expense by high adventurers. Give an interpretation of this interval.

    b. Use the confidence interval in part a to determine if there is sufficient evidence to indicate that the average expense by high adventurers differs from $4,000.

(Source: "Adventure Vacations Can Be Heart-Pounding and Cold," The Houston Chronicle, October 21, 2001, p. 7A.)

10.58 Dow Jones & Co. made plans to cut 4.9% of its Ottaway Newspapers, Inc., staff. The publisher said that it would take a third quarter charge in 1998 of $5 million to pay severance and related costs. Suppose that the company decided to poll 20 of its employees to ask the likelihood of accepting a buyout. The employees responded on a scale from 1 to 10, with 10 indicating that the employee would accept any reasonable buyout and 1 indicating that the employee would be totally unwilling to accept any type of buyout. The poll revealed a mean likelihood value of 6.5.

    a. To reach its goal of eliminating 4.9% of Ottaway Newspapers staff, a consultant believes that the likelihood value should be greater than 6. Is there sufficient evidence that the company's goal will be reached with respect to eliminating jobs? Assume that the sample standard deviation is 1.3 and that the significance level is .05.

    b. If you were a consultant being paid to advise Ottaway Newspapers on how to reach their goal of eliminating 4.9% of their staff, would you want to use a small significance level or a large significance level in part a? Explain.

(Source: "Dow Jones Proposes to Trim 125 Jobs at Its Ottaway Unit," The Wall Street Journal, June 30, 1998, p. B8.)

10.59 **[DATA SET EX10-59]** Variable Description:

FraudulentBill: Amount of fraudulent Medicare bill

The FBI investigates numerous fraudulent Medicare bills each year. A random sample of 100 fraudulent Medicare bills (in dollars) was selected for analysis. Is there evidence that the average fraudulent bill was greater than $600 using a 10% significance level? Remove the two largest bills, then repeat the analysis and compare the results.

10.60 **[DATA SET EX10-60]** Variable Description:

Contribution: Amount pledged by households during telethon

Appeals by Hollywood actors and musicians during an unprecedented telethon during October 2001 generated more than $150 million in pledges to benefit families of the World Trade Center and Pentagon attack victims. Pledges were for as little as $10 from households across the nation. The money was then distributed through the United Way. Suppose that the manager of the United Way Fund believes that the average household contributed more than $30. A random sample of 200 contributions is provided to test this belief.

    a. What are the results of a hypothesis test for the manager's belief? Use a 5% significance level.

    b. Construct a histogram of the data. Should the manager be concerned that the distribution of the data may not be normally distributed? What does the Central Limit Theorem say about the sample mean?

    c. Assume that the manager would like to use a bootstrap approach to find a 95% confidence interval on the mean contribution by households. Use 100 bootstrapped samples of size 200. Interpret this interval.

(Source: "Briefs," Dallas Morning News, September 25, 2001, p. 25A.)

10.61 Graph the power function for testing the null hypothesis of $\mu = 100$ against the alternative hypothesis of $\mu \neq 100$ when the true value of the mean ranges from 80 to 120. Do this for $n = 40$ and $n = 70$ when the population standard deviation is known to be 25. For which values of the mean does the power function change very little? To obtain a graph of the power function in Excel, put the values 80, 81, . . . , 120 in cells A2 to A42. Then in cells A1 through G1, put the titles presented below. In cells B2 through G2, put in the formulas presented below.

A	B	C	D	E	F	G
True Mean	Term needed in z1 and z2	z1	z2	P(Z > z1)	P(Z < z2)	Power
80	=(A2-100)*SQRT(40)/25	=1.96 - B2	=-1.96-B2	=1-NORMSDIST(C2)	=NORMSDIST(D2)	=E2 + F2

Now highlight the region: cells B1 through G1 and B2 through G2. Click on **Copy.** Now highlight rows 3 through 42 for columns B through G. Click on **Paste.** Use the line chart subtype option of the **Chart Wizard** to plot the power function. A graph of the power function for $n = 40$ is presented below.

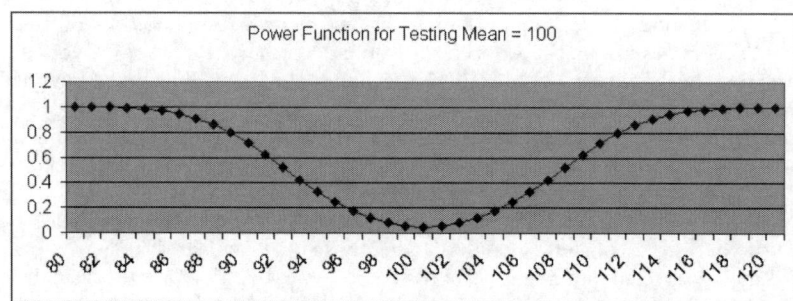

Computer Exercises Using the Databases

Exercise 1—Appendix F

Randomly select 100 observations from the database. Use a convenient statistical computer package to determine whether the sample evidence indicates that the mean of the variable **TOTLDEBT** (total indebtedness) exceeds $14,000 at the .05 significance level. Also determine whether the sample evidence indicates that the mean of the variable **HPAYRENT** exceeds $900 at the .05 significance level.

Exercise 2—Appendix F

Randomly select from the database 30 observations in which the location of residence is in the NE sector, and also randomly select another 30 observations in which

the location of residence is in the NW sector. Find separate 90% confidence intervals on the mean of the variable **INCOME1** (income of principal wage earner) from each of these two sets of data. Comment on the difference in the confidence intervals.

Exercise 3—Appendix G

Randomly select from the database 30 observations from companies with a bond rating of A and 30 observations from companies with a bond rating of C. Find separate 95% confidence intervals on the mean of sales minus cost of sales for each of these two random samples. Compare and comment on the differences.

Insights from Statistics in Action

Hillerich & Bradsby Company: Hitting the Quality Mark

The Statistics in Action introductory case study mentioned that H & B's top managers have learned to use statistical analysis in their decision making. In their operations, random samples of bats are frequently selected to determine if the operator's machinery needs adjusting. Even small deviations from the specs could be enough for a professional baseball player to refuse purchasing a bat. Consider two samples of 15 randomly selected turned bats given in StatInActChap9 to answer the following questions. These samples contain the weights in ounces of newly turned bats.

1. Construct 95% confidence intervals for the means of each of the two samples. Interpret these intervals.

2. Construct 90% confidence intervals for the means of each of the two samples. Interpret these intervals.

3. The newly turned bats being sampled are produced with a target weight of 33 ounces. For each of the two samples, determine if the mean weight of newly turned bats differs from 33 ounces. Use a significance level of .05. What conclusion would you tell the manager? Are the results of these tests consistent with the confidence intervals in question 1?

4. If the standard deviation of the weights of the bats exceeds .15 ounces, operators readjust their machinery. For each of the two samples, determine if the sample standard deviation of newly turned bats is greater than .15. What would you tell the manager?

5. The manager is considering changing the significance level in testing the mean weights of the bats. What advice would you give to the manager? What error, Type I or Type II, would you think is more important with respect to satisfying the customer?

(Source: "Go Figure," *Sports Illustrated,* May 10, 2004, p. 18. "Big League Quality," *Quality Progress,* August 2001, vol. 34, no. 8, p. 27–34. "Louisville Slugger Maker Cuts Errors with Shipping System Upgrade," *Frontline Solutions,* September 2001, vol. 2, no. 10, September 2001, p. 16–18.)

Data Analysis with Excel, MINITAB, and SPSS

Appendix

Excel

Hypothesis Test for a One-Population Mean with Known Population Standard Deviation

To obtain a Z test for the mean with known population standard deviation, click **KPK Data Analysis ➤ One Population Inference.** For example, with the data consisting of 60 kilowatt hours in Example 10.5 entered in A1:A61 with a label in A1, select **Population mean (z statistic)** for the test in the drop-down list box. Then, enter A1:A61 for the **Input Range,** 175 for the **Population Standard Deviation,** 1 for **Alpha** since the significance level is .01 in this example, and check **Labels.** Select Hypothesis Test for **Method,** select Right-tail test for **Hypothesis,** enter 918 for **Hypothesized Value of Mean,** and check

Graphical Display of Test to view a chart of the normal distribution with the rejection region and *p*-value region. Enter C1 (or some other location) for the **Output Range** and click **OK** to print the output.

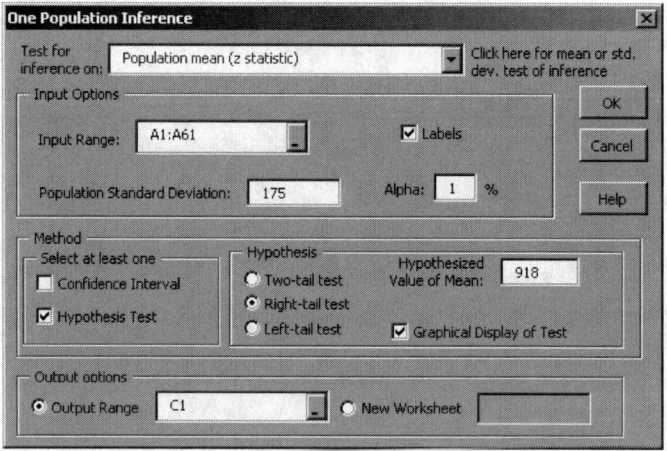

Hypothesis Test for a One-Population Mean with Unknown Population Standard Deviation

To obtain a *t* test for the mean with unknown population standard deviation, click **KPK Data Analysis ➤ One Population Inference.** Follow the same procedure for the case in which the population standard deviation is known, except select **Population mean with est. std. dev. (t statistic)** for the test in the drop-down list box. With this option, an edit box for the population standard deviation will not appear.

MINITAB

Hypothesis Test for a One-Population Mean with Known Population Standard Deviation

To obtain a Z test for the mean with known population standard deviation, click **Stat ➤ Basic Statistics ➤ 1-Sample Z.** For the data consisting of 60 kilowatt hours in Example 10.5 entered in C1, select **C1** for the **Samples in columns,** enter 175 for the population **Standard deviation,** and put 918 in the edit box for **Test mean** since this is the hypothesized mean. Click on **Options.** In the **Options** dialog box, enter 99 for the **Confidence level** since the significance level is .01 and select greater than from the drop-down list boxes for **Alternative.** Click **OK** for the output.

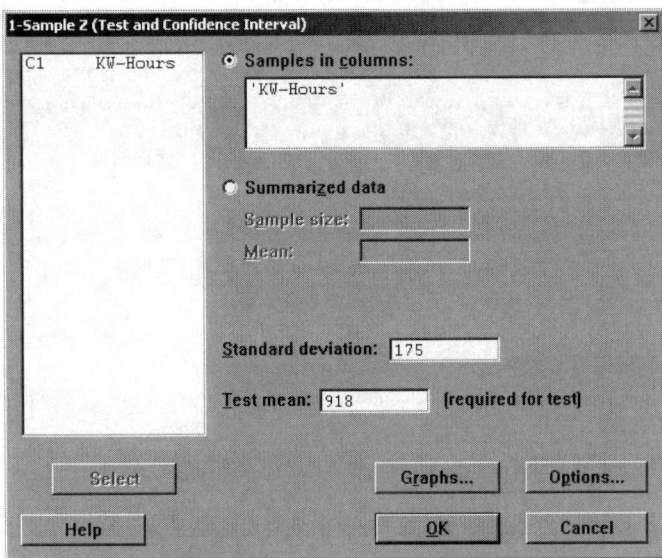

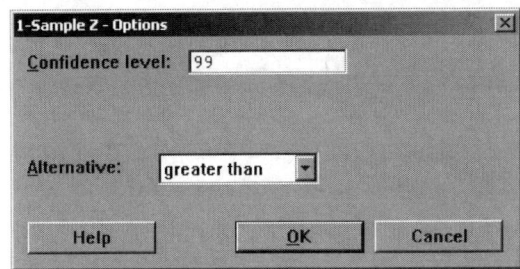

Hypothesis Test for a One-Population Mean with Unknown Population Standard Deviation

To obtain a *t* test for the mean with unknown population standard deviation, click **Stat ➤ Basic Statistics ➤ 1-Sample t.** Follow the same procedure for the case in which the population standard deviation is known. With this option, an edit box for the population standard deviation will not appear.

SPSS

Hypothesis Test for a One-Population Mean with Unknown Population Standard Deviation

To illustrate testing the mean of a single population, consider the output voltage of the 18 power supplies in Example 10.8. Enter these values in the first column of the data window and label this column voltage. Click **Analyze ➤ Compare Means ➤ One-Sample T Test.** Click on the pointer button to move the variable **voltage** into the **Test Variable(s)** box. In the **Test Value** box, enter 10 since this is the hypothesized value of the population mean. Click **OK** for the output. **Note:** For a one-tailed test, the *p*-value is obtained by dividing the SPSS p-value by two. This assumes that the sample mean agrees with the alternative hypothesis. For example, if the alternative hypothesis is H_a: $\mu > 10$, then the sample mean agrees with the alternative hypothesis provided the sample mean ($\bar{x}$) is greater than 10. If the sample mean does not agree with the alternative hypothesis (e.g., $\bar{x}$ is less than or equal to 10), the actual p-value is one minus one half of the SPSS two-tail p-value; that is, divide the SPSS p-value by two and subtract from one.

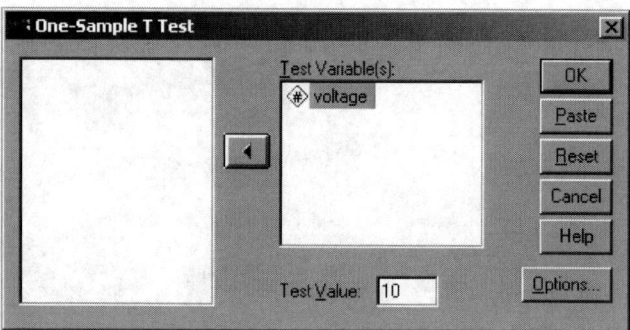

chapter

Comparing Two or More Populations

Statistics in Action
Rollovers with Sport-Utility Vehicles: Assessing the Impact

Once considered farm, work, or off-road vehicles, sport-utility vehicles (SUVs) have become increasingly popular on America's highways and are now made by nearly every automaker. Buyers of SUVs argue that these vehicles appeal to their sense of adventure, expression of personality, feeling of safety (since heavier vehicles typically fare better in accidents), and feeling of power with a higher seating position for a better view of the road. Although an SUV's size might make a driver feel safer, automakers are struggling with the publicity about the risk of rollovers.

The National Highway Traffic Safety Administration (NHTSA) uses the *static stability factor* (SSF) to assign rollover ratings to SUVs. The SSF is determined by dividing half a vehicle's track measurement by the height of its center of gravity. For example, an SSF of 1.13 to 1.24 qualifies for a three-star rating. This rating suggests a rollover risk between 20% and 30%. NHTSA is quick to point out that a low rating does not mean that a vehicle will spontaneously roll over. The popular Ford 2002 Explorer will qualify—but just barely—for an acceptable three-star rollover rating with an SSF of 1.13, and so will the Chevrolet 2002 Trail-Blazer with an SSF of 1.15. Only one SUV has a four-star rating, and that is the Pontiac Aztek.

Automakers do not believe the SSF is a reliable predictor of rollover, but they have given in to pressure from safety proponents. Some automotive analysts believe a safety rating should be computed by putting SUVs through numerous real-world tests that involve swerving, turning, and stopping abruptly at fairly high speeds. For exam-

ple, imagine the common accident scenario, where you've encountered a stopped semi truck 142 feet in front of you while going around a blind curve. If you are in a Porsche Boxster, a Dodge Caravan, a Pontiac Montana, a Ford Explorer, or a Chevrolet Suburban, the braking distance in feet is: 120 (yawn), 135 (Arrgh!), 141 (Whew!), 150 (SMASH!), and 155 (CRUNCH!!), respectively. These types of situations are difficult to incorporate into one safety score.

Automakers are not the only ones struggling with the rollover ratings. Insurance companies are interested in knowing if SUVs with less than a three-star rating have significantly more damage in collisions than SUVs with a three-star rating. When you have completed this chapter, you will be able to

- Determine what is meant by "significantly more damage" by SUVs with less than a three-star rating.

- Understand how to use independent and dependent samples to test hypotheses involving two populations such as SUVs *with less than* a three-star rating and those *with* a three-star rating.

- Construct and interpret a confidence interval for the difference in the amount of damage in a collision involving an SUV with three stars versus an SUV with less than three stars.

- Carry out a hypothesis test to make an inference about the means of three groups, such as the damage from a collision involving an SUV with one star, with two stars, and with three stars.

11.1 INDEPENDENT VERSUS DEPENDENT SAMPLES

When making comparisons between the means of two populations, we need to pay particular attention to how we intend to collect sample data. For example, how would you determine if tire brand A lasts longer than brand B? You might decide to put one of each brand on the rear wheels of ten cars and measure the tires' wear. Or you might randomly select 10 brand A and 10 brand B tires, attach them to a machine that wears them down for a certain time, and then measure the resulting tire wear. If you use the first procedure (putting both brands of tire on the same car), you obtain *dependent* samples; in the latter situation, you obtain *independent* samples.

Consider another situation. Suppose you are interested in male heights as compared with female heights. You obtain a sample of $n_1 = 50$ male heights and $n_2 = 50$ female heights. You obtain these data:

Observation	Male Heights	Observation	Female Heights
1	5.92 ft	1	5.36 ft
2	6.13 ft	2	5.64 ft
3	5.78 ft	3	5.44 ft
.	.	.	.
.	.	.	.
.	.	.	.
50	5.81 ft	50	5.52 ft

Is there any need to match up 5.92 with 5.36, 6.13 with 5.64, 5.78 with 5.44, and so on? The male heights were randomly selected and the female heights were obtained independently, so there is no reason to match up the first male height with the first female height, the second male height with the second female height, and so on. Nothing relates male 1 with female 1 other than the accident of their being selected first—these are **independent samples.**

What if you wish to know whether husbands are taller than their wives? To collect data, you select 50 married couples. Suppose you obtain the 100 observations from the previous male and female height example. Now, is there a reason to compare the first male height with the first female height, the second with the second, and so on? The answer is a definite yes, since each pair of heights belongs to a married couple. The resulting two samples are **dependent,** or **paired, samples.**

In summary,

1. If there is a definite reason for pairing (matching) corresponding data values, the two samples are *dependent* samples.

2. If the two samples were obtained independently and there is no reason for pairing the data values, the resulting samples are *independent* samples.

Why does this distinction matter? *If you are trying to decide whether male heights are, on the average, greater than female heights, the procedure that you use for testing this depends on whether the samples are obtained independently.*

Applications of dependent samples in a business setting include data from the following situations.

- *Comparisons of before versus after.* Sample 1: person's weight before a diet plan is begun. Sample 2: person's weight six months after starting the diet. Why do we pair the data? We pair them because each pair of observations belongs to the same person.

- *Comparisons of people with matching characteristics.* Sample 1: salary for a male employee at Company ABC. Sample 2: salary for a female employee at Company ABC, where the woman's education and job experience are equal to the man's. Why do we pair the data? We pair them because the two paired employees are identical in their job qualifications.

- *Comparisons of observations matched by location.* Sample 1: sales of brand A tires for a group of *n* stores. Sample 2: sales of brand B tires for the same group of stores. Why do we pair the data? We pair them because both observations were obtained from the same store. Your data consist of sales (weekly, monthly, and so on) from a sample of stores selling these two brands.

- *Comparisons of observations matched by time.* Sample 1: sales of restaurant A during a particular week. Sample 2: sales of restaurant B during this week. Why do we pair the data? We pair them because each pair of observations corresponds to the same week of the year.

X Exercises 11.1–11.8

Applying the New Concepts

11.1 Why does it matter if samples are independent or dependent?

11.2 A random sample of CPA accountants and another random sample of non–CPA accountants were used in a study to determine their job satisfaction. Do the data represent dependent or independent samples?

11.3 An industrial psychologist is interested in the changes in a worker's personality when stress is increased. A random sample of 50 employees of a manufacturing firm is selected. Each employee is put under a no-stress situation and a very stressful situation. Data are recorded on the employee's personality under each of these two conditions.
   a. Why would the sample of data collected under the no-stress situation and the sample of data collected under the very stressful situation be considered dependent samples?
   b. How could this experiment be conducted such that the samples were independent?

11.4 A pharmaceutical firm is interested in the efficacy of a new drug and of a standard drug. The research division of the firm randomly selects two groups of volunteers. One group is given the new drug and the other group is given the standard drug. Data are recorded on the effects of each drug. Is the research division using dependent or independent samples? Why?

11.5 The career placement center at Safire University conducts a survey of beginning salaries for MBAs with no on-the-job experience. Ten pairs of men and women are chosen randomly such that each pair of one man and one woman has nearly identical qualifications. Can the sample of observations from men be independent of the sample of observations from women?

11.6 A retail store would like to compare sales from two different arrangements of displaying its merchandise. Sales are recorded for a 30-day period with one arrangement and then sales are recorded for another 30-day period for the alternative arrangement. Would the data for each of the two 30-day periods be independent or dependent?

11.7 A marketing analyst would like to have two brands of sausage rated by consumers.
   a. Explain how the marketing analyst can use dependent samples to collect the data.
   b. Explain how the marketing analyst can use independent samples to collect the data.

11.8 List three different ways that dependent samples can be selected.

COMPARING TWO MEANS USING TWO INDEPENDENT SAMPLES (σ'S KNOWN)

When comparing the means of two independent samples from different populations, we can use Figure 11.1 to help visualize the situation. The two populations are shown to be normally distributed, but, whenever we use large samples from these populations, this is

FIGURE

11.1

Example of two
populations. Does
$\mu_1 = \mu_2$?

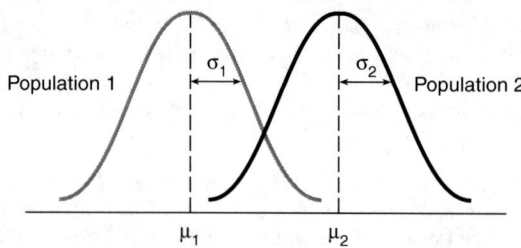

not a necessary assumption. Refer to Comment 3 on page 224 for a discussion of what is a "large" sample. Generally, $n_1 > 30$ and $n_2 > 30$ will suffice. For these populations,

μ_1 = mean of population 1

μ_2 = mean of population 2 } these are unknown

σ_1 = standard deviation of population 1

σ_2 = standard deviation of population 2 } these are known in section 11.2

For example, if we wished to compare U.S. adult male and female heights:

μ_1 = average of all female heights

μ_2 = average of all male heights } unknown

σ_1 = standard deviation of all female heights

σ_2 = standard deviation of all male heights } known

Comments

1. In this section, the population standard deviations (σ_1 and σ_2) are assumed to be known. When these standard deviations are unknown (the usual situation), use section 11.3.

2. The point estimates discussed in earlier chapters apply here as well—we simply have two of everything because we are dealing with two populations.

3. The procedure we follow is to obtain a random sample of size n_1 from population 1 and then obtain another sample of size n_2, completely independent of the first sample, from population 2. So, $\bar{X}_1$ is our best (point) estimate of μ_1. Likewise, $\bar{X}_2$ estimates μ_2.

Constructing a Confidence Interval for $\mu_1 - \mu_2$ (σ's Known)

Ace Delivery Service operates a fleet of delivery vans in the Houston area. They prefer to have all their drivers charge their gasoline using the same brand of credit card. Currently, they all use a Texgas credit card. Ace management has decided that perhaps Quik-Chek, a chain of convenience stores that also sells gasoline but does not accept credit cards, is worth investigating. A random sample of gas prices at 35 Texgas stations and 40 Quik-Chek stores in the Houston area is obtained. The cost of 1 gallon of regular gasoline is recorded; the data are summarized:

Sample 1 (Texgas)	Sample 2 (Quik-Chek)
$n_1 = 35$	$n_2 = 40$
$\bar{x}_1 = \$1.48$	$\bar{x}_2 = \$1.39$

Let μ_1 be the average price of regular gasoline at *all* Texgas stations in the Houston area, and let μ_2 be the average price of regular gasoline at all Quik-Chek stores in the Houston area. From past experience, it was assumed that $\sigma_1 = \$.12$ and $\sigma_2 = \$.10$.

When dealing with these two populations, the parameter of interest is $\mu_1 - \mu_2$, rather than the individual values of μ_1 and μ_2. Here, $\mu_1 - \mu_2$ represents the difference between the average gasoline prices at the Texgas stations and Quik-Chek stores. If we conclude that $\mu_1 - \mu_2 > 0$, then $\mu_1 > \mu_2$. In this case, the gasoline *is* more expensive at the Texgas stations.

The point estimator of $\mu_1 - \mu_2$ is the obvious one: $\bar{X}_1 - \bar{X}_2$. For our data, the (point) estimate of $\mu_1 - \mu_2$ is $\bar{x}_1 - \bar{x}_2 = 1.48 - 1.39 = .09$. How much more expensive is the gasoline from all of the Texgas stations, on the average? We do not know because this is $\mu_1 - \mu_2$, but we *do* have an estimate of this value—namely, 9¢.

What kind of random variable is $\bar{X}_1 - \bar{X}_2$? From Chapter 7, we know that $\bar{X}_1$ is approximately a normal random variable with mean μ_1 and variance σ_1^2/n_1 provided n_1 is large or population 1 is believed to be normally distributed. Under similar assumptions, $\bar{X}_2$ is approximately a normal random variable with mean μ_2 and variance σ_2^2/n_2. Because these are two independent samples, it follows that $\bar{X}_1 - \bar{X}_2$ is also approximately a normal random variable with mean $\mu_1 - \mu_2$ and variance $(\sigma_1^2/n_1) + (\sigma_2^2/n_2)$. Note that the variance of $\bar{X}_1 - \bar{X}_2$ is obtained by *adding* the variances for $\bar{X}_1$ and $\bar{X}_2$.

By standardizing this normal distribution, we obtain an approximate standard normal random variable defined by

$$Z = \frac{(\bar{X}_1 - \bar{X}_2) - (\mu_1 - \mu_2)}{\sqrt{\dfrac{\sigma_1^2}{n_1} + \dfrac{\sigma_2^2}{n_2}}}$$

11.1

We can now derive a confidence interval for $\mu_1 - \mu_2$. From Table A.4, we know that for the standard normal random variable Z,

$$P(-1.96 < Z < 1.96) = .95$$

Using equation 11.1 (and rearranging the inequalities), we can make the following statement about a random interval prior to obtaining the sample data:

$$P\left[(\bar{X}_1 - \bar{X}_2) - 1.96\sqrt{\frac{\sigma_1^2}{n_1} + \frac{\sigma_2^2}{n_2}} < \mu_1 - \mu_2 < (\bar{X}_1 - \bar{X}_2) + 1.96\sqrt{\frac{\sigma_1^2}{n_1} + \frac{\sigma_2^2}{n_2}}\right] = .95$$

This produces the following $(1 - \alpha) \cdot 100\%$ confidence interval for $\mu_1 - \mu_2$ (large samples, where σ_1 and σ_2 are known):

$$(\bar{X}_1 - \bar{X}_2) - Z_{\alpha/2}\sqrt{\frac{\sigma_1^2}{n_1} + \frac{\sigma_2^2}{n_2}} \quad \text{to} \quad (\bar{X}_1 - \bar{X}_2) + Z_{\alpha/2}\sqrt{\frac{\sigma_1^2}{n_1} + \frac{\sigma_2^2}{n_2}}$$

11.2

Notice that this interval is very similar to the confidence interval for a single population mean using a large sample, namely,

$$\text{(point estimate)} \pm Z_{\alpha/2} \cdot \text{(standard deviation of the point estimator)}$$

Using the data from the two gas-price samples, construct a 90% confidence interval for $\mu_1 - \mu_2$.

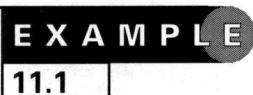

EXAMPLE

11.1

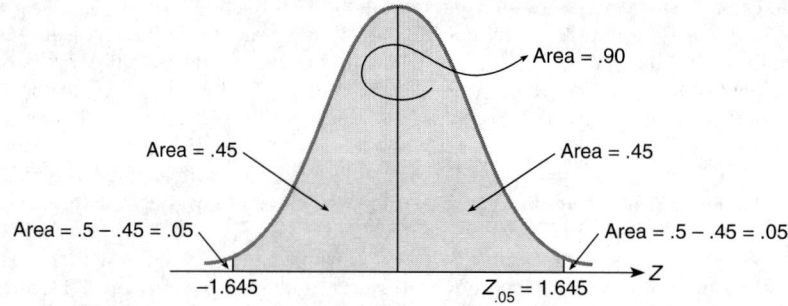

FIGURE

11.2

Finding the pair of Z values containing 90% of the area under the curve. The values are −1.645 and 1.645.

Solution

To begin with, the estimate of μ_1 is $\bar{x}_1 = \$1.48$, and the estimate of μ_2 is $\bar{x}_2 = \$1.39$. We are constructing a 90% confidence interval, so (using Table A.4) we find that $Z_{.05} = 1.645$ (Figure 11.2). The resulting 90% confidence interval for $\mu_1 - \mu_2$ is

$$(\bar{X}_1 - \bar{X}_2) - 1.645\sqrt{\frac{\sigma_1^2}{n_1} + \frac{\sigma_2^2}{n_2}} \quad \text{to} \quad (\bar{X}_1 - \bar{X}_2) + 1.645\sqrt{\frac{\sigma_1^2}{n_1} + \frac{\sigma_2^2}{n_2}}$$

$$= (1.48 - 1.39) - 1.645\sqrt{\frac{(.12)^2}{35} + \frac{(.10)^2}{40}} \text{ to } (1.48 - 1.39) + 1.645\sqrt{\frac{(.12)^2}{35} + \frac{(.10)^2}{40}}$$

$$= .09 - (1.645)(.0257) \quad \text{to} \quad .09 + (1.645)(.0257)$$

$$= .09 - .042 \quad \text{to} \quad .09 + .042$$

$$= .048 \quad \text{to} \quad .132$$

We can summarize this result in three ways:

1. We are 90% confident that $\mu_1 - \mu_2$ lies between .048 and .132.

2. We are 90% confident that the average price of Texgas regular gasoline is between 4.8¢ and 13.2¢ higher than the regular gasoline at Quik-Chek.

3. We are 90% confident that our estimate of $\mu_1 - \mu_2$ ($\bar{X}_1 - \bar{X}_2 = 9¢$) is within 4.2¢ of the actual value.

The confidence intervals defined in equations 11.2 and 11.3 will contain $\mu_1 - \mu_2$ 90% of the time. In other words, if you repeatedly obtained independent samples and repeated the procedure in Example 9.1, 90% of the corresponding confidence intervals would contain the unknown value of $\mu_1 - \mu_2$, and 10% of them would not.

Hypothesis Testing for μ_1 and μ_2 (σ's Known)

Are men on the average taller than women? How do you answer such a question? We know that we can start by getting a sample of male heights and independently obtaining a sample of female heights. Figure 11.3 illustrates the two corresponding populations.

We proceed as before and put the claim that we are trying to demonstrate into the *alternative* hypothesis. The resulting hypotheses are

$$H_0: \mu_1 \geq \mu_2 \quad \text{(men are not taller, on the average)}$$

$$H_a: \mu_1 < \mu_2 \quad \text{(men are taller, on the average)}$$

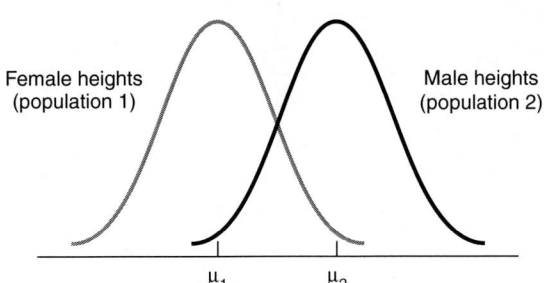

FIGURE

11.3

Hypothesis testing for two populations. Sample 1: size, n_1 and mean, $\bar{X}_1$. Sample 2: size, n_2 and mean, $\bar{X}_2$. Is $\mu_1 < \mu_2$?

We have estimators of μ_1 and μ_2, namely, $\bar{X}_1$ and $\bar{X}_2$. A sensible thing to do would be to reject H_0 if $\bar{X}_1$ is "significantly smaller" than $\bar{X}_2$. In this case, the obvious conclusion is that μ_1 (the average of all female heights in your population) is smaller than μ_2 (for male heights).

To define "significantly larger," we need to know what chance we are willing to take of rejecting H_0 when in fact it is true. This chance is α (the significance level) and, as before, it is determined prior to seeing any data. Typical values range from .01 to .1, with $\alpha = .05$ generally providing a good trade-off between Type I and Type II errors. The test statistic here is the same as the one used to derive a confidence interval for $\mu_1 - \mu_2$. We are dealing with the situation where σ_1 and σ_2 are known, so the test statistic is approximately a standard normal random variable, defined by

$$Z = \frac{\bar{X}_1 - \bar{X}_2}{\sqrt{\dfrac{\sigma_1^2}{n_1} + \dfrac{\sigma_2^2}{n_2}}}$$

provided n_1 and n_2 are large or we have reason to believe that the two populations of interest are *normal* populations.

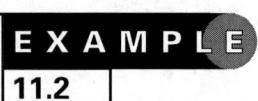

The Ace Delivery people suspected that the gasoline at the Quik-Chek stores was less expensive than that at Texgas before they obtained any data. (*Note:* This is important! Do not let the data dictate your hypotheses for you. If you do, you introduce a serious bias into your testing procedure, and the "true" significance level may no longer be the predetermined α.) Here, μ_1 represents the average price at all of the Texgas stations and μ_2 is the average price at the Quik-Chek stores in the area. Is $\mu_2 < \mu_1$? Or, put another way, is $\mu_1 > \mu_2$? Use a significance level of .05.

Solution

Step 1.   *Define the hypotheses.* The question is whether the data support the claim that $\mu_1 > \mu_2$, so we put this statement in the alternative hypothesis.

H_0: $\mu_1 \leq \mu_2$ (Texgas is less expensive or the same.)

H_a: $\mu_1 > \mu_2$ (Quik-Chek is less expensive.)

As in Chapter 8, the equals sign goes into H_0 for a one-tailed test. In other words, the case where $\mu_1 = \mu_2$ is contained in the null hypothesis.

FIGURE

11.4

Z curve showing rejection region for Example 11.2.

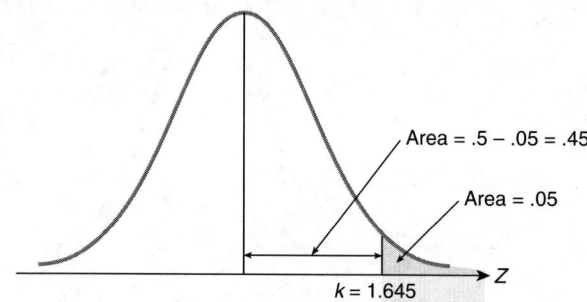

Area = .5 − .05 = .45

Area = .05

k = 1.645

Step 2. *Define the test statistic.* This is the statistic that you evaluate using the sample data. Its value will either support the alternative hypothesis or it will not. The test statistic for this situation is given by equation 11.3:

$$Z = \frac{\bar{X}_1 - \bar{X}_2}{\sqrt{\dfrac{\sigma_1^2}{n_1} + \dfrac{\sigma_2^2}{n_2}}}$$

Step 3. *Define the rejection region.* In Figure 11.4, where should the null hypothesis H_0 be rejected? We simply ask, what happens to Z when H_a is true? In this case ($\mu_1 > \mu_2$), we should see $\bar{X}_1 > \bar{X}_2$. In other words, Z will be positive. So we reject H_0 if Z is "too large," that is,

reject H_0 if $Z > k$ for some $k > 0$

Using $\alpha = .05$, we use Table A.4 to find the corresponding value of Z (that is, k). In Figure 11.4, $k = 1.645$. This is the same value and rejection region we obtained in Chapter 8 when using Z for a one-tailed test in the right tail. The test is

reject H_0 if $Z > 1.645$

Step 4. *Evaluate the test statistic and carry out the test.* The data collected showed $n_1 = 35$, $\bar{x}_1 = 1.48$ (from the Texgas sample) and $n_2 = 40$, $\bar{x}_2 = 1.39$ (from the Quik-Chek sample). In addition, the population standard deviations were believed to be $\sigma_1 = .12$ and $\sigma_2 = .10$. Based on these sample results, can we conclude that $\bar{x}_1 = 1.48$ is *significantly larger* than $\bar{x}_2 = 1.39$? If we can, the decision will be to reject H_0. The following value of the test statistic will answer our question.

$$Z = \frac{\bar{X}_1 - \bar{X}_2}{\sqrt{\dfrac{\sigma_1^2}{n_1} + \dfrac{\sigma_2^2}{n_2}}} = \frac{1.48 - 1.39}{\sqrt{\dfrac{(.12)^2}{35} + \dfrac{(.10)^2}{40}}}$$

$$= \frac{.09}{.0257} = 3.50 = Z*$$

Because $3.50 > 1.645$, we reject H_0; $\bar{x}_1$ is significantly larger than $\bar{x}_2$. Therefore, we claim that $\mu_1 > \mu_2$.

Step 5. *State a conclusion.* We conclude that the Quik-Chek stores *do* charge less for gasoline (on the average) than do the Texgas stations. If the locations of these stores are equally convenient to Ace Delivery Service, buying gas from Quik-Chek appears to be a money-saving alternative.

FIGURE
11.5

Z curve showing
p-value for
$Z^* = 3.50$.

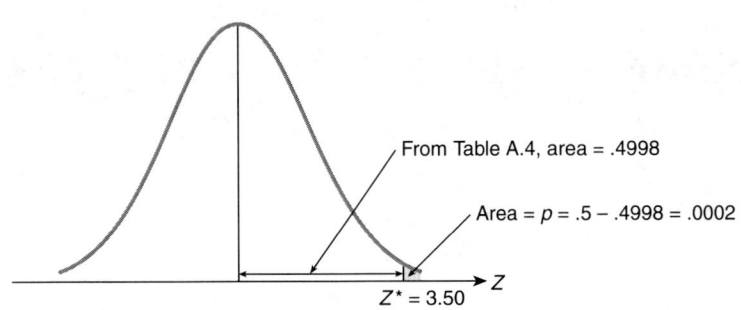

From Table A.4, area = .4998

Area = $p = .5 - .4998 = .0002$

$Z^* = 3.50$

Z

Using the corresponding p-value for the data in Example 11.2, what would you conclude using the classical approach (with $\alpha = .05$)? For this example, the p-value will be the area under the Z curve (Z is our test statistic) to the right (we reject H_0 in the right tail for this example) of the calculated test statistic, $Z^* = 3.50$. In general,

$$p = p\text{-value} = \begin{cases} \text{area to the right of } Z^* \text{ for } H_a: \mu_1 > \mu_2 \\ \text{area to the left of } Z^* \text{ for } H_a: \mu_1 < \mu_2 \\ 2 \cdot (\text{tail area of } Z^*) \text{ for } H_a: \mu_1 \neq \mu_2 \end{cases}$$

11.4

These three alternative hypotheses are your choices for this situation. Once again, $H_0: \mu_1 = \mu_2$ versus $H_a: \mu_1 \neq \mu_2$ is a two-tailed test, and the first two alternative hypotheses represent one-tailed tests.

Returning to our example, we can see from Figure 11.5 that the resulting p-value is $p = .0002$ (very small). Using the classical approach, because p is smaller than the significance level of .05, we reject H_0—the same conclusion as before. In fact, this procedure *always* leads to the same conclusion as the five-step solution, as we saw in Chapter 8.

If we elect not to select a significance level α and instead use only the p-value to make a decision, we proceed as before:

1. Reject H_0 if p is small ($p < .01$).

2. Fail to reject H_0 if p is large ($p > .1$).

3. Data are inconclusive if p is neither small nor large ($.01 \leq p \leq .1$).

For this example, $p = .0002$ is clearly small, and so we again reject H_0. The Quik-Chek gasoline definitely appears to be less expensive than the Texgas gasoline. As was pointed out in the previous chapter, you often encounter a result that is *statistically* significant but not significant in a *practical sense*. To illustrate, suppose that the p-value of .0002 was the result of two very large samples and that the difference in gasoline price for the two samples was $\bar{x}_1 - \bar{x}_2 = .008$. You might not view this difference (less than 1¢) as being worth the inconvenience of having to pay cash for all gasoline purchases.

Comments

There may well be situations where the severity of the Type I error requires a significance level smaller than .01 on the low end, or the impact of a Type II error dictates a significance level larger than .1 on the upper end. This rule is thus only a general yardstick that applies to most, but certainly not all, business applications.

INDEPENDENT SAMPLES TESTS
FOR μ_1 AND μ_2 (σ's KNOWN)

Two-Tailed Test

$$H_0: \mu_1 = \mu_2$$

$$H_a: \mu_1 \neq \mu_2$$

$$\text{reject } H_0 \text{ if } |Z| > Z_{\alpha/2}$$

where

$$Z = \frac{\bar{X}_1 - \bar{X}_2}{\sqrt{\dfrac{\sigma_1^2}{n_1} + \dfrac{\sigma_2^2}{n_2}}}$$

One-Tailed Test

$H_0: \mu_1 \leq \mu_2$	$H_0: \mu_1 \geq \mu_2$
$H_a: \mu_1 > \mu_2$	$H_a: \mu_1 < \mu_2$
reject H_0 if $Z > Z_\alpha$	reject H_0 if $Z < -Z_\alpha$

Two-Sample Procedure for Any Specified Value of $\mu_1 - \mu_2$

The two-tailed hypotheses for large sample tests for μ_1 and μ_2 can be written as

$$H_0: \mu_1 - \mu_2 = 0$$

$$H_a: \mu_1 - \mu_2 \neq 0$$

The right-sided one-tailed hypotheses are

$$H_0: \mu_1 - \mu_2 \leq 0$$

$$H_a: \mu_1 - \mu_2 > 0$$

The left-tailed hypotheses can be written in a similar manner. The point is that H_0 (so far) claims that $\mu_1 - \mu_2$ is equal to 0 or lies to one side of 0 (the one-tailed tests).

Suppose the claim is that $\mu_1 - \mu_2$ is more than 10. To demonstrate that this is true, we must make our alternative hypothesis $H_a: \mu_1 - \mu_2 > 10$; the corresponding null hypothesis is $H_0: \mu_1 - \mu_2 \leq 10$.

In general, to test that $\mu_1 - \mu_2 = $ some specified value, say D_0, the five-step procedure still applies, but the test statistic is now equation 11.5:

$$Z = \frac{(\bar{X}_1 - \bar{X}_2) - D_0}{\sqrt{\dfrac{\sigma_1^2}{n_1} + \dfrac{\sigma_2^2}{n_2}}}$$

11.5

Equation 11.5 applies to both one-tailed and two-tailed tests. It can be used to compare two means directly (for example, $H_0: \mu_1 = \mu_2$ versus $H_a: \mu_1 \neq \mu_2$) by setting $D_0 = 0$, as in Example 11.2.

In Example 11.2, we decided that Ace Delivery Service would save money if they purchased their gasoline from Quik-Chek because that store's average gasoline price appeared to be less than that of the Texgas stations. Because Quik-Chek does not accept credit cards, the owner of Ace is willing to purchase Quik-Chek gasoline only if their average price is more than 6¢ per gallon less than Texgas's. Do the data indicate that it is? (α is still .05.)

Solution

The question now is whether the data support the claim that the difference between the two means (Texgas and Quik-Chek) is larger than 6¢. So the hypotheses are $H_0: \mu_1 - \mu_2 \le .06$ and $H_a: \mu_1 - \mu_2 > .06$, where μ_1 is Texgas's mean and μ_2 is Quik-Chek's mean. The test statistic is

$$Z = \frac{(\bar{X}_1 - \bar{X}_2) - .06}{\sqrt{\dfrac{\sigma_1^2}{n_1} + \dfrac{\sigma_2^2}{n_2}}}$$

The computed value of Z is

$$Z^* = \frac{(1.48 - 1.39) - .06}{\sqrt{\dfrac{(.12)^2}{35} + \dfrac{(.10)^2}{40}}} = \frac{.03}{.0257} = 1.17$$

The testing procedure is exactly as it was previously—reject H_0 if $Z^* > 1.645$. Because $1.17 < 1.645$, we fail to reject H_0. The difference between the two sample means (9¢) was *not* significantly larger than the hypothesized value of 6¢.

These data provide insufficient evidence to conclude that Quik-Chek is more than 6¢ less expensive (on the average) than Texgas. If Ace's owner thinks that not using credit cards would be too much trouble for a savings of less than 6¢ per gallon, Ace should use the Texgas gasoline.

Using Excel to Carry Out a Two-Sample Z Test

Excel has a built-in function to carry out the two-sample Z test. This procedure will ask for the two population variances and assumes they are known. If, in fact, these two variances are estimated from the two samples, then a better way to go is to use an Excel two-sample t test procedure discussed in the next section.

To use Excel on Example 11.3, click on **Tools ➤ Data Analysis ➤ z-Test: Two-Sample for Means,** and use the instructions in the end-of-chapter appendix. The **Hypothesized Mean Difference** value is .06. If you were using Excel on Example 11.2, this value would be zero. After clicking on **OK,** you should obtain the output in cells C1:E12 in Figure 11.6.

In Figure 11.6, the calculated value of Z is 1.166487 and agrees with Example 11.3, where we obtained $Z^* = 1.17$. The arrow inserted into Figure 11.6 highlights the p-value, which is now .1217.* Since this is larger that .05, we fail to reject H_0 and arrive at the same conclusion reached in the solution to Example 11.3.

---

*In this chapter, Excel's one-tailed p-values are correct *provided* a true statement is obtained when the population means in the *alternative* hypothesis are replaced by the sample means. For this example, you would examine $\bar{x}_1 - \bar{x}_2 > .06$. Using $\bar{x}_1 = 1.48$ and $\bar{x}_2 = 1.39$, you obtain a true statement since $.09 > .06$. Consequently, the Excel p-value of .1217 is correct. If you had obtained a false statement, the correct p-value is 1 minus Excel's p-value (.8783 here).

FIGURE

11.6

Excel spreadsheet using **Tools ➤ Data Analysis ➤ z Test: Two-Sample for Means.**

	A	B	C	D	E
1	TEXGAS	QUIK-CHEK	z-Test: Two Sample for Means		
2	$1.50	$1.41			
3	$1.46	$1.46		*TEXGAS*	*QUIK-CHEK*
4	$1.58	$1.37	Mean	1.48	1.39
5	$1.68	$1.41	Known Variance	0.0144	0.01
6	$1.51	$1.30	Observations	35	40
7	$1.63	$1.60	Hypothesized Mean	0.06	
8	$1.49	$1.42	z	1.166487	
9	$1.75	$1.44	P(Z<=z) one-tail	0.121709	⬅
10	$1.31	$1.44	z Critical one-tail	1.644853	
11	$1.44	$1.41	P(Z<=z) two-tail	0.243418	
12	$1.53	$1.27	z Critical two-tail	1.95996	
13	$1.51	$1.40			

X Exercises 11.9–11.24

Understanding the Mechanics

11.9 An industrial engineer randomly samples 40 observations from each of two processes. The random sample from the first process yields a sample mean of 50. This population standard deviation is known to be 12. The random sample from the second process yields a sample mean of 56. This population standard deviation is known to be 14.

a. Compute the 90% confidence interval on the difference in the means of the two processes.

b. Is there evidence to indicate that the mean of the first process is less than the mean of the second process? Use a significance level of 10%.

11.10 Two independent random samples, each of size 80, were selected. Sample means were $\bar{x}_1 = 110$ and $\bar{x}_2 = 105$. The population variances are $\sigma_1^2 = 49$ and $\sigma_2^2 = 25$.

a. Find a 99% confidence interval for the difference of the population means.

b. Test that the difference in the population means is not equal to 3. Use a .05 significance level. Find the *p*-value.

11.11 A random sample results in $\bar{x}_1 = 20$ with $n_1 = 100$. The population standard deviation is $\sigma_1 = 6$. Another sample was selected independently resulting in $\bar{x}_2 = 22$ with $n_2 = 100$. The population standard deviation is $\sigma_2 = 7$. Test that the population means differ using a 1% significance level.

Applying the New Concepts

11.12 First National Bank and City National Bank are competing for customers who would like to open IRAs (individual retirement accounts). Thirty-two weeks are randomly selected for First National Bank and another 32 weeks are randomly selected for City National. The total amount deposited into IRAs is noted for each week. A summary of data (deposits in thousands of dollars) from

the survey is as follows. First National: $\bar{x}_1 = 4.1$, $\sigma_1 = 1.2$. City National: $\bar{x}_2 = 3.5$, $\sigma_2 = 0.9$. Use a 98% confidence interval to estimate the difference in the mean weekly deposits into IRAs for each bank.

11.13 Two discount stores in a popular shopping mall have their merchandise laid out differently. Both stores claim that the arrangement of goods in their store makes the customer buy more on impulse. A survey of 100 customers from each store is taken. Each customer is asked how much money he or she spent on merchandise he or she did not originally intend to buy before walking into the store. The results are as follows. Discount store 1: $\bar{x}_1 = \$15.50$, $\sigma_1 = 3.20$. Discount store 2: $\bar{x}_2 = \$19.40$, $\sigma_2 = \$4.80$. Find a 90% confidence interval for the difference in the mean amount of cash spent per customer on impulse buying for the two different stores. Is layout affecting impulse buying? How do you know?

11.14 Military managers have had to learn to make the military operations more economical by using the just-in-time system. Consider the following data measuring the time (in days) to deliver tank parts to NATO bases in Europe from the factory in 2000 and in 2005. Assume that the population variances for the two time frames are known to be 28 and 14 for time periods 2000 and 2005, respectively.

2000	2005
20	13
16	15
12	14
19	18
25	12
14	13
21	16
17	17
16	19
22	13

a. Is the mean time for 2005 less than that for 2000? Use a 10% significance level.

b. What assumptions do you need for the validity of the test in part a?

11.15 The manager of an information systems support group would like to test the hypothesis that easy listening music increases the productivity of programmers. Samples of two separate groups of 50 programmers were randomly selected from programmers across the company. The same computer programming task was given to each group and a rating on a scale from 1 to 100 was recorded for each individual programmer. The first group was given the task with easy listening music playing, whereas the second group did the task without music. The results revealed that the easy listening music group had a mean rating of 71. The population variance of this group is 30.2. The second group had a mean rating of 67. The population variance of the second group is 28.1. Use a significance level of 10% to test for the manager's belief.

11.16 Refer to Exercise 11.15.

a. Find a 90% confidence interval for the difference in the mean ratings of the two groups.

b. Can the information in part a be used to test the hypothesis in Exercise 11.15? Why or why not?

c. If the same programmers were used in each group in Exercise 11.15, would the assumptions for the validity of the test change?

11.17 A marketing analyst computes a 95% confidence interval on the difference between two population means to be –2.6 to 1.4. Can this interval be used to test that the mean of population 1 is greater than the mean of population 2 at the 5% significance level? Why or why not?

11.18 A production manager wishes to determine if there is a difference in the number of production units produced by the night shift and the day shift. A random sample of night and day shifts is selected, and the number of production units for each shift is recorded. The following statistics resulted.

	$\bar{x}$	σ	n
Day shift	27.4	6.4	60
Night shift	18.3	5.9	60

a. Find a 90% confidence interval on the difference in the mean number of production units for the two shifts.

b. Calculate a 99% confidence interval for part a.

c. Compare the two confidence intervals in parts a and b, and comment on the length of the intervals.

11.19 Eurostat, a statistical office of the European Union, reports that on average a person in Ireland bought one more movie ticket per year than a person in Britain. To confirm this report, a marketing entertainment researcher sampled 100 Irish and 150 British citizens. The researcher wished to test the belief that the difference in the average number of movie tickets ́purchased per year by British and Irish citizens was not equal to one. The results of the sample survey were as follows:

	$\bar{x}$	σ	n
Ireland	3.4	1.5	100
Britain	2.1	1.7	150

At the .10 significance level, do the data support the researchers belief that the difference in the average number of movie tickets purchased per year by British and Irish citizens was not equal to one. Report the p-value and interpret it.

(Source: "Irish Eyes Watching Movies," USA Today, May 26, 1998, p. 1D.)

11.20 Mad property tax disease is starting to grip business and homeowners in many provinces in Canada as properties get evaluated using market value assessment (MVA). Tenants in commercial buildings expected to see an approximate 10% to 30% jump in rents at the end of 1998. Suppose that an economist wished to show that the average percent increase in Toronto exceeds that in Quebec by more than 3 percent. A random sample of 100 properties in Quebec and 100 properties in Toronto affected by MVA revealed the average percent increase in rent.

City	$\bar{x}$	σ
Quebec	17	5
Toronto	24	10

Report the p-value for testing the economist's belief. Should the economist be concerned with the actual distribution of the data?

(Source: "Tax Revolt Sweeps Province Business Owners across Ontario," Toronto Sun, June 28, 1998, p. 69.)

11.21 The financial analyst of Hogan Securities believes there is no difference in the annual average returns for steel industry stocks and mineral industry stocks. Using the following information, test the hypothesis that there is no significant difference in the average returns for these two types of stocks. Steel industry stocks: $\bar{x}$ = 9%, n = 33, σ = 2.4%. Mineral industry stocks: $\bar{x}$ = 11%, n = 41, σ = 4%. Use a 10% significance level.

Using the Computer

11.22 **[DATA SET EX11-22]** Variable Description:

OccRateNorth: Occupancy rate of Holiday Hotel North

OccRateSouth: Occupancy rate of Holiday Hotel South

Occupancy rates (in percent) for 100 days were independently sampled for Holiday Hotel North and Holiday Hotel South. Historical standard deviations are 5% and 7% for the north and south hotels, respectively. Is there a significant difference in the occupancy rates for these two hotels? Use a 5% significance level.

11.23 **[DATA SET EX11-23]** Variable Description:

Loss1994: Loss from reselling leased car in 1994

Loss1997: Loss from reselling leased car in 1997

447

Automotive leasing companies usually resell returned leased cars at a loss from their national resale value when the lease terms expired. Automobile analysts believe that the loss from reselling these returned vehicles was at least $200 more in 1997 than in 1994. Suppose that a sample of 40 lease cars resold in 1994 and a sample of 40 lease cars resold in 1997 were randomly selected and their loss was recorded in dollars.

    a. Find the mean of both samples. Use the stacked histogram option on the KPK menu to view the two sets of data. What differences do you observe?

    b. Use the Z test for testing the hypothesis that the mean loss for 1997 is at least $200 more than in 1994. Assume the population standard deviations for the 1994 loss and 1997 loss are $413.07 and $408.50, respectively. Use a significance level of .10.

    c. Explain how practical significance of the results may differ from the statistical significance of the results for this problem.

(Source: "Lease Losses," USA Today, May 6, 1998, p. B1.)

11.24 [DATA SET EX11-24]Variable Description:

SalesCareer: Monthly sales by salespersons who say that they want to make a career out of sales

SalesNonCareer: Monthly sales by salespersons who say that they will eventually change to a profession that does not involve sales.

A sales manager believes that salespersons who wish to remain in sales as a career will sell at least $400 more than those who have decided that they will eventually change to a profession that does not involve sales. Across the company, 50 of each type of salesperson is selected, and each person's average monthly sales for the past six months is recorded in either the variables SalesCareer or SalesNon-Career. The units are in thousands of dollars. Test the sales manager's belief using a 5% significance level. What managerial conclusion can you give for this situation? Assume the population variances are .931 for the career group and 1.448 for the non–career group.

11.3

COMPARING TWO MEANS USING TWO INDEPENDENT SAMPLES (σ'S UNKNOWN)

In Chapters 8 and 10, we showed that when going from situations where the population standard deviation (σ) was known to situations where σ was unknown, the confidence interval and hypothesis-testing procedures both remained exactly the same, except that we used the t distribution rather than the Z distribution to describe the test statistic. We will use the same approach for the situation where the variances of the two populations are unknown.

Confidence Interval for $\mu_1 - \mu_2$ (σ's Unknown)

When using large samples from two populations with known variances to compare μ_1 and μ_2, we used the approximate Z-statistic defined by

$$Z = \frac{\bar{X}_1 - \bar{X}_2}{\sqrt{\dfrac{\sigma_1^2}{n_1} + \dfrac{\sigma_2^2}{n_2}}}$$

    The logical thing to do when the population variances are unknown is to replace each population variance (σ^2) by its estimate; namely, the corresponding sample variance (s^2). When replacing the first population variance (σ_1^2) with the variance of the first sample (s_1^2) and replacing σ_2^2 with s_2^2, the resulting statistic no longer approximates the standard normal. To make matters more complicated, it is not a t random variable, either. However, this expression is approximatelya t random variable if a somewhat complicated expression is used to derive the degrees of freedom (df). So we define

$$t' = \frac{\bar{X}_1 - \bar{X}_2}{\sqrt{\dfrac{s_1^2}{n_1} + \dfrac{s_2^2}{n_2}}}$$

11.6

This statistic approximately follows a t distribution with df given by equation 11.7:*

$$\text{df for } t' = \frac{\left[\dfrac{s_1^2}{n_1} + \dfrac{s_2^2}{n_2}\right]^2}{\dfrac{\left(\dfrac{s_1^2}{n_1}\right)^2}{n_1 - 1} + \dfrac{\left(\dfrac{s_2^2}{n_2}\right)^2}{n_2 - 1}}$$

11.7

Admittedly, equation 11.7 is a bit messy, but a good calculator or computer package makes this calculation relatively painless. If df as calculated is not an integer (1, 2, 3, . . .), it should be rounded to the nearest integer (procedure used by Excel). MINITAB always rounds *down* to the nearest integer (the conservative procedure) and SPSS does *not* round this value at all. As a check of your calculations, the df should be between A and B, where A is the smaller of $(n_1 - 1)$ and $(n_2 - 1)$ and B is $(n_1 - 1) + (n_2 - 1)$.

When finding the df, you can scale *both* s_1 and s_2 any way you wish, provided you scale them both the same way. By scaling, we mean that you can use s_1 and s_2 as is, or you can move the decimal point to the right or left. The resulting df will be the same *regardless* of the scaling used. However, when you evaluate the test statistic, t', or later perform a test of hypothesis, you must return to the *original* values of s_1 and s_2.

To derive an approximate confidence interval for $\mu_1 - \mu_2$, we use the same logic as in the previous (σ's known) procedure. Thus, a $(1 - \alpha) \cdot 100\%$ confidence interval for $\mu_1 - \mu_2$ (σ's unknown) is shown in equation 11.8:

$$(\bar{X}_1 - \bar{X}_2) - t_{\alpha/2,df}\sqrt{\frac{s_1^2}{n_1} + \frac{s_2^2}{n_2}} \quad \text{to} \quad (\bar{X}_1 - \bar{X}_2) + t_{\alpha/2,df}\sqrt{\frac{s_1^2}{n_1} + \frac{s_2^2}{n_2}}$$

11.8

Recall that df is specified in equation 11.7. If df is not an integer, round this value to the nearest integer.

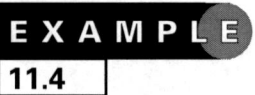

EXAMPLE 11.4

Checkers Cab Company is trying to decide which brand of tires to use for the coming year. Based on current price and prior experience, it has narrowed its choice to two brands, Beltex and Roadmaster. A recent study examined the durability of these tires by using a machine with a metallic device that wore down the tires. The time it took (in hours) for the tire to blow out was recorded.

Because the test for each tire took a great deal of time and the tire itself was ruined by the test, small samples (15 of each brand) were used. Notice that these are *independent* samples; there is no reason to match up the first Beltex tire with the first Roadmaster tire in the sample, the second Beltex with the second Roadmaster, and so on. (As discussed in Section 11.1, they would be dependent samples if the tires were tested by putting one of each brand on the rear wheels of 15 different cars.) To compensate for any machine fatigue, the order of selection for the 30 tires was determined randomly.

---

*For small sample sizes, we must have reason to believe that the two populations of interest are *normal* populations.

The blowout times (hours) were as follows:

Beltex	Roadmaster		Beltex	Roadmaster
3.82	4.16		2.84	3.65
3.11	3.92		3.26	3.82
4.21	3.94		3.74	4.55
2.64	4.22		3.04	3.82
4.16	4.15		2.56	3.85
3.91	3.62		2.58	3.62
2.44	4.11		3.15	4.88
4.52	3.45			

Construct a 90% confidence interval for $\mu_1 - \mu_2$, letting μ_1 be the average blowout time for *all* Beltex tires and μ_2 be the average blowout time for *all* Roadmaster tires. The blowout times for both tires are believed to be normally distributed.

Solution Here is a summary of the data from these two samples.

Sample 1 (Beltex)	Sample 2 (Roadmaster)
$n_1 = 15$	$n_2 = 15$
$\bar{x}_1 = 3.33$ hr	$\bar{x}_2 = 3.98$ hr
$s_1 = .68$ hr	$s_2 = .38$ hr

Your next step is to get a *t*-value from Table A.5. To do this, you first must calculate the correct df using equation 11.7:

$$df = \frac{\left[\dfrac{(.68)^2}{15} + \dfrac{(.38)^2}{15}\right]^2}{\dfrac{\left[\dfrac{(.68)^2}{15}\right]^2}{14} + \dfrac{\left[\dfrac{(.38)^2}{15}\right]^2}{14}}$$

$$= \frac{(.0404)^2}{.0000679 + .00000662} = 21.9$$

Rounding to the nearest integer, we use df = 22. Using Table A.5:

$$t_{.10/2,22} = t_{.05,22} = 1.717$$

The resulting 90% confidence interval for $\mu_1 - \mu_2$ is

$$\left(\bar{X}_1 - \bar{X}_2\right) - t_{.05,22}\sqrt{\frac{s_1^2}{n_1} + \frac{s_2^2}{n_2}} \text{ to } \left(\bar{X}_1 - \bar{X}_2\right) + t_{.05,22}\sqrt{\frac{s_1^2}{n_1} + \frac{s_2^2}{n_2}}$$

$$= \left(3.33 - 3.98\right) - 1.717\sqrt{\frac{(.68)^2}{15} + \frac{(.38)^2}{15}} \text{ to } \left(3.33 - 3.98\right) + 1.717\sqrt{\frac{(.68)^2}{15} + \frac{(.38)^2}{15}}$$

$$= -.65 - .35 \text{ to } -.65 + .35$$

$$= -1.00 \text{ hr to} -.30 \text{ hr}$$

So we are 90% confident that the average blowout time for the Beltex tires is between 18 minutes (.3 hours) and 1 hour *less* than the average for the Roadmaster tires. Based on these results, Roadmaster appears to be the better (longer-wearing) tire.

Hypothesis Testing for μ_1 and μ_2 (Independent Samples and σ's Unknown)

The five-step procedure for testing hypotheses concerning μ_1 and μ_2 with known variances also applies to the situation where the variances are unknown. The only difference is that Table A.5 is used (rather than Table A.4) to define the rejection region.

EXAMPLE 11.5

In Example 11.4 a confidence interval was constructed for the difference in average blowout times for Beltex and Roadmaster tires. Can we conclude that these average blowout times are in fact not the same? Use a significance level of .10.

Solution

Step 1. We are testing for a difference between the two means (not that Roadmaster is longer-wearing than Beltex or vice versa). The corresponding appropriate hypotheses are H_0: $\mu_1 = \mu_2$ and H_a: $\mu_1 \neq \mu_2$.

Step 2. The test statistic is

$$t' = \frac{\bar{X}_1 - \bar{X}_2}{\sqrt{\dfrac{s_1^2}{n_1} + \dfrac{s_2^2}{n_2}}}$$

which approximately follows a t distribution with df given by equation 11.7.

Step 3. You next need the df in order to determine your rejection region. In Example 11.4 we found that df = 22. Because H_a: $\mu_1 \neq \mu_2$, we will reject H_0 if t' is too large ($\bar{X}_1$ is significantly *larger* than $\bar{X}_2$) or if t' is too small ($\bar{X}_1$ is significantly *smaller* than $\bar{X}_2$). As in previous two-tailed tests using the Z or t statistic, H_0 is rejected if the absolute value of t exceeds the value from the table corresponding to $\alpha/2$. Using Table A.5, the rejection region for this situation will be

$$\text{reject } H_0 \text{ if } |t'| > t_{\alpha/2,\text{df}} = t_{.05,22} = 1.717$$

Step 4. The value of the test statistic is

$$t'^* = \frac{3.33 - 3.98}{\sqrt{\dfrac{(.68)^2}{15} + \dfrac{(.38)^2}{15}}} = \frac{-.65}{.20} = -3.25$$

Because $|t'^*| = 3.25 > 1.717$, we reject H_0. Consequently, the difference between the sample means (−.65) *is* significantly large (in absolute value), which leads to a rejection of the null hypothesis.

Step 5. There *is* a difference in the average blowout times for the two brands.

Comments

The hypotheses in Example 11.5 could be written as H_0 : $\mu_1 - \mu_2 = 0$ and H_a: $\mu_1 - \mu_2 \neq 0$. Having already determined a 90% confidence interval for $\mu_1 - \mu_2$, a much simpler way to perform this two-tailed test (using $\alpha = .10$) would be to reject H_0 if 0 does not lie in the 90% confidence interval for $\mu_1 - \mu_2$ and fail to reject H_0 otherwise. The confidence interval according to Example 11.4 is (−1.00, −.30), which does not contain zero, and so we reject H_0 (as before).

This alternative method of testing H_0 versus H_a holds only for a two-tailed test in which the significance level of the test, α, and the confidence level [$(1 - \alpha) \cdot 100\%$] of the confidence interval "match up." For example, a significance level of $\alpha = .05$ would correspond to a 95% confidence interval, a value of $\alpha = .10$ would correspond to a 90% confidence interval, and so on.

Notice that the procedure in this section for testing μ_1 versus μ_2 and constructing confidence intervals for $\mu_1 - \mu_2$ made no mention as to whether the population variances (or standard deviations) were equal or not. In fact, we can say that this procedure did not assume that $\sigma_1 = \sigma_2$; it also

did *not* assume that $\sigma_1 \neq \sigma_2$. Next, we will examine a special case where we have reason to believe that the standard deviations *are* equal. For this situation, we will define another t test to detect any difference between the population means.

Using Statistical Software to Carry Out a Two-Sample t Test

The Excel procedure to use here is the **Two-Sample t Test Assuming Unequal Variances.** The name of this procedure will make more sense after you read the Special Case of Equal Variances discussion to follow. Actually, a better title for the Excel procedure would have been "Two-Sample t Test Not Assuming Equal Variances," since using this procedure simply makes no assumptions about whether the population variances are the same.

Applying the Excel function to Example 11.5, click on **Tools ➤ Data Analysis ➤ Two-Sample t Test Assuming Unequal Variances.** The Excel output is shown in Figure 11.7. The MINITAB output in Figure 11.8 is obtained by clicking on **Stat ➤ Basic Statistics ➤ 2-Sample t.** Figure 11.9 contains the SPSS output using **Analyze ➤ Compare Means ➤ Independent-Samples T Test.** The lower portion of the SPSS output provides the solution when equal variances are not assumed. For all three computer outputs, the computed value of the test statistics is –3.25 (which agrees with the solution to Example 11.5) and the calculated p-value is .004. Based on this extremely small p-value, we once again reject H_0.

Special Case of Equal Variances

There are some situations in which we are willing to assume that the population variances (σ_1^2 and σ_2^2) are equal. This situation is common in many long-running production processes for which, based on past experience, you are convinced that the variation within population 1 is the same as the variation within population 2.

Another situation in which we may assume σ_1 and σ_2 are equal arises when we obtain two *additional* samples from the two populations, which we use strictly to determine if the population standard deviations are equal. If there is not sufficient evidence to indicate that $\sigma_1 \neq \sigma_2$, then there is no harm in assuming that $\sigma_1 = \sigma_2$. (A procedure for comparing the population standard deviations is discussed in Section 11.4.)

FIGURE 11.7

Excel spreadsheet using **Tools ➤ Data Analysis ➤ t Test: Two-Sample Assuming Unequal Variances.**

	A	B	C	D	E	F
1	Beltex	Roadmaster	t-Test: Two-Sample Assuming Unequal Variances			
2	3.82	4.16				
3	3.11	3.92		Beltex	Roadmaster	
4	4.21	3.94	Mean	3.332	3.984	
5	2.64	4.22	Variance	0.461246	0.142340	
6	4.16	4.15	Observations	15	15	
7	3.91	3.62	Hypothesized Mean	0		
8	2.44	4.11	df	22		
9	4.52	3.45	t Stat	-3.2503		
10	2.84	3.65	P(T<=t) one-tail	0.001835		
11	3.26	3.82	t Critical one-tail	1.321237		
12	3.74	4.55	P(T<=t) two-tail	0.00367		
13	3.04	3.82	t Critical two-tail	1.717144		
14	2.56	3.85				
15	2.58	3.62				
16	3.15	4.88				

FIGURE

11.8

MINITAB output using **Stat ➤ Basic Statistics ➤ 2-Sample t.**

Two-Sample T-Test and CI: Beltex, Roadmaster

```
Two-sample T for Beltex vs Roadmaster

             N   Mean   StDev   SE Mean
Beltex      15   3.332  0.679    0.18
Roadmaster  15   3.984  0.377    0.097


Difference = mu (Beltex) - mu (Roadmaster)
Estimate for difference:  -0.652000
90% CI for difference:  (-0.997175, -0.306825)
T-Test of difference = 0 (vs not =): T-Value = -3.25  P-Value = 0.004  DF = 21
```

Independent Samples Test

		Levene's Test for Equality of Variances		t-test for Equality of Means						
									90% Confidence Interval of the Difference	
		F	Sig.	t	df	Sig. (2-tailed)	Mean Difference	Std. Error Difference	Lower	Upper
TIME	Equal variances assumed	8.574	.007	-3.250	28	.003	-.6520	.2006	-.9932	-.3108
	Equal variances not assumed			-3.250	21.889	.004	-.6520	.2006	-.9965	-.3075

Why make the assumption that $\sigma_1 = \sigma_2$? Remember, we are still interested in the means, μ_1 and μ_2. As before, we would like to obtain a confidence interval for $\mu_1 - \mu_2$ and to perform a test of hypothesis. If, in fact, σ_1 is equal to σ_2, we can construct a slightly stronger test of μ_1 versus μ_2. By stronger, we mean that we are *more likely* to reject H_0 when it is actually false. This test is said to be more *powerful*.

For this case, because we believe that $\sigma_1^2 = \sigma_2^2 = \sigma^2$ (say), it makes sense to combine—or **pool**—our estimate of σ_1^2 (s_1^2) with the estimate of σ_2^2 (s_2^2) into one estimate of this common variance (σ^2). The resulting estimate of σ^2 is called the **pooled sample variance** and is written s_p^2. This estimate is merely a *weighted average* of s_1^2 and s_2^2, defined by

$$s_p^2 = \frac{(n_1 - 1)s_1^2 + (n_2 - 1)s_2^2}{n_1 + n_2 - 2}$$

11.9

Notice that s_p^2 gives more weight to the sample variance from the larger sample. Also, if the sample sizes are the same, then s_p^2 is simply the average of s_1^2 and s_2^2.

Constructing Confidence Intervals for $\mu_1 - \mu_2$

To construct the confidence interval, we make two changes in the previous procedure. First, t' is replaced by

$$t = \frac{\bar{X}_1 - \bar{X}_2}{\sqrt{\dfrac{s_p^2}{n_1} + \dfrac{s_p^2}{n_2}}}$$

11.10

$$= \frac{\bar{X}_1 - \bar{X}_2}{s_p \sqrt{\dfrac{1}{n_1} + \dfrac{1}{n_2}}}$$

11.11

Here (unlike the previous test statistic), t exactly follows a t distribution (assuming the two populations follow normal distributions).

Second, the df for t are much easier to derive:

$$df = n_1 + n_2 - 2$$

So you avoid the difficult df calculation in equation 11.7, but you need to derive the pooled variance, s_p^2, using the individual sample variances, s_1^2 and s_2^2.

As a check, your resulting pooled value for s_p^2 should be between s_1^2 and s_2^2, since it is a weighted average of these two values. It may be easier to check that s_p is between s_1 and s_2.

Hypothesis Testing for μ_1 and μ_2

In hypothesis testing for $\mu_1 - \mu_2$, the previous procedure applies, except that t' is replaced by t and the df used in Table A.5 is df $= n_1 + n_2 - 2$ rather than the df value from equation 11.7.

In Examples 11.4 and 11.5, we examined the blowout times for two brands of tires as measured by a machine performing a stress test of the sampled tires. Assume we have determined from previous tests that the *variation* of the blowout times is not affected by the tire brand. Assuming that σ_1^2 (Beltex) $= \sigma_2^2$ (Roadmaster), how can we construct a 90% confidence interval for $\mu_1 - \mu_2$ and determine whether there is a difference in the mean blowout times?

Sample 1 (Beltex)	Sample 2 (Roadmaster)
$n_1 = 15$	$n_2 = 15$
$\bar{x}_1 = 3.33$ hr	$\bar{x}_2 = 3.98$ hr
$s_1 = .68$ hr	$s_2 = .38$ hr

Our first step is to pool the sample variances:

$$s_p^2 = \frac{(15-1)(.68)^2 + (15-1)(.38)^2}{15+15-2} = \frac{(14)(.4624) + (14)(.1444)}{28}$$

$$= \frac{8.495}{28} = .303$$

$$s_p = \sqrt{.303} = .55 \text{ hr}$$

As a check, is .55 between .38 and .68? Yes. Consequently, $s_p^2 = .303$ is our estimate of the common variance (σ^2) of the two-tire populations. To find the 90% confidence interval for $\mu_1 - \mu_2$, we use

$$\left(\bar{X}_1 - \bar{X}_2\right) - t_{\alpha/2, df}\sqrt{\frac{s_p^2}{n_1} + \frac{s_p^2}{n_2}} \text{ to } \left(\bar{X}_1 - \bar{X}_2\right) + t_{\alpha/2, df}\sqrt{\frac{s_p^2}{n_1} + \frac{s_p^2}{n_2}}$$

11.12

where df $= n_1 + n_2 - 2$ and $\alpha = .10$.

Because $n_1 + n_2 - 2 = 28$, we find (from Table A.5) that $t_{.05,28} = 1.701$. Next,

$$\sqrt{\frac{s_p^2}{n_1} + \frac{s_p^2}{n_2}} = s_p\sqrt{\frac{1}{n_1} + \frac{1}{n_2}} = .55\sqrt{\frac{1}{15} + \frac{1}{15}} = .20$$

The resulting confidence interval is

$$(3.33 - 3.98) - (1.701)(.20) \quad \text{to} \quad (3.33 - 3.98) + (1.701)(.20)$$

$$= -.65 - .34 \quad \text{to} \quad -.65 + .34$$

$$= -.99 \quad \text{to} \quad -.31$$

Comparing this result to the confidence interval in Example 11.4, you see little difference in the two confidence intervals, although the interval using the pooled variance is a bit narrower. Oftentimes these intervals can differ considerably, depending on the relative sizes of n_1 and n_2 as well as the relative values of s_1^2 and s_2^2.

Now we wish to test H_0: $\mu_1 = \mu_2$ versus H_a: $\mu_1 \neq \mu_2$. For this particular example, we can, as noted earlier, reject H_0 (using $\alpha = .10$) because zero does not lie in the previously derived confidence interval for $\mu_1 - \mu_2$. In the five-step procedure, there are only two changes we need to make when using the pooled sample variances. First, when defining our rejection region, we use $n_1 + n_2 - 2 = 28$ df. From Table A.5, the test procedure is to

$$\text{reject } H_0 \text{ if } |t| > t_{\alpha/2,df}$$

where $t_{.05,28} = 1.701$.

Second, we determine the value of the test statistic using equation 11.11:

$$t = \frac{\bar{X}_1 - \bar{X}_2}{s_p \sqrt{\frac{1}{n_1} + \frac{1}{n_2}}} = \frac{3.33 - 3.98}{.55 \sqrt{\frac{1}{15} + \frac{1}{15}}} = \frac{-.65}{.20} = -3.25$$

Because $|-3.25| = 3.25 > 1.701$, we reject H_0; once again the two sample means are significantly different. We conclude that there is a difference in the population mean blowout times for the two brands of tires.

Using Excel to Carry Out a Two-Sample t Test Assuming Equal Variances

An Excel solution for the preceding example can be carried out by clicking on **Tools ➤ Data Analysis ➤ t Test: Two-Sample Assuming Equal Variances.** The output is shown in Figure 11.10 where (1) the calculated t value is -3.25, (2) the corresponding two-tailed p-value is .002997, and (3) the pooled standard deviation is the square root of the pooled variance—that is, $\sqrt{.301793} = .55$. As in Example 11.5 (Figure 11.7), we obtain a very small p-value when pooling the sample variances. For this particular example, we observe little difference in the two solutions.

FIGURE

11.10

Excel output using
**Tools ➤ Data
Analysis ➤
t Test: Two-
Sample Assuming
Equal Variances.**

t-Test: Two-Sample Assuming Equal Variances		
	Beltex	Roadmaster
Mean	3.332	3.984
Variance	0.461246	0.142340
Observations	15	15
Pooled Variance	0.301793	
Hypothesized Mean Difference	0	
df	28	
t Stat	-3.2503	
P(T<=t) one-tail	0.001499	
t Critical one-tail	1.312526	
P(T<=t) two-tail	0.002997	
t Critical two-tail	1.70113	

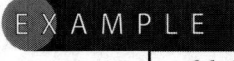

EXAMPLE
11.6

Using Statistical Software to Compare Two Population Means

In Examples 3.4 and 10.7, we examined the inside diameters of a certain machined part produced by Allied Manufacturing. Data set DATA9-6 contains the samples from Example 3.4 (100 measurements obtained before a quality-improvement effort) and Example 10.7 (100 measurements after this effort).

Column A contains the 100 measurements from Example 10.7.

Column B contains the 100 measurements from Example 3.4.

Prior to obtaining the second set of data, Allied wanted to know if there was sufficient evidence using a significance level of .05 to say that the mean of the process after the adjustment (data in column A) is less than the mean before the adjustment (data in column B).

What would you tell Allied? Did its adjustment to improve the quality of these parts produce a process having a smaller mean? Allied is not willing to assume the two population variances are equal. If you were to pool the sample variances (and assume equal population variances), would this change your conclusion?

Solution

A nice way to compare the two samples is to use the sample results to construct a pair of frequency polygons, plotted in the same graph (Figure 11.11). From this graph, it is readily apparent that there was a shift in the means after the adjustment. Also, the polygon for the after sample is wider than the before polygon, indicating more variation in the process after the adjustment. To determine if the after sample mean is significantly less than the before sample mean, the next step is to test the hypothesis.

Letting population 1 represent the process measurements after the adjustment and population 2 represent the measurements before the adjustment, the hypotheses under investigation are

$$H_0: \mu_1 \geq \mu_2$$

$$H_a: \mu_1 < \mu_2$$

An Excel solution not assuming equal variances is shown in Figure 11.12 (cells C1:E13). The calculated t statistic in cell D9 is −15.2393 and the p-value (in cell D10) is

FIGURE
11.11

Frequency polygons of the two samples obtained before and after the process adjustment.

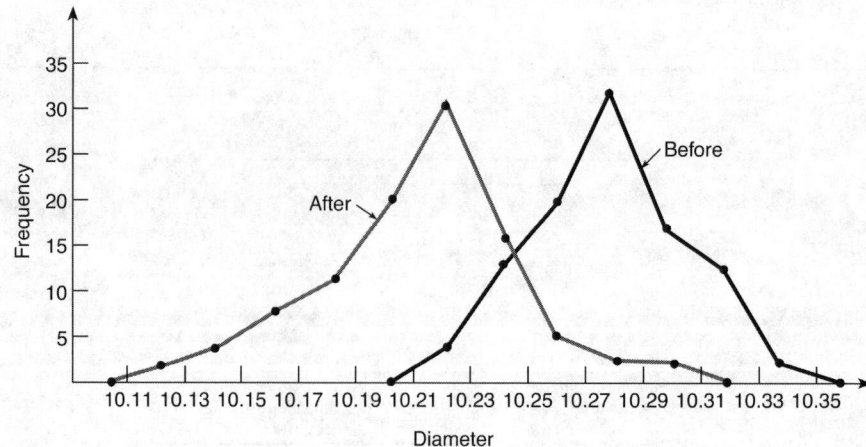

nearly zero.* The output using the equal variances procedure is contained in cells F1:G14 and is very similar to the previous solution—namely, the calculated test statistic is –15.2393, and the p-value (in cell G11) is nearly zero. The MINITAB solutions in Figure 11.13 and the SPSS solutions in Figure 11.14 provide the same computed value of the test statistic (–15.24) and corresponding p-value (nearly zero) for the two cases—where the variances are not assumed to be equal and where they are assumed to be equal.

Conclusion. Due to the extremely large sample sizes, both test statistics could be very closely approximated by the standard normal (Z) statistic. As a result, whether or not you pool is not a critical issue for very large sample sizes. The p-value is nearly zero (and less than $\alpha = .05$), and so we reject H_0. There is strong evidence to indicate that the process mean after the quality-improvement adjustment is less than the mean before the adjustment.

FIGURE

11.12

Excel spreadsheet for solutions to Example 11.6.

	A	B	C	D	E	F	G	H
1	After	Before	t-Test: Two-Sample Assuming Unequal Variances			t-Test: Two-Sample Assuming Equal Variances		
2	10.158	10.216						
3	10.244	10.221		After	Before		After	Before
4	10.202	10.226	Mean	10.21023	10.27539	Mean	10.21023	10.27539
5	10.206	10.228	Variance	0.001116	0.000712	Variance	0.001116	0.000712
6	10.257	10.230	Observations	100	100	Observations	100	100
7	10.149	10.230	Hypothesized Mean Difference	0		Pooled Variance	0.000914	
8	10.202	10.231	df	189		Hypothesized Mean Difference	0	
9	10.237	10.231	t Stat	-15.2393		df	198	
10	10.220	10.234	P(T<=t) one-tail	4.98E-35		t Stat	-15.2393	
11	10.223	10.237	t Critical one-tail	1.652957		P(T<=t) one-tail	1.65E-35	
12	10.165	10.239	P(T<=t) two-tail	9.97E-35		t Critical one-tail	1.652586	
13	10.166	10.239	t Critical two-tail	1.972594		P(T<=t) two-tail	3.30E-35	
14	10.210	10.240				t Critical two-tail	1.972016	
15	10.229	10.240						

DATA9-6

FIGURE

11.13

MINITAB solutions to Example 11.6.

Two-Sample T-Test and CI: After, Before

```
Two-sample T for After vs Before

          N     Mean    StDev   SE Mean
After    100   10.2102  0.0334   0.0033
Before   100   10.2754  0.0267   0.0027
```

not assuming equal variances

```
Difference = mu (After) - mu (Before)
Estimate for difference:  -0.065160
90% upper bound for difference:  -0.059661
T-Test of difference = 0 (vs <): T-Value = -15.24  P-Value = 0.000  DF = 188
```

assuming equal variances

```
Difference = mu (After) - mu (Before)
Estimate for difference:  -0.065160
90% upper bound for difference:  -0.059662
T-Test of difference = 0 (vs <): T-Value = -15.24  P-Value = 0.000  DF = 198
Both use Pooled StDev = 0.0302
```

---

*The value 4.98E-35 is written using *exponential notation,* which is very useful for representing very small or very large numbers. This particular value is actually 4.98, with the decimal place moved 35 places to the left—that is, a decimal point, followed by 34 zeros, followed by 498. This is a very small number (nearly zero). Also, be sure to refer to the footnote at the end of the previous section when interpreting Excel's one-tailed p-values.

FIGURE

11.14

SPSS solutions
to Example 11.6.

Independent Samples Test

		Levene's Test for Equality of Variances		t-test for Equality of Means						
									90% Confidence Interval of the Difference	
		F	Sig.	t	df	Sig. (2-tailed)	Mean Difference	Std. Error Difference	Lower	Upper
DIAMETER	Equal variances assumed	2.420	.121	-15.239	198	.000000	-6.516E-02	4.2758E-03	-7.2E-02	-5.8E-02
	Equal variances not assumed			-15.239	188.760	.000000	-6.516E-02	4.2758E-03	-7.2E-02	-5.8E-02

To Pool or Not to Pool? You might think, based on the previous examples, that it really does not matter whether you assume $\sigma_1 = \sigma_2$. The two confidence intervals were nearly the same and the tests of hypothesis results were very close, differing only in their df for the test statistic. However, this is not always the case. *Unless you have strong evidence that the variances are the same*, we suggest you not pool the sample variances *and use the test statistic defined in equation* 11.6. If you assume that $\sigma_1 = \sigma_2$ and use the t test statistic in equation 11.11 but, in fact, $\sigma_1 \neq \sigma_2$, your results can be unreliable. This test is quite sensitive to this particular assumption if the sample sizes (n_1 and n_2) are unequal. Also, if σ_1 and σ_2 *are* the same, we would expect s_1 and s_2 to be nearly the same. If, in addition, $n_1 = n_2$ (or nearly so), then the computed values of t' and t will be practically identical (including the df). What this means is that you have little to gain by pooling the variances (and using t) but a great deal to lose if your assumption is incorrect.

INDEPENDENT SAMPLES TESTS FOR μ_1 AND μ_2 (σ'S UNKNOWN)

Two-Tailed Test

$$H_0: \mu_1 - \mu_2 = D_0$$

$$H_a: \mu_1 - \mu_2 \neq D_0$$

$$(D_0 = 0 \text{ for } H_0: \mu_1 = \mu_2)$$

reject H_0 if $|T| > t_{\alpha/2,df}$

where, not assuming $\sigma_1 = \sigma_2$:

$$T = t' = \frac{(\bar{X}_1 - \bar{X}_2) - D_0}{\sqrt{\dfrac{s_1^2}{n_1} + \dfrac{s_2^2}{n_2}}}$$

$$df = \frac{\left[\dfrac{s_1^2}{n_1} + \dfrac{s_2^2}{n_2}\right]^2}{\dfrac{\left(\dfrac{s_1^2}{n_1}\right)^2}{n_1 - 1} + \dfrac{\left(\dfrac{s_2^2}{n_2}\right)^2}{n_2 - 1}}$$

Or, assuming $\sigma_1 = \sigma_2$:

$$T = t = \frac{(\bar{X}_1 - \bar{X}_2) - D_0}{s_p\sqrt{\dfrac{1}{n_1} + \dfrac{1}{n_2}}}$$

$$df = n_1 + n_2 - 2$$

where

$$s_p = \sqrt{\frac{(n_1 - 1)s_1^2 + (n_2 - 1)s_2^2}{n_1 + n_2 - 2}}$$

One-Tailed Test

$H_0: \mu_1 - \mu_2 \leq D_0$	$H_0: \mu_1 - \mu_2 \geq D_0$
$H_a: \mu_1 - \mu_2 > D_0$	$H_a: \mu_1 - \mu_2 < D_0$
($D_0 = 0$ for $H_0: \mu_1 \leq \mu_2$	($D_0 = 0$ for $H_0: \mu_1 \geq \mu_2$)
reject H_0 if $T > t_{\alpha, df}$	reject H_0 if $T < -t_{\alpha, df}$

X Exercises 11.25–11.36

Understanding the Mechanics

11.25 Independent random samples were selected from two normal populations. The following statistics were calculated.

Sample 1	Sample 2
$n_1 = 12$	$n_2 = 15$
$\bar{x}_1 = 10.0$	$\bar{x}_2 = 12.00$
$s_1 = 2.04$	$s_2 = 1.4$

a. Calculate the pooled estimate of the variance for the populations.
b. Find a 90% confidence interval for $\mu_1 - \mu_2$ using the pooled estimate of the variance for the populations.
c. Find a 90% confidence interval for $\mu_1 - \mu_2$ not assuming that the population variances are equal.

11.26 The observations below resulted from independent random samples selected from approximate normal populations.

Sample 1	Sample 2
4.5	6.5
7.0	5.4
3.1	7.8
6.2	8.1
5.8	7.9
6.1	

a. Conduct a test of hypothesis to determine if the mean of the second population is greater than the mean of the first population. Assume that the population variances are equal. Use a .05 significance level.
b. Perform the statistical test in part a, but don't assume that the population variances are equal.

Applying the New Concepts

11.27 The president of a personnel agency is interested in examining the annual mean salary differences between vice presidents of banks and vice presidents of savings and loan institutions. A random sample of eight of each kind of vice president was selected. Their annual salaries (in dollars) were as follows:

n	Banks	Savings and Loan Institutions	n	Banks	Savings and Loan Institutions
1	84,320	73,420	5	48,940	88,670
2	67,440	49,580	6	56,790	59,640
3	98,590	58,750	7	77,610	65,590
4	111,780	101,400	8	62,000	74,810

Conduct a test of hypothesis to determine if there is a significant difference in the average salary for the two vice president groups. The salaries for both groups are considered to be approximately normally distributed. Use a significance level of .05. Do not assume that the population variances are equal.

11.28 Construct a 90% confidence interval for the difference in the means of the salaries for vice presidents in the banking industry and for vice presidents of savings and loan institutions for Exercise 11.27. Do not assume that the population variances are equal.

11.29 Using the data in Exercise 11.27, test the same hypothesis, but assume that the population variances are equal.

11.30 The production supervisor of Dow Plast is conducting a test of the tensile strengths of two types of copper coils. The relevant data are as follows. Coil A: $\bar{x} = 118$, $s = 17$, $n = 9$. Coil B: $\bar{x} = 143$, $s = 24$, $n = 16$. The tensile strengths for the two types of copper coils are approximately normally distributed. Based on the p-value, do the data support the conclusion that the mean tensile strengths of the two coils are different at a significance level of 7%? Do not assume that the population variances are equal.

11.31 Construct a 99% confidence interval for $\mu_A - \mu_B$ in Exercise 11.30. Do not assume that the population variances are equal.

11.32 Using a pooled estimate of the variance, perform the test of hypothesis in Exercise 11.30. Compare the two answers.

Using the Computer

11.33 **[DATA SET EX11-33]** Variable Description:

MarketExp: Travel expenses for marketing dept.

R&DExp: Travel expenses for R&D dept.

The travel expenses of 17 employees from the marketing department and 17 employees from the research and development (R&D) department are provided. Test that the R&D's mean travel expenses exceeds that of the marketing department. Use a 10% significance level.

11.34 **[DATA SET EX11-34]** Variable Description:

SalaryIndustry: Manager's salary in private industry

SalaryGov: Manager's salary in government sector

Construct a 95% confidence interval for the difference in salaries for network planning managers working for private industry and for the government. Assume equal population variances. Use this interval to test for a difference in the mean salaries at the 5% significance level.

11.35 When assuming that population variances may not be equal, the degrees of freedom for the t-statistic decrease as one of the population variances becomes much larger than the other. To understand this relationship, put

a value of 10 in the first 15 rows of column A and the values 10 through 150 in increments of 10 in the first 15 rows of column B. Type the formulas presented at the top of the next page into the cells C1 through F1 and drag these down to row 15. Then plot the degrees of freedom that appear in column F with the variances that appear in column B. The graph should look like that given below. Comment on how quickly the degrees of freedom change as the variance of one group increases while the other group's variance remains constant.

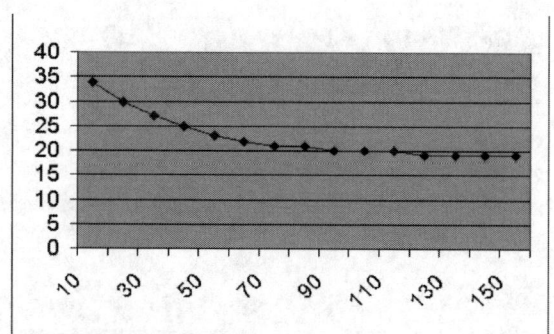

11.36 **[DATA SET EX11-36]** Variable Description:

PrivateUniv: Yearly tuition for a four-year private university in the South

PublicUniv: Yearly tuition for a four-year public university in the South

The American Council on Education claims that nationwide the average difference in tuition between four-year public universities and private universities is $11,500 per year. Suppose that a university administrator believes that the difference is less than this for universities in the South. A random sample of 15 public and 15 private four-year universities in the South is selected.

a. Construct two histograms for the yearly tuition at the selected universities in the South—one for private universities and one for public universities. Do the variances of the two data sets appear to be much different?

b. Using an appropriate t test, test that the tuition difference between private and public four-year universities in the South is less than $11,500. Use a 5% significance level.

(Source: "Why College Costs So Much," The New York Times, April 8, 2001, p. 47L.)

11.4

COMPARING THE VARIANCES OF TWO NORMAL POPULATIONS USING INDEPENDENT SAMPLES

Once again we concentrate on independent samples from two normal populations, only this time we focus our attention on the *variation* of these populations rather than on their averages (see Figure 11.15). When estimating and testing σ_1 versus σ_2, we will not be concerned about μ_1 and μ_2. They might be equal, or they might not—it simply does not matter for this test procedure.

In business applications, you may want to compare the variation of two different production processes or compare the risk involved with two proposed investment portfolios. As mentioned previously, when testing for population *means* using small, independent samples, you must pay attention to the population standard deviations (variances). Based on your belief that σ_1 does or does not equal σ_2, you select your corresponding test statistic for testing the means, μ_1 and μ_2. As a reminder, it is *not* a safe procedure to use the *same data set* to test both $\sigma_1 = \sigma_2$ and $\mu_1 = \mu_2$. A proper procedure would be to test σ_1 and σ_2 using one set of samples (as outlined in this section) and to obtain another set of samples *independently* of the first to test the means.

In the previous section, when trying to decide if $\mu_1 = \mu_2$, we examined the *difference* between the point estimators, $\bar{X}_1 - \bar{X}_2$. If $\bar{X}_1 - \bar{X}_2$ was large enough (in absolute value), we rejected H_0: $\mu_1 = \mu_2$. When looking at the variances, we use the *ratio of the sample variances*, s_1^2 and s_2^2, to derive a test of hypothesis and construct confidence intervals. We do this because the distribution of $s_1^2 - s_2^2$ is difficult to describe mathematically, but s_1^2/s_2^2 does have a recognizable distribution when in fact σ_1^2 and σ_2^2 are equal. So we define

$$F = \frac{s_1^2}{s_2^2}$$

11.13

If you were to obtain sets of two samples repeatedly, calculate s_1^2/s_2^2 for each set, and make a histogram of these ratios, the shape of this histogram would resemble the curve in Figure 11.16, the **F distribution.** Its shape does not resemble a normal curve—it is nonsymmetric, skewed right (right-tailed), and the corresponding random variable is never negative. There are many F curves, depending on the sample sizes, n_1 and n_2. The shape of the F curve becomes more symmetric as the sample sizes, n_1 and n_2, increase. As later chapters will demonstrate, the F distribution has a large variety of applications in statistics. Right-tail areas for this random variable have been tabulated in Table A.7. As a final note here, *the F-statistic in equation 11.13 is highly sensitive to the assumption of normal populations. For*

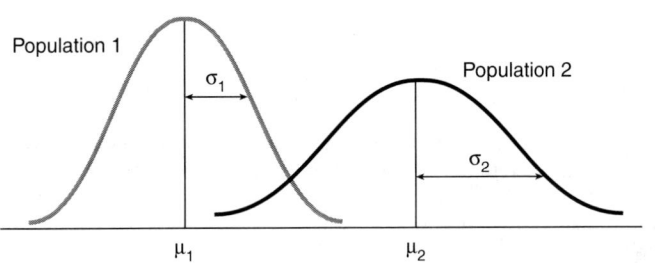

FIGURE

11.15

Compare two standard deviations. Does $\sigma_1 = \sigma_2$?

461

FIGURE
11.16

Shape of the *F*
distribution.

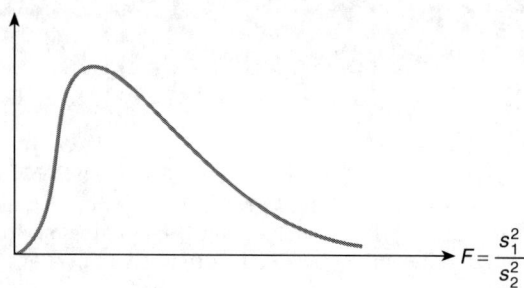

FIGURE
11.17

Unequal
population
variances.

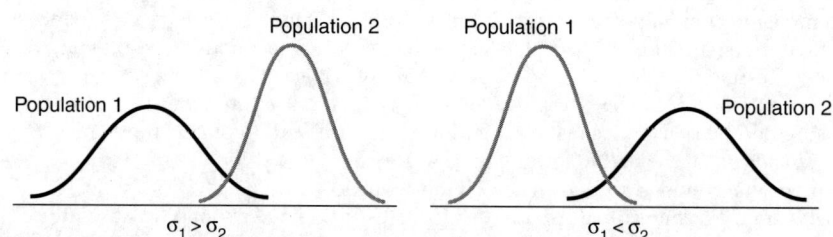

larger data sets, it is recommended that you examine the shape of the sample data when using this particular F-statistic.

When using the *t* statistic, we needed a way to specify the sample size(s) because the shapes of these curves change as the sample size changes. The same applies to the *F* distribution. There are two samples here, one from each population, and we need to specify *both* sample sizes. As before, we use the degrees of freedom (df) to accomplish this:

$$v_1 = \text{df for numerator} = n_1 - 1$$

$$v_2 = \text{df for denominator} = n_2 - 1$$

So, the *F* statistic shown in Figure 11.16 follows an *F* distribution with v_1 and v_2 df provided $\sigma_1^2 = \sigma_2^2$ ($\sigma_1 = \sigma_2$). What happens to *F* when $\sigma_1 \neq \sigma_2$? Suppose that $\sigma_1 > \sigma_2$? Then we would expect s_1 (the estimate of σ_1) to be larger than s_2 (the estimate of σ_2). We should see

$$s_1^2 > s_2^2$$

or

$$F = \frac{s_1^2}{s_2^2} > 1$$

Similarly, if $\sigma_1 < \sigma_2$, then we expect an *F* value < 1. We will use this reasoning to define a test of hypothesis for σ_1 versus σ_2.

Hypothesis Testing for $\sigma_1 = \sigma_2$

Does $\sigma_1 = \sigma_2$? We use the usual five-step procedure for testing a hypothesis concerning the two variances. Your choice of hypotheses is (as usual) a two-tailed test or a one-tailed test. For the two-tailed test the hypotheses are H_0: $\sigma_1 = \sigma_2$ ($\sigma_1^2 = \sigma_2^2$) and H_a: $\sigma_1 \neq \sigma_2$ ($\sigma_1^2 \neq \sigma_2^2$). For the one-tailed test the hypotheses are H_0: $\sigma_1 \leq \sigma_2$ and H_a: $\sigma_1 > \sigma_2$ [Figure 11.17(a)] or H_0: $\sigma_1 \geq \sigma_2$ and H_a: $\sigma_1 < \sigma_2$ [Figure 11.17(b)].

TABLE

11.1

Portion of F distribution table containing values with tail areas of .10 [Table A.7(a)].

V_2 \ V_1	1	2	3	4	5	6↓	7	8	9
1	39.86	49.50	53.59	55.83	57.24	58.20	58.91	59.44	59.86
2	8.53	9.00	9.16	9.24	9.29	9.33	9.35	9.37	9.38
3	5.54	5.46	5.39	5.34	5.31	5.28	5.27	5.25	5.24
4	4.54	4.32	4.19	4.11	4.05	4.01	3.98	3.95	3.94
5	4.06	3.78	3.62	3.52	3.45	3.40	3.37	3.34	3.32
6	3.78	3.46	3.29	3.18	3.11	3.05	3.01	2.98	2.96
7	3.59	3.26	3.07	2.96	2.88	2.83	2.78	2.75	2.72
→8	3.46	3.11	2.92	2.81	2.73	2.67	2.62	2.59	2.56
9	3.36	3.01	2.81	2.69	2.61	2.55	2.51	2.47	2.44
10	3.29	2.92	2.73	2.61	2.52	2.46	2.41	2.38	2.35

FIGURE

11.18

F curve with 6 and 8 df. Shaded area is the probability that F exceeds 2.67 [2.67 is from Table A.7(a)].

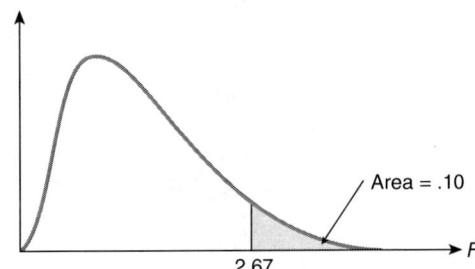

Area = .10

2.67

F

Finding Right-Tail F Values. Notice that the hypotheses can be written in terms of the standard deviations (σ_1 and σ_2) or the variances (σ_1^2 and σ_2^2); if $\sigma_1 > \sigma_2$, then $\sigma_1^2 > \sigma_2^2$.

Right-tail areas under an F curve are provided in Table A.7. Notice that we have a table for areas of .10 [Table A.7(a)], .05 [Table A.7(b)], .025 [Table A.7(c)], and .01 [Table A.7(d)]. These are the most commonly used values. For each table, the df for the numerator (v_1) run across the top, and the df for the denominator (v_2) run down the left margin. A portion of Table A.7(a) is shown in Table 11.1.

Suppose we want to know which F value has a right-tail area of .10 using 6 and 8 df. Let the F value whose right-tail area is a, where the df are v_1 and v_2, be

$$F_{a,v_1,v_2}$$

For example, using Table 11.1, $F_{.10,6,8} = 2.67$ (Figure 11.18).

Finding Left-Tail F Values. Notice that Table A.7 contains *right-tail* values only. However, we can use the following rule to determine left-tail values:

$$F \text{ value } (\text{df} = v_1, v_2) \text{ having a left-tail area of } a$$

$$= \frac{1}{F \text{ value } \left(\text{df} = v_2, v_1\right) \text{ having a right-tail area of } a}$$

FIGURE

11.19

F curve with 6 and 8 df for probability that *F* is less than .336.

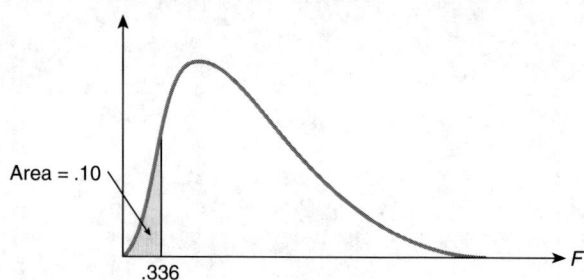

Take a look at Figure 11.19. From Figure 11.18, we know that the *F* value having a right-tail area of .10 is 2.67, where the df are 6 and 8. For this curve, what *F* value has a left-tail area equal to .10? First, you switch the df to 8 and 6. Using Table 11.1 [or Table A.7(a)], find the *F* value having a right-tail area = .10, where now the df are $v_1 = 8$ and $v_2 = 6$. This value is 2.98. Consequently, for the *F* curve with 6 and 8 df, the value having a *left*-tail area of .10 is $1/2.98 = .336$.

Since the area to the left of .336 is .10, the area to the right of this value is .90, and using the previously introduced notation we can say that

$$.336 = F_{1-.10,6,8} = F_{.9,6,8}$$

In general, we have

$$F_{1-a,v_1,v_2} = \frac{1}{F_{a,v_2,v_1}}$$

11.14

To test H_0 versus H_a, we use equation 11.13 as the test statistic. This procedure is summarized in the accompanying box.

HYPOTHESIS TESTS FOR σ_1 AND σ_2

Two-Tailed Test

$$H_0 : \sigma_1 = \sigma_2$$

$$H_a : \sigma_1 \neq \sigma_2$$

$$F = \frac{s_1^2}{s_2^2}$$

Reject H_0 if $F > F_{\alpha/2,v_1,v_2}$ (right tail)

or if $F < F_{1-\alpha/2,v_1,v_2}$ (left tail)

where $v_1 = n_1 - 1$ and $v_2 = n_2 - 1$.

One-Tailed Test

$$H_0 : \sigma_1 \le \sigma_2 \qquad\qquad H_0 : \sigma_1 \ge \sigma_2$$

$$H_a : \sigma_1 > \sigma_2 \qquad\qquad H_a : \sigma_1 < \sigma_2$$

$$F = \frac{s_1^2}{s_2^2} \qquad\qquad F = \frac{s_1^2}{s_2^2}$$

Reject H_0 if $F > F_{\alpha, v_1, v_2}$ Reject H_0 if $F < F_{1-\alpha, v_1, v_2}$

where $v_1 = n_1 - 1$ where $v_1 = n_1 - 1$

and $v_2 = n_2 - 1$.   and $v_2 = n_2 - 1$.

EXAMPLE 11.7

Managers at Case Automotive Products are considering the purchase of some new equipment that will fill 1-quart containers with a recently introduced radiator additive. They have narrowed their choices of brand of filling machine to brand 1 and brand 2. Although brand 1 is considerably less expensive than brand 2, they suspect that the contents delivered by the brand 1 machine will have more variation than would be obtained using brand 2. In other words, brand 1 is more apt to slightly (or severely) overfill or underfill containers. The Case people realize that they must use a container slightly larger than 1 quart in any event, to allow for heat expansion and overfill of their product.

The Case production department was able to obtain data on the performance of both brands for a sample of 25 containers using brand 1 and 20 containers using brand 2. Using their summary information, can you confirm Case's suspicions? Use $\alpha = .05$. All mean and standard deviation measurements are in fluid ounces.

Brand 1	Brand 2
$n_1 = 25$	$n_2 = 20$
$\bar{x}_1 = 31.8$	$\bar{x}_2 = 32.1$
$s_1 = 1.21$	$s_2 = .72$

Solution

Step 1. The purpose of the test is to determine if one standard deviation (or variance) is *larger* than the other; this calls for a one-tailed test. The suspicion is that σ_1 is larger than σ_2, so this statement is put in the alternative hypothesis. The resulting hypotheses are

$$H_0: \sigma_1 \le \sigma_2 \qquad H_a: \sigma_1 > \sigma_2$$

Step 2. The test statistic is

$$F = \frac{s_1^2}{s_2^2}$$

Step 3. Because the df are $v_1 = 25 - 1 = 24$ and $v_2 = 20 - 1 = 19$, we find $F_{.05,24,19} = 2.11$. The test of H_0 versus H_a will be to

$$\text{reject } H_0 \text{ if } F > 2.11$$

Step 4. The computed F value is

$$F^* = \frac{(1.21)^2}{(.72)^2} = 2.82$$

Because $2.82 > 2.11$, we reject H_0.

Step 5. On the basis of these data and this significance level, Case is correct in its belief that the variation in the containers filled by brand 1 exceeds that of the containers filled by brand 2.

EXAMPLE

11.8

Using Excel to Compare Two Population Variances

In Example 11.6, we compared the means of two processes—before and after a quality improvement adjustment to reduce the process mean. Allied Manufacturing would like to use these samples strictly to compare the two population variances to determine if they differ (assuming a significance level of .10). Column A in dataset DATA9-6 contains 100 sample values obtained *after* the adjustment, and column B contains 100 sample values obtained *before* the adjustment. To obtain an Excel solution, click on **Tools ➤ Data Analysis ➤ F Test: Two-Sample for Variances.**

Solution

The resulting output is contained in Figure 11.20. The one-tailed p-value is .013094 and is in cell D9. Since this is a two-tailed test (H_a states that the two standard deviations differ), you will need to double this value. To do this, type "p-value (2-tailed)" in cell C11 and "=2*D9" in cell D11. This produces the two-tailed p-value of .026188 in Figure 11.20. Since the p-value of .026188 is less than .10, we reject H_0 and conclude that the two population (process) variances *are* different. In fact, we see a noticeable increase in the process variation after the adjustment—a concern for the quality-improvement team at Allied.

Comments

1. If this had been the first step in our investigation of these two processes, and two additional samples were to be obtained to compare the two process means, the correct procedure would be to use the t' statistic described earlier, which does not assume that σ_1 and σ_2 are equal, provided both populations are believed to be normally distributed.*

2. To test for equal variances using MINITAB click on **Stat ➤ Basic Statistics ➤ 2 Variances** using data set DATA09-06.MTW. Select the **Samples in different columns** option.

FIGURE

11.20

Excel spreadsheet for **Tools ➤ Data Analysis ➤ F Test: Two-Sample for Variances** [*p*-value (2-tailed) added].

	A	B	C	D	E
1	After	Before	F-Test Two-Sample for Variances		
2	10.158	10.216			
3	10.244	10.221		After	Before
4	10.202	10.226	Mean	10.21023	10.27539
5	10.206	10.228	Variance	0.0011164	0.0007119
6	10.257	10.230	Observations	100	100
7	10.149	10.230	df	99	99
8	10.202	10.231	F	1.568194	
9	10.237	10.231	P(F<=f) one-tail	0.013094	
10	10.220	10.234	F Critical one-tail	1.29513	
11	10.223	10.237	p-value (2-tailed)	0.026188	
12	10.165	10.239			

---

*Recently, attention has been given to whether this F test is an effective "screening procedure" for determining which t test is appropriate for subsequent tests of the population means. (See the article by Markowski and Markowski in *The American Statistician*, November 1990, p. 322.) In particular, when the two sample sizes are unequal, the F test tends incorrectly to fail to reject H_0: $\sigma_1 = \sigma_2$ for situations where use of the t statistic in equation 11.10 (which assumes $\sigma_1 = \sigma_2$) is *not* appropriate.

Confidence Interval for $\frac{\sigma_1^2}{\sigma_2^2}$

Consider an F curve with v_1 and v_2 df. To construct a 95% confidence interval for σ_1^2/σ_2^2, you proceed as you did when performing a two-tailed test of σ_1 versus σ_2, by finding both left-tailed and right-tailed F values. Let F_L and F_R denote the left- and right-tailed F values, respectively. Using equation 11.14 and Figure 11.21,

$$F_R = F_{.025,v_1,v_2} \text{ and } F_L = \frac{1}{F_{.025,v_2,v_1}}$$

where $F_{.025,v_1,v_2}$ and $F_{.025,v_2,v_1}$ are obtained from Table A.7(c). *Remember:* Be sure to switch the df when finding the left-tailed value, F_L. The confidence interval for σ_1^2/σ_2^2 is then

$$\frac{s_1^2/s_2^2}{F_R} \text{ to } \frac{s_1^2/s_2^2}{F_L}$$

In general, we have a $(1 - \alpha) \cdot 100\%$ confidence interval for σ_1^2/σ_2^2 (independent samples):

$$\frac{s_1^2/s_2^2}{F_R} \text{ to } \frac{s_1^2/s_2^2}{F_L}$$

11.15

where

$$F_R = F_{\alpha/2,v_1,v_2}$$
$$F_L = \frac{1}{F_{\alpha/2,v_2,v_1}}$$
$$v_1 = n_1 - 1$$
$$v_2 = n_2 - 1$$

Using the Case Automotive Products data in Example 11.7, determine a 95% confidence interval for σ_1^2/σ_2^2.

EXAMPLE 11.9

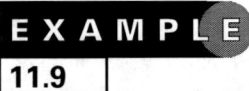

FIGURE 11.21

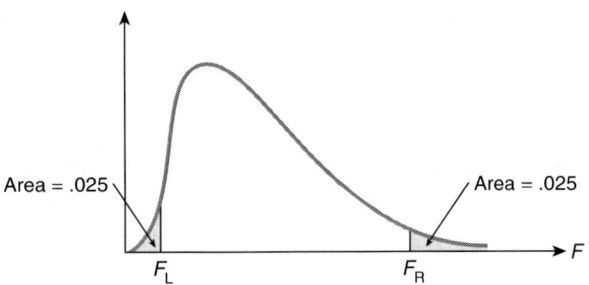

F curve with v_1 and v_2 df showing F values used for a 95% confidence interval.

Solution   Here, $n_1 = 25$, $s_1 = 1.21$, and $n_2 = 20$, $s_2 = .72$. So we need

$$F_R = F_{.025,24,19} = 2.45$$

$$F_L = \frac{1}{F_{.025,19,24}}$$

$$\approx \frac{1}{2.33} \left(\text{using } F_{.025,20,24} \right)$$

$$\approx .43$$

The 95% confidence interval for σ_1^2/σ_2^2 is

$$\frac{(1.21)^2/(.72)^2}{2.45} \text{ to } \frac{(1.21)^2/(.72)^2}{.43} = 1.15 \text{ to } 6.57$$

As a result, we are 95% confident that σ_1^2/σ_2^2 is between 1.15 and 6.57. This means that we are 95% confident that σ_1^2 is between 1.15 and 6.57 times as large as σ_2^2.

EXAMPLE 11.10   For the Case Automotive Products data in Example 11.7, determine a 95% confidence interval for σ_1/σ_2. Use the results of Example 11.9.

Solution   This is obtained simply by finding the *square root* of each endpoint of the confidence interval for σ_1^2/σ_2^2. Your 95% confidence interval for σ_1/σ_2 will be

$$\sqrt{1.15} \text{ to } \sqrt{6.57} = 1.07 \text{ to } 2.56 \text{ (fluid ounces)}$$

X Exercises 11.37–11.46

Understanding the Mechanics

11.37 Find the rejection region for each of the following situations.

   a. H_0: $\sigma_1^2 = \sigma_2^2$ versus H_a: $\sigma_1^2 \neq \sigma_2^2$, $n_1 = 20$, $n_2 = 15$, $\alpha = .05$
   b. H_0: $\sigma_1^2 \geq \sigma_2^2$ versus H_a: $\sigma_1^2 < \sigma_2^2$, $n_1 = 5$, $n_2 = 15$, $\alpha = .10$
   c. H_0: $\sigma_1 \leq \sigma_2$ versus H_a: $\sigma_1 > \sigma_2$, $n_1 = 19$, $n_2 = 11$, $\alpha = .01$

11.38 A random sample of size 10 from population A yielded a mean and standard deviation of 45 and 2.0, respectively. A random sample of size 25 from population B yielded a mean and standard deviation of 44 and 3.0, respectively.

   a. Test that the population standard deviations differ. Use a 5% significance level.
   a. Compute a 95% confidence interval for the ratio σ_A/σ_B. Is this confidence interval consistent with the conclusion in part a?

11.39 The following data were collected from normally distributed populations. Is there evidence that the standard deviation of the second population is less than that of the first? Use a 5% significance level.

Sample 1	Sample 2
7	7
9	6
8	9
2	6
3	7

Applying the New Concepts

11.40 The Water Pollution Prevention Council (WPPC) had recommended that the discharge of industrial waste and effluents into rivers in the district be done at a slow and steady rate of 100 pounds/hour (i.e., 2,400 pounds/day).

Industrial plants tended to concentrate their effluent discharge activity in the night shift. The WPPC found that although companies might technically achieve an average discharge rate of 2,400 pounds/day, the rivers could not cope with the erratic rate of discharge. The effluents needed to be released throughout the day, rather than all at night. It was recommended that the true variance of the discharge rate should not exceed 600. The following results were obtained from samples of 21 observations each.

Factory A: variance 585
Factory B: variance 618

At a 5% significance level, is there sufficient evidence to conclude that the variance for factory A is less than that for factory B?

11.41 A lot of investors have been reading about something called the "new-fund effect." That's the tendency of new funds to outperform their older peers because of any one of a number of factors: better access to initial public offerings, more motivated managers, or better spreads on trades. However, despite the potential growth benefits of new funds, their volatility makes many investors uncomfortable. Consider a sample of 10 newly created mid-cap mutual funds and a sample of 10 newly created small-cap mutual funds randomly selected from all mutual funds that are less than 18 months old. Is there sufficient evidence to conclude that there is a significant difference in the variance of newly created mid-cap and small-cap mutual funds? Use a .10 significance level.

Annualized Performance of New Mid-Cap Funds	Annualized Performance of New Small-Cap Funds
13.7	15.3
7.9	9.8
13.6	13.5
11.4	8.6
14.6	15.2
9.5	14.9
10.8	11.5
11.3	25.2
12.0	6.3
12.7	12.4

(Source: finance.yahoo.com)

11.42 The quality-improvement department of a company that manufactures wall clocks is studying the variability of two recently developed types of wall clocks. Using the following information, test the hypothesis that H_0: $\sigma_1 = \sigma_2$, using a significance level of .05. Assume that the samples are taken from populations that are approximately normally distributed. Clock 1: n = 25, s = 1.8. Clock 2: n = 21, s = 1.39.

11.43 The Honda Insight and Toyota Prius are the only mass-built hybrid cars available in the United States. These cars are able to get 50 to 60 miles per gallon (mpg) while emitting exhaust that is 90% cleaner than traditional low-emission vehicles, and neither has to be plugged in at night to recharge its battery. Suppose that an automotive analyst believes that the standard deviation in the mpg for the Prius is greater than the standard deviation in the mpg for the Insight. Test drives on a random sample of 25 Insights and 25 Prius yielded standard deviations of 2.30 and 3.25, respectively.

  a. At the 5% significance level, do the data support the analyst's belief?

  b. What assumptions are necessary for the test in part a to be valid?

(Source: "CHARGING UP: When Gas Prices Rise, So Do Sales of Hybrids," *Dallas Morning News*, July 5, 2001, p. 1D.)

11.44 The following is a summary of the mean annual return ($\bar{X}$) and variance (s^2) of the annual return for common stocks in three different industries. Computer industry: n = 16, $\bar{x}$ = 14.3%, s^2 = 5.6. Steel industry: n = 9, $\bar{x}$ = 8.5%, s^2 = 11.2. Oil-and-gas industry: n = 13, $\bar{x}$ = 11.8%, s^2 = 16.4. Using these data, can we conclude that computer stocks are less risky than oil and gas stocks? Use a significance level of .05. Assume that the mean annual returns for these industries are approximately normally distributed.

Using the Computer

11.45 **[DATA SET EX11-45]** Variable Description:

TraditStu: Grades in capstone MBA course for traditional students

NonTraditStu: Grades in capstone MBA course for nontraditional students

An associate dean at the University of North Texas was interested in whether the variation in scores for nontraditional students in the capstone MBA course is greater than that of the traditional student. A nontraditional student is one that has been out of school for more than 10 years. Fifty final grade scores were recorded for each of the types of students.

  a. Using a 5% significance level, can the associate dean conclude that the variation in scores is greater for nontraditional students? When using Excel's **F Test: Two-Sample for Variances** procedure, make sure that the group with the larger variance is designated as the first group.

  b. Subtract five points from each grade of the nontraditional student. Do you think that these new grades would affect the F test in part a? Try it.

11.46 Using the data set in Exercise 11.34, test for a difference in the population variances of the salaries in private industry and the government sector. Use a 5% significance level.

11.5

COMPARING THE MEANS OF TWO NORMAL POPULATIONS USING PAIRED SAMPLES

The final section of this chapter examines the situation in which the two samples are *not* obtained independently. All discussion up to this point has assumed that the two samples *are* independent. By not independent, we mean that the corresponding elements from the two samples are *paired*. Perhaps each pair of observations corresponds to the same city, the same week, the same married couple, or even the same person. Our discussion focuses on comparing the two population means for the situation in which two *dependent* samples are obtained from the two populations.

When attempting to estimate or test for the difference between two population means, your first question always should be, is there any natural reason to pair the first observation from sample 1 with the first observation from sample 2, the second with the second, and so on? If there is no reason to pair these data and the samples were obtained independently, the previous methods for finding confidence intervals and testing μ_1 versus μ_2 apply. If the data were gathered such that pairing the values is necessary, then it is *extremely* important that you recognize this and treat the data in a different manner. We can still determine confidence intervals and perform a test of hypothesis, but the procedure is different.

As an illustration, Metalloy manufactures metal hinges. The hardness of these hinges is tested by pressing a rod with a pointed tip into the hinge with a specified force and measuring the depth of the depression caused by the tip. Two tips are available for the hardness tester, and it is suspected that tip #1 produces higher hardness readings, on the average. To control for variation in the hardness of the hinges, it was decided to use paired samples in which *both* tips were used to test the hardness of the *same* metal hinge. The following coded data were obtained using 12 randomly selected hinges. The letter d represents the *difference* of each pair of hardness values (tip #1 – tip #2).

Hinge	1	2	3	4	5	6	7	8	9	10	11	12
Tip #1	39	32	42	49	45	47	45	48	38	48	41	47
Tip #2	35	34	38	48	47	43	41	47	35	46	37	44
d	4	–2	4	1	–2	4	4	1	3	2	4	3
d^2	16	4	16	1	4	16	16	1	9	4	16	9

$$\Sigma d = 4 - 2 + 4 + \ldots + 3 = 26$$
$$\Sigma d^2 = 16 + 4 + 16 + \ldots + 9 = 112$$

Each pair of values was obtained from the same metal hinge, so these data values clearly need to be paired—they are dependent samples. It seems reasonable to examine the difference of the two values for each hinge, so these differences (*d*), along with the d^2 values, are also shown. We have thus reduced the problem from two sets of values to a single set. The parameter of interest here is the *difference* of the population means, μ_d. Put another way, μ_d is the **mean of the population differences.**

Since we have a single set of sample values (the 12 differences) and a single parameter (μ_d), the results of Sections 8.4 and 10.4 can be used to construct a confidence interval and perform a test of hypothesis, *provided we have reason to believe that the population differences are normally distributed*. As a result, we need not worry about large versus small samples, because we will use the *t* distribution for our confidence intervals and tests of hypothesis, regardless of the sample sizes. Of course, if the number of differences is large (generally, $n > 30$), this distribution is closely approximated by the standard normal distribution.

Confidence Interval for μ_d Using Paired Samples

The statistic used to derive a confidence interval for μ_d and perform a test of hypothesis using *dependent samples* is

$$t_D = \frac{\bar{X}_1 - \bar{X}_2}{s_d / \sqrt{n}} = \frac{\bar{d}}{s_d / \sqrt{n}}$$

11.16

where

$$n = \text{the number of pairs of observations}$$

$$s_d = \text{the standard deviation of the } n \text{ differences}$$

$$= \sqrt{\frac{\sum d^2 - (\sum d)^2 / n}{n-1}}$$

$$\text{df for } t_D = n - 1$$

This is a *t random variable* with $n - 1$ df. Notice that the numerator of t_D is the same as before, namely, $\bar{X}_1 - \bar{X}_2$, which is also represented by $\bar{d} = \sum d / n$, the mean of the differences. The mean of the differences $\bar{d}$ always is equal to $\bar{X}_1 - \bar{X}_2$ (this can help you in checking your arithmetic when computing the d's).

Based on the discussion in Section 7.4, we obtain a $(1 - \alpha) \cdot 100\%$ confidence interval for μ_d:

$$\bar{d} - t_{\alpha/2, n-1} \frac{s_d}{\sqrt{n}} \text{ to } \bar{d} + t_{\alpha/2, n-1} \frac{s_d}{\sqrt{n}}$$

11.17

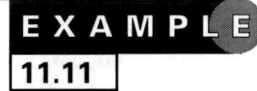

E X A M P L E

11.11

Using the hardness data, derive a 95% confidence interval for μ_d, where

$$\mu_d = \text{average difference in hardness}$$

Solution

We have

$$\bar{d} = \frac{\sum d}{n} = \frac{26}{12} = 2.167$$

Notice that

$$\bar{x}_1 = \frac{39 + 32 + \cdots + 47}{12} = 43.417$$

and

$$\bar{x}_2 = \frac{35 + 34 + \cdots + 44}{12} = 41.25$$

471

so $\bar{d} = \bar{x}_1 - \bar{x}_2 = 2.167$. It checks! Also,

$$s_d = \sqrt{\frac{\sum d^2 - (\sum d)^2 / n}{n-1}} = \sqrt{\frac{112 - (26)^2 / 12}{11}}$$

$$= \sqrt{\frac{55.667}{11}} = \sqrt{5.061} = 2.250$$

The resulting 95% confidence interval for μ_d is

$$\bar{d} - t_{.025,11}\frac{s_d}{\sqrt{n}} \quad \text{to} \quad \bar{d} + t_{.025,11}\frac{s_d}{\sqrt{n}}$$

$$= 2.167 - 2.201\frac{2.250}{\sqrt{12}} \quad \text{to} \quad 2.167 + 2.201\frac{2.250}{\sqrt{12}}$$

$$= 2.167 - 1.430 \quad \text{to} \quad 2.167 + 1.430$$

$$= .737 \quad \text{to} \quad 3.597$$

Based on these data, we are 95% confident that the hardness reading using tip #1 is between .737 and 3.597 *more* than the tip #2 reading. Notice that this is quite a wide confidence interval, due to the small sample sizes.

Hypothesis Testing Using Paired Samples

The test statistic for testing the means is the same as that in Section 8.4, except that we use the sample differences.

$$t_D = \frac{\bar{d} - D_0}{s_d / \sqrt{n}}$$

11.18

where D_0 is the hypothesized value of μ_d. When testing H_0: $\mu_d = D_0$ versus H_a: $\mu_d \neq D_0$, reject H_0 if $|t_D| > t_{\alpha/2,n-1}$. Here, $t_{\alpha/2,n-1}$ is obtained from Table A.5 using $n-1$ df. One-tailed tests are performed in a similar manner by placing α in either the right tail (H_a: $\mu_d > D_0$) or in the left tail (H_a: $\mu_d < D_0$). A summary is provided in the box on paired sample tests for μ_d and D_0 on page 337.

EXAMPLE 11.12

Consider the previous hardness data collected by Metalloy. Can you confirm the suspicion that the average difference in hardness readings (tip #1 – tip #2) is positive? Use a significance level of $\alpha = .05$.

Solution

Step 1. We are attempting to demonstrate that the average difference in hardness readings is positive; this claim goes into the alternative hypothesis. The resulting hypotheses are

$$H_0: \mu_d \leq 0$$

$$H_a: \mu_d > 0$$

Step 2. We are dealing with paired data, so the correct test statistic is

$$t_D = \frac{\bar{d}}{s_d / \sqrt{n}}$$

Step 3.   What happens to t_D when H_a is true? If $\mu_d > 0$, then we would expect $\bar{d}$ to be *positive*. So, the test procedure is to

$$\text{reject } H_0 \text{ if } t_D > k, \text{ for some } k > 0$$

What is k? As before, this depends on α, and in the usual manner, we have

$$\text{reject } H_0 \text{ if } t_D > t_{\alpha, n-1}$$

where $t_{\alpha, n-1}$ is obtained from Table A.5. For this situation, $t_{.05,11} = 1.796$, and so we

$$\text{reject } H_0 \text{ if } t_D > 1.796$$

Step 4.   Using the sample data,

$$t_D^* = \frac{2.167}{2.250 / \sqrt{12}} = 3.34$$

Because $3.34 > 1.796$, we reject H_0.

Step 5.   The average hardness reading using tip #1 is higher than that using tip #2.

Using Statistical Software to Compare Means Using Paired Samples

An Excel solution to Example 11.12 is provided in Figure 11.22 (cells C1:E14). First, you must enter the 12 values for tip #1 in cells A2:A13 and the 12 values for tip #2 in cells B2:B13. Type "Tip #1" in cell A1 and "Tip #2" in cell B1. To obtain the output in Figure 11.22, click on **Tools ➤ Data Analysis ➤ t Test: Paired Two-Sample for Means.** The resulting *p*-value (highlighted with an arrow) in cell D11 is .003318, which, using $\alpha = .05$, again results in rejecting H_0 since the *p*-value is less than α.

What happens if you fail to pair these observations and perform a regular two-sample *t* test, as we did in Section 11.3 for two, *independent* samples? The results are summarized in cells F1:H13 in Figure 11.22, where we observe an interesting result. The *t* value

---

FIGURE

11.22

Excel spreadsheet using **Tools ➤ Data Analysis ➤ t Test: Paired Two-Sample for Means** and **Tools ➤ Data Analysis ➤ t Test: Two-Sample Assuming Unequal Variances.**

	A	B	C	D	E	F	G	H
1	Tip #1	Tip #2	t-Test: Paired Two Sample for Means			t-Test: Two-Sample Assuming Unequal Variances		
2	39	35						
3	32	34		Tip #1	Tip #2		Tip #1	Tip #2
4	42	38	Mean	43.416667	41.25	Mean	43.416667	41.25
5	49	48	Variance	26.44697	27.659091	Variance	26.44697	27.659091
6	45	47	Observations	12	12	Observations	12	12
7	47	43	Pearson Correlation	0.906696		Hypothesized Mean Difference	0	
8	45	41	Hypothesized Mean Difference	0		df	22	
9	48	47	df	11		t Stat	1.020375	
10	38	35	t Stat	3.336426		P(T<=t) one-tail	0.159321	⬅
11	48	46	P(T<=t) one-tail	0.003318	⬅	t Critical one-tail	1.717144	
12	41	37	t Critical one-tail	1.795884		P(T<=t) two-tail	0.318641	
13	47	44	P(T<=t) two-tail	0.006635		t Critical two-tail	2.073875	
14			t Critical two-tail	2.200986				
15								

FIGURE

11.23

MINITAB output using **Stat ➤ Basic Statistics ➤ Paired t.**

Paired T-Test and CI: Tip 1, Tip 2

```
Paired T for Tip 1 - Tip 2

              N     Mean    StDev   SE Mean
Tip 1        12   43.4167  5.1427   1.4846
Tip 2        12   41.2500  5.2592   1.5182
Difference   12    2.16667 2.24958  0.64940


95% lower bound for mean difference: 1.00042
T-Test of mean difference = 0 (vs > 0): T-Value = 3.34   P-Value = 0.003
```

FIGURE

11.24

SPSS output using **Analyze ➤ Compare Means ➤ Paired-Samples T Test.**

Paired Samples Test

		Paired Differences							
					95% Confidence Interval of the Difference				
		Mean	Std. Deviation	Std. Error Mean	Lower	Upper	t	df	Sig. (2-tailed)
Pair 1	TIP1 - TIP2	2.167	2.250	.65	.737	3.596	3.34	11	.0066

(using the test statistic from equation 11.6) now is 1.02, with a corresponding p-value of $p = .159$ (highlighted with an arrow). This means that, using this test, we now *fail to reject* H_0. We are unable to demonstrate a difference between the average hardness readings, which, according to the paired sample test, is *not* a correct conclusion. The incorrect solution in cells F1:H13 shows convincingly that failing to pair the observations when you should can cause you to obtain an incorrect result. More importantly, there is nothing to warn you that this has occurred.

The MINITAB output in Figure 11.23 is obtained by clicking on **Stat ➤ Basic Statistics ➤ Paired t.** Figure 11.24 contains the SPSS solution obtained by clicking on **Analyze ➤ Compare Means ➤ Paired-Samples T Test.** Since this is a one-tailed test, the SPSS p-value of .0066 must be divided by 2. Consequently, both computer solutions provide a computed value of the test statistic equal to 3.34 (as in the Example 11.12 solution) with a corresponding p-value of .003. Since the p-value is less than .05, the null hypothesis is rejected.

EXAMPLE

11.13

The market research staff at Allied Foods is considering two different packaging designs for an instant breakfast cereal that Allied is about to introduce. The first type of container under consideration is a rectangular box, whereas the second container type has a cylindrical shape.

The staff decides to conduct a pilot study by placing the product in both containers and locating the two types at opposite ends of the breakfast cereal section in 10 different supermarkets. All the containers are placed at eye level to remove any effect due to the height of the display. The main question under consideration is whether there is any difference in the sales of the two types of container. From the following data, can you conclude that there is a difference in sales for the rectangular and cylindrical containers? Use $\alpha = .05$ to define your test.

Supermarket	1	2	3	4	5	6	7	8	9	10
Rectangular	194	152	160	172	118	110	137	126	176	145
Cylindrical	184	161	153	184	105	123	155	111	156	129

The data were gathered by collecting a pair of observations from each supermarket, so this is a clear-cut case of dependent sampling. Your next step should be to determine the paired differences. Define d to be the rectangular box sales minus the cylindrical box sales.

Solution

Supermarket	1	2	3	4	5	6	7	8	9	10	Total
d	10	−9	7	−12	13	−13	−18	15	20	16	29
d^2	100	81	49	144	169	169	324	225	400	256	1917

Step 1. We are attempting to detect a difference in the two means: a two-tailed test is in order. Let

$$\mu_d = \text{average difference in sales for the two container types}$$

The correct hypotheses are

$$H_0: \mu_d = 0$$

$$H_a: \mu_d \neq 0$$

Steps 2, 3. Using the t_D test statistic, the test will be to

$$\text{reject } H_0 \text{ if } |t_D| > t_{\alpha/2, n-1}$$

where $t_{\alpha/2, n-1} = t_{.025,9} = 2.262$.

Step 4. Using the sample data,

$$\bar{d} = \frac{\Sigma d}{n} = \frac{29}{10} = 2.9$$

$$s_d = \sqrt{\frac{\Sigma d^2 - (\Sigma d)^2 / n}{n-1}}$$

$$= \sqrt{\frac{1917 - (29)^2 / 10}{9}}$$

$$= \sqrt{\frac{1832.9}{9}} = 14.271$$

From these values we obtain

$$t_D^* = \frac{\bar{d}}{s_d / \sqrt{n}} = \frac{2.9}{14.271 / \sqrt{10}} = .643$$

Because $.643 < 2.262$, we fail to reject H_0.

Step 5. Based on these data, there is *insufficient evidence* to conclude that the container type has an effect on sales.

PAIRED SAMPLE TESTS FOR μ_d

Two-Tailed Test

$$H_0: \mu_d = D_0$$

$$H_a: \mu_d \neq D_0$$

$$\text{reject } H_0 \text{ if } |t_D^*| > t_{\alpha/2, n-1}$$

where
1. Each difference, d, is (sample 1 value – sample 2 value)

2. $t_D = \dfrac{\bar{d} - D_0}{s_d / \sqrt{n}}$

3. $\bar{d} = \bar{X}_1 - \bar{X}_2 = \dfrac{\Sigma d}{n}$

4. $s_d = \sqrt{\dfrac{\Sigma d^2 - (\Sigma d)^2 / n}{n-1}}$

5. df for $t_D = n - 1$

One-Tailed Test

$H_0: \mu_d \le D_0$	$H_0: \mu_d \ge D_0$
$H_a: \mu_d > D_0$	$H_a: \mu_d < D_0$
reject H_0 if $t_D^* > t_{\alpha, n-1}$	reject H_0 if $t_D^* < -t_{\alpha, n-1}$

X Exercises 11.47–11.55

Understanding the Mechanics

11.47 From each of two normally distributed populations, random samples were selected. The observations in the first sample are paired with the observations in the second sample. The following statistics were calculated: $\bar{x}_1 = 5.17$, $\bar{x}_2 = 3.16$, $s_d = 2.4$, $n = 13$.

  a. Do the data provide sufficient evidence that the mean of population 1 is greater than the mean of population 2? Use a .05 significance level.

  b. Find the p-value for the test statistic in part a.

11.48 The following data are the differences ($d = X_1 - X_2$) of pairs of observations from two normally distributed populations. Is there sufficient evidence to conclude that the mean of the first population is greater than the mean of the second population? Use a 5% significance level.

Pairs	1	2	3	4	5	6	7	8	9	10
d	10	–7	7	–10	13	–9	–18	15	20	16

11.49 Ten individuals were timed on two separate tasks. The times are as follows.

Person	Time for Task 1	Time for Task 2
1	10	6
2	12	14
3	15	10
4	13	11
5	14	16
6	15	11
7	16	12
8	12	11
9	18	15
10	13	11

  a. Construct a 90% confidence interval for the difference in the means of the times for the two tasks.

  b. Do the data support the conclusion that the means of the times for the two tasks differ? Use a 10% significance level.

Applying the New Concepts

11.50 The controller of a fast-food chain is interested in determining whether there is any difference in the weekly sales of restaurant 1 and restaurant 2. The weekly sales are approximately normally distributed. The sales, in dollars, for seven randomly selected weeks are:

Week	Restaurant 1	Restaurant 2
1	4100	3800
2	1800	4600
3	2200	5100
4	3400	3050
5	3100	2800
6	1100	1950
7	2200	3400

  a. Should this problem be analyzed using an independent or dependent sample t statistic?

  b. Using a significance level of .01, is there evidence to support the conclusion that there is a significant difference in the weekly sales of the two restaurants?

11.51 China's one-child policy, which limits most families to one baby to restrict population growth, seems to be making parents and grandparents in China willing to spend a larger portion of their disposable income on their children. Walt Disney Co. has been selling the Disney

Babies line of T-shirts since 1993 in China. Suppose that a market analyst believes that these T-shirts sell for $7.00 (dollar equivalent to the Chinese yuan) more than a local children's T-shirt. Suppose that 25 retail stores were randomly sampled in Shanghai and at each store, the price of a Disney T-shirt and the price of a local children's T-shirt were recorded. If the mean difference was $9.50 with a standard deviation of the differences, s_d, equal to $2.80, is there sufficient evidence to support the marketing analyst's belief? Use a significance level of .01.

(Source: "Chinese Babies Are Coveted Consumers," The Wall Street Journal, May 15, 1998, p. B1.)

11.52 Data on chief executive compensation indicate that top corporate officers continue to be handsomely rewarded, even though increases are relatively modest compared to the go-go years of the late 1990s. A recent survey indicated that average salary, bonus, and long-term compensation rose 9.1% to $8.1 million in 2003. The 25 top executive earners pulled down pay packages that were, on average, more than 900 times the yearly salary of a typical American worker. Suppose that 10 chief executives were randomly selected and the following bonuses were recorded.

Chief Executive Officer	Bonus in 2003 (in thousands)	Bonus in 2004 (in thousands)
1	195	196
2	183	160
3	208	220
4	190	195
5	220	200
6	235	250
7	175	180
8	150	145
9	245	240
10	210	230

a. Construct a 90% confidence interval on the average difference in the bonuses for the years 2003 and 2004. Interpret this interval.

b. Use part a to test that there is a difference in the average bonuses for the years 2003 and 2004. Use a 10% significance level.

(Source: "Executive Pay," Business Week, April 19, 2004.)

11.53 Twenty major mortgage institutions were selected and the amount of mortgage refinancing was recorded for 2005 and 2004. If the mean difference was $5.434 million with the standard deviation of the differences being $8.764 million, is there sufficient evidence to support that a difference exists in the amount of mortgage refinancing for 2005 and 2004? Use a 1% significance level.

Using the Computer

11.54 **[DATA SET EX11-54]** Variable Description:

District: Forty school districts in North Texas

Graduates2001: Number of high school graduates in the year 2001

Graduates2000: Number of high school graduates in the year 2000

The number of high school graduates in North Texas has shown an increase in the year 2001, thanks to efforts by educational counselors to keep high school students in school. Suppose educational researchers believe that, on average, the school districts have 30 more high school graduates in the year 2001 than in 2000.

a. Using a random sample of 40 school districts in North Texas, do the data indicate that the increase in the number of high school graduates differs from 30? What is the p-value? Would you reject the null hypothesis at the 10% significance level? At the 5% level? At the 1% level?

b. A t test for independent samples would not be valid to use in testing the hypothesis in part a. Why? Perform the hypothesis test using a t test for independent samples, assuming unequal variances to test this hypothesis. Compare the p-value for this test with the p-value obtained in part a.

(Source: "High School Attrition," Dallas Morning News, May 20, 2001, p. 17A.)

11.55 **[DATA SET EX11-55]** Variable Description:

PercentReworkPrior: Percent of materials that need rework prior to using quality control charts

PercentReworkPost: Percent of materials that need rework after use of quality control charts is implemented

The vice president of a manufacturing firm wishes to determine if the implementation of quality control charts at assembly lines will decrease the amount of rework required at each of the assembly lines. There are 35 assembly lines that the vice president selects randomly from plants at various locations. The percent of rework during the month prior to requiring workers to use control charts and the percent of rework afterward is recorded as a percent for variables PercentReworkPrior and PercentReworkPost, respectively.

a. Put PercentReworkPost-PercentReworkPrior in a separate column. Using a one population t statistic, test that the mean difference is less than zero. Use a 1% significance level.

b. Use the t statistic for paired samples to test that PercentReworkPost is less than PercentReworkPrior. Use a 1% significance level.

c. What similarities do you notice in the analyses in parts a and b?

d. What assumptions are necessary for the analysis in part b to be valid?

e. Do a what-if analysis by eliminating any pair that has a percentage of rework above 10%. How do the conclusions to part b change?

COMPARING MORE THAN TWO MEANS: ONE-FACTOR ANOVA

In Example 11.4, we compared the mean blowout times for two different brands of tires. In Section 11.3, we advised against assuming that the two population standard deviations (σ_1 and σ_2) were equal. As a result, we generally used a t test that did *not* pool the sample variances. However, when examining more than two normal populations (the topic of discussion in this section), the testing procedure for detecting a difference in the population means requires that the populations have the *same* distribution if, in fact, the population means are equal. Consequently, it can be used only when we are willing to assume that the *population variances are equal* (or approximately equal). The analysis of variance procedure is *not* extremely sensitive to departures from this assumption, especially if equal-sized samples are obtained from each population.

The Analysis of Variance Approach

We need to introduce two new terms. Example 11.4 examined the effect of one *factor* (brand), consisting of two *levels* (Beltex and Roadmaster). If you want to extend this to four brands (say, brands 1, 2, 3, and 4), then you still have *one* factor, but you now have *four* levels. The purpose of **analysis of variance (ANOVA)** is to determine whether this factor has a *significant effect* on the variable being measured (blowout times in Example 11.4). If, for instance, the brand factor *is* significant, the mean blowout times for the different brands will not be equal. Consequently, testing for equal means among the various brands is the same as attempting to answer this question: Is there a significant effect on blowout time due to this factor?

The 30 values in Example 11.4 are different, and we observe a variation in these values. We will look at two *sources of variation:* (1) variation *within* the samples (levels) and (2) variation *between* the samples.

Within-Sample Variation

When you obtain a sample, you usually obtain different values for each observation. The 15 Beltex values in Example 11.4 vary about the mean $\bar{x}_1 = 3.33$ hours, as measured by $s_1 = .68$ hour. Likewise, the 15 Roadmaster values also exhibit some variation ($s_2 = .38$ hour) about the mean ($\bar{x}_2 = 3.98$ hours). These are the **within-sample variations.** They are used when estimating the common population variance, say σ^2. This procedure tends to provide an accurate estimate of σ^2, whether or not the sample means are equal.

Between-Sample Variation

When you compare the two sample means in Example 11.4, observe that the Beltex values are smaller on average than the Roadmaster values. This is summarized in the sample means, where $\bar{x}_1 = 3.33$ hours appears to be considerably smaller than $\bar{x}_2 = 3.98$ hours. So there is a variation in the 30 values due to the *brand;* that is, due to the factor. This is **between-sample variation.** In general, if this variation is large, we expect considerable variation among the sample means. The between-sample variation is also used in another estimate of the common variance, σ^2, provided the population means are equal. In other words, if the means are equal, the between-sample and within-sample estimates of σ^2 should be nearly the same. As we will see later in this section, we can derive a test of hypothesis procedure for determining whether the means are equal by comparing these two estimates.

In general, one-factor ANOVA techniques can be used to study the effect of any single factor on performance, sales, and the like. This factor can consist of any number of levels—say, k levels. To determine if the levels of this factor affect our measured observations, we examine the hypotheses

$$H_0: \mu_1 = \mu_2 = \ldots = \mu_k$$

$$H_a: \text{not all } \mu\text{'s are equal}$$

Suppose we are interested in the average lifetimes of not two but four brands of batteries. Is there any difference in these four mean lifetimes? To answer this question, we test

$$H_0: \mu_1 = \mu_2 = \mu_3 = \mu_4$$

$$H_a: \text{not all } \mu\text{'s are equal}$$

Note that the complement of H_0 is *not* H_a: $\mu_1 \neq \mu_2 \neq \mu_3 \neq \mu_4$. This alternative hypothesis is "too strong," and the correct form of H_a is that at least two of the means differ or, as stated here, not all of the means are equal.

We have a single factor (brand) consisting of four levels (brand 1, brand 2, brand 3, brand 4). One possibility is to examine these samples one pair at a time using the t statistic discussed in the previous section. This appears to be a safe way to proceed here, although there are $_4C_2 = 6$ such pairs of tests to perform this way. The main problem with performing many tests of this nature is determining the probability of making an incorrect decision. In particular, what value does α have, where α is the probability of rejecting H_0: all μ's are equal, when in fact it is true? You set α in advance but, after performing 6 of these pairwise tests ($\mu_1 = \mu_2$, $\mu_1 = \mu_3$, . . .), for instance, what is your *overall* probability of concluding that at least one pair of means are not equal when they actually are? This is a difficult question. The overall probability is not the significance level, α, with which you selected for just one pair. *So we need an approach that will test for the equality of these four means using a single test.* This is what the ANOVA approach does.

Assumptions Behind the ANOVA Analysis

When using the ANOVA procedure, there are three key assumptions that must be satisfied. They are basically the same requirements that were necessary in Section 11.3 when testing two means using independent samples and the pooled variance approach:

1. The replicates (observations) are obtained *independently* and *randomly* from each of the populations. The value of one observation has no effect on any other replicates within the same sample or within the other samples.

2. The replicates from each population follow (approximately) a *normal* distribution.

3. The normal populations all have a *common variance,* σ^2. We expect the values in each sample to vary about the same amount. The ANOVA procedure will be much less sensitive to violations of this requirement when we obtain samples of equal size from each population.

Deriving the Sum of Squares

When examining k populations, for example, the data will be configured somewhat like this:

	Level 1	Level 2	. . .	Level k
	$\vdots$	$\vdots$		$\vdots$
	n_1 replicates	n_2 replicates	. . .	n_k replicates
	$\vdots$	$\vdots$		$\vdots$
Totals	T_1	T_2	. . .	T_k

These resemble the data from Example 11.4, where $k = 2$ and $n_1 = n_2 = 15$ replicates.

When using the ANOVA procedure, the two sources of variation are measured by calculating various **sums of squares, SS.** The sum of squares used to measure the between-sample variation is SS(factor) and the sum of squares for measuring the within-sample variation is SS(error). The final sum of squares is SS(total), which is the sum of SS(factor) and SS(error). The formulas for deriving each sum of squares are summarized in the following box and illustrated in Example 11.14.

Both SS(factor) and SS(error) will have corresponding degrees of freedom (df). The degrees of freedom for SS(factor) is $k - 1$, where k is the number of factor levels (2 in Example 11.4) and the degrees of freedom for SS(error) is $n - k$, where n is the total number of observations (30 in Example 11.4). The next step when using the ANOVA procedure is to determine something resembling an "average" sum of squares, referred to as a **mean square.** We compute a mean square for only SS(factor) and SS(error) by dividing each of the sums of squares by the corresponding degrees of freedom. The derivation of these two mean squares is contained in equations 11.23 and 11.24.

$$SS(\text{factor}) = \left[\frac{T_1^2}{n_1} + \frac{T_2^2}{n_2} + \cdots + \frac{T_k^2}{n_k} \right] - \frac{T^2}{n} \qquad \text{11.19}$$

$$SS(\text{total}) = \Sigma x^2 - \frac{T^2}{n} \qquad \text{11.20}$$

$$SS(\text{error}) = \Sigma x^2 - \left[\frac{T_1^2}{n_1} + \frac{T_2^2}{n_2} + \cdots + \frac{T_k^2}{n_k} \right] \qquad \text{11.21}$$

$$= SS(\text{total}) - SS(\text{factor}) \qquad \text{11.22}$$

Here, n = the total number of observations = $n_1 + n_2 + \ldots + n_k$, and $T = \Sigma x$ = the sum of all n observations = $T_1 + T_2 + \ldots + T_k$. Also, to find Σx^2, we square each of the n observations and sum the results.

Note that

$$MS(\text{factor}) = \frac{SS(\text{factor})}{\text{df for factor}} \qquad \text{11.23}$$

$$= \frac{SS(\text{factor})}{k-1}$$

$$MS(\text{error}) = \frac{SS(\text{error})}{\text{df for error}} \qquad \text{11.24}$$

$$= \frac{SS(\text{error})}{n-k}$$

The ANOVA Table

A convenient way of summarizing the various sums of squares, corresponding mean squares, and the value of the test statistic for testing the equality of the factor means is to use an **ANOVA table.** The format of this table follows. The total df are $n - 1$, which is the total of the factor df ($k - 1$) and the error df ($n - k$).

Source	df	SS	MS	F
Factor	$k - 1$	SS(factor)	MS(factor) = $\dfrac{SS(\text{factor})}{k-1}$	$\dfrac{MS(\text{factor})}{MS(\text{error})}$
Error	$n - k$	SS(error)	MS(error) = $\dfrac{SS(\text{error})}{n-k}$	
Total	$n - 1$	SS(total)		

The test statistic for testing H_0: $\mu_1 = \mu_2 = \ldots = \mu_k$ versus H_a: not all μ's are equal is

$$F = \frac{MS(\text{factor})}{MS(\text{error})}$$

which has an F distribution with $k - 1$ and $n - k$ df. The F distribution was introduced in Section 11.4.

The procedure is to reject H_0 when the variation among the sample means (measured by MS(factor)) is *large* compared to the variation within the samples (measured by MS(error)). Consequently, the test will be to reject H_0 whenever F lies in the *right-tailed* rejection region defined by the significance level, α.

EXAMPLE 11.14

The manufacturer of the small, battery-powered tape recorder (discussed at the start of this section) also manufactures battery-powered AM/FM radio sets that include the required batteries. This unit uses a smaller battery, and four suppliers (brands) of this battery are being considered. Past experience has indicated that the battery lifetimes are normally distributed. The supervising inspector of incoming quality again wants to know whether there is any difference among the average lifetimes of the four battery brands. Twenty-four batteries (six of each brand) are placed on a test device that slowly drains the battery power and records the battery lifetime. The following data (in hours) were obtained:

	Brand 1	Brand 2	Brand 3	Brand 4
	41	32	35	33
	35	37	30	27
	48	46	24	36
	40	53	26	35
	45	41	28	27
	52	43	31	25
Total (*T*)	261	252	174	183
Average ($\bar{X}$)	43.5	42.0	29.0	30.5
Variance (s^2)	37.1	52.8	15.2	22.3

The four sample averages are $\bar{x}_1 = 43.5$, $\bar{x}_2 = 42.0$, $\bar{x}_3 = 29.0$, and $\bar{x}_4 = 30.5$. Brands 1 and 2 appear to be outlasting brands 3 and 4. In other words, it appears that there is a significant *between-group variation*. But do these sample means provide sufficient evidence to reject H_0: $\mu_1 = \mu_2 = \mu_3 = \mu_4$, where each μ_i represents the average of *all* lifetimes for brand *i*? Use the ANOVA procedure to answer this question with $\alpha = .05$.

Solution

The requirements for this analysis are (1) the samples were obtained randomly and independently from each of the four populations, and (2) the battery lifetimes for each brand follow a *normal* distribution with a *common variance*, say, σ^2.

$$SS(\text{factor}) = \left[\frac{T_1^2}{n_1} + \frac{T_2^2}{n_2} + \frac{T_3^2}{n_3} + \frac{T_4^2}{n_4} \right] - \frac{T^2}{n}$$

So $n = n_1 + n_2 + n_3 + n_4 = 24$, and

$$T = \Sigma x = T_1 + T_2 + T_3 + T_4$$
$$= 261 + 252 + 174 + 183 = 870$$

Therefore,

$$SS(\text{factor}) = \frac{261^2}{6} + \frac{252^2}{6} + \frac{174^2}{6} + \frac{183^2}{6} - \frac{870^2}{24}$$
$$= 32,565 - 31,537.5 = 1027.5$$

$$SS(\text{total}) = \Sigma x^2 - \frac{T^2}{n}$$

$$= \left[41^2 + 35^2 + \cdots + 27^2 + 25^2 \right] - \frac{870^2}{24}$$

$$= 33,202 - 31,537.5 = 1664.5$$

$$SS(\text{error}) = SS(\text{total}) - SS(\text{factor})$$

$$= 1664.5 - 1027.5 = 637$$

The ANOVA table for this analysis follows:

Source	df	SS	MS	F
Factor	$k - 1 = 3$	1027.5	$1027.5/3 = 342.5$	$342.5/31.85 = 10.75$
Error	$n - k = 20$	637	$637/20 = 31.85$	
Total	23	1664.5		

The computed F value from the ANOVA table is $F^* = 10.75$. Since $\alpha = .05$, we use Table A.7 to find that $F_{.05,3,20} = 3.10$. Comparing these two values, $F^* = 10.75 > 3.10$, so we reject H_0.

We conclude that the average lifetimes for the four brands are not the same. This confirms our earlier suspicion based on the variation among the four sample means. Our results indicate that the brand factor *does* have a significant effect on battery lifetime.

Multiple Comparisons: A Follow-Up to the One-Factor ANOVA Procedure

If the one-factor ANOVA procedure leads to a rejection of H_0: all populations means are equal, a logic question would be, which means do differ? In other words, rejecting the ANOVA null hypothesis informs us that the means are not all the same but provides no clue as to which of the population means are different. Performing a series of t tests to compare all possible pairs of means is not a good idea, since the chances of making at least one Type I error (concluding that a difference exists between two population means when in fact they are the same) using such a procedure is much larger than the predetermined α used for each of the t tests.

What is needed is a technique that compares all possible pairs of means in such a way that the probability of making one or more Type I errors is α. This is a multiple comparisons procedure. There are several methods available for making multiple comparisons; the one presented here is **Tukey's multiple comparison test** (Tukey is pronounced too'-key).

Tukey's procedure is based on a statistical test that uses the largest and smallest sample means. The form of this statistic is

$$Q = \frac{\text{maximum}(\bar{X}_i) - \text{minimum}(\bar{X}_i)}{\sqrt{MS(\text{error})/n_r}}$$

11.25

where

1. Maximum $\bar{X}_i$ and minimum $\bar{X}_i$ are the largest and smallest means, respectively.

2. MS(error) is the pooled sample variance.

3. n_r is the number of replicates in each sample.

Notice that Tukey's procedure assumes that each sample contains the same number (n_r) of replicates. Critical values of the Q statistic are contained in Table A.9. Define

$Q_{\alpha,k,v}$ = critical value of the Q statistic from Table A.9 using a significance level of α; k is the number of sample means (groups), and v is the df associated with MS(error).

MULTIPLE COMPARISONS PROCEDURE: ONE-FACTOR ANOVA

1. Find $Q_{\alpha,k,v}$ using Table A9.
2. Determine

$$D = Q_{\alpha,k,v} \cdot \sqrt{\frac{MS(error)}{n_r}}$$

where MS(error) is the pooled sample variance and n_r is the number of replicates in each sample. For one-factor ANOVA, MS(error) is the same as s_p^2.
3. Place the sample means in order, from smallest to largest.
4. If two sample means differ by more than D, the conclusion is that the corresponding population means are unequal. In other words, if $|\bar{X}_i - \bar{X}_j| > D$, this implies that $\mu_i \neq \mu_j$.

To illustrate this procedure, reconsider Example 11.14. There we concluded that the average lifetime on a test device was not the same for the four brands of batteries. The four sample means were

$$\text{Brand 1:}\bar{x}_1 = 43.5$$
$$\text{Brand 2:}\bar{x}_2 = 42.0$$
$$\text{Brand 3:}\bar{x}_3 = 29.0$$
$$\text{Brand 4:}\bar{x}_4 = 30.5$$

For this study, there were $n_r = 6$ replicates in each sample, with a resulting pooled variance of $s_p^2 = MS(error) = 31.85$. The study contained $k = 4$ groups and the df for the error sum of squares was $v = n - k = 24 - 4 = 20$. Using a significance level of .05, we begin by finding $Q_{.05,4,20}$ in Table A.9. This value is 3.96. Next we determine

$$D = Q_{.05,4,20} \cdot \sqrt{\frac{MS(error)}{n_r}}$$

$$= 3.96\sqrt{\frac{31.85}{6}} = 9.12$$

The sample means, in order, are

$$\overline{29.0, 30.5,} \quad \overline{42.0, 43.5}$$

Any two sample means are significantly different using the Tukey procedure if they differ by an amount greater than $D = 9.12$. Here there are four significant differences, namely,

$$\bar{x}_1 - \bar{x}_3 = 43.5 - 29.0 = 14.5 > 9.12$$
$$\bar{x}_2 - \bar{x}_3 = 42.0 - 29.0 = 13.0 > 9.12$$
$$\bar{x}_1 - \bar{x}_4 = 43.5 - 30.5 = 13.0 > 9.12$$
$$\bar{x}_2 - \bar{x}_4 = 42.0 - 30.5 = 11.5 > 9.12$$

The conclusion from the multiple comparisons analysis is that $\mu_1 \neq \mu_3$, $\mu_1 \neq \mu_4$, $\mu_2 \neq \mu_3$, and $\mu_2 \neq \mu_4$. There is no evidence of a difference between the brand 1 and the brand 2 populations or between the brand 3 and the brand 4 populations. This is indicated by the two over-bars connecting these two pairs of sample means. In general, there is no evidence to indicate a difference in the population means for any group of sample means under such a bar.

Comment

The instructions for using Excel, MINITAB, or SPSS to carry out an ANOVA procedure and Tukey's test for multiple comparisons are contained in the end-of-chapter appendix.

X Exercises 11.56–11.66

Understanding the Mechanics

11.56 A sample from population A resulted in the observations 8, 6, 4, 6, and 3. A sample from population B resulted in the observations 2, 3, 4, 4, and 5.
  a. Compute the ANOVA table to test if the means of population A and B differ.
  b. Compute the two-sample t statistic, assuming equal population variances.
  c. What relationship do the MS(error) in part a and the pooled variance in part b have?
  d. What relationship do the F statistic in part a and the t statistic in part b have?

11.57 Use the following ANOVA table to answer the succeeding questions.

Source	df	SS	MS	F
Factor		180		
Error	36			
Total	39	241		

  a. Complete the ANOVA table, and determine the value of the F statistic for testing the null hypothesis that the means of the populations are equal.
  b. Do the data provide sufficient evidence to indicate that a difference exists in the means of the populations? Use a .01 significance level.
  c. If the number of observations from the random samples of each population are equal, what is the number of observations selected from each population?
  d. If $T_1 = 95$, $T_2 = 67$, $T_3 = 70$, and $T_4 = 64$, what pairs of population means are significantly different according to Tukey's multiple comparisons procedure? Use a .01 significance level.

11.58 Four independent samples are collected from four normally distributed populations. The data are as follows:

Group 1: 12 11 14 10 12 10
Group 2: 14 12 16 15
Group 3: 17 18 20 22 23
Group 4: 10   9 13 12

The SST is equal is 309.158. Conduct a test of the null hypothesis that the group means are equal. Use a 5% significance level.

11.59 Random samples of size 7 from populations A, B, C, and D resulted in sample mean values of 48, 47, 35, and 36, respectively. Assuming an MS(error) of 30, what are your conclusions regarding mean differences among populations A, B, C, and D using the Tukey multiple comparison procedure with a significance level of 5%?

Applying the New Concepts

11.60 A small engine-repair shop can special-order parts from any one of the three different warehouses and receive a substantial discount on the price. The manager of the shop is concerned with the length of time that it takes to special-order a part from one of the warehouses. The number of days it takes to special-order a part is recorded for 15 randomly selected orders from each of the three warehouses, as shown in the following table. Do the data indicate that there is a difference in the mean times that it takes to special-order a part from a warehouse? Use a .05 significance level. State the p-value.

Warehouse

A	13	17	14	10	9	15	18	11	13	18	16	13	15	12	16
B	7	12	8	15	6	10	12	10	8	14	10	6	9	13	11
C	10	12	18	19	9	15	20	11	15	13	17	13	10	14	16

11.61 A sales manager wanted to know whether there was a significant difference in the monthly sales of three sales representatives. John is strictly on commission. Randy is on commission and a small salary, and Ted is on a small commission and a salary. Eight months were chosen at random. The data represent monthly sales.

John	969	905	801	850	910	1030	780	810
Randy	738	773	738	805	850	800	690	720
Ted	751	764	701	810	840	790	720	735

  a. Using a significance level of .05, test the hypothesis that there is no difference in the mean monthly sales. (Coding the data may make the computations easier.)

b. What is the p-value?

c. Using a significance level of .05, perform a multiple comparisons procedure, if appropriate.

11.62 The Web site www.abia.org lets travelers use cyberspace to peek at the same arrival and departure screens seen by people at the Austin-Bergstrom International Airport and is updated every 30 seconds. This one Web site allows passengers to view the status of flights from several airlines. The mean time to locate information should be less than two minutes. Suppose that four random samples of 20 people each were selected to determine if the mean times that it takes to find the status of flights from American, Northwest, Delta, and Southwest Airlines are the same. How many t tests would have to be performed? What is the advantage of using an ANOVA procedure instead?

(Source: "Thanksgiving Travel Tips," The Austin American-Statesman, November 21, 2000, p. B2.)

11.63 The mean age of viewers of the major TV networks is very important to marketing strategists. CBS typically attracts the 50 year olds, NBC attracts the 40 year olds, and Fox attracts the 30 year olds. Suppose that a marketing strategist wanted to determine if the mean age of the following three programs differed: The Simpsons, That '70s Show, and Time of Your Life. Assume that a random sample of 100 viewers was selected for each of these three programs and that the sample means for The Simpsons, That '70s Show, and Time of Your Life were 31.38, 31.16, and 30.46 years of age. If the SSE was 3,247.40, construct the ANOVA table. What conclusion can the marketing strategist make? Use a 10% significance level.

(Source: "Too Old for Your Favorite Show? Viewer Median Age of Prime-Time," The Washington Post, January 3, 2000, p.7.)

Using the Computer

11.64 **[DATA SET EX11-64]**Variable Description:

LocationA: Programmer productivity metric at location A

LocationB: Programmer productivity metric at location B

LocationC: Programmer productivity metric at location C

A manager is using a new measure involving the creation of "function points" to measure the productivity for program-

mers. Function points require more creativity than simply replicating code. Fifty random days were selected from three locations and productivity metrics were measured.

a. Create three stacked histograms. Do you believe that there is any evidence of a difference in the means for the three locations?

b. Does an ANOVA table with a 5% significance level support your belief in part a?

c. Would you use a Tukey multiple comparison procedure for further analysis? Why or why not?

11.65 **[DATA SET EX11-65]**Variable Description:

Closing1: Rating of willingness to buy product after viewing closing technique 1

Closing2: Rating of willingness to buy product after viewing closing technique 2

Closing3: Rating of willingness to buy product after viewing closing technique 3

The effectiveness of closing techniques when selling a product has been debated among sales strategists. To determine the impact of three closing techniques, 60 potential customers (20 for each closing technique) were randomly selected to rate the closing techniques. Do the data provide sufficient evidence to conclude that the mean rating differs across closing techniques? Use a 5% significance level. Use Tukey's multiple comparison procedure to examine any differences.

11.66 **[DATA SET EX11-66]**Variable Description:

SpeedA: Number of nonconforming items at speed level A

SpeedB: Number of nonconforming items at speed level B

SpeedC: Number of nonconforming items at speed level C

A quality engineer believes that the speed level of a manufacturing process affects the number of nonconforming items produced. Use an ANOVA procedure and Tukey's multiple comparison procedure to assess any differences in the mean number of nonconforming items produced. Use a 1% significance level.

 Summary

This chapter has presented an introduction to statistical inference for two populations using both independent and dependent samples. When we used independent samples from two populations with known variances to test the population means, we defined a test statistic having approximately (or exactly) a standard normal distribution, and we also used this test statistic to define a confidence interval for $\mu_1 - \mu_2$. For independent samples from two populations with unknown variances (the usual situation), hypothesis testing on μ_1 versus μ_2 pays special attention to

whether we have reason to believe that the population standard deviations (σ_1 and σ_2) are equal.

To determine whether two population variances (or standard deviations) are the same, we introduced the F distribution. Using this distribution, we can perform one-tailed or two-tailed tests on the population variances (or standard deviations).

When two samples are obtained such that corresponding observations are paired (matched), the resulting samples are dependent, or paired. When using two such samples, we defined a t statistic to test the mean of the population differences, μ_d, and to construct a confidence interval for μ_d.

The analysis of variance (ANOVA) procedure is a method of detecting differences between the means of two or more normal populations. The various populations represent the levels of a factor under observation. The ratio of MS(factor) to MS(error) produces an F statistic that is used to test for equal population means. If the ANOVA procedure concludes that the population means are not the same, the follow-up Tukey multiple comparisons procedure should be conducted to determine which of the population means are unequal.

 # Summary of Formulas

Independent Samples (σ's Known)

1. Confidence interval for $\mu_1 - \mu_2$ (σ_1, σ_2 known):

$$\left(\bar{X}_1 - \bar{X}_2\right) \pm Z_{\alpha/2}\sqrt{\frac{\sigma_1^2}{n_1} + \frac{\sigma_2^2}{n_2}}$$

2. Hypothesis testing for μ_1 and μ_2: Test statistic is

$$Z = \frac{\left(\bar{X}_1 - \bar{X}_2\right) - D_0}{\sqrt{\frac{\sigma_1^2}{n_1} + \frac{\sigma_2^2}{n_2}}}$$

where D_0 is the hypothesized value of $\mu_1 - \mu_2$.

Independent Samples (σ's Unknown)

1. Confidence interval for $\mu_1 - \mu_2$ (not assuming $\sigma_1 = \sigma_2$):

$$\left(\bar{X}_1 - \bar{X}_2\right) \pm t_{\alpha/2,\text{df}}\sqrt{\frac{s_1^2}{n_1} + \frac{s_2^2}{n_2}}$$

where

$$\text{df} = \frac{\left[\frac{s_1^2}{n_1} + \frac{s_2^2}{n_2}\right]^2}{\frac{\left(\frac{s_1^2}{n_1}\right)^2}{n_1 - 1} + \frac{\left(\frac{s_2^2}{n_2}\right)^2}{n_2 - 1}}$$

2. Hypothesis testing for μ_1 and μ_2 (not assuming $\sigma_1 = \sigma_2$): Test statistic is

$$t' = \frac{\left(\bar{X}_1 - \bar{X}_2\right) - D_0}{\sqrt{\frac{s_1^2}{n_1} + \frac{s_2^2}{n_2}}}$$

where D_0 is the hypothesized value of $\mu_1 - \mu_2$ and where df are given in equation 1 above.

3. Confidence interval for $\mu_1 - \mu_2$ (assuming $\sigma_1 = \sigma_2$):

$$\left(\bar{X}_1 - \bar{X}_2\right) \pm t_{\alpha/2}s_p\sqrt{\frac{1}{n_1} + \frac{1}{n_2}}$$

where $\text{df} = n_1 + n_2 - 2$ and

$$s_p = \sqrt{\frac{(n_1-1)s_1^2 + (n_2-1)s_2^2}{n_1 + n_2 - 2}}$$

4. Hypothesis testing for μ_1 and μ_2 (assuming $\sigma_1 = \sigma_2$): Test statistic is

$$t = \frac{\left(\bar{X}_1 - \bar{X}_2\right) - D_0}{s_p\sqrt{\frac{1}{n_1} + \frac{1}{n_2}}}$$

where $\text{df} = n_1 + n_2 - 2$

Comparing Variances (or Standard Deviations)

1. Confidence interval for σ_1^2/σ_2^2:

$$\frac{s_1^2/s_2^2}{F_R} \quad \text{to} \quad \frac{s_1^2/s_2^2}{F_L}$$

where $F_R = F_{\alpha/2,v_1v_2}$, $F_L = 1/F_{\alpha/2,v_2v_1}$, $v_1 = n_1 - 1$, and $v_2 = n_2 - 1$.

2. Hypothesis testing for σ_1^2/σ_2^2. Test statistic is

$$F = \frac{s_1^2}{s_2^2}$$

Dependent (Paired) Samples

1. Confidence interval for μ_d:

$$\bar{d} \pm t_{\alpha/2, n-1} \frac{s_d}{\sqrt{n}}$$

where

n = number of paired observations

$\bar{d}$ = average of n differences

s_d = standard deviation of n differences

2. Hypothesis testing for μ_d: Test statistic is

$$t_D = \frac{\bar{d} - D_0}{s_d / \sqrt{n}} \quad (\text{df} = n - 1)$$

where D_0 is the hypothesized value of μ_d.

One-Factor ANOVA

$$SS(\text{factor}) = \left[\frac{T_1^2}{n_1} + \frac{T_2^2}{n_2} + \cdots + \frac{T_k^2}{n_k} \right] - \frac{T^2}{n}$$

$$SS(\text{total}) = \Sigma x^2 - \frac{T^2}{n}$$

$$SS(\text{error}) = SS(\text{total}) - SS(\text{factor})$$

$$MS(\text{factor}) = \frac{SS(\text{factor})}{k - 1}$$

$$MS(\text{error}) = \frac{SS(\text{error})}{n - k} = s_p^2$$

where

n = total number of observations

k = number of groups (populations) to be compared

T_i = total of sample values for the ith group

T = grand total = $T_1 + T_2 + \ldots + T_k$

1. Test statistic:

$$F = \frac{MS(\text{factor})}{MS(\text{error})}$$

2. Multiple comparisons:

$$\mu_i \neq \mu_j \ provided \ |\bar{X}_i - \bar{X}_j| > D$$

where

$$D = Q_{\alpha, k, v} \sqrt{\frac{MS(\text{error})}{n_r}}$$

v = df for error

n_r = number of replicates in each sample.

X Review Exercises 11.67–11.79

11.67 Independent random samples are selected from two normally distributed populations. Determine the value of the test statistic and the *p*-value from the hypothesis test in each of the following cases.

a. H_0: $\mu_1 - \mu_2 = 0$, H_a: $\mu_1 - \mu_2 \neq 0$, $n_1 = 64$, $n_2 = 38$, $\bar{x}_1 = 5.6$, $\bar{x}_2 = 6.9$, $\sigma_1 = 48$, $\sigma_2 = 17$

b. H_0: $\mu_1 - \mu_2 \leq 90$, H_a: $\mu_1 - \mu_2 > 90$, $n_1 = 24$, $n_2 = 26$, $\bar{x}_1 = 180$, $\bar{x}_2 = 80$, $s_1 = 24$, $s_2 = 20$

Do not assume the population standard deviations are equal

c. H_0: $\mu_1 - \mu_2 \geq 203$, H_a: $\mu_1 - \mu_2 < 203$, $n_1 = 100$, $n_2 = 100$, $\bar{x}_1 = 525$, $\bar{x}_2 = 325$, $\sigma_1 = 450$, $\sigma_2 = 165$

11.68 Dairy Castle wanted to boost the sales of its "Country Baskets." It thought that it might be helpful to hang posters that picture the item. It recorded the number of Country Baskets sold during lunchtime for one week at various stores. Dairy Castle repeated the sampling for another week when the poster advertising was used. Assume that weekly sales are normally distributed. Is there sufficient evidence to say that hanging the posters improved sales of the Country Baskets? Use a .05 significance level.

Store	Before	After	Store	Before	After
1218	215	240	1270	201	220
1224	180	220	1282	207	215
1236	150	190	1292	195	219
1252	180	175	1304	180	195

11.69 Global mutual funds invest anywhere in the world, and international mutual funds invest outside of the United States. A financial analyst wished to determine if a significant difference exists between the two. Random samples of 8 mutual funds from the global category and 10 from the international category were selected and their three-year performance was recorded. Using the following information, test for a difference in the mean performance of the two categories. Do not assume that the population variances are equal. Use a 10% significance level. What assumptions are necessary for this test to be valid?

Global mutual funds	26.3	32.2	48.1	25.5	29.3	31.5	36.7	39.1	
International mutual funds	29.5	60.3	29.6	44.3	48.1	37.5	32.3	27.5	54.2	36.2

11.70 Advertisers examine the average age of viewers of TV programs. For example, *60 Minutes* reportedly has one of the highest average ages at 57. Suppose that a marketing analyst believes that the age gap between *60 Minutes* and *Star Trek: Voyager* has narrowed to less than the historical 15 years. A random sample of 100 viewers from each of the TV programs was selected and the results are as follows.

	60 Minutes	**Star Trek: Voyager**
Sample mean	55.6	41.8
Population standard deviation	10.8	7.9
Sample size	100	100

a. Construct a 99% confidence interval on the difference of the average ages for the viewers of the two TV programs. How can you interpret this interval?

b. Test the hypothesis that the difference in the average age of viewers for these two programs is less than 15 years. Use a significance level of 1%.

c. Why can you not use the confidence interval in part a to test the hypothesis in part b?

(Source: "Too Old for Your Favorite Show? Viewer Median Age of Prime-Time," *The Washington Post*, January 3, 2000, p. 07.)

11.71 A study is designed to determine the effect of an office-training course on typing productivity. Ten typists are randomly selected and are asked to type 15 pages of equally difficult text before and after completing the training course. Their productivity is measured by the total number of errors made.

Typist	Before	After	Typist	Before	After
1	30	27	6	33	31
2	19	14	7	28	22
3	36	31	8	30	25
4	42	37	9	27	30
5	35	29	10	34	33

Assume that the total number of errors can be approximated by a normal distribution. Test the claim that taking the office-training course leads to a reduction in the average number of errors made by a typist. Use a significance level of .05.

11.72 A new packaging method that is proposed has an average output yield of finished units approximately the same as the existing packaging method. This new packaging method will be adopted if the variability in the number of finished units is less, thus providing greater process control. At a .05 significance level, is there sufficient evidence to conclude that the variance of the number of finished units is less for the new packaging method?

	Existing Packaging Method	New Packaging Method
Days sampled	9	9
s^2	1190	465

11.73 Suppose that a sample of size 16 is chosen from population 1 and a sample of size 26 is drawn from population 2. Assume that both populations are normally distributed. If a 90% confidence interval for the ratio of the variance of population 1 to the variance of population 2 is .367 to 1.753, what is the point estimate of the ratio of the two population variances?

11.74 A survey of four motels by 10 customers at each hotel yields 40 ratings, which resulted in the following partially complete ANOVA table. Test the null hypothesis that there is no difference in the average ratings of the four hotels. Use a 1% significance level.

Source	df	SS	MS	F
Factor				
Error			1,789	
Total		161.5		

11.75 A consulting firm wished to test if the leadership ability of supervisors, middle-level managers, and upper-level managers differs in a particular company. Using a metric to measure leadership, the consulting firm sampled five individuals and recorded the following data.

Supervisor	20	23	18	47	22
Middle-level manager	38	42	33	62	23
Upper-level manager	50	57	44	70	35

   a. Compute the ANOVA table. What conclusion can you make at the 5% significance level?
   b. Using a significance level of 5%, perform a multiple comparison procedure if appropriate.

11.76 **[DATA SET EX11-76]** Variable Description:

DallasGasIncrease: The amount in cents that gas prices in Dallas increased from spring to fall of 2004.

ElPasoGasIncrease: The amount in cents that gas prices in El Paso increased from spring to fall of 2004.

The price of oil jumped to more than $50 a barrel in the fall of 2004 for the first time. The price of gasoline rose also. In some cities, the price of gasoline rose more than in others. The price of gasoline in Dallas tends to be more variable than the price of gasoline in El Paso. Random samples of 50 gas stations in Dallas and 15 gas stations in El Paso were selected, and the increase in gasoline prices from spring to fall of 2004 were recorded.
   a. Test that the standard deviation of the increase in the price of gasoline in Dallas differs from that in El Paso. Use a 5% significance level.
   b. Test whether the increase in the price of gasoline in Dallas differs from the increase in the price of gasoline at gas pumps in El Paso. Use a 5% significance level.
   c. Did you assume equal variances for the populations in part b? Why?
   d. Would the conclusion change if you changed your answer to part c?

(Source:www.fueleconomy.gov/feg/gasprices/states/TX.shtml)

11.77   [DATA SET EX11-77] Variable Description:

Person: Number representing the person responding

BeforeDemo: Willingness to bank online before demonstration

AfterDemo: Willingness to bank online after demonstration

A financial analyst believes that more people would be willing to bank online if they viewed a demonstration showing that their transactions were secure and private. The analyst believes that an individual's willingness will increase by more than two points on a rating scale measuring an individual's willingness to bank online.

    a. Using the data before and after the demonstration, test the analyst's belief using a 5% significance level.

    b. Construct a 95% confidence interval on the difference of the ratings before and after the demonstration. Can this interval be used to answer part a?

11.78   [DATA SET EX11-78] Variable Description:

FishTaco: Rating for taco made with fish

ShrimpTaco: Rating for taco made with shrimp

CalamariTaco: Rating for taco made with calamari

American restaurants have become very creative in serving tacos. Sixty judges (20 for each of the three types of tacos) rated three taco dishes. Is there sufficient evidence that the mean ratings differ? Use a 5% significance level. Use Tukey's multiple comparison procedure at the 5% significance level to determine which mean ratings differ.

11.79   [DATA SET EX11-79] Variable Description:

HelpSysA: Time required to write a program using Help System A

HelpSysB: Time required to write a program using Help System B

HelpSysC: Time required to write a program using Help System C

A management information systems researcher wishes to determine if the time required to write a program differs according to the help system available to the programmer. Do the data support the conclusion that the mean time to write a program differs across the Help Systems A, B, and C? Use a 1% significance level. Perform a multiple comparison procedure, if appropriate, at the same significance level.

Computer Exercises Using the Databases

Exercise 1—Appendix F

Choose at random 10 observations from the database in which the family owns their home and 10 observations in which the family rents their home. (Refer to the variable OWNORENT.) Do the data support the conclusion that the home payment for homeowners is larger than the home payment for renters? Use a .05 significance level. What assumptions are necessary to ensure that the test procedure is valid? Do not assume equal population variances.

Exercise 2—Appendix F

Choose at random 10 observations from the database from a family of size 2 and 10 observations from a family of size 4. Do the data support the conclusion that the monthly utility expenditure (variable UTILITY) is larger for a family of size 4? Use a .05 significance level. Do not assume equal population variances.

Exercise 3—Appendix F

From the database, randomly select 10 observations each from the NE sector, the NW sector, and SE sector (variable LOCATION). Using a .05 significance level, is there sufficient evidence to conclude that the mean house payment or apartment/house rent (variable HPAYRENT) is significantly different for the three locations? Include a multiple comparisons procedure, if appropriate.

Exercise 4—Appendix G

From the database, choose a random sample of 12 companies with an A bond rating and another random sample of 12 companies with a C bond rating. Do the data support the conclusion that the net income of companies with a C bond rating is less than the net income of companies with an A rating? Use a .05 significance level. Do not assume equal population variances.

Exercise 5—Appendix G

From the database, choose a random sample of 15 companies with a B bond rating and another random sample of 15 companies with a C bond rating. Do the data support the conclusion that the variances of the current assets of the companies with B bond ratings and C bond ratings differ significantly at the .05 level?

Exercise 6—Appendix G

From the database, select at random 25 observations from each bond rating. (Refer to variable BONDRATE.) Determine the effect of bond rating on the assets (variable ASSETS). Use a .05 significance level. Include a multiple comparisons procedure, if appropriate.

Insights from Statistics in Action

Rollovers with Sport-Utility Vehicles: Assessing the Impact

The Statistics in Action introductory case discussed the increased attention being given to rollovers by SUVs. Insurance companies are asking themselves, Are the average repair costs for SUVs with less than a three-star rating larger than the repair costs for SUVs with a three-star rating for real-world collisions? This question can be answered by using statistical techniques designed to test for differences in the means of two populations.

1. If an automotive analyst wished to show that damage to SUVs with less than a three-star rating cost over $2,000 more than SUVs with a three-star rating, how would you set up the null and alternative hypotheses?

2. If a random sample of 25 SUVs with a three-star rating that were involved in collisions showed an average damage amount of $5,810 and a random sample of 25 SUVs with less than a three-star rating also involved in collisions showed an average damage amount of $8,000, would these data support the alternative hypothesis in question 1? Use a significance level of 5%. Assume that the data are from normally distributed populations with known population standard deviations of $1,450 for the SUVs with three-star ratings and $1,625 for the SUVs with less than three-star ratings.

3. Suppose that in question 2, the standard deviations of $1,450 and $1,625 were computed from the sample. Using a t test, would the results of the test change?

4. Construct a 95% confidence interval for the difference in the average damage amount for the two types of SUVs in question 2. Interpret this interval.

5. Suppose that an automotive analyst wished to compute a 95% confidence interval for the difference in the average damage amount of the two types of SUVs such that the margin of error is $500. Assume that the standard deviation of the amount of damage in real world collisions is $1,500 for each of the two types of SUVs. If the analyst wants to obtain equal sample sizes from the two types of SUVs, what sample sizes would be required?

(Sources: "GM Recalls All Saturn Vue SUVs for Suspension Failure," *Consumer Reports*, October 2004, vol. 69, p. 11. "Ford, GM Predict Better Rollover Ratings for '02 SUVs," *Ward's Auto World*, May 2001, vol. 37, issue 5, p. 28. "Sport Utility Vehicles—Safety Measures," *Consumer Reports*, September 2001, vol. 66, issue 9, p. 7.)

Appendix

Data Analysis with Excel, MINITAB, and SPSS

Excel

Comparing Two Independent Samples: *Z* Test for Differences in Two Means

To obtain a Z test for testing the difference in the means of two populations with independent samples, click **Tools ➤ Data Analysis ➤ z-test: Two Sample for Means** to obtain the **z-test** dialog box. If the Texgas and Quik-Chek data in Example 11.3 were in columns A and B with labels, the ranges **A1:A36** and **B1:B41** would be entered in the **Variable 1 Range** and **Variable 2 Range** edit boxes, respectively, and the **Labels** box would be checked. The **Hypothesized Mean Difference** would be entered as .06. Enter .0144 and .01 for the known variances in the **Variable 1 Variance** and **Variable 2 Variance** edit boxes. Enter .05 for the **Alpha** level and enter C1 (or some other location) for the **Output Range.**

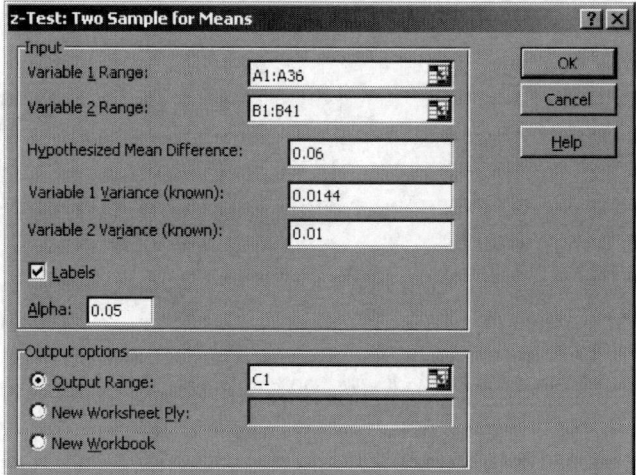

Comparing Two Independent Samples: *t* Test for Differences in Two Means

To obtain a *t* test for testing the difference in the means of two populations with independent samples, click **Tools ➤ Data Analysis ➤ t test: Two-Sample Assuming Unequal Variances ➤ OK** for the case in which the population variances are assumed to be unequal, or click **Tools ➤ Data Analysis ➤ t test: Two-Sample Assuming Equal Variances ➤ OK** for the case in which the population variances are assumed to be equal. These two dialog boxes look identical except for their titles. Enter data ranges in the first two edit boxes and check **Labels.** Enter 0 for the **Hypothesized Mean Difference,** .10 for the **Alpha** level, C1 for the **Output Range,** and click **OK.** To obtain the output in Figure 11.12, use this same procedure for the unequal variances case and use the dialog box for **t-Test: Two-Sample Assuming Equal Variances** to obtain the output in the figure assuming equal variances.

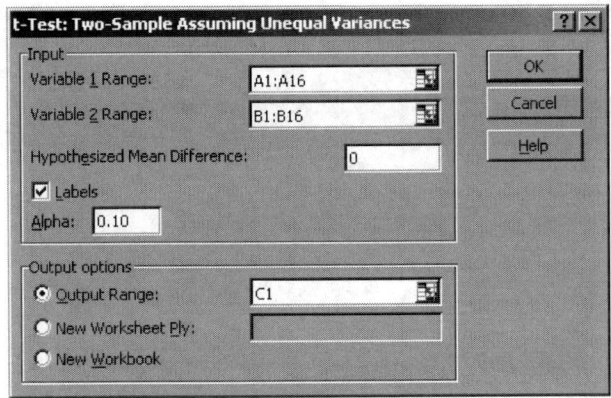

Comparing Two Paired Samples: *t* Test for Differences in Two Means

To obtain a *t* test for testing the difference in the means of two populations with paired samples, click **Tools ➤ Data Analysis ➤ Paired Two-Sample for Means ➤ OK.** The dialog box is identical to the **t-Test: Two-Sample Assuming Equal Variances** dialog box except that the title says **t-Test: Paired Two-Sample for Means.**

One-Factor ANOVA

To illustrate the one-factor ANOVA procedure with the battery brand data in Example 11.14, first put the data with labels in contiguous columns. Click on **KPK Data Analysis ➤ One-Factor ANOVA** to obtain the following dialog box. Enter the range of the data (including the labels) in the **Input Range** edit box and enter the **Alpha** level. Check **Tukey Test** for a multiple comparisons analysis and select either **5%** or **1%** significance levels. Click **OK** for the results of the ANOVA procedure and multiple comparison analysis.

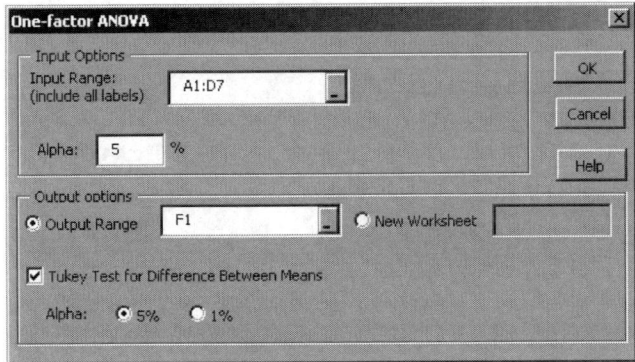

MINITAB

Comparing Two Independent Samples: *t* Test for Differences in Two Means

To obtain a *t* test for testing the difference in the means of two populations with independent samples, click **Stat ➤ Basic Statistics ➤ 2-Sample t.** For the after and before data in Example 11.6 in columns C1 and C2, respectively, click on **Samples in different columns** and enter the variables in **First** and **Second** edit boxes. Click the **Assume equal variances** check box only if equal variances are assumed. Click **Options** to enter the confidence level corresponding to the alpha level—in this example, .10. Enter 0 for the **Test difference** and **less than** for the **Alternative** edit box. Click **OK** on both of the displayed dialog boxes to obtain the output in Figure 11.13 assuming unequal variances.

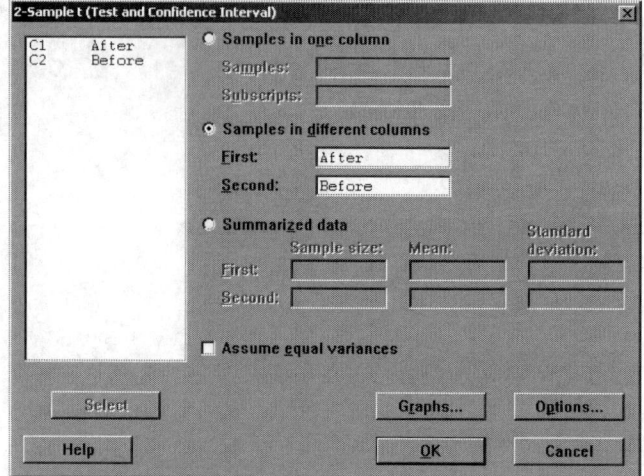

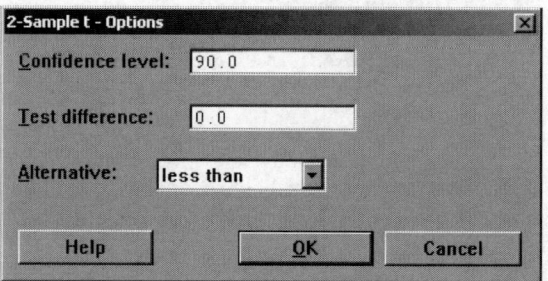

Comparing Two Paired Samples: *t* Test for Differences in Two Means

To obtain a *t* test for testing the difference in the means of two populations with paired samples, click **Stat ➤ Basic Statistics ➤ Paired t.** For the hardness data in Example 11.12, enter the variables in **First sample** and **Second sample** edit boxes, respectively. Click **Options** to obtain the same dialog box as for the **2-Sample t** dialog box. Enter the values for edit boxes in the **Options** dialog box and click **OK**. Click **OK** on the **Paired t** dialog box to obtain the output in Figure 11.23.

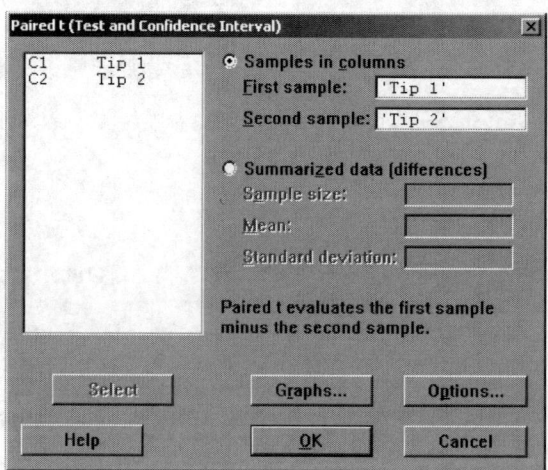

One-Factor ANOVA

The one-factor ANOVA procedure with the battery brand data in Example 11.14 will be used to illustrate the one-factor ANOVA procedure. With the data for each group in a separate column, click on **Stat ➤ ANOVA ➤ One-Way (unstacked)** to obtain the dialog box. Enter a confidence level for the confidence intervals for the mean of each population. Click on the **Comparisons** to select Tukey's multiple comparison analysis and enter the significance level. Click **OK** for the results of the ANOVA procedure and multiple comparisons procedure.

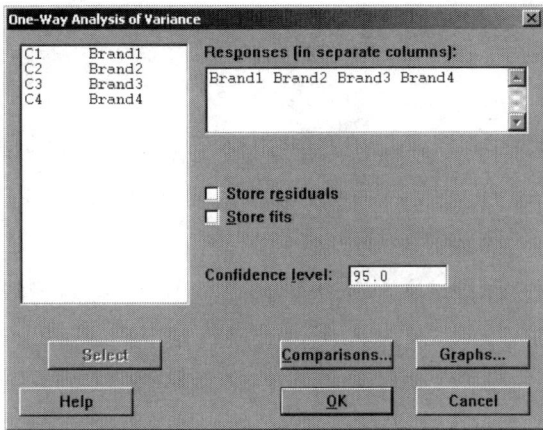

SPSS

Comparing Two Independent Samples: *t* Test for Differences in Two Means

To illustrate the inference procedure for testing the means of two populations with independent samples, consider the tire data in Example 11.5. The blowout times for the both brands are entered in the first column and the brand types (1 = Beltex, 2 = Roadmaster) are entered in the second column. By clicking on the **Variable View** tab, the columns can be named as shown. *Note:* The grouping variable (brand) must be created in order to use this SPSS procedure. If your data to be analyzed (e.g., time) are arranged in two columns (e.g., one for Beltex and one for Roadmaster), they must be stacked in one column and a grouping variable created, as illustrated.

In Example 11.5, the significance level was .10. Click **Analyze ➤ Compare Means ➤ Independent-Samples T Test** to obtain the **Independent-Samples T test** dialog box. Move the time variable from the left box to the **Test Variable(s)** box by clicking on the pointer. Move the brand variable to the **Grouping Variable** box by clicking on the second pointer. Click on **Define Groups,** and enter 1 in the **Group1** box and 2 in the **Group 2** box. Click on **Options** and enter 90 in the **Confidence Interval** box. By clicking on **OK,** the output in Figure 11.9 will appear. Note that *t* tests are displayed both for the case of equal variances and the case of unequal variances.

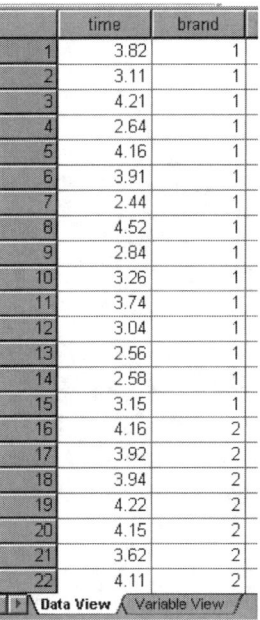

	time	brand
1	3.82	1
2	3.11	1
3	4.21	1
4	2.64	1
5	4.16	1
6	3.91	1
7	2.44	1
8	4.52	1
9	2.84	1
10	3.26	1
11	3.74	1
12	3.04	1
13	2.56	1
14	2.58	1
15	3.15	1
16	4.16	2
17	3.92	2
18	3.94	2
19	4.22	2
20	4.15	2
21	3.62	2
22	4.11	2

Data View / Variable View

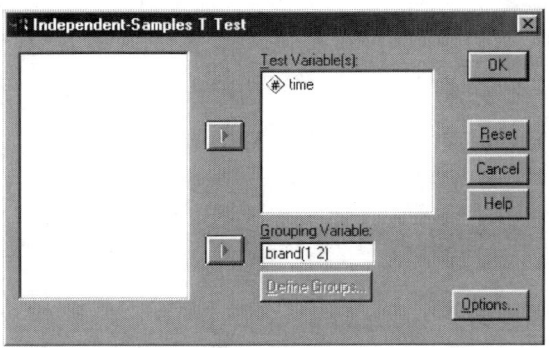

Comparing Two Paired Samples: *t* Test for Differences in Two Means

For the hardness data in Example 11.12, enter the data for tip #1 in the first column and for tip #2 in the second column. Click on the **Variable View** tab and name the variables. Click **Analyze ➤ Compare Means ➤ Paired-Samples T Test** to obtain the dialog box. Enter the variables tip1 and tip2 into the **Paired Variables** edit box. To obtain a 95% confidence interval on the differences in the population means, click on **Options** and enter 95 in the edit box. Click **OK** to obtain the results in Figure 11.24. For the right-tailed test in Example 11.12, the resulting *p*-value is half the value under **Sig. (2-tailed).**

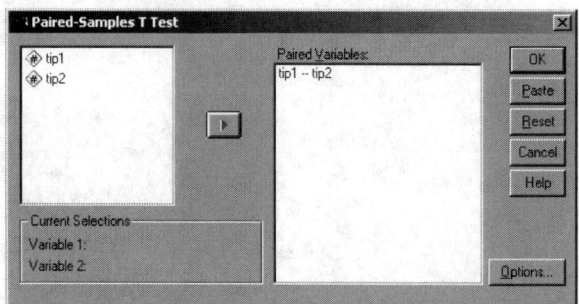

One-Factor ANOVA

Data for the one-factor ANOVA procedure must be entered the same way as for the independent samples *t* test. That is, there must be a grouping variable. Click on **Analyze ➤ Compare Means ➤ One-Way ANOVA** to obtain the displayed dialog box. For the battery brand data in Example 11.14, move the BatteryLife variable into the **Dependent List** box and move the grouping variable Brand into the **Factor** edit box. Click on **Post Hoc** to select **Tukey's** multiple comparison procedure and the significance level. Click **OK** for the results of the ANOVA procedure and multiple comparisons procedure.

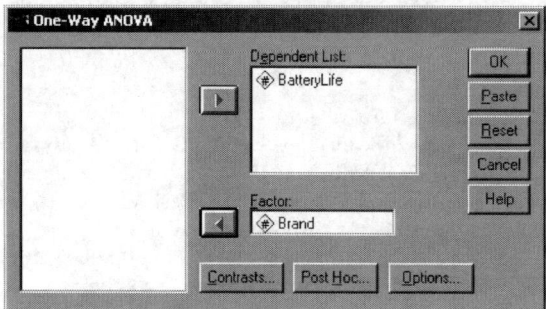

chapter

12

Analysis of Categorical Data X

Statistics in Action
Streaming Meemies: The Most Valuable Consumer Group on the Internet

Streamies, in marketing parlance, is an emerging group of highly interactive consumers who listen or view streaming media on the Internet. They engage in online radio listening and Webcast viewing. Many streamies use their office PCs to tune in to their favorite stations. Some use Web radio as a way to keep up with hometown news from a distance. In particular, sporting event broadcasts are very popular with streamies. Marketing analysts have noticed that the proportion of Internet users who are streamies is increasing.

Why are more Internet users dipping their toes in the stream? Radio is a great driver of online commerce. When consumers switch to broadband, their time spent online and with streaming media, especially video, surges. Internet radio is being compared to the arrival of FM in the 1960s. Many once-skeptical traditional radio stations are realizing that online access to one's favorite radio station is what the consumer wants.

Advertisers are thinking of creative ways to target the streamies. *Ad insertion*, a concept with its roots in the cable television industry, is being used to reach very active streamies. With ad insertion, a station can send its traditional broadcast over the Internet, with advertising that specifically targets a Web user. For example, streamies are targeted to buy music over the Internet immediately after hearing it. This makes Web radio a perfect

platform to generate CD sales. Advertisers estimate that approximately 44% of Internet users are streamies, and they want to target this consumer group because they are more highly educated and have higher incomes than nonstreamies.

Executives of various companies are making decisions on buying ads on Webcasts. They must assess if this tech-savvy, affluent group will purchase more of their product than the Internet surfers that are not streaming. Management must rely on surveys to determine the proportion of Internet users that will purchase their product online. When you have completed this chapter, you will be able to

- Construct a confidence interval for a single population proportion (e.g., the proportion of streamies who purchase a particular product).

- Construct a confidence interval for the difference in two population proportions (e.g., difference in the proportion of streamies and nonstreamies who purchase a particular product).

- Use hypothesis testing to determine if the proportion of a population differs from a hypothesized value.

- Use hypothesis testing to determine if the difference in two population proportions supports a claim that the population proportions differ.

12.1

ESTIMATION AND CONFIDENCE INTERVALS FOR A POPULATION PROPORTION

A test for a **population proportion** is a binomial situation. Using the definitions from Chapter 5, each member of your population is either a *success* or a *failure*. These words can be misleading; it is necessary only that each person (or object) in your population either have a certain attribute (a success) or not have it (a failure). So we define p to be the proportion of successes in the population—that is, the proportion that have a certain attribute.

Do not confuse the notation p = a population proportion with the previously used notation for a p-value. They do not mean the same thing. We hope that the context will make it clear which of the two p's is being described.

In Chapter 5 we assumed that p is known. For any binomial situation, perhaps p is known, or more likely, it was estimated in some way. This chapter examines how you can estimate p by using a sample from the population. Also, you can support (or fail to support) claims concerning the value of p. The final section in this chapter compares two samples from two separate populations.

Point Estimate for a Population Proportion

Auditors often deal with sample results concerned with a population proportion. This type of sampling is called *attribute sampling*, since the parameter of interest is the proportion of the population having a certain attribute. Suppose that Cassidy Electronics is under an audit investigation (perhaps, routine) to determine the proportion of payroll checks in the current fiscal year containing calculation errors. The proportion of interest is the proportion of payroll checks containing such an error. A random sample of 250 payroll checks turned up 14 containing calculation errors. What can you say about the proportion (p) of all payroll checks in this fiscal year that contain errors in calculation?

We view this as a binomial situation and define a "success" as a payroll check containing an error and a "failure" as a check containing no error. Consequently, p is the proportion of successes in the population (proportion of all payroll checks containing an error). Remember that p, like μ and σ previously, will remain *unknown* forever unless a complete 100% audit is conducted. To *estimate p*, we obtain a random sample and observe the proportion of successes in the sample. We use $\hat{p}$ (read as "p hat") to denote the estimate of p. Consequently, $\hat{p}$ (the proportion of successes in the sample) estimates p (the proportion of successes in the population). Here, $\hat{p}$ = proportion of payroll checks containing calculation errors = $14/250$ = .056.

In general,

> $\hat{p}$ = estimate of p
>
> = proportion of sample having a specified attribute
>
> = $\dfrac{x}{n}$

where n = sample size and x = the number of sample observations having this attribute.

The symbol ˆ is used to denote an *estimate*. Distinguish between $\hat{p}$ obtained from sample information and p, the population proportion being estimated by $\hat{p}$. This is the same type of difference that we previously recognized between a sample mean, $\bar{X}$ (often referred to as $\hat{\mu}$), and a population mean, μ.

The mean of the random variable $\hat{p}$ is the (unknown) value of p. In other words, the average value of $\hat{p}$ is the parameter it is estimating. Such an estimator is said to be **unbiased.** If we obtained random samples indefinitely, the resulting $\hat{p}$'s—on average—will equal p. This is a desirable property for a sample estimator to have. We have actually discussed two other unbiased estimators previously; $\bar{X}$ is an unbiased estimator of a population mean (μ) and s^2 is an unbiased estimator of a population variance (σ^2).

Confidence Intervals for a Population Proportion (Using a Large Sample)

When dealing with large samples, the Central Limit Theorem once again provides us with a reliable method of determining approximate confidence intervals for a population proportion. For each element in your sample, assign a value of 1 if this observation is a success (has the attribute) or 0 if this observation is a failure (does not have the attribute). Using the audit results at Cassidy Electronics to illustrate, for *each* payroll check in the sample we assign 1 if this check contains an error and 0 otherwise. So what is $\hat{p}$? We can write it as

$$\hat{p} = \frac{\overbrace{1+1+\cdots+1}^{14 \text{ times}}+\overbrace{0+0+\cdots+0}^{236 \text{ times}}}{250} = \frac{14}{250} = .056$$

In this sense, then, $\hat{p}$ is a *sample average:* it is an average of 0s and 1s. As a result, we can apply the Central Limit Theorem to $\hat{p}$ and conclude that $\hat{p}$ is (approximately) a normal random variable *for large samples*. This works reasonably well provided np and $n(1-p)$ are both greater than 5. So the distribution of $\hat{p}$ [large sample; $np > 5$ and $n(1-p) > 5$] can be summarized: $\hat{p}$ is (approximately) a normal random variable with

$$\text{mean} = p$$

$$\text{standard deviation (standard error)} = \sqrt{\frac{p(1-p)}{n}}$$

By standardizing this result, we have

$$Z = \frac{\hat{p}-p}{\sqrt{\dfrac{p(1-p)}{n}}}$$

12.2

which is approximately a standard normal random variable. This variable allows us to use Table A.4 to construct a confidence interval for p. This confidence interval is obtained in the identical manner used to construct previous confidence intervals with the standard normal distribution, namely,

(point estimate) $\pm Z_{\alpha/2} \cdot$ (standard deviation of point estimator)

12.3

The standard deviation of $\hat{p}$ (that is, the **standard error of $\hat{p}$**) in the denominator of equation 12.2 contains the unknown parameter, p. To estimate this standard error, it would seem logical to replace $p(1-p)/n$ with $\hat{p}(1-\hat{p})/n$. However, it can be shown that if we were to sample indefinitely, $\hat{p}(1-\hat{p})/n$ on the average *underestimates* $p(1-p)/n$. In fact, an unbiased estimator of $p(1-p)/n$ is obtained by using

$$\frac{\hat{p}(1-\hat{p})}{n-1}$$

and so the *estimated standard error* of $\hat{p}$ is

$$s_{\hat{p}} = \sqrt{\frac{\hat{p}(1-\hat{p})}{n-1}}$$

12.4

Using the estimated standard error, a $(1 - \alpha) \cdot 100\%$ confidence interval for p (large sample; $n\hat{p}$ and $n(1 - \hat{p})$ both > 5) is

$$\hat{p} - Z_{\alpha/2}\sqrt{\frac{\hat{p}(1-\hat{p})}{n-1}} \qquad \text{to} \qquad \hat{p} + Z_{\alpha/2}\sqrt{\frac{\hat{p}(1-\hat{p})}{n-1}}$$

12.5

EXAMPLE 12.1

Using the audit results (14 errors in 250 payroll checks), what is a 90% confidence interval for the proportion of all payroll checks in this fiscal year that contain calculation errors?

Solution Using Table A.4, $Z_{\alpha/2} = Z_{.05} = 1.645$. Also, $\hat{p} = 14/250 = .056$. So the 90% confidence interval for p is

$$.056 - 1.645\sqrt{\frac{(.056)(.944)}{249}} \quad \text{to} \quad .056 + 1.645\sqrt{\frac{(.056)(.944)}{249}}$$

$$= .056 - .024 \quad \text{to} \quad .056 + .024$$

$$= .032 \quad \text{to} \quad .080$$

Based on the sample results, we are 90% confident that the percentage of payroll checks containing calculation errors is between 3.2% and 8.0%.

EXAMPLE 12.2

Remember that in lot acceptance sampling, we either accept or reject a batch (lot) of components, parts, or assembled products based on tests using a random sample drawn from the lot.

Suppose we draw a sample of size 150 from a lot of calculators. We test each of the sampled calculators and find 13 defectives. Determine a 95% confidence interval for the proportion of defectives in the entire batch.

Solution Let p = proportion of defective calculators in the batch. Based on the sample of 150 calculators, we have

$$\hat{p} = \frac{13}{150} = .0867$$

Because $Z_{.025} = 1.96$, the 95% confidence interval for p is

$$.0867 - 1.96\sqrt{\frac{(.0867)(.9133)}{149}} \quad \text{to} \quad .0867 + 1.96\sqrt{\frac{(.0867)(.9133)}{149}}$$

$$= .0867 - .045 \quad \text{to} \quad .0867 + .045$$

$$= .042 \quad \text{to} \quad .132$$

Consequently, we are 95% confident that our estimate $\hat{p} = .0867$ is within .045 of the actual value of p. In other words, this sample estimates the actual percentage of defective calculators to within 4.5%, with 95% confidence.

Choosing the Sample Size (One Population)

Suppose that you want your point estimate, $\hat{p}$, to be within a certain amount of the actual proportion, p. In Example 12.2 the *margin of error, E,* was $E = .045$, that is, 4.5%. In general, larger samples will yield lower values of E. What if the buyer's specifications necessitate that we estimate the parameter p to within 2% with 95% confidence? Now,

$$E = 1.96\sqrt{\frac{\hat{p}(1-\hat{p})}{n-1}}$$

12.6

We have an earlier estimate of $p(\hat{p} = .0867)$ using the sample of size 150; this value can be used in equation 12.6. The purpose is to extend this sample in order to obtain this specific margin of error, E. The specified value of E is .02, so

$$E = .02 = 1.96\sqrt{\frac{(.0867)(.9133)}{n-1}}$$

Therefore,

$$\sqrt{\frac{(.0867)(.9133)}{n-1}} = \frac{.02}{1.96}$$

Squaring both sides and rearranging leads to

$$n = \frac{(1.96)^2(.0867)(.9133)}{(.02)^2} + 1 = 761.5$$

Rounding up *(always),* we come to the conclusion that a sample of size $n = 762$ calculators will be necessary to estimate p to within 2%.

By solving equation 12.6 for n, we arrive at the following equation, which provides the necessary sample size to estimate p with a specified margin of error, E, and confidence level $(1 - \alpha) \cdot 100\%$.

$$n = \frac{z_{\alpha/2}^2 \hat{p}(1-\hat{p})}{E^2} + 1$$

12.7

In this illustration, we used an estimate of p from a prior sample to determine the necessary sample size using equation 12.7. If the sample of size n based on this equation is our first and only sample, then *we have no estimate of p.* There is a conservative procedure we can follow here that will guarantee the accuracy (E) that we require. Look at the curve of different values of $\hat{p}(1 - \hat{p})$ in Figure 12.1. Consider these values:

$\hat{p}$	$\hat{p}(1 - \hat{p})$
.2	.16
.4	.24
.5	.25
.7	.21
.9	.09

Note that the largest value of $\hat{p}(1 - \hat{p})$ is .25.

FIGURE

12.1

Curve of values of $\hat{p}(1 - \hat{p})$.

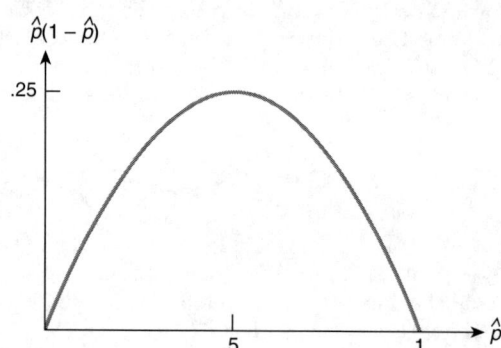

If we make $\hat{p}(1 - \hat{p})$ in equation 12.7 *as large as possible,* we will obtain a value of n that will result in a margin of error that is sure to be less than the specified value. So we can formulate this rule: If no prior estimate of p is available, a conservative procedure to determine the necessary sample size from equation 12.7 is to use $\hat{p} = .5$.

EXAMPLE

12.3

The insurance company underwriting the dental plan for Cassidy Electronics wishes to obtain a single sample that will estimate, to within 2% with 90% confidence, the proportion (p) of employees who would purchase the dental insurance. It has *no* prior knowledge of this proportion. Its intent is to obtain a large enough sample the first time so that the company can estimate the population proportion with this much accuracy. How large a sample is required?

Solution

We have no prior knowledge of p, so we use $\hat{p} = .5$ in equation 12.7 to obtain a sample size of

$$n = \frac{(1.645)^2(.5)(.5)}{(.02)^2} + 1 = 1692.3$$

To obtain an estimate of p with a maximum error of $E = .02$, we will need a sample size of $n = 1,693$ employees. With a sample of this size, we can safely say that the point estimate, $\hat{p}$, will be within 2% of the actual value of p, with 90% confidence (however, this is a very large sample).

X Exercises 12.1–12.15

Understanding the Mechanics

12.1 Construct 95% confidence intervals on the proportion for the following values of n and x, where n is the number of observations and x is the number of people having a specified attribute.

   a. $n = 15$ and $x = 7$
   b. $n = 20$ and $x = 11$
   c. $n = 30$ and $x = 15$
   d. $n = 50$ and $x = 25$

12.2 In each situation, determine whether the sample size is large enough to conclude that the Z statistic is appropriate to use in a confidence interval.

   a. $n = 12, \hat{p} = .6$
   b. $n = 20, \hat{p} = .45$
   c. $n = 100, \hat{p} = .98$
   d. $n = 200, \hat{p} = .98$
   e. $n = 500, \hat{p} = .98$
   f. $n = 15, \hat{p} = .50$

12.3 Find the necessary sample size so that a 95% confidence interval will have the following margin of error. Assume that a prior estimate of the proportion is .4.
- **a.** .10
- **b.** .05
- **c.** .03

12.4 From a sample of 90 people, 30% disagreed with a statement.
- **a.** Construct a 95% confidence interval for the proportion of people agreeing with the statement.
- **b.** Construct a 95% confidence interval for the proportion of people disagreeing with the statement.
- **c.** Compare the lengths of the confidence intervals in parts a and b.

12.5 From a sample of people, 25% favor an issue.
- **a.** Construct a 90% confidence interval for the proportion of individuals in favor of this issue assuming a sample size of 20.
- **b.** Repeat part a with a sample size of 100.
- **c.** Compare the lengths of the confidence intervals in parts a and b.

12.6 Using a historical estimate of p to be .20, what is the necessary sample size for a 90% confidence interval to have a margin of error of .10? .05? .02?

Applying the New Concepts

12.7 Distance learning has attracted the attention of many working people who do not want to lose time at work to go back to school. Approximately 70% of DSL (Digital Subscriber Line) subscribers who are full-time business employees say that they are interested in using their home computer DSL connection to take courses using the distance learning approach. Suppose that the dean of a college of business is interested in obtaining a 90% confidence interval for the proportion of local business professionals who would be interested in taking college courses using the distance learning approach.
- **a.** What sample size is required to obtain a margin of error of 4%?
- **b.** Suppose that the dean had no prior knowledge of the percentage of business professionals who would be interested in taking college courses using the distance learning approach. What would be the necessary sample size in part a?

(Source: "Can't Get Enough," American Demographics, June 2001, p. 27.)

12.8 Winthrop Boat Lines is exploring the possibility of offering a ferry service between the cities of Patna and Madura, provided there is sufficient demand to make it feasible. The firm randomly interviewed 210 commuters from the two cities, and 146 of them indicated they would patronize the ferry service instead of the current bus service. Estimate the population proportion p of commuters from the two cities who would prefer the ferry service. Construct a 95% confidence interval for p.

12.9 Employers maintain that drug testing in their company should be performed to lower injury rates and absenteeism costs. In 1987, only 22% of all U.S. companies performed any type of drug testing on their employees. Today, that figure is estimated to be above 60%.
- **a.** What sample size would be required to obtain a 99% confidence interval on the percentage of companies that require some type of drug testing for their employees? Assume that the margin of error is .021.
- **b.** Suppose that the confidence level is decreased to 90% in part a. How much lower is the required sample size?

(Source: "Accused Workers Challenge Drug-Test Results in Court," USA Today, July 16, 2001, p. 1B.)

12.10 About 2.8 million people are paid from the public purse at all levels of government across Canada. That was the average for the first quarter of 1998, according to data from Statistics Canada's Public Institutions Division show. The total includes all federal, provincial, and municipal workers, from mandarins to office cleaners, the military, crown corporation, and government business enterprise staffers, nurses, local police and fire personnel, teachers, public transit workers and on to drivers who chauffeur politicians around. It comes to about 18% of the labor force. Suppose that an economist wished to estimate the proportion of public employees in the Toronto area.
- **a.** What sample size is required to estimate the proportion of public employees in the Toronto area to within .01 with 99% confidence?
- **b.** How would the required sample size change if the estimate of the proportion in part a is to be within .005?

(Source: "2.8 Million Jobs Paid Out of Taxes," The Toronto Star, July 3, 1998, News section, p. 1.)

12.11 A manufacturer of microcomputers purchases electronic chips from a supplier that claims its chips are defective only 5% of the time. Determine the sample size that would be required to estimate the true proportion of defective chips if we wanted our estimate, $\hat{p}$, to be within 1.25% of the true proportion, with 99% confidence.

12.12 After George Bush and John Kerry's second debate, PollingReport.com revealed that Bush and Kerry were evenly split, each gathering the support of 45% of the voting population. Assuming that the confidence level is 95% and a margin of error of 4%, approximate the number of voters that were sampled in this poll.

Using the Computer

12.13 **[DATA SET EX12-13]** Variable Description:

Question: Which database is your favorite in relation to PHP development?

NumberOfResponses: Number of responses to each category

A leading Web infrastructure software company, named Zend Technologies Ltd, serves as a leader in sales for PHP (acronym for Hypertext Preprocessor). This data set is adapted from a survey obtained from their Web site (www.zend.com). Construct a 90% confidence interval for the proportion of responses selecting Oracle.

12.14 To gain insight into how the sample size changes as the margin of error decreases, first calculate the sample size, for a 95% confidence interval, using the following margin of error values: .02, .025, .03, .035, .04, .045, .05, .055, .06, .065, and .07. Assume no prior knowledge of the population proportion; that is, use .5 as the estimate of the proportion. Then graph the sample size versus the margin of error. The plot should look similar to the following graph. (In Excel, put the values of the margin of error in column A of a spreadsheet. Put the value of 1.96 in cell C1. In cell B1, type in "=(C1^2)*(0.5)*(1–0.5)/(A1^2)" and drag down to cell B11. These values are the required sample size.)

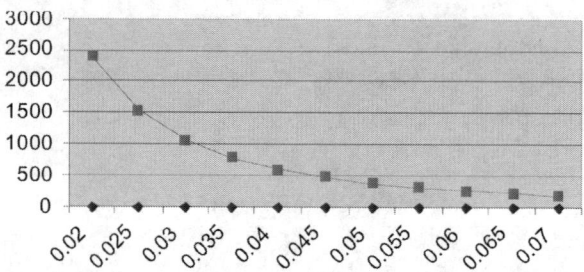

a. Do a what-if analysis and see how the graph changes when 90% and 99% confidence levels are used.

b. Do a what-if analysis by using a 95% confidence level and changing the estimate of the proportion to .3 and .1.

12.15 **[DATA SET EX12-15]** Variable Description:

Underfill_Overfill: A 1 is recorded if a machine overfills a container and a 0 is recorded if a container is underfilled

A production manager monitors a machine that tends to either slightly overfill or slightly underfill a container. The manager believes that the proportion of time that the machine overfills a bag is the same as the proportion of time that the machine underfills a bag. The manager collects 100 samples from this machine.

a. Compute a 90% confidence interval on the proportion of time that the machine overfills containers.

b. Change the confidence level to 99% in part a and compute the confidence interval. Contrast the margin of errors for the two confidence levels.

12.2

HYPOTHESIS TESTING FOR A POPULATION PROPORTION

How can you statistically reject a statement such as, at least 60% of all heavy smokers will contract a serious lung or heart ailment before age 65? Perhaps someone merely took a wild guess at the value of 60%, and it is your job to gather evidence that will either shoot down this claim or let it stand if there is insufficient evidence to conclude that this percentage actually is less than 60%. We set up hypotheses and test them much as we did before, only now we are concerned about a population proportion, p, rather than the mean of a particular population.

Hypothesis Testing Using a Large Sample

The standard five-step procedure is used for testing H_0 versus H_a when attempting to support a claim regarding a binomial parameter, p, using a large sample. The approximate standard normal random variable given by equation 12.2 is used as a test statistic for this situation.

The rejection region for this test is defined by determining the distribution of the test statistic, given that H_0 is true. This means that the unknown value of p in equation 12.2 is replaced by the value of p specified in H_0 (say, p_0). For a one-tailed test, the boundary value of p in H_0 is used. This procedure is summarized in the following box.

HYPOTHESIS TESTING (LARGE SAMPLE; np_0 AND $n(1 - p_0)$ BOTH GREATER THAN 5)

Two-Tailed Test

$$H_0: p = p_0$$

$$H_a: p \neq p_0$$

reject H_0 if $|Z| > Z_{\alpha/2}$

where

$$Z = \frac{\hat{p} - p_0}{\sqrt{\dfrac{p_0(1 - p_0)}{n}}}$$

One-Tailed Test

$H_0: p \leq p_0$	$H_0: p \geq p_0$
$H_a: p > p_0$	$H_a: p < p_0$
reject H_0 if $Z > Z_\alpha$	reject H_0 if $Z < -Z_\alpha$

Notice that the form of the test statistic is that used in many of the previous large sample test statistics, namely,

$$Z = \frac{(\text{point estimate}) - (\text{hypothesized value})}{(\text{standard deviation of point estimator})}$$

12.8

EXAMPLE 12.4

In Example 12.1, we estimated the proportion of payroll checks containing a calculation error. The audit plan also specifies that a more detailed inspection of the Cassidy Electronics payroll checks be conducted if there is evidence to indicate that this proportion* exceeds .03. Using a significance level of 10%, can you conclude that the percentage of checks in error exceeds 3%?

Solution

Step 1.   Your hypotheses should be

$$H_0: p \leq .03$$

$$H_a: p > .03$$

Step 2.   Since $np_0 = (250)(.03) = 7.5$ and $n(1 - p_0) = (250)(.97) = 242.5$ are both greater than 5, the large-sample test statistic can be used; namely,

$$Z = \frac{\hat{p} - p_0}{\sqrt{\dfrac{p_0(1 - p_0)}{n}}} = \frac{\hat{p} - .03}{\sqrt{\dfrac{(.03)(.97)}{250}}}$$

*Auditing textbooks often refer to this value as the *maximum tolerable error rate* (MTER).

FIGURE

12.2

Z curve showing
p-value for
Example 12.4.

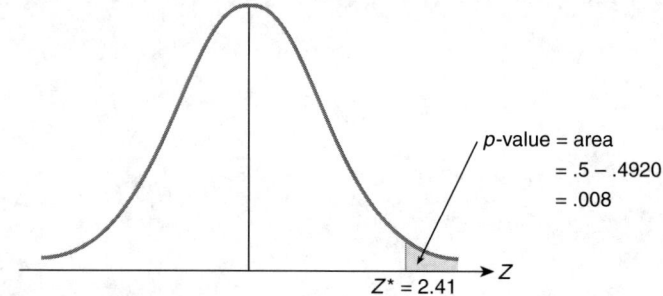

p-value = area
= .5 − .4920
= .008

$Z^* = 2.41$

Z

Step 3. The testing procedure, using $\alpha = .10$, will be to

$$\text{reject } H_0 \text{ if } Z > Z_{.10} = 1.28$$

Step 4. Using the sample data, $\hat{p} = 14/250 = .056$, so

$$Z^* = \frac{.056 - .03}{\sqrt{\dfrac{(.03)(.97)}{250}}} = \frac{.026}{.0108} = 2.41$$

Because $2.41 > 1.28$, we reject H_0 in favor of H_a.

Step 5. This sample indicates that the percentage of payroll checks in error *does* exceed 3%. In other words, at a significance level of $\alpha = .10$, the sample percentage containing an error (5.6%) *is* significantly greater than 3%, and, as a result, the alternative hypothesis is supported.

In Example 12.4, the computed test statistic was $Z^* = 2.41$. Figure 12.2 shows the Z curve and the calculated *p*-value, which is .008. Using the classical approach, because .008 is less than $\alpha = .10$, we reject H_0. If we choose to base our conclusion strictly on the *p*-value (without choosing a significance level, α), this value would be classified as "small"—it is less than .01. This means that using the classical approach, we would reject H_0 for both $\alpha = .10$ and $\alpha = .01$.

EXAMPLE

12.5

In Example 12.2, we estimated the proportion of calculators that were defective in a batch (lot). The company has determined that a good target for this defective percentage is 4%. The sample of 150 had 13 defectives. Can we conclude that the actual proportion of defective calculators is different from 4%? Use $\alpha = .05$.

Solution   **Step 1.** We wish to see if p is *different* from 4%, so we should use a two-tailed test with hypotheses

$$H_0: p = .04$$

$$H_a: p \neq .04$$

Step 2. Here $np_0 = (150)(.04) = 6$ and $n(1 - p_0) = (150)(.96) = 144$. Both are greater than 5, so the appropriate test statistic is

$$Z = (\hat{p} - p_0)/\sqrt{p_0(1 - p_0)/n} = (\hat{p} - .04)/\sqrt{(.04)(.96)/150}$$

FIGURE

12.3

Z curve showing
p-value (twice the
shaded area) for
Example 12.5.

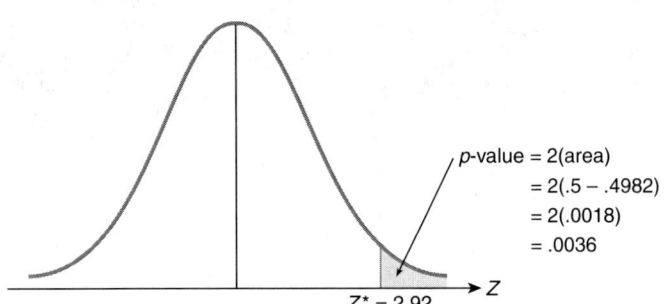

$p\text{-value} = 2(\text{area})$

$= 2(.5 - .4982)$

$= 2(.0018)$

$= .0036$

$Z^* = 2.92$

Z

FIGURE

12.4

(a) Excel solution
to Example 12.5
using **KPK Data
Analysis ➤
Inference on
Proportions ➤ One
Population
Proportion;** and
(b) MINITAB
solution for
Example 12.5
using **Stat ➤ Basic
Statistics ➤
1 Proportion.**

	A	B
1	Z Test for One Proportion	
2		
3	Sample Proportion	0.086667
4	Number of Observations	150
5	Ho:p = 0.04	Ha:p ≠ 0.04
6	Z*	2.9167
7	2 * P[Z ≥ |Z*|] two tail	0.00354
8	| Z Critical | , α = 0.05	1.959961
9		

Sheet1 ╱ Sheet2 ╱ Sheet3 ╱

(a)

Test and CI for One Proportion

Test of p = 0.04 vs p not = 0.04

Sample	X	N	Sample p	95% CI	Z-Value	P-Value
1	13	150	0.086667	(0.041643, 0.131691)	2.92	0.004

(b)

Step 3. With $\alpha = .05$, the test procedure of H_0 versus H_a will be to

$$\text{reject } H_0 \text{ if } |Z| > 1.96$$

Step 4. Using $\hat{p} = 13/150 = .0867$,

$$Z^* = \frac{.0867 - .04}{\sqrt{\dfrac{(.04)(.96)}{150}}} = \frac{.0467}{.016} = 2.92$$

Because $2.92 > 1.96$, we reject H_0.

Step 5. The company is *not* meeting its target percentage of defectives. As a reminder, because $\alpha = .05$, 5% of the time this particular test will reject H_0 when in fact it is true.

In Example 12.5, $Z^* = 2.92$. What is the *p*-value? This is a two-tailed test, so we need to *double* the right-tail area, as illustrated in Figure 12.3. So $p = 2 \cdot .0018 = .0036$. Thus, using either the classical procedure (comparing the *p*-value to $\alpha = .05$) or basing our decision strictly on the *p*-value, we reject H_0 because of this extremely small *p*-value.

An Excel solution to Example 12.5 using the macro from KPK Data Analysis is shown in Figure 12.4(a). To obtain this solution, click on **KPK Data Analysis ➤ Inference** on Proportions ➤ One Population Proportion. The MINITAB solution in Figure 12.4(b) is obtained by clicking on **Stat** ➤ **Basic Statistics** ➤ **1 Proportion.** Click on the **Summarized data** box and enter 150 (number of trials) and 13 (number of events). Click on **Options,** enter .04 in the **Test proportion** box, and click on the box indicating that the normal approximation should be used. The outputs in Figure 12.4 agree with the previous solution. The Excel p-value (.00354) is slightly more accurate than the one illustrated in Figure 12.3. Based on this small p-value, we conclude that the percentage of defective calculators is not 4%. *Note:* SPSS does not have a Z-test for a single-population proportion.

X Exercises 12.16–12.30

Understanding the Mechanics

12.16 Test that p differs from .75 using a sample size of 40 where $\hat{p} = .9$. Use a 10% significance level.

12.17 A random sample of 25 observations yielded a value of $\hat{p} = .60$. Test each of the following hypotheses and find the p-values.

    a. H_0: $p = .71$ versus H_a: $p \neq .71$
    b. H_0: $p \geq .71$ versus H_a: $p < .71$
    c. H_0: $p \leq .51$ versus H_a: $p > .51$

12.18 Is there sufficient evidence to indicate that the proportion of a population is less than .50 at a 1% significance level if $n = 400$ and $\hat{p} = .43$?

12.19 Is there sufficient evidence to indicate that the proportion of a population is more than .40 at a 10% significance level if $n = 200$ and $\hat{p} = .45$?

12.20 A random sample of size 20 revealed 12 respondents in favor of a proposal. Test the hypothesis that the proportion in favor differs from .52 using a 5% significance level.

12.21 In order for $np > 5$ and $n(1 - p) > 5$, how large must n be if $p = .03$?

12.22 Forty out of 250 randomly selected items need to be reworked. Test the hypothesis that less than 20% of the items in the population need to be reworked using a 10% significance level.

12.23 Test the belief that more than half of the respondents have a particular attribute. From a random sample, 86 out of 150 have this attribute. Use a 10% significance level. Would the conclusion change if only 84 out of 150 have this attribute?

Applying the New Concepts

12.24 More than 80% of retired Americans say that spending time with family and friends is their primary activity. However, approximately 50% say that they do extensive traveling. Suppose a researcher studying the habits of retired Americans believes that the percentage of retired Americans under the age of 80 who do extensive traveling is greater than 50%. The researcher finds that 40 out of 75 randomly sampled retired Americans under the age of 80 do extensive traveling. Test the researcher's belief using a significance level of 5%.

(Source: "Great Expectations for Aging," *USA Today*, August 7, 2001, p. 1B.)

12.25 A consumer group would like to determine the proportion of dealers who charge more than $450 monthly for a 36-month lease on a BMW 323i. The consumer group found a 90% confidence interval for the proportion of dealers in the midwest United States to be 24% to 38%. Suppose that the consumer group wished to find a 90% confidence interval to estimate the proportion to within 4% with 90% confidence. What sample size is necessary?

(Source: "Drive Buys," *The Wall Street Journal*, October 25, 1998, p. W7.)

12.26 In 2001, when gasoline prices were near the two-dollar mark in many parts of the United States, a nationwide survey revealed that only 28% of the population traveled less because of the high prices. Suppose that a survey in southern California was taken at the end of 2001, when gasoline prices returned to more normal levels. The survey revealed that 50 of 200 respondents were traveling less because of gasoline prices. Do these data support the hypothesis that less than 28% of the population traveled less because of gasoline prices? Use a 10% significance level.

(Source: "Few Drivers Yielding to Gas Costs," *USA Today*, May 24, 2001, p. 1B.)

12.27 Today, there are credit cards designed specifically for high school students: the Cobaltcard from American Express, Capital One's High School Student Card, and the Visa Buxx card. According to a *USA Today* survey, 22% of high-school seniors have credit cards. Suppose that a survey was taken in 2002 in Houston to determine if the percentage of high school seniors with credit cards differs from 22%. A random sample of 150 high school students in the Houston area found 34 students with credit cards. Is there sufficient evidence to say that the percentage of high school seniors in Houston differs from 22%? Base your conclusion on the p-value.

(Source: "Teen Credit Cards Actually Teach Responsibility," USA Today, July 31, 2001, p. 15A.)

12.28 The designers of cell phones are curious as to what percent of their customers use both thumbs when text messaging. The designers believe that the proportion is 40%. Suppose that a random sample of 300 customers revealed that 135 customers used both thumbs when text messaging.

    a. Find a 95% confidence interval for estimating the proportion of customers using both thumbs for text messaging.

    b. Test at the .05 significance level that the percentage of customers using both thumbs when text messaging differs from 40%. How can the confidence interval in part a. be used to test this?

(Source: "All Thumbs, Without the Stigma," The New York Times, August 12, 2004, p. G1.)

Using the Computer

12.29 **[DATA SET EX12-29]** Variable Description:

WatchHomShp: A Yes indicates that a family watches a televised home shopping program, and a No indicates that they do not.

A marketing agency wishes to determine if more than 50% of the families in the Chicago metropolitan area have ever watched a televised home shopping program. A random sample of 100 adults was selected through telephone interviews. A Yes reply indicated that the family has watched the program, and a No reply indicated that the family has never watched the program. These are the values for the variable WatchHomShp. Test to determine whether there is sufficient evidence to conclude that the true proportion is greater than 50%. Use the p-value to support your conclusion.

12.30 **[DATA SET EX12-30]** Variable Description:

ReadReport: A 1 indicates that a shareholder reads the annual report, and a 0 indicates that the shareholder does not.

The vice president of a public utilities company believes that less than 60% of the shareholders of the company read the annual report. From a random sample of 200 shareholders, a 1 or a 0 is listed for the variable ReadReport. Test the vice president's belief. Use a .01 significance level.

12.3

COMPARING TWO POPULATION PROPORTIONS (LARGE, INDEPENDENT SAMPLES)

Consider the following questions:

    Is the divorce rate higher in California than it is in New York?

    Is there a higher rate of lung cancer among cigarette smokers than there is among nonsmokers?

    Is there any difference in the proportion of engines rebuilt by Engine Masters that fail during the one-year warranty period and the proportion of engines rebuilt by Freed Motors that fail during the warranty period?

These questions are concerned with proportions from two populations. Our method of estimating these proportions will be exactly as it was for one population. We simply have two of everything—two populations, two samples, two estimates, and so on. In this section, it is assumed that the two samples are obtained independently.

    For example, consider the question concerning the proportion of engines that fail during the warranty period. Population 1 is all engines rebuilt by Engine Masters, with p_1 = proportion of all engines rebuilt by Engine Masters that fail during the warranty period, n_1 = sample size for the Engine Masters engines, and x_1 = number of engines in the Engine Masters sample that fail. Population 2 is all engines rebuilt by Freed Motors, where p_2, n_2, and x_2 are the corresponding values for this population.

Define a "success" to be that an engine fails during the warranty period. (Keep in mind that "success" is merely a label for the trait you are interested in. It need not be a desirable trait.) Our unbiased point estimator of p_1 will be as before:

$$\hat{p}_1 = \frac{\text{observed number of successes in the sample}}{\text{sample size}}$$

$$= \frac{\begin{array}{c}\text{number of engines in the Engine Masters sample}\\\text{that fail during the warranty period}\end{array}}{n_1}$$

That is, the unbiased point estimator of p_1 is

$$\hat{p}_1 = \frac{x_1}{n_1}$$

12.9

Similarly, the unbiased point estimator of p_2, obtained from the second sample, is

$$\hat{p}_2 = \frac{x_2}{n_2}$$

12.10

For the two-population case, the parameter of interest will be the *difference* between the two population proportions, $p_1 - p_2$. The next section discusses a method of estimating $p_1 - p_2$ by using a point estimate along with a corresponding confidence interval.

Confidence Interval for $p_1 - p_2$ (Large, Independent Samples)

The logical estimator of $p_1 - p_2$ is $\hat{p}_1 - \hat{p}_2$, the difference between the sample estimators. What kind of random variable is $\hat{p}_1 - \hat{p}_2$? We are dealing with large, independent samples (where $n_1\hat{p}_1$, $n_1(1 - \hat{p}_1)$, $n_2\hat{p}_2$, and $n_2(1 - \hat{p}_2)$ are each larger than 5), so it follows that $\hat{p}_1 - \hat{p}_2$ is (approximately) a normal random variable with

$$\text{mean} = p_1 - p_2$$

and

$$\text{standard deviation} = \sqrt{\frac{p_1(1-p_1)}{n_1} + \frac{p_2(1-p_2)}{n_2}}$$

In Section 12.1, we observed that $\hat{p}_1$ is a sample mean, where the sample consists of observations that are either a 1 (a particular event occurred) or a 0 (this event did not occur). Because the two samples are obtained independently, the results extend to this situation, leading to the approximate normal distribution for $\hat{p}_1 - \hat{p}_2$. Since $\hat{p}_1$ and $\hat{p}_2$ are unbiased estimators of p_1 and p_2, respectively, the mean of the estimator $\hat{p}_1 - \hat{p}_2$ is $p_1 - p_2$; that is, $\hat{p}_1 - \hat{p}_2$ is an unbiased estimator of $p_1 - p_2$. Notice that the variance of $\hat{p}_1 - \hat{p}_2$ is obtained by *adding* the variance of $\hat{p}_1$, or $p_1(1-p_1)/n_1$, to the variance of $\hat{p}_2$, or $p_2(1-p_2)/n_2$.

To derive a confidence interval for $p_1 - p_2$, we must estimate the unknown population parameters, p_1 and p_2, using the corresponding sample estimates, $\hat{p}_1$ and $\hat{p}_2$. The same argument used to derive the one-population estimated standard error in equation 12.4 can be used here to derive the estimated standard deviation of $\hat{p}_1 - \hat{p}_2$ (that is, the **standard error of $\hat{p}_1 - \hat{p}_2$**). This estimated standard error is

$$s_{\hat{p}_1 - \hat{p}_2} = \sqrt{\frac{\hat{p}_1(1-\hat{p}_1)}{n_1 - 1} + \frac{\hat{p}_2(1-\hat{p}_2)}{n_2 - 1}}$$

12.11

The resulting confidence interval for $p_1 - p_2$ using large samples [$n_1 \hat{p}_1$, $n_1(1-\hat{p}_1)$, $n_2 \hat{p}_2$, and $n_2(1-\hat{p}_2)$ each greater than 5] is

$$(\hat{p}_1 - \hat{p}_2) - Z_{\alpha/2}\sqrt{\frac{\hat{p}_1(1-\hat{p}_1)}{n_1 - 1} + \frac{\hat{p}_2(1-\hat{p}_2)}{n_2 - 1}}$$

$$\text{to} \quad (\hat{p}_1 - \hat{p}_2) + Z_{\alpha/2}\sqrt{\frac{\hat{p}_1(1-\hat{p}_1)}{n_1 - 1} + \frac{\hat{p}_2(1-\hat{p}_2)}{n_2 - 1}}$$

12.12

where $\hat{p}_1 = x_1/n_1$ and $\hat{p}_2 = x_2/n_2$ are the sample proportions. Observe that the construction of this confidence interval was the "usual" procedure employing Table A.4 and described in equation 12.3.

EXAMPLE 12.6

Of a random sample of 100 rebuilt engines from Engine Masters (population 1), 28 failed within the 12-month warranty period. A second sample, obtained independent of the first, consisted of 150 engines rebuilt by Freed Motors (population 2), 48 of which failed during the 12-month warranty period. Both sets of engines were subjected to the same weather conditions, engine stress, and maintenance program. Construct a 90% confidence interval for $p_1 - p_2$.

Solution

We have $\hat{p}_1 = 28/100 = .28$ and $\hat{p}_2 = 48/150 = .32$. Also, $Z_{\alpha/2} = Z_{.05} = 1.645$, using Table A.4. The resulting confidence interval for $p_1 - p_2$ is

$$(.28 - .32) - 1.645\sqrt{\frac{(.28)(.72)}{99} + \frac{(.32)(.68)}{149}}$$

$$\text{to} \quad (.28 - .32) + 1.645\sqrt{\frac{(.28)(.72)}{99} + \frac{(.32)(.68)}{149}}$$

$$= -.04 - .097 \quad \text{to} \quad -.04 + .097$$

$$= -.137 \quad \text{to} \quad .057$$

This confidence interval leaves us unable to conclude that either manufacturer produces a better engine. We are 90% confident that the percentage of Engine Masters engines failing during the warranty period is between 13.7% *lower* and 5.7% *higher* than for the Freed Motors engines.

EXAMPLE 12.7

The Redican Corporation manufactures one-quart metal cans to hold canned vegetable juice. A can is *nonconforming* if it is out of round or has a leak in the side weld. The cans are produced during two shifts, shift 1 (the day shift) and shift 2 (the night shift). The quality supervisor suspects that the proportion of nonconforming cans produced during the day shift (p_1) is *lower* than that for the night shift (p_2), since the day shift has better qualified workers. To investigate this, random samples of 500 cans were obtained from each shift. The results were as follows. Of the $n_1 = 500$ cans from the day shift, $x_1 = 70$ were nonconforming, and of the $n_2 = 500$ cans from the night shift, $x_2 = 110$ were nonconforming. Determine a 95% confidence interval for $p_1 - p_2$.

Solution   The proportion estimates are

$$\hat{p}_1 = \frac{70}{500} = .14 \qquad \hat{p}_2 = \frac{110}{500} = .22$$

The 95% confidence interval for $p_1 - p_2$ is

$$(.14 - .22) - 1.96\sqrt{\frac{(.14)(.86)}{499} + \frac{(.22)(.78)}{499}}$$

$$\text{to} \quad (.14 - .22) + 1.96\sqrt{\frac{(.14)(.86)}{499} + \frac{(.22)(.78)}{499}}$$

$$= -.08 - .047 \quad \text{to} \quad -.08 + .047$$

$$= -.127 \quad \text{to} \quad -.033$$

So we are 95% confident that (1) our estimate of the difference in proportions (shift 1 minus shift 2), namely, $\hat{p}_1 - \hat{p}_2 = -.08$, is within 4.7% of the actual value, and (2) the proportion of nonconforming cans during shift 1 is between 3.3% and 12.7% *lower* than for shift 2.

Hypothesis Testing for p_1 and p_2 (Large, Independent Samples)

Suppose that a recent report stated that, based on a sample of 500 people, 35% of all cigarette smokers had at some time in their lives developed a particular fatal disease. On the other hand, 25% of the nonsmokers in the sample acquired the disease. Can we conclude from this sample that, because $\hat{p}_1 = .35 > \hat{p}_2 = .25$, the proportion ($p_1$) of all smokers who will acquire the disease exceeds the proportion (p_2) for nonsmokers? In other words, is $\hat{p}_1$ *significantly* larger than $\hat{p}_2$? After all, even if $p_1 = p_2$, there is a 50–50 chance that $\hat{p}_1$ will be larger than $\hat{p}_2$, because for large samples, the distribution of $\hat{p}_1 - \hat{p}_2$ is approximately a bell-shaped (normal) curve centered at $p_1 - p_2$, which, if $p_1 = p_2$, would be zero.

Are the results of the sample significant, or are they due simply to the sampling error that is always present when estimating from a sample? Your alternative hypothesis can be that two proportions are *different* (a two-tailed test) or that one *exceeds* the other (a one-tailed test). As before, we will assume that the two random samples are obtained *independently*. The possible hypotheses are these:

FOR A TWO-TAILED TEST

$$H_0: p_1 = p_2$$
$$H_a: p_1 \neq p_2$$

FOR A ONE-TAILED TEST

$$H_0: p_1 \leq p_2 \qquad H_0: p_1 \geq p_2$$

or

$$H_a: p_1 > p_2 \qquad H_a: p_1 < p_2$$

One possible test statistic to use here would be the standard normal *(Z)* statistic that was used to derive a confidence interval for $p_1 - p_2$, namely,

$$Z = \frac{\hat{p}_1 - \hat{p}_2}{\sqrt{\dfrac{\hat{p}_1(1-\hat{p}_1)}{n_1 - 1} + \dfrac{\hat{p}_2(1-\hat{p}_2)}{n_2 - 1}}}$$

12.13

In previous tests of hypothesis, we always examined the distribution of the test statistic when H_0 was *true*. For a one-tailed test, we assumed the boundary condition of H_0, which in this case is $p_1 = p_2$. Because of this, whenever we obtained a value of the test statistic in one of the tails, our decision was to reject H_0 because this value would be very unusual if H_0 were true. This reasoning was used for test statistics that followed a Z, t, or F distribution.

We use the same approach here. If $p_1 = p_2 = p$ (for example), we can improve the test statistic in equation 12.13. For this situation, p is the proportion of successes in the combined population. Our best estimate of p is the proportion of successes in the *combined sample.* So define

$$\bar{p} = \frac{x_1 + x_2}{n_1 + n_2}$$

Thus, assuming $p_1 = p_2$, $\hat{p}_1 - \hat{p}_2$ is approximately a normal random variable with

$$\text{mean} = p_1 - p_2 = 0$$

and

$$\begin{aligned}
\text{standard deviation} &= \sqrt{\frac{p_1(1-p_1)}{n_1} + \frac{p_2(1-p_2)}{n_2}} \\
&\approx \sqrt{\frac{\bar{p}(1-\bar{p})}{n_1} + \frac{\bar{p}(1-\bar{p})}{n_2}}
\end{aligned}$$

The resulting test statistic for p_1 versus p_2 (large, independent samples; $n_1\hat{p}_1$, $n_1(1 - \hat{p}_1)$, $n_2\hat{p}_2$ and $n_2(1 - \hat{p}_2)$ are each greater than 5) is

$$Z = \frac{\hat{p}_1 - \hat{p}_2}{\sqrt{\dfrac{\bar{p}(1-\bar{p})}{n_1} + \dfrac{\bar{p}(1-\bar{p})}{n_2}}}$$

12.14

where

$$\hat{p}_1 = \frac{x_1}{n_1} \qquad \hat{p}_2 = \frac{x_2}{n_2} \qquad \bar{p} = \frac{x_1 + x_2}{n_1 + n_2}$$

Observe that the form of this test statistic is the same as for the single-population case described in equation 12.8. The test procedure is the standard routine when using the Z distribution.*

---

*As a final word here, always use the Z statistic in equation 12.14 to test two proportions. Equation 12.13 is included for discussion purposes only in this section and should never be used as the test statistic.

FOR A TWO-TAILED TEST

$$H_0: p_1 = p_2$$

$$H_a: p_1 \neq p_2$$

reject H_0 if $|Z| > Z_{\alpha/2}$

where Z is defined in equation 12.14.

FOR A ONE-TAILED TEST

$$H_0: p_1 \leq p_2 \qquad\qquad H_0: p_1 \geq p_2$$

$$H_a: p_1 > p_2 \quad \text{or} \quad H_a: p_1 < p_2$$

reject H_0 if $Z > Z_{\alpha}$ \qquad reject H_0 if $Z < -Z_{\alpha}$

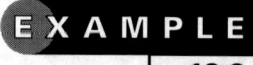

12.8

Using the engine failure data from Example 12.6, determine whether there is any difference between the proportion of Engine Masters engines (population 1) and the proportion of Freed Motors engines (population 2) that failed in the one-year warranty period. Let $\alpha = .10$.

Solution

The five-step procedure is the correct one. The confidence interval derived in Example 12.6 would produce the same result as the five-step procedure *if the test statistic were the one defined in equation 12.13. The correct procedure here is to use the Z-statistic in equation 12.14 as your test statistic.*

Step 1. Since we are looking for a difference between p_1 and p_2, define

$$H_0: p_1 = p_2$$

$$H_a: p_1 \neq p_2$$

Step 2. The test statistic is

$$Z = \frac{\hat{p}_1 - \hat{p}_2}{\sqrt{\dfrac{\bar{p}(1-\bar{p})}{n_1} + \dfrac{\bar{p}(1-\bar{p})}{n_2}}}$$

Step 3. Using $\alpha = .10$, then $Z_{\alpha/2} = Z_{.05} = 1.645$. The test procedure will be to

reject H_0 if $|Z| > 1.645$

Step 4. Since $n_1 = 100$, $x_1 = 28$, and $n_2 = 150$, $x_2 = 48$, then

$$\bar{p} = \frac{x_1 + x_2}{n_1 + n_2} = \frac{76}{250} = .304$$

Therefore, our estimate of the proportion of engines failing within the warranty period for the combined population (if $p_1 = p_2$) is $\bar{p} = .304$ (30.4%). Also, $\hat{p}_1 = 28/100 = .28$ and $\hat{p}_2 = 48/150 = .32$. The value of the test statistic is

FIGURE

12.5

Z curve showing
p-value (twice the
shaded area) for
Example 12.8.

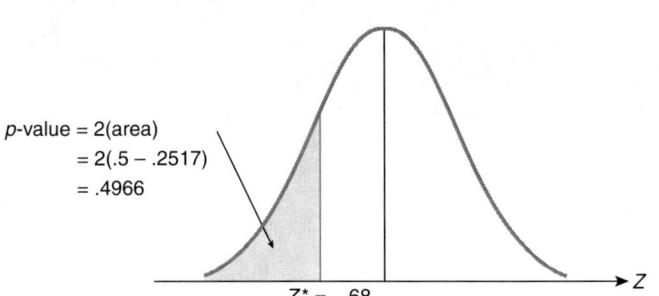

p-value = 2(area)
= 2(.5 − .2517)
= .4966

$Z^* = -.68$

$$Z^* = \frac{.28 - .32}{\sqrt{\dfrac{(.304)(.696)}{100} + \dfrac{(.304)(.696)}{150}}} = \frac{-.04}{.059} = -.68$$

Because $|Z^*| = .68 < 1.645$, we fail to reject H_0.

Step 5. There is *insufficient evidence* to conclude that a difference exists between the two brands of engines as far as engine durability during the warranty period is concerned.

The Z curve and calculated p-value for Example 12.8 are shown in Figure 12.5. The p-value is twice the shaded area (this was a two-tailed test) and is .4966, which is extremely large. Using the classical approach, because $.4966 > \alpha = .10$, we fail to reject H_0—there is insufficient evidence to indicate a difference in engine durability. As a reminder, this reasoning *always* leads to the same conclusion as the five-step procedure. Because .4966 exceeds *any* reasonable value of α, we fail to reject H_0 quite strongly for this application.

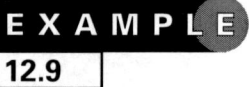

In Example 12.7, we examined the proportions of nonconforming metal cans produced by Redican during the day shift (p_1) and the night shift (p_2). Based on these data, can you conclude that the proportion of nonconforming cans during the day shift is lower than during the night shift? Use the p-value and a significance level of .05.

Solution

Step 1. We wish to know whether the data warrant the conclusion that p_1 is *smaller* than p_2. Placing this in the alternative hypothesis leads to

$$H_0: p_1 \geq p_2$$
$$H_a: p_1 < p_2$$

Steps 2, 3. Using the test statistic in equation 12.14, the resulting one-tailed test procedure would be to

reject H_0 if $Z < -Z_{.05} = -1.645$

This is the same as rejecting H_0 if the resulting p-value < .05.

Step 4. We have

$$\hat{p}_1 = \frac{70}{500} = .14 \qquad \text{and} \qquad \hat{p}_2 = \frac{110}{500} = .22$$

FIGURE

12.6

Z curve showing the calculated *p*-value for Example 12.9.

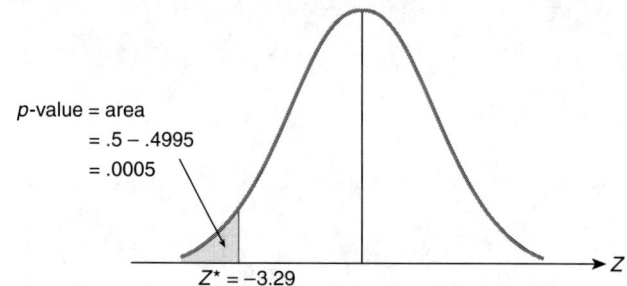

Also,

$$\bar{p} = \frac{(70+110)}{(500+500)} = \frac{180}{1000} = .18$$

Consequently,

$$Z^* = \frac{.14-.22}{\sqrt{\dfrac{(.18)(.82)}{500} + \dfrac{(.18)(.82)}{500}}} = \frac{-.08}{.0243} = -3.29$$

The *Z* curve and calculated *p*-value of .0005 are shown in Figure 12.6. H_0 is rejected since (1) −3.29 is less than −1.645 and, as a result, (2) the *p*-value of .0005 is less than α = .05. Condition (2) is actually a restatement of condition (1), since .0005 is the area to the left of −3.29 and .05 is the area to the left of −1.645.

Step 5.   There *is* evidence that the proportion of nonconforming cans is smaller during the day shift.

An Excel solution to Example 12.9 using the macro from KPK Data Analysis is shown in Figure 12.7(a). To obtain this solution, click on **KPK Data Analysis ➤ Inference on Proportions ➤ Two Population Proportions.** The MINITAB solution in Figure 12.7(b) is obtained by clicking on **Stat ➤ Basic Statistics ➤ 2 Proportions.** Click on the **Summarized data** box and enter 500 (number of trials) and 70 (number of events) for sample 1 and 500 (number of trials) and 110 (number of events) for sample 2. Click on **Options,** select "less than" as the alternative hypothesis, and click on the box indicating the pooled estimate of the population proportion should be used. The outputs in Figure 12.7 agree with the previous solution. In particular, the small *p*-value of .0005 supports the alternative hypothesis that the proportion of defective cans *is* smaller during the day shift. *Note:* SPSS does not have a Z-test for testing two population proportions.

X Exercises 12.31–12.39

Understanding the Mechanics

12.31 Two random samples reveal 40 successes out of 50 and 70 successes out of 80. Test that the population proportions of successes differ using a 5% significance level.

12.32 Construct a 90% confidence interval for the difference of two population proportions using $x_1 = 38$, $n_1 = 50$, and $x_2 = 45$, $n_2 = 50$.

12.33 If 100 out of 350 and 145 out of 400 individuals vote yes from populations 1 and 2, respectively, is there evi-

FIGURE

12.7

(a) Excel solution
to Example 12.9
using KPK Data
Analysis ➤
Inference on
Proportions ➤
Two Population
Proportions; and
(b) MINITAB
solution for
Example 12.9
using Stat ➤ Basic
Statistics ➤ 2
Proportions.

	A	B	C
1	**Z Test for Two Proportions**		
2		Variable 1	Variable 2
3	Sample Proportion	0.140	0.220
4	Number of Observations	500	500
5	Ho: p1 ≥ p2	Ha: p1 < p2	
6	Z*	-3.292432	
7	P[Z ≤ Z*]	0.0005	
8	Z Critical, α = 0.05	-1.644853	
9			

◄ ◄ ► ►◄ \Sheet1 / Sheet2 / Sheet3 / |◄|

(a)

Test and CI for Two Proportions

```
Sample   X    N    Sample p
1        70   500  0.140000
2        110  500  0.220000


Difference = p (1) - p (2)
Estimate for difference:  -0.08
95% upper bound for difference:  -0.0402503
Test for difference = 0 (vs < 0):  Z = -3.29   P-Value = 0.000
```

(b)

dence to support the hypothesis that the proportion of yes votes from population 1 is less than the proportion from population 2? Use a 1% significance level.

12.34   Random samples of size 300 from population A and B resulted in 36% and 28% successes, respectively. Construct a 95% confidence interval for $p_A - p_B$.

Applying the New Concepts

12.35   Test the hypothesis that more female teenagers use computer chat than male teenagers. Samples of 500 female and 500 male teenagers were selected, and 430 females and 390 males used computer chat in the past week. Use a 10% significance level.

12.36   Very few metropolitan areas in the United States have more than 25% of the adult population possessing a passport. New York City and San Francisco have the highest percentages of adults possessing a current U.S. passport. Suppose that a survey by a travel agency was conducted to determine if there is a significant difference in the proportion of adults in these two cities that possess a current passport. If a random sample of 300 adults from each city revealed that 105 and 90 adults from San Francisco and New York City, respectively, hold a current passport, what conclusion can the travel agency make? Use a 5% significance level.

(Adapted from "Passports at the Ready," USA Today, September 25–27, 1998, p. 1A.)

12.37   A quality engineer wishes to determine if there is a difference in the number of nonconforming bottle-top seals produced by two different assembly-line processes. A bottle-top seal is nonconforming if the seal is not airtight. To investigate this, the engineer samples 300 bottle-top seals from each assembly-line process. The samples reveal that one process produced eight nonconforming items and the other produced 12 nonconforming items. Based on these data, can the engineer conclude that there is a significant difference in the number of nonconforming bottle-top seals produced by the two assembly-line processes? Use the p-value to support your conclusion.

Using the Computer

12.38   **[DATA SET EX12-38]** Variable Description:

MalesInterested: A Yes indicates that a male is interested in a sales manager position, and a No indicates no interest

FemalesInterested: A Yes indicates that a female is interested in a sales manager position, and a No indicates no interest

The vice president at Global Life Insurance Company is interested in the proportion of male college business students and female college business students that would be willing to interview for a sales manager position at the company. Random samples of 170 males and 115 females from college business students were selected. Responses were recorded as Yes or No and are listed in variables MalesInterested and FemalesInterested. Test that the proportion of male students exceeds the proportion of female students interested in this position. Use the p-value of test statistic as the basis for your conclusion.

12.39 **[DATA SET EX12-39]** Variable Description:

ManufactA: A 1 indicates a defective motor and a 0 indicates that the motor is not defective from manufacturer A

ManufactB: A 1 indicates a defective motor and a 0 indicates that the motor is not defective from manufacturer B

Two manufacturers supply rebuilt motors to an air conditioning repair company. The manager at the air conditioning repair company believes that the proportion of defective motors from the two manufacturers differs. A random sample of 150 rebuilt motors from manufacturer A and 150 rebuilt motors from manufacturer B were selected. Variables ManufactA and ManufactB contain a 1 or a 0 to indicate a defective or nondefective motor.

a. Use the two-sample proportions test to test that there is sufficient evidence to indicate a difference. Use a 5% significance level.

b. What is the estimate of the pooled proportion, $\bar{p}$?

c. Use the Z statistic to test for a difference in the means of the two variables. Assign σ the value of $\sqrt{2\bar{p}(1-\bar{p})}$. What resemblance is there to the test in part a?

12.4

THE MULTINOMIAL SITUATION AND TESTING FOR INDEPENDENCE

A First Look at the Chi-Square Distribution

When constructing a confidence interval for a population mean (μ) with unknown standard deviation (σ) in Chapter 7, we used the t distribution. Such a distribution is referred to as a derived distribution because it was derived to describe the behavior of a particular test statistic. This type of distribution is not used to describe a population, as is the normal distribution in many applications. For example, you will not hear a statement such as, "Assume that these data follow a t distribution"—normal, exponential, uniform, maybe, but not a t distribution. The t random variable merely offers us a method of testing and constructing confidence intervals for the mean of a normal population when the standard deviation is unknown and is replaced by its estimate.

Another such continuous derived distribution is the **chi-square** (pronounced "ky square") distribution and is written as χ^2. The shape of this distribution is illustrated in Figure 12.8. Notice that, unlike the Z and t curves, the χ^2 distribution is not symmetric and is definitely skewed right.

For the chi-square distribution, as well as all continuous distributions, a probability corresponds to an area under a curve. Also, the shape of the chi-square curve, like that of its cousin the t distribution, must be specified by the corresponding degrees of freedom (df). Each application of the chi-square statistic will dictate what the degrees of freedom should be.

FIGURE

12.8

Shape of a chi-square distribution.

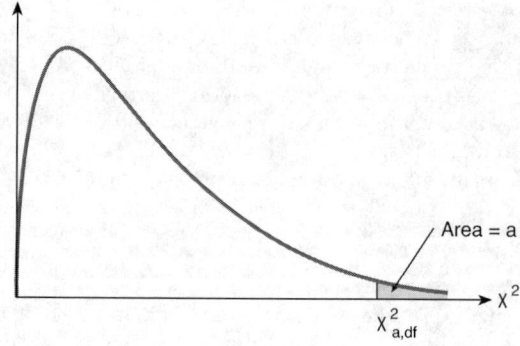

Area = a

χ^2

$\chi^2_{a,df}$

Let $\chi^2_{\alpha, \, df}$ be the χ^2 value whose area to the *right* is α, using the corresponding df. For example, what is $\chi^2_{.1, 12}$? This would be the chi-square value in Figure 12.9 whose right-tail area is .1 where the chi-square curve has 12 degrees of freedom. Tabulated values for the χ^2 distribution are contained in Table A.6. This table contains *right-tailed* probabilities. Based on this table and Figure 12.9, $P(\chi^2 > 18.5493)$ is .1; that is, $\chi^2_{.1, 12} = 18.5493$. A chi-square distributed statistic will be used to test a hypothesis for the multinomial situation, our next topic.

The Multinomial Situation

The multinomial situation is identical to the binomial situation, except that there are k possible outcomes on each trial rather than two. Here, k is any integer that is at least 2.

Suppose that the management of Tucker Industries is concerned with how company employees feel about management; in particular, do the employees feel that management is responsive to employee suggestions? A quality consultant has informed the Tucker team charged with examining this situation that traditionally the following percentages are observed in companies of this size:

Category	Description	Percentage of Employees in This Category
1	Management is extremely responsive to employee suggestions	.05
2	Management is somewhat responsive to employee suggestions	.30
3	No opinion	.20
4	Management is usually not responsive to employee suggestions	.40
5	Management is rarely responsive to employee suggestions	.05

The Tucker team would like to verify these percentages among its own employees and obtains responses to the question, "Is management responsive to employee suggestions?" from a random sample of 500 employees. Possible responses to this question are the five categories just listed, and the following frequencies are observed in each category for this sample:

Category	Frequency
1	32
2	142
3	87
4	221
5	18
	500

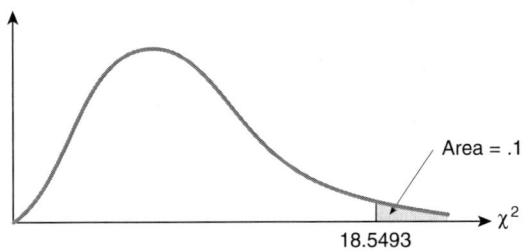

Area = .1

18.5493

χ^2

FIGURE

12.9

χ^2 curve with 12 df. The shaded area represents $P(\chi^2 > 18.5493)$.

The assumptions necessary for a multinomial experiment are as follows:

1. The experiment consists of n independent repetitions (trials).

2. Each trial outcome falls in exactly one of k categories.

3. The probabilities of the k outcomes are denoted by $p_1, p_2, \ldots, p_k$, where these probabilities (proportions) remain the same on each trial. Also, $p_1 + p_2 + \ldots + p_k = 1$.

For this situation, we can define k random variables as the k observed values, where

$$O_1 = \text{observed number of sample values in category 1}$$
$$O_2 = \text{observed number of sample values in category 2}$$
$$\vdots$$
$$O_k = \text{observed number of sample values in category } k$$

For our example, $n = 500$ trials, where each trial consists of obtaining an employee response to the question dealing with management response to employee suggestions. There are $k = 5$ possible responses (categories) for this experiment. Assuming these 500 Tucker Industries employees constitute a random sample, then these trials are independent. Also, let

$$p_1 = \text{proportion of people responding in category 1}$$
$$p_2 = \text{proportion of people responding in category 2}$$
$$\vdots$$
$$p_5 = \text{proportion of people responding in category 5}$$

The five random variables in our example are

$$O_1 = \text{observed number of Tucker employees in the sample responding in category 1}$$
$$\vdots$$
$$O_5 = \text{observed number of Tucker employees in the sample responding in category 5}$$

Thus, this example fits the assumptions for the multinomial situation.

Hypothesis Testing for a Multinomial Situation

The hypotheses for the Tucker Industries example are

$$H_0: p_1 = .05, p_2 = .30, p_3 = .20, p_4 = .40, p_5 = .05$$
$$H_a: \text{at least one of the } p_i\text{'s is incorrect}$$

Notice that H_a is *not* $p_1 \neq .05, p_2 \neq .30, \ldots, p_5 \neq .05$. This hypothesis is too strong and is not the opposite of H_0.

Let $p_{1,0}$ be any specified value of p_1, $p_{2,0}$, any specified value of p_2, and so on. The hypotheses to test the multinomial parameters are

$$H_0: p_1 = p_{1,0}, p_2 = p_{2,0}, \ldots, p_k = p_{k,0}$$
$$H_a: \text{at least one of the } p_i\text{'s is incorrect}$$

Using the observed values $(O_1, O_2, \ldots)$, the point estimates here are

$$\hat{p}_1 = \text{estimate of } p_1 = O_1/n$$
$$\hat{p}_2 = \text{estimate of } p_2 = O_2/n$$
$$\vdots$$

To test H_0 versus H_a, we use the chi-square statistic in equation 12.15. This test is called the **chi-square multinomial goodness-of-fit test.** To define the rejection region, notice that when H_a is true, we would expect the O's and E's to be "far apart," because the E's are determined by assuming that H_0 is true. In other words, if H_a is true, the chi-square test statistic should be large. Consequently, we always reject H_0 when χ^{2*} lies in the *right tail* when using this particular statistic.

To test H_0 versus H_a, compute

$$\chi^2 = \sum \frac{(O-E)^2}{E}$$

12.15

where

1. The summation is across all categories (outcomes).

2. The Os are the *observed* frequencies in each category using the sample.

3. The Es are the *expected* frequencies in each category if H_0 is true, so

$$E_1 = np_{1,0}$$
$$E_2 = np_{2,0}$$
$$E_3 = np_{3,0}$$
$$\vdots$$

4. The df for the chi-square statistic are $k - 1$, where k is the number of categories.

To carry out the test,

$$\text{reject } H_0 \text{ if } \chi^2 > \chi^2_{\alpha,\text{df}}$$

Notice that the hypothetical proportions (probabilities) for each of the categories are specified in H_0. Consequently, we will complete the analysis by concluding that at least one of the proportions is incorrect (we reject H_0) or that there is not enough evidence to conclude that these proportions are incorrect (we fail to reject H_0). We do not *accept* H_0; we never conclude that these specified proportions *are* correct. We act like the juror who acquits a defendant not because he or she is convinced that this person is innocent but because there was not sufficient evidence for conviction.

When we introduced the ANOVA technique, we mentioned that this procedure allowed us to determine whether many population means were equal using a *single* test. This technique was preferable to using many t tests to test the equality of two means, one pair at a time, because these tests would not be independent, and the overall significance level would be difficult to determine. We encounter the same situation here. *It is much better to use a chi-square goodness-of-fit test to test all of the proportions at once rather than using many Z tests to test the individual proportions.*

What do the observed number of Tucker Industries employees in each category for the sample of 500 employees tell us about the mix of responses to this question for all Tucker employees? Do they conform to the percentages cited by the quality consultant? Use a significance level of .05.

Solution

Step 1. Let p_1 = proportion of all Tucker employees that would respond in category 1 to this question; that is, they feel that management is extremely responsive to employee suggestions. Similarly, define p_2, p_3, p_4, and p_5 to be the corresponding percentages for categories 2, 3, 4, and 5. The hypotheses under investigation are

$$H_0: p_1 = .05, p_2 = .30, p_3 = .20, p_4 = .40, p_5 = .05$$

$$H_a: \text{at least one of these } p\text{'s is incorrect}$$

Step 2. The test statistic is

$$\chi^2 = \sum \frac{(O - E)^2}{E}$$

where the summation is over the five categories.

Step 3. Your test procedure here is to

$$\text{reject } H_0 \text{ if } \chi^2 > \chi^2_{d, df}$$

The df is (number of categories) −1, so df = 5 − 1 = 4. The chi-square value from Table A.6 is $\chi^2_{.05,4} = 9.49$, and we

$$\text{reject } H_0 \text{ if } \chi^2 > 9.49$$

Step 4. The observed values are

$$O_1 = 32, O_2 = 142, O_3 = 87, O_4 = 221, O_5 = 18$$

The expected values when H_0 is true are obtained by multiplying $n = 500$ by each of the proportions in H_0. So

$$E_1 = (500)(.05) = 25$$
$$E_2 = (500)(.30) = 150$$
$$E_3 = (500)(.20) = 100$$
$$E_4 = (500)(.40) = 200$$
$$E_5 = (500)(.05) = 25$$

In general, do not round the expected values, because they are averages. The computed value of the chi-square test statistic is

$$\chi^{2*} = \frac{(32 - 25)^2}{25} + \frac{(142 - 150)^2}{150} + \frac{(87 - 100)^2}{100} + \frac{(221 - 200)^2}{200} + \frac{(18 - 25)^2}{25}$$
$$= 8.242$$

Because 8.242 does not exceed 9.49, we fail to reject H_0.

Step 5. There is insufficient evidence to indicate that the proportion of Tucker employees in each response category differs from the proportions stated by the quality consultant. In other words, the observed values were "close enough" to the expected values under H_0 to let this hypothesis stand. Examining categories 4 and 5, this indicates that 45% of the Tucker employees feel that management is not responsive on some level to employee suggestions. Obviously, there is a great deal of room for improvement in this area of management relations.

Comment

Instructions for using Excel or MINITAB to perform a chi-square multinomial goodness-of-fit test are contained in the end-of-chapter appendix.

Pooling Categories

When using the chi-square procedure of comparing observed and expected values, we determine the difference between these two values for each category, square it, and *divide by the expected value, E.* If one value of E is very small (say, less than 5), then this computation produces an extremely *large* contribution to the final χ^2 value from this category. In other words, this small expected value produces an inflated chi-square value, with the result that we reject H_0 when perhaps we should not have. To prevent this from occurring, we use the following rule: When using equation 12.15, each expected value, E, should be at least 5.*

If you encounter an application where one or more of the expected values is less than 5, you can handle this situation by **pooling** your categories such that each of the new categories has an expected value that is at least 5.

Chi-Square Tests of Independence

In the previous section, we classified each member of a population into one of many categories. This classification was one-dimensional, because each member was classified using only *one* criterion (brand, color, and so on). In this section, we extend classification to a two-dimensional situation, in which each element in the population is classified according to two criteria, such as gender and income level (high, medium, or low). The question of interest is, are these two variables (classifications) *independent?* For example, if gender and income level are not independent, perhaps gender discrimination is present in the salary structure of a company. If a person's salary is not related to gender, these two classifications *would* be independent.

In Chapter 4, we examined a survey concerned with the age and gender of the purchasers of a recently released microcomputer. The results were summarized in a *contingency* (or *cross-tab*) table. This table consisted of **cells,** where each cell contains the *frequency* of people in the sample who satisfy each of the various cross-classifications:

Gender	Age <30	Age 30–45	Age >45	Total
Male	60	20	40	120
Female	40	30	10	80
Total	100	50	50	200

This 2×3 contingency table shows that there were 60 people who were both male *and* under 30. In Chapter 5, we determined various probabilities for a person selected at random from this group of 200, such as the probability that this person is both a male and over 45 years. Now we will view these data as the results of a particular experiment (survey) and attempt to determine whether the variables—age and gender—are independent

---

*This rule is somewhat arbitrary and a bit conservative, but is commonly used. Another procedure for pooling requires that all the expected values be 3 or more, while yet another procedure requires that no more than 20% of all the expected values be less than 5, with none less than 1.

for this application. Put another way, is the age structure of the male buyers the same as that of the female purchasers? The hypotheses are

H_0: the classifications (age and gender) are independent

H_a: the classifications are dependent

This problem can also be viewed as a multinomial experiment containing 200 trials and $(2)(3) = 6$ possible categories for each trial outcome.

Deriving a Test of Hypothesis for Independent Classifications. We want to decide whether the data about the purchasers exhibit random variation or a pattern of some type due to a dependency between age and gender. If these classifications *are* independent (H_0 is true), how many people would you expect in each cell? Consider the upper right cell, which shows males over 45 years. The expected number of sample observations in this cell is $200 \cdot P$(sampled purchaser is a male and over 45). Assuming independence, this is $200 \cdot P$(sampled purchaser is a male) $\cdot P$(sampled purchaser is over 45), using the multiplicative rule for independent events discussed in Chapter 4.

What is P(sampled purchaser is a male)? We do not know, because we do not have enough information to determine what percentage of *all* purchasers are male. However, we can *estimate* this probability using the percentage of males in the sample: $120/200 = .6$.

Similarly, P(sampled purchaser is over 45) can be estimated by the fraction of people over 45 in the sample—namely, $50/200$. So, our estimate of the expected number of observations for this cell is:

$$\hat{E} = 200 \cdot \frac{120}{200} \cdot \frac{50}{200} = \frac{(120)(50)}{200} = 30$$

So, for this cell, the observed frequency is $O = 40$, and our estimate of the expected frequency (if H_0 is true) is $\hat{E} = 30$. In general,

$$\hat{E} = \frac{(\text{row total for this cell}) \cdot (\text{column total for this cell})}{n}$$

where n = total sample size. A summary of the calculations can be tabulated as follows.

Gender	Age	Observed (O)	Expected ($\hat{E}$), if H_0 Is True
Male	<30	60	$(120)(100)/200 = 60$
	30–45	20	$(120)(50)/200 = 30$
	>45	40	$(120)(50)/200 = 30$
Female	<30	40	$(80)(100)/200 = 40$
	30–45	30	$(80)(50)/200 = 20$
	>45	10	$(80)(50)/200 = 20$
		200	200

The easiest way to represent these 12 values is to place the expected value in parentheses alongside the observed value in each cell:

Gender	Age <30	Age 30–45	Age >45	Total
Male	60 (60)	20 (30)	40 (30)	120
Female	40 (40)	30 (20)	10 (20)	80
Total	100	50	50	200

Pooling. As this point, you need to check your expected values. If any one of them is less than 5, you need to combine, or *pool,* the column (or row) in which this small value occurs with another column (or row) to comply with our earlier requirement that all expected values in the chi-square statistic are at least 5. The observed and expected values for this new column (row) are obtained by summing the values for the two columns (rows).

The Test Statistic. The test statistic for testing H_0: the classifications are independent versus H_a: the classifications are dependent is the usual chi-square statistic, which in this case compares each *observed* frequency with the corresponding *expected* frequency estimate.

$$\chi^2 = \sum \frac{(O - \hat{E})^2}{\hat{E}}$$

12.16

where the summation is over all cells of the contingency table.

Degrees of Freedom. In the multinomial situation, the degrees of freedom for the chi-square statistic were $k - 1$, where k = the number of categories (outcomes). In this situation, there were k values of $(O - \hat{E})$. However, because the sum of the observed frequencies is the same as the sum of the expected frequencies, the sum of the k values of $(O - \hat{E})$ is *always zero*. This means that, of these k values, only $k - 1$ are free to vary, resulting in $k - 1$ df for the chi-square statistic.

Take a close look at the observed and expected frequencies in the contingency table for age and gender of purchasers. Notice that (1) for each row, sum of O's = sum of $\hat{E}$'s and (2) for each column, sum of O's = sum of $\hat{E}$'s. In general, if classification 1 has c categories and classification 2 has r categories, you construct an $r \times c$ **contingency table** (Figure 12.10). Of the c values of $(O - \hat{E})$ in each row, only $c - 1$ are free to vary. Similarly, only $r - 1$ of the values in each column are free to assume any value. So, for this contingency table, only $(r - 1)(c - 1)$ values are free to vary. Therefore, for the chi-square test of independence,

$$df = (r - 1)(c - 1)$$

12.17

Testing Procedure. When H_0 is not true, the expected frequencies and observed frequencies will be very different, producing a large χ^2 value. We again reject H_0 if the value of the test statistic falls in the *right-tail* rejection region, so we

$$\text{reject } H_0 \text{ if } \chi^2 > \chi^2_{\alpha,df}$$

where $df = (r - 1)(c - 1)$.

In summary, the chi-square test of independence hypotheses are

H_0: the row and column classifications are independent (not related)

H_a: the classifications are dependent (related or associated in some way)

FIGURE

12.10

Expected value estimates for an $r \times c$ contingency table.

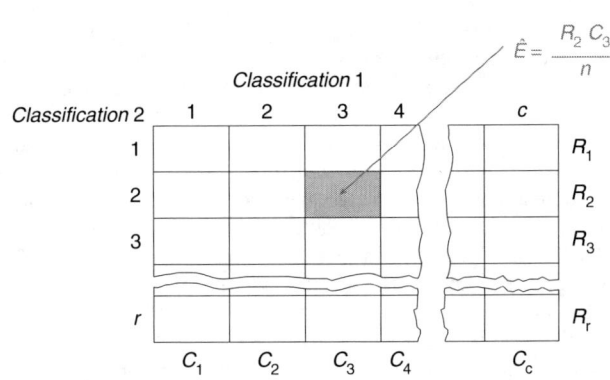

The test statistic is

$$\chi^2 = \sum \frac{(O - \hat{E})^2}{\hat{E}}$$

where

1. The summation is over all cells of the contingency table consisting of r rows and c columns.

2. O is the observed frequency in this cell.

3. $\hat{E}$ is the estimated expected frequency for this cell.

$$\hat{E} = \frac{\left(\begin{array}{c}\text{total of row in}\\\text{which the cell lies}\end{array}\right) \times \left(\begin{array}{c}\text{total of column in}\\\text{which the cell lies}\end{array}\right)}{(\text{total of all cells})}$$

4. The degrees of freedom for the chi-square statistic are df $= (r - 1)(c - 1)$. The test procedure is (using Table A.6):

$$\text{reject } H_0 \text{ if } \chi^2 > \chi^2_{\alpha,df}$$

We can now return to our question of whether the age and gender of microcomputer purchasers are independent. Step 1 (statement of hypotheses) and step 2 (definition of test statistic) of our five-step procedure have been discussed already. Assume that a significance level of $\alpha = .1$ was specified. For step 3, the df are $(2 - 1)(3 - 1) = 2$. Using Table A.6, $\chi^2_{.1,2} = 4.61$. So we will reject H_0 if $\chi^2 > 4.61$. For step 4, referring to the contingency table,

$$\chi^{2*} = \frac{(60-60)^2}{60} + \frac{(20-30)^2}{30} + \frac{(40-30)^2}{30} + \frac{(40-40)^2}{40}$$

$$+ \frac{(30-20)^2}{20} + \frac{(10-20)^2}{20}$$

$$= 0 + 3.33 + 3.33 + 0 + 5 + 5$$

$$= 16.66$$

This exceeds the table value of 4.61, so we reject H_0. We thus conclude that the age and gender classifications are *not* independent (step 5).

If the results of the chi-square test lead to a conclusion that the classifications are not independent, a closer look at the individual terms in the chi-square statistic can often reveal what the relationship is between these two variables.

Examining the six terms, we observe four large values, namely, 3.33 (male/age 30–45), 3.33 (male/age over 45), 5 (female/age 30–45), and 5 (female/age over 45). We obtained more men (and fewer women) over 45 years than we would expect if there was no dependency. Similarly, there were fewer men (and more women) between 30 and 45 years.

We can find the p-value for this situation also, given $\chi^{2*} = 16.66$. Using a χ^2 curve with 2 df, the area to the right of 16.66, using Table A.6, is $<.005$. The p-value indicates the *strength* of the dependency between two classifications. The *smaller* the p-value, the more you tend to support the alternative hypothesis, which indicates a stronger dependency between the two variables. For the age and gender illustration, $p < .005$, so we conclude that the age and gender of these purchasers are strongly related.

It is worth mentioning at this point that it is possible that examining one category (such as gender) can fail to show any differences among subcategories (male versus female), but when the category is examined along with another category (such as age classification), patterns can emerge. Such a technique is often useful in detecting job discrimination within companies. For example, no gender discrimination may be evident in a sample, but when it is examined along with race or age categories, certain discriminatory practices can be identified.

EXAMPLE 12.11

The personnel director at PCSoft, a computer software development firm, is interested in determining whether an employee's educational level has an effect on his or her job knowledge. An exam was given to a sample of 120 employees, and the director would like to know whether there is a difference in exam performance among three groups: (1) those with a high school diploma only, (2) those with a bachelor's degree only, and (3) those with a master's degree.

Rather than using the actual exam scores and performing a one-factor analysis of variance (ANOVA, discussed in Chapter 9), she rated each person's exam performance as high, average, or low. The results of the study are as follows:

	High	Average	Low	Total
Master's degree	4	20	11	35
Bachelor's degree	12	18	15	45
High school diploma	9	22	9	40
Total	25	60	35	120

Does job knowledge as measured by the exam appear to be related to the level of an employee's education, at this particular firm? Use $\alpha = .05$.

Solution

Step 1.   This problem calls for a chi-square test of independence, with hypotheses

H_0: exam performance is independent of educational level

H_a: these classifications are dependent

Steps 2 and 3.   Your test statistic is the chi-square statistic in equation 12.16. The table of frequencies here is a 3×3 contingency table, which means that the degrees of freedom are df $= (3-1)(3-1) = 4$. From Table A.6, we determine that $\chi^2_{.05,4} = 9.49$, so the testing procedure is to

reject H_0 if $\chi^2 > 9.49$

Step 4.   Computing the expected frequency estimates in the usual way, we arrive at the following table:

	High	Average	Low	Total
Master's degree	4 (7.29)	20 (17.5)	11 (10.21)	35
Bachelor's degree	12 (9.38)	18 (22.5)	15 (13.12)	45
High school diploma	9 (8.33)	22 (20.0)	9 (11.67)	40
Total	25	60	35	120

To illustrate the calculations, the 11.67 in the lower right cell is $(40 \times 35)/120$. The computed chi-square value is

$$\chi^{2*} = \frac{(4-7.29)^2}{7.29} + \frac{(20-17.5)^2}{17.5} + \cdots + \frac{(9-11.67)^2}{11.67} = 4.67$$

This value is less than 9.49, and so we fail to reject H_0.

Step 5.   We see no evidence of a relationship between job knowledge as measured by the exam and level of education.

We do not conclude that these data demonstrate that the two classifications are clearly *independent*, because this would amount to accepting H_0. We are simply unable to demonstrate that a relationship exists.

Comments

In Example 12.11, the personnel director recorded the exam performance as high, average, or low rather than listing the actual exam score. Why would anyone take *interval/ratio* data (the exam scores) and convert them to seemingly weaker *ordinal* data (the exam performance classifications)? Do you lose useful information by doing this? When using the ANOVA procedure in Chapter 9, we were forced to assume that these data came from *normal* populations with equal variances. In this chapter, *no* assumptions regarding the populations (aside from the randomness of the sample) were necessary. So, by converting the exam scores to a form suitable for a contingency table and using the chi-square test of independence, we can avoid the assumptions of normality and equal variances.

This question introduces *nonparametric statistics,* often called *distribution-free* statistics. The beauty of these procedures is that they require only very weak assumptions regarding the populations. However, if the data *do* satisfy the requirements of the ANOVA procedure (or nearly so), the nonparametric test is less sensitive to differences among the populations (such as educational level) and so is less *powerful* than the ANOVA *F* test.

Instructions for using Excel, MINITAB, or SPSS to perform a chi-square test of independence are contained in the end-of-chapter appendix.

X Exercises 12.40–12.52

Understanding the Mechanics

12.40 Using the following data, test with a significance level of 10% that the probabilities are the same in every category.

Category	A	B	C	D
Observed Frequency	58	37	44	61

12.41 Consider a multinomial experiment with five categories and a sample of size 50. Test H_0: $p_1 = .1$, $p_2 = .2$, $p_3 = .2$, $p_4 = .2$, $p_5 = .3$. Use a 5% significance level. Do all the cells have an expected frequency of at least 5?

Category	1	2	3	4	5
Observed Frequency	3	12	20	5	10

12.42 The following table contains observed frequencies for row and column categories.

	Column Categories	
Row Categories	Category 1	Category 2
Category 1	11	21
Category 2	9	12
Category 3	10	7

a. Formulate the hypotheses for a chi-square test of independence.
b. Calculate the expected cell frequencies.
c. Calculate the chi-square statistic.
d. At the 5% significance level, do the data support the conclusion that the categories are not independent?

12.43 Test the null hypothesis of independence of the two classifications A and B in the accompanying table. Combine any row or column to comply with the requirement that all expected cell frequencies are at least 5. Base your conclusions on the *p*-value.

A	B_1	B_2	B_3	B_4
A_1	10	6	3	2
A_2	13	7	8	4
A_3	3	15	2	1

(The table is headed by a spanning label **B**.)

Applying the New Concepts

12.44 Wal-Mart has accused Visa and MasterCard of improperly forcing them to swallow high fees on debit card transactions. Suppose that a Wal-Mart executive wished to determine if last year's percentages of 47%, 26%, 20%, and 7% for customers paying groceries using a credit card, debit card, check, and cash, respectively, still held. Assume that the executive randomly sampled 200 households and asked which form of payment was used when paying for groceries. The results were as follows.

Credit Card	Debit Card	Check	Cash
110	40	39	11

a. What is the expected value for each category? Should the expected values be above a certain value for the chi-square test to be valid?

b. Does this survey indicate that the population percentages using the different forms of payment differ from the previous year's percentages? Use a 10% significance level.

(Source: "WalMart to Limit Mastercard Use," The Wall Street Journal, December 3, 2003, p. A8.)

12.45 A stockbroker believes that when too many of the stock market newsletters are bullish on the market (that is, they predict that stock prices will go higher), the stock market will most likely fall. Thirty-two randomly selected stock market newsletters were each placed in one of three categories.

Bearish on Stock Market	Neutral on Stock Market	Bullish on Stock Market
9	10	13

Test the null hypothesis that the newsletters are equally divided among the three categories. Use a .05 significance level.

12.46 Economists believe that the average holiday spending for Americans is $800. The amount of time to pay off this holiday expense is two months or less for about 35% of the population and more than two months for the rest of the population. To check this claim, suppose that a random sample of 500 American adults was selected, and the following results were recorded.

Two Months or Less to Pay Off Holiday Bills	More than Two Months to Pay Off Holiday Bills
165	335

a. Is there sufficient evidence indicating that the percentage of the population paying off their holiday bills in two months or less differs from 35%?

b. Use the Z test to test the belief in part a. Use a 10% significance level.

c. What relationship exists between the test statistic in parts a and b?

(Source: "Holiday Hangover," USA Today, December 15, 1998, p. 1B.)

12.47 A quality manager was interested in whether a relationship exists between the number of defective items produced and the work shift. What conclusion can you give the manager using the following data? Use a 10% significance level.

	Product A	Product B	Product C
Shift1	120	130	140
Shift2	115	144	150
Shift3	155	120	118

12.48 Airlines have made an effort to serve healthy food on long flights. While rich brownies are still served, fruit and salads are appearing more frequently. The following table presents a poll of male and female travelers who were asked if they felt that the meal served on the airline was healthy.

	Thought the Meal Was Healthy	Did Not Think the Meal Was Healthy
Male	13	25
Female	20	42

a. State appropriate null and alternative hypotheses to test if a relationship exists between gender and thinking that the meal served in flight was healthy.

b. What conclusion can you make about the hypotheses in part a? Use the p-value to determine your response.

(Source: "Dining Out at 32,000 Feet," The Wall Street Journal, June 3, 2003, p. D1.)

12.49 The Meyers–Briggs Type Indicator (MBTI) is a personality scale that can be used to classify qualities like Extrovert (E), Introvert (I), Intuitive (N), Feeling (F), Sensing (S), Thinking (T), Judging (J), Perceptive (P). Thus, EN means extrovert-intuitive, SP means sensing-perceptive. Consider the following hypothetical frequencies for a cross-tabulation of four types of personality using the MBTI against profession.

Profession	EN	IF	SP	JT	Total
Computer Programmer	4	6	5	6	21
Accountant	3	7	5	5	20
Marketer	9	3	7	4	23
Educator	5	5	5	5	20
Total	21	21	22	20	84

a. From the table, can you conclude at a 1% significance level, whether personality type and profession are related?

b. State the p-value for your test.

Using the Computer

12.50 **[DATA SET EX12-50]** Variable Description:

CareerDev: Response indicating "Agree," "Indifferent," or "Disagree"

Two hundred employees were asked to state their reaction to the statement "Telecommuters have an equal chance of being promoted." Use the data in CareerDev to form a contingency table. Form a bar chart to display responses. Test the hypothesis that the proportions of responses from each response category are equal. Use a 5% significance level.

12.51 **[DATA SET EX12-51]** Variable Description:

Airport: Either New York Kennedy Airport, New York LaGuardia Airport, or Newark New Jersey Airport

IncidentCategory: One of four classifications of runway incidents denoted by an A, B, C, or D

The Federal Aviation Administration classifies runway incidents at airports into one of four categories. Category A incidents are incidents in which extreme action is taken to narrowly avoid a collision. Category B incidents are incidents in which there is substantial potential for a collision. Category C incidents are incidents in which there is ample time and distance to avoid a collision. Category D incidents are incidents in which there is little or no chance for collision but meets the definition of a runway incursion. Suppose that data are collected for the three major airports serving New York City.

a. Form a contingency table for these data and compute the expected values for each cell. Pool (combine) the necessary rows or columns so that no cell has an expected value less than five.

b. Using the table in part a, test that a relationship exists between the three major airports serving New York City and the type of incidents that can occur on a runway. Use a 10% significance level.

c. What would be the conclusion to part b had the frequency table been used without pooling any rows or columns?

(Source: "Runway Close Calls," Dallas Morning News, June 21, 2001, p. 20A.)

12.52 [DATA SET EX12-52] Variable Description:

Salary: Row categories listed under Salary are "Less than $40,0000," "Between $40,000 and less than $70,000," and "More than $70,000"

GM: Frequency of individuals preferring GM cars for each row

Ford: Frequency of individuals preferring Ford cars for each row

Imports: Frequency of individuals preferring import cars for each row

Market analysts are interested in the relationship between buyers' income and the type of car they prefer to drive. A study in which 500 recent automobile buyers were randomly selected revealed a possible relationship between a buyer's preference and his/her income bracket.

a. Is there sufficient evidence to indicate that a relationship exists between automobile preference and salary level using a 5% significance level?

b. Do a what-if analysis by considering only GM and Ford. Does this change your response to part a?

 # Summary

You will often encounter a situation in which you are concerned with a population proportion, rather than the mean or variance. The usual procedure of estimating a population parameter using the sample estimator, $\hat{p}$, allows you to derive a point estimate and construct a confidence interval for p. For large samples, the Central Limit Theorem can be applied to determine an approximate confidence interval provided $n\hat{p}$ and $n(1 - \hat{p})$ are greater than 5. When the desired accuracy of the point estimate, $\hat{p}$, is specified in advance, you can determine the sample size necessary to obtain this degree of accuracy for a specified confidence level. When you investigate a statement concerning a population proportion, you can use a statistical test of hypothesis.

To compare two population proportions (p_1 and p_2), two independent random samples are obtained, one from each population. Procedures for large, independent samples generally provide an accurate confidence interval or test of hypothesis whenever $n_1\hat{p}_1$, $n_1(1 - \hat{p}_1)$, $n_2\hat{p}_2$, and $n_2(1 - \hat{p}_2)$ each exceed 5. Two population proportions can be compared by first collecting two large, independent samples.

The multinomial situation is an extension of the binomial situation for Chapter 5. In the multinomial situation, each trial can result in any specified number of outcomes. To test that the population proportions are equal to a set of specified values, a random sample of observations is obtained, and a chi-square goodness-of-fit is carried out to reject or to fail to reject this set of probabilities (percentages). Finally, the chi-square test of independence can be used to determine whether two classifications (such as age and performance) are independent.

 # Summary of Formulas

Single Population

1. Point estimate of population proportion (p):

$$\tilde{p} = \frac{x}{n}$$

where

x = number of sample items having the selected attribute

n = sample size

2. Confidence interval for p (large sample):

$$\hat{p} \pm Z_{\alpha/2} \sqrt{\frac{\hat{p}(1-\hat{p})}{n-1}}$$

3. Sample size necessary to obtain margin of error (E) with $(1 - \alpha) \cdot 100\%$ confidence:

$$n = \frac{Z_{\alpha/2}^2 \hat{p}(1-\hat{p})}{E^2} + 1$$

4. Test statistic for hypothesis testing on p (large sample):

$$Z = \frac{\hat{p} - p_0}{\sqrt{\frac{p_0(1-p_0)}{n}}}$$

where p_0 is the hypothesized value of p.

Two Populations (Large, Independent Samples)

1. Confidence interval for $p_1 - p_2$:

$$(\hat{p}_1 - \hat{p}_2) \pm Z_{\alpha/2} \sqrt{\frac{\hat{p}_1(1-\hat{p}_1)}{n_1 - 1} + \frac{\hat{p}_2(1-\hat{p}_2)}{n_2 - 1}}$$

2. Test statistic for hypothesis testing on p_1 and p_2:

$$Z = \frac{\hat{p}_1 - \hat{p}_2}{\sqrt{\frac{\bar{p}(1-\bar{p})}{n_1} + \frac{\bar{p}(1-\bar{p})}{n_2}}}$$

where

$$\bar{p} = \frac{x_1 + x_2}{n_1 + n_2}$$

Chi-Square Test Statistic:

$$\chi^2 = \sum \frac{(O - E)^2}{E}$$

summed over all categories for a goodness-of-fit test and over all cells for a test of independence. In the latter case, each expected value (E) is replaced by its estimate, $\hat{E}$.

Estimated Expected Value for a Test of Independence

$$\hat{E} = \frac{(\text{row total for cell})(\text{column total for cell})}{n}$$

where n is the total of all cells in the contingency table.

X Review Exercises 12.53–12.67

12.53 A Gallup Poll of 1,025 adults revealed that 205 of these Americans do not own a credit card. Estimate the proportion of all Americans that do not own a credit card. Compute a 90% confidence interval for this proportion. What is the margin of error?

(Source: "Most Americans Have One or Two Credit Cards," *USA Today*, June 1, 2001, p. 1A.)

12.54 *People's Choice*, a monthly magazine, claimed that more than 40% of its subscribers had an annual income of $50,000 or more. In a random sample of 62 subscribers, 30 had incomes of $50,000 or more. Does this information substantiate the magazine's claim? Use a significance level of .10.

12.55 California has an unusually large number of small companies. Only 3% of all businesses in California are considered to have more than 100 employees. These businesses are especially vulnerable to California's rising electric utility costs. Suppose that a politician believes that the percent of businesses with more than 100 employees is higher in Southern California than the state average of 3%. What sample size is required to estimate the proportion of businesses in Southern California with more than 100 employees with a margin of error of 1% using a confidence level of 95%?

(Source: "California's Many Small Businesses," *USA Today*, July 5, 2001, p. 1B.)

12.56 Web site visitors are often loath to disclose personal information when making a purchase on the Internet. Despite safeguards, approximately 60% of all consumers who make purchases on the Internet do not feel comfortable giving their credit card number. Suppose that a random sample of 15 individuals who have made purchases over the Internet were selected at a shopping center and asked if they felt comfortable giving their credit card over the Internet. Assume that nine of the participants of this survey did not feel comfortable with this.

   a. At the 5% significance level, can it be concluded that more consumers who make purchases on the Internet do not feel comfortable giving their credit card number than those that do?

   b. Find a 95% confidence interval for the proportion of consumers who make purchases on the Internet that do not feel comfortable giving their credit card number.

   c. Assume that you have no prior knowledge of p (proportion of consumers who make purchases on the Internet that do not feel comfortable giving their credit card number). Estimate the sample size that is required to estimate p with 95% confidence, assuming a margin of error of 8%.

(Source: "Why Do You Ask?" *The Wall Street Journal*, June 25, 2001, p. R17.)

12.57 Holiday Inn ran a TV ad that showed ordinary people achieving extraordinary things like preventing a nuclear power plant accident, exploring a virus, studying the habits of the great white shark, or performing in a rock group. The heroes are not the people that they pretend to be, but when the truth is discovered, they all say that they got their smarts because they stayed at a Holiday Inn Express. Marketing analysts were surprised that only about 20% of the population really liked the ad. Suppose a marketing analyst believes that males think more highly of the ad than females. From a random sample of 500 males and 500 females, the analyst found that 114 males and 74 females really liked the ad a lot. Do the data support the market analyst's belief? Base your conclusion on the p-value.

(Source: "Stay Smart, Save the Day," *USA Today*, July 16, 2001, p. 4B.)

12.58 Marketing researchers like to contrast cities to gain insight into how consumers will react to different marketing strategies. One example is the difference between New York City and San Diego. The median age in San Diego is 43.8 versus 48.0 in New York City. Also New York City has about 15% of its population making over $100,000 annually versus 10% for San Diego. Suppose that a marketing researcher is interested in the percentage of adults that watch TV sports. A random sample of 250 for each city yielded 98 and 108 for New York City and San Diego, respectively. Can the marketing researcher conclude that the proportion of adults in San Diego that watch TV sports is greater than that in New York City? Use a 5% significance level.

(Source: "Tale of Two Cities," *USA Today*, October 20, 1998, p. 1A.)

12.59 A market-research firm is interested in testing the hypothesis that the proportion of students who own a car is the same for the local state university campus and a local private college. They interviewed 240 students from the state university and 270 from the private college. The number of students who did not own a car was 78 at the state university and 82 at the private college. Using a .02 significance level, test the hypothesis.

12.60 Almost 30% of undergraduates in college have taken out a student loan. This percentage is up from 19% ten years ago. The Education Department of the United States has noted that lenders have displayed more flexibility in allowing borrowers to pay off student loans. As a result, the default rate is declining. Suppose that the Education Department believes that the default rate is lower for students graduating from private schools. A random sample of 500 students from each sector yielded default rates of 8.0% and 8.8% from students having attended private and public schools, respectively.

   a. Test the Education Department's belief. What is the p-value?

   b. Suppose that the same proportions were found with sample sizes of 1,000 from each sector. How does the p-value change?

(Source: "College Bills: Student Loans Make the Grade," *Kiplinger's Personal Finance Magazine*, vol. 55, issue 10, October 2001, p. 24.)

12.61 Sears charges a 21% annual rate with the proprietary Sears credit card. Historically, 5% of all accounts end up not being closed out without being paid in full. Suppose that a financial analyst wished to determine if the current percentage of accounts that have not been paid in full is different from 5%.

    a. What conclusion can the analyst make using a 5% significance level if a random sample of 100 accounts revealed that eight accounts were closed out and had not been paid in full? Use the Z test.

    b. Use the chi-square goodness-of-fit test instead of the Z test in part a.

    c. What is the relationship between the test statistics in parts a and b?

(Adapted from "Come See the Softer Side of Sears—Its Earnings," *The Wall Street Journal*, July 23, 1998, p. B1.)

12.62 A large department store in New York City has five entrances and exits. It is believed that the proportion of shoppers entering or leaving the store is approximately the same for each of the five doorways on any single day. The number of customers entering or leaving the store is tallied at each doorway for three randomly selected days:

Doorways	Customers
1	150
2	123
3	126
4	163
5	152

Do the data justify the statement that all five entrances and exits are used equally often? Use a 5% significance level.

12.63 Six automotive manufacturers hold approximately 85% of the market share of automobiles sold in the United States. In September 2001, the market share held by General Motors, Ford, DaimlerChrysler, Toyota, Honda, and Nissan were 29.7%, 21.8%, 11.8%, 9.8%, 7.3%, and 4.6%, respectively. Suppose that with the slower economy in 2002, a survey of 1,000 recently sold automobiles shows the results in the following table. Would you conclude that the market share held by these six automotive manufacturers has changed? Use a 5% significance level.

General Motors	Ford	DaimlerChrysler	Toyota	Honda	Nissan	Other
325	201	120	102	64	39	149

(Source: "DaimlerChrysler Turnaround Seems to Be Going in Reverse," *The Wall Street Journal*, October 11, 2001, p. B4.)

12.64 Employers have expanded benefits for workers over the past several years to make recruiting easier and to increase morale. Among the benefits have been full or partial school tuition reimbursement and up to three months leave of absence unrelated to the Family Medical and Leave Act. Suppose that a study is conducted using 200 randomly selected companies, and their policy on tuition reimbursement, as well as their policy on family leave, are recorded.

	At Least 3 Months of Leave Allowed	Less than 3 Months of Leave Allowed
No tuition reimbursement	10	15
Partial tuition reimbursement	60	50
Full tuition reimbursement	50	15

    a. What null and alternative hypothesis would be of interest in determining if a relationship exists between a company's tuition reimbursement policy and its policy on family leave?

    b. Test the hypothesis developed in part a. What is your conclusion at the 5% significance level?

(Source: "Employers Expand Benefits," *USA Today*, June 28, 2001, p. 1B.)

12.65   In the field of organizational psychology, extensive study has been made of different leadership styles. One researcher refers to two extremes as authoritarian versus democratic; another refers to task-oriented versus people-oriented; yet others have their own labels for these qualities. Whatever the label, do these different styles affect the morale of the subordinates? To address this issue, a researcher established a ranking scale for worker morale, based on interviews, and grouped the workers into low, acceptable, and high morale categories. These were cross-classified against the leadership style of the supervisor. The following contingency table summarizes the results.

Worker Morale	Leadership Style		
	Authoritarian	Democratic	Total
Low	10	5	15
Acceptable	8	12	20
High	6	9	15
Total	24	26	50

a. Apply the chi-square test of independence to these data, at a 5% significance level.
b. State the p-value for your test.
c. Is worker morale related to the supervisor's leadership style, or are these qualities independent?

12.66   Kingston Pencils is considering a new bonus plan. Under the current bonus plan, the amount of bonus is not linked to production but only linked to profits. According to the proposed bonus plan, the amount of bonus will be linked to the quantity produced but will be subject to the amount of profits. The controller of Kingston is interested in examining whether employee opinion of the bonus plan is independent of job classification.

Employee	Favorable	Unfavorable
White collar	67	28
Blue collar	43	19

Calculate the p-value and interpret it.

12.67   **[DATA SET EX 12-67]** Variable Description:

DouglasorNoble: Indicates whether an online buyer purchases a Douglas fir or a Noble fir

OnlineSite: Indicates which of the four online sites that the buyer used in purchasing a Christmas tree

While Internet sales of Christmas trees still only represent about 5% of the Christmas tree market, experts say that this market segment could potentially grow rapidly. Some online buyers like the home-delivery aspect of the service, particularly if they are too busy to shop for a tree. To better understand the relationship between the type of tree and the online site where buyers purchase their trees, a random sample of 300 online buyers was selected, and the data in DouglasorNoble and OnlineSite were collected.

a. Form a contingency table of the data.
b. Can you conclude that the type of tree ordered and the online site are independent at the 5% significance level?
c. Do a what-if analysis by removing the site www.mtnstarfarms.com from the contingency table. Does this change your conclusion in part b?

Computer Exercises Using the Databases

Exercise 1—Appendix F

Randomly select 100 observations from the database. Find a 95% confidence interval on the proportion of households that own their homes. (Refer to the variable OWNORENT.)

Exercise 2—Appendix F

Randomly select 100 observations from the database. Estimate the proportion of observations from the NE sector in which the households own their homes. (Refer to the variable LOCATION and OWNORENT.) Also estimate the proportion of observations from the NW sector in which the households own their homes. Find a 95% confidence interval on the difference of the proportions of house owners for the two sectors.

Exercise 3—Appendix F

Randomly select 200 observations from the database. Are the categories own or rent one's residence (variable OWNORENT) and family size (variable FAMLSIZE) independent? Use a .05 significance level.

Exercise 4—Appendix G

Randomly select 100 observations from the database. Find a 95% confidence interval on the proportion of companies with a positive net income. (Refer to the variable NETINC.)

Exercise 5—Appendix G

Randomly select 100 observations from the database. Estimate the proportion of observations from companies with an A bond rating that have a positive net income. (Refer to the variables BONDRATE and NETINC.) Also estimate the proportion of observations from companies with a B bond rating that have a positive net income. Find a 95% confidence interval on the difference of the proportions of companies with positive net income between those with A bond ratings and those with B bond ratings.

Exercise 6—Appendix G

Randomly select 100 observations from the database. Are the categories bond rating (BONDRATE) and positive or negative net income (NETINC) independent? Use a .05 significance level.

Insights from Statistics in Action

Streaming Meemies: The Most Valuable Consumer Group on the Internet

The Statistics in Action introductory case discussed how company executives must make decisions on buying ads on Webcasts. They must assess whether streamies are more responsive to their product than nonstreamies. Surveys have illustrated that, in general, streamies are more likely to make online purchases. However, companies must feel assured before making an investment in advertising that the proportion of streamies making purchases of their company's product is significantly more than the Internet surfers that are not focusing on Internet audio or video. A company's decision makers can greatly benefit from using statistical techniques designed to make inferences about a population proportion.

Suppose that a survey of 200 Internet users determined whether the user was a streamie or a nonstreamie and whether the user was very likely to purchase a particular product online. The data are in StatInActChap10.xls. The data in the first column are labeled S for streamie or Non-S for nonstreamie and the data in the second column are labeled Yes, the user is likely to purchase the product online, or No, the user is not likely to purchase the product online. Use these data in answering the following questions.

Form a contingency table with the rows representing the categories of *streamie* or *nonstreamie* and the columns representing the categories of *Yes* or *No* as responses by users to their likelihood of purchasing the product online.

1. Find a 95% confidence interval on the proportion of Internet users that are likely to purchase the product online. Interpret this interval.

2. What sample size would be necessary to obtain a margin of error of 2% in estimating the proportion of Internet users that would purchase the product online?

3. Test that the proportion of Internet users that are streamies differs from the estimate of .44 obtained in a previous survey. Use a 5% significance level.

4. Test that the proportion of streamies who were likely to purchase the product online is greater than the proportion of non-streamies who were likely to purchase the product online. Use a 5% significance level.

(Source: "Wi-fi Your Hi-Fi," *Forbes*, September 2004, p. 61. "Online Stations Are Still Making Only Small Internet Waves," *The Financial Times*, April 4, 2001, p. 7. "Marketers Find Lucrative Audience in 'Streamies'," *Advertising Age*, 2000, vol. 71, issue 8, p. 48.)

Appendix

Data Analysis with Excel, MINITAB, and SPSS

Excel

Z test for Population Proportion

To obtain a Z test for a hypothesis test involving a population proportion click on **KPK Data Analysis ➤ Inference on Proportions ➤ One Population Proportion for the** dialog box. For example 12.5, insert the 13 for **Number of Successes,** 150 for **Sample Size,** 5 for **Alpha,** and .04 for **Hypothesized Value of Proportion** after choosing **Hypothesis Test** as **Method.** Click **Two-tail test** and enter the **Output Range** to be A1. Note that there is an option to obtain a **Graphical Display of Test.** Finally, click the **OK** button for the output.

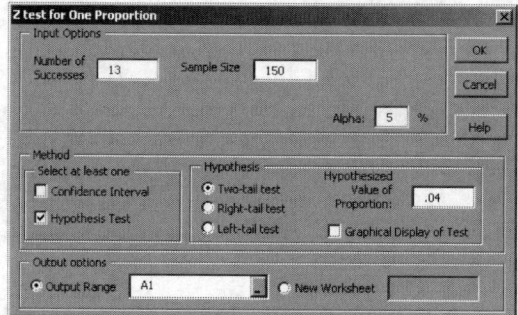

Z test for Comparing Two Population Proportions

To obtain a Z test for a hypothesis test involving two population proportions click on **KPK Data Analysis ➤ Inference on Proportions ➤ Two Population Proportions for the** dialog box. For example 12.9, insert 70 and 110 for the **Number of Successes** for **Sample 1** and **Sample 2,** respectively. Insert 500 for the **Sample Size** for both **Sample 1** and **Sample 2.** Next, enter 5 in the **Alpha** box and select the **Hypothesis Test** option. Click **Left-tail test** and enter A1 for the **Output Range.** Note that a **Graphical Display of Test** option is available with this test. Click **OK** for the output.

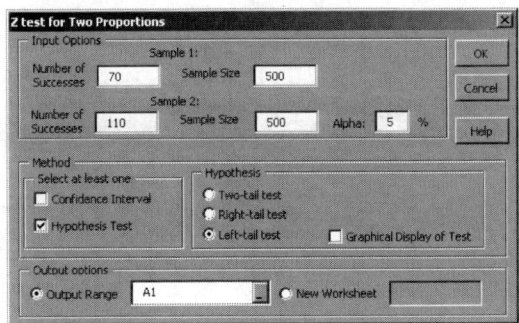

Chi-Square Multinomial Goodness-of-Fit Test

To perform a chi-square multinomial goodness-of-fit test, click on **KPK Data Analysis ➤ Chi-Square Tests** to obtain the dialog box. For **Select a test,** choose **Multinomial Goodness-of-Fit Test.** Say that the five observed values (32, 142, 87, 221, 18) and the five hypothesized proportions (.05, .30, .20, .40, .05) of Example 12.10 are in column A and B, respectively. Enter A1:A5 for the **Input Range of Observed Frequencies** and B1:B5 for the **Input Range of Hypothesized Proportions.** Enter 5 for **Alpha.** Select the **Output Range** and click **OK** for the output.

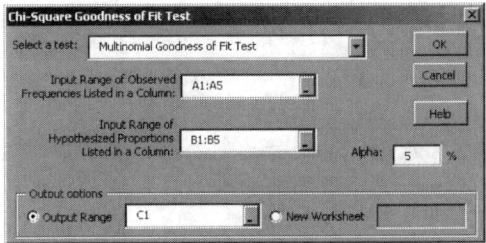

Chi-Square Test for Independence

To carry out a test of independence using the built-in Excel procedures, a table of expected frequencies needs to be computed. Using the KPK macros eliminates this computation. For example 12.11, first put the observed frequencies in, say, cells A1:C3. To obtain the dialog box for a chi-square test of independence, click on **KPK Data Analysis ➤ Chi Square Tests.** For **Select a test,** choose **Independence of Rows and Columns.** Enter A1:C3 for the **Input Range of Observed Frequencies.** Enter 5 for **Alpha.** Select the **Output Range,** say D1, and click **OK** for the output.

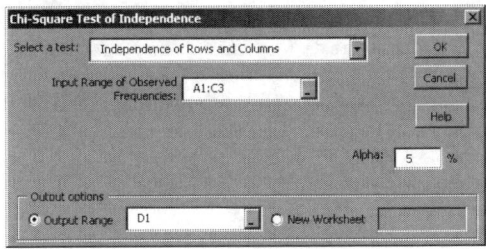

MINITAB

Z test for Population Proportion

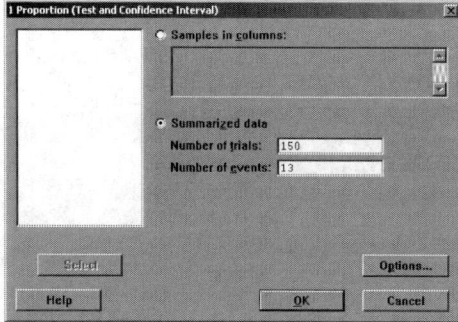
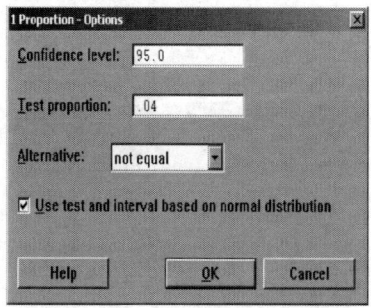

To obtain a *Z* test for a hypothesis test involving a population proportion, click on **Stat ➤ Basic Statistics ➤ 1 Proportion** to obtain the dialog box. For example 12.5, click the **Summarized data** option and enter 150 for **Number of trials** and 13 for **Number of events.** Click **Options** and enter 95 for the **Confidence level** since a .05 significance level is used in this example, .04 for the **Test proportion,** and not equal for **Alternative.** Check the option to **Use test and interval based on normal distribution** to obtain the *Z* test. Click the **OK** button to obtain the results.

Z test for Comparing Two Population Proportions

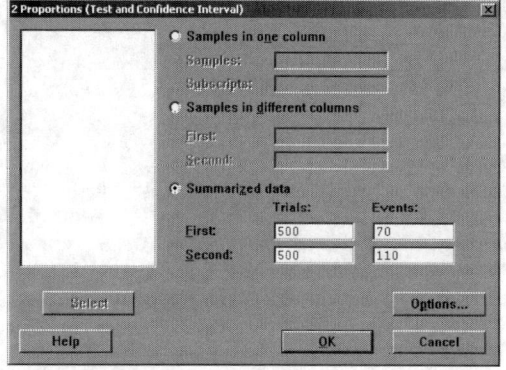
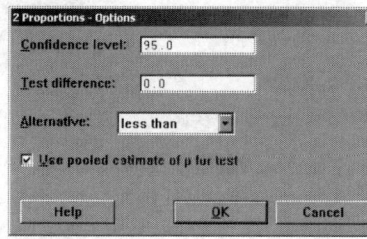

To obtain a *Z* test for a hypothesis test involving two population proportions, click on **Stat ➤ Basic Statistics ➤ 2 Proportions** to obtain the dialog box. For example 12.9, click the **Summarized data** option and enter 500 under **Trials** for **First** and **Second** samples. Enter 70 and 110 under **Events** for **First** and **Second** samples. Click **Options** and enter 95 for the **Confidence level** since a .05 significance level is used in this example, 0 for the **Test difference,** and less than for **Alternative.** Check the option to **Use pooled estimate of p for test.** Click **OK** button to obtain output.

Chi-Square Multinomial Goodness-of-Fit Test

MINITAB does not perform a chi-square goodness-of-fit test. However, if the observed frequencies are put in column C1 and the expected frequencies are put in column C2, then the following commands can be used to obtain the chi-square statistic and its p-value.

```
MTB > LET C3 = (C1 – C2)**2/C2
MTB > SUM C3, put into C4
MTB > CDF (C4);
SUBC > CHISQUARE(DF).
```

Chi-Square Test for Independence

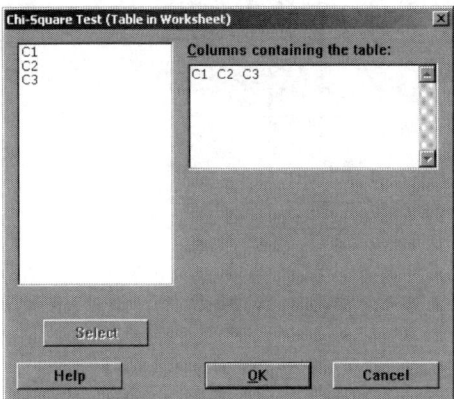

To perform a chi-square test of independence with a two-dimensional set of data, first list the observed frequencies for each cell in several columns. For Example 12.10, the observed frequencies would need to be placed in three columns, say, C1, C2, and C3. Click **Stat ➤ Tables ➤ Chi-Square Test.** Select C1, C2, and C3 for the **Columns containing the table.** Click **OK** for the output. If a contingency table needs to be first constructed click on **Stat ➤ Tables ➤ Cross Tabulation.**

SPSS

Chi-Square Test for Independence

The SPSS procedure to carry out a chi-square test of independence must begin with data that are not yet tabulated. If the data are already tabulated (as in Example 12.11), the first step is to construct two columns containing the untabulated data. For example 12.11, let

> M = employee's top level of education is a master's degree
>
> B = employee's top level of education is a bachelor's degree
>
> HS = employee's top level of education is a high school diploma

and

> H = employee's exam performance was rated as high
>
> A = employee's exam performance was rated as average
>
> L = employee's exam performance was rated as low

A data set containing 120 rows is constructed using the first two columns of the data sheet, as illustrated. Click on the **Variable View** tab and name these variables degree and perform. For example, the first four rows represent the four individuals with a master's degree and a high exam performance rating. The next 20 rows represent the 20 individuals with a master's degree and an average exam performance rating, and so on. The final nine rows contain "HS and L" for the nine individuals with a high school diploma and a low exam performance rating.

	degree	perform	var
1	M	H	
2	M	H	
3	M	H	
4	M	H	
5	M	A	
6	M	A	
7	M	A	
8	M	A	
9	M	A	
10	M	A	
11	M	A	
12	M	A	
13	M	A	
14	M	A	
15	M	A	
16	M	A	
17	M	A	
18	M	A	
19	M	A	
20	M	A	
21	M	A	
22	M	A	

◄ ► \ **Data View** ╱ Variable View ╱

Click on **Analyze ➤ Descriptive Statistics ➤ Crosstabs.** Move the degree variable into the **Row(s)** box and the perform variable into the **Column(s)** box. Click on the **Statistics** button and check **Chi-square statistic** in the dialog box that appears. To see the observed and expected frequency, click on **Cells** and check **Observed** and **Expected.** Click on **Continue** and then **OK.** Note that the chi-square value is labeled **Pearson Chi-Square** in the SPSS output.

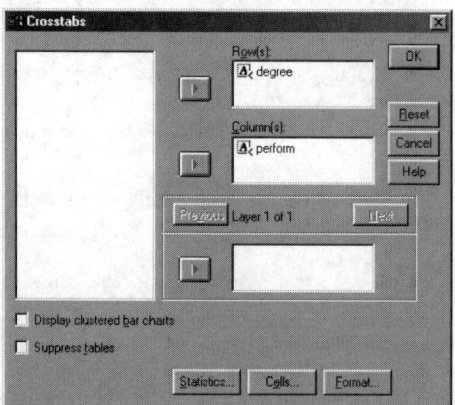

Correlation and Simple Linear Regression X

Statistics in Action
Alpha Beta Soup for the Investor's Soul: Recipe Includes Regression Analysis

The prospectus for Rydex Ursa reads: "Rydex Series Trust Ursa Fund seeks to provide investment results that inversely correlate with the performance of the S&P 500." This fund makes a market for itself by appealing to investors who believe that the S&P 500 stock index is ready to head south. The fund is able to move in a direction opposite to the S&P 500 index by engaging in short sales and futures contracts. In financial parlance, this mutual fund would have a negative beta. Knowing the alpha and beta of a mutual fund can assist investors in selecting mutual funds in accordance with their risk tolerance to hopefully prevent a bad case of financial heartburn.

Morningstar describes alpha as "a measure of the difference between a fund's actual returns and its expected performance, given its level of risk as measured by beta." The beta value of a stock characterizes the stock's response to fluctuations in the market portfolio. To better understand alpha and beta, consider the equation: mutual fund return = alpha + (beta × index return). This equation implies that the performance of a mutual fund can be measured against the performance of an index, typically the S&P 500 stock index. Suppose the market index return is 2% and a stock's beta is 1.5 and its alpha is 1. The stock return would then be 4% (i.e., 1% + (1.5 × 2%) = 4%). Thus, a higher beta value means that a mutual fund could outperform the general market if the market were to rally or it could underperform the market if the market were to decline.

Morningstar, started 14 years ago as a newsletter, now has annual revenues of $45 million. Its star ratings and information on the investment style of a fund are widely used by investors to assess a fund's performance. However, a mutual fund manager might change his or her investment approach over time. For example, a manager might switch to riskier stocks because the manager believes the economy is poised to rebound. Investors can detect this switch in a manager's investing style by monitoring the fund's beta.

Fidelity Dividend Growth fund had an alpha and a beta of 6.20 and .85, respectively, for the last three years. The beta value of .85 indicates that this fund is less volatile than the S&P 500. This type of fund would appeal to a somewhat conservative investor, perhaps one that understood that high-beta funds are a two-edged sword. The alpha value is positive for this fund, and this value represents the contribution made by the fund manager to the fund's performance. Mutual funds with high alpha values tend to be the higher-performing funds.

Statistical analysis provides investors with a variety of tools to evaluate their investment. When you have completed this chapter, you will be able to

- Use regression analysis to develop an equation with two variables, such as an equation involving the performance of a mutual fund and the performance of the S&P 500 index.

- Measure the strength of a linear relationship between two variables.

- Determine which observations, say values of mutual fund performance and S&P 500 performance, would be considered outliers and which observations, if removed, would have a dramatic effect on the best line through the observations.

13.1

BIVARIATE DATA AND CORRELATION

When each observation in your sample consists of data on two variables (such as a company's yearly sales and yearly advertising expenditures), this produces a sample consisting of **bivariate data.** For example, the sample data might consist of the age (X) and liquid assets (Y) for a number of individuals. Or it might contain the unemployment rate (X) and crime rate (Y) over a number of time periods in a particular large city. This topic was first introduced in Chapter 3, section 8, which explored the following example.

A real-estate developer wanted to determine whether there was a relationship between family income $(X$, in thousands of dollars) of the local residents and the square footage of their homes $(Y$, in hundreds of square feet). A random sample of 10 families produced the following results:

| Income (X) | 32 | 36 | 55 | 47 | 38 | 60 | 66 | 44 | 70 | 50 |
| Square footage (Y) | 16 | 17 | 26 | 24 | 22 | 21 | 32 | 18 | 30 | 20 |

A graphical representation of bivariate data is called a **scatter diagram.** In this graph, each observation is represented by a point, where the X values (income) are on the horizontal axis and the Y values (square footage) are on the vertical axis. The resulting scatter diagram is shown in Figure 13.1(a), where it appears that the larger incomes (X) are associated with larger home sizes (Y). These two variables are said to have a **positive (direct) relationship.** When larger values of X are associated with smaller values of Y, these variables have a **negative (inverse) relationship.** A classic example of a negative relationship is that between the prevailing interest rate (X) and the number of new housing starts (Y). As the interest rate increases, the construction of new homes typically decreases.

In Figure 13(b), a straight line is shown *slicing through* the 10 observations. Rarely will such a line actually pass through all the observations—in fact, such a situation is highly suspect unless there is an explicit (nonrandom) relationship between the two variables, such as that between the diameter of a circle (X) and the corresponding circumference of the circle (Y). The line in Figure 13(b) has a positive slope, indicating the positive (direct) relationship between household income and square footage. The strength of the linear relationship between two variables is measured by the coefficient of correlation.

FIGURE

13.1

Scatter diagram of real-estate data.
(a) Scatter diagram of sample data.
(b) Line through sample data.

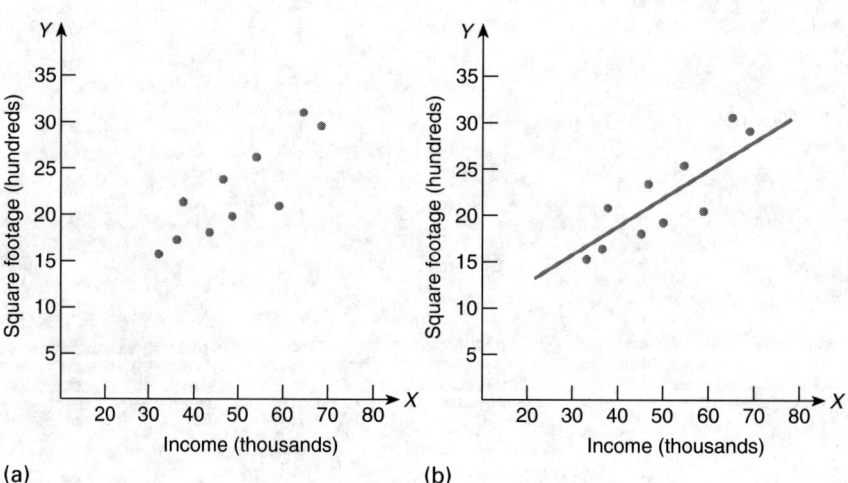

(a)

(b)

Coefficient of Correlation

The strength of the linear relationship between two variables can be computed from the sample data using a statistic called the **coefficient of correlation.** This statistic is called r and was first introduced in Chapter 3, section 8. The Chapter 3 discussion contained a formula for r and a number of scatter diagrams for various values of r (see Figure 3.15). Either of the following two equations can be used to calculate the sample coefficient of correlation:

$$r = \frac{\Sigma(x - \bar{x})(y - \bar{y})}{\sqrt{\Sigma(x - \bar{x})^2}\sqrt{\Sigma(y - \bar{y})^2}} \qquad \text{13.1}$$

$$= \frac{\Sigma xy - (\Sigma x)(\Sigma y)/n}{\sqrt{\Sigma x^2 - (\Sigma x)^2/n}\sqrt{\Sigma y^2 - (\Sigma y)^2/n}} \qquad \text{13.2}$$

where Σx = sum of X values, Σx^2 = sum of X^2 values, Σy = sum of Y values, Σy^2 = sum of Y^2 values, Σxy = sum of XY values, $\bar{x} = \Sigma x/n$, and $\bar{y} = \Sigma y/n$. Note that X and Y represent the variables on the horizontal and vertical axes, respectively, whereas x and y represent specific observations of the X and Y variables. When using a calculator to determine a coefficient of correlation, equation 13.2 provides a computationally easier procedure. Notice that the summations in the denominator of equation 13.1 are the numerators for the sample variances of x and y.

Sum of Squares

We will introduce a shorthand notation at this point, related to the notation in Chapter 9 for ANOVA.

$$SS_x = \text{sum of squares for } X \qquad \text{13.3}$$

$$= \Sigma(x - \bar{x})^2$$

$$= \Sigma x^2 - \frac{(\Sigma x)^2}{n}$$

$$SS_y = \text{sum of squares for } Y$$

$$= \Sigma(y - \bar{y})^2$$

$$= \Sigma y^2 - \frac{(\Sigma y)^2}{n} \qquad \text{13.4}$$

$$SCP_{XY} = \text{sum of cross products for } XY$$

$$= \Sigma(x - \bar{x})(y - \bar{y})$$

$$= \Sigma xy - \frac{(\Sigma x)(\Sigma y)}{n} \qquad \text{13.5}$$

Using this notation, we can write r as

$$r = \frac{SCP_{XY}}{\sqrt{SS_x}\sqrt{SS_y}} \qquad \text{13.6}$$

Comments

The discussion in Chapter 3, section 8, described some important properties of the sample correlation coefficient, r. There are four key things to remember:

1. r ranges from -1 to 1.

2. The larger $|r|$ (absolute value of r) is, the stronger is the linear relationship.

3. The sign of r tells you whether the relationship between X and Y is a positive (direct) or negative (inverse) one.

4. $r = 1$ or $r = -1$ implies that a perfect linear pattern exists between the two variables in the sample; that is, a single line will go *through each point*. Here we say that X and Y are **perfectly correlated.**

E X A M P L E 13.1

Determine the sample correlation coefficient for the real-estate data in Figure 13.1.

Solution   Your calculations can be organized as follows:

Family	X (Income)	Y (Square Footage)	XY	X²	Y²
1	32	16	512	1,024	256
2	36	17	612	1,296	289
3	55	26	1,430	3,025	676
4	47	24	1,128	2,209	576
5	38	22	836	1,444	484
6	60	21	1,260	3,600	441
7	66	32	2,112	4,356	1,024
8	44	18	792	1,936	324
9	70	30	2,100	4,900	900
10	50	20	1,000	2,500	400
	498	226	11,782	26,290	5,370

Using the totals from this table,

$$SS_X = 26,290 - \frac{(498)^2}{10} = 1489.6$$

$$SS_Y = 5370 - \frac{(226)^2}{10} = 262.4$$

$$SCP_{XY} = 11,782 - \frac{(498)(226)}{10} = 527.2$$

This value of the sample correlation coefficient is

$$r = \frac{SCP_{XY}}{\sqrt{SS_X}\sqrt{SS_Y}}$$

$$= \frac{527.2}{\sqrt{1489.6}\sqrt{262.4}} = \frac{527.2}{625.2} = .843$$

For large data sets, the easiest way to obtain a scatter diagram and calculate the value of r is to use a computer. The end-of-chapter appendix in Chapter 3 contains the necessary instructions when using Excel, MINITAB, or SPSS. By using Excel's Chart Wizard, the output in Figure 13.2 was generated. This figure was finetuned a bit by clicking on any of the values on the X axis, clicking on **Format Axis ➤ Scale,** and setting the minimum and maximum values to 30 and 75. This was repeated for the Y axis, where the minimum and maximum values were set to 15 and 35. In cell A11, Correlation Coefficient was entered. This value (.843) was computed in cell A12 by clicking on **Insert ➤ Function ➤ Statistical ➤ CORREL.**

FIGURE

13.2

Excel-generated
scatter diagram
and correlation
coefficient for the
real estate data.

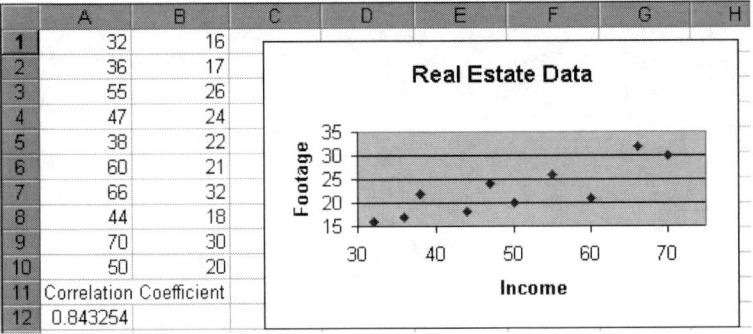

	A	B	C	D	E	F	G	H
1	32	16						
2	36	17						
3	55	26						
4	47	24						
5	38	22						
6	60	21						
7	66	32						
8	44	18						
9	70	30						
10	50	20						
11	Correlation Coefficient							
12	0.843254							

FIGURE

13.3

Vertical distances
from line L to real-
estate data
(Example 13.1),
represented by d_1,
$d_2, \ldots, d_{10}$.

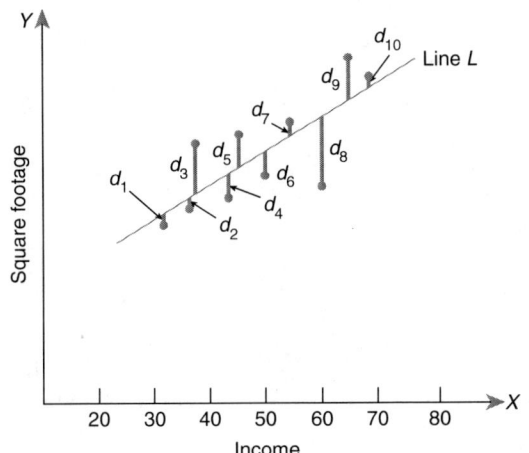

Least Squares Line

If we believe that two variables do exhibit an underlying linear pattern, how can we determine a straight line that best passes through these points? So far, we have demonstrated
only the calculations necessary to compute a correlation coefficient. We next illustrate how
to construct a line through a set of points exhibiting a linear pattern; we look at the
assumptions behind this procedure in the next section.

Look at the scatter diagram in Figure 13.1(b), which shows one possible line through
these points. The scatter diagram and line are repeated in Figure 13.3, which also shows
the vertical distances from each point to the line ($d_1, d_2, \ldots$).

Is line L the best line through these points? Because we would like the distances d_1, d_2,
$\ldots, d_{10}$ to be small, we define the best line to be the one that minimizes

$$\Sigma d^2 = d_1^2 + d_2^2 + d_3^2 + \ldots + d_{10}^2$$

13.7

We square each distance because some of these distances are positive (the point lies
above line L) and some are negative (the point lies *below* line L). If we did not square
each distance, d, the positive d's might cancel out the negative ones. This means that
using ($d_1 + d_2 + \ldots + d_{10}$) as a *measure of fit* is *not* a good idea. A better method is to

FIGURE

13.4

The least squares line for Example 13.1. Each $d = Y - \hat{Y}$, the error encountered by using the straight line to estimate the value of Y at the corresponding point.

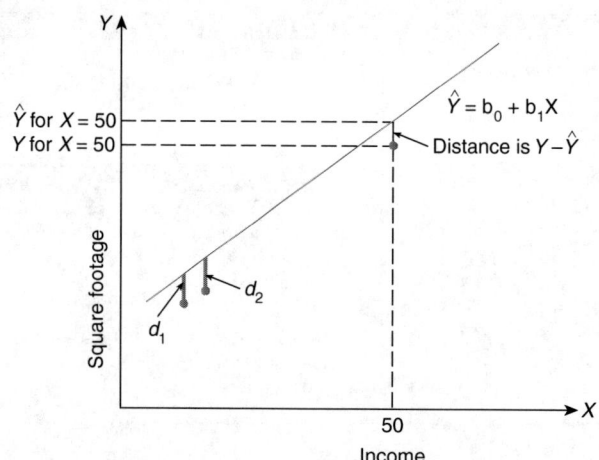

determine which line makes equation 13.7 as small as possible; this line is called the **least squares line.** Deriving this line in general requires the use of calculus (derivatives, in particular).*

Because we intend to use this line to predict Y for a particular value of X, we use the notation $\hat{Y}$ (Y-hat) to describe the equation of the line. We can now define, for the least squares line, the b_0 and b_1 that minimize $(d_1^2 + d_2^2 \ldots + d_n^2)$, given by

$$b_1 = \frac{\text{SCP}_{XY}}{\text{SS}_X}$$
   13.8

$$b_0 = \bar{y} - b_1 \bar{x}$$
   13.9

where SS_X and SCP_{XY} are as defined in equations 13.3 and 13.5. Also, $\bar{x} = \Sigma x / n$ and $\bar{y} = \Sigma y / n$. The resulting least squares line is

$$\hat{Y} = b_0 + b_1 X$$

In Figure 13.4, notice that each distance, d, is actually $Y - \hat{Y}$ and consists of the **residual,** encountered by using the straight line to estimate the value of Y at this point. So

$$\Sigma d^2 = \Sigma (y - \hat{y})^2$$

---

*For the mathematically curious, we provide a condensed derivation of these coefficients. To minimize Σd^2, first write this expression as

$$f(b_0, b_1) = \Sigma d^2 = \Sigma (y - \hat{y})^2$$
$$= \Sigma (y - b_0 - b_1 x)^2$$

because $\hat{y} = b_0 + b_1 x$.

To minimize this function, determine the partial derivatives with respect to b_0 (written as f_{b_0} and with respect to b_1 (written as f_{b_1}). These are

$$f_{b_0} = 2\Sigma(y - b_0 - b_1 x)(-1) = -2[\Sigma y - nb_0 - b_1 \Sigma x]$$
$$f_{b_1} = 2\Sigma(y - b_0 - b_1 x)(-x) = -2[\Sigma xy - b_0 \Sigma x - b_1 \Sigma x^2]$$

Setting $f_{b_0} = f_{b_1} = 0$ and solving for b_0 and b_1 results in equations 13.8 and 13.9.

This term is the **sum of squares of error** (or *residual sum of squares*) and is written **SSE**. Consequently, the least squares line is the one that makes SSE as small as possible.

$$SSE = \Sigma d^2 = \Sigma(y - \hat{y})^2$$

13.10

There is another method of determining SSE when using the least squares line, which avoids having to determine the value of $\hat{Y}$ at each point:

$$SSE = SS_Y - \frac{(SCP_{XY})^2}{SS_X}$$

13.11

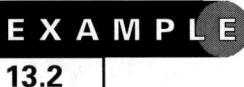

EXAMPLE 13.2

Determine the least squares line for the real-estate data we used in Example 13.1. What is the SSE?

Solution

Using the calculations from Example 13.1, $SCP_{XY} = 527.2$, $SS_X = 1489.6$, and $SS_Y = 262.4$, leading to

$$b_1 = \frac{SCP_{XY}}{SS_X}$$

$$= \frac{527.2}{1489.6} = .3539$$

and

$$b_0 = \bar{y} - b_1\bar{x}$$

$$= 22.6 - \left(\frac{527.2}{1489.6}\right)(49.8) = 4.975$$

because

$$\bar{y} = \frac{\Sigma y}{n} = \frac{226}{10} = 22.6 \quad \text{and} \quad \bar{x} = \frac{\Sigma x}{n} = \frac{498}{10} = 49.8$$

So the equation of the best (least squares) line through these points is

$$\hat{Y} = 4.975 + .3539X$$

This equation tells us that in the sample data an increase of $1,000 in income ($X$ increases by 1) is accompanied by an increase of 35.39 square feet in home size (Y increases by .3539), on the average. For this illustration (and many others in practice), the *intercept, b_0,* has no real meaning because it corresponds to an income of zero dollars. Furthermore, an income of zero is considerably outside the range of the incomes in the sample. It is unsafe to assume that the linear relationship between X and Y present over the range of sample incomes ($32,000 to $70,000) exists outside this range—in particular, all the way to an income of zero. The **slope,** b_1, generally is the more informative value.

In Figure 13.5, the actual value of Y (in the sample data) for $X = 50$ is $Y = 20$ (the last pair of X, Y values). The predicted value of Y using the least squares line is

$$\hat{Y} = 4.975 + (.3539)(50) = 22.670$$

FIGURE

13.5

Least squares line
for real-estate data
(Example 13.2).

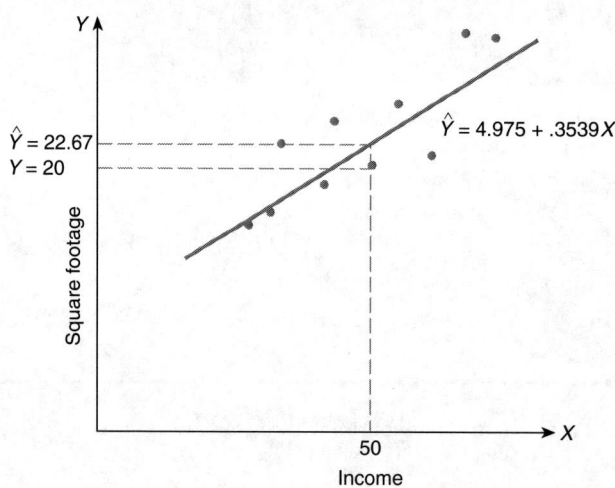

The residual at this point is

$$\text{residual} = Y - \hat{Y} = 20 - 22.670 = -2.670$$

Repeating this for the other nine points leads to the following results. Notice that the sum of the residuals when using the least squares line is zero. This is always true.

X	Y	$\hat{Y}$	$Y - \hat{Y}$	$(Y - \hat{Y})^2$
32	16	16.300	−0.300	0.090
36	17	17.715	−0.715	0.511
55	26	24.440	1.560	2.434
47	24	21.608	2.392	5.722
38	22	18.423	3.577	12.795
60	21	26.209	−5.209	27.134
66	32	28.332	3.668	13.454
44	18	20.547	−2.547	6.487
70	30	29.748	0.252	0.064
50	20	22.670	−2.670	7.129
			0	75.82

Rounded

As you can see, calculating the SSE (= 75.82) using the table and equation 13.10 is tedious. Using equation 13.11 instead leads to

$$SSE = 262.4 - \frac{(527.2)^2}{1489.6}$$

$$= 262.4 - 186.59$$

$$= 75.81$$

This calculated SSE value is slightly more accurate than the value obtained by summing the squared residuals and will be used in the examples to follow.

Remember, however, that equation 13.10 applies to *any* line that you choose to construct through these points, whereas equation 13.11 applies only to the SSE for the least squares line.

In Example 13.2, we attempted to predict the size of a home (Y) using the corresponding income (X). The variable Y is the **dependent variable,** and X is the **independent variable.** By passing a straight line through the sample points with Y as the dependent variable, we are **regressing** Y on X. *In linear regression, you regress the dependent variable, Y, which you are trying to predict, on the independent (or predictor or explanatory) variable, X.*

X Exercises 13.1–13.12

Understanding the Mechanics

13.1 Consider the following table.

X	Y	XY	X²	Y²
3	8			
10	22			
2	6			
5	9			
4	8			

Totals $\Sigma x =$ ___ $\Sigma y =$ ___ $\Sigma xy =$ ___ $\Sigma x^2 =$ ___ $\Sigma y^2 =$ ___

a. Find the totals for each column in the table.
b. Use the totals in the table to calculate the slope and the intercept for the least squares line.
c. Calculate the sample correlation of X and Y.

13.2 The following pairs of observations were collected.

X	1	2	3	4	5
Y	2	6	4	10	15

a. Plot the values of X and Y. What relationship does the scatter diagram suggest?
b. Find the least squares line.
c. Find the predicted value for each value of X.
d. Find the residual for each predicted value of Y.
e. Verify that the sum of the residuals in part d is zero.

Applying the New Concepts

13.3 Nationwide, about 27% of mortgage-paying homeowners spent 30% or more of their income on housing costs. Hawaiians paid the largest percentage at 41% and South Dakotans the smallest at 17.5%. Eight states were randomly selected, and the median household income (X) in thousands and the percentage of mortgage-paying homeowners whose housing costs exceed 30% of their income (Y) are as follows.

State	California	Hawaii	Idaho	Maine	Oklahoma	South Dakota	Utah	West Virginia
X	46.5	51.1	37.1	36.4	33.5	35.2	45.6	28.6
Y	37.2	41.0	20.6	24.3	22.0	17.5	30.0	23.0

a. Graph the data and draw a line through the points. Would you say that the data appear to demonstrate a linear relationship between X and Y?

b. Calculate the least squares line. How does it compare to the line in part a?

(Source: "Snapshot of U.S. Commuting, Income, Housing," *USA Today,* August 6, 2001, p. 2A.)

13.4 The supervisor of a group of assembly-line workers wanted to compare last year's productivity (X) to this year's productivity (Y) for each of the 20 employees that she supervises. In the past, an approximate linear relationship has existed between these two variables. Last year the average productivity per worker was 9.5 items per hour. This year, the average productivity per worker is 12.1 items per hour. The supervisor found the following sums for her 20 employees:

$$SCP_{XY} = 0.4$$
$$SS_X = 0.3$$
$$SS_Y = 0.8$$

a. Calculate the correlation coefficient.
b. Calculate the least squares line.
c. Calculate the sum of squares for error.

13.5 An investor regressed the three-year annualized return (Y) of 20 small-cap mutual funds on the five-year annualized return (X) of those funds. The resulting regression equation was $\hat{Y} = -10 + 1.1X$. Interpret the regression coefficients, assuming that the return is expressed in percent.

13.6 An accountant examined the relationship between the long-term debt (X) and the capital expenditure (Y) of a company, both in units of millions of dollars. The accountant computed $SS_X = 1,500$, $SS_Y = 250$, and $SCP_{XY} = 600$. Interpret the slope of the regression equation and the correlation coefficient.

13.7 Generale Bank agreed to a takeover from the Dutch–Belgian bank and insurance concern, named Fortis Group. This acquisition would propel Fortis to the top league of Europe's largest financial institutions and speed up other cross-border mergers in the European financial-services sector, an industry roiled by mounting competition and the launch of the euro. Generale Bank's management advisor is interested in the relationship between the market

549

capitalization of Europe's main bank insurance concerns and their total assets. The following data are listed as a random sample of these European companies with their market capitalization and total assets in billions of dollars.

European Bank Insurance Firm	Market Capitalization	Total Assets
Deutsche Bank	46.3	585.0
Credit Suisse	59.1	370.0
ING Group	49.4	309.4
Benelux Bank	23.8	168.0
Generale Bank	9.8	160.8
CGER-ASLK	33.6	328.8

a. Graph the data. Estimate the intercept and slope of the regression equation from viewing the graph. Also, estimate the correlation coefficient.

b. Calculate the least squares line. Interpret the coefficients of the regression equation. How closely do the calculated values of the least squares line agree with your estimates from part a?

c. Calculate the correlation coefficient and compare to your estimate from part a.

(Source: "Belgium's Largest Bank Agrees to Be Acquired by Fortis Group," The Wall Street Journal, May 13, 1998, p. C14.)

13.8 The following household income (X) and travel expenses (Y), both in units of thousands, were collected for 10 households.

X	50	45	70	82	95	60	48	65	100	75
Y	1.5	1.0	4.0	5.0	7.0	2.5	1.5	2.5	8.0	4.0

Compute the SSE using equations 13.10 and 13.11.

Using the Computer

13.9 **[DATA SET EX13-9]** Variable Description:

Year: Years 1992 to 2000

TexasLotto: Revenue in billions of dollars from Texas Lotto

TexasLottery: Revenue in billions of dollars from Texas Lottery

Lotteries remain the most pervasive form of gambling in the United States. The Texas Lottery Commission is interested in the revenue generated by the Texas Lotto, in which players pick six numbers, and the Texas Lottery, in which players pick less than six numbers (Cash 5, Pick 3, and Texas Two Step).

a. Estimate the correlation coefficient from a plot of the values of TexasLotto (X) and TexasLottery (X).

b. Compute the correlation and compare to your response in part a.

c. Interpret the coefficients of the regression equation.

13.10 **[DATA SET EX13-10]** Variable Description:

State: Name of U.S. state

2000Pop: Population of state at the end of the year 2000

1990Pop: Population of state at the end of the year 1990

For the first decade since 1870, every state in the United States gained population for the decade ending in 2000. Overall, the U.S. population grew by 13.2%. Not all states grew evenly; Nevada gained the most at 66.3% and North Dakota gained the least at .5%.

a. Plot Y = 2000Pop and X = 1990Pop. Would you say that the plot indicates a linear relationship between X and Y?

b. What is the correlation coefficient? Do you think that value indicates a linear trend?

c. Using the least squares line, what is the predicted value for the population of North Carolina at the end of the year 2000? Would you say this is a good estimate?

13.11 **[Simulation Exercise]** The method of least squares is a technique used to compute the "best" straight line fit to a set of data points plotted on a graph. To better visualize this technique, in Excel click in **KPK Data Analysis ➤ Simulation Exercise** and select **Draw Least Squares Line**. In this simulation exercise, the value of the correlation and the sample size of the data set to be generated is specified by the user. A graph of the data is presented to illustrate the shape of the data for the specified correlation and sample size. The user can move the line sitting above the graph inside the sample points so that it best slices through the data. Then the user can view the actual least squares line to see how closely it matches it to the user's line.

a. Using a sample size of 20, generate data having correlations of –.9, –.5, –.2, 0, .2, .5., and .9. Comment on the shape of the data for each correlation.

b. Select various combinations of high and low correlations with high and low sample sizes, and demonstrate your expertise at fitting a straight line through the data by moving the line sitting above the graph so that it appears to be the "best" linear predictor. Is the actual least squares line close to your line? For which combinations of correlations and sample sizes do you find this to be easy?

13.12 **[DATA SET EX13-12]** Variable Description:

AskPrice: Asking price of a car

SellPrice: Selling price of a car

A car dealer is interested in the relationship between the original asking price of a new car and the final selling price of the car. The car dealer selected a random sample of 50 car deals. The asking and selling prices were recorded as variables AskPrice and SellPrice, respectively. The units of the data are in thousands of dollars.

a. Graph the data. Estimate the intercept and slope of the regression equation from viewing the graph. Estimate the value of the correlation from viewing the graph.

b. Calculate the correlation coefficient and find the coefficients of the least squares line. Compare your answers to that in part a.

THE SIMPLE LINEAR REGRESSION MODEL

When we construct a straight line through a set of data points, we are attempting to predict the behavior of a dependent variable, Y, using a straight line equation with one predictor (independent) variable, X. Examples 13.1 and 13.2 examined the relationship in a particular community between the square footage (Y) of a particular home and the income of the owner (X).

Another applicant is attempting to predict the sales (Y) of a certain brand of shampoo using the amount of advertising expenditure (X) as the independent variable. We expect that as more advertising dollars are spent, the sales will increase. In other words, we expect a *positive* relationship for this situation.

Regression analysis is a method of studying the relationship between two (or more) variables, one purpose being to arrive at a method for predicting a value of the dependent variable. In **simple linear regression,** we use only *one* predictor variable, X, to describe the behavior of the dependent variable, Y. Also, the relationship between X and Y is assumed to be basically linear.

We have learned the mechanics of constructing a line through a set of bivariate sample values. We are now ready to introduce the concept of a statistical model.

Defining the Model

Return to Example 13.2 and Figure 13.2. This set of sample data contained a value of $X = 50$ and $Y = 20$. Consider the population of *all* houses in this community where the owner's income is 50 (that is, $50,000). Will they all have the same square footage? Unless this is a very boring-looking neighborhood, certainly not. Does this mean that the straight line predictor is of no use? The answer again is no; we do not expect things in this world to be that perfectly predictable. When you use the equation of a straight line to predict the square footage, you should be aware that there will be a certain amount of *error* present in this estimate. This is similar to the situation in which we estimate the mean, μ, of a population and the sample mean, $\bar{X}$, always estimates this parameter with a certain amount of inherent error.

When we elect to use a straight-line predictor, we employ a **statistical model** of the form

$$Y = \beta_0 + \beta_1 X + e$$

13.12

where (1) $\beta_0 + \beta_1 X$ is the *assumed* line about which *all* values of X and Y will fall, called the **deterministic** portion of the model, and (2) e is the error component, referred to as the **random error** part of the model.

In other words, there exists some (unknown) line about which all X, Y values can be expected to fall. Notice that we said "about which," not "on which"—hence the necessity of the error term, e, which is the unexplained error that is part of the simple linear model. Because this model considers only one independent variable, the effect of other predictor variables (perhaps unknown to the analyst) is contained in this error term. We will consider the effects of including additional independent variables in Chapter 14.

We emphasize that the deterministic portion, $\beta_0 + \beta_1 X$, refers to the straight line for the *population* and will remain unknown. However, by obtaining a random sample of bivariate data from this population, we are able to estimate the unknown parameters, β_0 and β_1. Thus b_0 is the *intercept* of the sample regression line and is the estimate of the population intercept, β_0. The value of b_0 can be calculated using equation 13.9. Similarly, b_1 is the *slope* of the sample regression line and is the estimate of the population slope, β_1. The value of b_1 can be calculated using equation 13.8.

FIGURE

13.6

Illustration of
assumption 1;
see text.

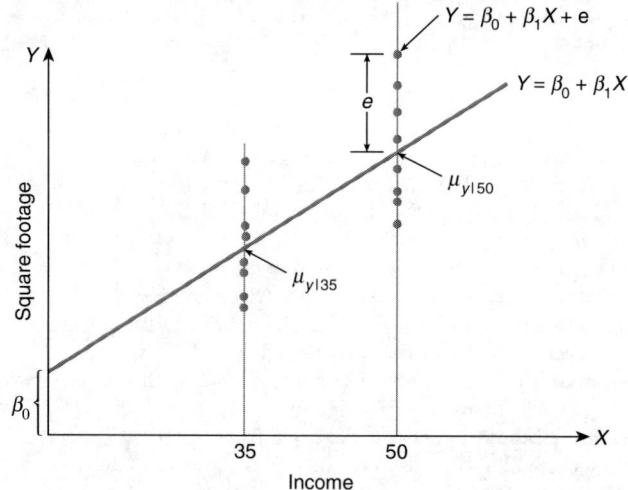

Assumptions for the Simple Linear Regression Model

We can construct a least squares line through *any* set of sample points, whether or not the pattern is linear. We could construct a least squares line through a set of sample data exhibiting no linear pattern at all. However, to have an effective predictor and a model that will enable us to make statistical decisions, certain assumptions are necessary.

We treat the values of X as fixed (nonrandom) quantities when using the simple linear regression model. For any given value of X, the only source of variation comes from the error component, e, which is a random variable. In fact, there are many random variables here, one for each possible value of X. The assumptions used with this model are concerned with the nature of these random variables.

The first three assumptions are concerned with the behavior of the error component for a fixed value of X. The fourth assumption deals with the manner in which the error components (random variables) affect each other.

Assumption 1. *The mean of each error component is zero.* This is the key assumption behind simple linear regression. Look at Figure 13.6, where we once again examine a value of $X = 50$. Considering all homes (in this community) whose owners have an income of \$50,000 ($X = 50$), we have already decided that these homes do not all have the same square footage, Y. In fact, the square-footage values will be scattered about the (unknown) line $Y = \beta_0 + \beta_1 X$, with some values lying above the line (e is positive) and some falling below it (e is negative). Consider the average of *all* Y values with $X = 50$. This is written as

$$\mu_{Y|50}$$

which is the mean of Y given $X = 50$. Our assumption here is that the point $(50, \mu_{Y|50})$ *lies on this line;* that is, for *any* value of X, the point $(x, \mu_{Y|x})$ *lies on the line* $Y = \beta_0 + \beta_1 X$ (such as $\mu_{Y|35}$ in Figure 13.6). Put another way, the error is zero, *on average.*

Assumption 2. *Each error component (random variable) follows an approximate normal distribution.* In our sample of 10 homes and incomes, we had one family with $X = 50$ and $Y = 20$. Figure 13.6 illustrates what we might expect if we were to examine other homes whose owners had an income of \$50,000. We assume here that if we were to obtain 100 homes, for example, whose owners had this income, a histogram of the resulting errors (e) would be bell-shaped in appearance. So we would expect a concentration of errors near zero (from assumption 1), with half of them positive and half of them negative.

FIGURE

13.7

A violation of
assumption 3;
see text.

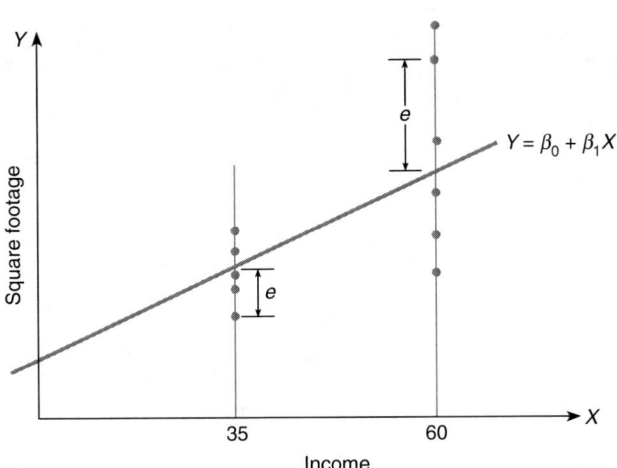

Assumption 3. *The variance of the error component, σ_e^2, is the same for each value of* X. For each value of X, the errors illustrated in Figure 13.6 have so far been assumed to follow a normal distribution with a mean of zero. So each error, e, is from such a normal population. The variance of this population is, σ_e^2. The assumption here is that, σ_e^2 *does not change* as the value of X changes. This is the assumption of **homoscedasticity.** A situation where this assumption is violated is illustrated in Figure 13.7, where we once again consider what might occur if we *were* to obtain (we will not, actually) many values of Y for $X = 35$ and also for $X = 60$. If Figure 13.7 were the result, assumption 3 would be violated, because the errors would be much larger (in absolute value) for the $60,000-income homes than they would for the $35,000-income homes. Figure 13.7 illustrates **heteroscedasticity,** which does pose a problem when we try to infer results from a linear regression equation.

You might argue that, proportionally, the errors for $X = 60$ seem about the same as those for $X = 35$, which means that you would expect larger errors for larger values of X here. If this is the case, the confidence intervals and tests of hypothesis that we are about to develop for the simple linear regression model are *not appropriate*. There are methods of "repairing" this situation, by applying a *transformation* to the dependent variable, Y, such as $\sqrt{Y}$ or log (Y). By using this "new" dependent variable rather than the original Y, the resulting errors often will exhibit a nearly constant variance. Such transformations, however, are beyond the scope of this text.

A summary of the first three assumptions is shown in Figure 13.8. Note that the distribution of errors is *identical* for each illustrated value of X; namely, it is a normal distribution with mean = 0 and variance σ_e^2.

Assumption 4. *The errors are independent of each other*. This implies that the error encountered for one value of Y is unaffected by the error for any other value of Y. To illustrate, consider the real-estate data and suppose that the sample is *not* random but that instead the sample houses are all located on a certain street. The first house has a positive error when predicting the square footage. If the probability is greater than .5 that the next house in the sample also has a positive error (that is, if its location makes it probable that it will be a certain size), then the assumption of independence is violated. In other words, the sample was poorly chosen because the houses on one street are likely to be more or less the same size and their owners are likely to have similar incomes. The nonrandom sample led to a violation of assumption 4.

We can draw two conclusions from these assumptions. First, each value of the dependent variable, Y, is a normal random variable with mean = $\beta_0 + \beta_1 X$ and variance σ_e^2. Second, the error components come from the same normal population, *regardless of the value* of X. In other words, it makes sense to examine the residuals resulting from each value of X in the sample, to construct a histogram of these residuals, and to determine whether its appearance is bell-shaped (normal), centered at zero. A key assumption when

FIGURE

13.8

Illustration
of assumptions
1, 2, 3; see text.

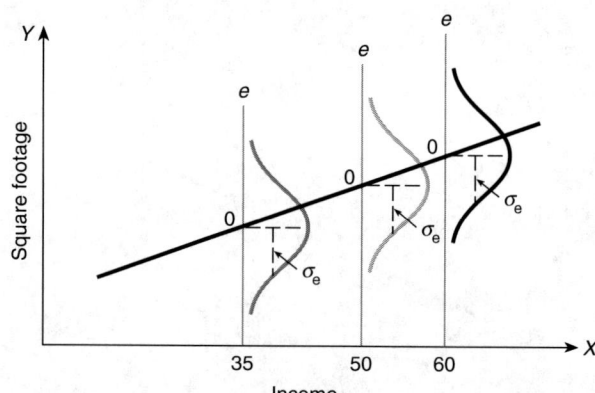

using simple linear regression is that the errors follow a normal distribution with a mean of zero. Constructing a histogram of the sample residuals provides a convenient method of determining whether this assumption is reasonable for a particular application.

This discussion is continued in section 13.6 ("Examining the Residuals"). This section will demonstrate graphical methods for checking these assumptions (including a histogram of the residuals), along with various numerical measures that identify *unusual* and *influential observations* in the sample data.

Estimating the Error Variance, σ_e^2

The variance of the error components, σ_e^2, measures the variation of the error terms resulting from the simple linear regression model. The value of σ_e^2 severely affects our ability to use this model as an effective predictor for a given situation. Suppose, for example, that σ_e^2 is very large in Figure 13.8. This means that if we were to obtain many observations (square footage values, Y) for a *fixed* value of X (say, income = $50,000), these Y values would vary a great deal, decreasing the accuracy of our model; we would prefer that these values were grouped closely about the mean, $\mu_{Y|50}$.

In practice, σ_e^2 typically is unknown and must be estimated from the sample. To estimate this variance, we first determine the sum of squares of error, SSE, using SSE $= \Sigma (y - \hat{y})^2$ or equation 13.11. Estimating β_0 and β_1 for the simple regression model results in a loss of 2 df, leaving $n - 2$ df for estimating the error variance. Consequently,

$$s^2 = \hat{\sigma}_e^2 = \text{estimate of } \sigma_e^2 = \frac{\text{SSE}}{n-2}$$

13.13

where

$$\text{SSE} = \Sigma(y - \hat{y})^2 = \text{SS}_Y - \frac{(\text{SCP}_{XY})^2}{\text{SS}_X}$$

Note that SSE is the expression that was minimized in Figure 13.3 when determining the "best" line through the sample points. In Figure 13.3, each distance d corresponds to $y - \hat{y}$.

We can determine the estimate of σ_e^2 and σ_e for the real-estate data in Example 13.2, where we calculated the value of SSE to be 75.81. Our estimate of σ_e^2 is

$$s^2 = \frac{SSE}{n-2} = \frac{75.81}{8} = 9.476$$

and so $s = \sqrt{9.476} = 3.078$ provides an estimate of σ_e. The values of s^2 and s are a measure of the variation of the Y values about the least squares line.

Comments

We know from the empirical rule that approximately 95% of the data from a normal population should lie within two standard deviations of the mean. For this example, this rule implies that approximately 95% of the residuals should lie within $2(3.078) = 6.16$ of the mean. In the table in Example 13.2, the sample residuals are in the fourth column. Their sum is *always* zero, when using the least squares line; therefore, their mean is *zero*. So, approximately 95% of the residuals should be no larger (in absolute value) than 6.16. In fact, all of them are less than 6.16—not a surprising result, given that we had only 10 values in the sample.

X Exercises 13.13–13.22

Understanding the Mechanics

13.13 The residuals of a least squares line are as follows.

$Y - \hat{Y}$:   .4 .2 3   −.1   .2   .1 −.3 −.4 −.2 −3 .1 .3 .4
             −3   .3 −.1 3   −.2 −.3 −.4

a. Find the estimate of the error variance, s^2.
b. Are approximately 95% of the residuals within $2s$ of the mean of the residuals? What does your answer indicate about the appropriateness of the data for a regression analysis procedure?

13.14 Consider the following set of residuals, resulting from a regression analysis.

$Y - \hat{Y}$	X	$Y - \hat{Y}$	X
.4	1.0	2.0	4.0
−.4	1.5	−3.0	5.0
−1.0	1.6	4.2	6.0
1.2	2.0	−3.4	7.0
−1.6	2.5	−5.0	8.0
−1.0	3.0	7.6	9.0

a. Construct a graph of the residuals versus the X values.
b. Does it appear that the equal variance assumption of regression analysis is violated?

Applying the New Concepts

13.15 The following data show the number of annual bankruptcies (X) in hundreds at a bankcruptcy court and the number of personnel who had to process the bankruptcies (Y).

X	210	380	410	1000	320	390	610
Y	15	18	18	59	14	18	24

Estimate the standard deviation of the error for the regression model.

13.16 Show that the mean of the residuals for the bankruptcy data in Ex 13.15 is zero.

13.17 The following is a list of sample errors $(Y - \hat{Y})$ from a linear regression application:

2.1, −.3, 1.4, −2.8, −3.9, 4.2, 3.6, 4.3, 1.8, −2.7, −.8, 1.2, .9, −1.1, −4.5, −5.2, −1.3, .5, .9, −.6, 1.5, 2.1, −2.2, .9

Do the data appear to conform to the empirical rule that approximately 95% of the errors should lie within two standard deviations of the mean? Construct a histogram for the residuals.

13.18 Let X be the distance an employee lives from his or her job. Let Y be the average time that it takes the employee to drive to work. Data from 30 employees gave the following sample statistics.

$$SCP_{XY} = 8.4 \qquad SS_X = 9.4 \qquad SS_Y = 12.2$$

a. Find the estimate of the error variance.
b. Find the interval in which approximately 68% of the error values should fall.

13.19 At Toys 'R' Us in Frankfurt, Germany, the manager converted toys that were previously priced in terms of marks into prices marked with euros. However, consumers believed that prices were not all converted evenly and that some prices were increased.

Retail Item	Original Price in Marks	Changed Price in Euros
Lego Life on Mars 7315	64.95	34.69
Black & Decker Drill KR 700	169	89.95
Wash & Go Shampoo 2 in 1	4.99	2.69
Original Kaisers Muffin Pan	16.95	8.99
Wileda Mop	9.99	5.49
Uno card game	16.99	8.99
Margaret Astor Powder Blush	16.95	8.99
Barbie Princess	32.95	18.49

a. Find the least squares line for predicting the changed price in euros using the original price in marks for the eight products listed.
b. Compute the correlation coefficient and interpret it.
c. Compute the residuals for each product. Based on the values of the residuals, which product would you say has been increased in price?

(Source: "Marketer's Friend, .99, Hits the Euro Zone," *The Wall Street Journal*, July 31, 2001, p. A14.)

13.20 Compute the variance of the error term in Exercise 13.19. Repeat with the retail item Barbie Princess removed. Compare.

Using the Computer

13.21 [DATA SET EX13-21] Variable Description:

InterpersonalScore: Employee's interpersonal skills rating

JobPerformScore: Employee's job performance rating

The Job Opportunities Build Success (JOBS) Coalition helps young underemployed workers keep their jobs by educating them about marketable skills. Suppose that the president of JOBS surveyed 70 of the workers that it has been educating on building a career. The survey requested employers of these workers to rate the employees on interpersonal skills (X) and on job performance (Y) on a scale from 1 to 10, with 10 representing perfect satisfaction.

   a. Determine the least squares line and interpret the slope of this line.

   b. Construct a histogram of the residuals. Do the residuals appear to follow a normal distribution?

(Source: "Skills D.C. Students Can Trade On." The Washington Post, September 19, 2004, p. B8.)

13.22 [DATA SET EX13-22] Variable Description:

SpecialNumber: Number of special parts ordered

SpecialCost: Dollar cost of special parts ordered

A sales manager for a car dealership mails an order for special parts each week. The manager is interested in the relationship between the number of special parts ordered and the total cost of the special order. One hundred special parts orders were randomly selected. The number of special parts and the total cost of these parts are recorded as variables SpecialNumber and SpecialCost, respectively.

   a. Find the least squares line and interpret the coefficients.

   b. What is the shape of the histogram of the residuals?

   c. Sometimes researchers make a transformation on the data to make the residuals conform better to a normal distribution. Suppose that the square of SpecialCost is used instead of the original values. Describe the shape of the histogram in which this value is used as the dependent variable. Would you say that the error component of this regression model follows an approximately normal distribution?

13.3

INFERENCE ON THE SLOPE, β_1

Performing a Test of Hypothesis on the Slope of the Regression Line

Under the assumptions of the simple linear regression model outlined in the previous section, we are now in a position to determine whether a linear relationship exists between the variables X and Y. Examining the estimate of the slope, b_1, will provide information as to the nature of this relationship.

Consider the population slope, β_1. Three possible situations are demonstrated in Figure 13.9. What can you say about using X as a predictor of Y in Figure 13.9a? When $\beta_1 = 0$, the population line is perfectly horizontal. As a result, the value of Y is the same for each value of X, and so X is not a good predictor of Y; the value of X provides no information regarding the value of Y. In the event $\beta_1 = 0$, the best predictor of Y is given by $\hat{Y} = \bar{y}$, and so $\beta_1 \neq 0$ is equivalent to saying that $\hat{Y}$ (using X as a predictor) is superior to using the sample mean ($\hat{Y} = \bar{y}$) as a predictor.

To determine whether X provides information in predicting Y, the hypotheses are

$$H_0: \beta_1 = 0 \qquad \text{(X provides no information)}$$
$$H_a: \beta_1 \neq 0 \qquad \text{(X does provide information)}$$

Other Alternative Hypotheses.   If we are attempting to demonstrate that a significant positive linear relationship exists between X and Y, the appropriate alternative hypothesis would be $H_a: \beta_1 > 0$. For example, do the data in Example 13.1 support the hypothesis that owners with large incomes have larger homes?

When the purpose of the analysis is to determine whether a negative linear relationship exists between X and Y, the alternative hypothesis should be $H_a: \beta_1 < 0$. For example, you would expect such a relationship between the number of new housing starts (Y) and

FIGURE

13.9

Three possible population slopes (β_1).

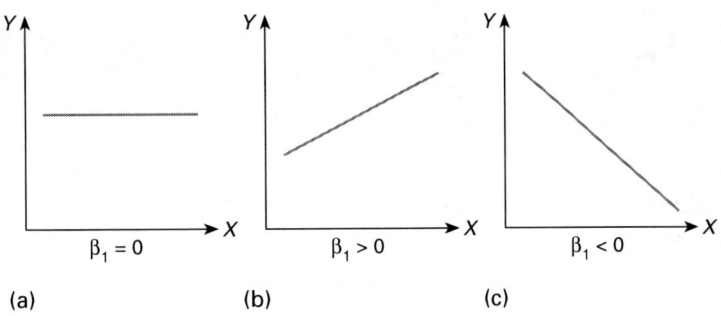

(a) $\beta_1 = 0$

(b) $\beta_1 > 0$

(c) $\beta_1 < 0$

the interest rate (X) (as the interest rate increases, you would expect the number of new houses under construction to decrease).

The Test Statistic. We use the point estimate of β_1 (that is, b_1) in the test statistic to determine the nature of β_1. What is b_1? a constant? a variable? Suppose that we obtained a different set of data and recalculated b_1. The new value would not be exactly the same as the previous value, implying that b_1 is actually a variable. To be more precise, under the assumptions of the previous section, b_1 is a *normal* random variable with mean = β_1 and variance = $\sigma_{b_1}^2 = \sigma_e^2/\mathrm{SS}_X$. Notice that b_1 is, on the average, equal to β_1; that is, b_1 is an *unbiased* estimator of β_1. The variance $\sigma_{b_1}^2$ is a parameter describing the variation in the b_1 values if we were to obtain random samples of n observations indefinitely.

If we replace the unknown σ_e^2 by its estimate, s^2, then the *estimated* variance of b_1 is $s_{b_1}^2 = s^2/\mathrm{SS}_X$. As a result

$$t = \frac{b_1 - \beta_1}{s/\sqrt{\mathrm{SS}_X}} = \frac{b_1 - \beta_1}{s_{b_1}}$$

13.14

has a t distribution with $n - 2$ df. If the null hypothesis is H_0: $\beta_1 = 0$, the test statistic becomes

$$t = \frac{b_1}{s/\sqrt{\mathrm{SS}_X}}$$

13.15

A summary of the testing procedure is shown in the accompanying box.

TEST OF HYPOTHESIS ON THE SLOPE OF THE REGRESSION LINE

Two-Tailed Test

$$H_0\text{: } \beta_1 = 0$$
$$H_a\text{: } \beta_1 \neq 0$$

Test statistic:

$$t = \frac{b_1}{s_{b_1}}$$

where $s_{b_1} = s/\sqrt{\mathrm{SS}_X}$ and df $= n - 2$.

Test:

$$\text{reject } H_0 \text{ if } |t| > t_{\alpha/2, n-2}$$

One-Tailed Test

$H_0: \beta_1 \le 0$	$H_0: \beta_1 \ge 0$
$H_a: \beta_1 > 0$	$H_a: \beta_1 < 0$
Test statistic:	Test statistic:
$t = \dfrac{b_1}{s_{b_1}}$	$t = \dfrac{b_1}{s_{b_1}}$
where $s_{b_1} = s/\sqrt{SS_X}$	where $s_{b_1} = s/\sqrt{SS_X}$
and $df = n-2$	and $df = n-2$
Test:	Test:
reject H_0 if $t > t_{\alpha,n-2}$	reject H_0 if $t < -t_{\alpha,n-2}$

EXAMPLE 13.3

Is there sufficient evidence, using the real-estate data in Example 13.1, to conclude that a positive linear relationship exists between income (X) and home size (Y)? Use $\alpha = .05$.

Solution

Step 1.   The hypotheses indicated here are

$$H_0: \beta_1 \le 0$$
$$H_a: \beta_1 > 0$$

Step 2.   The test statistic is

$$t = \frac{b_1}{s_{b_1}}$$

which has a t distribution with $n - 2 = 8$ df.

Step 3.   The testing procedure is to

$$\text{reject } H_0 \text{ if } t > t_{.05,8} = 1.860$$

The t curve is shown in Figure 13.10.

FIGURE 13.10

t curve with 8 df showing rejection region (shaded) for Example 13.3.

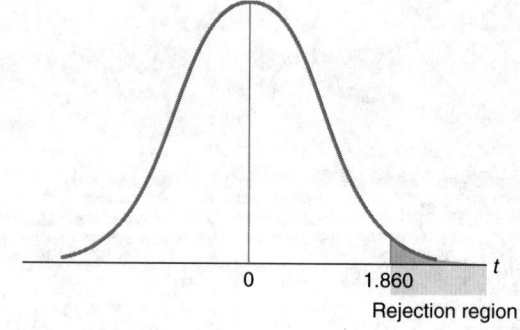

Step 4. We previously determined that $SS_X = 1489.6$, $b_1 = .3539$, and $s = 3.078$. The calculated test statistic is then

$$t^* = \frac{.3539}{3.078/\sqrt{1489.6}} = \frac{.3539}{.0797} = 4.44$$

where $s_{b_1} = .0797$. Because $4.44 > 1.86$, we reject H_0.

Step 5. Based on these 10 observations, we conclude that a positive linear relationship does exist between income and home size.

Using Statistical Software. The Excel solution to Example 13.3, shown in Figure 13.11, is obtained by clicking on **Tools ➤ Data Analysis ➤ Regression.** By clicking on the **Residuals** box, you will obtain the predicted Y values and the corresponding residuals shown in Figure 13.12. The MINITAB solution in Figure 13.13 can be obtained by clicking on **Stat ➤ Regression ➤ Regression.** The residuals and predicted values will be stored in two columns by clicking on **Storage** and checking the boxes alongside **Residuals** and **Fits.** The SPSS regression output in Figure 13.14 was obtained by clicking on **Analyze ➤ Regression ➤ Linear.** To capture the predicted values and residuals, click on **Save** and check the boxes alongside **Predicted Values (Unstandardized)** and **Residuals (Unstandardized).** Construction of the ANOVA tables, seen in the computer outputs, will be discussed in Chapter 14. Using the

FIGURE

13.11

Excel solution to Example 13.3.

	A	B	C	D	E	F
13	**Regression Statistics**					
14	Multiple R	0.843254475				
15	R Square	0.711078109				
16	Adjusted R Square	0.674962873				
17	Standard Error	3.078414856				
18	Observations	10				
19						
20	**ANOVA**					
21		df	SS	MS	F	Significance F
22	Regression	1	186.5868958	186.5869	19.68914	0.00217591
23	Residual	8	75.81310419	9.476638		
24	Total	9	262.4			
25						
26		Coefficients	Standard Error	t Stat	P-value	
27	Intercept	4.974758324	4.089663801	1.216422	0.258493	
28	X Variable 1	0.353920516	0.079761317	4.437245	0.002176	

FIGURE

13.12

Excel-generated predicted Y values and residuals.

	A	B	C
32	**RESIDUAL OUTPUT**		
33			
34	**Observation**	**Predicted Y**	**Residuals**
35	1	16.30021482	-0.30021482
36	2	17.71589689	-0.71589689
37	3	24.44038668	1.55961332
38	4	21.60902256	2.39097744
39	5	18.42373792	3.57626208
40	6	26.20998926	-5.20998926
41	7	28.33351235	3.66648765
42	8	20.54726101	-2.54726101
43	9	29.74919441	0.25080559
44	10	22.67078410	-2.67078410

FIGURE

13.13

MINITAB solution
to Example 13.3.

Regression Analysis: Footage versus Income

```
The regression equation is
Footage = 4.97 + 0.354 Income


Predictor     Coef   SE Coef      T      P
Constant     4.975     4.090   1.22  0.258
Income     0.35392   0.07976   4.44  0.002


S = 3.07841   R-Sq = 71.1%   R-Sq(adj) = 67.5%


Analysis of Variance

Source          DF      SS      MS      F      P
Regression       1  186.59  186.59  19.69  0.002
Residual Error   8   75.81    9.48
Total            9  262.40
```

FIGURE

13.14

SPSS solution to
Example 13.3.

Model Summary

Model	R	R Square	Adjusted R Square	Std. Error of the Estimate
1	.843a	.711	.675	3.078

ANOVAb

Model		Sum of Squares	df	Mean Square	F	Sig.
1	Regression	186.587	1	186.587	19.689	.002a
	Residual	75.813	8	9.477		
	Total	262.400	9			

Coefficientsa

Model		Unstandardized Coefficients B	Std. Error	Standardized Coefficients Beta	t	Sig.
1	(Constant)	4.975	4.0897		1.216	.2585
	INCOME	.3539	.07976	.843	4.437	.0022

a. Predictors: (Constant), INCOME

b. Dependent Variable: FOOTAGE

computer output for Excel, MINITAB, or SPSS, the following information can be obtained (and is highlighted in Figure 13.11).

1. The least squares equation is $\hat{Y} = 4.975 + .3539X$.

2. The standard deviation of b_1 is $s_{b_1} = .07976$.

3. The value of the test statistic is $t^* = b_1/s_{b_1} = 4.44$.

4. The p-value for the t test is .0022. Since this value is less than .05 (α), we can conclude that a positive linear relationship exists between income and home size.

5. The estimated standard deviation of the error components is $s = 3.078$.

6. The value of SSE is 75.81.

The 10 predicted Y values ($\hat{Y}$ values) and corresponding residuals ($Y - \hat{Y}$ values) are shown in Figure 13.12. These values were previously calculated without the use of a computer in the solution to Example 13.2. The Excel calculated residuals in Figure 13.12 contain more accuracy but do agree with the values in the Example 13.2 solution to two decimal places. MINITAB and SPSS will also provide these values as explained in the end-of-chapter appendix.

EXAMPLE 13.4

The firm of Smithson Financial Consultants has been hired by Blackburn Industries to determine whether a relationship exists between the age of unmarried male Blackburn employees (that is, never married, divorced, or widowed male employees) and the amount of individual liquid assets. The main question of interest is whether a linear relationship exists between these two variables, where X is defined as the age of the employee and Y is the *percentage* of annual income allocated to liquid assets (such as cash, savings accounts, and tradable stocks and bonds). A random sample of 12 unmarried male employees is selected, and the following data are obtained:

Age (X)	Liquid Assets (Y, Percentage of Annual Income)	Age (X)	Liquid Assets (Y, Percentage of Annual Income)
38	16	58	13
48	12	31	13
38	10	42	20
28	7	35	10
40	9	54	18
50	22	62	25

A scatter diagram of these 12 observations is provided in Figure 13.15, with a summary of the calculations. Using $\alpha = .10$, do you think that an employee's age provides useful information for predicting the percentage of total income allocated to liquid assets?

Solution

To derive the least squares regression line, we determine

$$b_1 = \frac{SCP_{XY}}{SS_X} = \frac{447.33}{1268.67} = .3526$$

and

$$b_0 = \bar{y} - b_1\bar{x}$$
$$= 14.583 - (.3526)(43.667) = -.814$$

Consequently, the least squares line is

$$\hat{Y} = -.814 + .3526X$$

Notice that the slope of this line is positive. As the following test of hypothesis will conclude, this slope is significant. Consequently, a higher percentage invested in liquid assets is associated with the *older* employees. According to these data, each additional year of age is accompanied by an increase of .35 percent of income allocated to liquid assets, on the average, for the unmarried male population at Blackburn.

To carry out a test of hypothesis, we follow the usual five-step procedure.

FIGURE

13.15

Scatter diagram and least squares line for age *(X)* and percentage of annual income invested in liquid assets *(Y)*.

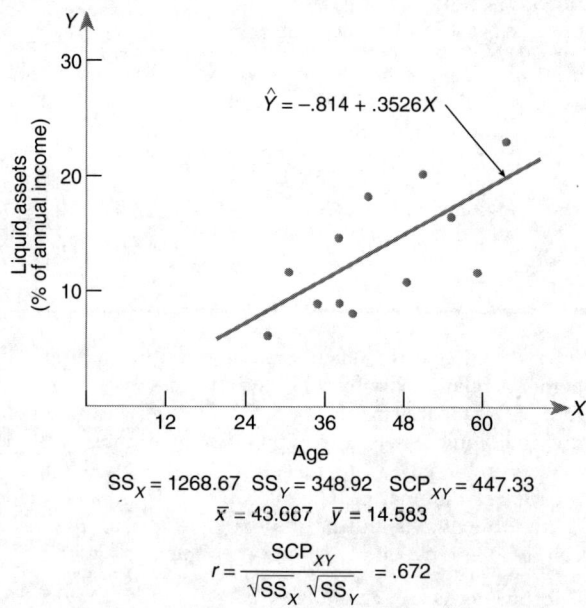

$$SS_X = 1268.67 \quad SS_Y = 348.92 \quad SCP_{XY} = 447.33$$
$$\bar{x} = 43.667 \quad \bar{y} = 14.583$$

$$r = \frac{SCP_{XY}}{\sqrt{SS_X}\,\sqrt{SS_Y}} = .672$$

Step 1. Because the suspected direction of the relationship between these two variables (positive or negative) is unknown before the data are obtained, a two-tailed test is appropriate. The hypotheses are

$$H_0: \beta_1 = 0$$
$$H_a: \beta_1 \neq 0$$

Step 2. The test statistic is $t = b_1/s_{b_1}$, which has $n - 2 = 10$ df.

Step 3. The test procedure is to

$$\text{reject } H_0 \text{ if } |t| > t_{.10/2,10} = t_{.05,10} = 1.812$$

Step 4. Based on the data summary in Figure 13.15 and using equation 13.11,

$$SSE = SS_Y - \frac{(SCP_{XY})^2}{SS_X}$$
$$= 348.92 - \frac{(447.33)^2}{1268.67}$$
$$= 348.92 - 157.73 = 191.19$$

Consequently,

$$s^2 = \frac{SSE}{n-2} = \frac{191.19}{10} = 19.12$$

and so

$$s_{b_1} = \frac{s}{\sqrt{SS_X}} = \frac{\sqrt{19.12}}{\sqrt{1268.67}} = .1228$$

The computed value of the test statistic is therefore:

$$t^* = \frac{b_1}{s_{b_1}}$$

$$= \frac{.3526}{.1228} = 2.87$$

Because $t^* = 2.87$ exceeds the table value of 1.812, we reject H_0 in support of H_a.

Step 5.   Our conclusion is that age is a useful (although imperfect) predictor of percentage of income invested in liquid assets for this particular population.

One thing to keep in mind is that *statistical* significance does not always imply *practical* significance. In other words, rejection of H_0: $\beta_1 = 0$ (statistical significance) does not mean that precise prediction (practical significance) follows. It *does* demonstrate to the researcher that, within the sample data at least, this particular independent variable has an association with the dependent variable.

Confidence Interval for β_1

Following our usual procedure of providing a confidence interval with a point estimate, we use the t distribution of the previous test statistic and equation 13.14 to define a confidence interval for β_1. The narrower this confidence interval is, the more faith we have in our estimate of β_1 and in our model as an accurate, reliable predictor of the dependent variable. A $(1 - \alpha) \times 100\%$ confidence interval for β_1 is

$$b_1 - t_{\alpha/2, n-2} s_{b_1} \qquad \text{to} \qquad b_1 + t_{\alpha/2, n-2} s_{b_1}$$

E X A M P L E

13.5

Construct a 90% confidence interval for the population slope, β_1, using the real-estate data in Examples 13.1 and 13.3.

Solution

All the necessary calculations have been completed; $b_1 = .3539$ and $s_{b_1} = .0797$ (from Example 13.3). Using $t_{.05,8} = 1.860$, the resulting confidence interval is

$$.3539 - (1.860)(.0797) \qquad \text{to} \qquad .3539 + (1.860)(.0797)$$
$$= .3539 - .148 \qquad \text{to} \qquad .3539 + .148$$
$$= .206 \qquad \text{to} \qquad .502$$

So we are 90% confident that the value of the estimated slope ($b_1 = .3539$) is within .148 of the actual slope, β_1. The large width of this interval is due in part to the lack of information (small sample size) used to derive the estimates; a larger sample would decrease the width of this confidence interval.

FIGURE

13.16

Curvilinear
relationship. The
horizontal line is
the least squares
line.

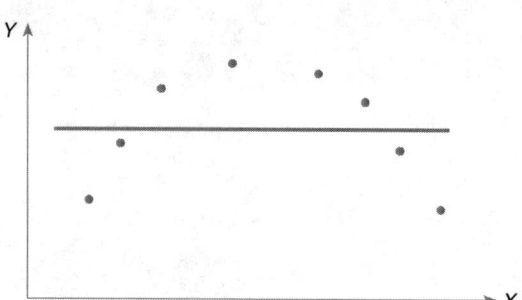

Comments

A failure to reject H_0 when performing a hypothesis test on β_1 does not always indicate that no relationship exists between the two variables. Some form of nonlinear relationship may exist between these variables. For example, in Figure 13.16, there is clearly a strong curved (*curvilinear*) relationship between X and Y. However, the least squares line through these points is horizontal, leading to a t value equal to zero and a failure to reject H_0. Furthermore, the sample correlation coefficient, r, for these data is zero.

Of course, you may fail to reject H_0 as the result of a type II error. In other words, you failed to reject H_0 when in fact a significant linear relationship does exist. This situation is more apt to occur when using a small sample to test the null hypothesis.

More often, a failure to reject H_0 occurs when there is no visible relationship between the two variables within the sample data. To determine whether there is no relationship or if there is a nonlinear one, you should inspect either a scatter diagram of the data, a scatter diagram of

the residuals, or, better yet, both. The latter diagram is a picture of the residuals $(Y - \hat{Y})$ plotted against the independent variable, X. Residual plots are discussed further in Section 13.6 and in Chapter 14.

In many situations, a business analyst has the opportunity to select the values of the independent variable, X, *before* the sample is obtained. At first glance, it might appear that the precision of b_1 (as an estimator of β_1) is unaffected by the X values. This is partially but not completely true. Because a narrow confidence interval for β_1 lends credibility to our model, we may choose to decrease the width of this confidence interval by decreasing s_{b_1}. Now $s_{b_1} = s/\sqrt{SS_X}$, so if we make SS_X large, the resulting s_{b_1} will be small. Therefore, given the opportunity, select a set of X values having a *large variance*. You can accomplish this by choosing a great many X values on the lower end of your range of interest, a large number of values at the upper end, and some values in between to detect any curvature that exists (as in Figure 13.16).

X Exercises 13.23–13.32

Understanding the Mechanics

13.23 The following statistics were obtained from 21 pairs of observations.

$$b_0 = -10.8 \qquad b_1 = 3.0 \qquad s_{b_1} = 1.6$$

a. Test that the slope of the population regression line differs from zero. Use a 1% significance level.
b. Find a 99% confidence interval for the slope of the population regression line.

13.24 Five observations collected in a regression study are as follows.

X	2	4	6	8	10
Y	1	3	4	15	20

a. Is there sufficient evidence using the observed data to conclude that a positive linear relationship exists between X and Y? Use a 5% significance level.
b. Compute the 95% confidence interval for the slope of the population regression line.

Applying the New Concepts

13.25 It is believed that the size of the U.S. population (X) is a variable that influences personal consumption expenditure for housing (Y). However, the relationship historically does not appear to be linear. Therefore, a log transformation of housing expenditure is used. Fifteen observations are taken over previous years. The units of Y are millions and the units of X are billions.

X	Log Y	X	Log Y	X	Log Y
183.69	3.935	196.56	4.241	207.66	4.631
186.54	4.001	198.71	4.305	209.90	4.722
189.24	4.060	200.71	4.379	211.91	4.818
191.89	4.117	202.68	4.465	213.85	4.923
194.30	4.182	205.05	4.542	215.97	5.009

From the data, does there appear to be a significant positive linear relationship between X and log Y? Use a significance level of .05.

13.26 The life of a lawnmower engine can be extended by frequent oil changes. An experiment was conducted in which 20 lawn mowers were used over many years with different time intervals between oil changes. Let X be the number of hours of operation between oil changes. Let Y be the number of years that the engine was able to perform adequately.

X	Y	X	Y	X	Y
11.25	12.1	22.0	9.5	25.5	6.1
15.5	11.8	22.5	9.2	26.0	5.4
17.5	11.5	23.0	8.4	26.5	4.8
20.5	10.1	23.5	8.8	27.0	4.6
19.5	9.9	24.0	7.1	28.0	4.8
18.5	9.7	24.5	7.2	30.0	4.1
21.5	10.1	25.0	5.8		

a. Graph the data and the least squares line.
b. Is there sufficient evidence to conclude, at the 10% significance level, that a negative linear relationship exists between Y and X? What is the critical region?

13.27 Gas mileage of vehicles depends on a number of factors such as weight of the vehicle, driving habits, and air system restrictions. As a general rule, more horsepower results in lower gas mileage. A random sample of seven large pickups was selected, and the horsepower and miles per gallon (mpg) were recorded. Is there sufficient evidence using the observed data to conclude that a negative relationship exists between horsepower and mpg? Use a 5% significance level.

Pickup	Horsepower (X)	Highway MPG (Y)
Cadillac Escalade	345	15
Chevrolet Silverado 1500	200	21
Dodge Ram 2500	245	17
Ford F-250	260	16
GMC Sierra 1500	270	21
Lincoln Blackwood	300	17
Toyota Tundra Regular	190	18

(Source: "Rolling On," *Kiplinger's Personal Finance*, December 2001, pp. 122–129.)

13.28 Monthly charges for wireless phone service have decreased as worldwide subscribers have increased. Is there sufficient evidence to conclude that a negative relationship exists between the monthly charges for wireless phone service and the number of worldwide subscribers,

using the following data? Use a 5% significance level. What are the necessary assumptions for your conclusions to be valid?

Year	Number of Wireless Subscribers	Monthly Charges for Wireless Phone Service
2001	610	35
2000	502	37
1999	410	38
1998	292	40
1997	255	45
1996	175	53
1995	150	60

(Source: "Emerging Mobile and Wireless Networks," *Communications of the ACM*, June 2000, pp. 73–81.)

13.29 Find a 95% confidence interval for the slope of the regression line predicting Monthly Charges for Wireless Phone Service using Number of Wireless Subscribers in Exercise 13.28. Interpret.

13.30 Use the confidence interval computed in Exercise 13.29 to test that a linear relationship exists between these variables in Exercise 13.28 at a 5% significance level.

Using the Computer

13.31 **[DATA SET EX13-31]** Variable Description:

FurniturePrice: Price of furniture sold

TimeToSell: Time that it took for a furniture item to sell

Experience: Length of time the salesperson has been in sales

The furniture store business can be tricky. "Furniture customers are fickle, with tastes varying widely across the country. They enter a store to get ideas and browse, not necessarily to buy," says Troy Peery Jr., president of Heilig-Meyers Company. Suppose that a furniture manager wished to determine if there is a linear relationship between the selling price of furniture and either the amount of time that it took for the furniture to sell or the number of years of experience of the salesperson who sold the furniture. The units for TimeToSell are months and the units for Experience are years.

a. Look at a plot of FurniturePrice and TimeToSell and a plot of FurniturePrice and Experience. Comment on the linear relationship in each plot. Which would you use to construct a prediction equation?
b. For the variables selected in part a to construct a prediction equation, is there sufficient evidence to conclude that a positive relationship exists at a 1% significance level?
c. Do a what-if analysis by multiplying TimeToSell by 2 and find the test statistic for testing whether a positive relationship exists. Compare this to your result in part b.

(Source: "Sofa with Your Stereo, Sir," *Forbes*, July 7, 1997, p. 46.)

13.32 [DATA SET EX13-32] Variable Description:

ExpenditureR&D: Percentage of total revenue spent on research and development (R&D)

PEratio: Price/earnings ratio for a company

A financial analyst is interested in the relationship between a company's P/E (price/earnings) ratio and the percentage of total revenue spent by the company on R&D. A random sample of 100 companies was selected

and the data were recorded in variables ExpenditureR&D and PEratio, respectively.

a. Plot the variables X = ExpenditureR&D and Y = PEratio. Estimate the intercept and slope and interpret these values.

b. Find 90%, 95%, and 99% confidence intervals for the slope of the regression line. How much does the width of the confidence interval change as the confidence level is increased?

13.4 MEASURING THE STRENGTH OF THE MODEL

We have already used the sample coefficient of correlation, r, as a measure of the amount of linear association within a sample of bivariate data. The value of r is given by

$$r = \frac{SCP_{XY}}{\sqrt{SS_X}\sqrt{SS_Y}}$$

13.16

The possible range for r is –1 to 1.

Comparing the equations for r and b_1 we see that

$$r = b_1 \sqrt{\frac{SS_X}{SS_Y}}$$

Because SS_X and SS_Y are always greater than zero, r and b_1 have the same sign. Thus, if a positive relationship exists between X and Y, then both r and b_1 will be greater than zero. Similarly, they are both less than zero if the relationship is negative.

When you determine r, you use a sample of observations; r is a statistic. What does r estimate? It is actually an estimate of ρ (rho, pronounced "roe"), the **population correlation coefficient.** To grasp what ρ is, imagine obtaining all possible X, Y values and using equation 13.16 to determine a correlation. The resulting value is ρ.

The population slope, β_1, and ρ are closely related. In particular, $\beta_1 = 0$ if and only if $\rho = 0$. This leads to another method of determining whether the simple linear regression model (using X to predict Y) is satisfactory. The hypotheses are

$$H_0: \rho = 0 \text{ (no linear relationship exists between X and Y)}$$

$$H_a: \rho \neq 0 \text{ (a linear relationship does exist)}$$

In a similar manner, alternative hypotheses can be set up to demonstrate a positive relationship ($H_a: \rho > 0$) or a negative relationship ($H_a: \rho < 0$). The test statistic uses the point estimate of ρ (that is, r) and is defined by

$$t = \frac{r}{\sqrt{\dfrac{1-r^2}{n-2}}}$$

13.17

where n = the number of observations in the sample. It is also a t statistic with $n - 2$ df. Although equations 13.15 and 13.17 appear to be unrelated, the two are algebraically equivalent and *their values for* t *are always the same.*

Thus, the t tests for H_0: $\beta_1 = 0$ *and* H_0: $\rho = 0$ produce identical results, *provided both tests use the same level of significance.* Performing both tests is therefore unnecessary; they both produce the same conclusion. Remember, if you have already computed the sample correlation coefficient, r, equation 13.17 offers a much easier method of determining whether the simple linear model is statistically significant. Notice also in equation 13.17 that the significance of the t value depends on the sample size, n. As a result, *if the sample size is large enough, then virtually any value of r can produce a significantly large value of* t.

E X A M P L E

13.6

Use equation 13.17 to determine whether a positive linear relationship exists between X = income and Y = home square footage, based on the real-estate data from Example 13.1. Use $\alpha = .05$.

Solution

The hypotheses to be used here are H_0: $\rho \leq 0$ versus H_a: $\rho \geq 0$. In Example 13.1, we found that $r = .843$. This leads to a computed test statistic value of

$$t^* = \frac{r}{\sqrt{\dfrac{1-r^2}{n-2}}} = \frac{.843}{\sqrt{\dfrac{1-(.843)^2}{8}}}$$

$$= \frac{.843}{.190} = 4.44$$

Because this value is the same as the one obtained in Example 13.3 (testing H_0: $\beta_1 \leq 0$ versus H_a: $\beta_1 > 0$), we draw the same conclusion. A positive linear relationship *does* exist between these two variables. In other words, r is large enough to justify this conclusion.

Remember, there is no harm in using equation 13.17 as a substitute for equation 13.15 with H_0: $\beta_1 = 0$ (or ≤ 0, or ≥ 0), particularly if you have already determined the value of r.

Danger of Assuming Causality

A word of warning is in order here—namely, that high statistical correlation does not imply *causality.* Even if the correlation between X and Y is extremely high (say, $r = .95$), a unit increase in X does not necessarily *cause* an increase in Y. All we know is that in the sample data, as X increased, so did Y. As a simple example, consider X = percentage of gray hairs and Y = blood pressure. One might expect to observe a high correlation between these two variables, but it is probably absurd to say that an additional gray hair will *cause* a person's blood pressure to increase. What is actually happening is that there is another variable, in this case age, that is causing both percentage of gray hair and blood pressure to increase.

In many business and economics applications, we observe highly correlated variables when each pair of observations corresponds to a particular time period. For example, we would expect a high correlation between average annual wages (X) and the U.S. gross national product (GNP; Y) when measured over time. Even though wages may be a good predictor of GNP, this correlation does not imply that an increase in wages *causes* an increase in GNP. It is much more likely that a third factor—inflation—caused both wages and GNP to increase.

Coefficient of Determination

In our earlier discussion of ANOVA techniques, we used the expression SS(total) $= \Sigma(y - \bar{y})^2$ to measure the tendency of a set of observations to group about the mean. If this value was large, then the observations (data) contained much variation and were *not* all clustered about the mean, $\bar{y}$.

In the simple linear regression model, $SS_Y = \Sigma(y - \bar{y})^2$ is computed in the same way and (as before) measures the total variation in the values of the dependent variable.

$$SS_Y = \text{total variation of the dependent variable observations}$$

When comparing the sum of squares of error, SSE, to the total variation, SS_Y, we use the ratio SSE/SS_Y. If all $\hat{Y}$ values are equal to their respective Y values, there is a perfect fit, with $SSE = 0$ and $r = 1$ or -1. Our model explains 100% of this total variation, and the unexplained variation is zero.

In general, SSE/SS_Y (expressed as a percentage) is the *percentage of unexplained variation*. Recall from equations 13.11 and 13.16 that

$$SSE = SS_Y - \frac{(SCP_{XY})^2}{SS_X} \quad \text{and} \quad r^2 = \frac{(SCP_{XY})^2}{SS_X SS_Y}$$

Thus

$$r^2 = 1 - \frac{SSE}{SS_Y}$$

As a result, r^2 may be interpreted as a measure of the *explained variation* in the dependent variable using the simple linear model; r^2 is the **coefficient of determination.**

$$r^2 = \text{coeficient of determination}$$
$$= 1 - \frac{SSE}{SS_Y}$$
= percentage of explained variation in the dependent variable using the simple linear regression model

13.18

For this model, we can determine r^2 simply by squaring the coefficient of correlation. In Chapter 14, we will predict the dependent variable, Y, using *more than one* predictor (independent) variable. To derive the coefficient of determination in this case, we must first calculate SSE and then use equation 13.18. So, although this definition may appear to be unnecessary, it will enable us to compute this value when we use a multiple linear regression model.

EXAMPLE 13.7

What percentage of the total variation of the home sizes is explained by means of the single predictor, income, using the real-estate data from Example 13.1?

Solution We previously calculated r to be .843, so the coefficient of determination is

$$r^2 = (.843)^2 = .711$$

Therefore, we have accounted for 71% of the total variation in the home sizes by using income as a predictor of home size.

Notice that we could have determined this value by using the calculations from Examples 13.1 and 13.2, where

FIGURE
13.17

Splitting $(y - \bar{y})$ into two deviations, $(\hat{y} - \bar{y}) + (y - \hat{y})$.

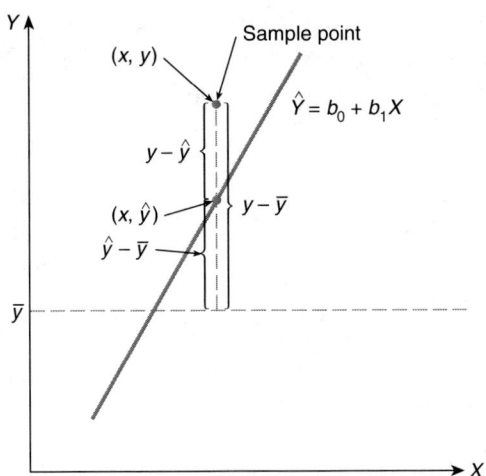

$$r^2 = 1 - \frac{SSE}{SS_Y}$$

$$= 1 - \frac{75.81}{262.4} = .711$$

Total Variation, SS_Y

In Chapter 11, when discussing the ANOVA procedure, we partitioned the total variation in the observations, measured by SS(total), into two sums of squares, namely, SS(factor) and SS(error). The resulting equation was

$$SS(total) = SS(factor) + SS(error)$$

In a similar fashion, we can partition the total variation of the Y values in linear regression, measured by SS_Y, into two other sums of squares. In Figure 13.17, notice that the value of $y - \bar{y}$ can be written as the sum of two deviations, namely,

$$y - \bar{y} = (\hat{y} - \bar{y}) + (y - \hat{y})$$

By squaring and summing over *all* the data points in the sample, we can show that*

$$\Sigma(y - \bar{y})^2 = \Sigma(\hat{y} - \bar{y})^2 + \Sigma(y - \hat{y})^2$$

The summation on the left of the equals sign is SS_Y. The second summation on the right is the sum of squares of error, SSE. The first summation on the right is defined to be the *sum of squares of regression,* SSR.

$$\Sigma(\hat{y} - \bar{y})^2 = SSR$$

As a result, we have

$$SS_Y = SSR + SSE$$

13.19

---

*This result follows since it can be shown that $\Sigma(\hat{y} - \bar{y})(y - \hat{y}) = 0$ when using the least squares line.

By comparing equations 13.11 and 13.19, we see that a simple way to calculate the sum of squares of regression is

$$SSR = \frac{(SCP_{XY})^2}{SS_X}$$

13.20

The regression sum of squares, SSR, measures the variation in the Y values that would exist if differences in X were the *only* cause of differences among the Y's. If this were the case, then all the (X, Y) points would lie exactly on the regression line. In practice, this does not happen when using a simple linear regression model. Otherwise, we would have a deterministic phenomenon, not an object of statistical investigation. Consequently, the sample points can be assumed to lie about the regression line rather than on this line. This variation *about* the regression line is measured by the error sum of squares, SSE.

X   Exercises 13.33–13.42

Understanding the Mechanics

13.33 The following data were collected on two variables X and Y.

X	1	2	4	6	10	12
Y	20	15	12	10	5	1

a. Specify the null and alternative hypotheses for testing that the population correlation is negative.
b. Calculate the estimate of the population correlation coefficient between X and Y.
c. Calculate the coefficient of determination.
d. Using a 5% significance level, test the hypothesis in part a.

Applying the New Concepts

13.34 The manager of a company that relies on traveling salespersons to sell the company's products wants to examine the relationship between sales and the amount of time a salesperson spends with each established customer who regularly orders the company's products. The manager collects data on 12 salespersons. Let Y represent sales per month and X represent hours spent with customers per month.

X	Y	X	Y	X	Y
3.2	412	6.1	715	5.1	570
4.6	500	4.2	500	7.1	800
3.9	450	5.6	610	6.5	725
5.3	610	5.3	600	7.8	850

Can one conclude that the population correlation coefficient between X and Y is positive? Use a 10% significance level. Can one conclude that spending more time with customers increases sales?

13.35 The financial industry has brought stability to the economics of many communities in terms of employment. The trend in the financial industry is to consolidate jobs and that means occasionally having layoffs such as the Bank of America's layoff of 4,500 jobs after taking over FleetBoston Financial Corp. Assume that the following is a record of the number of employees and the revenue associated with financial firms operating in the Boston metropolitan area from 1995 to 2004. What percentage of total variation in revenue is explained using number of employees? Does this indicate there is a linear relationship between revenue and number of employees? Use a 5% significance level.

Year	Number of Employees (in Thousands)	Revenue (in Billions)
1995	43.4	4.33
1996	50.4	4.74
1997	56.9	5.37
1998	61.5	6.02
1999	65.2	7.03
2000	71.0	8.16
2001	69.7	8.51
2002	81.5	9.96
2003	96.0	12.4
2004	100.5	14.4

(Source: "Bank of America Plans to Cut As Many as 4,500 More Jobs," *The Wall Street Journal*, October 8, 2004, p. C5)

13.36 Construction of apartment buildings in the New York City boroughs has been soaring in recent years. City and state programs have been subsidizing some of the construction. Consider the following data to be a random sample of yearly data listing the demand for new apartments and the supply of new units in the more affluent neighborhoods in the Bronx and Queens. The units are in thousands.

Demand for New Apartment Units	Supply of New Apartment Units	Demand for New Apartment Units	Supply of New Apartment Units
4.1	9.5	8.1	2.8
9.2	3.1	5.3	3.8
10.5	1.8	7.1	6.0
3.2	.7	11.0	12.1
−3.0	3.8	10.3	11.5
5.5	2.5	10.0	14.5

a. Compute the correlation between the demand for new apartment units and the supply of new apartment units.

b. Compute and interpret the coefficient of determination.

c. Do the data support that a nonzero correlation exists between these variables? Use a 10% significance level?

(Source: "New-Home Building Going Strong in the City," The New York Times, September 12, 2004, p. 11.2.)

13.37 Ten cards numbered 1 through 10 are shuffled, and a person is asked to pick one. The card is replaced and the deck reshuffled. Then the person is asked to draw a second card. If the second card is higher than the first, the dealer gives $.85 to the player. If the second card is not higher than the first, the player pays $1.15 to the dealer. A sample of 15 pairs of draws is taken to see whether there is any correlation between the first and the second cards.

a. Would you expect to observe significant correlation here? Why or why not?

b. Find the coefficient of determination for the following data, and test using a 5% significance level that there is no correlation between the first and the second cards. Interpret the value of the coefficient of determination.

First Card (X)	Second Card (Y)	First Card (X)	Second Card (Y)
7	3	10	5
3	10	3	6
8	2	4	3
5	8	6	1
2	7	7	8
7	9	8	4
9	4	2	6
1	1		

Using the Computer

13.38 [DATA SET EX13-38] Variable Description:

Time: Time period representing 36 months

MarketExp: Travel expenses of the marketing department

R&DExp: Travel expenses of the research and development (R&D) department.

Test that a linear relationship exists between the travel expenses of the R&D department and the natural log of the travel expenses of the marketing department. Use the p-value to make your conclusion. What assumptions need to be satisfied for the test procedure to be valid?

13.39 [DATA SET EX13-39] Variable Description:

2004Loans: Amount of mortgage loans in 2004 in millions of dollars

2000Loans: Amount of mortgage loans in 2000 in millions of dollars

Twenty major mortgage institutions were selected, and the amount of mortgage refinancing was recorded for 2004 and 2000. Test that a linear relationship exists between the variables 2004Loans and 2000Loans. Use a 10% significance level.

13.40 [DATA SET EX13-40] Variable Description:

CEO_Compens: Total compensation of the CEO in thousands of dollars

CompanyProfit: Annual company aftertax profit in millions of dollars

Test that a positive relationship exists between total compensation for CEOs and company profits. Use the p-value to determine if the data support a positive relationship.

13.41 [DATA SET EX13-41] Variable Description:

SatDishAdv: Amount spent on local advertising (excludes national advertising)

SatDishSales: Annual sales of satellite dishes

Tandy Corp.'s Radio Shack units have used its marketing muscle to promote many of its products. Through Radio Shack's ubiquitous neighborhood stores, Tandy has become a leading retailer for home satellite equipment. Suppose that a company analyst wished to determine if there is a linear relationship between the amount spent on local advertising (SatDishAdv) and the annual sales of satellite dishes (SatDishSales). Fifty stores are randomly selected and the data are recorded in units of thousands of dollars.

a. Find the correlation between X = SatDishAdv and Y = SatDishSales. Based on this value, do you think that the data will support the alternative hypothesis that the population correlation is positive? Use a 5% significance level.

b. Find the value of the t statistic for testing that the slope of the regression equation is greater than zero. What conclusion can you make using a 5% significance level? Compare the value of this t statistic with that calculated in part a.

c. Find the predicted values of SatDishSales. What is the correlation between these values and the original values of SatDishSales? Compare this to the correlation obtained in part a.

(Source: "Radio Shack Speeding Up Store Redesign Is Part of Plan to Lift Profits," The Wall Street Journal, September 9, 2004, p. 1)

13.42 [DATA SET EX13-42] Variable Description:

AnnualInc: Yearly income

VacationExp: Expenditure on vacation

A marketing analyst is interested in the relationship between the yearly income of recently married couples and their vacation expenditure for the year. A random sample of 100 married couples is selected, and the data are recorded in variables AnnualInc and VacationExp in units of thousands of dollars. If a relationship exists, the marketing analyst will use an estimate of a married couple's income to determine which type of promotional vacation information to mail to them.

a. Test whether a linear relationship exists between the variables $Y = \text{VacationExp}$ and $X = \text{AnnualInc}$. Use a 1% significance level.

b. Sometimes a transformation of one of the variables will result in a better linear relationship with the other variable. Take the natural log of AnnualInc. Find the correlation between these values and VacationExp. Is there sufficient evidence to conclude that a nonzero correlation exists at the 1% significance level?

13.5 ESTIMATION AND PREDICTION USING THE SIMPLE LINEAR MODEL

We have concentrated on predicting a value of the dependent variable (Y) for a given value of X. In the previous examples, we used a person's income, X, to predict the size of that person's home (Y). Notice in Figure 13.6 that we can also use the least squares line to estimate the *average (mean)* value of Y for a specified value of X. So we can use this line in two different situations.

Situation 1. The regression equation $\hat{Y} = b_0 + b_1 X$ estimates the *mean value* of Y for a specified value of the independent variable, X. For $X = x_0$, this value would be written $\mu_{Y|x_0}$ (the mean of Y given $X = x_0$).

For example, the least squares line passing through the real-estate data in Example 13.1 is $\hat{Y} = 4.975 + .3539X$. The average square footage for *all* homes in the population with an income of \$50,000 ($X = 50$) is $\mu_{Y|50}$. Its estimate is provided by the corresponding value on the least squares line, namely,

$$\hat{Y} = 4.975 + (.3539)(50) = 22.67$$

So the estimate of the average square footage of all such homes is 2,267 square feet (Figure 13.5).

Situation 2. An *individual* predicted value of Y also uses the regression equation $\hat{Y} = b_0 + b_1 X$ for a specified value of X. This value of Y is denoted Y_{x_0} for $X = x_0$. This application is the more common one in business, because a regression equation is generally used for individual forecasts.

For example, assume the Jenkins family resides in our sample community and has an income of \$50,000. A prediction of their home size (Y_{50}) is also

$$\hat{Y} = 4.975 + (.3539)(50) = 22.67$$

which is 2,267 square feet (Figure 13.5).

We see that the least squares line can be used to estimate average values (situation 1) or predict individual values (situation 2). Since $\mu_{Y|50}$ is a parameter, we use $\hat{Y}$ to estimate this value. On the other hand, Y_{50} represents a particular value of a dependent (random) variable, and so $\hat{Y}$ is used to predict this value. In the first situation, we can determine a confidence interval for $\mu_{Y|50}$; in the second situation, we determine a prediction interval for Y_{50}.

Confidence Interval for $\mu_{Y|x_0}$ (Situation 1)

We have already established that the point estimate of $\mu_{Y|x_0}$ is the corresponding value of $\hat{Y}$. The reliability of this estimate depends on (1) the number of observations in the sample, (2) the amount of variation in the sample, and (3) the value of $X = x_0$. A confidence interval for $\mu_{Y|x_0}$ takes all three factors into consideration.

A $(1 - \alpha) \times 100\%$ confidence interval for $\mu_{Y|x_0}$ is

$$\hat{Y} - t_{\alpha/2, n-2} s \sqrt{\frac{1}{n} + \frac{(x_0 - \bar{x})^2}{SS_X}} \quad \text{to} \quad \hat{Y} + t_{\alpha/2, n-2} s \sqrt{\frac{1}{n} + \frac{(x_0 - \bar{x})^2}{SS_X}}$$

13.21

EXAMPLE 13.8

Determine a 95% confidence interval for the average home size of families with an income of $45,000, using the real-estate data from Example 13.1.

Solution

We previously determined that $n = 10$, $\bar{x} = 49.8$, $SS_X = 1489.6$, and $s = 3.078$. The point estimate for the average square footage, $\mu_{Y|45}$, is

$$\hat{Y} = 4.975 + .3539(45)$$

$$= 20.90 \ (2{,}090 \text{ square feet})$$

Obtaining $t_{.025,8} = 2.306$ from Table A.5, the 95% confidence interval for $\mu_{Y|45}$ is

$$20.90 - (2.306)(3.078)\sqrt{\frac{1}{10} + \frac{(45 - 49.8)^2}{1489.6}} \quad \text{to} \quad 20.90 + (2.306)(3.078)\sqrt{\frac{1}{10} + \frac{(45 - 49.8)^2}{1489.6}}$$

$$= 20.90 - (2.306)(3.078)(.340) \quad \text{to} \quad 20.90 + (2.306)(3.078)(.340)$$

$$= 20.90 - 2.41 \quad \text{to} \quad 20.90 + 2.41$$

$$= 18.49 \quad \text{to} \quad 23.31$$

We are thus 95% confident that the average home size for families earning $45,000 is between 1,849 and 2,331 square feet.

Using Statistical Software to Construct Confidence and Prediction Intervals. Excel does not provide confidence and prediction intervals in its statistical tool package, but the KPK Data Analysis add-ins will allow you to compute these intervals. The income values were specified using the **Contiguous X Range** box.* The Excel output in Figure 13.18 was generated using **KPK Data Analysis ➤ Regression** and clicking on the check box inside the **Confidence Intervals for the Mean of Y and Prediction Intervals for Y** frame. The only available confidence level is 95%. The limits of the confidence intervals are in columns F and G. The corresponding prediction intervals (discussed next) are in columns H and I.

The MINITAB intervals in Figure 13.19 can be generated using **Stat ➤ Regression ➤ Regression,** clicking on **Storage** and checking the **Fits** box. Finally, click on **Options,** enter the Income variable in the **Prediction intervals for new observations** box, 95% as the **Confidence level,** and clicking on the check boxes alongside **Confidence limits** and **Prediction limits.**

---

*Chapter 12 will explore the use of more than one independent (explanatory) variable. These columns may or may not be adjacent (contiguous) in your spreadsheet. The KPK Data Analysis regression procedure, unlike the standard Excel procedure, allows for either option. In this chapter, always use the **Contiguous X Range** box.

FIGURE

13.18

Excel confidence and prediction intervals for the real-estate data using KPK Data Analysis (see Example 13.1).

	C	D	E	F	G	H	I
21							
22	X Variable 1	Predicted Value	Std Error Prediction	Lower 95% Mean	Upper 95% Mean	Lower 95% Predict	Upper 95% Predict
23	32	16.300	1.721	12.331	20.270	8.167	24.434
24	36	17.716	1.469	14.327	21.104	9.850	25.582
25	55	24.440	1.058	22.000	26.880	16.934	31.947
26	47	21.609	0.999	19.306	23.912	14.146	29.072
27	38	18.424	1.354	15.301	21.546	10.669	26.179
28	60	26.210	1.269	23.284	29.136	18.532	33.888
29	66	28.334	1.618	24.603	32.064	20.314	36.353
30	44	20.547	1.078	18.062	23.033	13.026	28.069
31	70	29.749	1.882	25.408	34.090	21.428	38.070
32	50	22.671	0.974	20.426	24.916	15.225	30.116

FIGURE

13.19

MINITAB confidence and prediction intervals for the real-estate data in Example 13.1

↓	C1 Income	C2 Footage	C3 FITS1	C4 CLIM1	C5 CLIM2	C6 PLIM1	C7 PLIM2
1	32	16	16.30021	12.3306	20.2699	8.1669	24.4336
2	36	17	17.7159	14.3274	21.1044	9.8498	25.5820
3	55	26	24.4404	22.0003	26.8805	16.9339	31.9469
4	47	24	21.6090	19.3059	23.9122	14.1459	29.0721
5	38	22	18.4237	15.3013	21.5462	10.6685	26.1790
6	60	21	26.2100	23.2844	29.1356	18.5319	33.8880
7	66	32	28.3335	24.6029	32.0642	20.3141	36.3529
8	44	18	20.5473	18.0618	23.0327	13.0259	28.0686
9	70	30	29.7492	25.4083	34.0901	21.4283	38.0701
10	50	20	22.6708	20.4256	24.9159	15.2254	30.1162

FIGURE

13.20

SPSS confidence and prediction intervals for the real-estate data in Example 13.1

	income	footage	pre_1	lmci_1	umci_1	lici_1	uici_1
1	32	16	16.300	12.331	20.270	8.167	24.434
2	36	17	17.716	14.327	21.104	9.850	25.582
3	55	26	24.440	22.000	26.880	16.934	31.947
4	47	24	21.609	19.306	23.912	14.146	29.072
5	38	22	18.424	15.301	21.546	10.669	26.179
6	60	21	26.210	23.284	29.136	18.532	33.888
7	66	32	28.334	24.603	32.064	20.314	36.353
8	44	18	20.547	18.062	23.033	13.026	28.069
9	70	30	29.749	25.408	34.090	21.428	38.070
10	50	20	22.671	20.426	24.916	15.225	30.116

The SPSS intervals in Figure 13.20 can be obtained by clicking on **Analyze ➤ Regression ➤ Linear,** clicking on **Save,** checking the box alongside **Predicted Values (Unstandardized),** and clicking on the boxes alongside **Mean** and **Individual** inside the **Prediction Intervals** frame. The value 95 should be entered in the **Confidence Interval** box.

The column labeled **Std. Error Prediction** in Figure 13.18 contains the standard deviation of the predicted Y values. Writing this as $s_{\hat{Y}}$,

$$s_{\hat{Y}} = s\sqrt{\frac{1}{n} + \frac{(x_0 - \bar{x})^2}{SS_x}}$$

13.22

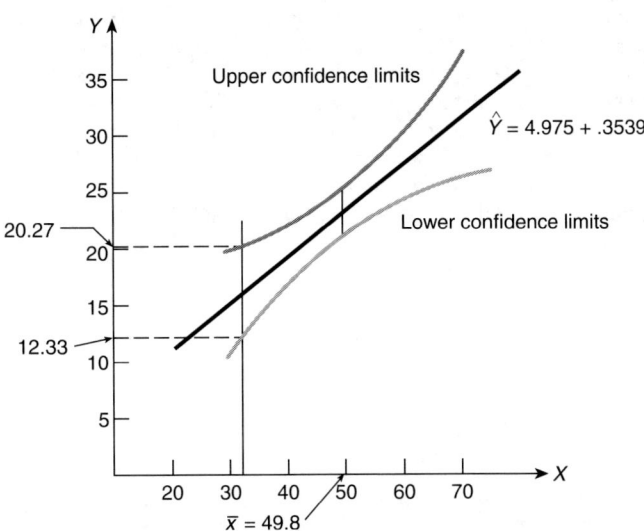

FIGURE

13.21

95% confidence intervals for the real-estate data.

For each value of X *in the sample* (say, x_0), the corresponding confidence interval for $\mu_{Y|x_0}$ is

$$\hat{Y} - t \cdot s_{\hat{Y}} \qquad \text{to} \qquad \hat{Y} + t \cdot s_{\hat{Y}}$$

where $t = t_{\alpha/2, n-2}$, as before, and $\hat{Y}$ is contained in the column labeled **Predicted Value** in Figure 13.18.

Using the Excel output in Figure 13.18, we can find the confidence intervals corresponding to X values of 32 and 50. The remaining eight confidence intervals are constructed in a similar manner.

For $X = 32$ in the first row, the confidence interval is

$$16.300 - (2.306)(1.721) \qquad \text{to} \qquad 16.300 + (2.306)(1.721)$$
$$= 12.33 \qquad \text{to} \qquad 20.27$$

For $X = 50$ in the last row, the confidence interval is

$$22.671 - (2.306)(.974) \qquad \text{to} \qquad 22.671 + (2.306)(.974)$$
$$= 20.43 \qquad \text{to} \qquad 24.92$$

Notice that the confidence interval is much wider for $X = 32$ than for $X = 50$.

All 10 confidence intervals are shown in columns F and G in Figure 13.18 under the headings **Lower 95% Mean** and **Upper 95% Mean.** The intervals in the first and last rows (for $X = 32$ and $X = 50$) agree with the previously calculated confidence intervals for the average square footage using these two incomes. For values of X not in the sample, simply construct a new column containing these values and enter this range in the **Contiguous X Range** box.

By connecting the upper end of the confidence intervals for all 10 data points and connecting the lower limits, we obtain Figure 13.21. Equation 13.21 indicates that the confidence interval is narrowest when $(x_0 - \bar{x})^2 = 0$, that is, at $X = x_0 = \bar{x}$. For values of X to the left or right of $\bar{x}$, the confidence interval is wider. In other words, the farther x_0 is from $\bar{x}$, *the less reliable is the estimate.*

The Danger of Extrapolation. *Extrapolation* is the process of calculating an estimate corresponding to a value of X outside the range of the data used to derive the prediction equation (the least squares line). For example, in Figure 13.21 the least squares line could be used to estimate the average home size for families with an income of $100,000. Although we *can* estimate $\mu_{Y|100}$, the corresponding confidence interval for this parameter will be extremely wide, so the point estimate, $\hat{Y}$, will have little practical value.

To use the simple regression model effectively for estimation, you need to stay within the range of the sampled values for the independent variable, X. This process is called *interpolation*. If you use values outside this range, you need to be aware that given *another* set of data, you would quite likely obtain a considerably different estimate. Furthermore, you have no assurance that the linear relationship still holds outside the range of your sample data.

Prediction Interval for Y_{x_0} (Situation 2)

The procedure of predicting individual values is used more often in business applications. The regression equation is generally used to *forecast* (predict) a future value of the dependent variable for a particular value of the independent variable. When attempting to predict a single value of the dependent variable, Y, using the simple linear regression model, we begin, as before, with $\hat{Y}$. Substituting $X = x_0$ into the regression equation provides the best prediction of Y_{x_0}. For example, if the Johnson family has an income of $45,000, our best guess as to their home size (using this particular model) is $\hat{Y}$ for $X = 45$. From the results of Example 13.8, this is 20.90, or 2,090 square feet.

We do not use the term *confidence interval* for this procedure because what we are estimating (Y_{x_0}) is not a parameter. It is a value of a random variable, so we use the term **prediction interval.**

The variability of the error in predicting a single value of Y is more than that for estimating the average value of Y (situation 1). It can be shown that an estimate of the variance of the error $(Y - \hat{Y})$, when using $\hat{Y}$ to predict an individual Y for $X = x_0$, is

$$s_{\hat{Y}}^2 = s^2\left(1 + \frac{1}{n} + \frac{(x_0 - \bar{x})^2}{SS_X}\right)$$

13.23*

This result can be used to construct a $(1 - \alpha) \times 100\%$ prediction interval for Y_{x_0}, as follows:

$$\hat{Y} - t_{\alpha/2, n-2}\, s\sqrt{1 + \frac{1}{n} + \frac{(x_0 - \bar{x})^2}{SS_X}} \quad \text{to}$$

$$\hat{Y} + t_{\alpha/2, n-2}\, s\sqrt{1 + \frac{1}{n} + \frac{(x_0 - \bar{x})^2}{SS_X}}$$

13.24

Notice that the only difference between this prediction interval and the confidence interval in equation 13.21 is the inclusion of "1+" under the square root sign. The other two terms under the square root are usually quite small, so this "1+" has a large effect on the width of the resulting interval. Be aware that our warning about extrapolating outside

---

*This follows because $Y = \hat{Y} + e$ and, as a result, $s_Y^2 = s_{\hat{Y}}^2 + s_e^2$. Substituting equation 13.22 for $s_{\hat{Y}}^2$ and s^2 for s_e^2 produces the desired results.

FIGURE

13.22

The 95% prediction and confidence intervals for the real-estate data. Calculated values on the *Y* axis are for *X* = 32.

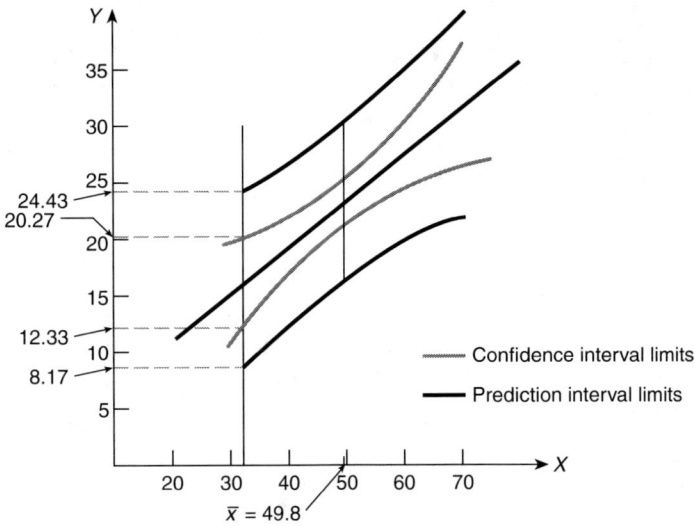

the range of the data applies here as well. In equations 13.23 and 13.24, the distance from the mean $(x_0 - \bar{x})$ is squared, which increases the risk of predicting beyond the range of the sampled data.

E X A M P L E

13.9

We previously determined that if the Johnson family has an income of $45,000, the best prediction of their home size is $\hat{Y} = 20.90$. Determine a 95% prediction interval for this situation.

Solution

We can use the calculations from Example 13.8 to derive the prediction interval for Y_{45}. The result is

$$20.90 - (2.306)(3.078)\sqrt{1 + \frac{1}{10} + \frac{(45 - 49.8)^2}{1489.6}} \quad \text{to}$$

$$20.90 + (2.306)(3.078)\sqrt{1 + \frac{1}{10} + \frac{(45 - 49.8)^2}{1489.6}}$$

$$= 20.90 - (2.306)(3.078)(1.056) \quad \text{to} \quad 20.90 + (2.306)(3.078)(1.056)$$

$$= 20.90 - 7.49 \quad \text{to} \quad 20.90 + 7.49$$

$$= 13.41 \quad \text{to} \quad 28.39$$

Comparing this interval to the confidence interval for $\mu_{Y|45}$ in Example 13.8, we see that individual predictions are considerably less accurate than estimations for the mean home size. Of course, we could reduce the width of this interval by obtaining additional data. Expecting accurate results from a sample of 10 observations is being a bit optimistic.

Figure 13.22 shows the prediction intervals for all 10 data points; the upper and lower limits have been connected. The increased width of a prediction interval versus a confidence interval is quite apparent from this graph. Also, like the width of a confidence interval, the width of a prediction interval increases as the value of X strays from $\bar{x}$.

FIGURE

13.23

Examination of the residuals. (a) The shotgun effect (no violation of assumptions 1 and 2). (b) A violation of the equal variance assumption (assumption 2).

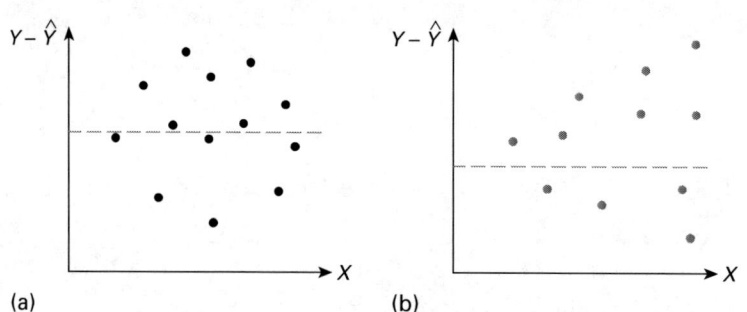

(a)　　　　　　　　　　　(b)

13.6

EXAMINING THE RESIDUALS

Checking the Model Assumptions

When using a linear regression model, you should keep two things in mind. First, no distributional assumptions are necessary to derive the least squares estimates of β_0 and β_1. The regression coefficients b_0 and b_1 from the sample regression line are the "best" estimates in the least squares sense.

Second, several key assumptions *are* required for the validity of any constructed confidence intervals and tests of hypothesis. If these assumptions are violated, you may still have an accurate prediction, $\hat{Y}$, but the validity of the inference procedures will be highly questionable.

Your final step in any regression analysis should be to verify your assumptions.

Assumption 1. *The errors are normally distributed with a mean of zero.* An easy method to determine whether the errors follow a normal distribution centered at zero is to let the computer construct a histogram of the sample residuals $(Y - \hat{Y})$. Since the residuals *always* sum to zero when using the least squares line, the residual histogram is typically centered at zero. The plot should reveal whether the distribution of residuals is severely skewed. Remember that an exact normal distribution is not necessary here; problems arise only when the distribution is severely skewed and does not resemble a normal distribution. (The Excel procedure to obtain this histogram is illustrated in upcoming Example 13.10.)

More sophisticated methods of checking this assumption involve the use of a *probability plot* or a *chi-square goodness-of-fit test*. We do not discuss the probability plot technique here, except to say that you plot the residuals in a specialized type of graph. If the resulting graph is linear in appearance, the normality assumption has been verified.

If you have reason to believe that this assumption of your model has been violated, then you need to search for another model. This new model may include additional predictor variables (the subject of Chapter 12) that have been overlooked. Another possibility is to transform the dependent variable (for example, use $\sqrt{Y}$ rather than Y) or to transform the independent variable. As your model tends to improve, you should observe the residuals tending toward a normal distribution.

Assumption 2. *The variance of the errors remains constant.* For example, you should not observe larger errors associated with larger values of X. When the residuals $(Y - \hat{Y})$ are plotted against the independent variable, X, we hope to observe *no pattern* (a *shotgun blast* appearance) in this graph, as in Figure 13.23(a). Remember—the assumption is essentially that the errors consist of what engineers call *noise*, with no observable pattern.

A common violation of this assumption of equal variances occurs when the value of the residual increases as X increases, as illustrated in Figure 13.23(b). In this graph, the

FIGURE

13.24

Autocorrelated
errors.

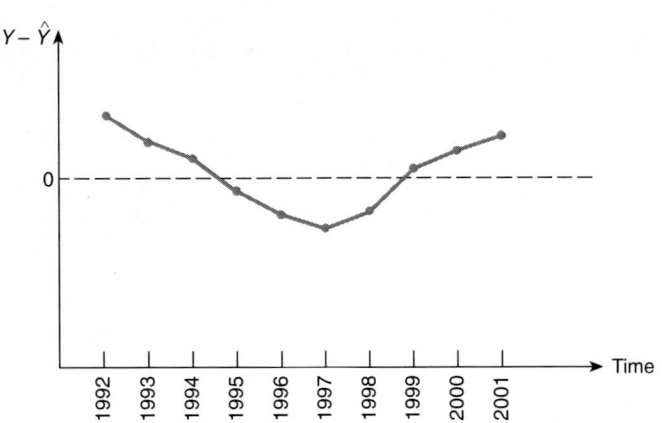

variance of the residual increases with X, producing a funnel appearance. This has a serious effect on the validity of the t tests discussed in this chapter, which determine the strength of the regression model.

When you encounter a violation of this type, you need to resort to more advanced modeling techniques, such as *weighted least squares* or *transformations* of your dependent variable.*

Assumption 3. *The errors are independent.* Examining this assumption after the regression equation has been determined involves using the residual from each of the sample observations. For given values of X, the actual error is

$$e = Y - (\beta_0 + \beta_1 X)$$

The β's are unknown, so we estimate the error by using the residual for this particular observation,

$$Y - \hat{Y} = Y - (b_0 + b_1 X)$$

When your regression data consist of *time-series* data, your errors often are not independent. This type of data has the following appearance:

Time	Y	X
1992	#	#
1993	#	#
1994	#	#
⋮	⋮	⋮

(# denotes a numeric value)

Also remember that your error component includes the effect of variables missing from your model. Chapter 12 deals with regression models containing more than one predictor variable. In many business applications, there is a positive relationship between time-related predictor variables, such as prices and wages, because they increase over time.

This relationship can produce a set of residuals in your regression analysis that are not independent of one another but instead display a pattern similar to the one in Figure 13.24. This plot contains the sample residuals on the vertical axis and time on the horizontal axis.

---

*See J. Neter, M. Kutner, and C. Nachtschein, *Applied Linear Regression Models*, 3rd ed. (Homewood, Ill.: Richard D. Irwin, 1996).

If this assumption were *not* violated here, we would observe the shotgun appearance as in Figure 13.23(a). Instead we notice that adjacent residuals have roughly the same value and so are correlated with each other. This is *autocorrelation*.

The problem of autocorrelated errors is the most difficult of the three assumptions to correct. The error term is not noise, as we originally assumed, but instead has a definite pattern (as in Figure 13.24).

To be more specific, the pattern in Figure 13.24 is one of *positive* autocorrelation. Negative autocorrelation exists when most of the neighboring residuals are very unequal in size (such as a positive residual, followed by a negative residual, followed by a positive residual, and so on). The amount of autocorrelation that exists in residuals is measured by the *Durbin–Watson statistic*, the next topic of discussion.

Autocorrelated Errors and the Durbin–Watson Statistic

The Durbin–Watson statistic frequently is used to test for significant autocorrelation in the residuals when the regression data consist of time-series data; that is, data recorded across time. Values of the dependent variable are denoted $y_1, y_2, y_3, \ldots , y_T$ and values of the independent (predictor) variable are denoted $x_1, x_2, x_3, \ldots , x_T$, where T is the total number of observations (time periods). The residual for time period t is $e_t = y_t - \hat{y}_t$, where $\hat{y}_t$ is the predicted value of the dependent variable for time period t. The assumption behind the Durbin–Watson test is that the errors follow a normal distribution.

If the value of the Durbin–Watson statistic is very small, then significant *positive* autocorrelation exists. This means that each value of e_t is very close to its neighbors, e_{t-1} and e_{t+1}. A large value indicates high *negative* autocorrelation, where each e_t value is very different from the adjacent residuals.

The value of the Durbin–Watson statistic (DW) is determined using each residual value, e_t and its previous value, e_{t-1}.

$$DW = \frac{\sum_{t=2}^{T}(e_t - e_{t-1})^2}{\sum_{t=1}^{T}e_t^2}$$

13.25

where T is the number of observations in the time series.

The range of possible values for the Durbin-Watson statistic is from 0 to 4. The **ideal value of DW** is 2. When DW = 2, the errors are completely uncorrelated, and there is no violation of the independent errors assumption. As DW decreases from 2, positive autocorrelation of the errors increases. Values between 2 and 4 indicate various degrees of negative autocorrelation.

The common problem of autocorrelated errors results from *positive* correlation between neighboring errors. When this situation occurs, the errors are not independent of one another; instead, each error is largely determined by its previous value. This implies that a similar behavior will exist for the estimated residuals in the regression model—that is, we can expect the estimated residuals to be positively correlated. The test for autocorrelation using the DW statistic is unique in that there is a certain range of DW values for which we can neither reject H_0: no autocorrelation exists, nor fail to reject it. The testing procedure uses Table A.9; the value of k in Table A.9 represents the number of predictor variables in the regression equation (k = 1 in this chapter) and n is equal to the number of sample observations. The significance level is assumed to be $\alpha = .05$. The hypotheses are

H_0: no autocorrelation exists

H_a: positive autocorrelation exists

FIGURE

13.25

Portion of output
using **KPK Data
Analysis ➤
Regression.**

	A	B	C	D	E	F	G	H
1	t	Loans	Int Rate	Predicted Loans	Residuals		Coefficients	
2	1	175	4.5	278.26	-103.26	Intercept	672.356	
3	2	198	4.7	260.74	-62.74	Int Rate	-87.577	
4	3	281	4.1	313.29	-32.29			
5	4	244	5.0	234.47	9.53	Durbin-Watson statistic = 0.884		
6	5	120	6.0	146.89	-26.89			
7	6	129	5.6	181.92	-52.92			
8	7	313	4.8	251.98	61.02			
9	8	290	4.9	243.23	46.77			
10	9	152	5.1	225.71	-73.71			
11	10	184	5.0	234.47	-50.47			
12	11	304	4.5	278.26	25.74			
13	12	331	4.2	304.53	26.47			
14	13	322	4.0	322.05	-0.05			
15	14	336	4.1	313.29	22.71			
16	15	350	5.0	234.47	115.53			
17	16	294	5.4	199.44	94.56			

The testing procedure uses the lower critical limit (d_L) and upper critical limit (d_U) of DW. Using the values of d_L and d_U from Table A.9, the testing procedure is

> Reject H_0 if DW $< d_L$.
>
> Fail to reject H_0 if DW $> d_U$.
>
> The test is inconclusive if $d_L \leq$ DW $\leq d_U$.

To illustrate the calculation of this statistic, consider the following data set which contains the number of new home loans (Y_t) and interest rate (X_t) at CitiBank over a four-year period. Observations are recorded quarterly for a total of 16 observations.

	2000				2001				2002				2003			
Qtr.	1	2	3	4	1	2	3	4	1	2	3	4	1	2	3	4
t	1	2	3	4	5	6	7	8	9	10	11	12	13	14	15	16
y_t	175	198	281	244	120	129	313	290	152	184	304	331	322	336	350	294
x_t	4.5	4.7	4.1	5.0	6.0	5.6	4.8	4.9	5.1	5.0	4.5	4.2	4.0	4.1	5.0	5.4

The computer output in Figure 13.25 was obtained by selecting portions of the output using the Excel **KPK Data Analysis ➤ Regression.** The input range for the dependent variable is B1:B17 and for the independent variable is C1:C17. The resulting prediction equation (using cells G2 and G3) is

$$\hat{y}_t = 672.356 - 87.577\, x_t$$

The predicted values for the number of loans are in column D and the residual values ($e_t = y_t - \hat{y}_t$) are contained in column E. The resulting Durbin–Watson statistic is

$$\frac{(-62.74+103.26)^2 + (-32.29+62.74)^2 + \cdots + (94.56-115.53)^2}{(-103.26)^2 + (-62.74)^2 + \cdots + (94.56)^2} = \frac{50{,}648.35}{57{,}315.65} = .884$$

This value agrees with the Excel-computed value in Figure 13.25. Using $\alpha = .05$, $n = 16$, $k = 1$, and Table A.9, $d_L = 1.10$ and $d_U = 1.37$. The test of hypothesis will be to

> Reject H_0 if DW < 1.10
>
> Fail to reject H_0 if DW > 1.37
>
> The test is inconclusive if $1.10 \leq$ DW ≤ 1.37.

Because DW = .884 lies in the rejection region, we conclude that the residuals are significantly autocorrelated at the 5% significance level and that assumption 3 has been violated. Consequently, any tests of hypothesis using this model are invalid and the next step should be to search for a regression model that *does* satisfy these three assumptions. Possible remedies for dealing with models containing significant autocorrelation are discussed in Section 14.4.

Comment

Practically all computer packages can provide the value of the Durbin–Watson statistic when performing a linear regression analysis. When your data are *not* collected over time (but rather from different families, cities, companies, or the like), this statistic is meaningless and should be ignored. For this situation, assumption 3 is not of vital concern and is often taken for granted.

Checking for Outliers and Influential Observations

A closer look at the regression data and computer solution can reveal some rather interesting and important details concerning the least squares line. Of particular interest is whether there are one or more **outliers** in the sample observations. These points are generally fairly obvious in a scatter diagram, since such points do not seem to "fit" with the remaining observations. An outlier can have a dramatic effect on the least squares line, because the regression line will be pulled in the direction of the outlier, reducing the effectiveness of the regression line as a predictor. Such observations need to be detected and studied to determine if an error was made in the recording of this data point and whether this observation should be corrected or removed from the sample data.

Also of interest is the determination of whether the sample outliers are very influential in determining the fitted regression line (the least squares line). A point is said to have a *strong influence* on the regression line if removal of this observation produces a dramatic shift in the regression line if the line is recalculated from the remaining points. These observations may be extreme in their X value, Y value, or both.

Figure 13.26 contains three outliers (points A, B, and C). Point A has an X value close to the average of the X values in the sample, but has an extremely large Y value. As we will demonstrate, this observation will not have a large influence on the regression line, due to the number of sample observations having similar X values. Point B has a large X value, but the Y value is consistent with the line determined from the remaining observations; it will not have a very strong influence on the regression line. Point C is another

FIGURE

13.26

Excel illustration of outliers and influential observations.

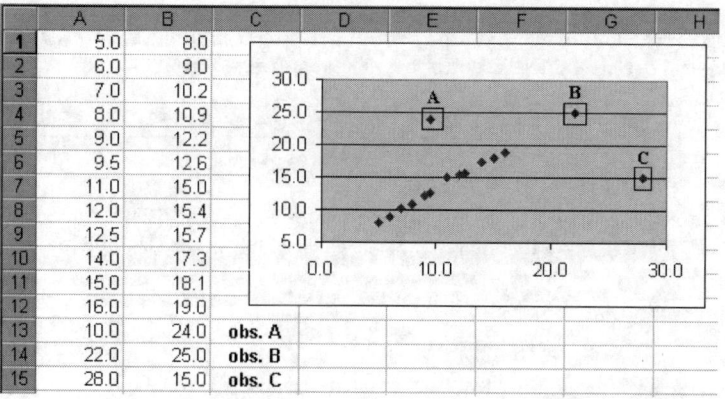

matter—it has an extremely large X value and a Y value that is not consistent with the regression line through the remaining observations. Removal of this observation would produce a drastically different least squares line; this point is an **influential observation.**

Identifying Outlying Values of the Independent Variable. Observations having extremely large or small values of the independent variable **(X)** can be detected by computing **sample leverages.** An observation whose value of the independent variable is distant from the sample mean of the X values $(\bar{x})$ is said to have high leverage. In Figure 13.26, point C would be a high-leverage observation and point B has a potentially high leverage. The leverage of the ith observation is measured by h_i, where

$$h_i = \frac{1}{n} + \frac{(x_i - \bar{x})^2}{SS_X}$$

13.26

and $SS_X = \Sigma x^2 - (\Sigma x)^2/n$.

Consider the real-estate data in Examples 13.1, 13.2, and 13.3. Suppose one additional observation is added to this data set. In Figure 13.27(a), this observation is $X = 115$ and $Y = 48$ (a family with a large income and a large house). In Figure 11.27(b), the additional observation is $X = 115$ and $Y = 29$ (a family with a large income and a small house for this income). The leverage value for the additional observation *will be the same* in both cases because it depends on the X value only. In either case, the average of the 11 X values in the sample is now

$$\bar{x} = 55.727$$

Also,

$$SS_X = 39,515 - \frac{(613)^2}{11} = 5354.18$$

Consequently, the leverage of the new observation is

$$h_{11} = \frac{1}{11} + \frac{(115 - 55.727)^2}{5354.18} = .747$$

Commonly accepted procedures for simple linear regression are to conclude that a sample observation has an outlying X value if its leverage value is larger than 4/n or larger than 6/n, where n is the number of sample observations. MINITAB uses the "larger than 6/n" rule, and we will accept that decision rule in our discussion. Here, $6/n = 6/11 = .545$; and since $.747 > .545$, we conclude that the 11th observation does have an unusually large income (X). Since the leverage value depends strictly on the X value, it is impossible to say whether the new observation exerts a large influence on the regression equation. We will demonstrate shortly that the new observation in Figure 13.27(a) is *not* an influential observation, whereas in Figure 13.27(b) it is.

Compare the leverage value in equation 13.26 and the confidence interval for the mean value of Y at $X = x_0$ given in equation 13.21. If a confidence interval is calculated at the ith observation (x_i, y_i), then the leverage for this observation, h_i, is the quantity under the square root sign in equations 13.21 and 13.22. As a result, the standard deviation of the predicted Y value in equation 13.22 can be written

$$s_{\hat{y}} = s\sqrt{h_i}$$

13.27

FIGURE

13.27

(a) Original real-estate data, with a new observation ($X = 115$, $Y = 48$). (b) Original real-estate data, with a new observation ($X = 115$, $Y = 29$).

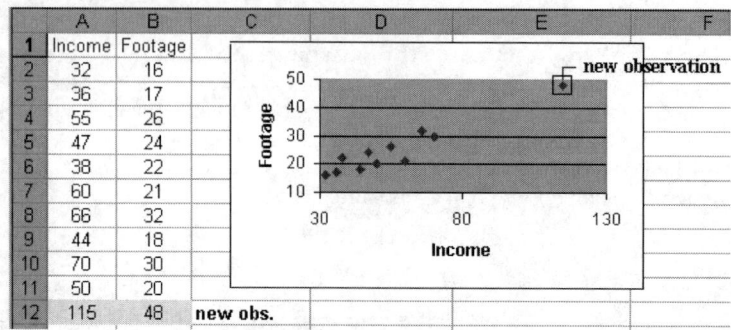

	A	B	C	D	E	F
1	Income	Footage				
2	32	16				
3	36	17				
4	55	26				
5	47	24				
6	38	22				
7	60	21				
8	66	32				
9	44	18				
10	70	30				
11	50	20				
12	115	48	new obs.			

(a)

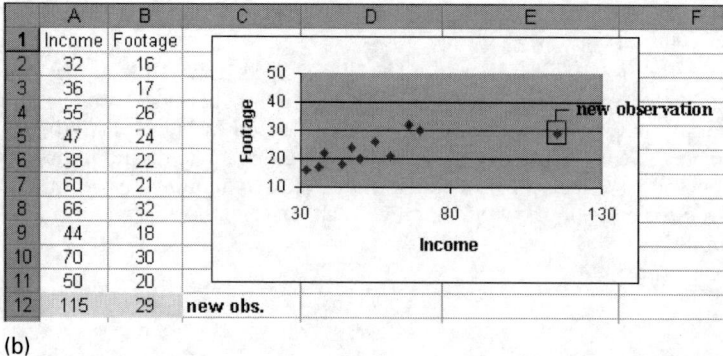

	A	B	C	D	E	F
1	Income	Footage				
2	32	16				
3	36	17				
4	55	26				
5	47	24				
6	38	22				
7	60	21				
8	66	32				
9	44	18				
10	70	30				
11	50	20				
12	115	29	new obs.			

(b)

The corresponding confidence interval for $\mu_{Y|x_i}$ is

$$\hat{Y} - t_{\alpha/2,n-2}s\sqrt{h_i} \quad \text{to} \quad \hat{Y} + t_{\alpha/2,n-2}s\sqrt{h_i}$$

13.28

and the prediction interval for Y_{x_i} in equation 13.24 is

$$\hat{Y} - t_{\alpha/2,n-2}s\sqrt{1+h_i} \quad \text{to} \quad \hat{Y} + t_{\alpha/2,n-2}s\sqrt{1+h_i}$$

13.29

Consequently, as the leverage of the ith observation increases (x_i moves farther from $\bar{x}$), the confidence interval for $\mu_{Y|x_i}$ and the prediction interval for Y_{x_i} become wider. The smallest possible leverage value is $h_i = 1/n$, and this occurs only if $x_i = \bar{x}$.

Identifying Outlying Values of the Dependent Variable. Sample observations having unusually large or small values of the dependent variable (Y) can generally be detected using the sample *standardized residuals*. Recall that the residual at the ith observation is $Y - \hat{Y}$, and that this residual estimates the error in the model at this observation. Since one of the model assumptions is that each error has a mean of zero, then to standardize the ith residual we simply divide by its estimated standard deviation. The estimated standard deviation of the ith residual can be written as

$$s\sqrt{1-h_i}$$

13.30

where h_i is the leverage for this observation, defined in equation 13.26, and s (rather, s^2) is defined in equation 13.13. Consequently,

$$\text{standardized residual} = \frac{Y_i - \hat{Y}_i}{s\sqrt{1 - h_i}}$$

13.31

A recommended procedure is to identify an observation as having an outlying value of Y if its standardized residual is larger than 2 or less than –2. MINITAB will automatically inform you which (if any) of your observations have standardized residuals larger than 2 in absolute value.

Using Excel, SPSS, or MINITAB and Figure 13.27(a), the following results can be obtained:

$$\text{Least squares line: } \hat{Y} = 3.752 + .3796X$$

$$SSE = 77.18 \quad \text{and} \quad s = \sqrt{\frac{77.18}{9}} = 2.93$$

For $X = 115$, $\hat{Y} = 47.41$, and

$$\text{Standardized residual of observation } 11 = \frac{48 - 47.41}{2.93\sqrt{1 - .747}} = .40$$

Consequently, observation 11 does not contain an extreme value of the dependent variable. We would still classify this observation as an outlier due to the large value of the independent variable ($X = 115$) and the correspondingly large leverage value ($h_{11} = .747$).

For Figure 13.27(b), the results are:

$$\text{Least squares line: } \hat{Y} = 13.746 + .1693X$$

$$SSE = 146.14 \quad \text{and} \quad s = \sqrt{\frac{146.14}{9}} = 4.03$$

For $X = 115$, $\hat{Y} = 33.22$, and

$$\text{Standardized residual of observation } 11 = \frac{29 - 33.22}{4.03\sqrt{1 - .747}} = -2.08$$

Since $-2.08 < -2$, observation 11 is extreme in both the Y value *and* the X value.

Identifying Influential Observations. On occasion, you may have one or two observations that have a very large impact on the sample regression line. If such an observation were deleted from the sample, the new values of the intercept (b_0) and/or the slope (b_1) would be much different. If such an observation exists, a little investigation may be in order to determine if this sample value should be modified or removed. If an error was made while recording this observation, then, if possible, the regression analysis should be rerun using the corrected value.

Often, it is impossible to recapture this observation. For example, it might have been recorded during an expensive experiment, which would necessitate rerunning the experiment. Perhaps, this observation occurred during a point in time that has since passed. For such situations, you could remove this observation and rerun the regression analysis.

By contrast, if this observation was recorded correctly, simply removing this observation from the data set is ill-advised. This observation might be revealing something; in particular, your model (using a straight line to predict Y) may be inappropriate, or the situation you're attempting to model is simply not as predictable as you expected. Perhaps additional independent variables should be considered (discussed in Chapter 14).

Determining influential observations uses the strategy for identifying outliers that was just discussed, since such observations are characterized by large leverage values (unusual values of X) and/or large standardized residuals (unusual values of Y).

A commonly used measure of influence is **Cook's distance measure,** which combines the leverage value and standardized residual into one overall value. Cook's distance measure for the ith observation is given by

$$D_i = \frac{1}{2}\frac{h_i}{1-h_i}\,(\text{standardized residual})^2$$

$$= \frac{(Y_i - \hat{Y}_i)^2}{2s^2}\left[\frac{h_i}{(1-h_i)^2}\right]$$

13.32

For example, in Figure 13.27(a), at observation 11,

$$Y = 48, \qquad \hat{Y} = 47.41, \qquad s = 2.93, \qquad h_{11} = .747$$

and so

$$D_{11} = \frac{(48-47.41)^2}{2(2.93)^2}\left[\frac{.747}{(1-.747)^2}\right] = .24$$

For Figure 13.27(b), at observation 11,

$$Y = 29, \qquad \hat{Y} = 33.22, \qquad s = 4.03, \qquad h_{11} = .747$$

and

$$D_{11} = \frac{(29-33.22)^2}{2(4.03)^2}\left[\frac{.747}{(1-.747)^2}\right] = 6.40$$

For simple linear regression, we recommend you conclude that the ith observation is influential if the corresponding D_i measure is larger than .8.* For Figure 13.27(a), the new observation is not considered influential: .24 < .8, and so, despite the large leverage value, this observation would not seriously affect the regression results if it were removed from the sample. In Figure 13.27(b), the new observation would be labeled as influential, because 6.40 > .8.

A final look at Figure 13.26 is contained in Figure 13.28, where the leverage value, standardized residual, and Cook's distance measure are shown for each of the three outliers. These results are summarized in Table 13.1, where the cutoff for the leverage values is $h_i = 6/n = 6/15 = .4$.

Statistical Software Application Use DATA13-10

A Full Simple Linear Regression Analysis

The editor of a monthly automotive magazine is interested in determining how well automotive manufacturers are meeting federal mandates concerning the average fuel economy that a manufacturer's fleet of cars must reach. The editor suspects that a linear relation-

---

*The cutoff value for Cook's distance measure in simple linear regression can also be defined using the F distribution: tail area = .5, df = 2 and n – 2. For nearly all sample sizes, the value .8 provides a reliable, and slightly conservative, approximation to this F-value.

FIGURE 13.28

Another look at Figure 13.26 with calculated leverages, standardized residuals, and Cook's distance measures.

	A	B	C	D	E	F	G	H
1	5.0	8.0						
2	6.0	9.0						
3	7.0	10.2						
4	8.0	10.9						
5	9.0	12.2						
6	9.5	12.6						
7	11.0	15.0						
8	12.0	15.4						
9	12.5	15.7						
10	14.0	17.3						
11	15.0	18.1						
12	16.0	19.0						
13	10.0	24.0	obs. A	0.077	2.47	0.255		
14	22.0	25.0	obs. B	0.243	1.44	0.334		
15	28.0	15.0	obs. C	0.530	-2.61	3.851		
16				h(i)	stan. res.	D(i)		

TABLE 13.1

Summary of Figures 13.26 and 13.28

Point	Outlying X Value (h > .fl)	Outlying Y Value (|stand.res.| > fl)	Influential Observation (D > .fl)
A	No	Yes	No
B	No	No	No
C	Yes	Yes	Yes

ship exists between X = engine capacity (in liters) and Y = miles per gallon (mpg). A sample of 60 different models was obtained (all models having a manual transmission) and is found in data set DATA13-10. The engine capacities (X values) are in column A, and the miles per gallon (Y values) are in column B.

Determine the appropriateness of the simple linear regression model, and examine the residuals (1) to detect any outliers, (2) to determine if any outliers would be classified as influential observations, and (3) to verify the model assumptions.

Solution

Begin by opening data file DATA13-10 using either Excel, MINITAB, or SPSS. The scatter diagram of the observations in Figure 13.29 was generated using Excel's **Chart Wizard ➤ XY (Scatter)**. From this diagram, it is clear that a negative relationship exists between X = capacity and Y = miles per gallon. There is one unusual observation (boxed). The MINITAB regression equation in Figure 13.30 was generated by clicking on **Stat ➤ Regression ➤ Regression** . The resulting regression equation from Figure 13.30 is Ŷ = 55.494 – 5.981X. Since the X coefficient is negative, there is indeed a negative relationship, and each additional liter of engine capacity in the data is accompanied by a decrease of approximately 6 miles per gallon (on the average).

The SPSS output in Figure 13.31 contains the predicted values, residuals, standardized residuals, leverage values, and Cook's D values. These columns are obtained by clicking on **Analyze ➤ Regression ➤ Linear,** and clicking on **Save.** The following boxes should be checked: **Predicted Values (Unstandardized)** in the **Predicted Values** frame, **Unstandardized** and **Studentized** in the **Residuals** frame, and **Cook's** and **Leverage** values in the **Distances** frame. Note: As mentioned in the end-of-chapter appendix, SPSS refers to the standardized residuals as studentized residuals, and 1/n (equal to 1/60 in this example) must be added to the computed leverage values.

A scan of the standardized residuals and Cook's distance measures reveals three "suspicious" or "interesting" observations—namely, observations 28, 51, and 60. These

FIGURE

13.29

Excel plot of X = engine capacity versus Y = miles per gallon (Example 13.10).

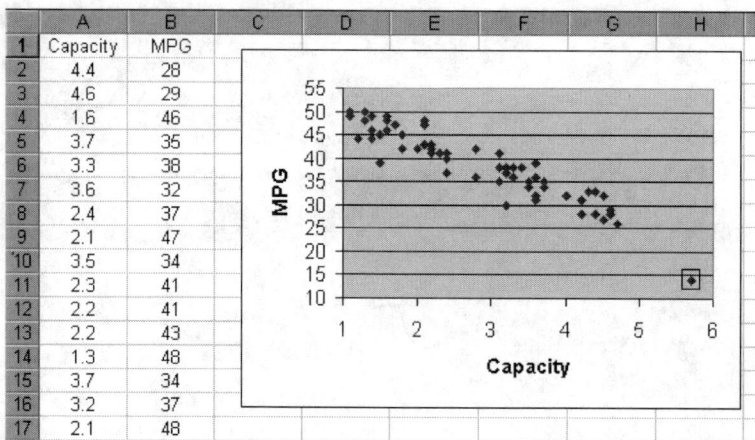

FIGURE

13.30

MINITAB regression output for Example 13.10.

Regression Analysis: MPG versus Capacity

The regression equation is
MPG = 55.5 - 5.98 Capacity

```
Predictor      Coef   SE Coef       T      P
Constant    55.4943    0.9373   59.21  0.000
Capacity    -5.9814    0.3074  -19.46  0.000


S = 2.75394   R-Sq = 86.7%   R-Sq(adj) = 86.5%


Analysis of Variance

Source         DF      SS      MS       F      P
Regression      1  2872.3  2872.3  378.72  0.000
Residual Error 58   439.9     7.6
Total          59  3312.2
```

three observations are indicated in Figure 13.31, which contains an abbreviated listing of the residuals, standardized residuals, leverages, and Cook's measures. The leverage cutoff here is 6/60 = .1 and a complete scan of the leverage column indicates that observation 28 is the only observation with a leverage value exceeding .1. It also has a standardized residual larger than 2 in absolute value, and so this observation contains outlying values of both the independent and dependent variables. This is, in fact, the "unusual" observation identified in the lower-right corner of the scatter diagram (Figure 13.29). Observations 51 and 60 also contain outlying values of Y, since their standardized residuals exceed 2 in absolute value.

All of the Cook's D values are under .8. Upon closer examination, it was discovered that observation 28 was from a Lamborghini and was, in fact, correctly recorded. No recording error was discovered for observations 51 and 60.

Figure 13.32 is a plot of the residuals, where the $Y - \hat{Y}$ values are plotted against the corresponding X values. The three boxed values correspond to observations 28 (labeled C), 51 (labeled B), and 60 (labeled A). In this plot, the three large residuals are obvious. No pattern is detected in the residual plot, and assumption 2 appears to be satisfied.

FIGURE

13.31

SPSS output
containing the
standardized
residuals,
leverages, and
Cook's distance
measures.

	capacity	mpg	predict	resid	stdresid	leverage	cook
1	4.4	28	29.1759	-1.1759	-.4376	.0477	.0048
2	4.6	29	27.9797	1.0203	.3813	.0561	.0043
3	1.6	46	45.9240	.0760	.0281	.0353	.0000
4	3.7	35	33.3630	1.6370	.6024	.0263	.0049
5	3.3	38	35.7555	2.2445	.8231	.0195	.0067
25	2.4	41	41.1388	-.1388	-.0509	.0189	.0000
26	3.6	31	33.9611	-2.9611	-1.0885	.0242	.0147
27	1.8	45	44.7277	.2723	.1004	.0297	.0002
28	5.7	14	21.4001	-7.4001	-2.8642	.1199	.5586
29	3.4	38	35.1574	2.8426	1.0431	.0208	.0116
30	1.1	50	48.9147	1.0853	.4051	.0536	.0046
50	4.5	27	28.5778	-1.5778	-.5884	.0518	.0094
51	3.2	30	36.3537	-6.3537	-2.3287	.0184	.0510
52	4.2	31	30.3722	.6278	.2327	.0403	.0011
53	1.7	47	45.3259	1.6741	.6180	.0323	.0064
54	4.6	28	27.9797	.0203	.0076	.0561	.0000
55	4.0	32	31.5685	.4315	.1594	.0340	.0004
56	2.4	40	41.1388	-1.1388	-.4175	.0189	.0017
57	1.3	50	47.7184	2.2816	.8480	.0455	.0171
58	2.1	43	42.9333	.0667	.0245	.0232	.0000
59	4.3	33	29.7741	3.2259	1.1980	.0439	.0329
60	1.5	39	46.5221	-7.5221	-2.7855	.0384	.1550

FIGURE

13.32

MINITAB
residual plot
(Example 13.10).

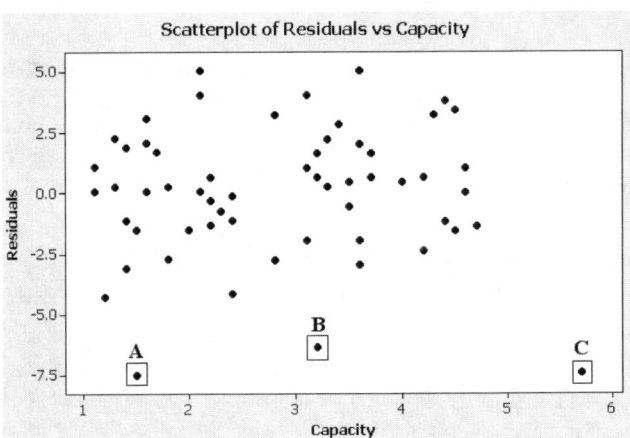

A histogram of the residuals is shown in Figure 13.33. To obtain the residual histogram in Figure 13.33, click on **KPK Data Analysis ➤ Quantitative Data Charts/Tables ➤ Histogram/Freq.**

Charts. The resulting histogram in Figure 13.33 appears to be approximately normally distributed with a mean of zero (assumption 1). The three residuals in the left-most two boxes correspond to observations 28, 51, and 60. There is no need to check assumption 3, because the regression data were not time-ordered.

Conclusion. The model appears to be an excellent one, providing a highly significant t statistic ($t = -19.46$, p-value ≈ 0) and $r^2 = 86.7\%$; that is, engine capacity explains 86.7% of the variation in the mpg values. All of the model assumptions appear to be satisfied. All

FIGURE

13.33

Histogram of
residuals using
KPK Data Analysis
(Example 13.10).

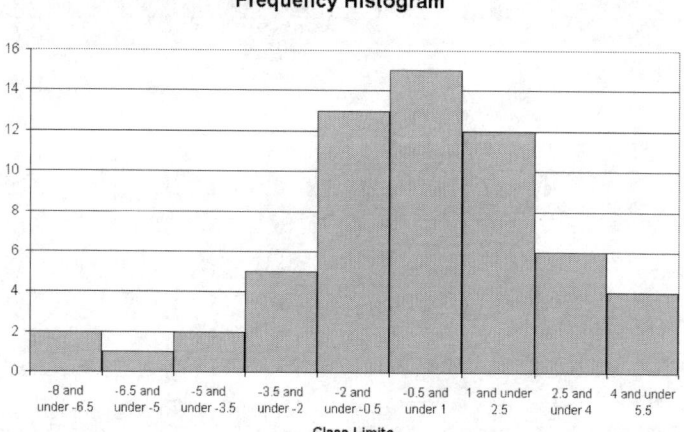

three of the apparent outliers could be retained in the model, since none of these observations produced a significant Cook's distance measure, and no error was made in the recording of these values. Consideration could be given to removing the Lamborghini from the population and from the sample, and restricting the discussion to less exotic automobiles.

X Exercises 13.43–13.57

Understanding the Mechanics

13.43 Data for X and Y are presented below.

X	12	15	20	25	30
Y	2	6	10	20	50

a. Calculate the least squares line.
b. Determine a 90% confidence interval for the mean value of Y using $X = 10$.
c. Determine a 90% prediction interval for Y using $X = 10$.
d. Calculate the standardized residual, the leverage value, and value of Cook's D for each observation.
e. Would any observation be considered influential?

13.44 Test that there is positive autocorrelation in a data set of 16 observations with four independent variables for each of the following values of the Durbin–Watson test statistic. Use a 5% significance level.
a. 2.50
b. .40
c. 1.01

Applying the New Concepts

13.45 For the data in Exercise 13.3, find a 95% confidence interval for the mean percentage of mortgage-paying homeowners whose housing costs exceed 30% for an X value equal to a median income of $35,000. Interpret this interval. For the same value of X, find a 95% prediction interval for the percentage of mortgage-paying homeowners whose housing costs exceed 30%. Interpret this interval.

13.46 Find a 90% confidence interval for the mean price charged by a commercial airline when distance traveled is 500 miles using the following data.

Distance (miles)	300	400	450	500	550	600	800	1000
Price Charged	140	220	230	250	255	288	350	480

13.47 Using the bankruptcy data in Ex 13.15, find the standardized residual, leverage value, and value of Cook's D for each observation. Comment on these values.

13.48 For the data in Exercise 13.19 in which the new price in euros is predicted using the original price in marks for eight products, calculate the standardized residual, the leverage value, and the value of Cook's D for each observation. Comment on these values. Would any observation be considered influential?

13.49 For the data in Exercise 13.25, find the 90% prediction interval for the log of personal consumption expenditure for an X value of 200 billion people. Transform the interval, by replacing each endpoint by 10^z, where z is the value of the endpoint. What does this transformed prediction interval represent?

13.50 **Consumer Reports** rates the performance of book-shelf speakers. Speakers are tested by placing them in an echo-free chamber and feeding them test signals containing all audible frequencies. Ratings range from 0 to 100, with 100 being a perfect score. Consumers often want to know if price is any reflection of the quality of the product. To understand if a linear relationship exists between the rating and the price of bookshelf speakers, the following data were collected.

Speakers	Price	Rating
NHT Model 1.5	600	76
B&W DM 602 S2	550	78
Polk Audio RT55i	550	61
JBL Northridge Series N28	400	75
Polk Audio RT35i	335	70
JBL Studio Series S26	300	61
DCM DCM6	200	50
Yamaha NS-A638	125	67
Bose 141	100	64
KLH 911B	100	47

a. Let the dependent variable be the price of a bookshelf speaker and the independent variable be the rating. Do the data support the conclusion that there is a linear relationship between these two variables? What is your conclusion at the 5% significance level? What would it be at the 1% significance level?

b. Based on the values of the standardized residuals, would you say that there are any outliers?

(Source: "Loudspeaker Ratings," Consumer Reports, August 2001, p. 36.)

13.51 For the data in Exercise 13.26, find the 99% confidence interval for the average number of years that a lawn mower will be able to function properly if the number of hours of operation between oil changes is 23 hours. What is the standard deviation for the predicted value of the number of years that a single lawnmower will be able to perform adequately if the number of hours of operation between oil changes is 23?

13.52 Since the economy has generally been growing from 1986 through 2004 (with the exception of short-lived recessions) economists are not surprised that the median personal income has trended upward. Find the regression equation for predicting median personal income (in units of thousands) using the variable year. Test for positive autocorrelation using a 5% significance level.

Year	1986	1987	1988	1989	1990	1991	1992
Income	31	32	34	35	34	33	33

Year	1993	1994	1995	1996	1997	1998	1999
Income	32	33	33	34	34	36	37

Year	2000	2001	2002	2003	2004
Income	38	36	37	38	39

13.53 A sample of 200 executives who work in Chicago was taken to find out how much of their own money the executives invest each year in stock of the company that they

work for. The following regression equation was developed, where X is the income (in thousands) of an executive and Y is the amount of money (in thousands) he or she invests each year in the company. The prediction equation is

$$\hat{Y} = 9.5 + 0.05X$$

Based on the regression equation, can the following statement be made? A Chicago-area executive who earns $95,000 a year would invest about $14,250 in company stock. Comment.

Using the Computer

13.54 **[DATA SET EX13-54]** Variable Description:

MortgageLender: Name of lending institution

Location: City and state of institution

MortgageLoans01: Amount of mortgage loans approved during 2001 in millions of dollars

MortgageLoans00: Amount of mortgage loans approved during 2000 in millions of dollars

In 2001, America's residential lenders were awash in refinancings. The total mortgage packages approved exceeded $1.5 trillion. However, refinancings were not uniform across the United States. Twenty major mortgage institutions were randomly selected, and the amount of mortgage refinancing was recorded for 2001 and 2000.

a. Plot Y = MortgageLoans01 and X = MortgageLoans00. Comment on how linearly related you think the two variables are.

b. Do the data support the hypothesis that there is a linear relationship between X and Y? Base your response on the p-value.

c. Determine a 95% prediction interval for the amount of mortgage loans approved in 2001 if the institution serviced $150,000 million of mortgages in 2000.

d. Determine if any observations are influential.

(Source: "Refi Boom Headaches," U.S. Banker, June 2001, p. 58.)

13.55 **[DATA SET EX13-55]** Variable Description:

Time: Monthly time periods numbered 1 through 60

GrossRev: Monthly gross revenue at Cinemark Theaters

The owner of Cinemark Theaters recorded the monthly gross revenue in thousands of dollars from 2000 through 2004. Regress GrossRev on the independent variable Time. What is the Durbin–Watson statistic for this regression model? Does positive autocorrelation exist at the 5% significance level?

13.56 **[DATA SET EX13-56]** Variable Description:

WebSalary: Salary paid to a Web manager

ComputerExp: Years experience working in a computer environment

What is the coefficient of determination between the salary paid to a Web manager and the years of experience? Remove the most influential observation and repeat.

13.57 **[DATA SET EX13-57]** Variable Description:

CEO_Compens: Total compensation of the chief executive officer (CEO)

CompanyProfit: Annual company after-tax profit.

Plot Y = CEO_Compens and X = CompanyProfit. Comment on the fit. Eliminate the most influential observation. What changes, if any, do you notice?

 # Summary

Whenever a sample of bivariate data contains a significant linear pattern, we determine the least squares line through the data points and generate an equation that can be used to predict values of the dependent variable. This model can be written as $Y = \beta_0 + \beta_1 X + e$, where $\beta_0 + \beta_1 X$ is the deterministic component and e represents the random (error) component. If a significant linear relationship exists within the sample data, both the direction (positive or negative) and the strength of this linear relationship can be measured using the sample coefficient of correlation, r.

By regressing Y on X we are able to determine the least squares line, $\hat{Y} = b_0 + b_1 X$. The value of b_0 is the intercept of the least squares line and estimates the population intercept β_0. The slope of the least squares line, b_1, estimates the population slope β_1.

Various methods for determining the utility of the model as a predictor of the dependent variable include: (1) a t test for detecting a significant slope, b_1; (2) a t test for determining whether the sample correlation, r, is significantly large; and (3) a confidence interval for the slope, β_1. The two t tests appear to be quite different, but their computed values (and df) are identical.

Another measure of how well the model provides estimates that fit the sample data is given by the coefficient of determination, r^2. For simple linear regression (one independent variable), this is the square of the correlation coefficient. For example, if $r^2 = .85$, then 85% of the variation in the sample Y values has been explained using this model.

The value of $\hat{Y}$ from the least squares regression line at a specific value of X can be used to estimate an average value of Y, given this value of X. The reliability of this estimate can be measured using the corresponding confidence interval. Similarly, we can use the $\hat{Y}$ value to center a prediction interval for an individual value of the dependent variable, given this specific value of X.

Examination of the residuals is an important step during a regression analysis. These values can be used to verify the model assumptions, as well as to indicate sample observations that appear to be outliers or observations that are very influential in determining the least squares line.

 # Summary of Formulas

Correlation Between Two Variables

$$r = \frac{SCP_{XY}}{\sqrt{SS_X}\,\sqrt{SS_Y}}$$

where

$$SCP_{XY} = \Sigma xy - \frac{(\Sigma x)(\Sigma y)}{n}$$

$$SS_X = \Sigma x^2 - \frac{(\Sigma x)^2}{n}$$

$$SS_Y = \Sigma y^2 - \frac{(\Sigma y)^2}{n}$$

Least Squares Line

$$\hat{Y} = b_0 + b_1 X$$

where

$$b_1 = \frac{SCP_{XY}}{SS_X} \quad \text{and} \quad b_0 = \bar{y} - b_1 \bar{x}$$

Estimate of the Residual Variance

$$\tilde{\sigma}_e^2 = s^2 = \frac{SSE}{n-2}$$

$$\text{SSE} = \Sigma(y - \hat{y})^2 = \text{SS}_Y - \frac{(\text{SCP}_{XY})^2}{\text{SS}_X}$$

t Statistic for Detecting a Significant Slope

$$t = \frac{b_1}{s_{b_1}} \quad (\text{df} = n-2), \text{ where}$$

$$s_{b_1} = \frac{s}{\sqrt{\text{SS}_X}}$$

Confidence Interval for the Slope, β_1

$$b_1 - t_{\alpha/2,n-2}s_{b_1} \quad to \quad b_1 + t_{\alpha/2,n-2}s_{b_1}$$

t Statistic for Detecting a Significant Correlation

$$t = \frac{r}{\sqrt{\dfrac{1-r^2}{n-2}}} \quad (\text{df} = n-2)$$

Coefficient of Determination

$$r^2 = \text{square of correlation coefficient}$$

$$= 1 - \frac{\text{SSE}}{\text{SS}_Y}$$

Confidence Interval for the Average Value of Y at a Specific Value of X (Say x_0)

$$\hat{Y} \pm t_{\alpha/2,n-2}s\sqrt{\frac{1}{n} + \frac{(x_0 - \bar{x})^2}{\text{SS}_X}}$$

Prediction Interval for a Particular Value of Y at a Specific Value of X (say, x_0)

$$\hat{Y} \pm t_{\alpha/2,n-2}s\sqrt{1 + \frac{1}{n} + \frac{(x_0 - \bar{x})^2}{\text{SS}_X}}$$

Leverage of the ith Observation

$$h_i = \frac{1}{n} + \frac{(x_i - \bar{x})^2}{\text{SS}_X}$$

Standardized Residual of the ith Observation

$$\frac{Y_i - \hat{Y}_i}{s\sqrt{1-h_i}}$$

Cook's Distance Measure for the ith Observation

$$D_i = \frac{(Y_i - \hat{Y}_i)^2}{2s^2}\left(\frac{h_i}{(1-h_i)^2}\right)$$

Durbin-Watson Statistic

$$\text{DW} = \frac{\sum_{t=2}^{T}(e_t - e_{t-1})^2}{\sum_{t=1}^{T}e_t^2}$$

X Review Exercises 13.58–13.73

13.58 The following statistics were calculated from pairs of observations where X represents the independent variable and Y represents the dependent variable.

$$\Sigma x = 511 \qquad \Sigma y = 314 \qquad \Sigma xy = 19,064$$
$$\Sigma x^2 = 34,234.5 \qquad \Sigma y^2 = 13,036 \qquad n = 8$$

a. Determine the least squares line.
b. Determine the sample correlation coefficient between X and Y.

c. Determine if there is a linear relationship between X and Y at the .10 significance level.

d. Find a 90% confidence interval for the slope of the regression line.

e. Find a 90% confidence interval for the mean of Y if $X = 60$.

f. Find a 90% prediction interval for Y if $X = 60$.

g. What are the necessary assumptions for the validity of the procedure in parts c, d, e, and f?

13.59 Arena football has experienced enormous growth since 1987, when only 12 indoor football games were played. To understand the relationship between the attendance (in millions) and number of games, data from 1995 to 2004 are listed below.

Year	1995	1996	1997	1998	1999	2000	2001	2002	2003	2004
Attendance	.41	.74	.69	.70	.88	1.13	1.07	1.04	1.06	1.15
Games	40	60	60	66	78	105	98	98	105	119

a. Find the least squares line for the data using $X =$ number of games and $Y =$ attendance (in millions). Interpret the slope of the regression equation.

b. Test that there is a linear relationship. Use the p-value to base your conclusion.

c. Find a 95% confidence interval for the slope of the regression line. Interpret the interval in the context of this problem.

d. Find a 95% prediction interval for the attendance when the number of games is 110.

e. What assumptions are necessary for the validity of the responses to parts b, c, and d?

13.60 Dolls-R-Us believes that television advertising is the most effective way to market its new line of dolls. The sales manager recorded the amount of money spent on advertising and the amount of sales for 20 randomly selected months. The average cost for television advertising for the 20 months was $110,000. The average sales volume for the 20 months was $675,000. The following sample statistics were found from the data for the 20 months.

$$SCP_{XY} = 198.4 \qquad SS_X = 205.3 \qquad SS_Y = 341.6$$

where Y represents the sales volume (in thousands) and X represents the television advertising costs (in thousands of dollars).

a. Calculate the least squares line.

b. Calculate the coefficient of determination.

c. Calculate the sum of squares of error.

d. What is the estimate of the variance of the error component for the model?

e. Is there sufficient evidence from the data to conclude at the .01 significance level that a positive relationship exists between X and Y?

f. Find a 95% prediction interval for the monthly sales volume if the television advertising expenditure during one particular month is $120,000.

13.61 A car rental agency has a fleet of 200 cars available for rent at Kennedy airport in New York City. The owner of the agency uses a regression equation for estimating the company's daily revenue based on the number of incoming flights that day. The regression equation is $\hat{Y} = 2500 + 21.4X$, where X is the number of daily incoming flights and Y is the daily revenue in dollars. The data used to find the least squares line are based on a sample of 100 randomly selected days in 2005. Can the following statement be made based on regression analysis? If Kennedy airport increases its daily incoming flights by 50 flights next year, then the car agency can expect to make an additional daily revenue of $1,070. Comment.

13.62 Each week, a realtor advertises the houses she manages that are available for rent. The number of telephone calls from people inquiring about the advertisement were recorded for several weeks, during which various sizes of the advertisement were used. Is there sufficient evidence from the following data to conclude at the .10 significance level, that a nonzero correlation exists?

X (Height of Ad, Inches)	Y (Number of Inquiries)	X (Height of Ad, Inches)	Y (Number of Inquiries)
0.5	3	2.5	10
1.0	4	3.0	14
1.5	6	3.5	12
2.0	5	4.0	18

13.63 The manager of a firm that specializes in assisting individuals in filling out federal income tax forms obtained data from the Internal Revenue Service pertaining to deductions for charitable contributions. The following table provides a distribution of charitable contributions of eight groups with different adjusted gross incomes.

Median Adjusted Gross Income (in Thousands of Dollars) (X)	Percentage in Group Making Charitable Contributions (Claiming Itemized Deductions) (Y)
5.0	17.0
7.5	36.0
12.5	40.5
17.5	38.5
25.0	29.2
40.0	14.0
75.0	4.2
100.0	1.5

  a. Obtain the least squares line for these data.
  b. Identify the values of the intercept, the slope, and the variance of the error for the simple linear regression model.
  c. Find the residuals for all the Y values.
  d. If the correlation between X and Y above was very strong, would it then be correct to conclude that an increase in income causes people to become less charitable?

13.64 The toughness of a paint is usually a good indication of how long it will last. Generally, the low-luster paints tend to be tougher than the flat paints, especially in their ability to resist staining. *Consumer Reports* rates paints on their toughness and also provides an overall rating for each paint. Twelve flat paints and their overall rating (higher scores are better) and their toughness rating (lower scores are better) are shown below. Find a 95% prediction interval for the overall score of a paint with a toughness rating of 6. Interpret this interval.

Flat Paints	Overall Score	Toughness
Valspar American Tradition (Lowe's)	80	3
Sherwin Williams Everclean Interior	70	4
Ralph Lauren Premium Quality	63	5
Sears Best Easy Living	63	8
Glidden Dulux Inspirations	62	4
Behr Premium Plus (The Home Depot)	61	5
Martha Stewart Everyday Colors	61	5
Color Place Premium (Wal-Mart)	60	7
Dutch Boy Fresh Look (Kmart)	60	8
Benjamin Moore Regal Wall Satin	60	9
Kelly Moore Super	55	7
Glidden Evermore (The Home Depot)	52	12

(Source: "Picking the Best Paint," *Consumer Reports*, June 2001, pp. 36–38.)

13.65 What is the variance of the error term for predicting overall score using toughness in Exercise 13.64? Remove the most influential observation. What is the variance of the error term now?

13.66 Stock brokerage firms receive a score called their batting average. This value is obtained by dividing the firm's total number of awards for various categories such as forecasting earnings of companies by the number of analysts used by that firm. The following data represent the stock-picking awards of eight stock brokerage firms and their batting average.

Securities Firm	Number of Stock-Picking Awards	Batting Average
Salomon Smith Barney	21	.574
Merrill Lynch	8	.359
Morgan Stanley	15	.410
Lehman Brothers	11	.522
Goldman Sachs	11	.344
A.G. Edwards	10	.477
Credit Suisse First Boston	8	.273
J.P. Morgan Chase	6	.313

a. Plot Y = batting average and X = number of stock picking awards. Do you think that the data demonstrate a linear relationship between X and Y?
b. Calculate the coefficient of determination. Interpret this value.
c. Find a 90% prediction interval for the batting average of a securities firm that has 12 stock-picking awards. Interpret this interval.

(Source: "Firm by Firm: Tally of Awards Ranks 82 Research Houses," The Wall Street Journal, June 26, 2001, p. R16.)

13.67 Diane's Beauty Salon is currently hiring beauticians at its new location in a popular mall. Diane wants to know what percentage of commission to pay the beauticians based on experience. A survey of 12 licensed beauticians was taken with the following results.

Percentage of Commission (Y)	Years of Experience (X)	Percentage of Commission (Y)	Years of Experience (X)
24	2	25	4
18	1	44	12
30	5	33	8
41	10	24	3
35	8	20	1
35	7	40	10

a. Find the least squares line.
b. Calculate the sum of squares due to error.
c. Test the null hypothesis that there is no linear relationship between years of experience and percentage of commissions paid. Use a significance level of .05.
d. Find a 90% confidence interval for the slope of the regression line.

13.68 Plot the residuals for the least squares line in Exercise 13.67. Do the residuals appear to be random? Compute the necessary statistics to determine if there are any influential observations.

13.69 **[DATA SET EX13-69]** Variable Description:

ChinaEmissions: China's carbon dioxide emissions in millions of metric tons of carbon

US_Emissions: United States' carbon dioxide emissions in millions of metric tons of carbon

Only a few years ago, many studies projected that China would emerge as the world's leading source of carbon dioxide by 2020, but recent developments appear to have put off that day by years. Although the United States has improved its energy efficiency since the oil crises of the 1970s, the growth in gas-guzzling vehicles continues to push the carbon dioxide emissions of the United States to new highs. China is second to the United States because it makes such enormous inefficient use of coal. Data are collected on the carbon dioxide emissions of both countries from 1980 to 1999.
a. Plot the values of the carbon dioxide emissions of China and the carbon dioxide emissions of the United States.
b. Develop a regression equation to predict the carbon dioxide emissions of China using the carbon dioxide emissions of the United States.

c. For which years does the regression equation appear to predict well?

d. What observations (if any) would you identify as influential?

(Source: "China Said to Reduce Carbon Dioxide Emissions," New York Times, June 15, 2001, p. 65.)

13.70 **[DATA SET EX13-70]** Variable Description:

Year: Year from 1970 to 2001

MinWage: Minimum wage adjusted for inflation

After adjusting for inflation, the real value of the minimum wage has actually decreased over the past few years. This is in contrast to the 1970s, in which the real value of the minimum wage generally increased. Find the regression equation for predicting MinWage using the variable year. What is the value of the Durbin–Watson statistic? Test for positive autocorrelation of the error terms using a 5% significance level.

(Source: "A Bumpy Road for Those at the Bottom," The Wall Street Journal, July 19, 2001, p. A10.)

13.71 **[DATA SET EX13-71]** Variable Description:

Total: Total amount of soup purchased using coupons

Campbell: Amount of Campbell soup purchased using coupons

Heinz: Amount of Heinz soup purchased using coupons

Private: Amount of soup with a private store label purchased using coupons

Roughly 258 billion coupons are distributed annually with about 80% of all coupons distributed through inserts in newspapers. However, only about 2 percent of all coupons are ever redeemed. Supposed that an analyst for the food industry is interested in the relationship of the total purchase of soup by a family household using coupons and the purchase of three brands of soup also using a coupon. The analyst randomly selected 50 soup-eating families who use coupons to buy soup. Over a six-month period, each family's total purchase of soups and the purchase of either Campbells, Heinz, or a private store brand of soup all with coupons were recorded.

a. Construct a correlation table for these four variables. (In Excel, use Correl function.) Interpret the correlations. Which correlations differ from zero at the 5% significance level?

b. Would you say that the variable Campbell is a good predictor of Private? Why?

c. Which variable would you say is the best predictor of the total amount of soup purchased over the past six months?

(Source: "Use of Coupons Cuts Both Ways," The Washington Post, September 12, 2004, p. F1.)

13.72 **[DATA SET EX13-72]** Variable Description:

OverallScore: Overall rating for portable CD players

HeadPhone ErrCorr: Score on headphones and error detection for portable CD players

BumpImm_Controls: Score on bump immunity and controls for portable CD players

Consumer Reports rates portable CD players so that a consumer can judge which CD player is the best value. An overall rating is given to each CD player that is tested. Ratings are also given to headphones and error correction to reflect a CD player's accuracy in reproducing sound and how well the CD handled damaged discs. In addition, ratings are provided on "bump immunity" and controls to reflect how well a CD resisted skipping when jostled and the ease of using the buttons and reading the LCD panel.

a. Develop the estimated regression equation that can be used to predict the overall rating for a portable CD player using the score on headphones and error detection. Assess the fit of this equation using a 5% significance level.

b. Repeat part a using the score on bump immunity and controls to predict the overall rating.

c. Compare the regression equations in parts a and b. Which variable, score on headphones and error detection or score on bump immunity and controls, would you say is a better predictor of the overall score for portable CD players?

d. For the equation that you selected in part c, find the observation with the largest standardized residual. Remove that observation and estimate the regression equation on the remaining data. By how much does the coefficient of determination change?

(Source: "Portable CD Players," Consumer Reports, July, 2001, p. 214.)

13.73 [DATA SET EX13-73] Variable Description:

Model: Model name of luxury automobile

SugRetailPrice: Suggested retail price of the automobile model.

DealerCost: Dealer's cost for the automobile model

Generally, subtracting 10% of the suggested retail price of an automobile is an approximation of the dealer's cost. However, the dealer's cost for luxury models tends to vary more.

a. What is the predicted value for the dealer's cost for a Mercedes-Benz CL500 using a SugRetailPrice as a predictor variable?

b. Remove the observation with the largest value of Cook's D. Repeat part a and compare the predicted values.

Computer Exercises Using the Databases

Exercise 1—Appendix F

From the database, randomly select 50 observations. Compute the sample correlation between the variable HPAYRENT (house payment or rent) and the variable UTILITY (monthly utility expenditure). Is there evidence to conclude that a positive correlation exists? Use a .05 significance level.

Exercise 2—Appendix F

Randomly select 50 observations from the database. Plot the values of total indebtedness (TOTLDEBT) and total income (INCOME1 + INCOME2). Also plot the values of TOTLDEBT and HPAYRENT (house payment or rent). Choose the graph that appears to have a stronger linear relationship between the graphed variables. Test to determine if the predictor variable significantly contributes to the prediction of total indebtedness. Use a significance level of .10.

Exercise 3—Appendix G

Randomly select 50 observations from the database. Compute the sample correlation between the variable NETINC (net income) and each of the variables SALES (gross sales) and COSTSALE (cost of sale). Select the variable from the latter two that has the highest correlation with net income. Regress net income on this variable and determine if this variable significantly contributes to the prediction of net income. Use a .05 significance level.

Exercise 4—Appendix G

Randomly select 50 observations from the database. Compute the regression line for predicting total assets (TOTAL) from current assets (ASSETS). Also compute the regression line for predicting total assets using current liabilities (LIABIL). Test for the adequacy of the fit of these two regression lines to the data. Use a .10 significance level. Which of these two regression lines has a higher value for the coefficient of determination and what does the higher value indicate?

Insights from Statistics in Action

Alpha Beta Soup for the Investor's Soul: Recipe Includes Regression Analysis

The Statistics in Action introductory case study mentioned that investors use the alpha and beta of a mutual fund to assess the volatility of the fund. These values are the intercept and slope, respectively, of a regression equation in which a mutual fund's performance is regressed on the S&P 500 index. If beta were zero (or not significantly different from zero), the performance of a mutual fund when compared to the performance of the S&P 500 stock index would be represented as having a constant rate of return. If the beta were between 0 and 1, the mutual fund (e.g., a mutual fund investing in utility stocks) would be less volatile than the stock market. A beta equal to 1 would indicate a match in performance with the S&P 500 and a value above 1 indicates a fund that is more volatile than the general market. Suppose that an investor is monitoring two mutual funds, the Heritage Fund and the Eagle Fund, and wishes to compare their performance to the S&P 500 index. Each of these funds has returned 31% over the past 30 weeks, and the weekly percentage increase or decrease in performance is recorded for each fund and for the S&P 500 index in the data file StatInActChap14.xls.

1. Graph the data for the Heritage Fund and the S&P 500 index. Also graph the data for the Eagle Fund and the S&P 500 index. Do you believe that a linear trend exists for each graph?

2. Find the regression equation for each graph in part a. Do you consider the regression lines to be an acceptable fit to the data? Use the p-value as a basis for your conclusion.

3. How would you interpret the intercept and slope for each regression line? Which mutual fund would a conservative investor prefer?

4. Using the regression analysis for the Heritage Fund and the regression analysis for Eagle Fund, which observation has the largest standardized residual? Delete this observation from the data set and find the resulting regression equation.

5. Compare the r^2 for the regression line with and without the deleted observation in part 4. Look at the observation that was deleted. Why do you believe that it is an influential observation?

(Source: "Family Finance: Morningstar Plans to Offer Retirement Advice," *The Wall Street Journal*, September 22, 2004, p. D2. "Quoth the Mavens," *The Washington Post*, February 29, 2004, "The Alpha Advantage," *Financial Planning*, September 2001, vol. 31, issue 8, p. 59.)

Appendix

Data Analysis with Excel, MINITAB, and SPSS

Excel

Simple Linear Regression Using Excel's Regression Procedure

Click on **Tools ➤ Data Analysis ➤ Regression** to obtain the dialog box for Excel's regression procedure. For the real-estate data in Example 13.3, enter "B1:B10" for the **Input Y Range** so that square footage is the dependent variable and enter "A1:A10" for the **Input X Range** so that income is the independent variable. If labels are included in the input range, then **Labels** needs to be checked. Check **Residuals** to obtain the predicted and residual values of each observation. Enter the **Output Range** and click **OK** to obtain the output in Figures 13.11 and 13.12.

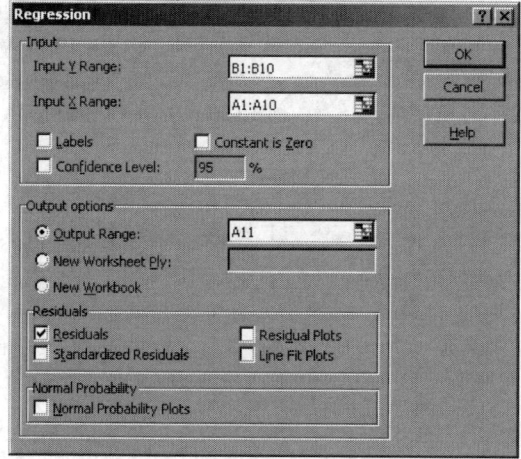

Simple Linear Regression Using KPK Data Analysis

To implement many of the regression options discussed in this chapter, use the KPK Data Analysis macros. Click on **KPK Data Analysis ➤ Regression** to obtain the dialog box. For example, using DATA11-10 in Example 13.10, enter B1:B61 and A1:A61 in the **Y Range** and the **Contiguous X Range.** Be sure that a label is included as the first cell in each range. Check **Residuals, Standardized Residuals, Leverages,** and **Cook's Ds** to identify influential observations. Enter the **Output Range** and click **OK** to obtain the output.

To obtain a histogram of the residuals as in Figure 13.33, check **Residual Histogram.** To obtain confidence intervals and prediction intervals at the 95th confidence level as in Figure 13.18, check **Enter range of new observations for confidence intervals and prediction intervals.** In the adjacent edit box, enter the range of X values in column format. Click on the **Durbin-Watson Statistic** to display the value of this statistic for autocorrelated errors, as illustrated in Figure 13.25.

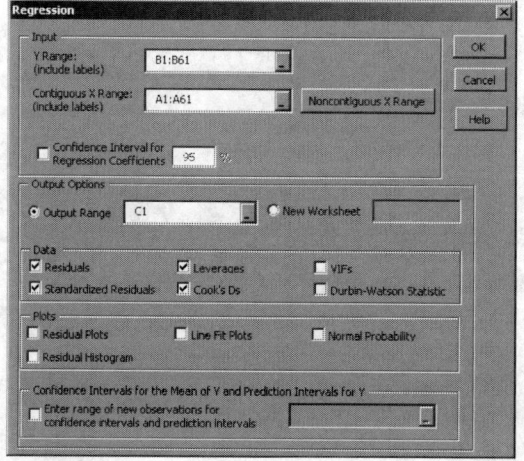

MINITAB

Simple Linear Regression

Click on **Stat ➤ Regression ➤ Regression** to obtain the dialog box for Minitab's regression procedure. For the real-estate data in Example 13.3, enter footage for the **Response** (dependent) variable and income for the **Predictors** variable. Clicking on **Storage** produces a **Regression — Storage** dialog box that allows the option of storing regression

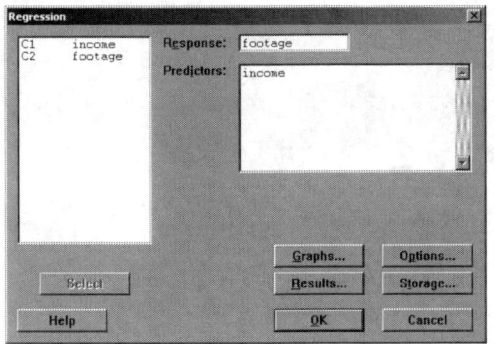
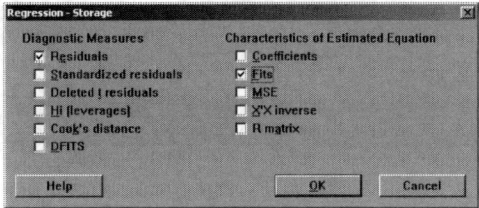

diagnostic statistics and characteristics of the estimated equation. Check **Residuals** and **Fits,** click **OK,** and then **OK** on the **Regression** dialog box to obtain the output in Figure 13.13 with the residuals and predicted variables stored in the data window. Check **Residuals, Standardized residuals, Hi,** and **Cook's distance** in the **Regression — Storage** dialog box to identify influential observations.

To obtain confidence intervals and prediction intervals as in Figure 13.19, click **Options** on the **Regression** dialog box to display the **Regression — Options** dialog box. Enter the income variable into the **Prediction intervals for new observations** box, enter 95 as the **Confidence level,** and check the **Confidence limits** and **Prediction limits** boxes. Check **Fit intercept** at the top of the dialog box to include the intercept term in the regression equation. Click **OK,** and then **OK** in the **Regression** dialog box to display the output. In the **Regression — Options** dialog box, click on the **Durbin-Watson statistic** to compute this statistic for autocorrelated errors. Another option is to click on **Graphs** on the **Regression** dialog box to display a screen to select a histogram of the residuals.

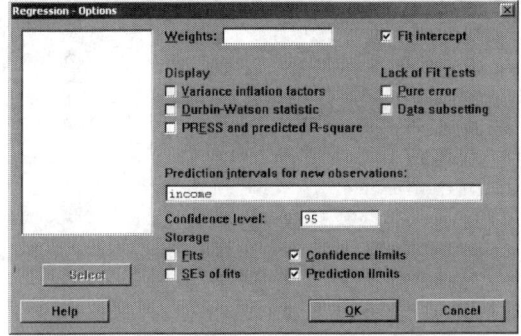

SPSS

Simple Linear Regression

The dialog box for regression analysis can be obtained by clicking on **Analyze ➤ Regression ➤ Linear.** For the real-estate data in Example 13.3, move the variable footage into the **Dependent** box and the variable income into the **Independent(s)** box. Click **OK** to obtain the output in Figure 13.14.

By clicking on the **Save** option before clicking the **OK** button, a dialog box will appear displaying statistics that can be saved as shown in Figures 13.20 and 13.31.

To obtain:

1. The predicted *Y* values, click on **Unstandardized** in the **Predicted Values** frame.

2. The standardized residuals, click on **Studentized** in the **Residuals** frame. *Note:* SPSS refers to the standardized residuals defined in equation 13.31 as studentized residuals, rather than standardized residuals.

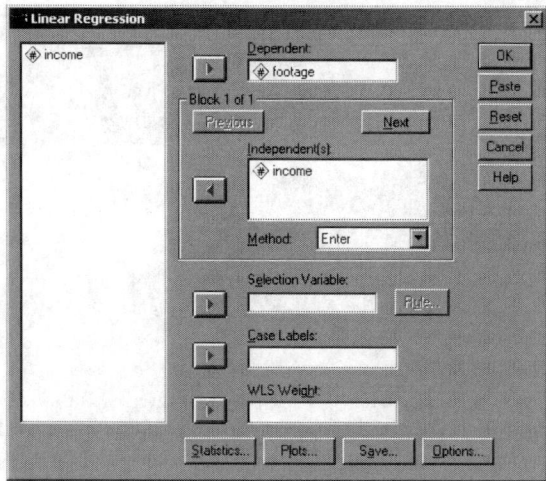

3. The Cook's distance measures, click on **Cook's** in the **Distances** frame.

4. The sample leverages, click on **Leverage values** in the **Distances** frame.

5. The confidence intervals on the mean value of y or prediction intervals, click on **Mean** and **Individual** in the **Prediction Intervals** frame. To obtain an interval for a specific value of the predictor variable, enter the predictor variable's value in a row, but leave the corresponding value under the predicted variable blank.

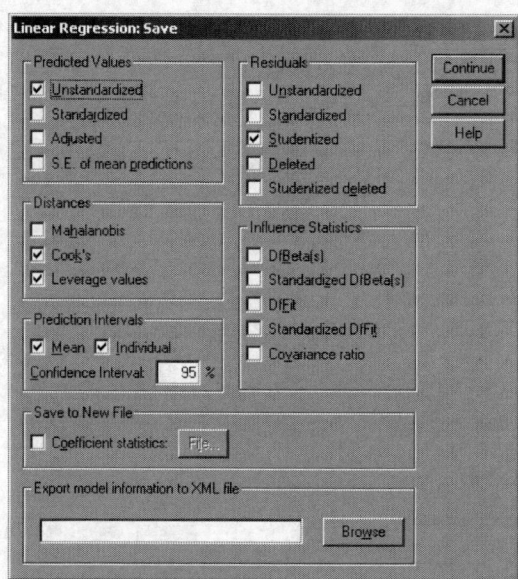

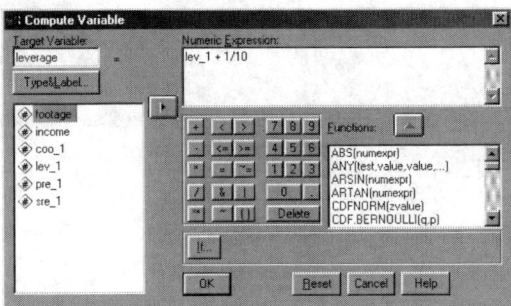

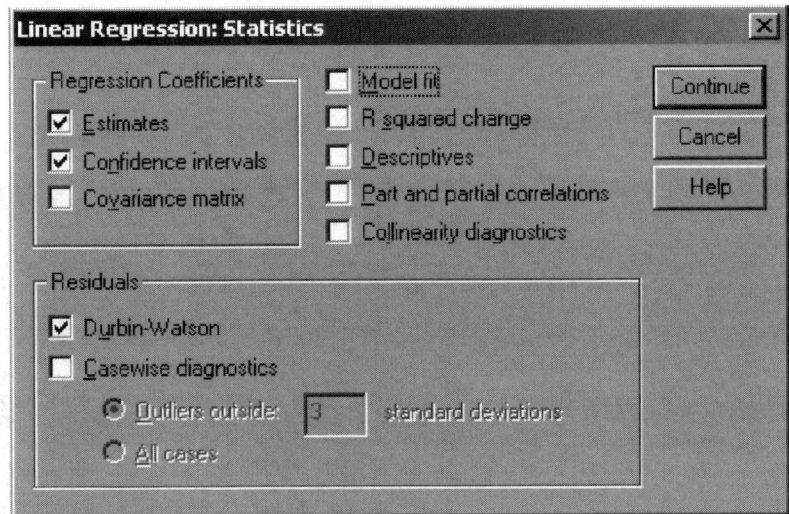

Note on the SPSS leverage values: SPSS does not include the term $1/n$ in equation 13.26 when defining sample leverages. Consequently, the SPSS sample leverage for the ith observation is $(x_i - \bar{x})^2/SS_X$. To obtain the leverage values that agree with equation 13.26 (used in the KPK Excel macros and Minitab), click on **Transform ➤ Compute.** Enter leverage in the **Target Variable** box and lev_1 + 1/10 in the **Numeric Expression** box. Click **OK** to obtain the leverage values.

To obtain a confidence interval for the regression coefficient as in Example 13.5, or the Durbin–Watson statistic as in section 13.6, click on **Statistics** and check **Estimates** and **Confidence intervals** under **Regression Coefficients,** or check **Durbin-Watson** under **Residuals.** Click **Continue** to return to the **Linear Regression** dialog box.

14

Multiple Linear Regression

Statistics in Action
Getting Framed Right Before Your Eyes: Evaluating the Price You Will Pay

Nearly 60 percent of Americans, 161 million people, depend on prescription eyewear. Choosing eyewear can be a complicated process: Working within the constraints of prescription requirements, consumers try to find a style that is both flattering and fashionable. Often, they have the added complication of not being able to actually *see* what they look like in the frames when making their purchasing decision. That is, the eyewear must be glazed with the prescription lenses before the consumer can truly view what they have bought. If the eyewear doesn't feel right or the buyer believes that the spectacles really do have that nerd look, then a potential conflict can brew with customer service. Some frame companies are using the Internet to help consumers see themselves in their frames before they buy them. They allow consumers to upload a picture of themselves and then "try the frames" on their photo.

Eyewear is big business. In 2001, the market for eyeglasses was approximately $14 billion according to Jobson Optical Group, a trade publisher and research company for the optical industry. Most optical stores tout product selection, insurance benefits, competitive prices, high quality, and fast service. Doctors of optometry are even located inside some of the stores. Companies are conducting research in which a wearer can one day adjust the lenses to fit his or prescription in minutes.

Three companies—Luxottica, Safilo, and Marchon—make almost half of all eyeglass frames

in the United States. Many of these frames are quite similar. Consumers often see one frame cost $250 and a look-alike frame cost about $125. In some cases, the metal can be more expensive, such as the case with titanium frames. But often, the price differential comes from the way the eyewear is marketed or from the frame design. Hypoallergenic frames typically command a higher price.

Statistical analysis can be used to determine those variables that make a difference in the pricing of eyewear. *Consumer Reports* surveyed 64,000 consumers to evaluate variables such as service, quality, satisfaction, and speed in delivering the product. When you have completed this chapter, you will be able to

- Construct a prediction equation involving more than one predictor, such as predicting the price of eyeglasses using several variables recorded in a consumer survey.

- Construct a regression model that includes interactions between the predictor variables and includes transformations of predictor variables, such as the square of a variable.

- Classify an observation as *influential*.

- Verify model assumptions necessary for the validity of testing the contribution of independent variables in a prediction equation.

THE MULTIPLE LINEAR REGRESSION MODEL

Prediction Using More than One Variable

To explain or predict the behavior of a certain dependent variable using more than one predictor variable, we use a **multiple linear regression** model. The form of this model is

$$Y = \beta_0 + \beta_1 X_1 + \beta_2 X_2 + \cdots + \beta_k X_k + e$$

where $X_1, X_2, \ldots, X_k$ are the k independent (predictor) variables and e is the error associated with this model.

Notice that equation 12.1 is similar to the equation for the simple linear regression model (equation 13.12) except that the *deterministic component* is now

$$\beta_0 + \beta_1 X_1 + \cdots + \beta_k X_k$$

rather than $\beta_0 + \beta_1 X$. Once again the error term, e, is included to provide for deviations about the deterministic component.

What is the appearance of the deterministic portion in equation 14.2? In Chapter 13, where we discussed simple linear regression, the deterministic portion was a straight line. In the case of multiple linear regression, the deterministic portion is more difficult (usually impossible) to represent graphically. If your model contains two predictor variables, X_1 and X_2, the deterministic component becomes a plane, as shown in Figure 14.1. Consequently, the key assumption behind the use of this particular model is that the Y values will lie in this plane, *on the average*, for any particular values of X_1 and X_2.

In Chapter 13, we examined the relationship between the square footage of a home (Y) and the corresponding household income (X). The results were:

- least squares line: $\hat{Y} = 4.975 + .3539X$

- correlation between X and Y: $r = .843$

- coefficient of determination: $r^2 = .711$

- a significant linear relationship exists

FIGURE 14.1

The multiple linear regression model (two independent variables).

605

We now want to include two additional variables in this model. The real-estate developer performing the study suspects that (1) larger families have larger homes and (2) the size of the home is affected by the amount of formal education (years of college) of the wage earner(s) in the home. We now have three independent variables:

X_1 = annual income (thousands of dollars)

X_2 = family size

X_3 = combined years of formal education (beyond high school) for all household wage earners

The same 10 families introduced in Example 13.1 were used in the study, but data were collected on the two additional variables, X_2 and X_3.*

Family	Y (Home Square Footage)	X_1 (Income)	X_2 (Family Size)	X_3 (Years of Formal Education)
1	16	32	2	4
2	17	36	2	8
3	26	55	3	7
4	24	47	4	0
5	22	38	4	2
6	21	60	3	10
7	32	66	6	8
8	18	44	3	8
9	30	70	5	2
10	20	50	3	6

The data configuration now has four columns (including Y) and 10 rows (called *observations*). Our task is to use the data on all *three* variables (X_1, X_2, and X_3) to provide a better estimate of home size (Y).

The Least Squares Estimate. Using Figure 14.1, we proceed as we did for simple regression and determine an estimate of the β's that will make the sum of squares of the residuals as small as possible. A *residual* is defined as the difference between the actual Y value and its estimate; that is, $Y - \hat{Y}$. In other words, we attempt to find the $b_0, b_1, \ldots, b_k$ that minimize the sum of squares of error,

$$SSE = \Sigma(Y - \hat{Y})^2$$

14.3

where now $\hat{Y} = b_0 + b_1X_1 + b_2X_2 + \ldots + b_kX_k$ and $b_0, b_1, \ldots, b_k$ are called the *least squares estimates* of $\beta_0, \beta_1, \ldots, \beta_k$.

By determining the estimated *regression coefficients* ($b_0, b_1, \ldots, b_k$) that minimize SSE rather than $\Sigma(Y - \hat{Y})$, we once again avoid the problem of positive errors canceling out negative ones. Another advantage of this procedure is that, by means of a little calculus, we can show that a fairly simple expression exists for these sample regression coefficients. Because this expression involves the use of *matrix notation,* we omit this result.[†]

There is only one way to solve a multiple regression problem in practice, and that is with the help of a computer. All computer packages determine the values of $b_0, b_1, \ldots, b_k$ in the same way—namely, by minimizing SSE. As a result, these values will be identical (except for numerical rounding errors), regardless of which computer program you use.

---

*A sample of size 10 is unrealistically small in practice.

†Information on this expression is presented in T. Sincich and W. Mendenhall, *A Second Course in Business Statistics: Regression Analysis,* 5th ed. (Upper Saddle River, NJ: Prentice-Hall, 1996); and J. Neter, M. Kutner, and C. Nachtscheim, *Applied Linear Regression Models,* 3rd ed. (Homewood, Ill.: Richard D. Irwin, 1996).

	A	B	C	D	E	F	G	H	I	J
1	Footage	Income	FamSize	YrsEduc	**SUMMARY OUTPUT**					
2	16	32	2	4						
3	17	36	2	8	**Regression Statistics**					
4	26	55	3	7	Multiple R	0.95145				
5	24	47	4	0	R Square	0.90527				
6	22	38	4	2	Adjusted R Square	0.85790				
7	21	60	3	10	Standard Error	2.03545				
8	32	66	6	8	Observations	10				
9	18	44	3	8						
10	30	70	5	2	**ANOVA**					
11	20	50	3	6		df	SS	MS	F	Significance F
12					Regression	3	237.54155279	79.18052	19.1115	0.001792476
13					Residual	6	24.85844721	4.143075		
14					Total	9	262.4			
15										
16						Coefficients	Standard Error	t Stat	P-value	
17					Intercept	5.656717014	2.8342039	1.995875	0.093	
18					Income	0.193878366	0.0876996	2.210711	0.069	
19					FamSize	2.338108367	0.9077909	2.575602	0.042	
20					YrsEduc	-0.162770718	0.2440711	-0.666899	0.530	

FIGURE 14.2

Excel multiple regression solution for predicting house size using three predictor variables.

Regression Analysis: Footage versus Income, FamSize, YrsEduc

The regression equation is
Footage = 5.66 + 0.194 Income + 2.34 FamSize - 0.163 YrsEduc

```
Predictor     Coef    SE Coef      T       P
Constant     5.657     2.834    2.00   0.093
Income     0.19388   0.08770    2.21   0.069
FamSize     2.3381    0.9078    2.58   0.042
YrsEduc    -0.1628    0.2441   -0.67   0.530


S = 2.03545   R-Sq = 90.5%   R-Sq(adj) = 85.8%


Analysis of Variance

Source           DF      SS       MS      F      P
Regression        3  237.542   79.181  19.11  0.002
Residual Error    6   24.858    4.143
Total             9  262.400
```

FIGURE 14.3

MINITAB multiple regression solution for predicting house size using three predictor variables.

In the example where we attempt to predict home size using the three predictor variables, the prediction equation is

$$\hat{Y} = b_0 + b_1X_1 + b_2X_2 + b_3X_3$$

where

$\hat{Y}$ = predicted home size

X_1 = income

X_2 = family size

X_3 = years of education

and b_0, b_1, b_2, and b_3 are the least squares estimates of β_0, β_1, β_2, and β_3.

Using the data just presented, the Excel solution in Figure 14.2 can be obtained by clicking on **Tools ➤ Data Analysis ➤ Regression**. Enter B1:D11 as the **Input X Range** and A1:A11 as the **Input Y Range**. The MINITAB solution in Figure 12.3 can be obtained by

FIGURE

14.4

SPSS multiple regression solution for predicting house size using three predictor variables.

Model Summary

Model	R	R Square	Adjusted R Square	Std. Error of the Estimate
1	.951[a]	.905	.858	2.035

ANOVA[b]

Model		Sum of Squares	df	Mean Square	F	Sig.
1	Regression	237.542	3	79.181	19.112	.00179[a]
	Residual	24.858	6	4.143		
	Total	262.400	9			

Coefficients[a]

Model		Unstandardized Coefficients		Standardized Coefficients		
		B	Std. Error	Beta	t	Sig.
1	(Constant)	5.657	2.8342		1.996	.093
	INCOME	.194	.0877	.462	2.211	.069
	FAMSIZE	2.338	.9078	.550	2.576	.042
	YRSEDUC	-.163	.2441	-.100	-.667	.530

a. Predictors: (Constant), YRSEDUC, INCOME, FAMSIZE

b. Dependent Variable: FOOTAGE

clicking on **Stat ➤ Regression ➤ Regression.** The SPSS regression output in Figure 14.4 was obtained by clicking on **Analyze ➤ Regression ➤ Linear.** Using the computer outputs, the best prediction equation (in the least squares sense) for home size is

$$\hat{Y} = 5.657 + .194X_1 + 2.338X_2 - .163X_3$$

So this solution minimizes SSE. But what is the SSE here? We need to determine how well this equation "fits" the 10 observations in the data set. Consider the first family, where $X_1 = 32$ (income = $32,000), $X_2 = 2$ (family size = 2, such as an adult couple with no children), and $X_3 = 4$ (combined years of college = 4). The predicted home size here is

$$\hat{Y} = 5.657 + .194(32) + 2.338(2) - .163(4) = 15.886$$

Consequently, the predicted home size is 1,589 square feet. The actual square footage for this observation is 1,600 ($Y = 16$), so the sample residual here is $Y - \hat{Y} = 16 - 15.886 = .114$.

Using this procedure on the remaining nine observations, we get the following results:

Y	$\hat{Y}$	$Y - \hat{Y}$	$(Y - \hat{Y})^2$
16	15.886	0.114	0.01300
17	16.010	0.990	0.98010
26	22.195	3.805	14.47803
24	24.121	−0.121	0.01464
22	22.051	−0.051	0.00260
21	22.676	−1.676	2.80898
32	31.179	0.821	0.67404
18	19.900	−1.900	3.61000
30	30.593	−0.593	0.35165
20	21.388	−1.388	1.92654
		0	24.86 = SSE

approximately

The computed value for the error sum of square is SSE = 24.86. This value also is highlighted in cell G13 in Figure 12.2. This result implies that for any other values of b_0, b_1, b_2, and b_3, if we were to find the corresponding $\hat{Y}$'s and the resulting SSE = $\Sigma\ (Y - \hat{Y})^2$ using these values, this new SSE would be larger than 24.86. Thus, $b_0 = 5.657$, $b_1 = .194$, $b_2 = 2.338$, and $b_3 = -.163$ minimize the error sum of squares, SSE. Put still another way, these values of b_0, b_1, b_2, and b_3 provide the best fit to our data.

Using only income (X_1) as a predictor in Chapter 13, we found the SSE to be 75.81 in our table. By including the additional two variables, the SSE has been reduced from 75.81 to 24.86 (a 67% reduction). It appears that either family size (X_2), years of education (X_3), or both contribute, perhaps significantly, to the prediction of Y.

Interpreting the Regression Coefficients.   When using a multiple linear regression equation, such as $Y = \beta_0 + \beta_1 X_1 + \beta_2 X_2 + \beta_3 X_3 + e$, what does β_2 represent? Very simply, it reflects the change in Y that can be expected to accompany a change of one unit in X_2, provided all other variables (namely, X_1 and X_3) are held constant.

In the previous example, the sample estimate of β_2 was $b_2 = 2.338$. Can we expect an increase of 2.338 on the average as X_2 (the family size) increases by one if X_1 and X_3 are held constant? This type of argument is filled with problems, as we demonstrate later. The primary problem is that a change in one of the predictor variables (such as X_2) always (or almost always) is accompanied by a change in one of the other predictors (say, X_1) in the sample observations. Consequently, variables X_1 and X_2 are related in some manner, such as $X_1 = 1 + 5X_2$. In other words, a situation in which X_2, for instance, changed and the others remained constant would not be observed in the sample data.

In the case (typically not observed in business applications) where the predictor variables are totally unrelated, a unit change in X_2, for example, can be expected to be accompanied by a change in the dependent variable equal to the value of β_2.

In general, it is not safe to assume that the predictor variables are unrelated. As a result, the b's usually do not reflect the true "partial effects" of the predictor variables, and you should avoid such conclusions. Section 14.3 discusses methods of dealing with this type of situation.

The Assumptions Behind the Multiple Linear Regression Model

The form of the multiple linear regression model is given by equation 14.1, which contains a linear combination of the k **predictor (independent) variables** as well as the error component, e, to predict the behavior of a particular **dependent variable, Y.** The assumptions for the case of k > 1 predictors are exactly the same as for k = 1 independent variable (simple linear regression). Two assumptions were discussed in Chapter 13:

1. The errors follow a normal distribution, centered at zero, with common variance, σ_e^2.

2. The errors are (statistically) independent.

The case for k = 2 predictor variables can be represented graphically, as shown in Figures 14.1 and 14.5. Using Figure 14.5, consider the situation in which $X_1 = 30$ and $X_2 = 8$. If you were to obtain repeated values of Y for these values for X_1 and X_2, you would obtain some Y's above the plane and some below. The assumptions are that the average value of Y with $X_1 = 30$ and $X_2 = 8$ lies on the plane and that, moreover, these errors are normally distributed.

The final part of assumption 1 is that the variation about this plane does not depend on the values of X_1 and X_2. You should see roughly the same amount of variation if you obtain repeated values of Y corresponding to $X_1 = 50$ and $X_2 = 2$ as you observed for $X_1 = 30$ and $X_2 = 8$. The variance of these errors, if you could observe Y indefinitely, is σ_e^2.

Finally, assumption 2 means that the error encountered at $X_1 = 50$ and $X_2 = 2$, for instance, is not affected by a known error at any other point, such as $X_1 = 30$ and $X_2 = 8$. The error associated with one pair of X_1, X_2 values has no effect on any other error.

FIGURE

14.5

The errors in
multiple linear
regression ($k = 2$).

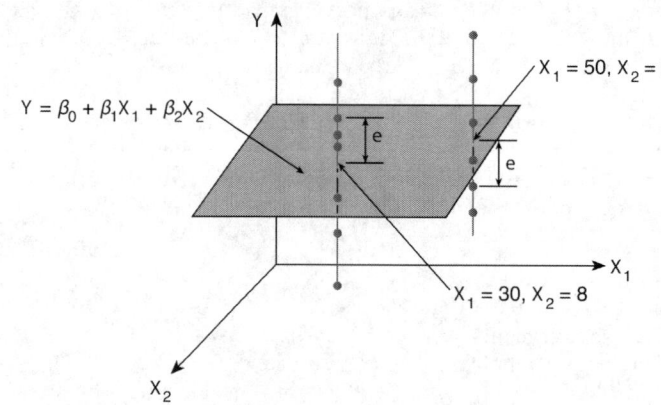

An Estimate of σ_e^2. When using a straight line to model a relationship between Y and a single predictor, the estimate of σ_e^2 was given by equation 13.13, where

$$s^2 = \tilde{\sigma}_e^2 = \frac{SSE}{n-2}$$

In general, for k predictors and n observations, the estimate of this variance is

$$s^2 = \hat{\sigma}_e^2 = \frac{SSE}{n - (k+1)} = \frac{SSE}{n-k-1}$$

14.4

   The value of s^2 is critical in determining the reliability and usefulness of the model as a predictor. If $s^2 = 0$, then SSE = 0, implying that $Y = \hat{Y}$ for each of the observations in the sample data. This rarely happens in practice, but it does point out that a small s^2 is desirable. As s^2 increases, you can expect more error when predicting a value of Y for specified values of $X_1, X_2, \ldots, X_k$. In the next section, we use s^2 as a key to determining whether the model is satisfactory and which of the independent variables are useful in the prediction of the dependent variable.
   The square root of this estimated variance is the **residual standard deviation.**

$$s = \sqrt{\frac{SSE}{n-k-1}}$$

14.5

In the Excel solution in Figure 12.2, the value of s is highlighted in cell F7. The residual standard deviation is often called the **standard error.**

EXAMPLE

14.1

Determine the estimate of σ_e^2 and the residual standard deviation (standard error) for the real-estate data on page 606.

Solution

This example contained n = 10 observations and k = 3 predictor variables. The resulting error sum of squares was SSE = 24.86 (from Figures 14.2, 14.3 and 14.4). Therefore,

$$s^2 = \tilde{\sigma}_e^2$$

$$= \frac{24.86}{10-3-1} = \frac{24.86}{6} = 4.14$$

and

$$s = \sqrt{4.14} = 2.035$$

That is, the residual standard deviation is 203.5 square feet.

   If a particular regression model meets all the required assumptions, then the next question of interest is whether this set of independent variables provides an accurate method of predicting the dependent variable, Y. The next section shows how to calculate the predictive ability of your model and determine which variables contribute significantly to an accurate prediction of Y.

X   Exercises 14.1–14.8

Understanding the Mechanics

14.1   The least squares regression equation using 20 observations is $\hat{Y} = 3 - 10X_1 + 20X_2 - X_3$.
   a. What is the error degrees of freedom?
   b. If X_1 is increased by 1, X_2 increased by 2, and X_3 remains unchanged, what is the net change in the predicted value of Y?

14.2   The following data were collected.

Y	X_1	X_2
5.4	11	3.1
7.7	14	5.1
9.1	17	5.4
8.8	17	4.4
6.2	11	3.5
7.0	12	3.8
8.4	14	4.9
7.1	13	4.0

The regression equation for this data is $\hat{Y} = .214 + .341X_1 + .608X_2$. Calculate the estimate of the variance of the error component of the model.

Applying the New Concepts

14.3   An oil-service company decided to fit a least squares equation to a set of data to predict the total cost of building a well. The independent variables are X_1 = drilling days, X_2 = total depth, and X_3 = intermediate casing depth. After calculating the least squares equation, the residuals were calculated to find out whether the assumptions of regression analysis are satisfied. The following are the residuals from 20 observations:

   −0.8, 1.5, −3.7, 4.1, −3.1, −5.2, 4.3, −2.1, −1.6, 4.1, 0.9, −0.3, 4.5, −4.2, 3.2, −2.7, 1.7, −2.2, 3.4, −1.8

Do the residuals $Y - \hat{Y}$ appear to conform to the empirical rule that approximately 95% of the data should lie within two standard deviations of the mean?

14.4   What are the standard assumptions about the error component of a multiple linear regression model for inference results about the model to be valid?

14.5   Tony owns a used-car lot. He would like to predict monthly sales volume. Tony believes that sales volume (given in thousands) is directly related to the number of salespeople employed and the number of cars on the lot for sale. The following data were collected over a period of 10 months:

Monthly Sales Volume (Y)	Salespeople (X_1)	Cars (X_2)
5.8	4	20
7.5	5	15
11.4	7	25
7.0	3	17
5.1	2	18
8.1	4	25
13.3	8	30
15.0	9	35
8.3	5	20
6.8	4	23

   a. Using a computerized statistical package, determine the least squares prediction equation for these data.
   b. Find the value of SSE.

14.6   Using the regression equation $\hat{Y} = 100 - 4X_1 + 12X_2 - 2X_3$, where do you expect the average value of Y to be for $X_1 = 10$, $X_2 = 5$, and $X_3 = 20$?

Using the Computer

14.7   **[DATA SET EX14-7]** Variable Description:

Model: Brand and description of laptop

Price: Retail price of laptop

Rating: Overall score by Consumer Reports

Features: A score of 1, 2, or 3 with low values indicating more features

Laptops now belong in the same league as desktop computers, thanks to brighter and larger displays, faster processors, and more-efficient batteries. Expanding a laptop's advantages is the growing availability of high-speed wireless Internet access. For recommendations on which laptop to purchase, consumers look toward the ratings provided by Consumer Reports A sample of 12 laptops was selected and the rating and score on the laptop's features are recorded.

a. Find the prediction equation for the price of a laptop using rating and features. What is the value of the residual standard deviation?

b. If the value of SSE were equal to zero for this problem, what would that imply?

(Source: "Is This Your Next Computer?" Consumer Reports, 66, issue 6, June 2001, p. 20.)

14.8 [DATA SET EX14-8] Variable Description:

SuburbCity: A suburban city in California

City: The largest city that lies closest to the suburban city

Age: The age of the suburban city

InitialPop: The population of the suburban city when the suburb was first recognized as a suburban city

2000Pop: Population of the suburban city in the year 2000

Many suburbs in California have grown into large cities, but are often not thought of as cities because they are in the shadow of a major city. Urban experts recognize suburbs having either a large population or having a substantial growth spurt as suburban cities. These suburban cities often have more homes than jobs and are sometimes called boomburbs.Fourteen suburban cities were sampled, and their age as a suburban city, the initial population of the suburban city when it was first recognized as a city, and the population size of the city in the year 2000 were recorded.

a. Find the regression equation to predict 2000Pop using the predictors Age and InitialPop. If InitialPop is held constant but the age of the suburban city changes by one year, by how much does the predicted population size change?

b. Verify that the sum of the residuals is zero. What is the mean of the residuals? Do approximately 95% of the residuals lie within two standard deviations of the mean?

(Source: "Boomburbs' Growth Skyrockets," USA Today, June 22, 2001, p. 11A.)

14.2

HYPOTHESIS TESTING AND CONFIDENCE INTERVALS FOR THE β PARAMETERS

Multiple linear regression is a popular tool in the application of statistical techniques to business decisions. However, this modeling procedure does not always result in an accurate and reliable predictor. When the independent variables that you have selected account for very little of the variation in the values of the dependent variable, the model (as is) serves no useful purpose.

The first thing we demonstrate is how to determine whether your overall model is satisfactory. We begin by summarizing a regression analysis in an analysis of variance (ANOVA) table, much as we did in Section 9.6.

The ANOVA Table

The summary ANOVA table contains the usual headings.

Source	df	SS	MS	F
Regression	k	SSR	MSR	MSR/MSE
Residual	n – k – 1	SSE	MSE	
Total	n – 1	SST		

where n = number of observations and k = number of independent variables.

$$SST = \text{total sum of squares}$$

14.6

$$= SS_Y$$

$$= \Sigma(Y - \bar{Y})^2 = \Sigma Y^2 - \frac{(\Sigma Y)^2}{n}$$

$$SSE = \text{sum of squares for error}$$

14.7

$$= \Sigma(Y - \hat{Y})^2$$

$$SSR = \text{sum of squares for regression}$$

14.8

$$= \Sigma(\hat{Y} - \bar{Y})^2$$

$$= SST - SSE$$

$$MSR = \text{mean square for regression}$$

14.9

$$= \frac{SSR}{k}$$

$$MSE = \text{mean square for error}$$

14.10

$$= \frac{SSE}{n-k-1}$$

Practically all computer packages provide you with this ANOVA summary as part of the standard output. Referring to the ANOVA section in any of the computer outputs in the previous section, notice that

$$SST = SS_Y$$

$$= (16^2 + 17^2 + \cdots + 20^2) - \frac{(16 + 17 + \cdots + 20)^2}{10}$$

This is the same value of SS_Y we obtained for the same example in Chapter 13, when we used only income (X_1) as the predictor variable. This is hardly surprising because *this value is strictly a function of the Y values* and is unaffected by the model that we are using to predict Y. The total sum of squares (SST) measures the total variation in the values of the dependent variable. Its value is the same, regardless of which predictor variables are included in the model.

The df for the regression source of variation is k = the number of predictor variables in the analysis. The df for the error sum of squares is $n - k - 1$, where n = the number of observations in the sample data.

As in the case of simple linear regression, the sum of squares of regression (SSR) measures the variation *explained* by the model—the variation in the Y values that would exist if differences in the values of the predictor variables were the only cause of differences among the Y's. By contrast, the sum of squares of error (SSE) represents the variation *unexplained* by the model. The easiest way to determine the sum of squares of regression is to subtract:

$$SSR = SST - SSE$$

The error mean square is $MSE = SSE/(n - k - 1) = 24.858/(10 - 4) = 4.14$. This is the same as the *estimate* of σ_e^2 determined in Example 12.1. So,

$$s^2 = \hat{\sigma}_e^2 = MSE$$

A Test for H_0: All β's = 0

We have yet to make use of the F value calculated in the ANOVA table, where

$$F = \frac{\text{MSR}}{\text{MSE}}$$

14.11

When using the simple regression model, we previously argued that one way to determine whether X is a significant predictor of Y is to test H_0: $\beta_1 = 0$, where β_1 is the coefficient of X in the model $Y = \beta_0 + \beta_1 X + e$. If you reject H_0, the conclusion is that the independent variable X *does* contribute significantly to the prediction of Y. For example, in Example 13.3, by rejecting H_0: $\beta_1 = 0$, we concluded that income (X_1) was a useful predictor of home size (Y) using the simple linear model.

We use a similar test as the first step in the multiple regression analysis, where we examine the hypotheses

$$H_0: \beta_1 = \beta_2 = \cdots = \beta_k = 0$$

$$H_a: \text{at least one of the } \beta\text{'s} \neq 0$$

If we *reject* H_0, we can conclude that at least one (but maybe not all) of the independent variables contributes significantly to the prediction of Y. If we *fail to reject* H_0, we are unable to demonstrate that any of the independent variables (or combination of them) helps explain the behavior of the dependent variable, Y. For example, in our housing example, if we were to fail to reject H_0, this would imply that we are unable to demonstrate that the variation in the home sizes (Y) can be explained by the effect of income, family size, and years of education.

Test Statistic for H_0 versus H_a.   The test statistic used to determine whether our multiple regression model contains at least one explanatory variable is the F statistic from the preceding ANOVA table.

When testing H_0: all β's = 0 (this set of predictor variables is no good at all) versus H_a: at least one $\beta \neq 0$ (at least one of these variables is a good predictor), the test statistic is

$$F = \frac{\text{MSR}}{\text{MSE}}$$

which has an F distribution with k and $n - k - 1$ df. The expression $n - k - 1$ can be written as $n - (k + 1)$, where $k + 1$ is the number of coefficients (β's) estimated including the constant term.

Notice that the df for the F statistic comes directly from the ANOVA table. The testing procedure is to

$$\text{reject } H_0 \text{ if } F > F_{\alpha, v_1, v_2}$$

where (1) $v_1 = k$, $v_2 = n - k - 1$ and (2) F_{α, v_1, v_2} is the corresponding F value in Table A.7 having a *right-tail area* = α (Figure 14.6).

EXAMPLE 14.2

Using the real-estate data and the model we developed, what can you say about the predictive ability of the independent variables, income (X_1), family size (X_2), and years of education (X_3)? Use $\alpha = .10$.

FIGURE

14.6

F curve with *k* and *n* − *k* − 1 df. The lightly shaded area is the rejection region.

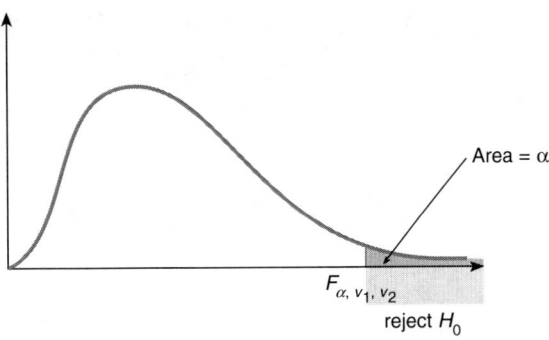

Area = α

F_{α, v_1, v_2}

reject H_0

Solution

Step 1. The hypotheses are

$$H_0: \beta_1 = \beta_2 = \beta_3 = 0$$

$$H_a: \text{at least one } \beta \neq 0$$

Remember that your hope here is to reject H_0. If you are unable to demonstrate that any of your independent variables have any predictive ability, then you will fail to reject H_0.

Step 2. The test statistic is

$$F = \frac{\text{MSR}}{\text{MSE}}$$

The mean squares are obtained from the ANOVA summary of the regression analysis (refer to the computer outputs in Section 12.1).

Step 3. The df for the F statistic are $k = 3$ and $n - k - 1 = 10 - 3 - 1 = 6$. So we will

$$\text{reject } H_0 \text{ if } F > F_{.10,3,6} = 3.29$$

Step 4. The computer outputs for Excel, MINITAB, and SPSS in Section 12.1 agree that the computed F value is

$$F^* = \frac{79.18}{4.14} = 19.1$$

Because $F^* > 3.29$, we reject H_0.

Step 5. The three independent variables *as a group* constitute a good predictor of home size. This does *not* imply that all three variables have significant predictive ability; however, at least one of them does. The next section shows how you can tell *which* of these predictor variables significantly contributes to the prediction of home size.

A Test for $H_0: \beta_i = 0$

Assuming that you rejected the null hypothesis that all of the β's are zero, the next logical question would be, which of the independent variables contributes to the prediction of *Y*?

In Example 14.2, we rejected the null hypothesis, so at least one of these three independent variables affects the variation of the 10 home sizes in the sample. To determine the contribution of each variable, we perform three separate t tests:

$$H_0: \beta_1 = 0 \; (X_1 \text{ does not contribute})$$

$$H_a: \beta_1 \neq 0 \; (X_1 \text{ does contribute})$$

$$H_0: \beta_2 = 0 \; (X_2 \text{ does not contribute})$$

$$H_a: \beta_2 \neq 0 \; (X_2 \text{ does contribute})$$

$$H_0: \beta_3 = 0 \; (X_3 \text{ does not contribute})$$

$$H_a: \beta_3 \neq 0 \; (X_3 \text{ does contribute})$$

One-tailed tests also can be used here, but we will demonstrate this procedure using two-tailed tests. This means that we are testing to see whether this particular X contributes to the prediction of Y, but we are not concerned about the direction (positive or negative) of this relationship.

When income (X_1) was the only predictor of home size (Y), we used a t test to determine whether the simple linear regression model was adequate. In Example 13.3, the value of the test statistic was derived:

$$t = \frac{b_1}{s_{b_1}}$$

14.12

Also, b_1 is the estimate of β_1 in the simple regression model, and s_{b_1} is the (estimated) standard deviation of b_1. Excel refers to s_{b_1} as the **Standard Error** of b_1 (as in Figure 12.2). MINITAB refers to this value as **SE Coef** (see Figure 14.3), and the same value can be found in the SPSS output under the heading **Std. Error** (refer to Figure 12.4).

All computer packages provide both the estimated coefficient (b_1) and its standard error (s_{b_1}). In Example 13.3, the computed value of this t statistic was $t^* = 4.44$. This result led us to conclude that income was a good predictor of home size because a significant positive relationship existed between these two variables.

We use the same t statistic procedure to test the effect of the individual variables in a multiple regression model. When examining the effect of an individual independent variable, X_i, on the prediction of a dependent variable, the hypotheses are

$$H_0: \beta_i = 0$$

$$H_a: \beta_i \neq 0$$

The test statistic is

$$t = \frac{b_i}{s_{b_i}}$$

where (1) b_i is the estimate of β_i, (2) s_{b_i} is the (estimated) standard error of b_i, and (3) the df for the t statistic is $n - k - 1$.

The test of H_0 versus H_a is to

$$\text{reject } H_0 \text{ if } \alpha t\alpha > t_{\alpha/2, n-k-1}$$

where $t_{\alpha/2, n-k-1}$ is obtained from Table A.5.

We can now reexamine the real-estate data in Example 14.2.

X_1 = Income. Consider the hypotheses

$$H_0: \beta_1 = 0$$

$$H_a: \beta_1 \neq 0$$

As in Example 14.2, we use $\alpha = .10$.

According to the computer outputs in the previous section, $b_1 = .194$ and $s_{b_1} = .0877$. Also contained in the output is the computed value of

$$t^* = \frac{b_1}{s_{b_1}} = \frac{.194}{.0877} = 2.21$$

Why is this value of t^* not the same as the value of t calculated for this variable in Chapter 13, when income was the only predictor of Y? When there are three predictors in the model, t^* for income is 2.21. When income is the only predictor in the model, $t^* = 4.44$. The difference in the two values is simply that $t^* = 2.21$ provides a measure of the contribution of X_1 = income, *given that X_2 and X_3 already have been included in the model*. A large value of t^* indicates that X_1 contributes significantly to the prediction of Y, even if X_2 and X_3 have been included previously as predictors.

The hypotheses can better be stated as

H_0: income *does not* contribute to the prediction of home size, *given* that family size and years of education already have been included in the model

H_a: income *does* contribute to this prediction, *given* that family size and years of education already have been included in the model

or as

$$H_0: \beta_1 = 0 \quad \text{(if } X_2 \text{ and } X_3 \text{ are included)}$$

$$H_a: \beta_1 \neq 0$$

Because $t^* = 2.21$ exceeds the table value of $t_{\alpha/2, n-k-1} = t_{.05, 10-3-1} = t_{.05, 6} = 1.943$, we conclude that income contributes significantly to the prediction of home size and should be kept in the model. An easier procedure to use here is to compare the corresponding p-value to the significance level (α). The p-value in the previous computer outputs is equal to .069. Since this is less than $\alpha = .10$, we reject H_0 and again conclude that income is a significant predictor.

X_2 = Family Size. Using a similar argument, the following test of hypothesis will determine the contribution of family size, X_2, as a predictor of the home square footage, given that X_1 and X_3 already have been included. The hypotheses here are

$$H_0: \beta_2 = 0 \quad \text{(if } X_1 \text{ and } X_3 \text{ are included)}$$

$$H_a: \beta_2 \neq 0$$

Referring to the previous computer outputs, the computed t statistic here is

$$t^* = \frac{b_2}{s_{b_2}} = \frac{2.3381}{.9078} = 2.576$$

This value also exceeds $t_{.05, 6} = 1.943$ (p-value of .042 is less than .10), and so family size provides useful information in predicting the square footage of a home. We conclude that we should keep X_2 in the model.

X_3 = **Years of Education.** To test

$$H_0: \beta_3 = 0 \qquad \text{(if } X_1 \text{ and } X_2 \text{ are included)}$$
$$H_a: \beta_3 \neq 0$$

we once again use the t statistic.

$$t = \frac{b_3}{s_{b_3}}$$

According to the previous computer outputs, the computed value of this statistic is

$$t^* = \frac{-.1628}{.2441} = -.67$$

Because $|t^*| = .67$, which does not exceed $t_{.05,6} = 1.943$, we fail to reject H_0. Here, the p-value of .530 exceeds the significance level of .10. We conclude that, given the values of X_1 = income and X_2 = family size, the level of a family's education appears not to contribute to the prediction of the size of their home. This means that X_3 can be ignored in the final prediction equation, leaving only X_1 and X_2.

Comments

As a word of warning, you should *not* simply remove this term from the equation containing all three variables. Since the predictor variables are typically related in some manner, the sample regression coefficients ($b_0, b_1, \ldots$) change as variables are added to or deleted from the model. Refer-ring to the computer outputs in the previous section, the final prediction equation is not $\hat{Y} = 5.657 + .194X_1 + 2.338X_2$. Instead, the coefficients of X_1 and X_2 should be derived by repeating the analysis using only these two variables. The resulting prediction equation is $\hat{Y} = 5.091 + .165X_1 + 2.657X_2$.

A Confidence Interval for β_i

Using what you believe to be the "best" model, you can easily construct a $(1 - \alpha) \times 100\%$ confidence interval for β_i based on the previous t statistic:

$$b_i - t_{\alpha/2,n-k-1}s_{b_i} \qquad \text{to} \qquad b_i + t_{\alpha/2,n-k-1}s_{b_i}$$

14.13

Once again, k represents the number of predictor variables used to estimate β_i.

EXAMPLE 14.3

Suppose you decide to retain only X_1 = income and X_2 = family size in the prediction equation. Referring to Figure 14.7, construct a 90% confidence interval for β_2, the coefficient for X_2.

Solution Since this model contains $k = 2$ predictor variables, we first find $t_{\alpha/2,n-k-1} = t_{.05,7} = 1.895$. Using cells F19 and G19 (highlighted) in Figure 14.7, the confidence interval for β_2 is

$$2.6569 - (1.895)(.7405) \qquad \text{to} \qquad 2.6569 + (1.895)(.7405)$$
$$= 2.6569 - 1.4032 \qquad \text{to} \qquad 2.6569 + 1.4032$$
$$= 1.25 \qquad \text{to} \qquad 4.06$$

FIGURE

14.7

E	F	G	H	I	J	K	L	M
SUMMARY OUTPUT								
Regression Statistics								
Multiple R	0.94776							
R Square	0.89824							
Adjusted R Square	0.86917							
Standard Error	1.95306							
Observations	10							
ANOVA								
	df	SS	MS	F	Significance F			
Regression	2	235.6989	117.8495	30.8956	0.000336			
Residual	7	26.7011	3.8144					
Total	9	262.4						
	Coefficients	Standard Error	t Stat	P-value	Lower 95%	Upper 95%	Lower 90.0%	Upper 90.0%
Intercept	5.0911	2.5948	1.9620	0.0906	-1.0448	11.2269	0.1749	10.0072
Income	0.1649	0.0731	2.2565	0.0586	-0.0079	0.3376	0.0264	0.3033
FamSize	2.6569	0.7405	3.5882	0.0089	0.9060	4.4079	1.2541	4.0598

Excel prediction equation and ANOVA table using X_1 and X_2.

Therefore, we are 90% confident that the estimate of β_2 (that is, $b_2 = 2.6569$) is within 1.4032 of the actual value of β_2. Notice that this is an extremely wide confidence interval. As usual, increasing the sample size would help to reduce the width of this confidence interval. When creating Figure 14.7, if you enter 90% as the confidence level, Excel will determine this confidence interval for you (cells L19 and M19 in Figure 14.7).

Statistical Software Application Use DATA14-4

Multiple Regression Analysis Using Statistical Software

EXAMPLE

14.4

The management of BB Investments decided to develop a model to predict the amount of money invested by various clients in their portfolio of high-risk securities. It was generally agreed that the income of the investor should be a major factor in predicting his or her annual investment and would explain a major portion of the variability in the amount invested. In addition, the investor's willingness to assume risk also was influenced by the investor's view of current and future economic conditions. On the assumption that the investors would use economic forecasts and economists' indices of future expectations, the financial group at BB Investments constructed an economic index that ranged from 0 to 100. When applied to any particular point in time, this index was tied to the expected increase in interest rates and borrowing levels, the expected increase in manufacturing costs because of the rate of inflation, and the expected level of price inflation at the retail level. This meant that the lower the index, the better the future economic conditions were expected to be.

Data were obtained by randomly selecting 50 high-risk portfolio customers and recording their incomes and the amounts of their investments. The income figures represent annual incomes and the economic index values are the index values at the time the investment was made. Determine the adequacy of this model and the predicted investment for an investor with an income of $48,500 at a time when the economic index has a value of 72.

The Excel regression solution can be obtained by clicking on **Tools ➤ Data Analysis ➤ Regression** and is shown in Figure 14.8. The **Input Y Range** is A1:A51, and the **Input X Range** is B1:C51. The MINITAB solution is shown in Figure 14.9, obtained by clicking on **Stat ➤ Regression ➤ Regression**. The SPSS regression output in Figure 14.10 was obtained by clicking on **Analyze ➤ Regression ➤ Linear**. In all three figures, the regression coefficients, value of R^2, value of MSR, value of MSE, and the p-value for the F test are highlighted.

Solution

FIGURE

14.8

Excel regression solution for Example 14.4.

	A	B	C	D	E	F	G	H	I
1	Invest	Index	Income	**SUMMARY OUTPUT**					
2	2500	86	55800						
3	3700	54	60400	Regression Statistics					
4	3900	21	72700	Multiple R	0.9478				
5	1700	91	41700	R Square	**0.8984**				
6	1000	72	35200	Adjusted R Square	0.8941				
7	1700	16	41800	Standard Error	283.0331				
8	2500	81	43700	Observations	50				
9	3400	32	67900						
10	2500	37	53700	**ANOVA**					
11	2900	89	57400		df	SS	MS	F	Significance F
12	2100	48	47100	Regression	2	33294135.6	**16647068**	207.81	**4.5877E-24**
13	2600	61	55300	Residual	47	3765064.4	80108		
14	1700	33	40000	Total	49	37059200			
15	2100	82	40200						
16	1500	95	36900		Coefficients	Standard Error	t Stat	P-value	
17	1700	73	40700	Intercept	**-1183.318**	219.3704	-5.3942	2.19E-06	
18	1400	9	35100	Index	**-.127**	1.5471	-0.0822	0.934847	
19	2400	42	50900	Income	**0.072**	0.0036	20.0643	1.1E-24	

FIGURE

14.9

MINITAB regression solution for Example 14.4.

Regression Analysis

```
The regression equation is
Invest = - 1183 - 0.13 Index + 0.0720 Income

Predictor      Coef       StDev        T        P
Constant      -1183.3     219.4      -5.39    0.000
Index         -0.127      1.547      -0.08    0.935
Income        0.071995    0.003588   20.06    0.000

S = 283.0      R-Sq = 89.8%      R-Sq(adj) = 89.4%

Analysis of Variance

Source          DF      SS         MS        F        P
Regression      2     33294136   16647068   207.81   0.000
Residual Error  47    3765064    80108
Total           49    37059200
```

FIGURE

14.10

SPSS regression solution for Example 14.4.

Model Summary

Model	R	R Square	Adjusted R Square	Std. Error of the Estimate
1	.9478[a]	.8984	.894	283.03

ANOVA[b]

Model		Sum of Squares	df	Mean Square	F	Sig.
1	Regression	33294136	2	**16647068**	207.81	**.00000**[a]
	Residual	3765064	47	80108		
	Total	37059200	49			

Coefficients[a]

Model		Unstandardized Coefficients		Standardized Coefficients		
		B	Std. Error	Beta	t	Sig.
1	(Constant)	-1183.318	219.370		-5.394	.000
	INDEX	-.127	1.547	-.004	-.082	.935
	INCOME	.072	.004	.947	20.064	.000

a. Predictors: (Constant), INCOME, INDEX

b. Dependent Variable: INVEST

The least squares equation is

$$\hat{Y} = -1183.3 - .127X_1 + .072X_2$$

The predicted investment is

$$\hat{Y} = -1183.3 - .127(72) + .072(48,500)$$
$$= -1183.3 - 9.1 + 3492.0 = 2299.6$$

that is, approximately \$2,300. Note that, following the same argument used in Chapter 13, \$2,300 also serves as an estimate of the average investment whenever $X_1 = 72$ and $X_2 = \$48,500$. This topic is explored further in Section 14.4, where we discuss the construction of a confidence interval for an average investment or a prediction interval for an individual investment.

The first test of hypothesis determines whether these two variables as a group provide a useful model for predicting the amount of an investment:

$$H_0: \beta_1 = \beta_2 = 0$$
$$H_a: \beta_1 \neq 0, \beta_2 \neq 0, \text{ or both} \neq 0$$

Using the ANOVA table, the value of the F statistic is

$$F^* = \frac{MSR}{MSE} = \frac{16,647,068}{80,108} = 207.81$$

The df here are $v_1 = k = 2$ and $v_2 = n - k - 1 = 50 - 2 - 1 = 47$. Because $F_{.10,2,47}$ is not in Table A.7a, we use the nearest value, $F_{.10,2,40} = 2.44$. The computed F^* exceeds this value, so we reject H_0 and conclude that at least one of these two independent variables is a significant predictor of investment amounts. We could have avoided any table look-up here by simply comparing the p-value for the F test (nearly zero) to the significance level of $a = .10$. Since the p-value is less than a, H_0 is rejected rather soundly and we arrive at the same conclusion.

The t Tests. Because we rejected $H_0: \beta_1 = \beta_2 = 0$, the next step is to examine the t tests to determine which of the two independent variables are useful predictors. The t value from Table A.5 is $t_{a/2,n-k-1} = t_{.05,47} \approx 1.684$. We can either compare the t values to 1.684 or compare the corresponding p-values to $a = .10$. The p-value for $X_1 =$ economic index is $.935 > .10$, and the p-value for $X_2 =$ income is approximately zero and is $< .10$. The large p-value (and small t statistic) for X_1 implies that, given the presence of X_2 in the model, X_1 does not contribute useful information to the prediction of the amount of an investment. Conversely, for X_2, the small p-value (and large t statistic of 20.06) indicates that the investor's income is an excellent predictor of the amount of an investment. It was the contribution of this variable and not of X_1 that produced the extremely large F value obtained previously.

As we have seen, a quick glance at the computer output allows you to determine whether your model is useful as a whole and, furthermore, which variables are useful predictors. But beware—the analysis is not over! Before you form your conclusions from this analysis and make critical decisions based on several tests of hypotheses, you need to be sure that none of the assumptions of the multiple linear regression model (discussed earlier) have been violated. We will discuss this problem in the final section of this chapter, where we conclude the analysis by examining the sample residuals, $Y - \hat{Y}$.

The use of t tests allows you to determine the predictive contribution of each independent variable, provided you want to examine the contribution of one such variable while assuming that the remaining variables are included in the equation. The next section shows you how to extend this procedure to a situation in which you wish to determine the contribution of any set of predictor variables by using a single test.

X Exercises 14.9–14.20

Understanding the Mechanics

14.9 The following regression equation was calculated from a data set of 20 observations: $\hat{Y} = -1.0 + 2.5X_1 + 4.0X_2$. The value of MSR and MSE are .465 and .004, respectively. The standard deviations of the regression coefficients of X_1 and X_2 are .26 and .21, respectively.

    a. Test the hypothesis that at least one of the regression coefficients is not equal to zero. Use a .05 significance level.

    b. Test H_0: $\beta_1 = 0$ versus H_a: $\beta_1 \neq 0$. Use a .05 significance level.

    c. Test H_0: $\beta_2 = 0$ versus H_a: $\beta_2 \neq 0$. Use a .05 significance level.

14.10 A researcher wished to test that a model with five independent variables contributed to the prediction of a certain dependent variable. From 51 observations, the researcher calculated SST to be equal to 215 and SSE to be equal to 180. Construct an ANOVA table.

Applying the New Concepts

14.11 Many chief executives (CEOs) have been under serious criticism from organized labor for the fat paychecks that CEOs take home. Many of the CEOs have advocated sacrifice and leaner paychecks for large groups of employees of their companies. An experiment was set up in which 15 observations were taken on the variables:

$$Y = \text{CEOs pay (in thousands of dollars)}$$

$$X_1 = \text{company's net profit (in millions of dollars)}$$

$$X_2 = \text{number of employees (in thousands)}$$

A computer package gave the following sample statistics:

$$b_1 = .1336 \qquad b_2 = -.86$$

$$s_{b_1} = .0424 \qquad s_{b_2} = .39$$

    a. Given that X_2 is in the model, does X_1 contribute to predicting the dependent variable at the .05 significance level?

    b. Given that X_1 is in the model, does X_2 contribute to predicting the dependent variable at the .05 significance level?

14.12 Brown and Gilbert's law firm would like to predict the salary for a legal secretary based on years of college education (X_1), typing speed in words per minute (X_2), and years of experience (X_3). The following data were collected:

Y	X_1	X_2	X_3	Y	X_1	X_2	X_3
15,120	2	65	2	12,500	0	45	.5
12,500	1	45	2	15,800	2.5	60	2
26,000	3.5	85	9	19,600	1	70	3
19,000	0	55	11	21,800	3	75	6
16,000	4	85	1	12,400	0	60	.5
15,000	0	65	1	22,500	2	75	7

    a. Using a computerized statistical package, determine the least squares prediction equation.

    b. What is the value of the residual standard deviation?

    c. Do the variables X_1, X_2, and X_3 contribute to predicting salaries at the .10 significance level?

    d. Find a 90% confidence interval for β_1.

    e. Test the null hypothesis that $\beta_1 = 0$ at the 10% significance level.

    f. Interpret the results of the hypothesis test in part e.

14.13 Highway miles per gallon (mpg) for large pickups range from 14 to 21. Typically, the more horsepower and the larger the engine size, the lower the mpg. A random sample of eight pickups is selected. Find the 95% confidence intervals for the regression coefficients of a model using horsepower and engine size to predict mpg. Interpret these two confidence intervals.

Pickup	MPG	Horsepower	Engine Size
Chevrolet Avalanche	15	285	5.3
Chevrolet Silverado 2500	16	300	6.0
Dodge Ram 1500	19	215	3.7
F-150 Regular Cab	21	202	4.2
GMC1500 Regular Cab	23	200	4.3
GMC Sierra Denali	14	325	6.0
Lincoln Blackwood	17	300	5.4
Toyota Tundra Regular	19	190	3.4

(Source: "2002 Car Guide," *Kiplinger's Personal Finance*, December 2001, p. 128.)

14.14 The regression equation $\hat{Y} = 11 + .5X_1 + .2X_2$ was computed using 20 data points to predict the price/earnings ratio (P/E) of a stock from the independent variables gross profit margin (X_1) and the sales growth of the company (X_2). The independent variables are expressed in terms of percentages. Assume that the standard deviations of the estimates for β_1 and β_2 are .16 and .21, respectively.

    a. What is the 95% confidence interval for β_1? Interpret this interval.

    b. What is the 95% confidence interval for β_2? Interpret this interval.

14.15 The tensile strength (Y) of a paper product is related both to the amount of hardwood in the pulp (X_1) and to the amount of time the paper spent soaking in a preparatory solution prior to cutting (X_2). A quality engineer collected ten samples of the variables Y, X_1, and X_2. Complete the following ANOVA table to test the null hypothesis that the independent variables X_1 and X_2 are not useful predictors of the tensile strength of the paper product.

Source	df	SS	MS	F
Regression			582.83	
Error				
Total		1300.90		

14.16 Datamatics Equipment, a Seattle-based electronics firm, is interested in identifying variables in the manufacturing environment that have a linear relationship with the number of line shortages on the manufacturing floor. The sample data used in a regression analysis are as follows:

Week	Y	X_1	X_2	X_3	Week	Y	X_1	X_2	X_3
1	293	205	5.936	343	9	420	365	4.780	453
2	348	215	5.815	259	10	407	329	4.905	460
3	416	227	4.983	250	11	397	345	5.009	426
4	445	301	4.841	236	12	430	249	4.869	408
5	453	362	4.755	243	13	497	356	4.791	324
6	392	358	4.775	303	14	534	424	4.754	330
7	382	302	4.813	411	15	547	430	4.598	283
8	365	246	4.909	420					

where

Y = number of line shortages with back-order status for a given week

X_1 = number of delinquent purchase orders for a given week

X_2 = inventory level (in millions of dollars) for prior weeks

X_3 = number of purchased items for prior weeks

The least squares regression equation was found to be:

$$\hat{Y} = 710.9 + 0.4767X_1 - 70.90X_2 - 0.2525X_3$$

a. Does the complete model significantly contribute to predicting the dependent variable? Use a 10% significance level.
b. If s_{b_2} is 36.886, find a 95% confidence interval for β_2.
c. Interpret the results of the hypothesis test in part a, and interpret the confidence interval in part b.

14.17 A district manager is interested in predicting district sales of an exclusively sold home water filter. As part of a marketing feasibility study, the manager selects 10 home improvement stores to market the water filter and collects data on the sales (Y), the size of the target population (X_1), and the per capita income of the local area (X_2). The sample residuals were: 350, 1,250, –3,500, 290, 1,500, –150, 4,500, –1,480, –1,250, –1,510. Given that the value of SST is 91,231,286, test the hypothesis that the variables X_1 and X_2 contribute to predicting sales. Use a 5% significance level.

Using the Computer

14.18 **[DATA SET EX14-18]** Variable Description:

FinancialAnalyst: Numbered 1 through 12 for 12 analysts

ActualReturn: Percent return on stock recommendation

TargetReturn: Expected return on stock recommendation

EarningsGrowth: Percent earnings growth over 5 years

Financial analysts typically recommend stocks with high earnings growth, hoping that the growth rate will entice investors to bid the stock higher. What is the regression equation used to predict ActualReturn using TargetReturn and EarningsGrowth? Interpret the t tests for testing that the independent variables TargetReturn and Earnings-Growth contribute to the prediction of the variable Actual-Return. Use a 5% significance level.

14.19 **[DATA SET EX14-19]** Variable Description:

CellularBill: Bill for monthly use of cellular smart phone

MinutesTalked: Total number of talking minutes on cellular smart phone

MonthlyCharge: Fixed monthly charge for cellular smart phone

PalmSource, maker of Palm operating system for hand-held devices, has introduced an operating system designed specially for smart phones. The smart phone can run programs typically found on desktop computers, and customers are billed monthly to use the operating system. Suppose that a communications consultant wished to determine the relationship between the variable CellularBill and the independent variables MinutesTalked and MonthlyCharge.
  a. Perform a regression analysis on these data and explain what conclusions the data support at a 5% significance level.
  b. Construct a histogram of the residuals and comment on the shape of the distribution.

(Source: "Maker of Palm Software to Unveil Operating System for Smart Phones," New York Times, September 27, 2004, p. C4.)

14.20 **[DATA SET EX14-20]** Variable Description:

ProficiencyStart: Proficiency of newly hired employee

Proficiency6mo: Proficiency of employee after six months

Proficiency1yr: Proficiency of employee after one year

An operations manager is interested in predicting the proficiency of an employee after being on the job for one year. The manager uses two predictors—proficiency when hired and proficiency after six months.
  a. Find the estimated regression equation using ProficiencyStart and Proficiency6mo to predict Proficiency1yr.

b. Test that ProficiencyStart does not contribute to the prediction of Proficiency1yr, given that Proficiency6mo is included in the model. Use a 5% significance level.

c. Find the regression coefficient for Proficiency6mo and interpret this interval. Use a 95% confidence interval.

d. Test that Proficiency6mo does not contribute to the prediction of Proficiency1yr, given that ProficiencyStart is included in the model. Use a 5% significance level.

e. Find a 95% confidence interval for the regression coefficient of ProficiencyStart and interpret this interval.

14.3   DETERMINING THE PREDICTIVE ABILITY OF CERTAIN INDEPENDENT VARIABLES

We can extend the procedure we used to examine the contribution of each independent variable, one at a time, using a t test.

Assume that the personnel director of an accounting firm has developed a regression model to predict an individual's performance on the CPA exam. The multiple linear regression model contains eight independent variables, three of which (say, X_6, X_7, X_8) describe the physical attributes of each individual (say, height, weight, and age). Can all three of these variables be removed from the analysis without seriously affecting the predictive ability of the model?

To answer this question, we return to a statistic described in Chapter 13 that measures how well a model captures the variation in the values of the dependent variable.

Coefficient of Determination

The total variation of the sampled dependent variable is determined by

$$SST = \text{total sum of squares}$$
$$= SS_Y$$
$$= \Sigma(Y - \bar{Y})^2$$
$$= \Sigma Y^2 - \frac{(\Sigma Y)^2}{n}$$

where n = number of observations. To determine what percentage of this variation has been explained by the predictor variables in the regression equation, we determine the **coefficient of determination, R^2.**

$$R^2 = 1 - \frac{SSE}{SST}$$

14.14

The range for R^2 is 0 to 1. If $R^2 = 1$, then 100% of the total variation has been explained, because in this case SSE $= \Sigma(Y - \hat{Y})^2 = 0$, and so $Y = \hat{Y}$ for each observation in the sample; that is, the model provides a *perfect predictor*. This does not occur in practice, but the main point is that a large value of R^2 is generally desirable for a regression application. It should be mentioned that $R^2 = 1$ whenever the number of observations (n) is equal to the number of estimated coefficients $(k + 1)$. This does not mean that you have a "wonderful" model; rather, you have inadequate data. As a result, you need to guard against using too small a sample in your regression analysis. *A general rule of thumb is to use a sample containing at least three times as many (unique) observations as the number of predictor variables* (k) *in the model.*

H_0: All β's = 0.   A test statistic for testing H_0: all β's = 0 was introduced in equation 12.11, which used the ratio of two mean squares from the ANOVA table. Another way to calculate this F value is to use

$$F = \frac{R^2 k}{(1 - R^2)/(n - k - 1)}$$

14.15

This version of the F statistic is used to answer the question, Is the value of R^2 significantly large? If H_0 is rejected, then the answer is yes, and so this group of predictor variables has at least some predictive ability for predicting Y.

The F value computed in this way will be exactly the same as the one computed using F = MSR/MSE, except for possible rounding error (see Example 14.5).

Once again, remember that statistical significance does not always imply practical significance. A large value of R^2 (rejecting H_0) does not imply that precise prediction (practical significance) will follow. However, it does inform the researcher that these predictor variables, as a group, are associated with the dependent variable.

EXAMPLE
14.5

In Example 13.7, we determined that X = income explained 71% of the total variation of the home sizes (Y) in the sample, since the computed value of r^2 was .711. What percentage is explained using all three predictors (income, family size, and years of education)?

Solution

The coefficient of determination using X_1 only is .71. Using the computer solutions in Section 14.1, the coefficient of determination using X_1, X_2, and X_3 is

$$R^2 = 1 - \frac{SSE}{SST}$$
$$= 1 - \frac{24.858}{262.4} = .905$$

Consequently, 90.5% of this variation has been explained using the three independent variables.

The F value determined in Example 14.2 for testing H_0: $\beta_1 = \beta_2 = \beta_3 = 0$ can be duplicated using equation 14.15 because

$$F^* = \frac{.905/3}{(1 - .905)/(10 - 3 - 1)} = \frac{.905/3}{.095/6} = 19.1 \text{ (as before)}$$

Comments

1. In Example 14.5, notice that the value of R^2 increased when we went from using one independent variable to using three. As you add variables to your regression model, R^2 never decreases. However, the increase may not be a significant one. If adding 10 more predictor variables to your model causes R^2 to increase from .91 to .92, this is not a significant increase. Therefore, do not include these 10 variables; they clutter up your model and are likely to add spurious predictive ability to it.

2. Nearly every computer package (including Excel, SPSS, and MINITAB) will provide a value in the output, referred to as the **adjusted** R^2. This particular statistic does not necessarily increase as additional predictor variables are added to the model, and many

researchers use this value to determine the predictive contribution of a variable added to the model. The adjusted R^2 is found by dividing SSE and SST by their respective degrees of freedom.

$$R^2(\text{adj}) = 1 - \frac{SSE/(n - k - 1)}{SST/(n - 1)}$$

14.16

Referring to Example 14.5 and the computer outputs in Section 14.1, the adjusted R^2 value is

$$R^2(\text{adj}) = 1 - \frac{24.858/6}{262.4/9} = 1 - \frac{4.143}{29.156} = .858$$

How can we tell if adding (or removing) a certain set of X variables causes a significant increase (or decrease) in R^2?

The Partial F Test

Consider the situation in which the personnel director is trying to determine whether to retain three variables (X_6 = height, X_7 = weight, X_8 = age) as predictors of a person's performance on a CPA exam. We know one thing—R^2 will be higher with these three variables included in the model. If we do not observe a significant increase, however, our advice would be to remove these variables from the analysis. To determine the extent of this increase, we use another F test.

We define two models—one contains X_6, X_7, and X_8, and one does not:

Complete model uses all predictor variables, including X_6, X_7, and X_8

Reduced model uses the same predictor variables as the complete model except X_6, X_7, and X_8

Also, let

$$R_c^2 = \text{the value of } R^2 \text{ for the complete model}$$
$$R_r^2 = \text{the value of } R^2 \text{ for the reduced model}$$

Do X_6, X_7, and X_8 contribute to the prediction of Y? We will test

$$H_0: \beta_6 = \beta_7 = \beta_8 = 0 \text{ (they do not contribute)}$$
$$H_a: \text{at least one of the } \beta\text{'s} \neq 0 \text{ (at least one of them does contribute)}$$

The test statistic here is

$$F = \frac{(R_c^2 - R_r^2)/v_1}{(1 - R_c^2)/v_2}$$

14.17

where v_1 = number of β's in H_0 and $v_2 = n - 1 - $ (number of X's in the complete model).

For this illustration, $v_1 = 3$ because there are three β's in H_0. Assuming that there are eight predictor variables in the complete model, then $v_2 = n - 1 - 8 = n - 9$. Here, n is the total number of observations (rows) in the data. This F statistic measures the partial effect of these three variables; it is a partial F test.

Equation 14.17 resembles the F statistic given in equation 14.15, which we used to test H_0: all β's = 0. If all the β's are zero, then the reduced model consists of only a constant term, and the resulting R^2 will be zero; that is, $R_r^2 = 0$. Setting $R_r^2 = 0$ in equation 14.17 produces equation 14.15, where $v_1 = k$ and $v_2 = n - k - 1$.

These variables (as a group) contribute significantly if the computed partial F value in equation 14.17 exceeds F_{a,v_1,v_2} from Table A.7.

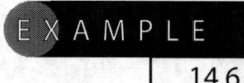

EXAMPLE
14.6

The personnel director gathered data from 30 individuals using all eight independent variables. These data were entered into a computer, and a multiple linear regression analysis was performed. The resulting R^2 was .857.

Next, variables X_6, X_7, and X_8 were omitted, and a second regression analysis was performed. The resulting R^2 was .824. Do the variables X_6, X_7, and X_8 (height, weight, and age) appear to have any predictive ability? Use $\alpha = .10$.

Here, $n = 30$ and

$$R_c^2 = .857 \text{ (complete model)}$$

$$R_r^2 = .824 \text{ (reduced model)}$$

Based on the previous discussion, the value of the partial F statistic is

$$F^* = \frac{(.857 - .824)/3}{(1 - .857)/(30 - 1 - 8)} = \frac{.033/3}{.143/21} = 1.61$$

The procedure is to reject H_0: $\beta_6 = \beta_7 = \beta_8 = 0$ if $F^* > F_{.10,3,21} = 2.36$. The computed F value does not exceed the table value, so we fail to reject H_0. We conclude that these variables should be removed from the analysis because including them in the model fails to produce a significantly larger R^2.

Comments

The partial F test also can be used to determine the effect of adding a *single* variable to the model. To determine the predictive ability of an individual independent variable, we can compute the partial F statistic or the somewhat simpler t statistic discussed in Section 14.2. Some computer packages use the F statistics to summarize the individual predictors, whereas others (such as Excel, SPSS, and MINITAB) use the t values to measure the influence of each predictor. You should use whatever is provided (the F statistic or t statistic) to measure the partial effect of each variable; both sets of statistics accomplish the same thing.

Using Curvilinear Models: Polynomial Regression

Motormax produces electric motors for use in home furnaces. The company has formed a team of employees to examine the relationship between the dollars spent per week in inspecting finished products (X) and the number of motors produced during that week that were returned to the factory by the customer (Y). Motormax suspects that the number of returned motors will decrease as the amount spent on inspection increases but that after a certain point the decrease will slow down— that is, the number of returned motors will continue to decrease but at a slower rate. In other words, after spending a certain amount on inspecting finished product, they will reach a point where there will be little decrease in the number of returned motors, even though they spend a much larger amount on inspection.

The following data were gathered from company records covering 15 (nonconsecutive) weeks (the inspection expenditure (X) is in thousands of dollars):

Week	Units Returned (Y)	Inspection Expenditures (X)	Week	Units Returned (Y)	Inspection Expenditures (X)
1	32	5.1	9	25	8.5
2	16	13.5	10	26	6.8
3	48	2.1	11	28	6.4
4	24	8.0	12	15	14.7
5	21	10.6	13	38	3.6
6	14	15.4	14	23	9.7
7	42	2.8	15	21	11.5
8	18	12.8			

The sample values and scatter diagram are shown in Figure 14.11. This MINITAB chart can be obtained by clicking on **Graph ➤ Scatterplot ➤ With Regression**. The last five values are above the trend line, and so it appears that Motormax has a point—the number of returned motors does appear to level off after a certain amount of inspection expense.

14.11

MINITAB scatter diagram of data and least squares line for inspection expense example.

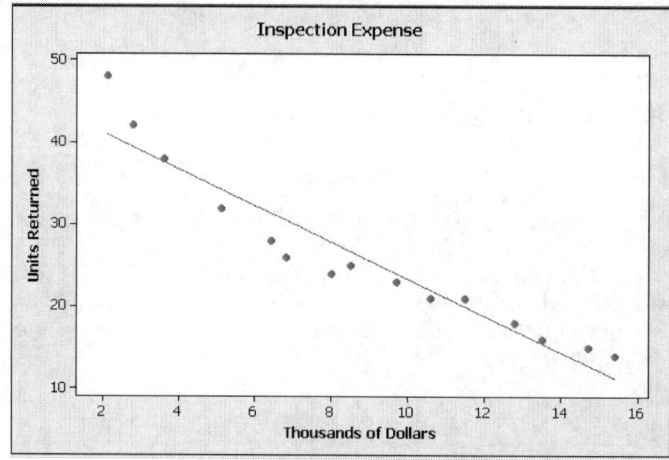

FIGURE

14.12

Quadratic curves. (a) Graph of $Y = 34 - 12X + 2X^2$. In general, this is the shape of $Y = \beta_0 + \beta_1 X + \beta_2 X^2$, where $\beta_2 > 0$. (b) Graph of $Y = 6 + 12X - 2X^2$. In general, this is the shape of $Y = \beta_0 + \beta_1 X + \beta_2 X^2$, where $\beta_2 < 0$.

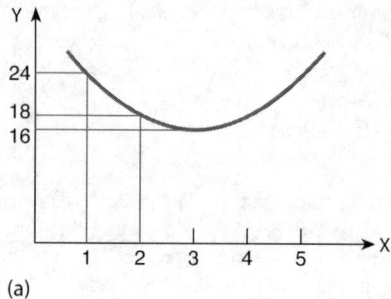

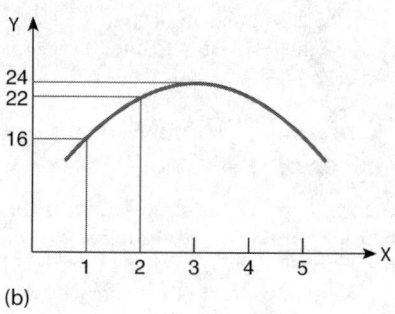

Does the simple linear model $Y = \beta_0 + \beta_1 X + e$ capture the relationship between inspection expenditure (X) and number of units returned (Y)? Although Y does decrease as X increases here, the linear model does not capture the "slowing down" of Y for larger values of X. The least squares line (contained in Figure 14.11) overpredicts Y for the middle range of X but underpredicts Y for small or large values of X.

Figure 14.12 shows **quadratic curves** rather than straight lines. If we include X^2 in the model, we can describe the curved relationship that seems to exist between the number of returned motors and inspection expense. More specifically, the left half of Figure 14.12(a) resembles the shape of the scatter diagram in Figure 14.11.

Consider the model

$$Y = \beta_0 + \beta_1 X + \beta_2 X^2 + e$$

14.18

Is this a linear regression model? At first glance, it would appear not to be. However, by the word linear we really mean that the model is linear in the unknown β's, not in X. In equation 14.18, there is no term such as β_1 / β_2 or $\beta_1 \beta_2$. So the model is linear in the β's, and this is a (multiple) linear regression application.

The model in equation 14.18 is a **curvilinear model** and is an example of polynomial regression. Such models are very useful when a particular independent variable and dependent variable exhibit a definite increasing and/or decreasing relationship that is nonlinear.

FIGURE

14.13

Excel solution to Example 14.7 using $Y = \beta_0 + \beta_1 X + \beta_2 X^2$.

	A	B	C	D	E	F	G	H	I
1	Returned	Dollars	DollarsSQ	SUMMARY OUTPUT					
2	32	5.1	26.01						
3	16	13.5	182.25	Regression Statistics					
4	48	2.1	4.41	Multiple R	0.98709				
5	24	8.0	64.00	R Square	0.97434	←—R^2			
6	21	10.6	112.36	Adjusted R Square	0.97007				
7	14	15.4	237.16	Standard Error	1.74059				
8	42	2.8	7.84	Observations	15				
9	18	12.8	163.84						
10	25	8.5	72.25	ANOVA					
11	26	6.8	46.24		df	SS	MS	F	Significance F
12	28	6.4	40.96	Regression	2	1380.5775	690.2887	227.844	2.853E-10
13	15	14.7	216.09	Residual	12	36.3559	3.0297		
14	38	3.6	12.96	Total	14	1416.9333			
15	23	9.7	94.09						
16	21	11.5	132.25		Coefficients	Standard Error	t Stat	P-value	
17				Intercept	54.8053	1.9878	27.5714	3.2E-12	
18				Dollars	-4.9555	0.5121	-9.6772	5.1E-07	
19				DollarsSQ	0.1561	0.0287	5.4478	0.00015	

Solving for β_0, β_1, and β_2. Equation 14.18 represents a multiple regression model containing two predictors, namely, $X_1 = X$ and $X_2 = X^2$. The data for the model then are

Y	X_1	X_2
32	5.1	26.01 (= 5.1^2)
16	13.5	182.25 (= 13.5^2)
48	2.1	4.41
⋮	⋮	⋮
23	9.7	94.09
21	11.5	132.25

These data for Y, X_1, and X_2 are your input to the multiple linear regression computer program. You can simplify this task by letting the computer build the $X_2 = X^2$ column of data by squaring the entries in the $X_1 = X$ column.

EXAMPLE

14.7

Determine the solution using the model $Y = \beta_0 + \beta_1 X + \beta_2 X^2 + e$ for the Motormax data shown in Figure 14.13. Also,

1. Predict the number of returned motors for a week in which Motormax spends $20,000 on inspecting final product.

2. What do the F test and t test tell you about this model? Use $\alpha = .10$.

Solution 1

To obtain the Excel solution in Figure 14.13, enter the data and labels in cells A1:B16 as shown. In cell C1, type DollarsSQ and in cell C2, type = B2*B2. Drag cell C2 down through cell C16. This will produce the X^2 values in column C. Next, click on **Tools ➤ Data Analysis ➤ Regression,** and enter A1:A16 as the **Input Y Range,** B1:C16 as the **Input X Range,** and D1 as the **Output Range.** Finally, click on the box alongside **Labels** (since there are labels in the first row) and on **OK.**

The regression coefficients are in cells E17:E19 (highlighted). The predicted number returned for $X_1 = 20$ (thousand) is

$$\hat{Y} = 54.8 - 4.96(20) + .156(20)^2 = 18.0$$

The model predicts that 18 motors will be returned during this particular week.

Solution 2   We first examine the F test. Our first test of hypothesis determines whether the overall model has predictive ability.

$$H_0: \beta_1 = \beta_2 = 0$$

$$H_a: \text{at least one of the } \beta\text{'s} \neq 0$$

Using the R^2 value from Figure 14.13 (in cell E5) and equation 14.15,

$$F^* = \frac{.97434/2}{.02566/(15-2-1)} = \frac{.97434/2}{.02566/12} = 227.8$$

As we might have suspected, this model does have significant predictive ability; $F^* = 227.8$ exceeds $F_{\alpha,k,n-k-1} = F_{.10,2,12} = 2.81$ from Table A.7.

Now we want to look at the t tests (same as partial F tests). Here, we examine each variable in the model, namely, X and X^2. The t value from Table A.5 is $t_{.10,12} = 1.356$ for a one-tailed test. We want to determine first whether $X_1 =$ inspection expenditure should be included in the model. Increased expenditure should be associated with decreased returns, so β_1 should be less than zero. We will therefore use a one-tailed procedure to test $H_0: \beta_1 \geq 0$ versus $H_a: \beta_1 < 0$.

According to Figure 14.13, the computed t statistic is $t^* = b_1/(\text{standard deviation of } b_1) = -9.68$ (highlighted). Now, $t^* = -9.68 < -1.356$, which means that the expenditure variable should be retained as a predictor of returns.

Next, we want to determine whether $X_2 = (\text{inspection expenditures})^2$ contributes significantly to the prediction of number returned. We are asking whether including the *quadratic term* was necessary. If this model is the correct one, then according to Figure 14.12(a), β_2 should not only be unequal to zero but also, more specifically, should be greater than zero. This follows because if the number of returned motors does, in fact, level off after a certain amount of inspection expenditures, the curve should resemble the left half of the quadratic curve in Figure 14.12(a).

The appropriate hypotheses are

$$H_0: \beta_2 \leq 0$$

$$H_a: \beta_2 > 0$$

We reject H_0 if $t > t_{.10,12} = 1.356$.

From Figure 14.13, we see that $t^* = b_2/(\text{standard deviation of } b_2) = 5.45$ (highlighted). This value lies in the rejection region, so we conclude that $\beta_2 > 0$, which means that the quadratic term, X^2, contributes significantly and in the correct direction.

Comments

There are three points you should note about the curvilinear model.

1. Curvilinear models often are used for situations in which the rate of increase or decrease in the dependent variable is not constant when plotted against a particular independent variable. The use of X^2 (and in some cases, X^3) in your model allows you to capture this nonlinear relationship between your variables.

2. There are other methods available for modeling a nonlinear relationship, including

$$Y = \beta_0 + \beta_1 \left(\frac{1}{X}\right) + \text{error}$$

and

$$Y = \beta_0 + \beta_1 e^{-x} + \text{error}$$

These models also are (simple, here) linear regressions; they are linear in the unknown parameters. Unlike the quadratic model discussed previously, these models involve a *transformation* of the independent variable, X. When replacing X by the transformed X (such as $1/X$ or e^{-x}) in the model, one obtains many other curvilinear models that may better fit a set of sample data displaying a nonlinear pattern.

3. Avoid using the model $Y = \beta_0 + \beta_1 X + \beta_2 X^2 + e$ for values of X outside the range of data used in the analysis.

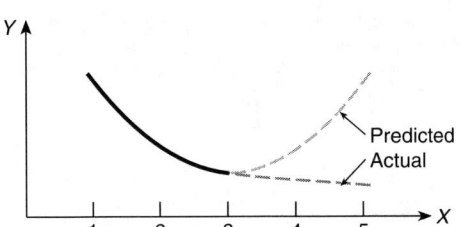

FIGURE

14.14

Error resulting
from extrapolation.
See text and
Figure 14.12(a).

Extrapolation is extremely dangerous when using this modeling technique. Consider Figure 14.12(a), and suppose that values of X between 1 and 3 were used to derive the estimate of β_0, β_1, and β_2. Figure 14.14 shows the results. For values of X larger than 3, the predicting equation will turn up, whereas the actual relationship will probably continue to level off. So this model works for interpolation (for values of X between 1 and 3, here) but is extremely unreliable for extrapolation.

The Problem of Multicollinearity

It is an easy exercise (and often seen in practice) to construct a data set where all the t values in a multiple regression analysis are not significant (say, all the p-values are > .10) yet the F statistic testing the overall model is quite significant (say, has a p-value = .005). At first glance, these results seem to be contradictory since the overall model appears to be very adequate yet none of the predictor variables have a significant contribution. This situation demonstrates the problem of **multicollinearity.** In multiple regression models, it is desirable for each independent (predictor) variable, X, to be highly correlated with Y, but it is *not* desirable for the X's to be highly correlated *with each other.* In business applications of multiple linear regression, the independent variables typically have a certain amount of pairwise correlation (usually positive). Extremely high correlation between any pair of variables can cause a variety of problems, including the seemingly contradictory results of insignificant t values and a highly significant F value.

The (sample) correlation between independent variables X_i and X_j is

$$r_{ij} = \frac{\Sigma X_i X_j - (\Sigma X_i)(\Sigma X_j)/n}{\sqrt{\Sigma X_i^2 - (\Sigma X_i)^2/n}\sqrt{\Sigma X_j^2 - (\Sigma X_j)^2/n}}$$

If a careful look at the data set reveals that nearly every time X_i increases, so does X_j, then the value of r_{ij} will be large (near one). This implies that X_i and X_j are highly correlated and these data contain a great deal of multicollinearity.

Consider a linear regression model with two independent variables, X_1 and X_2. Suppose the p-value for X_1 is .99, the p-value for X_2 is .27 and the p-value for the F statistic is .006. A closer look at the correlation between X_1 and X_2 reveals a value of $r_{12} = .970$. First of all, the correlation of X_1 and X_2 explains the small t values. Remember that each t value describes the contribution of that particular independent variable *after* all other independent variables have been included in the model. X_1 is very nearly a linear function of X_2 (as evidenced by $r_{12} = .970$), so it contributes very little to the prediction of Y, given that X_2 is in the model. The same argument applies to X_2. This means that neither X_1 nor X_2 is a strong predictor, given that the other variable is included—not that each one is a weak predictor by itself.

The second implication of the multicollinearity is that the situation in which X_1 increases by 1 while X_2 remains constant never occurred in the sample data—as X_1 increased by 1, X_2 always changed also, because X_1 and X_2 are highly correlated.

Finally, the sample coefficients (b_1 and b_2) of our independent variables have very large variances. If we took another sample from this population, the values of b_1 and b_2 probably would change dramatically—this is not a good situation. In fact, these coefficients can appear to have the "wrong" sign, a sign different from that obtained when regressing X_1 or X_2 alone on Y.

FIGURE

14.15

Excel solution
using age and
years of
experience to
predict salary.

	A	B	C	D	E	F	G	H	I	J	K
1	Salary	Age	YearsExp	SUMMARY OUTPUT							
2	62	52	33								
3	45	47	21	Regression Statistics							
4	55	38	14	Multiple R	0.87897						
5	38	25	3	R Square	0.77259						
6	52	44	18	Adjusted R Square	0.70762						
7	70	55	30	Standard Error	5.48362						
8	41	36	8	Observations	10						
9	48	40	15								
10	43	32	7	ANOVA							
11	58	50	27		df	SS	MS	F	Significance F		
12				Regression	2	715.1095	357.5548	11.8907	0.0056		
13				Residual	7	210.4905	30.0701				
14				Total	9	925.6					
15											
16					Coefficients	Standard Error	t Stat	P-value	Lower 95%	Upper 95%	VIF
17				Intercept	36.1169	20.9639	1.7228	0.1286	-13.4547	85.6885	
18				Age	-0.0140	0.7948	-0.0176	0.9865	-1.8933	1.8653	16.9494
19				YearsExp	0.8903	0.7409	1.2016	0.2686	-0.8617	2.6423	16.9494

Detecting Multicollinearity: Variance Inflation Factors

Whenever you perform a multiple regression analysis, it is always a good idea to examine the pairwise correlations between all of your variables, including the dependent variable. In this way, you can often detect two variables that are contributing to the multicollinearity problem.

An examination of pairwise correlations is not a foolproof method of detecting multicollinearity problems, since a particular independent variable may be nearly a linear combination of several other independent variables, but still not be highly correlated pairwise with any of them. Consequently, an examination of the correlation matrix would fail to detect this relationship.

Suppose a regression analysis contains 10 predictor variables and that variable X_6 is nearly a linear combination of X_3, X_5, and X_9. Consequently,

$$X_6 \approx a_0 + a_1 X_3 + a_2 X_5 + a_3 X_9$$

for some set of constants a_0, a_1, a_2, and a_3. How can we detect if such a relationship exists? This is accomplished very simply, by treating X_6 as a dependent variable and using variables X_3, X_5, and X_9 as independent variables in a regression analysis. If this relationship is present in the data, the resulting R^2 will be very high. This large value of R^2 is your warning that this independent variable is contributing to the multicollinearity problem. Fortunately, it is not necessary to examine each independent variable in this way. Most computer packages will compute a statistic referred to as a **variance inflation factor** for each independent variable. The variance inflation factor for variable X_j is defined as

$$\text{VIF}_j = \frac{1}{1 - R_j^2}$$

14.19

where R_j^2 is the coefficient of determination obtained by regressing X_j on the remaining $k - 1$ independent variables. If R_j^2 is large (close to 1.0), then VIF_j will be large. *A commonly used procedure here is to conclude that severe multicollinearity exists in the sample data if the maximum VIF_j is larger than 10.*

Consider the sample of 10 employees at Bellaire Industries, illustrated in Figure 14.15. The intent of this analysis was to determine if age (X_1) and years of experience (X_2) could be used to predict an employee's salary (Y). The Excel solution is also shown in Figure 14.15, where it can be observed that the p-values for both predictor variables are large (.9865 for age and .2686 for years of experience), yet the F statistic is significant (p-value of .0056). The Excel regression procedure does not provide the variance inflation factors, but these values are

FIGURE

14.16

MINITAB solution
using age and
years of
experience to
predict salary.

Regression Analysis: Salary versus Age, YearsExp

```
The regression equation is
Salary = 36.1 - 0.014 Age + 0.890 YearsExp


Predictor      Coef   SE Coef      T      P    VIF
Constant      36.12     20.96   1.72  0.129
Age         -0.0140    0.7948  -0.02  0.986   16.9
YearsExp     0.8903    0.7409   1.20  0.269   16.9

S = 5.48362   R-Sq = 77.3%   R-Sq(adj) = 70.8%

Analysis of Variance

Source          DF      SS      MS      F      P
Regression       2  715.11  357.55  11.89  0.006
Residual Error   7  210.49   30.07
Total            9  925.60
```

FIGURE

14.17

SPSS solution
using age and
years of
experience to
predict salary.

ANOVA[b]

Model		Sum of Squares	df	Mean Square	F	Sig.
1	Regression	715.110	2	357.555	11.891	.006[a]
	Residual	210.490	7	30.070		
	Total	925.600	9			

Coefficients[a]

Model		Unstandardized Coefficients		Standardized Coefficients			Collinearity Statistics	
		B	Std. Error	Beta	t	Sig.	Tolerance	VIF
1	(Constant)	36.117	20.964		1.723	.129		
	AGE	-1.40E-02	.795	-.013	-.018	.986	.059	16.949
	YEARSEXP	.890	.741	.892	1.202	.269	.059	16.949

a. Predictors: (Constant), YEARSEXP, AGE

b. Dependent Variable: SALARY

available when using **KPK Data Analysis ➤ Regression.** MINITAB will provide the VIFs by clicking on **Options ➤ Variance inflation factors** (see Figure 14.16), and SPSS computes VIFs by clicking on **Statistics ➤ Collinearity diagnostics** (as illustrated in Figure 14.17). The VIFs are highlighted within the computer outputs and are both equal to 16.9.

Note that the VIFs for both X_1 and X_2 are equal (such is always the case when using only two predictor variables), and both exceed 10. For this data set, the correlation between X_1 and X_2 is .970. When regressing X_1 on X_2 (or vice versa), the resulting R^2 is the square of this correlation; that is, $R_1^2 = R_2^2 = (.970)^2 = .941$. The resulting values for VIF_1 and VIF_2 are

$$VIF_1 = VIF_2 = \frac{1}{1-.941} = 16.9$$

which agree with the computer-derived values. The easiest way out of this dilemma is to remove one of these predictor variables from the model. The best procedure here would be to retain X_2 = years of experience, because it has the highest correlation with Y.

A Final Look at Multicollinearity

Another method of eliminating correlated predictor variables is to use a **stepwise** selection procedure. This technique of selecting the variables to be used in a multiple linear regression equation is discussed in the next section. Essentially, it selects variables one at a time and generally (although not always) does not insert into the regression equation a variable that is highly correlated with a variable already in the equation. In the previous example, a stepwise procedure would have selected variable X_2 (the single best predictor of Y) and then informed the user that X_1 did not significantly improve the prediction of Y, given that X_2 was already included in the prediction equation.

Other, more advanced methods of detecting and treating the multicollinearity problem are beyond the scope of this text. One of the more popular procedures is *ridge regression*.*

We have seen that the problem of multicollinearity enters into our regression analysis when an independent variable is highly correlated with one or more other independent variables. Multicollinearity produces inflated regression coefficients that can even have the wrong sign. Also, the resulting t statistics can be small, making it difficult to determine the predictive ability of an individual variable. Therefore, $b_1, b_2, \ldots$ tell us nothing about the partial effect of each variable, unless we can demonstrate that there is no correlation among our predictor variables. In business applications, correlation (in particular, *positive* correlation) among the independent variables is far from unusual.

As a final note, care should be taken in the selection of a model not to include variables that will be likely to produce multicollinearity. The detection and correction of the multicollinearity problem is often difficult to accomplish, and the methods discussed in this section are open to debate. The treatments of multicollinearity discussed so far are highly data dependent; that is, a new set of data could very well produce different results. Also, examining pairwise correlations may well miss the presence of multicollinearity, since multicollinearity will exist when one predictor variable is nearly a linear combination of two or more predictor variables and is not highly correlated with either of them. *In short, there is no easy way out of the multicollinearity problem.*

☒ Exercises 14.21–14.30

Understanding the Mechanics

14.21 The SSE and SST for a regression equation with three independent variables were found to be 26 and 250, respectively. The number of observations was 10.
  a. Calculate the R^2 value.
  b. Calculate the adjusted R^2 value.

14.22 A researcher collected data from 28 individuals. Seven independent variables were used to predict a dependent variable. The value of R^2 for this model was .87. When the variables X_1 and X_3 were omitted from the model, R^2 was .84. Do the variables X_1 and X_3 contribute to the prediction of the dependent variable? Use a .10 significance level.

Applying the New Concepts

14.23 The manager of the personnel department of a computer firm is interested in knowing the relationship between the pay raise (Y) given to an employee of the firm and the following variables: yearly performance evaluation (X_1), years with the company (X_2), and number of credit hours of computer courses that the employee has taken in college (X_3). After observing 50 employees under different values of X_1, X_2, and X_3, the manager wishes to test that X_2 and X_3 contribute to predicting the variation in pay raises. The coefficient of determination for the model involving just Y and X_1 is .71. The coefficient of determination for the model with X_1, X_2, and X_3 is .82. Do the additional independent variables contribute significantly to the model? Use a 5% significance level.

14.24 The computer programming courses of COBOL, C, C++, Java, and Visual Basic will be among the dominant programming languages expected of future information systems graduates. Suppose that a career placement director wished to determine the relationship between a student's starting salary and two independent variables: a proficiency score in programming languages and a score measuring interpersonal skills. Data collected from 83 graduates of an information systems program yielded a coefficient of determination of .64.
  a. Using a significance level of 1%, what conclusion can you make about the contribution that these two prediction scores make to the prediction of starting salaries?
  b. What is the value of the adjusted R^2? How does this compare with the value of R^2?

14.25 The dean of the college of business at Fargo University would like to see whether several variables affect a

---

*For an excellent discussion of this topic, see J. Neter, M. Kutner, and C. Nachtscheim, *Applied Linear Regression Models*, 3rd ed. (Homewood, Ill.: Richard D. Irwin, 1996).

student's grade point average. Thirty first-year students were randomly selected and data were collected on the following variables:

Y = grade point average for the first year

X_1 = average time spent per month at fraternity or sorority functions

X_2 = average time spent per month working part time

X_3 = total number of hours of coursework attempted

The SSE for the least squares line involving only Y and X_1 was found to be 5.21. The SSE for the complete model was found to be 4.31. The SST is 24.1. At the 5% significance level, test the null hypothesis that the independent variables X_2 and X_3 do not contribute to predicting the variation in Y, given that X_1 is already in the model.

14.26 After a series of hurricanes struck Florida in 2004 and the price of oil exceeded $50 a barrel, the federal government negotiated with oil companies to lend them oil from the U.S. Strategic Petroleum Reserve. The market capitalization of major oil companies is mostly driven by their oil/gas reserves. Suppose that an energy consultant collected data on 10 major oil companies to determine the relationship between an oil company's reserves, X (in units of billions of barrels), and market capitalization, Y (in units of billions of dollars).

   a. The R^2 for the regression equation $\hat{Y} = -18.035 + 10.856X$ is 91.78%. Test that the variable oil reserves contributes to the prediction of market capitalization. Use a 1% significance level.

   b. The R^2 for the regression equation $\hat{Y} = -9.045 + 7.857X + .150X^2$ is 92.29%. Test that the variable oil reserves and the square of this variable contribute to the prediction of market capitalization. Use a 1% significance level.

   c. What is the adjusted value of R^2 for the model in parts a and b? Since the value of the adjusted R^2 does not increase in value for the model in part b, what conclusion can you make about the appropriateness of adding the quadratic term to the model?

(Source: "U.S. Considers Refiners' Request to Tap Oil Reserves," *The Wall Street Journal*, September 24, 2004, p. A3.)

14.27 Professor Xenophon Koufteros of The University of Texas at El Paso and Professors Mark Vonderembse and William Doll of The University of Toledo have performed a large-scale study to understand the impact that manufacturing practices have on throughput time reduction. A random sample of 244 firms was used to collect data on throughput time (TT) as well as on pull production (PP) and quality improvement effort (QI). For the regression equation predicting TT using PP and QI, the MSE was .85851 and the total sum of squares was 242.67012. Use the following table to determine which independent variables should be included in the model assuming a 5% signifi-

cance level. What is the value of R^2? How does this compare to the value of the adjusted R^2?

Variable	Coefficient	Standard Deviation
Pull Production (PP)	−.1268	.0586
Quality Improvement Effort (QI)	−.291539	.2061

(Source: "How to Cut Manufacturing Throughput Time," 1998 *Proceedings of the Decision Sciences Institute*, pp. 1433–35.)

14.28 An economist would like to examine the relationship between personal savings and the following independent variables:

X_1 = total personal income

X_2 = yield on U.S. government securities

X_3 = consumer price index

The following data were collected for 14 randomly selected months:

Y	X_1	X_2	X_3	Y	X_1	X_2	X_3
80.2	2077.2	12.036	233.2	107.4	2179.4	9.259	249.4
91.6	2086.4	12.814	236.4	116.8	2205.7	10.321	252.7
87.4	2101.0	15.526	239.8	102.1	2234.3	11.580	253.9
104.9	2102.1	14.003	242.5	97.9	2257.6	13.888	256.2
116.2	2114.1	9.150	244.9	93.3	2276.6	15.661	258.4
109.1	2127.1	6.995	247.6	83.6	2300.7	14.724	260.5
110.1	2161.2	8.126	247.8	91.0	2318.2	14.905	263.2

   a. Using a computerized statistical package, determine the least squares equation for these data.

   b. Use only the variables X_1 and X_2. What is the new prediction equation?

   c. Does the variable X_3 contribute to predicting the variation in personal savings, given that X_1 and X_2 are in the model? Use a 10% significance level.

Using the Computer

14.29 **[DATA SET EX14-29]** Variable Description:

CompPerf: Performance with computer software on a scale from 1 to 100

CompEffic: Self-perception of computer self-efficacy on a scale from 1 to 7

Loyalty: Self-perception of loyalty to company on a scale from 1 to 7

CompanyYrs: Number of years with the company

Using the data collected by an information technology researcher, test and interpret the contribution of the variables CompEffic, Loyalty, and CompanyYrs to predict CompPerf. Use a 5% significance level.

14.30 **[DATA SET EX14-30]** Variable Description:

XBoxSpend: Amount of money spent by a family on Xbox

GamesSpend: Amount of money spent by a family on games other than Xbox

TimeOwnGames: Length of time that a family has owned computer games

Microsoft has rolled out software to speed the job of designing Xbox games and also to bridge the software worlds of the PC and the Xbox. Microsoft believes that the PC will be the next consumer digital hub. While 37 million homes have a PlayStation, 83 million have a personal computer. Suppose that an analyst wished to determine the relationship between the amount a family spends on Xbox

and the independent variables GamesSpend and Time-OwnGames. A random sample of 35 families was selected.

a. Do the variables GamesSpend and TimeOwnGames contribute to the prediction of XboxSpend? Use a 5% significance level.

b. Take the natural logarithm of XboxSpend and use this variable as the dependent variable in part a. Do you believe that this model explains the relationship between the dependent and independent variables better in part a?

(Source: "Business World: Just How Crazy is Xbox?" *The Wall Street Journal*, September 22, 2004, p. A29.)

X Exercises 14.31–14.38

Understanding the Mechanics

14.31 Which independent variables appear to contribute to high multicollinearity? Use the following correlation matrix.

	Y	X_1	X_2	X_3	X_4	X_5
Y	1.00	.80	.95	.32	.41	.50
X_1	.80	1.00	.98	.03	.25	.41
X_2	.95	.98	1.00	.12	.22	.03
X_3	.32	.03	.12	1.00	.10	.27
X_4	.41	.25	.22	.10	1.00	.97
X_5	.50	.41	.03	.27	.97	1.00

14.32 A regression equation uses three independent variables to predict Y. The coefficient of determination for regressing X_1 on variables X_2 and X_3 is .95. The coefficient of determination for regressing X_2 on variables X_1 and X_3 is .85.

a. What is the VIF for X_1?

b. What is the VIF for X_2?

c. Would you say multicollinearity may present a problem for this regression equation?

Applying the New Concepts

14.33 A marketing analyst regressed the percentage of the market share (Y) of primetime television programs on the program's rating (X) and on the square of X (X^2). The correlation between X and X^2 was .99077. Calculate the VIF for each of the variables and comment on whether multicollinearity is a concern.

14.34 A manager collected 40 observations on three variables to predict worker proficiency. The manager computed the least squares equation to be $\hat{Y} = 30 - 501X_1 + 300X_2 + 1.8X_3$. The manager collected another set of observations using the same variables and found the least squares equation to be $\hat{Y} = -20 + 204X_1 - 98X_2 + 1.9X_3$. Is there any explanation for these two different prediction equations?

14.35 A financial analyst uses four independent variables to predict the earnings of a company. Construct a correla-

tion matrix to determine if multicollinearity appears to be a problem with using all four independent variables. Compute the least squares equation using independent variables that do not contribute to the multicollinearity problem.

Y	X_1	X_2	X_3	X_4
40	3	5	12	18
40	4	6	14	21
47	5	8	15	23
47	6	9	13	22
45	5	7	17	27
36	4	6	21	34
27	6	9	32	48
29	8	12	42	63
36	3	5	18	27
35	4	6	25	40

14.36 Consider the following set of data for 12 emerging growth-oriented companies. Y represents the growth rate of a company for the current year, X_1 represents the growth rate of the company for the previous year, and X_2 represents the percent of the market that does not use the company's product or a similar product. All values are percentages.

Y	X_1	X_2	Y	X_1	X_2
20	10	30	30	15	60
24	12	35	36	42	38
18	15	25	47	45	40
33	30	40	35	32	32
27	19	32	28	24	31
20	24	20	32	20	50

a. Construct the correlation matrix for the variables. Does multicollinearity appear to be a problem?

b. Find the coefficient of determination for the model with only X_1 included in the model.

c. Find the coefficient of determination for the model with only X_2 in the model.

d. The coefficient of determination for the complete model is .896. Does it appear from observing the values of the coefficient of determination in parts a and b that both variables X_1 and X_2 should stay in the model?

Using the Computer

14.37   **DATA SET EX[14-37]** Variable Description:

StockPercent: Percentage of portfolio in stocks

BondPercent: Percentage of portfolio in bonds

Performance: Percentage return of the portfolio six months later

The Web site www.fool.comprovides advice to the individual investor that is often quite different from that provided by brokerage firms. For example, they advise 100% stock allocation if a person plans to be invested for 8 to 10 years. Most brokerage firm recommend that 10% to 40% of a portfolio always be in bonds. Suppose 50 financial strategist were asked what percentage of their portfolio should be invested in stocks and bonds. The performance of the corresponding portfolio was recorded six months later.

   a. Regress Performance on StockPercent and BondPercent. Does the model contribute to the prediction of Performance using a 5% significance level?

   b. Does each of the independent variables contribute to the prediction of Performance assuming the other independent variable is in the model? Use a 5% significance level.

   c. Find the VIF of StockPercent and BondPercent. Do you believe that there is a multicollinearity problem within the data?

14.38   **[DATA SET EX14-38]** Variable Description:

SalesMonth: Sales of discount department store during the previous month

AgeStore: Age of the store

ExperManager: Years of experience of store manager

A regional executive is interested in predicting SalesMonth using AgeStore and ExperManager as independent variables. Comment on the fit of this model using a 5% significance level. Add the squares of the variables AgeStore and ExperManager to the model. Find the VIFs for the independent variables using this model and comment on whether multicollinearity is a concern.

14.4

DUMMY VARIABLES AND ADDITIONAL TOPICS IN MULTIPLE LINEAR REGRESSION

The use of **dummy**, or **indicator**, **variables** in a regression analysis allows you to include qualitative variables in the model. For example, if you wanted to include an employee's gender as a predictor variable in a regression model, define

$$X_1 = \begin{cases} 1 & \text{if female} \\ 0 & \text{if male} \end{cases}$$

Note that the choice of which gender is assigned the value of 1, male or female, is arbitrary. The estimated value of Y will be the same, regardless of which coding procedure is used.

   Returning to the data we used in Example 14.2, the real-estate developer noticed that all the houses in the population were from three neighborhoods, A, B, and C. Taking note of which neighborhood each of the sampled houses was from led to the following data (in the discussion following Example 14.2, X_3 = years of education was shown to be a weak predictor and so is removed from the model here):

Family	Home Square Footage (Y)	Income (X_1)	Family Size (X_2)	Neighborhood
1	16	32	2	B
2	17	36	2	C
3	26	55	3	A
4	24	47	4	C
5	22	38	4	B
6	21	60	3	C
7	32	66	6	B
8	18	44	3	B
9	30	70	5	A
10	20	50	3	A

Using these data, we can construct the necessary dummy variables and determine whether they contribute significantly to the prediction of home size (Y).

One way to code neighborhoods would be to define

$$X_3 = \begin{cases} 0 & \text{if neighborhood A} \\ 1 & \text{if neighborhood B} \\ 2 & \text{if neighborhood C} \end{cases}$$

However, this type of coding has many problems. First, because $0 < 1 < 2$, the codes imply that neighborhood A is smaller than neighborhood B, which is smaller than neighborhood C. Furthermore, any difference between neighborhoods A and C receives twice the weight (because $2 - 0 = 2$) of any difference between neighborhoods A and B or B and C. So this coding transforms data that are actually *nominal* to data that are *interval,* a much stronger type.

A better procedure is to use the necessary number of dummy variables (coded 0 or 1) to represent the neighborhoods. We needed one dummy variable with two categories (male and female) to specify a person's gender. To represent the three neighborhoods, we use two dummy variables by letting

$$X_3 = \begin{cases} 1 & \text{if house is in A} \\ 0 & \text{otherwise} \end{cases} \quad \text{and} \quad X_4 = \begin{cases} 1 & \text{if house is in B} \\ 0 & \text{otherwise} \end{cases}$$

Note that as for the male/female dummy variable, this coding is arbitrary as far as the prediction, $\hat{Y}$, is concerned. We could have assigned $X_3 = 0$ and $X_4 = 0$ to neighborhood A, with $X_3 = 1$ for B and $X_4 = 1$ for C.

What happened to neighborhood C? It is not necessary to develop a third dummy variable here because we have the following scheme:

House Is in Neighborhood	X_3	X_4
A	1	0
B	0	1
C	0	0

In fact, it can be shown that a third dummy variable is not only unnecessary, it is very important that you not include it. If you attempted to use three such dummy variables in your model, you would receive a message in your computer output informing you that "no solution exists" for this model. Suppose we had introduced a third dummy variable (say, X_5) that was equal to 1 if the house was in neighborhood C. For each observation in the sample, we would have

$$X_5 = 1 - X_3 - X_4$$

Whenever any one predictor variable is a linear function (including a constant term) of one or more other predictors, then mathmematically *no solution* exists for the least squares coefficients, since you have multicollinearity at its worst. To arrive at a usable equation, any such predictor variable must not be included.

The resulting model here is*

$$Y = \beta_0 + \beta_1 X_1 + \beta_2 X_2 + \beta_3 X_3 + \beta_4 X_4 + e$$

---

*Models that include dummy variables typically contain terms that reflect any interaction between the dummy variables and the other quantitative variables. For this model, this would amount to adding four additional terms to the model, namely, $X_1 X_3$, $X_1 X_4$, $X_2 X_3$, and $X_2 X_4$. Such a model would require a larger sample size (n) than that used in this illustration, since the model would then contain $k = 8$ predictor variables. This topic is explored further in Section 14.5.

FIGURE

14.18

Excel solution
(partial output) to
real-estate dummy
variable problem.
(a) Solution using
X_1, X_2, X_3, and X_4.
(b) Solution using
variables X_1 and X_2

	A	B	C	D	E	F	G	H	I	J	K
1	Footage	Income	FamSize	NbhoodA	NbhoodB	Summary Output for A					
2	16	32	2	0	1						
3	17	36	2	0	0	Regression Statistics					
4	26	55	3	1	0	Multiple R	0.960				
5	24	47	4	0	0	R Square	0.921	←	R-Squared (complete model)		
6	22	38	4	0	1	Adjusted R Square	0.858				
7	21	60	3	0	0	Standard Error	2.036				
8	32	66	6	0	1	Observations	10				
9	18	44	3	0	1						
10	30	70	5	1	0	Summary Output for B					
11	20	50	3	1	0						
12						Regression Statistics					
13						Multiple R	0.948				
14						R Square	0.898	←	R-Squared (reduced model)		
15						Adjusted R Square	0.869				
16						Standard Error	1.953				
17						Observations	10				

The final array of data (ready for input into a computer program) is

Row	Y	X_1	X_2	X_3	X_4	Row	Y	X_1	X_2	X_3	X_4
1	16	32	2	0	1	6	21	60	3	0	0
2	17	36	2	0	0	7	32	66	6	0	1
3	26	55	3	1	0	8	18	44	3	0	1
4	24	47	4	0	0	9	30	70	5	1	0
5	22	38	4	0	1	10	20	50	3	1	0

where Y = square footage of home, X_1 = income, X_2 = family size, X_3 = 1 if neighborhood A, and X_4 = 1 if neighborhood B.

An abbreviated Excel solution using all four predictors is shown in Figure 14.18(a). To determine whether the particular neighborhood has any effect on the prediction of home size, we test

$$H_0: \beta_3 = \beta_4 = 0 \qquad \text{(if } X_1 \text{ and } X_2 \text{ are included)}$$

$$H_a: \beta_3 \text{ or } \beta_4 \text{ (or both)} \neq 0$$

In the complete model, the variables are X_1, X_2, X_3, and X_4, and from Figure 14.18(a),

$$R_c^2 = .921$$

In the reduced model, the variables are X_1 and X_2 only, and from Figure 14.18(b),

$$R_r^2 = .898$$

At first glance, it does not appear that X_3 and X_4 produced a significant increase in R^2. The partial F test will determine whether this is true.

$$F = \frac{(R_c^2 - R_r^2)/(\text{number of } \beta\text{'s in } H_0)}{(1 - R_c^2)/[n - 1 - (\text{number of } X\text{'s in the complete model})]}$$

$$= \frac{(.921 - .898)/2}{(1 - .921)/(10 - 1 - 4)} = \frac{.023/2}{.079/5} = .73$$

Using $\alpha = .10$, this result is considerably less than $F_{.10,2,5} = 3.78$, so there is no evidence that the neighborhood dummy variables significantly improve the prediction of home size.

In this example, the dummy variables were not significant predictors in the model. However, do not let this mislead you. In many business applications, dummy variables representing location, weather conditions, yes/no situations, time, and many other variables can have a tremendous effect on improving the results of a multiple regression model.

Stepwise Procedures

Assume you wish to predict annual divisional profits for a large corporation using, among other techniques, a multiple linear regression model. Your strategy is to consider any variable that you think *could* have an effect on these profits. You have identified 12 such variables.

One possibility is to include all these variables in your model and to use the *t* tests to decide which variables are significant predictors. However, this procedure invites multi-collinearity, because your model is more apt to include correlated predictors, severely hindering the interpretation of your model. In particular, two independent variables that are very highly correlated may both have small *t* values (as we saw in Section 14.3), causing you possibly to discard both of them from the model—this is *not* the right thing to do because you possibly should have retained one of them.

A better way to proceed here is to use one of the several stepwise selection procedures. These techniques either choose or eliminate variables, one at a time, in an effort not to include those variables that either have no predictive ability or are highly correlated with other predictor variables. A word of caution—these procedures do not provide a guarantee against multicollinearity; however, they greatly reduce the chances of including a large set of correlated independent variables.

These procedures consist of three different selection techniques: (1) forward regression, (2) backward regression, and (3) stepwise regression.

Forward Regression. The **forward regression** method of model selection puts variables into the equation, one at a time, beginning with that variable having the highest correlation (or R^2) with Y. For sake of argument, call this variable X_1.

Next, it examines the remaining variables for the variable that, when included with X_1, has the highest R^2. That predictor (with X_1) is inserted into the model. This procedure continues until adding the "best" remaining variable at that stage results in an insignificant increase in R^2 according to the partial F test.

Backward Regression. **Backward regression** is the opposite of forward regression: it begins with *all* variables in the model and, one by one, removes them. It begins by finding the "worst" variable—the one that causes the smallest decrease in R^2 when removed from the complete model. If the decrease is insignificant, this variable is removed, and the process continues.

The variable among those remaining in the model that causes the smallest decrease in the new R^2 is considered next. You continue this procedure of removing variables until a significant drop in R^2 is obtained, at which point you replace this significant predictor and terminate the selection.

Will the model resulting from a backward regression be the same as that obtained using forward regression? Not necessarily; usually, however, the resulting models are very similar. Of course, if two variables are highly correlated, the forward procedure could choose one of the correlated predictors, whereas the backward procedure could choose the other.

Stepwise Regression. The **stepwise regression** method is a modification of forward regression. *It is the most popular and flexible of the three selection techniques.* It proceeds exactly as does forward regression, except that at each stage it can *remove* any variable whose partial F value indicates that this variable does not contribute, given the present set of independent variables in the model. Like forward regression, it stops when the "best" variable among those remaining produces an insignificant increase in R^2.

Figure 14.19 illustrates this procedure for the example on predicting divisional profits (the data are not shown). Data from all 12 independent variables, as well as from Y, are used as input to a stepwise regression program. One possible outcome from this analysis is shown in Figure 14.19.

The stepwise input for the data we used to predict home size in Section 14.4 is contained in the end-of-chapter appendix. As we previously determined, X_3 and X_4 do not contribute significantly, and so the resulting prediction equation includes only $X_1 =$ income and $X_2 =$ family size. This equation, provided in Figure 14.7, is

$$\hat{Y} = 5.091 + .165X_1 + 2.66X_2$$

FIGURE

14.19

Possible solution using stepwise regression on divisional profits data.

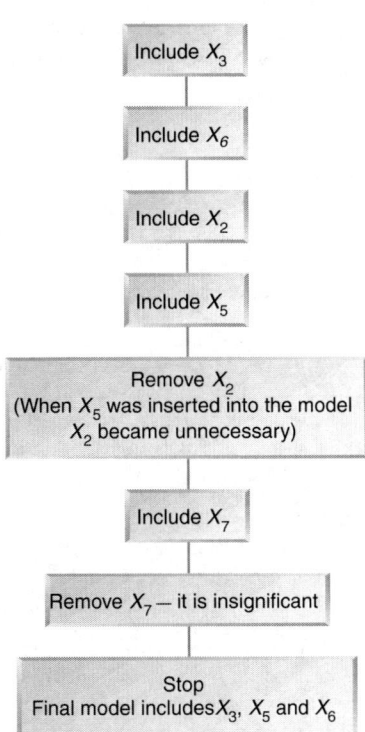

Using Dummy Variables in Forward or Stepwise Regression. We emphasized that $C - 1$ dummy variables should be used to represent C categories if *all* the dummy variables were to be inserted into the regression equation. When using a forward or stepwise regression procedure, this may not be the best way to proceed, as the following illustration shows.

Suppose you are using nine dummy (indicator) variables to represent 10 cities. The dependent variable is monthly sales, and the purpose is to determine which city (or cities) exhibits very large or very small sales. If a forward or stepwise selection procedure is used, then including one of these dummy variables indicates that specifying this particular city significantly improves the prediction of sales. In other words, it indicates that sales for this city are not just average but are much higher (its coefficient will be positive) or lower (its coefficient will be negative) than average.

When you use the forward or stepwise techniques, you probably will not include all nine dummy variables in the model. Your ability to predict sales (Y) is unaffected by not defining a tenth dummy variable and, in fact, as pointed out earlier, the regression analysis will not accept all 10 dummy variables.

For this situation, however, there is the danger of not detecting extremely high or low sales in the tenth city, which did not receive a dummy variable. When including these variables one at a time in the regression equation using a forward or stepwise procedure, we can allow the regression model to examine the effect of all 10 cities. We do this by defining 10 such dummy variables, one for each city.*

---

*This problem is discussed in D. Dorsett and J. T. Webster, "Guidelines for Variable Selection Problems When Dummy Variables Are Used," *The American Statistician,* 37, no. 4 (1983): p. 337.

Because a forward regression procedure generally will not attempt to include all 10 dummy variables, you are able to investigate the existence of high or low sales in each of the 10 cities. When using dummy variables in a forward or stepwise regression procedure, it is perfectly acceptable to use C such variables to represent C categories.

Examining the Residuals

The topic of examining the sample residuals (values of $Y - \hat{Y}$) was introduced in Section 13.6 for the linear regression model containing one predictor variable. These values can be plotted in **residual plots** to verify the model assumptions discussed on page 609 as well as to identify outliers and observations that are very influential in determining the least squares prediction equation. The process for constructing a residual plot is discussed as it pertains to verifying the model assumptions.

Checking the Model Assumptions.   An important step in a regression analysis is to verify the model assumptions. If one or more of these assumptions are violated, the results of the F test and the t tests discussed in this chapter are, at best, questionable. The procedure for verifying these assumptions is nearly identical to that used in simple linear regression, described in detail in Section 13.6.

- **Checking Assumption 1:** The errors are normally distributed, with a mean of zero. Construct a histogram of the sample residuals. This plot should resemble a normal curve centered at zero. Remember that an exact normal curve is not necessary here, but the inference results from this chapter are suspect if this distribution is severely skewed.

- **Checking Assumption 2:** The variance of the errors remains constant. In Chapter 13, the sample residuals were plotted against the independent variable, X. For the multiple regression analysis, there is more than one independent variable and so one alternative is to plot the residuals versus the predicted ($\hat{Y}$) values. This plot should contain no pattern. This is the shotgun blast appearance illustrated in Figure 11.23(a), where now the horizontal axis is $\hat{Y}$ rather than X. Beware of situations where the larger residuals are associated with the larger $\hat{Y}$ values, as illustrated in Figure 11.23(b), where again the horizontal axis is $\hat{Y}$.

- **Checking Assumption 3:** The errors are independent. This is an important assumption whenever the sample data are obtained in a sequential manner—in particular, across time. Such data are referred to as **time series data,** where, for example, each row (value of Y and the predictor variables) corresponds to a particular year. This assumption can be tested using the Durbin–Watson statistic, introduced in Section 13.6. Equation 13.25 can be used for both single and multiple linear regression and is used to test for significant autocorrelation in the residuals using Table A.9 where k represents the number of independent (predictor) variables.

All is not lost if the Durbin–Watson test concludes that significant autocorrelation is present in the residuals. We do not attempt to describe all the remedies for this situation.* However, the following procedures are often used to modify the model such that the "new" residuals are uncorrelated:

1. Improve the existing model by attempting to discover other significant predictor variables. Because the residuals include the effect of these missing variables, residual autocorrelation often can be improved by including these additional variables. This procedure offers the best solution to the autocorrelation problem but, unfortunately, is easier said than done.

---

*For discussions of these methods, consult B. L. Bowerman and R. T. O'Connell, Forecasting and Time Series: An Applied Approach, 3rd ed., Pacific Grove, Calif: Brooks/Cole, a part of Cengage Learning 2000 and S. Makridakis S. C. Wheelwright, and R. J. Hyndman, Forecasting: Methods and Applications,3rd ed. (New York: Wiley, 1997).

2. Replace y_t by the *first difference* where the new dependent variable is $y_t' = y_t - y_{t-1}$.

3. Replace y_t by the *percentage change* during year t,

$$z_t = \left(\frac{y_t - y_{t-1}}{y_{t-1}} \right) 100$$

Detecting Sample Outliers. As in Chapter 13, we will:

- Detect sample observations with outlying values of the predictor variables using **sample leverages.**

- Detect observations with outlying values of the dependent variable, Y, using the **standardized residuals.**

- Classify an observation as "influential" using the corresponding **Cook's distance measure.**

For the multiple linear regression model, no simple formula exists for the leverage value (h_i) of the ith observation. Nearly all computerized statistical packages will provide you with these leverage values via a simple command. The instructions when using SPSS and MINITAB are contained in the end-of-chapter appendix for Chapter 13. The output using Excel will be shown in upcoming Example 14.8. A *suggested procedure* here is to conclude that an observation has outlying values of the predictor variables *if its leverage value is larger than* $2(k + 1)/n$ *or larger than* $3(k + 1)/n$, where k is the number of predictor variables and n is the number of observations (rows of data). Since MINITAB and the KPK Data Analysis regression procedure within Excel use the "larger than $3(k + 1)/n$" rule, we will use this decision rule in the discussion to follow.

The standardized residual, as in Chapter 13, is defined as

$$\text{Standardized residual} = \frac{Y_i - \hat{Y}_i}{s\sqrt{1 - h_i}}$$

14.20

where $s = \sqrt{\text{MSE}}$ and MSE is as defined in equation 14.10. *A recommended procedure* is to identify an observation as having an outlying value of Y *if its standardized residual is larger than 2 or less than −2*. MINITAB will flag automatically any observation having such a standardized residual.

Influential observations are those that, if removed, result in a considerably different regression equation. Such observations may have been improperly recorded (an error was made) or, if recorded correctly, may be a signal that your model is inadequate. A search for additional predictor variables could be made that, when inserted into the existing model, results in a better "model fit." Influential observations will be identified by using Cook's distance measure, where this measure for the ith observation is defined as

$$D_i = \left(\frac{1}{k+1} \right) \left(\frac{h_i}{1-h_i} \right) (\text{standardized residual})^2$$

$$= \frac{(Y_i - \hat{Y}_i)^2}{(k+1)s^2} \left[\frac{h_i}{(1-h_i)^2} \right]$$

14.21

A *suggested procedure here* is to conclude that the ith observation is influential *if the corresponding* D_i *measure is larger than* DMAX, where DMAX depends on the number of predictor variables and is as specified in Table 14.1. For a more accurate procedure, you can set DMAX $= F_{.5, k+1, n-k-1}$. The values in Table 14.1 closely approximate these median F values.

TABLE

14.1

Critical values for Cook's distance measure, D_i using k predictor variables. An observation is classified as influential if $D_i >$ DMAX.

k	1 or 2	3 or 4	≥ 5
DMAX	.8	.9	1.0

FIGURE

14.20

Excel regression output using KPK Data Analysis (Example 14.8).

	A	B	C	D	E	F	G	H	I
	Invest	Index	Income	SUMMARY OUTPUT				**Maximum**	
1	2500	86	55800					Stand. Resid.	**1.99005**
2	3700	54	60400	Regression Statistics				Leverage	**0.13557**
3	3900	21	72700	Multiple R	0.9478			Cook's D	**0.11589**
4	1700	91	41700	R Square	0.8984				
5	1000	72	35200	Adjusted R Square	0.8941				
6	1700	16	41800	Standard Error	283.0331				
7	2500	81	43700	Observations	50				
8	3400	32	67900						
9	2500	37	53700	ANOVA					
10	2900	89	57400		df	SS	MS	F	Significance F
11	2100	48	47100	Regression	2	33294135.56	16647067.78	207.808	4.5877E-24
12	2600	61	55300	Residual	47	3765064.438	80107.754		
13	1700	33	40000	Total	49	37059200			
14	2100	82	40200						
15	1500	95	36900		Coefficients	Standard Error	t Stat	P-value	
16	1700	73	40700	Intercept	-1183.3183	219.3704	-5.3942	2.194E-06	
17	1400	9	35100	Index	-0.1271	1.5471	-0.0822	9.348E-01	
18	2400	42	50900	Income	0.0720	0.0036	20.0643	1.096E-24	
19	1000	74	36300						
20	3200	31	63700						
21	2500	12	46800						
22	4500	25	75200	RESIDUAL OUTPUT					
23	2400	24	42400						
24	2000	88	42000	Observation	Predicted Invest	Residuals	Standardized Residuals	Leverages	Cook's D
25	2900	53	54600	1	2823.0588	-323.0588	-1.1797	0.0639	0.0317
26	3600	40	61600	2	3158.3038	541.6962	1.9445	0.0312	0.0406
27	2800	81	60000	3	4048.0362	-148.0362	-0.5500	0.0958	0.0107
28	2200	44	50600	4	1807.2959	-107.2959	-0.3951	0.0793	0.0045
29	3800	36	66300	5	1341.7453	-341.7453	-1.2549	0.0742	0.0420
30	4300	50	70900	6	1824.0315	-124.0315	-0.4572	0.0812	0.0062
31	3300	95	66600	7	1952.5570	547.4430	1.9901	0.0553	0.0773

EXAMPLE

14.8

Residual Analysis Using Statistical Software

An analysis of the residuals using the investment data in Example 14.4 follows. Since this sample consists of a random sample of 50 investment clients, and is not time ordered, assumption 3 was not investigated.

Solution

To obtain the Excel output in Figure 14.20, click on **KPK Data Analysis ➤ Regression.** Be sure to click on the boxes for **Residuals, Standardized Residuals, Leverages,** and **Cook's Ds.** The maximum standardized residual, leverage value, and Cook's D are provided in cells I2:I4. To obtain these values, first type in the labels in cells H1:H4 of Figure 14.20. In cell I2, type "=max(G26:G75)" to obtain the maximum standardized residual, since these values occupy cells G26:G75 in Figure 14.20. Repeat this using "=max(H26:H75)" in cell I3 for the maximum leverage and "=max(I26:I75)" in cell I4 for the maximum Cook's D.

A MINITAB histogram of the residuals is shown in Figure 14.21. This graph can be obtained as part of the regression analysis by clicking on **Graphs ➤ Individual Plots** and checking **Histogram of residuals.** Except for a slight positive skew, the residuals appear

FIGURE

14.21

MINITAB histogram of the residuals (Example 14.8).

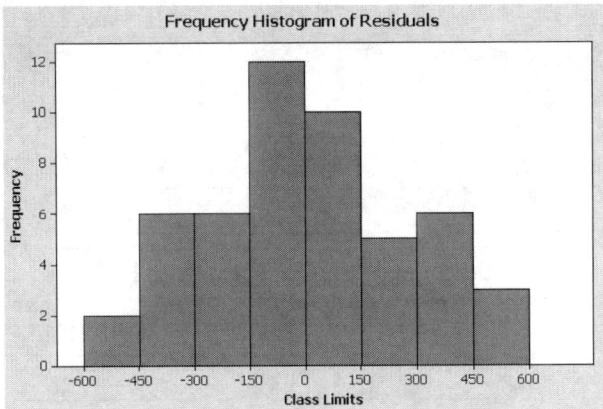

FIGURE

14.22

SPSS residual plot for Example 14.8.

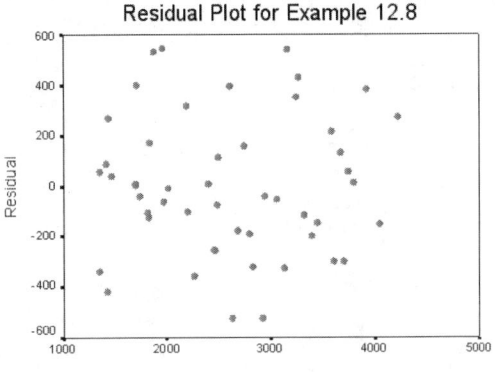

to be approximately normally distributed, centered at zero, and so we conclude that assumption 1 is satisfied.

An SPSS plot of the residuals versus the predicted Y values ($\hat{Y}$ values) is shown in Figure 14.22. When you click on **Save** and check **Unstandardized Predicted Values** and **Unstandardized Residuals,** these values will be stored as two additional columns in the data window. The scatterplot can be obtained by clicking on **Graphs ➤ Scatter ➤ Simple.** No pattern is observed in this plot and assumption 2 appears to be satisfied.

Using the maximum values in the upper right corner of Figure 14.20, we see that none of the standardized residuals is greater than 2 in absolute value, and so there are no observations with an outlying Y value. None of the leverage (h_i) values exceed $3(2 + 1)/50 = 9/50 = .18$, and so there are no observations with unusually large or small values of the predictor variables. Finally, there are no influential observations, since all of the Cook's distance measures are less than .8 (from Table 14.1).

Prediction Using Multiple Regression

Once a regression equation has been derived, its primary application generally is to derive predicted values of the dependent variable. Computer packages provide an easy method of deriving such an estimate. To illustrate, consider the regression equation we developed for the real-estate data. For this illustration we include X_3 = years of formal education,

FIGURE

14.23

Prediction for new data using Excel and KPK Data Analysis.

Refer to Figure 14.2 for the input data.

	E	F	G	H	I	J	K	L	M
1	SUMMARY OUTPUT								
2									
3	Regression Statistics								
4	Multiple R	0.9515							
5	R Square	0.9053							
6	Adjusted R Square	0.8579							
7	Standard Error	2.0355							
8	Observations	10							
9									
10	ANOVA								
11		df	SS	MS	F	Significance F			
12	Regression	3	237.5416	79.1805	19.1115	0.00179			
13	Residual	6	24.8584	4.1431					
14	Total	9	262.4						
15									
16		Coefficients	Standard Error	t Stat	P-value	Lower 95%	Upper 95%		
17	Intercept	5.6567	2.8342	1.9959	0.0930	-1.2783	12.5918		
18	Income	0.1939	0.0877	2.2107	0.0691	-0.0207	0.4085		
19	FamSize	2.3381	0.9078	2.5756	0.0420	0.1168	4.5594		
20	YrsEduc	-0.1628	0.2441	-0.6669	0.5296	-0.7600	0.4345		
21									
22									
23									
24	X Variable 1	X Variable 2	X Variable 3	Predicted Value	Std Error Prediction	Lower 95% Mean	Upper 95% Mean	Lower 95% Predict	Upper 95% Predict
25	46	4	8	22.625	1.3555	19.309	25.942	16.641	28.609

although, as we demonstrated in Section 14.2, this variable could be dropped without any significant loss in the prediction of home size. The resulting prediction equation was

$$\hat{Y} = 5.657 + .194X_1 + 2.338X_2 - .163X_3$$

Consider a situation in which

$$X_1 = \text{income} = 46 \text{ (thousands of dollars)}$$

$$X_2 = \text{family size} = 4$$

$$X_3 = \text{years of formal education} = 8 \text{ (years)}$$

The predicted home size (Y) here is

$$\hat{Y} = 5.657 + .194(46) + 2.338(4) - .163(8) = 22.63 \text{ (2,263 square feet)}$$

Using Statistical Software to Construct Confidence and Prediction Intervals. Excel does not provide confidence and prediction intervals in its statistical tool package, but the KPK Data Analysis add-ins will allow you to compute these intervals. Referring to Figure 14.2, the new observation ($X_1 = 46$, $X_2 = 4$, $X_3 = 8$) can be typed into cells B12, C12, and D12. Click on **KPK Data Analysis ➤ Regression** and enter B1:D11 as the **Contiguous X Range** and A1:A11 as the **Y Range.** The Excel output in Figure 14.23 was generated by clicking on the check box inside the **Confidence Intervals for the Mean of Y and Prediction Intervals for Y** frame and entering B12:D12 as the range of new observations. The only available confidence level is 95%.

The MINITAB intervals in Figure 14.24 can be generated using **Stat ➤ Regression ➤ Regression.** Insert the new observations in the final row of the data and use * as the missing Y value. Click on **Options,** enter the three predictor variables in the **Prediction intervals for new observations box,** and check the four boxes under **Storage.** The output in Figure 14.24 contains the predicted values (PFIT1), the standard errors of the predicted values (PSDF1), the 95% confidence limits for the mean (CLIM1 and CLIM2), and the 95% prediction limits (PLIM1 and PLIM2).

The SPSS intervals in Figure 14.25 can be obtained by clicking on **Analyze ➤ Regression ➤ Linear.** Enter the new observations in the final row of the data, leaving the Y value blank. Click on **Save** and check the boxes alongside **Predicted Values (Unstandardized)** and **S.E. of mean predictions.** Click on the boxes alongside **Mean** and **Individual** inside the **Prediction Intervals** frame. The value 95 should be entered in the **Confidence Interval** box. The output in Figure 14.25 contains the predicted values (pre_1), the standard errors

FIGURE

14.24

Prediction for new data using MINITAB.

↓	C1	C2	C3	C4	C5	C6	C7	C8	C9	C10
	Footage	Income	FamSize	YrsEduc	PFIT1	PSDF1	CLIM1	CLIM2	PLIM1	PLIM2
1	16	32	2	4	15.886	1.193	12.967	18.805	10.113	21.659
2	17	36	2	8	16.010	1.161	13.170	18.851	10.277	21.744
3	26	55	3	7	22.195	0.975	19.810	24.580	16.673	27.717
4	24	47	4	0	24.121	1.300	20.940	27.303	18.211	30.031
5	22	38	4	2	22.051	1.371	18.695	25.407	16.045	28.057
6	21	60	3	10	22.676	1.331	19.420	25.932	16.725	28.627
7	32	66	6	8	31.179	1.854	26.644	35.715	24.443	37.915
8	18	44	3	8	19.900	0.949	17.577	22.222	14.404	25.395
9	30	70	5	2	30.593	1.608	26.660	34.527	24.247	36.940
10	20	50	3	6	21.388	0.767	19.512	23.264	16.066	26.710
11	*	46	4	8	22.625	1.355	19.309	25.942	16.641	28.609

FIGURE

14.25

Prediction for new data using SPSS.

	footage	income	famsize	yrseduc	pre_1	sep_1	lmci_1	umci_1	lici_1	uici_1
1	16	32	2	4	15.886	1.193	12.967	18.805	10.113	21.659
2	17	36	2	8	16.010	1.161	13.170	18.851	10.277	21.744
3	26	55	3	7	22.195	.975	19.810	24.580	16.673	27.717
4	24	47	4	0	24.121	1.300	20.940	27.303	18.211	30.031
5	22	38	4	2	22.051	1.371	18.695	25.407	16.045	28.057
6	21	60	3	10	22.676	1.331	19.420	25.932	16.725	28.627
7	32	66	6	8	31.179	1.854	26.644	35.715	24.443	37.915
8	18	44	3	8	19.900	.949	17.577	22.222	14.404	25.395
9	30	70	5	2	30.593	1.608	26.660	34.527	24.247	36.940
10	20	50	3	6	21.388	.767	19.512	23.264	16.066	26.710
11		46	4	8	22.625	1.355	19.309	25.942	16.641	28.609

of the predicted values (sep_1), the 95% confidence limits for the mean (lmci_1 and umci_1), and the 95% prediction limits (lici_1 and uici_1).

In all three computer outputs, the predicted Y value is $\hat{Y} = 22.625$. This agrees with the previous result.

Confidence and Prediction Intervals.   In the preceding illustration, what does $\hat{Y} = 22.625$ estimate? For ease of notation, let X_0 represent the set of X values used for this estimate; that is, $X_0 = (46, 4, 8)$, where $X_1 = 46$, $X_2 = 4$, and $X_3 = 8$. This value of $\hat{Y}$ estimates (1) the averagehome size of all families with this specific set of X values, written $\mu_{Y|X_0}$ and (2) the home size for an individual family having this specific set of X values, written Y_{X_0}.

Using the notation from Chapter 13, let

$s_{\hat{Y}}$ = standard deviation (standard error) of the predicted Y mean

To determine the reliability of this particular point estimate, $\hat{Y}$, you can (1) derive a **confidence interval** for $\mu_{Y|X_0}$ if your intent is to estimate the averagevalue of Y given X_0 (not the usual situation) or (2) derive a **prediction interval** for Y_{X_0} if the purpose is to forecast an individual value of Y given this specific set of values for the predictor variables. In business applications, deriving a specific forecast is, by far, the more popular use of linear regression.

These intervals are summarized as follows. A $(1 - \alpha) \cdot 100\%$ confidence interval for $\mu_{Y|X_0}$ is

$$\hat{Y} - t_{\alpha/2,n-k-1} s_{\hat{Y}} \quad \text{to} \quad \hat{Y} + t_{\alpha/2,n-k-1} s_{\hat{Y}}$$

14.22

A $(1 - \alpha) \cdot 100\%$ prediction interval for Y_{X_0} is

$$\hat{Y} - t_{\alpha/2,n-k-1}\sqrt{s^2 + s_{\hat{Y}}^2} \quad \text{to} \quad \hat{Y} + t_{\alpha/2,n-k-1}\sqrt{s^2 + s_{\hat{Y}}^2}$$

14.23

where s^2 is the MSE value in the regression ANOVA table and is defined in equation 14.4.

The standard deviation of the predicted Y mean is labeled StdErrorPrediction (Excel), PSDF1 (MINITAB), or sep_1 (SPSS). Using the three preceding computer outputs, this value is highlighted and is equal to $s_{\hat{Y}} = 1.3555$. The 95% confidence interval for $\mu_{Y|X_0}$ is derived by first using Table A.5 to obtain $t_{\alpha/2,n-k-1} = t_{.025,10-3-1} = t_{.025,6} = 2.447$. The resulting confidence interval is

$$22.625 - (2.447)(1.3555) \quad \text{to} \quad 22.625 + (2.447)(1.3555)$$
$$= 22.625 - 3.317 \quad \text{to} \quad 22.625 + 3.317$$
$$= 19.308 \quad \text{to} \quad 25.942$$

Consequently, we have estimated the average home size for families with $X_1 = 46$, $X_2 = 4$, $X_3 = 8$ to within 331.7 square feet of the actual mean with 95% confidence. This interval is highlighted in the three preceding computer printouts. Note that the more accurate lower limit is 19.309.

The prediction interval from equation 14.23 is derived by using MSE = 4.1431 from Figure 14.23 to obtain

$$22.625 - 2.447\sqrt{4.1431 + (1.3555)^2} \quad \text{to} \quad 22.625 + 2.447\sqrt{4.1431 + (1.3555)^2}$$
$$= 22.625 - 5.984 \quad \text{to} \quad 22.625 + 5.984$$
$$= 16.641 \quad \text{to} \quad 28.609$$

This means that we have predicted the home size of an individual family with $X_1 = 46$, $X_2 = 4$, and $X_3 = 8$ to within 598.4 square feet of the actual value with 95% confidence. This interval is also highlighted in the three preceding computer printouts.

X Exercises 14.39–14.54

Understanding the Mechanics

14.39 Let Y be the annual salary, in thousands of dollars, of a salesperson. Let X_1 be the years of experience of the salesperson. A salesperson's pay can come from salary, commission, or a combination of the two. Let $X_2 = 1$ if the salesperson is strictly on commission and $X_2 = 0$ if not. Let $X_3 = 1$ if the salesperson is on a combination of salary and commission and $X_3 = 0$ if not. From 20 observations a prediction equation was found to be $\hat{Y} = 7 + 5X_1 + 4X_2 + 7X_3$.
   a. What is the predicted salary of a salesperson with five years' experience who is working strictly on commissions?
   b. What is the predicted salary of a salesperson with five years' experience who is working on a combination of salary and commissions?
   c. What is the predicted salary of a salesperson with five years' experience who is working strictly on salary?
   d. Test the hypothesis that the dummy variables improve the prediction of a salesperson's salary. Assume that R^2 for the model including only X_1 is .70 and that R^2 for the complete model is .80. Use a .05 significance level.

Applying the New Concepts

14.40 If an economist is interested in examining the relationship between household income and household recreational expenses over time, then the economist would use *time series* data. However, if an economist is interested in estimating household recreational expenses as a function of household income, then he or she would use *cross-sectional* data. A set of cross-sectional data were collected from a sample of 30 households in a large metropolitan area. The independent variables are yearly household income (in thousands), X_1, and house payment (either rent or mortgage), X_2. The dependent variable was annual household recreational expenses. The least squares line is $\hat{Y} = 51.3 + 12.3X_1 + .11X_2$. Given that the standard deviations of the estimates of the coefficients of X_1 and X_2 are 5.59 and .048, test the hypothesis that the variable X_1 contributes to the prediction of Y, given that X_2 is in the model. Also, test that X_2 contributes to the prediction of Y, given that X_1 is in the model. Use a .05 significance level.

14.41 An operations manager has collected data on four variables used to predict the cost of employee turnover (Y). Perform a backward regression procedure using a significance level of 10% to determine which variables contribute to the prediction of Y. Start by developing a model with all the independent variables in the model. Then remove the independent variable with the largest p-value provided that the p-value is greater than .10 and create a new model with the remaining independent variables. Repeat this procedure with the new model by removing the independent variable with the largest p-value that is greater than .10 and again developing a new model with the remaining variables. When all the independent variables have p-values less than .10, then this is the final model selected using the backward regression procedure.

Y	X_1	X_2	X_3	X_4
27	3	3	12	23
23	5	4	14	25
30	6	5	17	20
24	7	6	22	22
27	7	7	28	33
22	5	7	45	39
11	4	8	34	50
22	3	3	25	60
16	2	6	22	76
11	1	8	25	88

14.42 Data are collected for the variables Y, X_1, and X_2. A computer printout of the correlation matrix is:

$$\begin{array}{c c c c} & Y & X_1 & X_2 \\ Y & \begin{bmatrix} 1 \\ X_1 & .49 \\ X_2 & .30 \end{bmatrix} & \begin{matrix} .49 & .30 \\ 1 & .12 \\ .12 & 1 \end{matrix} \end{array}$$

a. Which independent variable, X_1 or X_2, would be selected first in a forward regression procedure?
b. Which independent variable, X_1 or X_2, would be a better predictor of Y? Why?

14.43 The following is a correlation matrix for three independent variables and one dependent variable:

$$\begin{array}{c c c c c} & Y & X_1 & X_2 & X_3 \\ Y & \begin{bmatrix} 1 \\ X_1 & .25 \\ X_2 & .36 \\ X_3 & .59 \end{bmatrix} & \begin{matrix} .25 & .36 & .59 \\ 1 & .54 & .22 \\ .54 & 1 & .31 \\ .22 & .31 & 1 \end{matrix} \end{array}$$

a. Which independent variable would be chosen for the first stage of a forward regression procedure?
b. Which independent variable would be chosen for the first step of a stepwise regression procedure?

14.44 The least squares regression equation

$$\hat{Y} = 1.5 + 3.5X_1 + 7.5X_2 - 150X_3$$

has the following t values for the independent variables:

Null Hypothesis	t Statistic
$\beta_1 = 0$	4.5
$\beta_2 = 0$	1.89
$\beta_3 = 0$	1.52

Twenty observations were used in calculating the least squares equation. In the first stage of a backward selection procedure, which independent variable would be eliminated first? Use a 5% level of significance.

14.45 Describe the main difference between the forward selection procedure and the stepwise selection procedure in regression analysis.

14.46 Football team valuation experts assess the value of a team on several factors, including the stadium in which they play. Several teams have increased their value by moving into taxpayer-paid stadiums. Gate receipts contribute to revenue and player costs affect operating income. The following table presents the current value of 10 randomly selected football franchises, their current value, annual revenue in millions of dollars, and operating income in millions of dollars.

Franchise	Current Value	Revenue	Operating Income
Tampa Bay Buccaneers	582	146	35.5
Tennessee Titans	536	134	41.5
Cincinnati Bengals	479	120	14.5
St. Louis Rams	448	124	25.2
New York Jets	423	121	17.1
San Francisco 49ers	419	120	26.1
Philadelphia Eagles	405	116	6.7
Chicago Bears	362	113	3.3
Arizona Cardinals	342	107	5.1
Atlanta Falcons	338	113	5.0

a. Do the variables revenue and operating income contribute to the prediction of the current value of a football franchise. Use a 5% significance level.
b. Compute the coefficient of determination for the model obtained in part a and interpret it.
c. Find the standardized residual for each observation.
d. Remove any observation having a standardized residual less than –2 or greater than 2 and use the remaining observations to compute the least squares line. How does the coefficient of variation for this model compare to that obtained in part b?
e. Using the model obtained in part d, find a 95% prediction interval for the current value of a franchise with a revenue of $120 million and operating income of $20 million.

(Source: "Team Valuations," *Forbes*, September 2001, pp. 82–86.)

14.47 Which of the standard assumptions of regression appear to have been violated in the data from the following table, which lists the dependent variable and the residual values?

Y	$Y - \hat{Y}$	$\hat{Y}$	$Y - \hat{Y}$
1.5	.12	5.0	−1.45
2.1	−.70	5.5	1.61
3.5	−.91	6.0	1.79
4.0	1.02	7.0	−2.40
4.5	−1.18	7.5	2.10

14.48 How should a graph of the residuals $(Y - \hat{Y})$ plotted against the predicted values $\hat{Y}$ look if the standard assumptions of regression are satisfied?

14.49 A set of 20 observations is used to obtain the least squares line

$$\hat{Y} = 1.5 + 3.6X_1 + 4.9X_2$$

a. Given that the estimated standard deviation of Y at X_1 = 1.0 and X_2 = 2.0 is 3.4, find a 90% confidence interval for the mean value of Y at X_1 = 1.0 and X_2 = 2.0.

b. Given that the MSE from this analysis is 21.5, then, using the information in part a, find a 90% prediction interval for an individual value of Y at X_1 = 1.0 and X_2 = 2.0.

14.50 The first quarter of 1998 saw the Standard & Poor's 500 Index surge nearly 14%. Nine of the 14 major brokerage firms did even better than the index in recommending companies to investors. Investors are often interested in whether a brokerage firm's previous performance can be used to predict current performance. Let Y represent the current quarter's performance. Let X_1 and X_2 represent the performance for one year and five years, respectively. Consider the performance data below for 14 major brokerage houses. Performance is measured in percentage.

Firm	Quarter Ending 3/31/98 (Y)	One Year Performance (X_1)	Five-Year Performance (X_2)
Lehman Brothers	16.6	62.4	162.4
Everen	12.5	59.4	177.0
A. G. Edwards	18.0	58.1	239.7
Wheat First	22.6	57.8	175.0
Edwards Jones	15.8	56.8	152.4
Raymond James	16.5	56.4	247.4
Prudential	14.7	56.0	127.6
Paine Weber	21.0	53.1	292.2
Goldman Sachs	12.6	50.1	169.4
Merril Lynch	14.5	46.2	200.1
Credit Suisse F. B.	11.6	46.2	178.3
Bear Stearns	14.4	45.7	177.9
Salomon S. B.	11.5	44.3	172.0
Morgan Stanley	13.6	39.0	125.4

a. The prediction equation for these data is $\hat{Y} = -.342 + .1982X_1 + .0291X_2$. Predict Y for each of the brokerage houses.

b. Calculate the residuals $Y - \hat{Y}$ for each firm.

c. Calculate the residual standard deviation.

d. How many residuals lie within two standard deviations of the mean of the error terms? How many observations would you expect to lie outside of two standard deviations, assuming that the residuals are approximately normally distributed?

(Source: "Brokerage Houses' Stock Picks Sparkle," Wall Street Week, May 7, 1998, p. C1.)

14.51 Explain the difference between a confidence interval for the mean value of Y at particular values of the independent variables and a prediction interval for a future value of Y at particular values of the independent variables. Will the prediction interval for Y always be larger than the corresponding confidence interval for particular values of the independent variables?

Using the Computer

14.52 **[DATA SET EX14-52]** Variable Description:

Location: Location of exclusive property in the Houston and surrounding area

Price: Price for exclusive property advertised in The Wall Street Journal

Bedrooms: Number of bedrooms in the house

Sqfootage: Square footage of living space in the house

Real-estate agents use The Wall Street Journal to advertise exceptional properties to gain maximum exposure to potential buyers outside a local area. A random sample of 20 properties in the Houston metropolitan area are selected, and the price, number of bedrooms, and square footage are recorded.

a. Create a dummy variable that is equal to 1 if the property has five or more bedrooms and 0 if it has less than five bedrooms. Do Sqfootage and the dummy variable contribute to the prediction of the price of the property? Use a 10% significance level.

b. What is a 95% prediction interval for a six-bedroom house with 4,700 square feet?

c. Can you identify any observations with a standardized residual larger than 2 or less than −2?

(Source: "Distinctive Properties & Estates," The Wall Street Journal, June 22, 2001, p. W15F.)

14.53 **[DATA SET EX14-53]** Variable Description:

Magazine: Name of widely circulated magazine

TotalRev: Total revenue for the magazine from all sources

AdRev: Revenue from advertisements in the magazine

SubscriberRev: Revenue for the magazine from subscribers

Magazines obtain revenue from advertisements, subscribers, newsstands, and general circulation. The amount of revenue from advertisements and subscribers tends to be rather stable for most widely circulated magazines. To understand the relationship between AdRev and SubscriberRev in predicting TotalRev, 16 widely circulated magazines were randomly selected. Data for each of the variables were recorded in units of thousands of dollars.

    a. Using a significance level of 1%, comment on the contribution of AdRev and SubscriberRev in predicting TotalRev.

    b. Interpret the 95% prediction interval for a magazine's total revenue given that the revenue from advertisements is $200,000 and the revenue from subscribers is $100,000.

    c. Are there any influential observations? If so, eliminate the most influential observation and comment on the increase or decrease in the coefficient of determination.

(Source: "Top 300 Magazines by Gross Revenue," *Advertising Age*, June 16, 1997, p. S6.)

14.54 **[DATA SET EX14-54]** Variable Description:

Funding: Level of funding approved for research proposal

Theory: Score on theoretical soundness

Usefulness: Score on usefulness of applications

Reviewer: 1 if reviewer is from the business research center and 0 if the reviewer is external to the center

A business research center collects data on research proposals submitted for funding. Using the variables in this data set, find and interpret a 95% confidence interval for the mean level of funding for a proposal with scores of 7 for theoretical soundness and 7 for usefulness in applications reviewed within the research center. Check the distribution of the residuals of the least squares line for predicting Funding with the variables Theory, Usefulness, and Reviewer by constructing a histogram of the residuals.

14.5

MODEL BUILDING

Linear regression models can provide you with a variety of predictive equations that attempt to explain the behavior of a particular dependent variable. These go beyond the straight line obtained in Chapter 13 and the flat plane of this chapter, using two independent (predictor) variables, illustrated in Figure 14.1. This section will introduce you to the more flexible linear models, which include the effect of **interaction terms** and **quadratic terms.**

Interaction Effects

An interaction effect between two predictor variables, say, X_1 and X_2, implies that how these two variables occur together has an impact on the prediction of the dependent variable. A linear regression model containing two predictor variables and an interaction term can be written

$$Y = \beta_0 + \beta_1 X_1 + \beta_2 X_2 + \beta_3 X_1 X_2 + e$$

14.24

where the interaction term is the product of X_1 and X_2, and e is the error associated with the model. Since the error term is assumed to have a mean of zero, an alternate form of this model is

$$\mu_Y = \beta_0 + \beta_1 X_1 + \beta_2 X_2 + \beta_3 X_1 X_2$$

14.25

where μ_Y is the mean of the random variable Y.

    To illustrate an interaction effect, consider the model

$$\mu_Y = 10 + 15X_1 + 4X_2 - 5X_1 X_2$$

FIGURE

14.26

Illustration of
interaction effect.
(a) Interaction is
present in the
model $\mu_Y = 10 + 15X_1 + 4X_2 - 5X_1X_2$.
(b) Interaction is
absent in the
model $\mu_Y = 10 + 15X_1 + 4X_2$.

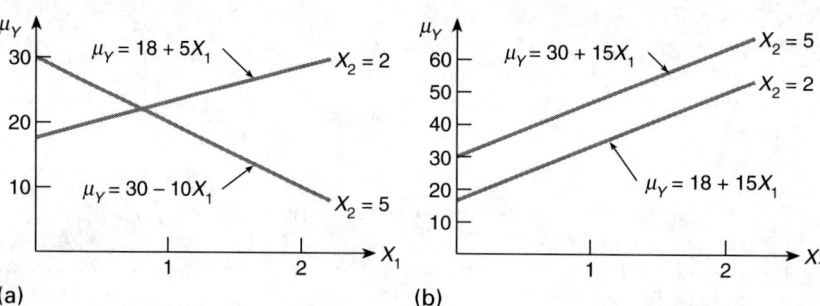

(a)   (b)

Suppose we set $X_2 = 2$. Then we have

$$\mu_Y = 10 + 15X_1 + 4(2) - 5X_1(2)$$
$$= 10 + 15X_1 + 8 - 10X_1$$
$$= 18 + 5X_1$$

For $X_2 = 5$, the model becomes

$$\mu_Y = 10 + 15X_1 + 4(5) - 5X_1(5)$$
$$= 10 + 15X_1 + 20 - 25X_1$$
$$= 30 - 10X_1$$

These two lines are shown in Figure 14.26(a). Due to presence of the interaction term, the relationship between Y and X_1 is highly dependent on the value of X_2. This is not the case if the interaction effect is missing from the model, illustrated in Figure 14.26(b). Without the interaction term, the model becomes

$$\mu_Y = 10 + 15X_1 + 4X_2$$

where for $X_2 = 2$, we have $\mu_Y = 10 + 15X_1 + 4(2) = 18 + 15X_1$ and for $X_2 = 5$, the model becomes $\mu_Y = 10 + 15X_1 + 4(5) = 30 + 15X_1$. Notice in Figure 14.26(b) that the two lines are parallel, indicating the absence of an interaction effect between these two variables.

Quadratic Effects

Quadratic effects were discussed in Section 14.3, which introduced curvilinear models. An example of a curvilinear model using a single predictor variable (say, X_1) is

$$Y = \beta_0 + \beta_1X_1 + \beta_2X_1^2 + e$$

Such a model is useful whenever the effect of X_1 is nonlinear; in particular, the change in Y for a given change in X_1 tends to increase or decrease as X_1 gets larger. Such a relationship can be seen in Figure 14.11, where the change in Y tends to slow down for larger values of the predictor variable. Including quadratic terms in the multiple regression model allows you to capture such relationships between the dependent variable and the various predictor variables.

Second-Order Models

The multiple linear regression model introduced in equation 14.1 is

$$Y = \beta_0 + \beta_1 X_1 + \beta_2 X_2 + \ldots + \beta_k X_k + e$$

This model is referred to as a **first-order model,** since no interaction terms or quadratic terms are included.

A **complete second-order model** is one that includes all possible interaction and quadratic terms. For the cases of two and three predictor variables, this model becomes

$$Y = \beta_0 + \beta_1 X_1 + \beta_2 X_2 + \beta_3 X_1 X_2 + \beta_4 X_1^2 + \beta_5 X_2^2 + e$$

$$Y = \beta_0 + \beta_1 X_1 + \beta_2 X_2 + \beta_3 X_3 + \beta_4 X_1 X_2 + \beta_5 X_1 X_3 + \beta_6 X_2 X_3$$
$$+ \beta_7 X_1^2 + \beta_8 X_2^2 + \beta_9 X_3^2 + e$$

14.27 14.28

Such a model is linear in the unknown β parameters, and so is considered to be a multiple linear regression model. It will provide you with a much more powerful modeling tool than will a first-order model. Construction of a second-order model is illustrated in Example 14.9.

Statistical Software Application Use DATA14-9

Construction of a Second-Order Model

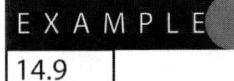

E X A M P L E

14.9

A financial analyst at a major lending institution is interested in predicting the annual sales for defense-related companies. As a possible set of predictor variables, she decides to use the number of employees, current assets, current liabilities, and total assets. Data from a random sample of 50 such industries is contained in dataset DATA14-9, where each column of data is described as follows:

Column	Contains
A	Y = annual sales (units of $10,000,000)
B	X_1 = number of employees (units of 100)
C	X_2 = current assets (units of $100,000)
D	X_3 = current liabilities (units of $100,000)
E	X_4 = total assets (units of $100,000)

Construct an appropriate second-order model based on this set of sample data. Use a significance level of .10.

The first look at the data will be a first-order model containing all four predictor variables. The Excel solution using these variables is shown in Figure 14.27. This output, which includes the four variance inflation factors, can be obtained by clicking on **KPK Data Analysis ➤ Regression.** The **Y Range** is A1:A51, and the (contiguous) **X Range** is B1:E51. Both ranges must include labels in the first row. It will be necessary to click on the box alongside **VIFs.** The variance inflation factors for X_1 and X_3 (highlighted) are both larger than 10, indicating a high correlation between these two variables. This correlation (highlighted in cell G23) is .949. This correlation can be obtained by typing = correl(B2:B51,D2:D51) in cell G23. As a result, it was decided to drop X_3 (current liabilities) from the model, since the analyst, rather arbitrarily, elected to keep the number of employees (X_1) in the prediction equation.

The regression analysis was repeated using X_1, X_2, and X_4 in Figure 14.28. All of the variance inflation factors are now well under 10. Due to the large p-value for X_4 = total assets (highlighted), this variable was dropped from the model. Note: It is possible that an interaction effect exists between X_1 and X_4 or between X_2 and X_4, which will not be detected once X_4 is dropped from the model.

Solution

FIGURE 14.27

Excel regression solution using KPK Data Analysis and all four predictor variables.

	A	B	C	D	E	F	G	H	I	J	K	L	M
1	Sales	Employees	CurAssets	CurLiabil	TotAssets	**SUMMARY OUTPUT**							
2	2.6	17.9	37.0	6.6	67.4								
3	5.1	24.9	8.8	7.4	26.1	Regression Statistics							
4	1.9	12.9	13.3	2.5	40.1	Multiple R	0.96224						
5	2.2	11.3	17.7	3.3	56.6	R Square	0.92590						
6	4.4	18.8	21.8	6.2	80.7	Adjusted R Square	0.91931						
7	2.4	13.6	17.9	2.8	12.3	Standard Error	0.52817						
8	3.1	16.1	27.2	5.6	75.9	Observations	50						
9	5.1	25.4	15.8	7.6	24.7								
10	5.3	23.4	15.1	7.0	13.4	**ANOVA**							
11	2.3	15.5	24.5	5.2	27.8		*df*	*SS*	*MS*	*F*	*Significance F*		
12	6.8	32.9	23.7	10.3	28.3	Regression	4	156.8559	39.2140	140.5677	0.000000		
13	2.5	13.1	49.3	3.2	100.5	Residual	45	12.5536	0.2790				
14	4.7	24.4	23.9	8.2	39.3	Total	49	169.4095					
15	4.8	20.4	17.7	5.9	71.6								
16	3.8	17.9	3.2	6.6	69.9		Coefficients	Standard Error	t Stat	P-value	Lower 95%	Upper 95%	VIF
17	4.4	23.9	9.4	5.8	48.3	Intercept	-0.0098	0.3016	-0.0326	0.9741	-0.6172	0.5975	
18	1.9	10.8	20.5	4.1	78.5	Employees	0.2178	0.0302	7.2193	0.0000	0.1571	0.2786	**10.9718**
19	2.7	13.6	37.2	5.3	23.9	CurAssets	-0.0162	0.0075	-2.1631	0.0359	-0.0313	-0.0011	1.0738
20	4.6	21.6	10.7	8.5	55.0	CurLiabil	-0.0102	0.0883	-0.1151	0.9089	-0.1879	0.1676	**10.8690**
21	5.9	27.9	14.8	8.8	20.7	TotAssets	0.0020	0.0033	0.6261	0.5344	-0.0045	0.0086	1.1321
22	4.8	18.5	18.6	5.6	46.9								
23	9.4	42.8	23.4	13.8	72.2	Corr(X1 and X3)	**0.949**						
24	3.6	19.0	29.2	5.9	57.5								

FIGURE 14.28

SPSS regression solution using X_1, X_2, and X_4.

Coefficients[a]

Model		Unstandardized Coefficients		Standardized Coefficients			Collinearity Statistics	
		B	Std. Error	Beta	t	Sig.	Tolerance	VIF
1	(Constant)	-.0035	.293		-.012	.991		
	Employees	.2145	.009	.956	23.693	.000	.990	**1.010**
	CurAssets	-.0163	.007	-.091	-2.201	.033	.936	**1.068**
	TotAssets	.0020	.003	.026	.623	**.537**	.931	**1.075**

a. Dependent Variable: SALES

FIGURE 14.29

MINITAB regression solution using X_1, X_2, X_1X_2, and quadratic terms.

Regression Analysis

```
The regression equation is
Sales = 1.11 + 0.133 Employees - 0.0394 CurAssets + 0.00231 Emp*Assets
        +0.000686 EmpSQ -0.000289 AssetsSQ

Predictor        Coef        StDev         T        P
Constant       1.1075       0.6910      1.60    0.116
Employee      0.13281      0.04442      2.99    0.005
CurAsset     -0.03944      0.04186     -0.94    0.351
Emp*Assets   0.002313     0.001505      1.54    0.131
EmpSQ       0.0006865    0.0008813      0.78    0.440
AssetsSQ   -0.0002890    0.0005442     -0.53    0.598

S = 0.5066      R-Sq = 93.3%       R-Sq(adj) = 92.6%

Analysis of Variance

Source            DF          SS          MS          F        P
Regression         5     158.119      31.624     123.24    0.000
Residual Error    44      11.291       0.257
Total             49     169.410
```

In Figure 14.29, the interaction effect between X_1 and X_2 (that is, X_1X_2) along with the quadratic terms (X_1^2 and X_2^2) were included. *Note:* The end-of-chapter appendix contains instructions for building interaction and quadratic terms when using Excel, MINITAB, or SPSS. Referring to the highlighted *p*-values in Figure 14.29, the *p*-values for the quadratic terms appear quite large, and so the analyst decided to re-run the regression analysis without these terms in the model. This output is shown in Figure 14.30.

FIGURE

14.30

Excel regression solution using X_1, X_2, and X_1X_2.

The R^2 value using the five predictors in Figure 14.29 is .933 (highlighted). The R^2 value with the quadratic terms removed is .932 (highlighted in Figure 14.30). Consequently, the two quadratic terms do not contribute significantly to the prediction of sales. This is confirmed using the partial F value, where

$$F^* = \frac{(.933 - .932)/2}{(1 - .933)/(50 - 1 - 5)} = .33$$

which is less than $F_{.10,2,44} \approx 2.44$. The p-values for the remaining three predictors are less than .10, and so the resulting prediction equation is

$$\hat{Y} = 1.0820 + 0.1543X_1 - 0.0622X_2 + 0.0029X_1X_2$$

The final step in the analysis would be to examine the residuals, as outlined in Example 14.8.

X Exercises 14.55–14.60

Understanding the Mechanics

14.55 Consider a regression model with a continuous independent variable X_1 and with an independent variable X_2 that is equal to 1 for training method A and 0 for training method B. Twenty observations were used to yield the following prediction equation.

$$\hat{Y} = 10.1 + 5X_1 + 8X_2 - 10X_1X_2$$

a. For training method A, what is the prediction equation?

b. For training method B, what is the prediction equation?

c. Are the prediction lines parallel in parts a and b?

14.56 Consider the following two regression models that were fit using 25 observations:

Model 1: $\hat{Y} = 13 + 2X_1 + 3X_2 + 6X_1^2 + 7X_2^2 - 20X_1X_2$

Model 2: $\hat{Y} = 10 + 14X_1 + 2X_2$

a. What terms in Model 1 indicate a quadratic effect?

b. If the coefficients of determination for Model 1 and Model 2 are .61 and .52, respectively, do the second-order terms contribute to the prediction of Y in Model 1? Use a .05 significance level.

Applying the New Concepts

14.57 A marketing researcher is interested in how advertising (X_1) and price (X_2) affect sales (Y). In a computer printout of a regression analysis, the p-values for X_1 and X_2 are .002 and .011, respectively. In a regression model with interaction, the p-values for X_1, X_2, and X_1X_2 are .082, .351, and .013, respectively. Why do you think that the p-value associated with X_1 and X_2 changed?

14.58 Stocks with fast-growing earnings are usually classified as growth stocks. Stocks that have low P/E ratios and that are believed to be undervalued are categorized as value stocks. A sample of 16 top-performing midcap mutual funds—eight value-oriented mutual funds and eight growth-oriented mutual funds—are selected. The following table displays the percent return of these mutual funds during the second quarter of 2001 and during the first six months of 2001.

Midcap Growth	Six-Month Return	Quarterly Return
Baron Growth	9.4	18.7
Wasatch Ultra Growth	9.4	36.5
Westcore Select	9.3	21.4
Federated Kaufmann K	7.5	14.4
Oak Ridge Sm Cap Eqty A	3.5	14.7
Value Line Emerg Opptys	2.5	18.2
Heritage Aggr Growth A	1.9	13.7
Quant Sm Cap Shs	1.8	14.3
Midcap Value		
CGM Tr Focus Fund	26.0	19.7
Columbia Strategic Value	24.4	16.5
Al Frank Fund	22.8	14.9
MassMutual Inst Foc VI A	21.8	14.1
TCW Galileo Val Op Instl	20.4	16.7
Diamond Hill Focus A	19.7	12.0
Merrill Mid Cap Val A	18.1	15.2
Legg Maso Inv Oppty Prm	17.7	11.5

a. Is there sufficient evidence that a dummy variable representing the classification of growth or value orientation and the variable representing quarterly return contribute to the prediction of a mutual fund's six-month return? Use a 5% significance level.

b. Add the square of quarterly return and the interaction of the dummy variable representing growth or value classifications with quarterly return to the model in part a. Test that these additional terms contribute to the model when the dummy variable and the quarterly return variable are in the model. Use a 5% significance level.

(Source: "USA Today's Midyear Stock Mutual Fund Report," USA Today, July 5, 2001, p. 7B.)

14.59 [DATA SET EX14-59] Variable Description:

Age: Age in years of person applying for term insurance

InsuranceLevel: Indicator variable equal to 0 or 1 for $100,000 or $500,000 of insurance, respectively

Gender: Indicator variable equal to 0 or 1 for male or female, respectively

MonthlyRate: Monthly premium for insurance

Term insurance rates have trended lower over the past couple of decades as the life expectancy of Americans has increased. A sample of term insurance quotes for 63 randomly selected individuals was collected. These rates assume that individuals are healthy and are nonsmokers.

a. Construct quadratic and interaction terms to predict the monthly premium of an individual. In the model include the independent variables Age, InsuranceLevel, Gender, the square of Age, the interaction of Age and InsuranceLevel, and the interaction of Age and Gender. Use the p-values to determine whether these independent variables contribute to the prediction of the monthly premium.

b. Remove the two observations that you believe are the most influential and repeat part a. Compare the MSE for this model with the regression model in part a.

(Source: "Affordable Life Insurance," Kiplinger's Personal Finance, August 2001, p. 61.)

14.60 [DATA SET EX14-60] Variable Description:

Tasktime: Time required to complete a task

Aptitude: Score on aptitude test

Exper: On-the-job experience

A manager in charge of a production process is interested in the amount of time, Y, in minutes (Tasktime) that it takes a production worker to perform a certain task relative to his or her score on an aptitude test (Aptitude) and relative to the person's on-the-job experience (Exper) in years. The manager uses a first-order regression model with Aptitude and Exper to predict Tasktime. In addition, the manager uses a second-order regression model with Aptitude, the square of Aptitude, Exper, the square of Exper, and the interaction of Aptitude and Exper. Test that the second-order terms contribute to the model using a 5% significance level.

 Summary

Multiple linear regression offers a method of predicting (or modeling) the behavior of a particular dependent variable (Y) using two or more independent (predictor) variables. To use this technique properly, you must pay special attention to the assumptions behind it: (1) the regression errors follow a normal distribution, centered at zero, with a common variance, and (2) the errors are statistically independent.

To determine the adequacy of the regression model, you can test the entire set of predictor variables using an F test and the contribution of an individual predictor variable can be tested using a t statistic. The coefficient of determination, R^2, describes the percentage of the total variation in the sample Y values explained by this set of predictor variables. To determine the contribution of a particular subset of the predictor variables, R^2 is computed with all variables included and then with the subset of variables excluded from the regression equation. A partial F test is then used to determine whether the resulting decrease in R^2 is significant.

When a curvilinear pattern exists between two variables, X and Y, this nonlinear relationship often can be modeled by including a quadratic (X^2) term in the regression equation. A linear regression model containing a strictly linear combination of the predictor variables is called a *first order model*. A complete second-order model includes quadratic terms and interaction terms.

The problem of multicollinearity arises in the application of multiple linear regression whenever one or more of the predictor variables are a nearly linear combination of the remaining predictor variables. The most common form of multicollinearity occurs when two predictor variables are highly correlated. The presence of multicollinearity within a specific data set can be detected by computing a variance inflation factor for each predictor variable.

Stepwise techniques allow you to insert variables one at a time into the equation (forward regression), remove them one at a time after initially including all variables in the equation (backward regression), or perform a combination of the two by inserting variables one at a time but removing a variable that has become redundant at any stage (stepwise regression). Once the variables for the model have been selected, residual plots should be obtained (1) to examine the underlying assumptions that are necessary in a regression analysis, and (2) to search for outlying and influential observations.

Dummy variables can be used in a regression application to represent the categories of a qualitative variable (such as city). If all dummy variables are to be inserted into the equation, then $C - 1$ such variables should be defined to represent C categories. If a forward or stepwise selection procedure is used to define the final regression equation, then a better procedure is to define C dummy variables to represent this situation.

A confidence interval is derived whenever the predicted Y value is used to estimate the average value of the dependent variable for a specific set of X values. When the predicted Y value is used to predict an individual value of Y for a specific set of X values, a prediction interval can be used to place bounds on the actual Y value.

✓ Summary of Formulas

$$H_0: \text{all } \beta's = 0$$

$$H_a: \text{at least one } \beta \neq 0$$

$$F = \frac{\text{MSR}}{\text{MSE}} = \frac{R^2/k}{(1-R^2)/(n-k-1)}$$

$$(\text{df} = k \text{ and } n-k-1)$$

$$H_0: \beta_i = 0$$

$$H_a: \beta_i \neq 0$$

$$(\text{or } H_a: \beta_i > 0)$$

$$(\text{or } H_a: \beta_i < 0)$$

$$t = \frac{b_i}{s_{b_i}}$$

$$(\text{df} = n-k-1)$$

Confidence Interval for β_i

$$b_i - t_{\alpha/2,n-k-1}s_{b_i} \quad \text{to} \quad b_i + t_{\alpha/2,n-k-1}s_{b_i}$$

Coefficient of Determination

$$R^2 = 1 - \frac{\text{SSE}}{\text{SST}}$$

where

$$\text{SST} = \Sigma(Y - \bar{Y})^2 = \Sigma Y^2 - \frac{(\Sigma Y)^2}{n}$$

and

$$\text{SSE} = \Sigma(Y - \hat{Y})^2$$

Coefficient of Determination (Adjusted)

$$R^2(\text{adj}) = 1 - \frac{\text{SSE}/(n-k-1)}{\text{SST}/(n-1)}$$

Partial F test

$$H_0: X_i, X_{i+1}, \ldots, X_j \text{ do not contribute}$$

$$H_a: \text{at least one of them contributes}$$

$$F = \frac{(R_c^2 - R_r^2)/v_1}{(1-R_c^2)/v_2}$$

where (1) R_c^2 is the R^2 including the variables in H_0 (the complete model), (2) R_r^2 is the R^2 excluding the variables in H_0 (the reduced model), (3) v_1 = the number of β's in H_0, (4) $v_2 = n - 1 -$ (number of X's in the complete model), and (5) the degrees of freedom for the F statistic are v_1 and v_2.

Variance Inflation Factor for the jth Predictor Variable

$$VIF_j = \frac{1}{1 - R_j^2}$$

where R_j^2 is the coefficient of determination obtained by regressing the jth predictor variable on the remaining $k - 1$ predictor variables.

Standardized Residual

$$\text{Standardized residual} = \frac{Y_i - \hat{Y}_i}{s\sqrt{1 - h_i}}$$

where h_i is the corresponding leverage value, $s = \sqrt{MSE}$, and $MSE = SSE/(n - k - 1)$.

Cook's Distance Measure

$$D_i = \frac{(Y_i - \hat{Y}_i)^2}{(k+1)s^2}\left[\frac{h_i}{(1 - h_i)^2}\right]$$

X Review Exercises 14.61–14.74

14.61 The following information is selected from a computer printout of a multiple regression analysis:

Predictor	Coefficient	S.D.
Constant	–1.0	.396
X_1	4.8	.512
X_2	5.9	.42

Analysis of Variance

Source	df	SS	MS	F
Model	2		147.65	
Residual				
Total	19	314.80		

a. Write the multiple regression equation.
b. What percentage of the total variation in Y is explained by the model?
c. Does the model with X_1 and X_2 contribute to the prediction of Y? Use a .05 significance level.
d. Does X_1 contribute to this model given that X_2 is in the model? Use a .05 significance level.
e. Does X_2 contribute to this model given that X_1 is in the model? Use a .05 significance level.

14.62 A company has opened several outdoor ice-skating rinks and would like to know what factors affect the attendance at the rinks. The manager believes that the following variables affect attendance:

$$X_1 = \text{temperature (forecasted high)}$$

$$X_2 = \text{wind speed (forecasted high)}$$

$$X_3 = 1 \text{ if weekend and 0 otherwise}$$

$$X_4 = X_1 X_2$$

The following least squares model was found from 30 days of data:

$$\hat{Y} = 250 + 4.8X_1 - 30X_2 + 1.3X_3 + 35X_4$$

a. What is the predicted attendance on a weekend if the forecasted high temperature is 28°F and the forecasted high wind speed is 12 miles per hour?

b. If the coefficient of determination for the model is .67, test that the overall model contributes to predicting the attendance at the ice-skating rinks. Use a .05 significance level. What is the value of the adjusted R^2?

c. If the standard deviation of the estimate of the coefficient of X_2 is 2.01, does the variable wind speed contribute to predicting the variation in attendance, assuming that the variables X_1, X_3, and X_4 are in the model? Use a .05 significance level.

14.63 A manager examined a regression analysis with two predictor variables, X_1 and X_2, of the number of videos rented monthly (Y) for 10 months. The regression equation was $\hat{Y} = 97.86 - 1.48X_1 + .38X_2$. The standard errors of the regression coefficients of X_1 and X_2 are .28 and .24, respectively. The values of SST and SSE are 23652.91 and 3597.14, respectively. What conclusions can you make regarding the contribution of the model to predicting Y? What conclusions can you make regarding the contribution of each predictor variable given that the other predictor variable is in the model? Use a 5% significance level.

14.64 A real-estate agent wanted to explore the feasibility of using multiple regression analysis in appraising the value of single-family homes within a certain community. The following variables were used:

$$Y = \text{selling price of a house (in dollars)}$$

$$X_1 = \text{total living area (in square feet)}$$

$$X_2 = \begin{cases} 1 & \text{if in neighborhood 1} \\ 0 & \text{if not} \end{cases}$$

$$X_3 = \begin{cases} 1 & \text{if in neighborhood 2} \\ 0 & \text{if not} \end{cases}$$

$$X_4 = \begin{cases} 1 & \text{if lot size is larger than the typical house lot} \\ 0 & \text{if not} \end{cases}$$

The data are as follows:

Y	X_1	X_2	X_3	X_4	Y	X_1	X_2	X_3	X_4
63,000	2,020	1	0	1	31,350	640	0	1	0
36,000	980	1	0	0	49,400	1,910	0	0	1
44,000	1,230	0	0	1	31,000	900	1	0	0
37,000	980	0	1	0	56,000	1,890	1	0	0
28,000	640	0	1	0	63,500	1,900	0	0	1
28,000	720	0	1	0	49,000	2,080	1	0	1
56,000	2,400	1	0	1	63,000	1,900	0	0	1
28,600	670	0	1	0					

Using a computerized statistical package, find the following:

a. The least squares equation

b. The 95% confidence interval for the coefficient of total living area

c. The 95% prediction interval for selling price given that $X_1 = 1,800$, $X_2 = 1$, $X_3 = 0$, and $X_4 = 0$

d. The overall F test for the model and the resulting conclusion using a 5% significance level.

14.65 To understand how two seemingly unrelated variables can be used to construct a regression equation in which the independent variable is a significant predictor, consider the following. Randomly generate 30 observations for 50 normally distributed random variables having a mean and standard deviation of 0 and 1. Using a statistical computer package, find the correlation matrix for the 50 variables. Pick the two variables with the highest correlations and find the p-value for the F statistic to test if one variable contributes to the prediction of the other. From this result, what precaution would you recommend to someone who is using forward regression to select one variable being regressed on 50 variables?

14.66 The owner of a photographic laboratory would like to explore the relationship between her weekly profits (Y) and

X_1 = number of rolls of film sold

X_2 = number of enlargements given out free for advertising purposes

X_3 = number of prints

X_4 = number of reprints

Several weeks were selected randomly, and the following data were collected.

Y	X_1	X_2	X_3	X_4	Y	X_1	X_2	X_3	X_4
350	50	15	130	50	358	62	17	125	35
414	61	18	150	39	392	55	19	150	36
385	71	12	125	45	415	59	24	157	44
429	86	21	141	36	380	63	28	140	38
415	90	22	133	40					

Use a computerized statistical package.
  a. Find the least squares prediction equation.
  b. Test the null hypothesis that X_4 does not contribute to predicting the variation in Y given that X_1, X_2, and X_3 are already in the model. Use a .05 significance level.
  c. Find the 90% confidence interval for the mean value of Y given $X_1 = 85$, $X_2 = 20$, $X_3 = 135$, and $X_4 = 37$.
  d. Find the coefficient of determination for the complete model and interpret its value.
  e. Examine the residuals. Do you detect any outliers or influential observations?

14.67 When an additional independent variable is added to a regression model, the coefficient of determination can never decrease. Use the following data with the model (a) predicting Y using X_1, (b) predicting Y using X_1 and X_2, and (c) predicting Y using X_1, X_2, and X_3. Record the values of SSE, SST, R^2, R^2 (adj), and MSE. Comment on how these values change each time that a new independent variable is added to the model.

Y	X_1	X_2	X_3
2	4	1	35
3	10	6	15
4	20	11	40
5	22	18	10
6	25	25	45
12	30	31	5

14.68 An operations manager uses five independent variables to predict the productivity of a plant. Suppose that for 26 days the manager collects data and uses these 26 observations to fit a regression equation. Assume that the regression sum of squares is 95.6 and that the error sum of squares is 159.0.
  a. Construct an ANOVA table. Does the overall model contribute to predicting the productivity of the plant? Use a 5% significance level.
  b. Compute the R^2 and interpret its value. What is the value of the adjusted R^2?

14.69 The vice president of operations at an airline company collects performance ratings of each of its supervisors in charge of maintenance of aircraft. Data are collected on the number of hours per month spent studying new maintenance procedures (X_1), their education level (X_2), and the number of years that they have been on the job (X_3). Using 25 supervisors in the field, the operations vice president used a statistical package to obtain an error sum of squares of 43.4005 using all three independent variables to predict the ratings of each supervisor. When only X_1 was used, an error sum of squares of 56.685 was obtained. Assume that the total sum of squares was 70.26. Do the variables X_2 and X_3 contribute to the prediction of supervisor performance ratings? Use a 5% significance level.

14.70 · **[DATA SET EX14-70]** Variable Description:

AskPrice: Asking price of a used Chevrolet Camaro

Age: Car's age in years

Mileage: Car's mileage in thousands of miles

ConditionAverage: Dummy variable equal to 1 for average condition and 0 if not

ConditionPoor: Dummy variable equal to 1 if poor condition and 0 if not

Dealer_Indiv: Dummy variable equal to 1 if dealer sold car and 0 if seller is an individual

Use a forward regression analysis to obtain a model in which the predictor variables contribute to the prediction of AskPrice. Use a 10% significance level. Examine the residuals and determine if any outliers or influential observations are present.

14.71 **[DATA SET EX14-71]** Variable Description:

Company: Name of mid-size US banking company

ROE3yr: Return on Equity by a banking company for the past three years

EPS_GR3yr: Earnings per share growth rate for a banking company for the past three years

Banking companies must adapt to changes in the economy to stay competitive. Many banks monitor the companies to which they make major loans, constantly evaluating cash flow and collateral values. That is, if a bank has an early warning system in place, it can cut its losses to maintain profitability. The ROE (return on equity) represents how well a bank can balance profitability, asset management, and financial leverage.

   a. What is the prediction equation for predicting ROE3yr using EPS_GR3yr and the square of EPS_GR3yr? Does the F test indicate that the model contributes to the prediction of ROE3yr? Use a 5% significance level.
   b. Do the t tests for the individual predictors (EPS_GR3yr and the square of this term) indicate that each of them contribute to the prediction of ROE3yr? Do you suspect that multicollinearity is present? What are the values of the VIF for the independent variables?
   c. Remove the observation that you consider to be most influential. Repeat part a with this observation removed. Did you realize that removing an influential observation could change the conclusion when testing that a model adequately predicts its dependent variable?

(Source: "Mid-Size U.S. Banking Companies Fiscal 1998–2000," U.S. Banker, June 2001, p. 46.)

14.72 **[DATA SET EX14-72]** Variable Description:

SecurityFirm: Name of stock brokerage firm

BattingAverage: A firm's total awards divided by the number of employed analysts

Stock-PickingAwards: Number of awards for picking stocks that outperformed the market

Earnings-ForecastingAwards: Number of awards for being the most accurate firm in forecasting the earnings of certain stocks

Twenty stock brokerage firms were selected, and each firm's batting average, number of stock-picking awards, and earnings-forecasting awards were recorded. The batting average is a score obtained by dividing the firm's total number of awards for many different categories by the number of analysts used by that firm.

a. Develop a complete second order model to predict BattingAverage using Stock-PickingAwards and Earnings-ForecastingAwards. That is, form second-order terms involving quadratic terms and the interaction term and include these in the regression model. At the 5% significance level, is there sufficient evidence to say that the model contributes to the prediction of a firm's batting average?

b. Interpret the R^2 and the R^2 (adj) for this model.

c. Form a model called the reduced model by using only Stock-PickingAwards and Earnings-ForecastingAwards in the model. What is the coefficient of determination for this model?

d. Using the reduced model in part c and the complete model in part a, test that the second order terms contribute to the prediction of a firm's batting average. Use a 5% significance level.

(Source: "Firm by Firm: Tally of Awards Ranks 82 Research Houses," The Wall Street Journal, June 26, 2001, p. R16.)

14.73   [DATA SET EX14-73] Variable Description:

State: Name of State

MedianIncome: Median household income

HousingCostsExceed30%: Percentage of mortgage-paying homeowners whose housing costs exceed 30% of income

EightRoomsOrMore: Percentage of homes with 8 or more rooms

Thirty states are randomly selected and the median household income (Y), percentage of mortgage-paying homeowners whose housing costs exceed 30% of income (X_1), and percentage of homes with eight or more rooms (X_2) are recorded.

a. Test that the regression model using X_1 and X_2 contributes to the prediction of Y. Use the p-value to base your conclusion.

b. Predict the median household income for a state that has 18% of its mortgage-paying homeowners with housing costs exceeding 30% of their income, and 16% of the homes with eight or more rooms.

c. What are the VIF values for the independent variables? Is multicollinearity a problem?

d. Plot the residuals versus X_1. Also, plot the residuals versus X_2. Would you say that the plots appear to be random?

(Source: "Snapshot of U.S. Commuting, Income, Housing," USA Today, August 6, 2001, p. 2A.)

14.74   [DATA SET EX14-74] Variable Description:

Company_Country: Company name and its location

AnnualRevenue: Current yearly revenue in millions of dollars

RevPriorYear: Yearly revenue in millions of dollars during the prior year

ExpandingAgg: An indicator variable that is equal to 1 if the company is expanding aggressively at the international level and 0 if not

A sample of 25 international companies that are heavily invested in the United States are listed with their current and prior years' annual revenue in millions of dollars. An indicator variable is used to denote if the company is expanding aggressively worldwide.

a. Form an interaction term with RevPriorYear and ExpandingAgg by multiplying these two variables. Test that the variables RevPriorYear, ExpandingAgg, and the interaction term contribute to the prediction of current yearly revenue. Use the p-value as a basis for your conclusion.

b. Find a 95% prediction interval for a company's current yearly revenue, given that its prior year's revenue was $18,000 million and the company was expanding aggressively worldwide. Interpret this interval.

c. Which observations would you classify as being influential? Why?

(Source: "The International 500," Forbes, July 23, 2001, p. 136.)

Computer Exercises Using the Databases

Exercise 1—Appendix F

From the database, randomly select 50 observations. Regress the variable HPAYRENT (house payment or apartment/house rent) on the prediction variables INCOME1 (primary income), INCOME2 (secondary income), and FAMLSIZE (size of family). Find the coefficient of determination for the complete model. Find a 90% confidence interval on the mean value of HPAYRENT for families having a principal income of $45,000, a secondary income of $22,000, and a family size equal to three.

Exercise 2—Appendix F

Using the data from the previous problem along with dummy variables representing the LOCATION of the residences, do both a forward regression analysis and a backward regression analysis with a significance level of .10. Compare the two resulting models.

Exercise 3—Appendix G

From the database, randomly select 50 observations. Consider a multiple regression model, where the dependent variable is SALES and predictor variables are COSTSALE (sales cost), EMPLOYEE (number of employees), NETINC (net income), ASSETS, and TOTAL. Using these predictor variables, what percentage of the variation in the SALES values has been explained? Construct a histogram of the residuals. Do the regression assumptions appear to be satisfied?

Exercise 4—Appendix G

Using the data from the previous exercise, perform both a forward regression analysis and a backward regression analysis, with a significance level of .10. Compare the resulting models.

Insights from Statistics in Action

Getting Framed Right Before Your Eyes: Evaluating the Price You Will Pay

The Statistics in Action introductory case study mentioned that *Consumer Reports* surveyed 64,000 consumers to evaluate variables such as service, quality, satisfaction, and speed in delivering a product. *Consumer Reports* lists the median price that consumers paid for a pair of glasses at each of 19 optical stores. Service, quality, satisfaction, and speed in manufacturing the glasses is meas-ured on a five-point scale by consumers. Multiple regression analysis can be used to determine which of these consumer-provided variables differentiate the price of eyewear at the various optical stores. Use the data provided in StatInActChap15.xls to answer the following questions. Lower values for the consumer variables indicate a better rating.

1. From your own experience, which predictor variables—service, quality, satisfaction, and speed—do you believe would be the best predictors of price? Which predictor variable do you believe would make the least contribution to the prediction of price?

2. Conduct a multiple regression analysis using all four predictor variables. Does the overall model contribute to the prediction of price? Use the *p*-value as the basis for your conclusion.

3. Which predictor variables are significant at the 5% level? Find the regression equation removing those independent variables that are not significant at the 5% level.

4. What is the coefficient of determination for the model in question 2? Compare this to the coefficient of determination in question 3, with the nonsignificant variables removed. Is there much of a change in the coefficient of determination? Would you have expected the coefficient of determination to change much?

5. Find a 95% confidence interval for the mean value of the price of eyewear for optical stores in which quality and satisfaction were rated 3 and 2. Interpret this interval.

(Sources: "Need Reading Glasses? Welcome to Middle Age," *The New York Times*, June 8, 2004, p. F5. "Clear Choices," *Consumer Reports*, June 2001, p. 10–15. "Glasses That Change With Your Prescription," *Business Week*, March 12, 2001, p. 97.)

Appendix

Data Analysis with Excel, MINITAB, and SPSS

Excel

Multiple Linear Regression

Performing multiple linear regression is similar to performing simple linear regression. The same dialog boxes are used. The independent variables must be in contiguous columns unless the **Regression** dialog box in **KPK Data Analysis** is used and the **Noncontiguous X Range** button is clicked. A check box is provided on the **Regression** dialog box to display **VIFs.**

Building Quadratic and Interaction Terms

Quadratic and interaction terms can be easily constructed in Excel. As displayed in the spreadsheet, type the formulas for the square and interaction of two variables to create these terms. Drag the formula to compute the square and interaction terms for each observation.

	A	B	C	D
1	Income	FamilySize	IncomeSq	Income_FamilySize
2	32	2	=A2*A2	=A2*B2
3	36	2	=A3*A3	=A3*B3
4	55	3	=A4*A4	=A4*B4
5	47	4	=A5*A5	=A5*B5
6	38	4	=A6*A6	=A6*B6
7	60	3	=A7*A7	=A7*B7

Stepwise Procedures

Excel does not have an automatic stepwise, backward, or forward regression procedure. However, for models with few variables, these procedures can be implemented manually by using the **Noncontiguous X Range** button to select variables to enter into the model.

Minitab

Multiple Linear Regression

Perform multiple linear regression by using the same procedure as in performing simple linear regression. Simply enter several independent variables instead of a single variable in the **Predictors** edit box. A check box is provided on the **Options** dialog box to display **Variance inflation factors.**

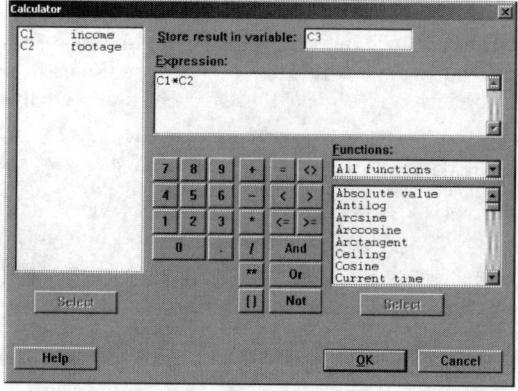

Building Quadratic and Interaction Terms

To construct quadratic and interaction terms, click **Calc ➤ Calculator.** In the **Expression** edit box enter the formula for constructing the new variable. For example, to compute the interaction of the variables in C1 and C2, enter the product of C1 and C2.

Stepwise Procedures

Forward, backward, and stepwise regression procedures can be obtained by clicking on **Stat ➤ Regression ➤ Stepwise.** Using the data in Section 14.4, move footage into the **Response** variable and income, FamSize, NbhoodA, and NbhoodB into the **Predictors** edit box. Click on **Methods** to select either **Stepwise, Forward,** or **Backward** regression procedures. Select either Use alpha values or Use F values for these procedures. The remove value of alpha (F value) must be no smaller (no larger) than the enter value.

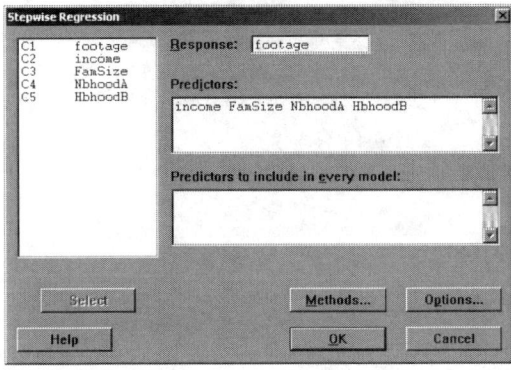 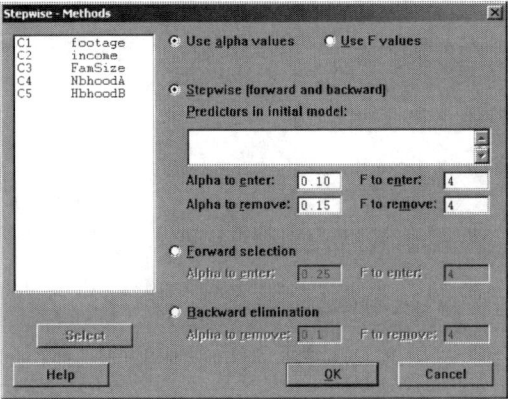

SPSS

Multiple Linear Regression

The dialog box for multiple regression analysis is the same as illustrated in the appendix of Chapter 13. In the **Linear Regression** dialog box enter multiple independent variables into the **Independent(s)** edit box instead of just one variable. Diagnostic statistics such as the residuals, standardized residuals, Cook's D, leverage values, and confidence and prediction intervals, can be obtained using the same procedure as explained in the appendix of Chapter 13. To display VIFs, click on **Collinearity diagnostics** in the **Linear Regression: Statistics** dialog box.

Building Quadratic and Interaction Terms

Quadratic and interaction terms can be constructed in SPSS using **Transform ➤ Compute.** For example, to include the quadratic term for income; that is, $(income)^2$, enter the information in the **Target Variable** and **Numeric Expression** boxes as shown.

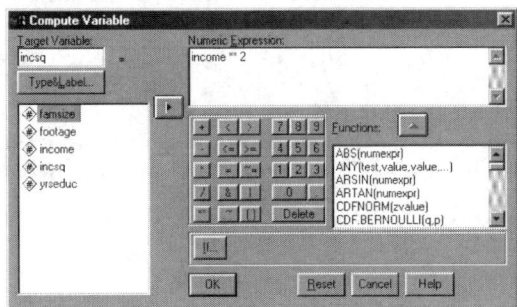

To construct an interaction term for income and family size, enter "incxfam" in the **Target Variable** box and "income*famsize" in the **Numeric Expression** box. The resulting columns are shown in the data window below.

Stepwise Procedures

Forward, backward, and stepwise regression procedures can be obtained by clicking on **Analyze ➤ Regression ➤ Linear.** Using the data in Section 14.4, first move footage into the **Dependent** edit box and Income, FamSize, NbhoodA, and NbhoodB into the **Independents** edit box.

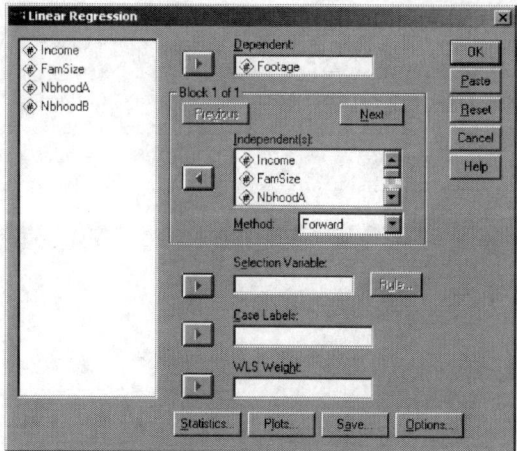

Forward Regression: In the shown dialog box, select **Forward** in the **Method** box. By clicking on **Options,** the significance level of the F statistics can be set. In the **Options** dialog box, increasing the significance level in the **Entry** box makes it easier for variables to enter the model. The Removal significance level must always be greater than the Entry significance level.

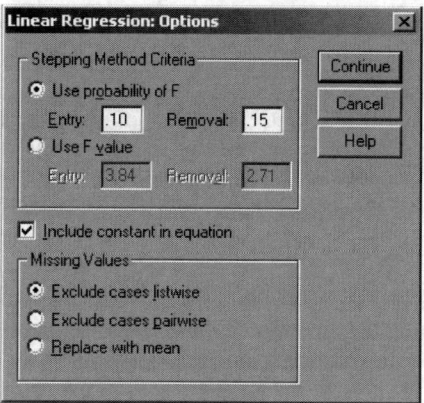

Backward Regression and Stepwise Regression: In the **Linear Regression** dialog box, for backward regression, select **Backward** in the **Method** box. For stepwise regression, select **Stepwise** in the **Method** box.

Note: **Use F value** in the **Options** dialog box to specify values of the F statistic for entering and removing a variable into/from the model. The **Removal** value must be less than the **Entry** value.

APPENDIX B ANSWERS TO ODD-NUMBERED EXERCISES

Chapter 1

1.1 The following populations are examples of populations that would be of interest to a business manager: **a.** Consumers of a certain product. **b.** Employees of a company. **c.** All electrical components manufactured by a factory. A business manager would prefer to sample from a population rather than take a census because of the cost and time involved.

1.3 Inferential statistics

1.5 a. Quantitative, ratio **b.** Qualitative, ordinal **c.** Qualitative, nominal **d.** Quantitative, interval **e.** Qualitative, ordinal

1.7 This would be a primary source.

1.9 a. Primary **b.** Secondary **c.** Primary **d.** Secondary

1.11 A random sample of 20 Zip codes provides a better representation of the population of all 70 Zip codes.

1.13 Give five categories of income and ask the respondent to which category does he/she belong.

1.15 Some comments motivating a person to fill out the questionnaire should be included. A closing statement may thank respondents for their time.

1.17 a. This is a leading question. **b.** Ask the question about the "Nightly Business Report" after the respondent lists his/her favorite television programs. **c.** It is not clear whether "large" refers to population or area.

1.19 a. Population consists of all individuals with a high net worth. **b.** Ask the general questions first and then ask the specific questions. **c.** The individual may not base his/her decision on whether the economy is slowing down.

1.21 a. The firms that buy computer chips from the company. **b.** Excel, SPSS, or MINITAB can be used to generate random numbers. **c.** Satisfaction by firms that buy from the company. **d.** The average of the responses can be used as the statistic to estimate the parameter in part (c).

1.23 a. The population is customers using America Online. **b.** A random sample could be selected by numbering all accounts and then randomly selecting a subset. **c.** Selecting customers by using a random sample would provide a more representative sample.

1.25 a. Represents a sample of employees at General Motors if randomly selected from the population of all employees at General Motors. **b.** Sample **c.** Sample **d.** Population of all possible ways of choosing two cards from a deck of 52 cards. **e.** Sample

1.27 1. Ratio – Quantitative, 2. Ratio – Quantitative, 3. Nominal – Qualitative, 4. Ordinal – Qualitative, 5. Ordinal – Qualitative, 6. Ratio – Quantitative

1.29 a. Computer buyers who have purchased Apple's new product. **b.** A random sample can be selected from warranties on file. **c.** Demographics: 1. What is your age? 2. Your highest level of education is high school, college, or graduate school? 3. How many children in your household?

Questions on satisfaction: 1. On a scale from 1 to 10 (perfect), how would you rate your satisfaction with your new TiBook?

2. Do you consider the TiBook to be attractively priced? 3. What feature do you like most about the TiBook?

d. A discount on future purchases could be offered.

e. For those purchasers that did not respond to the survey, the company might try to contact them by telephone or perhaps further entice their participation by offering frequent-flyer miles.

1.31 A possible systematic approach would be to select a number between 1 and 5 at random. Select the company with this rank. Next add 5 to that rank and select the next company. Continue adding 5 to the rank of the previous company selected until 20 companies have been selected.

1.33 Advantages of Telephone: Can get clarification on response; response rate is usually higher, more control over who responds. Disadvantages of Telephone: Usually more costly; takes longer to complete; requires interviewers to conduct the survey in a similar manner over the phone.

Advantages of Mail: Reach more respondents; cost is lower than for telephone or door-to-door.

Disadvantages of Mail: Response rate is usually lower; may not know who filled out the survey.

Advantages of E-mail: Reach respondents quickly; cost is the least.

Disadvantages of E-mail: Do not know who really is filling out the survey; requires respondent to have an e-mail address; e-mail addresses change more readily than home addresses or phone numbers.

Advantages of door-to-door: Know who the respondent is; can clarify questions.

Disadvantages of door-to-door: May not be a cost-effective approach; requires interviewers to be trained in collecting information in a similar fashion.

Chapter 2

2.1 a. 1,000

b.

Lower Class Limit	Upper Class Limit
0	1000
1000	2000
2000	3000
3000	4000
4000	5000
5000	6000
6000	7000
7000	8000

c. $1200/8062 = .1488$
$1500/8062 = .1861$
$2500/8062 = .3101$
$2300/8062 = .2853$
$500/8062 = .0620$
$50/8062 = .0062$
$10/8062 = .0012$
$2/8062 = .0002$

2.3 a. (224,000 – 111,000)/5 = 22,600. Use a class width of 25,000.

Class Number	Class
1	110,000 and under 135,000
2	135,000 and under 160,000
3	160,000 and under 185,000
4	185,000 and under 210,000
5	210,000 and under 235,000

b. (224,000 – 111,000)/6 = 18,833. Use a class width of 20,000.

Class Number	Class
1	110,000 and under 130,000
2	130,000 and under 150,000
3	150,000 and under 170,000
4	170,000 and under 190,000
5	190,000 and under 210,000
6	210,000 and under 230,000

c. (224,000 – 111,000)/12 = 9,416.7. Use a class width of 10,000.

Class Number	Class
1	110,000 and under 120,000
2	120,000 and under 130,000
3	130,000 and under 140,000
4	140,000 and under 150,000
5	150,000 and under 160,000
6	160,000 and under 170,000
7	170,000 and under 180,000
8	180,000 and under 190,000
9	190,000 and under 200,000
10	200,000 and under 210,000
11	210,000 and under 220,000
12	220,000 and under 230,000

2.5 a. Frequency distributions are easier to examine than the raw data.

b.

Weekly Earnings	Frequency	Relative Frequency
$ 0 and under $211	1462	.2183
$211 and under $334	1295	.1934
$334 and under $493	1354	.2022
$493 and under $730	1297	.1937
$730 and higher	1288	.1924

c. .1937 + .1924 = .3861

2.7 a. PE

Frequency Distribution Table

Class	Class Limits	Frequency
1	15 and under 20	5
2	20 and under 25	4
3	25 and under 30	6
4	30 and under 35	2
5	35 and under 40	3
6	40 and under 45	4
7	45 and under 50	2
8	50 and under 55	1
9	55 and under 60	1

b. **Frequency Distribution Table**

Class	Class Limits	Frequency
1	15 and under 22	7
2	22 and under 29	6
3	29 and under 36	5
4	36 and under 43	5
5	43 and under 50	3
6	50 and under 57	2

c. By showing a histogram, it is hoped that the person viewing the histogram will quickly understand the shape of the data distribution.

2.9 c.

Class Number	Frequency	Cumulative Frequency	Relative Frequency	Cumulative Relative Frequency
1	15	15	.375	.375
2	10	25	.25	.625
3	8	33	.20	.825
4	5	38	.125	.95
5	2	40	.05	1.00
	40			

2.11 b. CW = .5; Number of classes = 7; Class intervals are 1 and under 1.5, . . . , 4 and under 4.5.

2.13 Number of Times Used WWW

Frequency Distribution Table

Class	Class Limits	Frequency
1	0 and under 4	3
2	4 and under 8	6
3	8 and under 12	8
4	12 and under 16	9
5	16 and under 20	6
6	20 and under 24	3
7	24 and under 28	1

2.15 The most commonly quoted price is 99.

2.17 a. Class intervals are 15–24, . . . , 95–104; Cumulative relative frequencies are .03, .20, .33, .46, .56, .69, .82, .92, .99.

2.19 Eight class intervals can be constructed starting at 0 with a width of 1500. The respective relative frequencies are .51, .19, .19, .03, .03, .00, .03, and .01. Using the frequency distribution, 51% of the companies have lost less than 1500 million.

2.21 Eight class intervals can be constructed starting at 30 with a width of 10. The respective relative frequencies are .24, .26, .16, .08, .16, .04, .02, and .04.

2.23 The shape can be described as being approximately bell-shaped.

2.25

a.

Class Limits	Relative Freq
15 and under 17	.10
17 and under 19	.48
19 and under 21	.24
21 and under 23	.14
23 and under 25	.05

b.

Class Limits	Relative Freq
15 and under 17	.08
17 and under 19	.46
19 and under 21	.27
21 and under 23	.14
23 and under 25	.05

2.31 c. The percentages for all the companies increase considerably when the two top companies are omitted.

2.33 a. Most of the loans are being borrowed by Mexico, China, Brazil, and Indonesia. **b.** Bar charts and pie charts do not order the categories and do not have a cumulative scale.

2.37 a. The four largest bars show that Phillips, RCA, Sanyo, and Sony are the four largest companies in consumer electronics.

2.39 The "Yes" group is obviously larger for the "46-55 year olds" and the "No" group is larger for the "18-29 year olds."

2.41 Percentages for the pie chart for the "Not at All Concerned," "Not Too Concerned," "Somewhat Concerned," and "Very Concerned" are 17%, 21%, 33%, and 29%, respectively.

2.43 The three-dimensional pie chart makes BEA appear to have a more impressive share of the market although the percentages are the same as in the two-dimensional pie chart.

2.45 The first four companies listed in the Pareto chart are responsible for approximately 70% of the dollar transactions.

2.49 Europe and the United States account for almost 70% of the responses.

2.51 **a.** There are no outliers. **b.** The distribution is uniformly shaped from 20 to under 30. The interval 15 and under 20 and the interval 30 and under 35 only have a single observation. The interval from 10 and under 15 is close to the frequency of the values from 20 and under 30.

2.55 **a.** The stem-and-leaf diagram and the histogram show similar shapes.

2.57 **b.** Ford, General Motors, and DaimlerChrylser make up approximately 67% of the market. Note that General Motors and Ford make up more than half of the market and that the top six automakers make up over 90% of the market.

2.59 Both histograms are similar in that they start off high and then the relative frequency decreases as the values for the class intervals increase.

Chapter 3

3.1 **a.** mean = 19.2; median = 12; midrange = 26. **b.** mean = 4.8; median = 3; midrange = 6.5

3.3 **a.** 1, 2, 7, 8, 9 **b.** 1, 3, 10, 18, 19

3.5 No, the median does not have to change by the same amount that the mean changes.

3.7 Mean = 326,944/13 = 25,150 ;
Median = 20,247
If 61,175 is omitted, the value of the mean will change more than if any other value is omitted. After omitting 61,175, the mean is 265,769/12 = 22,147.

3.9 Mean = 4,155.7/99 = 41.98;
Median = 36.02; Modes = 26.45, 36.02, 48.78;
Midrange = 68.535

3.11 **a.** mean = 50,345,266.5; median = 31,314,038.5; midrange = 80,421,913.5. **b.** mean = 32,811,477.5; median = 26,613,436; midrange = 59,783,055.5. **c.** The new mean and median would be equal to the mean and median of the raw data multiplied by 120. **d.** The mean is 6,041,431,980. The median is 3,757,684,620.

3.13 **a.** Range = 8; $\bar{x}$ = 30/5 = 6; s = 3.16; CV = 52.7%.
b. Range = 80; $\bar{x}$ = 300/5 = 60; s = 31.62; CV = 52.7%.
c. Range = .08; $\bar{x}$ = .3/5 = .06; s = .0316; CV = 52.7%.

3.15 CV = 6.89% for Team 1 and 11.54% for Team 2.

3.17 Full data set: s = 9.751
Data set with 2 smallest and 2 largest values removed: s = 2.897

3.19 **a.** The mean should be a value close to the middle of the ordered data set. An approximation to the standard deviation is $(948 - 84.9)/4 \doteq 216$. **b.** Mean = 493.85; s = 346.79; **c.** Remove the values 84.9 and 948. The mean may shift somewhat, but the standard deviation is smaller. **d.** Mean = 482.55; s = 275.27

3.21 **a.** Mean is 85.2, standard deviation is 47.6, coefficient of variation is 100(47.6/85.2) = 55.87%, and the variance is 2266.182.

b. The mean should change by dividing its value by 60. The standard deviation should change by dividing its value by 60. The variance should change by dividing its value by 3600. **c.** Mean is 1.42, standard deviation is .793, and the variance is .6295.

3.23 Median is 1.5, Mean is 10/10 = 1 and s^2 = $(20 - (10)^2/10)/9 = 1.111$; s = 1.054; Sk = $3(\bar{x} - \text{Md})/s$ = $3(1 - 1.5)/1.054 = -1.423$

3.25 **a.** –2 **b.** 3 **c.** 55 **d.** 37.5

3.27 **a.** 73.5 **b.** 105.5 **c.** 75 = 25th percentile; 103 = 75th percentile. **d.** $\bar{x}$ = 90.6333; median = 87.5; s = 19.71781; Sk = 0.47673. **e.** The data are slightly skewed to the right.

3.31 Sk = 1.244

3.33 **b.** The mean, median, and standard deviation are 971.4, 457.5, and 1149.799. Pearson's coefficient of skewness = 1.34. **c.** The mean, median, and standard deviation are 626.029, 388.0, and 550.013. Pearson's coefficient of skewness = 1.30.

3.35 **a.** 80 to 120 **b.** 100 ± 3(20)

3.37 **a.** $\bar{x}$ = 44.8; s = 10.5283. **b.** 44.8 ± 2(10.5283). **c.** 44.8 ± 3(10.5283). **d.** Yes.

3.39 $\bar{x}$ = 50.5; s = 9.7512; n = 30; $\bar{x} \pm s$ = 40.749 to 60.2512, 90% of the data values fall in this interval; $\bar{x} \pm 2s$ = 30.997 to 70.002, 93.33% of the data values fall in this interval; $\bar{x} \pm 3s$ = 21.246 to 79.753, 93.33% of data values fall in this interval.

3.41 $\bar{x} \pm 2s$ = 90.633 ± 2(19.71781); 96.667% of the data actually lie within this interval.

3.43 Chebyshev's rule says that at least 75% of the data must be within 2 standard deviations of the mean. Therefore, the bounds are 109.29 and 216.49.

Chebyshev's rule says that at least 89% of the data must be within 3 standard deviations of the mean. Therefore, the bounds are 82.49 and 243.29.

3.45 **a.** The following interval contains at least 75% of the data. $\bar{x} - 2s$ to $\bar{x} + 2s$; 18335.76 – 2(2268.515) to 18335.76 + 2(2268.515); $13,798.73 to $22,872.79. The following interval contains at least 89% of the data. $\bar{x} - 3s$ to $\bar{x} + 3s$; 18,335.76 – 3(2268.515) to 18335.76 + 3(2268.515); $11,530.22 to $25,141.31

b. 196 observations (98%) of the data lie within 2 standard deviations of the mean. The minimum number expected by Chebyshev's inequality is 150. 199 observations (99.5%) of the data lie within 2 standard deviations of the mean. The minimum number expected by Chebyshev's inequality is 178.

3.47 **a.** 6 **b.** 8 **c.** 10 **d.** 18 **e.** No extreme outliers

3.49 Approximately 25% of the customers are served in 10 minutes or more.

3.51 The data are skewed left. No outliers were detected.

3.53 r = .955

3.55 r = –.948

3.57 r = –.986

3.59 r = .950

3.61 Mean = 315.0, s = 133.2, Sk = .3378

3.63 Approximately 95% of the data should lie within 2 standard deviations of the mean which is the interval 25.89 to 79.61.

3.65 Z = 2.8 for X = 200.

3.67 r = .730

3.69 **a.** The data are approximately bell-shaped. **b.** Sk = .32. **c.** By the empirical rule, approximately 68% of the values should fall between –1.155 and 1.655.

3.71 $45 to $105

3.73 The supervisor should accept the shipment.

3.75 The mean, median, and standard deviation are .249, .20, and .158, respectively. The coefficient of skewness is .930.

3.77 **b.** The data appear to have come from a bell-shaped distribution. **c.** $\bar{x}$ = 50.2167, s = 15.913, and Sk = .04

Chapter 4

4.1 The amplitudes of the seasonal and cyclical effects become more dramatic after a long period of time.

4.3 On a seasonal basis, the demand in July is typically greater than in March. If the number of housing starts is the same for March and July, then demand is slowing down.

4.5 **a.** Cyclical variation **b.** Seasonal variation **c.** Trend **d.** Irregular activity

4.7 **b.** b_0 = –5.33; b_1 = 56.286 **c.** 388.667

4.9 It is difficult to predict whether future observations will follow the curvature of the quadratic trend curve.

4.11 $\bar{y}_t$ = –24.418 + 6.2429t

4.13 b_0 = .3714, b_1 = –1.1036, and b_2 = .5964; $\bar{y}_8$ = 29.714

4.15 **a.** A quadratic trend would provide a better fit than a linear trend. **b.** 139.95 million

4.17 Cyclical components for time periods 1 through 10: .67, .73, 1.25, 1.04, .92, 1.03, 1.11, 1.07, .98, and .92

4.19 **c.** Approximately 4 years.

4.21 **a.** b_0 = 6.360, b_1 = .117 **c.** The cycle appears to be longer than 5 years.

4.23 **a.** Cyclical components: .976, 1.01, 1.02, .996, .97, 1.02, 1.05, .99, .96, 1.01 **b.** The length of the cycle is slightly more than 3 years.

4.25 **a.** Cyclical components: .96, .99, 1.06, 1.01, .94, 1.01, 1.09, .98, .92, .99, 1.12, .99, .90, 1.01, 1.13, .99, .93 **b.** The length of the cycles are 3 years, 5 years, and 3 years.

4.27 At times 1, 2, 3, and 4, $\bar{y}_t$ is 37.5, 36, 26.5, and 35.

4.29 1st quarter: 65.4; 2nd quarter: 78.9; 3rd quarter: 87.1; 4th quarter: 84.1.

4.31 For times 37 through 48, predicted data values are: 9.9, 16.24, 12.48, 27.69, 23.98, 31.22, 54.72, 72.23, 7.14, 4.86, 4.96, 2.53.

4.33 Deseasonalized FDI figures can be obtained by dividing FDI by the appropriate seasonal index. For 2000, figures are 26.00, 26.02, 26.00, and 25.98.

4.35 Centered moving averages are 18.5, 20.875, 22.875, 24.50. Ratio to moving average: 1.24, 1.44, .87, .61.

4.37 Moving averages contain less noise than the original time series.

4.39 Seasonal indexes are .8710, .8256, .8458, .9291, 1.0276, 1.0503, 1.0730, 1.1614, 1.1411, 1.0629, 1.0452, .9670.

4.41 Seasonal indexes are 1.0913, 1.2155, .8573, .8358.

4.43 Seasonal indexes are .889, 1.081, 1.009, .965, 1.053, 1.001, .945, 1.077, 1.043, 1.000, .976, .961.

4.45 I_t = 1.0185

4.47 .859, .890, 1.176, 1.224

4.49 Trend line through the deseasonalized data is TR(t) = 458.655 + 6.853t, TR(49) = 794.45

4.51 The plot of the irregular (noise) components over time reveals no obvious patterns.

4.53 **a.** 12.636, 15.252, 20.468, 19.26 **b.** 49.83, 86.94, 101.745, 96.835 **c.** 26.4, 25.52, 18.0, 15.12

4.55 Forecast for Qtr.3, 2005: 145.8; Forecast for Qtr.4, 2005: 157.4

4.57 Forecasts for the four quarters are: 218.8, 322.7, 266.3, 514.6

4.59 **a.** Residuals: 1.422, .980, and .982. **b.** Residuals: .847, .293, and .305.

4.61 116.261

4.63 **a.** Index numbers are: 100, 116.67, 141.67, 183.33, 208.33. **b.** Index numbers are: 85.71, 100.00, 121.43, 157.14, 178.57

4.65 **a.** 120.6 **b.** 119.0 **c.** 118.7

4.67 **a.** 135.6 **b.** 136.11 **c.** 135.9

4.71 **a.** Laspeyres index = 96.78 **b.** Paasche Index = 97.59

4.73 **a.** Trend **b.** Irregular **c.** Seasonal **d.** Irregular

4.75 **a.** $\bar{y}_t$ – 32.697 + .213t for t = 1, 2, 3, . . . **b.** $\bar{y}_{14}$ = 32.697 + .213(14) = 35.68.

4.77 b_0 = –10.40 b_1 = 6.80

4.79 $\bar{y}_t$ = 6.139 + 1.745t – 0.149t² is the trend component.

4.81 **a.** Seasonal indexes are 1.20, 1.15, 1.07, .92, .91, .95, .96, .96, .92, .93, .99, 1.05. **b.** $\bar{d}_t$ = 151.806 + 1.094t **c.** Cyclical components are 1.02, 1.01, 1.00, .99, .97, .98, .98, .99, .98, 1.00, 1.00, 1.01. **d.** June, irregular = 1.00; July, irregular = 1.00.

4.83 **a.** Laspeyres index = 109.13 **b.** Paasche Index = 108.41

4.85 157.147

4.87 137.215.

Chapter 5

5.1 **a.** P(B) = 1.25 cannot be a probability. **b.** The sum of the probabilities do not sum to one. **c.** The sum of the probabilities cannot be greater than one.

5.3 **a.** .10 **b.** .25 **c.** .60 **d.** .70

5.5 A and B are mutually exclusive.

5.7 **a** .2667 **b.** .5867

5.9 **a.** .541 **b.** .015 **c.** .5 **d.** .949 **e.** 0

5.11 **a.** .7 **b.** .2 **c.** .9 **d.** .5

5.13 The joint probability of "Pay Ticket" and "Fight Ticket" is equal to zero. The joint probability of "Run Red Light" and "Speeding" is equal to zero.

5.15 **a.** .875 **b.** .35 **c.** .917 **d.** If the events of no tuition reimbursement and at least 3 months of leave had a frequency value of 0 in the table, then these two events would be mutually exclusive.

5.17 **b.** .1 **c.** .3 **d.** .6667

5.19 **a.** .8 **b.** .857 **c.** .1 **d.** .333

5.21 P(C or D) = .5

5.23 $P(A \mid \bar{B})$ = .2857

5.25 A and B are not mutually exclusive.

5.27 P(A | B) refers to the probability of event A occurring given that event B has occurred.

5.29 **a.** .54 **b.** .86 **c.** .675

5.31 .90

5.33 P(High Consumption | 1998) = 6/12 = .5
P(High Consumption | 1999) = 9/12 = .75
P(High Consumption | 2000) = 11/12 = .917

5.35 **a.** Try different numbers of people to see how large a group of people is necessary for the relative frequency to be at least .5 (approximately).

5.37 **a.** .34 **b.** .25

5.39 E_1 = drug user; B = test is positive; P(B) = .1044; $P(E_1 \boxtimes B)$ = .9569

5.41 .048

5.43 **a.** .0395 **b.** .405

5.45 .12

5.47 If P(A or B or C) is less than one, then other events are possible. The largest that P(A or B or C) can be is P(A) + P(B) + P(C) = .4 + .3 + .1 = .8.

5.49 .333

5.51 .008

5.53 .012

5.55 **a.** .091 **b.** .125 **c.** .273

5.57 **a.** .64 **b.** .24 **c.** .216 **d.** .784 **e.** .28

5.59 **a.** 0.15 **b.** .3

5.61 **a.** The event of a Delta airline flight being delayed is not independent of Southwest airline being delayed. **b.** .5576.

Chapter 6

6.1 **a.** P(Circuit board needs to be returned to factory) = 2/8 = .25 **b.** P(Circuit board is in good working condition) = 3/8 = .375

6.3 **b.** P(X > 1) = .75 **c.** P(X = 1 or X = 3) = .75

6.5 Yes, it is a discrete distribution. The values of X could be 0, 1, 2, 3, ...

6.7 Assume the business manager works for a video store. Continuous: 1. Amount of money a customer spends on each purchase, 2. Time it takes for a customer to check out. Discrete: 1. Number of customers who come in per hour, 2. Number of videos each customer buys/rents.

6.9 **a.** Valid **b.** Not valid **c.** Valid **d.** Not valid **e.** Not valid

6.11 Yes

6.13 Yes

6.15 Yes, this function is a probability mass function since all probability values are between 0 and 1 and they sum to 1.0.

6.17 P(X = x) = 1/3 for x = 2, 4, 6

6.19 **b.** The sum = 7 has a probability of 6/36 = .1667. **c.** The probability that the sum of dice will be between 5 and 8 should be approximately 20/36 = .556.

6.21 **a.** μ = 33.33; σ = 9.428. **b.** μ = 17.909; σ = 7.704.

6.23 μ = 3; σ^2 = 3.

6.25 μ = .7; σ^2 = 1.01; σ = 1.005

6.27 μ = .35; σ^2 = .0065; σ = .0806

6.29 **a.** P(X = 2) = .044 **b.** P(X > 2) = .945 **c.** P(X $\leq$ 2) = .055 **d.** P(X < 2) = .011 **e.** P(X $\geq$ 2) = .989

6.31 .3647

6.33 .506

6.35 **a.** .382782 **b.** .22057 **c.** mean for part (a) is 3.0, mean for part (b) is 3.7

6.37 **a.** .001 **b.** 3 **c.** σ = 1.55 **d.** .982

6.39 .7636

6.41 **a.** n = 100 and p = .5 P(X $\geq$ 50) = .5398 **b.** n = 100 and p = .7 P(X $\geq$ 50) = 1.000 **c.** n = 100 and p = .662 P(X $\geq$ 50) = .9997 **d.** Expected number of families that are owners from New York is 50, from Indiana is 70, and from across the USA is 66.2. **e.** Standard deviation for the number of families that are owners from New York is 5, from Indiana is 4.58, and from across the USA is 4.73.

6.43 P(X>7) = .5470; P(X $\leq$ 7) = .4530

6.45 Mean is 2: P(X = 0) = .1353; Mean is 5: P(X = 0) = .0067.

6.47 .2783

6.49 **a.** P(X $\geq$ 8) = .7797 **b.** P(X $\leq$ 12) = .7916 **c.** The mean is 10 and the standard deviation is sqrt(10) = 3.16. **d.** The conditions for a Poisson distribution can be justified.

6.51 **a.** .5831 **b.** .0487

6.53 **a.** .9004 **b.** 2.83

6.55 **a.** .1992 **b.** 1.732

6.57 Only b is a property of a discrete probability distribution.

6.59 **a.** X can be equal to 1, 3, 4, 5, or 7. **b.** P(X = 1) = P(X = 3) = P(X = 5) = P(X = 7) = 1/6 and P(X = 4) = 2/6. **c.** μ = 4 **d.** σ^2 = 3.332

6.61 This is not a likely occurrence.

6.63 Binomial distribution with p = .6; P(X $\geq$ 5) = .8338

6.65 **b.** The mean is 2.68; the standard deviation is 2.328.

6.67 **a.** Let X be a binomial random variable with n = 8 and p = .50. The expected number of travel agencies that provide the cheapest airfare for the Chicago to Santa Ana route is np = 4. **b.** σ^2 = 2 and σ = 1.414. **c.** P(X = 0) = .004 This event would be considered unusual. **d.** This problem is assuming that the trials are independent. Also, this problem assumes that the probability of a success (providing the cheapest fare for the route from Chicago to Santa Ana) is .5.

6.69 **a.** Let X be a binomial random variable with n = 50 and p = .10. P(X $\geq$ 5) = .5688 **b.** For p = .13, P(X $\geq$ 5) = .7956. For p = .15, P(X $\geq$ 5) = .8879. For p = .20, P(X $\geq$ 5) = .9815. **c.** Let X be a Poisson random variable with a mean of 10. P(X > 8) = .6671 **d.** For the Poisson random variable, the standard deviation is 3.162.

Chapter 7

7.3 **a.** .4772 **b.** .1102 **c.** .8591

7.5 **a.** 0.8907 **b.** 0.8907 **c.** 0.8907 **d.** 0.475 **e.** .3344

7.7 **a.** 1.03 **b.** 1.03 **c.** −1.76 **d.** 2.0 **e.** −2.0

7.9 **a.** P(Z > 2) = .0228 **b.** P(Z > 3.4) = .0003 **c.** P(Z < −1.8) = .0359 **d.** P(Z < −3.8) = .000007

7.11 **a.** .1587 **b.** 0.0228 **c.** .3830

7.13 0.0808

7.15 82.5

7.17 **a.** $P(X > 3) = .1841$ **b.** $P(X > 3) = .2266$ **c.** $P(X > 3) = .2810$

7.19 **a.** $P(X < 2000) = .8413$ **b.** $P(X < 1200) = .0013$.

7.21 **a.** 10 **b.** 2

7.23 **a.** The refund damage value of $117.51 yields a probability less than .01.

7.25 The histogram of data with a standard deviation of 5 shows that the data are more dispersed than a histogram of data with a standard deviation of 1 or 3.

7.27 Mean = 150 σ = 28.87

7.29 A = 4, Mean = .25 hr, P(X < .6 hour) = .9093

7.31 **a.** $\mu = 62.5$; $\sigma = 4.33$; Probability is .58. **b.** 66.94

7.33 **a.** 0.524 **b.** 23.15 **c.** 1.819

7.35 .51 (Note that the mean is 300.)

7.37 0.2997

7.39 Let X be an exponentially distributed random variable with $\mu = 200$. $P(X > 200) = .368$

7.41 **a.** The uniform distribution most closely approximates the distribution of BotErr and TopErr. **b.** The approximate shape of TotalErr is normal.

7.43 **a.** The normal distribution is symmetric about its mean, so the probability is 50%. **b.** The uniform distribution is symmetric about its mean, so the probability is 50%. **c.** .3679

7.45 5

7.47 **a.** $P(X < x) = .50$ implies that x = mean = $150. **b.** X = $171. **c.** X = $171.

7.49 **a.** 452 **b.** 480

7.51 60% of the time, the price of the yen to the dollar will be between 125.8 and 134.2.

7.53 87.12

7.55 Probability is .344; σ = 30

7.57 .2231

7.59 4.32 and 7.68

7.61 .3935

7.63 **a.** Between 5,000 and 7,000 (approximately) **b.** .4772

Chapter 8

8.1 **a.** .8413 **b.** .1359 **c.** .9332

8.3 **a.** The Central Limit Theorem tells us that the distribution of the sample mean is approximately normally distributed with a mean of 4 and a standard deviation of $1/\sqrt{50}$. **b.** If the sample size were increased to 100, the approximation of the normal distribution would be much closer for the distribution of $\bar{X}$. The mean would be 4 and the standard deviation would be $1/\sqrt{100}$.

8.5 .0022

8.7 **a.** .6826 **b.** .7888

8.9 **a.** As the sample size increases, the histogram should look more like a normal distribution.

8.11 49.10 to 54.30

8.13 327.98 to 432.02

8.15 9.29 to 10.31

8.17 21.224 to 23.576

8.19 As the sample size increases, the confidence interval gets narrower. A 90% confidence interval is wider than an 80% confidence interval.

8.21 90% confident that the true population mean lies between 1010.22 and 1059.56.
99% confident that the true population mean lies between 996.25 and 1073.53.

8.23 **a.** .005 **b.** .95 **c.** .10 **d.** .95

8.25 1.79 to 2.31

8.27 12.99 to 18.49 years

8.29 We are 99% confident that the population mean lies between $32,723.56 and $39,252.24. We are 90% confident that the population mean lies between $34,146.61 and $37,829.19.

8.31 1937.31 to 2986.02

8.33 82.1908 to 86.0701

8.35 **a.** n = 61 **b.** σ = 12.5; n = 67

8.37 17

8.39 17

8.41 20

8.43 At 86%, n = 240; at 99%, n = 666

8.45 Answers will vary due to the random nature of the bootstrap method.

8.47 Answers will vary due to the random nature of the bootstrap method.

8.51 Answers will vary due to the random nature of the bootstrap method.

8.53 Answers will vary due to the random nature of the bootstrap method.

8.55 14.286 to 17.628

8.57 4.47 to 5.61

8.59 2.54 to 4.25

8.61 **a.** .1587 **b.** .3745

8.63 **a.** The point estimate of the average weight is 50. **b.** The sample standard deviation is .2.

8.65 59

8.67 The Central Limit Theorem says that as the sample size becomes larger, the distribution of the estimate of the proportion of days when breads are sold will become approximately normally distributed.

8.69 62

8.71 We are 90% confident that the true population mean lies between 151.90 and 173.88.

8.73 **a.** 2.5627 to 3.1271 **b.** 2.5679 to 3.1219 **c.** The normal approximation is reasonably good.

Chapter 9

9.3 **a.** quality characteristic **b.** control chart **c.** process

9.7 Roughly half the MBNQA point total (450 out of 1000) comes from Category 7: Results

9.11 The flowchart should have several decision nodes, such as "Is the bank interest rate competitive?" and "Do the applicants qualify for the amount of the loan?"

9.13 A Pareto chart can be used to display the results.

9.15 Main branches might consist 1. Waiting to be seated, 2. Ordering the meal, 3. Enjoying the meal, and 4. Filing complaints or compliments. Secondary branches can be attached to these main branches.

9.21 Xbar chart: UCL = 449.49; CL = 427.05; LCL = 404.61. R chart: UCL = 82.23; CL = 38.90; LCL = 0.

9.23 **a.** UCL = 2.45; CL = 1.32; LCL = 0.18

9.25 **a.** UCL = .0219; CL = .01175; LCL = .0016. **b.** Observations appear to decrease and then increase.

9.27 For Northern: UCL = 1454.2; CL = 848.47; LCL = 242.7. For Southern: UCL = 1551.123; CL = 757.633; LCL = -35.857.

9.29 For Xbar chart: UCL = 24.84; CL = 19.71; LCL = 14.58. For R chart: UCL = 16.07; CL = 7.04; LCL = 0.

9.31 For Xbar chart: UCL = 10.86; CL = 10.01; LCL = 9.16. For R chart: UCL = 2.14; CL = 0.83; LCL = 0.

9.35 UCL = .115; CL = .05; LCL = 0.

9.37 **a.** pbar = .307; UCL = .58; CL = .307; LCL = .03. **b.** No

9.39 UCL = 6.822; CL = 2.286; LCL = 0.

9.41 For the c chart, UCL = 11.29; CL = 4.75; LCL = 0.

9.43 For c chart, UCL = 13,578; CL = 6.143; LCL = 0. **b.** No, since two plotted values exeed the UCL.

9.47 Process A: $C_p = 0.78$ (inadequate); Process B: $C_p = 1.13$ (adequate); Process C: $C_p = 2.16$ (good); Process D: $C_p = 1.11$ (adequate)

9.51 **a.** s' = 7.28; $C_{pm} = 0.97$. **b.** s' = 6.20; $C_{pm} = 1.14$. **c.** C_{pm} converges to C_p

9.53 Process A **b.** For Process A, $C_{pk} = 1.08$; for Process B, $C_{pk} = 1.22$. **c.** Process B, since it is more capable.

9.55 **a.** $C_p = 1.41$ **b.** $C_{pk} = 1.38$.

9.63 Since the variation about the target value is expected to be larger than the usual variance, C_p is usually larger than C_p

9.65 The process is considered out of control because the first six points are increasing and also the sixth observation is above 84.

9.67 **a.** Scatter diagram **b.** Flowchart **c.** Control chart **d.** Pareto chart **e.** Cause-and-effect diagram

9.69 For Xbar chart: UCL = 86.66; CL = 82.475; LCL = 78.286. For R chart: UCL = 13.123; CL = 5.750; LCL = 0.

9.71 **a.** c chart **b.** UCL = 6.14; CL = 1.195; LCL = 0. **c.** In control.

9.73 **a.** The xbar chart contains patterns 2, 5, and 6. **b.** The R chart gives out of control signals.

Chapter 10

10.1 **a.** H_0: The containers are filled to 24 ounces; H_a: The containers are filled to an amount different from 24 ounces.

10.3 **a.** True **b.** True **c.** True **d.** False

10.5 $Z^* = 4.65$; reject H_0.

10.7 **b.** $Z^* = 2.17$; fail to reject H_0. **c.** $Z^* = 3.06$; reject H_0.

10.9 Since the 95% confidence interval does not contain 1.2, reject H_0.

10.11 **a.** 408.615 to 451.385 **b.** $Z^* = -5.38$; reject H_0.

10.13 **a.** .5912 **b.** 1.0

10.15 **a.** The histogram appears to have a bell-shaped appearance. **b.** $Z^* = -1.059$; fail to reject H_0. **c.** 130.515 to 155.818.

10.17 **a.** H_0: $\mu \geq \mu_0$; H_a: $\mu < \mu_0$. **b.** H_0: $\mu \geq 30$; H_a: $\mu < 30$. **c.** H_0: $\mu = 15$; H_a: $\mu \neq 15$.

10.19 **a.** $Z^* = 2$; reject H_0. **b.** $Z^* = 0$; fail to reject H_0.

10.21 $Z^* = 1.67$; reject H_0.

10.23 .7642

10.25 **a.** $Z^* = 2.34$; reject H_0.

10.27 **a.** fail to reject H_0 **b.** reject H_0 **c.** fail to reject H_0 **d.** reject H_0

10.29 $Z^* = 3.0$; p-value = .0026

10.31 $Z^* = 2.67$; p-value = .0076

10.33 $Z^* = -1.29$; p-value = .0985; fail to reject H_0.

10.35 **a.** p-value = .205; fail to reject H_0.

10.37 **a.** $t^* = .968$; fail to reject H_0. **b.** $t^* = .968$; fail to reject H_0. **c.** $t^* = -4.6$; reject H_0. **d.** $t^* = -1.4$; fail to reject H_0.

10.39 $t^* = -.13$; fail to reject H_0.

10.41 $t^* = 2.67$; reject H_0.

10.43 $t^* = 3.2$; reject H .

10.45 **a.** p-value = .094

10.47 Only b and d can be acceptable alternative hypotheses.

10.49 **a.** True **b.** True **c.** True **d.** False **e.** True

10.51 **a.** .2274 **b.** .1279 **c.** .9830

10.53 $Z^* = -3.5$; p-value is .0004; reject H_0.

10.55 $Z^* = 2.0$; reject H_0. No.

10.57 **a.** 4087.84 to 4912.16 **b.** Since the 99% confidence interval does not contain the hypothesized value of 4000, reject H_0.

10.59 $t^* = 1.645$; reject H_0; after removing two largest values, $t^* = 1.015$; fail to reject H_0.

10.61 The increase in the power begins to level off for $\mu > 114$ and $\mu < 86$.

Chapter 11

11.1 The data should be examined to see if they are independent or dependent in order to choose the correct analysis procedure.

11.3 **a.** Dependent samples **b.** The samples are independent.

11.5 The sample of men and the sample of women are dependent.

11.7 **a.** The marketing analyst can have each person rate both brands of sausage. **b.** The marketing analyst can have each person rate only one of the brands of sausage.

11.9 **a.** -10.80 to -1.20 **b.** $Z^* = -2.06$; reject H_0.

11.11 $Z^* = -2.17$; fail to reject H .

11.13 -4.849 to -2.951

11.15 $Z^* = 3.70$; reject H_0.

11.17 The confidence interval can be used to form a conclusion about a two-sided hypothesis test. However, the confidence interval cannot be used for one-sided tests.

11.19 $Z^* = 1.47$; p-value = .1416; fail to reject H_0.

11.21 $Z^* = -2.66$; reject H_0.

11.23 **b.** $Z^* = -1.52$; reject H_0.

11.25 **a.** $s_p = 1.711$ **b.** -3.132 to $-.868$ **c.** -3.3982 to $-.8018$

11.27 t⊠ $= .4595$; fail to reject H_0.

11.29 $t^* = 0.4595$; fail to reject H_0.

11.31 -48.364 to -1.636

11.33 $t^* = -.380$; fail to reject H_0.

11.35 The degrees of freedom decrease as the variance of one population becomes substantially higher than the other population variance.

11.37 **a.** $F_{.025,19,14} \doteq F_{.025,20,14} = 2.84$; $F_{.975,19,14} \doteq 1/F_{.025,15,19} = .3816$. **b.** $F_{.90,4,14} \doteq 1/F_{.10,15,4} = .258$. **c.** $F_{.01,18,10} \doteq F_{.01,20,10} = 4.41$.

11.39 **a.** $F^* = 6.46$; reject H_0 .

11.41 $F^* = .156$; reject H_0.

11.43 **a.** $F^* = .501$; reject H_0 .

11.45 **a.** $F^* = 1.37$; fail to reject H_0. **b.** The results in part (a) remain the same when 5 points are subtracted from each grade.

11.47 **a.** $t^* = 3.02$; reject H_0. **b.** $.005 < $ p-value $ < .01$

11.49 **a.** $.668$ to 3.53 **b.** $t_D^* = 2.689$; reject H_0.

11.51 $t^* = 4.46$; reject H_0.

11.53 $t^* = 2.77$; fail to reject H_0.

11.55 **a.** $t^* = -1.89$; fail to reject H_0. **b.** $t^* = -1.89$; fail to reject H_0.

11.57 **a.** $F^* = 35.50$; **b.** Since $F^* = 35.50 > F_{.01,3,36} \doteq F_{.01,3,40} = 4.31$, reject H_0. **c.** $n = 40$. The number of observations from each group is 10. **d.** $D = 1.932$; Conclusion: The population mean of group 1 is different from the population mean of groups 2, 3, and 4.

11.59 $\bar{x}_A = 48$ $\bar{x}_B = 47$ $\bar{x}_C = 35$ $\bar{x}_D = 36$; $D = 8.07$; Conclude that $\mu_B \neq \mu_D$ and $\mu_B \neq \mu_C$ and $\mu_A \neq \mu_D$ and $\mu_A \neq \mu_C$.

11.61 **a.** $F^* = 8.7670$; reject H_0 . The monthly sales are not the same for the three salesmen. **b.** p-value is less than .01 **c.** $\bar{x}_J = 881.875$ $\bar{x}_R = 764.25$ $\bar{x}_T = 763.88$; $D = 82.2414$; So conclude that $\mu_J \neq \mu_R$ and $\mu_J \neq \mu_T$.

11.63 $F^* = 2.111$; fail to reject the null hypothesis that the mean ages for the three programs are equal.

11.65 $F^* = 6.468$; reject H_0 closing techniques 2 and 3 differ.

11.67 **a.** $Z^* = .197$; p-value $= .8414$. **b.** df $= 44$; $t^* = 1.59$; $.05 < $ p-value $ < .10$. **c.** $Z^* = 0.063$; p-value $= .4761$.

11.69 $t^* = -1.43$; fail to reject H_0.

11.71 $t^* = 3.90$; reject H_0.

11.73 .767

11.75 $F^* = 4.55$; reject H_0 $D = 5.91$; conclude that all pairs of means differ.

11.77 **a.** $t_D^* = 1.928$; reject H_0. **b.** A 95% confidence interval is 1.956 to 3.511. A 99% confidence interval is 1.685 to 3.781.

11.79 $F^* = 5.886$; reject H_0. Tukey's procedure reveals that HelpSysA and HelpSysC differ.

Chapter 12

12.1 **a.** .206 to .728; **b.** .326 to .774 **c.** .318 to .682 **d.** .36 to .64

12.3 **a.** $n = 94$ **b.** $n = 370$ **c.** $n = 1026$

12.5 **a.** .087 to .413 **b.** .178 to .322 **c.** In part a, the length of the confidence interval is .326. In part b, the length of the confidence interval is .144.

12.7 **a.** $n = 357$ **b.** $n = 424$

12.9 **a.** $n = 3613$ **b.** $n = 1474$

12.11 2019

12.13 .09896 to .11376

12.15 **a.** .468 to .632 **b.** .421 to .679

12.17 **a.** $Z^* = -1.212$; p-value $= .2262$. **b.** $Z^* = -1.212$ from part (a); p-value $= .1131$. **c.** $Z^* = .90$; p-value $= .184$; fail to reject H_0.

12.19 $Z^* = 1.44$; reject H_0.

12.21 n must be greater than or equal to 167.

12.23 $\hat{p} = .5733$; $Z^* = 1.795$; reject H_0. $\hat{p} = .56$; $Z^* = 1.470$; reject H_0.

12.25 $n = 363$

12.27 $Z^* = .207$; fail to reject H_0.

12.29 $Z^* = .20$; fail to reject H_0.

12.31 $Z^* = -1.15$; fail to reject H_0.

12.33 $Z^* = -2.24$; fail to reject H_0.

12.35 $Z^* = -3.29$; reject H_0.

12.37 $Z^* = -.91$; p-value $= .3628$; fail to reject H_0.

12.39 **a.** $Z^* = .795$; fail to reject H_0. **b.** $\bar{p} = .05$ **c.** $Z^* = .7947$

12.41 H_0: $p_1 = .1$ $p_2 = .2$ $p_3 = .2$ $p_4 = .2$ $p_5 = .3$ H_a: at least one of the proportions is incorrect $\chi^{2*} = 15.37$; reject H_0.

12.43 H_0: the classifications of the A's are independent of the classification of the B's. H_a: the classifications of the A's are not independent of the classification of the B's. $\chi^{2*} = 15.3383$; reject H_0.

12.45 H_0: $p_1 = 1/3$ $p_2 = 1/3$ $p_3 = 1/3$ H_a: at least one of the p_i's is incorrect $\chi^{2*} = .8125$; fail to reject H_0.

12.47 $\chi^{2*} = 12.9253$; reject H_0.

12.49 **a.** H_0: personality type and profession are independent H_a: personality type and profession are dependent $\chi^{2*} = 6.004$; fail to reject H_0. **b.** p-value $> .10$.

12.51 **a.** H_0: Type of incident and major airports are independent H_a: Type of incident and major airports are dependent $\chi^{2*} = 9.80$; reject H_0. **b.** If categories A and B were not combined, $\chi^{2*} = 10.05$; fail to reject H_0.

12.53 .179 to .221. The margin of error is .021.

12.55 $n = 1,119$

12.57 $Z^* = 3.24$; p-value $= .0006$; reject H_0.

12.59 $Z^* = -.512$; fail to reject H_0.

12.61 $Z^* = 1.3765$; fail to reject H_0.

12.63 $\chi^{2*} = 6.35$; fail to reject H_0.

12.65 **a.** $\chi^{2*} = 2.9915$; fail to reject H_0.

12.67 **(a and b)** $\chi^{2*} = 10.88$ (p-value $= .012$); reject H_0. **c.** $\chi^{2*} = .586$ (p-value $= .746$); fail to reject H_0.

Chapter 13

13.1 **a.** $\Sigma x = 24$; $\Sigma y = 53$; $\Sigma xy = 333$; $\Sigma x^2 = 154$; $\Sigma y^2 = 729$. **b.** $b_1 = 2.0258$; $b_0 = 0.876$. **c.** $r = 0.9759$.

13.3 **b.** $b_1 = .954$ $b_0 = -10.5$

13.5 Be careful when interpreting the coefficients: There may not have been any small cap mutual funds with a return this low in the data set.

13.7 **b.** $\tilde{Y} = 11.278 + .0803X$ **c.** $r = .688$

13.9 **b.** $r = .601$ **c.** $b_1 = 1.395$ $b_0 = .835$

13.11 When the magnitude of the correlation and the sample size is large, it should be relatively easy to draw the least squares line.

13.13 **a.** $s = 1.4376$ **b.** 16 residuals (80%) fall within 2s of the mean of the residuals.

13.15 $s = 5.09$ is the estimated standard deviation of the error for the regression model.

13.17 $s = 2.6624$; all the sample residuals are within two standard deviations of the mean.

13.19 **a.** $b_1 = .532$ $b_0 = .164$ **b.** $r = .9999$

13.21 **a.** $\tilde{Y} = .7195 + .75097X$. **b.** Yes, although there is a slight left skew.

13.23 **a.** $t^* = 1.875$; fail to reject H_0. **b.** -1.578 to 7.578

13.25 $t^* = 27.1601$; reject H_0.

13.27 **a.** $t^* = -1.54$; fail to reject H_0.

13.29 $-.0776$ and $-.0175$.

13.31 **a.** r^2 with Experience is .12. r^2 with TimeToSell is .66. **b.** For TimeToSell, regression model is $\tilde{Y} = 265.16 + 99.27X$; $t^* = 11.9$, yes. **c.** $t^* = 11.9$, reject H_0

13.33 **a.** $H_0: \rho \geq 0$ vs. $H_a: \rho < 0$ **b.** $r = -.981$ **c.** coefficient of determination $= .962$ **d.** $t^* = -10.06$; reject H_0.

13.35 $r^2 = .97$, $t^* = 17.45$, reject H_0.

13.37 **b.** $t^* = -.4450$; fail to reject H_0.

13.39 $t^* = 12.922$; reject H_0.

13.41 **a.** $.95$, $t^* = 20.73$, reject H_0 **b.** $t^* = 20.73$, reject H_0 **c.** $.95$

13.43 **a.** $b_1 = 2.433$ $b_0 = -32.041$ **b.** -24.987 to 9.573 **c.** -34.5538 to 19.1398 **e.** The fifth observation is considered influential.

13.45 95% confidence interval for the mean of Y at $X = 35$: 18.465 to 27.325; 95% prediction interval for the value of Y at $X = 35$: 11.249 to 34.540

13.47 Observation 4 is an outlier and an influential observation. Note that the standardized residual is greater than 2, and Cook's $D > .8$.

13.49 4.3177 to 4.4877

13.51 7.2049 to 8.4543; $s_{\tilde{y}} = 0.9897$.

13.53 If the value of $95,000$ is outside the range of values for the independent variable X, then this may not be a valid statement. It may be that all executives in the sample had incomes greater than $95,000.

13.55 $DW = .265$; the Durbin-Watson test indicates that positive autocorrelation exists.

13.57 Observation 27 has a Cook's D of 157.16 and is influential. R-square is .334. Without observation 27, the R-square is .962, a substantial increase.

13.59 **a.** $b_1 = .009317$ $b_0 = .1146$ **b.** $t^* = 13.45$; reject H_0. **c.** .00772 to .01091 **d.** 95% prediction interval for the value of Y at $X = 110$: 1.003 to 1.276

13.61 It may not be appropriate to try to predict revenue for a year different from 1984.

13.63 **a.** $\tilde{Y} = 35.606 - .368X$ **b.** $s^2 = 90.878$

13.65 Variance of the error term is 25.49. With a Cook's D of .98, observation 1 is the most influential observation. Variance of the error term without observation 1 is 11.03.

13.67 **a.** $t^* = 19.0454$; reject H_0. **b.** 2.028 to 2.455

13.69 **b.** $b_1 = 1.087$ $b_0 = -775.381$ **c.** The regression equation appears to predict well for observations 5, 6, 9, and 10, as these observations have very small standardized residuals.

d. Observation 20 is considered influential since Cook's D is greater than .8.

13.71 **a.** Conclude that all population correlations are different from 0 except for the pair Campbell and Private and the pair Heinz and Private. **b.** No, since there is not sufficient evidence to indicate that a nonzero correlation exists between Campbell and Private. **c.** Campbell

13.73 **a.** $78,278.00 **b.** With observation 18 removed, $82,732.29.

Chapter 14

14.1 **a.** 16 **b.** 30

14.3 $\tilde{\sigma}_e = 3.4565$

14.5 **a.** $\tilde{Y} = 0.0090 + 1.1102X_1 + 0.13855X_2$ **b.** $SSE = 4.7289$

14.7 **a.** $\tilde{Y} = -878.386 + 42.019X_2 + 46.505X_2$. **b.** If $SSE = 0$, then the prediction equation would be a perfect predictor.

14.9 **a.** $F^* = 116.25$; reject H_0. **b.** $t^* = 9.615$; reject H_0. **c.** $t^* = 19.05$; reject H_0.

14.11 **a.** $t^* = 3.1509$; reject H_0. **b.** $t^* = -2.205$; reject H_0.

14.13 We are 95% confident that the regression coefficient for Horsepower is between $-.172$ to $-.024$. We are 95% confident that the regression coefficient for Engine Size is between -1.207 to 6.870.

14.15

ANOVA TABLE

Source	df	SS	MS	F
Regression	2	1165.66	582.83	30.17
Residual	7	135.24	19.32	
Total	9	1300.90		

14.17 $F^* = 4$; fail to reject H_0.

14.19 **a.** $F^* = 182.5$, reject H_0; $t^* = 15.25$, reject H_0 for MinutesTalked; $t^* = 15.87$, reject H_0 for MonthlyCharge

14.21 $R^2 = .896$; $R^2(\text{adj}) = .844$.

14.23 $F^* = 14.056$; reject H_0.

14.25 $F^* = 2.718$; fail to reject H_0.

14.27 For PP, $t^* = -2.16$ and for QI, $t^* = -1.414$. Since $t_{.025,241} \gtreqless 1.96$, PP contributes to the prediction of TT. $SSR = 35.769$, $SSE = 206.9$, $F^* = 20.83$. Since $F_{.05,2,241} \doteq 3.00$; reject H_0.

14.29 $\tilde{Y} = -11.62 + 4.60X_1 + 9.14X_2 + 2.53X_3$; $R^2 = .982$; The t-statistics for the variables CompEffic, Loyalty, and CompanyYrs are 12.996, 31.197, and 12.286, respectively. Each t-statistic squared is equal to the value of the corresponding partial F statistic. Each variable significantly contributes to the model given that the other variables are in the model.

14.31 X_1 and X_2 are highly correlated. X_4 and X_5 are highly correlated.

14.33 $VIF = 1/(1-(.9908)^2) = 54.6$ for each of the two variables. Multicollinearity is a concern.

14.35 X_1 and X_2 are highly correlated (.991) and X_3 and X_4 are highly correlated (.997). Variables X_1 and X_4 will be eliminated from the model. The prediction equation using X_2 and X_3 is $\tilde{Y} = 43.532 + 1.824X_2 - .892X_3$.

14.37 $F^* = 34.51$, reject H_0. **b.** No **c.** 17.7

14.39 **a.** 36 **b.** 39 **c.** 32 **d.** $F^* = 4$; reject H_0.

14.41 The final model is $\tilde{Y} = 24.126 + 2.152X_1 - 2.120X_2$.

14.43 **a.** X_3 **b.** X_3

14.45 Stepwise regression can remove any variable whose partial F value indicates that a variable does not contribute to the model. Forward regression cannot remove any variable from the model once it is included.

14.47 Assumption of equal variances for the error terms appears to have been violated.

14.49 **a.** 8.984 to 20.816 **b.** 4.895 to 24.905

14.51 The width of the prediction interval is always at least as wide as the width of the confidence interval for the mean of Y.

14.53 **a.** $t^* = 14.8$ and $t^* = 8.5$ for AdRev and SubscriberRev, respectively. Reject H_0. **b.** 237.47 to 405.93 **c.** Observation 1 is influential. $R^2 = .977$ with observation 1 and $R^2 = .998$ without observation 1.

14.55 **a.** $\tilde{Y} = 18.1 - 5X_1$ **b.** $\tilde{Y} = 10.1 + 5X_1$ **c.** No, the prediction lines are not parallel.

14.57 This change is due to the multicollinearity in the model introduced by the interaction term.

14.59 **b.** Observations 46 and 47 appear to be the most influential with standardized residuals of 3.75 and 4.43 and Cook's D values of .4 and .6, respectively.

14.61 **a.** $\tilde{Y} = -1.0 + 4.8X_1 + 5.9X_2$

b.

ANOVA TABLE

Source	df	SS	MS	F
Model	2	295.3	147.65	128.4
Residual	17	19.5	1.15	
Total	19	314.8		

$R^2 = .938$ **c.** $F^* = 128.4$; reject H_0. **d.** $t^* = 9.375$; reject H_0. **e.** $t^* = 14.05$; reject H_0.

14.63 For the model $F^* = 19.51$; together the variables X_1 and X_2 significantly contribute to the model. X_1 contributes to the model given X_2 in the model since $t^* = -5.28$. X_2 does not contribute to the model given X_1 in the model since $t^* = 1.58$.

14.65 This exercise illustrates that sometimes independent variables may be selected as good predictors although they are statistically independent of the dependent variable.

14.67 **a.** SSE decreases and R-square increases while SST remains unchanged.

14.69 **a.** $F^* = 3.21$; the data do not indicate that X_2 and X_3 contribute to the prediction of performance ratings.

14.71 **a.** $F^* = 4.999$; reject H_0. **b.** VIFs are both equal to 34.758.

14.73 **b.** $\tilde{Y} = 34,976$ **c.** Both VIFs are equal to 1.220.

Areas of the standard normal distribution

The entries in this table are the probabilities that a standard normal random variable is between 0 and z (the shaded area).

Second Decimal Place in z

z	0.00	0.01	0.02	0.03	0.04	0.05	0.06	0.07	0.08	0.09
0.0	0.0000	0.0040	0.0080	0.0120	0.0160	0.0199	0.0239	0.0279	0.0319	0.0359
0.1	0.0398	0.0438	0.0478	0.0517	0.0557	0.0596	0.0636	0.0675	0.0714	0.0753
0.2	0.0793	0.0832	0.0871	0.0910	0.0948	0.0987	0.1026	0.1064	0.1103	0.1141
0.3	0.1179	0.1217	0.1255	0.1293	0.1331	0.1368	0.1406	0.1443	0.1480	0.1517
0.4	0.1554	0.1591	0.1628	0.1664	0.1700	0.1736	0.1772	0.1808	0.1844	0.1879
0.5	0.1915	0.1950	0.1985	0.2019	0.2054	0.2088	0.2123	0.2157	0.2190	0.2224
0.6	0.2257	0.2291	0.2324	0.2357	0.2389	0.2422	0.2454	0.2486	0.2517	0.2549
0.7	0.2580	0.2611	0.2642	0.2673	0.2704	0.2734	0.2764	0.2794	0.2823	0.2852
0.8	0.2881	0.2910	0.2939	0.2967	0.2995	0.3023	0.3051	0.3078	0.3106	0.3133
0.9	0.3159	0.3186	0.3212	0.3238	0.3264	0.3289	0.3315	0.3340	0.3365	0.3389
1.0	0.3413	0.3438	0.3461	0.3485	0.3508	0.3531	0.3554	0.3577	0.3599	0.3621
1.1	0.3643	0.3665	0.3686	0.3708	0.3729	0.3749	0.3770	0.3790	0.3810	0.3830
1.2	0.3849	0.3869	0.3888	0.3907	0.3925	0.3944	0.3962	0.3980	0.3997	0.4015
1.3	0.4032	0.4049	0.4066	0.4082	0.4099	0.4115	0.4131	0.4147	0.4162	0.4177
1.4	0.4192	0.4207	0.4222	0.4236	0.4251	0.4265	0.4279	0.4292	0.4306	0.4319
1.5	0.4332	0.4345	0.4357	0.4370	0.4382	0.4394	0.4406	0.4418	0.4429	0.4441
1.6	0.4452	0.4463	0.4474	0.4484	0.4495	0.4505	0.4515	0.4525	0.4535	0.4545
1.7	0.4554	0.4564	0.4573	0.4582	0.4591	0.4599	0.4608	0.4616	0.4625	0.4633
1.8	0.4641	0.4649	0.4656	0.4664	0.4671	0.4678	0.4686	0.4693	0.4699	0.4706
1.9	0.4713	0.4719	0.4726	0.4732	0.4738	0.4744	0.4750	0.4756	0.4761	0.4767
2.0	0.4772	0.4778	0.4783	0.4788	0.4793	0.4798	0.4803	0.4808	0.4812	0.4817
2.1	0.4821	0.4826	0.4830	0.4834	0.4838	0.4842	0.4846	0.4850	0.4854	0.4857
2.2	0.4861	0.4864	0.4868	0.4871	0.4875	0.4878	0.4881	0.4884	0.4887	0.4890
2.3	0.4893	0.4896	0.4898	0.4901	0.4904	0.4906	0.4909	0.4911	0.4913	0.4916
2.4	0.4918	0.4920	0.4922	0.4925	0.4927	0.4929	0.4931	0.4932	0.4934	0.4936
2.5	0.4938	0.4940	0.4941	0.4943	0.4945	0.4946	0.4948	0.4949	0.4951	0.4952
2.6	0.4953	0.4955	0.4956	0.4957	0.4959	0.4960	0.4961	0.4962	0.4963	0.4964
2.7	0.4965	0.4966	0.4967	0.4968	0.4969	0.4970	0.4971	0.4972	0.4973	0.4974
2.8	0.4974	0.4975	0.4976	0.4977	0.4977	0.4978	0.4979	0.4979	0.4980	0.4981
2.9	0.4981	0.4982	0.4982	0.4983	0.4984	0.4984	0.4985	0.4985	0.4986	0.4986
3.0	0.4987	0.4987	0.4987	0.4988	0.4988	0.4989	0.4989	0.4989	0.4990	0.4990
3.1	0.4990	0.4991	0.4991	0.4991	0.4992	0.4992	0.4992	0.4992	0.4993	0.4993
3.2	0.4993	0.4993	0.4994	0.4994	0.4994	0.4994	0.4994	0.4995	0.4995	0.4995
3.3	0.4995	0.4995	0.4995	0.4996	0.4996	0.4996	0.4996	0.4996	0.4996	0.4997
3.4	0.4997	0.4997	0.4997	0.4997	0.4997	0.4997	0.4997	0.4997	0.4997	0.4998
3.5	0.4998									
4.0	0.49997									
4.5	0.499997									
5.0	0.4999997									

Critical values of *t*

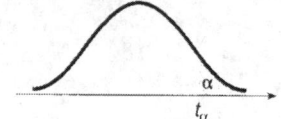

Degrees of Freedom	t.100	t.050	t.025	t.010	t.005
1	3.078	6.314	12.706	31.821	63.657
2	1.886	2.920	4.303	6.965	9.925
3	1.638	2.353	3.182	4.541	5.841
4	1.533	2.132	2.776	3.747	4.604
5	1.476	2.015	2.571	3.365	4.032
6	1.440	1.943	2.447	3.143	3.707
7	1.415	1.895	2.365	2.998	3.499
8	1.397	1.860	2.306	2.896	3.355
9	1.383	1.833	2.262	2.821	3.250
10	1.372	1.812	2.228	2.764	3.169
11	1.363	1.796	2.201	2.718	3.106
12	1.356	1.782	2.179	2.681	3.055
13	1.350	1.771	2.160	2.650	3.012
14	1.345	1.761	2.145	2.624	2.977
15	1.341	1.753	2.131	2.602	2.947
16	1.337	1.746	2.120	2.583	2.921
17	1.333	1.740	2.110	2.567	2.898
18	1.330	1.734	2.101	2.552	2.878
19	1.328	1.729	2.093	2.539	2.861
20	1.325	1.725	2.086	2.528	2.845
21	1.323	1.721	2.080	2.518	2.831
22	1.321	1.717	2.074	2.508	2.819
23	1.319	1.714	2.069	2.500	2.807
24	1.318	1.711	2.064	2.492	2.797
25	1.316	1.708	2.060	2.485	2.787
26	1.315	1.706	2.056	2.479	2.779
27	1.314	1.703	2.052	2.473	2.771
28	1.313	1.701	2.048	2.467	2.763
29	1.311	1.699	2.045	2.462	2.756
30	1.310	1.697	2.042	2.457	2.750
35	1.306	1.690	2.030	2.438	2.724
40	1.303	1.684	2.021	2.423	2.704
50	1.299	1.676	2.009	2.403	2.678
60	1.296	1.671	2.000	2.390	2.660
120	1.289	1.658	1.980	2.358	2.617
∞	1.282	1.645	1.960	2.326	2.576